NUMERICAL ANALYSIS WITH APPLICATIONS IN MECHANICS AND ENGINEERING

NUMERICAL ANALYSIS WITH APPLICATIONS IN MECHANICS AND ENGINEERING

PETRE TEODORESCU
NICOLAE-DORU STĂNESCU
NICOLAE PANDREA

IEEE PRESS

WILEY

For general information on our other products and services or for technical support, please contact our Customer Care Department within the United States at (800) 762-2974, outside the United States at (317) 572-3993 or fax (317) 572-4002.

Wiley also publishes its books in a variety of electronic formats. Some content that appears in print may not be available in electronic formats. For more information about Wiley products, visit our web site at www.wiley.com.

Library of Congress Cataloging-in-Publication Data:

Teodorescu, P. P.
  Numerical Analysis with Applications in Mechanics and Engineering / Petre Teodorescu,
Nicolae-Doru Stanescu, Nicolae Pandrea.
     pages cm
  ISBN 978-1-118-07750-4 (cloth)
 1. Numerical analysis. 2. Engineering mathematics. I. Stanescu, Nicolae-Doru. II. Pandrea,
Nicolae. III. Title.
  QA297.T456 2013
  620.001′518−dc23
                                    2012043659

Printed in the United States of America

ISBN: 9781118077504

10 9 8 7 6 5 4 3 2 1

CONTENTS

PREFACE

In writing this book, it is the authors' wish to create a bridge between mathematical and technical disciplines, which requires knowledge of strong mathematical tools in the area of numerical analysis. Unlike other books in this area, this interdisciplinary work links the applicative part of numerical methods, where mathematical results are used without understanding their proof, to the theoretical part of these methods, where each statement is rigorously demonstrated.

Each chapter is followed by problems of mechanics, physics, or engineering. The problem is first stated in its mechanical or technical form. Then the mathematical model is set up, emphasizing the physical magnitudes playing the part of unknown functions and the laws that lead to the mathematical problem. The solution is then obtained by specifying the mathematical methods described in the corresponding theoretical presentation. Finally, a mechanical, physical, and technical interpretation of the solution is provided, giving rise to complete knowledge of the studied phenomenon.

The book is organized into 10 chapters. Each of them begins with a theoretical presentation, which is based on practical computation—the "know-how" of the mathematical method—and ends with a range of applications.

The book contains some personal results of the authors, which have been found to be beneficial to readers.

The authors are grateful to Mrs. Eng. Ariadna–Carmen Stan for her valuable help in the presentation of this book. The excellent cooperation from the team of John Wiley & Sons, Hoboken, USA, is gratefully acknowledged.

The prerequisites of this book are courses in elementary analysis and algebra, acquired by a student in a technical university. The book is addressed to a broad audience—to all those interested in using mathematical models and methods in various fields such as mechanics, physics, and civil and mechanical engineering; people involved in teaching, research, or design; as well as students.

Petre Teodorescu
Nicolae-Doru Stănescu
Nicolae Pandrea

1

ERRORS IN NUMERICAL ANALYSIS

In this chapter, we deal with the most encountered errors in numerical analysis, that is, enter data errors, approximation errors, round-off errors, and propagation of errors.

1.1   ENTER DATA ERRORS

Enter data errors appear, usually, if the enter data are obtained from measurements or experiments. In such a case, the errors corresponding to the estimation of the enter data are propagated, by means of the calculation algorithm, to the exit data.

We define in what follows the notion of stability of errors.

Definition 1.1   A calculation process P is stable to errors if, for any $\varepsilon > 0$, there exists $\delta > 0$ such that if for any two sets I_1 and I_2 of enter data we have $\|I_1 - I_2\|_i < \delta$, then the two exit sets S_1 and S_2, corresponding to I_1 and I_2, respectively, verify the relation $\|S_1 - S_2\|_e < \varepsilon$.

Observation 1.1   The two norms $\|\ \|_i$ and $\|\ \|_e$ of the enter and exit quantities, respectively, which occur in Definition 1.1, depend on the process considered.

Intuitively, according to Definition 1.1, the calculation process is stable if, for small variations of the enter data, we obtain small variations of the exit data.

Hence, we must characterize the stable calculation process. Let us consider that the calculation process P is characterized by a family $\mathbf{f_k}$ of functions defined on a set of enter data with values in a set of exit data. We consider such a vector function $\mathbf{f_k}$ of vector variable $\mathbf{f_k} : \mathcal{D} \to \mathbb{R}^n$, where $\mathcal{D}$ is a domain in $\mathbb{R}^m$ (we propose to have m enter data and n exit data).

Definition 1.2 $\mathbf{f} : \mathcal{D} \to \mathbb{R}^n$ is a Lipschitz function (has the Lipschitz property) if there exists $m > 0$, constant, so as to have $\|\mathbf{f(x)} - \mathbf{f(y)}\| < m\|\mathbf{x} - \mathbf{y}\|$ for any $\mathbf{x}, \mathbf{y} \in \mathcal{D}$ (the first norm is in $\mathbb{R}^n$ and the second one in $\mathbb{R}^m$).

Numerical Analysis with Applications in Mechanics and Engineering, First Edition.
Petre Teodorescu, Nicolae-Doru Stănescu, and Nicolae Pandrea.
© 2013 The Institute of Electrical and Electronics Engineers, Inc. Published 2013 by John Wiley & Sons, Inc.

It is easy to see that a calculation process characterized by Lipschitz functions is a stable one.

In addition, a function with the Lipschitz property is continuous (even uniform continuous) but the converse does not hold; for example, the function $f : \mathbb{R}_+ \to \mathbb{R}_+$, $f(x) = \sqrt{x}$, is continuous but it is not Lipschitz. Indeed, let us suppose that $f(x) = \sqrt{x}$ is Lipschitz, hence that it has a positive constant $m > 0$ such that

$$|f(x) - f(y)| < m|x - y|, \quad (\forall) x, y \in \mathbb{R}_+. \tag{1.1}$$

Let us choose x and y such that $0 < y < x < 1/4m^2$. Expression (1.1) leads to

$$\sqrt{x} - \sqrt{y} < m(\sqrt{x} - \sqrt{y})(\sqrt{x} + \sqrt{y}), \tag{1.2}$$

from which we get

$$1 < m(\sqrt{x} + \sqrt{y}). \tag{1.3}$$

From the choice of x and y, it follows that

$$\sqrt{x} + \sqrt{y} < \sqrt{\frac{1}{4m^2}} + \sqrt{\frac{1}{4m^2}} = \frac{1}{m}, \tag{1.4}$$

so that relations (1.3) and (1.4) lead to

$$1 < m\frac{1}{m} = 1, \tag{1.5}$$

which is absurd. Hence, the continuous function $f : \mathbb{R}_+ \to \mathbb{R}_+$, $f(x) = \sqrt{x}$ is not a Lipschitz one.

1.2   APPROXIMATION ERRORS

The approximation errors have to be accepted by the conception of the algorithms because of various objective considerations.

Let us determine the limit of a sequence using a computer; it is supposed that the sequence is convergent. Let the sequence $\{x_n\}_{n \in \mathbb{N}}$ be defined by the relation

$$x_{n+1} = \frac{1}{1 + x_n^2}, \quad n \in \mathbb{N}, \; x_0 \in \mathbb{R}. \tag{1.6}$$

We observe that the terms of the sequence are positive, excepting eventually x_0. The limit of this sequence, denoted by $\overline{x}$, is the positive root of the equation

$$x = \frac{1}{1 + x^2}. \tag{1.7}$$

If we wish to determine $\overline{x}$ with two exact decimal digits, then we take an arbitrary value of x_0, for example, $x_0 = 0$, and calculate the successive terms of the sequence $\{x_n\}$ (Table 1.1).

TABLE 1.1   Calculation of $\bar{x}$ with Two Exact Decimal Digits

n	x_n	n	x_n	n	x_n	n	x_n
0	0	4	0.6028	8	0.6705	12	0.6804
1	1	5	0.7290	9	0.6899	13	0.6836
2	0.5	6	0.6530	10	0.6775	14	0.6815
3	0.8	7	0.7011	11	0.6854	15	0.6828

We obtain $\bar{x} = 0.68 \ldots$

1.3   ROUND-OFF ERRORS

Round-off errors are due to the mode of representation of the data in the computer. For instance, the number 0.8125 in base 10 is represented in base 2 in the form $0.8125 = \overline{0.1101}_2$ and the number 0.75 in the form $\overline{0.11}_2$. Let us suppose that we have a computer that works with three significant digits. The sum $0.8125 + 0.75$ becomes

$$1.5625 = \overline{0.1101}_2 + \overline{0.11}_2 \approx \overline{0.110}_2 + \overline{0.11}_2 = \overline{1.100}_2 = 1.5. \tag{1.8}$$

Such errors may also appear because of the choice of inadequate types of data in the programming realized on the computer.

1.4   PROPAGATION OF ERRORS

Let us consider the number x and let $\bar{x}$ be an approximation of it.

Definition 1.3

(i) We call absolute error the expression

$$E = x - \bar{x}. \tag{1.9}$$

(ii) We call relative error the expression

$$R = \frac{x - \bar{x}}{x}. \tag{1.10}$$

1.4.1   Addition

Let $x_1, x_2, \ldots, x_n$ be the numbers for which the relative errors are $R_1, R_2, \ldots, R_n$, while their absolute errors read $E_1, E_2, \ldots, E_n$.

The relative error of the sum is

$$R\left(\sum_{i=1}^{n} x_i\right) = \frac{\sum_{i=1}^{n} E_i}{\sum_{i=1}^{n} x_i} \tag{1.11}$$

and we may write the relation

$$\min_{i=\overline{1,n}} |R_i| \leq \left| R\left(\sum_{i=1}^{n} x_i\right) \right| \leq \max_{i=\overline{1,n}} |R_i|, \tag{1.12}$$

that is, the modulus of the relative error of the sum is contained between the lower and the higher values in the modulus of the relative errors of the component members.

Thus, if the terms $x_1, x_2, \ldots, x_n$ are positive and of the same order of magnitude,

$$\frac{\max\limits_{i=\overline{1,n}} x_i}{\min\limits_{i=\overline{1,n}} x_i} < 10, \tag{1.13}$$

then we must take the same number of significant digits for each term x_i, $i = \overline{1, n}$, the same number of significant digits occurring in the sum too.

If the numbers $x_1, x_2, \ldots, x_n$ are much different among them, then the number of the significant digits after the comma is given by the greatest number x_i (we suppose that $x_i > 0$, $i = \overline{1, n}$). For instance, if we have to add the numbers

$$x_1 = 100.32, \quad x_2 = 0.57381, \tag{1.14}$$

both numbers having five significant digits, then we will round off x_2 to two digits (as x_1) and write

$$x_1 + x_2 = 100.32 + 0.57 = 100.89. \tag{1.15}$$

It is observed that addition may result in a compensation of the errors, in the sense that the absolute error of the sum is, in general, smaller than the sum of the absolute error of each term.

We consider that the absolute error has a Gauss distribution for each of the terms x_i, $i = \overline{1, n}$, given by the distribution density

$$\phi(x) = \frac{1}{\sigma\sqrt{2\pi}} e^{-\frac{x^2}{2\sigma^2}}, \tag{1.16}$$

from which we obtain the distribution function

$$\Phi(x) = \int_{-\infty}^{x} \phi(x)\mathrm{d}x, \tag{1.17}$$

with the properties

$$\Phi(-\infty) = 0, \quad \Phi(\infty) = 1, \quad \Phi(x) \in (0, 1), \quad -\infty < x < \infty. \tag{1.18}$$

The probability that x is contained between $-x_0$ and x_0, with $x_0 > 0$ is

$$P(|x| < x_0) = \Phi(x_0) - \Phi(-x_0) = \int_{-x_0}^{x_0} \phi(t)\mathrm{d}t = \frac{\sqrt{2}}{\sigma\sqrt{\pi}} \int_{0}^{x_0} e^{-\frac{t^2}{2\sigma^2}} \mathrm{d}t. \tag{1.19}$$

Because $\phi(x)$ is an even function, it follows that the mean value of a variable with a normal Gauss distribution is

$$x_{\mathrm{med}} = \int_{-\infty}^{\infty} x\phi(x)\mathrm{d}x = 0, \tag{1.20}$$

while its mean square deviation reads

$$(x^2)_{\mathrm{max}} = \int_{-\infty}^{\infty} x^2\phi(x)\mathrm{d}x = \sigma^2. \tag{1.21}$$

Usually, we choose σ as being the mean square root

$$\sigma = \sigma_{\mathrm{RMS}} = \sqrt{\frac{1}{n}\sum_{i=1}^{n} R_i^2}. \tag{1.22}$$

1.4.2 Multiplication

Let us consider two numbers x_1, x_2 for which the relative errors are R_1, R_2, while the approximations are $\overline{x}_1$, $\overline{x}_2$, respectively. We have

$$\overline{x}_1\overline{x}_2 = x_1(1 + R_1)x_2(1 + R_2) = x_1x_2(1 + R_1 + R_2 + R_1R_2). \qquad (1.23)$$

Because R_1 and R_2 are small, we may consider $R_1R_2 \approx 0$, hence

$$\overline{x}_1\overline{x}_2 = x_1x_2(1 + R_1 + R_2), \qquad (1.24)$$

so that the relative error of the product of the two numbers reads

$$R(x_1x_2) = R_1 + R_2. \qquad (1.25)$$

Similarly, for n numbers $x_1, x_2, \dots, x_n$, of relative errors $R_1, R_2, \dots, R_n$, we have

$$R\left(\prod_{i=1}^{n} x_i\right) = \sum_{i=1}^{n} R_i. \qquad (1.26)$$

Let x be a number that may be written in the form

$$x = x^* \times 10^r, \quad 1 \le x^* < 10, \quad 10^r \le x < 10^{r+1}, \quad x^* \in \mathbb{Z}. \qquad (1.27)$$

The absolute error is

$$|E| \le 10^{r-n}, \qquad (1.28)$$

while the relative one is

$$|R| = \frac{|E|}{x} \le \frac{10^{r-n+1}}{x^* \times 10^r} = \frac{10^{-n+1}}{x^*} \le 10^{-n+1}, \qquad (1.29)$$

where we have supposed that x has n significant digits.

If $\overline{x}$ is the round-off of x at n significant digits, then

$$|E| \le 5 \times 10^{r-n}, \quad |R| \le \frac{5}{\overline{x}} \times 10^{r-n}. \qquad (1.30)$$

The error of the last significant digit, the nth, is

$$\varepsilon = \frac{E}{10^{r-n+1}} = \frac{xR}{10^{r-n+1}} = x^* R \times 10^{n-1}. \qquad (1.31)$$

Let x_1, x_2 now be two numbers of relative errors R_1, R_2 and let R be the relative error of the product x_1x_2. We have

$$R = \frac{x_1x_2 - \overline{x}_1\overline{x}_2}{x_1x_2} = R_1 + R_2 - R_1R_2. \qquad (1.32)$$

Moreover, $|R|$ takes its greatest value if R_1 and R_2 are negative; hence, we may write

$$|R| \le 5\left(\frac{1}{x_1^*} + \frac{1}{x_2^*}\right) \times 10^{-n} + \frac{25}{x_1^*x_2^*} \times 10^{-2n}, \qquad (1.33)$$

where the error of the digit on the nth position is

$$|\varepsilon(x_1 x_2)| \leq \frac{(x_1 x_2)^*}{2} \left(\frac{1}{x_1^*} + \frac{1}{x_2^*} \right) + \frac{5}{2} \frac{(x_1 x_2)^*}{x_1^* x_2^*} \times 10^{-n}. \tag{1.34}$$

On the other hand,

$$(x_1 x_2)^* = x_1^* x_2^* \times 10^{-p}, \tag{1.35}$$

where $p = 0$ or $p = 1$, the most disadvantageous case being that described by $p = 0$.
The function

$$\phi(x_1^*, x_2^*) = \frac{10^p}{2}(x_1^* + x_2^* + 5 \times 10^{-n}) \tag{1.36}$$

defined for $1 \leq x_1^* < 10$, $1 \leq x_2^* < 10$, $1 \leq x_1^* x_2^* < 10$ will attain its maximum on the frontier of the above domain, that is, for $x_1^* = 1$, $x_2^* = 10$ or $x_1^* = 10$, $x_2^* = 1$. It follows that

$$\phi(x_1^*, x_2^*) \leq \frac{10^{-p}}{2}(11 + 5 \times 10^{-n}), \tag{1.37}$$

and hence

$$|\varepsilon(x_1, x_2)| \leq \frac{11}{2} + \frac{5}{2} \times 10^{-n} < 6, \tag{1.38}$$

so that the error of the nth digit of the response will have at the most six units.
If $x_1 = x_2 = x$, then the most disadvantageous case is given by

$$(x^*)^2 = (x^2)^* = 10 \tag{1.39}$$

when

$$|\varepsilon(\overline{x}^2)| \leq 10^{\frac{1}{2}} + \frac{5}{2} \times 10^{-n} < 4, \tag{1.40}$$

that is, the nth digit of x^2 is given by an approximation of four units.
Let $x_1, \ldots, x_m$ now be m numbers; then

$$\left| \varepsilon \left(\prod_{i=1}^m \overline{x}_i \right) \right| \leq \frac{(\overline{x}_1 \cdots \overline{x}_m)^*}{2 \times 5 \times 10^{-n}} \left[\prod_{i=1}^m \left(1 + \frac{5 \times 10^{-n}}{x_i^*} \right) - 1 \right], \tag{1.41}$$

the most disadvantageous case being that in which $m - 1$ numbers x_i^* are equal to 1, while one number is equal 10. In this case, we have

$$\left| \varepsilon \left(\prod_{i=1}^m \overline{x}_i \right) \right| \leq \frac{5}{5 \times 10^{-n}} \left[(1 + 5 \times 10^{-n})^{m-1} \left(1 + \frac{5 \times 10^{-n}}{10} \right) - 1 \right]. \tag{1.42}$$

If all the m numbers are equal, $x_i = x$, $i = \overline{1, m}$, then the most disadvantageous situation appears for $(x^*)^m = (x^m)^* = 10$, and hence it follows that

$$|\varepsilon(\overline{x}^m)| \leq \frac{5}{5 \times 10^{-n}} \left[\left(1 + \frac{5 \times 10^{-m}}{10} \right)^m - 1 \right]. \tag{1.43}$$

1.4.3   Inversion of a Number

Let x be a number, $\bar{x}$ its approximation, and R its relative error. We may write

$$\frac{1}{\bar{x}} = \frac{1}{x(1+R)} = \frac{1}{x}(1 - R + R^2 - R^3 + \cdots) \approx \frac{1}{x}(1 - R), \qquad (1.44)$$

hence

$$R\left(\frac{1}{x}\right) = \frac{\frac{1}{x} - \frac{1}{\bar{x}}}{\frac{1}{x}} = R, \qquad (1.45)$$

so that the relative error remains the same.

In general,

$$E\left(\frac{1}{\bar{x}}\right) = -\frac{E}{\bar{x}^2}. \qquad (1.46)$$

1.4.4   Division of Two Numbers

We may imagine the division of x_1 by x_2 as the multiplication of x_1 by $1/x_2$, so that

$$R\left(\frac{x_1}{x_2}\right) = R(x_1) + R(x_2); \qquad (1.47)$$

hence, the relative errors are summed up.

1.4.5   Raising to a Negative Entire Power

We may write

$$R\left(\frac{1}{x^m}\right) = R\left(\frac{1}{x}\frac{1}{x}\cdots\frac{1}{x}\right) = \sum_{i=1}^{m} R\left(\frac{1}{x}\right) = \sum_{i=1}^{m} R(x), \quad m \in \mathbb{N}, \ m \neq 0, \qquad (1.48)$$

so that the relative errors are summed up.

1.4.6   Taking the Root of pth Order

We have, successively,

$$\bar{x}^{\frac{1}{p}} = (x + R)^{\frac{1}{p}} = x^{\frac{1}{p}}(1 + R)^{\frac{1}{p}}$$

$$= x^{\frac{1}{p}}\left[1 + \frac{R}{p} + \frac{1}{p}\left(\frac{1}{p} - 1\right)\frac{R^2}{2!} + \frac{1}{p}\left(\frac{1}{p} - 1\right)\left(\frac{1}{p} - 2\right)\frac{R^3}{3!} + \cdots\right], \qquad (1.49)$$

$$R\left(x^{\frac{1}{p}}\right) = \frac{x^{\frac{1}{p}} - \bar{x}^{\frac{1}{p}}}{x^{\frac{1}{p}}} \approx -\frac{R}{p}. \qquad (1.50)$$

The maximum error for the nth digit is now obtained for $x = 10^{(k-m)/m}$, $x^* = 1$, $(x^*)^m = 10^{1-m}$, $m = 1/p$, k entire, and is given by

$$\left|\varepsilon\left(x^*\right)^{\frac{1}{p}}\right| \leq \frac{10^{1-m}}{2 \times 5 \times 10^{-n}}[(1 + 5 \times 10^{-n})^m - 1] = 10^{n-m}[(1 + 5 \times 10^{-n})^m - 1]. \qquad (1.51)$$

1.4.7   Subtraction

Subtraction is the most disadvantageous operation if the result is small with respect to the minuend and the subtrahend.

Let us consider the subtraction $20.003 - 19.998$ in which the first four digits of each number are known with precision; concerning the fifth digit, we can say that it is determined with a precision of 1 unit. It follows that for 20.003 the relative error is

$$R_1 \leq \frac{10^{-3}}{20.003} < 5 \times 10^{-5}, \tag{1.52}$$

while for 19.998 the relative error is

$$R_1 \leq \frac{10^{-3}}{19.998} < 5.1 \times 10^{-5}. \tag{1.53}$$

The result of the subtraction operation is 5×10^{-3}, while the last digit may be wrong with two units, so that the relative error of the difference is

$$R = \frac{2 \times 10^{-3}}{5 \times 10^{-3}} = 400 \times 10^{-3}, \tag{1.54}$$

that is, a relative error that is approximately 8000 times greater than R_1 or R_2.

It follows the rule that the difference of two quantities must be directly calculated, without previously calculating the two quantities.

1.4.8   Computation of Functions

Starting from Taylor's relation

$$f(x) - f(\overline{x}) = (x - \overline{x}) f'(\xi), \tag{1.55}$$

where ξ is a point situated between x and $\overline{x}$, it follows that the absolute error is

$$|E(f)| \leq |E| \sup_{\xi \in \text{Int}(x, \overline{x})} |f'(\xi)|, \tag{1.56}$$

while the relative error reads

$$|R(f)| \leq \frac{|E|}{|f(x)|} \sup_{\xi \in \text{Int}(x, \overline{x})} |f'(\xi)|, \tag{1.57}$$

where $\text{Int}(x, \overline{x})$ defines the real interval of ends x and $\overline{x}$.

1.5   APPLICATIONS

Problem 1.1

Let us consider the sequence of integrals

$$I_n = \int_0^1 x^n e^x dx, \quad n \in \mathbb{N}. \tag{1.58}$$

(i) Determine a recurrence formula for $\{I_n\}_{n \in \mathbb{N}}$.

Solution: To calculate I_n, $n \geq 1$, we use integration by parts and have

$$I_n = \int_0^1 x^n e^x dx = x^n e^x \big|_0^1 - n \int_0^0 x^{n-1} e^x dx = e - I_{n-1}. \tag{1.59}$$

(ii) Show that $\lim_{n \to \infty} I_n$ does exist.

Solution: For $x \in [0, 1]$ we have

$$x^{n+1} e^x \leq x^n e^x, \tag{1.60}$$

hence $I_{n+1} \leq I_n$ for any $n \in \mathbb{N}$. It follows that $\{I_n\}_{n \in \mathbb{N}}$ is a decreasing sequence of real numbers.
   On the other hand,

$$x^n e^x \geq 0, \quad x \in [0, 1], \quad n \in \mathbb{N}, \tag{1.61}$$

so that $\{I_n\}_{n \in \mathbb{N}}$ is a positive sequence of real numbers.
   We get

$$0 \leq \cdots \leq I_{n+1} \leq I_n \leq \cdots \leq I_1 \leq I_0, \tag{1.62}$$

so that $\{I_n\}_{n \in \mathbb{N}}$ is convergent and, moreover,

$$0 \leq \lim_{n \to \infty} I_n \leq I_0 = \int_0^1 e^x dx = e - 1. \tag{1.63}$$

(iii) Calculate I_{13}.

Solution: To calculate the integral we have two methods.

Method 1.

$$I_0 = \int_0^1 e^x dx = e^x \big|_0^1 = e - 1, \tag{1.64}$$

$$I_1 = e - 1 I_0 = 1, \tag{1.65}$$

$$I_2 = e - 2 I_1 = e - 2, \tag{1.66}$$

$$I_3 = e - 3 I_2 = 6 - 2e, \tag{1.67}$$

$$I_4 = e - 4 I_3 = 9e - 24, \tag{1.68}$$

$$I_5 = e - 5 I_4 = 120 - 44e, \tag{1.69}$$

$$I_6 = e - 6 I_5 = 265e - 720, \tag{1.70}$$

$$I_7 = e - 7 I_6 = 5040 - 1854e, \tag{1.71}$$

$$I_8 = e - 8 I_7 = 14833e - 40320, \tag{1.72}$$

$$I_9 = e - 9 I_8 = 362880 - 133496e, \tag{1.73}$$

$$I_{10} = e - 10 I_9 = 1334961e - 3628800, \tag{1.74}$$

$$I_{11} = e - 11 I_{10} = 39916800 - 14684570e, \tag{1.75}$$

$$I_{12} = e - 12 I_{11} = 176214841e - 479001600, \tag{1.76}$$

$$I_{13} = e - 13 I_{12} = 6227020800 - 2290792932e. \tag{1.77}$$

It follows that

$$I_{13} = 0.1798. \tag{1.78}$$

Method 2. In this case, we replace directly the calculated values, thus obtaining

$$I_0 = e - 1 = 1.718281828, \tag{1.79}$$

$$I_1 = e - 1I_0 = 1, \tag{1.80}$$

$$I_2 = e - 2I_1 = 0.718281828, \tag{1.81}$$

$$I_3 = e - 3I_2 = 0.563436344, \tag{1.82}$$

$$I_4 = e - 4I_3 = 0.464536452, \tag{1.83}$$

$$I_5 = e - 5I_4 = 0.395599568, \tag{1.84}$$

$$I_6 = e - 6I_5 = 0.34468442, \tag{1.85}$$

$$I_7 = e - 7I_6 = 0.305490888, \tag{1.86}$$

$$I_8 = e - 8I_7 = 0.274354724, \tag{1.87}$$

$$I_9 = e - 9I_8 = 0.249089312, \tag{1.88}$$

$$I_{10} = e - 10I_9 = 0.227388708, \tag{1.89}$$

$$I_{11} = e - 11I_{10} = 0.21700604, \tag{1.90}$$

$$I_{12} = e - 12I_{11} = 0.114209348, \tag{1.91}$$

$$I_{13} = e - 13I_{12} = 1.233560304. \tag{1.92}$$

We observe that, because of the propagation of errors, the second method cannot be used to calculate I_n, $n \geq 12$.

Problem 1.2

Let the sequences $\{x_n\}_{n\in\mathbb{N}}$ and $\{y_n\}_{n\in\mathbb{N}}$ be defined recursively:

$$x_{n+1} = \frac{1}{2}\left(x_n + \frac{0.5}{x_n}\right), \quad x_0 = 1, \tag{1.93}$$

$$y_{n+1} = y_n - \lambda(y_n^2 - 0.5), \quad y_0 = 1. \tag{1.94}$$

(i) Calculate $x_1, x_2, \ldots, x_7$.

Solution: We have, successively,

$$x_1 = \frac{1}{2}\left(x_0 + \frac{0.5}{x_0}\right) = \frac{3}{4}, \tag{1.95}$$

$$x_2 = \frac{1}{2}\left(x_1 + \frac{0.5}{x_1}\right) = \frac{17}{24}, \tag{1.96}$$

$$x_3 = \frac{1}{2}\left(x_2 + \frac{0.5}{x_2}\right) = \frac{577}{816}, \tag{1.97}$$

$$x_4 = \frac{1}{2}\left(x_3 + \frac{0.5}{x_3}\right) = 0.707107, \tag{1.98}$$

$$x_5 = \frac{1}{2}\left(x_4 + \frac{0.5}{x_4}\right) = 0.707107, \tag{1.99}$$

$$x_6 = \frac{1}{2}\left(x_5 + \frac{0.5}{x_5}\right) = 0.707107, \tag{1.100}$$

$$x_7 = \frac{1}{2}\left(x_6 + \frac{0.5}{x_6}\right) = 0.707107. \tag{1.101}$$

(ii) Calculate $y_1, y_2, \ldots, y_7$ for $\lambda = 0.49$.

Solution: There result the values

$$y_1 = y_0 - 0.49(y_0^2 - 0.5) = 0.755, \tag{1.102}$$

$$y_2 = y_1 - 0.49(y_1^2 - 0.5) = 0.720688, \tag{1.103}$$

$$y_3 = y_2 - 0.49(y_2^2 - 0.5) = 0.711186, \tag{1.104}$$

$$y_4 = y_3 - 0.49(y_3^2 - 0.5) = 0.708351, \tag{1.105}$$

$$y_5 = y_4 - 0.49(y_4^2 - 0.5) = 0.707488, \tag{1.106}$$

$$y_6 = y_5 - 0.49(y_5^2 - 0.5) = 0.707224, \tag{1.107}$$

$$y_7 = y_8 - 0.49(y_8^2 - 0.5) = 0.707143. \tag{1.108}$$

(iii) Calculate $y_1, y_2, \ldots, y_7$ for $\lambda = 49$.

Solution: In this case, we obtain the values

$$y_1 = y_0 - 49(y_0^2 - 0.5) = -23.5, \tag{1.109}$$

$$y_2 = y_1 - 49(y_1^2 - 0.5) = -27059.25, \tag{1.110}$$

$$y_3 = y_2 - 49(y_2^2 - 0.5) = -3.587797 \times 10^{10}, \tag{1.111}$$

$$y_4 = y_3 - 49(y_3^2 - 0.5) = -6.307422 \times 10^{22}, \tag{1.112}$$

$$y_5 = y_4 - 49(y_4^2 - 0.5) = -1.949395 \times 10^{47}, \tag{1.113}$$

$$y_6 = y_5 - 49(y_5^2 - 0.5) = -1.862070 \times 10^{96}, \tag{1.114}$$

$$y_7 = y_8 - 49(y_8^2 - 0.5) = -1.698979 \times 10^{194}. \tag{1.115}$$

We observe that the sequences $\{x_n\}_{n \in \mathbb{N}}$ and $\{y_n\}_{n \in \mathbb{N}}$ converge to $\sqrt{0.5} = 0.707107$ for $\lambda = 0.49$, while the sequence $\{y_n\}_{n \in \mathbb{N}}$ is divergent for $\lambda = 49$.

Problem 1.3

If the independent aleatory variables X_1 and X_2 have the density distributions $p_1(x)$ and $p_2(x)$, respectively, then the aleatory variable $X_1 + X_2$ has the density distribution

$$p(x) = \int_{-\infty}^{\infty} p_1(x - s) p_2(s) \mathrm{d}s. \tag{1.116}$$

(i) Demonstrate that if the aleatory variables X_1 and X_2 have a normal distribution by zero mean and standard deviations σ_1 and σ_2, then the aleatory variable $X_1 + X_2$ has a normal distribution.

Solution: From equation (1.116) we have

$$p(x) = \int_{-\infty}^{\infty} \frac{1}{\sigma_1 \sqrt{2\pi}} \mathrm{e}^{-\frac{(x-s)^2}{2\sigma_1^2}} \frac{1}{\sigma_2 \sqrt{2\pi}} \mathrm{e}^{-\frac{s^2}{2\sigma_2^2}} \mathrm{d}s = \frac{1}{2\pi\sigma_1\sigma_2} \int_{-\infty}^{\infty} \mathrm{e}^{-\frac{(x-s)^2}{2\sigma_1^2}} \mathrm{e}^{-\frac{s^2}{2\sigma_2^2}} \mathrm{d}s. \tag{1.117}$$

We require the values λ_1, λ_2, and a real, such that

$$\frac{(x-s)^2}{2\sigma_1^2} + \frac{s^2}{2\sigma_2^2} = \frac{x^2}{\lambda_1^2} + \frac{(s-ax)^2}{\lambda_2^2}, \tag{1.118}$$

from which

$$\frac{x^2}{\sigma_1^2} = \frac{x_2^2}{\lambda_1^2} + \frac{a^2 x^2}{\lambda_2^2}, \quad \frac{s^2}{\sigma_1^2} + \frac{s^2}{\sigma_2^2} = \frac{s^2}{\lambda_2^2}, \quad -\frac{2xs}{\sigma_1^2} = -\frac{2asx}{\lambda_2^2}, \tag{1.119}$$

with the solution

$$\lambda_2^2 = \frac{\sigma_1^2 \sigma_2^2}{\sigma_1^2 + \sigma_2^2}, \quad a = \frac{\sigma_2^2}{\sigma_1^2 + \sigma_2^2}, \quad \lambda_1^2 = \sigma_1^2 + \sigma_2^2. \tag{1.120}$$

We make the change of variable

$$s - ax = \sqrt{2}\lambda_2 t, \quad ds = \sqrt{2}\lambda_2 dt \tag{1.121}$$

and expression (1.118) becomes

$$p(x) = \frac{1}{2\pi\sigma_1\sigma_2} \int_{-\infty}^{\infty} e^{-\frac{x^2}{2\lambda_1^2}} e^{-t^2} \lambda_2 dt = \frac{1}{\sqrt{\sigma_1^2 + \sigma_2^2}\sqrt{2\pi}} e^{-\frac{x^2}{2(\sigma_1^2 + \sigma_2^2)}}. \tag{1.122}$$

(ii) Calculate the mean and the standard deviation of the aleatory variable $X_1 + X_2$ of point (i).

Solution: We calculate

$$\int_{-\infty}^{\infty} xp(x)dx = \frac{1}{\sqrt{\sigma_1^2 + \sigma_2^2}\sqrt{2\pi}} \int_{-\infty}^{\infty} xe^{-\frac{x^2}{2(\sigma_1^2 + \sigma_2^2)}} dx = 0, \tag{1.123}$$

$$\int_{-\infty}^{\infty} x^2 p(x)dx = \frac{1}{\sqrt{\sigma_1^2 + \sigma_2^2}\sqrt{2\pi}} \int_{-\infty}^{\infty} x^2 e^{-\frac{x^2}{2(\sigma_1^2 + \sigma_2^2)}} dx$$

$$= \left(-\frac{\sqrt{\sigma_1^2 + \sigma_2^2}}{\sqrt{2\pi}} xe^{-\frac{x^2}{\sigma_1^2 + \sigma_2^2}} \right) \Bigg|_{-\infty}^{\infty} + \frac{\sqrt{\sigma_1^2 + \sigma_2^2}}{\sqrt{2\pi}} \int_{-\infty}^{\infty} e^{-\frac{x^2}{2(\sigma_1^2 + \sigma_2^2)}} dx$$

$$= \sigma_1^2 + \sigma_2^2. \tag{1.124}$$

(iii) Let X be an aleatory variable with a normal distribution, a zero mean, and standard deviation σ. Calculate

$$I_1 = \frac{1}{\sigma\sqrt{2\pi}} \int_{-\infty}^{\infty} e^{-\frac{x^2}{2\sigma^2}} dx \tag{1.125}$$

and

$$I_2 = \frac{1}{\sigma\sqrt{2\pi}} \int_{-\sigma}^{\sigma} e^{-\frac{x^2}{2\sigma^2}} dx. \tag{1.126}$$

Solution: Through the change of variable

$$x = \sigma\sqrt{2}u, \quad dx = \sigma\sqrt{2}du, \tag{1.127}$$

it follows that

$$I_1 = \frac{1}{\sigma\sqrt{2\pi}} \int_{-\infty}^{\infty} e^{-u^2} \sigma\sqrt{2} du = 1. \tag{1.128}$$

Similarly, we have

$$I_2 = \frac{1}{\sqrt{\pi}} \int_{-\sigma}^{\sigma} e^{-u^2} du. \tag{1.129}$$

On the other hand,

$$\int_{-\sigma}^{\sigma} e^{-u^2} du = \sqrt{\int_0^{2\pi} \int_0^{\sigma} e^{-\rho^2} \rho \, d\rho \, d\theta} = \sqrt{\pi(1 - e^{-\sigma^2})}, \tag{1.130}$$

so that

$$I_2 = \sqrt{1 - e^{-\sigma^2}}. \tag{1.131}$$

(iv) Let $0 < \varepsilon < 1$, fixed. Determine $R > 0$ so that

$$\frac{1}{\sqrt{\pi}} \int_{-R}^{R} e^{-x^2} dx < \varepsilon. \tag{1.132}$$

Solution: Proceeding as with point (iii), it follows that

$$\int_{-R}^{R} e^{-x^2} dx = \sqrt{\pi(1 - e^{-R^2})}, \tag{1.133}$$

so that we obtain the inequality

$$\sqrt{1 - e^{-R^2}} < \varepsilon, \tag{1.134}$$

from which

$$R < \sqrt{-\ln(1 - \varepsilon^2)}. \tag{1.135}$$

(v) Calculate

$$I_3 = \frac{1}{\sigma\sqrt{2\pi}} \int_{-R}^{R} e^{-\frac{x^2}{2\sigma^2}} dx \tag{1.136}$$

and

$$I_4 = \frac{1}{\sigma\sqrt{2\pi}} \int_{R}^{\infty} e^{-\frac{x^2}{2\sigma^2}} dx \tag{1.137}$$

Solution: We again make the change of variable (1.127) and obtain

$$I_3 = \frac{1}{\sqrt{\pi}} \int_{-\frac{R}{\sigma\sqrt{2}}}^{\frac{R}{\sigma\sqrt{2}}} e^{-u^2} du. \tag{1.138}$$

Point (ii) shows that

$$\int_{-A}^{A} e^{-x^2} dx = \sqrt{\pi(1 - e^{-A^2})}, \quad A > 0; \tag{1.139}$$

hence, it follows that

$$I_3 = \sqrt{1 - e^{-\frac{R^2}{2\sigma^2}}}. \tag{1.140}$$

On the other hand, we have seen that $I_1 = 1$ and we may write

$$I_1 = \frac{1}{\sigma\sqrt{2\pi}} \left(2\int_R^\infty e^{-\frac{x^2}{\sigma^2}} dx + \int_{-R}^R e^{-\frac{x^2}{2\sigma^2}} dx \right) = 2I_4 + I_3. \tag{1.141}$$

Immediately, it follows that

$$I_4 = \frac{I_1 - I_3}{2} = \frac{1 - \sqrt{1 - e^{-\frac{R^2}{2\sigma^2}}}}{2}. \tag{1.142}$$

(vi) Let X_1 and X_2 be two aleatory variables with a normal distribution, a zero mean, and standard deviation σ. Determine the density distribution of the aleatory variable $X_1 + X_2$, as well as its mean and standard deviation.

Solution: It is a particular case of points (i) and (ii); hence, we obtain

$$p(x) = \frac{1}{2\sigma\sqrt{\pi}} e^{-\frac{x^2}{4\sigma^2}}, \tag{1.143}$$

that is, a normal aleatory variable of zero mean and standard deviation $\sigma\sqrt{2}$.

(vii) Let N_1 and N_2 be numbers estimated with errors ε_1 and ε_2, respectively, considered to be aleatory variables with normal distribution, zero mean, and standard deviation σ. Calculate the sum $N_1 + N_2$ so that the error is less than a value $\varepsilon > 0$.

Solution: The requested probability is given by

$$I = \int_{-\infty}^\varepsilon \frac{1}{2\sigma\sqrt{\pi}} e^{-\frac{x^2}{4\sigma^2}} dx = \int_{-\infty}^{-\varepsilon} \frac{1}{2\sigma\sqrt{\pi}} e^{-\frac{x^2}{4\sigma^2}} dx + \int_{-\varepsilon}^\varepsilon \frac{1}{2\sigma\sqrt{\pi}} e^{-\frac{x^2}{4\sigma^2}} dx. \tag{1.144}$$

Taking into account the previous results, we obtain

$$\int_{-\infty}^{-\varepsilon} \frac{1}{2\sigma\sqrt{\pi}} e^{-\frac{x^2}{4\sigma^2}} dx = \frac{1 - \sqrt{1 - e^{-\frac{\varepsilon^2}{4\sigma^2}}}}{2}, \tag{1.145}$$

$$\int_{-\varepsilon}^\varepsilon \frac{1}{2\sigma\sqrt{\pi}} e^{-\frac{x^2}{4\sigma^2}} dx = \sqrt{1 - e^{-\frac{\varepsilon^2}{4\sigma^2}}}, \tag{1.146}$$

so that

$$I = \frac{1}{2} \left(1 + \sqrt{1 - e^{-\frac{\varepsilon^2}{4\sigma^2}}} \right). \tag{1.147}$$

FURTHER READING

Acton FS (1990). Numerical Methods that Work. 4th ed. Washington: Mathematical Association of America.

Ackleh AS, Allen EJ, Hearfott RB, Seshaiyer P (2009). Classical and Modern Numerical Analysis: Theory, Methods and Practice. Boca Raton: CRC Press.

Atkinson KE (1989). An Introduction to Numerical Analysis. 2nd ed. New York: John Wiley & Sons, Inc.

Atkinson KE (2003). Elementary Numerical Analysis. 2nd ed. New York: John Wiley & Sons, Inc.

Bakhvalov N (1976). Méthodes Numérique. Moscou: Editions Mir (in French).

Berbente C, Mitran S, Zancu S (1997). Metode Numerice. Bucureşti: Editura Tehnică (in Romanian).

Burden RL, Faires L (2009). Numerical Analysis. 9th ed. Boston: Brooks/Cole.

Chapra SC (1996). Applied Numerical Methods with MATLAB for Engineers and Scientists. Boston: McGraw-Hill.

Cheney EW, Kincaid DR (1997). Numerical Mathematics and Computing. 6th ed. Belmont: Thomson.

Dahlquist G, Björck Å (1974). Numerical Methods. Englewood Cliffs: Prentice Hall.

Démidovitch B, Maron I (1973). Éléments de Calcul Numérique. Moscou: Editions Mir (in French).

Epperson JF (2007). An Introduction to Numerical Methods and Analysis. Hoboken: John Wiley & Sons, Inc.

Gautschi W (1997). Numerical Analysis: An Introduction. Boston: Birkhäuser.

Greenbaum A, Chartier TP (2012). Numerical Methods: Design, Analysis, and Computer Implementation of Algorithms. Princeton: Princeton University Press.

Hamming RW (1987). Numerical Methods for Scientists and Engineers. 2nd ed. New York: Dover Publications.

Hamming RW (2012). Introduction to Applied Numerical Analysis. New York: Dover Publications.

Heinbockel JH (2006). Numerical Methods for Scientific Computing. Victoria: Trafford Publishing.

Higham NJ (2002). Accuracy and Stability of Numerical Algorithms. 2nd ed. Philadelphia: SIAM.

Hildebrand FB (1987). Introduction to Numerical Analysis. 2nd ed. New York: Dover Publications.

Hoffman JD (1992). Numerical Methods for Engineers and Scientists. New York: McGraw-Hill.

Kharab A, Guenther RB (2011). An Introduction to Numerical Methods: A MATLAB Approach. 3rd ed. Boca Raton: CRC Press.

Krîlov AN (1957). Lecţii de Calcule prin Aproximaţii. Bucureşti: Editura Tehnică (in Romanian).

Kunz KS (1957). Numerical Analysis. New York: McGraw-Hill.

Levine L (1964). Methods for Solving Engineering Problems Using Analog Computers. New York: McGraw-Hill.

Marinescu G (1974). Analiză Numerică. Bucureşti: Editura Academiei Române (in Romanian).

Press WH, Teukolski SA, Vetterling WT, Flannery BP (2007). Numerical Recipes: The Art of Scientific Computing. 3rd ed. Cambridge: Cambridge University Press.

Quarteroni A, Sacco R, Saleri F (2010). Numerical Mathematics. 2nd ed. Berlin: Springer-Verlag.

Ralston A, Rabinowitz P (2001). A First Course in Numerical Analysis. 2nd ed. New York: Dover Publications.

Ridgway Scott L (2011). Numerical Analysis. Princeton: Princeton University Press.

Sauer T (2011). Numerical Analysis. 2nd ed. London: Pearson.

Simionescu I, Dranga M, Moise V (1995). Metode Numerice în Tehnică. Aplicaţii în FORTRAN. Bucureşti: Editura Tehnică (in Romanian).

Stănescu ND (2007). Metode Numerice. Bucureşti: Editura Didactică şi Pedagogică (in Romanian).

Stoer J, Bulirsh R (2010). Introduction to Numerical Analysis. 3rd ed. New York: Springer-Verlag.

2

SOLUTION OF EQUATIONS

We deal with several methods of approximate solutions of equations, that is, the bipartition method, the chord (secant) method, the tangent method (Newton), and the Newton–Kantorovich method. These are followed by applications.

2.1   THE BIPARTITION (BISECTION) METHOD

Let us consider the equation[1]

$$f(x) = 0, \tag{2.1}$$

where $f : [a, b] \to \mathbb{R}$, $a, b \in \mathbb{R}$, $a < b$, f continuous on $[a, b]$, with a single root α, $f(\alpha) = 0$, on the interval $[a, b]$.

First, we verify if $f(a) = 0$ or $f(b) = 0$; if this occurs, then the algorithm stops. Otherwise, we consider the middle of the interval $[a, b]$, $c = (a + b)/2$. We verify if c is a solution of equation (2.1); if $f(c) = 0$, the algorithm stops; if not, we calculate $f(c)$. If $f(a) \times f(c) < 0$, then we consider the interval $[a, c]$ on which we have the true solution; if not, we consider the interval $[c, b]$. Thus, the interval $[a, b]$ is diminished to $[a, c]$ or $[c, b]$, its new length being equal to $(a + b)/2$. We thus obtain a new interval $[a, b]$, where $a = c$ or $b = c$, and we apply the procedure described above. The procedure stops when a certain criterion (e.g., the length of the interval $[a, b]$ is less than a given ε) is fulfilled.

---

[1]The bipartition method is the simplest and most popular method for solving equations. It was known by ancient mathematicians.

Numerical Analysis with Applications in Mechanics and Engineering, First Edition.
Petre Teodorescu, Nicolae-Doru Stănescu, and Nicolae Pandrea.
© 2013 The Institute of Electrical and Electronics Engineers, Inc. Published 2013 by John Wiley & Sons, Inc.

As we can see from this exposition, the bipartition method consists in the construction of three sequences $\{a_n\}$, $\{b_n\}$, and $\{c_n\}$, $n \in \mathbb{N}$, as follows:

$$a_0 = 0, \quad b_0 = b, \quad c_n = \frac{a_n + b_n}{2}, \quad n \geq 0, \quad a_{n+1} = \begin{cases} a_n & \text{for } f\left(a_n\right) \times f(c_n) < 0 \\ c_n & \text{otherwise} \end{cases},$$

$$b_{n+1} = \begin{cases} b_n & \text{for } f\left(c_n\right) \times f(b_n) < 0 \\ c_n & \text{otherwise} \end{cases}. \tag{2.2}$$

The bipartition method is based on the following theorem.

Theorem 2.1   The sequences $\{a_n\}$, $\{b_n\}$, $\{c_n\}$, $n \in \mathbb{N}$, given by formulae (2.2), are convergent, and their limit is the value of the unique real root α of equation (2.1) on the interval $[a, b]$.

Demonstration. Let us show that

$$b_n - a_n = \frac{b - a}{2^n}, \tag{2.3}$$

for any $n \in \mathbb{N}$.

To fix the ideas, we suppose that $f(a) < 0$ and $f(b) > 0$. If $f(c_{n-1}) < 0$, then

$$b_n - a_n = b_{n-1} - c_{n-1} = b_{n-1} - \frac{a_{n-1} + b_{n-1}}{2} = \frac{b_{n-1} - a_{n-1}}{2}, \tag{2.4}$$

whereas if $f(c_{n-1}) > 0$, we get

$$b_n - a_n = c_{n-1} - a_{n-1} = \frac{a_{n-1} + b_{n-1}}{2} - a_{n-1} = \frac{b_{n-1} - a_{n-1}}{2}. \tag{2.5}$$

Hence, in general,

$$b_n - a_n = \frac{b_{n-1} - a_{n-1}}{2} = \frac{b_{n-2} - a_{n-2}}{2^2} = \cdots = \frac{b_0 - a_0}{2^n} = \frac{b - a}{2^n}. \tag{2.6}$$

It is obvious that

$$a_n < c_n < b_n, \quad n \in \mathbb{N}. \tag{2.7}$$

From the definition of the sequence $\{a_n\}$, $n \in \mathbb{N}$, it follows that $a_{n+1} = a_n$ or $a_{n+1} = c_n = (a_n + b_n)/2 > a_n$. We may write

$$a_{n+1} \geq a_n, \quad n \in \mathbb{N}; \tag{2.8}$$

hence, the sequence $\{a_n\}$, $n \in \mathbb{N}$, is monotone increasing. Analogically, we obtain the relation

$$b_{n+1} \leq b_n, \quad n \in \mathbb{N}; \tag{2.9}$$

this means that the sequence $\{b_n\}$, $n \in \mathbb{N}$, is monotone decreasing.

Let us have the sequence of relations

$$a = a_0 \leq a_1 \leq \cdots \leq a_n \leq \cdots \leq b_n \leq \cdots \leq b_1 \leq b_0 = b, \tag{2.10}$$

where the sequence $\{a_n\}$, $n \in \mathbb{N}$, is superior bounded by any value b_n, $n \in \mathbb{N}$; in particular, we can take $b_n = b$. The sequence $\{b_n\}$, $n \in \mathbb{N}$, is inferior bounded by any value a_n, $n \in \mathbb{N}$, in particular by $a_n = a$.

We have stated thus that $\{a_n\}$, $n \in \mathbb{N}$, is a monotone increasing and superior bounded (by b) sequence, and hence it is convergent, while the sequence $\{b_n\}$, $n \in \mathbb{N}$ is a monotone decreasing and inferior bounded (by a) sequence, and hence it is convergent, too.

Let $A = \lim\limits_{n\to\infty} a_n$ and $B = \lim\limits_{n\to\infty} b_n$. Let us show that $A = B$, that is, that the sequences $\{a_n\}$, $\{b_n\}$, $n \in \mathbb{N}$, have the same limit. We have

$$A - B = \lim_{n\to\infty} a_n - \lim_{n\to\infty} b_n = \lim_{n\to\infty} (a_n - b_n). \tag{2.11}$$

On the other hand, taking into account relation (2.6), we get

$$\lim_{n\to\infty} (a_n - b_n) = \lim_{n\to\infty} \frac{a - b}{2^n} = 0. \tag{2.12}$$

The last two expressions show that $A - B = 0$, hence $A = B$.

Let $A = \lim\limits_{n\to\infty} a_n = \lim\limits_{n\to\infty} b_n$. Applying now the tongs theorem for the sequences $\{a_n\}$, $\{b_n\}$, and $\{c_n\}$, $n \in \mathbb{N}$, and taking into account (2.7), it follows that the sequence $\{c_n\}$, $n \in \mathbb{N}$, is convergent and $\lim\limits_{n\to\infty} c_n = A$.

Let us show that $f(A) = 0$. We have

$$f(A) = f\left(\lim_{n\to\infty} a_n\right) = \lim_{n\to\infty} f(a_n) \leq 0, \tag{2.13}$$

$$f(A) = f\left(\lim_{n\to\infty} b_n\right) = \lim_{n\to\infty} f(b_n) \geq 0, \tag{2.14}$$

where if f is continuous, then the function commutes into the limit. The last two expressions lead to $f(A) = 0$, and hence A is the root α of the equation $f(x) = 0$ on the interval $[a, b]$.

To determine the corresponding error, we can proceed in two modes.

In the first method, we start from the evident relations

$$|a_n - b_n| = 2|a_n - c_n|, \, |a_n - b_n| = 2|b_n - c_n|, \tag{2.15}$$

where $a_n = c_{n-1}$, or $b_n = c_{n-1}$, from which we obtain

$$|a_n - b_n| = 2|c_{n-1} - c_n|, \tag{2.16}$$

so that

$$|c_n - \alpha| < |a_n - b_n| = 2|c_{n-1} - c_n|. \tag{2.17}$$

To determine the solution α with an error ε, we must calculate the terms of the sequence $\{c_n\}$, $n \in \mathbb{N}$, until the relation

$$2|c_{n-1} - c_n| < \varepsilon \tag{2.18}$$

is fulfilled. We then have an *a posteriori estimation of the error*.

In the second method, we start from the relation

$$|c_n - \alpha| < b_n - a_n = \frac{b - a}{2^n}. \tag{2.19}$$

To determine now the solution α with an error ε, we must calculate n terms of the sequence $\{c_n\}$, $n \in \mathbb{N}$, so that

$$\frac{b - a}{2^n} < \varepsilon \Rightarrow n = \left[\frac{\ln\left(\frac{b-a}{\varepsilon}\right)}{\ln 2}\right] + 1, \tag{2.20}$$

where the brackets represent the entire part of the fraction. We then have an *a priori estimation of the error*.

Observation 2.1 If equation (2.1) has several roots on the interval $[a, b]$, the above algorithm leads to one of these roots.

2.2   THE CHORD (SECANT) METHOD

Let us consider the equation[2]

$$f(x) = 0, \tag{2.21}$$

where $f : [a, b] \subset \mathbb{R} \to \mathbb{R}$, f continuous on $[a, b]$, with a single root on the interval $[a, b]$. We construct a point $c \in [a, b]$ using the following rule. Let us consider the straight line AB, where $A(a, f(a))$ and $B(b, f(b))$. The equation of this line, denoted by (d) in Figure 2.1, is

$$\frac{y - f(a)}{f(b) - f(a)} = \frac{x - a}{b - a}. \tag{2.22}$$

The value of the abscissa c of the intersection point of the straight line (d) with the Ox-axis is given by the equation

$$\frac{-f(a)}{f(b) - f(a)} = \frac{c - a}{b - a}, \tag{2.23}$$

from which we obtain

$$c = \frac{af(b) - bf(a)}{f(b) - f(a)}. \tag{2.24}$$

The method consists firstly in verifying if a or b is solution of equation (2.21). If $f(a) = 0$ or $f(b) = 0$, then the procedure stops. Otherwise, we determine c using formula (2.24). If $f(c) = 0$, then the algorithm ends, the required solution of equation (2.21) being found. If $f(c) \neq 0$, then we calculate the products. If $f(a) \cdot f(c) < 0$, then the solution is in the interval $[a, c]$, and if $f(a) \cdot f(c) > 0$, then, obviously, we consider the interval $[c, b]$. Thus, the interval $[a, b]$ is replaced by one of the intervals $[a, c]$ or $[c, b]$, the length of which is strictly smaller than that of the interval $[a, b]$.

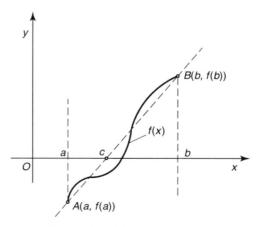

Figure 2.1   The chord method.

[2]The method was known by the Babylonian and Egyptian mathematicians in different forms. It also appears (as regula falsi) in the papers of Abu Kamil (tenth century), Qusta ibn Luqa (tenth century), and Leonardo of Pisa (Fibonacci, 1202).

The chord method involves the construction of three sequences $\{a_n\}$, $\{b_n\}$, and $\{c\}$, $n \in \mathbb{N}$, defined recurrently as follows:

$$a_0 = a, \quad b_0 = b, \quad c_n = \frac{a_n f(b_n) - b_n f(a_n)}{f(b_n) - f(a_n)}, \quad a_{n+1} = \begin{cases} a_n & \text{if } f(a_n) \cdot f(c_n) < 0 \\ c_n & \text{otherwise} \end{cases};$$

$$b_{n+1} = \begin{cases} b_n & \text{if } f(c_n) \cdot f(b_n) < 0 \\ c_n & \text{otherwise} \end{cases}.$$

(2.25)

Theorem 2.2 Let $f : [a, b] \to \mathbb{R}$, $f \in C^0([a, b])$, f with a single root in the interval $[a, b]$. Under these conditions, the sequence $\{c_n\}$, defined by relations (2.25), converges to α, the unique solution of equation (2.21) in the interval $[a, b]$.

Demonstration. The sequences $\{a_n\}$ and $\{b_n\}$, $n \in \mathbb{N}$, satisfy the relation

$$a_n < b_n, \quad (\forall) \; n \; \in \; \mathbb{N}. \tag{2.26}$$

Indeed, for $n = 0$ we have $a_0 = a < b = b_0$.
On the other hand, if $f(c_{n-1}) \neq 0$, then we have

$$a_n - b_n = c_{n-1} - b_n = \frac{a_{n-1} f(b_{n-1}) - b_{n-1} f(a_{n-1})}{f(b_{n-1}) - f(a_{n-1})} - b_{n-1} = \frac{f(b_{n-1})(a_{n-1} - b_{n-1})}{f(b_{n-1}) - f(a_{n-1})}$$

(2.27)

for $a_n = c_{n-1}$, and

$$a_n - b_n = a_{n-1} - c_{n-1} = a_{n-1} - \frac{a_{n-1} f(b_{n-1}) - b_{n-1} f(a_{n-1})}{f(b_{n-1}) - f(a_{n-1})} = -\frac{f(a_{n-1})}{f(b_{n-1}) - f(a_{n-1})}$$

(2.28)

for $b_n = c_{n-1}$, respectively.
Let us suppose that $f(a) < 0$ and $f(b) > 0$, which leads to $f(a_n) < 0$ and $f(b_n) > 0$, $(\forall) \; n \in \mathbb{N}$, respectively. In this case, it follows that $a_n - b_n$ has the same sign as $a_{n-1} - b_{n-1}$. By complete induction we obtain $a_n < b_n$, hence relation (2.26) is true.
We have

$$a_n < c_n < b_n, \quad (\forall) n \in \mathbb{N}. \tag{2.29}$$

Indeed, we can write

$$a_n - c_n = a_n - \frac{a_n f(b_n) - b_n f(a_n)}{f(b_n) - f(a_n)} = -\frac{f(a_n)(a_n - b_n)}{f(b_n) - f(a_n)} < 0 \tag{2.30}$$

and

$$b_n - c_n = b_n - \frac{a_n f(b_n) - b_n f(a_n)}{f(b_n) - f(a_n)} = -\frac{f(b_n)(b_n - a_n)}{f(b_n) - f(a_n)} > 0, \tag{2.31}$$

respectively, hence relation (2.29) is true.
We thus show that the sequence $\{a_n\}_{n \in \mathbb{N}}$ is monotone increasing and superior bounded by any element b_n of the sequence $\{b_n\}_{n \in \mathbb{N}}$, in particular by $b_0 = b$. Hence, the sequence $\{a_n\}_{n \in \mathbb{N}}$ is convergent, and let A be its limit. Analogically, the sequence $\{b_n\}_{n \in \mathbb{N}}$ is monotone decreasing and inferior bounded by any element of the sequence $\{a_n\}_{n \in \mathbb{N}}$, particularly by $a_0 = a$; hence, the sequence $\{b_n\}_{n \in \mathbb{N}}$ is convergent, and let B be its limit. We thus obtain

$$\lim_{n \to \infty} a_n = A, \quad \lim_{n \to \infty} b_n = B, \quad A \leq B, \quad A, B \in [a, b]. \tag{2.32}$$

Let us show now that the sequence $\{c_n\}$ is convergent.

Case 2.1   We suppose that $A = B$. Using inequality (2.29) and passing to the limit, we obtain

$$A = \lim_{n \to \infty} a_n \leq \lim_{n \to \infty} c_n \leq \lim_{n \to \infty} b_n = B \tag{2.33}$$

and the theorem of tongs leads to

$$\lim_{n \to \infty} c_n = A = B. \tag{2.34}$$

On the other hand,

$$f(A) = f(\lim_{n \to \infty} a_n) = \lim_{n \to \infty} f(a_n) \leq 0 \tag{2.35}$$

and

$$f(B) = f(\lim_{n \to \infty} b_n) = \lim_{n \to \infty} f(b_n) \geq 0; \tag{2.36}$$

because of the continuity of f, the limit commutes with the function. It follows from equation (2.35) and equation (2.36) that $f(A) = f(\lim_{n \to \infty} c_n) = 0$ and, because f has a single root in the interval $[a, b]$, we deduce that $A = \alpha$, hence $\lim_{n \to \infty} c_n = \alpha$.

Case 2.2   We suppose that $A \neq B$. Let us assume at the very beginning that it is not possible to have $f(A) = f(B) = 0$ because f has only one root in the interval $[a, b]$. Hence, $f(A) \neq f(B)$. Let us now pass to the limit for

$$c_n = \frac{a_n f(b_n) - b_n f(a_n)}{f(b_n) - f(a_n)}. \tag{2.37}$$

We get

$$\lim_{n \to \infty} c_n = \lim_{n \to \infty} \frac{a_n f(b_n) - b_n f(a_n)}{f(b_n) - f(a_n)} = \frac{Af(B) - Bf(A)}{f(B) - f(A)}. \tag{2.38}$$

If $f(A) = 0$ and $f(B) \neq 0$, then relation (2.38) leads to

$$\lim_{n \to \infty} c_n = \frac{Af(B) - B \cdot 0}{f(B) - 0} = A, \tag{2.39}$$

hence $c_n \to \alpha$. If $f(B) = 0$ and $f(A) \neq 0$, then relation (2.38) leads to

$$\lim_{n \to \infty} c_n = \frac{A \cdot 0 - Bf(A)}{0 - f(A)} = B, \tag{2.40}$$

so that we get once more $c_n \to \alpha$. Finally, if $f(A) \neq 0$ and $f(B) \neq 0$, it is obvious that $f(A) < 0$ and $f(B) > 0$.

On the other hand, the inequalities

$$A < \frac{Af(B) - Bf(A)}{f(B) - f(A)} < B \tag{2.41}$$

hold, which is evident because they lead to

$$-Af(A) < -Bf(A) \quad \text{and} \quad Af(B) < Bf(B). \tag{2.42}$$

Passing now to the limit in equation (2.37) and taking into account inequality (2.41), we get

$$A < \lim_{n \to \infty} c_n < B, \tag{2.43}$$

so that we have $a_{n+1} = c_n$ or $b_{n+1} = c_n$ for any $n \geq 0$. Hence,

$$\{c_n | n \in \mathbf{N}\} \subset \{a_m | m \in \mathbf{N}^*\} \cup \{b_m | m \in \mathbf{N}^*\} \subset (-\infty, A) \cup (B, +\infty), \tag{2.44}$$

from which

$$\lim_{n \to \infty} c_n \in (-\infty, A] \cup [B, \infty). \tag{2.45}$$

Relations (2.43) and (2.45) are in contradiction so that this case is not possible, and the theorem is proved.

Theorem 2.3 (*a posteriori* estimation of the error). Let $f : [a, b] \to \mathbb{R}$, f continuous on $[a, \ b]$ and derivable on $(a, \ b)$; we suppose that f has a single root α on $[a, b]$ and that there exist the real and strict positive constants $m > 0$, $M > 0$ such that

$$m \leq |f'(x)| \leq M, \quad (\forall)x \in (a, b). \tag{2.46}$$

Under these conditions, the relation

$$|c_{n-1} - \alpha| \leq \frac{M}{m}|c_n - c_{n-1}|, \tag{2.47}$$

which represents the a posteriori estimation of the error in the chord method, holds.

Demonstration. Assuming that $f(c_{n-1}) \neq 0$, we can write

$$c_n - c_{n-1} = \frac{a_n f(b_n) - b_n f(a_n)}{f(b_n) - f(a_n)} - a_n = \frac{f(a_n)(a_n - b_n)}{f(b_n) - f(a_n)} \tag{2.48}$$

if $f(c_{n-1}) < 0$ and

$$c_n - c_{n-1} = \frac{a_n f(b_n) - b_n f(a_n)}{f(b_n) - f(a_n)} - b_n = \frac{f(b_n)(a_n - b_n)}{f(b_n) - f(a_n)} \tag{2.49}$$

if $f(c_{n-1}) > 0$, respectively.

Let us apply now Lagrange's finite increments formula to the function f on the interval $[a_n, \ b_n]$. Hence, there exists $\xi \in (a_n, \ b_n)$ such that

$$f(b_n) - f(a_n) = f'(\xi)(b_n - \ a_n). \tag{2.50}$$

From equation (2.48), equation (2.49), and equation (2.50) we get

$$c_n - c_{n-1} = -\frac{f(a_n)}{f'(\xi)} \quad \text{for } f(c_{n-1}) < 0 \tag{2.51}$$

or

$$c_n - c_{n-1} = -\frac{f(b_n)}{f'(\xi)} \quad \text{for } f(c_{n-1}) > 0. \tag{2.52}$$

Let us now apply Lagrange's formula to the restriction of the function f on the interval $[a_n, \alpha]$. Hence, there exists $\xi_n \in (a_n, \alpha)$ such that

$$f(\alpha) - f(a_n) = f'(\xi_n)(\alpha - a_n); \tag{2.53}$$

because $f(\alpha) = 0$, we get

$$-f(a_n) = f'(\xi_n)(\alpha - a_n). \tag{2.54}$$

Obviously, in the case $f(c_{n-1}) > 0$, we apply Lagrange's formula to the restriction of function f in the interval (α, b_n), the calculation being analogous. From equation (2.51) and equation (2.54), it follows that

$$c_n - c_{n-1} = -\frac{f'(\xi_n)(\alpha - a_n)}{f'(\xi_n)}. \tag{2.55}$$

On the other hand, we can write the relations

$$|c_n - c_{n-1}| \geq |\alpha - c_{n-1}|, \quad |\alpha - a_n| \leq |c_n - c_{n-1}|, \tag{2.56}$$

$$|f'(\xi_n)| \leq M, \quad |f'(\xi_n)| \geq m, \tag{2.57}$$

so that, by applying the modulus, expression (2.55) leads to

$$|\alpha - c_{n-1}| \leq \frac{M}{m}|c_n - c_{n-1}|. \tag{2.58}$$

Theorem 2.4 (a priori estimation of the error). Let $f : [a, b] \to \mathbb{R}$, f having a single root on $[a, b]$. If f is convex, strictly increasing, and derivable on $[a, b]$ and if $f'(a) > 0$, then the relation

$$\alpha - c_n \leq \left[1 - \frac{f'(a)}{f'(b)}\right]^n (\alpha - c_0) \leq \left[1 - \frac{f'(a)}{f'(b)}\right]^n (b - a) \tag{2.59}$$

holds.

Demonstration. Because f is convex, we deduce that f' is strictly increasing on $[a, b]$ so that we have

$$f'(a) < f'(x) < f'(b), \quad (\forall)x \in (a, b). \tag{2.60}$$

From equation (2.37), taking into account that f is convex and supposing that $f(a) < 0$, $f(b) > 0$, we obtain

$$\alpha - c_n = \alpha - \frac{c_{n-1}f(b) - bf(c_{n-1})}{f(b) - f(c_{n-1})} = \frac{f(b)(\alpha - c_{n-1}) - f(c_{n-1})(\alpha - b)}{f(b) - f(c_{n-1})}. \tag{2.61}$$

We now apply Lagrange's theorem to the function f on the interval $[\alpha, b]$; hence, there exists $\xi \in (\alpha, b)$ such that

$$f(b) - f(\alpha) = f'(\xi)(b - \alpha). \tag{2.62}$$

Analogically, applying Lagrange's formula to the function f on the interval $[c_{n-1}, \alpha]$, it results in the existence of $\zeta \in (c_{n-1}, \alpha)$, for which we can write

$$f(\alpha) - f(c_{n-1}) = f'(\zeta)(\alpha - c_{n-1}). \tag{2.63}$$

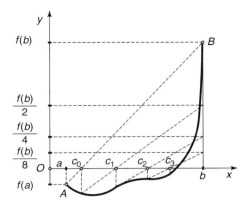

Figure 2.2   Modified chord method.

Because $f(\alpha) = 0$, expressions (2.62) and (2.63) take a simpler form

$$f(b) = f'(\xi)(b - \alpha), \tag{2.64}$$

$$-f(c_{n-1}) = f'(\zeta)(\alpha - c_{n-1}), \tag{2.65}$$

respectively.Replacing the last two relations in formula (2.61), we obtain

$$\alpha - c_n = \frac{f'(\xi) - f'(\zeta)}{f(b) - f(c_{n-1})}(b - \alpha)(\alpha - c_{n-1}). \tag{2.66}$$

Because $\zeta < \xi$ and f' is strictly increasing, we get

$$f'(\xi) - f'(\zeta) > 0. \tag{2.67}$$

On the other hand, $f(b) > 0$ and $f(c_{n-1}) < 0$. Relation (2.66) leads now to

$$\alpha - c_n \leq \frac{f'(\xi) - f'(\zeta)}{f(b)}(b - \alpha)(\alpha - c_{n-1}). \tag{2.68}$$

Replacing relation (2.64) in the last formula, we get

$$\alpha - c_n \leq \frac{f'(\xi) - f'(\zeta)}{f'(\xi)}(\alpha - c_{n-1}) = \left[1 - \frac{f'(\zeta)}{f'(\xi)}\right](\alpha - c_{n-1}) \leq \left[1 - \frac{f'(a)}{f'(b)}\right](\alpha - c_{n-1}). \tag{2.69}$$

If we write relation (2.69) for $n - 1, n - 2, \dots, 1$, it results in

$$\alpha - c_n \leq \left[1 - \frac{f'(a)}{f'(b)}\right]^n (\alpha - c_0) \leq \left[1 - \frac{f'(a)}{f'(b)}\right]^n (b - a), \tag{2.70}$$

and the theorem is proved.

A variant of this method supposes the division by 2, at each step, of the value of the function at the end at which it is maintained. The situation is presented in a graphical form in Figure 2.2.

In the case considered in the figure, we obtain the results

$$c_0 = \frac{af(b) - bf(a)}{f(b) - f(a)}, \quad c_1 = \frac{c_0 \frac{f(b)}{2} - bf(c_0)}{\frac{f(b)}{2} - f(c_0)}, \quad c_2 = \frac{c_1 \frac{f(b)}{4} - bf(c_1)}{\frac{f(b)}{4} - f(c_1)}, \quad c_3 = \frac{c_2 \frac{f(b)}{8} - bf(c_2)}{\frac{f(b)}{8} - f(c_2)}. \tag{2.71}$$

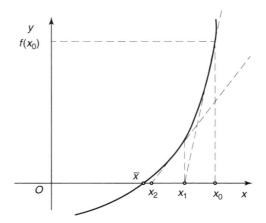

Figure 2.3   The tangent method.

2.3   THE TANGENT METHOD (NEWTON)

Let us consider the equation[3]

$$f(x) = 0, \tag{2.72}$$

with the root $\overline{x}$, and let $(\overline{x} - \Delta, \overline{x} + \Delta)$ be the interval on which equation (2.72) has a single solution (obviously $\overline{x}$).

Let us consider the point $x_0 \in (\overline{x} - \Delta, \; \overline{x} + \Delta)$ and let us construct the tangent to the graph of the function f at the point $(x_0, f(x_0))$ (Fig. 2.3); the corresponding equation is

$$y - f(x_0) = f'(x_0)(x - x_0). \tag{2.73}$$

The point of intersection with the Ox-axis is given by

$$-f(x_0) = f'(x_0)(x_1 - x_0), \tag{2.74}$$

from which

$$x_1 = x_0 - \frac{f(x_0)}{f'(x_0)}. \tag{2.75}$$

The last formula allows the construction of a recurrent sequence $\{x_n\}_{n \in \mathbb{N}}$ in the form

$$x_0 \in (\overline{x} - \Delta, \overline{x} + \Delta), \quad x_{n+1} = x_n - \frac{f(x_n)}{f'(x_n)}. \tag{2.76}$$

The tangent method consists in the construction of the terms of the sequence $\{x_n\}_{n \in \mathbb{N}}$ until a certain criterion of stopping is satisfied, that is, until we obtain $\overline{x}$ or until the modulus of the difference between two consecutive terms x_n and x_{n+1} of the sequence is smaller than an ε a priori given.

[3]The method is sometimes called the Newton–Raphson method. It appears in *De analysi per aequationes numero terminorum infinitas* (1711) by Isaac Newton (1642–1727) used for finding polynomials roots, in *De metodis fluxionum et serierum infinitarum* (1736) by Isaac Newton, again for polynomials roots, in *A Treatise of Algebra both Historical and Practical* by John Wallis (1690), and in *Analysis aequationum universalis* (1690) by Joseph Raphson (circa 1648–circa 1715). The general case of the method for arbitrary equations was given by Thomas Simpson in 1740.

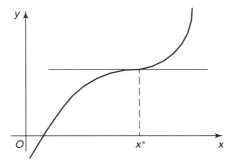

Figure 2.4 The tangent at the point x^* at the graph of the function f is horizontal and it does not intersect the Ox-axis.

Therefore, we state the following theorem.

Theorem 2.5 Let us consider the function $f : (\overline{x} - \Delta, \overline{x} + \Delta) \to \mathbb{R}$, with $f(\overline{x}) = 0$, which has a single root in the interval $(\overline{x} - \Delta, \overline{x} + \Delta)$. Let us suppose that f is twice derivable on $(\overline{x} - \Delta, \overline{x} + \Delta)$ and that there exist the real, strictly positive constants $\alpha > 0$, $\beta > 0$ so as to have $|f'(x)| \geq \alpha$, $|f'(x)| \leq \beta$ for any $x \in (\overline{x} - \Delta, \overline{x} + \Delta)$. If we denote by λ the value $\min\{\Delta, 2\alpha/\beta\}$, then, for any $x_0 \in (\overline{x} - \lambda, \overline{x} + \lambda)$, the sequence $\{x_n\}_{n \in \mathbb{N}}$, defined by relations (2.76), converges to $\overline{x}$.

Demonstration. Let us observe firstly that, because of the hypothesis of the existence of the constant $\alpha > 0$, the derivative f' does not vanish on the interval $(\overline{x} - \Delta, \overline{x} + \Delta)$. Hence, the situation considered in Figure 2.4, in which the tangent to the graph of the function f at the point x^* is horizontal, cannot be accepted in the hypothesis considered.

Taking into account the existence of the constant $\beta > 0$, we can state that if $\widetilde{x} \in (\overline{x} - \Delta, \overline{x} + \Delta)$ such that $|f'(\widetilde{x})| < \infty$ exists, then we have $|f'(x)| < \infty$ for any $x \in (\overline{x} - \Delta, \overline{x} + \Delta)$. Therefore, let us apply Lagrange's formula of finite increments to the function f' on the interval defined by the ends $\widetilde{x}$ and x. We deduce the existence of a point ξ in this interval for which we have

$$|f'(x) - f'(\widetilde{x})| = |x - \widetilde{x}| \cdot |f''(\xi)| \leq \beta |x - \widetilde{x}| \leq \beta \Delta, \tag{2.77}$$

from which

$$2\beta \Delta + f'(\widetilde{x}) \leq f'(x) \leq 2\beta \Delta + f'(\widetilde{x}), \tag{2.78}$$

hence $|f'(x)| < \infty$. Thus, the hypotheses of the theorem avoid the situation in Figure 2.5, which leads to $x = x^*$ in the iteration sequence (2.76) ($x_n = x_{n+k}$, for any $k \geq 1$).

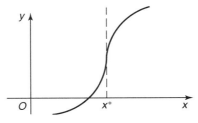

Figure 2.5 The tangent at the point x^* at the graph of the function f is vertical and, by iteration of relation (2.76) for $x = x^*$ we get $x_n = x_{n+k}$ for any $k \geq 1$.

We cannot have $|f'(x)| = \infty$ for any $x \in (\overline{x} - \Delta, \overline{x} + \Delta)$ because the graph of f would be a vertical straight line passing through x^* so that f can no more be a function in the sense of the known definition.

The sequence $\{x_n\}_{n \in N}$ satisfies the relation

$$|\overline{x} - x_{n+1}| \leq \frac{\beta}{2\alpha} |\overline{x} - x_n|^2. \tag{2.79}$$

Indeed, we may write successively

$$|\overline{x} - x_{n+1}| = \left| \overline{x} - x_n + \frac{f(x_n)}{f'(x_n)} \right| = \left| \frac{f'(x_n)(\overline{x} - x_n) + f(x_n)}{f'(x_n)} \right| = \left| \frac{-f'(x_n)(\overline{x})x_n - f(x_n)}{f'(x_n)} \right|, \tag{2.80}$$

so that

$$|\overline{x} - x_{n+1}| = \left| \frac{f(\overline{x}) - f(x_n) - f'(x_n)(\overline{x} - x_n)}{f'(x_n)} \right|, \tag{2.81}$$

because $f(\overline{x}) = 0$.

On the other hand, by representing the function f by means of a Taylor series around the point x_n, we have

$$f(\overline{x}) = f(x_n) + \frac{\overline{x} - x_n}{1!} f'(x_n) + \frac{(\overline{x} - x_n)^2}{2!} f''(\xi), \tag{2.82}$$

where ξ is a point situated between $\overline{x}$ and x_n.

From relations (2.81) and (2.82) we get

$$|\overline{x} - x_{n+1}| = \left| \frac{(\overline{x} - x_n)^2 f''(\xi)}{2!} \right| \left| \frac{1}{f'(x_n)} \right| \tag{2.83}$$

and, taking into account that $|f'(x_n)| \geq \alpha$, $|f''(\xi)| \leq \beta$, we obtain equation (2.79).

To show that the sequence $\{x_n\}_{n \in N}$ has its terms in the interval $(\overline{x} - \lambda, \overline{x} + \lambda)$, we use an induction method. The affirmation is obvious for $n = 0$ because of the choice of x_0. Let us now suppose that $x_n \in (\overline{x} - \lambda, \overline{x} + \lambda)$. From equation (2.79) we get

$$|\overline{x} - x_{n+1}| \leq \frac{\beta}{2\alpha} |\overline{x} - x_n|^2 < \frac{\beta}{2\alpha} \cdot \lambda^2 = \left(\frac{\beta}{2\alpha} \lambda \right) \cdot \lambda \leq \lambda, \tag{2.84}$$

which leads to

$$-\lambda < \overline{x} - x_{n+1} < \lambda, \quad \overline{x} - \lambda < x_{n+1} < \overline{x} + \lambda, \tag{2.85}$$

hence $x_{n+1} \in (\overline{x} - \lambda, \overline{x} + \lambda)$. Therefore, if $x_n \in (\overline{x} - \lambda, \overline{x} + \lambda)$, then $x_{n+1} \in (\overline{x} - \lambda, \overline{x} + \lambda)$ and also $x_0 \in (\overline{x} - \lambda, \overline{x} + \lambda)$. It follows that $x_n \in (\overline{x} - \lambda, \overline{x} + \lambda)$ for any $n \in \mathbb{N}$.

To show that $\{x_n\}_{n \in \mathbb{N}}$ converges to $\overline{x}$, we multiply expression (2.79) by $\beta/(2\alpha)$. We obtain

$$\frac{\beta}{2\alpha} |\overline{x} - x_{n+1}| \leq \left[\frac{\beta}{2\alpha} (\overline{x} - x_n) \right]^2. \tag{2.86}$$

Let us denote by $\{z_n\}_{n \in \mathbb{N}}$ the sequence defined by

$$z_n = \frac{\beta}{2\alpha} (\overline{x} - x_n), \quad n \in \mathbb{N}, \tag{2.87}$$

so that equation (2.86) can now be written as

$$z_{n+1} \leq z_n^2. \tag{2.88}$$

Written for $n - 1$, $n - 2$, $\ldots$, 0, relation (2.88) leads to

$$z_{n+1} \leq z_0^{2^{n+1}}.$$ (2.89)

On the other hand,

$$z_0 = \frac{\beta}{2\alpha} |\bar{x} - x_0| < \frac{\beta}{2\alpha} \lambda \leq 1,$$ (2.90)

corresponding to the definition of λ. Finally, there results

$$\lim_{n \to \infty} z_n = 0, \quad \lim_{n \to \infty} \frac{\beta}{2\alpha} |\bar{x} - x_n| = 0,$$ (2.91)

from which

$$\lim_{n \to \infty} x_n = \bar{x},$$ (2.92)

so that the sequence $\{x_n\}_{n \in \mathbb{N}}$ converges to the single root $\bar{x} \in (\bar{x} - \Delta, \bar{x} + \Delta)$ of the equation $f(x) = 0$.

Proposition 2.1 (*a priori* estimation of the tangent method). If $\lambda < 2\alpha/\beta$, then the relation

$$|\bar{x} - x_n| \leq \frac{2\alpha}{\beta} \left(\frac{\beta}{2\alpha} \lambda \right)^{2^n}$$ (2.93)

exists under the conditions of Theorem 2.5.

Demonstration. We can easily obtain

$$\frac{\beta}{2\alpha}(\bar{x} - x_n) \leq \left[\frac{\beta}{2\alpha} (\bar{x} - x_0) \right]^{2^n} < \left(\frac{\beta}{2\alpha} \lambda \right)^{2^n},$$ (2.94)

from relation (2.79), and the proposition is proved.

Observation 2.2   To obtain the root $\bar{x}$ with a precision ε we get, from formula (2.93), the estimation

$$\frac{2\alpha}{\beta} \left(\frac{\beta}{2\alpha} \lambda \right)^{2^n} < \varepsilon,$$ (2.95)

from which we get the number of iteration steps

$$n = \left[\ln \left[\ln \left(\frac{\varepsilon \beta}{2\alpha} \right) / \ln \left(\frac{\beta \lambda}{2\alpha} \right) \right] / \ln 2 \right] + 1,$$ (2.96)

whereby the entire part of the function within square brackets is proved.

Proposition   2.2 (*a posteriori* estimation of the error in the tangent method). We   have   the expression

$$|x_{n+1} - \bar{x}| \leq \frac{\beta}{2\alpha} |x_{n+1} - x_n|^2,$$ (2.97)

in the frame of Theorem 2.5.

Demonstration. By expansion into a Taylor series of the function f around x_n, we get

$$f(x_{n+1}) = f(x_n) + \frac{x_{n+1} - x_n}{1!} f'(x_n) + \frac{(x_{n+1} - x_n)^2}{2!} f''(\zeta), \qquad (2.98)$$

from which

$$f(x_{n+1}) - f(x_n) - \frac{x_{n+1} - x_n}{1} f'(x_n) = \frac{(x_{n+1} - x_n)^2}{2} f''(\zeta), \qquad (2.99)$$

where ζ is a point situated between x_n and x_{n+1}. Applying the modulus to equation (2.99) and taking into account equation (2.76), we get

$$|f(x_{n+1})| = \frac{(x_{n+1} - x_n)^2}{2} |f''(\zeta)|. \qquad (2.100)$$

On the other hand, from the hypotheses of Theorem 2.5 we obtain

$$|f''(\zeta)| \leq \beta, \qquad (2.101)$$

and relation (2.100) may be transcribed into the form

$$|f(x_{n+1})| \leq \frac{\beta}{2} |x_{n+1} - x_n|^2. \qquad (2.102)$$

Applying the formula of finite increments to the function f between the points x_{n+1} and $\bar{x}$ (the root of the equation $f(x) = 0$ in the interval $(\bar{x} - \Delta, \bar{x} + \Delta)$), the existence of a point ξ between x_{n+1} and $\bar{x}$ such that

$$f(x_{n+1}) - f(\bar{x}) = f'(\xi)(x_{n+1} - \bar{x}) \qquad (2.103)$$

is proved.

Taking into account that $f(\bar{x}) = 0$, relations (2.102) and (2.103) lead to

$$|f'(\xi)||x_{n+1} - \bar{x}| \leq \frac{\beta}{2} |x_{n+1} - x_n|^2 \qquad (2.104)$$

and, taking into account that $|f'(\xi)| \geq \alpha$, we obtain relation (2.97), which we had to prove.

Observation 2.3   To obtain the root $\bar{x}$ with precision ε, formula (2.97) leads to

$$\frac{\beta}{2\alpha} |x_{n+1} - x_n|^2 < \varepsilon, \qquad (2.105)$$

from which

$$|x_{n+1} - x_n| < \sqrt{\frac{2\alpha\varepsilon}{\beta}}; \qquad (2.106)$$

the iteration algorithm continues until the modulus of the difference of two consecutive iterations becomes smaller than $\sqrt{2\alpha\varepsilon/\beta}$.

Theorem 2.6   Let $f : [a, \ b] \to \mathbb{R}$ a function that satisfies the following conditions:

    (i) f' is strictly positive on $(a, \ b)$, that is, $f'(x) > 0$, $(\forall) \ x \in (a, \ b)$;
   (ii) f'' is strictly positive on $(a, \ b)$, hence $f''(x) > 0$, $(\forall) \ x \in (a, \ b)$;
  (iii) f has a single root $\bar{x}$ in the interval $(a, \ b)$.

In the above hypotheses, the sequence $\{x_n\}_{n\in\mathbb{N}}$, defined by relation (2.76) with $f(x_0) > 0$, is a sequence of real numbers that converges to $\bar{x}$.

Demonstration. The sequence $\{x_n\}_{n\in\mathbb{N}}$ is a decreasing one. To prove this, we write Taylor's relation for the points x_{n+1} and x_n so that

$$f(x_{n+1}) = f(x_n) + \frac{x_{n+1} - x_n}{1!} f'(x_n) + \frac{(x_{n+1} - x_n)^2}{2!} f''(\xi), \qquad (2.107)$$

where ξ is a point between x_n and x_{n+1}.

On the other hand, from relation (2.76) we obtain

$$f(x_n) + f'(x_n)(x_{n+1} - x_n) = 0, \qquad (2.108)$$

which, replaced in formula (2.107), leads to

$$f(x_{n+1}) = \frac{f''(\xi)}{2} (x_{n+1} - x_n)^2. \qquad (2.109)$$

Taking into account hypothesis (ii), we get $f(x_{n+1}) > 0$, $(\forall)\ n \geq 0$, and because $f(x_0) > 0$ it follows that $f(x_n) > 0$, $(\forall)\ n\ \in\ \mathbb{N}$.

Relation (2.76) may be written in the form

$$x_{n+1} - x_n = -\frac{f(x_n)}{f'(x_n)} \qquad (2.110)$$

and because $f(x_n) > 0$, $f'(x_n) > 0$ (hypothesis (i)), we have

$$x_{n+1} - x_n < 0, \qquad (2.111)$$

and hence the sequence $\{x_n\}_{n\in\mathbb{N}}$ is a decreasing one (even strictly decreasing).

The sequence $\{x_n\}_{n\in\mathbb{N}}$ is inferior bounded by $\bar{x}$, the unique solution of the equation $f(x) = 0$ in the interval $(a,\ b)$. Indeed, because $f(x_n) \geq 0$, $(\forall)\ n\ \in\ \mathbb{N}$, and the function f is strictly increasing on $(a,\ b)$ (hypothesis (i)) and $f(\bar{x}) = 0$, we obtain $x_n \geq \bar{x}$, $(\forall)\ n \in \mathbb{N}$, and hence the sequence $\{x_n\}_{n\in\mathbb{N}}$ is inferior bounded by $\bar{x}$.

From the previous two steps, we deduce that $\{x_n\}_{n\in\mathbb{N}}$ is convergent; let x^* be its limit. Passing to the limit for $n \to \infty$ in the definition relation (2.76), we get

$$\lim_{n\to\infty} x_{n+1} = \lim_{n\to\infty} x_n - \lim_{n\to\infty} \frac{f(x_n)}{f'(x_n)}, \qquad (2.112)$$

from which

$$x^* = x^* - \frac{f(x^*)}{f'(x^*)}, \qquad (2.113)$$

hence $f(x^*) = 0$. But $f(\bar{x}) = 0$ and f have a single root in $(a,\ b)$ such that $x^* = \bar{x}$; hence the theorem is proved.

Observation 2.4

(i) Theorem 2.6 makes sure that, in the conditions of the hypotheses, the sequence $\{x_n\}_{n\in\mathbb{N}}$ is convergent to $\bar{x}$ with $f(\bar{x}) = 0$, and x_0 can be taken arbitrarily in the interval $(a,\ b)$, with the condition $f(x_0) > 0$. In particular, if the conditions (i) and (ii) are satisfied at the point b, we can take $x_0 = b$.

(ii) If the function f is strictly concave and decreasing, then we can consider the function $-f$, which has the same root $\bar{x}$, attaining the hypotheses of Theorem 2.6.

(iii) If f is strictly convex and decreasing, then we can take $x_0 = a$, assuming that the hypotheses (i) and (ii) of Theorem 2.6 are satisfied at the point a.

(iv) If the function f is strictly concave and increasing, then we consider the function $-f$, which satisfies the conditions of point (iii) of this observation.

Observation 2.5   We can no more give formulae for an a priori or an a posteriori estimation of the error in the conditions of Theorem 2.6. Therefore, the sequence of iterations stops usually when $|x_{n+1} - x_n|^2 < \varepsilon$, where ε is the imposed error.

Observation 2.6   Newton's method presented here has at least two deficiencies. The first one consists in the choice of intervals of the form $(\bar{x} - \mu, \bar{x} + \mu)$, where $\bar{x}$ is the required solution, that is, intervals centered just at the point $\bar{x}$, which is unknown. This deficiency can be easily eliminated for functions twice differentiable as shown later. The second deficiency arises because in any iteration step we must calculate $f(x_n)$ as well as $f'(x_n)$. We can construct a simplified Newton's method in which we need not calculate $f'(x_n)$ every time, but always use $f'(x_0)$. Such a method is given by Theorem 2.8.

Theorem 2.7 (general procedure of choice of the start point x_0). Let $f : [a, b] \to \mathbb{R}$ be a function twice differentiable for which $f(a) < 0$ and $f(b) > 0$. Let us suppose that there exist the strict positive constants α and β such that $|f'(x)| \geq \alpha$ and $|f''(x)| \leq \beta$ for any $x \in [a,\ b]$. We apply the bisection method to the equation $f(x) = 0$ on the interval $[a,\ b]$ until we obtain an interval $[m_1,\ m_2]$ for which $a < m_1$, $m_2 < b$ and $m_2 - m_1 < 2\alpha/\beta$. Choosing $x_0 \in (m_1,\ m_2)$, the sequence of successive iterations given by Newton's method converges to the unique solution $\bar{x}$ of the equation $f(x) = 0$ in the interval $[a,\ b]$.

Demonstration. From the condition $|f'(x)| \geq \alpha$, $\alpha > 0$ and because f is twice differentiable, it follows that $f'(x)$ does not change the sign in the interval $[a,\ b]$. But $f(a) < 0$ and $f(b) > 0$, and hence f is strictly increasing ($f'(x) > 0$, $(\forall)x \in [a, b]$). Hence, f has a single solution $\bar{x}$ in the interval $[a,\ b]$ so that such a hypothesis is not necessary.

Let $[\gamma'_n, \gamma''_n]$ be the interval obtained at the nth iteration in the bipartition method. It is known that the sequences $\{\gamma'_n\}_{n \in \mathbb{N}}$ and $\{\gamma''_n\}_{n \in \mathbb{N}}$ converge to $\bar{x}$. Let us introduce the value

$$\varepsilon = \min \left\{ \bar{x} - a, b - \bar{x}, \frac{2\alpha}{\beta} \right\}; \tag{2.114}$$

we observe that $\varepsilon > 0$.

There result the following statements:

- there exists n' such that $|\gamma'_n - \bar{x}| < \varepsilon$ for $n > n'$;
- there exists n'' such that $|\gamma''_n - \bar{x}| < \varepsilon$ for $n > n''$;
- there exists n''' such that $|\gamma'''_n - \bar{x}| < \varepsilon$ for $n > n'''$.

Let us denote $n_\varepsilon = \max\{n',\ n'',\ n'''\}$. From the above three statements, we obtain

$$|\gamma'_n - \bar{x}| < \varepsilon, |\gamma''_n - \bar{x}| < \varepsilon, |\gamma'''_n - \bar{x}| < \varepsilon, \quad \text{with } n > n_\varepsilon. \tag{2.115}$$

We denote by $[m_1, \ m_2]$ the interval $[\gamma'_n, \gamma''_n]$ corresponding to $n = n_\varepsilon + 1$. The first inequality (2.115) leads to

$$-\varepsilon < \overline{x} - m_1 < \varepsilon; \tag{2.116}$$

hence, because $a - \overline{x} > \varepsilon$, we get $m_1 > a$. Analogically, from the second relation (2.115) we obtain $m_2 < b$, and hence the last relation (2.115) leads to

$$m_2 - m_1 < \varepsilon < \frac{2\alpha}{\beta}. \tag{2.117}$$

On the other hand, the interval $[m_1, \ m_2]$ can be written in the form

$$\left[a + i\frac{b-a}{2^{n_\varepsilon+1}}, a + (i+1)\frac{b-a}{2^{n_\varepsilon+1}} \right], \tag{2.118}$$

with $i \in \mathbb{N}$, $i > 0$ (because $m_1 > a$) and $i + 1 < 2^{n_\varepsilon+1}$ (because $m_2 < b$). We have

$$m_1 - (m_2 - m_1) = a + (i-1)\frac{b-a}{2^{n_\varepsilon+1}} \geq a, \tag{2.119}$$

$$m_2 - (m_2 - m_1) = a + (i+2)\frac{b-a}{2^{n_\varepsilon+1}} \leq b. \tag{2.120}$$

Considering that $\overline{x} \in (m_1, \ m_2)$, we get

$$m_1 > \overline{x} - (m_2 - m_1), \ m_2 < \overline{x} + (m_2 - m_1), \ \overline{x} - (m_2 - m_1) > a, \ \overline{x} + (m_2 - m_1) < b. \tag{2.121}$$

Introducing the notation

$$\Delta = m_2 - m_1, \tag{2.122}$$

we are led to the sequence of inclusions

$$(m_1, \ m_2) \subset (\overline{x} - \Delta, \ \overline{x} + \Delta) \subset [a, \ b]. \tag{2.123}$$

On the other hand, $m_2 - m_1 < 2\alpha/\beta$, hence $\lambda = m_2 - m_1 = \Delta$ in Theorem 2.5.

Theorem 2.8 (simplified Newton's method). Let $f : (\overline{x} - \Delta, \overline{x} + \Delta) \to \mathbb{R}$ be a function for which $\overline{x}$ is its single root in the interval $(\overline{x} - \Delta, \overline{x} + \Delta)$. Let us suppose that f is twice differentiable on $(\overline{x} - \Delta, \overline{x} + \Delta)$ and that there exist two strictly positive constants α and β such that $|f'(\alpha)| \geq \alpha$ and $|f''(x)| \leq \beta$ for any $x \in (\overline{x} - \Delta, \overline{x} + \Delta)$. Also, let λ be such that $0 < \lambda < \min\{\Delta, \alpha/(2\beta)\}$. Under these conditions, the sequence $\{x_n\}_{n \in \mathbb{N}}$ defined by

$$x_0 \in (\overline{x} - \lambda, \overline{x} + \lambda), \ x_{n+1} = x_n - \frac{f(x_n)}{f'(x_0)}, \quad \text{with } f'(x_0) \neq 0 \tag{2.124}$$

converges to $\overline{x}$ (Fig. 2.6).

Demonstration. Let us show that $x_n \in (\overline{x} - \lambda, \overline{x} + \lambda)$ for any $n \in \mathbb{N}$ using the induction method. By the choice of x_0, it follows that the statement is true for $n = 0$. Let us suppose that the affirmation is true for n and let us state it for $n + 1$. We have, successively,

$$|\overline{x} - x_{n+1}| = \left| \overline{x} - x_n + \frac{f(x_n)}{f'(x_0)} \right| = \left| \frac{f'(x_0)(\overline{x} - x_n) + f(x_n)}{f'(x_0)} \right|. \tag{2.125}$$

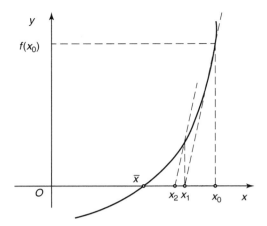

Figure 2.6   Simplified Newton's method.

On the other hand, $f(\overline{x}) = 0$, and the previous relation leads to

$$|\overline{x} - x_{n+1}| = \frac{1}{|f'(x_0)|}|f'(x_0)(\overline{x} - x_n) + f(x_n) - f(\overline{x})|. \tag{2.126}$$

Let us now apply Lagrange's formula of finite increments to the function f on the interval defined by the points x_n and $\overline{x}$. It results in the existence of a point ξ situated between x_n and $\overline{x}$ such that

$$f(x_n) - f(\overline{x}) = f'(\xi)(x_n - \overline{x}). \tag{2.127}$$

Relation (2.126) becomes

$$|\overline{x} - x_{n+1}| = \frac{1}{|f'(x_0)|}|[f'(x_0) - f'(\xi)](\overline{x} - x_n)|. \tag{2.128}$$

We now apply Lagrange's formula to the function f' on the interval defined by the points x_0 and ξ; let us deduce that there exists a point ζ in this interval such that

$$f'(x_0) - f'(\xi) = f''(\zeta)(x_0 - \xi). \tag{2.129}$$

Relation (2.128) now becomes

$$|\overline{x} - x_{n+1}| = \frac{1}{|f'(x_0)|}|f''(\zeta)||x_0 - \xi||\overline{x} - x_n|. \tag{2.130}$$

Taking into account the hypotheses of the theorem concerning the derivatives f' and f'' and the constants $\alpha > 0$ and $\beta > 0$, relation (2.130) leads to

$$|\overline{x} - x_{n+1}| \le \frac{\beta}{\alpha}|x_0 - \xi||\overline{x} - x_n|. \tag{2.131}$$

We may now write the following sequence of relations

$$|x_0 - \xi| = |x_0 - \overline{x} + \overline{x} - \xi| \le |x_0 - \overline{x}| + |\overline{x} - \xi| \le \lambda + \lambda = 2\lambda; \tag{2.132}$$

from equation (2.131) and equation (2.132) we obtain

$$|\overline{x} - x_{n+1}| \leq \frac{2\beta\lambda}{\alpha}|\overline{x} - x_n|. \tag{2.133}$$

By the choice of λ in the hypotheses of the theorem, we get $2\beta\lambda/\alpha < 1$; hence,

$$|\overline{x} - x_{n+1}| < |\overline{x} - x_n|. \tag{2.134}$$

The induction hypothesis $|\overline{x} - x_n| < \lambda$ leads to $|\overline{x} - x_{n+1}| < \lambda$, hence $x_{n+1} \in (\overline{x} - \lambda, \overline{x} + \lambda)$, and the induction principle states that $x_n \in (\overline{x} - \lambda, \overline{x} + \lambda)$ for any $n \in \mathbb{N}$.

Let us show that $x_n \to \overline{x}$ for $n \to \infty$. We write relation (2.133) for $n - 1, n - 2, \ldots, 0$, hence

$$|\overline{x} - x_{n+1}| \leq \left(\frac{2\beta\lambda}{\alpha}\right)^{n+1} |\overline{x} - x_0|; \tag{2.135}$$

because $2\beta\lambda/\alpha < 1$, we get

$$|\overline{x} - x_{n+1}| \to 0 \quad \text{for } n \to \infty, \tag{2.136}$$

that is, $\lim\limits_{n \to \infty} x_n = \overline{x}$, and the theorem is proved.

Proposition 2.3 (*a priori* estimation of the error in Newton's simplified method). The relation

$$|\overline{x} - x_n| \leq \left(\frac{2\beta\lambda}{\alpha}\right)^n \lambda \tag{2.137}$$

exists under the conditions of Theorem 2.8.

Demonstration. If we write relation (2.135) for n, that is,

$$|x - x_n| \leq \left(\frac{2\beta\lambda}{\alpha}\right)^n |\overline{x} - x_0|, \tag{2.138}$$

and if we consider that $x_0 \in (\overline{x} - \lambda, \overline{x} + \lambda)$, hence $|\overline{x} - x_0| < \lambda$, we obtain the formula required.

Observation 2.7   If we wish to determine $\overline{x}$ with an imposed accuracy ε, then we have to consider

$$|\overline{x} - x_n| \leq \left(\frac{2\beta\lambda}{\alpha}\right)^n \lambda < \varepsilon; \tag{2.139}$$

we thus obtain the necessary iteration steps in the simplified Newton's method

$$n = \left[\ln\left(\frac{\varepsilon}{\lambda}\right) / \ln\left(\frac{2\beta\lambda}{\alpha}\right)\right] + 1, \tag{2.140}$$

where, as is usual, the square brackets denote the entire part of the function.

Proposition 2.4 (*a posteriori* estimation of the error in the simplified Newton method). The relation

$$|x_{n+1} - \overline{x}| \leq \frac{2\beta\lambda}{\alpha}|x_{n+1} - x_n| \tag{2.141}$$

exists under the conditions of Theorem 2.8.

Demonstration. Let us write Taylor's formula for the function f at the points x_{n+1} and x_n. We have

$$f(x_{n+1}) = f(x_n) + \frac{x_{n+1} - x_n}{1!} f'(x_n) + \frac{(x_{n+1} - x_n)^2}{2!} f''(\xi),$$ (2.142)

where ξ is a point between x_n and x_{n+1}. From the definition of the sequence $\{x_n\}_{n \in \mathbb{N}}$, we obtain the relation

$$f(x_n) = f'(x_0)(x_n - x_{n+1}),$$ (2.143)

which, when replaced in equation (2.142), leads to

$$f(x_{n+1}) = [f'(x_0) - f'(x_n)](x_n - x_{n+1}) + \frac{(x_{n+1} - x_n)^2}{2} f''(\xi).$$ (2.144)

Let us now apply Lagrange's formula to the function $f'(x)$ for the points x_0 and x_n. It follows that there exists ζ such that

$$f'(x_0) - f'(x_n) = f''(\zeta)(x_0 - x_n).$$ (2.145)

From equation (2.145) and equation (2.144), we get

$$f(x_{n+1}) = f''(\zeta)(x_0 - x_n)(x_n - x_{n+1}) + \frac{(x_{n+1} - x_n)^2}{2} f''(\xi).$$ (2.146)

In modulus, we obtain

$$|f(x_{n+1})| = \left| f''(\zeta)(x_0 - x_n)(x_n - x_{n+1}) + \frac{(x_{n+1} - x_n)^2}{2} f''(\xi) \right|$$

$$\leq \left[|f''(\zeta)| |x_0 - x_n| + \frac{|f''(\xi)|}{2} |x_{n+1} - x_n| \right] |x_{n+1} - x_n|.$$ (2.147)

On the other hand, we have

$$|x_0 - x_n| = |x_0 - \bar{x} + \bar{x} - x_n| \leq |x_0 - \bar{x}| + |\bar{x} - x_n| < 2\lambda$$ (2.148)

and

$$|x_{n+1} - x_n| = |x_{n+1} - \bar{x} + \bar{x} - x_n| \leq |x_{n+1} - \bar{x}| + |\bar{x} - x_n| < 2\lambda.$$ (2.149)

Hence,

$$|f(x_{n+1})| \leq \left[|f''(\zeta)| |x_0 - x_n| + \frac{|f''(\xi)|}{2} |x_{n+1} - x_n| \right] |x_{n+1} - x_n|$$

$$< [2\lambda |f''(\zeta)| + \lambda |f''(\xi)|] |x_{n+1} - x_n|.$$ (2.150)

The condition of boundedness of $|f''(x)|$ on $(\bar{x} - \Delta, \bar{x} + \Delta)$, expressed by $|f''(x)| < \beta$ with $\beta > 0$, and relation (2.150) lead to

$$|f(x_{n+1})| < 3\beta\lambda |x_{n+1} - x_n|.$$ (2.151)

Let us now apply Lagrange's formula to the function f and for the points x_{n+1} and $\bar{x}$,

$$f(x_{n+1}) - f(\bar{x}) = f'(\gamma)(x_{n+1} - \bar{x}),$$ (2.152)

where γ is a point situated between x_{n+1} and $\bar{x}$.

On the other hand, $f(\overline{x}) = 0$ so that

$$f(x_{n+1}) = f'(\gamma)(x_{n+1} - \overline{x}), \tag{2.153}$$

which, when introduced in relation (2.151), leads to

$$|f'(\gamma)||x_{n+1} - \overline{x}| < 3\beta\lambda|x_{n+1} - x_n|. \tag{2.154}$$

Considering that $|f'(x)| \geq \alpha$ for any $x \in (\overline{x} - \Delta, \overline{x} + \Delta)$, the above formula leads to relation (2.141) so that the proposition is proved.

Observation 2.8   If we wish to determine $\overline{x}$ with an imposed precision ε, then we must continue the sequence of iterations (2.124) until

$$|x_{n+1} - x_n| < \frac{\alpha\varepsilon}{3\beta\lambda}. \tag{2.155}$$

Observation 2.9   The statements in Observation 2.4 remain valid in this case too.

2.4   THE CONTRACTION METHOD

Let us consider the equation

$$f(x) = 0 \tag{2.156}$$

with $f : I \to \mathbb{R}$, where I is an interval of the real axis.

We suppose that we can rewrite the formula in the form

$$x = \phi(x), \tag{2.157}$$

assuming that $\overline{x}$ is a solution of equation (2.156) if and only if it is a solution of equation (2.157).

Definition 2.1   The roots of equation (2.157) are called *fixed points of the function* ϕ.

Observation 2.10   The passing from equation (2.156) to equation (2.157) is not unique. Indeed, let us consider that

$$\phi(x) = x - \lambda f(x), \tag{2.158}$$

where λ is a real arbitrary parameter. In this case, any root $\overline{x}$ of equation (2.156) is also a root of equation (2.157) and the converse is also true.

Let us consider an approximation x_0 of the root of equation (2.157) and let us construct the sequence $\{x_n\}_{n \in \mathbb{N}}$ defined by the relation of recurrence

$$x_{n+1} = \phi(x_n), \quad n \geq 0. \tag{2.159}$$

We have to state sufficient conditions for this sequence so as to converge to the root $\overline{x}$ of equation (2.157).

Definition 2.2   Let $\mathcal{B}$ be a Banach space and $\phi : \mathcal{B} \to \mathcal{B}$ an application for which there exists $q \in (0, \ 1)$ such that for any two elements x and y of $\mathcal{B}$ we have

$$\|\phi(x) - \phi(y)\| \leq q\|x - y\|. \tag{2.160}$$

Such a function is called *contraction*.

Theorem 2.9 (Stefan Banach (1892–1945)). Let $\mathcal{B}$ be a Banach space and ϕ a contraction on it. In this case, the sequence $\{x_n\}_{n\in\mathbb{N}}$ defined by equation (2.159) is convergent to the unique root $\bar{x}$ for any $x_0 \in \mathcal{B}$.

Demonstration. Let us consider two successive terms x_n and x_{n+1} of the sequence $\{x_n\}_{n\in\mathbb{N}}$ for which we can write

$$\|x_{n+1} - x_n\| = \|\phi(x_n) - \phi(x_{n-1})\| \leq q\|x_n - x_{n-1}\| \leq q^2\|x_{n-1} - x_{n-2}\| \leq \cdots \leq q^n\|x_1 - x_0\|. \tag{2.161}$$

On the other hand,

$$
\begin{aligned}
\|x_{n+p} - x_n\| &= \|x_{n+p} - x_{n+p-1} + x_{n+p-1} - x_{n+p-2} + \cdots + x_{n+1} - x_n\| \\
&\leq \|x_{n+p} - x_{n+p-1}\| + \|x_{n+p-1} - x_{n+p-2}\| + \cdots + \|x_{n+1} - x_n\| \\
&\leq q^{n+p-1}\|x_1 - x_0\| + q^{n+p-2}\|x_1 - x_0\| + \cdots + q^n\|x_1 - x_0\| \\
&= q^n\|x_1 - x_0\|(q^{p-1} + q^{p-2} + \cdots + 1) = q^n\|x_1 - x_0\|\frac{1 - q^p}{1 - q} < \frac{q^n}{1 - q}\|x_1 - x_0\|.
\end{aligned}
\tag{2.162}
$$

The sequence $\{x_n\}_{n\in\mathbb{N}}$ is a Cauchy one. Indeed, for any $\varepsilon > 0$ there exists $n_\varepsilon \in \mathbb{N}$ such that for any $n \geq n_\varepsilon$ and for any $p > 0$, $p \in \ \mathbb{N}$, to have the relation

$$\|x_{n+p} - x_n\| < \varepsilon. \tag{2.163}$$

It is sufficient to assume

$$\frac{q^n}{1 - q}\|x_1 - x_0\| < \varepsilon, \tag{2.164}$$

as relation (2.162) suggests; hence, $\{x_n\}_{n\in\mathbb{N}}$ is a Cauchy sequence. Because $\mathcal{B}$ is a Banach space, we state that $\{x_n\}_{n\in\mathbb{N}}$ is convergent, and let

$$x^* = \lim_{n\to\infty} x_n. \tag{2.165}$$

We observe that ϕ satisfies condition (2.160) because it is a contraction, and hence it is continuous. We may write

$$x^* = \lim_{n\to\infty} \phi(x_n) = \phi(\lim_{n\to\infty} x_n) = \phi(x^*), \tag{2.166}$$

Hence, $x^* = \bar{x}$ is a root of equation (2.157).

Let us show that $\bar{x}$ is the unique solution of equation (2.157). Per absurdum, let us suppose that $\bar{x}$ is not the unique solution of equation (2.157) and let $\bar{\bar{x}}$ be another solution of the same. We have

$$\|\bar{x} - \bar{\bar{x}}\| = \|\phi(\bar{x}) - \phi(\bar{\bar{x}})\| \leq q\|\bar{x} - \bar{\bar{x}}\| < \|\bar{x} - \bar{\bar{x}}\|, \tag{2.167}$$

because ϕ is a contraction, and hence $\bar{x}$ is unique.

Corollary 2.1   Let $\phi : [a, b] \to \mathbb{R}$ so that

(a) for any $x \in [a, \ b]$, we have $\phi(x) \in [a, b]$;

(b) there exists $q \in (0, 1)$, such that for any x, y of $[a, \ b]$ we have

$$|\phi(x) - \phi(y)| \leq q|x - y|. \tag{2.168}$$

Under these conditions,

(i) if $x_0 \in [a, \ b]$, then $x_n \in [a, \ b]$ for any $n \in \mathbb{N}$ and the sequence $\{x_n\}_{n \in \mathbb{N}}$ is convergent;

(ii) if $\overline{x} = \lim\limits_{n \to \infty} x_n$, then $\overline{x}$ is the unique root of equation (2.157) in $[a, \ b]$.

Demonstration. We can apply Banach's theorem 2.9 because the set of real numbers $\mathbb{R}$ is a Banach space and relation (2.170) shows that ϕ is a contraction.

On the other hand, $\phi(x) \in [a, b]$ for any $x \in [a, b]$ and, because $x_0 \in [a, b]$, we successively deduce that $x_1 = \phi(x_0) \in [a, b]$, $x_2 \in [a, b]$, $\ldots$, $x_n \in [a, b]$, $\ldots$; hence the corollary is proved.

Corollary 2.2   Let $\phi : [a, b] \to \mathbb{R}$ so that

(a) we have $\phi(x) \in [a, b]$ for any $x \in [a, b]$;

(b) ϕ is differentiable on $[a, b]$ and there exists $q \in (0, \ 1)$ such that

$$|\phi'(x)| \leq q < 1, \quad \text{for any } x \in [a, \ b]. \tag{2.169}$$

Under these conditions,

(i) if $x_0 \in [a, b]$, then $x_n \in [a, b]$ for any $n \in \mathbb{N}$ and the sequence $\{x_n\}_{n \in \mathbb{N}}$ is convergent;

(ii) if $\overline{x} = \lim\limits_{n \to \infty} x_n$, then $\overline{x}$ is the only root of equation (2.170) in $[a, b]$.

Demonstration. Let us consider $x \in [a, b]$, $y \in [a, b]$, $x < y$. Under these conditions, we can apply Lagrange's formula of finite increments to the function ϕ on the interval $[x, y]$. Hence, there exists $\xi \in (x, y)$ such that

$$\phi(y) - \phi(x) = \phi'(\xi)(x - y). \tag{2.170}$$

Applying the modulus, we get

$$|\phi(x) - \phi(y)| = |\phi'(\xi)||x - y|, \tag{2.171}$$

from which

$$|\phi(x) - \phi(y)| \leq \sup_{\xi \in [a,b]} |\phi'(\xi)||x - y| \leq q|x - y|, \tag{2.172}$$

so that we can use Corollary 2.1.

Observation 2.11   To apply a method using the above considerations, we must solve the following problems:

(i) the determination of the interval $[a, b]$ so as to have $\phi(x) \in [a, b]$ for any $x \in [a, b]$;

(ii) ϕ is a contraction on the interval $[a, b]$.

Proposition 2.5   Let $\phi : [a - \lambda, a + \lambda] \to \mathbb{R}$ be a contraction of the contraction constant q. If $|\phi(a) - a| \leq (1 - q)\lambda$, then there exists the relation $\phi([a - \lambda, a + \lambda]) \subseteq [a - \lambda, a + \lambda]$.

Demonstration. Let $x \in [a - \lambda, a + \lambda]$. We have

$$|\phi(x) - a| = |\phi(x) - \phi(a) + \phi(a) - a| \leq |\phi(x) - \phi(a)| + |\phi(a) - a|. \tag{2.173}$$

On the other hand, ϕ is a contraction, hence

$$|\phi(x) - \phi(a)| \leq q|x - a|. \tag{2.174}$$

If we take into account the hypothesis and relation (2.174), then relation (2.173) leads to

$$|\phi(x) - a| \leq q|x - a| + (1 - q)\lambda. \tag{2.175}$$

Because $x \in [a - \lambda, a + \lambda]$, it follows that

$$|x - a| \leq \lambda \tag{2.176}$$

so that relation (2.175) allows

$$|\phi(x) - a| \leq q\lambda + (1 - q)\lambda = \lambda, \tag{2.177}$$

that is,

$$\phi(x) \in [a - \lambda, a + \lambda], \quad \text{for any } x \in [a - \lambda, \ a + \lambda], \tag{2.178}$$

and the proposition is proved.

Proposition 2.6   Let $\phi : [a, b] \to \mathbb{R}$. If ϕ satisfies the conditions

  (a) ϕ is differentiable on $[a, b]$;
  (b) the equation $x = \phi(x)$ has a root $\overline{x} \in (\alpha, \beta)$, with

$$\alpha = a + \frac{b - a}{3}, \quad \beta = b - \frac{b - a}{3}; \tag{2.179}$$

  (c) there exists $q \in (0, \ 1)$ such that

$$|\phi'(x)| \leq q < 1, \quad \text{for any } x \in [a, \ b]; \tag{2.180}$$

  (d) $x_0 \in (\alpha, \beta)$;

then

   (i) the sequence $\{x_n\}_{n \in \mathbb{N}}$ has all the terms in the interval $(a, \ b)$;
   (ii) the sequence $\{x_n\}_{n \in \mathbb{N}}$ is convergent and $\lim\limits_{n \to \infty} x_n = \overline{x}$;
   (iii) $\overline{x}$ is the unique solution of the equation $x = \phi(x)$ in (a, b).

Demonstration. The points (ii) and (iii) are obvious consequences of Corollary 2.2.

To demonstrate point (i), let $x_1 = \phi(x_0)$. Applying the finite increments formula to the function ϕ between the points x_0 and $\overline{x}$, it follows that there exists ξ between x_0 and $\overline{x}$ such that

$$|x_1 - \overline{x}| = |\phi(x_0) - \phi(\overline{x})| = |\phi'(\xi)||x_0 - \overline{x}|. \tag{2.181}$$

On the other hand,

$$|\phi'(\xi)| \leq \sup_{\xi \in [a,b]} |\phi'(\xi)| \leq q < 1 \tag{2.182}$$

and relation (2.181) allows

$$|x_1 - \overline{x}| \leq q|x_0 - \overline{x}| \leq q(\beta - \alpha) < \frac{b-a}{3}; \tag{2.183}$$

hence, $x_1 \in (a, b)$. Let us suppose that $x_{n-1} \in (a, b)$ and $|x_{n-1} - \overline{x}| < (b-a)/3$. We wish to show that $|x_n - \overline{x}| < (b-a)/3$. We have

$$|x_n - \overline{x}| = |\phi(x_{n-1}) - \phi(\overline{x})|. \tag{2.184}$$

We now apply Lagrange's finite increments formula between the points x_{n-1} and $\overline{x}$ so that

$$|\phi(x_{n-1}) - \phi(\overline{x})| = |x_{n-1} - \overline{x}||\phi'(\zeta)| \leq |x_{n-1} - \overline{x}| \sup_{\zeta \in [a,b]} |\phi'(\zeta)| \leq q\frac{b-a}{3} < \frac{b-a}{3}; \tag{2.185}$$

hence, $x_n \in (a, b)$; this is valid for any $n \in \mathbb{N}$, taking into account the mathematical induction principle.

Proposition 2.7 (*a priori* estimation of the error in the contractions method). Let $x = \phi(x)$ with $\phi : [a, b] \to [a, b]$, ϕ contraction, and let $\overline{x}$ be its unique root in $[a, b]$. Let $\{x_n\}_{n \in \mathbb{N}}$ be the sequence of successive approximations defined by the recurrence relation (2.159). Under these conditions, there exists the relation

$$|x_n - \overline{x}| \leq q^n(b-a), \tag{2.186}$$

where q is the contraction constant of ϕ, $0 < q < 1$.

Demonstration. Formula (2.186) is an obvious consequence of the successive relations

$$|x_n - \overline{x}| = |\phi(x_{n-2}) - \phi(\overline{x})| \leq q|x_{n-1} - \overline{x}|$$
$$= q|\phi(x_{n-2}) - \phi(\overline{x})| \leq q^2|x_{n-2} - \overline{x}| \leq \cdots \leq q^n|x_0 - \overline{x}|, \tag{2.187}$$

where

$$|x_0 - \overline{x}| \leq b - a. \tag{2.188}$$

Observation 2.12 To determine the solution $\overline{x}$ of equation (2.157) with precision ε, we must determine the necessary number n_ε of iterations from

$$q^n(b-a) < \varepsilon, \tag{2.189}$$

from which

$$n_\varepsilon = \left[\frac{\ln\left[\varepsilon/(b-a)\right]}{\ln q} \right] + 1, \tag{2.190}$$

where the square brackets represent the entire part function.

Proposition 2.8 (*a posteriori* **estimation of the error in the contractions method**). Let $x = \phi(x)$ with $\phi : [a, b] \to [a, b]$ a contraction of the contraction constant q, $0 < q < 1$, and let $\bar{x}$ be the unique root of this equation in $[a, b]$. Let us also consider the sequence $\{x_n\}_{n \in \mathbb{N}}$ of successive approximations defined by the recurrence relation (2.159). Under these conditions, there exists the relation

$$|x_n - \bar{x}| \leq \frac{1}{1 - q} |x_{n+1} - x_n| \tag{2.191}$$

for any $n \in \mathbb{N}$.

Demonstration. Formula (2.162) leads to the relation

$$|x_{n+p} - x_n| = |x_{n+p} - x_{n+p-1} + x_{n+p-1} - x_{n+p-2} + \cdots + x_{n+1} - x_n|$$
$$\leq |x_{n+p} - x_{n+p-1}| + |x_{n+p-1} - x_{n+p-2}| + \cdots + |x_{n+1} - x_n|$$
$$\leq q^{p-1}|x_{n+1} - x_n| + q^{p-2}|x_{n+1} - x_n| + \cdots + |x_{n+1} - x_n| = \frac{1 - q^p}{1 - q}|x_{n+1} - x_n|. \tag{2.192}$$

We pass to the limit for $p \to \infty$ in relation (2.192), hence

$$\lim_{p \to \infty} |x_{n+p} - x_n| \leq \lim_{p \to \infty} \frac{1 - q^p}{1 - q}|x_{n+1} - x_n| \tag{2.193}$$

and, because $\lim_{p \to \infty} x_{n+p} = \bar{x}$ and $\lim_{p \to \infty} q^p = 0$, we obtain formula (2.191), which had to be proved.

Observation 2.13   To determine the solution of equation (2.157) with precision ε, we must calculate the terms of the sequence $\{x_n\}_{n \in \mathbb{N}}$ until

$$\frac{1}{1 - q}|x_{n+1} - x_n| < \varepsilon, \tag{2.194}$$

from which

$$|x_{n+1} - x_n| < \varepsilon(1 - q). \tag{2.195}$$

2.5   THE NEWTON–KANTOROVICH METHOD

We now deal with a variant[4] of Newton's method, where the successive iterations sequence is defined by a contraction.

Theorem 2.10   Let $f : [x^* - \lambda, x^* + \lambda] \to \mathbb{R}$, $f(x^*) \neq 0$, be a twice differentiable function. Let us denote this as

$$a = |f'(x^*)|, \tag{2.196}$$

$$c = |f(x^*)|. \tag{2.197}$$

We also suppose that there exists $b > 0$ such that

$$|f''(x)| \leq b, \quad \text{for any } x \in [x^* - \lambda, x^* + \lambda] \tag{2.198}$$

---

[4]The theorem was stated by Leonid Vitaliyevich Kantorovich (1912–1986) in 1940.

and let us denote

$$\mu = \frac{bc}{2a^2}. \tag{2.199}$$

If $\mu < 1/4$, under these conditions, the application

$$g(x) = x - \frac{f(x)}{f'(x^*)} \tag{2.200}$$

is a contraction from $[x^* - ky^*, x^* + ky^*]$ to $[x^* - ky^*, x^* + ky^*]$, where

$$k = \frac{c}{a}, \tag{2.201}$$

and y^* is the smallest solution of the equation

$$\mu y^2 - y + 1 = 0, \tag{2.202}$$

that is,

$$y^* = \frac{1 - \sqrt{1 - 4\mu}}{2\mu}. \tag{2.203}$$

Demonstration. Firstly, we show that $g([x^* - ky^*, x^* + ky^*]) \subseteq [x^* - ky^*, x^* + ky^*]$. Let us calculate $|g(x) - x^*|$. We have

$$|g(x) - x^*| = \left| x - \frac{f(x)}{f'(x^*)} - x^* \right| = \left| x - x^* - \frac{f(x)}{f'(x^*)} + \frac{f(x^*)}{f'(x^*)} - \frac{f(x^*)}{f'(x^*)} \right|$$

$$= \left| \frac{f'(x^*)(x - x^*) - f(x) + f(x^*)}{f'(x^*)} - \frac{f(x^*)}{f'(x^*)} \right|$$

$$\leq \frac{1}{|f'(x^*)|} |f'(x^*)(x - x^*) - f(x) + f(x^*)| + \left| \frac{f(x^*)}{f'(x^*)} \right|. \tag{2.204}$$

If we take into account relations (2.196), (2.197), and (2.201), then relation (2.204) leads to

$$|g(x) - x^*| \leq \frac{1}{a} |f'(x^*)(x - x^*) - f(x) + f(x^*)| + k. \tag{2.205}$$

Taylor's formula written for the points x and x^* leads to

$$f(x) = f(x^*) + f'(x^*)(x - x^*) + \frac{1}{2} f''(\xi)(x - x^*)^2, \tag{2.206}$$

where ξ is a point situated between x and x^*. Obviously, it follows that

$$|f'(x^*)(x - x^*) - f(x) + f(x^*)| \leq \frac{1}{2} |f''(\xi)|(x - x^*)^2 \tag{2.207}$$

and, taking into account condition (2.198), we have

$$|f'(x^*)(x - x^*) - f(x) + f(x^*)| \leq \frac{1}{2} b(x - x^*)^2. \tag{2.208}$$

We obtain

$$|g(x) - x^*| \leq \frac{b}{2a}|x - x^*|^2 + k \tag{2.209}$$

from relations (2.205) and (2.206). On the other hand, $x \in [x^* - ky^*, x^* + ky^*]$, hence

$$|x - x^*| \leq ky^* \tag{2.210}$$

and relation (2.209) leads to

$$|g(x) - x^*| \leq \frac{b}{2a}k^2(y^*)^2 + k = k\left[\frac{bc}{2a^2}(y^*)^2 + 1\right]. \tag{2.211}$$

From relations (2.199) and (2.202), we get

$$\frac{bc}{2a^2}(y^*)^2 + 1 = \mu(y^*)^2 + 1 = y^*, \tag{2.212}$$

hence

$$|g(x) - x^*| \leq ky^*. \tag{2.213}$$

Concluding, $g([x^* - ky^*, x^* + ky^*]) \subset [x^* - ky^*, x^* + ky^*]$.
    Let us show now that g is a contraction. We have

$$|g(x)| = \left|1 - \frac{f'(x)}{f'(x^*)}\right| = \left|\frac{1}{f'(x^*)}\right||f'(x^*) - f'(x)|. \tag{2.214}$$

Applying the finite increments formula to the function f' for the points x and x^*, it follows that there exists η between x and x^* such that

$$f'(x^*) - f'(x) = f''(\eta)(x^* - x) \tag{2.215}$$

and, applying the modulus to the last relation, we get

$$|f'(x^*) - f'(x)| = |f''(\eta)||x^* - x|. \tag{2.216}$$

Taking into account equation (2.198), relation (2.216) leads to

$$|f'(x^*) - f'(x)| \leq b|x^* - x|. \tag{2.217}$$

Relations (2.214) and (2.217) imply that

$$|g'(x)| \leq \frac{1}{|f'(x^*)|}b|x^* - x| \tag{2.218}$$

and, taking into account equation (2.197), we obtain

$$|g'(x)| \leq b|x^* - x|. \tag{2.219}$$

Applying now formulae (2.210), (2.201), and (2.199), we get

$$|g'(x)| \leq \frac{b}{a}ky^* = 2\mu y^* = 1 - \sqrt{1 - 4\mu}. \tag{2.220}$$

Because $0 < \mu < 1/4$, we get $|g'(x)| < 1$ and can choose as contraction constant

$$q = 1 - \sqrt{1 - 4\mu} < 1, \tag{2.221}$$

proving that g is a contraction.

Observation 2.14   We must obviously have

$$[x^* - ky^*, x^* + ky^*] \subset [x^* - \lambda, x^* + \lambda]. \tag{2.222}$$

To fulfill condition (2.222), it is sufficient that

$$ky^* \le \lambda, \tag{2.223}$$

from which

$$k \le \frac{\lambda}{y^*} = \frac{2\lambda\mu}{1 - \sqrt{1 - 4\mu}}. \tag{2.224}$$

Observation 2.15   The solution $\bar{x}$ of the equation

$$x = g(x), \tag{2.225}$$

which is the same as that of the equation

$$f(x) = 0, \tag{2.226}$$

is obtained by constructing the sequence

$$x_0 \in [x^* - ky^*, x^* + ky^*] \text{ arbitrary}, \quad x_{n+1} = g(x_n), \quad n \ge 0. \tag{2.227}$$

Observation 2.16   The formulae that define the *a priori* estimation of the error

$$|\bar{x} - x_n| \le \frac{q^n}{1 - q}|x_1 - x_0| \tag{2.228}$$

and the *a posteriori* estimation of the error

$$|\bar{x} - x_n| \le \frac{1}{1 - q}|x_{n+1} - x_n|, \tag{2.229}$$

respectively, are obviously those in the contractions method, specifying that q is given by equation (2.221).

2.6 NUMERICAL EXAMPLES

Consider the equation

$$f(x) = x - \frac{1 - \sin x}{2} = 0, \quad x \in [0, 1]. \tag{2.230}$$

We observe that $f(0) = -0.5$ and $f(1) = 0.9207$; we also have

$$f'(x) = 1 + 0.5 \cos x, \tag{2.231}$$

hence $f'(x) > 0$ for $x \in [0, 1]$. We conclude that the equation $f(x) = 0$ has only one root in the interval $[0, 1]$.

Let us apply the bipartition method to solve equation (2.230). The calculation is given in Table 2.1.

We may state that

$$\overline{x} \in [0.333984375, 0.3359375]. \tag{2.232}$$

We now apply the method of the chord to solve equation (2.230); the calculation may be found in Table 2.2.

It follows that

$$\overline{x} \approx 0.335418. \tag{2.233}$$

The recurrence formula in the tangent method reads

$$x_{n+1} = x_n - \frac{x_n - 0.5(1 - \sin x_n)}{1 + 0.5 \cos x_n}. \tag{2.234}$$

Because

$$f'(x) = 1 + 0.5 \cos x, \quad f''(x) = -0.5 \sin x \tag{2.235}$$

TABLE 2.1   Solution of Equation (2.229) by the Bipartition Method

Step	a_n	b_n	c_n	$f(a_n)$	$f(b_n)$	$f(c_n)$
0	0	1	0.5	−0.5	0.9207	0.2397 > 0
1	0	0.5	0.25	−0.5	0.2397	−0.1263 < 0
2	0.25	0.5	0.375	−0.1263	0.2397	0.0581 > 0
3	0.25	0.375	0.3125	−0.1263	0.0581	−0.0338 < 0
4	0.3125	0.375	0.34375	−0.0338	0.0581	0.0123 > 0
5	0.3125	0.34375	0.328125	−0.0338	0.0123	−0.0107 < 0
6	0.328125	0.34375	0.3359375	−0.0107	0.0123	0.0008 > 0
7	0.328125	0.3359375	0.33203125	−0.0107	0.0008	−0.005 < 0
8	0.33203125	0.3359375	0.333984375	−0.005	0.0008	−0.0021 < 0

TABLE 2.2   Solution of Equation (2.229) by the Chord Method

Step	a_n	b_n	c_n	$f(a_n)$	$f(b_n)$	$f(c_n)$
0	0	1	0.351931	−0.5 < 0	0.920735	0.024287 > 0
1	0	0.351931	0.335628	−0.5 < 0	0.024287	0.000309 > 0
2	0	0.335628	0.335421	−0.5 < 0	0.000309	4×10^{-6} > 0
3	0	0.335421	0.335418	−0.5 < 0	4×10^{-6} > 0	≈ 0

and $f'(x) > 0$, $f''(x) \leq 0$ for $x \in [0, \ 1]$, we deduce that the function f is strictly increasing and concave on the interval $[0, \ 1]$. We may thus choose

$$x_0 = a = 0. \tag{2.236}$$

The calculations are given in Table 2.3.
We obtain

$$\overline{x} \approx 0.335418. \tag{2.237}$$

Let us solve the same problem by means of the modified Newton method, for which

$$x_{n+1} = x_n - \frac{x_n - 0.5(1 - \sin x)}{1.5}. \tag{2.238}$$

The calculations are given in Table 2.4.
We get

$$\overline{x} \approx 0.335418. \tag{2.239}$$

To solve equation (2.230) by the contractions method, we write it in the form

$$x = 0.5(1 - \sin x) = \phi(x). \tag{2.240}$$

Taking into account that the derivative

$$\phi'(x) = -0.5 \cos x, \quad |\phi'(x)| \leq 0.5 < 1, \tag{2.241}$$

it follows that $\phi(x)$ is a contraction such that the recurrence formula is of the form

$$x_{n+1} = \phi(x_n) = 0.5(1 - \sin x_n); \tag{2.242}$$

the calculation is given in Table 2.5.

TABLE 2.3   Solution of Equation (2.229) by the Tangent Method

Step	x_n	$f(x_n)$	$f'(x_n)$
0	0	−0.5	1.5
1	0.333333	−0.003070	1.472479
2	0.335418	-4.7675×10^{-8}	1.472136
3	0.335418	−	−

TABLE 2.4   Solution of Equation (2.229) by Means of the Modified Newton Method

Step	x_n	$f(x_n)$
0	0	−0.5
1	0.333333	−0.003070
2	0.335380	−0.000056
3	0.335417	-2×10^{-6}
4	0.335418	-4.7675×10^{-8}
5	0.335418	−

TABLE 2.5   Solution of Equation (2.229) by the Contractions Method

Step	x_n	$\phi(x_n)$
0	0.5	0.260287
1	0.260287	0.371321
2	0.371321	0.318577
3	0.318577	0.343392
4	0.343392	0.331650
5	0.331659	0.337194
6	0.337194	0.334580
7	0.334580	0.335814
8	0.335814	0.335231
9	0.335231	0.335506
10	0.335506	0.335377
11	0.335377	0.335437
12	0.335437	0.335409
13	0.335409	0.335422
14	0.335422	0.335416
15	0.335416	0.335419
16	0.335419	0.335418
17	0.335418	0.335418

We obtain

$$\overline{x} \approx 0.335418. \tag{2.243}$$

To apply the Newton–Kantorovich method, let us consider

$$x^* = 0.5. \tag{2.244}$$

$$c = |f(x^*)| = |0.5 - 0.5(1 - \sin 0.5)| = 0.239713, \tag{2.245}$$

$$a = |f(x^*)| = |1 + \cos 0.5| = 1.438791, \tag{2.246}$$

$$|f''(x)| = |-0.5 \sin x| = 0.5 \sin x \leq 0.5 \sin 1 = 0.420735; \tag{2.247}$$

we may thus take

$$|f''(x)| \leq b = 0.43, \tag{2.248}$$

$$\mu = \frac{bc}{2a^2} = 0.024896 < \frac{1}{4}, \tag{2.249}$$

$$\lambda = 0.5. \tag{2.250}$$

Hence, we can apply the Newton–Kantorovich method, with

$$k = \frac{c}{a} = 0.166607, \tag{2.251}$$

$$y^* = \frac{1 - \sqrt{1 - 4\mu}}{2\mu} = 1.026219, \tag{2.252}$$

$$ky^* = 0.170975 \tag{2.253}$$

and the function $g : [0.329025, 0.670975] \rightarrow [0.329025, 0.670975]$

$$g(x) = x - \frac{f(x)}{f'(x^*)}. \tag{2.254}$$

TABLE 2.6   Solution of Equation (2.229) by the Newton–Kantorovich Method

Step	x_n	$f(x_n)$
0	0.5	0.239713
1	0.333393	−0.002981
2	0.335465	0.000069
3	0.335417	−0.000002
4	0.335418	-4.7675×10^{-8}
5	0.335418	−

The calculation is given in Table 2.6.
We deduce that

$$\bar{x} \approx 0.335418. \tag{2.255}$$

The following conclusions result:

(i) the most unfavorable method is that of bisection, for which a relatively large number of steps are necessary to determine the solution with a good approximation;

(ii) the number of steps in the contractions method depends on the value of the contraction constant; if this constant is close to 1, then the number of iteration steps increases;

(iii) Newton's method is quicker than the modified Newton method;

(iv) the Newton–Kantorovich method has both the advantages and the disadvantages of Newton's and contractions methods;

(v) the chord method is quicker than the bisection one, but less quick than Newton's method.

2.7   APPLICATIONS

Problem 2.1

Let us consider a material point of mass m, which moves on the Ox-axis (Fig. 2.7), under the action of a force

$$F = -\frac{F_0}{b} x e^{\frac{x}{b}}. \tag{2.256}$$

Determine the displacement $x_{\max}$, knowing the initial conditions: $t = 0$, $x = x_0$, $\dot{x} = v_0$. Numerical application: $x_0 = 0$, $v_0 = 40 \text{ ms}^{-1}$, $F_0 = 50 \text{ N}$, $b = 2 \text{ m}$, $m = 1 \text{ kg}$.

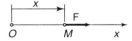

Figure 2.7   Problem 2.1.

Solution:

1. Theory
The theorem of variation of the kinetic energy is

$$\frac{mv^2}{2} - \frac{mv_0^2}{2} = W, \tag{2.257}$$

where v is the velocity of the material point, while

$$W = \int_{x_0}^{x} F(x)\mathrm{d}x \tag{2.258}$$

is the work of the force F; imposing the condition $v = 0$, we obtain x_{max} as the solution of the equation

$$-\frac{mv_0^2}{2} = \int_{x_0}^{x} F(x)\mathrm{d}x. \tag{2.259}$$

In the considered case, by using the notations

$$\xi = \frac{x}{b}, \quad k = \frac{mv_0^2}{2bF_0} + \frac{x_0}{b}\mathrm{e}^{\frac{x_0}{b}} - \mathrm{e}^{\frac{x_0}{b}}, \tag{2.260}$$

we obtain the equation

$$\xi\mathrm{e}^{\xi} - \mathrm{e}^{\xi} - k = 0. \tag{2.261}$$

2. Numerical Calculation
In the case of the numerical application, equation (2.260) takes the form

$$\xi\mathrm{e}^{\xi} - \mathrm{e}^{\xi} - 7 = 0, \tag{2.262}$$

the solution of which is

$$\xi \approx 1.973139, \tag{2.263}$$

that is,

$$x_{max} = b\xi \approx 3.946278 \text{ m}. \tag{2.264}$$

Problem 2.2

Two particles move on the Ox-axis corresponding to the laws (Fig. 2.8)

$$x_1 = A_1 \cos(\omega_1 t), \tag{2.265}$$

$$x_2 = d + A \cos(\omega_2 t + \phi), \tag{2.266}$$

where ω_1, ω_2, ϕ, A_1, and A_2 are positive constants, while t is the time.

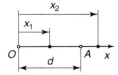

Figure 2.8 Problem 2.2.

Let us determine the first positive value of the time at which the two particles meet.
Numerical application: $\omega_1 = 2 \text{ s}^{-1}$, $\omega_2 = \pi \text{ s}^{-1}$, $\phi = \pi/6 \text{ rad}$, $d = 1 \text{ m}$, $A_1 = 0.6 \text{ m}$, $A_2 = 0.8 \text{ m}$.

Solution: The meeting condition reads

$$x_1 = x_2, \tag{2.267}$$

from which

$$A_1 \cos(\omega_1 t) = d + A_2 \cos(\omega_2 t + \phi) \tag{2.268}$$

or

$$\cos(\omega_1 t) = \frac{d}{A_1} + \frac{A_2}{A_1} \cos(\omega_2 t + \phi). \tag{2.269}$$

Because $-1 \le \cos(\omega_1 t) \le 1$, we obtain a condition that must verify the parameters of the problem

$$-1 \le \frac{d}{A_1} + \frac{A_2}{A_1} \cos(\omega_2 t + \phi) \le 1. \tag{2.270}$$

In the numerical case considered, it follows that

$$\cos 2t = \frac{1}{0.6} + \frac{0.8}{0.6} \cos\left(\pi t + \frac{\pi}{6}\right). \tag{2.271}$$

Let us represent graphically the functions $f : \mathbb{R}_+ \to \mathbb{R}$, $g : \mathbb{R}_+ \to \mathbb{R}$ (Fig. 2.9)

$$f(t) = 0.6 \cos 2t, \quad g(t) = 1 + 0.8 \cos\left(\pi t + \frac{\pi}{6}\right). \tag{2.272}$$

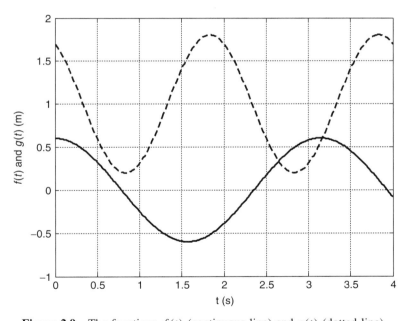

Figure 2.9   The functions $f(t)$ (continuous line) and $g(t)$ (dotted line).

From the figure, we obtain the first point of meeting for t_1 contained between 2.5 and 3 s. Solving the equation

$$0.6 \cos 2t - 1 - 0.8 \cos\left(\pi t + \frac{\pi}{6}\right) = 0, \tag{2.273}$$

we obtain the required solution

$$t_1 \approx 2.6485 \text{ s.} \tag{2.274}$$

FURTHER READING

Acton FS (1990). Numerical Methods that Work. 4th ed. Washington: Mathematical Association of America.

Ackleh AS, Allen EJ, Hearfott RB, Seshaiyer P (2009). Classical and Modern Numerical Analysis: Theory, Methods and Practice. Boca Raton: CRC Press.

Atkinson KE (1989). An Introduction to Numerical Analysis. 2nd ed. New York: John Wiley & Sons, Inc.

Atkinson KE (2003). Elementary Numerical Analysis. 2nd ed. Hoboken: John Wiley & Sons, Inc.

Bakhvalov N (1976). Méthodes Numérique. Moscou: Editions Mir (in French).

Berbente C, Mitran S, Zancu S (1997). Metode Numerice. Bucureşti: Editura Tehnică (in Romanian).

Burden RL, Faires L (2009). Numerical Analysis. 9th ed. Boston: Brooks/Cole.

Butt R (2009). Introduction to Numerical Analysis Using MATLAB. Boston: Jones and Bartlett Publishers.

Chapra SC (1996). Applied Numerical Methods with MATLAB for Engineers and Scientists. Boston: McGraw-Hill.

Cheney EW, Kincaid DR (1997). Numerical Mathematics and Computing. 6th ed. Belmont: Thomson.

Cira O, Măruşter Ş (2008). Metode Numerice pentru Ecuaţii Neliniare. Bucureşti: Editura Matrix Rom (in Romanian).

Dahlquist G, Björck Å (1974). Numerical Methods. Englewood Cliffs: Prentice Hall.

Démidovitch B, Maron I (1973). Éléments de Calcul Numérique. Moscou: Editions Mir (in French).

Dennis JE Jr, Schnabel RB (1987). Numerical Methods for Unconstrained Optimization and Nonlinear Equations. Philadelphia: SIAM.

DiBenedetto E (2010). Classical Mechanics: Theory and Mathematical Modeling. New York: Springer-Verlag.

Epperson JF (2007). An Introduction to Numerical Methods and Analysis. Hoboken: John Wiley & Sons, Inc.

Fung YC, Tong P (2011). Classical and Computational Solid Mechanics. Singapore: World Scientific Publishing.

Gautschi W (1997). Numerical Analysis: An Introduction. Boston: Birkhäuser.

Godunov SK, Reabenki VS (1977). Scheme de Calcul cu Diferenţe Finite. Bucureşti: Editura Tehnică (in Romanian).

Greenbaum A, Chartier TP (2012). Numerical Methods: Design, Analysis, and Computer Implementation of Algorithms. Princeton: Princeton University Press.

Hamming RW (1987). Numerical Methods for Scientists and Engineers. 2nd ed. New York: Dover Publications.

Hamming RW (2012). Introduction to Applied Numerical Analysis. New York: Dover Publications.

Heinbockel JH (2006). Numerical Methods for Scientific Computing. Victoria: Trafford Publishing.

Higham NJ (2002). Accuracy and Stability of Numerical Algorithms. 2nd ed. Philadelphia: SIAM.

Hildebrand FB (1987). Introduction to Numerical Analysis. 2nd ed. New York: Dover Publications.

Hoffman JD (1992). Numerical Methods for Engineers and Scientists. New York: McGraw-Hill.

Kharab A, Guenther RB (2011). An Introduction to Numerical Methods: A MATLAB Approach. 3rd ed. Boca Raton: CRC Press.

Kelley CT (1987a). Iterative Methods for Linear and Nonlinear Equations. Philadelphia: SIAM.

Kelley CT (1987b). Solving Nonlinear Equations with Newton's Method. Philadelphia: SIAM.

Kleppner D, Kolenkow RJ (2010). An Introduction to Mechanics. Cambridge: Cambridge University Press.

Kress R (1996). Numerical Analysis. New York: Springer-Verlag.

Krîlov AN (1957). Lecţii de Calcule prin Aproximaţii. Bucureşti: Editura Tehnică (in Romanian).

Kunz KS (1957). Numerical Analysis. New York: McGraw-Hill.

Lange K (2010). Numerical Analysis for Statisticians. 2nd ed. New York: Springer-Verlag.

Lurie AI (2002). Analytical Mechanics. New York: Springer-Verlag.

Marinescu G (1974). Analiză Numerică. Bucureşti: Editura Academiei Române (in Romanian).

Meriam JL, Kraige LG (2012). Engineering Mechanics: Dynamics. Hoboken: John Wiley & Sons, Inc.

Otto SR, Denier JP (2005). An Introduction to Programming and Numerical Methods in MATLAB. London: Springer-Verlag.

Pandrea N (2000). Elemente de Mecanica Solidului în Coordonate Plückeriene. Bucureşti: Editura Academiei Române (in Romanian).

Pandrea N, Stănescu ND (2002). Mecanică. Bucureşti: Editura Didactică şi Pedagogică (in Romanian).

Popovici P, Cira O (1992). Rezolvarea Numerică a Ecuaţiilor Neliniare. Timişoara: Editura Signata (in Romanian).

Postolache M (2006). Modelare Numerică. Teorie şi Aplicaţii. Bucureşti: Editura Fair Partners (in Romanian).

Press WH, Teukolski SA, Vetterling WT, Flannery BP (2007). Numerical Recipes: The Art of Scientific Computing. 3rd ed. Cambridge: Cambridge University Press.

Quarteroni A, Sacco R, Saleri F (2010). Numerical Mathematics. 2nd ed. Berlin: Springer-Verlag.

Ralston A, Rabinowitz P (2001). A First Course in Numerical Analysis. 2nd ed. New York: Dover Publications.

Ridgway Scott L (2011). Numerical Analysis. Princeton: Princeton University Press.

Salvadori MG, Baron ML (1962). Numerical Methods in Engineering. Englewood Cliffs: Prentice Hall.

Sauer T (2011). Numerical Analysis. 2nd ed. London: Pearson.

Simionescu I, Dranga M, Moise V (1995). Metode Numerice în Tehnică. Aplicaţii în FORTRAN. Bucureşti: Editura Tehnică (in Romanian).

Stănescu ND (2007). Metode Numerice. Bucureşti: Editura Didactică şi Pedagogică (in Romanian).

Stoer J, Bulirsh R (2010). Introduction to Numerical Analysis. 3rd ed. New York: Springer-Verlag.

Süli E, Mayers D (2003). An Introduction to Numerical Analysis. Cambridge: Cambridge University Press.

Teodorescu PP (2010). Mechanical Systems: Classical Models. Volume 1: Particle Mechanics. Dordrecht: Springer-Verlag.

Udrişte C, Iftode V, Postolache M (1996). Metode Numerice de Calcul. Algoritmi şi Programe Turbo Pascal. Bucureşti: Editura Tehnică (in Romanian).

3

SOLUTION OF ALGEBRAIC EQUATIONS

In this chapter, we deal with the determination of limits of the roots of polynomials, including their separation. Three methods are considered, namely, Lagrange's method, the Lobachevski–Graeffe method, and Bernoulli's method.

3.1 DETERMINATION OF LIMITS OF THE ROOTS OF POLYNOMIALS

Let

$$f(X) = a_0 X^n + a_1 X^{n-1} + \cdots + a_n \tag{3.1}$$

be a polynomial in $\mathbb{R}(X)$, where $n \in \mathbb{N}^*$, $a_i \in \mathbb{R}$, $i = \overline{0, n}$. Let us consider the algebraic equation

$$f(x) = a_0 x^n + a_1 x^{n-1} + \cdots + a_n = 0. \tag{3.2}$$

Theorem 3.1 All the roots of the algebraic equation (3.2) are in the circular annulus of the complex plane, defined by the inequalities

$$\frac{|a_n|}{a' + |a_n|} \leq |x| \leq 1 + \frac{a}{|a_0|}, \tag{3.3}$$

where a and a' are specified by

$$a = \max\{|a_1|, \ldots, |a_n|\}, \quad a' = \max\{|a_0|, \ldots, |a_{n-1}|\}. \tag{3.4}$$

Demonstration. We now show that

$$|x| \leq 1 + \frac{a}{|a_0|}. \tag{3.5}$$

Numerical Analysis with Applications in Mechanics and Engineering, First Edition.
Petre Teodorescu, Nicolae-Doru Stănescu, and Nicolae Pandrea.
© 2013 The Institute of Electrical and Electronics Engineers, Inc. Published 2013 by John Wiley & Sons, Inc.

We may write

$$|a_1 x^{n-1} + a_2 x^{n-2} + \cdots + a_n| \leq |a_1||x^{n-1}| + |a_2||x^{n-2}| + \cdots$$

$$+ |a_n| \leq a(|x^{n-1}| + |x^{n-2}| + \cdots + 1) = a\frac{|x|^n - 1}{|x| - 1}. \tag{3.6}$$

If $|x| > 1$, then

$$a\frac{|x|^n - 1}{|x| - 1} < a\frac{|x|^n}{|x| - 1} \tag{3.7}$$

and relation (3.6) leads to

$$|a_1 x^{n-1} + a_2 x^{n-2} + \cdots + a_n| < a\frac{|x|^n}{|x| - 1}. \tag{3.8}$$

Let x be a root of equation (3.2). Thus,

$$|f(x)| = |a_0 x^n + a_1 x^{n-1} + \cdots + a_n| = 0 \tag{3.9}$$

and

$$|f(x)| \geq |a_0 x^n| - |a_1 x^{n-1} + \cdots + a_n|, \tag{3.10}$$

from which

$$|a_0 x^n| \leq |a_1 x^{n-1} + \cdots + a_n|. \tag{3.11}$$

Taking into account relations (3.6) and (3.7), the latter formula leads to the relation

$$|a_0||x|^n < a\frac{|x|^n}{|x| - 1}, \tag{3.12}$$

and hence inequality (3.5) is proved.

To arrive at the other inequality, we perform the transformation $x \mapsto 1/y$, hence

$$f(y) = a_n y^n + a_{n-1} y^{n-1} + \cdots + a_0. \tag{3.13}$$

Let y be a root of this polynomial. Taking into account equation (3.5), we get

$$|y| \leq 1 + \frac{a'}{|a_n|}, \tag{3.14}$$

that is,

$$\frac{1}{|x|} \leq 1 + \frac{a'}{|a_n|}, \tag{3.15}$$

hence

$$|x| \geq \frac{|a_n|}{|a_n| + a'}. \tag{3.16}$$

Observation 3.1   Let

$$L = 1 + \frac{a}{|a_0|}, \quad l = \frac{|a_n|}{a' + |a_n|}. \tag{3.17}$$

We have $l < 1$, $L > 1$, and $L > l$.

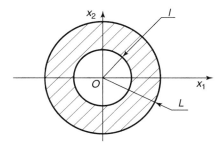

Figure 3.1   Domain where the roots of equation (3.2) lie.

Observation 3.2   The roots of equation (3.2) are in the hatched domain of the complex plane (Fig. 3.1).

Observation 3.3   If equation (3.2) has positive, real roots, then formula (3.3) can be written for these roots in the form

$$\frac{|a_n|}{a + |a_n|} \leq x \leq 1 + \frac{a}{|a_0|}. \tag{3.18}$$

Observation 3.4   We can always assume that $a_n \neq 0$. In the opposite case, we may obtain an equation of the form

$$a_0 x^p + a_1 x^{p-1} + \cdots + a_p = 0, \tag{3.19}$$

where $a_p \neq 0$.

Definition 3.1   The real number $L > 0$ is called a *superior bound* of the positive roots of equation (3.2) if for any such root $\overline{x}$, we have $\overline{x} < L$.

Definition 3.2   The real number $l > 0$ is called an *inferior bound* of the positive roots of equation (3.2) if for any such root $\overline{x}$, we have $\overline{x} > l$.

Observation 3.5

(i) The value $-l < 0$ will be a superior bound of the negative roots of equation (3.2) if $l > 0$ is an inferior bound of the positive roots of the same equation.

(ii) The value $-L < 0$ will be an inferior bound of the negative roots of equation (3.2) if $L > 0$ is a superior bound of the positive roots of the same equation.

(iii) The real roots of equation (3.2) are in the set $(-L, -l) \cup (l, L)$.

Observation 3.6

(i) Let us consider the equation

$$f_1(x) = (-1)^n f(-x) = 0, \tag{3.20}$$

for which L_1 denotes a superior bound of its positive roots. If $\alpha < 0$, is a negative root of equation (3.2), then $-\alpha > 0$ will be a root of equation (3.20), hence $-\alpha < L_1$, from which $\alpha > -L_1$.

(ii) Let us consider the equation

$$f_2(x) = x^n f\left(\frac{1}{x}\right) = 0 \tag{3.21}$$

and let L_2 denote a superior bound of its positive roots. If $\alpha > 0$ is a positive root of equation (3.2), then $1/\alpha > 0$ is a solution of equation (3.21) for which $1/\alpha < L_2$, hence $\alpha > 1/L_2$.

(iii) Let us now consider the equation

$$f_3(x) = (-1)^n x^n f\left(-\frac{1}{x}\right) = 0. \tag{3.22}$$

Let L_3 be a superior bound of its positive roots. If $\alpha < 0$ is a negative root of equation (3.2), then $-1/\alpha > 0$ is a positive root of equation (3.22), for which the relation $-1/\alpha < L_3$ is true. Hence, it follows that $\alpha < -1/L_3$.

(iv) From the above considerations, it follows that the real roots of equation (3.2) belong to the set $(-L_1, -1/L_3) \cup (1/L_2, L)$.

Theorem 3.2 Let A be the greatest absolute value of the negative coefficients of the algebraic equation (3.2) for which $a_0 > 0$ (eventually, by multiplying it by -1). In these conditions, a superior limit of the positive roots of this equation is given by

$$L = 1 + \left(\frac{A}{a_0}\right)^{\frac{1}{k}}, \tag{3.23}$$

where k is the index of the first negative coefficient in the expression of the polynomial function (3.1).

Demonstration. Let us specify the terms which appear in equation (3.23). Thus, A is given by

$$A = \max_{1 \le i \le n} \{|a_i| \, | \, a_i < 0\}, \tag{3.24}$$

while k is given by

$$k = \min\{i \, | \, a_i < 0, a_j \ge 0, (\forall) \, j < i\}. \tag{3.25}$$

Let $x > 0$. Then, $f(x)$ can be written in the form

$$f(x) = a_0 x^n + \cdots + a_{k-1} x^{n-k+1} + (a_k x^{n-k} + \cdots + a_n) \ge a_0 x^n - A(x^{n-k} + \cdots + 1)$$

$$= a_0 x^n - B \frac{x^{n-k+1} - 1}{x - 1}. \tag{3.26}$$

For $x > 1$, the last formula leads to

$$f(x) = a_0 x^n - A \frac{x^{n-k+1}}{x - 1}. \tag{3.27}$$

Let $\bar{x}$ be a positive root of equation (3.2). Relation (3.27) leads to

$$0 > a_0 \bar{x}^n - A \frac{\bar{x}^{n-k+1}}{\bar{x} - 1}, \tag{3.28}$$

from which

$$a_0 < A \frac{\overline{x}^{-(k-1)}}{\overline{x} - 1} = \frac{A}{\overline{x}^{k-1}(\overline{x} - 1)} < \frac{A}{(\overline{x} - 1)^k}, \tag{3.29}$$

so that

$$\overline{x} < 1 + \left(\frac{A}{a_0}\right)^{\frac{1}{k}}. \tag{3.30}$$

Observation 3.7   If all the coefficients of equation (3.2) are positive, then this equation has no positive roots.

Observation 3.8   We notice that Theorem 3.2 gives more restricted bounds for the limits of the real roots of equation (3.2).

Theorem 3.3 (Newton). Let f be the polynomial function given by equation (3.1), with $a_0 > 0$, and let $a \in \mathbb{R}$, $a > 0$, a number such that $f(a) > 0$, $f'(a) > 0$, $\ldots$, $f^{(n)}(a) > 0$. In these conditions, a is a superior bound of the positive roots of equation (3.2).

Demonstration. The expansion of f into a Taylor series around a is of the form

$$f(x) = f(a) + (x - a)\frac{f'(a)}{1!} + (x - a)^2 \frac{f''(a)}{2!} + \cdots + (x - a)^n \frac{f^{(n)}(a)}{n!} \cdots. \tag{3.31}$$

We observe that if $x \geq a$, then $f(x) > 0$ because $f^{(i)}(a) > 0$ and $x - a > 0$. It thus follows that f cannot have roots greater than a, hence a is a superior bound of the roots of the equation $f(x) = 0$.
   Let us show that there exists such an a. We have

$$f^{(n)}(x) = a_0 n! > 0, \tag{3.32}$$

because $a_0 > 0$, by hypothesis. It follows that $f^{(n-1)}(x)$ is strictly increasing, and hence there exists $a_1 \in \mathbb{R}$ so that $f^{(n-1)}(x) > 0$ for $x \geq a_1$. Obviously, we may consider $a_1 > 0$. We pass now to $f^{(n-1)}(x)$, which is strictly positive for $x > a_1$. It follows that there exists a_2, where $a_2 \geq a_1$, such that $f^{(n-2)}(x) > 0$ for $x \geq a_2$. The procedure continues until a_n, with $a_n \geq a_{n-1} \geq \cdots \geq a_1$, so that $f^{(i)}(a_n) \geq 0$ for any $i = \overline{0, n}$. We now take $a = a_n$.

Theorem 3.4   Let f be a polynomial function of the form (3.1) and let us suppose that $a_0 > 0$ and that the polynomial has only one variation of sign in the sequence of its coefficients, that there exists i, $1 \leq i < n$, so that $a_j > 0$ for any j, $0 \leq j \leq i$, and $a_j < 0$ for any j, $i < j \leq n$. Let us suppose that there exists $a \in \mathbb{R}$, so that $f(a) \geq 0$. Then $f(x) > 0$ for any $x > a$.

Demonstration. Let us write the polynomial f in the form

$$f(x) = (a_0 x^n + \cdots + a_i x^{n-i}) - (a_{i+1} x^{n-i-1} + \cdots + a_n). \tag{3.33}$$

It follows that

$$f(x) = x^{n-i} \left[(a_0 x^{n-i} + \cdots + a_i) - \left(\frac{a_{i+1}}{x} + \cdots + \frac{a_n}{x^{n-i}} \right) \right]. \tag{3.34}$$

If x increases starting from a, the expression in first parentheses will increase, while that in the second parentheses will decrease. Hence $f(x)$ is increasing and, because $f(a) \geq 0$, it follows that $f(x) > 0$ for $x > a$. Hence a is a superior bound of the positive roots of the equation $f(x) = 0$.

Observation 3.9   The previous theorem suggests a method to determine a superior bound of the positive roots of equation (3.2). To do this, we group the terms of the polynomial so that

(i) the powers of x are decreasing in any group;

(ii) the first coefficient of a group is positive;

(iii) we have only one variation of sign in the interior of each group.

We now determine a superior bound of the positive roots for each group; hence, the superior bound of the positive roots of equation (3.2) will be the maximum of the superior bounds of the positive roots of the groups.

Observation 3.10   The method presented above, called *the method of terms grouping*, is sensible to the choice of the groups.

3.2   SEPARATION OF ROOTS

Definition 3.3   Let $\{b_i\}_{i=\overline{0,m}}$ be a finite sequence of real numbers, so that $b_i < b_{i+1}$, $i = \overline{0, m}$. We say that this sequence separates the roots of the algebraic equation $f(x) = 0$ with

$$f(x) = a_0 x^n + \cdots + a_n, \tag{3.35}$$

if we have a single root of this equation in any interval (b_i, b_{i+1}), $i = \overline{0, m}$.

Observation 3.11   The sequence $\{b_i\}_{i=\overline{0, m}}$ can be chosen as consisting of a part of Rolle's sequence.

Proposition 3.1   Let f be a polynomial of even degree n, $n = 2k$, for which $a_0 a_{2k} < 0$. The equation

$$f(x) = a_0 x^{2k} + a_1 x^{2k-1} + \cdots + a_{2k} = 0 \tag{3.36}$$

has at least one positive root and one negative root in these conditions.

Demonstration. To fix the ideas, let us suppose that $a_0 > 0$. Because

$$\lim_{x \to \infty} f(x) = +\infty, \tag{3.37}$$

it follows that there exists $m_1 > 0$, so that $f(x) > 0$ for any $x > m_1$. Analogically, we have

$$\lim_{x \to -\infty} f(x) = \infty, \tag{3.38}$$

hence there exist $m_2 < 0$, so that $f(x) > 0$ for any $x < m_2$. Let $M = \max\{|m_1|, |m_2|\}$. Hence, for any x, $|x| > M$, we will have $f(x) > 0$.

On the other hand, $f(0) = a_{2k} < 0$ according to $a_0 a_{2k} < 0$ and $a_0 > 0$. It follows that there exists $\xi_1 \in (-M, 0)$ and $\xi_2 \in (0, M)$, so that $f(\xi_1) = 0$ and $f(\xi_2) = 0$. Hence, equation (3.36) has at least one positive root, the proposition being proved.

Observation 3.12   Proposition 3.1 specifies only the existence of a positive root and a negative one, but there can exist several positive and negative roots.

Proposition 3.2   Let f be a polynomial with real coefficients and (a, b) an interval of the real axis. Let us suppose that f has a single root $\overline{x}$ of multiplicity order k on this interval. Under these conditions,

(i) $f(a)f(b) > 0$ if k is an even number;

(ii) $f(a)f(b) < 0$ if k is an odd number.

Demonstration. We write f in the form

$$f(x) = (x - \overline{x})^k g(x), \tag{3.39}$$

where $g(x)$ is a polynomial with real coefficients, without solution in the interval (a, b). We have

$$f(a) = (a - \overline{x})^k g(a), \quad f(b) = (b - \overline{x})^k g(b). \tag{3.40}$$

We mention that $g(a)$ and $g(b)$ have the same sign, because g has no roots in the interval (a, b).
On the other hand,

$$a - \overline{x} < 0, \quad b - \overline{x} > 0, \tag{3.41}$$

because $\overline{x} \in (a, b)$. We may write

$$f(a)f(b) = (a - \overline{x})^k (b - \overline{x})^k g(a)g(b) = [(a - \overline{x})(b - \overline{x})]^k g(a)g(b). \tag{3.42}$$

The sign of $f(a)f(b)$ is given by $[(a - \overline{x})(b - \overline{x})]^k$. If k is an even number (eventually 0), then $[(a - \overline{x})(b - \overline{x})]^k > 0$, hence $f(a)f(b) > 0$. Analogically, if k is an odd number, then $[(a - \overline{x})(b - \overline{x})]^k < 0$, so that $f(a)f(b) < 0$.

Proposition 3.3 Let f be a polynomial of degree n with real coefficients and (a, b) an interval of the real axis. Let us suppose that, in the interval (a, b), f has s roots denoted by $\overline{x}_1, \overline{x}_2, \ldots, \overline{x}_s$, of multiplicity orders $k_1, k_2, \ldots, k_s$. In these conditions,

(i) if $f(a)f(b) < 0$, then $\sum_{i=1}^{s} k_i$ is an odd number;

(ii) if $f(a)f(b) > 0$, then $\sum_{i=1}^{s} k_i$ is an even number (eventually 0).

Demonstration. Let us suppose that the roots $\overline{x}_1, \overline{x}_2, \ldots, \overline{x}_s$ have been increasingly ordered on the interval (a, b), so that $\overline{x}_1 < \overline{x}_2 < \cdots < \overline{x}_s$. Let $\overline{x}$ be one of these roots of multiplicity order k and h a real number. We may write

$$f(\overline{x} + h) = h^k \frac{f^{(k)}(\overline{x})}{k!} + h^{k+1} \frac{f^{(k+1)}(\xi_1)}{(k+1)!}, \tag{3.43}$$

where $\xi_1 \in (\overline{x}, \overline{x} + h)$. Analogically,

$$f(\overline{x} - h) = (-1)^k h^k \frac{f^{(k)}(\overline{x})}{k!} + (-1)^{k+1} h^{k+1} \frac{f^{(k+1)}(\xi_2)}{(k+1)!}, \tag{3.44}$$

with $\xi_2 \in (\overline{x} - h, \overline{x})$. Hence, it follows that

$$
\begin{aligned}
f(\overline{x} + h)f(\overline{x} - h) = {}& (-1)^k \left[h^k \frac{f^{(k)}(\overline{x})}{k!} \right]^2 + (-1)^k \frac{h^{2k+1}}{k!(k+1)!} \\
& \times f^{(k)}(\overline{x}) f^{(k+1)}(\xi_1) + (-1)^{k+1} \frac{h^{2k+1}}{k!(k+1)!} f^{(k)}(\overline{x}) f^{(k+1)}(\xi_2) \\
& + (-1)^{k+1} \frac{h^{2k+2}}{[(k+1)!]^2} f^{(k+1)}(\xi_1) f^{(k+1)}(\xi_2)
\end{aligned} \tag{3.45}
$$

or

$$f(\overline{x} + h)f(\overline{x} - h) = (-1)^k \left[h^k \frac{f^{(k)}(\overline{x})}{k!} \right]^2 + h^{2k+1}\phi(\overline{x}, \xi_1, \xi_2), \tag{3.46}$$

where the notation for the function ϕ is obvious. We can immediately show that, for h sufficiently small, the sign of $f(\overline{x} + h)f(\overline{x} - h)$ is given by the sign of $(-1)^k$ and it is $+1$ for k even and -1 for k odd, respectively. It follows that f has the sign of $f(a)$ on the interval $(a, \overline{x}_1)$, has the sign of $(-1)^{k_1}f(a)$ on the interval $(\overline{x}_1, \overline{x}_2)$, has the sign of $(-1)^{k_1+k_2}f(a)$ on the interval $(\overline{x}_2, \overline{x}_3)$, $\ldots$, and has the sign of $(-1)^{k_1+\cdots+k_s}f(a)$ on the interval $(\overline{x}_s, b)$. Hence, we can state that if $f(a)f(b) < 0$, then $\sum_{i=1}^{s} k_i$ is an odd number, while if $f(a)f(b) > 0$, then the sum is an even number (eventually 0).

Theorem 3.5 (Edward Waring, 1736–1798). Let f be a polynomial with real coefficients and $\overline{x}_1$ and $\overline{x}_2$ be two consecutive roots of the polynomial (i.e., no other root of the polynomial exists between $\overline{x}_1$ and $\overline{x}_2$). Let $\overline{x}_1$ be of order of multiplicity k_1, and $\overline{x}_2$ of order of multiplicity k_2. Under these conditions, the polynomial $g = f' + \lambda f$, $\lambda \in \mathbb{R}$, has, on the interval $(\overline{x}_1, \overline{x}_2)$, a number of real roots, the sum of multiplicity orders of which is odd. Moreover, $\overline{x}_1$ and $\overline{x}_2$ are roots of the polynomial g, of multiplicity orders $k_1 - 1$ and $k_2 - 1$, respectively.

Demonstration. Let us write the polynomial f in the form

$$f(x) = (x - \overline{x}_1)^{k_1}(x - \overline{x}_2)^{k_2}h(x), \tag{3.47}$$

where $h(x)$ does not change in sign in the interval $(\overline{x}_1, \overline{x}_2)$. Hence,

$$\begin{aligned} f'(x) &= k_1(x - \overline{x}_1)^{k_1-1}(x - \overline{x}_2)^{k_2}h(x) \\ &\quad + k_2(x - \overline{x}_1)^{k_1}(x - \overline{x}_2)^{k_2-1}h(x) + (x - \overline{x}_1)^{k_1}(x - \overline{x}_2)^{k_2}h'(x) \\ &= (x - \overline{x}_1)^{k_1-1}(x - \overline{x}_2)^{k_2-1}[k_1(x - \overline{x}_2)h(x) + k_2(x - \overline{x}_1)h(x) \\ &\quad + (x - \overline{x}_1)(x - \overline{x}_2)h'(x)]. \end{aligned} \tag{3.48}$$

Denoting by $p(x)$ the polynomial

$$p(x) = k_1(x - \overline{x}_2)h(x) + k_2(x - \overline{x}_1)h(x) + (x - \overline{x}_1)(x - \overline{x}_2)h'(x), \tag{3.49}$$

relation (3.48) leads to

$$f'(x) = (x - \overline{x}_1)^{k_1-1}(x - \overline{x}_2)^{k_2-1}p(x). \tag{3.50}$$

The polynomial $g(x)$ can be written in the form

$$\begin{aligned} g(x) &= (x - \overline{x}_1)^{k_1-1}(x - \overline{x}_2)^{k_2-1}p(x) + \lambda(x - \overline{x}_1)^{k_1}(x - \overline{x}_2)^{k_2}h(x) \\ &= (x - \overline{x}_1)^{k_1-1}(x - \overline{x}_2)^{k_2-1}[p(x) + \lambda(x - \overline{x}_1)(x - \overline{x}_2)h(x)]. \end{aligned} \tag{3.51}$$

Denoting by $q(x)$ the polynomial

$$q(x) = p(x) + \lambda(x - \overline{x}_1)(x - \overline{x}_2)h(x), \tag{3.52}$$

formula (3.51) leads to

$$g(x) = (x - \overline{x}_1)^{k_1-1}(x - \overline{x}_2)^{k_2-1}q(x). \tag{3.53}$$

Note that $g(x)$ has the roots $\bar{x}_1$ and $\bar{x}_2$ of multiplicity orders $k_1 - 1$ and $k_2 - 1$ (a root of multiplicity order 0 is, in fact, not a root), respectively. The roots of $g(x)$, other than $\bar{x}_1$ and $\bar{x}_2$, are the roots of $q(x)$. But

$$q(\bar{x}_1) = p(\bar{x}_1) = k_1(\bar{x}_1 - \bar{x}_2)h(\bar{x}_1), \quad q(\bar{x}_2) = p(\bar{x}_2) = k_2(\bar{x}_2 - \bar{x}_1)h(\bar{x}_2), \tag{3.54}$$

hence

$$q(\bar{x}_1)q(\bar{x}_2) = -k_1 k_2 (\bar{x}_1 - \bar{x}_2)^2 h(\bar{x}_1)h(\bar{x}_2). \tag{3.55}$$

On the other hand, $h(\bar{x}_1)$ and $h(\bar{x}_2)$ have the same sign on $(\bar{x}_1, \bar{x}_2)$, $k_1 > 0$, $k_2 > 0$, $(\bar{x}_1 - \bar{x}_2)^2 > 0$, and we obtain

$$q(\bar{x}_1)q(\bar{x}_2) < 0. \tag{3.56}$$

Taking into account Proposition 3.3, the theorem is proved.

Corollary 3.1 Let f be a polynomial with real coefficients, the roots of which are $\bar{x}_1, \ldots, \bar{x}_s$, of multiplicity orders $k_1, \ldots, k_s$, respectively.

  (i) If all the roots of f are real, then all the roots of f' are also real.
 (ii) If all the roots of f are simple, then all the roots of f' are also simple and separate the roots of f.

Demonstration.

  (i) We may write

$$\sum_{i=1}^{s} k_i = n, \tag{3.57}$$

where n is the degree of f. Waring's theorem shows that $\bar{x}_i$, $i = \overline{1, s}$, are roots of the polynomial $f' + \lambda f$, $\lambda \in \mathbb{R}$, also of multiplicity orders $k_i - 1$. It follows that the sum of the multiplicity orders of the roots of $f' + \lambda f$ is given by

$$\sum_{i=1}^{s}(k_i - 1) = \sum_{i=1}^{s} k_i - s = n - s. \tag{3.58}$$

On the other hand, there exists at least one root between $\bar{x}_i$ and $\bar{x}_{i+1}$. The addition of these $s - 1$ roots to the sum equation (3.58) shows that the sum of multiplicity orders of the roots of polynomial $f' + \lambda f$ is at least equal to

$$n - s + (s - 1) = n - 1. \tag{3.59}$$

Let us note that, from Waring's theorem, from formula (3.59), and because the sum of the multiplicity orders of the polynomial $f' + \lambda f$ is equal to n, it follows that each of the roots of $f' + \lambda f$, situated between $\bar{x}_i$ and $\bar{x}_{i+1}$, are simple roots. Accordingly, it follows that the last root of $f' + \lambda f$ is situated either in the interval $(-\infty, \bar{x}_1)$, or in the interval $(\bar{x}_s, \infty)$ and that this root is simple. This last root cannot be complex, without being real, $\xi \in \mathbb{C} - \mathbb{R}$, because the polynomial $f' + \lambda f$ being with real coefficients, it would result that the conjugate $\bar{\xi}$ of ξ is also a root. The sum of the multiplicity orders of the other roots of the polynomial $f' + \lambda f$, which are real, in accordance with Waring's theorem, would be equal to $n - 2$, in contradiction to formula (3.59). The s roots of f' are $\bar{x}_1, \ldots, \bar{x}_s$, of multiplicity orders $k_1 - 1, \ldots, k_s - 1$, respectively, as well as the $s - 1$ roots situated between $\bar{x}_i$ and $\bar{x}_{i+1}$, $i = \overline{1, s-1}$. The sum of the multiplicity orders of these roots is equal to

$$\sum_{i=1}^{s}(k_i - 1) + (s - 1) = n - 1 \qquad (3.60)$$

and, because the degree of f' is equal to $n - 1$, it is sufficient to make $\lambda = 0$, obtaining thus all the roots of f', all of which are real.

(ii) It is a particular case of point (i) for

$$k_1 = k_2 = \cdots = k_s = 1. \qquad (3.61)$$

Proposition 3.4 Let $a_1, \ldots, a_n$ be a finite sequence of nonzero numbers. If we leave out the intermediate terms $a_2, \ldots, a_{n-1}$, the extremes a_1 and a_n remaining unchanged, then the number of sign variations in the sequence of two elements obtained differs from the number of sign variations of the initial sequence by an even number (eventually 0).

Demonstration. Let us consider a sequence of three consecutive elements of the initial sequence, that is, a_i, a_{i+1}, a_{i+2}, $i \geq 1$, $i \leq n - 2$, and let us eliminate the intermediate element a_{i+1}. To fix the ideas, let us suppose that $a_i > 0$. The following situations are possible:

(a) $a_{i+1} > 0$, $a_{i+2} > 0$. The number of sign variations is equal to zero in the initial sequence and in the last one also it is equal to zero; hence, the difference of the two numbers is an even number;

(b) $a_{i+1} > 0$, $a_{i+2} < 0$. The number of sign variations is equal to one in the initial sequence, and in the last one it is equal to one too; the difference of the two numbers is zero, hence an even number;

(c) $a_{i+1} < 0$, $a_{i+2} > 0$. In this case, we have two sign variations in the initial sequence, while in the last sequence we have none; the difference is equal to two, hence an even number;

(d) $a_{i+1} < 0$, $a_{i+2} < 0$. We have one variation of sign in both sequences; the difference is thus equal to zero, hence an even number.

The considered property thus holds for this sequence of three elements.

In the general case, by eliminating any intermediate term from a_2 to a_{n-1}, the number of sign variations differs by two or remains the same and the proposition is proved.

Corollary 3.2 Let

$$f(x) = a_0 x^n + a_1 x^{n-1} + \cdots + a_{n-1} x + a_n \qquad (3.62)$$

be a polynomial of degree n with real coefficients. The number of sign variations of the sequence of the coefficients of f has the same parity as the sum of the orders of multiplicity of the positive real roots of the equation $f(x) = 0$.

Demonstration. Let us suppose that $a_0 > 0$. There are two cases. If $a_n < 0$, then $f(0) = a_n < 0$ and $\lim_{x \to \infty} f(x) = +\infty$. According to Proposition 3.3, it follows that the sum of the orders of multiplicity of the positive roots of the equation $f(x) = 0$ is an odd number, and hence Proposition 3.4 shows that the number of sign variations in the sequence of the coefficients of f is an odd number. If $a_n > 0$, then $f(0) = a_n > 0$ and $\lim_{x \to \infty} f(x) = +\infty$. As the number of sign variations in the sequence of the coefficients of f is even, Proposition 3.3 shows that the sum of the orders of multiplicity of the positive roots of the equation $f(x) = 0$ is an even number.

Corollary 3.3 Let f be a polynomial of degree n with real coefficients, the positive real roots of which are all simple. In this case, the number of sign variations in the sequence of the coefficients of f has the same parity as the number of positive roots of the equation $f(x) = 0$.

Demonstration. In the given conditions, the sum of the multiplicity orders of the positive roots of the equation $f(x) = 0$ is equal just to the number of these roots and we apply Corollary 3.2.

Lemma 3.1 Let α be a nonzero positive number and let $f(x)$ be a polynomial of degree n. Let us consider the polynomial $g(x) = (x - \alpha)f(x)$. In these conditions, the number of sign variations in the sequence of the coefficients of the polynomial g differs from the number of sign variations of the coefficients of f by a positive odd number.

Demonstration. Let us consider the polynomial

$$f(x) = a_n x^n + a_{n-1} x^{n-1} + \cdots + a_1 x + a_0, \tag{3.63}$$

which we write in the form

$$f(x) = a_n x^n + \cdots + a_i x^i - a_j x^j - \cdots - a_k x^k + a_l x^l + \cdots, \tag{3.64}$$

where we have marked groups of terms of the same sign. The polynomial $g(x)$ is now written in the form

$$g(x) = (x - \alpha)(a_n x^n + \cdots + a_i x^i) + (x - \alpha)(-a_j x^j - \cdots - a_k x^k) + (x - \alpha)(a_l x^l + \cdots) - \cdots$$

$$= a_n x^{n+1} + \cdots + a_i x^{i+1} - \alpha a_n x^n - \cdots - \alpha a_i x^i - a_j x^{j+1} - \cdots - a_k x^{k+1} + \alpha a_j x^j$$

$$+ \cdots + \alpha a_k x^k + a_l x^{l+1} + \cdots - \alpha a_l x^l - \cdots \tag{3.65}$$

The following situations may occur:

(a) $i > j + 1$. We have only one sign variation in this case.
(b) $i = j + 1$. We introduce the terms $-\alpha a_i$ and $-a_j$ in the same group and have once more a sign variation between the first and the last term in the group.
(c) $k > l + 1$. We have a sign variation too.
(d) $k = l + 1$. The coefficient of x^{l+1} is positive and we have a sign variation in this case.

Let a_n and a_p be the coefficients of the extreme terms of the polynomial f. It follows that the extreme terms of g are a_n and αa_p. If $a_n a_p > 0$, then $-\alpha a_n a_p < 0$, whereas if $a_n a_p < 0$, then $-\alpha a_n a_p > 0$. It follows that the number of sign variations in the sequence of the coefficients of g is greater than the number of variations in the sequence of variations of f; we mention also that the difference between the two numbers is an odd number.

Theorem 3.6 (Descartes[1]). Let us suppose that the equation $f(x) = 0$ has only simple roots, the number of positive roots of which is p. In this case, p is either equal to the number of sign variations in the sequence of coefficients of f or is less than minus from this one by an even number.

Demonstration. Let $\bar{x}_1, \ldots, \bar{x}_p$ be the p positive simple roots of the equation $f(x) = 0$. We may write

$$f(x) = (x - \bar{x}_1) \cdots (x - \bar{x}_p)g(x), \tag{3.66}$$

---

[1]The theorem was presented by René Descartes (1596–1650) in *La Géométrie* (1637) and is also known as the rule of signs.

where $g(x)$ has no positive roots. Let n_1 be the number of sign variations of the coefficients of the polynomial $g(x)$. According to the Corollary 3.3, n_1 is an even number

$$n_1 = 2m, \quad m \in \mathbb{N}. \tag{3.67}$$

We now apply the Lemma 3.1 p times, so that every time number of the sign variations in the sequence of the coefficients of the obtained polynomials will increase by an odd number. It follows that the number of sign variations in the sequence of the coefficients of the polynomial g is given by

$$N_v = n_1 + \sum_{i=1}^{p}(2k_i + 1) = 2\left(m + \sum_{i=1}^{p} k_i\right) + p. \tag{3.68}$$

We obtain

$$p = N_v - 2\left(m + \sum_{i=1}^{p} k_i\right) \tag{3.69}$$

and the theorem is proved.

Observation 3.13   Taking into account the polynomial $f_1(x) = (-1)^n f(-x)$, we may apply Descartes' theorem for the negative roots of f too.

Definition 3.4   Let f be a polynomial with real coefficients, which does not have multiple roots, and let $[a, b]$ be an interval of the real axis. A finite sequence $f_0, f_1, \ldots, f_k$ of polynomials associated with the polynomial f on this interval is called a *Sturm sequence* if

(i) the last polynomial $f_k(x)$ has no real roots;
(ii) two consecutive polynomials $f_i(x)$ and $f_{i+1}(x)$ have no common roots;
(iii) if $\overline{x} \in \mathbb{R}$ and $f_i(\overline{x}) = 0$, then $f_{i-1}(\overline{x}) f_{i+1}(\overline{x}) < 0$, $i = \overline{0, k-1}$;
(iv) $f_i(a) \neq 0$; $f_i(b) \neq 0$ for any $i = \overline{0, k}$.

Proposition 3.5   For any polynomial f with real coefficients, without multiple roots, and for any interval $[a, b]$ with $f(a) \neq 0$, $f(b) \neq 0$, there exists a Sturm sequence associated with f on $[a, b]$.

Demonstration. Let us construct the sequence f_i so that

$$f_0 = f, \quad f_1 = f', \tag{3.70}$$

while for $i \geq 2$ we have

$$f_0 = f_1 q_1 - f_2, f_1 = f_2 q_2 - f_3, \ldots, f_{i-2} = f_{i-1} q_{i-1} - f_i, \ldots \tag{3.71}$$

Because the degrees of the polynomials decrease, it follows that there exist only a finite number of such polynomials.

In the following, we verify that the sequence of these polynomials f_i, $i = \overline{0, k}$, previously defined is a Sturm sequence associated with f on $[a, b]$.

(i) Because $f = f_0$ and $f' = f_1$ have no common factors (f has no multiple roots), it follows that the last polynomial f_k of the sequence is a constant.

(ii) If f_i and f_{i-1}, $1 \leq i \leq k$, have a common root, then from relation (3.71) it would follow that f_{i-2} has the same root. Finally, we can show that the root is common to $f_0 = f$ and $f_1 = f'$, so that the polynomial f would then have multiple roots, which is a contradiction to the hypothesis. Therefore, f_i and f_{i-1} have no common roots, $1 \leq i \leq k$.

(iii) Let $\overline{x} \in \mathbb{R}$ be so that $f_i(\overline{x}) = 0$ for a certain index i, $1 \leq i \leq k - 1$. From

$$f_{i-1}(\overline{x}) = f_i(\overline{x})q_i(\overline{x}) - f_{i+1}(\overline{x}), \qquad (3.72)$$

we get

$$f_{i-1}(\overline{x}) = -f_{i+1}(\overline{x}), \qquad (3.73)$$

because $f_i(\overline{x}) = 0$; hence

$$f_{i-1}(\overline{x})f_{i+1}(\overline{x}) < 0. \qquad (3.74)$$

(iv) From (ii) and (iii) it follows that $f_i(a)$ may be equal to zero only for a finite number of indices i_1, i_2, ..., i_p between 0 and k, as well as for any two neighboring indices $i_{k+1} - i_k > 1$. We can replace the value a with the value $a + \varepsilon$, ε sufficiently small, so that the properties (i), (ii) and (iii) are not violated, and $f_i(a) \neq 0$ for any $i = \overline{0, k}$. Analogically, we may also replace the value b with the value $b - \mu$, μ sufficiently small, to get all the properties required by the Sturm sequence.

Theorem 3.7 (Sturm[2]). Let f be a polynomial with real coefficients and without multiple roots. The number of real roots of the polynomial f in the interval $[a, b]$ is given by $W_s(a) - W_s(b)$, where $W_s(x^*)$ is the number of the sign variations in the sequence $f_0(x^*)$, $f_1(x^*)$, ..., $f_k(x^*)$.

Demonstration. Let f_i, $0 \leq i \leq k - 1$, be an arbitrary term (but not the last) of the Sturm sequence and let us denote by $\overline{x}_1$, $\overline{x}_2$, ..., $\overline{x}_s$ the roots of this polynomial in the interval $[a, b]$.

We shall show that $W_s(x^*)$ remains constant for $x^* \in (\overline{x}_k, \overline{x}_{k+1})$. Let us suppose *per absurdum* that $W_s(x^*)$ is not constant. Then there exist two real numbers, $\overline{y}_1$ and $\overline{y}_2$, in the interval $(\overline{x}_k, \overline{x}_{k+1})$ so that $f_i(\overline{y}_1)f_i(\overline{y}_2) < 0$. It follows that there exists $\xi \in (\overline{y}_1, \overline{y}_2)$, $\overline{y}_1 < \overline{y}_2$, so that $f_i(\xi) = 0$. But ξ is not a root of f_i because $\xi \in (\overline{x}_k, \overline{x}_{k+1})$ and $\overline{x}_k$ and $\overline{x}_{k+1}$ are consecutive roots. Hence, $W_s(x^*)$ is constant for $x^* \in (\overline{x}_k, \overline{x}_{k+1})$.

Let us consider $\overline{y} \in [a, b]$ and $f_i(\overline{y}) = 0$, $1 \leq i \leq k - 1$, that is $\overline{y}$ is not a root for f. We shall show that $W_s(a) = W_s(b)$. From property (iii) of the Sturm sequence, it follows that $f_{i-1}(\overline{y})f_{i+1}(\overline{y}) < 0$, that is, $f_{i-1}(\overline{y})$ and $f_{i+1}(\overline{y})$ have opposite signs. These signs do not change if we replace $\overline{y}$ by a and b, respectively. Hence, it follows that the number of sign variations in the triples $f_{i-1}(a)$, $f_i(a)$, $f_{i+1}(a)$ and $f_{i-1}(b)$, $f_i(b)$, $f_{i+1}(b)$, respectively is every time equal to unity. We conclude that if $\overline{y}$ is not a root of f, then $W_s(a) = W_s(b)$.

Let $\overline{y} \in [a, b]$, $\overline{y}$ a root of f. In this case, $f(a)f(b) < 0$, and hence $f'(a)$ and $f'(b)$ have the same sign as $f(b)$. It results $W_s(a) - W_s(b) = 1$. It follows that each root adds a unity to $W_s(a) - W_s(b)$. Thus the theorem is proved.

Theorem 3.8 (Budan[3] or Budan–Fourier). Let f be a polynomial in the variable x, and a and b two real numbers, not necessarily finite. Let us denote by δf the sequence f, f', ..., $f^{(n)}$ and by $W(\delta f, p)$ the number of variations of sign in the sequence $f(p)$, $f'(p)$, ..., $f^{(n)}(p)$. In these conditions, if $R(f, a, b)$ is the number of real roots of f in the interval $[a, b]$, each root being

---

[2]The idea is a generalization of Euclid's algorithm in the case of polynomials and was proved in 1829 by Jacques Charles François Sturm (1803–1855).

[3]Ferdinand François Désiré Budan de Boislaurent (1761–1840) proved this theorem in 1807. The proof was lost and was replaced by another statement of an equivalent theorem belonging to Jean Baptiste Joseph Fourier (1768–1830), published in 1836.

counted as many times as its order of multiplicity, then $W(\delta f, a) - W(\delta f, b)$ is at least equal to $R(f, a, b)$, while the difference between them is a positive even number, that is,

$$W(\delta f, a) - W(\delta f, b) = R(f, a, b) + 2k, \quad k \in \mathbb{N}. \tag{3.75}$$

Demonstration. First, let us remark that $W(\delta f, x)$ may change its value only if x passes through a root $\overline{x}$ of a polynomial of the sequence δf. We can find an $\varepsilon > 0$ so that, in the interval $[\overline{x} - \varepsilon, \overline{x} + \varepsilon]$, no function of the sequence δf has roots, other than $\overline{x}$. Let us denote by m the order of multiplicity of $\overline{x}$.

If we show that

$$W(\delta f, \overline{x}) = W(\delta f, \overline{x} + \varepsilon) \tag{3.76}$$

and

$$W(\delta f, \overline{x} - \varepsilon) - [W(\delta f, \overline{x}) + m] = 2k, \quad k \in \mathbb{N}, \tag{3.77}$$

then the theorem is proved.

Indeed, when x goes through the interval $[a, b]$, $R(f, a, b)$ and $W(\delta f, x)$ are modified only if x becomes equal to a root $\overline{x}$ of f or of one of its derivatives. At such a point, $R(f, a, b)$ increases with the order of multiplicity of $\overline{x}$ for f, while $W(\delta f, x)$ decreases with the sum of m and an even natural number (Proposition 3.4). It follows therefore that the sum $R(f, a, b) + W(\delta f, x)$ may be changed only by the roots $\overline{x}$ of f or of its derivatives, in which case the value of the sum decreases by an even natural number. We thus obtain the above theorem, because this sum is equal to $W(\delta f, a)$ for $x = a$.

Let us now prove relations (3.76) and (3.77). The proof is obtained by induction on the degree of f.

If f is of first degree, then

$$W(\delta f, \overline{x} - \varepsilon) = 1, \quad W(\delta f, \overline{x}) = W(\delta f, \overline{x} + \varepsilon) = 0 \tag{3.78}$$

and the induction hypothesis is verified.

Let us suppose now that the degree of f is at least equal to 2 and that m is the order of multiplicity of $\overline{x}$ for f. We begin by assuming that $f(\overline{x}) = 0$, from which $m > 0$ and $\overline{x}$ is the root of an order of multiplicity $m - 1$ of f'. The induction hypothesis leads to

$$W(\delta f', \overline{x}) = W(\delta f', \overline{x} + \varepsilon), \quad W(\delta f', \overline{x} - \varepsilon) - [W(\delta f', \overline{x}) + (m - 1)] = 2k_1, \quad k_1 \in \mathbb{N}. \tag{3.79}$$

From Lagrange's mean theorem, applied to the intervals $[\overline{x} - \varepsilon, \overline{x}]$ and $[\overline{x}, \overline{x} + \varepsilon]$, we deduce that f and f' do not have the same sign in $\overline{x} - \varepsilon$ but have the same sign in $\overline{x} + \varepsilon$, hence

$$W(\delta f \overline{x}) = W(\delta f', \overline{x}) = W(\delta f', \overline{x} + \varepsilon) = W(\delta f, \overline{x} + \varepsilon), \tag{3.80}$$

$$W(\delta f, \overline{x} - \varepsilon) = W(\delta f', \overline{x} - \varepsilon) + 1 \geq W(\delta f', \overline{x}) + (m - 1) + 1$$

$$= W(\delta f', \overline{x}) + m, \tag{3.81}$$

$$W(\delta f, \overline{x} - \varepsilon) - [W(\delta f, \overline{x}) + m] = 2k, \quad k \in \mathbb{N}, \tag{3.82}$$

so that the theorem is proved in this case.

If $f(\overline{x}) \neq 0$, that is $m = 0$, then we denote by m' the order of multiplicity of $\overline{x}$ for f'. From the induction hypothesis, we have

$$W(\delta f', \overline{x}) = W(\delta f', \overline{x} + \varepsilon), \tag{3.83}$$

$$W(\delta f', \overline{x} - \varepsilon) - [W(\delta f', \overline{x}) - m'] = 2k_1, \quad k_1 \in \mathbb{N}. \tag{3.84}$$

On the other hand, $f(\overline{x}) \neq 0$ and $f'(\overline{x}) = 0$, $f''(\overline{x}) = 0$, $\ldots$, $f^{(m')}(\overline{x}) = 0$, $f^{(m'+1)}(\overline{x}) \neq 0$. We may suppose that $f^{(m'+1)}(\overline{x}) > 0$ (eventually, multiplying f by -1). The following situations may occur:

- m' is an even number. In this case, $f'(\overline{x} - \varepsilon)$ and $f'(\overline{x} + \varepsilon)$ are positive, hence, for each x of the set $\{\overline{x} - \varepsilon, \overline{x}, \overline{x} + \varepsilon\}$, the first nonzero term of the sequence $f'(x)$, $f''(x)$, $\ldots$, $f^{(k)}(x)$ is positive. If $f(\overline{x}) > 0$, then $W(\delta f, x) = W(\delta f', x)$, while if $f(\overline{x}) < 0$, then $W(\delta f, x) = W(\delta f', x) + 1$. The theorem is proved, because it follows that

$$W(\delta f, \overline{x}) = W(\delta f, \overline{x} + \varepsilon), \tag{3.85}$$

$$W(\delta f, \overline{x} - \varepsilon) - W(\delta f, \overline{x}) = W(\delta f', \overline{x} - \varepsilon) - W(\delta f', \overline{x}), \tag{3.86}$$

the term on the right being greater than m' by an even number; and because m' is an even number, it follows that this term is also an even number.

- m' is an odd number. We get

$$f'(\overline{x} - \varepsilon) < 0 < f'(\overline{x} + \varepsilon), \tag{3.87}$$

hence the first nonzero term of the sequence $f'(x)$, $f''(x)$, $\ldots$, $f^{(k)}(x)$ will have the signs $+$, $-$, $+$ at the points $\overline{x} - \varepsilon$, $\overline{x}$, $\overline{x} + \varepsilon$, respectively. If $f(\overline{x}) > 0$, then $W(\delta f, \overline{x} - \varepsilon) = W(\delta f', \overline{x} - \varepsilon) + 1$, so that the other two variations of sign remain unchanged. If $f(\overline{x}) < 0$, then the number of variations of sign does not change for $\overline{x} - \varepsilon$, but increases by unity for $\overline{x}$ and $\overline{x} + \varepsilon$. We obtain

$$W(\delta f, \overline{x}) = W(\delta f, \overline{x} + \varepsilon), \tag{3.88}$$

$$W(\delta f, \overline{x} - \varepsilon) - W(\delta f, \overline{x}) = W(\delta f', \overline{x} - \varepsilon) - W(\delta f', \overline{x}) \pm 1. \tag{3.89}$$

On the other hand, $W(\delta f', \overline{x} - \varepsilon) - W(\delta f', \overline{x})$ is equal to m' to which we add an even natural number (i.e., an odd number, because m' is odd). It follows therefore that if we add or subtract 1 to this difference, we obtain an even natural number which is just $W(\delta f, \overline{x} - \varepsilon) - W(\delta f, \overline{x})$ and the theorem is proved.

Observation 3.14 Descartes' theorem is a particular case of Budan's theorem. Indeed, if

$$f = a_0 x^n + a_1 x^{n-1} + \cdots + a_n, \tag{3.90}$$

then

$$\operatorname{sgn} f(0) = \operatorname{sgn} a_n, \ \operatorname{sgn} f'(0) = sgn a_{n-1}, \ \ldots, \ \operatorname{sgn} f^{(n)}(0) = a_0, \tag{3.91}$$

$$\operatorname{sgn} f(\infty) = \operatorname{sgn} f'(\infty) = \cdots = \operatorname{sgn} f^{(n)}(\infty) = \operatorname{sgn} a_0 \tag{3.92}$$

and from Budan's theorem, for $a = 0$, $b = \infty$, it follows that $W(\delta f, 0)$ is just the number of variations of sign in the sequence a_0, a_1, $\ldots$, a_n, $W(\delta f, \infty) = 0$. Hence we obtain Descartes' theorem.

3.3   LAGRANGE'S METHOD

Let us consider the equation[4]

$$f(x) = a_0 x^n + a_1 x^{n-1} + \cdots + a_0 = 0, \tag{3.93}$$

---

[4]The method was named in the honor of Joseph Louis Lagrange (Giuseppe Luigi Lagrancia or Giuseppe Luigi Lagrangia) (1736–1813) who studied the problem in 1770.

TABLE 3.1   The Generalized Horner's Schema

a_0	a_1	a_2	$\cdots$	a_{n-2}	a_{n-1}	a_n
α	a_0	a_{11}	a_{12}	$\cdots$	$a_{1,n-2}$	$a_{1,n-1}$
α	a_0	a_{21}	a_{22}	$\cdots$	$a_{2,n-2}$	
$\cdots$	$\cdots$	$\cdots$	$\cdots$	$\cdots$		
α	a_0	$a_{n-1,1}$				
α	a_0					

the coefficients a_i, $i = \overline{0, n}$, of which are real numbers and let $\alpha \in \mathbb{R}$ be an arbitrary value. We may write Taylor's formula around α in the form

$$f(x) = f(\alpha) + \frac{x - \alpha}{1!} f'(\alpha) + \frac{(x - \alpha)^2}{2!} f''(\alpha) + \cdots + \frac{(x - \alpha)^n}{n!} f^{(n)}(\alpha). \tag{3.94}$$

Hence, it follows that the remainder of the division of $f(x)$ by $x - \alpha$ is just $f(\alpha)$, while the quotient is given by

$$Q_1(x) = f'(\alpha) + \frac{x - \alpha}{2!} f''(\alpha) + \cdots + \frac{(x - \alpha)^{n-1}}{n!} f^{(n)}(\alpha). \tag{3.95}$$

The remainder of the division of $Q_1(x)$ by $x - \alpha$ is $f'(\alpha)$, while the quotient becomes

$$Q_2(x) = \frac{f''(\alpha)}{2!} + \frac{x - \alpha}{3!} f'''(\alpha) + \cdots + \frac{(x - \alpha)^{n-2}}{n!} f^{(n)}(\alpha). \tag{3.96}$$

In general,

$$Q_i(x) = \frac{f^{(i)}(\alpha)}{i!} + \frac{x - \alpha}{(i + 1)!} f^{(i+1)}(\alpha) + \cdots + \frac{(x - \alpha)^{n-i}}{n!} f^{(n)}(\alpha), \tag{3.97}$$

while the remainder of the division of $Q_i(x)$ by $x - \alpha$ is

$$R_i(x) = \frac{f^{(i)}(\alpha)}{i!}. \tag{3.98}$$

Hence, we have the following relations between the coefficients a_0, ..., a_n of $f(\alpha)$ and the coefficients a'_0, ..., a'_{n-1} of $f'(\alpha)$:

$$a'_0 = a_0, \quad a'_1 = a'_0 \alpha + a_1, \ldots, a'_{n-1} = a'_{n-2}\alpha + a_{n-1}. \tag{3.99}$$

Analogically, the coefficients a'_0, ..., a'_{n-1} of $f'(\alpha)$ and the coefficients a''_0, ..., a''_{n-2} of $f''(\alpha)/2$ are related as follows:

$$a''_0 = a'_0, \quad a''_1 = a''_0 \alpha + a'_1, \quad \ldots, \quad a''_{n-2} = a''_{n-3}\alpha + a'_{n-2}. \tag{3.100}$$

The above relations may be systematized in Table 3.1.

The first row gives the coefficients of $f(\alpha)$, that is, a_0, ..., a_n, the second gives the coefficients of $f'(\alpha)/1!$, that is, $a'_0 = a_0$, $a'_1 = a_{11}$, ..., $a'_{n-1} = a_{1,n-1}$, the third the coefficients of $f''(\alpha)/2!$, that is, $a''_0 = a_0$, $a''_1 = a_{21}$, ..., $a''_{n-2} = a_{2,n-2}$, ..., the nth row has the coefficients of $f^{(n-1)}(\alpha)/(n - 1)!$, that is, $a_0^{(n-1)} = a_0$, $a_1^{(n-1)} = a_{n-1,1}$, and the last row, the $(n + 1)$th, the coefficients of $f^{(n)}(\alpha)/n!$, that is, $a_0^{(n)} = a_0$. This table is known as the *generalized Horner's schema*.

Let us suppose that equation (3.93) is the one that has a positive real root $\bar{x}$. The case of the negative root is similar to the previous one if we consider the equation

$$g(x) = (-1)^n f(-x) = 0. \tag{3.101}$$

Let us suppose that we have found a natural number a_1, so that

$$a_1 < \bar{x} < a_1 + 1; \tag{3.102}$$

hence $\bar{x}$ becomes

$$\bar{x} = a_1 + \frac{1}{x_1}, \tag{3.103}$$

with $x_1 \in \mathbb{R}_+^*$. We then have

$$f_1(x_1) = x_1^n f(a_1) + x_1^{n-1} \frac{f'(a_1)}{1!} + x_1^{n-2} \frac{f''(a_1)}{2!} + \cdots + \frac{f^{(n)}(a_1)}{n!} = 0. \tag{3.104}$$

We now search for a natural number a_2, so that

$$x_1 = a_2 + \frac{1}{x_2}, \tag{3.105}$$

and hence

$$f_2(x_2) = x_2^n f(a_2) + x_2^{n-1} \frac{f'(a_2)}{1!} + x_2^{n-2} \frac{f''(a_2)}{2!} + \cdots + \frac{f^{(n)}(a_2)}{n!} = 0. \tag{3.106}$$

The procedure continues by searching for a_3, so that

$$x_2 = a_3 + \frac{1}{x_3}. \tag{3.107}$$

Finally, we obtain

$$\bar{x} = a_1 + \cfrac{1}{a_2 + \cfrac{1}{a_3 + \cfrac{1}{\ddots}}}, \tag{3.108}$$

a decomposition of $\bar{x}$ in a continued fraction.

Let us denote

$$R_n = a_1 + \cfrac{1}{a_2 + \cfrac{1}{a_3 + \cfrac{1}{\ddots + \cfrac{1}{a_n}}}} = \frac{A_n}{B_n}. \tag{3.109}$$

Dirichlet's theorem shows that

$$|\bar{x} - R_n| < \frac{1}{B_n^2}, \tag{3.110}$$

thus obtaining the error of approximation in the solution $\bar{x}$.

The method presented above is called *Lagrange's method*.

Observation 3.15 To apply Lagrange's method, it is necessary to have one and only one solution of equation (3.93) between a_1 and $a_1 + 1$.

3.4   THE LOBACHEVSKI–GRAEFFE METHOD

Let us consider the algebraic equation[5]

$$a_0 x^n + a_1 x^{n-1} + \cdots + a_{n-1}x + a_n = 0, \tag{3.111}$$

where $a_i \in \mathbb{R}$, $i = \overline{0, n}$, and let us denote by $\overline{x}_i$, $i = \overline{1, n}$, its roots.

3.4.1   The Case of Distinct Real Roots

Let us suppose that the n distinct roots are obtained as follows

$$|\overline{x}_1| > |\overline{x}_2| > \cdots > |\overline{x}_n|. \tag{3.112}$$

The corresponding Viète's relations are

$$\overline{x}_1 + \overline{x}_2 + \cdots + \overline{x}_n = -\frac{a_1}{a_0}, \quad \overline{x}_1\overline{x}_2 + \cdots + \overline{x}_1\overline{x}_n + \cdots + \overline{x}_{n-1}\overline{x}_n = \frac{a_2}{a_0},$$

$$\overline{x}_1\overline{x}_2\overline{x}_3 + \cdots + \overline{x}_1\overline{x}_2\overline{x}_n + \cdots + \overline{x}_{n-2}\overline{x}_{n-1}\overline{x}_n = -\frac{a_3}{a_0}, \quad \ldots, \quad \overline{x}_1\overline{x}_2\cdots\overline{x}_n = (-1)^n\frac{a_n}{a_0}. \tag{3.113}$$

If

$$|\overline{x}_1| \gg |\overline{x}_2| \gg |\overline{x}_3| \gg \cdots \gg |\overline{x}_n|, \tag{3.114}$$

then the roots $\overline{x}_i$, $i = \overline{1, n}$, may be given by the approximate formulae

$$\overline{x}_1 \approx -\frac{a_1}{a_0}, \quad \overline{x}_2 \approx -\frac{a_2}{a_1}, \quad \overline{x}_3 \approx -\frac{a_3}{a_2}, \quad \ldots, \overline{x}_n \approx -\frac{a_n}{a_{n-1}}. \tag{3.115}$$

Let us see now how we can transform equation (3.111) into another one for which the roots $\overline{y}_i$, $i = \overline{1, n}$, satisfy condition (3.114); there exist certain relations between the roots $\overline{x}_k$, $k = \overline{1, n}$, and $\overline{y}_i$, $i = \overline{1, n}$. We now introduce the polynomial function

$$f(x) = a_0 x^n + a_1 x^{n-1} + \cdots + a_{n-1}x + a_n; \tag{3.116}$$

we can then write

$$f(x) = a_0(x - \overline{x}_1)(x - \overline{x}_2)\cdots(x - \overline{x}_n) \tag{3.117}$$

because of the supposition that the roots $\overline{x}_i$, $i = \overline{1, n}$, are real and distinct.
   On the other hand,

$$f(-x) = (-1)^n a_0(x + \overline{x}_1)(x + \overline{x}_2)\cdots(x + \overline{x}_n), \tag{3.118}$$

hence

$$f(x)f(-x) = (-1)^n a_0^2(x^2 - \overline{x}_1^2)(x^2 - \overline{x}_2^2)\cdots(x^2 - \overline{x}_n^2). \tag{3.119}$$

From relation (3.116), we get

$$f(-x) = (-1)^n a_0 x^n + (-1)^{n-1}a_1 x^{n-1} + \cdots + (-1)a_{n-1}x + a_n, \tag{3.120}$$

[5]This method was presented by Germinal Pierre Dandelin (1794–1847) in 1826, Karl Heinrich Graeffe (Karl Heinrich Gräffe) (1799–1873) in 1837, and Nikolai Ivanovich Lobachevski (1792–1856) in 1834.

and hence

$$f(x)f(-x) = (-1)^n[a_0^2 x^{2n} - (a_1^2 - 2a_0a_2)x^{2n-2} + (a_2^2 - 2a_1a_3 + 2a_0a_4)x^{2n-2} + \cdots + (-1)^n a_n^2].$$

$$(3.121)$$

By the transformation

$$y = x^2, \tag{3.122}$$

the equation

$$f(x)f(-x) = 0 \tag{3.123}$$

becomes

$$a_0' y^n + a_1' y^{n-1} + \cdots + a_{n-1}' y + a_n' = 0, \tag{3.124}$$

where

$$a_0' = a_0^2, \quad a_1' = -(a_1^2 - 2a_0a_2), \quad a_2' = a_2^2 - 2a_1a_3 + 2a_0a_4, \quad \ldots, \quad a_n' = (-1)^n a_n^2. \tag{3.125}$$

We can write these relations in the form

$$a_j' = \left[a_j^2 + 2\sum_{i=1}^n (-1)^i a_{j-1} a_{j+1} \right] (-1)^j, \quad j = \overline{0, n}, \tag{3.126}$$

where $a_j = 0$ for $j < 0$ or $j > n$.

Observation 3.16

   (i) Equation (3.123) has $2n$ roots, namely, $\pm \overline{x}_1, \pm \overline{x}_2, \ldots, \pm \overline{x}_n$.
  (ii) By solving equation (3.124), we obtain the roots $\overline{y}_1, \overline{y}_2, \ldots, \overline{y}_n$. The roots $\overline{x}_1, \overline{x}_2, \ldots, \overline{x}_n$ are no more unique, because $\overline{x}_i = \sqrt{-\overline{y}_i}$ or $\overline{x}_i = -\sqrt{-\overline{y}_i}$, $i = \overline{1, n}$.

The procedure described above can be repeated for equation (3.124) in y. In general, the procedure is repeated p times, obtaining thus an equation of the form

$$a_0^{(p)} z^n + a_1^{(p)} z^{n-1} + \cdots + a_{n-1}^{(p)} z + a_n^{(p)} = 0, \tag{3.127}$$

the roots of which are $\overline{z}_1, \overline{z}_2, \ldots, \overline{z}_n$. The connection between $\overline{z}_i$ and $\overline{x}_i$ is given by

$$\overline{x}_i = \sqrt[2^p]{-\overline{z}_i} \quad \text{or} \quad \overline{x}_i = -\sqrt[2^p]{-\overline{z}_i}, \quad i = \overline{1, n}. \tag{3.128}$$

The roots of equation (3.127) are given by the formulae of the form (3.115), hence

$$\overline{z}_1 = -\frac{a_1^{(p)}}{a_0^{(p)}}, \quad \overline{z}_2 = -\frac{a_2^{(p)}}{a_1^{(p)}}, \quad \ldots, \quad \overline{z}_i = -\frac{a_{i+1}^{(p)}}{a_i^{(p)}}, \quad \ldots, \quad \overline{z}_n = -\frac{a_n^{(p)}}{a_{n-1}^{(p)}}, \tag{3.129}$$

so relations (3.128) may also be written in the form

$$\overline{x}_i = \sqrt[2^p]{-\frac{a_i^{(p)}}{a_{i-1}^{(p)}}} \quad \text{or} \quad \overline{x}_i = -\sqrt[2^p]{-\frac{a_i^{(p)}}{a_{i-1}^{(p)}}}, \quad i = \overline{1, n}. \tag{3.130}$$

Relations (3.130) must satisfy the initial equation $f(x) = 0$, retaining only its solutions.

3.4.2 The Case of a Pair of Complex Conjugate Roots

Let us again consider equation (3.111), supposing that two of its roots, say $\overline{x}_k$ and $\overline{x}_{k+1}$, are conjugate complex ones. We can write relation (3.112) in the form

$$|\overline{x}_1| > |\overline{x}_2| > \cdots > |\overline{x}_k| = |\overline{x}_{k+1}| > |\overline{x}_{k+2}| > \cdots > |\overline{x}_n|. \tag{3.131}$$

We denote by

$$r = |\overline{x}_k| = |\overline{x}_{k+1}|, \tag{3.132}$$

the modulus of the conjugate complex roots, where

$$\overline{x}_k = \alpha + i\beta, \qquad \overline{x}_{k+1} = \alpha - i\beta, \qquad r = \sqrt{\alpha^2 + \beta^2}. \tag{3.133}$$

From Viète's relation,

$$\overline{x}_1 + \overline{x}_2 + \cdots + \overline{x}_k + \overline{x}_{k+1} + \cdots + \overline{x}_n = -\frac{a_1}{a_0}, \tag{3.134}$$

we easily obtain

$$\alpha = -\frac{a_1}{2a_0} - \frac{1}{2} \sum_{\substack{j=1 \\ j \neq k; j \neq k+1}}^{n} \overline{x}_j, \tag{3.135}$$

by taking into account relations (3.133). Squaring equation (3.111) and proceeding as from equation (3.111), we obtain the equation

$$a_0^{(p)} z^n + a_1^{(p)} z^{n-1} + \cdots + a_{k-1}^{(p)} z^{n-k+1} + a_k^{(p)} z^{n-k} + a_{k+1}^{(p)} z^{n-k-1} + \cdots + a_1^{(p)} z + a_0^{(p)} = 0. \tag{3.136}$$

The roots $\overline{z}_k$ and $\overline{z}_{k+1}$ satisfy the relation

$$a_{k-1}^{(p)} z^2 + a_k^{(p)} z + a_{k+1}^{(p)} = 0. \tag{3.137}$$

Then

$$\overline{z}_k \overline{z}_{k+1} = \frac{a_{k+1}^{(p)}}{a_{k-1}^{(p)}}. \tag{3.138}$$

On the other hand,

$$\overline{z}_k \overline{z}_{k+1} = (\overline{x}_k \overline{x}_{k+1})^{2^p} = (r^2)^{2^p}, \tag{3.139}$$

from which

$$r^2 = \sqrt[2^p]{\frac{a_{k+1}^{(p)}}{a_{k-1}^{(p)}}}. \tag{3.140}$$

From relations (3.135) and (3.140), we get

$$\beta^2 = r^2 - \alpha^2 = \sqrt[2^p]{\frac{a_{k+1}^{(p)}}{a_{k-1}^{(p)}}} - \left[-\frac{a_1}{2a_0} - \frac{1}{2} \sum_{\substack{j=1 \\ j \neq k; j \neq k+1}}^{n} \overline{x}_j \right]. \tag{3.141}$$

Knowing α and β, we obtain the roots $\overline{x}_k$ and $\overline{x}_{k+1}$.

Observation 3.17

(i) If all the roots of equation (3.111) are real and distinct, then all the products of the form $a_{j-i}a_{j+i}$ become negligible with respect to a_j^2, hence all the coefficients $a_j^{(s)}$ become perfect quasi-squares beginning from a certain rank.

(ii) If a certain $a_j^{(s)}$, $1 \leq j \leq n - 1$, does not become a perfect square, but is situated between two perfect squares $a_{j-1}^{(s)}$ and $a_{j+1}^{(s)}$, then the ratio

$$(r^2)^{2^s} = \frac{a_{j+1}^{(s)}}{a_{j-1}^{(s)}}, \tag{3.142}$$

where r is the modulus of the pair of conjugate complex roots or even the value of a double real root (if the imaginary part of the conjugate complex roots vanishes).

(iii) More generally, if $2l - 1$ coefficients $a_{k-2l+1}^{(s)}, a_{k-2l+2}^{(s)}, \ldots, a_k^{(s)}$ are situated between two perfect squares $a_{k-2l}^{(s)}$ and $a_k^{(s)}$, then there exist l pairs of roots that have the same modulus r.

3.4.3 The Case of Two Pairs of Complex Conjugate Roots

Let $\overline{x}_k$, $\overline{x}_{k+1}$ and $\overline{x}_l$, $\overline{x}_{l+1}$ be two pairs of conjugate complex roots, so that

$$\overline{x}_k = \alpha_1 + i\beta_1, \quad \overline{x}_{k+1} = \alpha_1 - i\beta_1, \quad \overline{x}_l = \alpha_2 + i\beta_2, \quad \overline{x}_{l+1} = \alpha_2 - i\beta_2, \tag{3.143}$$

with $\beta_1 \neq 0$, $\beta_2 \neq 0$. We may write the sequence of inequalities

$$|\overline{x}_1| > |\overline{x}_2| > \cdots > |\overline{x}_{k-1}| > |\overline{x}_k| = |\overline{x}_{k+1}| > |\overline{x}_{k+2}| > \cdots$$

$$> |\overline{x}_{l-1}| > |\overline{x}_l| = |\overline{x}_{l+1}| > |\overline{x}_{l+2}| > \cdots > |\overline{x}_n|, \tag{3.144}$$

where $\overline{x}_1, \ldots, \overline{x}_n$ are the roots of equation (3.111), all real, except for $\overline{x}_k$, $\overline{x}_{k+1}$, $\overline{x}_l$, and $\overline{x}_{l+1}$. We obtain thus two equations of second degree, that is,

$$a_{k-1}^{(p)}z^2 + a_k^{(p)}z + a_{k+1}^{(p)} = 0, \quad a_{l-1}^{(p)}z^2 + a_l^{(p)}z + a_{l+1}^{(p)} = 0. \tag{3.145}$$

Let us denote by r_1 and r_2 the moduli of the two pairs of complex roots

$$r_1 = |\overline{x}_k| = |\overline{x}_{k+1}|, \quad r_2 = |\overline{x}_l| = |\overline{x}_{l+1}|. \tag{3.146}$$

We can write the relations

$$r_1^2 = \overline{x}_k\overline{x}_{k+1} = \alpha_1^2 + \beta_1^2, \quad r_2^2 = \overline{x}_l\overline{x}_{l+1} = \alpha_2^2 + \beta_2^2; \tag{3.147}$$

and from equation (3.145), we obtain

$$r_1^2 = \sqrt[2^p]{\frac{a_{k+1}^{(p)}}{a_{k-1}^{(p)}}}, \quad r_2^2 = \sqrt[2^p]{\frac{a_{l+1}^{(p)}}{a_{l-1}^{(p)}}}. \tag{3.148}$$

From the first Viète relation for equation (3.111), we have

$$\sum_{i=1}^{n} \overline{x}_i = -\frac{a_1}{a_0} \tag{3.149}$$

or

$$\overline{x}_1 + \overline{x}_2 + \cdots + \overline{x}_{k-1} + \overline{x}_{k+1} + \overline{x}_{k+2} + \cdots + \overline{x}_{l-1} + \overline{x}_l + \overline{x}_{l+1} + \overline{x}_{l+2} + \cdots + \overline{x}_n = -\frac{a_1}{a_0}, \quad (3.150)$$

because

$$\overline{x}_k + \overline{x}_{k+1} = 2\alpha_1, \quad \overline{x}_l + \overline{x}_{l+1} = 2\alpha_2, \quad (3.151)$$

we have

$$\alpha_1 + \alpha_2 = -\frac{1}{2}\left[\frac{a_1}{a_0} + \sum_{\substack{i=1 \\ i \neq k; i \neq k+1 \\ i \neq l; i \neq l+1}}^{n} \overline{x}_i\right]. \quad (3.152)$$

Let us consider now the last two Viète relations,

$$\overline{x}_1 \overline{x}_2 \ldots \overline{x}_{n-1} + \overline{x}_1 \overline{x}_2 \ldots \overline{x}_{n-2} \overline{x}_n + \cdots + \overline{x}_2 \overline{x}_3 \ldots \overline{x}_n = (-1)^{n-1}\frac{a_{n-1}}{a_0}, \quad (3.153)$$

$$\overline{x}_1 \overline{x}_2 \ldots \overline{x}_n = (-1)^n \frac{a_n}{a_0}. \quad (3.154)$$

By division, we get

$$\frac{1}{\overline{x}_1} + \cdots + \frac{1}{\overline{x}_{k-1}} + \frac{1}{\overline{x}_k} + \frac{1}{\overline{x}_{k+1}} + \frac{1}{\overline{x}_{k+2}} + \cdots + \frac{1}{\overline{x}_{l-1}} + \frac{1}{\overline{x}_l} + \frac{1}{\overline{x}_{l+1}} + \frac{1}{\overline{x}_{l+2}} + \cdots + \frac{1}{\overline{x}_n} = -\frac{a_{n-1}}{a_n}. \quad (3.155)$$

On the other hand,

$$\frac{1}{\overline{x}_k} + \frac{1}{\overline{x}_{k+1}} = \frac{\overline{x}_k + \overline{x}_{k+1}}{\overline{x}_k \overline{x}_{k+1}} = \frac{2\alpha_1}{r_1^2}, \quad \frac{1}{\overline{x}_l} + \frac{1}{\overline{x}_{l+1}} = \frac{\overline{x}_l + \overline{x}_{l+1}}{\overline{x}_l \overline{x}_{l+1}} = \frac{2\alpha_2}{r_2^2}, \quad (3.156)$$

leading to

$$\frac{\alpha_1}{r_1^2} + \frac{\alpha_2}{r_2^2} = -\frac{1}{2}\left[\frac{a_{n-1}}{a_n} + \sum_{\substack{i=1 \\ i \neq k; i \neq k+1 \\ i \neq l; i \neq l+1}}^{n} \frac{1}{\overline{x}_i}\right]. \quad (3.157)$$

We obtain α_1 and α_2 from relations (3.152) and (3.157). Taking into account $r_1, r_2, \alpha_1, \alpha_2$, it follows that

$$\beta_1 = \sqrt{r_1^2 - \alpha_1^2}, \quad \beta_2 = \sqrt{r_2^2 - \alpha_2^2}. \quad (3.158)$$

3.5   THE BERNOULLI METHOD

Let us consider the equation[6]

$$f(x) = x^n + a_1 x^{n-1} + \cdots + a_n = 0, \quad (3.159)$$

---

[6]Daniel Bernoulli (1700–1782) used this method for the first time in 1724.

to which we associate the recurrence formula

$$\mu_n + a_1\mu_{n-1} + \cdots + a_n = 0. \tag{3.160}$$

If the roots of equation (3.195) are $\xi_1, \xi_2, \ldots, \xi_n$ and if equation (3.160) is considered to be a difference equation, then the solution of the latter is of the form

$$\mu_k = C_1\xi_1^k + C_2\xi_2^k + \cdots + C_n\xi_n^k, \quad k = \overline{1, n}, \tag{3.161}$$

where C_i, $i = \overline{1, n}$, are constants that do not depend on k, while the roots ξ_i, $i = \overline{1, n}$, are assumed to be distinct.

Let us further suppose that the roots ξ_i, $i = \overline{1, n}$, are indexed such that

$$|\xi_1| > |\xi_2| > \cdots > |\xi_n|. \tag{3.162}$$

Writing expression (3.161) in the form

$$\mu_k = C_1\xi_1^k \left(1 + C_2\frac{\xi_2^k}{\xi_1^k} + \cdots + C_n\frac{\xi_n^k}{\xi_1^k} \right) \tag{3.163}$$

and making $k \mapsto k - 1$, from which

$$\mu_{k-1} = C_1\xi_1^{k-1} \left(1 + C_2\frac{\xi_2^{k-1}}{\xi_1^{k-1}} + \cdots + C_n\frac{\xi_n^{k-1}}{\xi_1^{k-1}} \right), \tag{3.164}$$

it follows that

$$\xi_1 = \lim_{k \to \infty} \frac{\mu_k}{\mu_{k-1}}, \tag{3.165}$$

supposing that $\mu_1, \mu_2, \ldots, \mu_n$ are chosen so as not to have $C_1 = 0$. Such a choice is given by

$$\mu_1 = \mu_2 = \cdots = \mu_{n-1} = 0, \quad \mu_n = -a_0. \tag{3.166}$$

Another choice for the n values is given by

$$\mu_r = -(a_1\mu_{r-1} + a_2\mu_{r-2} + \cdots + a_{r-1}\mu_1 + a_r), \quad r = \overline{1, n}, \tag{3.167}$$

where we suppose that $\mu_i = 0$ if $i \le 0$. In the case of this choice, we obtain $C_i = 1$, $i = \overline{1, n}$, and

$$\mu_k = \xi_1^k + \xi_2^k + \cdots + \xi_n^k, \quad k \ge 1. \tag{3.168}$$

Moreover, we also obtain also the approximate relations

$$\xi_1 \approx \frac{\mu_k}{\mu_{k-1}}, \quad \xi_1 \approx \sqrt[k]{\mu_k}, \tag{3.169}$$

with k sufficiently large.

If ξ_1 is a complex root, then $\xi_2 = \bar{\xi}_1$, $|\xi_1| = |\xi_2|$. We may write

$$\xi_1 = \zeta_1 + i\eta_1 = \beta_1 e^{i\phi_1}, \quad \xi_1 = \zeta_1 - i\eta_1 = \beta_1 e^{-i\phi_1}, \tag{3.170}$$

where

$$\beta_1 = \sqrt{\xi_1^2 + \eta_1^2} > 0. \tag{3.171}$$

The sum $C_1\xi_1^k + C_2\xi_2^k$ may be replaced by

$$\beta_1^k(C_1\cos k\phi_1 + C_2\sin k\phi_1), \tag{3.172}$$

where we have made the substitutions

$$C_1 \mapsto \frac{C_1 - iC_2}{2}, \quad C_2 \mapsto \frac{C_1 + iC_2}{2}. \tag{3.173}$$

Hence it follows that, for k sufficiently large, we may write

$$\mu_k \approx \beta_1^k(C_1\cos k\phi_1 + C_2\sin k\phi_1). \tag{3.174}$$

Moreover, μ_k must satisfy the recurrence relation

$$\mu_{k+1} - 2\mu_k\beta_1\cos\phi_1 + \beta_1^2\mu_{k-1} = 0. \tag{3.175}$$

Making $k \mapsto k - 1$, we obtain the second relation of recurrence

$$\mu_k - 2\mu_{k-1}\beta_1\cos\phi_1 + \beta_1^2\mu_{k-2} = 0. \tag{3.176}$$

By eliminating $\cos\phi_1$ between these relations, it follows that

$$(\mu_{k-1}^2 - \mu_k\mu_{k-2})\beta_1^2 = \mu_k^2 - \mu_{k+1}\mu_{k-1}, \tag{3.177}$$

whereas by eliminating β_1^2, we obtain

$$2(\mu_{k-1}^2 - \mu_k\mu_{k-2})\cos\phi_1 = \mu_k\mu_{k-1} - \mu_{k+1}\mu_{k-2}. \tag{3.178}$$

Denoting

$$s_k = \mu_k^2 - \mu_{k+1}\mu_{k-1}, \quad t_k = \mu_k\mu_{k-1} - \mu_{k+1}\mu_{k-2}, \tag{3.179}$$

we obtain the values

$$\beta_1^2 \approx \frac{s_k}{s_{k-1}}, \quad 2\beta_1\cos\phi_1 \approx \frac{t_k}{t_{k-1}}, \tag{3.180}$$

for k sufficiently large and $C_1 \neq 0$, $C_2 \neq 0$ (a case that may be eliminated).

If ξ_1 is a double root, $\xi_1 = \xi_2$, then in the sum (3.161) we obtain the expression $\xi_1^k(C_1 + C_2k)$. It follows that μ_k satisfies the relation

$$\mu_{k+1} - 2\mu_k\xi_1 + \mu_{k-1}\xi_1^2 = 0, \tag{3.181}$$

for $k \to \infty$.

Proceeding as above, we obtain the relation

$$2\xi_1 \approx \frac{t_k}{s_{k-1}}. \tag{3.182}$$

3.6   THE BIERGE–VIÈTE METHOD

Let us consider the polynomial[7]

$$f(x) = x^n + a_1 x^{n-1} + \cdots + a_n \tag{3.183}$$

which we divide by $x - \xi$. It follows that

$$f(x) = x^n + a_1 x^{n-1} + \cdots + a_n = (x - \xi)(x^{n-1} + b_1 x^{n-2} + \cdots + b_{n-1}) + R, \tag{3.184}$$

where R is the remainder. In particular,

$$R = f(\xi). \tag{3.185}$$

Dividing now the quotient of relation (3.184) by $x - \xi$, we obtain

$$x^{n-1} + b_1 x^{n-2} + \cdots + b_{n-1} = (x - \xi)(x^{n-2} + c_1 x^{n-3} + \cdots + c_{n-2}) + R', \tag{3.186}$$

while the remainder R' verifies the relation

$$R' = f'(\xi). \tag{3.187}$$

Obviously, the procedure may continue.

Between the coefficients a_i, $i = \overline{1, n}$, and b_j, $j = \overline{1, n - 1}$, there take place the relations

$$a_1 = b_1 - \xi, \quad a_2 = b_2 - \xi b_1, \quad \ldots, \quad a_{n-1} = b_{n-1} - \xi b_{n-2}, \quad a_n = R - \xi b_{n-1} \tag{3.188}$$

and similarly for b_j, $j = \overline{1, n - 1}$, and c_k, $k = \overline{1, n - 2}$.

It follows that

$$R = f(\xi) = b_n = a_n + \xi b_{n-1}, \tag{3.189}$$

$$R' = f'(\xi) = c_{n-1} = b_{n-1} + \xi c_{n-2}. \tag{3.190}$$

Thus, we obtain the relation of recurrence

$$\xi^* = \xi - \frac{R}{R'} = \xi - \frac{a_n + \xi b_{n-1}}{b_{n-1} + \xi c_{n-2}}. \tag{3.191}$$

As a matter of fact, the Bierge–Viète method is a variant of Newton's method, in which the computation of the functions $f(\xi)$ and $f'(\xi)$ is avoided.

3.7   LIN METHODS

The first Lin method[8] derives from the Bierge–Viète one, for which the relation $f(\xi) = 0$ is equivalent to

$$a_n + \xi b_{n-1} = 0, \tag{3.192}$$

the notations being those in the previous paragraph.

---

[7]This method is the Newton–Raphson method in the case of polynomials. It was named in the honor of François Viète (1540–1603) who stated it for the first time, in a primary form, in 1600.

[8]The methods were presented for the first time by Sir Leonard Bairstow (1880–1963) in 1920. They were mathematically developed by S. N. Lin in 1941 and 1943.

In this case, b_{n-1} is seen as a function of ξ, hence relation (3.192) is written in the form

$$\xi = -\frac{a_n}{b_{n-1}(\xi)}. \tag{3.193}$$

We obtain thus an iterative formula in which

$$\xi^* = -\frac{a_n}{b_{n-1}(\xi)}, \tag{3.194}$$

from which

$$\Delta\xi = \xi^* - \xi = -\frac{a_n + \xi b_{n-1}(\xi)}{b_{n-1}(\xi)} \tag{3.195}$$

or, equivalently,

$$\xi^* = \xi - \frac{R}{b_{n-1}(\xi)}. \tag{3.196}$$

On the other hand, we have seen in the previous paragraph that

$$b_{n-1}(\xi) = \frac{f(\xi) - a_n}{\xi} \tag{3.197}$$

and the recurrence relation (3.193) becomes

$$\xi^* = -\frac{a_n \xi}{f(\xi) - a_n}. \tag{3.198}$$

Hence, it follows that the first Lin method is equivalent to the application of the method of contractions to the function

$$F(\xi) = -\frac{a_n \xi}{f(\xi) - a_n}; \tag{3.199}$$

this method is convergent if

$$|F'(x)| = \left| a_n \frac{x f'(x) - f(x) + a_n}{[f(x) - a_n]^2} \right| < 1. \tag{3.200}$$

On the other hand, if ξ is a root of the equation $f(x) = 0$, then we may write

$$\mu_r = F'(\xi_r) = 1 + \frac{\xi_r}{a_n} f'(\xi_r) = 1 + \frac{\xi_r f'(\xi_r)}{f(0)} \tag{3.201}$$

and the convergence is ensured if

$$|\mu_r| = \left| 1 + \frac{\xi_r}{a_n} f'(\xi_r) \right| < 1, \tag{3.202}$$

that is, if the start value for the iterations sequence is sufficiently close to ξ_r.

The second method of Lin starts from the idea of dividing the polynomial

$$f(x) = x^n + a_1 x^{n-1} + \cdots + a_n \tag{3.203}$$

by the quadratic factor $x^2 + px + q$, obtaining

$$x^n + a_1 x^{n-1} + \cdots + a_n = (x^2 + px + q)(x^{n-2} + b_1 x^{n-3} + \cdots + b_{n-2}) + Rx + S. \tag{3.204}$$

It follows therefore that $x^2 + px + q$ is a divisor of f if and only if $R = 0$ and $S = 0$.

Expanding the computations in equation (3.204), we obtain the relations

$$a_1 = b_1 + p, \quad a_2 = b_2 + pb_1 + q, \quad a_3 = b_3 + pb_2 + qb_1, \quad \ldots,$$

$$a_{n-2} = b_{n-2} + pb_{n-3} + qb_{n-4}, \quad a_{n-1} = R + pb_{n-2} + qb_{n-3}, \quad a_n = S + qb_{n-2}. \quad (3.205)$$

Using the recurrence formula

$$b_k = a_k - pb_{k-1} - qb_{k-2}, \quad k = \overline{1, n}, \quad b_0 = 1, \quad b_{-1} = 0, \quad (3.206)$$

it follows that R and S are given by

$$R = b_{n-1} = a_{n-1} - pb_{n-2} - q_{n-3}, \quad S = b_n + pb_{n-1} = a_n - qb_{n-2}. \quad (3.207)$$

Using the condition $R = 0$, $S = 0$, so that $x^2 + px + q$ divides f, we obtain

$$a_{n-1} - pb_{n-2} - qb_{n-3} = 0, \quad a_n - qb_{n-2} = 0. \quad (3.208)$$

Lin's idea consists in applying the method of successive iterations to the sequences defined by

$$p = \frac{a_{n-1} - qb_{n-3}}{b_{n-2}}, \quad q = \frac{a_n}{b_{n-2}}, \quad (3.209)$$

so that the new values p^*, q^* after iteration become

$$p^* = \frac{a_{n-1} - qb_{n-3}}{b_{n-2}}, \quad q^* = \frac{a_n}{b_{n-2}}, \quad (3.210)$$

$$\Delta p = p^* - p = \frac{a_{n-1} - pb_{n-2} - qb_{n-3}}{b_{n-2}}, \quad \Delta q = q^* - q = \frac{a_n - qb_{n-2}}{b_{n-2}} \quad (3.211)$$

or, equivalently,

$$p^* = p + \frac{R}{b_{n-2}}, \quad q^* = q + \frac{S}{b_{n-2}}. \quad (3.212)$$

Because $\overline{x}_1$ and $\overline{x}_2$ are the roots of the equation $x^2 + px + q$, we have

$$Rx_1 + S = f(x_1), \quad Rx_2 + S = f(x_2), \quad (3.213)$$

resulting in the expressions

$$x_1(p^* - p) + (q^* - q) = \frac{qf(x_1)}{a_n - S}, \quad x_2(p^* - p) + (q^* - q) = \frac{qf(x_2)}{a_n - S}. \quad (3.214)$$

Denoting the roots of the equation $x^2 + p^*x + q^* = 0$ by x_1^*, x_2^*, we obtain the relations

$$(x_2 - x_1)(x_1^* - x_1) = \frac{qf(x_1)}{a_n - S} - (x_1^* - x_1)(x_2^* - x_2),$$

$$(x_2 - x_1)(x_2^* - x_2) = -\frac{qf(x_2)}{a_n - S} + (x_1^* - x_1)(x_2^* - x_2). \quad (3.215)$$

If (x_1^*, x_2^*) is sufficiently close to (x_1, x_2), then Lagrange's theorem of finite increments leads to

$$x_1 - x_1^* \approx \left[1 + \frac{\xi_1 \xi_2}{\xi_2 - \xi_1} \frac{f'(\xi_1)}{a_n} \right] (\xi_1 - x_1), \quad x_2 - x_2^* \approx \left[1 - \frac{\xi_1 \xi_2}{\xi_2 - \xi_1} \frac{f'(\xi_2)}{a_n} \right] (\xi_2 - x_2),$$
(3.216)

where ξ_1 and ξ_2 are the roots of equation $f(x) = 0$.

Hence, the method is convergent if the moduli of the expressions in the brackets of relation (3.50) are strictly subunitary. Moreover, it is necessary that the start values for p and q be sufficiently close to $-(\xi_1 + \xi_2)$ and $\xi_1 \xi_2$, respectively.

3.8   NUMERICAL EXAMPLES

Example 3.1   Let us consider the polynomial

$$P(x) = X^5 + 3X^4 - 2X^3 + 6X^2 + 5X - 7$$
(3.217)

for which we wish to determine the limits between which its roots can be found.

Using the notation in Section 3.1, we have

$$a = \max\{|3|, \ |-2|, |6|, |5|, |-7|\} = 7, \quad a_0 = 1,$$
(3.218)

$$a' = \max\{|1|, |3|, |-2|, |6|, |5|\} = 6, \quad a_5 = -7,$$
(3.219)

so that the roots of the equation $P(x) = 0$ can be found in the interval

$$\frac{7}{13} = \frac{7}{6+7} \leq |\bar{x}| \leq 1 + \frac{7}{1} = 8.$$
(3.220)

The positive roots of the equation $P(x) = 0$ has as upper limit, the value

$$L = 8.$$
(3.221)

Let us consider the equations

$$P(-x) = 0,$$
(3.222)

$$x^5 P \left(\frac{1}{x} \right) = 0,$$
(3.223)

and

$$-x^5 P \left(-\frac{1}{x} \right) = 0,$$
(3.224)

which may be written also in the forms

$$x^5 - 3x^4 - 2x^3 - 6x^2 + 5x + 7 = 0,$$
(3.225)

$$7x^5 - 5x^4 - 6x^3 + 2x^2 - 3x - 1 = 0,$$
(3.226)

and

$$7x^5 + 5x^4 - 6x^3 - 2x^2 - 3x + 1 = 0.$$
(3.227)

The upper limits of the positive roots of these equations are given by

$$L_1 = 1 + \frac{7}{1} = 8, \quad L_2 = 1 + \frac{6}{7} = \frac{13}{7}, \quad L_3 = 1 + \frac{6}{7} = \frac{13}{7}, \tag{3.228}$$

so that the real roots of the equation $P(x) = 0$ are to be found in the set

$$M_1 = \left[-L_1, -\frac{1}{L_3}\right] \cup \left[\frac{1}{L_2}, L\right] = \left[-8, -\frac{7}{13}\right] \cup \left[\frac{7}{13}, 8\right]. \tag{3.229}$$

If we solve the problem by using the second method of determination of the upper limit of the roots of the equation, we get

(i) for the equation $P(x) = 0$: $a_0 = 1$, $A = 7$, $k = 2$, $L = 1 + (a_0/A)^{1/k} = 1 + \sqrt{1/7}$;
(ii) for equation (3.225): $a_0 = 1$, $A = 6$, $k = 1$, $L_1 = 1 + 1/6 = 7/6$;
(iii) for equation (3.226): $a_0 = 7$, $A = 5$, $k = 1$, $L_2 = 1 + 7/5 = 12/5$;
(iv) for equation (3.227): $a_0 = 7$, $A = 6$, $k = 2$, $L_3 = 1 + (7/6)^{1/2} = 1 + \sqrt{7/6}$.

In this case, the real roots of the equation $P(x) = 0$ have to be found in the set

$$M_2 = \left[-\frac{7}{6}, -\frac{1}{1 + \sqrt{7/6}}\right] \cup \left[\frac{5}{12}, 1 + \sqrt{1/7}\right]. \tag{3.230}$$

Let us denote by $f(x)$, $f_1(x)$, $f_2(x)$, and $f_3(x)$ the functions

$$f(x) = x^5 + 3x^4 - 2x^3 + 6x^2 + 5x - 7, \quad f_1(x) = x^5 - 3x^4 - 2x^3 - 6x^2 + 5x + 7,$$

$$f_2(x) = 7x^5 - 5x^4 - 6x^3 + 2x^2 - 3x - 1, \quad f_3(x) = 7x^5 + 5x^4 - 6x^3 - 2x^2 - 3x + 1, \tag{3.231}$$

for which the derivatives are

$$f'(x) = 5x^4 + 12x^3 - 6x^2 + 12x + 5, \quad f''(x) = 20x^3 + 36x^2 - 12x + 12,$$

$$f'''(x) = 60x^2 + 72x - 12, \quad f^{(iv)}(x) = 120x + 72, \quad f^{(v)}(x) = 120, \tag{3.232}$$

$$f_1'(x) = 5x^4 - 12x^3 - 6x^2 - 12x + 5, \quad f_1''(x) = 20x^3 - 36x^2 - 12x - 12,$$

$$f_1'''(x) = 60x^2 - 72x - 12, \quad f_1^{(iv)}(x) = 120x - 72, \quad f_1^{(v)}(x) = 120, \tag{3.233}$$

$$f_2'(x) = 35x^4 - 20x^3 - 18x^2 + 4x - 3, \quad f_2''(x) = 140x^3 - 60x^2 - 36x + 4,$$

$$f_2'''(x) = 420x^2 - 120x - 36, \quad f_2^{(iv)}(x) = 840x - 120, \quad f_2^{(v)}(x) = 840, \tag{3.234}$$

$$f_3'(x) = 35x^4 + 20x^3 - 18x^2 - 4x - 3, \quad f_3''(x) = 140x^3 + 60x^2 - 36x - 4,$$

$$f_3'''(x) = 420x^2 + 120x - 36, \quad f_3^{(iv)}(x) = 840x + 120, \quad f_3^{(v)}(x) = 840. \tag{3.235}$$

To apply Newton's method, we search first for a value $M > 0$ so that $f^{(v)}(M) > 0$. Obviously, M may be any positive real number. We choose $M = 0.1$. We search now for a value $M' \geq M$ so that $f^{(iv)}(M') > 0$. We choose $M' = M$. The procedure is continued for the value M'' and the derivative $f'''(x)$, obtaining $M'' = M' = M$. Step by step, it follows that we may choose the value $L = 1$ for the function $f(x)$.

Analogically, we get the following values

- for $f_1(x)$: $L_1 = 4$;
- for $f_2(x)$: $L_2 = 2$;
- for $f_3(x)$: $L_3 = 1$.

It follows that the real roots of the equation $f(x) = 0$ have to be found in the set

$$M_3 = [-4, -1] \bigcup \left[\frac{1}{2}, 1 \right]. \tag{3.236}$$

Let us solve the same problem by the method of grouping the terms.
For $f(x)$ we may make a group of the form

$$(x^5 + 3x^4 - 2x^3) + (6x^2 + 5x - 7), \tag{3.237}$$

for which we find as upper bounds of the positive roots the values $M_1 = 2$, $M_2 = 1$, so that an upper bound of these roots is given by $M_1 = 2$.
In the same case of the function $f(x)$ we may make also the group

$$(x^5 - 2x^3) + (3x^4 + 6x^2 + 5x - 7), \tag{3.238}$$

for which the upper bounds of the positive roots are the values $M_3 = 2$ and $M_4 = 1$, from which we deduce that the upper bound of the positive roots is given by the value $M_3 = 2$.
In conclusion, the upper limit of the positive roots of the equation $f(x) = 0$ is $L = \max\{M_1, M_3\} = 2$.
By an analogous procedure, it follows that:

- for $f_1(x)$ there is only one possibility of grouping

$$(x^5 - 3x^4 - 2x^3 - 6x^2) + (5x + 7), \tag{3.239}$$

hence the value $L_1 = 4$;
- for $f_2(x)$, there is only one possibility of grouping

$$(7x^5 - 5x^4 - 6x^3) + (2x^2 - 3x - 1) \tag{3.240}$$

to which corresponds $L_2 = 2$;
- for $f_3(x)$ the possibilities of grouping

$$(7x^5 + 5x^4 - 6x^3 - 2x^2 - 3x) + (1), \tag{3.241}$$

with $L_3' = 1$,

$$(7x^5 - 6x^3) + (5x^4 - 2x^2 - 3x) + (1), \tag{3.242}$$

with $L_3'' = 2$,

$$(7x^5 - 6x^3 - 2x^2) + (5x^4 - 3x) + (1), \tag{3.243}$$

with $L_3''' = 2$,

$$(7x^5 - 6x^3 - 3x) + (5x^4 - 2x^2) + (1), \tag{3.244}$$

with $L_3^{(iv)} = 2$,

$$(7x^5 - 2x^2 - 3x) + (5x^4 - 6x^3) + (1), \tag{3.245}$$

with $L_3^{(v)} = 2$,

$$(7x^5 - 2x^2) + (5x^4 - 6x^3 - 3x) + (1), \tag{3.246}$$

with $L_3^{(vi)} = 2$,

$$(7x^5 - 3x) + (5x^4 - 6x^3 - 2x^2) + (1), \tag{3.247}$$

with $L_3^{(vii)} = 2$, so that $L_3 = 2$.

In conclusion, the real roots of the equation $f(x) = 0$ may be found in the set

$$M_4 = \left[-4, -\frac{1}{2}\right] \cup \left[\frac{1}{2}, 2\right]. \tag{3.248}$$

We observe that the four methods lead to different results.

Moreover, Newton's method and the method of grouping of terms lead to sufficiently laborious expressions for the determination of the values L, L_1, L_2, and L_3, because they imply polynomials of a great degree for which we have no formulas to calculate the roots. In the example presented here, we have preferred to determine these limits by entire numbers, although sometimes they can be found as roots of some algebraic equations of small degrees (1 or 2). The first two methods are simpler to apply, the second one having a more restricted area of values for the real roots.

Example 3.2   We wish to determine, as a function of the real parameter λ, the number of negative and positive roots of the equation

$$x^4 - 2x^2 - \lambda = 0. \tag{3.249}$$

To do this, we denote by $f : \mathbb{R} \to \mathbb{R}$ the polynomial function

$$f(x) = x^4 - 2x^2 - \lambda, \tag{3.250}$$

the derivative of which is

$$f'(x) = 4x^3 - 4x, \tag{3.251}$$

so that the first two polynomials of the Sturm sequence are

$$f_0(x) = x^4 - 2x^2 - \lambda, \tag{3.252}$$

$$f_1(x) = x^3 - x. \tag{3.253}$$

Dividing f_0 by f_1, we obtain the quotient x and the remainder $(-x^2 - \lambda)$, so that the following polynomial in the Sturm sequence reads

$$f_2(x) = x^2 + \lambda. \tag{3.254}$$

Now dividing f_1 by f_2 results in the quotient x and the remainder $-(\lambda + 1)x$, from we get the polynomial

$$f_3(x) = (\lambda + 1)x. \tag{3.255}$$

We continue this process with the polynomials f_2 and f_3, for which we obtain the quotient $x/(\lambda + 1)$ and the remainder λ; hence, the last polynomial of the Sturm sequence is

$$f_4(x) = -\lambda. \tag{3.256}$$

Case 1 $\lambda \in (-\infty, -1)$ We construct the following table, where $\varepsilon > 0$ is a sufficiently small value.

	f_0	f_1	f_2	f_3	f_4	W_S
$-\infty$	$+$	$-$	$+$	$+$	$+$	2
$-\varepsilon$	$+$	$+$	$-$	$+$	$+$	2
ε	$+$	$-$	$-$	$-$	$+$	2
∞	$+$	$+$	$+$	$-$	$+$	2

The number of negative roots of the equation $f(x) = 0$ is given by

$$W_S(-\infty) - W_S(-\varepsilon) = 2 - 2 = 0, \tag{3.257}$$

while the number of positive roots of the same equation is

$$W_S(\varepsilon) - W_S(\infty) = 0. \tag{3.258}$$

In conclusion, for $\lambda \in (-\infty, -1)$ our equation has no real roots.

Case 2 $\lambda = -1$ In this case, the equation $f(x) = 0$ becomes

$$x^4 - 2x^2 + 1 = (x^2 - 1)^2 = 0 \tag{3.259}$$

and has the double roots $x_1 = -1$ and $x_2 = 1$.

Case 3 $\lambda \in (-1, 0)$ We construct the following table, where ε is a sufficiently small positive value.

	f_0	f_1	f_2	f_3	f_4	W_S
$-\infty$	+	−	+	−	+	4
$-\varepsilon$	+	+	−	−	+	2
ε	+	−	−	+	+	2
∞	+	+	+	+	+	0

It follows that the number of negative values of the equation $f(x) = 0$ is

$$W_S(-\infty) - W_S(-\varepsilon) = 4 - 2 = 2, \tag{3.260}$$

while the number of positive roots of the same equation is given by

$$W_S(\varepsilon) - W_S(\infty) = 2 - 0 = 2. \tag{3.261}$$

Case 4 $\lambda = 0$ The equation $f(x) = 0$ now takes the form

$$x^4 - 2x^2 = x^2(x^2 - 2) = 0 \tag{3.262}$$

and has the double root $x_1 = 0$ and the simple roots $x_2 = -\sqrt{2}$ and $x_3 = \sqrt{2}$.

Case 5 $\lambda \in (0, \infty)$ We construct the following table, in which $\varepsilon > 0$ is a sufficiently small value.

	f_0	f_1	f_2	f_3	f_4	W_S
$-\infty$	+	−	+	−	+	4
$-\varepsilon$	+	+	−	−	+	2
ε	+	−	−	+	+	2
∞	+	+	+	+	+	0

In this case, the number of negative roots of the equation $f(x) = 0$ is

$$W_S(-\infty) - W_S(-\varepsilon) = 3 - 2 = 1, \tag{3.263}$$

while the number of positive roots is

$$W_S(\varepsilon) - W_S(\infty) = 2 - 1 = 1. \tag{3.264}$$

If we were to apply Descartes' theorem to solve the same problem, then we would find that for $\lambda > 0$, we have only one variation of sign in the sequence of the coefficients of the polynomial $x^4 - 2x^2 - \lambda$, which means that equation (3.249) has only one positive root. Making $x \mapsto -x$, we obtain the same equation (3.249) and, analogically it follows that it has a negative root. If $\lambda < 0$, then Descartes' theorem shows that equation (3.249) has zero or two positive roots and zero or two negative roots.

The same conclusion is obtained from Budan's theorem.

Example 3.3 Let us consider the equation

$$f(x) = x^3 + x - 3 = 0, \tag{3.265}$$

the roots of which we wish to determine.

We begin by presenting an exact method of solving the equation of third degree, that is, the method of Hudde (Johann van Waveren Hudde, 1628–1704).

Let us observe that any equation of third degree,

$$a_0 y^3 + a_1 y^2 + a_2 y + a_3 = 0, \qquad a_0 \neq 0, \tag{3.266}$$

may be brought to the canonical form

$$x^3 + ax + b = 0, \tag{3.267}$$

by dividing it by a_0 and by the transformation

$$y = x - \frac{a_1}{3a_0}. \tag{3.268}$$

We search for solutions of the form

$$x = u + v, \quad u, v \in \mathbb{C}, \tag{3.269}$$

for equation (3.267). It follows that

$$(u + v)^3 + a(u + v) + b = 0 \tag{3.270}$$

or, equivalently,

$$u^3 + v^3 + 3uv(u + v) + a(u + v) + b = 0. \tag{3.271}$$

We shall determine u and v so that

$$u^3 + v^3 = -b, \quad uv = -\frac{a}{3}. \tag{3.272}$$

The last relation (3.272) leads to

$$u^3 + v^3 = -\frac{a^3}{27}, \tag{3.273}$$

hence u^3 and v^3 are solutions of second-degree equation

$$z^2 + bz - \frac{a^3}{27} = 0, \tag{3.274}$$

from which

$$z_{1,2} = \frac{-b \pm \sqrt{b^2 + \frac{4a^3}{27}}}{2}.$$

(3.275)

We get the values

$$u = \sqrt[3]{\frac{-b - \sqrt{b^2 + \frac{4a^3}{27}}}{2}}, \quad v = \sqrt[3]{\frac{-b + \sqrt{b^2 + \frac{4a^3}{27}}}{2}}.$$

(3.276)

Let us denote by Δ the expression

$$\Delta = \frac{4a^3}{27} + b^2,$$

(3.277)

called the *discriminant* of the equation of third degree. Three situations may occur:

Case 1 $\Delta = 0$. In this case, all the roots of equation (3.267) are real, one of them being a double; this is just the condition for such a root. Indeed, denoting by $g(x)$ the function

$$g(x) = x^3 + ax + b,$$

(3.278)

the derivative of which is

$$g'(x) = 3x^2 + a.$$

(3.279)

From the condition that $g(x)$ and $g'(x)$ have a common root, we deduce

$$3x^3 + 3ax + 3b = 0, \quad 3x^3 + ax = 0,$$

(3.280)

from which

$$2ax + 3b = 0.$$

(3.281)

Hence the common root is

$$\overline{x} = -\frac{3b}{2a}.$$

(3.282)

Replacing $\overline{x}$ in equation (3.267), we get

$$-\frac{27b^3}{8a^3} - \frac{3b}{2} + b = 0,$$

(3.283)

from which

$$\frac{27b^3}{4a^3} + b = 0,$$

(3.284)

that is, the condition $\Delta = 0$.

Case 2 $\Delta < 0$. In this situation, expressions (3.276) become

$$u = \sqrt[3]{\frac{-b - i\sqrt{|\Delta|}}{2}}, \quad v = \sqrt[3]{\frac{-b + i\sqrt{|\Delta|}}{2}}$$

(3.285)

or, taking into account the trigonometric representation of complex numbers,

$$u = \sqrt[3]{A}(\cos\theta - i\sin\theta), \quad v = \sqrt[3]{A}(\cos\theta + i\sin\theta),$$

(3.286)

where

$$A = \frac{1}{2}\sqrt{b^2 + \Delta^2} \tag{3.287}$$

and θ is the argument, $\theta \in [0, 2\pi)$. We deduce the values

$$u_1 = \sqrt[3]{A}\left(\cos\frac{\theta}{3} - i\sin\frac{\theta}{3}\right), \quad u_2 = \sqrt[3]{A}\left(\cos\frac{\theta+2\pi}{3} - i\sin\frac{\theta+2\pi}{3}\right),$$

$$u_3 = \sqrt[3]{A}\left(\cos\frac{\theta+4\pi}{3} - i\sin\frac{\theta+4\pi}{3}\right), \tag{3.288}$$

$$v_1 = \sqrt[3]{A}\left(\cos\frac{\theta}{3} + i\sin\frac{\theta}{3}\right), \quad v_2 = \sqrt[3]{A}\left(\cos\frac{\theta+2\pi}{3} + i\sin\frac{\theta+2\pi}{3}\right),$$

$$v_3 = \sqrt[3]{A}\left(\cos\frac{\theta+4\pi}{3} + i\sin\frac{\theta+4\pi}{3}\right), \tag{3.289}$$

and the roots of equation (3.267) are

$$x_1 = u_1 + v_1 = 2\sqrt[3]{A}\cos\frac{\theta}{3}, \quad x_2 = u_2 + v_2 = 2\sqrt[3]{A}\cos\frac{\theta+2\pi}{3},$$

$$x_3 = u_3 + v_3 = 2\sqrt[3]{A}\cos\frac{\theta+4\pi}{3}. \tag{3.290}$$

All these roots are real and distinct.

Case 3 $\Delta > 0$. In this situation, expressions (3.276) read

$$u = \sqrt[3]{\frac{-b-\sqrt{\Delta}}{2}}, \quad v = \sqrt[3]{\frac{-b+\sqrt{\Delta}}{2}} \tag{3.291}$$

or, equivalently,

$$u = \sqrt[3]{\frac{|b+\sqrt{\Delta}|}{2}}(\cos\lambda\pi + i\sin\lambda\pi), \quad v = \sqrt[3]{\frac{|b-\sqrt{\Delta}|}{2}}(\cos\mu\pi + i\sin\mu\pi), \tag{3.292}$$

where λ and μ are two entire parameters with the values 0 or 1, function of the sign of the expressions $-b - \sqrt{\Delta}$ and $-b + \sqrt{\Delta}$.

It follows that

$$u_1 = \sqrt[3]{\frac{|b+\sqrt{\Delta}|}{2}}\left(\cos\frac{\lambda\pi}{3} + i\sin\frac{\lambda\pi}{3}\right), \quad u_2 = \sqrt[3]{\frac{|b+\sqrt{\Delta}|}{2}}\left(\cos\frac{\lambda\pi+2\pi}{3} + i\sin\frac{\lambda\pi+2\pi}{3}\right),$$

$$u_3 = \sqrt[3]{\frac{|b+\sqrt{\Delta}|}{2}}\left(\cos\frac{\lambda\pi+4\pi}{3} + i\sin\frac{\lambda\pi+4\pi}{3}\right), \tag{3.293}$$

$$v_1 = \sqrt[3]{\frac{|b-\sqrt{\Delta}|}{2}}\left(\cos\frac{\mu\pi}{3} + i\sin\frac{\mu\pi}{3}\right), \quad v_2 = \sqrt[3]{\frac{|b-\sqrt{\Delta}|}{2}}\left(\cos\frac{\mu\pi+2\pi}{3} + i\sin\frac{\mu\pi+2\pi}{3}\right),$$

$$v_3 = \sqrt[3]{\frac{|b-\sqrt{\Delta}|}{2}}\left(\cos\frac{\mu\pi+4\pi}{3} + i\sin\frac{\mu\pi+4\pi}{3}\right). \tag{3.294}$$

We obtain nine combinations for the roots of equation (3.267) from which only three lead to roots, one real and two complex conjugate.

Returning to equation (3.265), it has already been brought to the canonical form with $a = 1$ and $b = -3$. It follows that

$$\Delta = \frac{4a^3}{27} + b^2 = \frac{247}{27} > 0, \tag{3.295}$$

and hence equation (3.265) has a real root and two complex conjugate.
We have

$$u = \sqrt[3]{\frac{3 - \sqrt{\frac{247}{27}}}{2}}, \quad v = \sqrt[3]{\frac{3 + \sqrt{\frac{247}{27}}}{2}}, \tag{3.296}$$

so that

$$u_1 = -0.230806, \quad u_2 = 0.115403 + 0.199883i, \quad u_3 = 0.115403 - 0.199883i, \tag{3.297}$$

$$v_1 = 1.444217, \quad v_2 = -0.722109 + 1.250729i, \quad v_3 = -0.722109 - 1.250729i. \tag{3.298}$$

These result in the solutions

$$x_1 = u_1 + v_1 = 1.213411, \quad x_2 = u_2 + v_2 = -0.606706 + 1.450612i,$$

$$x_3 = u_3 + v_3 = -0.606706 - 1.450612i. \tag{3.299}$$

Applying Descartes theorem to the function $f(x)$, we deduce that equation (3.265) has only one positive root. Now making $x \mapsto -x$ in equation (3.265), we deduce the equation

$$x^3 + x + 3 = 0, \tag{3.300}$$

so that equation (3.265) has no negative roots. In conclusion, equation (3.265) has a positive root and two complex conjugate roots.

Let us apply now Lagrange's method to determine the positive root of equation (3.265). We have $f(1) = -1 < 0$, $f(2) = 7 > 0$, hence the positive root of equation (3.265) lies between 1 and 2. We construct the following table:

		1	**0**	**1**	**−3**
1		1	1	2	−1
1		1	2	4	
1		1	3		
1		1			

It results in the equation

$$f_1(x) = x^3 - 4x^2 - 3x - 1 = 0, \tag{3.301}$$

while the solution reads

$$\overline{x} = 1 + \frac{1}{\cdots}. \tag{3.302}$$

As $f_1(4) = -13 < 0$, $f_1(5) = 9 > 0$, the equation $f_1(x) = 0$ has a root between 4 and 5, while the solution $\overline{x}$ reads as

$$\overline{x} = 1 + \cfrac{1}{4 + \cfrac{1}{\vdots}}. \tag{3.303}$$

We construct the following table:

	1	−4	−3	−1
4	1	0	−3	−13
4	1	4	13	
4	1	8		
4	1			

and obtain the equation

$$f_2(x) = 13x^3 - 13x^2 - 8x - 1 = 0,$$ (3.304)

for which $f_2(1) = -9 < 0$, $f_2(2) = 35 > 0$. Now, the solution becomes

$$\bar{x} = 1 + \cfrac{1}{4 + \cfrac{1}{1 + \cfrac{1}{\cdots}}}.$$ (3.305)

It results in the table

	13	−13	−8	−1
1	13	0	−8	−9
1	13	13	5	
1	13	26		
1	13			

and the new equation

$$f_3(x) = 9x^3 - 5x^2 - 26x - 13 = 0,$$ (3.306)

for which $f_3(2) = -13 < 0$, $f_3(3) = 107 > 0$; the equation $f_3(x) = 0$ has a root between 2 and 3. Moreover, the solution $\bar{x}$ takes the form

$$\bar{x} = 1 + \cfrac{1}{4 + \cfrac{1}{1 + \cfrac{1}{2 + \cfrac{1}{\vdots}}}}$$ (3.307)

and we obtain the following table.

	9	−5	−26	−13
2	9	13	0	−13
2	9	31	62	
2	9	49		
2	9			

It results in the equation

$$f_4(x) = 13x^3 - 62x^2 - 49x - 9 = 0,$$ (3.308)

TABLE 3.2 Solving of Equation (2.49) by the Lobachevski–Graeffe Method

Step	a_0	a_1	a_2	a_3
0	1	0	1	-3
1	1	2	1	-9
2	1	-2	37	-81
3	1	70	1045	-6561
4	1	-2810	2010565	-43046721
5	1	-3874970	3.800449×10^{12}	-1.853020×10^{15}
6	1	-7.414495×10^{12}	1.412905×10^{25}	-3.433684×10^{30}
7	1	-2.671664×10^{25}	2.081974×10^{50}	-1.179018×10^{61}

for which $f_4(5) = -179 < 0$, $f_4(6) = 273 > 0$; the solution $\overline{x}$ takes the form

$$\overline{x} = 1 + \cfrac{1}{4 + \cfrac{1}{1 + \cfrac{1}{2 + \cfrac{1}{5 + \cfrac{1}{\vdots}}}}}. \tag{3.309}$$

We stop here and write

$$\overline{x} \approx 1 + \cfrac{1}{4 + \cfrac{1}{1 + \cfrac{1}{2 + \cfrac{1}{5 + 1}}}} = \frac{108}{89} = 1.213483, \tag{3.310}$$

the precision of determination of the solution being

$$\left| \overline{x} - \frac{108}{89} \right| < \frac{1}{89^2} = \frac{1}{7921}. \tag{3.311}$$

Let us solve now equation (3.265) using the Lobachevski–Graeffe method. We may pass from the coefficients $a_i^{(p)}$, $i = \overline{0, 3}$, at the step p, to the coefficients $a_i^{(p+1)}$, $i = \overline{0, 3}$, using the formulae

$$a_0^{(p+1)} = [a_0^{(p)}]^2, \quad a_1^{(p+1)} = -\{[a_1^{(p)}]^2 - 2a_0^{(p)}a_2^{(p)}\}, \quad a_2^{(p+1)} = [a_2^{(p)}]^2 - 2a_1^{(p)}a_3^{(p)},$$
$$a_3^{(p+1)} = -[a_3^p]^2. \tag{3.312}$$

It results in Table 3.2.

The changes of sign in the column of a_1 indicates the presence of a pair of complex roots. The real root is determined by the relation

$$x_3 = \pm \sqrt[2^7]{-\frac{a_3^{(7)}}{a_2^{(7)}}} = \pm 1.21341; \tag{3.313}$$

we observe that equation (3.265) is verified by

$$x_3 = 1.21341. \tag{3.314}$$

Searching for the complex roots of the form

$$x_1 = \alpha + i\beta, \quad x_2 = \alpha - i\beta, \tag{3.315}$$

we obtain, from the Viète relation,

$$\alpha = -\frac{a_1}{2a_0} - \frac{1}{2}x_3 = -0.60671. \tag{3.316}$$

If r is the modulus of the two complex roots (3.315), then

$$r^2 = \sqrt[2^7]{\frac{a_2^{(7)}}{a_0^{(7)}}} = 2.472368, \tag{3.317}$$

hence

$$\beta^2 = r^2 - \alpha^2 = 2.104271, \quad \beta = 1.45061. \tag{3.318}$$

The required roots are

$$x_1 = -0.60671 + 1.45061i, \quad x_2 = -0.60671 - 1.45061i, \quad x_3 = 1.21341. \tag{3.319}$$

We shall use now the Bernoulli method to solve equation (3.265).
We choose parameters μ_k, $k \in \mathbb{N}$, using the recurrence formula

$$\mu_k = -(a_1\mu_{k-1} + a_2\mu_{k-2} + \cdots + a_{k-1}\mu_1 + a_k), \tag{3.320}$$

where $a_0 = 1$, $a_1 = 0$, $a_2 = 1$, $a_3 = -3$, $a_i = 0$ for $i < 0$ or $i > 3$ and $\mu_i = 0$ for $i \leq 0$.
Successively, we get

$$\mu_1 = x_1 + x_2 + x_3 = 0, \tag{3.321}$$

$$\mu_2 = x_1^2 + x_2^2 + x_3^2 = -2, \tag{3.322}$$

$$\mu_3 = x_1^3 + x_2^3 + x_3^3 = 9, \tag{3.323}$$

$$\mu_4 = -(a_1\mu_3 + a_2\mu_2 + a_3\mu_1) = 2, \tag{3.324}$$

$$\mu_5 = -15, \quad \mu_6 = 25, \quad \mu_7 = 21, \quad \mu_8 = -70, \quad \mu_9 = 54, \quad \mu_{10} = 133, \quad \mu_{11} = -264,$$

$$\mu_{12} = 29, \quad \mu_{13} = 663, \quad \mu_{14} = -821, \quad \mu_{15} = -576, \quad \mu_{16} = 2810, \quad \mu_{17} = -1887, \tag{3.325}$$

$$s_{16} = \mu_{16}^2 - \mu_{15}\mu_{17} = 6809188, \quad s_{15} = \mu_{15}^2 - \mu_{14}\mu_{16} = 2638786,$$

$$t_{16} = \mu_{16}\mu_{15} - \mu_{17}\mu_{14} = -3167787, \quad t_{15} = \mu_{15}\mu_{14} - \mu_{16}\mu_{13} = -1390134, \tag{3.326}$$

so that

$$|x_2|^2 = |x_3|^2 \approx \frac{s_{16}}{s_{15}} = 2.580424, \quad |x_2| = |x_3| \approx 1.60637, \tag{3.327}$$

$$2|x_2|\cos\phi = 2|x_3|\cos\phi \approx \frac{t_{16}}{t_{15}} = 2.278764, \quad \cos\phi = 0.709. \tag{3.328}$$

Although the modulus of the two complex conjugate roots determined is relatively correct, their argument ($\cos\phi$) is obtained as positive; but, in reality, this has a negative value.

Let us apply now the Bierge–Viète method to determine the real root of equation (3.265). To do this, let ξ be a real number. Dividing $f(x)$ twice by $x - \xi$, we obtain the following data.

	1	0	1	−3
ξ	1	$\xi = b_1$	$\xi^2 + 1 = b_2$	$\xi^3 + \xi - 3$
ξ	1	$2\xi = c_1$	$3\xi^2 + 1$	

The following recurrence relation results:

$$\xi^* = \xi - \frac{-3 + \xi(\xi^2 + 1)}{\xi^2 + 1 + \xi \times 2\xi} = \xi - \frac{\xi^3 + \xi - 3}{3\xi^2 + 1}. \tag{3.329}$$

As a matter of fact, we have obtained thus the same Newton method, the results of which have been presented before.

We have seen that the application of the first Lin method is equivalent to the application of the contractions method to the function

$$F(\xi) = -\frac{a_n \xi}{f(\xi) - a_n} = \frac{3}{\xi^2 + 1}. \tag{3.330}$$

The method is convergent if

$$\left| 1 + \frac{x_1}{a_n} f'(x_1) \right| < 1, \tag{3.331}$$

that is,

$$\left| 1 - \frac{1.213411}{3} \left(3 \times 1.213411^2 + 1 \right) \right| < 1, \tag{3.332}$$

which is absurd because it leads to $1.191 < 1$.

The convergence is assured in the case of the second Lin method if we have simultaneously

$$\left| 1 + \frac{x_2 x_3}{x_3 - x_2} \frac{f'(x_2)}{a_n} \right| < 1, \quad \left| 1 - \frac{x_2 x_3}{x_3 - x_2} \frac{f'(x_3)}{a_n} \right| < 1. \tag{3.333}$$

We obtain

$$\left| 1 - \frac{2.472367}{2.901224} \frac{1}{-3} \left[3(-0.606706 - 1.450612i)^2 + 1 \right] \right| < 1,$$

$$\left| 1 - \frac{2.472367}{2.901224} \frac{1}{-3} \left[3(-0.606706 + 1.450612i)^2 + 1 \right] \right| < 1, \tag{3.334}$$

that is,

$$|-0.195481 + 1.5i| < 1, \quad |-0.195481 - 1.5i| < 1, \tag{3.335}$$

which is absurd; hence neither the second Lin method also cannot be applied.

3.9 APPLICATIONS

Problem 3.1

A material point of mass m moves along the Ox-axis (Fig. 3.2) acted upon by a force

$$F = -F_0 P \left(\frac{x}{b} \right), \tag{3.336}$$

where P is a polynomial of nth degree, while b is a given constant.

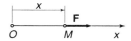

Figure 3.2   Problem 3.1.

Determine the displacements of extreme values, knowing the following initial conditions: $t = 0$, $x = x_0$, $\dot{x} = v_0$.

Solution:

1. Theory
   From the theorem of kinetic energy,

$$\frac{mv^2}{2} - \frac{mv_0^2}{2} = W, \tag{3.337}$$

where v is the velocity of the material point, while W is the work done by force F.

$$W = \int_{x_0}^{x} F(x)\,\mathrm{d}x, \tag{3.338}$$

and with the initial condition $v = 0$, we obtain the extreme values of the distance x as solutions of the equation

$$-\frac{mv_0^2}{2} = \int_{x_0}^{x} F(x)\,\mathrm{d}x. \tag{3.339}$$

With the help of the notations

$$\xi = \frac{x}{b}, \quad \xi_0 = \frac{x_0}{b}, \tag{3.340}$$

we obtain from equation (3.339) the algebraic equation

$$\widetilde{P}(\xi) - k = 0, \tag{3.341}$$

where $\widetilde{P}(\xi)$ is a primitive of the polynomial $P(\xi)$, while k is given by

$$k = \frac{mv_0^2}{2bF_0} + \widetilde{P}(\xi). \tag{3.342}$$

Numerical application: $m = 4$ kg, $x_0 = 0$, $v_0 = 20$ ms^{-1}, $F_0 = 50$ N, $P(x/b) = A_2(x/b)^2 + A_1(x/b) + A_0$, $A_0 = -2$, $A_1 = 2$, $A_2 = 3$, $b = 1$ m.
2. Numerical computation
   We obtain the following successively:

$$P(\xi) = 3\xi^2 + 2\xi - 2, \tag{3.343}$$

$$\widetilde{P}(\xi) = \xi^3 + \xi^2 - 2\xi, \quad \widetilde{P}(\xi_0) = 0; \tag{3.344}$$

it results in the equation

$$\xi^3 + \xi^2 - 2\xi - 16 = 0 \tag{3.345}$$

with the solutions

$$\xi_1 = -2.459120, \quad \xi_2 = -3.45912 - 3.749674i, \quad \xi_3 = -3.45912 + 3.749674i. \tag{3.346}$$

Problem 3.2

Consider the system illustrated in Figure 3.3 (the schema of half of an automobile), formed by two equal masses m_1 and a mass m_2. The nonlinear springs (denoted by k_1, ε_1) give an elastic force

$$F_e = k_1 z + \varepsilon_1 z^2, \tag{3.347}$$

where z is the elongation.

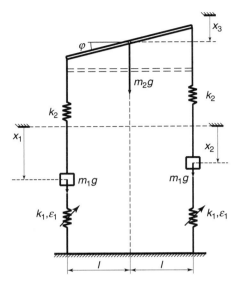

Figure 3.3   Problem 3.2.

The system moves in a vertical plane, the rotation of the bar of mass m_2 (denoted by ϕ) being considered sufficiently small to admit the approximations $\sin \phi \approx \phi$, $\cos \phi \approx 1$.

Let us suppose that both the nonlinear and the linear springs are contracted. Determine

- the positions of equilibrium;
- their stability as a function of the parameter ε_1, assuming that k_1, k_2, m_1, m_2 are known.

Numerical application: $m_1 = 50$ kg, $m_2 = 750$ kg, $l = 2$ m, $k_2 = 20000$ Nm^{-1}, $k_1 = 10^5$ Nm^{-1}, $J = [m_2(2l)^2]/12 = 1000$ kg m^2, $g = 9.8065$ m s^{-2}.

Solution:

1. Theory

   1.1. Equations of equilibrium

   Isolating the three bodies, we obtain the representations in Figure 3.4.

   The equations of equilibrium are

$$\varepsilon_1 x_{10}^2 + k_1 x_{10} - k_2(x_{30} + l\phi_0 - x_{10}) - m_1 g = 0, \tag{3.348}$$

$$\varepsilon_1 x_{20}^2 + k_1 x_{20} - k_2(x_{30} - l\phi_0 - x_{20}) - m_1 g = 0, \tag{3.349}$$

$$k_2(x_{30} + l\phi_0 - x_{10}) + k_2(x_{30} - l\phi_0 - x_{20}) - m_2 g = 0, \tag{3.350}$$

$$k_2 l(x_{30} - l\phi_0 - x_{20}) + k_2 l(x_{30} + l\phi_0 - x_{10}) = 0, \tag{3.351}$$

where the index 0 corresponds to the position of equilibrium.

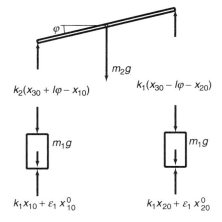

Figure 3.4 Isolation of the rigid bodies.

The above equations may be put in the form

$$\varepsilon_1 x_{10}^2 + (k_1 + k_2)x_{10} - k_2 x_{30} - k_2 l \phi_0 = m_1 g, \tag{3.352}$$

$$\varepsilon_1 x_{20}^2 + (k_1 + k_2)x_{20} - k_2 x_{30} + k_2 l \phi_0 = m_1 g, \tag{3.353}$$

$$-k_2 x_{10} - k_2 x_{20} + 2k_2 x_{30} = m_2 g, \tag{3.354}$$

$$x_{10} - x_{20} - 2l \phi_0 = 0. \tag{3.355}$$

1.2. Positions of equilibrium
From relation (3.355), we obtain

$$\phi_0 = \frac{x_{10} - x_{20}}{2l}, \tag{3.356}$$

which, replaced in relations (3.352) and (3.354), leads to

$$\varepsilon_1 x_{10}^2 + (k_1 + k_2)x_{10} - k_2 x_{30} - \frac{k_2}{2}(x_{10} - x_{20}) = m_1 g, \tag{3.357}$$

$$\varepsilon_1 x_{20}^2 + (k_1 + k_2)x_{20} - k_2 x_{30} + \frac{k_2}{2}(x_{10} - x_{20}) = m_1 g. \tag{3.358}$$

From equation (3.354), we get

$$x_{30} = \frac{m_2 g}{2k_2} + \frac{x_{10} + x_{20}}{2}. \tag{3.359}$$

Subtracting relation (3.357) from (3.358), term by term, it follows that

$$\varepsilon_1(x_{10}^2 - x_{20}^2) + k_1(x_{10} - x_{20}) = 0, \tag{3.360}$$

from which it follows that

$$x_{10} = x_{20} \text{ or } x_{10} + x_{20} = -\frac{k_1}{\varepsilon_1}. \tag{3.361}$$

If $x_{10} = x_{20}$, then from equation (3.356) we obtain $\phi_0 = 0$, so that from equation (3.359) we get

$$x_{30} = \frac{m_2 g}{2k_2} + x_{10} = \frac{m_2 g}{2k_2} + x_{20}. \tag{3.362}$$

If $x_{10} + x_{20} = -k_1/\varepsilon_1$, then we may write

$$x_{10} = -\frac{k_1}{\varepsilon_1} - x_{20}, \quad x_{20} = -\frac{k_1}{\varepsilon_1} - x_{10}. \tag{3.363}$$

Relation (3.359) leads to

$$x_{30} = \frac{m_2 g}{2k_2} - \frac{k_1}{2\varepsilon_1}, \tag{3.364}$$

while from equation (3.356) we obtain

$$\phi_0 = \frac{x_{10}}{l} + \frac{k_1}{2l\varepsilon_1}, \quad \phi_0 - \frac{x_{20}}{l} - \frac{k_1}{2l\varepsilon_1}. \tag{3.365}$$

Equation (3.357) now takes the form

$$\varepsilon_1 x_{10}^2 + (k_1 - k_2)x_{10} - \frac{k_1 k_2}{2\varepsilon_1} - \left(m_1 + \frac{m_2}{2}\right)g = 0, \tag{3.366}$$

while equation (3.358) becomes

$$\varepsilon_1 x_{20}^2 + (k_1 - k_2)x_{20} - \frac{k_1 k_2}{2\varepsilon_1} - \left(m_1 + \frac{m_2}{2}\right)g = 0. \tag{3.367}$$

As a matter of fact, equations (3.366) and (3.367) are the same. The discriminant of these equations is

$$\Delta = k_1^2 + k_2^2 + 4\varepsilon_1 \left(m_1 + \frac{m_2}{2}\right)g \tag{3.368}$$

and the condition $\Delta \geq 0$ leads to the inequality

$$\varepsilon_1 \geq -\frac{k_1^2 + k_2^2}{4\left(m_1 + \frac{m_2}{2}\right)g}. \tag{3.369}$$

The sum of the roots of equation (3.366) (of equation (3.367) too) is

$$S = \frac{k_1 - k_2}{\varepsilon_1} \neq -\frac{k_1}{\varepsilon_1}, \tag{3.370}$$

which means that the position of equilibrium (if it exists) is given by

$$x_{10} = x_{20} = \frac{k_2 - k_1 - \sqrt{\Delta}}{2\varepsilon_1} \quad \text{or} \quad x_{10} = x_{20} = \frac{k_2 - k_1 + \sqrt{\Delta}}{2\varepsilon_1}. \tag{3.371}$$

As $x_{10} > 0$, $x_{20} > 0$ (the springs are compressed), from $x_{10} + x_{20} = -k_1/\varepsilon_1$ it follows that $\varepsilon_1 < 0$.

It follows, from the first equality (3.371), that

$$k_2 = \Delta, \tag{3.372}$$

from which

$$k_1^2 + k_2^2 + 4\varepsilon_1 \left(m_1 + \frac{m_2}{2}\right) g = k_2^2, \tag{3.373}$$

that is,

$$\varepsilon_1 = -\frac{k_1^2}{4\left(m_1 + \frac{m_2}{2}\right) g}, \tag{3.374}$$

which verifies inequalities (3.369) and $\varepsilon_1 < 0$.

It follows that the position of equilibrium is

$$x_{10} = x_{20} = -\frac{k_1}{2\varepsilon_1} > 0, \tag{3.375}$$

ε_1 being given by equation (3.374).

For the second equation (3.371), we obtain

$$k_2 = -\sqrt{\Delta}, \tag{3.376}$$

which is absurd.

Let us remark that equation (3.375) is a particular case of the first relation (3.361), and hence at equilibrium $x_{10} = x_{20}$.

1.3. Equations of motion

Using the schema in Figure 3.3, these equations are

$$m_1 \ddot{x}_1 = k_2(x_3 + l\phi - x_1) - k_1 x_1 - \varepsilon_1 x_1^2 + m_1 g, \tag{3.377}$$

$$m_1 \ddot{x}_2 = k_2(x_3 - l\phi - x_2) - k_1 x_2 - \varepsilon_1 x_2^2 + m_1 g, \tag{3.378}$$

$$m_2 \ddot{x}_3 = k_2(-x_3 - l\phi + x_1) + k_2(-x_3 + l\phi + x_2) + m_2 g, \tag{3.379}$$

$$J \ddot{\phi} = k_2 l(-x_3 - l\phi + x_1) - k_2 l(-x_3 + l\phi + x_2). \tag{3.380}$$

Denoting $x_1 = \xi_1$, $x_2 = \xi_2$, $x_3 = \xi_3$, $\phi = \xi_4$, $\dot{x}_1 = \xi_5$, $\dot{x}_2 = \xi_6$, $\dot{x}_3 = \xi_7$, $\dot{\phi} = \xi_8$,

$$a_{10} = -\frac{\varepsilon_1}{m_1}, \quad a_{11} = -\frac{k_1 + k_2}{m_1}, \quad a_{13} = \frac{k_2}{m_1}, \quad a_{14} = \frac{k_2 l}{m_1}, \tag{3.381}$$

$$a_{20} = -\frac{\varepsilon_1}{m_1}, \quad a_{22} = -\frac{k_1 + k_2}{m_1}, \quad a_{23} = \frac{k_2}{m_1}, \quad a_{24} = -\frac{k_2 l}{m_1}, \tag{3.382}$$

$$a_{31} = \frac{k_2}{m_2}, \quad a_{32} = \frac{k_2}{m_2}, \quad a_{33} = -\frac{2k_2}{m_2}, \tag{3.383}$$

$$a_{41} = \frac{k_2 l}{J}, \quad a_{42} = -\frac{k_2 l}{J}, \quad a_{44} = -\frac{2k_2 l^2}{J}, \tag{3.384}$$

we obtain the system

$$\dot{\xi}_1 = \xi_5, \quad \dot{\xi}_2 = \xi_6, \quad \dot{\xi}_3 = \xi_7, \quad \dot{\xi}_4 = \xi_8, \quad \dot{\xi}_5 = a_{10}\xi_1^2 + a_{11}\xi_1 + a_{13}\xi_3 + a_{14}\xi_4 + g,$$

$$\dot{\xi}_6 = a_{20}\xi_2^2 + a_{22}\xi_2 + a_{23}\xi_3 + a_{24}\xi_4 + g, \quad \dot{\xi}_7 = a_{31}\xi_1 + a_{32}\xi_2 + a_{33}\xi_3 + g,$$

$$\dot{\xi}_8 = a_{41}\xi_1 + a_{42}\xi_2 + a_{44}\xi_4. \tag{3.385}$$

1.4. Stability of the positions of equilibrium

Denoting by $f_k(\xi_1, \ldots, \xi_8)$, $k = \overline{1,8}$, the expressions of the right member of relations (3.385) and by $j_{kl} = \partial f_k/\partial \xi_l$, $k, l = \overline{1,8}$, their partial derivatives, the characteristic equation is

$$\begin{vmatrix} -\lambda & 0 & 0 & 0 & 1 & 0 & 0 & 0 \\ 0 & -\lambda & 0 & 0 & 0 & 1 & 0 & 0 \\ 0 & 0 & -\lambda & 0 & 0 & 0 & 1 & 0 \\ 0 & 0 & 0 & -\lambda & 0 & 0 & 0 & 1 \\ j_{51} & 0 & j_{53} & j_{54} & -\lambda & 0 & 0 & 0 \\ 0 & j_{62} & j_{63} & j_{64} & 0 & -\lambda & 0 & 0 \\ j_{71} & j_{72} & j_{73} & 0 & 0 & 0 & -\lambda & 0 \\ j_{81} & j_{82} & 0 & j_{84} & 0 & 0 & 0 & -\lambda \end{vmatrix} = 0, \qquad (3.386)$$

from which

$$\begin{vmatrix} j_{51} - \lambda^2 & 0 & j_{53} & j_{54} \\ 0 & j_{62} - \lambda^2 & j_{63} & j_{64} \\ j_{71} & j_{72} & j_{73} - \lambda^2 & 0 \\ j_{81} & j_{82} & 0 & j_{84} - \lambda^2 \end{vmatrix} = 0. \qquad (3.387)$$

We obtain the algebraic equation of eighth degree in λ

$$\lambda^8 + A\lambda^6 + B\lambda^4 + C\lambda^2 + D = 0, \qquad (3.388)$$

where

$$A = -j_{51} - j_{62} - j_{73} - j_{74}, \qquad (3.389)$$

$$B = j_{62}j_{73} + j_{62}j_{84} + j_{73}j_{84} - j_{64}j_{82} - j_{63}j_{72}$$
$$+ j_{51}j_{62} + j_{51}j_{73} + j_{51}j_{84} - j_{53}j_{71} - j_{54}j_{81}, \qquad (3.390)$$

$$C = -j_{62}j_{73}j_{84} + j_{64}j_{73}j_{82} + j_{63}j_{72}j_{84} - j_{51}j_{62}j_{73} - j_{51}j_{62}j_{84} - j_{51}j_{73}j_{84}$$
$$+ j_{51}j_{64}j_{82} + j_{51}j_{63}j_{72} + j_{53}j_{62}j_{71} + j_{53}j_{71}j_{84} + j_{54}j_{62}j_{81}$$
$$+ j_{54}j_{73}j_{81}, \qquad (3.391)$$

$$D = j_{51}j_{62}j_{73}j_{84} - j_{51}j_{64}j_{73}j_{82} - j_{51}j_{63}j_{72}j_{84} + j_{53}j_{64}j_{71}j_{82} - j_{53}j_{64}j_{72}j_{81}$$
$$- j_{53}j_{62}j_{71}j_{84} - j_{54}j_{62}j_{73}j_{81} - j_{54}j_{63}j_{71}j_{82} + j_{54}j_{63}j_{72}j_{81}. \qquad (3.392)$$

Equation (3.388), with the notation $u = \lambda^2$, may be written in the form

$$u^4 + Au^3 + Bu^2 + Cu + D = 0 \qquad (3.393)$$

and, for the position of stable equilibrium, it is necessary and sufficient that all the roots of equation (3.393) be negative and distinct (see 1.10. Discussion).

The following situations may occur:

- The roots are distinct.
- There is a double root.
- There is a triple root.
- There is a root of an order of multiplicity equal to four.
- There are two double roots.

1.5. Case of distinct roots

Making $u \mapsto -u$ in equation (3.393), we obtain

$$u^4 - Au^3 + Bu^2 - Cu + D = 0 \tag{3.394}$$

and, from Descartes' theorem, we deduce the necessary condition for the existence of four negative roots

$$A > 0, \quad B > 0, \quad C > 0, \quad D > 0. \tag{3.395}$$

We construct the Sturm sequence associated to the polynomial

$$f(u) = u^4 + Au^3 + Bu^2 + Cu + D. \tag{3.396}$$

We choose

$$f_0(u) = u^4 + Au^3 + Bu^2 + Cu + D, \tag{3.397}$$

$$f_1 = u^3 + \frac{3A}{4}u^2 + \frac{B}{2}u + \frac{C}{4}. \tag{3.398}$$

Dividing f_0 by f_1, we obtain the remainder

$$R_2 = \frac{8B - 3A^2}{16}u^2 + \frac{6C - AB}{8}u + \frac{16D - AC}{16}. \tag{3.399}$$

We find that it is necessary that $8B - 3A^2 \neq 0$; in the opposite case, R_2 would have a degree at most equal to 1 (as with the polynomial f_2 in the Sturm sequence) and would result in only four terms in the Sturm sequence (f_0, f_1, f_2, and f_3 (the last term being a constant)), so that in the sequence $f_0(-\infty)$, $f_1(-\infty)$, $f_2(-\infty)$, $f_3(-\infty)$, we would have at most three variations of sign. It would follow that equation (3.393) has at most three negative roots, which is not convenient. As a conclusion, it results in the necessary condition

$$8B - 3A^2 \neq 0. \tag{3.400}$$

Writing

$$R_2 = -\alpha_2' u^2 - \beta_2' u - \gamma_2', \tag{3.401}$$

we may choose the following term of Sturm's sequence in the form

$$f_2(u) = u^2 + \beta_2 u + \gamma_2, \tag{3.402}$$

where

$$\beta_2 = \frac{\beta_2'}{\alpha_2'} = \frac{2(6C - AB)}{8B - 3A^2}, \quad \gamma_2 = \frac{\gamma_2'}{\alpha_2'} = \frac{16D - AC}{8B - 3A^2}. \tag{3.403}$$

Dividing f_1 by f_2, we obtain the remainder

$$R_3 = -\beta_3' u - \gamma_3', \tag{3.404}$$

where

$$\beta_3' = \gamma_2 - \frac{B}{2} + \beta_2\left(\frac{3}{4}A - \beta_2\right), \quad \gamma_3' = -\frac{C}{4} + \gamma_2\left(\frac{3}{4}A - \beta_2\right). \tag{3.405}$$

TABLE 3.3   Table of the Variations of Sign in the Sturm Sequence

u	f_0	f_1	f_2	f_3	f_4	W_S
$-\infty$	$+$	$-$	$+$	$-$	$\operatorname{sgn} f_4$	3 or 4
0	$+$	$+$	$\operatorname{sgn}\gamma_2$	$\operatorname{sgn}\gamma_3$	$\operatorname{sgn} f_4$	0, 1, 2, or 3

Similar considerations lead to the condition $\beta_3' \neq 0$, from which

$$\frac{16D - AC}{8B - 3A^2} - \frac{B}{2} + \frac{2(6C - AB)}{8B - 3A^2}\left[\frac{3}{4}A - \frac{2(6C - AB)}{8B - 3A^2}\right] \neq 0. \tag{3.406}$$

We choose

$$f_3(u) = u + \gamma_3, \tag{3.407}$$

with

$$\gamma_3 = \frac{\gamma_3'}{\beta_3'}. \tag{3.408}$$

Dividing f_2 by f_3 results in the remainder

$$R_4 = \gamma_2 - \gamma_3(\beta_2 - \gamma_3) \tag{3.409}$$

and the polynomial

$$f_4(u) = \gamma_3(\beta_2 - \gamma_3) - \gamma_2, \tag{3.410}$$

which must be nonzero (the roots are distinct!), from which we obtain the condition

$$\frac{-\frac{C}{4} + \gamma_2\left(\frac{3}{4}A - \beta_2\right)}{\gamma_2 - \frac{B}{2} + \beta_2\left(\frac{3}{4}A - \beta_2\right)}\left[\beta_2 - \frac{-\frac{C}{4} + \gamma_2\left(\frac{3}{4}A - \beta_2\right)}{\gamma_2 - \frac{B}{2} + \beta_2\left(\frac{3}{4}A - \beta_2\right)}\right] - \gamma_2 \neq 0. \tag{3.411}$$

We may construct Table 3.3.

The only possibility to have four negative distinct roots is that $W_S(-\infty) = 4$ and $W_S(0) = 0$, from which result the conditions

$$f_4 > 0, \quad \gamma_2 > 0, \quad \gamma_3 > 0. \tag{3.412}$$

1.6. The case of a double root

If the polynomial $f(u)$ given by (L) has a double root, say $\bar{u}$, then $\bar{u}$ is also a root for the derivative $f'(u)$, that is,

$$\bar{u}^4 + A\bar{u}^3 + B\bar{u}^2 + C\bar{u} + D = 0, \quad 4\bar{u}^3 + 3A\bar{u}^2 + 2B\bar{u} + C = 0. \tag{3.413}$$

Relations (3.413) multiplied by 4 and $-\bar{u}$, respectively, summed, lead to

$$A\bar{u}^3 + 2B\bar{u}^2 + 3C\bar{u} + 4D = 0. \tag{3.414}$$

We multiply the second relation (3.413) by A, relation (3.141) by -4 and make the sum, obtaining

$$(3A^2 - 8B)\bar{u}^2 + (2AB - 12C)\bar{u} + AC - 16D = 0. \tag{3.415}$$

Summing relation (3.414), multiplied by $(8B - 3A^2)$, with relation (3.415), multiplied by $A\overline{u}$, we get the relation

$$(4B^2 + A^2B - 3AC)\overline{u}^2 + (6BC - 2A^2C - 4AD)\overline{u} + D(3A^2 - 8B) = 0. \quad (3.416)$$

Multiplying expressions (3.415) and (3.416) by $(4B^2 - A^2B - 3AC)$ and $(8B - 3A^2)$, respectively, and summing the results thus obtained, we get

$$(8AB^3 - 2A^3B^2 - 28A^2BC + 36AC^2 - 32ABD - 6A^4C + 12A^3D)\overline{u}$$
$$+ 4AB^2C - A^3BC - 3A^2C^2 - 128B^2D + 64A^2BD + 48ACD - 9A^4D = 0 \quad (3.417)$$

and the condition

$$4AB^3 - A^3B^2 - 14A^2BC + 18AC^2 - 16ABD - 3A^4C + 6A^3D \neq 0. \quad (3.418)$$

We now construct Horner's schema in Table 3.4.
The other roots result from

$$u^2 + (A + 2\overline{u})u + 3\overline{u}^2 + 2A\overline{u} + B = 0 \quad (3.419)$$

which must have two negative roots, distinct and different from $\overline{u}$, from which result the conditions

$$\Delta = (A + 2\overline{u})^2 - 4(3\overline{u}^2 + 2A\overline{u} + B) > 0,$$

$$A + 2\overline{u} > 0, \quad 3\overline{u}^2 + 2A\overline{u} + B > 0, \quad \frac{-(A + 2\overline{u}) \pm \sqrt{\Delta}}{2} \neq \overline{u}. \quad (3.420)$$

Writing relation (3.418) in the form $E_1\overline{u} + E_2 = 0$, the notations being obvious, we also obtain the condition

$$\frac{E_2}{E_1} > 0. \quad (3.421)$$

1.7. Case of a triple root

Let us denote this root by $\overline{\overline{u}}$; then, it must satisfy the conditions

$$\overline{\overline{u}}^4 + A\overline{\overline{u}}^3 + B\overline{\overline{u}}^2 + C\overline{\overline{u}} + D = 0, \quad 4\overline{\overline{u}}^3 + 3A\overline{\overline{u}}^2 + 2B\overline{\overline{u}} + C = 0, \quad 6\overline{\overline{u}}^2 + 3A\overline{\overline{u}} + B = 0. \quad (3.422)$$

Multiplying the second relation (3.422) by 3, the third one by $-2\overline{\overline{u}}$ and summing, we obtain the equation

$$3A\overline{\overline{u}}^2 + 4B\overline{\overline{u}} + 3C = 0. \quad (3.423)$$

Summing now the last relation (3.422), multiplied by A, to relation (3.423), multiplied by -2, it follows that

$$(3A^2 - 8B)\overline{\overline{u}} + AB - 6C = 0, \quad (3.424)$$

TABLE 3.4   Horner's Schema for a Double Root

1	A	B	C	D	
$\overline{u}$	1	$A + \overline{u}$	$\overline{u}^2 + A\overline{u} + B$	$\overline{u}^3 + A\overline{u}^2 + B\overline{u} + C$	0
$\overline{u}$	1	$A + 2\overline{u}$	$3\overline{u}^2 + 2A\overline{u} + B$	0	

from which

$$\overline{\overline{u}} = \frac{6C - AB}{3A^2 - 8B} < 0, \quad 3A^2 - 8B \neq 0. \tag{3.425}$$

We construct now Horner's schema in Table 3.5.
We obtain thus the last root

$$u^* = -A - 3\overline{\overline{u}} < 0. \tag{3.426}$$

1.8. Case of the root of order of multiplicity equal to four
   Let $\overline{\overline{\overline{u}}}$ be this root. It will satisfy the relations

$$\overline{\overline{\overline{u}}}^4 + A\overline{\overline{\overline{u}}}^3 + B\overline{\overline{\overline{u}}}^2 + C\overline{\overline{\overline{u}}} + D = 0, \quad 4\overline{\overline{\overline{u}}}^3 + 3A\overline{\overline{\overline{u}}}^2 + 2B\overline{\overline{\overline{u}}} + C = 0,$$

$$6\overline{\overline{\overline{u}}}^2 + 3A\overline{\overline{\overline{u}}} + B = 0, \quad 4\overline{\overline{\overline{u}}} + A = 0, \tag{3.427}$$

from which

$$\overline{\overline{\overline{u}}} = -\frac{A}{4} < 0; \tag{3.428}$$

it follows

$$\left(u + \frac{A}{4}\right)^4 = u^4 + Au^3 + Bu^2 + Cu + D, \tag{3.429}$$

from which

$$B = \frac{3A^2}{8}, \quad C = \frac{A^3}{16}, \quad D = \frac{A^4}{256}. \tag{3.430}$$

1.9. Case of two double roots
   Let $\overline{u} < 0$ and $\overline{\overline{u}} < 0$ be the two double roots. We may write

$$u^4 + Au^3 + Bu^2 + Cu + D = (u - \overline{u})^2(u - \overline{\overline{u}})^2, \tag{3.431}$$

from which

$$A = -2(\overline{u} + \overline{\overline{u}}), \quad B = (\overline{u} + \overline{\overline{u}})^2, \quad C = -2\overline{u}\overline{\overline{u}}(\overline{u} + \overline{\overline{u}}), \quad D = (\overline{u}\overline{\overline{u}})^2,$$

$$A > 0, \quad B > 0, \quad C > 0, \quad D > 0. \tag{3.432}$$

It follows that $\overline{u}$ and $\overline{\overline{u}}$ are solutions of the equation

$$z^2 + \frac{A}{2}z + \sqrt{D} = 0, \tag{3.433}$$

that is,

$$z_{1,2} = -\frac{A}{4} \pm \frac{1}{2}\sqrt{A^2 - 16\sqrt{D}}, \tag{3.434}$$

TABLE 3.5   Horner's Schema for a Triple Root

	1	A	B	C	D
$\overline{\overline{u}}$	1	$A + \overline{\overline{u}}$	$\overline{\overline{u}}^2 + A\overline{\overline{u}} + B$	$\overline{\overline{u}}^3 + A\overline{\overline{u}}^2 + B\overline{\overline{u}} + C$	0
$\overline{\overline{u}}$	1	$A + 2\overline{\overline{u}}$	$3\overline{\overline{u}}^2 + 2A\overline{\overline{u}} + B$	0	
$\overline{\overline{u}}$	1	$A + 3\overline{\overline{u}}$	0		

obtaining thus a new condition

$$\frac{A^4}{256} > D. \tag{3.435}$$

Denoting by

$$\overline{u} = -\frac{A}{4} + \frac{1}{2}\sqrt{A^2 - 16\sqrt{D}}, \quad \overline{\overline{u}} = -\frac{A}{4} - \frac{1}{2}\sqrt{A^2 - 16\sqrt{D}}, \tag{3.436}$$

it follows that

$$\overline{u} + \overline{\overline{u}} = -\frac{A}{2}, \quad \overline{u}\overline{\overline{u}} = \sqrt{D}, \quad (\overline{u} + \overline{\overline{u}})^2 = \frac{A^2}{4} = B, \quad -2\overline{u}\overline{\overline{u}}(\overline{u} + \overline{\overline{u}}) = A\sqrt{D} = C. \tag{3.437}$$

1.10. **Discussion**

Let $\overline{u} = \alpha + i\beta$, $\alpha \neq 0$, $\beta \neq 0$ be a root of equation (3.413), which will be written in the trigonometric form

$$\overline{u} = |\overline{u}|(\cos\theta + i\sin\theta), \tag{3.438}$$

from which

$$\lambda = \overline{u}^{\frac{1}{2}} = \sqrt{|\overline{u}|}\left(\cos\frac{\theta}{2} + i\sin\frac{\theta}{2}\right) \quad \text{or}$$

$$\lambda = \overline{u}^{\frac{1}{2}} = \sqrt{|\overline{u}|}\left[\cos\left(\frac{\theta}{2} + \pi\right) + i\sin\left(\frac{\theta}{2} + \pi\right)\right]. \tag{3.439}$$

Let us remark that, irrespective of the value of θ, we get either $\cos(\theta/2) > 0$, or $\cos(\theta/2 + \pi) > 0$, hence equation (3.388) will have at least one root with a positive real part, that is, the position of equilibrium is unstable. Let us suppose now that a root of equation (3.393) is of the form

$$\overline{u} = i\beta, \quad \beta \neq 0, \tag{3.440}$$

that is,

$$\overline{u} = |\beta|\left(\cos\frac{\pi}{2} + i\sin\frac{\pi}{2}\right) \quad \text{or} \quad \overline{u} = |\beta|\left(\cos\frac{3\pi}{2} + i\sin\frac{3\pi}{2}\right). \tag{3.441}$$

We deduce

$$\lambda = \overline{u}^{\frac{1}{2}} = \sqrt{|\beta|}\left(\cos\frac{\pi}{4} + i\sin\frac{\pi}{4}\right) \quad \text{or} \quad \lambda = \overline{u}^{\frac{1}{2}} = \sqrt{|\beta|}\left(\cos\frac{3\pi}{4} + i\sin\frac{3\pi}{4}\right) \quad \text{or}$$

$$\lambda = \overline{u}^{\frac{1}{2}} = \sqrt{|\beta|}\left(\cos\frac{5\pi}{4} + i\sin\frac{5\pi}{4}\right), \tag{3.442}$$

hence at least one root of the characteristic equation (3.388) has its real part positive, so that the equilibrium is unstable.

The case $\alpha = 0$, $\beta = 0$ leads to the root $\overline{u} = 0$, from which it follows that $\lambda = 0$ is a double root of the characteristic equation (3.388). The linear approximation of the motion around the position of equilibrium will contain a term of the form Kt, where K is a constant, hence the equilibrium also is unstable.

Thus, the only possibility of stability of equilibrium is that described by the fact that all the roots of equation (3.393) are negative.

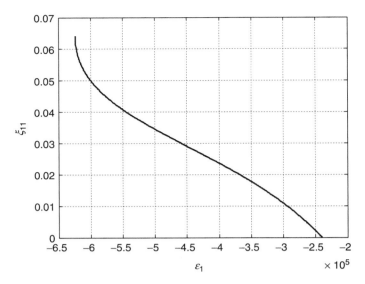

Figure 3.5   The first branch of stability described by ξ_{11} for $\varepsilon_1 < 0$.

If such a root $\bar{u} < 0$ is double, then for the characteristic equation, we obtain the double roots $\lambda_1 = i\sqrt{|\bar{u}|}$, $\lambda_2 = -i\sqrt{|\bar{u}|}$. Each such root leads, in the linear approximation of the motion around the position of equilibrium, to terms of the form $Kt\sqrt{|\bar{u}|}\sin(\pi t/2)$; the equilibrium is unstable too.

Hence, it follows that the equilibrium is stable (in fact, simply stable) if and only if the four roots of equation (3.393) are negative and distinct.

2. Numerical computation

We obtain the values

$$a_{11} = -2400, \quad a_{13} = 400, \quad a_{14} = 53.333, \quad a_{22} = -2400, \quad a_{23} = 400,$$

$$a_{24} = -53.333, \quad a_{31} = 26.667, \quad a_{32} = 26.667, \quad a_{33} = -53.333, \quad a_{41} = 40,$$

$$a_{42} = -40, \quad a_{44} = -160, \tag{3.443}$$

$$a_{10} = -\frac{\varepsilon_1}{50}, \quad a_{20} = -\frac{\varepsilon_1}{50}, \tag{3.444}$$

$$j_{51} = -\frac{\varepsilon_1\xi_1}{25} - 2400, \quad j_{53} = 400, \quad j_{54} = 53.333,$$

$$j_{62} = -\frac{\varepsilon_1\xi_2}{25} - 2400 = -\frac{\varepsilon_1\xi_1}{25} - 2400, \quad j_{63} = 400, \quad j_{64} = -53.333,$$

$$j_{71} = 26.667, \quad j_{72} = 26.667, \quad j_{73} = -53.333, \quad j_{81} = 40,$$

$$j_{82} = -40, \quad j_{84} = -160. \tag{3.445}$$

The stability diagrams are plotted in Figure 3.5, Figure 3.6, and Figure 3.7. We have to consider two branches for $\varepsilon_1 < 0$. The first branch is given by

$$\xi_{11} = \frac{k_2 - k_1 + \sqrt{k_1^2 + k_2^2 + 4\varepsilon_1\left(m_1 + \dfrac{m_2}{2}\right)g}}{2\varepsilon_1} \tag{3.446}$$

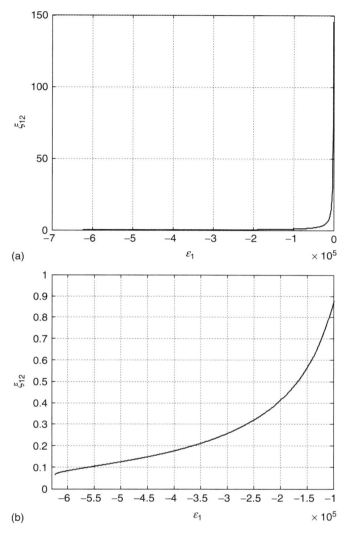

Figure 3.6 (a) The second branch of stability described by ξ_{12} for $\varepsilon_1 < 0$ and (b) detail of this branch.

and the second one by

$$\xi_{12} = \frac{k_2 - k_1 - \sqrt{k_1^2 + k_2^2 + 4\varepsilon_1 \left(m_1 + \dfrac{m_2}{2}\right) g}}{2\varepsilon_1}. \tag{3.447}$$

They exist only if the expression under the radical is positive. The two branches start from the same point for which the expression under the radical vanishes.

The first branch may lead, for values of ε_1 sufficiently close to zero, to negative roots ξ_{11}, a fact which is not in concordance with the hypothesis that all the springs are compressed. The branch contains simply stable positions of equilibrium and is presented in Figure 3.5.

The second branch leads to solutions valid for any $\varepsilon_1 < 0$. Moreover, these solutions define simply stable positions of equilibrium. For $\varepsilon_1 \to 0$, we obtain $\xi_{12} \to \infty$. This branch is presented in Figure 3.6.

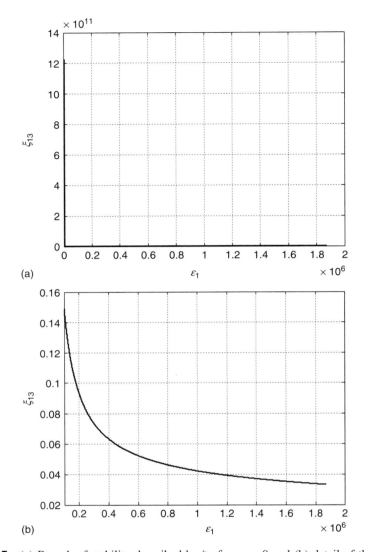

Figure 3.7   (a) Branch of stability described by ξ_1 for $\varepsilon_1 > 0$ and (b) detail of this branch.

If $\varepsilon_1 > 0$, then we have to consider only one branch, described by

$$\xi_1 = \frac{k_2 - k_1 + \sqrt{k_1^2 + k_2^2 + 4\varepsilon_1 \left(m_1 + \dfrac{m_2}{2}\right) g}}{2\varepsilon_1}. \tag{3.448}$$

This branch leads to $\xi_1 \to \infty$ for $\varepsilon_1 \to 0$ too. It is presented in Figure 3.7.
   If $\varepsilon_1 = 0$, then we obtain the linear case described by

$$\xi_1 = \frac{\left(m_1 + \dfrac{m_2}{2}\right) g}{k_1}, \tag{3.449}$$

which is a simply stable position of equilibrium.

Obviously, the stability diagram in the general case is much more complicated and to draw it we must take into consideration all the possibilities of compression or expansion of the springs. Moreover, because the function that describes the elastic force in the nonlinear springs is not an odd function, the situations to be studied cannot be obtained one from the other by simple changes of sign. The diagrams that are presented are only parts of the stability diagram of the mechanical system considered.

FURTHER READING

Acton FS (1990). Numerical Methods that Work. 4th ed. Washington: Mathematical Association of America.

Ackleh AS, Allen EJ, Hearfott RB, Seshaiyer P (2009). Classical and Modern Numerical Analysis: Theory, Methods and Practice. Boca Raton: CRC Press.

Atkinson KE (1989). An Introduction to Numerical Analysis. 2nd ed. New York: John Wiley & Sons, Inc.

Atkinson KE (2003). Elementary Numerical Analysis. 2nd ed. Hoboken: John Wiley & Sons, Inc.

Bakhvalov N (1976). Méthodes Numérique. Moscow: Editions Mir (in French).

Berbente C, Mitran S, Zancu S (1997). Metode Numerice. Bucureşti: Editura Tehnică (in Romanian).

Burden RL, Faires L (2009). Numerical Analysis. 9th ed. Boston: Brooks/Cole.

Butt R (2009). Introduction to Numerical Analysis Using MATLAB. Boston: Jones and Bartlett Publishers.

Chapra SC (1996). Applied Numerical Methods with MATLAB for Engineers and Scientists. Boston: McGraw-Hill.

Cheney EW, Kincaid DR (1997). Numerical Mathematics and Computing. 6th ed. Belmont: Thomson.

Cira O, Măruşter Ş (2008). Metode Numerice pentru Ecuaţii Neliniare. Bucureşti: Editura Matrix Rom (in Romanian).

Dahlquist G, Björck Å (1974). Numerical Methods. Englewood Cliffs: Prentice-Hall, Inc.

Démidovitch B, Maron I (1973). Éléments de Calcul Numérique. Moscow: Editions Mir (in French).

DiBenedetto E (2010). Classical Mechanics: Theory and Mathematical Modeling. New York: Springer-Verlag.

Epperson JF (2007). An Introduction to Numerical Methods and Analysis. Hoboken: John Wiley & Sons, Inc.

Fung YC, Tong P (2011). Classical and Computational Solid Mechanics. Singapore: World Scientific Publishing.

Gautschi W (1997). Numerical Analysis: An Introduction. Boston: Birkhäuser.

Godunov SK, Reabenki VS (1977). Scheme de Calcul cu Diferenţe Finite. Bucureşti: Editura Tehnică (in Romanian).

Greenbaum A, Chartier TP (2012). Numerical Methods: Design, Analysis, and Computer Implementation of Algorithms. Princeton: Princeton University Press.

Hamming RW (1987). Numerical Methods for Scientists and Engineers. 2nd ed. New York: Dover Publications.

Hamming RW (2012). Introduction to Applied Numerical Analysis. New York: Dover Publications.

Heinbockel JH (2006). Numerical Methods for Scientific Computing. Victoria: Trafford Publishing.

Hildebrand FB (1987). Introduction to Numerical Analysis. 2nd ed. New York: Dover Publications.

Hoffman JD (1992). Numerical Methods for Engineers and Scientists. New York: McGraw-Hill.

Jazar RN (2008). Vehicle Dynamics: Theory and Applications: New York: Springer-Verlag.

Kharab A, Guenther RB (2011). An Introduction to Numerical Methods: A MATLAB Approach. 3rd ed. Boca Raton: CRC Press.

Kleppner D, Kolenkow RJ (2010). An Introduction to Mechanics. Cambridge: Cambridge University Press.

Kress R (1996). Numerical Analysis. New York: Springer-Verlag.

Krîlov AN (1957). Lecţii de Calcule prin Aproximaţii. Bucureşti: Editura Tehnică (in Romanian).

Kunz KS (1957). Numerical Analysis. New York: McGraw-Hill.

Lange K (2010). Numerical Analysis for Statisticians. 2nd ed. New York: Springer-Verlag.

Lurie AI (2002). Analytical Mechanics. New York: Springer-Verlag.

Marinescu G (1974). Analiză Numerică. Bucureşti: Editura Academiei Române (in Romanian).

Meriam JL, Kraige LG (2012). Engineering Mechanics: Dynamics. Hoboken: John Wiley & Sons, Inc.

Otto SR, Denier JP (2005). An Introduction to Programming and Numerical Methods in MATLAB. London: Springer-Verlag.

Pandrea N (2000). Elemente de Mecanica Solidului în Coordonate Plückeriene. Bucureşti: Editura Academiei Române (in Romanian).

Pandrea N, Pârlac S, Popa D (2001). Modele pentru Studiul Vibraţiilor Automobilelor. Piteşti: Tiparg (in Romanian).

Pandrea N, Stănescu ND (2002). Mecanică. Bucureşti: Editura Didactică şi Pedagogică (in Romanian).

Popovici P, Cira O (1992). Rezolvarea Numerică a Ecuaţiilor Neliniare. Timişoara: Editura Signata (in Romanian).

Postolache M (2006). Modelare Numerică. Teorie şi Aplicaţii. Bucureşti: Editura Fair Partners (in Romanian).

Press WH, Teukolski SA, Vetterling WT, Flannery BP (2007). Numerical Recipes: The Art of Scientific Computing. 3rd ed. Cambridge: Cambridge University Press.

Quarteroni A, Sacco R, Saleri F (2010). Numerical Mathematics. 2nd ed. Berlin: Springer-Verlag.

Ralston A, Rabinowitz P (2001). A First Course in Numerical Analysis. 2nd ed. New York: Dover Publications.

Ridgway Scott L (2011). Numerical Analysis. Princeton: Princeton University Press.

Salvadori MG, Baron ML (1962). Numerical Methods in Engineering. Englewood Cliffs: Prentice-Hall, Inc.

Sauer T (2011). Numerical Analysis. 2nd ed. London: Pearson.

Simionescu I, Dranga M, Moise V (1995). Metode Numerice în Tehnică. Aplicaţii în FORTRAN. Bucureşti: Editura Tehnică (in Romanian).

Stănescu ND (2007). Metode Numerice. Bucureşti: Editura Didactică şi Pedagogică (in Romanian).

Stănescu ND (2011). Mechanical Systems with neo–Hookean Elements: Stability and Behavior. Saarbrucken: LAP.

Stoer J, Bulirsh R (2010). Introduction to Numerical Analysis. 3rd ed. New York: Springer-Verlag.

Süli E, Mayers D (2003). An Introduction to Numerical Analysis. Cambridge: Cambridge University Press.

Teodorescu PP (2010). Mechanical Systems: Classical Models. Volume 1: Particle Mechanics. Dordrecht: Springer-Verlag.

Udrişte C, Iftode V, Postolache M (1996). Metode Numerice de Calcul. Algoritmi şi Programe Turbo Pascal. Bucureşti: Editura Tehnică (in Romanian).

4

LINEAR ALGEBRA

4.1 CALCULATION OF DETERMINANTS

4.1.1 Use of Definition

Let $\mathbf{A}$ be a square matrix of order n, $\mathbf{A} \in \mathcal{M}_n(\mathbb{R})$, the elements of which are a_{ij}, $i, j = \overline{1, n}$, hence

$$\mathbf{A} = [a_{ij}]_{\substack{i=\overline{1,n} \\ j=\overline{1,n}}}. \tag{4.1}$$

The determinant of matrix $\mathbf{A}$, denoted by $\det \mathbf{A}$, is given by

$$\det \mathbf{A} = \sum_{\sigma \in \Sigma_n} \operatorname{sgn} \sigma \prod_{i=1}^{n} a_{i\sigma(i)}, \tag{4.2}$$

where σ is a permutation of the set $\{1, 2, \ldots, n\}$, $\sum_n$ is the set of all these permutations, while $\operatorname{sgn} \sigma$ is the signature of the permutation σ, having the value 1 if σ is an even permutation and the value -1 if σ is an odd permutation.

Observation 4.1 In the calculation of the determinant $\det \mathbf{A}$, there appear $n!$ terms in formula (4.2).

Observation 4.2 As $n!$ is a quickly increasing function with respect to n, it follows that the number of terms that must be calculated becomes very large, even for small values of n. For each generated permutation, one must calculate its signature too. It follows that the calculation time increases considerably, even for small values of n. For instance, $7! = 5040$, so that a determinant of seventh order will generate 5040 permutations, and it is necessary to determine the signature of every one of them.

Observation 4.3 Formula (4.2) must be applied even in the case in which the value of the determinant can be exactly obtained by other methods.

Numerical Analysis with Applications in Mechanics and Engineering, First Edition.
Petre Teodorescu, Nicolae-Doru Stănescu, and Nicolae Pandrea.
© 2013 The Institute of Electrical and Electronics Engineers, Inc. Published 2013 by John Wiley & Sons, Inc.

4.1.2   Use of Equivalent Matrices

This method starts from the following properties of the determinants:

- if two rows (columns) of a square matrix $\mathbf{A}$ commute into each other, then a new matrix $\mathbf{A}'$ is obtained for which $\det \mathbf{A}' = -\det \mathbf{A}$;
- if a row (column) of a square matrix is multiplied by λ, then a new matrix $\mathbf{A}'$ is obtained for which $\det \mathbf{A}' = \lambda \det \mathbf{A}$;
- if a row (column) of a square matrix $\mathbf{A}$ is multiplied by λ and this is added to another row (column) of $\mathbf{A}$, then a new matrix $\mathbf{A}'$ is obtained for which $\det \mathbf{A}' = \det \mathbf{A}$.

The idea of the method consists in applying some such transformation to the matrix $\mathbf{A}$, in order to obtain a new matrix $\mathbf{A}'$ of a particular form, for which $\det \mathbf{A}'$ is easier to calculate (directly). We must take into account the factors $\lambda_1, \ldots, \lambda_m$ that may occur because of the transformations made, so that

$$\det \mathbf{A} = \prod_{i=1}^{n} \lambda_i \det \mathbf{A}'. \tag{4.3}$$

Observation 4.4   Let us consider a permutation σ of the set $\{1, 2, \ldots, n\}$ and let us suppose that σ is unlike the identical one. Let us now write this permutation in the form

$$\sigma = \begin{pmatrix} 1 & 2 & \cdots & i & \cdots & n \\ \sigma(1) & \sigma(2) & \cdots & \sigma(i) & \cdots & \sigma(n) \end{pmatrix}. \tag{4.4}$$

Then there exists an index $i \in \{1, 2, \ldots, n\}$ so that $\sigma(i) = j < i$.

Demonstration. Let us suppose that this affirmation is not true. Then, for any $i \in \{1, 2, \ldots, n\}$ we have $\sigma(i) = j \geq i$. First, we take $i = n$. We deduce $\sigma(n) = j \geq n$, hence $\sigma(n) = n$. Let us suppose now that $i = n - 1$. It follows that $\sigma(n - 1) = j \geq n - 1$, from which $\sigma(n - 1) = n - 1$ or $\sigma(n - 1) = n$. But $\sigma(n) = n$, hence $\sigma(n - 1) \neq n$. We obtain $\sigma(n - 1) = n - 1$. Proceeding analogically for $i = n - 2$, $i = n - 3$, $\ldots$, $i = 1$, it follows that $\sigma(i) = i$ for any i, $1 \leq i \leq n$. But, by definition, σ is different from the identical permutation. Hence, there is a contradiction, so that the supposition made is false and the observation is proved.

The previous observation shows that any term in formula (4.2), excepting the one obtained by using the identical permutation, will contain a factor a_{ij}, $i < j$, that is, an element situated under the principal diagonal in the matrix $\mathbf{A}$. It follows that for a matrix $\mathbf{A}$ of the form

$$\mathbf{A} = \begin{bmatrix} a_{11} & a_{12} & \cdots & a_{1,n-1} & a_{1n} \\ 0 & a_{22} & \cdots & a_{2,n-1} & a_{2n} \\ \vdots & \vdots & \vdots & \vdots & \vdots \\ 0 & 0 & \cdots & a_{n-1,n-1} & a_{n-1,n} \\ 0 & 0 & \cdots & 0 & a_{nn} \end{bmatrix}, \tag{4.5}$$

the determinant is easy to calculate; it is given by

$$\det \mathbf{A} = \prod_{i=1}^{n} a_{ii}. \tag{4.6}$$

By this method, we try to obtain a matrix $\mathbf{A}'$ of the form (4.5) so as to have

$$\det \mathbf{A} = \pm \det \mathbf{A}', \tag{4.7}$$

where we take the sign $+$ in case of an even number of row permutations or the sign$-$ in case of an odd number of such permutations.

Observation 4.5 Let us suppose that at a certain transformation step we obtain $a_{ii} = 0$, for a certain i, and that for any j, $1 < j \leq n$, we have $a_{ji} = 0$. In this case, $\det \mathbf{A} = 0$ and it is no more necessary to obtain the form (4.5).

Observation 4.6 The procedure presented above may be modified to obtain a matrix $\mathbf{A}$ of the form

$$\mathbf{A} = \begin{bmatrix} 0 & 0 & \cdots & 0 & a_{1n} \\ 0 & 0 & \cdots & a_{2,n-1} & a_{2n} \\ \cdots & \cdots & \cdots & \cdots & \cdots \\ 0 & a_{n-1,2} & \cdots & a_{n-1,n-1} & a_{n-1,n} \\ a_{n1} & a_{n2} & \cdots & a_{n,n-1} & a_{nn} \end{bmatrix}, \tag{4.8}$$

for which

$$\det \mathbf{A} = -\prod_{i=1}^{n} a_{i,n+1-i}. \tag{4.9}$$

4.2 CALCULATION OF THE RANK

Let $\mathbf{A}$ be a matrix with m rows and n columns and real elements, $\mathbf{A} \in \mathcal{M}_{m,n}(\mathbb{R})$. Let us suppose that $m \leq n$.

By definition, the rank of the matrix $\mathbf{A}$ is the order of the greatest nonzero minor; but, to obtain this rank, we must consider a great number of determinants.

Observation 4.7 We have

$$\text{rank}\mathbf{A} \leq \min\{m, n\}. \tag{4.10}$$

for a matrix $\mathbf{A} \in \mathcal{M}_{m,n}(\mathbb{R})$.

To calculate this rank we use its following properties:

- The rank of the matrix $\mathbf{A}$ is equal to the rank of its transpose $\mathbf{A}^{\mathrm{T}}$.
- The rank of the matrix $\mathbf{A}$ is not modified by multiplying a row (column) by a nonzero number.
- The rank of the matrix $\mathbf{A}$ does not change by commuting two of its rows (columns) into each other.
- The rank of the matrix $\mathbf{A}$ is not modified by multiplying one of its rows (columns) by λ and by adding the result to another row (column) of $\mathbf{A}$.

The idea of the method consists in obtaining a matrix $\mathbf{A}'$ of the same rank as $\mathbf{A}$ but of the particular form ($m \leq n$)

$$\mathbf{A}' = \begin{bmatrix} a_{11} & 0 & \cdots & 0 & 0 & \cdots & 0 & 0 \\ 0 & a_{22} & \cdots & 0 & 0 & \cdots & 0 & 0 \\ \cdots & \cdots & \cdots & \cdots & \cdots & \cdots & \cdots & \cdots \\ 0 & 0 & \cdots & a_{m-1,m-1} & 0 & \cdots & 0 & 0 \\ 0 & 0 & \cdots & 0 & a_{m,m} & \cdots & 0 & 0 \end{bmatrix}, \tag{4.11}$$

where the greatest nonzero minor is obtained by selecting those rows and columns for which $a_{ii} \neq 0$, $1 \leq i \leq m$.

Hence, it follows that the rank of the matrix $\mathbf{A}$ is equal to the number of nonzero elements of the principal pseudo diagonal of matrix $\mathbf{A}'$ in formula (4.11).

Observation 4.8 We need to continue calculating until we obtain the form (4.11). If we try to obtain only a superior triangular matrix, then we may obtain an incorrect result.

4.3 NORM OF A MATRIX

Definition 4.1 Let $\mathbf{A}$ and $\mathbf{B}$ be two matrices with m rows and n columns and real elements. We say that $\mathbf{A} \leq \mathbf{B}$ if for any i and j, $1 \leq i \leq m$, $1 \leq j \leq n$, we have

$$a_{ij} \leq b_{ij}. \tag{4.12}$$

Definition 4.2 Let $\mathbf{A} \in \mathcal{M}_{m,n}(\mathbb{R})$. We define the modulus of the matrix $\mathbf{A} = [a_{ij}]_{\substack{i=\overline{1,m}\\j=\overline{1,n}}}$ by the relation

$$|\mathbf{A}| = [|a_{ij}|]_{\substack{i=\overline{1,m}\\j=\overline{1,n}}}. \tag{4.13}$$

Proposition 4.1 The application of modulus has the following properties:

(i) If $\mathbf{A}$ and $\mathbf{B}$ are two matrices with m rows and n columns and real elements, then

$$|\mathbf{A} + \mathbf{B}| \leq |\mathbf{A}| + |\mathbf{B}|. \tag{4.14}$$

(ii) If $\mathbf{A} \in \mathcal{M}_{m,n}(\mathbb{R})$ and $\mathbf{B} \in \mathcal{M}_{n,p}(\mathbb{R})$, then

$$|\mathbf{AB}| \leq |\mathbf{A}| \cdot |\mathbf{B}|. \tag{4.15}$$

(iii) If $\mathbf{A} \in \mathcal{M}_{m,n}(\mathbb{R})$ and $\alpha \in \mathbb{R}$, then

$$|\alpha\mathbf{A}| = |\alpha| \cdot |\mathbf{A}|. \tag{4.16}$$

Demonstration.

(i) Let $\mathbf{A} = [a_{ij}]_{\substack{i=\overline{1,m}\\j=\overline{1,n}}}$, $\mathbf{B} = [b_{ij}]_{\substack{i=\overline{1,m}\\j=\overline{1,n}}}$ and let us denote by $\mathbf{C} = [c_{ij}]_{\substack{i=\overline{1,m}\\j=\overline{1,n}}}$ the matrix sum, $\mathbf{C} = \mathbf{A} + \mathbf{B}$. An element of this matrix is given by

$$c_{ij} = a_{ij} + b_{ij}, \tag{4.17}$$

hence, by applying the modulus, we obtain

$$|c_{ij}| = |a_{ij} + b_{ij}| \leq |a_{ij}| + |b_{ij}|. \tag{4.18}$$

Because i and j have been chosen arbitrarily, $1 \leq i \leq m$, $1 \leq j \leq n$, we have the result (4.14).

(ii) Let us denote by $\mathbf{C} = [c_{ij}]_{i=\overline{1,m} \atop j=\overline{1,n}}$ the matrix product $\mathbf{C} = \mathbf{A} \cdot \mathbf{B}$. An element of this matrix is given by

$$c_{ij} = \sum_{k=1}^{n} a_{ik} b_{kj}. \tag{4.19}$$

Analogically, we denote by $\mathbf{D} = [d_{ij}]_{i=\overline{1,m} \atop j=\overline{1,p}}$ the matrix $\mathbf{D} = |\mathbf{A}| \cdot |\mathbf{B}|$, an element of which is given by

$$d_{ij} = \sum_{k=1}^{n} |a_{ik}||b_{kj}|. \tag{4.20}$$

Comparing relations (4.18) and (4.19) and taking into account that i and j are arbitrary, $1 \leq i \leq m$, $1 \leq j \leq p$, we obtain the relation (4.15).

(iii) Let $\mathbf{B} = [b_{ij}]_{i=\overline{1,m} \atop j=\overline{1,n}}$ be the matrix $\mathbf{B} = |\alpha\mathbf{A}|$, an element of which is

$$b_{ij} = |\alpha a_{ij}| = |\alpha||a_{ij}|. \tag{4.21}$$

We obtain the relation (4.16) immediately.

Corollary 4.1 Let $\mathbf{A} \in \mathcal{M}_n(\mathbb{R})$ be a square matrix of order n with real elements. Then, for $p \in \mathbb{N}$ arbitrary, one has the relation

$$|\mathbf{A}^p| \leq |\mathbf{A}|^p. \tag{4.22}$$

Demonstration. If $p = 0$, then relation (4.22) is obvious because

$$|\mathbf{A}^0| = \mathbf{I}_n \text{ and } |\mathbf{A}|^0 = \mathbf{I}_n. \tag{4.23}$$

Let us suppose that the relation is true for p and let us state it now for $p + 1$. We have

$$|\mathbf{A}^{p+1}| = |\mathbf{A}^p \cdot \mathbf{A}|. \tag{4.24}$$

Applying the property (ii) of Proposition 4.1, we get

$$|\mathbf{A}^p \cdot \mathbf{A}| \leq |\mathbf{A}^p| \cdot |\mathbf{A}| \tag{4.25}$$

and relation (4.24) becomes

$$|\mathbf{A}^{p+1}| = |\mathbf{A}^p \cdot \mathbf{A}| \leq |\mathbf{A}^p| \cdot |\mathbf{A}| \leq |\mathbf{A}|^p \cdot |\mathbf{A}| = |\mathbf{A}|^{p+1}. \tag{4.26}$$

The principle of mathematical induction shows thus that relation (4.24) is true for any $p \in \mathbb{N}$ and the corollary is proved.

Definition 4.3 Let $\mathbf{A} \in \mathcal{M}_{m,n}(\mathbb{R})$. A real number satisfying the following properties is called the *norm* of the matrix $\mathbf{A}$, and is denoted by $\|\mathbf{A}\|$:

(i) $\|\mathbf{A}\| \geq 0$ and $\|\mathbf{A}\| = 0$ if and only if $\mathbf{A} = \mathbf{0}_{m,n}$.
(ii) $\|\alpha\mathbf{A}\| = |\alpha|\|\mathbf{A}\|$ for any $\alpha \in \mathbb{R}$.

(iii) $\|\mathbf{A} + \mathbf{B}\| \leq \|\mathbf{A}\| + \|\mathbf{B}\|$ for any matrix $\mathbf{B} \in \mathcal{M}_{m,n}(\mathbb{R})$.

(iv) $\|\mathbf{AB}\| \leq \|\mathbf{A}\| \cdot \|\mathbf{B}\|$ for any matrix $\mathbf{B} \in \mathcal{M}_{n,p}(\mathbb{R})$.

Observation 4.9

(i) If we put $\alpha = -1$ in the property (ii) of Definition 4.3, it follows that

$$\|-\mathbf{A}\| = \|\mathbf{A}\| \text{ for any } \mathbf{A} \in \mathcal{M}_{m,n}(\mathbb{R}). \tag{4.27}$$

(ii) From

$$\|\mathbf{A}\| = \|\mathbf{B} + \mathbf{A} - \mathbf{B}\| \leq \|\mathbf{B}\| + \|\mathbf{A} - \mathbf{B}\| \tag{4.28}$$

it follows that

$$\|\mathbf{A}\| - \|\mathbf{B}\| \leq \|\mathbf{A} - \mathbf{B}\| \tag{4.29}$$

and, taking into account equation (4.27), we get

$$\|\mathbf{B}\| - \|\mathbf{A}\| \leq \|\mathbf{A} - \mathbf{B}\| \tag{4.30}$$

too. The last two relations lead to

$$\|\mathbf{A} - \mathbf{B}\| \geq |\|\mathbf{A}\| - \|\mathbf{B}\||. \tag{4.31}$$

Definition 4.4 A norm of a matrix is called *canonical* if, in addition to the four properties of Definition 4.3, it also fulfills the following conditions:

(i) For any matrix $\mathbf{A} \in \mathcal{M}_{m,n}(\mathbb{R})$, $\mathbf{A} = [a_{ij}]_{\substack{i=\overline{1,m} \\ j=\overline{1,n}}}$, we have $|a_{ij}| \leq \|\mathbf{A}\|$ for any $i = \overline{1,m}$, $j = \overline{1,n}$;

(ii) for any $\mathbf{A}$, $\mathbf{B} \in \mathcal{M}_{m,n}(\mathbb{R})$ with $|\mathbf{A}| \leq |\mathbf{B}|$, we have $\|\mathbf{A}\| \leq \|\mathbf{B}\|$.

Proposition 4.2 Let $\mathbf{A} \in \mathcal{M}_{m,n}(\mathbb{R})$ be a matrix with m rows and n columns and real elements. We define

$$\|\mathbf{A}\|_{\infty} = \max_{1 \leq i \leq m} \sum_{j=1}^{n} |a_{ij}|, \tag{4.32}$$

$$\|\mathbf{A}\|_{1} = \max_{1 \leq j \leq m} \sum_{i=1}^{m} |a_{ij}|, \tag{4.33}$$

$$\|\mathbf{A}\|_{k} = \sqrt{\sum_{i=1}^{m} \sum_{j=1}^{n} a_{ij}^2}. \tag{4.34}$$

Under these conditions, $\|\cdot\|_{\infty}$, $\|\cdot\|_{1}$, and $\|\cdot\|_{k}$ are canonical norms.

Demonstration. One must verify six properties:

(i) It is obvious that $\|\mathbf{A}\| \geq 0$ and $\|\mathbf{A}\| = 0$ if and only if $\mathbf{A} = \mathbf{0}_{m,n}$ for any of the three norms.

(ii) The relation $\|\alpha \mathbf{A}\| = |\alpha| \|\mathbf{A}\|$ is immediate because the modulus of the product is equal to the product of the moduli.

(iii) Let $\mathbf{B} \in \mathcal{M}_{n,p}(\mathbb{R})$ be arbitrary. We may write successively

$$\|\mathbf{A} + \mathbf{B}\|_\infty = \max_{1 \le i \le m} \sum_{j=1}^{n} |a_{ij} + b_{ij}| \le \max_{1 \le i \le m} \left(\sum_{j=1}^{n} |a_{ij}| + \sum_{j=1}^{n} |b_{ij}| \right)$$

$$\le \max_{1 \le i \le m} \sum_{j=1}^{n} |a_{ij}| + \max_{1 \le i \le m} \sum_{j=1}^{n} |b_{ij}| = \|\mathbf{A}\|_\infty + \|\mathbf{B}\|_\infty, \tag{4.35}$$

$$\|\mathbf{A} + \mathbf{B}\|_1 = \max_{1 \le j \le m} \sum_{i=1}^{m} |a_{ij} + b_{ij}| \le \max_{1 \le j \le m} \left(\sum_{i=1}^{m} |a_{ij}| + \sum_{i=1}^{m} |b_{ij}| \right)$$

$$\le \max_{1 \le j \le m} \sum_{i=1}^{m} |a_{ij}| + \max_{1 \le j \le m} \sum_{i=1}^{m} |b_{ij}| = \|\mathbf{A}\|_1 + \|\mathbf{B}\|_1, \tag{4.36}$$

$$\|\mathbf{A} + \mathbf{B}\|_k = \sqrt{\sum_{i=1}^{m} \sum_{j=1}^{n} (a_{ij} + b_{ij})^2} = \sqrt{\sum_{i=1}^{m} \sum_{j=1}^{n} |a_{ij} + b_{ij}|^2} \le \sqrt{\sum_{i=1}^{m} \sum_{j=1}^{n} (|a_{ij}| + |b_{ij}|)^2}$$

$$= \sqrt{\sum_{i=1}^{m} \sum_{j=1}^{n} |a_{ij}|^2 + \sum_{i=1}^{m} \sum_{j=1}^{n} |b_{ij}|^2 + 2 \sum_{i=1}^{m} \sum_{j=1}^{n} |a_{ij}| |b_{ij}|}. \tag{4.37}$$

The Cauchy–Buniakowski–Schwarz inequality states that for any real numbers $x_i, y_i, i = \overline{1, r}$, one has

$$\left| \sum_{i=1}^{r} x_i y_i \right|^2 \le \sum_{i=1}^{r} |x_i|^2 \sum_{i=1}^{r} |y_i|^2, \tag{4.38}$$

hence

$$\sum_{i=1}^{m} \sum_{j=1}^{n} |a_{ij}| |b_{ij}| \le \sqrt{\sum_{i=1}^{m} \sum_{j=1}^{n} |a_{ij}|^2 \sum_{i=1}^{m} \sum_{j=1}^{n} |b_{ij}|^2}. \tag{4.39}$$

From equations (4.37) and (4.39) we obtain

$$\|\mathbf{A} + \mathbf{B}\|_k \le \sqrt{\sum_{i=1}^{m} \sum_{j=1}^{n} |a_{ij}|^2 + \sum_{i=1}^{m} \sum_{j=1}^{n} |b_{ij}|^2 + 2 \sqrt{\sum_{i=1}^{m} \sum_{j=1}^{n} |a_{ij}|^2 \sum_{i=1}^{m} \sum_{j=1}^{n} |b_{ij}|^2}}$$

$$= \sqrt{\sum_{i=1}^{m} \sum_{j=1}^{n} |a_{ij}|^2} + \sqrt{\sum_{i=1}^{m} \sum_{j=1}^{n} |b_{ij}|^2} = \|\mathbf{A}\|_k + \|\mathbf{B}\|_k. \tag{4.40}$$

(iv) Let $\mathbf{B} \in \mathcal{M}_{n,p}(\mathbb{R})$ be arbitrary. We have

$$\|\mathbf{AB}\|_\infty = \max_{1 \le i \le m} \left\{ \sum_{j=1}^{p} \left| \sum_{l=1}^{n} a_{il} b_{lj} \right| \right\} \le \max_{1 \le i \le m} \sum_{j=1}^{p} \sum_{l=1}^{n} |a_{il} b_{lj}| = \max_{1 \le i \le m} \sum_{l=1}^{n} |a_{il}| \sum_{j=1}^{p} |b_{lj}|. \tag{4.41}$$

But

$$\max \sum_{l=1}^{n} |a_{il}| = \|\mathbf{A}\|_\infty \tag{4.42}$$

and

$$\sum_{j=1}^{p} |b_{lj}| \le \|\mathbf{B}\|_{\infty}, \tag{4.43}$$

because it is a sum of moduli on the row l. It follows that

$$\|\mathbf{AB}\|_{\infty} \le \|\mathbf{A}\|_{\infty}\|\mathbf{B}\|_{\infty}. \tag{4.44}$$

Then

$$\|\mathbf{AB}\|_1 = \max_{1 \le l \le p}\left\{\sum_{i=1}^{m}\left|\sum_{j=1}^{n} a_{il}b_{lj}\right|\right\} \le \max_{1 \le l \le p}\sum_{i=1}^{m}\sum_{j=1}^{n}|a_{il}b_{lj}|$$

$$\le \max_{1 \le l \le p}\sum_{j=1}^{n}|b_{lj}|\sum_{i=1}^{m}|a_{ij}| = \|\mathbf{B}\|_1\sum_{i=1}^{m}|a_{ij}| \le \|\mathbf{B}\|_1\|\mathbf{A}\|_1 = \|\mathbf{A}\|_1\|\mathbf{B}\|_1. \tag{4.45}$$

We also have

$$\|\mathbf{A}\cdot\mathbf{B}\|_k = \sqrt{\sum_{i=1}^{m}\sum_{j=1}^{p}\left|\sum_{l=1}^{n} a_{il}b_{lj}\right|^2} \le \sqrt{\sum_{i=1}^{m}\sum_{j=1}^{p}\left(\sum_{l=1}^{n}|a_{il}|\,|b_{lj}|\right)^2}. \tag{4.46}$$

From the Cauchy–Buniakowski–Schwarz inequality, we obtain

$$\left(\sum_{l=1}^{n}|a_{il}|\,|b_{lj}|\right)^2 \le \sum_{l=1}^{n}|a_{il}|^2 \cdot \sum_{l=1}^{n}|b_{lj}|^2 \tag{4.47}$$

and relation (4.46) becomes

$$\|\mathbf{A}\cdot\mathbf{B}\|_k \le \sqrt{\sum_{i=1}^{m}\sum_{l=1}^{n}|a_{il}|^2}\sqrt{\sum_{j=1}^{p}\sum_{l=1}^{n}|b_{lj}|^2} = \|\mathbf{A}\|_k\|\mathbf{B}\|_k. \tag{4.48}$$

(v) Let a_{lc} be an arbitrary element of matrix $\mathbf{A}$. We may write

$$\|\mathbf{A}\|_{\infty} = |a_{i1}| + |a_{i2}| + \cdots + |a_{in}| \ge |a_{lc}|, \tag{4.49}$$

$$\|\mathbf{A}\|_1 = |a_{1j}| + |a_{2j}| + \cdots + |a_{mj}| \ge |a_{lc}|, \tag{4.50}$$

in these conditions, where i and j are the row and the column, respectively, on which the sum of the moduli is maximum

$$\|\mathbf{A}\|_k = \sqrt{\sum_{i=1}^{m}\sum_{j=1}^{n}|a_{ij}|^2} \ge \sqrt{|a_{lc}|^2} = |a_{lc}|. \tag{4.51}$$

(vi) This is an immediate consequence of (v). From $|\mathbf{A}| < |\mathbf{B}|$ it follows that $\|\mathbf{A}\| \le \|\mathbf{B}\|$, where $\|\,\|$ corresponds to any of the three norms.

Definition 4.5   Let $\{\mathbf{A}_k\}_{k \in \mathbb{N}^*}$ be a sequence of matrices of the same order $\mathbf{A}_k \in \mathcal{M}_{m,n}(\mathbb{R})$, for any $k \in \mathbb{N}^*$. We call the limit of the sequence of matrices $\{\mathbf{A}_k\}_{k \in \mathbb{N}}$ a matrix

$$\mathbf{A} = \lim_{k \to \infty} \mathbf{A}_k, \quad \mathbf{A} \in \mathcal{M}_{m,n}(\mathbb{R}), \tag{4.52}$$

for which the elements of $\mathbf{A} = [a_{ij}]_{\substack{i=\overline{1,m} \\ j=\overline{1,n}}}$ are given by

$$a_{ij} = \lim_{k \to \infty} a_{ij}^{(k)}, \tag{4.53}$$

where $\mathbf{A}_k = [a_{ij}^{(k)}]_{\substack{i=\overline{1,m} \\ j=\overline{1,n}}}$.

Proposition 4.3

(i) The necessary and sufficient condition for the sequence $\{\mathbf{A}_k\}_{k \in \mathbb{N}}$ to be convergent to the matrix $\mathbf{A}$ is

$$\lim_{k \to \infty} \|\mathbf{A} - \mathbf{A}_k\| \to 0, \tag{4.54}$$

where $\|\,\|$ is a certain canonical norm. Moreover,

$$\lim_{k \to \infty} \|\mathbf{A}_k\| = \|\mathbf{A}\|. \tag{4.55}$$

(ii) *The Cauchy criterion for convergence*: The necessary and sufficient condition for the sequence of matrices $\{\mathbf{A}_k\}_{k \in \mathbb{N}}$ to be convergent is that for any $\varepsilon > 0$, there exists $N(\varepsilon) \in \mathbb{N}$ so that for any $k > N(\varepsilon)$ and any $p \in \mathbb{N}^*$, $\|\mathbf{A}_{k+p} - \mathbf{A}_k\| < \varepsilon$, where $\|\,\|$ takes the place of any canonical norm.

Demonstration.

(i) *The necessity.* If $\mathbf{A}_k = [a_{ij}^{(k)}]_{\substack{i=\overline{1,m} \\ j=\overline{1,n}}} \to [a_{ij}]_{\substack{i=\overline{1,m} \\ j=\overline{1,n}}}$, then for any $\varepsilon > 0$, there exists $N(\varepsilon) \in \mathbb{N}$ so that for any $k > N(\varepsilon)$,

$$|a_{ij} - a_{ij}^{(k)}| < \varepsilon \tag{4.56}$$

or, equivalently,

$$|\mathbf{A} - \mathbf{A}_k| < \varepsilon \mathbf{1}_{m,n}, \tag{4.57}$$

where $\mathbf{1}_{m,n}$ is the matrix with m rows and n columns and all elements equal to 1.

Passing to the norm in relation (4.47) and taking into account that $\|\,\|$ is a canonical norm, we have

$$\|\mathbf{A} - \mathbf{A}_k\| < \varepsilon\|\mathbf{1}_{m,n}\|, \tag{4.58}$$

for any $k > N(\varepsilon)$. We get the relation

$$\lim_{k \to \infty} \|\mathbf{A} - \mathbf{A}_k\| = 0, \tag{4.59}$$

because $\|\mathbf{1}_{m,n}\|$ is a finite real number.

The sufficiency. From $\|\mathbf{A} - \mathbf{A}_k\| \to 0$ for $k \to \infty$ it follows that for any $\varepsilon > 0$, there exists $N(\varepsilon) \in \mathbb{N}$ so that for any $k > N(\varepsilon)$,

$$\|\mathbf{A} - \mathbf{A}_k\| < \varepsilon. \tag{4.60}$$

Taking into account that $\| \|$ is a canonical norm, we get

$$|a_{ij} - a_{ij}^{(k)}| \leq \|\mathbf{A} - \mathbf{A}_k\| < \varepsilon \tag{4.61}$$

for $k > N(\varepsilon)$. Therefore, it follows that

$$\lim_{n \to \infty} a_{ij}^{(k)} = a_{ij}, \tag{4.62}$$

hence

$$\lim_{k \to \infty} \mathbf{A}_k = \mathbf{A}. \tag{4.63}$$

On the other hand, one has

$$|\|\mathbf{A}_k\| - \|\mathbf{A}\|| \leq \|\mathbf{A} - \mathbf{A}_k\| < \varepsilon \tag{4.64}$$

and one obtains

$$\lim_{k \to \infty} \|\mathbf{A}_k\| = \|\mathbf{A}\|. \tag{4.65}$$

(ii) *The necessity.* If $\lim_{k \to \infty} \mathbf{A}_k = \mathbf{A}$, then from (i) it follows that $\lim_{k \to \infty} \|\mathbf{A} - \mathbf{A}_k\| = 0$. In that case,

$$\|\mathbf{A}_{k+p} - \mathbf{A}_k\| = \|\mathbf{A}_{k+p} - \mathbf{A} + \mathbf{A} - \mathbf{A}_k\| \leq \|\mathbf{A}_{k+p} - \mathbf{A}\| + \|\mathbf{A} - \mathbf{A}_k\|. \tag{4.66}$$

Let $\varepsilon > 0$. Because $\lim_{k \to \infty} \|\mathbf{A} - \mathbf{A}_k\| = 0$, there exists $N(\varepsilon) \in \mathbb{N}^*$ so that $\|\mathbf{A}_k - \mathbf{A}\| < \varepsilon/2$ for any $k > N(\varepsilon)$. We may choose $N(\varepsilon)$ so that

$$\|\mathbf{A}_{k+p} - \mathbf{A}\| < \frac{\varepsilon}{2}, \quad \|\mathbf{A} - \mathbf{A}_k\| < \frac{\varepsilon}{2} \tag{4.67}$$

for any $p \in \mathbb{N}$; then equation (4.68) leads to

$$\|\mathbf{A}_{k+p} - \mathbf{A}_k\| < \varepsilon. \tag{4.68}$$

The sufficiency. If $\|\mathbf{A}_{k+p} - \mathbf{A}_k\| < \varepsilon$, because $\| \|$ is a canonical norm, we have

$$|a_{ij}^{(k+p)} - a_{ij}^{(k)}| < \varepsilon \tag{4.69}$$

for any i, j, $1 \leq i \leq m$, $1 \leq j \leq n$. It follows that $a_{ij}^{(k)}$ is a Cauchy sequence of real numbers, hence convergent; let us denote its limit by a_{ij}. Taking into account (i), the proposition is proved.

Definition 4.6   Let $\{\mathbf{A}_k\}_{k \in \mathbb{N}^*}$ be a sequence of matrices with $\mathbf{A}_k \in \mathcal{M}_{m,n}(\mathbb{R})$ for any $k \in \mathbb{N}^*$. In that case,

$$\sum_{k=1}^{\infty} \mathbf{A}_k = \lim_{N \to \infty} \sum_{k=1}^{N} \mathbf{A}_k. \tag{4.70}$$

Definition 4.7

(i) We say that the series $\mathbf{S}_N = \sum_{k=1}^{N} \mathbf{A}_k$, with $\mathbf{A}_k \in \mathcal{M}_{m,n}(\mathbb{R})$, is convergent if the sequence $\{\mathbf{S}_N\}_{N \in \mathbb{N}^*}$ is convergent.

(ii) The series is called *absolute convergent* if the series $\mathbf{S}_N = \sum_{k=1}^{N} |\mathbf{A}_k|$ is convergent.

Proposition 4.4

(i) If the series $\mathbf{S}_N = \sum_{k=1}^{N} \mathbf{A}_k$, $\mathbf{A}_k \in M_{m,n}(\mathbb{R})$, is convergent, then $\lim_{k \to \infty} \mathbf{A}_k = \mathbf{0}$.

(ii) If a series of matrices is absolute convergent, then it is convergent.

(iii) Let $\| \|$ be a canonical norm. If the numerical series $\sum_{k=1}^{\infty} \|\mathbf{A}_k\|$ is convergent, then the series $\sum_{k=1}^{\infty} \mathbf{A}_k$ is absolute convergent.

(iv) Let r be the convergence radius of the series $\sum_{k=1}^{\infty} \|\mathbf{A}_k\| \mathbf{x}^k$, where $\| \|$ is a canonical norm. In this case, if $\|\mathbf{x}\| < r$, then the series $\sum_{k=1}^{\infty} \mathbf{A}_k \mathbf{x}^k$ and $\sum_{k=1}^{\infty} \mathbf{x}^k \mathbf{A}_k$ are convergent, where $\mathbf{x}$ is chosen so that we may calculate $(\sum_{k=1}^{\infty} \mathbf{A}_k \mathbf{x}^k$ $(\mathbf{x} \in \mathcal{M}_n(\mathbb{R}))$ or $\sum_{k=1}^{\infty} \mathbf{x}^k \mathbf{A}_k$ $(\mathbf{x} \in \mathcal{M}_m(\mathbb{R}))$, respectively).

(v) If $\|\mathbf{x}\| < 1$, then the series $\sum_{k=1}^{\infty} \mathbf{A}\mathbf{x}^k$ and $\sum_{k=1}^{\infty} \mathbf{x}^k \mathbf{A}$, where the matrices $\mathbf{A}$ and $\mathbf{x}$ are of such a nature that one may effect the calculations, are convergent.

(vi) Let $\mathbf{x} \in \mathcal{M}_n(\mathbb{R})$ and $\mathbf{A} \in \mathcal{M}_{m,n}(\mathbb{R})$, with $\|\mathbf{x}\| < 1$. Under these conditions,

$$\sum_{k=1}^{\infty} \mathbf{A}\mathbf{x}^k = \mathbf{A}(\mathbf{I}_n - \mathbf{x})^{-1}. \tag{4.71}$$

If $\mathbf{x} \in \mathcal{M}_m(\mathbb{R})$ and $\|\mathbf{x}\| < 1$, then

$$\sum_{k=1}^{\infty} \mathbf{x}^k \mathbf{A} = (\mathbf{x} - \mathbf{I}_n)^{-1} \mathbf{A}. \tag{4.72}$$

Demonstration.

(i) Let $\mathbf{S}_N = \sum_{k=1}^{N} \mathbf{A}_k$. As $\mathbf{S}_N$ is convergent, there exists $\mathbf{S} \in \mathcal{M}_{m,n}(\mathbb{R})$ so that $\mathbf{S} = \lim_{N \to \infty} \mathbf{S}_N$. On the other hand, $\mathbf{A}_{N+1} = \mathbf{S}_{N+1} - \mathbf{S}_N$ and we pass to the limit after N. We have

$$\lim_{N \to \infty} \mathbf{A}_{N+1} = \lim_{N \to \infty} \mathbf{S}_{N+1} - \lim_{N \to \infty} \mathbf{S}_N = \mathbf{S} - \mathbf{S} = \mathbf{0}. \tag{4.73}$$

(ii) Let the series $\sum_{k=1}^{\infty} \mathbf{A}_k$ be absolute convergent, that is, $\sum_{k=1}^{\infty} |\mathbf{A}_k|$ is convergent. But

$$\sum_{k=1}^{\infty} |\mathbf{A}_k| = \left[\sum_{k=1}^{\infty} \left| a_{ij}^{(k)} \right| \right]_{\substack{i=\overline{1,m} \\ j=\overline{1,n}}}. \tag{4.74}$$

It follows that that any series $\sum_{k=1}^{\infty} |a_{ij}^{(k)}|$ is convergent, hence any series $\sum_{k=1}^{\infty} a_{ij}^{(k)}$ is absolute convergent. Moreover, the series $\sum_{k=1}^{\infty} \mathbf{A}_k = \left[\sum_{k=1}^{\infty} \left| a_{ij}^{(k)} \right| \right]_{\substack{i=\overline{1,m} \\ j=\overline{1,n}}}$ is absolute convergent.

(iii) Let $\mathbf{A}_k = [a_{ij}^{(k)}]_{\substack{i=\overline{1,m} \\ j=\overline{1,n}}}$. As $\| \|$ is a canonical norm, it follows that $|a_{ij}^{(k)}| \leq \|\mathbf{A}_k\|$ for any i, j, $1 \leq i \leq m$, $1 \leq j \leq n$. Hence, any series $\sum_{k=1}^{\infty} a_{ij}^{(k)}$ is absolute convergent and $\sum_{k=1}^{\infty} \mathbf{A}_k$ is also absolute convergent.

(iv) We may write successively

$$\left\| \sum_{k=1}^{N+p} \mathbf{A}_k \mathbf{x}^k - \sum_{k=1}^{N} \mathbf{A}_k \mathbf{x}^k \right\| = \| \mathbf{A}_{N+1} \mathbf{x}^{N+1} + \cdots + \mathbf{A}_{N+p} \mathbf{x}^{N+p} \|$$

$$\leq \| \mathbf{A}_{N+1} \| \| \mathbf{x}^{N+1} \| + \cdots + \| \mathbf{A}_{N+p} \| \| \mathbf{x}^{N+p} \|$$

$$\leq \| \mathbf{x} \|^{N+1} (\| \mathbf{A}_{N+1} \| + \cdots + \| \mathbf{A}_{N+p} \| \| \mathbf{x} \|^{p-1})$$

$$\leq r^{N+1} (\| \mathbf{A} \| + \cdots + \| \mathbf{A}_{N+p} \| r^{p-1}); \tag{4.75}$$

As the series $\sum_{k=1}^{\infty} \|\mathbf{A}_k\| \|\mathbf{x}\|^k$ is convergent for $\|\mathbf{x}\| < r$, it follows that

$$\left\| \sum_{k=1}^{N+p} \mathbf{A}_k \mathbf{x}^k - \sum_{k=1}^{N} \mathbf{A}_k \mathbf{x}^k \right\| < \varepsilon, \quad N > N(\varepsilon), \quad p \in \mathbb{N}. \tag{4.76}$$

Cauchy's criterion states that $\sum_{k=1}^{\infty} \mathbf{A}_k \mathbf{x}^k$ is convergent.

Analogically, we state that $\sum_{k=1}^{\infty} \mathbf{x}^k \mathbf{A}_k$ is convergent.

(v) The series $\sum_{k=0}^{\infty} \mathbf{A}\mathbf{x}^k$ is convergent for $\|\mathbf{x}\| < 1$, as a consequence of (iv) with $r = 1$, the geometric series with subunitary ratio being convergent. Analogically, this follows for the series $\sum_{k=0}^{\infty} \mathbf{x}^k \mathbf{A}$.

(vi) Starting from the relation

$$\mathbf{A}(\mathbf{I}_n + \mathbf{x} + \mathbf{x}^2 + \cdots + \mathbf{x}_k)(\mathbf{I}_n - \mathbf{x}) = \mathbf{A}(\mathbf{I}_n - \mathbf{x}^{k+1}), \tag{4.77}$$

passing to the limit for $k \to \infty$ and taking into account that $\mathbf{x}^{k+1} \to \mathbf{0}$, because $\|\mathbf{x}\| < 1$, we obtain

$$\left(\sum_{k=0}^{\infty} \mathbf{A}\mathbf{x}^k \right)(\mathbf{I}_n - \mathbf{x}) = \mathbf{A}. \tag{4.78}$$

Let us consider the particular case $\mathbf{A} = \mathbf{I}_n$. One has

$$\left(\sum_{k=0}^{\infty} \mathbf{x}^k \right)(\mathbf{I}_n - \mathbf{x}) = \mathbf{I}_n, \tag{4.79}$$

hence

$$\det\left(\sum_{k=0}^{\infty} \mathbf{x}^k \right) \det(\mathbf{I}_n - \mathbf{x}) = \det(\mathbf{I}_n) = 1, \tag{4.80}$$

from which

$$\det(\mathbf{I}_n - \mathbf{x}) \neq 0, \tag{4.81}$$

the matrix $\mathbf{I}_n - \mathbf{x}$ being invertible. Hence, equation (4.78) leads to

$$\sum_{k=0}^{\infty} \mathbf{A}\mathbf{x}^k = \mathbf{A}(\mathbf{I}_n - \mathbf{x})^{-1}. \tag{4.82}$$

The second relation is analogous.

Corollary 4.2

(i) If $\|\mathbf{x}\| < 1$, $\mathbf{x} \in \mathcal{M}_n(\mathbb{R})$, then

$$\sum_{k=0}^{\infty} \mathbf{x}_k = (\mathbf{I}_n - \mathbf{x})^{-1}. \tag{4.83}$$

(ii) Under the same conditions as in (i), we have

$$\|(\mathbf{I}_n - \mathbf{x})^{-1}\| \leq \|\mathbf{I}_n\| + \frac{\|\mathbf{x}\|}{1 - \|\mathbf{x}\|}. \tag{4.84}$$

Demonstration.
   (i) It is a consequence of point (vi) of the previous proposition for $\mathbf{A} = \mathbf{I}_n$.
   (ii) We have

$$\|(\mathbf{I}_n - \mathbf{x})^{-1}\| = \left\| \sum_{k=0}^{\infty} \mathbf{x}^k \right\| \leq \|\mathbf{I}_n\| + \sum_{k=1}^{\infty} \|\mathbf{x}\|^k \leq \|\mathbf{I}_n\| + \|\mathbf{x}\| \frac{1}{1 - \|\mathbf{x}\|}. \tag{4.85}$$

Observation 4.10 If $\|\mathbf{I}_n\| = 1$, then relation (4.84) becomes

$$\|(\mathbf{I}_n - \mathbf{x})^{-1}\| \leq \frac{1}{1 - \|\mathbf{x}\|}. \tag{4.86}$$

Proposition 4.5 (Evaluation of the Remainders). Let us denote by $\mathbf{R}_k$ the remainder of the series $\sum_{k=0}^{\infty} \mathbf{A}\mathbf{x}^k$, $\|\mathbf{x}\| < 1$, that is,

$$\mathbf{R}_k = \sum_{i=k+1}^{\infty} \mathbf{A}\mathbf{x}^k. \tag{4.87}$$

Under these conditions,

$$\|\mathbf{R}_k\| \leq \frac{\|\mathbf{A}\| \|\mathbf{x}\|^{k+1}}{1 - \|\mathbf{x}\|}. \tag{4.88}$$

Demonstration. We may write

$$\|\mathbf{R}_n\| = \left\| \sum_{i=k+1}^{\infty} \mathbf{A}\mathbf{x}^i \right\| \leq \|\mathbf{A}\| \left\| \sum_{i=k+1}^{\infty} \mathbf{x}^i \right\| \leq \|\mathbf{A}\| \sum_{i=k+1}^{\infty} \|\mathbf{x}\|^i = \frac{\|\mathbf{A}\| \|\mathbf{x}\|^{k+1}}{1 - \|\mathbf{A}\|}. \tag{4.89}$$

4.4 INVERSION OF MATRICES

4.4.1 Direct Inversion

Let the matrix

$$\mathbf{A} = [a_{ij}]_{i,j=\overline{1,n}}, \quad \mathbf{A} \in \mathcal{M}_n(\mathbb{R}) \tag{4.90}$$

for which

$$\det \mathbf{A} \neq 0; \tag{4.91}$$

that is, the matrix $\mathbf{A}$ is a nonsingular square matrix of order n with real elements.
   Under these conditions, the inverse of the matrix $\mathbf{A}$ is given by

$$\mathbf{A}^{-1} = \frac{1}{\det \mathbf{A}} \left[(-1)^{i+j} \Gamma_{ji} \right]_{i,j=\overline{1,n}}, \tag{4.92}$$

where Γ_{lk} is the determinant of the matrix $\mathbf{A}_{lk}$ obtained from the matrix $\mathbf{A}$ by eliminating the row l and the column k, hence a square matrix of order $n - 1$,

$$\mathbf{A} = \begin{bmatrix} a_{11} & \cdots & a_{1,k-1} & a_{1,k+1} & \cdots & a_{1n} \\ a_{21} & \cdots & a_{2,k-1} & a_{2,k+1} & \cdots & a_{2n} \\ \cdots & \cdots & \cdots & \cdots & \cdots & \cdots \\ a_{l-1,1} & \cdots & a_{l-1,k-1} & a_{l-1,k+1} & \cdots & a_{l-1,n} \\ a_{l+1,1} & \cdots & a_{l+1,k-1} & a_{l+1,k+1} & \cdots & a_{l+1,n} \\ \cdots & \cdots & \cdots & \cdots & \cdots & \cdots \\ a_{n1} & \cdots & a_{n,k-1} & a_{n,k+1} & \cdots & a_{nn} \end{bmatrix}. \tag{4.93}$$

4.4.2 The Gauss–Jordan Method

This method[1] is based on

Lemma 4.1 (Substitution Lemma). Let $\mathcal{V}$ be a finite-dimensional vector space of dimension n and let $\mathcal{B} = \{\mathbf{v}_1, \mathbf{v}_2, \ldots, \mathbf{v}_n\}$ a basis of the vapor space. Let $\mathbf{x}$, $\mathbf{x} \neq 0$, be a vector of $\mathcal{V}$. Then $\mathbf{x}$ may replace any vector $\mathbf{v}_i$ of the basis $\mathcal{B}$ if, by expressing it as a linear combination of the basis' vectors, the scalar α_i which multiplies $\mathbf{v}_i$ is nonzero. Moreover, in this case, the set $\mathcal{B}' = \{\mathbf{v}_1, \ldots, \mathbf{v}_{i-1}, \mathbf{x}, \mathbf{v}_{i+1}, \ldots, \mathbf{v}_n\}$ is a basis of the vector space $\mathcal{V}$.

Demonstration. There exist scalars $\alpha_1, \alpha_2, \ldots, \alpha_n$, not all equal to zero, so that

$$\mathbf{x} = \sum_{i=1}^{n} \alpha_i \mathbf{v}_i, \tag{4.94}$$

because $\mathcal{B}$ is a basis. Let us suppose that $\alpha_1 \neq 0$. It follows that

$$\mathbf{v}_1 = \frac{1}{\alpha_1} \left(\mathbf{x} - \sum_{i=2}^{n} \alpha_i \mathbf{v}_i \right). \tag{4.95}$$

Let us show that the vectors $\mathbf{x}, \mathbf{v}_2, \ldots, \mathbf{v}_n$ are linearly independent. We suppose firstly that this is not so; in this case, there can exist scalars $\beta_1, \ldots, \beta_n$, not all zero, so that

$$\beta_1 \mathbf{x} + \beta_2 \mathbf{v}_2 + \cdots + \beta_n \mathbf{v}_n = \mathbf{0}. \tag{4.96}$$

Taking into account equation (4.94), we have

$$\beta_1 (\alpha_1 \mathbf{v}_1 + \alpha_2 \mathbf{v}_2 + \cdots + \alpha_n \mathbf{v}_n) + \beta_2 \mathbf{v}_2 + \cdots + \beta_n \mathbf{v}_n = \mathbf{0}, \tag{4.97}$$

from which

$$\beta_1 \alpha_1 \mathbf{v}_1 + (\beta_1 \alpha_1 + \beta_2) \mathbf{v}_2 + \cdots + (\beta_1 \alpha_n + \beta_n) \mathbf{v}_n = \mathbf{0}. \tag{4.98}$$

As $\mathcal{B}$ is a basis, one obtains the system

$$\beta_1 \alpha_1 = 0, \quad \beta_1 \alpha_2 + \beta_2 = 0, \ldots, \beta_1 \alpha_n + \beta_n = 0 \tag{4.99}$$

with the solution $\mathcal{B}$, $i = \overline{1, n}$. The vectors $\mathbf{x}, \mathbf{v}_2, \ldots, \mathbf{v}_n$ are thus linearly independent. Let us now show that they constitute a system of generators. Let $\mathbf{y}$ be a vector of $\mathcal{V}$. As $\mathcal{B}$ is a basis, there exist scalars γ_i, $i = \overline{1, n}$, so that

$$\mathbf{y} = \gamma_1 \mathbf{v}_1 + \gamma_2 \mathbf{v}_2 + \cdots + \gamma_n \mathbf{v}_n. \tag{4.100}$$

Taking into account equation (4.95), we get

$$\mathbf{y} = \gamma_1 \left[\frac{1}{\alpha_1} \mathbf{x} - (\alpha_2 \mathbf{v}_2 + \alpha_3 \mathbf{v}_3 + \cdots + \alpha_n \mathbf{v}_n) \right] + \gamma_2 \mathbf{v}_2 + \cdots + \gamma_n \mathbf{v}_n, \tag{4.101}$$

from which we have

$$\mathbf{y} = \frac{\gamma_1}{\alpha_1} \mathbf{x} + (\gamma_2 - \gamma_1 \alpha_2) \mathbf{v}_2 + (\gamma_3 - \gamma_1 \alpha_3) \mathbf{v}_3 + \cdots + (\gamma_n - \gamma_1 \alpha_n) \mathbf{v}_n. \tag{4.102}$$

---

[1]The method is named after Carl Friedrich Gauss (1777–1855) who discovered it in 1810, and Wilhelm Jordan (1842–1899) who described it in 1887. The method was known by the Chinese (tenth–second century BC). It also appears in 1670 attributed to Isaac Newton.

As **y** is arbitrary, the vectors **x**, $\mathbf{v}_2$, ..., $\mathbf{v}_n$ form a system of generators $\mathcal{B}'$, which is a new basis for $\mathcal{V}$, hence the lemma is proved.

If the matrix **A** is nonsingular, then its columns are linearly independent. Let us write **A** in the form

$$\mathbf{A} = [\mathbf{c}_1 \quad \mathbf{c}_2 \quad \cdots \quad \mathbf{c}_n], \tag{4.103}$$

where $\mathbf{c}_i$ is the column i

$$\mathbf{c}_i = [a_{1i} \quad a_{2i} \quad \cdots \quad a_{ni}]^{\mathrm{T}}. \tag{4.104}$$

Let us consider now an arbitrary column vector of dimension n

$$\mathbf{b} = [b_1 \quad b_2 \quad \cdots \quad b_n]^{\mathrm{T}}. \tag{4.105}$$

One can associate to every column $\mathbf{c}_i$, $i = \overline{1,n}$, a vector $\mathbf{v}_i$ of $\mathbb{R}^n$. The vectors $\mathbf{v}_i$, $i = \overline{1,n}$, are linearly independent too, because $\mathbf{c}_i$, $i = \overline{1,n}$, are linearly independent. One has $\dim \mathbb{R}^n = n$, so that $\mathbf{v}_i$ and $\mathbf{c}_i$, respectively, form a basis. Hence, the vector **b** given by equation (4.105) will be generated by the columns of matrix **A**

$$\mathbf{b} = \alpha_1 \mathbf{c}_1 + \alpha_2 \mathbf{c}_2 + \cdots + \alpha_n \mathbf{c}_n. \tag{4.106}$$

In particular, **b** may be a column of the unit matrix.

Let us construct the table

$$\left.\begin{array}{cccc|cccc} a_{11} & a_{12} & \cdots & a_{1n} & 1 & 0 & \cdots & 0 \\ a_{21} & a_{22} & \cdots & a_{2n} & 0 & 1 & \cdots & 0 \\ \cdots & \cdots & \cdots & \cdots & \cdots & \cdots & \cdots & \cdots \\ a_{n1} & a_{n2} & \cdots & a_{nn} & 0 & 0 & \cdots & 1 \end{array}\right. . \tag{4.107}$$

On the left side of the table are given the columns of the matrix **A**, while on the right side is the unit matrix. Thus, a row of the table has $2n$ elements. We multiply the rows of the table by numbers conveniently chosen, we commute them into one another or we add one to another, so as to obtain the unit matrix on the left side; and we obtain the inverse matrix $\mathbf{A}^{-1}$ on the right. The procedure is an application of the substitution lemma because, obviously, the columns of the matrix **A** (supposed to be nonsingular) as well as the column of the unit matrix are bases in the space $\mathbb{R}^n$.

Observation 4.11   If, at a given point, on the left side of the table, on trying to obtain the column i, we have $a'_{ii} = 0$, $a'_{i+1,i} = 0$, ..., $a'_{ni} = 0$, then $\det \mathbf{A} = 0$ and we cannot obtain the inverse matrix.

Observation 4.12   Usually, one tries to have on the position of a'_{ii} the greatest modulus between $|a'_{ii}|$, $|a'_{i+1,i}|$, ..., $|a'_{n,i}|$, so as to reduce the errors of calculation.

4.4.3   The Determination of the Inverse Matrix by its Partition

Let us consider the nonsingular square matrix of nth order $\mathbf{A} \in \mathcal{M}_n(\mathbb{R})$, with real elements. Let us partition the matrix

$$\mathbf{A} = \begin{bmatrix} \mathbf{A}_1 & \mathbf{A}_3 \\ \mathbf{A}_2 & \mathbf{A}_4 \end{bmatrix}, \tag{4.108}$$

where $\mathbf{A}_1 \in \mathcal{M}_p(\mathbb{R})$ is a square matrix of order p, $p < n$, $\mathbf{A}_2 \in \mathcal{M}_{n-p,p}(\mathbb{R})$ is a matrix with $n - p$ rows and p columns, $\mathbf{A}_3 \in \mathcal{M}_{p,n-p}(\mathbb{R})$ is a matrix with p rows and $n - p$ columns, while $\mathbf{A}_4 \in \mathcal{M}_{n-p}(\mathbb{R})$ is a square matrix of order $n - p$.

Let us denote by

$$\mathbf{B} = \begin{bmatrix} \mathbf{B}_1 & \mathbf{B}_3 \\ \mathbf{B}_2 & \mathbf{B}_4 \end{bmatrix} \tag{4.109}$$

the inverse of the matrix $\mathbf{A}$, of the same form (4.108), where the dimensions of the matrices $\mathbf{B}_i$ are the same as those of the matrices $\mathbf{A}_i$, $i = \overline{1,4}$. As the matrix $\mathbf{B}$ is the inverse of the matrix $\mathbf{A}$, one has

$$\mathbf{A} \cdot \mathbf{B} = \mathbf{I}_n, \tag{4.110}$$

where $\mathbf{I}_n$ is the unit matrix of order n. Taking into account relations (4.108) and (4.109), relation (4.110) leads to

$$\begin{bmatrix} \mathbf{A}_1 & \mathbf{A}_3 \\ \mathbf{A}_2 & \mathbf{A}_4 \end{bmatrix} \begin{bmatrix} \mathbf{B}_1 & \mathbf{B}_3 \\ \mathbf{B}_2 & \mathbf{B}_4 \end{bmatrix} = \begin{bmatrix} \mathbf{I}_p & \mathbf{0}_{p,n-p} \\ \mathbf{0}_{n-p,p} & \mathbf{I}_{n-p} \end{bmatrix}, \tag{4.111}$$

from which

$$\mathbf{A}_1\mathbf{B}_1 + \mathbf{A}_3\mathbf{B}_2 = \mathbf{I}_p, \quad \mathbf{A}_1\mathbf{B}_3 + \mathbf{A}_3\mathbf{B}_4 = \mathbf{0}_{p,n-p}, \quad \mathbf{A}_2\mathbf{B}_1 + \mathbf{A}_4\mathbf{B}_2 = \mathbf{0}_{n-p,p},$$
$$\mathbf{A}_2\mathbf{B}_3 + \mathbf{A}_4\mathbf{B}_4 = \mathbf{I}_{n-p}. \tag{4.112}$$

The second relation (4.112) leads to

$$\mathbf{B}_3 = -\mathbf{A}_1^{-1}\mathbf{A}_3\mathbf{B}_4, \tag{4.113}$$

which, replaced in the last relation (4.112), leads to

$$-\mathbf{A}_2\mathbf{A}_1^{-1}\mathbf{A}_3\mathbf{B}_4 + \mathbf{A}_4\mathbf{B}_4 = \mathbf{I}_{n-p}, \tag{4.114}$$

hence

$$\mathbf{B}_4 = (\mathbf{A}_4 - \mathbf{A}_2\mathbf{A}_1^{-1}\mathbf{A}_3)^{-1}. \tag{4.115}$$

On the other hand, one may write the relation

$$\mathbf{B} \cdot \mathbf{A} = \mathbf{I}_n \tag{4.116}$$

too; it follows that the system

$$\mathbf{B}_1\mathbf{A}_1 + \mathbf{B}_3\mathbf{A}_2 = \mathbf{I}_p, \quad \mathbf{B}_1\mathbf{A}_3 + \mathbf{B}_3\mathbf{A}_4 = \mathbf{0}_{p,n-p}, \quad \mathbf{B}_2\mathbf{A}_1 + \mathbf{B}_4\mathbf{A}_2 = \mathbf{0}_{n-p,p},$$
$$\mathbf{B}_2\mathbf{A}_3 + \mathbf{B}_4\mathbf{A}_4 = \mathbf{I}_{n-p}. \tag{4.117}$$

The third relation (4.117) leads to

$$\mathbf{B}_2 = -\mathbf{B}_4\mathbf{A}_3\mathbf{A}_1^{-1}, \tag{4.118}$$

while from the first relation (4.112), one obtains

$$\mathbf{B}_1 = \mathbf{A}_1^{-1} - \mathbf{A}_1^{-1}\mathbf{A}_3\mathbf{B}_2. \tag{4.119}$$

Finally, the formulae (4.113), (4.115), (4.118), and (4.119) lead to

$$\mathbf{B}_4 = (\mathbf{A}_4 - \mathbf{A}_2\mathbf{A}_1^{-1}\mathbf{A}_3)^{-1}, \quad \mathbf{B}_3 = -\mathbf{A}_1^{-1}\mathbf{A}_3(\mathbf{A}_4 - \mathbf{A}_2\mathbf{A}_1^{-1}\mathbf{A}_3)^{-1},$$
$$\mathbf{B}_2 = -(\mathbf{A}_4 - \mathbf{A}_2\mathbf{A}_1^{-1}\mathbf{A}_3)^{-1}\mathbf{A}_2\mathbf{A}_1^{-1}, \quad \mathbf{B}_1 = \mathbf{A}_1^{-1} + \mathbf{A}_1^{-1}\mathbf{A}_3(\mathbf{A}_4 - \mathbf{A}_2\mathbf{A}_1^{-1}\mathbf{A}_3)^{-1}\mathbf{A}_2\mathbf{A}_1^{-1}. \tag{4.120}$$

4.4.4   Schur's Method of Inversion of Matrices

Let $\mathbf{A}$ be a quadratic matrix of nth order, which we partition in the form[2]

$$\mathbf{A} = \begin{bmatrix} \mathbf{A}_1 & \mathbf{A}_2 \\ \mathbf{A}_3 & \mathbf{A}_4 \end{bmatrix}, \tag{4.121}$$

where $\mathbf{A}_1$ is a quadratic matrix of pth order, $p < n$, $\mathbf{A}_2$ is a matrix with p rows and $n - p$ columns, $\mathbf{A}_3$ is a matrix with $n - p$ rows and p columns, while $\mathbf{A}_4$ is a quadratic matrix of $(n - p)$th order. Let us also suppose that $\mathbf{A}_4$ and $\mathbf{A}_1 - \mathbf{A}_2\mathbf{A}_4^{-1}\mathbf{A}_3$ are invertible matrices.

Definition 4.8   The matrix $\mathbf{A}_1 - \mathbf{A}_2\mathbf{A}_4^{-1}\mathbf{A}_3$ is called the Schur complement of the matrix $\mathbf{A}$.

Proposition 4.6   Under the above conditions, the decomposition

$$\begin{bmatrix} \mathbf{A}_1 & \mathbf{A}_2 \\ \mathbf{A}_3 & \mathbf{A}_4 \end{bmatrix} = \begin{bmatrix} \mathbf{I}_p & \mathbf{A}_2\mathbf{A}_4^{-1} \\ \mathbf{0}_{n-p,p} & \mathbf{I}_{n-p} \end{bmatrix} \begin{bmatrix} \mathbf{A}_1 - \mathbf{A}_2\mathbf{A}_4^{-1}\mathbf{A}_3 & \mathbf{0}_{p,n-p} \\ \mathbf{0}_{n-p,p} & \mathbf{A}_4 \end{bmatrix} \begin{bmatrix} \mathbf{I}_p & \mathbf{0}_{p,n-p} \\ \mathbf{A}_4^{-1}\mathbf{A}_3 & \mathbf{I}_{n-p} \end{bmatrix} \tag{4.122}$$

takes place, where $\mathbf{I}_p$ and $\mathbf{I}_{n-p}$ are the unit matrices of orders p and $n - p$, respectively, while $\mathbf{0}_{p,n-p}$ or $\mathbf{0}_{n-p,p}$ mark zeros with p rows and $n - p$ columns or with $n - p$ rows and p columns, respectively.

Demonstration.   The result is evident, being an elementary multiplication of matrices.

Corollary 4.3   Under the same conditions, the inverse of the matrix $\mathbf{A}$ is

$$\mathbf{A}^{-1} = \begin{bmatrix} \mathbf{I}_p & \mathbf{0}_{p,n-p} \\ -\mathbf{A}_4^{-1}\mathbf{A}_3 & \mathbf{I}_{n-p} \end{bmatrix} \begin{bmatrix} \left(\mathbf{A}_1 - \mathbf{A}_2\mathbf{A}_4^{-1}\mathbf{A}_3\right)^{-1} & \mathbf{0}_{p,n-p} \\ \mathbf{0}_{n-p,p} & \mathbf{A}_4^{-1} \end{bmatrix} \begin{bmatrix} \mathbf{I}_p & -\mathbf{A}_2\mathbf{A}_4^{-1} \\ \mathbf{0}_{n-p,p} & \mathbf{I}_{n-p} \end{bmatrix}. \tag{4.123}$$

Demonstration.   The result is obvious.

Observation 4.13

(i) We may consider that the matrix $\mathbf{A}_1$ is invertible, in which case, the Schur complement of the matrix $\mathbf{A}$ is given by $\mathbf{A}_4 - \mathbf{A}_3\mathbf{A}_1^{-1}\mathbf{A}_2$.

(ii) If $\mathbf{A}_1$ and $\mathbf{A}_4 - \mathbf{A}_3\mathbf{A}_1^{-1}\mathbf{A}_2$ are invertible, then we may write

$$\mathbf{A} = \begin{bmatrix} \mathbf{I}_p & \mathbf{0}_{p,n-p} \\ \mathbf{A}_3\mathbf{A}_1^{-1} & \mathbf{I}_{n-p} \end{bmatrix} \begin{bmatrix} \mathbf{A}_1 & \mathbf{0}_{p,n-p} \\ \mathbf{0}_{n-p,p} & \mathbf{A}_4 - \mathbf{A}_3\mathbf{A}_1^{-1}\mathbf{A}_2 \end{bmatrix} \begin{bmatrix} \mathbf{I}_p & \mathbf{A}_1^{-1}\mathbf{A}_2 \\ \mathbf{0}_{n-p,p} & \mathbf{I}_{n-p} \end{bmatrix} \tag{4.124}$$

and

$$\mathbf{A}^{-1} = \begin{bmatrix} \mathbf{I}_p & -\mathbf{A}_1^{-1}\mathbf{A}_2 \\ \mathbf{0}_{n-p,p} & \mathbf{I}_{n-p} \end{bmatrix} \begin{bmatrix} \mathbf{A}_1^{-1} & \mathbf{0}_{p,n-p} \\ \mathbf{0}_{n-p,p} & \left(\mathbf{A}_4 - \mathbf{A}_3\mathbf{A}_1^{-1}\mathbf{A}_2\right)^{-1} \end{bmatrix} \begin{bmatrix} \mathbf{I}_p & \mathbf{0}_{p,n-p} \\ -\mathbf{A}_3\mathbf{A}_1^{-1} & \mathbf{I}_{n-p} \end{bmatrix}, \tag{4.125}$$

respectively.

[2]The method was found by Isaai Schur (1875–1941).

Observation 4.14

(i) If $\mathbf{A}$, $\mathbf{A}_2$, $\mathbf{A}_3$, and $\mathbf{A}_4$ are invertible, while $\mathbf{A}_1 = \mathbf{0}_p$, then the Schur complement is given by $-\mathbf{A}_2\mathbf{A}_4^{-1}\mathbf{A}_3$ and the inverse of the matrix $\mathbf{A}$ is given, corresponding to formula (4.123), by

$$\mathbf{A}^{-1} = \begin{bmatrix} -\mathbf{A}_3^{-1}\mathbf{A}_4\mathbf{A}_2^{-1} & \mathbf{A}_3^{-1} \\ \mathbf{A}_2^{-1} & \mathbf{0}_{n-p} \end{bmatrix}. \tag{4.126}$$

(ii) If $\mathbf{A}$, $\mathbf{A}_1$, $\mathbf{A}_2$ and $\mathbf{A}_3$ are invertible, while $\mathbf{A}_4 = \mathbf{0}_{n-p}$, then the Schur complement becomes $-\mathbf{A}_3\mathbf{A}_1^{-1}\mathbf{A}_2$ and relation (4.127) leads to

$$\mathbf{A}^{-1} = \begin{bmatrix} \mathbf{0}_p & \mathbf{A}_3^{-1} \\ \mathbf{A}_2^{-1} & -\mathbf{A}_2^{-1}\mathbf{A}_1\mathbf{A}_3^{-1} \end{bmatrix}. \tag{4.127}$$

In multibody dynamics, matrices of the form

$$\mathbf{A} = \begin{bmatrix} \mathbf{A}_1 & -\mathbf{A}_3^{\mathrm{T}} \\ \mathbf{A}_3 & \mathbf{0} \end{bmatrix}, \tag{4.128}$$

for which the decomposition, corresponding to relation (4.124), is

$$\mathbf{A} = \begin{bmatrix} \mathbf{I}_p & \mathbf{0}_{p,n-p} \\ \mathbf{A}_3\mathbf{A}_1^{-1} & \mathbf{I}_{n-p} \end{bmatrix} \begin{bmatrix} \mathbf{A}_1 & \mathbf{0}_{p,n-p} \\ \mathbf{0}_{n-p,p} & \mathbf{A}_3\mathbf{A}_1^{-1}\mathbf{A}_3^{\mathrm{T}} \end{bmatrix} \begin{bmatrix} \mathbf{I}_p & -\mathbf{A}_1^{-1}\mathbf{A}_3^{\mathrm{T}} \\ \mathbf{0}_{n-p,p} & \mathbf{I}_{n-p} \end{bmatrix}, \tag{4.129}$$

are of interest. Using relation (4.125), the inverse of this matrix is of the form

$$\mathbf{A}^{-1} = \begin{bmatrix} \mathbf{I}_p & \mathbf{A}_1^{-1}\mathbf{A}_3^{\mathrm{T}} \\ \mathbf{0}_{n-p,p} & \mathbf{I}_{n-p} \end{bmatrix} \begin{bmatrix} \mathbf{A}_1 & \mathbf{0}_{p,n-p} \\ \mathbf{0}_{n-p,p} & \left(\mathbf{A}_3\mathbf{A}_1^{-1}\mathbf{A}_3^{\mathrm{T}}\right)^{-1} \end{bmatrix} \begin{bmatrix} \mathbf{I}_p & \mathbf{0}_{p,n-p} \\ -\mathbf{A}_3\mathbf{A}_1^{-1} & \mathbf{I}_{n-p} \end{bmatrix}, \tag{4.130}$$

4.4.5   The Iterative Method (Schulz)

Let $\mathbf{A} \in \mathcal{M}_n(\mathbb{R})$ be nonsingular and $\mathbf{B}_0$ be an approximate value of $\mathbf{A}^{-1}$. Let us consider the matrix[3]

$$\mathbf{C}_0 = \mathbf{I}_n - \mathbf{A}\mathbf{B}_0, \tag{4.131}$$

where $\mathbf{I}_n$ is the unit matrix of order n. If $\mathbf{C}_0 = 0$, then $\mathbf{B}_0 = \mathbf{A}^{-1}$ and the procedure stops. Let us suppose that $\mathbf{C}_0 \neq 0$. We construct the sequence

$$\mathbf{B}_k = \mathbf{B}_{k-1} + \mathbf{B}_{k-1}\mathbf{C}_{k-1}, \quad k \geq 1, \tag{4.132}$$

where

$$\mathbf{C}_{k-1} = \mathbf{I}_n - \mathbf{A}\mathbf{B}_{k-1}. \tag{4.133}$$

Proposition 4.7   The relation

$$\mathbf{C}_k = \mathbf{C}_0^{2^k}, \quad k \geq 1. \tag{4.134}$$

takes place for the sequence $\{\mathbf{C}_k\}_{k \geq 1}$ defined by relations (4.132) and (4.133).

---

[3]The method was published by G. Schulz in 1933.

Demonstration. We have

$$\mathbf{C}_1 = \mathbf{I}_n - \mathbf{A} \cdot \mathbf{B}_1 = \mathbf{I}_n - \mathbf{A}(\mathbf{B}_0 + \mathbf{B}_0\mathbf{C}_0) = \mathbf{I}_n - \mathbf{A}\mathbf{B}_0(\mathbf{I}_n + \mathbf{C}_0) \tag{4.135}$$

for $k = 1$. On the other hand,

$$\mathbf{A}\mathbf{B}_0 = \mathbf{I}_n - \mathbf{C}_0, \tag{4.136}$$

hence

$$\mathbf{C}_1 = \mathbf{I}_n - (\mathbf{I}_n - \mathbf{C}_0)(\mathbf{I}_n + \mathbf{C}_0) = \mathbf{C}_0^2. \tag{4.137}$$

Let us now suppose that $\mathbf{C}_k = \mathbf{C}_0^{2^k}$ and let us show that $\mathbf{C}_{k+1} = \mathbf{C}_0^{2^{k+1}}$. We may write

$$\mathbf{C}_{k+1} = \mathbf{I}_n - \mathbf{A}\mathbf{B}_{k+1} = \mathbf{I}_n - \mathbf{A}(\mathbf{B}_k + \mathbf{B}_k\mathbf{C}_k) = \mathbf{I}_n - \mathbf{A}\mathbf{B}_k(\mathbf{I}_n + \mathbf{C}_k). \tag{4.138}$$

Then

$$\mathbf{A}\mathbf{B}_k = \mathbf{I}_n - \mathbf{C}_k, \tag{4.139}$$

corresponding to relation (4.133); relation (4.138) leads to

$$\mathbf{C}_{k+1} = \mathbf{I}_n - (\mathbf{I}_n - \mathbf{C}_k)(\mathbf{I}_n + \mathbf{C}_k) = \mathbf{C}_k^2 = \mathbf{C}_0^{2^{k+1}}. \tag{4.140}$$

Taking into account the principle of mathematical induction, relation (4.134) is true for any $k \geq 1$.

Proposition 4.8 If there exists $q \in \mathbb{R}$, $0 < q < 1$, so that $\|\mathbf{C}_0\| \leq q$, then

$$\lim_{k \to \infty} \mathbf{B}_k = \mathbf{A}^{-1}. \tag{4.141}$$

Demonstration. We may write successively

$$\|\mathbf{C}_k\| = \|\mathbf{C}_0^{2^k}\| \leq \|\mathbf{C}_0\|^{2^k} \leq q^{2^k}, \tag{4.142}$$

hence

$$\lim_{k \to \infty} \|\mathbf{C}_k\| = 0. \tag{4.143}$$

On the other hand,

$$\mathbf{C}_k = \mathbf{I}_n - \mathbf{A}\mathbf{B}_k \tag{4.144}$$

and relation (4.143) leads to

$$\lim_{k \to \infty} \mathbf{C}_k = \lim_{k \to \infty} (\mathbf{I}_n - \mathbf{A}\mathbf{B}_k) = 0. \tag{4.145}$$

The last relation implies

$$\mathbf{I}_n = \lim_{k \to \infty} \mathbf{A}\mathbf{B}_k, \tag{4.146}$$

hence

$$\lim_{k \to \infty} \mathbf{B}_k = \mathbf{A}^{-1}. \tag{4.147}$$

Proposition 4.9 Taking into account the previous notations, the following relation exists:

$$\|\mathbf{A}^{-1} - \mathbf{B}_k\| \leq \|\mathbf{B}_0\| \left(\|\mathbf{I}_n\| + \frac{q}{1-q} \right) q^{2^k}. \tag{4.148}$$

Demonstration. The relation $\|\mathbf{A}^{-1} - \mathbf{B}_k\|$ may be written in the form

$$\|\mathbf{A}^{-1} - \mathbf{B}_k\| = \|\mathbf{A}^{-1} - \mathbf{A}^{-1}(\mathbf{A}\mathbf{B}_k)\| = \|\mathbf{A}^{-1}(\mathbf{I}_n - \mathbf{A}\mathbf{B}_k)\|$$
$$\leq \|\mathbf{A}^{-1}\|\|\mathbf{I}_n - \mathbf{A}\mathbf{B}_k\| = \|\mathbf{A}^{-1}\|\|\mathbf{C}_k\| = \|\mathbf{A}^{-1}\|\|\mathbf{C}_0^{2^k}\| \leq \|\mathbf{A}^{-1}\|\|\mathbf{C}_0\|^{2^k} \leq \|\mathbf{A}^{-1}\|q^{2^k}.$$
(4.149)

Then

$$\mathbf{A}^{-1} = \mathbf{B}_0(\mathbf{I}_n - \mathbf{C}_0)^{-1}, \tag{4.150}$$

hence

$$\|\mathbf{A}^{-1}\| \leq \|\mathbf{B}_0\|\|(\mathbf{I}_n - \mathbf{C}_0)^{-1}\| = \|\mathbf{B}_0\|\|\mathbf{I}_n + \mathbf{C}_0 + \mathbf{C}_0^2 + \cdots\|$$
$$\leq \|\mathbf{B}_0\|(\|\mathbf{I}_n\| + \|\mathbf{C}_0\| + \|\mathbf{C}_0^2\| + \cdots) \leq \|\mathbf{B}_0\|(\|\mathbf{I}_n\| + q + q^2 + q^{2^2} + q^{2^3} + \cdots)$$
$$\leq \|\mathbf{B}_0\|(\|\mathbf{I}_n\| + q + q^2 + q^3 + \cdots) \leq \|\mathbf{B}_0\|\left(\|\mathbf{I}_n\| + q\frac{1}{1-q}\right). \tag{4.151}$$

It follows that

$$\|\mathbf{A}^{-1} - \mathbf{B}_k\| \leq \|\mathbf{B}_0\|\left(\|\mathbf{I}_n\| + \frac{q}{1+q}\right)q^{2^k}. \tag{4.152}$$

Observation 4.15   If $\|\mathbf{I}_n\| = 1$, then relation (4.148) becomes

$$\|\mathbf{A}^{-1} - \mathbf{B}_k\| \leq \frac{\|\mathbf{B}_0\|}{1-q}q^{2^k}. \tag{4.153}$$

Observation 4.16   If we wish to obtain the matrix $\mathbf{A}^{-1}$ with a precision ε, then we stop at the point that

$$\frac{\|\mathbf{B}_0\|}{1-q}q^{2^k} < \varepsilon \tag{4.154}$$

if $\|\mathbf{I}_n\| = 1$, or when

$$\|\mathbf{B}_0\|\left(\|\mathbf{I}_n\| + \frac{q}{1-q}\right)q^{2^k} < \varepsilon. \tag{4.155}$$

Each of the relations (4.154) and (4.155) indicates the number of necessary iteration steps. We have thus to deal with an a priori estimation of the error.

Observation 4.17   One uses sometimes a stopping condition of the form

$$\|\mathbf{B}_k - \mathbf{B}_{k-1}\| < \varepsilon, \tag{4.156}$$

which results because the sequence $\mathbf{B}_k$ is convergent.

4.4.6   Inversion by Means of the Characteristic Polynomial

Let $\mathbf{A} \in \mathcal{M}_n(\mathbb{R})$ a square matrix with $\det \mathbf{A} \neq 0$ and the secular equation

$$\det[\mathbf{A} - \lambda \mathbf{I}_n] = 0, \tag{4.157}$$

which may be transcribed in the form

$$\begin{vmatrix} a_{11} - \lambda & a_{12} & a_{13} & \cdots & a_{1,n-1} & a_{1n} \\ a_{21} & a_{22} - \lambda & a_{23} & \cdots & a_{2,n-1} & a_{2n} \\ \cdots & \cdots & \cdots & \cdots & \cdots & \cdots \\ a_{n-1,1} & a_{n-1,2} & a_{n-1,3} & \cdots & a_{n-1,n-1} - \lambda & a_{n-1,n} \\ a_{n1} & a_{n2} & a_{n3} & \cdots & a_{n,n-1} & a_{nn} - \lambda \end{vmatrix} = 0 \tag{4.158}$$

or, equivalently,

$$(-1)^n \lambda^n + \sigma_1 \lambda^{n-1} + \sigma_2 \lambda^{n-2} + \cdots + \sigma_n = 0. \tag{4.159}$$

Replacing λ by $\mathbf{A}$ in the characteristic equation (4.157), one gets

$$\det[\mathbf{A} - \mathbf{A}] = 0 \tag{4.160}$$

which, obviously, is true. Hence,

$$(-1)^n \mathbf{A}^n + \sigma_1 \mathbf{A}^{n-1} + \sigma_2 \mathbf{A}^{n-2} + \cdots + \sigma_n \mathbf{I}_n = \mathbf{0}. \tag{4.161}$$

On multiplying relation (4.161) on the right by $\mathbf{A}^{-1}$, we get

$$(-1)^n \mathbf{A}^{n-1} + \sigma_1 \mathbf{A}^{n-2} + \cdots + \sigma_{n-1} \mathbf{I}_n = -\sigma_n \mathbf{A}^{-1}, \tag{4.162}$$

obtaining

$$\mathbf{A}^{-1} = -\frac{1}{\sigma_n} [(-1)^n \mathbf{A}^{n-1} + \sigma_1 \mathbf{A}^{n-2} + \cdots + \sigma_{n-1} \mathbf{I}_n]. \tag{4.163}$$

4.4.7   The Frame–Fadeev Method

The Frame–Fadeev method[4] is a different reading from the previous one, where the coefficients σ_i, $i = \overline{1, n}$, of various powers of λ in the secular equation are obtained as traces of certain matrices.

We multiply the characteristic equation

$$(-1)^n \lambda^n + \sigma_1 \lambda^{n-1} + \sigma_2 \lambda^{n-2} + \cdots + \sigma_{n-1} \lambda + \sigma_n = 0 \tag{4.164}$$

by $(-1)^n$ to bring it in the form

$$\lambda^n + \sigma_1^* \lambda^{n-1} + \sigma_2^* \lambda^{n-2} + \cdots + \sigma_{n-1}^* \lambda + \sigma_n^* = 0. \tag{4.165}$$

Following sequences

$$\mathbf{A}_1 = \mathbf{A}, \quad \sigma_1^* = -Tr\mathbf{A}_1, \quad \mathbf{B}_1 = \mathbf{A}_1 + \sigma_1^* \mathbf{I}_n, \tag{4.166}$$

$$\mathbf{A}_2 = \mathbf{A}\mathbf{B}_1, \quad \sigma_2^* = -\frac{1}{2} Tr\mathbf{A}_2, \quad \mathbf{B}_2 = \mathbf{A}_2 + \sigma_2^* \mathbf{I}_n \tag{4.167}$$

[4]This method was published by J. S. Frame in 1949 and then in 1964, and by D. K. Fadeev (Faddeev) in 1952 in Russian and then in 1963 in English.

and, in general,

$$\mathbf{A}_k = \mathbf{A}\mathbf{B}_{k-1}, \quad \sigma_k^* = -\frac{1}{k}Tr\mathbf{A}_k, \quad \mathbf{B}_k = \mathbf{A} + \sigma_k^*\mathbf{I}_n, \tag{4.168}$$

until

$$\mathbf{A}_n = \mathbf{A}\mathbf{B}_{n-1}, \quad \sigma_n^* = -\frac{1}{n}Tr\mathbf{A}_n, \quad \mathbf{B}_n = \mathbf{A}_n + \sigma_n^*\mathbf{I}_n \tag{4.169}$$

are obtained.

The last relation (4.169) is just the Hamilton–Cayley equation, hence

$$\mathbf{B}_n = \mathbf{A}_n + \sigma_n^*\mathbf{I}_n = 0, \tag{4.170}$$

from which

$$\mathbf{A}_n = -\sigma_n^*\mathbf{I}_n. \tag{4.171}$$

The first formula (4.169) leads now to

$$\mathbf{A}\mathbf{B}_{n-1} = -\sigma_n^*\mathbf{I}_n, \tag{4.172}$$

hence

$$\mathbf{A}^{-1} = -\frac{1}{\sigma_n^*}\mathbf{B}_{n-1}. \tag{4.173}$$

4.5   SOLUTION OF LINEAR ALGEBRAIC SYSTEMS OF EQUATIONS

4.5.1   Cramer's Rule

Let us consider the linear system of n equations with n unknowns[5]

$$\begin{cases} a_{11}x_1 + a_{12}x_2 + \cdots + a_{1n}x_n = b_1, \\ a_{21}x_1 + a_{22}x_2 + \cdots + a_{2n}x_n = b_2, \\ \vdots \\ a_{n1}x_1 + a_{n2}x_2 + \cdots + a_{nn}x_n = b_n, \end{cases} \tag{4.174}$$

which may be written in the form

$$\mathbf{A}\mathbf{x} = \mathbf{b}, \tag{4.175}$$

where $\mathbf{A} = [a_{ij}]_{i,j=\overline{1,n}}$, $\mathbf{x} = \begin{bmatrix} x_1 & x_2 & \cdots & x_n \end{bmatrix}^T$, $\mathbf{b} = \begin{bmatrix} b_1 & b_2 & \cdots & b_n \end{bmatrix}^T$, $\mathbf{A} \in \mathcal{M}_n(\mathbb{R})$, $\mathbf{x} \in \mathcal{M}_{n,1}(\mathbb{R})$, $\mathbf{b} \in \mathcal{M}_{n,1}(\mathbb{R})$.

We suppose that the system is determined compatible, that is $\det \mathbf{A} \neq 0$. In this case, the solution of the system is given by

$$x_i = \frac{\Delta_i}{\Delta}, \quad i = \overline{1,n}, \tag{4.176}$$

where

$$\Delta = \begin{vmatrix} a_{11} & a_{12} & \cdots & a_{1n} \\ a_{21} & a_{22} & \cdots & a_{2n} \\ \cdots & \cdots & \cdots & \cdots \\ a_{n1} & a_{n2} & \cdots & a_{nn} \end{vmatrix}, \tag{4.177}$$

[5]The method was named after Gabriel Cramer (1704–1752) who published it in 1750.

$$\Delta_i = \begin{vmatrix} a_{11} & a_{12} & \cdots & a_{1,i-1} & b_1 & a_{1,i+1} & \cdots & a_{1n} \\ a_{21} & a_{22} & \cdots & a_{2,i-1} & b_2 & a_{2,i+1} & \cdots & a_{2n} \\ \cdots & \cdots & \cdots & \cdots & \cdots & \cdots & \cdots & \cdots \\ a_{n-1,1} & a_{n-1,2} & \cdots & a_{n-1,i-1} & b_{n-1} & a_{n-1,i+1} & \cdots & a_{n-1,n} \\ a_{n1} & a_{n2} & \cdots & a_{n,i+1} & b_n & a_{n,i+1} & \cdots & a_{nn} \end{vmatrix}. \tag{4.178}$$

Formulae (4.176) form the so-called Cramer's rule.

The obvious disadvantage of this method consists in the fact that one must calculate $n+1$ determinants of $n+1$ distinct matrices of nth order.

If $\det \mathbf{A} = 0$, then the system may be undetermined compatible or incompatible.

Obviously, the first step consists in the calculation of $\Delta = \det \mathbf{A}$. If $\Delta \neq 0$, then one may apply formula (4.176); in the contrary case, the algorithm stops.

4.5.2   Gauss's Method

The idea of Gauss's method consists in bringing the system of n linear algebraic equations with n unknowns

$$\begin{cases} a_{11}x_1 + a_{12}x_2 + \cdots + a_{1n}x_n = b_1, \\ a_{21}x_1 + a_{22}x_2 + \cdots + a_{2n}x_n = b_2, \\ \vdots \\ a_{n1}x_1 + a_{n2}x_2 + \cdots + a_{nn}x_n = b_n \end{cases} \tag{4.179}$$

to a canonical form in which the unknowns may easily be obtained. Such a form is the triangular one in which the system (4.179) is written in the form

$$\begin{cases} a'_{11}x_1 + a'_{12}x_2 + a'_{13}x_3 + \cdots + a'_{1,n-1}x_{n-1} + a'_{1n}x_n = b'_1, \\ a'_{22}x_2 + a'_{23}x_3 + \cdots + a'_{1,n-1}x_{n-1} + a'_{2n}x_n = b'_2, \\ a'_{33}x_3 + \cdots + a'_{3,n-1}x_{n-1} + a'_{3n}x_n = b'_3, \\ \vdots \\ a'_{n-1,n-1}x_{n-1} + a'_{n-1,n}x_n = b'_{n-1}, \\ a'_{nn}x_n = b'_n. \end{cases} \tag{4.180}$$

The solution of this system is given by

$$x_n = \frac{1}{a'_{nn}}b'_n, \quad x_{n-1} = \frac{1}{a'_{n-1,n-1}}(b'_{n-1} - a'_{n-1,n}x_n), \quad \ldots, \quad x_i = \frac{1}{a'_{ii}}\left(b'_i - \sum_{j=i+1}^{n} a'_{ij}\right), \quad \ldots,$$

$$x_1 = \frac{1}{a'_{11}}\left(b'_1 - \sum_{j=2}^{n} a'_{1j}x_j\right) \tag{4.181}$$

and is obtained step by step, starting from x_n, continuing with $x_{n-1}, x_{n-2}, \ldots$, until x_1.

Observation 4.18   Obviously, equation (4.180) is not the only possible form in which the solution can be immediately obtained. We may take, for instance, an inferior triangular form of the system, the determination of the unknowns beginning with x_1, continuing with $x_2, x_3, \ldots$, until x_n.

Observation 4.19   We observe from equation (4.181) that all the coefficients a'_{ii}, $i = \overline{1, n}$, must be nonzero.

In Gauss's method, we multiply successively the first row with suitable values, adding then to the rows 2, 3, $\ldots, n$, so as to obtain a zero value for all a_{i1}, $2 \leq i \leq n$, remaining with $a_{11} \neq 0$. If

$a_{11} = 0$ in the initial system, then we look for a nonzero coefficient between a_{21}, a_{31}, ..., a_{n1}. If all a_{i1}, $i = \overline{1,n}$, vanish, then the procedure stops, and the variable x_1 disappears in all n equations (if not, we have a system of n equations with at most $n - 1$ unknowns). We continue then with the second row and multiply it (we suppose $a_{22} \neq 0$) with suitable values so that all elements a_{32}, a_{42}, ..., a_{n2} do vanish. Obviously, if $a_{22} = 0$, then we commute the second row with another row i for which $a_{i2} \neq 0$. After the first step, the system (4.181) becomes

$$\begin{cases} a_{11}^{(1)} x_1 + a_{12}^{(1)} x_2 + a_{13}^{(1)} x_3 + \cdots + a_{1n}^{(1)} x_n = b_1^{(1)}, \\ \qquad\quad a_{22}^{(1)} x_2 + a_{23}^{(1)} x_3 + \cdots + a_{2n}^{(1)} x_n = b_2^{(1)}, \\ \qquad\quad a_{32}^{(1)} x_2 + a_{33}^{(1)} x_3 + \cdots + a_{3n}^{(1)} = b_3^{(1)}, \\ \qquad\qquad\qquad\qquad\qquad\qquad\qquad\vdots \\ \qquad\quad a_{n2}^{(1)} x_2 + a_{n3}^{(1)} x_3 + \cdots + a_{nn}^{(1)} x_n = b_n^{(1)}, \end{cases} \qquad (4.182)$$

while, after the second step, the form of the system will be

$$\begin{cases} a_{11}^{(2)} x_1 + a_{12}^{(2)} x_2 + a_{13}^{(2)} x_3 + \cdots + a_{1n}^{(2)} x_n = b_1^{(2)}, \\ \qquad\quad a_{22}^{(2)} x_2 + a_{23}^{(2)} x_3 + \cdots + a_{2n}^{(2)} x_n = b_2^{(2)}, \\ \qquad\quad a_{32}^{(2)} x_2 + a_{33}^{(2)} x_3 + \cdots + a_{3n}^{(2)} = b_3^{(2)}, \\ \qquad\qquad\qquad\qquad\qquad\qquad\qquad\vdots \\ \qquad\quad a_{n2}^{(2)} x_2 + a_{n3}^{(2)} x_3 + \cdots + a_{nn}^{(2)} x_n = b_n^{(2)}. \end{cases} \qquad (4.183)$$

The procedure will continue until we obtain the form (4.180).

Observation 4.20   To reduce the calculation errors at step i, $i = \overline{1, n - 1}$, we do not make the pivot with $a_{ii}^{(i)}$ but bring to position the element among $a_{ii}^{(i)}$, $a_{i+1,i}^{(i)}$, ..., $a_{ni}^{(i)}$ that is greatest in modulus. If all these elements vanish (the maximum is equal to zero), then the algorithm stops.

4.5.3   The Gauss–Jordan Method

The Gauss–Jordan method is a similar one to Gauss's method, specifying that the row i, after multiplying it with suitable values, is added not only to the rows $i + 1$, $i + 2$, ..., n, but to the rows 1, 2, ..., $i - 1$ too. Thus, the matrix of the system becomes a diagonal one

$$\begin{cases} a_{11}' x_1 + 0 \cdot x_2 + 0 \cdot x_3 + \cdots + 0 \cdot x_{n-1} + 0 \cdot x_n = b_1', \\ \qquad\quad a_{22}' x_2 + 0 \cdot x_3 + \cdots 0 \cdot x_{n-1} + 0 \cdot x_n = b_2', \\ \qquad\qquad\quad a_{33}' x_3 + \cdots + 0 \cdot x_{n-1} + 0 \cdot x_n = b_3', \\ \qquad\qquad\qquad\qquad\qquad\qquad\qquad\quad\vdots \\ \quad a_{n-1,n-1}' x_{n-1} + 0 \cdot x_{n-1} + 0 \cdot x_n = b_{n-1}', \\ \qquad\qquad\qquad\qquad\qquad\qquad a_{nn}' x_n = b_n'. \end{cases} \qquad (4.184)$$

In this case, the solution of the system (4.184) becomes

$$x_i = \frac{b_i'}{a_{ii}'}, \quad a_{ii}' \neq 0, \quad i = \overline{1, n}. \qquad (4.185)$$

The observations to Gauss's method remain valid.

4.5.4   The LU Factorization

The idea of the method[6] consists in writing the matrix $\mathbf{A}$ of the linear system $\mathbf{Ax} = \mathbf{b}$, $\mathbf{A} \in \mathcal{M}_n(\mathbb{R})$, $\mathbf{x} \in \mathcal{M}_{n,1}(\mathbb{R})$, $b \in \mathcal{M}_{n,1}(\mathbb{R})$, in the form

$$\mathbf{A} = \mathbf{LU}, \tag{4.186}$$

where $\mathbf{L} \in \mathcal{M}_n(\mathbb{R})$ is an inferior triangular matrix

$$\mathbf{L} = \begin{bmatrix} l_{11} & 0 & 0 & \cdots & 0 & 0 \\ l_{21} & l_{22} & 0 & \cdots & 0 & 0 \\ l_{31} & l_{32} & l_{33} & \cdots & 0 & 0 \\ \cdots & \cdots & \cdots & \ddots & \cdots & \cdots \\ l_{n-1,1} & l_{n-1,2} & l_{n-1,3} & \cdots & l_{n-1,n-1} & 0 \\ l_{n,1} & l_{n,2} & l_{n,3} & \cdots & l_{n,n-1} & l_{n,n} \end{bmatrix}, \tag{4.187}$$

while $\mathbf{U} \in \mathcal{M}_n(\mathbb{R})$ is a superior triangular matrix

$$\mathbf{U} = \begin{bmatrix} u_{11} & u_{12} & u_{13} & \cdots & u_{1,n-1} & u_{1n} \\ 0 & u_{22} & u_{23} & \cdots & u_{2,n-1} & u_{2,n} \\ 0 & 0 & u_{33} & \cdots & u_{3,n-1} & u_{3,n} \\ \cdots & \cdots & \cdots & \ddots & \cdots & \cdots \\ 0 & 0 & 0 & \cdots & u_{n-1,n-1} & u_{n-1,n} \\ 0 & 0 & 0 & \cdots & 0 & u_{n,n} \end{bmatrix}. \tag{4.188}$$

Taking into account the previous relations, we may determine the values of the elements of the matrices $\mathbf{L}$ and $\mathbf{U}$

$$l_{11}u_{11} = a_{11}, \quad l_{11}u_{12} = a_{12}, \ldots, l_{11}u_{1n} = a_{1n}, \quad l_{21}u_{11} = a_{21}, l_{21}u_{12} + l_{22}u_{22} = a_{22}, \ldots,$$
$$l_{21}u_{1n} + l_{22}u_{2n} = a_{2n}, \ldots, \quad l_{n1}u_{11} = a_{n1}, \quad l_{n1}u_{12} + l_{n2}u_{22} = a_{n2},$$
$$l_{n1}u_{1n} + l_{n2}u_{2n} + \ldots + l_{nn}u_{nn} = a_{nn}. \tag{4.189}$$

The system

$$\mathbf{Ax} = \mathbf{b} \tag{4.190}$$

now takes the form

$$\mathbf{LUx} = \mathbf{b}. \tag{4.191}$$

We denote

$$\mathbf{Ux} = \mathbf{y} \tag{4.192}$$

and we now have to solve two systems, that is,

$$\mathbf{Ly} = \mathbf{b}, \tag{4.193}$$

with $\mathbf{L}$ an inferior triangular matrix, which has the solution

$$y_i = \frac{1}{l_{ii}} \left(b_i - \sum_{j=1}^{i-1} l_{ji} y_j \right), \quad i = \overline{1, n}, \tag{4.194}$$

---

[6]The method was introduced by Alan Mathison Turing (1912–1954).

and the system

$$\mathbf{Ux} = \mathbf{y}, \tag{4.195}$$

where $\mathbf{U}$ is a superior triangular matrix, having the solution

$$x_i = \frac{1}{u_{ii}} \left(y_i - \sum_{j=i+1}^{n} u_{ji} x_j \right), \quad i = \overline{1, n}, \tag{4.196}$$

respectively.

Observation 4.21   We observe that the system (4.189) has n^2 equations and $n^2 + n$ unknowns. To be determined, n unknowns must be a priori specified. Depending on the specified unknowns, the method must be used in various readings that will be presented in the following.

A. *The Doolittle Method*   In the frame of this method,[7] the values

$$l_{ii} = 1, \quad i = \overline{1, n} \tag{4.197}$$

are established and the system (4.189) becomes

$$u_{11} = a_{11}, u_{12} = a_{12}, \dots, u_{1n} = a_{1n}, \quad l_{21}u_{11} = a_{21}, l_{21}u_{12} + u_{22} = a_{22}, \dots, l_{21}u_{1n} + u_{2n} = a_{2n},$$
$$\dots, l_{n1}u_{11} = a_{n1}, l_{n1}u_{12} + l_{n2}u_{22} = a_{n2}, \dots, l_{n1}u_{1n} + l_{n2}u_{2n} + \dots + u_{nn} = a_{nn}. \tag{4.198}$$

The solution of this system becomes

$$l_{ii} = 1, \quad i = \overline{1, n}, \quad u_{1j} = a_{1j}, \quad j = \overline{1, n}, \quad l_{21} = \frac{a_{21}}{a_{11}}, \quad u_{2k} = a_{2k} - l_{21}u_{1k}, \quad k = \overline{2, n}, \dots,$$
$$l_{n1} = \frac{a_{n1}}{u_{11}}, \quad l_{n2} = \frac{1}{u_{22}}(a_{n2} - l_{n1}u_{12}), \dots, u_{nn} = a_{nn} - l_{n1}u_{n1} - l_{n2}u_{n2} - \dots - l_{n,n-1}u_{n,n-1}. \tag{4.199}$$

B. *The Crout Method*   In the Crout method,[8] the values

$$u_{ii} = 1 \; i = \overline{1, n}, \tag{4.200}$$

are imposed, so that the system (4.189) becomes

$$l_{11} = a_{11}, \quad l_{11}u_{12} = a_{12}, \quad \dots, \quad l_{11}u_{1n} = a_{1n}, \quad l_{21} = a_{21}, \quad l_{21}u_{12} + l_{22} = a_{22}, \quad \dots,$$
$$l_{21}u_{1n} + l_{22}u_{2n} = a_{2n}, \quad \dots, \quad l_{n1} = a_{n1}, \quad l_{n1}u_{12} + l_{n2} = a_{n2}, \quad \dots,$$
$$l_{n1}u_{1n} + l_{n2}u_{2n} + \dots + l_{n,n-1}u_{n-1,n} + l_{n,n} = a_{nn}, \tag{4.201}$$

with the solution

$$u_{ii} = 1, \quad i = \overline{1, n}, \quad l_{j1} = a_{j1}, \quad j = \overline{1, n}, \quad u_{12} = \frac{a_{12}}{l_{11}}, \quad l_{k2} = a_{k2} - l_{k1}u_{12}, \quad k = \overline{2, n}, \dots,$$
$$u_{1n} = \frac{a_{1n}}{l_{11}}, \quad u_{2n} = \frac{1}{l_{22}}(a_{2n} - l_{21}u_{1n}), \dots, l_{nn} = a_{nn} - l_{n1}u_{1n} - \dots - l_{n,n-1}u_{n-1,n}. \tag{4.202}$$

---

[7]The method was described by Myrick Hascall Doolittle (1830–1913).
[8]The method was named after Prescott Durand Crout (1907–1984).

C. *The Cholesky Method*   We suppose that the matrix **A** is symmetric and positive definite,[9] that is

$$\mathbf{A}^T = \mathbf{A} \tag{4.203}$$

and

$$\mathbf{x}^T \mathbf{A} \mathbf{x} > 0 \tag{4.204}$$

for any $\mathbf{x} \in \mathcal{M}_{n,1}(\mathbb{R})$, $\mathbf{x} \neq 0$. We may choose the matrices **L** and **U** so that

$$\mathbf{U} = \mathbf{L}^T, \tag{4.205}$$

in these conditions. The condition $\mathbf{A} = \mathbf{L}\mathbf{U}$, written now in the form

$$\mathbf{A} = \mathbf{L}\mathbf{L}^T, \tag{4.206}$$

or, equivalently,

$$
\begin{bmatrix}
a_{11} & a_{12} & a_{13} & \cdots & a_{1n} \\
a_{21} & a_{22} & a_{23} & \cdots & a_{2n} \\
\cdots & \cdots & \cdots & \cdots & \cdots \\
a_{n1} & a_{n2} & a_{n3} & \cdots & a_{nn}
\end{bmatrix}
=
\begin{bmatrix}
l_{11} & 0 & 0 & \cdots & 0 \\
l_{21} & l_{22} & 0 & \cdots & 0 \\
\cdots & \cdots & \cdots & \cdots & \cdots \\
l_{n1} & l_{n2} & l_{n3} & \cdots & l_{nn}
\end{bmatrix}
\begin{bmatrix}
l_{11} & l_{21} & \cdots & l_{n1} \\
0 & l_{22} & \cdots & l_{n2} \\
\cdots & \cdots & \cdots & \cdots \\
0 & \cdots & \cdots & l_{nn}
\end{bmatrix}, \tag{4.207}
$$

leads to

$$l_{11}^2 = a_{11}, \quad l_{11}l_{21} = a_{12}, \quad \ldots, \quad l_{11}l_{n1} = a_{1n}, \quad l_{21}l_{11} = a_{21}, \quad l_{21}^2 + l_{22}^2 = a_{22}, \ldots, l_{21}l_{n1} + l_{22}l_{n2}$$

$$= a_{2n}, \ldots, l_{n1}l_{11} = a_{n1}, \quad l_{n1}l_{21} + l_{n2}l_{22} = a_{n2}, \ldots, l_{n1}^2 + l_{n2}^2 + \ldots + l_{nn}^2 = a_{nn}, \tag{4.208}$$

the solution of which is

$$l_{ii} = \sqrt{a_{ii} - \sum_{j=1}^{i-1} l_{ji}^2}, \quad j = \overline{1,n}, \quad l_{ij} = \frac{1}{l_{ii}}\left(a_{ij} - \sum_{k=1}^{i-1} l_{ki}l_{kj}\right), \quad j > i. \tag{4.209}$$

4.5.5 The Schur Method of Solving Systems of Linear Equations

Let us consider the linear system

$$
\begin{cases}
a_{11}x_1 + a_{12}x_2 + \cdots + a_{1n}x_n = b_1, \\
\vdots \\
a_{n1}x_1 + a_{n2}x_2 + \cdots + a_{nn}x_n = b_n,
\end{cases}
\tag{4.210}
$$

which we write in a condensed form as

$$\mathbf{A}\mathbf{x} = \mathbf{b}. \tag{4.211}$$

We suppose that the system is compatible determined and that the matrix **A** allows a partition of the form

$$\mathbf{A} = \begin{bmatrix} \mathbf{A}_1 & \mathbf{A}_2 \\ \mathbf{A}_3 & \mathbf{A}_4 \end{bmatrix}, \tag{4.212}$$

where $\mathbf{A}_1 \in \mathcal{M}_p(\mathbb{R})$, $\mathbf{A}_2 \in \mathcal{M}_{p,n-p}(\mathbb{R})$, $\mathbf{A}_3 \in \mathcal{M}_{n-p,p}(\mathbb{R})$, and $\mathbf{A}_4 \in \mathcal{M}_{n-p}(\mathbb{R})$.

---

[9]The method was presented by André–Louis Cholesky (1876–1918).

We partition the column vectors $\mathbf{x}$ and $\mathbf{b}$ in the form

$$\mathbf{x} = \begin{bmatrix} \mathbf{x}_1 \\ \mathbf{x}_2 \end{bmatrix}, \quad \mathbf{b} = \begin{bmatrix} \mathbf{b}_1 \\ \mathbf{b}_2 \end{bmatrix}, \tag{4.213}$$

where

$$\mathbf{x}_1 = [x_1 \cdots x_p]^T, \quad \mathbf{x}_2 = [x_{p+1} \cdots x_n]^T, \quad \mathbf{b}_1 = [b_1 \cdots b_p]^T, \quad \mathbf{b}_2 = [b_{p+1} \cdots b_n]^T. \tag{4.214}$$

The system (4.211) is now written in the form

$$\mathbf{A}_1\mathbf{x}_1 + \mathbf{A}_2\mathbf{x}_2 = \mathbf{b}_1, \quad \mathbf{A}_3\mathbf{x}_1 + \mathbf{A}_4\mathbf{x}_2 = \mathbf{b}_2. \tag{4.215}$$

If the matrix $\mathbf{A}_4$ is invertible, then the second equation (4.213) becomes

$$\mathbf{A}_4^{-1}\mathbf{A}_3\mathbf{x}_1 + \mathbf{x}_2 = \mathbf{A}_4^{-1}\mathbf{b}_2, \tag{4.216}$$

from which

$$\mathbf{x}_2 = \mathbf{A}_4^{-1}\mathbf{b}_2 - \mathbf{A}_4^{-1}\mathbf{A}_3\mathbf{x}_1. \tag{4.217}$$

Substituting now relation (4.217) in the first equation (4.215), we get

$$\mathbf{A}_1\mathbf{x}_1 + \mathbf{A}_2\mathbf{A}_4^{-1}\mathbf{b}_2 - \mathbf{A}_2\mathbf{A}_4^{-1}\mathbf{A}_3\mathbf{x}_1 = \mathbf{b}_1 \tag{4.218}$$

or, equivalently,

$$(\mathbf{A}_1 - \mathbf{A}_2\mathbf{A}_4^{-1}\mathbf{A}_3)\mathbf{x}_1 = \mathbf{b}_1 - \mathbf{A}_2\mathbf{A}_4^{-1}\mathbf{b}_2. \tag{4.219}$$

Now, if $\mathbf{A}_1 - \mathbf{A}_2\mathbf{A}_4^{-1}\mathbf{A}_3$ is invertible, then it follows

$$\mathbf{x}_1 = (\mathbf{A}_1 - \mathbf{A}_2\mathbf{A}_4^{-1}\mathbf{A}_3)^{-1}(\mathbf{b}_1 - \mathbf{A}_2\mathbf{A}_4^{-1}\mathbf{b}_2). \tag{4.220}$$

Relations (4.220) and (4.217) give the solution of the system (4.211).

The conditions of invertibility of the matrices $\mathbf{A}_4$ and $\mathbf{A}_1 - \mathbf{A}_2\mathbf{A}_4^{-1}\mathbf{A}_3$ are just the Schur conditions for the determination of the matrix $\mathbf{A}^{-1}$.

If the matrix $\mathbf{A}_1$ is invertible, then the first equation (4.215) leads to

$$\mathbf{x}_1 = \mathbf{A}_1^{-1}\mathbf{b}_1 - \mathbf{A}_1^{-1}\mathbf{A}_2\mathbf{x}_2, \tag{4.221}$$

while from the second equation (4.215) we obtain

$$\mathbf{A}_3\mathbf{A}_1^{-1}\mathbf{b}_1 - \mathbf{A}_3\mathbf{A}_1^{-1}\mathbf{A}_2\mathbf{x}_2 + \mathbf{A}_4\mathbf{x}_2 = \mathbf{b}_2, \tag{4.222}$$

from which, if $\mathbf{A}_4 - \mathbf{A}_3\mathbf{A}_1^{-1}\mathbf{A}_2$ is an invertible matrix, we get

$$\mathbf{x}_2 = (\mathbf{A}_4 - \mathbf{A}_3\mathbf{A}_1^{-1}\mathbf{A}_2)^{-1}(\mathbf{b}_2 - \mathbf{A}_3\mathbf{A}_1^{-1}\mathbf{b}_1). \tag{4.223}$$

In this case too, the invertibility conditions of the matrices $\mathbf{A}_1$ and $\mathbf{A}_4 - \mathbf{A}_3\mathbf{A}_1^{-1}\mathbf{A}_2$ are Schur's conditions to determine the inverse of the matrix $\mathbf{A}$.

Let us suppose now that the matrix $\mathbf{A}_4$ is invertible, while $\mathbf{Q}$ is a nonsingular quadratic matrix. Moreover, we verify the relations

$$\mathbf{Q}\mathbf{b}_2 = 0, \quad \mathbf{x}_2 = \mathbf{Q}^T\boldsymbol{\lambda}. \tag{4.224}$$

Under these conditions, the equation

$$\begin{bmatrix} \mathbf{A}_1 & \mathbf{A}_2 \\ \mathbf{A}_3 & \mathbf{A}_4 \end{bmatrix} \begin{bmatrix} \mathbf{x}_1 \\ \mathbf{x}_2 \end{bmatrix} = \begin{bmatrix} \mathbf{b}_1 \\ \mathbf{b}_2 \end{bmatrix} \tag{4.225}$$

may be written in the form

$$\begin{bmatrix} \mathbf{I} & \mathbf{0} \\ \mathbf{0} & \mathbf{Q} \end{bmatrix} \begin{bmatrix} \mathbf{A}_1 & \mathbf{A}_2 \\ \mathbf{A}_3 & \mathbf{A}_4 \end{bmatrix} \begin{bmatrix} \mathbf{I} & \mathbf{0} \\ \mathbf{0} & \mathbf{Q}^{\mathrm{T}} \end{bmatrix} \begin{bmatrix} \mathbf{x}_1 \\ \boldsymbol{\lambda} \end{bmatrix} = \begin{bmatrix} \mathbf{b}_1 \\ \mathbf{0} \end{bmatrix}, \tag{4.226}$$

which may be easily verified by performing the requested products and taking into account the relations (4.224). It follows that

$$\begin{bmatrix} \mathbf{A}_1 & \mathbf{A}_2\mathbf{Q}^{\mathrm{T}} \\ \mathbf{Q}\mathbf{A}_3 & \mathbf{Q}\mathbf{A}_4\mathbf{Q}^{\mathrm{T}} \end{bmatrix} \begin{bmatrix} \mathbf{x}_1 \\ \boldsymbol{\lambda} \end{bmatrix} = \begin{bmatrix} \mathbf{b}_1 \\ \mathbf{0} \end{bmatrix}, \tag{4.227}$$

from which

$$\mathbf{A}_1\mathbf{x}_1 + \mathbf{A}_2\mathbf{Q}^{\mathrm{T}}\boldsymbol{\lambda} = \mathbf{b}_1, \quad \mathbf{Q}\mathbf{A}_3\mathbf{x}_1 + \mathbf{Q}\mathbf{A}_4\mathbf{Q}^{\mathrm{T}}\boldsymbol{\lambda} = \mathbf{0}. \tag{4.228}$$

From the second relation (4.228) one obtains

$$\boldsymbol{\lambda} = -(\mathbf{Q}^{\mathrm{T}})^{-1}\mathbf{A}_4^{-1}\mathbf{A}_3\mathbf{x}_1, \tag{4.229}$$

which, replaced in the first relation (4.228), leads to

$$(\mathbf{A}_1 - \mathbf{A}_2\mathbf{A}_4^{-1}\mathbf{A}_3)\mathbf{x}_1 = \mathbf{b}_1. \tag{4.230}$$

If the expression between parentheses in equation (4.230) defines a nonsingular matrix, then relations (4.230) and (4.229) give the required solution, because $\mathbf{Q}\mathbf{A}_4\mathbf{Q}^{\mathrm{T}}$ is always invertible.

Let us consider now the case in which $\mathbf{A}_4$ is not invertible, a situation that may be frequently encountered in the mechanics of multibody systems, when $\mathbf{A}_4 = \mathbf{0}$. From the first relation (4.228), we get

$$\mathbf{x}_1 = \mathbf{A}_1^{-1}(\mathbf{b}_1 - \mathbf{A}_2\mathbf{Q}^{\mathrm{T}}\boldsymbol{\lambda}), \tag{4.231}$$

which, replaced in the second relation (4.228), leads to

$$(\mathbf{A}_4 - \mathbf{A}_3\mathbf{A}_1^{-1}\mathbf{A}_2)\mathbf{Q}^{\mathrm{T}}\boldsymbol{\lambda} = -\mathbf{A}_3\mathbf{A}_1^{-1}\mathbf{b}_1. \tag{4.232}$$

If the expression from the parentheses in equation (4.232), as well as $\mathbf{A}_1$, are nonsingular matrices, then relations (4.232) and (4.231) lead to the solution of the system (4.225) with the conditions (4.224).

In the particular case frequently encountered, for which $\mathbf{A}_4 = \mathbf{0}$, the relation (4.70) is simplified in the form

$$\mathbf{Q}\mathbf{A}_3\mathbf{A}_2\mathbf{Q}^{\mathrm{T}}\boldsymbol{\lambda} = -\mathbf{Q}\mathbf{A}_3\mathbf{A}_1^{-1}\mathbf{b}_1, \tag{4.233}$$

from which

$$\boldsymbol{\lambda} = (\mathbf{A}_3\mathbf{A}_2\mathbf{Q}^{\mathrm{T}})^{-1}\mathbf{A}_3\mathbf{A}_1^{-1}\mathbf{b}_1, \tag{4.234}$$

and the relation (4.69) now leading to

$$\mathbf{x}_1 = \mathbf{A}_1^{-1}[\mathbf{I} - \mathbf{A}_2\mathbf{Q}^{\mathrm{T}}(\mathbf{A}_3\mathbf{A}_2\mathbf{Q}^{\mathrm{T}})^{-1}\mathbf{A}_3\mathbf{A}_1^{-1}]\mathbf{b}_1. \tag{4.235}$$

Let us now consider the case of the system

$$\begin{bmatrix} \mathbf{A}_1 & \mathbf{A}_2 \\ \mathbf{A}_3 & \mathbf{A}_4 \end{bmatrix} \begin{bmatrix} \mathbf{x}_1 \\ \mathbf{x}_2 \end{bmatrix} + \begin{bmatrix} \mathbf{c}_1 \\ \mathbf{c}_2 \end{bmatrix} = \begin{bmatrix} \mathbf{b}_1 \\ \mathbf{b}_2 \end{bmatrix}, \tag{4.236}$$

the relations (4.224) continuing to remain valid. Proceeding analogically, we obtain the relation

$$\begin{bmatrix} \mathbf{A}_1 & \mathbf{A}_2\mathbf{Q}^T \\ \mathbf{Q}\mathbf{A}_3 & \mathbf{Q}\mathbf{A}_4\mathbf{Q}^T \end{bmatrix} \begin{bmatrix} \mathbf{x}_1 \\ \boldsymbol{\lambda} \end{bmatrix} = \begin{bmatrix} \mathbf{b}_1 - \mathbf{c}_1 \\ -\mathbf{Q}\mathbf{c}_2 \end{bmatrix}, \tag{4.237}$$

resulting in the system

$$\mathbf{A}_1\mathbf{x}_1 + \mathbf{A}_2\mathbf{Q}^T\boldsymbol{\lambda} = \mathbf{b}_1 - \mathbf{c}_1, \quad \mathbf{Q}\mathbf{A}_3\mathbf{x}_1 + \mathbf{Q}\mathbf{A}_4\mathbf{Q}^T\boldsymbol{\lambda} = -\mathbf{Q}\mathbf{c}_2. \tag{4.238}$$

If $\mathbf{A}_4$ is invertible, then the last relation (4.238) leads to

$$\boldsymbol{\lambda} = -(\mathbf{Q}^T)^{-1}\mathbf{A}_4^{-1}(\mathbf{c}_2 + \mathbf{A}_3\mathbf{c}_1), \tag{4.239}$$

which, replaced in the first equation (4.238), allows to write

$$(\mathbf{A}_1 - \mathbf{A}_2\mathbf{A}_4^{-1}\mathbf{A}_3)\mathbf{x}_1 = \mathbf{b}_1 - \mathbf{c}_1 + \mathbf{A}_2\mathbf{A}_4^{-1}\mathbf{c}_2. \tag{4.240}$$

If the expression between parentheses of equation (4.240) defines a nonsingular matrix, then formulae (4.240) and (4.239) give the required solution.

If $\mathbf{A}_1$ is invertible, then the first relation (4.238) leads to

$$\mathbf{x}_1 = \mathbf{A}_1^{-1}(\mathbf{b}_1 - \mathbf{c}_1 - \mathbf{A}_2\mathbf{Q}^T\boldsymbol{\lambda}), \tag{4.241}$$

which, replaced in the second equation (4.238), allows to write

$$(\mathbf{A}_4 - \mathbf{A}_3\mathbf{A}_1^{-1}\mathbf{A}_2)\mathbf{Q}^T\boldsymbol{\lambda} = -[\mathbf{c}_2 + \mathbf{A}_3\mathbf{A}_1^{-1}(\mathbf{b}_1 - \mathbf{c}_1)]. \tag{4.242}$$

If the expression between the parentheses, in the left-hand term of the formula (4.242) defines an invertible matrix, then relations (4.242) and (4.241) give the solution we require.

In the particular case defined by $\mathbf{A}_4 = \mathbf{0}$, we obtain, from relations (4.242) and (4.241), the formulae

$$\boldsymbol{\lambda} = (\mathbf{A}_3\mathbf{A}_1^{-1}\mathbf{A}_2\mathbf{Q}^T)^{-1}[\mathbf{c}_2 + \mathbf{A}_3\mathbf{A}_1^{-1}(\mathbf{b}_1 - \mathbf{c}_1)], \tag{4.243}$$

$$\mathbf{x}_1 = \mathbf{A}_1^{-1}\{\mathbf{b}_1 - \mathbf{c}_1 - \mathbf{A}_2(\mathbf{A}_3\mathbf{A}_1^{-1}\mathbf{A}_2)^{-1}[\mathbf{c}_2 + \mathbf{A}_3\mathbf{A}_1^{-1}(\mathbf{b}_1 - \mathbf{c}_1)]\}. \tag{4.244}$$

Let us now modify the second condition (4.224) in the form

$$\mathbf{x}_2 = \mathbf{Q}^T\boldsymbol{\lambda} + \boldsymbol{\beta}. \tag{4.245}$$

The system (4.236) now becomes

$$\begin{bmatrix} \mathbf{A}_1 & \mathbf{A}_2\mathbf{Q}^T \\ \mathbf{Q}\mathbf{A}_3 & \mathbf{Q}\mathbf{A}_4\mathbf{Q}^T \end{bmatrix} \begin{bmatrix} \mathbf{x}_1 \\ \boldsymbol{\lambda} \end{bmatrix} = \begin{bmatrix} \mathbf{b}_1 - \mathbf{c}_1 - \mathbf{A}_2\boldsymbol{\beta} \\ -\mathbf{Q}\mathbf{c}_2 - \mathbf{Q}\mathbf{A}_4\boldsymbol{\beta} \end{bmatrix}, \tag{4.246}$$

from which we get

$$\mathbf{A}_1\mathbf{x}_1 + \mathbf{A}_2\mathbf{Q}^T\boldsymbol{\lambda} = \mathbf{b}_1 - \mathbf{c}_1 - \mathbf{A}_2\boldsymbol{\beta}, \quad \mathbf{Q}\mathbf{A}_3\mathbf{x}_1 + \mathbf{Q}\mathbf{A}_4\mathbf{Q}^T\boldsymbol{\lambda} = -\mathbf{Q}\mathbf{c}_2 - \mathbf{Q}\mathbf{A}_4\boldsymbol{\beta}. \tag{4.247}$$

If $\mathbf{A}_4$ is invertible, then the last relation (4.247) leads to

$$\boldsymbol{\lambda} - (\mathbf{A}_4 \mathbf{Q}^T)^{-1}(\mathbf{A}_3 \mathbf{x}_1 + \mathbf{c}_2 + \mathbf{A}_4 \boldsymbol{\beta}), \tag{4.248}$$

which, replaced in the first equation (4.247), allows to write

$$(\mathbf{A}_1 - \mathbf{A}_2 \mathbf{A}_4^{-1} \mathbf{A}_3)\mathbf{x}_1 = \mathbf{b}_1 - \mathbf{c}_1 - \mathbf{A}_2 \boldsymbol{\beta} + \mathbf{A}_2 \mathbf{A}_4^{-1}(\mathbf{c}_1 + \mathbf{A}_4 \boldsymbol{\beta}). \tag{4.249}$$

If the expression between the parentheses on the left-hand side of this formula defines an invertible matrix, then relations (4.249) and (4.248) give the required answer.

If $\mathbf{A}_1$ is invertible, then the first relation (4.247) leads to

$$\mathbf{x}_1 = \mathbf{A}_1^{-1}(\mathbf{b}_1 - \mathbf{c}_1 - \mathbf{A}_2 \boldsymbol{\beta}) - \mathbf{A}_1^{-1} \mathbf{A}_2 \mathbf{Q}^T \boldsymbol{\lambda}, \tag{4.250}$$

which, replaced in the last relation (4.247), allows to write

$$(\mathbf{A}_4 - \mathbf{A}_3 \mathbf{A}_1^{-1} \mathbf{A}_2)\mathbf{Q}^T \boldsymbol{\lambda} = -\mathbf{c}_2 - \mathbf{A}_4 \boldsymbol{\beta} - \mathbf{A}_3 \mathbf{A}_1^{-1}(\mathbf{b}_1 - \mathbf{c}_1 - \mathbf{A}_2 \boldsymbol{\beta}). \tag{4.251}$$

If the parentheses of the left-hand side of the previous relation define a nonsingular matrix, then the relations (4.251) and (4.250) constitute the required answer.

In the particular case given by $\mathbf{A}_4 = \mathbf{0}$, formulae (4.251) and (4.250) are simplified in the form

$$\boldsymbol{\lambda} = (\mathbf{Q}^T \mathbf{A}_3 \mathbf{A}_1^{-1} \mathbf{A}_2)^{-1}[-\mathbf{c}_2 - \mathbf{A}_3 \mathbf{A}_1^{-1}(\mathbf{b}_1 - \mathbf{c}_1 - \mathbf{A}_2 \boldsymbol{\beta})], \tag{4.252}$$

$$\mathbf{x}_1 = \mathbf{A}_1^{-1}(\mathbf{b}_1 - \mathbf{c}_1 - \mathbf{A}_2 \boldsymbol{\beta}) - \mathbf{A}_1^{-1} \mathbf{A}_2 (\mathbf{A}_3 \mathbf{A}_1^{-1} \mathbf{A}_2)^{-1}[-\mathbf{c}_2 - \mathbf{A}_3 \mathbf{A}_1^{-1}(\mathbf{b}_1 - \mathbf{c}_1 - \mathbf{A}_2 \boldsymbol{\beta})]. \tag{4.253}$$

Observation 4.22   The theory presented above remains valid also in the case in which we renounce the condition that $\mathbf{Q}$ be invertible. The only condition asked is that $\mathbf{Q}$ should be a full rank matrix.

Considering now the system (4.247), if $\mathbf{A}_4$ is invertible, then the last equation (4.247) leads to

$$\boldsymbol{\lambda} = (\mathbf{Q}\mathbf{A}_4 \mathbf{Q}^T)^{-1}(-\mathbf{Q}\mathbf{c}_2 - \mathbf{Q}\mathbf{A}_4 \boldsymbol{\beta} - \mathbf{Q}\mathbf{A}_3 \mathbf{x}_1), \tag{4.254}$$

while the first relation (4.247) gives

$$[\mathbf{A}_1 - \mathbf{A}_2 \mathbf{Q}^T (\mathbf{Q}\mathbf{A}_4 \mathbf{Q}^T)^{-1} \mathbf{Q}\mathbf{A}_3]\mathbf{x}_1 = \mathbf{b}_1 - \mathbf{c}_1 - \mathbf{A}_2 \boldsymbol{\beta} + \mathbf{A}_2 \mathbf{Q}^T (\mathbf{Q}\mathbf{A}_4 \mathbf{Q}^T)^{-1}(\mathbf{Q}\mathbf{c}_1 + \mathbf{Q}\mathbf{A}_4 \boldsymbol{\beta}). \tag{4.255}$$

If the square brackets on the left-hand side of this formula define an invertible matrix, then formulae (4.255) and (4.254) give the allowed answer.

If $\mathbf{A}_1$ is invertible, then, from the first relation (4.247), we get

$$\mathbf{x}_1 = \mathbf{A}_1^{-1}(\mathbf{b}_1 - \mathbf{c}_1 - \mathbf{A}_2 \boldsymbol{\beta} - \mathbf{A}_2 \mathbf{Q}^T \boldsymbol{\lambda}), \tag{4.256}$$

which, replaced in the second formula (4.247), leads to

$$(\mathbf{Q}\mathbf{A}_4 \mathbf{Q}^T + \mathbf{Q}\mathbf{A}_3 \mathbf{A}_1^{-1} \mathbf{A}_2 \mathbf{Q}^T)\boldsymbol{\lambda} = \mathbf{Q}\mathbf{c}_2 + \mathbf{Q}\mathbf{A}_4 \boldsymbol{\beta} + \mathbf{Q}\mathbf{A}_3(\mathbf{b}_1 - \mathbf{c}_1 - \mathbf{A}_2 \boldsymbol{\beta}). \tag{4.257}$$

If the parentheses on the left-hand side of equation (4.257) define a nonsingular matrix, then the formulae (4.257) and (4.256) give the searched answer.

If $\mathbf{A}_4 = \mathbf{0}$, then the relation (4.257) may be written in the form

$$\mathbf{Q}\mathbf{A}_3\mathbf{A}_1^{-1}\mathbf{A}_2\mathbf{Q}^T\boldsymbol{\lambda} = \mathbf{Q}\mathbf{c}_2 + \mathbf{Q}\mathbf{A}_3(\mathbf{b}_1 - \mathbf{c}_1 - \mathbf{A}_2\boldsymbol{\beta}). \tag{4.258}$$

If $\boldsymbol{\beta} = \mathbf{0}$, then the relations (4.254)–(4.258) become

$$\boldsymbol{\lambda} = (\mathbf{Q}\mathbf{A}_4\mathbf{Q}^T)^{-1}(-\mathbf{Q}\mathbf{c}_2 - \mathbf{Q}\mathbf{A}_3\mathbf{x}_1), \tag{4.259}$$

$$[\mathbf{A}_1 - \mathbf{A}_2\mathbf{Q}^T(\mathbf{Q}\mathbf{A}_4\mathbf{Q}^T)^{-1}\mathbf{Q}\mathbf{A}_3]\mathbf{x}_1 = \mathbf{b}_1 - \mathbf{c}_1 + \mathbf{A}_2\mathbf{Q}^T(\mathbf{Q}\mathbf{A}_4\mathbf{Q}^T)^{-1}\mathbf{Q}\mathbf{c}_2, \tag{4.260}$$

$$\mathbf{x}_1 = \mathbf{A}_1^{-1}(\mathbf{b}_1 - \mathbf{c}_1 - \mathbf{A}_2\mathbf{Q}^T\boldsymbol{\lambda}), \tag{4.261}$$

$$(\mathbf{Q}\mathbf{A}_4\mathbf{Q}^T + \mathbf{Q}\mathbf{A}_3\mathbf{A}_1^{-1}\mathbf{A}_2\mathbf{Q}^T)\boldsymbol{\lambda} = \mathbf{Q}\mathbf{c}_2 + \mathbf{Q}\mathbf{A}_3(\mathbf{b}_1 - \mathbf{c}_1), \tag{4.262}$$

$$\mathbf{Q}\mathbf{A}_3\mathbf{A}_1^{-1}\mathbf{A}_2\mathbf{Q}^T\boldsymbol{\lambda} = \mathbf{Q}\mathbf{c}_2 + \mathbf{Q}\mathbf{A}_3(\mathbf{b}_1 - \mathbf{c}_1). \tag{4.263}$$

If we also have $\mathbf{c}_1 = \mathbf{0}$, $\mathbf{c}_2 = \mathbf{0}$, then the last relations are simplified and, furthermore, we are led to

$$\boldsymbol{\lambda} = -(\mathbf{Q}\mathbf{A}_4\mathbf{Q}^T)^{-1}\mathbf{Q}\mathbf{A}_3\mathbf{x}_1, \tag{4.264}$$

$$[\mathbf{A}_1 - \mathbf{A}_2\mathbf{Q}^T(\mathbf{Q}\mathbf{A}_4\mathbf{Q}^T)^{-1}\mathbf{Q}\mathbf{A}_3]\mathbf{x}_1 = \mathbf{b}_1, \tag{4.265}$$

$$\mathbf{x}_1 = \mathbf{A}_1^{-1}(\mathbf{b}_1 - \mathbf{A}_2\mathbf{Q}^T\boldsymbol{\lambda}), \tag{4.266}$$

$$(\mathbf{Q}\mathbf{A}_4\mathbf{Q}^T + \mathbf{Q}\mathbf{A}_3\mathbf{A}_1^{-1}\mathbf{A}_2\mathbf{Q}^T)\boldsymbol{\lambda} = \mathbf{Q}\mathbf{A}_3\mathbf{b}_1, \tag{4.267}$$

$$\mathbf{Q}\mathbf{A}_3\mathbf{A}_1^{-1}\mathbf{A}_2\mathbf{Q}^T\boldsymbol{\lambda} = \mathbf{Q}\mathbf{A}_3\mathbf{b}_1. \tag{4.268}$$

4.5.6   The Iteration Method (Jacobi)

Let us consider the system of linear equations[10]

$$\begin{cases} a_{11}x_1 + a_{12}x_2 + \cdots + a_{1n}x_n = b_1, \\ a_{21}x_1 + a_{22}x_2 + \cdots + a_{2n}x_n = b_2, \\ \vdots \\ a_{i1}x_1 + a_{12}x_2 + \cdots + a_{in}x_n = b_i, \\ \vdots \\ a_{n1}x_1 + a_{n2}x_2 + \cdots + a_{nn}x_n = b_n, \end{cases} \tag{4.269}$$

which may also be written in the matrix form

$$\mathbf{A}\mathbf{x} = \mathbf{b}, \tag{4.270}$$

where

$$\mathbf{A} = \begin{bmatrix} a_{11} & a_{12} & \cdots & a_{1n} \\ a_{21} & a_{22} & \cdots & a_{2n} \\ \cdots & \cdots & \cdots & \cdots \\ a_{n1} & a_{n2} & \cdots & a_{nn} \end{bmatrix}, \quad \mathbf{b} = \begin{bmatrix} b_1 & b_2 & \cdots & b_n \end{bmatrix}^T, \quad \mathbf{x} = \begin{bmatrix} x_1 & x_2 & \cdots & x_n \end{bmatrix}^T. \tag{4.271}$$

We suppose that $a_{ii} \neq 0$, $i = \overline{1, n}$, in the system (4.269) and that $\mathbf{A}$ is nonsingular.

---

[10]The method was named after Carl Gustav Jacob Jacobi (1804–1851).

If one includes the unknown x_i in the equation i of the system (4.269), then one may write

$$
\begin{cases}
x_1 = \dfrac{b_1}{a_{11}} - \dfrac{a_{12}}{a_{11}}x_2 - \dfrac{a_{13}}{a_{11}}x_3 - \cdots - \dfrac{a_{1n}}{a_{11}}x_n, \\[2mm]
x_2 = \dfrac{b_2}{a_{22}} - \dfrac{a_{21}}{a_{22}}x_1 - \dfrac{a_{23}}{a_{22}}x_3 - \cdots - \dfrac{a_{2n}}{a_{22}}x_n, \\[2mm]
\qquad\vdots \\[1mm]
x_i = \dfrac{b_i}{a_{ii}} - \dfrac{a_{i1}}{a_{ii}}x_1 - \dfrac{a_{i2}}{a_{ii}}x_2 - \cdots - \dfrac{a_{in}}{a_{ii}}x_n, \\[2mm]
\qquad\vdots \\[1mm]
x_n = \dfrac{b_n}{a_{nn}} - \dfrac{a_{n1}}{a_{nn}}x_1 - \dfrac{a_{n2}}{a_{nn}}x_2 - \cdots - \dfrac{a_{n,n-1}}{a_{nn}}x_{n-1}.
\end{cases}
\tag{4.272}
$$

Let us denote

$$
\beta_i = \frac{b_i}{a_{ii}}, \quad i = \overline{1, n},
\tag{4.273}
$$

$$
\alpha_{ij} = -\frac{a_{ij}}{a_{ii}}, \quad i = \overline{1, n}, \quad i \neq j, \quad \alpha_{ij} = 0, \quad i = j.
\tag{4.274}
$$

It follows that

$$
\boldsymbol{\alpha} =
\begin{bmatrix}
0 & \alpha_{12} & \cdots & \alpha_{1,n-1} & \alpha_{1n} \\
\alpha_{21} & 0 & \cdots & \alpha_{2,n-1} & \alpha_{2n} \\
\cdots & \cdots & \cdots & \cdots & \cdots \\
\alpha_{n1} & \alpha_{n2} & \cdots & \alpha_{n,n-1} & 0
\end{bmatrix},
\quad
\boldsymbol{\beta} =
\begin{bmatrix}
\beta_1 \\ \beta_2 \\ \vdots \\ \beta_n
\end{bmatrix},
\tag{4.275}
$$

so that the system (4.272) becomes

$$
\mathbf{x} = \boldsymbol{\beta} + \boldsymbol{\alpha}\mathbf{x}.
\tag{4.276}
$$

Let $\mathbf{x}^{(0)} \in \mathcal{M}_{n,1}(\mathbb{R})$ be an initial solution of the system (4.276). We define the sequence of iterations

$$
\mathbf{x}^{(1)} = \boldsymbol{\beta} + \boldsymbol{\alpha}\mathbf{x}^{(0)}, \quad \mathbf{x}^{(2)} = \boldsymbol{\beta} + \boldsymbol{\alpha}\mathbf{x}^{(1)}, \quad \ldots, \quad \mathbf{x}^{(k+1)} = \boldsymbol{\beta} + \boldsymbol{\alpha}\mathbf{x}^{(k)}, \quad \ldots,
\tag{4.277}
$$

where $k \in \mathbb{N}^*$. Let us suppose that the sequence $\mathbf{x}^{(0)}, \mathbf{x}^{(1)}, \ldots, \mathbf{x}^{(k)}, \ldots$, is convergent and let

$$
\overline{\mathbf{x}} = \lim_{k \to \infty} \mathbf{x}^{(k)}
\tag{4.278}
$$

be its limit. It follows that

$$
\overline{\mathbf{x}} = \boldsymbol{\beta} + \boldsymbol{\alpha}\overline{\mathbf{x}},
\tag{4.279}
$$

hence $\overline{\mathbf{x}}$ is the solution of the system (4.276).

Proposition 4.10 A sufficient condition of convergence of the sequence of successive iterations

$$
\mathbf{x}^{(k+1)} = \boldsymbol{\beta} + \boldsymbol{\alpha}\mathbf{x}^{(k)}, \quad k \in \mathbb{N}^*, \quad \mathbf{x}^{(0)} \text{ arbitrary},
\tag{4.280}
$$

is $\|\boldsymbol{\alpha}\| < 1$, where $\|\;\|$ is one of the canonical norms.

Demonstration. We may write

$$
\mathbf{x}^{(k)} = \boldsymbol{\beta} + \boldsymbol{\alpha}\mathbf{x}^{(k-1)} = \boldsymbol{\beta} + \boldsymbol{\alpha}(\boldsymbol{\beta} + \boldsymbol{\alpha}\mathbf{x}^{(k-2)}) = (\mathbf{I}_n + \boldsymbol{\alpha})\boldsymbol{\beta} + \boldsymbol{\alpha}^2\mathbf{x}^{(k-2)}.
\tag{4.281}
$$

We get, in general,

$$\mathbf{x}^{(k)} = (\mathbf{I}_n + \boldsymbol{\alpha} + \boldsymbol{\alpha}^2 + \cdots + \boldsymbol{\alpha}^{k-1})\boldsymbol{\beta} + \boldsymbol{\alpha}^k \mathbf{x}^{(0)}, \tag{4.282}$$

where $\mathbf{I}_n$ is the unit matrix of nth order.

On the other hand, from $\|\boldsymbol{\alpha}\| < 1$ and because $\|\ \|$ is canonical, we also have

$$\|\boldsymbol{\alpha}^k\| \le \|\boldsymbol{\alpha}\|^k. \tag{4.283}$$

It follows that $\|\boldsymbol{\alpha}^k\| \to 0$ for $k \to \infty$, because $\|\boldsymbol{\alpha}\|^k \to 0$ for $k \to \infty$. One obtains

$$\lim_{k \to \infty} \boldsymbol{\alpha}^k = \mathbf{0}. \tag{4.284}$$

Then

$$\lim_{k \to \infty} (\mathbf{I}_n + \boldsymbol{\alpha} + \cdots + \boldsymbol{\alpha}^{k-1}) = (\mathbf{I}_n - \boldsymbol{\alpha})^{-1} \tag{4.285}$$

and, passing to the limit in (4.282), it follows that

$$\overline{\mathbf{x}} = (\mathbf{I}_n - \boldsymbol{\alpha})^{-1}\boldsymbol{\beta}, \tag{4.286}$$

from which

$$(\mathbf{I}_n - \boldsymbol{\alpha})\overline{\mathbf{x}} = \boldsymbol{\beta}; \tag{4.287}$$

which is just the relation (4.279), showing that $\overline{\mathbf{x}}$ is a solution of the system (4.276), hence of the system (4.269).

Observation 4.23   Instead of the sequence of successive iterations $\mathbf{x}^{(0)}$, $\mathbf{x}^{(1)}$, ..., $\mathbf{x}^{(k)}$, ..., we may consider the sequence

$$\mathbf{y}^{(0)} = \mathbf{x}^{(0)}, \quad \mathbf{y}^{(k)} = \mathbf{x}^{(k)} - \mathbf{x}^{(k-1)}, \quad k \in \mathbb{N}^*. \tag{4.288}$$

We get

$$\mathbf{y}^{(k+1)} = \mathbf{x}^{(k+1)} - \mathbf{x}^{(k)} = \boldsymbol{\beta} + \boldsymbol{\alpha}\mathbf{x}^{(k)} - \boldsymbol{\beta} - \boldsymbol{\alpha}\mathbf{x}^{(k-1)}, \tag{4.289}$$

from which

$$\mathbf{y}^{(k+1)} = \boldsymbol{\alpha}(\mathbf{x}^{(k)} - \mathbf{x}^{(k-1)}), \quad k \in \mathbb{N}^*, \tag{4.290}$$

hence

$$\mathbf{y}^{(k+1)} = \boldsymbol{\alpha}\mathbf{y}^{(k)}, \quad k \in \mathbb{N}^*. \tag{4.291}$$

On the other hand,

$$\mathbf{x}^{(k+1)} = \sum_{i=0}^{k+1} \mathbf{y}^{(i)} = \mathbf{x}^{(0)} + \sum_{i=1}^{k+1} \boldsymbol{\alpha}^i \mathbf{y}^{(1)}. \tag{4.292}$$

Observation 4.24

(i) If $\mathbf{x}^{(0)} = \boldsymbol{\beta}$, then the sequence of successive iterations becomes a particular form

$$\mathbf{x}^{(0)} = \boldsymbol{\beta}, \ \mathbf{x}^{(1)} = \boldsymbol{\beta} + \boldsymbol{\alpha}\mathbf{x}^{(0)} = (\mathbf{I}_n + \boldsymbol{\alpha})\boldsymbol{\beta},$$

$$\mathbf{x}^{(2)} = \boldsymbol{\beta} + \boldsymbol{\alpha}\mathbf{x}^{(1)} = \boldsymbol{\beta} + \boldsymbol{\alpha}\boldsymbol{\beta} + \boldsymbol{\alpha}^2\boldsymbol{\beta} = (\mathbf{I}_n + \boldsymbol{\alpha} + \boldsymbol{\alpha}^2)\boldsymbol{\beta}, \ \ldots, \mathbf{x}^{(k)}$$

$$= (\mathbf{I}_n + \boldsymbol{\alpha} + \boldsymbol{\alpha}^2 + \cdots + \boldsymbol{\alpha}^n)\boldsymbol{\beta}, \ \ldots \tag{4.293}$$

(ii) For $\mathbf{x}^{(0)} = \boldsymbol{\beta}$, relation (4.292) is written in the form

$$\mathbf{x}^{(k+1)} = \sum_{i=0}^{k+1} \boldsymbol{\alpha}^i \boldsymbol{\beta}, \tag{4.294}$$

where $\boldsymbol{\alpha}^0 = \mathbf{I}_n$.

Proposition 4.11 (Estimation of the Error). Under the above conditions, the relation

$$\|\mathbf{x}^{(k)} - \overline{\mathbf{x}}\| \le \frac{1}{1 - \|\boldsymbol{\alpha}\|} \|\mathbf{x}^{(k+1)} - \mathbf{x}^{(k)}\| \le \frac{\|\boldsymbol{\alpha}\|^k \|\mathbf{x}^{(1)} - \mathbf{x}^{(0)}\|}{1 - \|\boldsymbol{\alpha}\|} \tag{4.295}$$

follows.

Demonstration. Let $\mathbf{x}^{(m+1)}$ and $\mathbf{x}^{(m)}$ be two consecutive iterations, with $m \in \mathbb{N}^*$. We have

$$\mathbf{x}^{(m+1)} - \mathbf{x}^{(m)} = \boldsymbol{\beta} + \boldsymbol{\alpha}\mathbf{x}^{(m)} - \boldsymbol{\beta} - \boldsymbol{\alpha}\mathbf{x}^{(m-1)} = \boldsymbol{\alpha}(\mathbf{x}^{(m)} - \mathbf{x}^{(m-1)}). \tag{4.296}$$

It follows that

$$\mathbf{x}^{(m+1)} - \mathbf{x}^{(m)} = \boldsymbol{\alpha}^{m-k}(\mathbf{x}^{(k+1)} - \mathbf{x}^{(k)}) = \boldsymbol{\alpha}^m(\mathbf{x}^{(1)} - \mathbf{x}^{(0)}) \tag{4.297}$$

for any $1 \le k < m$. Passing to the norm in the relation (4.297), it follows that

$$\|\mathbf{x}^{(m+1)} - \mathbf{x}^{(m)}\| \le \|\boldsymbol{\alpha}\|^{m-k}\|\mathbf{x}^{(k+1)} - \mathbf{x}^{(k)}\| \le \|\boldsymbol{\alpha}\|^m\|\mathbf{x}^{(1)} - \mathbf{x}^{(0)}\|. \tag{4.298}$$

Let $p \in \mathbb{N}^*$, arbitrary. We calculate

$$\|\mathbf{x}^{(k+p)} - \mathbf{x}^{(k)}\| = \|\mathbf{x}^{(k+p)} - \mathbf{x}^{(k+p-1)} + \mathbf{x}^{(k+p-1)} - \cdots - \mathbf{x}^{(k+1)} + \mathbf{x}^{(k)}\|$$
$$\le \|\mathbf{x}^{(k+p)} - \mathbf{x}^{(k+p-1)}\| + \|\mathbf{x}^{(k+p-1)} - \mathbf{x}^{(k+p-2)}\| + \cdots + \|\mathbf{x}^{(k+1)} - \mathbf{x}^{(k)}\|. \tag{4.299}$$

From (4.298), we get

$$\|\mathbf{x}^{(k+p)} - \mathbf{x}^{(k+p-1)}\| \le \|\boldsymbol{\alpha}\|^{p-1}\|\mathbf{x}^{(k+1)} - \mathbf{x}^{(k)}\|, \|\mathbf{x}^{(k+p-1)} - \mathbf{x}^{(k+p-2)}\|$$
$$\le \|\boldsymbol{\alpha}\|^{p-2}\|\mathbf{x}^{(k+1)} - \mathbf{x}^{(k)}\|, \ldots, \|\mathbf{x}^{(k+2)} - \mathbf{x}^{(k+1)}\| \le \|\boldsymbol{\alpha}\|\|\mathbf{x}^{(k+1)} - \mathbf{x}^{(k)}\|, \tag{4.300}$$

so that the relation (4.298) leads to

$$\|\mathbf{x}^{(k+p)} - \mathbf{x}^{(k)}\| \le \|\boldsymbol{\alpha}\|^{p-1}\|\mathbf{x}^{(k+1)} - \mathbf{x}^{(k)}\| + \|\boldsymbol{\alpha}\|^{p-2}\|\mathbf{x}^{(k+1)} - \mathbf{x}^{(k)}\| + \cdots + \|\mathbf{x}^{(k+1)} - \mathbf{x}^{(k)}\|$$
$$= \frac{1 - \|\boldsymbol{\alpha}\|^p}{1 - \|\boldsymbol{\alpha}\|}\|\mathbf{x}^{(k+1)} - \mathbf{x}^{(k)}\| \le \frac{1}{1 - \|\boldsymbol{\alpha}\|}\|\mathbf{x}^{(k+1)} - \mathbf{x}^{(k)}\|. \tag{4.301}$$

Taking into account that

$$\|\mathbf{x}^{(k+1)} - \mathbf{x}^{(k)}\| \le \|\boldsymbol{\alpha}\|\|\mathbf{x}^{(k)} - \mathbf{x}^{(k-1)}\| \le \|\boldsymbol{\alpha}\|^2\|\mathbf{x}^{(k-1)} - \mathbf{x}^{(k-2)}\| \le \cdots \le \|\boldsymbol{\alpha}\|^k\|\mathbf{x}^{(1)} - \mathbf{x}^{(0)}\|, \tag{4.302}$$

we get

$$\|\mathbf{x}^{(k+p)} - \mathbf{x}^{(k)}\| \le \frac{1}{1 - \|\boldsymbol{\alpha}\|}\|\mathbf{x}^{(k+1)} - \mathbf{x}^{(k)}\| \le \frac{\|\boldsymbol{\alpha}\|^k}{1 - \|\boldsymbol{\alpha}\|}\|\mathbf{x}^{(1)} - \mathbf{x}^{(0)}\| \tag{4.303}$$

from the formula (4.301).

We pass now to the limit for $p \to \infty$ in the last relation and take into account $\lim\limits_{p \to \infty} \mathbf{x}^{(k+p)} = \bar{\mathbf{x}}$, obtaining the relation (4.295), which had to be proved.

Corollary 4.4   If $\mathbf{x}^{(0)} = \boldsymbol{\beta}$, then the relation (4.295) becomes

$$\|\mathbf{x}^{(k)} - \bar{\mathbf{x}}\| \le \frac{1}{1 - \|\boldsymbol{\alpha}\|}\|\mathbf{x}^{(k+1)} - \mathbf{x}^{(k)}\| \le \frac{\|\boldsymbol{\alpha}\|^{k+1}}{1 - \|\boldsymbol{\alpha}\|}\|\boldsymbol{\beta}\|. \tag{4.304}$$

Demonstration. We have

$$\mathbf{x}^{(0)} = \boldsymbol{\beta}, \quad \mathbf{x}^{(1)} = (\mathbf{I}_n + \boldsymbol{\alpha})\boldsymbol{\beta}, \quad \mathbf{x}^{(2)} = (\mathbf{I}_n + \boldsymbol{\alpha} + \boldsymbol{\alpha}^2)\boldsymbol{\beta}, \ldots, \quad \mathbf{x}^{(m)} = (\mathbf{I}_n + \boldsymbol{\alpha} + \boldsymbol{\alpha}^2 + \cdots + \boldsymbol{\alpha}^m)\boldsymbol{\beta} \tag{4.305}$$

for $\mathbf{x}^{(0)} = \boldsymbol{\beta}$, so that

$$\|\mathbf{x}^{(k+1)} - \mathbf{x}^{(k)}\| = \|\boldsymbol{\alpha}^{k+1}\boldsymbol{\beta}\| \le \|\boldsymbol{\alpha}\|^{k+1}\|\boldsymbol{\beta}\| \tag{4.306}$$

and the relation (4.304) is obvious.

Observation 4.25

(i) *A priori* estimation of the error: The formula (4.295), written in the form

$$\|\mathbf{x}^{(k)} - \bar{\mathbf{x}}\| \le \frac{\|\boldsymbol{\alpha}\|^k \|\mathbf{x}^{(1)} - \mathbf{x}^{(0)}\|}{1 - \|\boldsymbol{\alpha}\|} < \varepsilon, \tag{4.307}$$

leads to the a priori estimation of the error in the iterations method. So, to determine the solution $\bar{\mathbf{x}}$ with an imposed precision ε, we must make a number of iterations given by

$$k = \left[\frac{\ln\left[\varepsilon\left(1 - \|\boldsymbol{\alpha}\|\right)/\|\mathbf{x}^{(1)} - \mathbf{x}^{(0)}\|\right]}{\ln(\|\boldsymbol{\alpha}\|)}\right] + 1, \tag{4.308}$$

where the external brackets mark the entire part of the function.

(ii) *A posteriori* estimation of the error: This estimation is given by the formula (4.295) written in the form

$$\|\mathbf{x}^{(k)} - \bar{\mathbf{x}}\| \le \frac{1}{1 - \|\boldsymbol{\alpha}\|}\|\mathbf{x}^{(k+1)} - \mathbf{x}^{(k)}\| < \varepsilon. \tag{4.309}$$

Hence, to determine $\bar{\mathbf{x}}$ with an imposed precision ε, we must iterate until the difference between two successive iterations $\mathbf{x}^{(k)}$ and $\mathbf{x}^{(k+1)}$ verifies the relation

$$\|\mathbf{x}^{(k+1)} - \mathbf{x}^{(k)}\| < \varepsilon(1 - \|\boldsymbol{\alpha}\|). \tag{4.310}$$

Observation 4.26   A sufficient condition to have $\|\boldsymbol{\alpha}\| < 1$ is given by the relation

$$|a_{ii}| > \sum_{\substack{j=1 \\ j \ne i}}^{n}|a_{ij}|, \quad i = \overline{1, n}. \tag{4.311}$$

Thus, it follows $\|\boldsymbol{\alpha}\|_\infty < 1$. Analogically, if

$$|a_{ii}| > \sum_{\substack{j=1 \\ j \ne i}}^{n}|a_{ij}|, \quad i = \overline{1, n}, \tag{4.312}$$

then we get $\|\boldsymbol{\alpha}\|_1 < 1$.

4.5.7 The Gauss–Seidel Method

The Gauss–Seidel method[11] is a variant of the iterations method; indeed, at the step $k + 1$ for the determination of $x_i^{(k+1)}$ one uses the values $x_1^{(k+1)}$, ..., $x_{i-1}^{(k+1)}$ (obtained at this step) and the values $x_{i+1}^{(k)}$, ..., $x_n^{(k)}$ (determined in the preceding step). We may write

$$x_1^{(k+1)} = \beta_1 + \sum_{j=1}^{n} \alpha_{ij} x_j^{(k)}, \quad x_2^{(k+1)} = \beta_2 + \alpha_{21} x_1^{(k+1)} \sum_{j=2}^{n} \alpha_{2j} x_j^{(k)}, \quad \ldots,$$

$$x_i^{(k+1)} = \beta_i + \sum_{j=1}^{i-1} \alpha_{ij} x_j^{(k+1)} + \sum_{j=i+1}^{n} \alpha_{ij} - x_j^{(k)}, \quad \ldots, \quad x_n^{(k+1)} = \beta_n + \sum_{j=1}^{n-1} \alpha_{nj} x_j^{(k)}. \quad (4.313)$$

Proposition 4.12 Let $\mathbf{x} = \alpha\mathbf{x} + \beta$, where $\|\alpha\|_\infty < 1$ be the linear system. Under these conditions, the iterative Gauss–Seidel process described by the relations (4.313) is convergent to the unique solution of the system for any choice of the initial value $\mathbf{x}^{(0)}$.

Demonstration. The component $x_i^{(k)}$ is given by

$$x_i^{(k)} = \sum_{j=1}^{i-1} \alpha_{ij} x_j^{(k)} + \sum_{j=i+1}^{n} \alpha_{ij} x_j^{(k-1)} + \beta_i, \quad i = \overline{1, n}. \quad (4.314)$$

On the other hand,

$$\overline{x}_i = \sum_{j=1}^{n} \alpha_{ij} \overline{x}_j + \beta_i, \quad i = \overline{1, n}, \quad (4.315)$$

and, by subtracting the relation (4.314) from relation (4.315) term by term, we obtain

$$\overline{x}_i - x_i^{(k)} = \sum_{j=1}^{i-1} \alpha_{ij} (\overline{x}_j - x_j^{(k)}) + \sum_{j=i+1}^{n} \alpha_{ij} (\overline{x}_j - x_j^{(k-1)}). \quad (4.316)$$

We apply the modulus in the last relation and obtain the result

$$|\overline{x}_i - x_i^{(k)}| \le \sum_{j=1}^{i-1} |\alpha_{ij}| |\overline{x}_j - x_j^{(k)}| + \sum_{j=i+1}^{n} |\alpha_{ij}| |\overline{x}_j - x_j^{(k-1)}|, \quad i = \overline{1, n}. \quad (4.317)$$

But

$$|\overline{x}_i - x_i^{(k)}| \le \|\overline{\mathbf{x}} - \mathbf{x}^{(k)}\|_\infty, \quad (4.318)$$

because $\|\,\|_\infty$ is a canonical norm, and hence

$$|\overline{x}_i - x_i^{(k)}| \le \sum_{j=1}^{i-1} |\alpha_{ij}| \|\overline{\mathbf{x}} - \mathbf{x}^{(k)}\| + \sum_{k=i+1}^{n} |\alpha_{ij}| \|\overline{\mathbf{x}} - \mathbf{x}^{(k-1)}\|. \quad (4.319)$$

Let us denote by m the value of the index $i = \overline{1, n}$ for which $|\overline{x}_m - x_m^{(k)}|$ is the norm $\|\alpha\|_\infty$, hence

$$|\overline{x}_m - x_m^{(k)}| = \max_{1 \le i \le n} |\overline{x}_i - x_i^{(k)}| = \|\alpha\|_\infty. \quad (4.320)$$

---

[11]The method is named after Carl Friedrich Gauss (1777–1855) and Philipp Ludwig von Seidel (1821–1896).

We have

$$\|\overline{\mathbf{x}} - \mathbf{x}^{(k)}\| \leq \lambda_i \|\overline{\mathbf{x}} - \mathbf{x}^{(k)}\| + \mu_i \|\overline{\mathbf{x}} - \mathbf{x}^{(k-1)}\|, \tag{4.321}$$

hence

$$\|\overline{\mathbf{x}} - \mathbf{x}^{(k)}\| \leq \frac{\mu_i}{1 - \lambda_i} \|\overline{\mathbf{x}} - \mathbf{x}^{(k-1)}\|. \tag{4.322}$$

Let

$$q = \max_{1 \leq i \leq n} \frac{\mu_i}{1 - \lambda_i}. \tag{4.323}$$

Let us show that $q \leq \|\boldsymbol{\alpha}\|_\infty < 1$. Now,

$$\lambda_i + \mu_i = \sum_{j=1}^n |\alpha_{ij}| \leq \|\boldsymbol{\alpha}\|_\infty, \tag{4.324}$$

from which

$$\mu_i \leq \|\boldsymbol{\alpha}\|_\infty - \lambda_i, \quad i = \overline{1, n}, \tag{4.325}$$

with $\|\boldsymbol{\alpha}\|_\infty < 1$. We may also write

$$\frac{\mu_i}{1 - \lambda_i} \leq \frac{\|\boldsymbol{\alpha}\|_\infty - \lambda_i}{1 - \lambda_i} \leq \frac{\|\boldsymbol{\alpha}\|_\infty - \lambda_i \|\boldsymbol{\alpha}\|_\infty}{1 - \lambda_i} = \|\boldsymbol{\alpha}\|_\infty < 1, \tag{4.326}$$

hence $q \leq \|\boldsymbol{\alpha}\|_\infty$.

The relation (4.322) leads now to the sequence of inequalities

$$\|\overline{\mathbf{x}} - \mathbf{x}^{(k)}\| \leq q\|\overline{\mathbf{x}} - \mathbf{x}^{(k-1)}\| \leq q^2 \|\overline{\mathbf{x}} - \mathbf{x}^{(k-2)}\| \leq \cdots \leq q^k \|\overline{\mathbf{x}} - \mathbf{x}^{(0)}\| \tag{4.327}$$

and, by passing to the limit as $k \to \infty$, we get

$$\lim_{k \to \infty} \mathbf{x}^{(k)} = \overline{\mathbf{x}} \tag{4.328}$$

and the proposition is thus proved.

Proposition 4.13 (Error Estimation). Under the above conditions, the inequalities result:

$$\|\mathbf{x}^{(k)} - \overline{\mathbf{x}}\|_\infty \leq \frac{1}{1 - q} \|\mathbf{x}^{(k+1)} - \mathbf{x}^{(k)}\|_\infty \leq \frac{q^k}{1 - q} \|\mathbf{x}^{(1)} - \mathbf{x}^{(0)}\|_\infty \tag{4.329}$$

Demonstration. The proof is analogical to that of Proposition 4.11.

Observation 4.27   Obviously, the formulae for error estimation are

$$\|\mathbf{x}^{(k)} - \overline{\mathbf{x}}\|_\infty \leq \frac{q^k}{1 - q} \|\mathbf{x}^{(1)} - \mathbf{x}^{(0)}\|_\infty < \varepsilon \tag{4.330}$$

and

$$\|\mathbf{x}^{(k)} - \overline{\mathbf{x}}\|_\infty \leq \frac{1}{1 - q} \|\mathbf{x}^{(k+1)} - \mathbf{x}^{(k)}\|_\infty, \tag{4.331}$$

respectively.

4.5.8   The Relaxation Method

Let the linear system be given by

$$
\begin{cases}
a_{11}x_1 + a_{12}x_2 + \cdots + a_{1n}x_n = b_1, \\
a_{21}x_1 + a_{22}x_2 + \cdots + a_{2n}x_n = b_2, \\
\qquad\qquad \cdots \\
a_{n1}x_1 + a_{n2}x_2 + \cdots + a_{nn}x_n = b_n,
\end{cases}
\tag{4.332}
$$

which we assume to be compatible determined and with $a_{ii} \neq 0$, $i = \overline{1,n}$. Dividing row i by a_{ii}, $i = \overline{1,n}$, one obtains the system

$$
\begin{cases}
-x_1 + \gamma_{12}x_2 + \cdots + \gamma_{1n}x_n + \delta_1 = 0, \\
\gamma_{21}x_1 - x_2 + \cdots + \gamma_{2n}x_n - \delta_2 = 0, \\
\qquad\qquad \cdots \\
\gamma_{n1}x_1 + \gamma_{n2}x_2 + \cdots - x_n + \delta_n = 0,
\end{cases}
\tag{4.333}
$$

where

$$
\gamma_{ij} = -\frac{a_{ij}}{a_{ii}}, \quad \delta_i = \frac{b_i}{a_{ii}}, \quad i,j = \overline{1,n}, \quad i \neq j.
\tag{4.334}
$$

Let $\mathbf{x}^{(0)} = \begin{bmatrix} x_1^{(0)} & x_2^{(0)} & \cdots & x_n^{(0)} \end{bmatrix}^{\mathrm{T}}$ be an approximation of the solution of the system (4.323), which we replace in that one. We thus obtain rests of the form

$$
R_1^{(0)} = -x_1^{(0)} + \sum_{j=2}^{n} \gamma_{1j}x_j^{(0)} + \delta_1, \quad R_2^{(0)} = -x_2^{(0)} + \sum_{j=2}^{n} \gamma_{2j}x_j^{(0)} + \delta_2, \quad \ldots,
$$

$$
R_n^{(0)} = -x_n^{(0)} + \sum_{j=2}^{n} \gamma_{nj}x_j^{(0)} + \delta_n.
\tag{4.335}
$$

Let

$$
|R_k^{(0)}| = \max\{|R_1^{(0)}|, |R_2^{(0)}|, \ldots, |R_n^{(0)}|\},
\tag{4.336}
$$

be the maximum of the moduli of these rests and let us give to x_k the value $x_k + R_k^{(0)}$. At this point, $R_k^{(1)} = 0$ and the other rests are

$$
R_i^{(1)} = R_i^{(0)} + \gamma_{ik}R_k^{(0)}, \quad i = \overline{1,n}, \quad i \neq k.
\tag{4.337}
$$

Between the rests $R_i^{(1)}$, $i = \overline{1,n}$, one of them will be maximum in modulus, say, $R_l^{(1)}$. We give to x_i the increment $R_l^{(1)}$; it follows that $R_l^{(2)} = 0$ and

$$
R_i^{(2)} = R_i^{(1)} + \gamma_{il}R_l^{(1)}, \quad i = \overline{1,n}, \quad i \neq l.
\tag{4.338}
$$

The process may continue either until one obtains the desired precision, or until $R_i^{(p)} = 0$, $i = \overline{1,n}$, at some step.

The solution of the system is given by

$$
x_i = x_i^{(0)} + \sum_{k=1}^{p} R_i^{(k)},
\tag{4.339}
$$

where p is the number of the iteration steps performed.

4.5.9 The Monte Carlo Method

Let us consider the linear system[12]

$$\mathbf{Ax} = \mathbf{b}, \quad \mathbf{A} \in \mathcal{M}_n(\mathbb{R}), \quad \mathbf{x}, \mathbf{b} \in \mathcal{M}_{n,1}(\mathbb{R}), \tag{4.340}$$

which can be written in the form

$$\mathbf{x} = \alpha\mathbf{x} + \beta, \tag{4.341}$$

where $\|\alpha\| < 1$, $\|\|$ being one of the canonical norms.

Let us choose the factors v_{ij}, $i, j = \overline{1, n}$, so that

$$\alpha_{ij} = p_{ij} v_{ij}, \tag{4.342}$$

where

$$p_{ij} \geq 0, \quad \text{with } p_{ij} > 0 \text{ for } \alpha_{ij} > 0, \quad i, j = \overline{1, n}, \tag{4.343}$$

$$\sum_{j=1}^{n} p_{ij} < 1, \quad i = \overline{1, n}. \tag{4.344}$$

We construct the matrix $\mathbf{H}$ so that $h_{ij} = p_{ij}$, $i, j = \overline{1, n}$, $h_{n+1,j} = 0$, $j = \overline{1, n}$, $h_{i,n+1} = 1 - \sum_{j=1}^{n} p_{ij}$, $i = \overline{1, n}$, $h_{n+1,n+1} = 1$, that is,

$$\mathbf{H} = \begin{bmatrix} p_{11} & p_{12} & \cdots & p_{1n} & p_{1,n+1} = 1 - \sum_{j=1}^{n} p_{1j} \\ p_{21} & p_{22} & \cdots & p_{2n} & p_{2,n+1} = 1 - \sum_{j=1}^{n} p_{2j} \\ \cdots & \cdots & \cdots & \cdots & \cdots \\ p_{n1} & p_{n2} & \cdots & p_{nn} & p_{n,n+1} = 1 - \sum_{j=1}^{n} p_{nj} \\ 0 & 0 & \cdots & 0 & 1 \end{bmatrix}. \tag{4.345}$$

Moreover, we choose a sequence $S_1, S_2, \ldots, S_{n+1}$ of states possible and incompatible with one another, in which S_{n+1} is the frontier or the absorbent barrier. Thus, p_{ij} represents the probability of passing of a particle from the state S_i to the state S_j independently of the previous states, the further states being non-definite. The state S_{n+1} is a singular one and supposes the stopping of the particle, which is evidenced by $p_{n+1,j} = 0$, $j = \overline{1, n}$.

Thus, a particle starts from an initial state S_i, $i = \overline{1, n}$, then passes into another state S_j and so on until it attains the final state S_{n+1}. Obviously, the number of states through which the particle passes is finite, but the number is different from simulation to simulation, that is, there are a number of paths from the initial state S_i, $i = \overline{1, n}$, to the final one S_{n+1}. It appears as a simple, homogeneous Markov chain with a finite number of states.

Let S_{i_0}, $i_0 = \overline{1, n}$, be an initial state and one such Markov chain that defines the trajectory of the particle be given by

$$T_i = \{S_{i_0}, S_{i_1}, \ldots, S_{i_m}, S_{i_{m+1}}\}, \tag{4.346}$$

where $S_{i_{m+1}} = S_{n+1}$, that is, the final state.

---

[12]The Monte Carlo method was stated in the 1940s by John von Neumann (1903–1957), Stanislaw Marcin Ulam (1909–1984), and Nicholas Constantine Metropolis (1915–1999). The name of the method comes from the famous Monte Carlo Casino.

We associate with this trajectory the aleatory variable X_i, the value of which is

$$\xi(T_i) = \beta_{i_0} + v_{i_0 i_1}\beta_{i_0} + v_{i_1 i_2}\beta_{i_1} + \cdots + v_{i_{m-1} i_m}\beta_{i_m}. \tag{4.347}$$

Theorem 4.1   The mathematical expectation

$$MX_i = \sum_{T_i}\xi(T_i)P(T_i) = \sum_i\sum_{T_{ij}}\xi(T_{ij})P(T_{ij}) = x_i \tag{4.348}$$

is a solution of the system (4.341).

Demonstration. The trajectories of T_i type may be divided into distinct classes as functions of the state through which the particle passes for the first time. We have

$$T_{i_1} = \{S_i, S_1, \ldots\}, \quad T_{i_2} = \{S_i, S_2, \ldots\}, \quad T_{i_n} = \{S_i, S_n, \ldots\}, \quad T_{i_{n+1}} = \{S_i, S_{n+1}\}. \tag{4.349}$$

Thus, T_i is the trajectory from one of the sets (4.349), if T_i is given by (4.346), then the associate aleatory variable X_i will have the value

$$\xi(T_{ij}) = \beta_i + v_{ij}\beta_j + v_{ji_2}\beta_{i_2} + \cdots + v_{i_{m-1}i_m}\beta_{i_m} = \beta_i + v_{ij}\xi(T_j). \tag{4.350}$$

Obviously, for the trajectory $T_{i_{n+1}} = \{S_i, S_{n+1}\}$, we have

$$\xi(T_{i_{n+1}}) = \beta_i. \tag{4.351}$$

If $j < n + 1$, then the trajectory T_i is composed from the segment (S_i, S_j), to which we add a trajectory from the set T_j defined by (4.349). It follows that

$$P(T_{ij}) = p_{ij}P(T_j). \tag{4.352}$$

If $j = n + 1$, then

$$P(T_{i_{n+1}}) = p_{i,n+1}. \tag{4.353}$$

It follows that

$$MX_i = \sum_{i=1}^{n}T_j[\beta_i + v_{ij}\xi(T_{ij})]p_{ij}P(T_j) + \beta_i p_{i,n+1} \tag{4.354}$$

or

$$MX_i = \sum_{j=1}^{n}p_{ij}v_{ij}\sum_{T_j}\xi(T_j) + \beta_i\left[\sum_{j=1}^{n}p_{ij}\sum_{T_j}P(T_j) + p_{i,n+1}\right]. \tag{4.355}$$

On the other hand,

$$\sum_{T_j}\xi(T_j)P(T_j) = MX_j, \quad j = \overline{1, n}, \tag{4.356}$$

$$\sum_{T_j}P(T_j) = 1, \tag{4.357}$$

$$\sum_{j=1}^{n}p_{ij}\sum_{T_j}P(T_j) + p_{i,n+1} = \sum_{j=1}^{n+1}p_{ij} = 1, \tag{4.358}$$

so that the formula (4.355) becomes

$$MX_i = \sum_{j=1}^{n} \alpha_{ij} MX_j + \beta_i, \quad i = \overline{1, n},\tag{4.359}$$

and the theorem is proved.

Chebyshev's theorem ensures that the inequality

$$\left| x_i - \frac{1}{N} \sum_{k=1}^{N} \xi\left(T_i^{(k)}\right) \right| < \varepsilon \tag{4.360}$$

is realized with a probability tending to 1 for $N \to \infty$. Thus it follows that

$$x_i \approx \frac{1}{N} \sum_{k=1}^{N} \xi(T_i^{(k)}).\tag{4.361}$$

Practically, the problem is solved in a simpler manner. One constructs the matrix **H**. Let us observe that if $\|\alpha\| < 1$, then we may choose $p_{ij} = |\alpha_{ij}|$ and $v_{ij} = 1$ if $\alpha_{ij} > 0$ or $v_{ij} = -1$ if $\alpha_{ij} < 0$. Let us suppose that we wish to determine x_i, hence we start with the state S_i. Thus, a uniformly distributed aleatory number is generated in the interval $(0, 1)$, let the number be π_1. On the line i of the matrix **H**, an index j is required, so that

$$\sum_{k=1}^{j} p_{ik} \leq \pi_1 \text{ and } \sum_{k=1}^{j+1} p_{ik} > \pi_1.\tag{4.362}$$

This index defines the new state S_j through which the particle passes. Obviously, this state may also be S_{n+1}, the case in which the trajectory stops. If $j \neq n + 1$, then we use the row j of the matrix **H**, for which a new uniformly distributed aleatory number is generated in the interval $(0, 1)$. The process continues until the final state S_{n+1} is attained. Thus, $\xi(T_i^{(1)})$, where the upper index (1) marks the first simulation, is calculated. The procedure is repeated N times, the approximate value of x_i being given by the formula (4.361).

Observation 4.28   The process gives also a possibility to calculate the inverse of the matrix **A**, with $\|\mathbf{A}\| < 1$, because determining the inverse $\mathbf{A}^{-1}$ is equivalent to solving a system of n^2 linear equations with n^2 unknowns.

4.5.10   Infinite Systems of Linear Equations

We have considered until now a linear system of n equations with n unknowns, where n is a finite integer. We try to generalize this for $n \to \infty$.

Let us consider the infinite system

$$\mathbf{Ax} = \mathbf{b},\tag{4.363}$$

where $\mathbf{x} = [x_k]_{k \in \mathbb{N}}^{\mathrm{T}}$, $\mathbf{A} = [a_{jk}]_{j,k \in \mathbb{N}}$, $\mathbf{b} = [b_j]_{j \in \mathbb{N}}^{\mathrm{T}}$.

Definition 4.9   The system is called *regular* if the matrix **A** is diagonally dominant, that is,

$$|a_{jj}| \geq \sum_{\substack{k \in \mathcal{K} \\ k \neq j}} |a_{jk}|, \quad j \in \mathbb{N},\tag{4.364}$$

and *completely regular* if the above inequality (4.364) is strict, that is, **A** is strictly diagonally dominant.

The well-known theorem that asserts the existence and the uniqueness of the solution of a finite, linear algebraic system, whose associated matrix is strictly diagonally dominant can be extended to completely regular infinite systems. If the system is regular, but not completely regular, only the existence of the solution is ensured.

The condition (4.364) may be written also in the form

$$\rho = 1 - \frac{\sum_{\substack{k \in \mathbb{N} \\ k \neq j}}}{|a_{jk}||a_{jj}|} \geq 0. \tag{4.365}$$

In case of a regular system, one may use the method of sections, considering that n is a finite integer, that is, one solves a finite system formed by the first n equations with the first n unknowns, by the methods presented above. Obviously, the accuracy of the solution depends on the number n.

4.6   DETERMINATION OF EIGENVALUES AND EIGENVECTORS

4.6.1   Introduction

Let $\mathbf{A} \in \mathcal{M}_n(\mathbb{C})$ be a matrix with complex elements and $\mathcal{V} \subset \mathbb{C}^n$ a vector space. The matrix **A** defines a linear transformation by the relation

$$\mathbf{x} \in \mathcal{V} \mapsto \mathbf{A}\mathbf{x} \in \mathcal{V}. \tag{4.366}$$

Let us consider a subspace $\mathcal{V}_1$ of $\mathcal{V}$ and let us suppose that $\mathcal{V}_1$ is invariant with respect to the linear transformation induced by the matrix **A**, hence for any $\mathbf{x} \in \mathcal{V}_1$ it follows that $\mathbf{A}\mathbf{x} \in \mathcal{V}_1$. It follows that the subspace $\mathcal{V}_1$ is defined by the equation

$$\mathbf{A}\mathbf{x} = \lambda\mathbf{x}, \tag{4.367}$$

where λ is an element of the corpus that defines the product by scalars over $\mathcal{V}$.

Definition 4.10   Any nonzero element **x** that satisfies the relation (4.367) is called an *eigenvector of the matrix* **A**, while the element λ is called an *eigenvalue of the matrix* **A**.

Definition 4.11   The set of all the eigenvalues of the matrix **A** is called the *spectrum of this matrix* and is denoted by Sp**A** or $\mathbf{\Lambda}(\mathbf{A})$.

Observation 4.29

(i) If λ is an eigenvalue of the matrix **A**, then the matrix $\mathbf{A} - \lambda\mathbf{I}_n$, where $\mathbf{I}_n$ is the unit matrix of order n, is a singular matrix and, conversely, if the matrix $\mathbf{A} - \lambda\mathbf{I}_n$ is singular, then λ is an eigenvalue for the matrix **A**.

(ii) The eigenvalues of the matrix **A** are obtained by solving the algebraic equation

$$\det[\mathbf{A} - \lambda\mathbf{I}_n] = 0, \tag{4.368}$$

called the *characteristic equation* or *secular equation*.

(iii) Equation (4.368) is an algebraic equation of nth degree, which, corresponding to the basic theorem of algebra, has n roots in $\mathbb{C}$. These roots may be distinct or one may have various orders of multiplicity. Hence, it follows that to an eigenvector there corresponds only one eigenvalue, but to an eigenvalue there may correspond several eigenvectors.

(iv) If $\mathbf{A} \in \mathcal{M}_n(\mathbb{R})$, then the eigenvalues are real or conjugate complex.

(v) If the matrix $\mathbf{A} \in \mathcal{M}_n(\mathbb{C})$ has n distinct eigenvalues λ_i, $i = \overline{1, n}$, then any vector $\mathbf{y} \in \mathbb{C}^n$ may be written in the form

$$\mathbf{y} = \sum_{i=1}^{n} \mu_i \mathbf{x}_i, \tag{4.369}$$

where $\mu_i \in \mathbb{C}$, $i = \overline{1, n}$, the formula being unique.

(vi) As

$$\mathbf{A}\mathbf{x}_i = \lambda_i \mathbf{x}_i, \quad i = \overline{1, n}, \tag{4.370}$$

by multiplying the relation (4.369) on the left by $\mathbf{A}^k$, we obtain

$$\mathbf{A}^k \mathbf{y} = \sum_{i=1}^{n} \mathbf{A}^k \mu_i \mathbf{x}_i = \sum_{i=1}^{n} \mu_i \mathbf{A}^k \mathbf{x}_i = \sum_{i=1}^{n} \mu_i \mathbf{A}^{k-1}(\mathbf{A}\mathbf{x}_i)$$

$$= \sum_{i=1}^{n} \mu_i \mathbf{A}^{k-1} \lambda_i \mathbf{x}_i = \cdots = \sum_{i=1}^{n} \lambda_i^k \mu_i \mathbf{x}_i. \tag{4.371}$$

(vii) Let us suppose that we have the relation

$$|\lambda_1| > |\lambda_i|, \quad i = \overline{2, n}, \tag{4.372}$$

for the matrix $\mathbf{A}$; that is, λ_1 is the greatest eigenvalue in modulus. The expression (4.371) may also be written in the form

$$\mathbf{A}^k \mathbf{y} = \sum_{i=1}^{n} \lambda_i^k \mu_i \mathbf{x}_i = \lambda_1^k \mu_1 \mathbf{x}_1 + \lambda_2^k \mu_2 \mathbf{x}_2 + \cdots + \lambda_n^k \mu_n \mathbf{x}_n$$

$$= \lambda_1^k \mu_1 \left(\mathbf{x}_1 + \frac{\lambda_2^k}{\lambda_1^k} \frac{\mu_2}{\mu_1} \mathbf{x}_2 + \cdots + \frac{\lambda_n^k}{\lambda_1^k} \frac{\mu_n}{\mu_1} \mathbf{x}_n \right), \tag{4.373}$$

where we suppose that $\mu_1 \neq 0$. Passing to the limit after k in the last relation, we get

$$\lim_{k \to \infty} \mathbf{A}^k \mathbf{y} = \lim_{k \to \infty} \lambda_1^k \mu_1 \mathbf{x}_1. \tag{4.374}$$

(viii) Let $\mathbf{A} \in \mathcal{M}_n(\mathbb{C})$ and $k \in \mathbb{N}^*$. Under these conditions, if the eigenvalues of $\mathbf{A}$ are distinct $\lambda_i \in \mathbb{C}, i = \overline{1, n}, \lambda_i \neq \lambda_j$ for $i \neq j, j = \overline{1, n}$, then the spectrum of the matrix $\mathbf{A}^k$ is given by

$$\Lambda(\mathbf{A}^k) = \{\lambda_i^k\}, \quad i = \overline{1, n}. \tag{4.375}$$

It follows that if $\mathbf{A}$ is idempotent (that is $\mathbf{A}^2 = \mathbf{A}$), then $\Lambda(\mathbf{A}) = \{0, 1\}$, and if $\mathbf{A}$ is nilpotent (that is there exists $k \in \mathbb{N}$ so that $\mathbf{A}^k = \mathbf{0}$), then $\Lambda(\mathbf{A}) = \{0\}$.

(ix) If $\mathbf{x}$ is an eigenvector of the matrix $\mathbf{A}$ corresponding to the eigenvalue λ, that is, if

$$\mathbf{A}\mathbf{x} = \lambda\mathbf{x}, \tag{4.376}$$

while $\mathbf{y}$ is a vector in $\mathbb{C}^n$, which depends on the variable $t \in \mathbb{R}$ (in general, t is the time), corresponding to the law

$$\mathbf{y}(t) = e^{\lambda t}\mathbf{x}, \tag{4.377}$$

then $\mathbf{y}$ verifies the differential equation

$$\frac{d\mathbf{y}}{dt} = \mathbf{A}\mathbf{y}. \tag{4.378}$$

Indeed, one may write

$$\frac{d\mathbf{y}}{dt} = \lambda e^{\lambda t}\mathbf{x} = e^{\lambda t}\lambda\mathbf{x} = e^{\lambda t}\mathbf{A}\mathbf{x} = \mathbf{A}e^{\lambda t}\mathbf{x} = \mathbf{A}\mathbf{y}. \tag{4.379}$$

It follows that the particular solution of a system of ordinary differential equations may be immediately written if one knows the eigenvectors and the eigenvalues of the matrix $\mathbf{A}$.

Definition 4.12   The matrices $\mathbf{A}$ and $\mathbf{B}$ of $\mathcal{M}_n(\mathbb{C})$ are said to be *similar* if there exists a nonsingular matrix $\mathbf{P} \in \mathcal{M}_n(\mathbb{C})$, so that

$$\mathbf{B} = \mathbf{P}^{-1}\mathbf{A}\mathbf{P}. \tag{4.380}$$

Observation 4.30   Let λ be an eigenvalue of the matrix $\mathbf{A}$ and $\mathbf{x}$ be the corresponding eigenvector. If $\mathbf{B}$ is a matrix similar to $\mathbf{A}$, by means of the matrix $\mathbf{P}$, then λ is an eigenvalue of $\mathbf{A}$ if and only if it is eigenvalue of $\mathbf{B}$ with the eigenvector $\mathbf{P}^{-1}\mathbf{x}$. Indeed, we obtain

$$\mathbf{B}(\mathbf{P}^{-1}\mathbf{x}) = \mathbf{P}^{-1}\mathbf{A}\mathbf{P}\mathbf{P}^{-1}\mathbf{x} = \mathbf{P}^{-1}\mathbf{A}\mathbf{x} = \mathbf{P}^{-1}\lambda\mathbf{x} = \lambda\mathbf{P}^{-1}\mathbf{x} \tag{4.381}$$

from $\mathbf{A}\mathbf{x} = \lambda\mathbf{x}$.

4.6.2   Krylov's Method

Let us denote by $P(\lambda)$ the characteristic polynomial[13]

$$P(\lambda) = \det[\mathbf{A} - \lambda\mathbf{I}_n], \tag{4.382}$$

where $\mathbf{A} \in \mathcal{M}_n(\mathbb{R})$, $\mathbf{I}_n$ being as usual the unit matrix of order n. We may write

$$P(\lambda) = (-1)^n\lambda^n + p_1\lambda^{n-1} + p_2\lambda^{n-2} + \cdots + p_n. \tag{4.383}$$

Multiplying the relation (4.383) by $(-1)^n$ we obtain a polynomial of nth degree, for which the dominant coefficient is equal to 1,

$$P_1(\lambda) = \lambda^n + q_1\lambda^{n-1} + q_2\lambda^{n-2} + \cdots + q_n, \tag{4.384}$$

in which

$$q_i = (-1)^n p_i, \quad i = \overline{1, n-1}. \tag{4.385}$$

---

[13]The method is credited to Aleksey Nikolaevich Krylov (1863–1945) who first presented it in 1931.

The Hamilton–Cayley theorem allows to state that the matrix $\mathbf{A}$ equates the characteristic polynomial to zero. Hence, we obtain

$$\mathbf{A}^n + q_1\mathbf{A}^{n-1} + q_2\mathbf{A}^{n-2} + \cdots + q_n\mathbf{I}_n = \mathbf{0}. \tag{4.386}$$

Let

$$\mathbf{y}^{(0)} = \begin{bmatrix} y_1^{(0)} & y_2^{(0)} & \cdots & y_n^{(0)} \end{bmatrix}^{\mathsf{T}} \tag{4.387}$$

be a nonzero vector in $\mathbb{R}^n$. Let us multiply the relation (4.386) on the right by $\mathbf{y}^{(0)}$. It results

$$\mathbf{A}^n\mathbf{y}^{(0)} + q_1\mathbf{A}^{n-1}\mathbf{y}^{(0)} + q_2\mathbf{A}^{n-2}\mathbf{y}^{(0)} + \cdots + q_n\mathbf{y}^{(0)} = \mathbf{0}. \tag{4.388}$$

We denote

$$\mathbf{A}^k\mathbf{y}^{(0)} = \mathbf{y}^{(k)}, \quad k = \overline{0, n} \tag{4.389}$$

and the relation (4.388) becomes

$$\mathbf{y}^{(n)} + q_1\mathbf{y}^{(n-1)} + q_2\mathbf{y}^{(n-2)} + \cdots + q_n\mathbf{y}^{(0)} = \mathbf{0}, \tag{4.390}$$

an equation in which the unknowns are $q_1, q_2, \ldots, q_n$. The relation (4.390) may be also written in the form

$$q_1\mathbf{y}^{(n-1)} + q_2\mathbf{y}^{(n-2)} + \cdots + q_n\mathbf{y}^{(0)} = -\mathbf{y}^{(n)} \tag{4.391}$$

or in components,

$$\begin{bmatrix} y_1^{(n-1)} & y_1^{(n-2)} & \cdots & y_1^{(0)} \\ y_2^{(n-1)} & y_2^{(n-2)} & \cdots & y_2^{(0)} \\ \cdots & \cdots & \cdots & \cdots \\ y_n^{(n-1)} & y_n^{(n-2)} & \cdots & y_n^{(0)} \end{bmatrix} \begin{bmatrix} q_1 \\ q_2 \\ \cdots \\ q_n \end{bmatrix} = - \begin{bmatrix} y_1^{(n)} \\ y_2^{(n)} \\ \cdots \\ y_n^{(n)} \end{bmatrix}. \tag{4.392}$$

The coefficients $q_1, q_2, \ldots, q_n$ of the characteristic polynomial are determined by solving the linear system (4.392) of n equations with n unknowns.

Observation 4.31   The relation (4.389) that defines the vector $\mathbf{y}^{(k)}$ may also be written recursively

$$\mathbf{y}^{(0)} \in \mathbf{R}^n \text{ arbitrary}, \quad \mathbf{y}^{(0)} \neq 0, \quad \mathbf{y}^{(k)} = \mathbf{A}\mathbf{y}^{(k-1)}, \quad k \geq 1. \tag{4.393}$$

Observation 4.32   If the roots of the characteristic polynomial are real and distinct, then Krylov's method also leads to the corresponding eigenvectors. Indeed, the n eigenvectors $\mathbf{x}_1, \ldots, \mathbf{x}_n$ form a basis in $\mathbb{R}^n$; then any vector of $\mathbb{R}^n$ may be written as a linear combination of these vectors of the basis. In particular, there exist the constants $c_1, c_2, \ldots, c_n$, not all zero, so that

$$\mathbf{y}^{(0)} = c_1\mathbf{x}_1 + c_2\mathbf{x}_2 + \cdots + c_n\mathbf{x}_n. \tag{4.394}$$

The relations (4.393) are transcribed now in the form

$$\mathbf{y}^{(0)} = \mathbf{A}\mathbf{y}^{(0)} = \mathbf{A}(c_1\mathbf{x}_1 + \cdots + c_n\mathbf{x}_n) = c_1\lambda_1\mathbf{x}_1 + c_2\lambda_2\mathbf{x}_2 + \cdots + c_n\lambda_n\mathbf{x}_n,$$
$$\mathbf{y}^{(2)} = c_1\lambda_1^2\mathbf{x}_1 + c_2\lambda_2^2\mathbf{x}_2 + \cdots + c_n\lambda_n^2\mathbf{x}_n, \quad \ldots, \quad \mathbf{y}^{(n)} = c_1\lambda_1^n\mathbf{x}_1 + c_2\lambda_2^n\mathbf{x}_2 + \cdots + c_n\lambda_n^n\mathbf{x}_n. \tag{4.395}$$

Let us introduce the polynomials

$$\phi_i(\lambda) = \lambda^{n-1} + q_{1i}\lambda^{n-2} + \cdots + q_{n-1,i}, \quad i = \overline{1,n}, \tag{4.396}$$

hence, it follows that

$$y^{(n-1)} + q_{1i}y^{(n-2)} + \cdots + q_{n-1,i}y^{(0)} = c_1\phi_i(\lambda_1)x_1 + \cdots + c_n\phi_i(\lambda_n)x_n. \tag{4.397}$$

On the other hand, we consider

$$\phi_i(\lambda) = \frac{P_1(\lambda)}{\lambda - \lambda_i}, \tag{4.398}$$

so that the coefficients q_{ij}, $i = \overline{1,n}$, $j = \overline{1,n-1}$, are given by Horner's schema

$$q_{0j} = 1, \quad q_{ij} = \lambda_j q_{i-1,j} + q_i. \tag{4.399}$$

Under these conditions,

$$\phi_i(\lambda_j) = 0 \text{ for any } i \text{ and } j \text{ with } i \neq j \tag{4.400}$$

and

$$\phi_i(\lambda_j) = P'(\lambda_j) \neq 0. \tag{4.401}$$

We thus obtain

$$y^{(n-1)} + q_{1i}y^{(n-2)} + \cdots + q_{n-1,i}y^{(0)} = c_i\phi_i(\lambda_i)x_i, \quad i = \overline{1,n} \tag{4.402}$$

and if $c_i \neq 0$, then we get the eigenvectors $c_i\phi_i(\lambda_i)x_i$, $i = \overline{1,n}$.

4.6.3 Danilevski's Method

Let[14]

$$P(\lambda) = \begin{vmatrix} a_{11} - \lambda & a_{12} & \cdots & a_{1n-1} & a_{1n} \\ a_{21} & a_{22} - \lambda & \cdots & a_{2n-1} & a_{2n} \\ \cdots & \cdots & \cdots & \cdots & \cdots \\ a_{n-1,1} & a_{n-1,2} & \cdots & a_{n-1,n-1} - \lambda & a_{n-1,n} \\ a_{n1} & a_{n2} & \cdots & a_{n,n-1} & a_{n,n} - \lambda \end{vmatrix} = (-1)^n \left[\lambda^n - \sum_{i=1}^{n} p_i \lambda^{n-i} \right]. \tag{4.403}$$

be the characteristic polynomial of the matrix $\mathbf{A} \in \mathcal{M}_n(\mathbb{R})$. The idea of the method consists in the transformation of the matrix

$$\mathbf{A} - \lambda\mathbf{I}_n = \begin{bmatrix} a_{11} - \lambda & a_{12} & \cdots & a_{1n-1} & a_{1n} \\ a_{21} & a_{22} - \lambda & \cdots & a_{2n-1} & a_{2n} \\ \cdots & \cdots & \cdots & \cdots & \cdots \\ a_{n-1,1} & a_{n-1,2} & \cdots & a_{n-1,n-1} - \lambda & a_{n-1,n} \\ a_{n1} & a_{n2} & \cdots & a_{n,n-1} & a_{n,n} - \lambda \end{bmatrix} \tag{4.404}$$

[14]The method was stated by A. M. Danilevski (Danilevsky) in Russian in 1937, and then in 1959 it was translated into English.

into the matrix

$$\mathbf{B} - \lambda \mathbf{I}_n = \begin{bmatrix} p_1 - \lambda & p_2 & p_3 & \cdots & p_{n-2} & p_{n-1} & p_n \\ 1 & -\lambda & 0 & \cdots & 0 & 0 & 0 \\ 0 & 1 & -\lambda & \cdots & 0 & 0 & 0 \\ \cdots & \cdots & \cdots & \cdots & \cdots & \cdots & \cdots \\ 0 & 0 & 0 & \cdots & 0 & 1 & -\lambda \end{bmatrix} \tag{4.405}$$

of a normal Frobenius form.[15]

On the other hand, the determinant of the matrix $\mathbf{B} - \lambda \mathbf{I}_n$, calculated by developing after the first row, is

$$\det[\mathbf{B} - \lambda \mathbf{I}_n] = (-1)^{n-1} \left(\sum_{i=1}^{n} p_i \lambda^{n-i} - \lambda^n \right) = P(\lambda). \tag{4.406}$$

To bring the matrix $\mathbf{A}$ to the Frobenius form $\mathbf{B}$, we proceed as follows:

- We multiply the $(n-1)$th column of the matrix $\mathbf{A}$ by $a_{n1}/a_{n,n-1}$, $a_{n2}/a_{n,n-1}$, ..., $a_{n,n-2}/a_{n,n-1}$, $a_{nn}/a_{n,n-1}$, respectively, and subtract it from the columns 1, 2, ..., $n-2$, n, respectively. This is equivalent to the multiplication on the right of the matrix $\mathbf{A}$ by the matrix

$$\mathbf{M}_1 = \begin{bmatrix} 1 & 0 & \cdots & 0 & 0 & 0 \\ 0 & 1 & \cdots & 0 & 0 & 0 \\ \cdots & \cdots & \cdots & \cdots & \cdots & \cdots \\ -\dfrac{a_{n,1}}{a_{n,n-1}} & -\dfrac{a_{n,2}}{a_{n,n-1}} & \cdots & -\dfrac{a_{n,n-2}}{a_{n,n-1}} & \dfrac{1}{a_{n,n-1}} & -\dfrac{a_{nn}}{a_{n,n-1}} \\ 0 & 0 & \cdots & 0 & 0 & 1 \end{bmatrix}. \tag{4.407}$$

The inverse of the matrix $\mathbf{M}_1$ is

$$\mathbf{M}_1^{-1} = \begin{bmatrix} 1 & 0 & \cdots & 0 & 0 & 0 \\ 0 & 1 & \cdots & 0 & 0 & 0 \\ \cdots & \cdots & \cdots & \cdots & \cdots & \cdots \\ a_{n1} & a_{n2} & \cdots & a_{n,n-2} & a_{n,n-1} & a_{n,n} \\ 0 & 0 & \cdots & 0 & 0 & 1 \end{bmatrix}. \tag{4.408}$$

- To obtain a similar matrix, we must consider, in the following step, the matrix

$$\mathbf{A}_2 = \mathbf{M}_1^{-1} \mathbf{A}_1 \mathbf{M}_1, \quad \mathbf{A}_1 = \mathbf{A}. \tag{4.409}$$

- the procedure is repeated for the $(n-1)$th row and the matrix $\mathbf{A}_2$ until we obtain the $(n-1)$th row of the Frobenius matrix;
- the procedure continues until the second row, when the Frobenius matrix directly results.

Observation 4.33 If the element $a_{i,i-1}$ is equal to zero (this means, on the computer, $|a_{i,i-1}| < \varepsilon$, ε given a priori), then one searches on the row i for a nonzero element among a_{i1}, a_{i2}, ..., $a_{i,i-2}$,

---

[15]This form was introduced by Ferdinand Georg Frobenius (1849–1917).

let it be a_{ij}, $j < i - 1$, adding the columns i and j of the initial matrix. This means multiplication on the right by the matrix

$$
\mathbf{M}_{ij}^* =
\begin{bmatrix}
1 & 0 & 0 & \cdots & 0 & \cdots & 0 & \cdots & 0 & \cdots & 0 \\
0 & 1 & 0 & \cdots & 0 & \cdots & 0 & \cdots & 0 & \cdots & 0 \\
0 & 0 & 1 & \cdots & 0 & \cdots & 0 & \cdots & 0 & \cdots & 0 \\
\cdots & \cdots & \cdots & \cdots & \cdots & \cdots & \cdots & \cdots & \cdots & \cdots & \cdots \\
0 & 0 & 0 & \cdots & m_{jj}^* = 1 & \cdots & 0 & \cdots & m_{ji}^* = 1 & \cdots & 0 \\
\cdots & \cdots & \cdots & \cdots & \cdots & \cdots & \cdots & \cdots & \cdots & \cdots & \cdots \\
0 & 0 & 0 & \cdots & 0 & \cdots & 0 & \cdots & 0 & \cdots & 1
\end{bmatrix},
\tag{4.410}
$$

the inverse of which is

$$
(\mathbf{M}_{ij}^*)^{-1} =
\begin{bmatrix}
1 & 0 & 0 & \cdots & 0 & \cdots & 0 & \cdots & 0 & \cdots & 0 \\
0 & 1 & 0 & \cdots & 0 & \cdots & 0 & \cdots & 0 & \cdots & 0 \\
0 & 0 & 1 & \cdots & 0 & \cdots & 0 & \cdots & 0 & \cdots & 0 \\
\cdots & \cdots & \cdots & \cdots & \cdots & \cdots & \cdots & \cdots & \cdots & \cdots & \cdots \\
0 & 0 & 0 & \cdots & \left(m_{jj}^*\right)^{-1} = 1 & \cdots & 0 & \cdots & (m_{ji}^*)^{-1} = -1 & \cdots & 0 \\
0 & 0 & 0 & \cdots & 0 & \cdots & 0 & \cdots & 0 & \cdots & 1
\end{bmatrix}.
\tag{4.411}
$$

Observation 4.34

(i) If $\mathbf{y}$ is an eigenvector of the Frobenius matrix $\mathbf{B}$, then the eigenvector of the matrix $\mathbf{A}$ is

$$
\mathbf{x} = \mathbf{M}_1 \mathbf{M}_2 \cdots \mathbf{M}_{n-1}\mathbf{y},
\tag{4.412}
$$

where we suppose that, by passing from the matrix $\mathbf{A}$ to the Frobenius matrix $\mathbf{B}$, addition of columns have not been necessary (if not, matrices of the form (4.410) would appear in the product (4.412)).

(ii) Let us consider that the Frobenius matrix has distinct eigenvalues and let λ be one such value (which is eigenvalue for the matrix $\mathbf{A}$ too, the matrix $\mathbf{A}$ also having distinct eigenvalues). The eigenvector $\mathbf{y}$, corresponding to the eigenvalue λ for the Frobenius matrix, satisfies the relation

$$
\begin{bmatrix}
p_1 & p_2 & \cdots & p_{n-1} & p_n \\
1 & 0 & \cdots & 0 & 0 \\
0 & 1 & \cdots & 0 & 0 \\
\cdots & \cdots & \cdots & \cdots & \cdots \\
0 & 0 & \cdots & 1 & 0
\end{bmatrix}
\begin{bmatrix}
y_1 \\ y_2 \\ y_3 \\ \cdots \\ y_n
\end{bmatrix}
= \lambda
\begin{bmatrix}
y_1 \\ y_2 \\ y_3 \\ \cdots \\ y_n
\end{bmatrix},
\tag{4.413}
$$

from which

$$
y_{n-j} = \lambda y_{n-j+1}, \quad j = \overline{1, n-1}
\tag{4.414}
$$

and

$$
\sum_{i=1}^{n} p_i y_i = \lambda y_1.
\tag{4.415}
$$

The relation (4.414) leads to

$$
y_{n-1} = \lambda y_n, \quad y_{n-2} = \lambda y_{n-1} = \lambda^2 y_n, \quad \ldots, \quad y_1 = \lambda^{n-1} y_n
\tag{4.416}
$$

and, by replacing in (4.415), we obtain

$$y_n \left(\lambda^n - \sum_{i=1}^{n} p_i \lambda^{n-i} \right) = 0; \qquad (4.417)$$

hence, the characteristic polynomial of the matrix $\mathbf{A}$ is the same as that of the Frobenius matrix $\mathbf{B}$. Moreover, because $y_n \neq 0$ (if not, it would follow that $\mathbf{y} = \mathbf{0}$), one obtains also the eigenvector of the Frobenius matrix $\mathbf{B}$,

$$\mathbf{y} = [\lambda^{n-1} \quad \lambda^{n-2} \quad \cdots \quad \lambda \quad 1]^{\mathrm{T}}, \qquad (4.418)$$

where we have supposed that $y_n = 1$.

Observation 4.35   To reduce the errors in calculation, we usually consider as pivot not the element $a_{i,i-1}$ but the greatest element in modulus from among $a_{i1}, a_{i2}, \ldots, a_{i,i-1}$. Let that element be a_{ij}, that is

$$|a_{ij}| = \max_{k=\overline{1,i-1}} |a_{ik}|. \qquad (4.419)$$

A commutation one into the other of the columns i and j is necessary, under these conditions; one thus uses a matrix

$$P_{ij} = P_{ij}^{-1} = \begin{bmatrix} 1 & 0 & \cdots & 0 & \cdots & 0 & \cdots & 0 \\ 0 & 1 & \cdots & 0 & \cdots & 0 & \cdots & 0 \\ \cdots & \cdots & \cdots & \cdots & \cdots & \cdots & \cdots & \cdots \\ 0 & 0 & \cdots & p_{ii}=0 & \cdots & p_{ij}=1 & \cdots & 0 \\ \cdots & \cdots & \cdots & \cdots & \cdots & \cdots & \cdots & \cdots \\ 0 & 0 & \cdots & p_{ji}=1 & \cdots & p_{jj}=0 & \cdots & 0 \\ \cdots & \cdots & \cdots & \cdots & \cdots & \cdots & \cdots & \cdots \\ 0 & 0 & \cdots & 0 & \cdots & 0 & \cdots & 1 \end{bmatrix}. \qquad (4.420)$$

Observation 4.36   If at a certain point, all the elements $a_{ij}^{(n+1-i)}$, $j = \overline{1, i-1}$, vanish, that is, at the step $n + 1 - i$ we will not be able to find a pivot on the row i, then the determinant of the matrix $\mathbf{A}$ is written, according to Laplace's theorem, as the product of two determinants and the matrix $\mathbf{A}$ is decomposed into blocks.

4.6.4   The Direct Power Method

Let us consider the matrix $\mathbf{A} \in \mathcal{M}_n(\mathbb{R})$ for which we suppose that the eigenvalues are distinct and ordered as follows:

$$|\lambda_1| > |\lambda_2| > \cdots > |\lambda_n|. \qquad (4.421)$$

The n eigenvectors $\mathbf{x}_1, \mathbf{x}_2, \ldots, \mathbf{x}_n$, corresponding to the eigenvalues $\lambda_1, \lambda_2, \ldots, \lambda_n$ are linearly independent, hence they form a basis in $\mathbb{R}^n$.

Let $\mathbf{y} \in \mathbb{R}^n$ be arbitrary. Under these conditions, $\mathbf{y}$ has a unique representation with respect to the basis' vectors $\mathbf{x}_1, \ldots, \mathbf{x}_n$; hence there exist the real constants $a_1, \ldots, a_n$, uniquely determinate, so that

$$\mathbf{y} = \sum_{j=1}^{n} a_j \mathbf{x}_j. \qquad (4.422)$$

On the other hand,

$$\mathbf{A}\mathbf{y} = \mathbf{A}\sum_{j=1}^{n} a_j \mathbf{x}_j = \sum_{j=1}^{n} a_j (\mathbf{A}\mathbf{x}_j) \qquad (4.423)$$

and because

$$\mathbf{A}\mathbf{x}_j = \lambda_j \mathbf{x}_j, \quad j = \overline{1, n}, \qquad (4.424)$$

it results in the representation

$$\mathbf{A}\mathbf{y} = \sum_{j=1}^{n} a_j \lambda_j \mathbf{x}_j. \qquad (4.425)$$

Analogically, we obtain the relations

$$\mathbf{A}^2 \mathbf{y} = \sum_{j=1}^{n} a_j \lambda_j^2 \mathbf{x}_j, \qquad (4.426)$$

$$\mathbf{A}^3 \mathbf{y} = \sum_{j=1}^{n} a_j \lambda_j^3 \mathbf{x}_j \qquad (4.427)$$

and, in general,

$$\mathbf{A}^n \mathbf{y} = \sum_{j=1}^{n} a_j \lambda_j^n \mathbf{x}_j \qquad (4.428)$$

for any $m \in \mathbb{N}^*$.

Let us denote

$$\mathbf{y}^{(m)} = \mathbf{A}^m \mathbf{y} = [y_1^{(m)} \quad y_2^{(m)} \quad \cdots \quad y_n^{(m)}]^{\mathrm{T}}; \qquad (4.429)$$

the relation (4.428) becomes

$$\mathbf{y}^{(m)} = \sum_{j=1}^{n} a_j \lambda_j^m \mathbf{x}_j. \qquad (4.430)$$

Let $\mathcal{V}$ be the subspace of $\mathbb{R}^n$ generated by the set of vectors

$$\mathbf{Y} = \{\mathbf{y}^{(1)}, \quad \mathbf{y}^{(2)}, \quad \ldots, \quad \mathbf{y}^{(m)}, \quad \ldots\} \qquad (4.431)$$

and let $\mathcal{B}$

$$\mathcal{B} = \{\mathbf{e}_1, \quad \mathbf{e}_2, \quad \ldots, \quad \mathbf{e}_n\}. \qquad (4.432)$$

be a basis of it or an extension of one of its bases in $\mathbb{R}^n$.

Observation 4.37

(i) All the previous considerations are valid for $\mathbf{y} \neq \mathbf{0}$. Obviously, if $\mathbf{y} = \mathbf{0}$, then $\mathbf{y}^{(m)} = \mathbf{0}$ for any $m \in \mathbb{N}^*$. Moreover, if $\mathbf{A} = \mathbf{0}$, then $\mathbf{y}^{(m)} = \mathbf{0}$ for any $m \in \mathbb{N}^*$, irrespective of the $\mathbf{y}$ initially chosen. We will suppose that $\mathbf{A} \neq \mathbf{0}$ and $\mathbf{y} \neq \mathbf{0}$.

(ii) Obviously, the space $\mathbf{Y}$ may have a dimension less than n. As $\mathbf{y}^{(m)} \in \mathbb{R}^n$ for any $m \in \mathbb{N}^*$, it follows that $\mathbf{Y} \subset \mathbb{R}^n$ and $\dim \mathbf{Y} \leq \dim \mathbb{R}^n$. If $\dim \mathbf{Y} = n$, then, obviously, $\mathcal{B}$ is given by the formula (4.432). If $\dim \mathbf{Y} < n$, then one can add to the basis' vectors, let us say in terms of k, $n - k$ vectors to form the basis $\mathcal{B}$ in $\mathbb{R}^n$. As $\mathcal{B}$ is such a basis, it follows that any vector of $\mathbb{R}^n$ may be written in the form of a unique linear combination of vectors of $\mathcal{B}$. In particular,

$$\mathbf{x}_j = \sum_{i=1}^{n} x_{ij} \mathbf{e}_j, \quad j = \overline{1, n}. \tag{4.433}$$

Under these conditions, the vector $\mathbf{y}^{(m)}$ becomes

$$\mathbf{y}^{(m)} = \sum_{j=1}^{n} \left[a_j \lambda_j^m \left(\sum_{i=1}^{n} x_{ij} \mathbf{e}_i \right) \right] = \sum_{i=1}^{n} \left[\mathbf{e}_i \left(\sum_{j=1}^{n} a_j x_{ij} \lambda_j^m \right) \right]. \tag{4.434}$$

But

$$\sum_{j=1}^{n} a_j x_{ij} \lambda_j^m = y_i^{(m)}, \tag{4.435}$$

so that

$$y_i^{(m)} = \sum_{j=1}^{n} a_j x_{ij} \lambda_j^m. \tag{4.436}$$

Writing the previous relation for $m + 1$,

$$y_i^{(m+1)} = \sum_{j=1}^{n} a_j x_{ij} \lambda_j^{m+1}, \tag{4.437}$$

and making the ratio of (4.436) to (4.437), we obtain

$$\frac{y_i^{(m+1)}}{y_i^{(m)}} = \frac{\displaystyle\sum_{j=1}^{n} a_j x_{ij} \lambda_j^{m+1}}{\displaystyle\sum_{j=1}^{n} a_j x_{ij} \lambda_j^m}. \tag{4.438}$$

On the other hand,

$$\begin{aligned} y_i^{(m+1)} &= \sum_{j=1}^{n} a_j x_{ij} \lambda_j^{m+1} = a_1 x_{i1} \lambda_1^{m+1} + \cdots + a_n x_{in} \lambda_n^{m+1} \\ &= \lambda_1^{m+1} \left[a_1 x_{i1} + a_2 x_{i2} \left(\frac{\lambda_2}{\lambda_1} \right)^{m+1} + \cdots + a_n x_{in} \left(\frac{\lambda_n}{\lambda_1} \right)^{m+1} \right] \end{aligned} \tag{4.439}$$

and, analogically,

$$y_i^{(m)} = \lambda_1^m \left[a_1 x_{i1} + a_2 x_{i2} \left(\frac{\lambda_2}{\lambda_1} \right)^m + \cdots + a_n x_{in} \left(\frac{\lambda_n}{\lambda_1} \right)^m \right]. \tag{4.440}$$

Taking into account the relations (4.421), (4.439), and (4.440) and making $m \to \infty$ in the relation (4.438), we get

$$\lim_{m \to \infty} \frac{y_i^{(m+1)}}{y_i^{(m)}} = \lambda_1. \tag{4.441}$$

Observation 4.38

(i) The formula (4.441) suggests that the index i, $1 \le i \le n$, chosen for the ratio $y_i^{(m+1)}/y_i^{(m)}$, does not matter because we obtain λ_1, as the limit. The statement is erroneous.

(ii) It is also possible that the limit in the relation (4.441) is infinite or does not exist, which may lead to erroneous values for the approximation of λ_1.

(iii) It follows from (i) and (ii) that the method is sensitive to the choice of the start vector $\mathbf{y}$.

(iv) Instead of the ratio (4.441), we may choose

$$\lambda_1 = \lim_{m \to \infty} \frac{\sum_{i=1}^{n} y_i^{(m+1)}}{\sum_{i=1}^{n} y_i^{(m)}}, \tag{4.442}$$

so as to obtain the approximate formula

$$\lambda_1 \approx \frac{\sum_{i=1}^{n} y_i^{(m+1)}}{\sum_{i=1}^{n} y_i^{(m)}}. \tag{4.443}$$

(v) The procedure may be accelerated with regard to the convergence, by using powers of 2 as values of m, so that

$$\mathbf{A}^2 = \mathbf{AA}, \quad \mathbf{A}^4 = \mathbf{A}^2 \mathbf{A}^2, \quad \dots, \quad \mathbf{A}^{2^k} = \mathbf{A}^{2^{k-1}} \mathbf{A}^{2^{k-1}}. \tag{4.444}$$

The value of λ_1 is given by the ratio

$$\lambda_1 = \lim_{k \to \infty} \frac{y_i^{(2^k)}}{y_i^{(2^{k-1})}}. \tag{4.445}$$

(vi) The vector

$$\mathbf{y}^{(m)} = \mathbf{A}^m \mathbf{y} \tag{4.446}$$

is the approximate value of the eigenvector of the matrix $\mathbf{A}$, associated with the eigenvalue λ_1. Indeed, one may write

$$\mathbf{A}^m \mathbf{y} = a_1 \lambda_1^m \mathbf{x}_1 + \sum_{j=2}^{n} a_j \lambda_j^m \mathbf{x}_j = a_1 \lambda_1^m \left\{ \mathbf{x}_1 + \sum_{j=2}^{n} \left[\frac{a_j}{a_1} \left(\frac{\lambda_j}{\lambda_1} \right)^m \mathbf{x}_j \right] \right\}. \tag{4.447}$$

But

$$\lim_{m \to \infty} \left(\frac{\lambda_j}{\lambda_1} \right)^m = 0, \tag{4.448}$$

It follows

$$\mathbf{A}^m \mathbf{y} \approx a_1 \lambda_1^m \mathbf{x}_1, \tag{4.449}$$

hence the vector $\mathbf{A}^m \mathbf{y}$ differs from the eigenvector $\mathbf{x}_1$ only by a multiplicative factor.

(vii) One can also choose

$$\lambda_1 = \frac{1}{n} \sum_{i=1}^{n} \frac{y_i^{(m+1)}}{y_i^{(m)}}. \tag{4.450}$$

If the greatest modulus of the roots is multiple, of order of multiplicity p, that is,

$$|\lambda_1| = |\lambda_2| = \cdots = |\lambda_p| > |\lambda_{p+1}| > \cdots > |\lambda_n|, \tag{4.451}$$

then

$$\frac{y_i^{(m+1)}}{y_i^{(m)}} = \frac{\lambda_1^{m+1} \sum_{j=1}^{p} a_j x_{ij} + \sum_{j=p+1}^{n} a_j x_{ij} \lambda_j^{m+1}}{\lambda_1^{m} \sum_{j=1}^{p} a_j x_{ij} + \sum_{j=p+1}^{n} a_j x_{ij} \lambda_j^{m}}. \tag{4.452}$$

Assuming that

$$\sum_{j=1}^{p} a_j x_{ij} \neq 0, \tag{4.453}$$

we obtain

$$\frac{y_i^{(m+1)}}{y_i^{(m)}} = \lambda_1 \frac{1 + \sum_{j=p+1}^{n} \left[\frac{a_j x_{ij}}{\sum_{j=1}^{p} a_j x_{ij}} \left(\frac{\lambda_j}{\lambda_1} \right)^{m+1} \right]}{1 + \sum_{j=p+1}^{n} \left[\frac{a_j x_{ij}}{\sum_{j=1}^{p} a_j x_{ij}} \left(\frac{\lambda_j}{\lambda_1} \right)^{m} \right]}. \tag{4.454}$$

Passing to the limit for m and taking into account that $(\lambda_j/\lambda_1)^m \to 0$ for $m \to \infty$, we obtain

$$\lim_{m \to \infty} \frac{y_i^{(m+1)}}{y_i^{(m)}} = \lambda_1. \tag{4.455}$$

Now, $\mathbf{A}^m \mathbf{y} = \mathbf{y}^{(m)}$ is one of the eigenvectors associated with the eigenvalue λ_1.

Observation 4.39

(i) Let us form the sequence of matrices $\mathbf{A}, \mathbf{A}^2, \mathbf{A}^{2^2}, \ldots, \mathbf{A}^{2^k}$. As

$$\sum_{i=1}^{n} \lambda_i^m = Tr(\mathbf{A}^m), \quad m = 2^k, \tag{4.456}$$

where $Tr(\cdot)$ denotes the trace of $(\cdot)$, we obtain the equality

$$\lambda_1^m + \lambda_2^m + \cdots + \lambda_n^m = \lambda_1^m \left[1 + \left(\frac{\lambda_2}{\lambda_1} \right)^m + \cdots + \left(\frac{\lambda_n}{\lambda_1} \right)^m \right] = Tr(\mathbf{A}^m) \tag{4.457}$$

for the simple eigenvalue λ_1. Passing to the limit for $m \to \infty$, it follows that

$$\mathrm{Tr}(\mathbf{A}^m) = \lambda_1^m, \tag{4.458}$$

from which

$$\lambda_1 = \sqrt[m]{\mathrm{Tr}(\mathbf{A}^m)}. \tag{4.459}$$

(ii) If now we write

$$\mathbf{A}^{m+1} = \mathbf{A}^m \cdot \mathbf{A}, \tag{4.460}$$

$$\lambda_1^{m+1} + \cdots + \lambda_n^{m+1} = \mathrm{Tr}(\mathbf{A}^{m+1}), \tag{4.461}$$

$$\lambda_1^m + \cdots + \lambda_n^m = \mathrm{Tr}(\mathbf{A}^m). \tag{4.462}$$

Dividing the last two relations and making $m \to \infty$, it follows that

$$\lambda_1 = \frac{\mathrm{Tr}(\mathbf{A}^{m+1})}{\mathrm{Tr}(\mathbf{A}^m)}. \tag{4.463}$$

4.6.5   The Inverse Power Method

The inverse power method is used to find the smallest eigenvalue in the modulus of the matrix $\mathbf{A} \in \mathcal{M}_n(\mathbb{R})$, in the case in which $\mathbf{A}$ is nonsingular. In the latter case, $\det \mathbf{A} \neq 0$ and, in the characteristic polynomial

$$P(\lambda) = (-1)^n \lambda^n + p_{n-1} \lambda^{n-1} + \cdots + p_1 \lambda + p_0, \tag{4.464}$$

the free term is nonzero

$$p_0 = \det \mathbf{A} \neq 0. \tag{4.465}$$

Hence, $\lambda = 0$ is not an eigenvalue for the matrix $\mathbf{A}$.

Let $\mathbf{x}$ be an eigenvector corresponding to the eigenvalue λ of the matrix $\mathbf{A}$. One can successively write ($\lambda \neq 0$)

$$\mathbf{x} = \lambda^{-1} \lambda \mathbf{x} = \lambda^{-1} \mathbf{A} \mathbf{x}, \tag{4.466}$$

from which

$$\mathbf{A}^{-1} \mathbf{x} = \lambda^{-1} \mathbf{x}; \tag{4.467}$$

hence, the eigenvalues of the inverse $\mathbf{A}^{-1}$ are the inverses of the eigenvalues of the original matrix $\mathbf{A}$. Thus, if λ_1 is the smallest eigenvalue in modulus of the matrix $\mathbf{A}$, that is,

$$0 < |\lambda_1| < |\lambda_2| \leq \cdots \leq |\lambda_n|, \tag{4.468}$$

then $1/\lambda_1$ is the greatest eigenvalue in modulus for $\mathbf{A}^{-1}$ and we can use the method of direct power for the matrix $\mathbf{A}^{-1}$.

Obviously, all the commentaries and discussions made in the direct power method remain valid.

4.6.6   The Displacement Method

The idea of the displacement method is based on the observation that if the matrix $\mathbf{A}$ has the eigenvalues λ_1, λ_2, $\ldots$, λ_n, then the matrix $\mathbf{A} - q\mathbf{I}_n$, $\mathbf{A} \in \mathcal{M}_n(\mathbb{R})$, $q \in \mathbb{R}$, has the eigenvalues $\lambda_1 - q$, $\lambda_2 - q$, $\ldots$, $\lambda_n - q$. Thus, one can find also eigenvalues other than the maximum or the minimum ones in the modulus for the matrix $\mathbf{A}$.

Let us suppose that λ_1 is the maximum value in the modulus of the matrix $\mathbf{A}$, while λ_n is the minimum value in modulus of the matrix $\mathbf{A}$. After a displacement q, considering the matrix $\mathbf{A} - q\mathbf{I}_n$, the maximum and the minimum eigenvalues in the modulus of this new matrix are given by

$$\lambda_1' = \max_{1 \le i \le n} |\lambda_i - q|, \quad \lambda_{n1}' = \min_{1 \le i \le n} |\lambda_i - q|. \tag{4.469}$$

4.6.7   Leverrier's Method

Let $\mathbf{A} \in \mathcal{M}_n(\mathbb{R})$, with the characteristic polynomial[16]

$$P(\lambda) = \det(\lambda\mathbf{I}_n - \mathbf{A}) = \lambda^n + p_1\lambda^{n-1} + p_2\lambda^{n-2} + \cdots + p_n. \tag{4.470}$$

The roots of $P(\lambda)$ are λ_1, λ_2, $\ldots$, λ_n. Let us denote

$$S_k = \lambda_1^k + \lambda_2^k + \cdots + \lambda_n^k. \tag{4.471}$$

The following Newton formulae are known

$$S_k + S_{k-1}p_1 + \cdots + S_1p_{k-1} = -kp_k. \tag{4.472}$$

We obtain the relations

$$k = 1 \Rightarrow S_1 = -p_1 \Rightarrow p_1 = -S_1, \quad k = 2 \Rightarrow S_2 + p_1S_1 = -2p_2 \Rightarrow p_2 = -\frac{1}{2}(S_2 + p_1S_1),$$

$$\ldots, \quad k = n \Rightarrow p_n = -\frac{1}{n}(S_n + S_{n-1}p_1 + S_{n-2} + \cdots + S_1p_{n-1}), \tag{4.473}$$

for $k = 1, 2, \ldots, n$. On the other hand,

$$S_1 = \lambda_1 + \cdots + \lambda_n = Tr(\mathbf{A}), \quad S_2 = \lambda_1^2 + \cdots + \lambda_n^2 = Tr(\mathbf{A}^2), \quad \ldots,$$

$$S_k = \lambda_1^k + \cdots + \lambda_n^k = Tr(\mathbf{A^k}), \quad \ldots, \quad S_n = \lambda_1^n + \cdots + \lambda_n^n = \mathrm{Tr}(\mathbf{A}^n). \tag{4.474}$$

The coefficients p_1, p_2, $\ldots$, p_n are given by the formulae (4.472) and (4.473).

4.6.8   The L–R (Left–Right) Method

This method is based on the fact that any matrix $\mathbf{A} \in \mathcal{M}_n(\mathbb{R})$ may be decomposed as a product of two matrices

$$\mathbf{A} = \mathbf{LR}, \tag{4.475}$$

in which $\mathbf{L} \in \mathcal{M}_n(\mathbb{R})$ is an inferior triangular matrix, while $\mathbf{R} \in \mathcal{M}_n(\mathbb{R})$ is a superior triangular matrix. The decomposition leads to the sequence of matrices $\mathbf{A}_1$, $\mathbf{A}_2$, $\ldots$, $\mathbf{A}_k$ in which

$$\mathbf{A}_i = \mathbf{L}_i\mathbf{R}_i, \quad i = \overline{1, k}, \tag{4.476}$$

---

[16]The method was named in the honor of Urbain Jean Joseph Le Verrier (Leverrier) (1811–1877).

where the matrices $\mathbf{L}_i$ are inferior triangular, with the elements on the principal diagonal equal to unity

$$l_{jj}^{(i)} = 1, \quad j = \overline{1, n}, \tag{4.477}$$

while the matrices $\mathbf{R}_i$ are superior triangular.

The recurrence formula of the sequence is given by

$$\mathbf{A}_{i+1} = \mathbf{R}_i \mathbf{L}_i, \quad \mathbf{A}_1 = \mathbf{A}. \tag{4.478}$$

One obtains thus a similar transformation, because

$$\mathbf{L}_1 = \mathbf{A}_1 \mathbf{R}_1^{-1}, \quad \mathbf{A}_2 = \mathbf{R}_1 \mathbf{L}_1 = \mathbf{R}_1 \mathbf{A}_1 \mathbf{R}_1^{-1} = \mathbf{L}_1^{-1} \mathbf{A}_1 \mathbf{L}_1,$$

$$\mathbf{A}_3 = \mathbf{R}_2 \mathbf{L}_2 = \mathbf{R}_2 \mathbf{R}_1 \mathbf{A}_1 (\mathbf{R}_2 \mathbf{R}_1)^{-1} = (\mathbf{L}_1 \mathbf{L}_2)^{-1} \mathbf{A}_1 (\mathbf{L}_1 \mathbf{L}_2), \quad \dots,$$

$$\mathbf{A}_k = (\mathbf{R}_{k-1} \mathbf{R}_{k-2} \cdots \mathbf{R}_1) \mathbf{A}_1 (\mathbf{R}_{k-1} \mathbf{R}_{k-2} \cdots \mathbf{R}_1)^{-1} = (\mathbf{L}_1 \mathbf{L}_2 \cdots \mathbf{L}_{k-1})^{-1} \mathbf{A}_1 (\mathbf{L}_1 \mathbf{L}_2 \cdots \mathbf{L}_{k-1}) \tag{4.479}$$

Moreover, all the matrices $\mathbf{A}_1, \dots, \mathbf{A}_k$ have the same eigenvalues.

Observation 4.40

(i) The matrix

$$\mathbf{S}_{k-1} = \prod_{j=1} \mathbf{L}_j \tag{4.480}$$

is an inferior triangular matrix with

$$s_{ii}^{(k-1)} = 1 \tag{4.481}$$

and

$$\lim_{i \to \infty} \mathbf{L}_i = \mathbf{I}_n, \tag{4.482}$$

where $\mathbf{I}_n$ is the unit matrix of order n, while the matrix

$$\mathbf{D}_{k-1} = \prod_{j=1}^{k-1} \mathbf{R}_j \tag{4.483}$$

is a superior triangular matrix.

(ii) The elements of the principal diagonal of the matrix $\mathbf{R}_i$ tend to the eigenvalues of the matrix $\mathbf{A}$ for $i \to \infty$.

(iii) The elements of the matrices $\mathbf{L}_i$ and $\mathbf{R}_i$ are the solutions of the system of equations (4.476), that is,

$$r_{1i} = a_{1i}, \ i = \overline{1, n}, \ r_{ij} = 0 \text{ for } i > j, \ l_{i1} = \frac{a_{1i}}{a_{11}}, \ i = \overline{2, n}, \ a_{11} \neq 0, \ r_{ij} = a_{ij} - \sum_{k=1}^{i-1} l_{ik} r_{kj},$$

$$i \leq j, \ l_{ij} = \frac{1}{r_{ii}} \left(a_{ij} - \sum_{k=1}^{j-1} l_{ik} r_{kj} \right), \ r_{ii} \neq 0, \ i > j, \ l_{ii} = 1, \ i = \overline{1, n}, \ l_{ij} = 0, \ i < j.$$

$$\tag{4.484}$$

(iv) If the sequence $\mathbf{A}_1, \mathbf{A}_2, \ldots, \mathbf{A}_k$ is convergent, then the matrix $\mathbf{A}_k$ is superior triangular and the elements situated on the principal diagonal are the eigenvalues of the matrix $\mathbf{A}$, that is,

$$a_{ii}^{(k)} = \lambda_i, \quad i = \overline{1, n}. \tag{4.485}$$

(v) The condition for stopping the algorithm is given by

$$\|\mathbf{A}_k - \mathbf{A}_{k-1}\| < \varepsilon, \tag{4.486}$$

where ε is a positive error imposed a priori, while $\|\,\|$ is one of the canonical norms of the matrix.

4.6.9 The Rotation Method

The rotation method applies to the symmetric matrices $\mathbf{A} \in \mathcal{M}_n(\mathbb{R})$ and supplies both the eigenvectors and the eigenvalues of the matrix.

The idea consists in the construction of sequence of matrices $\mathbf{A}_0 = \mathbf{A}, \mathbf{A}_1, \ldots, \mathbf{A}_p, \ldots$, obtained by the rule

$$\mathbf{A}_{p+1} = \mathbf{R}_{ij}^{-1} \mathbf{A}_p \mathbf{R}_{ij}, \tag{4.487}$$

the transformations being unitary and orthogonal.

To do this, we choose the matrix $\mathbf{R}_{ij}$ in the form of a rotation matrix

$$\mathbf{R}_{ij} = \begin{bmatrix} 1 & 0 & \cdots & 0 & \cdots & 0 & \cdots & 0 & 0 \\ 0 & 1 & \cdots & 0 & \cdots & 0 & \cdots & 0 & 0 \\ \cdots & \cdots & \cdots & \cdots & \cdots & \cdots & \cdots & \cdots & \cdots \\ 0 & 0 & \cdots & \cos\alpha & \cdots & -\sin\alpha & \cdots & 0 & 0 \\ \cdots & \cdots & \cdots & \cdots & \cdots & \cdots & \cdots & \cdots & \cdots \\ 0 & 0 & \cdots & \sin\alpha & \cdots & \cos\alpha & \cdots & 0 & 0 \\ \cdots & \cdots & \cdots & \cdots & \cdots & \cdots & \cdots & \cdots & \cdots \\ 0 & 0 & \cdots & 0 & \cdots & 0 & \cdots & 1 & 0 \\ 0 & 0 & \cdots & 0 & \cdots & 0 & \cdots & 0 & 1 \end{bmatrix}, \tag{4.488}$$

that is, a unitary matrix in which the elements $r_{ii}, r_{ij}, r_{ji}, r_{jj}$ have been modified in the form $r_{ii} = \cos\alpha$, $r_{ij} = -\sin\alpha$, $r_{ji} = \sin\alpha$, $r_{jj} = \cos\alpha$. Obviously,

$$\mathbf{R}_{ij}^{-1} = \mathbf{R}_{ij}^{\mathrm{T}}. \tag{4.489}$$

By multiplying a matrix $\mathbf{A}_p$ by $\mathbf{R}_{ij}^{-1}$ on the left and by $\mathbf{R}_{ij}$ on the right, respectively,

$$\mathbf{A}_{p+1} = \mathbf{R}_{ij}^{-1} \mathbf{A}_p \mathbf{R}_{ij}, \tag{4.490}$$

we obtain a new matrix, which has the property

$$a_{ij}^{(p+1)} = a_{ji}^{(p+1)} = 0, \tag{4.491}$$

that is, two new extradiagonal elements equal to zero have been created.

On the other hand, the Euclidian norm $\|\ \|_k$ remains unchanged to transformations similar to rotation matrices, so that

$$\sum_{k\neq l}\left[a_{kl}^{(p+1)}\right]^2 = \sum_{k\neq l}\left[a_{kl}^{(p)}\right]^2 - 2\left[a_{ij}^{(p)}\right]^2 + \frac{1}{2}\left[\left(a_{jj}^{(p)} - a_{ii}^{(p)}\right)\sin 2\alpha + 2a_{ij}^{(p)}\cos 2\alpha\right]^2. \tag{4.492}$$

It follows therefore that the Euclidian norm of the new matrix, calculated only with the extradiagonal elements, will diminish the most if

$$|a_{ij}^{(p)}| = \max_{k\neq l}|a_{kl}^{(p)}| \tag{4.493}$$

and

$$\tan 2\alpha = \frac{2a_{ij}^{(p)}}{a_{jj}^{(p)} - a_{ii}^{(p)}}, \quad |\alpha| \leq \frac{\pi}{4}. \tag{4.494}$$

If we denote such a norm by $\|\ \|_{k'}$, then

$$\left[\|\mathbf{A}_{p+1}\|_{k'}\right]^2 = \left[\|\mathbf{A}_p\|_{k'}\right]^2 - 2\left[a_{i_p j_p}^{(p)}\right]^2 \tag{4.495}$$

and, furthermore,

$$\left[a_{i_p j_p}^{(p)}\right]^2 \geq \frac{\left[\|\mathbf{A}_p\|_{k'}\right]^2}{n(n-1)}, \tag{4.496}$$

because $a_{i_p j_p}^{(p)}$ is the maximal element in modulus out of the principal diagonal in the matrix $\mathbf{A}_p$.

It results in the sequence of inequalities

$$[\|\mathbf{A}_{p+1}\|_{k'}]^2 \leq [\|\mathbf{A}_p\|_{k'}]^2\left[1 - \frac{2}{n(n-1)}\right] \leq \cdots \leq [\|\mathbf{A}_0\|_{k'}]^2\left[1 - \frac{2}{n(n-1)}\right]^{p+1}, \tag{4.497}$$

hence

$$\lim_{p\to\infty}\|\mathbf{A}_{p+1}\|_{k'} = 0. \tag{4.498}$$

One obtains thus a matrix $\mathbf{A}^*$, all the extradiagonal elements of which are equal to zero, while on the principal diagonal, it has the eigenvalues of the matrix $\mathbf{A}$.

Moreover, for a matrix $\mathbf{A}_p$, $p \in \mathbb{N}$, the elements of the principal diagonal approximate the eigenvalues of the matrix $\mathbf{A}$, while the columns of the matrix

$$\mathbf{R} = \mathbf{R}_{i_1 j_1}\mathbf{R}_{i_2 j_2}\cdots\mathbf{R}_{i_{p-1} j_{p-1}} \tag{4.499}$$

approximate the eigenvectors of the matrix $\mathbf{A}$.

4.7 QR DECOMPOSITION

Definition 4.13 Let $\mathbf{v} \in \mathcal{M}_{n,1}(\mathbb{R})$, $\mathbf{v} \neq 0$. The matrix

$$\mathbf{H} = \mathbf{I}_n - \frac{2\mathbf{v}\mathbf{v}^{\mathrm{T}}}{\mathbf{v}^{\mathrm{T}}\mathbf{v}} \tag{4.500}$$

is called the *Householder*[17] *reflexion* or *Householder matrix* or *Householder transformation*, while the vector $\mathbf{v}$ is called the *Householder vector*, $\mathbf{I}_n$ being the unit matrix of order n.

[17]Introduced by Alston Scott Householder (1904–1993) in 1958.

Let a vector $\mathbf{x} \in \mathcal{M}_{n,1}(\mathbb{R})$,

$$\mathbf{x} = [x_1 \quad x_2 \cdots x_n]^\mathrm{T} \tag{4.501}$$

and let us calculate

$$\mathbf{Hx} = \left(\mathbf{I}_n - \frac{2\mathbf{v}\mathbf{v}^\mathrm{T}}{\mathbf{v}^\mathrm{T}\mathbf{v}}\right)\mathbf{x} = \mathbf{x} - \frac{2\mathbf{v}^\mathrm{T}\mathbf{x}}{\mathbf{v}^\mathrm{T}\mathbf{v}}\mathbf{v}. \tag{4.502}$$

Let $\mathbf{e}_1$ be the first column of the unit matrix $\mathbf{I}_n$. If $\mathbf{Hx}$ is in the vector subspace generated by $\mathbf{e}_1$, then it follows results that $\mathbf{v}$ is in the vector subspace generated by $\mathbf{x}$ and $\mathbf{e}_1$. Let us take

$$\mathbf{v} = \mathbf{x} + \lambda\mathbf{e}_1, \tag{4.503}$$

where $\lambda \in \mathbb{R}$. It follows that

$$\mathbf{v}^\mathrm{T}\mathbf{x} = \mathbf{x}^\mathrm{T}\mathbf{x} + \lambda x_1, \tag{4.504}$$

$$\mathbf{v}^\mathrm{T}\mathbf{v} = \mathbf{x}^\mathrm{T}\mathbf{x} + 2\lambda x_1 + \lambda^2, \tag{4.505}$$

$$\mathbf{Hx} = \left(1 - 2\frac{\mathbf{x}^\mathrm{T}\mathbf{x} + \lambda x_1}{\mathbf{x}^\mathrm{T}\mathbf{x} + 2\lambda x_1 + \lambda^2}\right) - 2\lambda\frac{\mathbf{v}^\mathrm{T}\mathbf{x}}{\mathbf{v}^\mathrm{T}\mathbf{v}}\mathbf{e}_1; \tag{4.506}$$

the condition that $\mathbf{Hx}$ be in the vector subspace generated by $\mathbf{e}_1$ leads to

$$1 - 2\frac{\mathbf{x}^\mathrm{T}\mathbf{x} + \lambda x_1}{\mathbf{x}^\mathrm{T}\mathbf{x} + 2\lambda x_1 + \lambda^2} = 0, \tag{4.507}$$

that is,

$$\lambda^2 = \mathbf{x}^\mathrm{T}\mathbf{x}, \quad \lambda = \pm\sqrt{\mathbf{x}^\mathrm{T}\mathbf{x}}. \tag{4.508}$$

Definition 4.14   Let $\mathbf{A} \in \mathcal{M}_{m,n}(\mathbb{R})$. We call the following expression the **QR** *factorization* of the matrix $\mathbf{A}$:

$$\mathbf{A} = \mathbf{QR}, \tag{4.509}$$

where $\mathbf{Q} \in \mathcal{M}_m(\mathbb{R})$ is an orthogonal matrix.

$$\mathbf{Q}^\mathrm{T}\mathbf{Q} = \mathbf{I}_m, \tag{4.510}$$

and $\mathbf{R} \in \mathcal{M}_{m,n}(\mathbb{R})$ is an upper triangular matrix.

Let

$$\mathbf{A} = \begin{bmatrix} a_{11} & a_{12} & a_{13} & \cdots & a_{1n} \\ a_{21} & a_{22} & a_{23} & \cdots & a_{2n} \\ \cdots & \cdots & \cdots & \cdots & \cdots \\ a_{m1} & a_{m2} & a_{m3} & \cdots & a_{mn} \end{bmatrix}. \tag{4.511}$$

We find a Householder matrix $\mathbf{H}_1 \in \mathcal{M}_m(\mathbb{R})$, so that

$$\mathbf{H}_1\mathbf{A} = \begin{bmatrix} a'_{11} & a'_{12} & a'_{13} & \cdots & a'_{1n} \\ 0 & a'_{22} & a'_{23} & \cdots & a'_{2n} \\ \cdots & \cdots & \cdots & \cdots & \cdots \\ 0 & a'_{m2} & a'_{m3} & \cdots & a'_{mn} \end{bmatrix}. \tag{4.512}$$

We determine now a new Householder matrix $\mathbf{H}_2 \in \mathcal{M}_{m-1}(\mathbb{R})$ with the property

$$\overline{\mathbf{H}}_2 \begin{bmatrix} a'_{22} \\ a'_{23} \\ \vdots \\ a'_{m2} \end{bmatrix} = \begin{bmatrix} a''_{22} \\ 0 \\ \vdots \\ 0 \end{bmatrix} \tag{4.513}$$

and choose

$$\mathbf{H}_2 = \begin{bmatrix} 1 & \mathbf{O} \\ 0 & \overline{\mathbf{H}}_2 \end{bmatrix}. \tag{4.514}$$

Thus,

$$\mathbf{H}_2 \mathbf{H}_1 \mathbf{A} = \begin{bmatrix} a''_{11} & a''_{12} & a''_{13} & \cdots & a''_{1n} \\ 0 & a''_{22} & a''_{23} & \cdots & a''_{2n} \\ 0 & 0 & a''_{33} & \cdots & a''_{3n} \\ \cdots & \cdots & \cdots & \cdots & \cdots \\ 0 & 0 & a''_{m3} & \cdots & a''_{mn} \end{bmatrix}. \tag{4.515}$$

The procedure is continuing with the determination of the matrix $\overline{\mathbf{H}}_3$ with the property

$$\overline{\mathbf{H}}_3 \begin{bmatrix} a''_{33} \\ a''_{43} \\ \vdots \\ a''_{m3} \end{bmatrix} = \begin{bmatrix} a'''_{33} \\ 0 \\ \vdots \\ 0 \end{bmatrix} \tag{4.516}$$

and with the choice of the matrix

$$\mathbf{H}_3 = \begin{bmatrix} \mathbf{I}_2 & 0 \\ 0 & \overline{\mathbf{H}}_3 \end{bmatrix}. \tag{4.517}$$

Thus, we determine the Householder matrices $\mathbf{H}_1$, $\mathbf{H}_2$, $\mathbf{H}_3$, ..., $\mathbf{H}_p$, where $p = \min\{m, n\}$. Moreover,

$$\mathbf{R} = \mathbf{H}_p \mathbf{H}_{p-1} \ldots \mathbf{H}_2 \mathbf{H}_1 \mathbf{A} \tag{4.518}$$

and

$$\mathbf{Q} = \mathbf{H}_1 \mathbf{H}_2 \ldots \mathbf{H}_{p-1} \mathbf{H}_p. \tag{4.519}$$

Another possibility to obtain the **QR** decomposition is by the use of the Givens rotation matrices.

Definition 4.15   The matrix denoted by $\mathbf{G}(i, j, \theta)$, which is different from the unit matrix $\mathbf{I}_n$, and whose elements are given by

$$g_{ii} = \cos\theta, \quad g_{ij} = \sin\theta, \quad g_{ji} = -\sin\theta, \quad g_{jj} = \cos\theta. \tag{4.520}$$

is called the *Givens rotation*[18] matrix of order n.

---

[18]Defined by James Wallace Givens Jr. (1910–1993) in 1950.

Let $\mathbf{y}$ be the product

$$\mathbf{y} = \begin{bmatrix} y_1 \\ y_2 \\ \vdots \\ y_n \end{bmatrix} = \mathbf{G}(i, j, \theta) \begin{bmatrix} x_1 \\ x_2 \\ \vdots \\ x_n \end{bmatrix}. \tag{4.521}$$

It follows that

$$y_k = \begin{cases} x_i \cos\theta - x_j \sin\theta, & \text{for } k = i \\ x_i \sin\theta + x_j \cos\theta, & \text{for } k = j \\ x_k, \text{otherwise}, \end{cases} \tag{4.522}$$

so that $y_k = 0$ for

$$\cos\theta = \frac{x_i}{\sqrt{x_i^2 + x_j^2}}, \quad \sin\theta = -\frac{x_j}{\sqrt{x_i^2 + x_j^2}}. \tag{4.523}$$

Multiplying the matrix $\mathbf{A}$ on the left by various Givens matrices $\mathbf{G}_1^{\mathrm{T}}, \mathbf{G}_2^{\mathrm{T}}, \ldots, \mathbf{G}_r^{\mathrm{T}}$, results, in a finite number of steps, in the matrix

$$\mathbf{R} = \mathbf{G}_r^{\mathrm{T}} \mathbf{G}_{r-1}^{\mathrm{T}} \cdots \mathbf{G}_2^{\mathrm{T}} \mathbf{G}_1^{\mathrm{T}} \mathbf{A}, \tag{4.524}$$

an upper triangular matrix. The matrix $\mathbf{Q}$ is given by

$$\mathbf{Q} = \mathbf{G}_1 \mathbf{G}_2 \cdots \mathbf{G}_{r-1} \mathbf{G}_r. \tag{4.525}$$

4.8   THE SINGULAR VALUE DECOMPOSITION (SVD)

Definition 4.16

(i) Let $\mathbf{x}_1, \mathbf{x}_2, \ldots, \mathbf{x}_p$ be vectors in $\mathbb{R}^n$, $p \leq n$. We say that the vectors $\mathbf{x}_i$, $i = \overline{1, p}$, are orthogonal if

$$\mathbf{x}_i^{\mathrm{T}} \mathbf{x}_j = 0, \tag{4.526}$$

for any $1 \leq i, j \leq p, i \neq j$.
(ii) If, in addition,

$$\mathbf{x}_i^{\mathrm{T}} \mathbf{x}_i = 1 \tag{4.527}$$

for any $1 \leq i \leq p$, then the vectors $\mathbf{x}_1, \mathbf{x}_2, \ldots, \mathbf{x}_p$ are called *orthonormal* vectors.

Observation 4.41

(i) If $\mathbf{x}_i$, $i = \overline{1, p}$, are orthogonal, then they are also linear independent.
(ii) The system of orthogonal vectors $\mathbf{x}_i$, $i = \overline{1, p}$, of $\mathbb{R}^n$, $p < n$, may be completed by the vectors $\mathbf{x}_{p+1}, \ldots, \mathbf{x}_n$, so that the new system of vectors $\mathbf{x}_1, \ldots, \mathbf{x}_n$ is orthogonal.
(iii) There exists $\mathbf{A}_1 \in \mathcal{M}_{n,(n-p)}(\mathbb{R})$, $p < n$, so that the matrix

$$\mathbf{A} = \begin{bmatrix} \mathbf{A}_1 & \mathbf{A}_2 \end{bmatrix} \tag{4.528}$$

has orthonormal columns.

Theorem 4.2   (Singular Value Decomposition (SVD)[19]). If $\mathbf{A} \in \mathcal{M}_{m,n}(\mathbb{R})$ then there exist orthogonal matrices $\mathbf{U} \in \mathcal{M}_m(\mathbb{R})$ and $\mathbf{V} \in \mathcal{M}_n(\mathbb{R})$ so that

$$\mathbf{U}^\mathrm{T}\mathbf{A}\mathbf{V} = \begin{bmatrix} \sigma_1 & 0 & \cdots & 0 \\ 0 & \sigma_2 & \cdots & 0 \\ \cdots & \cdots & \cdots & \cdots \\ 0 & 0 & \cdots & \sigma_p \end{bmatrix}, \tag{4.529}$$

where $p = \min\{m, n\}$.

Demonstration. Let $\mathbf{x} \in \mathbb{R}^n$ and $y \in \mathbb{R}^m$ be two vectors of unitary norm that fulfill the relation

$$\mathbf{A}\mathbf{x} = \|\mathbf{A}\|_2 \mathbf{y} = \sigma\mathbf{y}. \tag{4.530}$$

Taking into account the previous observation, we know that matrices $\mathbf{V}_2 \in \mathcal{M}_{n,n-1}(\mathbb{R})$ and $\mathbf{U}_2 \in \mathcal{M}_{m,m-1}(\mathbb{R})$ exist, so that the matrices $V = [\mathbf{x}\mathbf{V}_2] \in \mathcal{M}_n(\mathbb{R})$ and $U = [\mathbf{y}\mathbf{U}_2] \in \mathcal{M}_m(\mathbb{R})$ are orthogonal.

On the other hand,

$$\mathbf{U}^\mathrm{T}\mathbf{A}\mathbf{V} = \begin{bmatrix} \sigma & \mathbf{w}^\mathrm{T} \\ 0 & \mathbf{B} \end{bmatrix} = \mathbf{A}_1. \tag{4.531}$$

But

$$\left\| \mathbf{A}_1 \begin{bmatrix} \sigma \\ \mathbf{w} \end{bmatrix} \right\|_2^2 \geq (\sigma^2 + \mathbf{w}^\mathrm{T}\mathbf{w})^2 \tag{4.532}$$

and

$$\left\| \mathbf{A}_1 \begin{bmatrix} \sigma \\ \mathbf{w} \end{bmatrix} \right\|_2 \leq \|\mathbf{A}_1\|_2 \left\| \begin{bmatrix} \sigma \\ \mathbf{w} \end{bmatrix} \right\|_2. \tag{4.533}$$

Then

$$\|\mathbf{X}\|_2 = \|\mathbf{X}^\mathrm{T}\|_2, \tag{4.534}$$

for any matrix $\mathbf{X}$, and hence,

$$\left\| \begin{bmatrix} \sigma \\ \mathbf{w} \end{bmatrix} \right\|_2 = \sqrt{\left\| \begin{bmatrix} \sigma \\ \mathbf{w} \end{bmatrix} \right\|_2 \left\| \begin{bmatrix} \sigma \\ \mathbf{w} \end{bmatrix}^\mathrm{T} \right\|_2} \geq \sqrt{\left\| \begin{bmatrix} \sigma & \mathbf{w} \end{bmatrix} \begin{bmatrix} \sigma \\ \mathbf{w} \end{bmatrix} \right\|_2} = \sqrt{(\sigma^2 + \mathbf{w}^\mathrm{T}\mathbf{w})}, \tag{4.535}$$

so that

$$\|\mathbf{A}_1\|_2^2 \geq \sigma^2 + \mathbf{w}^\mathrm{T}\mathbf{w}. \tag{4.536}$$

But $\mathbf{U}$ and $\mathbf{V}$ are orthogonal; we have

$$\|\mathbf{U}\mathbf{A}\mathbf{V}\|_2 = \|\mathbf{U}^\mathrm{T}\mathbf{A}\mathbf{V}\|_2 = \|\mathbf{A}\|_2 \tag{4.537}$$

and we deduce

$$\sigma^2 = \|\mathbf{A}\|_2^2 = \|\mathbf{U}^\mathrm{T}\mathbf{A}\mathbf{V}\|_2^2 = \|\mathbf{A}_1\|_2^2. \tag{4.538}$$

[19]The algorithm for SVD was given by Gene Howard Golub (1932–2007) and William Morton Kahan (1933–) in 1970.

Comparing relations (4.536) and (4.538), it follows that

$$\mathbf{w}^{\mathbf{T}}\mathbf{w} = \|\mathbf{w}\|_2^2 = 0, \tag{4.539}$$

and hence,

$$\mathbf{w} = 0. \tag{4.540}$$

The procedure is continued for the matrix $\mathbf{B} \in \mathcal{M}_{m-1,n-1}(\mathbb{R})$ and so on, the theorem being proved.

In the demonstration, we used $\|\ \|_2$ defined as follows:

- for $\mathbf{x} \in \mathbb{R}^n$,

$$\|\mathbf{x}\|_2 = \sqrt{x_1^2 + x_2^2 + \cdots + x_n^2}. \tag{4.541}$$

- for $\mathbf{A} \in \mathcal{M}_{m,n}(\mathbb{R})$,

$$\|\mathbf{A}\|_2 = \sup_{\mathbf{x} \neq 0} \frac{\|\mathbf{A}\mathbf{x}\|_2}{\|\mathbf{x}\|_2} = \max_{\|\mathbf{x}\|_2 = 1} \|\mathbf{A}\mathbf{x}\|_2. \tag{4.542}$$

4.9 USE OF THE LEAST SQUARES METHOD IN SOLVING THE LINEAR OVERDETERMINED SYSTEMS

We consider the linear system

$$\mathbf{A}\mathbf{x} = \mathbf{b}, \tag{4.543}$$

where $\mathbf{A} \in \mathcal{M}_{m,n}(\mathbb{R})$, $m \geq n$, $\mathbf{x} \in \mathcal{M}_{n,1}(\mathbb{R})$, $\mathbf{b} \in \mathcal{M}_{m,1}(\mathbb{R})$.

Definition 4.17 System (4.543) is called an *overdetermined* system.

Obviously, system (4.543) has an exact solution only in some particular cases.

An idea of solving consists in finding the vector $\mathbf{x}$ so as to minimize the expression $\|\mathbf{A}\mathbf{x} - \mathbf{b}\|$, where $\|\ \|$ is one of the norms of the matrix, that is

$$\min_{\mathbf{x} \in \mathcal{M}_{n,1}(\mathbb{R})} \|\mathbf{A}\mathbf{x} - \mathbf{b}\|. \tag{4.544}$$

It is obvious that the answer depends on the chosen norm.

Usually, we consider the norm $\|\ \|_2$, which leads to the least squares method.

To begin, let us consider the case in which the columns of the matrix $\mathbf{A}$ are linearly independent. We start from the equality

$$\|\mathbf{A}(\mathbf{x} + \alpha\mathbf{z}) - \mathbf{b}\|_2^2 = \|\mathbf{A}\mathbf{x} - \mathbf{b}\|_2^2 + 2\alpha\mathbf{x}^{\mathbf{T}}\mathbf{A}^{\mathbf{T}}(\mathbf{A}\mathbf{x} - \mathbf{b}) + \alpha^2\|\mathbf{A}\mathbf{z}\|_2^2, \tag{4.545}$$

where α is a real parameter, while $\mathbf{z} \in \mathcal{M}_{n,1}(\mathbb{R})$.

If $\mathbf{x}$ is a solution of relation (4.544), then

$$\mathbf{A}^{\mathbf{T}}(\mathbf{A}\mathbf{x} - \mathbf{b}) = \mathbf{0}. \tag{4.546}$$

Indeed, if relation (4.546) is not satisfied, then we choose

$$\mathbf{z} = -\mathbf{A}^{\mathbf{T}}(\mathbf{A}\mathbf{x} - \mathbf{b}) \tag{4.547}$$

and from equation (4.545) we get

$$\|A(x + \alpha z) - b\|_2^2 < \|Ax - b\|_2^2, \qquad (4.548)$$

that is, x does not minimize expression (4.544), which is absurd.

It follows therefore that if the columns of the matrix A are linearly independent, then the solution of system (4.543) in the sense of the least squares, denoted by x_{LS}, is obtained from the linear system

$$A^T A x_{LS} = A^T b. \qquad (4.549)$$

Definition 4.18

(i) System (4.549) is called the *system of normal equations*.

(ii) The expression

$$r_{LS} = b - A x_{LS} \qquad (4.550)$$

is called the *minimum residual*.

If A has the **QR** decomposition, where $Q \in \mathcal{M}_m(\mathbb{R})$ is orthogonal, while R is upper triangular, then

$$Q^T A = R = \begin{bmatrix} r_{11} & r_{12} & \cdots & r_{1n} \\ 0 & r_{22} & \cdots & r_{2n} \\ \cdots & \cdots & \cdots & \cdots \\ 0 & 0 & \cdots & r_{nn} \\ 0 & 0 & \cdots & 0 \\ \cdots & \cdots & \cdots & \cdots \\ 0 & 0 & \cdots & 0 \end{bmatrix}. \qquad (4.551)$$

We also denote

$$Q^T b = \begin{bmatrix} c \\ d \end{bmatrix}, \qquad (4.552)$$

where

$$c = [c_1 \quad c_2 \quad \cdots \quad c_n]^T, \quad d = [d_1 \quad d_2 \quad \cdots \quad d_{m-n}]^T. \qquad (4.553)$$

Thus, it follows that

$$\|Ax - b\|_2^2 = \|Q^T Ax - Q^T b\|_2^2 = \|R_1 x - c\|_2^2 + \|d\|_2^2, \qquad (4.554)$$

with

$$R_1 = \begin{bmatrix} r_{11} & r_{12} & \cdots & 0 \\ 0 & r_{22} & \cdots & r_{2n} \\ \cdots & \cdots & \cdots & \cdots \\ 0 & 0 & \cdots & r_{nn} \end{bmatrix}, \quad R_1 \in \mathcal{M}_n(\mathbb{R}). \qquad (4.555)$$

As

$$\text{rank}(A) = \text{rank}(R_1) = n, \qquad (4.556)$$

the solution of system (4.543) in the sense of the least squares is obtained from the system

$$R_1 x_{LS} = c. \qquad (4.557)$$

The case in which the columns of the matrix $\mathbf{A}$ are not linearly independent is somewhat more complicated.

Let us denote by $\bar{\mathbf{x}}$ a solution of equation (4.544) and let $\mathbf{z} \in \text{null}(\mathbf{A})$. It follows that $\bar{\mathbf{x}} + \mathbf{z}$ is also a solution of equation (4.544), hence condition (4.544) does not have a unique solution. Moreover, the set of all $\mathbf{x} \in \mathcal{M}_{n,1}(\mathbb{R})$ for which $\|\mathbf{A}\mathbf{x} - \mathbf{b}\|_2$ is minimum is a convex set. We define in this set $\mathbf{x}_{\text{LS}}$ as being that $\mathbf{x}$ for which $\|\mathbf{x}\|_2$ is minimum. Let us show that $\mathbf{x}_{\text{LS}}$ is unique.

We denote by $\mathbf{Q}$ and $\mathbf{Z}$ two orthogonal matrices for which

$$\mathbf{Q}^{\text{T}}\mathbf{A}\mathbf{Z} = \mathbf{T} = \begin{bmatrix} t_{11} & t_{12} & \cdots & t_{1r} & 0 & \cdots & 0 \\ t_{21} & t_{22} & \cdots & t_{2r} & 0 & \cdots & 0 \\ \cdots & \cdots & \cdots & \cdots & \cdots & \cdots & \cdots \\ t_{r1} & t_{r2} & \cdots & t_{rr} & 0 & \cdots & 0 \\ 0 & 0 & \cdots & 0 & 0 & \cdots & 0 \\ \cdots & \cdots & \cdots & \cdots & \cdots & \cdots & \cdots \\ 0 & 0 & \cdots & 0 & 0 & \cdots & 0 \end{bmatrix}, \tag{4.558}$$

where $r = \text{rank}(\mathbf{A})$.

Under these conditions,

$$\|\mathbf{A}\mathbf{x} - \mathbf{b}\|_2^2 = \|(\mathbf{Q}^{\text{T}}\mathbf{A}\mathbf{Z})\mathbf{Z}^{\text{T}}\mathbf{x} - \mathbf{Q}^{\text{T}}\mathbf{b}\|_2^2 = \|\mathbf{T}_1\mathbf{w} - \mathbf{c}\|_2^2 + \|\mathbf{d}\|_2^2, \tag{4.559}$$

where

$$\mathbf{Z}^{\text{T}}\mathbf{x} = \begin{bmatrix} \mathbf{w} \\ \mathbf{y} \end{bmatrix}, \quad \mathbf{Q}^{\text{T}}\mathbf{b} = \begin{bmatrix} \mathbf{c} \\ \mathbf{d} \end{bmatrix}, \tag{4.560}$$

$$\mathbf{w} = [w_1 \quad w_2 \quad \cdots \quad w_r]^{\text{T}}, \quad \mathbf{y} = [y_1 \quad y_2 \quad \cdots \quad y_{n-r}]^{\text{T}},$$

$$\mathbf{c} = [c_1 \quad c_2 \quad \cdots \quad c_r]^{\text{T}}, \quad \mathbf{d} = [d_1 \quad d_2 \quad \cdots \quad d_{n-r}]^{\text{T}}, \tag{4.561}$$

$$\mathbf{T}_1 = \begin{bmatrix} t_{11} & t_{12} & \cdots & t_{1r} \\ t_{21} & t_{22} & \cdots & t_{2r} \\ \cdots & \cdots & \cdots & \cdots \\ t_{r1} & t_{r2} & \cdots & t_{rr} \end{bmatrix}. \tag{4.562}$$

If we choose $\mathbf{x}$ such that equation (4.559) be minimum, then

$$\mathbf{w} = \mathbf{T}_1^{-1}\mathbf{c} \tag{4.563}$$

and

$$\mathbf{x}_{\text{LS}} = \mathbf{Z}\begin{bmatrix} \mathbf{T}_1^{-1}\mathbf{c} \\ 0 \end{bmatrix}. \tag{4.564}$$

If we use SVD for the matrix $\mathbf{A}$, then

$$\mathbf{x}_{\text{LS}} = \sum_{i=1}^{r} \frac{\mathbf{u}_i^{\text{T}}\mathbf{b}}{\sigma_i}\mathbf{v}_i, \tag{4.565}$$

where

$$\mathbf{U}^{\mathrm{T}}\mathbf{A}\mathbf{V} = \boldsymbol{\Sigma} = \begin{bmatrix} \sigma_1 & 0 & \cdots & 0 & 0 & \cdots & 0 \\ 0 & \sigma_2 & \cdots & 0 & 0 & \cdots & 0 \\ \cdots & \cdots & \cdots & \cdots & \cdots & \cdots & \cdots \\ 0 & 0 & \cdots & \sigma_r & 0 & \cdots & 0 \\ 0 & 0 & \cdots & 0 & 0 & \cdots & 0 \\ \cdots & \cdots & \cdots & \cdots & \cdots & \cdots & \cdots \\ 0 & 0 & \cdots & 0 & 0 & \cdots & 0 \end{bmatrix}, \quad \boldsymbol{\Sigma} \in \mathcal{M}_{m,n}(\mathbb{R}), \tag{4.566}$$

$$\mathbf{U} = [\mathbf{u}_1 \quad \mathbf{u}_2 \quad \cdots \quad \mathbf{u}_m], \qquad \mathbf{V} = [\mathbf{v}_1 \quad \mathbf{v}_2 \quad \cdots \quad \mathbf{v}_n]. \tag{4.567}$$

4.10 THE PSEUDO-INVERSE OF A MATRIX

Let $\mathbf{A} \in \mathcal{M}_{m,n}(\mathbb{R})$ for which we know the SVD,

$$\mathbf{U}^{\mathrm{T}}\mathbf{A}\mathbf{V} = \boldsymbol{\Sigma} \in \mathcal{M}_{m,n}(\mathbb{R}) \tag{4.568}$$

and let $r = \mathrm{rank}(\mathbf{A})$.

Definition 4.19   The matrix $\mathbf{A}^+ \in \mathcal{M}_{n,m}(\mathbb{R})$ is defined by

$$\mathbf{A}^+ = \mathbf{V}\boldsymbol{\Sigma}^+\mathbf{U}^{\mathrm{T}}, \tag{4.569}$$

where $\boldsymbol{\Sigma}^+ \in \mathcal{M}_{n,m}(\mathbb{R})$ and

$$\boldsymbol{\Sigma}^+ = \begin{bmatrix} \dfrac{1}{\sigma_1} & 0 & \cdots & 0 & 0 & \cdots & 0 \\ 0 & \dfrac{1}{\sigma_2} & \cdots & 0 & 0 & \cdots & 0 \\ \cdots & \cdots & \cdots & \cdots & \cdots & \cdots & \cdots \\ 0 & 0 & \cdots & \dfrac{1}{\sigma_r} & 0 & \cdots & 0 \\ 0 & 0 & \cdots & 0 & 0 & \cdots & 0 \\ \cdots & \cdots & \cdots & \cdots & \cdots & \cdots & 0 \\ 0 & 0 & \cdots & 0 & 0 & \cdots & 0 \end{bmatrix}. \tag{4.570}$$

Let us observe that

$$\mathbf{x}_{\mathrm{LS}} = \mathbf{A}^+\mathbf{b}; \tag{4.571}$$

hence $\mathbf{A}^+$ is the unique solution of the problem

$$\min_{\mathbf{X} \in \mathcal{M}_{n,m}(\mathbb{R})} \|\mathbf{A}\mathbf{X} - \mathbf{I}_m\|_k. \tag{4.572}$$

4.11 SOLVING OF THE UNDERDETERMINED LINEAR SYSTEMS

Definition 4.20 The linear system

$$\mathbf{Ax} = \mathbf{b}, \tag{4.573}$$

where $\mathbf{A} \in \mathcal{M}_{m,n}(\mathbb{R})$, $\mathbf{b} \in \mathcal{M}_{m,1}(\mathbb{R})$, $\mathbf{x} \in \mathcal{M}_{n,1}(\mathbb{R})$ and $m < n$ is called an *underdetermined linear system*.

Let us consider the QR decomposition of the matrix $\mathbf{A}^{\mathrm{T}}$,

$$\mathbf{A}^{\mathrm{T}} = \mathbf{QR} = \mathbf{Q} \begin{bmatrix} \mathbf{R}_1 \\ \mathbf{0}_{n-m,m} \end{bmatrix}, \tag{4.574}$$

where $\mathbf{R}_1 \in \mathcal{M}_m(\mathbb{R})$, while $\mathbf{0}_{n-m,m}$ is a matrix of $\mathcal{M}_{n-m,m}(\mathbb{R})$ with all elements equal to zero.

System (4.573) is now written in the form

$$(\mathbf{QR})^{\mathrm{T}}\mathbf{x} = \begin{bmatrix} \mathbf{R}_1^{\mathrm{T}} & \mathbf{0}_{m,n-m} \end{bmatrix} \begin{bmatrix} \mathbf{z}_1 \\ \mathbf{z}_2 \end{bmatrix} = \mathbf{b}, \tag{4.575}$$

where $\mathbf{z}_1 \in \mathcal{M}_{m,1}(\mathbb{R})$, $\mathbf{z}_2 \in \mathcal{M}_{n-m,1}(\mathbb{R})$ and

$$\mathbf{Q}^{\mathrm{T}}\mathbf{x} = [\mathbf{z}_1 \quad \mathbf{z}_2]^{\mathrm{T}}. \tag{4.576}$$

The minimum in norm solution is obtained if we impose the condition $\mathbf{z}_2 = 0$.

In general, an underdetermined system either does not have a solution or has an infinite number of solutions.

4.12 NUMERICAL EXAMPLES

Example 4.1 Let us calculate the determinant of the matrix

$$\mathbf{A} = \begin{bmatrix} 1 & 2 & -3 \\ 5 & 0 & 4 \\ 2 & 1 & 7 \end{bmatrix}. \tag{4.577}$$

If we calculate the determinant by means of the definition, then we have to consider $3! = 6$ permutations. These permutations, together with their signs and the corresponding products are given below.

Permutation	Sign	Product
$p_1 = (1, 2, 3)$	+	$P_1 = a_{11}a_{22}a_{33} = 0$
$p_2 = (1, 3, 2)$	−	$P_2 = a_{11}a_{23}a_{32} = 4$
$p_3 = (2, 1, 3)$	−	$P_3 = a_{12}a_{21}a_{33} = 70$
$p_4 = (2, 3, 1)$	+	$P_4 = a_{12}a_{23}a_{31} = 16$
$p_5 = (3, 1, 2)$	+	$P_5 = a_{13}a_{21}a_{32} = -15$
$p_6 = (3, 2, 1)$	−	$P_6 = a_{13}a_{22}a_{31} = 0$

We obtain

$$\det \mathbf{A} = P_1 - P_2 - P_3 + P_4 + P_5 - P_6 = -73. \tag{4.578}$$

The same problem may be solved by means of equivalent matrices. Let us denote by Δ the required determinant and let us commute the rows 1 and 2 of the matrix **A** with each other in order to realize the pivoting with the maximum element in modulus of the column 1. We have

$$\Delta = - \begin{vmatrix} 5 & 0 & 4 \\ 1 & 2 & -3 \\ 2 & 1 & 7 \end{vmatrix}. \tag{4.579}$$

We multiply row 1 by $-1/5$ and $-2/5$, and we add it to the rows 2 and 3, respectively, obtaining

$$\Delta = - \begin{vmatrix} 5 & 0 & -4 \\ 0 & 2 & -\dfrac{19}{5} \\ 0 & 1 & \dfrac{27}{5} \end{vmatrix}. \tag{4.580}$$

We now multiply row 2 by $-1/2$ and we add it to row 3, obtaining

$$\Delta = - \begin{vmatrix} 5 & 0 & -4 \\ 0 & 2 & -\dfrac{19}{5} \\ 0 & 0 & \dfrac{73}{10} \end{vmatrix} = -73. \tag{4.581}$$

Example 4.2 Let us calculate the rank of the matrix

$$\mathbf{A} = \begin{bmatrix} 1 & 2 & 3 & 0 \\ 3 & 5 & 8 & 1 \\ 6 & 11 & 17 & 1 \end{bmatrix}. \tag{4.582}$$

We observe that the minor of second order

$$\Delta_2 = \begin{vmatrix} 1 & 2 \\ 3 & 5 \end{vmatrix} = -1 \tag{4.583}$$

has a non zero value, hence the rank of **A** is at least equal to two.

Let us now border this minor by elements so as to obtain all the minors of order 3. As a matter of fact we have only two such minors, that is

$$\Delta_{31} = \begin{vmatrix} 1 & 2 & 3 \\ 3 & 5 & 8 \\ 6 & 11 & 17 \end{vmatrix} = 0, \tag{4.584}$$

$$\Delta_{32} = \begin{vmatrix} 1 & 2 & 0 \\ 3 & 5 & 1 \\ 6 & 11 & 1 \end{vmatrix} = 0, \tag{4.585}$$

so it follows that

$$\text{rank } \mathbf{A} = 2. \tag{4.586}$$

We may solve this problem by using equivalent matrices too. Thus, the rank of the matrix $\mathbf{A}$ is the same with the rank of the matrix obtained from the matrix $\mathbf{A}$ by commuting rows 1 and 3 with each other,

$$\mathbf{A} = \begin{bmatrix} 1 & 2 & 3 & 0 \\ 3 & 5 & 8 & 1 \\ 6 & 11 & 17 & 1 \end{bmatrix} \sim \begin{bmatrix} 6 & 11 & 17 & 1 \\ 3 & 5 & 8 & 1 \\ 1 & 2 & 3 & 0 \end{bmatrix}. \tag{4.587}$$

We now multiply, in the new matrix, row 1 by $-1/2$ and $-1/6$, and add it to rows 2 and 3, respectively, obtaining

$$\mathbf{A} \sim \begin{bmatrix} 6 & 11 & 17 & 1 \\ 0 & -\dfrac{1}{2} & -\dfrac{1}{2} & \dfrac{1}{2} \\ 0 & \dfrac{1}{6} & \dfrac{1}{6} & -\dfrac{1}{6} \end{bmatrix}. \tag{4.588}$$

We now multiply the rows 2 and 3 by 2 and 6, respectively, obtaining

$$\mathbf{A} \sim \begin{bmatrix} 6 & 11 & 17 & 1 \\ 0 & -1 & -1 & 1 \\ 0 & 1 & 1 & -1 \end{bmatrix}. \tag{4.589}$$

We multiply column 1 by $-11/6$, by $-17/6$ and by $-1/6$ and add it to columns 2, 3, and 4, respectively, obtaining

$$\mathbf{A} \sim \begin{bmatrix} 6 & 0 & 0 & 0 \\ 0 & -1 & -1 & 1 \\ 0 & 1 & 1 & -1 \end{bmatrix}. \tag{4.590}$$

We add now the second row to the third one, resulting

$$\mathbf{A} \sim \begin{bmatrix} 6 & 0 & 0 & 0 \\ 0 & -1 & -1 & -1 \\ 0 & 0 & 0 & 0 \end{bmatrix}. \tag{4.591}$$

The last step consists in the subtraction of the second column from the third one and by addition of the second column to the fourth one, deducing

$$\mathbf{A} \sim \begin{bmatrix} 6 & 0 & 0 & 0 \\ 0 & -1 & 0 & 0 \\ 0 & 0 & 0 & 0 \end{bmatrix} = \mathbf{B}. \tag{4.592}$$

To determine the rank of the matrix $\mathbf{A}$ it is now sufficient to number the non-zero elements of the principal quasi-diagonal of the matrix $\mathbf{B}$, that is, the elements $b_{11} = 6$, $b_{22} = -1$ and $b_{33} = 0$. It follows that

$$\text{rank } \mathbf{A} = 2. \tag{4.593}$$

Example 4.3   Let the matrix

$$\mathbf{A} = \begin{bmatrix} 1 & 2 & -1 \\ 0 & 3 & 4 \\ 5 & 6 & -2 \end{bmatrix}. \tag{4.594}$$

We pose the problem of calculating the inverse of this matrix.
The direct method supposes the calculation of the determinant

$$\det \mathbf{A} = 25 \tag{4.595}$$

and of the minors

$$\Gamma_{11} = \begin{vmatrix} 3 & 4 \\ 6 & -2 \end{vmatrix} = -30, \quad \Gamma_{12} = \begin{vmatrix} 0 & 4 \\ 5 & -2 \end{vmatrix} = -20, \quad \Gamma_{13} = \begin{vmatrix} 0 & 3 \\ 5 & 6 \end{vmatrix} = -15,$$

$$\Gamma_{21} = \begin{vmatrix} 2 & -1 \\ 6 & -2 \end{vmatrix} = 2, \quad \Gamma_{22} = \begin{vmatrix} 1 & -1 \\ 5 & -2 \end{vmatrix} = 3, \quad \Gamma_{23} = \begin{vmatrix} 1 & 2 \\ 5 & 6 \end{vmatrix} = -4, \quad \Gamma_{31} = \begin{vmatrix} 2 & -1 \\ 3 & 4 \end{vmatrix} = 11,$$

$$\Gamma_{32} = \begin{vmatrix} 1 & -1 \\ 0 & 4 \end{vmatrix} = 4, \quad \Gamma_{33} = \begin{vmatrix} 1 & 2 \\ 0 & 3 \end{vmatrix} = 3, \tag{4.596}$$

from which

$$\mathbf{A}^{-1} = \frac{1}{25} \begin{bmatrix} -30 & -2 & 11 \\ 20 & 3 & -4 \\ -15 & 4 & 3 \end{bmatrix}. \tag{4.597}$$

We now pass on to the Gauss–Jordan method for which we construct the table

$$\left. \begin{array}{ccc} 1 & 2 & -1 \\ 0 & 3 & 4 \\ 5 & 6 & -2 \end{array} \right| \begin{array}{ccc} 1 & 0 & 0 \\ 0 & 1 & 0 \\ 0 & 0 & 1 \end{array}. \tag{4.598}$$

We commute rows 1 and 3 with each other,

$$\left. \begin{array}{ccc} 5 & 6 & -2 \\ 0 & 3 & 4 \\ 1 & 2 & -1 \end{array} \right| \begin{array}{ccc} 0 & 0 & 1 \\ 0 & 1 & 0 \\ 1 & 0 & 0 \end{array}, \tag{4.599}$$

we divide row 1 by 5,

$$\left. \begin{array}{ccc} 1 & \dfrac{6}{5} & -\dfrac{2}{5} \\ 0 & 3 & 4 \\ 1 & 2 & -1 \end{array} \right| \begin{array}{ccc} 0 & 0 & \dfrac{1}{5} \\ 0 & 1 & 0 \\ 1 & 0 & -\dfrac{1}{5} \end{array}. \tag{4.600}$$

and then we subtract row 1 from row 3, obtaining

$$\left. \begin{array}{ccc} 1 & \dfrac{6}{5} & -\dfrac{2}{5} \\ 0 & 3 & 4 \\ 0 & \dfrac{4}{5} & -\dfrac{3}{5} \end{array} \right| \begin{array}{ccc} 0 & 0 & \dfrac{1}{5} \\ 0 & 1 & 0 \\ 1 & 0 & -\dfrac{1}{5} \end{array}. \tag{4.601}$$

We now divide row 2 by 3,

$$\left. \begin{array}{ccc} 1 & \dfrac{6}{5} & -\dfrac{2}{5} \\ 0 & 1 & \dfrac{4}{3} \\ 0 & \dfrac{4}{5} & -\dfrac{3}{5} \end{array} \right| \begin{array}{ccc} 0 & 0 & \dfrac{1}{5} \\ 0 & \dfrac{1}{3} & 0 \\ 1 & 0 & -\dfrac{1}{5} \end{array}, \tag{4.602}$$

and then multiply the new row 2 by $-6/5$ and $-4/5$, and add the results to rows 1 and 3, respectively, obtaining

$$
\left[
\begin{array}{ccc|ccc}
1 & 0 & -2 & 0 & -\dfrac{2}{5} & \dfrac{1}{5} \\[2ex]
0 & 1 & \dfrac{4}{3} & 0 & \dfrac{1}{3} & 0 \\[2ex]
0 & 0 & -\dfrac{3}{5} & 1 & -\dfrac{14}{5} & -\dfrac{1}{5}
\end{array}
\right].
\tag{4.603}
$$

Further, we divide the third row by $-5/3$,

$$
\left[
\begin{array}{ccc|ccc}
1 & 0 & -2 & 0 & -\dfrac{2}{5} & \dfrac{1}{5} \\[2ex]
0 & 1 & \dfrac{4}{3} & 0 & \dfrac{1}{3} & 0 \\[2ex]
0 & 0 & 1 & -\dfrac{3}{5} & \dfrac{4}{25} & \dfrac{3}{25}
\end{array}
\right],
\tag{4.604}
$$

and multiply the new row 3 by 2 and $-4/3$, and add it to the rows 1 and 2, respectively,

$$
\left[
\begin{array}{ccc|ccc}
1 & 0 & 0 & -\dfrac{6}{5} & -\dfrac{2}{25} & \dfrac{11}{25} \\[2ex]
0 & 1 & 0 & \dfrac{4}{5} & \dfrac{3}{25} & -\dfrac{4}{25} \\[2ex]
0 & 0 & 1 & -\dfrac{3}{5} & \dfrac{4}{25} & \dfrac{3}{25}
\end{array}
\right].
\tag{4.605}
$$

We have thus, in the right part of table (4.605), the searched required inverse, given before in equation (4.597).

We shall solve now the same problem by the method of partitioning the matrix $\mathbf{A}$.

If

$$
\mathbf{A} = \begin{bmatrix} \mathbf{A}_1 & \mathbf{A}_3 \\ \mathbf{A}_2 & \mathbf{A}_4 \end{bmatrix}, \quad \mathbf{A}^{-1} = \mathbf{B} = \begin{bmatrix} \mathbf{B}_1 & \mathbf{B}_3 \\ \mathbf{B}_2 & \mathbf{B}_4 \end{bmatrix},
\tag{4.606}
$$

then we have

$$
\mathbf{B}_4 = (\mathbf{A}_4 - \mathbf{A}_2\mathbf{A}_1^{-1}\mathbf{A}_3)^{-1}, \quad \in \mathbf{B}_3 = -\mathbf{A}_1^{-1}\mathbf{A}_3\mathbf{B}_4, \quad \mathbf{B}_2 = -\mathbf{B}_4\mathbf{A}_2\mathbf{A}_1^{-1}, \quad \mathbf{B}_1 = \mathbf{A}_1^{-1} - \mathbf{A}_1^{-1}\mathbf{A}_3\mathbf{B}_2,
\tag{4.607}
$$

with the conditions that $\mathbf{A}_4 - \mathbf{A}_2\mathbf{A}_1^{-1}\mathbf{A}_3$ and $\mathbf{A}_1$ be invertible matrices.

Let us choose

$$
\mathbf{A}_1 = [1], \quad \mathbf{A}_2 = \begin{bmatrix} 0 \\ 5 \end{bmatrix}, \quad \mathbf{A}_3 = [2 \quad -1], \quad \mathbf{A}_4 = \begin{bmatrix} 3 & 4 \\ 6 & -2 \end{bmatrix},
\tag{4.608}
$$

from which

$$\mathbf{A}_1^{-1} = [1], \tag{4.609}$$

$$\mathbf{B}_4 = \mathbf{A}_4 - \mathbf{A}_2\mathbf{A}_1^{-1}\mathbf{A}_3 = \begin{bmatrix} 3 & 4 \\ 6 & -2 \end{bmatrix} - \begin{bmatrix} 0 \\ 5 \end{bmatrix}[1]\begin{bmatrix} 2 & -1 \end{bmatrix} = \begin{bmatrix} 3 & 4 \\ -4 & 3 \end{bmatrix}, \tag{4.610}$$

$$(\mathbf{A}_4 - \mathbf{A}_2\mathbf{A}_1^{-1}\mathbf{A}_3)^{-1} = \frac{1}{25}\begin{bmatrix} 3 & -4 \\ 4 & 3 \end{bmatrix}, \tag{4.611}$$

$$\mathbf{B}_3 = -[1]\begin{bmatrix} 2 & -1 \end{bmatrix}\frac{1}{25}\begin{bmatrix} 3 & -4 \\ 4 & 3 \end{bmatrix} = \frac{1}{25}\begin{bmatrix} 2 & 11 \end{bmatrix}, \tag{4.612}$$

$$\mathbf{B}_2 = -\frac{1}{25}\begin{bmatrix} 3 & -4 \\ 4 & 3 \end{bmatrix}\begin{bmatrix} 0 \\ 5 \end{bmatrix} = \frac{1}{25}\begin{bmatrix} 20 \\ -15 \end{bmatrix}, \tag{4.613}$$

$$\mathbf{B}_1 = -[1] - [1]\begin{bmatrix} 2 & -1 \end{bmatrix}\frac{1}{25}\begin{bmatrix} 20 \\ -15 \end{bmatrix} = -\begin{bmatrix} 6 \\ 5 \end{bmatrix}. \tag{4.614}$$

We obtained thus the same inverse (4.597).

To determine the inverse using the iterative method (Schulz) we shall consider an approximation $\mathbf{B}_0$ of $\mathbf{A}^{-1}$, given by

$$\mathbf{B}_0 = \begin{bmatrix} -1.23 & -0.1 & 0.46 \\ 0.77 & 0.13 & -0.15 \\ -0.62 & 0.17 & 0.11 \end{bmatrix}. \tag{4.615}$$

We deduce

$$\mathbf{C}_0 = \mathbf{I}_3 - \mathbf{A}\mathbf{B}_0 = \begin{bmatrix} 0.07 & 0.01 & -0.05 \\ 0.17 & -0.07 & 0.01 \\ 0.29 & 0.06 & -0.18 \end{bmatrix}, \tag{4.616}$$

$$\|\mathbf{C}_0\|_\infty = 0.53, \tag{4.617}$$

so that we may apply Schulz's method.

There follows, successively,

$$\mathbf{B}_1 = \mathbf{B}_0 + \mathbf{B}_0\mathbf{C}_0 = \begin{bmatrix} -1.1997 & -0.0777 & 0.4377 \\ 0.8025 & 0.1196 & -0.1602 \\ -0.6026 & 0.1595 & 0.1229 \end{bmatrix}, \tag{4.618}$$

$$\mathbf{C}_1 = \mathbf{I}_3 - \mathbf{A}\mathbf{B}_1 = \begin{bmatrix} -0.0079 & -0.002 & 0.0056 \\ 0.0029 & 0.0032 & -0.011 \\ -0.0217 & -0.0101 & 0.0185 \end{bmatrix}, \tag{4.619}$$

$$\mathbf{B}_2 = \mathbf{B}_1 + \mathbf{B}_1\mathbf{C}_1 = \begin{bmatrix} -1.199946 & -0.079970 & 0.439934 \\ 0.799983 & 0.119996 & -0.159985 \\ -0.600044 & 0.159974 & 0.120045 \end{bmatrix}. \tag{4.620}$$

The procedure may, obviously, continue, the exact value of the inverse being

$$\mathbf{A}^{-1} = \lim_{n \to \infty} \mathbf{B}_n = \begin{bmatrix} -1.2 & -0.08 & 0.44 \\ 0.8 & 0.12 & -0.16 \\ -0.6 & 0.16 & 0.12 \end{bmatrix}. \tag{4.621}$$

Another possibility to determine $\mathbf{A}^{-1}$ consists in the use of the characteristic polynomial of the matrix $\mathbf{A}$. To do this, we calculate

$$\begin{vmatrix} 1-\lambda & 2 & -1 \\ 0 & 3-\lambda & 4 \\ 5 & 6 & -2-\lambda \end{vmatrix} = -\lambda^3 + 2\lambda^2 + 24\lambda + 25, \tag{4.622}$$

which leads to the equation

$$\mathbf{A}^3 + 2\mathbf{A}^2 + 24\mathbf{A} + 25\mathbf{I}_3 = \mathbf{O}_3, \tag{4.623}$$

from which, multiplying by $\mathbf{A}^{-1}$, we get

$$-\mathbf{A}^2 + 2\mathbf{A} + 24\mathbf{I}_3 = -25\mathbf{A}^{-1}; \tag{4.624}$$

hence

$$\mathbf{A}^{-1} = \frac{1}{25}(\mathbf{A}^2 - 2\mathbf{A} - 24\mathbf{I}_3). \tag{4.625}$$

But

$$\mathbf{A}^2 = \begin{bmatrix} 1 & 2 & -1 \\ 0 & 3 & 4 \\ 5 & 6 & -2 \end{bmatrix} \begin{bmatrix} 1 & 2 & -1 \\ 0 & 3 & 4 \\ 5 & 6 & -2 \end{bmatrix} = \begin{bmatrix} -4 & 2 & 9 \\ 20 & 33 & 4 \\ -5 & 16 & 23 \end{bmatrix} \tag{4.626}$$

and it follows that

$$\mathbf{A}^{-1} = \frac{1}{25}\left(\begin{bmatrix} -4 & 2 & 9 \\ 20 & 33 & 4 \\ -5 & 16 & 23 \end{bmatrix} - 2\begin{bmatrix} 1 & 2 & -1 \\ 0 & 3 & 4 \\ 5 & 6 & -2 \end{bmatrix} - 24\begin{bmatrix} 1 & 0 & 0 \\ 0 & 1 & 0 \\ 0 & 0 & 1 \end{bmatrix} \right) = -\frac{1}{25}\begin{bmatrix} -30 & -2 & 11 \\ 20 & 3 & -4 \\ -15 & 4 & 3 \end{bmatrix}. \tag{4.627}$$

Let us now calculate the inverse of $\mathbf{A}$, using the Frame–Fadeev method. We have successively

$$\mathbf{A}_1 = \mathbf{A} = \begin{bmatrix} 1 & 2 & -1 \\ 0 & 3 & 4 \\ 5 & 6 & -2 \end{bmatrix}, \quad \sigma_1 = -\mathrm{Tr}(\mathbf{A}_1) = -2,$$

$$\mathbf{B}_1 = \mathbf{A}_1 + \sigma_1\mathbf{I}_3 = \begin{bmatrix} -1 & 2 & -1 \\ 0 & 1 & 4 \\ 5 & 6 & -4 \end{bmatrix}, \tag{4.628}$$

$$\mathbf{A}_2 = \mathbf{A}\mathbf{B}_1 = \begin{bmatrix} -6 & -2 & 11 \\ 20 & 27 & -4 \\ -15 & 4 & 27 \end{bmatrix}, \quad \sigma_2 = -\frac{1}{2}\mathrm{Tr}(\mathbf{A}_2) = -24,$$

$$\mathbf{B}_2 = \mathbf{A}_2 + \sigma_2\mathbf{I}_3 = \begin{bmatrix} -30 & -2 & 11 \\ 20 & 3 & -4 \\ -15 & 4 & 3 \end{bmatrix}, \tag{4.629}$$

$$\mathbf{A}_3 = \mathbf{A}\mathbf{B}_2 = \begin{bmatrix} 25 & 0 & 0 \\ 0 & 25 & 0 \\ 0 & 0 & 25 \end{bmatrix}, \quad \sigma_3 = -\frac{1}{3}\mathrm{Tr}(\mathbf{A}_3) = -25,$$

$$\mathbf{B}_3 = \mathbf{A}_3 + \sigma_3\mathbf{I}_3 = \begin{bmatrix} 0 & 0 & 0 \\ 0 & 0 & 0 \\ 0 & 0 & 0 \end{bmatrix}; \tag{4.630}$$

hence

$$\mathbf{A}^{-1} = -\frac{1}{\sigma_3}\mathbf{B}_2 = \frac{1}{25}\begin{bmatrix} -30 & -2 & 11 \\ 20 & 3 & -4 \\ -15 & 4 & 3 \end{bmatrix}. \tag{4.631}$$

To determine the inverse of **A** by Schur's method, let us consider

$$\mathbf{A} = \begin{bmatrix} \mathbf{A}_1 & \mathbf{A}_2 \\ \mathbf{A}_3 & \mathbf{A}_4 \end{bmatrix}, \tag{4.632}$$

where

$$\mathbf{A}_1 = [1], \quad \mathbf{A}_2 = [2 \quad -1], \quad \mathbf{A}_3 = \begin{bmatrix} 0 \\ 5 \end{bmatrix}, \quad \mathbf{A}_4 = \begin{bmatrix} 3 & 4 \\ 6 & -2 \end{bmatrix}. \tag{4.633}$$

We have

$$\mathbf{A}_4^{-1} = -\frac{1}{30}\begin{bmatrix} -2 & -4 \\ -6 & 3 \end{bmatrix}, \tag{4.634}$$

$$\mathbf{A}_2\mathbf{A}_4^{-1} = -\frac{1}{30}[2 \quad -1]\begin{bmatrix} -2 & -4 \\ -6 & 3 \end{bmatrix} = -\frac{1}{30}[2 \quad -11], \tag{4.635}$$

$$\mathbf{A}_4^{-1}\mathbf{A}_3 = -\frac{1}{30}\begin{bmatrix} -2 & -4 \\ -6 & 3 \end{bmatrix}\begin{bmatrix} 0 \\ 5 \end{bmatrix} = -\frac{1}{30}\begin{bmatrix} -20 \\ 15 \end{bmatrix}, \tag{4.636}$$

$$\mathbf{A}_2\mathbf{A}_4^{-1}\mathbf{A}_3 = -\frac{1}{30}[2 \quad -11]\begin{bmatrix} 0 \\ 5 \end{bmatrix} = \begin{bmatrix} 11 \\ 6 \end{bmatrix}, \tag{4.637}$$

$$\mathbf{A}_1 - \mathbf{A}_2\mathbf{A}_4^{-1}\mathbf{A}_3 = \begin{bmatrix} -\frac{5}{6} \end{bmatrix}, \quad (\mathbf{A}_1 - \mathbf{A}_2\mathbf{A}_4^{-1}\mathbf{A}_3)^{-1} = \begin{bmatrix} -\frac{6}{5} \end{bmatrix}. \tag{4.638}$$

We may write

$$\mathbf{A} = \begin{bmatrix} 1 & 2 & -1 \\ 0 & 3 & 4 \\ 5 & 6 & -2 \end{bmatrix} = \begin{bmatrix} 1 & -\frac{2}{30} & \frac{11}{30} \\ 0 & 1 & 0 \\ 0 & 0 & 1 \end{bmatrix}\begin{bmatrix} -\frac{5}{6} & 0 & 0 \\ 0 & 3 & 4 \\ 0 & 6 & -2 \end{bmatrix}\begin{bmatrix} 1 & 0 & 0 \\ \frac{2}{3} & 1 & 0 \\ -\frac{1}{2} & 0 & 1 \end{bmatrix}, \tag{4.639}$$

$$\mathbf{A}^{-1} = \begin{bmatrix} 1 & 0 & 0 \\ -\frac{2}{3} & 1 & 0 \\ \frac{1}{2} & 0 & 1 \end{bmatrix}\begin{bmatrix} -\frac{6}{5} & 0 & 0 \\ 0 & \frac{1}{15} & \frac{2}{15} \\ 0 & \frac{1}{5} & -\frac{1}{10} \end{bmatrix}\begin{bmatrix} 1 & \frac{1}{15} & -\frac{11}{30} \\ 0 & 1 & 0 \\ 0 & 0 & 1 \end{bmatrix} = \begin{bmatrix} -\frac{6}{5} & -\frac{2}{25} & \frac{11}{25} \\ \frac{4}{5} & \frac{3}{25} & -\frac{4}{25} \\ -\frac{3}{5} & \frac{4}{25} & \frac{3}{25} \end{bmatrix}. \tag{4.640}$$

Example 4.4   Let the linear system be

$$10x_1 + 2x_2 - x_3 = 7, \quad 2x_1 + 8x_2 + x_3 = -5, \quad x_1 + x_2 + 10x_3 = 8, \tag{4.641}$$

the solution of which is required.

If we wish to apply Cramer's rule, then we must calculate the determinants

$$\Delta = \begin{vmatrix} 10 & 2 & -1 \\ 2 & 8 & 1 \\ -1 & 1 & 10 \end{vmatrix} = 738, \quad \Delta_1 = \begin{vmatrix} 7 & 2 & -1 \\ -5 & 8 & 1 \\ 8 & 1 & 10 \end{vmatrix} = 738,$$

$$\Delta_2 = \begin{vmatrix} 10 & 7 & -1 \\ 2 & -5 & 1 \\ -1 & 8 & 10 \end{vmatrix} = -738, \quad \Delta_3 = \begin{vmatrix} 10 & 2 & 7 \\ 2 & 8 & -5 \\ -1 & 1 & 8 \end{vmatrix} = 738, \tag{4.642}$$

wherefrom

$$x_1 = \frac{\Delta_1}{\Delta} = 1, \quad x_2 = \frac{\Delta_2}{\Delta} = -1, \quad x_3 = \frac{\Delta_3}{\Delta} = 1. \tag{4.643}$$

To solve the same problem by Gauss's method, we multiply the first equation in system (4.641) by $-1/5$ and by $1/10$ and we will add it to the second and third equations (4.642) and (4.643), respectively, obtaining

$$10x_1 + 2x_2 - x_3 = 7, \quad \frac{38}{5}x_2 + \frac{6}{5}x_3 = -\frac{32}{5}, \quad \frac{6}{5}x_2 + \frac{99}{10}x_3 = \frac{87}{10}. \tag{4.644}$$

We now multiply the second equation in system (4.644) by $-3/19$ and add it to the third equation (4.644), resulting in the system

$$10x_1 + 2x_2 - x_3 = 7, \quad \frac{38}{5}x_2 + \frac{6}{5}x_3 = -\frac{32}{5}, \quad \frac{369}{38}x_3 = \frac{369}{38}, \tag{4.645}$$

with the solution

$$x_3 = 1, \quad x_2 = -1, \quad x_1 = 1. \tag{4.646}$$

The first step in solving by the Gauss–Jordan method leads to the same system (4.644). We now multiply the second equation by $-5/19$ and by $-3/19$ and add it to the first and to the third equations of system (4.644), respectively, obtaining

$$10x_1 - \frac{25}{19}x_3 = \frac{165}{19}, \quad \frac{38}{5}x_2 + \frac{6}{5}x_3 = -\frac{32}{5}, \quad \frac{369}{38}x_3 = \frac{369}{38}. \tag{4.647}$$

We now multiply the third equation of system (4.647) by $50/369$ and $-76/615$, and add it to the first and second equations (4.641) and (4.642), respectively, obtaining

$$10x_1 = 10, \quad \frac{38}{5}x_2 = -\frac{38}{5}, \quad \frac{369}{38}x_3 = \frac{369}{38} \tag{4.648}$$

and the solution

$$x_1 = 1, \quad x_2 = -1, \quad x_3 = 1. \tag{4.649}$$

Applying the Doolittle method of factorization LU, we are led to

$$\begin{bmatrix} 1 & 0 & 0 \\ l_{21} & 1 & 0 \\ l_{31} & l_{32} & 1 \end{bmatrix} \begin{bmatrix} u_{11} & u_{12} & u_{13} \\ 0 & u_{22} & u_{23} \\ 0 & 0 & u_{33} \end{bmatrix} = \begin{bmatrix} 10 & 2 & -1 \\ 2 & 8 & 1 \\ -1 & 1 & 10 \end{bmatrix}, \tag{4.650}$$

wherefrom we obtain the system

$$u_{11} = 10, \quad u_{12} = 2, \quad u_{13} = -1, \quad l_{21}u_{11} = 2, \quad l_{21}u_{12} + u_{22} = 8, \quad l_{21}u_{13} + u_{23} = 1,$$

$$l_{31}u_{11} = -1, \quad l_{31}u_{12} + l_{32}u_{22} = 1, \quad l_{31}u_{13} + l_{32}u_{23} + u_{33} = 10, \tag{4.651}$$

with the solution

$$u_{11} = 10, \ u_{12} = 2, \ u_{13} = -1, \ l_{21} = \frac{1}{5}, \ u_{22} = \frac{38}{5}, \ u_{23} = \frac{6}{5}, \ l_{31} = -\frac{1}{10}, \ l_{32} = \frac{3}{19},$$

$$u_{33} = \frac{369}{38}. \tag{4.652}$$

There results

$$L = \begin{bmatrix} 1 & 0 & 0 \\ \dfrac{1}{5} & 1 & 0 \\ -\dfrac{1}{10} & \dfrac{3}{19} & 1 \end{bmatrix}, \quad U = \begin{bmatrix} 10 & 2 & -1 \\ 0 & \dfrac{38}{5} & \dfrac{6}{5} \\ 0 & 0 & \dfrac{369}{38} \end{bmatrix}. \tag{4.653}$$

We denote

$$Ux = y \tag{4.654}$$

and solve the system

$$Ly = b, \tag{4.655}$$

that is

$$y_1 = 7, \quad \frac{1}{5}y_1 + y_2 = -5, \quad -\frac{1}{10}y_1 + \frac{3}{19}y_2 + y_3 = 8, \tag{4.656}$$

wherefrom

$$y_1 = 7, \quad y_2 = -\frac{32}{5}, \quad y_3 = \frac{369}{38}. \tag{4.657}$$

Expression (4.654) leads to the system

$$10x_1 + 2x_2 - x_3 = 7, \quad \frac{38}{5}x_2 + \frac{6}{5}x_3 = -\frac{32}{5}, \quad \frac{369}{38}x_3 = \frac{369}{38}, \tag{4.658}$$

with the known solution (4.649).

The Crout method leads to

$$\begin{bmatrix} l_{11} & 0 & 0 \\ l_{21} & l_{22} & 0 \\ l_{31} & l_{32} & l_{33} \end{bmatrix} \begin{bmatrix} 1 & u_{12} & u_{13} \\ 0 & 1 & u_{23} \\ 0 & 0 & 1 \end{bmatrix} = \begin{bmatrix} 10 & 2 & -1 \\ 2 & 8 & 1 \\ -1 & 1 & 10 \end{bmatrix}, \tag{4.659}$$

wherefrom

$$l_{11} = 10, \quad l_{11}u_{12} = 2, \quad l_{11}u_{13} = -1, \quad l_{21} = 2, \quad l_{21}u_{12} + l_{22} = 8, \quad l_{21}u_{13} + l_{22}u_{23} = 1,$$

$$l_{31} = -1, \quad l_{31}u_{12} + l_{32} = 1, \quad l_{31}u_{13} + l_{32}u_{23} + l_{33} = 10, \tag{4.660}$$

with the solution

$$l_{11} = 10, \quad u_{12} = \frac{1}{5}, \quad u_{13} = -\frac{1}{10}, \quad l_{22} = \frac{38}{5}, \quad u_{23} = \frac{3}{19}, \quad l_{31} = -1; \tag{4.661}$$

hence

$$L = \begin{bmatrix} 10 & 0 & 0 \\ 2 & \dfrac{38}{5} & 0 \\ -1 & \dfrac{6}{5} & \dfrac{369}{38} \end{bmatrix}, \quad U = \begin{bmatrix} 1 & \dfrac{1}{5} & -\dfrac{1}{10} \\ 0 & 1 & \dfrac{3}{19} \\ 0 & 0 & 1 \end{bmatrix}. \tag{4.662}$$

This results in the system

$$10y_1 = 7, \quad 2y_1 + \frac{38}{5}y_2 = -5, \quad -y_1 + \frac{6}{5}y_2 + \frac{369}{38}y_3 = 8, \tag{4.663}$$

with the solution

$$y_1 = \frac{7}{10}, \quad y_2 = -\frac{16}{19}, \quad y_3 = 1, \tag{4.664}$$

and the system

$$x_1 + \frac{1}{5}x_2 - \frac{1}{10}x_3 = \frac{7}{10}, \quad x_2 + \frac{3}{19}x_3 = -\frac{16}{19}, \quad x_3 = 1, \tag{4.665}$$

with the same solution (4.649).

To apply the Cholesky method, we must verify that the matrix $\mathbf{A}$ is symmetric (obviously!) and positive definite.

We have

$$\mathbf{A} = \begin{bmatrix} 10 & 2 & -1 \\ 2 & 8 & 1 \\ -1 & 1 & 10 \end{bmatrix}, \tag{4.666}$$

$$\mathbf{x}^T\mathbf{A}\mathbf{x} = \begin{bmatrix} x_1 & x_2 & x_3 \end{bmatrix} \begin{bmatrix} 10 & 2 & -1 \\ 2 & 8 & 1 \\ -1 & 1 & 10 \end{bmatrix} \begin{bmatrix} x_1 \\ x_2 \\ x_3 \end{bmatrix}$$

$$= (2x_1 + x_2)^2 + (x_1 - x_3)^2 + (x_2 + x_3)^2 + 5x_1^2 + 6x_2^2 + 8x_3^2 > 0, \tag{4.667}$$

for any $\mathbf{x} \neq 0$.

Hence, we may apply the Cholesky method in which

$$\mathbf{L} = \begin{bmatrix} l_{11} & 0 & 0 \\ l_{21} & l_{22} & 0 \\ l_{31} & l_{32} & l_{33} \end{bmatrix}, \quad \mathbf{U} = \begin{bmatrix} l_{11} & l_{21} & l_{31} \\ 0 & l_{22} & l_{32} \\ 0 & 0 & l_{33} \end{bmatrix}. \tag{4.668}$$

It results the system

$$l_{11}^2 = 10, \quad l_{11}l_{21} = 2, \quad l_{11}l_{31} = -1, \quad l_{21}l_{11} = 2, \quad l_{21}^2 + l_{22}^2 = 8, \quad l_{21}l_{31} + l_{22}l_{32} = 1,$$
$$l_{31}l_{11} = -1, \quad l_{31}l_{21} + l_{32}l_{22} = 1, \quad l_{31}^2 + l_{32}^2 + l_{33}^2 = 10, \tag{4.669}$$

with the solution

$$l_{11} = \sqrt{10}, \quad l_{21} = \frac{2}{\sqrt{10}}, \quad l_{31} = -\frac{1}{\sqrt{10}}, \quad l_{22} = \sqrt{\frac{38}{5}}, \quad l_{32} = \frac{6}{\sqrt{190}}, \quad l_{33} = \sqrt{\frac{369}{38}}, \tag{4.670}$$

so that

$$\mathbf{L} = \begin{bmatrix} \sqrt{10} & 0 & 0 \\ \frac{2}{\sqrt{10}} & \sqrt{\frac{38}{5}} & 0 \\ -\frac{1}{\sqrt{10}} & \frac{6}{\sqrt{190}} & \sqrt{\frac{369}{38}} \end{bmatrix}, \quad \mathbf{U} = \begin{bmatrix} \sqrt{10} & \frac{2}{\sqrt{10}} & -\frac{1}{\sqrt{10}} \\ 0 & \sqrt{\frac{38}{5}} & \frac{6}{\sqrt{190}} \\ 0 & 0 & \sqrt{\frac{369}{38}} \end{bmatrix}. \tag{4.671}$$

We obtain the systems

$$\sqrt{10}y_1 = 7, \quad \frac{2}{\sqrt{10}}y_1 + \sqrt{\frac{38}{5}}y_2 = -5, \quad -\frac{1}{\sqrt{10}}y_1 + \frac{6}{\sqrt{190}}y_2 + \sqrt{\frac{369}{38}}y_3 = 8, \tag{4.672}$$

with the solution

$$y_1 = \frac{7}{\sqrt{10}}, \quad y_2 = -\frac{32}{\sqrt{190}}, \quad y_3 = \sqrt{\frac{369}{38}}, \tag{4.673}$$

and

$$\sqrt{10}x_1 + \frac{2}{\sqrt{10}}x_2 - \frac{1}{\sqrt{10}}x_3 = \frac{7}{\sqrt{10}}, \quad \sqrt{\frac{38}{5}}x_2 + \frac{6}{\sqrt{190}}x_3 = -\frac{32}{\sqrt{190}}, \quad \sqrt{\frac{369}{38}}x_3 = \sqrt{\frac{369}{38}},$$
$$\tag{4.674}$$

respectively, wherefrom results solution (4.649).

To solve system (4.641) by the iteration (Jacobi) method, we write it in the form

$$x_1 = 0.7 - 0.2x_2 + 0.1x_3, \quad x_2 = -0.625 - 0.25x_1 - 0.125x_3, \quad x_3 = 0.8 + 0.1x_1 - 0.1x_2,$$
$$\tag{4.675}$$

the matrices $\boldsymbol{\alpha}$ and $\boldsymbol{\beta}$ having the expressions

$$\boldsymbol{\alpha} = \begin{bmatrix} 0 & -0.2 & 0.1 \\ -0.25 & 0 & -0.125 \\ 0.1 & -0.1 & 0 \end{bmatrix}, \quad \boldsymbol{\beta} = \begin{bmatrix} 0.7 \\ -0.625 \\ 0.8 \end{bmatrix}. \tag{4.676}$$

We choose

$$\mathbf{x}^{(0)} = \boldsymbol{\beta}, \tag{4.677}$$

the iteration formula being

$$\mathbf{x}^{(n+1)} = \boldsymbol{\alpha}\mathbf{x}^{(n)} + \boldsymbol{\beta}. \tag{4.678}$$

Let us observe that

$$\|\boldsymbol{\alpha}\|_\infty = 0.375 < 1, \tag{4.679}$$

so that the Jacobi method may be applied.

We have successively

$$\mathbf{x}^{(1)} = \boldsymbol{\alpha}\mathbf{x}^{(0)} + \boldsymbol{\beta} = \begin{bmatrix} 0 & -0.2 & 0.1 \\ -0.25 & 0 & -0.125 \\ 0.1 & -0.1 & 0 \end{bmatrix} \begin{bmatrix} 0.7 \\ -0.625 \\ 0.8 \end{bmatrix} + \begin{bmatrix} 0.7 \\ -0.625 \\ 0.8 \end{bmatrix} = \begin{bmatrix} 0.905 \\ -0.9 \\ 0.9325 \end{bmatrix}, \tag{4.680}$$

$$\mathbf{x}^{(2)} = \boldsymbol{\alpha}\mathbf{x}^{(1)} + \boldsymbol{\beta} = \begin{bmatrix} 0 & -0.2 & 0.1 \\ -0.25 & 0 & -0.125 \\ 0.1 & -0.1 & 0 \end{bmatrix} \begin{bmatrix} 0.905 \\ -0.9 \\ 0.9325 \end{bmatrix} + \begin{bmatrix} 0.7 \\ -0.625 \\ 0.8 \end{bmatrix} = \begin{bmatrix} 0.97325 \\ -0.9678125 \\ 0.9805 \end{bmatrix},$$
$$\tag{4.681}$$

$$\mathbf{x}^{(3)} = \boldsymbol{\alpha}\mathbf{x}^{(2)} + \boldsymbol{\beta} = \begin{bmatrix} 0.9916125 \\ -0.990875 \\ 0.99410625 \end{bmatrix}, \quad \mathbf{x}^{(4)} = \boldsymbol{\alpha}\mathbf{x}^{(3)} + \boldsymbol{\beta} = \begin{bmatrix} 0.997585625 \\ -0.997166406 \\ 0.99824875 \end{bmatrix}. \tag{4.682}$$

The procedure may continue, so that at the limit, we obtain

$$\overline{\mathbf{x}} = \lim_{n \to \infty} \mathbf{x}^{(n)} = \begin{bmatrix} 1 \\ -1 \\ 1 \end{bmatrix}. \tag{4.683}$$

The solution of system (4.641) may be determined by means of the Gauss–Seidel method too. In this case, the iteration formulae read

$$x_1^{(n+1)} = 0.7 - 0.2x_2^{(n)} + 0.1x_3^{(n)}, \quad x_2^{(n+1)} = -0.625 - 0.25x_1^{(n+1)} - 0.125x_3^{(n)},$$
$$x_3^{(n+1)} = 0.8 + 0.1x_1^{(n+1)} - 0.1x_2^{(n+1)}. \tag{4.684}$$

It results successively in

$$x_1^{(1)} = 0.7 + 0.2 \cdot 0.625 + 0.1 \cdot 0.8 = 0.905,$$

$$x_2^{(1)} = -0.625 - 0.2 \cdot 0.905 + 0.125 \cdot 0.8 = -0.95125,$$

$$x_3^{(1)} = 0.8 + 0.1 \cdot 0.905 + 0.1 \cdot 0.95125 = 0.985625, \tag{4.685}$$

$$x_1^{(2)} = 0.7 + 0.2 \times 0.95125 + 0.1 \times 0.985625 = 0.9888125,$$

$$x_2^{(2)} = -0.625 - 0.25 \times 0.9888125 - 0.125 \times 0.985625 = -0.99540625,$$

$$x_3^{(2)} = 0.8 + 0.1 \times 0.9888125 + 0.1 \times 0.99540625 = 0.998421875, \tag{4.686}$$

$$x_1^{(3)} = 0.998923437, \quad x_2^{(3)} = -0.999533593, \quad x_3^{(3)} = 0.999845703, \tag{4.687}$$

$$x_1^{(4)} = 0.999891288, \quad x_2^{(4)} = -0.999953534, \quad x_3^{(4)} = 0.999984482. \tag{4.688}$$

The procedure continues by obtaining at the limit, for $n \to \infty$, solution (4.649).

If we wish to solve the problem by the relaxation method, then we write system (4.641) in the form

$$x_1 + 0.2x_2 - 0.1x_3 - 0.7 = 0, \quad x_2 + 0.25x_1 + 0.125x_3 + 0.625 = 0,$$
$$x_3 - 0.1x_1 + 0.1x_2 - 0.8 = 0. \tag{4.689}$$

Let us replace in equation (4.689) the values given by $\mathbf{x}^{(0)}$. It follows that

$$0.7 - 0.2 \times 0.625 - 0.1 \times 0.8 - 0.7 = -0.205 = R_1^{(0)},$$

$$-0.625 + 0.25 \times 0.7 + 0.125 \times 0.8 + 0.625 = -0.275 = R_2^{(0)},$$

$$0.8 - 0.1 \times 0.7 - 0.1 \times 0.625 - 0.8 = -0.1325 = R_3^{(0)}. \tag{4.690}$$

The greatest remainder in modulus is $R_2^{(0)}$, so that

$$\mathbf{x}^{(1)} = \mathbf{x}^{(0)} + \begin{bmatrix} 0 \\ -0.275 \\ 0 \end{bmatrix} = \begin{bmatrix} 0.7 \\ -0.9 \\ 0.8 \end{bmatrix}. \tag{4.691}$$

We now replace in system (4.689) the values given by $\mathbf{x}^{(1)}$, obtaining the remainders

$$0.7 - 0.2 \times 0.9 - 0.1 \times 0.8 - 0.7 = -0.26 = R_1^{(1)},$$

$$-0.9 - 0.25 \times 0.7 + 0.125 \times 0.8 + 0.625 = 0 = R_2^{(1)},$$

$$0.8 - 0.1 \times 0.7 - 0.1 \times 0.9 - 0.8 = -0.16 = R_3^{(1)}; \tag{4.692}$$

the greatest remainder in modulus is $R_1^{(1)}$, hence

$$\mathbf{x}^{(2)} = \mathbf{x}^{(1)} + \begin{bmatrix} 0.26 \\ 0 \\ 0 \end{bmatrix} = \begin{bmatrix} 0.96 \\ -0.9 \\ 0.8 \end{bmatrix}. \tag{4.693}$$

Continuing the procedure, we obtain the values

$$\mathbf{x}^{(3)} = \begin{bmatrix} 0.96 \\ -0.9 \\ 0.986 \end{bmatrix}, \quad \mathbf{x}^{(4)} = \begin{bmatrix} 0.96 \\ -0.98825 \\ 0.986 \end{bmatrix}, \quad \mathbf{x}^{(5)} = \begin{bmatrix} 0.99625 \\ -0.98825 \\ 0.986 \end{bmatrix}, \quad \mathbf{x}^{(6)} = \begin{bmatrix} 0.99625 \\ -0.98825 \\ 0.99845 \end{bmatrix},$$

$$\mathbf{x}^{(7)} = \begin{bmatrix} 0.99625 \\ -0.9988687 \\ 0.99845 \end{bmatrix}, \dots \tag{4.694}$$

To apply Schur's method, we write the matrix

$$\mathbf{A} = \begin{bmatrix} 10 & 2 & -1 \\ 2 & 8 & 1 \\ -1 & 1 & 10 \end{bmatrix} \tag{4.695}$$

in the form

$$\mathbf{A} = \begin{bmatrix} \mathbf{A}_1 & \mathbf{A}_2 \\ \mathbf{A}_3 & \mathbf{A}_4 \end{bmatrix}, \tag{4.696}$$

where

$$\mathbf{A}_1 = \begin{bmatrix} 10 & 2 \\ 2 & 8 \end{bmatrix}, \quad \mathbf{A}_2 = \begin{bmatrix} -1 \\ 1 \end{bmatrix}, \quad \mathbf{A}_3 = [-1 \quad 1], \quad \mathbf{A}_4 = [10]. \tag{4.697}$$

The vectors

$$\mathbf{x} = \begin{bmatrix} x_1 \\ x_2 \\ x_3 \end{bmatrix}, \quad \mathbf{b} = \begin{bmatrix} 7 \\ -5 \\ 8 \end{bmatrix}, \tag{4.698}$$

are written in the form

$$\mathbf{x} = \begin{bmatrix} \mathbf{x}_1 \\ \mathbf{x}_2 \end{bmatrix}, \quad \mathbf{b} = \begin{bmatrix} \mathbf{b}_1 \\ \mathbf{b}_2 \end{bmatrix}, \tag{4.699}$$

where

$$\mathbf{x}_1 = \begin{bmatrix} x_1 \\ x_2 \end{bmatrix}, \quad \mathbf{x}_2 = [x_3], \quad \mathbf{b}_1 = \begin{bmatrix} 7 \\ -5 \end{bmatrix}, \quad \mathbf{b}_2 = [8]. \tag{4.700}$$

It follows that

$$\mathbf{x}_1 = (\mathbf{A}_1 - \mathbf{A}_2 \mathbf{A}_4^{-1} \mathbf{A}_3)^{-1} (\mathbf{b}_1 - \mathbf{A}_2 \mathbf{A}_4^{-1} \mathbf{b}_2), \tag{4.701}$$

$$\mathbf{x}_2 = \mathbf{A}_4^{-1} \mathbf{b}_2 - \mathbf{A}_4^{-1} \mathbf{A}_3 \mathbf{x}_1. \tag{4.702}$$

Effecting the necessary calculations, we obtain

$$\mathbf{A}_4^{-1} = \begin{bmatrix} \dfrac{1}{10} \end{bmatrix}, \tag{4.703}$$

$$\mathbf{A}_1 - \mathbf{A}_2\mathbf{A}_4^{-1}\mathbf{A}_3 = \frac{1}{10}\begin{bmatrix} 99 & 21 \\ 21 & 79 \end{bmatrix}, \quad (\mathbf{A}_1 - \mathbf{A}_2\mathbf{A}_4^{-1}\mathbf{A}_3)^{-1} = \frac{1}{738}\begin{bmatrix} 79 & -21 \\ -21 & 99 \end{bmatrix}, \quad (4.704)$$

$$\mathbf{b}_1 - \mathbf{A}_2\mathbf{A}_4^{-1}\mathbf{b}_2 = \frac{1}{10}\begin{bmatrix} 78 \\ -58 \end{bmatrix}, \quad (4.705)$$

$$\mathbf{x}_1 = \frac{1}{7380}\begin{bmatrix} 79 & -21 \\ -21 & 99 \end{bmatrix}\begin{bmatrix} 78 \\ -58 \end{bmatrix} = \begin{bmatrix} 1 \\ -1 \end{bmatrix} \quad (4.706)$$

$$\mathbf{x}_2 = \frac{1}{10}[8] - \frac{1}{10}[-1 \quad 1]\begin{bmatrix} 1 \\ -1 \end{bmatrix} = [1]. \quad (4.707)$$

System (4.641) may be solved by the Monte Carlo method too. To do this, we write it in the form

$$x_1 = -0.2x_2 + 0.1x_3 + 0.7, \quad x_2 = -0.25x_1 - 0.125x_3 - 0.625, \quad x_3 = 0.1x_1 - 0.1x_2 + 0.8 \quad (4.708)$$

and the matrix $\mathbf{H}$ becomes

$$\mathbf{H} = \begin{bmatrix} 0 & 0.2 & 0.1 & 0.7 \\ 0.25 & 0 & 0.125 & 0.625 \\ 0.1 & 0.1 & 0 & 0.8 \\ 0 & 0 & 0 & 1 \end{bmatrix}. \quad (4.709)$$

For the initial state S_1, we may write as follows:

- If $0 \le x < 0.2$, then we pass to the state S_2.
- If $0.2 \le x < 0.3$, then we pass to the state S_3.
- If $0.3 \le x < 1$, then we pass in the final state S_4.

For the initial state S_2, we have the following:

- If $0 \le x < 0.25$, then we pass to the state S_1.
- If $0.25 \le x < 0.375$, then we pass to the state S_3.
- If $0.375 \le x < 1$, then we pass to the final state S_4.

Finally, for the initial state S_3 we get the following:

- If $0 \le x < 0.1$, then we pass to the state S_1.
- If $0.1 \le x < 0.2$, then we pass to the state S_2.
- If $0.2 \le x < 1$, then we pass to the final state S_4.

Moreover,

$$v_{11} = 0, \quad v_{12} = -1, \quad v_{13} = 1, \quad v_{21} = -1, \quad v_{22} = 0, \quad v_{23} = -1, \quad v_{31} = 1,$$

$$v_{32} = -1, \quad v_{33} = 0. \quad (4.710)$$

There have been 1000 simulations made for each unknown x_i, $i = \overline{1, 3}$, of the following form:

Nr.	Random number	Trajectory	The value of the aleatory variable X
1	0.263		
	0.194		
	0.925	S_1, S_3, S_2, S_4	$0.7 - 0.8 + 0.325 - 0.625$

We obtain the values

$$x_1 \approx 0.98, \quad x_2 \approx -1.03, \quad x_3 \approx 1.06. \tag{4.711}$$

Example 4.5   Let $\mathbf{x} \in \mathcal{M}_{2,1}(\mathbb{R})$. We define the norm

$$\|\mathbf{x}\|_2 = \sqrt{x_1^2 + x_2^2}, \tag{4.712}$$

where

$$\mathbf{x} = \begin{bmatrix} x_1 & x_2 \end{bmatrix}^{\mathrm{T}}. \tag{4.713}$$

For a matrix $\mathbf{A} \in \mathcal{M}_2(\mathbb{R})$ we define the norm

$$\|\mathbf{A}\|_2 = \sup_{\mathbf{x} \neq 0} \frac{\|\mathbf{A}\mathbf{x}\|_2}{\|\mathbf{x}\|_2}. \tag{4.714}$$

Let us consider

$$\mathbf{A} = \begin{bmatrix} 1 & 2 \\ 0 & -1 \end{bmatrix}. \tag{4.715}$$

We wish to calculate $\|\mathbf{A}\|_2$.

Let us show that expression (4.712) defines a norm. First of all $\|\mathbf{x}\|_2 \geq 0$ for any $\mathbf{x} \in \mathcal{M}_{2,1}(\mathbb{R})$. Moreover, $\|\mathbf{x}\|_2 = 0$ leads to $x_1^2 + x_2^2 = 0$, with the unique solution $x_1 = x_2 = 0$, hence $\mathbf{x} = 0$.

Let $\mathbf{y} \in \mathcal{M}_{2,1}(\mathbb{R})$,

$$\mathbf{y} = \begin{bmatrix} y_1 & y_2 \end{bmatrix}^{\mathrm{T}}. \tag{4.716}$$

We have successively

$$\|\mathbf{x} + \mathbf{y}\|_2 = \sqrt{(x_1 + y_1)^2 + (x_2 + y_2)^2} = \sqrt{x_1^2 + x_2^2 + y_1^2 + y_2^2 + 2x_1 y_1 + 2x_2 y_2}, \tag{4.717}$$

$$\|x\|_2 + \|y\|_2 = \sqrt{x_1^2 + x_2^2} + \sqrt{y_1^2 + y_2^2} \tag{4.718}$$

and the inequality

$$\|\mathbf{x} + \mathbf{y}\|_2 \leq \|\mathbf{x}\|_2 + \|\mathbf{y}\|_2 \tag{4.719}$$

is equivalent to

$$x_1 y_1 + x_2 y_2 \leq \sqrt{x_1^2 + x_2^2}\sqrt{y_1^2 + y_2^2}. \tag{4.720}$$

If $x_1 y_1 + x_2 y_2 < 0$, then inequality (4.720) is obviously satisfied.

If $x_1 y_1 + x_2 y_2 > 0$, then we square both members of inequality (4.720) and obtain the equivalent relation

$$2x_1 x_2 y_1 y_2 \leq x_1^2 y_2^2 + x_2^2 y_1^2, \tag{4.721}$$

Which is obviously true.

We also may write

$$\|\alpha \mathbf{x}\|_2 = \sqrt{\alpha^2 x_1^2 + \alpha^2 x_2^2} = |\alpha| \|\mathbf{x}\|_2, \tag{4.722}$$

where $\alpha \in \mathbb{R}$, hence $\|\mathbf{x}\|_2$ is a norm.

On the other hand,

$$\|\mathbf{A}\|_2 = \sup_{\mathbf{x} \neq 0} \frac{\|\mathbf{A}\mathbf{x}\|_2}{\|\mathbf{x}\|_2} = \sup_{\mathbf{x} \neq 0} \left\| \mathbf{A} \frac{\mathbf{x}}{\|\mathbf{x}\|_2} \right\| = \max_{\|\mathbf{x}\|_2 = 1} \|\mathbf{A}\mathbf{x}\|_2. \tag{4.723}$$

From $\|\mathbf{x}\|_2 = 1$, it follows that there exists $\theta \in [0, 2\pi)$ with the property

$$\mathbf{x} = \begin{bmatrix} x_1 & x_2 \end{bmatrix}^{\mathrm{T}} = \begin{bmatrix} \cos \theta & \sin \theta \end{bmatrix}^{\mathrm{T}}. \tag{4.724}$$

If

$$\mathbf{A} = \begin{bmatrix} a_{11} & a_{12} \\ a_{21} & a_{22} \end{bmatrix}, \tag{4.725}$$

then

$$\mathbf{A}\mathbf{x}|_{\|\mathbf{x}\|_2 = 1} = \begin{bmatrix} a_{11} \cos \theta + a_{12} \sin \theta \\ a_{21} \cos \theta + a_{22} \sin \theta \end{bmatrix} \tag{4.726}$$

and

$$\|\mathbf{A}\mathbf{x}\|_2 = [(a_{11}^2 + a_{21}^2)\cos^2 \theta + (a_{12}^2 + a_{22}^2)\sin^2 \theta + 2(a_{11}a_{12} + a_{21}a_{22}) \sin \theta \cos \theta]^{\frac{1}{2}}. \tag{4.727}$$

It follows that

$$\|\mathbf{A}\|_2 = \max_{\theta \in [0, 2\pi)} \left[\frac{a_{11}^2 + a_{21}^2 - a_{12}^2 - a_{22}^2}{2} \cos 2\theta + \left(a_{11}a_{12} + a_{21}a_{22} \right) \sin 2\theta \right.$$
$$\left. + \frac{a_{11}^2 + a_{21}^2 + a_{12}^2 + a_{22}^2}{2} \right]^{\frac{1}{2}}. \tag{4.728}$$

We verify immediately that $\| \ \|_2$ is norm.

For the matrix $\mathbf{A}$ given by equation (4.715), we get

$$\|\mathbf{A}\|_2 = \max_{\theta \in [0, 2\pi)} [-2 \cos 2\theta + 2 \sin 2\theta + 3]^{\frac{1}{2}}. \tag{4.729}$$

We denote $f : [0, 2\pi) \to \mathbb{R}$,

$$f(\theta) = -2 \cos 2\theta + 2 \sin 2\theta + 3, \tag{4.730}$$

and we may write

$$f'(\theta) = 4 \sin 2\theta + 4 \cos 2\theta. \tag{4.731}$$

The equation $f'(\theta) = 0$ leads to the solution

$$\tan 2\theta = -1, \tag{4.732}$$

wherefrom

$$\sin 2\theta = \frac{\sqrt{2}}{2}, \quad \cos 2\theta = \frac{-\sqrt{2}}{2}. \tag{4.733}$$

It follows that

$$\|\mathbf{A}\|_2 = \sqrt{3 + 2\sqrt{2}}. \tag{4.734}$$

Example 4.6   Let the matrix

$$\mathbf{A} = \begin{bmatrix} 2 & 1 & -1 & 3 \\ 0 & 3 & 2 & 5 \\ 2 & 4 & 1 & 8 \end{bmatrix}, \tag{4.735}$$

for which we calculate the QR factorization.
   We have

$$\mathbf{x}_1 = \begin{bmatrix} 2 & 0 & 2 \end{bmatrix}^T, \quad \|\mathbf{x}\|_2 = 2\sqrt{2} = \lambda_1 \tag{4.736}$$

and choose

$$\mathbf{v}_1 = \mathbf{x}_1 + 2\sqrt{2}\mathbf{e}_1 = 2\begin{bmatrix} 1 + \sqrt{2} & 0 & 1 \end{bmatrix}^T. \tag{4.737}$$

It follows successively that

$$\mathbf{v}_1\mathbf{v}_1^T = 4\begin{bmatrix} 3 + 2\sqrt{2} & 0 & 1 + \sqrt{2} \\ 0 & 0 & 0 \\ 1 + \sqrt{2} & 0 & 1 \end{bmatrix}, \tag{4.738}$$

$$\mathbf{v}_1^T\mathbf{v}_1 = 8(2 + \sqrt{2}), \tag{4.739}$$

$$2\frac{\mathbf{v}_1\mathbf{v}_1^T}{\mathbf{v}_1^T\mathbf{v}_1} = \frac{1}{2 + \sqrt{2}}\begin{bmatrix} 3 + 2\sqrt{2} & 0 & 1 + \sqrt{2} \\ 0 & 0 & 0 \\ 1 + \sqrt{2} & 0 & 1 \end{bmatrix}, \tag{4.740}$$

$$\mathbf{H}_1 = \frac{1}{2 + \sqrt{2}}\begin{bmatrix} -1 - \sqrt{2} & 0 & -1 - \sqrt{2} \\ 0 & 2 + \sqrt{2} & 0 \\ -1 - \sqrt{2} & 0 & 1 + \sqrt{2} \end{bmatrix}, \tag{4.741}$$

$$\mathbf{H}_1\mathbf{A} = \begin{bmatrix} -2.828427 & -3.535534 & 0 & -7.778175 \\ 0 & 3 & 2 & 5 \\ 0 & 2.121320 & 1.414215 & 3.535534 \end{bmatrix}. \tag{4.742}$$

We also find

$$\mathbf{x}_2 = \begin{bmatrix} 3 & 2.121320 \end{bmatrix}^T, \quad \|\mathbf{x}_2\|_2 = 3.674234 = \lambda_2. \tag{4.743}$$

$$\mathbf{v}_2 = \mathbf{x}_2 + 3.674234\mathbf{e}_2 = \begin{bmatrix} 6.674234 & 2.121320 \end{bmatrix}^T, \tag{4.744}$$

$$\mathbf{v}_2\mathbf{v}_2^T = \begin{bmatrix} 44.545399 & 14.158186 \\ 14.158186 & 4.5 \end{bmatrix}, \tag{4.745}$$

$$\mathbf{v}_2^T\mathbf{v}_2 = 49.045399, \tag{4.746}$$

$$2\frac{\mathbf{v}_2\mathbf{v}_2^T}{\mathbf{v}_2^T\mathbf{v}_2} = \begin{bmatrix} 1.816497 & 0.577350 \\ 0.577350 & 0.183503 \end{bmatrix}, \tag{4.747}$$

$$\overline{\mathbf{H}}_2 = \begin{bmatrix} -0.816497 & -0.577350 \\ -0.577350 & 0.816497 \end{bmatrix}, \tag{4.748}$$

$$\mathbf{H}_2 = \begin{bmatrix} 1 & 0 & 0 \\ 0 & -0.816497 & -0.577350 \\ 0 & -0.577350 & 0.816497 \end{bmatrix}, \tag{4.749}$$

$$\mathbf{H_2 H_1 A} = \begin{bmatrix} -2.828427 & -3.535534 & 0 & -7.778175 \\ 0 & -3.674235 & -2.449491 & -6.123726 \\ 0 & 0 & 0 & 0 \end{bmatrix} = \mathbf{R}, \qquad (4.750)$$

$$\mathbf{Q} = \mathbf{H_1 H_2} = \begin{bmatrix} -0.707107 & 0.408248 & -0.577350 \\ 0 & -0.816497 & -0.577350 \\ -0.707107 & -0.408248 & 0.577350 \end{bmatrix}. \qquad (4.751)$$

The same factorization may be found by u with the Givens matrices too.

At the beginning, we equate to zero the element $a_{31} = 2$. To do this, we choose the Givens matrix

$$\mathbf{G_1} = \begin{bmatrix} 1 & 0 & 0 \\ 0 & \cos\theta & \sin\theta \\ 0 & -\sin\theta & \cos\theta \end{bmatrix}, \qquad (4.752)$$

such that

$$\mathbf{G_1^T} \begin{bmatrix} 2 \\ 0 \\ 2 \end{bmatrix} = \begin{bmatrix} 2 \\ -2\sin\theta \\ 2\cos\theta \end{bmatrix}. \qquad (4.753)$$

The element $2\cos\theta$ vanishes for $\theta = \pi/2$ and we obtain

$$\mathbf{G_1} = \begin{bmatrix} 1 & 0 & 0 \\ 0 & 0 & 1 \\ 0 & -1 & 0 \end{bmatrix}, \quad \mathbf{G_1^T} = \begin{bmatrix} 1 & 0 & 0 \\ 0 & 0 & -1 \\ 0 & 1 & 0 \end{bmatrix}, \qquad (4.754)$$

$$\mathbf{G_1^T A} = \begin{bmatrix} 2 & 1 & -1 & 3 \\ -2 & -4 & -1 & -8 \\ 0 & 3 & 2 & 5 \end{bmatrix}. \qquad (4.755)$$

We now equate to zero the element -2 of row 2 and column 1 in the matrix $\mathbf{G_1^T A}$. For this, we choose

$$\mathbf{G_2} = \begin{bmatrix} \cos\theta & \sin\theta & 0 \\ -\sin\theta & \cos\theta & 0 \\ 0 & 0 & 1 \end{bmatrix}, \quad \mathbf{G_2^T} = \begin{bmatrix} \cos\theta & -\sin\theta & 0 \\ \sin\theta & \cos\theta & 0 \\ 0 & 0 & 1 \end{bmatrix} \qquad (4.756)$$

and obtain

$$\mathbf{G_2^T} \begin{bmatrix} 2 \\ -2 \\ 0 \end{bmatrix} = \begin{bmatrix} 2\cos\theta + 2\sin\theta \\ 2\sin\theta - 2\cos\theta \\ 0 \end{bmatrix}. \qquad (4.757)$$

The element $2\sin\theta - 2\cos\theta$ vanishes for $\theta = \pi/4$ and we obtain

$$\mathbf{G_2} = \begin{bmatrix} \dfrac{\sqrt{2}}{2} & \dfrac{\sqrt{2}}{2} & 0 \\ -\dfrac{\sqrt{2}}{2} & \dfrac{\sqrt{2}}{2} & 0 \\ 0 & 0 & 1 \end{bmatrix}, \qquad (4.758)$$

$$
\mathbf{G}_2^T\mathbf{G}_1^T\mathbf{A} =
\begin{bmatrix}
\dfrac{\sqrt{2}}{2} & -\dfrac{\sqrt{2}}{2} & 0 \\[2mm]
\dfrac{\sqrt{2}}{2} & \dfrac{\sqrt{2}}{2} & 0 \\[2mm]
0 & 0 & 1
\end{bmatrix}
\begin{bmatrix}
2 & 1 & -1 & 3 \\
-2 & -4 & -1 & -8 \\
0 & 3 & 2 & 5
\end{bmatrix}
=
\begin{bmatrix}
2\sqrt{2} & 5\dfrac{\sqrt{2}}{2} & 0 & 11\dfrac{\sqrt{2}}{2} \\[2mm]
0 & -3\dfrac{\sqrt{2}}{2} & -\sqrt{2} & -5\dfrac{\sqrt{2}}{2} \\[2mm]
0 & 3 & 2 & 5
\end{bmatrix}.
$$

$$(4.759)$$

Obviously, the procedure may be continued, obtaining again the known factorization.

Example 4.7   Let us consider the matrix

$$
\mathbf{A} =
\begin{bmatrix}
1 & 2 \\
0 & 2
\end{bmatrix},
\tag{4.760}
$$

for which we want to calculate the SVD.

Let $\mathbf{u} \in \mathcal{M}_{2,1}(\mathbb{R})$,

$$
\mathbf{u} = \begin{bmatrix} \cos\theta & \sin\theta \end{bmatrix}^T, \quad \theta \in [0, 2\pi), \quad \|\mathbf{u}\|_2 = 1.
\tag{4.761}
$$

To determine $\|\mathbf{A}\|_2$ we have to calculate

$$
\mathbf{A}\mathbf{u} =
\begin{bmatrix}
\cos\theta + 2\sin\theta \\
2\sin\theta
\end{bmatrix}
\tag{4.762}
$$

and

$$
\|\mathbf{A}\mathbf{u}\|_2 = \sqrt{\frac{9}{2} + 2\sin 2\theta - \frac{7}{2}\cos 2\theta}.
\tag{4.763}
$$

Let $f : [0, 2\pi) \to \mathbb{R}$,

$$
f(\theta) = \frac{9}{2} + 2\sin 2\theta - \frac{7}{2}\cos 2\theta,
\tag{4.764}
$$

for which

$$
f'(\theta) = 4\cos 2\theta + 7\sin 2\theta.
\tag{4.765}
$$

The equation $f'(\theta) = 0$ leads to the solution

$$
\tan 2\theta = -\frac{4}{7}, \quad \sin 2\theta = \frac{4}{\sqrt{65}}, \quad \cos 2\theta = -\frac{7}{\sqrt{65}},
\tag{4.766}
$$

hence

$$
\|\mathbf{A}\|_2 = \sqrt{\frac{9}{2} + \frac{\sqrt{65}}{2}} = 2.92081
\tag{4.767}
$$

The equation

$$
\mathbf{A}\mathbf{x} = \sigma\mathbf{y} = \|\mathbf{A}\|_2\mathbf{y}
\tag{4.768}
$$

leads to

$$
\begin{bmatrix}
1 & 2 \\
0 & 2
\end{bmatrix}
\begin{bmatrix}
x_1 \\
x_2
\end{bmatrix}
= \sigma
\begin{bmatrix}
y_1 \\
y_2
\end{bmatrix}
\tag{4.769}
$$

wherefrom

$$
x_1 + 2x_2 = \sigma y_1, \quad 2x_2 = \sigma y_2;
\tag{4.770}
$$

moreover,

$$x_1^2 + x_2^2 = 1, \quad y_1^2 + y_2^2 = 1. \tag{4.771}$$

Relation (4.720) leads to

$$(x_1 + x_2)^2 + (2x_2)^2 = \sigma^2, \tag{4.772}$$

hence

$$x_1^2 + 4x_1 x_2 + 8x_2^2 = \sigma^2. \tag{4.773}$$

It follows that

$$4x_1 x_2 + 7x_2^2 = \sigma^2 - 1. \tag{4.774}$$

We obtain successively

$$x_1 = \frac{\sigma^2 - 1 - 7x_2^2}{4x_2}, \tag{4.775}$$

$$\left(\frac{\sigma^2 - 1 - 7x_2^2}{4x_2} \right)^2 + x_2^2 = 1, \tag{4.776}$$

$$65x_2^4 - [14(\sigma^2 - 1) + 16]x_2^2 + (\sigma^2 - 1)^2 = 0, \tag{4.777}$$

$$x_2^2 = 0.93412, \quad x_2 = \pm 0.9665. \tag{4.778}$$

We choose

$$x_2 = 0.9665, \quad x_1 = 0.2567, \tag{4.779}$$

wherefrom

$$y_1 = 0.7497, \quad y_2 = 0.6618. \tag{4.780}$$

We now determine the vector $\mathbf{v}_2$ so that $\mathbf{x} = \begin{bmatrix} x_1 & x_2 \end{bmatrix}^T$ and $\mathbf{v}_2 = \begin{bmatrix} v_1 & v_2 \end{bmatrix}^T$ are orthogonal. We deduce

$$0.2567 v_1 + 0.9665 v_2 = 0 \tag{4.781}$$

and may choose

$$v_1 = -0.9665, \quad v_2 = 0.2567, \tag{4.782}$$

resulting in the matrix

$$\mathbf{V} = \begin{bmatrix} 0.2567 & -0.9665 \\ 0.9665 & 0.2567 \end{bmatrix}. \tag{4.783}$$

Analogically, we get

$$\mathbf{U} = \begin{bmatrix} 0.7497 & -0.6618 \\ 0.6618 & 0.7497 \end{bmatrix}. \tag{4.784}$$

Moreover,

$$\mathbf{U}^T \mathbf{A} \mathbf{V} = \begin{bmatrix} 2.92 & 0 \\ 0 & 0.68 \end{bmatrix} \tag{4.785}$$

and the problem is solved.

Example 4.8   Let the matrix

$$\mathbf{A} = \begin{bmatrix} -1 & -3 & -4 \\ 8 & 12 & 14 \\ -4 & -5 & -5 \end{bmatrix}, \tag{4.786}$$

for which we wish to determine the eigenvalues and eigenvectors.

We begin solving with Krylov's method. To do this, we consider the vector

$$\mathbf{y}^{(0)} = \begin{bmatrix} 1 & 0 & 1 \end{bmatrix}^{\mathrm{T}} \tag{4.787}$$

and calculate successively

$$\mathbf{y}^{(1)} = \mathbf{A}\mathbf{y}^{(0)} = \begin{bmatrix} -1 & -3 & -4 \\ 8 & 12 & 14 \\ -4 & -5 & -5 \end{bmatrix} \begin{bmatrix} 1 \\ 0 \\ 1 \end{bmatrix} = \begin{bmatrix} -5 \\ 22 \\ -9 \end{bmatrix}, \tag{4.788}$$

$$\mathbf{y}^{(2)} = \mathbf{A}\mathbf{y}^{(1)} = \begin{bmatrix} -1 & -3 & -4 \\ 8 & 12 & 14 \\ -4 & -5 & -5 \end{bmatrix} \begin{bmatrix} -5 \\ 22 \\ -9 \end{bmatrix} = \begin{bmatrix} -25 \\ 98 \\ -45 \end{bmatrix}, \tag{4.789}$$

$$\mathbf{y}^{(3)} = \mathbf{A}\mathbf{y}^{(2)} = \begin{bmatrix} -1 & -3 & -4 \\ 8 & 12 & 14 \\ -4 & -5 & -5 \end{bmatrix} \begin{bmatrix} -5 \\ 22 \\ -9 \end{bmatrix} = \begin{bmatrix} -89 \\ 346 \\ -165 \end{bmatrix}. \tag{4.790}$$

It results in the linear system

$$\begin{bmatrix} -25 & -5 & 1 \\ 98 & 22 & 0 \\ -45 & -9 & 1 \end{bmatrix} \begin{bmatrix} q_1 \\ q_2 \\ q_3 \end{bmatrix} = - \begin{bmatrix} -89 \\ 346 \\ -165 \end{bmatrix}, \tag{4.791}$$

with the solution

$$q_1 = -6, \quad q_2 = 11, \quad q_3 = -6 \tag{4.792}$$

and the characteristic polynomial

$$P(\lambda) = \lambda^3 - 6\lambda^2 + 11\lambda - 6. \tag{4.793}$$

The eigenvalues of the matrix $\mathbf{A}$ result from the equation $P(\lambda) = 0$ and are

$$\lambda_1 = 3, \quad \lambda_2 = 2, \quad \lambda_3 = 1. \tag{4.794}$$

The polynomials $\phi_i(\lambda)$, $i = \overline{1, 3}$, are obtained by dividing $P(\lambda)$ by $\lambda - \lambda_i$; we have

$$\phi_1(x) = \lambda^2 - 3\lambda + 2, \quad \phi_2(\lambda) = \lambda^2 - 4\lambda + 3, \quad \phi_3(\lambda) = \lambda^2 - 5\lambda + 6. \tag{4.795}$$

The eigenvectors are

$$c_i \phi_i(\lambda_i)\mathbf{x}_i = \mathbf{y}^{(2)} + q_{1i}\mathbf{y}^{(1)} + q_{21}\mathbf{y}^{(0)}, \quad i = \overline{1, 3}, \tag{4.796}$$

where

$$\phi_1(\lambda_1) = 2, \quad \phi_2(\lambda_2) = -1, \quad \phi_3(\lambda_3) = 2. \tag{4.797}$$

It follows that

$$2c_1\mathbf{x}_1 = \begin{bmatrix} -25 \\ 98 \\ -45 \end{bmatrix} - 3 \begin{bmatrix} -5 \\ 22 \\ -9 \end{bmatrix} + 2 \begin{bmatrix} 1 \\ 0 \\ 1 \end{bmatrix} = \begin{bmatrix} -8 \\ 32 \\ -16 \end{bmatrix}, \tag{4.798}$$

$$-c_2 \mathbf{x}_2 = \begin{bmatrix} -25 \\ 98 \\ -45 \end{bmatrix} - 4 \begin{bmatrix} -5 \\ 22 \\ -9 \end{bmatrix} + 3 \begin{bmatrix} 1 \\ 0 \\ 1 \end{bmatrix} = \begin{bmatrix} -2 \\ 10 \\ -6 \end{bmatrix}, \tag{4.799}$$

$$2c_3 \mathbf{x}_3 = \begin{bmatrix} -25 \\ 98 \\ -45 \end{bmatrix} - 5 \begin{bmatrix} -5 \\ 22 \\ -9 \end{bmatrix} + 6 \begin{bmatrix} 1 \\ 0 \\ 1 \end{bmatrix} = \begin{bmatrix} 6 \\ -12 \\ 6 \end{bmatrix}. \tag{4.800}$$

To apply the Danilevski method, we must obtain the Frobenius form of the matrix $\mathbf{A}$. We multiply the matrix $\mathbf{A}$ on the left by the matrix

$$\mathbf{M}_1 = \begin{bmatrix} 1 & 0 & 0 \\ -\dfrac{4}{5} & -\dfrac{1}{5} & -1 \\ 0 & 0 & 1 \end{bmatrix}, \tag{4.801}$$

the inverse of which is

$$\mathbf{M}_1^{-1} = \begin{bmatrix} 1 & 0 & 0 \\ -4 & -5 & -5 \\ 0 & 0 & 1 \end{bmatrix}, \tag{4.802}$$

and obtain

$$\mathbf{A}_2 = \mathbf{M}_1^{-1} \mathbf{A} \mathbf{M}_1 = \begin{bmatrix} \dfrac{7}{5} & \dfrac{3}{5} & -1 \\ \dfrac{12}{5} & \dfrac{23}{5} & -6 \\ 0 & 1 & 0 \end{bmatrix}. \tag{4.803}$$

We now multiply the matrix $\mathbf{A}_2$ on the left by the matrix

$$\mathbf{M}_2 = \begin{bmatrix} \dfrac{5}{12} & -\dfrac{23}{12} & \dfrac{5}{2} \\ 0 & 1 & 0 \\ 0 & 0 & 1 \end{bmatrix}, \tag{4.804}$$

the inverse of which is

$$\mathbf{M}_2^{-1} = \begin{bmatrix} \dfrac{12}{5} & \dfrac{23}{12} & -6 \\ 0 & 1 & 0 \\ 0 & 0 & 1 \end{bmatrix}, \tag{4.805}$$

obtaining

$$\mathbf{A}_3 = \mathbf{M}_2^{-1} \mathbf{A}_2 \mathbf{M}_2 = \begin{bmatrix} 6 & -11 & 6 \\ 1 & 0 & 0 \\ 0 & 1 & 0 \end{bmatrix}. \tag{4.806}$$

The matrix $\mathbf{A}_3$ is just the required Frobenius form. The characteristic polynomial is

$$-\lambda^3 + 6\lambda^2 - 11\lambda + 6 = 0 \tag{4.807}$$

and has the roots given by equation (4.720).

We obtain the eigenvectors of the Frobenius matrix in the form

$$\mathbf{y}_i = \begin{bmatrix} \lambda_i^2 & \lambda_i & 1 \end{bmatrix}^T, \quad i = \overline{1,3}, \tag{4.808}$$

that is

$$\mathbf{y}_1 = \begin{bmatrix} 9 & 3 & 1 \end{bmatrix}^T, \quad \mathbf{y}_2 = \begin{bmatrix} 4 & 2 & 1 \end{bmatrix}^T, \quad \mathbf{y}_3 = \begin{bmatrix} 1 & 1 & 1 \end{bmatrix}^T. \tag{4.809}$$

The eigenvectors of the matrix $\mathbf{A}$ are

$$\mathbf{x}_i = \mathbf{M}_1 \mathbf{M}_2 \mathbf{y}_i, \quad i = \overline{1,3}, \tag{4.810}$$

and it follows successively that

$$\mathbf{M}_1 \mathbf{M}_2 = \begin{bmatrix} \dfrac{5}{12} & -\dfrac{23}{12} & \dfrac{5}{2} \\ -\dfrac{1}{3} & \dfrac{4}{3} & -3 \\ 0 & 0 & 1 \end{bmatrix}, \tag{4.811}$$

$$\mathbf{x}_1 = \begin{bmatrix} \dfrac{5}{12} & -\dfrac{23}{12} & \dfrac{5}{2} \\ -\dfrac{1}{3} & \dfrac{4}{3} & -3 \\ 0 & 0 & 1 \end{bmatrix} \begin{bmatrix} 9 \\ 3 \\ 1 \end{bmatrix} = \begin{bmatrix} \dfrac{1}{2} \\ -2 \\ 1 \end{bmatrix}, \tag{4.812}$$

$$\mathbf{x}_2 = \begin{bmatrix} \dfrac{5}{12} & -\dfrac{23}{12} & \dfrac{5}{2} \\ -\dfrac{1}{3} & \dfrac{4}{3} & -3 \\ 0 & 0 & 1 \end{bmatrix} \begin{bmatrix} 4 \\ 2 \\ 1 \end{bmatrix} = \begin{bmatrix} \dfrac{1}{3} \\ -\dfrac{5}{3} \\ 1 \end{bmatrix}, \tag{4.813}$$

$$\mathbf{x}_3 = \begin{bmatrix} \dfrac{5}{12} & -\dfrac{23}{12} & \dfrac{5}{2} \\ -\dfrac{1}{3} & \dfrac{4}{3} & -3 \\ 0 & 0 & 1 \end{bmatrix} \begin{bmatrix} 1 \\ 1 \\ 1 \end{bmatrix} = \begin{bmatrix} 1 \\ -2 \\ 1 \end{bmatrix}. \tag{4.814}$$

The maximum eigenvalue in modulus and the corresponding eigenvector may be determined by means of the direct power method.

To do this, we use the vector $\mathbf{y}^{(0)}$ defined by relation (4.713) and calculate successively

$$\mathbf{y}^{(1)} = \mathbf{y}^{(0)} = \begin{bmatrix} 1 & 0 & 1 \end{bmatrix}^T, \tag{4.815}$$

$$\mathbf{y}^{(2)} = \mathbf{A}\mathbf{y}^{(1)} = \begin{bmatrix} -1 & -3 & -4 \\ 8 & 12 & 14 \\ -4 & -5 & -5 \end{bmatrix} \begin{bmatrix} 1 \\ 0 \\ 1 \end{bmatrix} = \begin{bmatrix} -5 \\ 22 \\ -9 \end{bmatrix}, \tag{4.816}$$

$$\mathbf{y}^{(3)} = \mathbf{A}\mathbf{y}^{(2)} = \begin{bmatrix} -1 & -3 & -4 \\ 8 & 12 & 14 \\ -4 & -5 & -5 \end{bmatrix} \begin{bmatrix} -5 \\ 22 \\ -9 \end{bmatrix} = \begin{bmatrix} -25 \\ 98 \\ -45 \end{bmatrix}, \tag{4.817}$$

$$\mathbf{y}^{(4)} = \mathbf{A}\mathbf{y}^{(3)} = \begin{bmatrix} -1 & -3 & -4 \\ 8 & 12 & 14 \\ -4 & -5 & -5 \end{bmatrix} \begin{bmatrix} -25 \\ 98 \\ -45 \end{bmatrix} = \begin{bmatrix} -89 \\ 346 \\ -165 \end{bmatrix}, \tag{4.818}$$

$$\mathbf{y}^{(5)} = \mathbf{A}\mathbf{y}^{(4)} = \begin{bmatrix} -1 & -3 & -4 \\ 8 & 12 & 14 \\ -4 & -5 & -5 \end{bmatrix} \begin{bmatrix} -89 \\ 346 \\ -165 \end{bmatrix} = \begin{bmatrix} -289 \\ 1130 \\ -549 \end{bmatrix}, \tag{4.819}$$

$$\mathbf{y}^{(6)} = \mathbf{A}\mathbf{y}^{(5)} = \begin{bmatrix} -1 & -3 & -4 \\ 8 & 12 & 14 \\ -4 & -5 & -5 \end{bmatrix} \begin{bmatrix} -289 \\ 1130 \\ -549 \end{bmatrix} = \begin{bmatrix} -905 \\ 3562 \\ -1749 \end{bmatrix}, \tag{4.820}$$

$$\mathbf{y}^{(7)} = \mathbf{A}\mathbf{y}^{(6)} = \begin{bmatrix} -1 & -3 & -4 \\ 8 & 12 & 14 \\ -4 & -5 & -5 \end{bmatrix} \begin{bmatrix} -905 \\ 3562 \\ -1749 \end{bmatrix} = \begin{bmatrix} -2785 \\ 11018 \\ -5445 \end{bmatrix}, \tag{4.821}$$

$$\mathbf{y}^{(8)} = \mathbf{A}\mathbf{y}^{(7)} = \begin{bmatrix} -1 & -3 & -4 \\ 8 & 12 & 14 \\ -4 & -5 & -5 \end{bmatrix} \begin{bmatrix} -2785 \\ 11018 \\ -5445 \end{bmatrix} = \begin{bmatrix} -8489 \\ 33706 \\ -16725 \end{bmatrix}, \tag{4.822}$$

$$\mathbf{y}^{(9)} = \mathbf{A}\mathbf{y}^{(8)} = \begin{bmatrix} -1 & -3 & -4 \\ 8 & 12 & 14 \\ -4 & -5 & -5 \end{bmatrix} \begin{bmatrix} -8489 \\ 33706 \\ -16725 \end{bmatrix} = \begin{bmatrix} -25729 \\ 102410 \\ -50949 \end{bmatrix}, \tag{4.823}$$

$$\mathbf{y}^{(10)} = \mathbf{A}\mathbf{y}^{(9)} = \begin{bmatrix} -1 & -3 & -4 \\ 8 & 12 & 14 \\ -4 & -5 & -5 \end{bmatrix} \begin{bmatrix} -8489 \\ 33706 \\ -16725 \end{bmatrix} = \begin{bmatrix} -25729 \\ 102410 \\ -50949 \end{bmatrix}. \tag{4.824}$$

It follows that

$$\lambda_1 \approx \frac{y_1^{(10)}}{y_1^{(9)}} = 3.02, \quad \lambda_1 \approx \frac{y_2^{(0)}}{y_2^{(9)}} = 3.025, \quad \lambda_1 \approx \frac{y_3^{(10)}}{y_3^{(9)}} = 3.029. \tag{4.825}$$

The eigenvector is $\mathbf{y}^{(10)}$ on normalization gives

$$\overline{\mathbf{y}}^{(10)} = \begin{bmatrix} -0.219 & 0.873 & -0.435 \end{bmatrix}^{\mathrm{T}}. \tag{4.826}$$

The eigenvalue $\lambda_3 = 1$ may be obtained by using the inverse power method. We have

$$\mathbf{A}^{-1} = \frac{1}{6} \begin{bmatrix} 10 & 5 & 6 \\ -16 & -11 & -18 \\ 8 & 7 & 12 \end{bmatrix} \tag{4.827}$$

and, using the same vector $\mathbf{y}^{(0)}$ given by equation (4.787), we have

$$\mathbf{y}^{(1)} = \mathbf{A}^{-1}\mathbf{y}^{(0)} = \frac{1}{6} \begin{bmatrix} 10 & 5 & 6 \\ -16 & -11 & -18 \\ 8 & 7 & 12 \end{bmatrix} \begin{bmatrix} 1 \\ 0 \\ 1 \end{bmatrix} = \frac{1}{6} \begin{bmatrix} 16 \\ -34 \\ 20 \end{bmatrix}, \tag{4.828}$$

$$\mathbf{y}^{(2)} = \mathbf{A}^{-1}\mathbf{y}^{(1)} = \frac{1}{36} \begin{bmatrix} 10 & 5 & 6 \\ -16 & -11 & -18 \\ 8 & 7 & 12 \end{bmatrix} \begin{bmatrix} 16 \\ -34 \\ 20 \end{bmatrix} = \frac{1}{36} \begin{bmatrix} 110 \\ -242 \\ 110 \end{bmatrix}, \tag{4.829}$$

$$\mathbf{y}^{(3)} = \mathbf{A}^{-1}\mathbf{y}^{(2)} = \frac{1}{6^3}\begin{bmatrix} 10 & 5 & 6 \\ -16 & -11 & -18 \\ 8 & 7 & 12 \end{bmatrix}\begin{bmatrix} 110 \\ -242 \\ 110 \end{bmatrix} = \frac{1}{6^3}\begin{bmatrix} 550 \\ -1078 \\ 506 \end{bmatrix}, \tag{4.830}$$

$$\mathbf{y}^{(4)} = \mathbf{A}^{-1}\mathbf{y}^{(3)} = \frac{1}{6^4}\begin{bmatrix} 10 & 5 & 6 \\ -16 & -11 & -18 \\ 8 & 7 & 12 \end{bmatrix}\begin{bmatrix} 550 \\ -1078 \\ 506 \end{bmatrix} = \frac{1}{6^4}\begin{bmatrix} 3146 \\ 6050 \\ 2926 \end{bmatrix}, \tag{4.831}$$

$$\mathbf{y}^{(5)} = \mathbf{A}^{-1}\mathbf{y}^{(4)} = \frac{1}{6^5}\begin{bmatrix} 10 & 5 & 6 \\ -16 & -11 & -18 \\ 8 & 7 & 12 \end{bmatrix}\begin{bmatrix} 3146 \\ 6050 \\ 2926 \end{bmatrix} = \frac{1}{6^5}\begin{bmatrix} 18766 \\ -36454 \\ 17930 \end{bmatrix}, \tag{4.832}$$

$$\mathbf{y}^{(6)} = \mathbf{A}^{-1}\mathbf{y}^{(5)} = \frac{1}{6^6}\begin{bmatrix} 10 & 5 & 6 \\ -16 & -11 & -18 \\ 8 & 7 & 12 \end{bmatrix}\begin{bmatrix} 18766 \\ -36454 \\ 17930 \end{bmatrix} = \frac{1}{6^6}\begin{bmatrix} 112970 \\ -222002 \\ 110110 \end{bmatrix}, \tag{4.833}$$

$$\mathbf{y}^{(7)} = \mathbf{A}^{-1}\mathbf{y}^{(6)} = \frac{1}{6^7}\begin{bmatrix} 10 & 5 & 6 \\ -16 & -11 & -18 \\ 8 & 7 & 12 \end{bmatrix}\begin{bmatrix} 112970 \\ -222002 \\ 110110 \end{bmatrix} = \frac{1}{6^7}\begin{bmatrix} 680350 \\ -1347478 \\ 671066 \end{bmatrix}, \tag{4.834}$$

$$\mathbf{y}^{(8)} = \mathbf{A}^{-1}\mathbf{y}^{(7)} = \frac{1}{6^8}\begin{bmatrix} 10 & 5 & 6 \\ -16 & -11 & -18 \\ 8 & 7 & 12 \end{bmatrix}\begin{bmatrix} 680350 \\ -1347478 \\ 671066 \end{bmatrix} = \frac{1}{6^8}\begin{bmatrix} 4092506 \\ -8142530 \\ 4063246 \end{bmatrix}, \tag{4.835}$$

$$\mathbf{y}^{(9)} = \mathbf{A}^{-1}\mathbf{y}^{(8)} = \frac{1}{6^9}\begin{bmatrix} 10 & 5 & 6 \\ -16 & -11 & -18 \\ 8 & 7 & 12 \end{bmatrix}\begin{bmatrix} 4092506 \\ -8142530 \\ 4063246 \end{bmatrix} = \frac{1}{6^9}\begin{bmatrix} 245914886 \\ -49050694 \\ 24501290 \end{bmatrix}, \tag{4.836}$$

$$\mathbf{y}^{(10)} = \mathbf{A}^{-1}\mathbf{y}^{(9)} = \frac{1}{6^{10}}\begin{bmatrix} 10 & 5 & 6 \\ -16 & -11 & -18 \\ 8 & 7 & 12 \end{bmatrix}\begin{bmatrix} 245914886 \\ -49050694 \\ 24501290 \end{bmatrix} = \frac{1}{6^{10}}\begin{bmatrix} 147673130 \\ -294935762 \\ 147395710 \end{bmatrix}. \tag{4.837}$$

It follows that

$$\lambda_3 \approx \frac{y_1^{(10)}}{y_1^{(9)}} = 1.0008, \quad \lambda_3 \approx \frac{y_2^{(10)}}{y_2^{(9)}} = 1.0021, \quad \lambda_3 \approx \frac{y_3^{(10)}}{y_3^{(9)}} = 1.0026, \tag{4.838}$$

and we obtain the eigenvector $\mathbf{y}^{(10)}$ or, when normalized,

$$\bar{\mathbf{y}}^{(10)} = \begin{bmatrix} 0.4088 & -0.8164 & 0.4080 \end{bmatrix}^{\mathsf{T}}. \tag{4.839}$$

The eigenvalue λ_2 may be found by means of the displacement method. To do this, we consider the matrix

$$\mathbf{B} = \mathbf{A} - 1.9\mathbf{I}_3 = \begin{bmatrix} -2.9 & -3 & -4 \\ 8 & 10.1 & 14 \\ -4 & -5 & -6.9 \end{bmatrix}, \tag{4.840}$$

the inverse of which is

$$\mathbf{B}^{-1} = \begin{bmatrix} -3.131313 & 7.070707 & 16.161616 \\ 8.080808 & -40.505051 & -86.868687 \\ -4.040404 & 25.252525 & 53.434343 \end{bmatrix}. \tag{4.841}$$

We successively calculate

$$\mathbf{B}^{-2} = \begin{bmatrix} 1.64269 & 99.58167 & 198.75522 \\ -1.63249 & -495.85751 & -992.55170 \\ 0.81624 & 297.92876 & 596.27586 \end{bmatrix}, \tag{4.842}$$

$$\mathbf{B}^{-4} = \begin{bmatrix} 2.364 & 10000.159 & 19999.477 \\ -3.360 & -49997.593 & -99994.870 \\ 1.679 & 29998.797 & 59997.436 \end{bmatrix}, \tag{4.843}$$

$$\mathbf{B}^{-8} = \begin{bmatrix} -15.8 & 100000011.4 & 200000020.9 \\ 92.6 & -499999600.9 & -1000000199 \\ -56.3 & 3000000505 & 600000099.5 \end{bmatrix}. \tag{4.844}$$

It follows that for $\mathbf{B}^{-8}$, the eigenvalue

$$\overline{\lambda} \approx \sqrt[8]{\mathrm{Tr}(\mathbf{B}^{-8})} = 10.0; \tag{4.845}$$

hence, the matrix $\mathbf{B}$ has the eigenvalue

$$\lambda = \frac{1}{\overline{\lambda}} = 0.1. \tag{4.846}$$

We deduce from equation (4.840) that the matrix $\mathbf{A}$ has the eigenvalue

$$\lambda_2 = \lambda + 1.9 = 2.0. \tag{4.847}$$

The eigenvalues of the matrix $\mathbf{A}$ may be determined by the Leverier method too. We calculate

$$\mathbf{A} = \begin{bmatrix} -1 & -3 & -4 \\ 8 & 12 & 14 \\ -4 & -5 & -5 \end{bmatrix}, \quad S_1 = \mathrm{Tr}(\mathbf{A}) = 6, \tag{4.848}$$

$$\mathbf{A}^2 = \begin{bmatrix} -7 & -13 & -18 \\ 32 & 50 & 66 \\ -16 & -23 & -29 \end{bmatrix}, \quad S_2 = \mathrm{Tr}(\mathbf{A}^2) = 14, \tag{4.849}$$

$$\mathbf{A}^3 = \begin{bmatrix} -25 & -45 & -64 \\ 104 & 174 & 242 \\ -52 & -83 & -113 \end{bmatrix}, \quad S_3 = \mathrm{Tr}(\mathbf{A}^3) = 36, \tag{4.850}$$

the coefficients of the characteristic polynomial being given by

$$p_1 = -S_1 = -6, \tag{4.851}$$

$$p_2 = -\frac{1}{2}(S_2 + p_1 S_1) = 11, \tag{4.852}$$

$$p_3 = -\frac{1}{3}(S_3 + p_1 S_2 + p_2 S_1) = -6. \tag{4.853}$$

We obtain the characteristic equation

$$\lambda^3 - 6\lambda^2 + 11\lambda - 6 = 0, \tag{4.854}$$

whose roots are given by equation (4.794).

Another method to determine the eigenvalues is the Left–Right one.
We write the matrix $\mathbf{A}$ in the form

$$\mathbf{A} = \begin{bmatrix} 1 & 0 & 0 \\ l_{21} & 1 & 0 \\ l_{31} & l_{32} & 1 \end{bmatrix} \begin{bmatrix} r_{11} & r_{12} & r_{13} \\ 0 & r_{22} & r_{23} \\ 0 & 0 & r_{33} \end{bmatrix} ; \tag{4.855}$$

it results in the system

$$r_1 = -1, \quad r_{12} = -3, \quad r_{13} = -4, \quad l_{21}r_{11} = 8, \quad l_2r_{12} + r_{22} = 12, \quad l_{21}r_{13} + r_{23} = 14,$$

$$l_{31}r_{11} = -4, \quad l_{31}r_{12} + l_{32}r_{22} = -5, \quad l_{31}r_{13} + l_{32}r_{23} + r_{33} = -5, \tag{4.856}$$

with the solution

$$r_{11} = -1, \quad r_{12} = -3, \quad r_{13} = -4, \quad l_{21} = -8, \quad r_{22} = -12, \quad r_{23} = -18, \quad l_{31} = 4,$$

$$l_{32} = -\frac{7}{12}, \quad r_{33} = \frac{1}{2}, \tag{4.857}$$

hence the matrices

$$\mathbf{L}_1 = \begin{bmatrix} 1 & 0 & 0 \\ -8 & 1 & 0 \\ 4 & -\frac{7}{12} & 1 \end{bmatrix}, \quad \mathbf{R}_1 = \begin{bmatrix} -1 & -3 & -4 \\ 0 & -12 & -18 \\ 0 & 0 & \frac{1}{2} \end{bmatrix}, \tag{4.858}$$

$$\mathbf{A}_2 = \mathbf{R}_1\mathbf{L}_1 = \begin{bmatrix} -1 & -3 & -4 \\ 0 & -12 & -18 \\ 0 & 0 & \frac{1}{2} \end{bmatrix} \begin{bmatrix} 1 & 0 & 0 \\ -8 & 1 & 0 \\ 4 & -\frac{7}{12} & 1 \end{bmatrix} = \begin{bmatrix} 7 & -\frac{2}{3} & -4 \\ 24 & -\frac{3}{2} & -18 \\ 2 & -\frac{7}{24} & \frac{1}{2} \end{bmatrix}. \tag{4.859}$$

The procedure can continue, the data obtained being given in Table 4.1.
This results in the following eigenvalues

$$\lambda_1 \approx 3.0002, \quad \lambda_2 \approx 1.9888, \quad \lambda_3 \approx 1.0056. \tag{4.860}$$

Example 4.9   Let the linear system be

$$2x_1 + 3x_2 + x_3 + 3x_4 = 9, \quad x_1 - 2x_2 - x_3 + 5x_4 = 3, \quad 3x_1 + 6x_2 + x_3 - 2x_4 = 8,$$

$$-2x_1 - x_2 + 6x_3 + 4x_4 = 7, \quad x_1 + 2x_2 + 5x_3 - 7x_4 = 1. \tag{4.861}$$

We wish to determine the solution of this system in the sense of the least squares method. We have

$$\mathbf{A} = \begin{bmatrix} 2 & 3 & 1 & 3 \\ 1 & -2 & -1 & 5 \\ 3 & 6 & 1 & -2 \\ -2 & -1 & 6 & 4 \\ 1 & 2 & 5 & -7 \end{bmatrix}. \tag{4.862}$$

We shall first determine the rank of the matrix $\mathbf{A}$.
We commute rows 1 and 2 with each other,

$$\mathbf{A} \sim \begin{bmatrix} 1 & -2 & -1 & 5 \\ 2 & 3 & 1 & 3 \\ 3 & 6 & 1 & -2 \\ -2 & -1 & 6 & 4 \\ 1 & 2 & 5 & -7 \end{bmatrix} ; \tag{4.863}$$

TABLE 4.1   Determination of the Eigenvalues by the L–R Method

Step	A	L	R
1	$\begin{bmatrix} -1 & -3 & -4 \\ 8 & 12 & 14 \\ -4 & -5 & -5 \end{bmatrix}$	$\begin{bmatrix} 1 & 0 & 0 \\ -8 & 11 & 0 \\ 4 & 0.583333 & 1 \end{bmatrix}$	$\begin{bmatrix} -1 & -3 & -4 \\ 0 & -12 & -18 \\ 0 & 0 & 0.5 \end{bmatrix}$
2	$\begin{bmatrix} 7 & -0.6667 & -4 \\ 24 & -1.5 & -18 \\ 2 & 0.2917 & 0.5 \end{bmatrix}$	$\begin{bmatrix} 1 & 0 & 0 \\ 3.4286 & 1 & 0 \\ 0.2857 & -0.1288 & 1 \end{bmatrix}$	$\begin{bmatrix} 7 & -0.6667 & -4 \\ 0 & 0.7857 & -4.2857 \\ 0 & 0 & 1.0909 \end{bmatrix}$
3	$\begin{bmatrix} 3.5714 & -0.1515 & -4 \\ 1.4694 & 1.3377 & -4.2857 \\ 0.3117 & -0.1405 & 1.0909 \end{bmatrix}$	$\begin{bmatrix} 1 & 0 & 0 \\ 0.4114 & 1 & 0 \\ 0.0873 & -0.0909 & 1 \end{bmatrix}$	$\begin{bmatrix} 3.5714 & -0.1515 & -4 \\ 0 & 1.4 & -2.64 \\ 0 & 0 & 1.2 \end{bmatrix}$
4	$\begin{bmatrix} 3.16 & 0.2121 & -4 \\ 0.3456 & 1.64 & -2.64 \\ 0.1047 & -0.1091 & 1.2 \end{bmatrix}$	$\begin{bmatrix} 1 & 0 & 0 \\ 0.1094 & 1 & 0 \\ 0.0331 & -0.0718 & 1 \end{bmatrix}$	$\begin{bmatrix} 3.16 & 0.2121 & -4 \\ 0 & 1.16168 & -2.2025 \\ 0 & 0 & 1.1744 \end{bmatrix}$
5	$\begin{bmatrix} 3.0506 & 0.4994 & -4 \\ 0.1038 & 1.7750 & -2.2025 \\ 0.0389 & -0.0843 & 1.1744 \end{bmatrix}$	$\begin{bmatrix} 1 & 0 & 0 \\ 0.0348 & 1 & 0 \\ 0.0128 & -0.0516 & 1 \end{bmatrix}$	$\begin{bmatrix} 3.0506 & 0.4994 & -4 \\ 0 & 1.7580 & -2.0664 \\ 0 & 0 & 1.1188 \end{bmatrix}$
6	$\begin{bmatrix} 3.0166 & 0.7058 & -4 \\ 0.0335 & 1.8646 & -2.0664 \\ 0.0143 & -0.0577 & 1.1188 \end{bmatrix}$	$\begin{bmatrix} 1 & 0 & 0 \\ 0.0111 & 1 & 0 \\ 0.0047 & -0.0329 & 1 \end{bmatrix}$	$\begin{bmatrix} 3.0166 & 0.7058 & -4 \\ 0 & 1.8568 & -2.0220 \\ 0 & 0 & 1.0712 \end{bmatrix}$
7	$\begin{bmatrix} 3.0055 & 0.8374 & -4 \\ 0.0110 & 1.9233 & -2.0220 \\ 0.0051 & -0.0352 & 1.0712 \end{bmatrix}$	$\begin{bmatrix} 1 & 0 & 0 \\ 0.0037 & 1 & 0 \\ 0.0017 & -0.0191 & 1 \end{bmatrix}$	$\begin{bmatrix} 3.0055 & 0.8374 & -4 \\ 0 & 1.9202 & -2.0073 \\ 0 & 0 & 1.0396 \end{bmatrix}$
8	$\begin{bmatrix} 3.0018 & 0.9137 & -4 \\ 0.0037 & 1.9585 & -2.0073 \\ 0.0018 & -0.0198 & 1.0396 \end{bmatrix}$	$\begin{bmatrix} 1 & 0 & 0 \\ 0.0012 & 1 & 0 \\ 0.0006 & -0.0104 & 1 \end{bmatrix}$	$\begin{bmatrix} 3.0018 & 0.9137 & -4 \\ 0 & 1.9574 & -2.0024 \\ 0 & 0 & 1.0211 \end{bmatrix}$
9	$\begin{bmatrix} 3.0006 & 0.9553 & -4 \\ 0.0012 & 1.9783 & -2.0024 \\ 0.0006 & -0.0106 & 1.0211 \end{bmatrix}$	$\begin{bmatrix} 1 & 0 & 0 \\ 0.0004 & 1 & 0 \\ 0.0002 & -0.0055 & 1 \end{bmatrix}$	$\begin{bmatrix} 3.0006 & 0.9553 & -4 \\ 0 & 1.9779 & -2.0008 \\ 0 & 0 & 1.0110 \end{bmatrix}$
10	$\begin{bmatrix} 3.0002 & 0.9772 & -4 \\ 0.0004 & 1.9888 & -2.0008 \\ 0.0002 & -0.0055 & 1.0110 \end{bmatrix}$	$\begin{bmatrix} 1 & 0 & 0 \\ 0.0001 & 1 & 0 \\ 0.0001 & -0.0028 & 1 \end{bmatrix}$	$\begin{bmatrix} 3.0002 & 0.9772 & -4 \\ 0 & 1.9887 & -2.0003 \\ 0 & 0 & 1.0056 \end{bmatrix}$

then we multiply row 1 by -2, -3, 2 and -1, and add it to rows 2, 3, 4, 5, respectively, obtaining

$$\mathbf{A} \sim \begin{bmatrix} 1 & -2 & -1 & 5 \\ 0 & 7 & 3 & -7 \\ 0 & 12 & 4 & -17 \\ 0 & -5 & 4 & -6 \\ 0 & 4 & 6 & -12 \end{bmatrix}. \tag{4.864}$$

We multiply column 1 by 2, 1, -5 and add this to columns 2, 3, 4, respectively, to get

$$\mathbf{A} \sim \begin{bmatrix} 1 & 0 & 0 & 0 \\ 0 & 7 & 3 & -7 \\ 0 & 12 & 4 & -17 \\ 0 & -5 & 4 & -6 \\ 0 & 4 & 6 & -12 \end{bmatrix}; \tag{4.865}$$

We also multiply row 2 by $-12/7$, $5/7$ and $-4/7$, and add this to rows 3, 4, 5, respectively

$$\mathbf{A} \sim \begin{bmatrix} 1 & 0 & 0 & 0 \\ 0 & 7 & 3 & -7 \\ 0 & 0 & -\dfrac{8}{7} & -5 \\ 0 & 0 & \dfrac{43}{7} & -11 \\ 0 & 0 & \dfrac{30}{7} & -8 \end{bmatrix}. \tag{4.866}$$

We now multiply column 2 by $-3/7$ and 1, and add this to columns 3, 4, respectively

$$\mathbf{A} \sim \begin{bmatrix} 1 & 0 & 0 & 0 \\ 0 & 7 & 0 & 0 \\ 0 & 0 & -\dfrac{8}{7} & -5 \\ 0 & 0 & \dfrac{43}{7} & -11 \\ 0 & 0 & \dfrac{30}{7} & -8 \end{bmatrix}. \tag{4.867}$$

We now multiply row 3 by $43/8$ and $30/8$, and add this to rows 4, 5, respectively

$$\mathbf{A} \sim \begin{bmatrix} 1 & 0 & 0 & 0 \\ 0 & 7 & 0 & 0 \\ 0 & 0 & -\dfrac{8}{7} & -5 \\ 0 & 0 & 0 & -\dfrac{303}{7} \\ 0 & 0 & 0 & -\dfrac{107}{4} \end{bmatrix}. \tag{4.868}$$

Finally, we multiply row 4 by $-749/1212$ and add this to row 5

$$\mathbf{A} \sim \begin{bmatrix} 1 & 0 & 0 & 0 \\ 0 & 7 & 0 & 0 \\ 0 & 0 & -\dfrac{8}{7} & -5 \\ 0 & 0 & 0 & -\dfrac{303}{7} \\ 0 & 0 & 0 & 0 \end{bmatrix}. \tag{4.869}$$

It follows that

$$\text{rank}(\mathbf{A}) = 4, \tag{4.870}$$

so that we must solve the linear system

$$\mathbf{A}^{\mathrm{T}} \mathbf{A} \mathbf{x}_{\mathrm{LS}} = \mathbf{A}^{\mathrm{T}} \mathbf{b}, \tag{4.871}$$

that is

$$
\begin{bmatrix}
2 & 1 & 3 & -2 & 1 \\
3 & -2 & 6 & -1 & 2 \\
1 & -1 & 1 & 6 & 5 \\
3 & 5 & -2 & 4 & -7
\end{bmatrix}
\begin{bmatrix}
2 & 3 & 1 & 3 \\
1 & -2 & -1 & 5 \\
3 & 6 & 1 & -2 \\
-2 & -1 & 6 & 4 \\
1 & 2 & 5 & -7
\end{bmatrix}
\begin{bmatrix}
x_1 \\ x_2 \\ x_3 \\ x_4
\end{bmatrix}
=
\begin{bmatrix}
2 & 1 & 3 & -2 & 1 \\
3 & -2 & 6 & -1 & 2 \\
1 & -1 & 1 & 6 & 5 \\
3 & 5 & -2 & 4 & -7
\end{bmatrix}
\begin{bmatrix}
9 \\ 3 \\ 8 \\ 7 \\ 1
\end{bmatrix}
$$

(4.872)

or, equivalently,

$$
\begin{bmatrix}
19 & 26 & -3 & -10 \\
26 & 54 & 15 & -31 \\
-3 & 15 & 64 & -15 \\
-10 & -31 & -15 & 103
\end{bmatrix}
\begin{bmatrix}
x_1 \\ x_2 \\ x_3 \\ x_4
\end{bmatrix}
=
\begin{bmatrix}
32 \\ 64 \\ 61 \\ 47
\end{bmatrix}.
$$

(4.873)

The solution of this system is

$$
\mathbf{x}_{LS} = \begin{bmatrix} x_1 & x_2 & x_3 & x_4 \end{bmatrix}^T = \begin{bmatrix} 1 & 1 & 1 & 1 \end{bmatrix}^T.
$$

(4.874)

Example 4.10   Let us again take the matrix $\mathbf{A}$ of Example 4.7 for which we have found

$$
\mathbf{U} = \begin{bmatrix} 0.7497 & -0.6618 \\ 0.6618 & 0.7497 \end{bmatrix}, \quad
\mathbf{V} = \begin{bmatrix} 0.2567 & -0.9665 \\ 0.9665 & 0.2567 \end{bmatrix},
$$

(4.875)

$$
\mathbf{A} = \begin{bmatrix} 1 & 2 \\ 0 & 2 \end{bmatrix},
$$

(4.876)

$$
\mathbf{\Sigma} = \mathbf{U}^T \mathbf{A} \mathbf{V} = \begin{bmatrix} 2.92 & 0 \\ 0 & 0.68 \end{bmatrix}.
$$

(4.877)

Its pseudo-inverse (in fact, it is just the inverse) is given by

$$
\mathbf{A}^+ = \mathbf{V}\mathbf{\Sigma}^+\mathbf{U}^T = \begin{bmatrix} 0.2567 & -0.9665 \\ 0.9665 & 0.2567 \end{bmatrix} \begin{bmatrix} \frac{1}{2.92} & 0 \\ 0 & \frac{1}{0.68} \end{bmatrix} \begin{bmatrix} 0.7497 & 0.6618 \\ -0.6618 & 0.7497 \end{bmatrix} = \begin{bmatrix} 1 & -1 \\ 0 & 0.5 \end{bmatrix}.
$$

(4.878)

Example 4.11   Let the underdetermined linear system be

$$
2x_1 + 3x_2 + x_3 = 6, \quad x_1 + 4x_2 + 3x_3 = 8.
$$

(4.879)

The matrix $\mathbf{A}$ has the expression

$$
\mathbf{A} = \begin{bmatrix} 2 & 3 & 1 \\ 1 & 4 & 3 \end{bmatrix}, \quad
\mathbf{A}^T = \begin{bmatrix} 2 & 1 \\ 3 & 4 \\ 1 & 3 \end{bmatrix}.
$$

(4.880)

We find now the QR decomposition of the matrix $\mathbf{A}^T$.
We have

$$
x_1 = \begin{bmatrix} 2 & 3 & 1 \end{bmatrix}^T, \quad \|x_1\|_2 = \sqrt{14} = \lambda_1
$$

(4.881)

and choose

$$
\mathbf{v}_1 = \mathbf{x}_1 + \lambda_1 \mathbf{e}_1 = \begin{bmatrix} 2 + \sqrt{14} & 3 & 1 \end{bmatrix}^T.
$$

(4.882)

Then

$$\mathbf{v}_1\mathbf{v}_1^{\mathsf{T}} = \begin{bmatrix} 18+4\sqrt{14} & 6+3\sqrt{14} & 2+\sqrt{14} \\ 6+3\sqrt{14} & 9 & 3 \\ 2+\sqrt{14} & 3 & 1 \end{bmatrix}, \tag{4.883}$$

$$\mathbf{v}_1^{\mathsf{T}}\mathbf{v}_1 = 28+4\sqrt{14}, \tag{4.884}$$

$$2\frac{\mathbf{v}_1\mathbf{v}_1^{\mathsf{T}}}{\mathbf{v}_1^{\mathsf{T}}\mathbf{v}_1} = \begin{bmatrix} 1.53452 & 0.80178 & 0.26726 \\ 0.80178 & 0.41893 & 0.13964 \\ 0.26726 & 0.13964 & 0.04655 \end{bmatrix}, \tag{4.885}$$

$$\mathbf{H}_1 = \begin{bmatrix} -0.53452 & -0.80178 & -0.26726 \\ -0.80178 & 0.58107 & -0.13964 \\ -0.26726 & -0.13964 & 0.95345 \end{bmatrix}, \tag{4.886}$$

$$\mathbf{H}_1\mathbf{A}^{\mathsf{T}} = \begin{bmatrix} -0.53452 & -0.80178 & -0.26726 \\ -0.80178 & 0.58107 & -0.13964 \\ -0.26726 & -0.13964 & 0.95345 \end{bmatrix}\begin{bmatrix} 2 & 1 \\ 3 & 4 \\ 1 & 3 \end{bmatrix} = \begin{bmatrix} -3.74164 & -4.54342 \\ 0 & 1.10358 \\ 0 & 2.03453 \end{bmatrix}. \tag{4.887}$$

The next vector is

$$\mathbf{x}_2 = \begin{bmatrix} 1.10358 & 2.03453 \end{bmatrix}^{\mathsf{T}}, \tag{4.888}$$

for which

$$\|\mathbf{x}_2\|_2 = 2.31456. \tag{4.889}$$

We choose

$$\mathbf{v}_2 = \mathbf{x}_2 + \|\mathbf{x}_2\|_2\mathbf{e}_2 = \begin{bmatrix} 3.418174 & 2.03453 \end{bmatrix}^{\mathsf{T}}, \tag{4.890}$$

for which

$$\mathbf{v}_2\mathbf{v}_2^{\mathsf{T}} = \begin{bmatrix} 11,68368 & 6,95431 \\ 6,95431 & 4,13931 \end{bmatrix}, \tag{4.891}$$

$$\mathbf{v}_2^{\mathsf{T}}\mathbf{v}_2 = 15,82299, \tag{4.892}$$

$$2\frac{\mathbf{v}_2\mathbf{v}_2^{\mathsf{T}}}{\mathbf{v}_2^{\mathsf{T}}\mathbf{v}_2} = \begin{bmatrix} 1,47680 & 0,87901 \\ 0,87901 & 0,52320 \end{bmatrix}, \tag{4.893}$$

$$\mathbf{H}_2 = \begin{bmatrix} 1 & 0 & 0 \\ 0 & -0.47680 & -0.87901 \\ 0 & -0.87901 & 0.47680 \end{bmatrix}, \tag{4.894}$$

$$\mathbf{H}_2\mathbf{H}_1\mathbf{A}^{\mathsf{T}} = \begin{bmatrix} -3.74164 & -4.54342 \\ 0 & -2.31456 \\ 0 & 0 \end{bmatrix} = \mathbf{R}, \tag{4.895}$$

$$\mathbf{Q} = \mathbf{H}_1\mathbf{H}_2 = \begin{bmatrix} -0.53452 & 0.61721 & 0.57735 \\ -0.80178 & -0.15431 & -0.57735 \\ -0.26726 & -0.77151 & 0.57735 \end{bmatrix}. \tag{4.896}$$

It results in the system

$$\begin{bmatrix} -3.74164 & 0 & 0 \\ -4.54342 & -2.31456 & 0 \end{bmatrix}\begin{bmatrix} z_1 \\ z_2 \\ z_3 \end{bmatrix} = \begin{bmatrix} 6 \\ 8 \end{bmatrix}, \tag{4.897}$$

with the solution

$$z_1 = -1.60357, \quad z_2 = -0.30861, \quad z_3 = 0. \tag{4.898}$$

The vector $\mathbf{x}$ is given by the system

$$\begin{bmatrix} 0.53452 & -0.80178 & -0.26726 \\ 0.61721 & -0.15431 & -0.77151 \\ 0.57735 & -0.57735 & 0.57735 \end{bmatrix} \begin{bmatrix} x_1 \\ x_2 \\ x_3 \end{bmatrix} = \begin{bmatrix} -1.60357 \\ -0.30861 \\ 0 \end{bmatrix} \tag{4.899}$$

and it follows that

$$x_1 = 0.66667, \quad x_2 = 1.33334, \quad x_3 = 0.66667, \quad \|\mathbf{x}\|_2 = 1.633. \tag{4.900}$$

If we consider $z_3 = 0.57785$, then we obtain $\overline{x}_1 = 1$, $\overline{x}_2 = 1$, $\overline{x}_3 = 1$, $\|\overline{\mathbf{x}}\|_2 = \sqrt{3} = 1.73205 > \|\mathbf{x}\|_2$.

Example 4.12   Let

$$\mathbf{A} = \begin{bmatrix} 1 & 2 \\ 2 & 2 \end{bmatrix}, \tag{4.901}$$

be the matrix for which we wish to determine the eigenvalues and eigenvectors by means of the rotation method.

To do this, we construct the matrix $\mathbf{R}_1$ given by

$$\mathbf{R}_1 = \begin{bmatrix} \cos \alpha & -\sin \alpha \\ \sin \alpha & \cos \alpha \end{bmatrix}, \quad \mathbf{R}_1^{-1} = \mathbf{R}_1^{T}, \tag{4.902}$$

where

$$\tan 2\alpha = \frac{2a_{12}}{a_{11} - a_{22}} = -4. \tag{4.903}$$

It follows that

$$\alpha = -0.66291, \tag{4.904}$$

$$\mathbf{R}_1 = \begin{bmatrix} 0.78821 & 0.61541 \\ -0.61541 & 0.78821 \end{bmatrix} \tag{4.905}$$

and the new matrix

$$\mathbf{A}_2 = \mathbf{R}_1^{-1}\mathbf{A}\mathbf{R}_1 = \begin{bmatrix} -0.56156 & 0 \\ 0 & 3.56157 \end{bmatrix}. \tag{4.906}$$

We observe that the matrix $\mathbf{A}_2$ is a diagonal one, the eigenvalues of the matrix $\mathbf{A}$ being given by

$$\lambda_1 \approx 0.56156, \quad \lambda_2 = 3.56157, \tag{4.907}$$

while the eigenvectors read

$$\mathbf{v}_1 = \begin{bmatrix} 0.78821 & -0.61541 \end{bmatrix}^{T}, \quad \mathbf{v}_2 = \begin{bmatrix} 0.61541 & 0.78821 \end{bmatrix}^{T}. \tag{4.908}$$

The exact eigenvalues of the matrix $\mathbf{A}$ are

$$\overline{\lambda}_1 = \frac{3 - \sqrt{17}}{2} = -0.56155, \quad \overline{\lambda}_2 = \frac{3 + \sqrt{17}}{2} = 3.56155. \tag{4.909}$$

4.13 APPLICATIONS

Problem 4.1

Let us show that the motion of the system in Figure 4.1 is stable if the force F is given by

$$\ddot{F} = -40\dot{x} - 25x, \tag{4.910}$$

the constants of the system being $m = 4$ kg, $c = 20$ N s m^{-1}, $k = 41$ N m^{-1}.

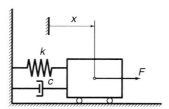

Figure 4.1 Problem 4.1.

Solution: Differentiating twice the differential equation of motion

$$m\ddot{x} + c\dot{x} + kx = F \tag{4.911}$$

with respect to time and taking into account the numerical values, we obtain

$$4\overset{....}{x} + 20\overset{...}{x} + 41\ddot{x} + 40\dot{x} + 25x = 0; \tag{4.912}$$

the characteristic equation is

$$b_0 r^4 + b_1 r^3 + b_2 r^2 + b_3 r + b_4 = 0, \tag{4.913}$$

where $b_0 = 4$, $b_1 = 20$, $b_2 = 41$, $b_3 = 40$, $b_4 = 25$.

The motion is asymptotically stable if the solutions of equation (4.913) are either strictly negative or complex with a strict negative real part. To this end, the conditions of the Routh–Hurwitz criterion must be fulfilled, that is,

$$b_i > 0, \quad i = \overline{1,4}, \quad \det \mathbf{A}_1 > 0, \quad \det \mathbf{A}_2 > 0, \tag{4.914}$$

where

$$\mathbf{A}_1 = \begin{bmatrix} b_1 & b_0 \\ b_3 & b_2 \end{bmatrix}, \quad \mathbf{A}_2 = \begin{bmatrix} b_1 & b_0 & 0 \\ b_3 & b_2 & b_1 \\ 0 & b_4 & b_3 \end{bmatrix} \tag{4.915}$$

or, equivalent,

$$\mathbf{A}_1 = \begin{bmatrix} 20 & 4 \\ 40 & 41 \end{bmatrix}, \quad \mathbf{A}_2 = \begin{bmatrix} 20 & 4 & 0 \\ 40 & 41 & 20 \\ 0 & 25 & 40 \end{bmatrix}. \tag{4.916}$$

In case of the numerical application, we obtain the values $\det \mathbf{A}_1 = 660$, $\det \mathbf{A}_2 = 16{,}400$, conditions (4.914) are fulfilled and, as a consequence, the motion is asymptotically stable.

Moreover, the roots of equation (4.913) are $r_{1,2} = -2 \pm i$, $r_{3,4} = -1/2 \pm i$, obtaining a solution obviously asymptotically stable:

$$x = C_1 e^{-2t} \cos(t + \phi_1) + C_2 e^{-\frac{t}{2}} \cos(t + \phi_2), \tag{4.917}$$

where C_1, C_2, ϕ_1, ϕ_2 are integration constants that may be determined by the initial conditions.

Problem 4.2

We consider a rigid solid acted upon by five forces of intensities F_i, $i = \overline{1,5}$, the supports of which being the straight lines of equations

$$b_i x - a_i y = 0, \quad z - z_i = 0, \quad a_i^2 + b_i^2 = 1, \quad i = \overline{1,5}. \tag{4.918}$$

If we show that if the rank of the matrix

$$\mathbf{A} = \begin{bmatrix} a_1 & a_2 & a_3 & a_4 & a_5 \\ b_1 & b_2 & b_3 & b_4 & b_5 \\ a_1 z_1 & a_2 z_2 & a_3 z_3 & a_4 z_4 & a_5 z_5 \\ b_1 z_1 & b_2 z_2 & b_3 z_3 & b_4 z_4 & b_5 z_5 \end{bmatrix} \tag{4.919}$$

is equal to four, then we may determine the intensities F_i, $i = \overline{1,5}$, so that the solid is in equilibrium.

Solution: The equations of equilibrium

$$\sum_{i=1}^{5} F_i a_i = 0, \quad \sum_{i=1}^{5} F_i b_i = 0, \quad \sum_{i=1}^{5} F_i a_i z_i = 0, \quad \sum_{i=1}^{5} F_i b_i z_i = 0 \tag{4.920}$$

form a system of homogeneous algebraic equations, which admits solutions if $\mathrm{rank}\mathbf{A} = 4$. Because the determinant

$$\begin{vmatrix} a_1 & a_2 & a_3 & a_4 \\ b_1 & b_2 & b_3 & b_4 \\ a_1 z_1 & a_2 z_2 & a_3 z_3 & a_4 z_4 \\ b_1 z_1 & b_2 z_2 & b_3 z_3 & b_4 z_4 \end{vmatrix} = \begin{vmatrix} 1 & 0 & \dfrac{\sqrt{2}}{2} & \dfrac{3}{5} \\ 0 & 1 & \dfrac{\sqrt{2}}{2} & \dfrac{4}{5} \\ 0 & 0 & \dfrac{\sqrt{2}}{2} & -\dfrac{3}{10} \\ 0 & \dfrac{1}{2} & \dfrac{\sqrt{2}}{2} & -\dfrac{2}{5} \end{vmatrix} = \dfrac{3\sqrt{2}}{40} \neq 0, \tag{4.921}$$

system (4.920) admits the solution

$$\frac{F_1}{\begin{vmatrix} a_2 & a_3 & a_4 & a_5 \\ b_2 & b_3 & b_4 & b_5 \\ a_2 z_2 & a_3 z_3 & a_4 z_4 & a_5 z_5 \\ b_2 z_2 & b_3 z_3 & b_4 z_4 & b_5 z_5 \end{vmatrix}} = \frac{F_2}{\begin{vmatrix} a_3 & a_4 & a_5 & a_1 \\ b_3 & b_4 & b_5 & b_1 \\ a_3 z_3 & a_4 z_4 & a_5 z_5 & a_1 z_1 \\ b_3 z_3 & b_4 z_4 & b_5 z_5 & b_1 z_1 \end{vmatrix}} = \frac{F_3}{\begin{vmatrix} a_4 & a_5 & a_1 & a_2 \\ b_4 & b_5 & b_1 & b_2 \\ a_4 z_4 & a_5 z_5 & a_1 z_1 & a_2 z_2 \\ b_4 z_4 & b_5 z_5 & b_1 z_1 & b_2 z_2 \end{vmatrix}}$$

$$= \frac{F_4}{\begin{vmatrix} a_5 & a_1 & a_2 & a_3 \\ b_5 & b_1 & b_2 & b_3 \\ a_5 z_5 & a_1 z_1 & a_2 z_2 & a_3 z_3 \\ b_5 z_5 & b_1 z_1 & b_2 z_2 & b_3 z_3 \end{vmatrix}} = \frac{F_5}{\begin{vmatrix} a_1 & a_2 & a_3 & a_4 \\ b_1 & b_2 & b_3 & b_4 \\ a_1 z_1 & a_2 z_2 & a_3 z_3 & a_4 z_4 \\ b_1 z_1 & b_2 z_2 & b_3 z_3 & b_4 z_4 \end{vmatrix}} \tag{4.922}$$

or, equivalent,

$$
\frac{F_1}{\begin{vmatrix} 0 & \dfrac{\sqrt{2}}{2} & \dfrac{3}{5} & \dfrac{3}{5} \\[2mm] 1 & \dfrac{\sqrt{2}}{2} & \dfrac{4}{5} & \dfrac{4}{5} \\[2mm] 0 & \dfrac{\sqrt{2}}{2} & -\dfrac{3}{10} & \dfrac{3}{5} \\[2mm] \dfrac{1}{2} & \dfrac{\sqrt{2}}{2} & -\dfrac{2}{5} & -\dfrac{4}{5} \end{vmatrix}}
=
\frac{F_2}{\begin{vmatrix} \dfrac{\sqrt{2}}{2} & \dfrac{3}{5} & -\dfrac{3}{5} & 1 \\[2mm] \dfrac{\sqrt{2}}{2} & \dfrac{4}{5} & \dfrac{4}{5} & 0 \\[2mm] \dfrac{\sqrt{2}}{2} & -\dfrac{3}{10} & \dfrac{3}{5} & 0 \\[2mm] \dfrac{\sqrt{2}}{2} & -\dfrac{2}{5} & -\dfrac{4}{5} & 0 \end{vmatrix}}
=
\frac{F_3}{\begin{vmatrix} \dfrac{3}{5} & -\dfrac{3}{5} & 1 & 0 \\[2mm] \dfrac{4}{5} & \dfrac{4}{5} & 0 & 1 \\[2mm] -\dfrac{3}{10} & \dfrac{3}{5} & 0 & 0 \\[2mm] -\dfrac{2}{5} & -\dfrac{4}{5} & 0 & \dfrac{1}{2} \end{vmatrix}}
$$

$$
=
\frac{F_4}{\begin{vmatrix} -\dfrac{3}{5} & 1 & 0 & \dfrac{\sqrt{2}}{2} \\[2mm] \dfrac{4}{5} & 0 & 1 & \dfrac{\sqrt{2}}{2} \\[2mm] \dfrac{3}{5} & 0 & 0 & \dfrac{\sqrt{2}}{2} \\[2mm] -\dfrac{4}{5} & 0 & \dfrac{1}{2} & \dfrac{\sqrt{2}}{2} \end{vmatrix}}
=
\frac{F_5}{\begin{vmatrix} 1 & 0 & \dfrac{\sqrt{2}}{2} & \dfrac{3}{5} \\[2mm] 0 & 1 & \dfrac{\sqrt{2}}{2} & \dfrac{4}{5} \\[2mm] 0 & 0 & \dfrac{\sqrt{2}}{2} & -\dfrac{3}{10} \\[2mm] 0 & \dfrac{1}{2} & \dfrac{\sqrt{2}}{2} & -\dfrac{2}{5} \end{vmatrix}},
\tag{4.923}
$$

from which

$$
\frac{F_1}{-\dfrac{213\sqrt{2}}{200}} = \frac{F_2}{-\dfrac{19\sqrt{2}}{25}} = \frac{F_3}{\dfrac{21}{25}} = \frac{F_4}{\dfrac{19\sqrt{2}}{20}} = \frac{F_5}{-\dfrac{13\sqrt{2}}{40}}.
\tag{4.924}
$$

Denoting now by λ (arbitrary real number) the common value of the ratios in relations (4.924), we obtain the forces

$$
F_1 = -\frac{213\sqrt{2}}{200}\lambda, \quad F_2 = -\frac{19\sqrt{2}}{25}\lambda, \quad F_3 = \frac{21}{25}\lambda, \quad F_4 = \frac{19\sqrt{2}}{20}\lambda, \quad F_5 = -\frac{13\sqrt{2}}{40}\lambda.
\tag{4.925}
$$

Problem 4.3

Let us consider a rigid solid (Fig. 4.2), suspended by $n = 6$ bars with spherical hinges.

Let $\mathbf{u}_i$ be the unit vectors in the directions $A_i A_{0i}$, $\mathbf{r}_i$ the position vectors of the points A_i, the vectors $\mathbf{m}_i = \mathbf{r}_i \cdot \mathbf{u}_i$, (a_i, b_i, c_i), (d_i, e_i, f_i) the projections of the vectors $\mathbf{u}_i$, $\mathbf{m}_i$, $i = \overline{1,6}$, on the axes of the $OXYZ$-trihedron, while $\mathbf{A}$ is the matrix defined by

$$
\mathbf{A} = \begin{bmatrix} a_1 & a_2 & a_3 & a_4 & a_5 & a_6 \\ b_1 & b_2 & b_3 & b_4 & b_5 & b_6 \\ c_1 & c_2 & c_3 & c_4 & c_5 & c_6 \\ d_1 & d_2 & d_3 & d_4 & d_5 & d_6 \\ e_1 & e_2 & e_3 & e_4 & e_5 & e_6 \\ f_1 & f_2 & f_3 & f_4 & f_5 & f_6 \end{bmatrix}.
\tag{4.926}
$$

Let us show that if $\text{rank}\mathbf{A} = 6$, then the equilibrium of the rigid solid is a statically determined (isostatic) problem, hence the efforts N_i in the bars $A_i A_{0i}$, $i = \overline{1,6}$, may be determined for any system of forces $(\mathbf{F}, \mathbf{M}_O)$ that acts upon the rigid solid.

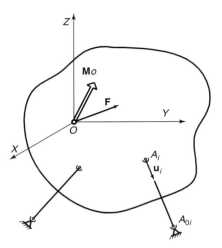

Figure 4.2   Problem 4.3.

As a numerical application, we consider the cube in Figure 4.3 of side $l = 2$ m, acted upon by the force of components $F_X = 2000$ N, $F_Y = 2000$ N, $F_Z = 4000$ N, by the moment of projections $M_{OX} = 3000$ Nm, $M_{OY} = 1000$ N m, $M_{OZ} = 2000$ N m, the bars $A_1 A_{01}$, $A_5 A_{05}$ being parallel to the OX-axis, the bars $A_2 A_{02}$, $A_6 A_{06}$ being parallel to the OY-axis, while the bars $A_3 A_{03}$, $A_4 A_{04}$ are parallel to the OZ-axis.

Solution: By means of the vectors $\mathbf{u}_i$, $\mathbf{m}_i$, $i = \overline{1, 6}$, the equations of equilibrium

$$\sum_{i=1}^{6} \mathbf{N}_i + \mathbf{F} = \mathbf{0}, \quad \sum_{i=1}^{6} \mathbf{r}_i \cdot \mathbf{N}_i + \mathbf{M}_O = \mathbf{0} \tag{4.927}$$

are obtained in the form

$$\sum_{i=1}^{6} N_i \mathbf{u}_i + \mathbf{F} = \mathbf{0}, \quad \sum_{i=1}^{6} N_i \mathbf{m}_i + \mathbf{M}_O = \mathbf{0}. \tag{4.928}$$

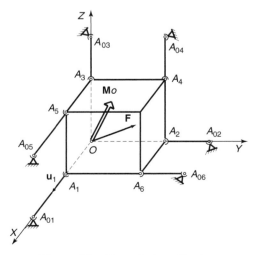

Figure 4.3   Numerical application.

If we denote by (F_X, F_Y, F_Z), (M_{OX}, M_{OY}, M_{OZ}) the projections of the vectors $\mathbf{F}$, $\mathbf{M}_O$ on the axes OX, OY, OZ and by $\{F\}$, $\{N\}$ the column matrices

$$\{\mathbf{F}\} = \begin{bmatrix} F_X & F_Y & F_Z & M_{OX} & M_{OY} & M_{OZ} \end{bmatrix}^{\mathrm{T}},$$
$$\{\mathbf{N}\} = \begin{bmatrix} N_1 & N_2 & N_3 & N_4 & N_5 & N_6 \end{bmatrix}^{\mathrm{T}}, \tag{4.929}$$

then system (4.928) leads to the matrix equation

$$\mathbf{A}\{\mathbf{N}\} + \{\mathbf{F}\} = \{\mathbf{0}\}, \tag{4.930}$$

which has a solution if $rank\,\mathbf{A} = 6$ and the problem is isostatic.

Observation 4.42 If the number of bars $n > 6$, then equation (4.930) may have as well a solution if rank$\mathbf{A} = 6$. In this case, the problem is statically undetermined (hyperstatic); the determination of the reactions N_i, $i = \overline{1, n}$, is possible by taking into account the elastic equilibrium equations.

In the numerical case, it follows that

$$\mathbf{A} = \begin{bmatrix} 1 & 0 & 0 & 0 & 1 & 0 \\ 0 & 1 & 0 & 0 & 0 & 1 \\ 0 & 0 & 1 & 1 & 0 & 0 \\ 0 & 0 & 0 & 2 & 0 & 0 \\ 0 & 0 & 0 & 0 & 2 & 0 \\ 0 & 0 & 0 & 0 & 0 & 2 \end{bmatrix}, \tag{4.931}$$

$$\det \mathbf{A} = 8 \neq 0, \quad rank\mathbf{A} = 6; \tag{4.932}$$

and because

$$\{\mathbf{F}\} = 1000 \begin{bmatrix} 2 & 2 & 4 & 3 & 1 & 2 \end{bmatrix}^{\mathrm{T}}, \tag{4.933}$$

we obtain the matrix equation

$$\begin{bmatrix} 1 & 0 & 0 & 0 & 1 & 0 \\ 0 & 1 & 0 & 0 & 0 & 1 \\ 0 & 0 & 1 & 1 & 0 & 0 \\ 0 & 0 & 0 & 2 & 0 & 0 \\ 0 & 0 & 0 & 0 & 2 & 0 \\ 0 & 0 & 0 & 0 & 0 & 2 \end{bmatrix} \begin{bmatrix} N_1 \\ N_2 \\ N_3 \\ N_4 \\ N_5 \\ N_6 \end{bmatrix} = \begin{bmatrix} -2000 \\ -2000 \\ -4000 \\ -3000 \\ -1000 \\ -2000 \end{bmatrix}, \tag{4.934}$$

from which the values

$$N_1 = -1500 \text{ N}, \quad N_2 = -1000 \text{ N}, \quad N_3 = -2500 \text{ N},$$
$$N_4 = -1500 \text{ N}, \quad N_5 = -500 \text{ N}, \quad N_6 = -1000 \text{ N}. \tag{4.935}$$

Problem 4.4

A homogeneous straight bar AB, of constant cross section, of mass m and length $2l$ is moving, under the action of its own weight, in the vertical plane OXY (Fig. 4.4), with the end A on the hyperbola of equation

$$F(X, Y) = (X - 2l)Y - 8l^2 = 0. \tag{4.936}$$

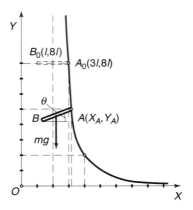

Figure 4.4   Problem 4.4.

Knowing that at the initial moment the bar is in rest and parallel to the OX-axis, the end A being of coordinates $(3l, 8l)$, determine the reaction N_A at this moment, the acceleration of the gravity center C, as well as the angular acceleration.

Numerical application for $m = 3$ kg, $l = 1$ m.

Solution: Denoting by (X, Y) the coordinates of the center of gravity C and by θ the angle made by the bar with the OX-axis, we may write the relations

$$X_A = X + l\cos\theta, \quad Y_A = Y + l\sin\theta, \quad \dot{X}_A = \dot{X} - l\dot{\theta}\sin\theta, \quad \dot{Y}_A = \dot{Y} + l\dot{\theta}\cos\theta,$$
$$\ddot{X}_A = \ddot{X} - l\ddot{\theta}\sin\theta - l\dot{\theta}^2\cos\theta, \quad \ddot{Y}_A = \ddot{Y} + l\ddot{\theta}\cos\theta - l\dot{\theta}^2\sin\theta, \tag{4.937}$$

from which, for the initial moment $(X = 3l, Y = 8l, \theta = 0, \dot{\theta} = 0, \dot{X} = 0, \dot{Y} = 0)$, we obtain

$$\dot{X}_A = 0, \quad \dot{Y}_A = 0, \quad \ddot{X}_A = \ddot{X}, \quad \ddot{Y}_A = \ddot{Y} + l\ddot{\theta}. \tag{4.938}$$

By successive differentiation of equation (4.936) with regard to time, we get the relations

$$\dot{X}_A Y_A + (X_A - 2l)\dot{Y}_A = 0, \quad \ddot{X}_A Y_A + (X_A - 2l)\ddot{Y}_A + 2\dot{X}_A \dot{Y}_A = 0. \tag{4.939}$$

Taking into account the relations at the initial moment, it follows that

$$8l\ddot{X} + l\ddot{Y} + l^2\ddot{\theta} = 0. \tag{4.940}$$

The reaction N_A has the components

$$N_{AX} = \lambda\left.\frac{\partial F}{\partial X}\right|_{\substack{X=X_A \\ Y=Y_A}}, \quad N_{AY} = \lambda\left.\frac{\partial F}{\partial Y}\right|_{\substack{X=X_A \\ Y=Y_A}} \tag{4.941}$$

or

$$N_{AX} = \lambda Y_A, \quad N_{AY} = \lambda(X_A - 2l), \tag{4.942}$$

which, at the initial moment, become

$$N_{AX} = 8\lambda l, \quad N_{AY} = \lambda l. \tag{4.943}$$

Under these conditions, the theorem of momentum leads to the equations

$$m\ddot{X} = 8\lambda l, \quad m\ddot{Y} = -mg + \lambda l, \tag{4.944}$$

while the theorem of moment of momentum with respect to the point C allows to write

$$\frac{ml^2}{3}\ddot{\theta} = \lambda l^2. \tag{4.945}$$

Using the notation

$$\mathbf{A} = \begin{bmatrix} m & 0 & 0 & -8l \\ 0 & m & 0 & -l \\ 0 & 0 & \dfrac{ml^2}{3} & -l^2 \\ 8l & l & l^2 & 0 \end{bmatrix}, \tag{4.946}$$

equation (4.944) and equation (4.945), equation (4.940) can be written in the matrix form

$$\mathbf{A}\begin{bmatrix} \ddot{X} \\ \ddot{Y} \\ \ddot{\theta} \\ \lambda \end{bmatrix} = \begin{bmatrix} 0 \\ -mg \\ 0 \\ 0 \end{bmatrix}, \tag{4.947}$$

from which, by inverting the matrix $\mathbf{A}$, the matrix

$$\begin{bmatrix} \ddot{X} \\ \ddot{Y} \\ \ddot{\theta} \\ \lambda \end{bmatrix} = -mg\mathbf{A}^{-1}\begin{bmatrix} 0 \\ 1 \\ 0 \\ 0 \end{bmatrix} \tag{4.948}$$

is obtained.

For the numerical application, we have

$$\mathbf{A} = \begin{bmatrix} 3 & 0 & 0 & -8 \\ 0 & 3 & 0 & -1 \\ 0 & 0 & 1 & -1 \\ 8 & 1 & 1 & 0 \end{bmatrix}, \quad \mathbf{A}^{-1} = \begin{bmatrix} 0.019608 & -0.039216 & -0.117647 & 0.117647 \\ -0.039216 & 0.328431 & -0.014706 & 0.014706 \\ -0.117647 & -0.014706 & 0.955882 & 0.044118 \\ -0.117647 & -0.014706 & -0.044118 & 0.044118 \end{bmatrix}, \tag{4.949}$$

$$\begin{bmatrix} \ddot{X} \\ \ddot{Y} \\ \ddot{\theta} \\ \lambda \end{bmatrix} = \begin{bmatrix} 1.153715 \\ -9.662276 \\ 0.432643 \\ 0.432643 \end{bmatrix}, \tag{4.950}$$

$$N_{AX} = 3.461144 \text{ N}, \quad N_{AY} = 0.432643 \text{ N}. \tag{4.951}$$

Problem 4.5

We consider a system of two homogeneous straight bars, of constant cross sections, lengths $2l_1$ and $2l_2$ and masses m_1 and m_2 (Fig. 4.5), respectively, acted upon by their own weights m_1g and m_2g (a double pendulum). The fixed reference system is OXY, the OX-axis being vertical.

Taking as generalized coordinates the coordinates (X_1, Y_1), (X_2, Y_2) of the center of gravity C_1 and C_2, respectively, as well as the angles θ_1 and θ_2 made by the bars with the OX-axis, it is required

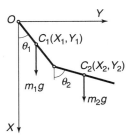

Figure 4.5   Problem 4.5.

(a) to write the differential equation of motion, using the multibody method;

(b) the dimensions $l_1 = l_2 = 0.5$ m and the initial conditions at $t = 0$: $X_1 = l_1$, $Y_1 = 0$, $\theta_1 = 0$, $X_2 = 2l_1$, $Y_2 = l_2$, $\theta_2 = \pi/2$, $\dot{X}_1 = \dot{X}_2 = \dot{Y}_1 = \dot{Y}_2 = 0$, $\dot{\theta}_1 = \dot{\theta}_2 = 0$ being given, determine the accelerations $\ddot{X}_1$, $\ddot{Y}_1$, $\ddot{\theta}_1$, $\ddot{X}_2$, $\ddot{Y}_2$, $\ddot{\theta}_2$ and the reactions, by inverting the matrix in two cases, that is, $m_1 = m_2 = 3$ kg and $m_1 = 0$, $m_2 = 3$ kg.

Solution: Differentiating the constraints functions with respect to time,

$$X_1 - l_1\cos\theta_1 = 0, \quad Y_1 - l_1\sin\theta_1 = 0,$$

$$-X_1 - l_1\cos\theta_1 + X_2 - l_2\cos\theta_2 = 0,$$

$$-Y_1 - l_1\sin\theta_1 + Y_2 - l_2\sin\theta_2 = 0, \tag{4.952}$$

and using the notations

$$[\mathbf{B}] = \begin{bmatrix} 1 & 0 & l_1\sin\theta_1 & 0 & 0 & 0 \\ 0 & 1 & -l_1\cos\theta_1 & 0 & 0 & 0 \\ -1 & 0 & l_1\sin\theta_1 & 1 & 0 & l_2\sin\theta_2 \\ 0 & -1 & -l_1\cos\theta_1 & 0 & 1 & -l_2\cos\theta_2 \end{bmatrix}, \tag{4.953}$$

$$\{q\} = \begin{bmatrix} X_1 & Y_1 & \theta_1 & X_2 & Y_2 & \theta_2 \end{bmatrix}^{\mathrm{T}}, \tag{4.954}$$

$[\mathbf{B}]$ being the constraints matrix and $\{q\}$ the column matrix of the generalized coordinates, we obtain the relation

$$[\mathbf{B}]\{\dot{q}\} = \{\mathbf{0}\}. \tag{4.955}$$

We apply Lagrange's equations

$$\frac{\mathrm{d}}{\mathrm{d}t}\left(\frac{\partial T}{\partial \dot{q}_k}\right) - \frac{\partial T}{\partial q_k} + \frac{\partial V}{\partial q_k} = \sum_{i=1}^{4} B_{ik}\lambda_i, \quad k = \overline{1, 6}, \tag{4.956}$$

where λ_i, $i = \overline{1, 4}$, are Lagrange's multipliers, while the kinetic energy T and the potential energy V are given by the relations

$$T = \frac{1}{2}\sum_{i=1}^{2}\left[m_i\left(\dot{X}_i^2 + \dot{Y}_i^2\right) + \frac{m_i l_i^2}{3}\dot{\theta}_i^2\right], \tag{4.957}$$

$$V = -g\sum_{i=1}^{2} m_i X_i, \tag{4.958}$$

respectively.

Using the notations

$$[\mathbf{M}] = \begin{bmatrix} m_1 & 0 & 0 & 0 & 0 & 0 \\ 0 & m_1 & 0 & 0 & 0 & 0 \\ 0 & 0 & \dfrac{m_1 l_1^2}{3} & 0 & 0 & 0 \\ 0 & 0 & 0 & m_2 & 0 & 0 \\ 0 & 0 & 0 & 0 & m_2 & 0 \\ 0 & 0 & 0 & 0 & 0 & \dfrac{m_2 l_2^2}{3} \end{bmatrix}, \quad \{\mathbf{F}\} = \begin{bmatrix} m_1 g \\ 0 \\ 0 \\ m_2 g \\ 0 \\ 0 \end{bmatrix}, \quad \{\boldsymbol{\lambda}\} = \begin{bmatrix} \lambda_1 \\ \lambda_2 \\ \lambda_3 \\ \lambda_4 \end{bmatrix}, \quad (4.959)$$

we obtain the matrix equation

$$[\mathbf{M}]\{\ddot{\mathbf{q}}\} = \{\mathbf{F}\} + [\mathbf{B}]^{\mathrm{T}}\{\boldsymbol{\lambda}\}. \quad (4.960)$$

Relation (4.960) and relation (4.955), differentiated with respect to time, are expressed together in the matrix equation of motion of the mechanical system

$$\begin{bmatrix} [\mathbf{M}] & -[\mathbf{B}]^{\mathrm{T}} \\ [\mathbf{B}] & [\mathbf{0}] \end{bmatrix} \begin{bmatrix} \{\ddot{\mathbf{q}}\} \\ \{\boldsymbol{\lambda}\} \end{bmatrix} = \begin{bmatrix} \{\mathbf{F}\} \\ -[\dot{\mathbf{B}}]\{\dot{\mathbf{q}}\} \end{bmatrix}. \quad (4.961)$$

We obtain

$$\begin{bmatrix} \{\ddot{\mathbf{q}}\} \\ \{\boldsymbol{\lambda}\} \end{bmatrix} = \begin{bmatrix} [\mathbf{M}]^{-1} - [\mathbf{M}]^{-1}[\mathbf{B}]^{\mathrm{T}}[[\mathbf{B}][\mathbf{M}]^{-1}[\mathbf{B}]^{\mathrm{T}}]^{-1}[\mathbf{B}][\mathbf{M}]^{-1} & [\mathbf{M}]^{-1}[\mathbf{B}]^{\mathrm{T}}[[\mathbf{B}][\mathbf{M}]^{-1}[\mathbf{B}]^{\mathrm{T}}]^{-1} \\ -[[\mathbf{B}][\mathbf{M}]^{-1}[\mathbf{B}]^{\mathrm{T}}]^{-1}[\mathbf{B}][\mathbf{M}]^{-1} & [[\mathbf{B}][\mathbf{M}]^{-1}[\mathbf{B}]^{\mathrm{T}}]^{-1} \end{bmatrix}$$

$$\times \begin{bmatrix} \{\mathbf{F}\} \\ -[\dot{\mathbf{B}}]\{\dot{\mathbf{q}}\} \end{bmatrix} \quad (4.962)$$

if the matrix $[\mathbf{M}]$ is invertible.

For the first numerical application, we obtain the values

$$[\mathbf{M}] = \begin{bmatrix} 3 & 0 & 0 & 0 & 0 & 0 \\ 0 & 3 & 0 & 0 & 0 & 0 \\ 0 & 0 & 0.25 & 0 & 0 & 0 \\ 0 & 0 & 0 & 3 & 0 & 0 \\ 0 & 0 & 0 & 0 & 3 & 0 \\ 0 & 0 & 0 & 0 & 0 & 0.25 \end{bmatrix}, \quad [\mathbf{M}]^{-1} = \begin{bmatrix} \dfrac{1}{3} & 0 & 0 & 0 & 0 & 0 \\ 0 & \dfrac{1}{3} & 0 & 0 & 0 & 0 \\ 0 & 0 & 4 & 0 & 0 & 0 \\ 0 & 0 & 0 & \dfrac{1}{3} & 0 & 0 \\ 0 & 0 & 0 & 0 & \dfrac{1}{3} & 0 \\ 0 & 0 & 0 & 0 & 0 & 4 \end{bmatrix}, \quad (4.963)$$

$$[\mathbf{B}] = \begin{bmatrix} 1 & 0 & 0 & 0 & 0 & 0 \\ 0 & 1 & -0.5 & 0 & 0 & 0 \\ -1 & 0 & 0 & 1 & 0 & 0.5 \\ 0 & -1 & -0.5 & 0 & 1 & 0 \end{bmatrix}, \quad [\mathbf{B}]^{\mathrm{T}} = \begin{bmatrix} 1 & 0 & -1 & 0 \\ 0 & 1 & 0 & -1 \\ 0 & -0.5 & 0 & -0.5 \\ 0 & 0 & 1 & 0 \\ 0 & 0 & 0 & 1 \\ 0 & 0 & 0.5 & 0 \end{bmatrix}, \quad (4.964)$$

$$\{\mathbf{F}\} = \begin{bmatrix} 29.4195 & 0 & 0 & 29.4195 & 0 & 0 \end{bmatrix}^{\mathrm{T}}, \quad (4.965)$$

$$[\dot{\mathbf{B}}]\{\dot{\mathbf{q}}\} = \begin{bmatrix} 0 & 0 & 0 & 0 \end{bmatrix}^{\mathrm{T}}, \quad (4.966)$$

$$\begin{bmatrix} \{\ddot{\mathbf{q}}\} \\ \{\boldsymbol{\lambda}\} \end{bmatrix} = \begin{bmatrix} \ddot{X}_1 & \ddot{Y}_1 & \ddot{\theta}_1 & \ddot{X}_2 & \ddot{Y}_2 & \ddot{\theta}_2 & \lambda_1 & \lambda_2 & \lambda_3 & \lambda_4 \end{bmatrix}^{\mathrm{T}}$$

$$= \begin{bmatrix} 0 & 0 & 0 & 7.354875 & 0 & -14.709750 & -36.774375 & 0 & -7.354875 & 0 \end{bmatrix}^{\mathrm{T}} \quad (4.967)$$

for the initial moment, where λ_1, λ_2 are the reactions at the hinge O, while λ_3, λ_4 are the reactions at the hinge O_1.

For the second numerical application, the matrix $[\mathbf{M}]$ is not invertible, so that it is necessary to proceed to the inversion of the total matrix

$$[\mathbf{A}] = \begin{bmatrix} [\mathbf{M}] & -[\mathbf{B}]^{\mathrm{T}} \\ [\mathbf{B}] & [\mathbf{0}] \end{bmatrix}. \quad (4.968)$$

Hence, it follows that

$$\begin{bmatrix} \{\ddot{\mathbf{q}}\} \\ \{\boldsymbol{\lambda}\} \end{bmatrix} = \begin{bmatrix} \ddot{X}_1 & \ddot{Y}_1 & \ddot{\theta}_1 & \ddot{X}_2 & \ddot{Y}_2 & \ddot{\theta}_2 & \lambda_1 & \lambda_2 & \lambda_3 & \lambda_4 \end{bmatrix}^{\mathrm{T}}$$

$$= \begin{bmatrix} 0 & 0 & 0 & 7.354875 & 0 & -14.709750 & -7.354875 & 0 & -7.354875 & 0 \end{bmatrix}^{\mathrm{T}}. \quad (4.969)$$

Problem 4.6

Consider a rigid solid, as illustrated in Figure 4.6, upon which a percussion $\mathbf{P}$ is applied at the point A. We denote by

- $Oxyz$ —the reference system rigidly connected to the solid;
- m —the mass;
- $[\mathbf{J}_O]$ —the matrix of the moments of inertia

$$[\mathbf{J}_O] = \begin{bmatrix} J_x & -J_{xy} & -J_{xz} \\ -J_{xy} & J_y & -J_{yz} \\ -J_{xz} & -J_{yz} & J_z \end{bmatrix}; \quad (4.970)$$

- $\mathbf{r}_C$ —the position vector of the center of gravity C;
- x_C, y_C, z_C —the coordinates of the gravity center C;
- $\mathbf{r}_A$ —the position vector of the point A;
- x_A, y_A, z_A —the coordinates of the point A;

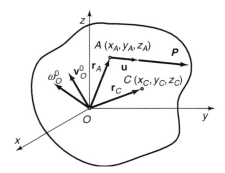

Figure 4.6   Problem 4.6.

- **u**—the unit vector of the percussion **P**;
- a, b, c—the components of the unit vector **u**;
- d, e, f—the projections on the axes of the vector $\mathbf{r}_A \cdot \mathbf{u}$;
- P—the intensity of the percussion **P**;
- $\mathbf{v}_O^0$—the velocity of the point O before the application of the percussion;
- v_{Ox}^0, v_{Oy}^0, v_{Oz}^0—the projections of the velocity $\mathbf{v}_O^0$ on the axes;
- $\boldsymbol{\omega}^0$—the angular velocity of the rigid solid before the application of the percussion;
- ω_x^0, ω_y^0, ω_z^0—the projections of the vector $\boldsymbol{\omega}^0$ on the axes;
- $\mathbf{v}_O$—the velocity of the point O after application of the percussion;
- v_{Ox}, v_{Oy}, v_{Oz}—projections of the velocity $\mathbf{v}_O$ on the axes;
- $\boldsymbol{\omega}$—the angular velocity after percussion;
- ω_x, ω_y, ω_z—the projections of the vector $\boldsymbol{\omega}$ on the axes;
- $\{\mathbf{v}_O^0\}$, $\{\boldsymbol{\omega}^0\}$, $\{\mathbf{v}_O\}$, $\{\boldsymbol{\omega}\}$—the column matrices defined by

$$\{\mathbf{v}_O^0\} = \begin{bmatrix} v_{Ox}^0 & v_{Oy}^0 & v_{Oz}^0 \end{bmatrix}^T, \quad \{\boldsymbol{\omega}^0\} = \begin{bmatrix} \omega_x^0 & \omega_y^0 & \omega_z^0 \end{bmatrix}^T,$$

$$\{\mathbf{v}_O\} = \begin{bmatrix} v_{Ox} & v_{Oy} & v_{Oz} \end{bmatrix}^T, \quad \{\boldsymbol{\omega}\} = \begin{bmatrix} \omega_x & \omega_y & \omega_z \end{bmatrix}^T; \tag{4.971}$$

- $\{\mathbf{u}\}$, $\{\mathbf{m_u}\}$—the column matrices defined by

$$\{\mathbf{u}\} = \begin{bmatrix} a & b & c \end{bmatrix}^T, \quad \{\mathbf{m_u}\} = \begin{bmatrix} d & e & f \end{bmatrix}^T; \tag{4.972}$$

- $\{\mathbf{V}\}$, $\{\mathbf{V}^0\}$, $\{\mathbf{U}\}$—the column matrices defined by

$$\{\mathbf{V}\} = \begin{bmatrix} v_{Ox} & v_{Oy} & v_{Oz} & \omega_x & \omega_y & \omega_z \end{bmatrix}^T,$$

$$\{\mathbf{V}^0\} = \begin{bmatrix} v_{Ox}^0 & v_{Oy}^0 & v_{Oz}^0 & \omega_x^0 & \omega_y^0 & \omega_z^0 \end{bmatrix}^T, \tag{4.973}$$

$$\{\mathbf{U}\} = \begin{bmatrix} a & b & c & d & e & f \end{bmatrix}^T;$$

- $[\mathbf{m}]$, $[\mathbf{S}]$, $[\mathbf{M}]$—the matrices defined by

$$[\mathbf{m}] = \begin{bmatrix} m & 0 & 0 \\ 0 & m & 0 \\ 0 & 0 & m \end{bmatrix}, \quad [\mathbf{S}] = \begin{bmatrix} 0 & -mz_C & my_C \\ mz_C & 0 & -mx_C \\ -my_C & mx_C & 0 \end{bmatrix}, \quad [\mathbf{M}] = \begin{bmatrix} [\mathbf{m}] & [\mathbf{S}]^T \\ [\mathbf{S}] & [\mathbf{J}_O] \end{bmatrix}. \tag{4.974}$$

Determine the velocities v_{Ox}, v_{Oy}, v_{Oz}, ω_x, ω_y, ω_z after the application of the percussion.

For the numerical application, we take $m = 80$, $J_x = 2$, $J_{xy} = 0.8$, $J_{xz} = 0.4$, $J_y = 2$, $J_{yz} = 0.4$, $J_z = 3.2$, $x_C = 0.05$, $y_C = 0.05$, $z_C = 0.025$, $x_A = 0.2$, $y_A = 0.2$, $z_A = 0.1$, $a = 2/3$, $b = 1/3$, $c = 2/3$, $v_{Ox}^0 = 10$, $v_{Oy}^0 = 8$, $v_{Oz}^0 = 7$, $\omega_x^0 = 4$, $\omega_y^0 = 3$, $\omega_z^0 = 5$, $P = 100$ (quantities given in SI).

Solution: The theorem of momentum for collisions, in matrix form, leads to

$$[\mathbf{m}]\left\{\{\mathbf{v}_O\} - \{\mathbf{v}_O^0\}\right\} + [\mathbf{S}]^T\{\{\boldsymbol{\omega}\} - \{\boldsymbol{\omega}^0\}\} = P\{\mathbf{u}\}. \tag{4.975}$$

Analogically, the theorem of moment of momentum for collisions about the point O, in matrix form, reads

$$[\mathbf{S}]\{\{\mathbf{v}_O\} - \{\mathbf{v}_O^0\}\} + [\mathbf{J}_O]\{\{\boldsymbol{\omega}\} - \{\boldsymbol{\omega}^0\}\} = P\{\mathbf{m_u}\}. \tag{4.976}$$

Equation (4.975) and equation (4.976) may be written together in a matrix form

$$[\mathbf{M}]\{\{\mathbf{V}\} - \{\mathbf{V}^0\}\} = P\{\mathbf{U}\}; \tag{4.977}$$

inverting the matrix $[\mathbf{M}]$

$$\{\mathbf{V}\} = \{\mathbf{V}^0\} + P[\mathbf{M}]^{-1}\{\mathbf{U}\}. \tag{4.978}$$

For the numerical application, we obtain

$$\mathbf{r}_A = 0.2\mathbf{i} + 0.2\mathbf{j} + 0.1\mathbf{k}, \quad \mathbf{u} = \frac{2}{3}\mathbf{i} + \frac{1}{3}\mathbf{j} + \frac{2}{3}\mathbf{k},$$

$$\mathbf{r}_A \cdot \mathbf{u} = \begin{vmatrix} \mathbf{i} & \mathbf{j} & \mathbf{k} \\ 0.2 & 0.2 & 0.1 \\ \dfrac{2}{3} & \dfrac{1}{3} & \dfrac{2}{3} \end{vmatrix} = 0.1\mathbf{i} - \frac{0.2}{3}\mathbf{j} - \frac{0.2}{3}\mathbf{k}, \tag{4.979}$$

$$[\mathbf{S}] = \begin{bmatrix} 0 & -2 & 4 \\ 2 & 0 & -4 \\ -4 & 4 & 0 \end{bmatrix}, \tag{4.980}$$

$$\{\mathbf{U}\} = \begin{bmatrix} \dfrac{2}{3} & \dfrac{1}{3} & \dfrac{2}{3} & 0.1 & -\dfrac{0.2}{3} & -\dfrac{0.2}{3} \end{bmatrix}^{\mathrm{T}}, \quad \{\mathbf{V}^0\} = \begin{bmatrix} 10 & 8 & 7 & 4 & 3 & 5 \end{bmatrix}^{\mathrm{T}}, \tag{4.981}$$

$$[\mathbf{M}] = \begin{bmatrix} 80 & 0 & 0 & 0 & 2 & -4 \\ 0 & 80 & 0 & -2 & 0 & 4 \\ 0 & 0 & 80 & 4 & -4 & 0 \\ 0 & -2 & 4 & 2 & -0.8 & -0.4 \\ 2 & 0 & -4 & -0.8 & 2 & -0.4 \\ -4 & 4 & 0 & -0.4 & -0.4 & 3.2 \end{bmatrix}, \tag{4.982}$$

$$[\mathbf{M}]^{-1} = \begin{bmatrix} -0.013620 & -0.000854 & -0.000532 & -0.001260 & -0.011898 & 0.016447 \\ -0.000854 & 1.013620 & -0.000532 & 0.011898 & 0.001260 & -0.016447 \\ -0.000532 & -0.000532 & -0.014628 & -0.021277 & 0.021277 & 0 \\ -0.001260 & 0.011898 & -0.021277 & 0.673292 & 0.247760 & 0.098681 \\ -0.011898 & 0.001260 & 0.021277 & 0.247760 & 0.673292 & 0.098681 \\ 0.016447 & -0.016447 & 0 & 0.098681 & 0.098681 & 0.378289 \end{bmatrix}, \tag{4.983}$$

from which

$$\{\mathbf{V}\} = \begin{bmatrix} v_{Ox} & v_{Oy} & v_{Oz} & \omega_x & \omega_y & \omega_z \end{bmatrix}^{\mathrm{T}}$$
$$= \begin{bmatrix} 8.985140 & 8.581827 & 5.616983 & 7.317427 & 0.998380 & 3.355253 \end{bmatrix}^{\mathrm{T}}. \tag{4.984}$$

Problem 4.7

The matrix of the moments of inertia of a rigid solid is

$$[\mathbf{J}] = \begin{bmatrix} J_{xx} & -J_{xy} & -J_{xz} \\ -J_{xy} & J_{yy} & -J_{yz} \\ -J_{xz} & -J_{yz} & J_{zz} \end{bmatrix} = \begin{bmatrix} 2.178606 & 0.313753 & -0.219693 \\ 0.313753 & 3.209143 & 0.553764 \\ -0.219693 & 0.553764 & 3.612250 \end{bmatrix};$$

let us determine the principal moments of inertia J_x, J_y, J_z, as well as the principal directions.

Solution:

1. Theory

The principal moments of inertia are just the eigenvalues of the matrix $[\mathbf{J}]$, which are given by the third-degree equation

$$\det[[\mathbf{J}] - \lambda[\mathbf{I}]] = 0, \tag{4.985}$$

where $[\mathbf{I}]$ is the unit matrix of third order, hence

$$J_x = \lambda_1, \quad J_y = \lambda_2, \quad J_z = \lambda_3. \tag{4.986}$$

The principal directions a_i, b_i, c_i, $a_i^2 + b_i^2 + c_i^2 = 1$, $i = \overline{1, 3}$, are given by the system

$$(J_{xx} - \lambda_i)a_i - J_{xy}b_i - J_{xz}c_i = 0, \quad -J_{xy}a_i + (J_{yy} - \lambda_i)b_i - J_{yz}c_i = 0. \tag{4.987}$$

Using the notations

$$\Delta_{1i} = \begin{vmatrix} -J_{xy} & -J_{xz} \\ J_{yy} - \lambda_i & -J_{yz} \end{vmatrix}, \quad \Delta_{2i} = \begin{vmatrix} -J_{xz} & J_{xx} - \lambda_i \\ -J_{yz} & -J_{xy} \end{vmatrix}, \quad \Delta_{3i} = \begin{vmatrix} J_{xx} - \lambda_i & -J_{xy} \\ J_{xy} & J_{yy} - \lambda_i \end{vmatrix}, \tag{4.988}$$

we obtain the equalities

$$\frac{a_i}{\Delta_{1i}} = \frac{b_i}{\Delta_{2i}} = \frac{c_i}{\Delta_{3i}} = \mu_i; \tag{4.989}$$

the condition $a_i^2 + b_i^2 + c_i^2 = 1$ leads to

$$\mu_i = \frac{1}{\sqrt{\Delta_{1i}^2 + \Delta_{2i}^2 + \Delta_{3i}^2}}, \tag{4.990}$$

so that the solution is

$$a_i = \mu_i \Delta_{1i}, \quad b_i = \mu_i \Delta_{2i}, \quad c_i = \mu_i \Delta_{3i}, \quad i = \overline{1, 3}. \tag{4.991}$$

2. Numerical calculation

Solving system (4.985), we obtain the eigenvalues

$$\lambda_1 = 2, \quad \lambda_2 = 3, \quad \lambda_3 = 4, \tag{4.992}$$

hence relations (4.988) lead to

$$\Delta_{11} = 0.439385, \quad \Delta_{21} = -0.167835, \quad \Delta_{31} = 0.117519, \tag{4.993}$$

$$\Delta_{12} = 0.219692, \quad \Delta_{22} = 0.385929, \quad \Delta_{32} = -0.270230, \tag{4.994}$$

$$\Delta_{13} = -0.000001, \quad \Delta_{23} = 0.939693, \quad \Delta_{33} = 1.342021, \tag{4.995}$$

$$\mu_1 = 2.062672, \quad a_1 = 0.906308, \quad b_1 = -0.346188, \quad c_1 = 0.242404, \tag{4.996}$$

$$\mu_2 = 1.923681, \quad a_2 = 0.422618, \quad b_2 = 0.742405, \quad c_2 = -0.519836, \tag{4.997}$$

$$\mu_3 = 0.610387, \quad a_3 = 4 \times 10^{-7}, \quad b_3 = 0.573576, \quad c_3 = 0.819152. \tag{4.998}$$

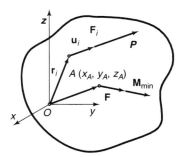

Figure 4.7   Problem 4.8.

Problem 4.8

Consider a rigid solid (Fig. 4.7) in the reference frame $Oxyz$ and the straight lines that pass through the points A_i of position vectors $\mathbf{r}_i(x_i, y_i, z_i)$, $i = \overline{1,3}$, the unit vectors along which are $\mathbf{u}_i(a_i, b_i, c_i)$, $i = \overline{1,3}$. Upon this solid act three forces of unknown intensities F_1, F_2, F_3, the supports of which are the three straight lines. Let us determine the intensities F_1, F_2, F_3 of the forces so that, at the point A of position vector $\mathbf{r}_A(x_A, y_A, z_A)$, the system of forces is reduced to a minimal torsor.

Numerical application: $x_1 = 0$, $y_1 = 0$, $z_1 = 8a$, $x_2 = a$, $y_2 = 0$, $z_2 = 0$, $x_3 = 0$, $y_3 = -6a$, $z_3 = 0$, $a_1 = 1$, $b_1 = 0$, $c_1 = 0$, $a_2 = 0$, $b_2 = 1$, $c_2 = 0$, $a_3 = 0$, $b_3 = 0$, $c_3 = 1$, $x_A = 0$, $y_A = 0$, $z_A = 7a$, $a = 1$ m.

Solution:

1. Theory

Reduced at O, the system of three forces is of components

$$\mathbf{F} = \sum_{i=1}^{3} F_i \mathbf{u}_i, \quad \mathbf{M}_O = \sum_{i=1}^{3} F_i \mathbf{r}_i \cdot \mathbf{u}_i; \tag{4.999}$$

by reducing it at A, we obtain the components

$$\mathbf{F} = \sum_{i=1}^{3} F_i \mathbf{u}_i, \quad \mathbf{M}_A = \sum_{i=1}^{3} F_i \mathbf{r}_i \cdot \mathbf{u}_i - \mathbf{r}_A \cdot \sum_{i=1}^{3} F_i \mathbf{u}_i. \tag{4.1000}$$

The conditions to have the minimal moment is transcribed in the relation

$$\mathbf{M}_A = \lambda \mathbf{F}. \tag{4.1001}$$

Using the notations

$$\{\widetilde{\mathbf{F}}\} = \begin{bmatrix} F_x & F_y & F_z \end{bmatrix}^T, \quad \{\mathbf{M}_A\} = \begin{bmatrix} M_{Ax} & M_{Ay} & M_{Az} \end{bmatrix}^T, \quad \{\mathbf{F}\} = \begin{bmatrix} F_1 & F_2 & F_3 \end{bmatrix}^T, \tag{4.1002}$$

$$d_i = y_i c_i - z_i b_i, \quad e_i = z_i a_i - x_i c_i, \quad f_i = x_i b_i - y_i a_i, \quad i = \overline{1,3}, \tag{4.1003}$$

$$[\mathbf{U}] = \begin{bmatrix} a_1 & a_2 & a_3 \\ b_1 & b_2 & b_3 \\ c_1 & c_2 & c_3 \end{bmatrix}, \quad [\mathbf{V}] = \begin{bmatrix} d_1 & d_2 & d_3 \\ e_1 & e_2 & e_3 \\ f_1 & f_2 & f_3 \end{bmatrix}, \quad [\mathbf{r}_A] = \begin{bmatrix} 0 & -z_A & y_A \\ z_A & 0 & -x_A \\ -y_A & x_A & 0 \end{bmatrix}, \tag{4.1004}$$

$$[\mathbf{A}] = [\mathbf{V}] - [\mathbf{r}_A][\mathbf{U}], \quad [\mathbf{B}] = [\mathbf{U}]^{-1}[\mathbf{A}], \tag{4.1005}$$

in a matrix form, relations (4.1000) become

$$\{\widetilde{\mathbf{F}}\} = [\mathbf{U}]\{\mathbf{F}\}, \quad \{\mathbf{M}_A\} = [\mathbf{A}]\{\mathbf{F}\} \tag{4.1006}$$

and condition (4.1001) reads

$$[\mathbf{B}]\{\mathbf{F}\} = \lambda\{\mathbf{F}\}; \tag{4.1007}$$

the problem becomes one of eigenvalues and eigenvectors.

The eigenvalues λ_1, λ_2, λ_3 are given by the equation

$$\det[[\mathbf{B}] - \lambda[\mathbf{I}]] = 0, \tag{4.1008}$$

while the intensities of the forces are given by the first two secular equations of the matrix equation (4.1007).

We obtain thus three directions, hence three minimal torsors to which the considered system of forces is reduced.

2. Numerical calculation

It follows, successively, that

$$d_1 = 0, \quad e_1 = 6a, \quad f_1 = 0, \quad d_2 = 0, \quad e_2 = 0, \quad f_2 = a, \quad d_3 = 6a, \quad e_3 = 0, \quad f_3 = 0, \tag{4.1009}$$

$$[\mathbf{U}] = \begin{bmatrix} 1 & 0 & 0 \\ 0 & 1 & 0 \\ 0 & 0 & 1 \end{bmatrix}, \quad [\mathbf{V}] = \begin{bmatrix} 0 & 0 & 6a \\ 6a & 0 & 0 \\ 0 & a & 0 \end{bmatrix}, \quad [\mathbf{r}_A] = \begin{bmatrix} 0 & -7a & 0 \\ 7a & 0 & 0 \\ 0 & 0 & 0 \end{bmatrix}, \tag{4.1010}$$

$$[\mathbf{A}] = [\mathbf{B}] = \begin{bmatrix} 0 & 7a & -6a \\ a & 0 & 0 \\ 0 & a & 0 \end{bmatrix} = \begin{bmatrix} 0 & 7 & -6 \\ 1 & 0 & 0 \\ 0 & 1 & 0 \end{bmatrix}, \tag{4.1011}$$

while equation (4.1008) is

$$\lambda^3 - 7\lambda + 6 = 0, \tag{4.1012}$$

with the solutions

$$\lambda_1 = 1, \quad \lambda_2 = 2, \quad \lambda_3 = -3. \tag{4.1013}$$

Equation (4.1007), written in the form

$$\begin{bmatrix} -\lambda_i & 7 & -6 \\ 1 & -\lambda_i & 0 \\ 0 & 1 & -\lambda_i \end{bmatrix} \begin{bmatrix} F_1 \\ F_2 \\ F_3 \end{bmatrix} = \{\mathbf{0}\}, \tag{4.1014}$$

leads to the solutions

$$F_2 = \frac{F_1}{\lambda_i}, \quad F_3 = \frac{F_1}{\lambda_i^2}, \tag{4.1015}$$

that is, to the set of values of the components of the resultant along the axes

$$\begin{bmatrix} F_1 & F_1 & F_1 \end{bmatrix}^{\mathrm{T}}, \quad \begin{bmatrix} F_1 & \frac{F_1}{2} & \frac{F_1}{4} \end{bmatrix}^{\mathrm{T}}, \quad \begin{bmatrix} F_1 & -\frac{F_1}{3} & \frac{F_1}{9} \end{bmatrix}^{\mathrm{T}}, \tag{4.1016}$$

F_1 being an arbitrary value.

Finally, it results in

- the first minimal torsor: resultant $F = F_1\sqrt{3}$, minimum moment $M_{1\,\min} = F_1 a\sqrt{3} = F_1\sqrt{3}$, direction of the resultant $\begin{bmatrix} 1/\sqrt{3} & 1/\sqrt{3} & 1/\sqrt{3} \end{bmatrix}^{\mathrm{T}}$;

- the second minimal torsor: resultant $F = F_1\sqrt{21}/4$, minimum moment $M_{1\,min} = F_1a\sqrt{21}/2 = F_1\sqrt{21}/2$, direction of the resultant $\begin{bmatrix} 4/\sqrt{21} & 2/\sqrt{21} & 1/\sqrt{21} \end{bmatrix}^{\mathrm{T}}$;
- the third minimal torsor: resultant $F = F_1\sqrt{91}/4$, minimum moment $M_{1\,min} = -F_1a\sqrt{91}/3 = -F_1\sqrt{91}/3$, direction of the resultant $\begin{bmatrix} 9/\sqrt{91} & -3/\sqrt{91} & 1/\sqrt{21} \end{bmatrix}^{\mathrm{T}}$.

Problem 4.9

To study the free vibrations of an automobile, let us consider the model in Figure 4.8. Thus, for this model (half of an automobile) let the notations be as follows:

k_1, k_2—stiffness of the tires;
k_3, k_4—stiffness of the suspension springs;
k_5, k_6—stiffness of the passengers' chairs;
m_1, m_2—the masses of the wheels (to which are added the masses of the pivot pins);
m_3—half of the suspended mass of the automobile;
m_5, m_6—the masses of the chairs, to which are added 75% of the passengers' masses;
J—moment of inertia of the suspended mass with respect to the gravity center C.

It is required

- to determine the deflections of the springs in the state of equilibrium;
- to write the matrix equation of the free vibrations;
- to determine the eigenpulsations and the modal matrix;
- to discuss the results thus obtained.

Solution:

1. Theory

Denoting by z_{i0}, $i = \overline{1,6}$, the deflections of the springs in the state of equilibrium and taking into account the forces represented in Figure 4.9, we obtain the equilibrium equations

$$k_1z_{10} - k_3z_{30} = m_1g, \quad k_2z_{20} - k_4z_{40} = m_2g, \quad k_3z_{30} + k_4z_{40} - k_5z_{50} - k_6z_{60} = m_3g,$$

$$k_3z_{30}l_1 - k_5z_{50}l_{s1} - k_4z_{40}l_2 + k_6z_{60}l_{s2} = 0, \quad k_5z_{50} = m_5g, \quad k_6z_{60} = m_6g, \qquad (4.1017)$$

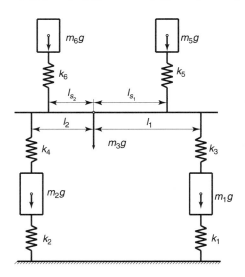

Figure 4.8   Problem 4.9.

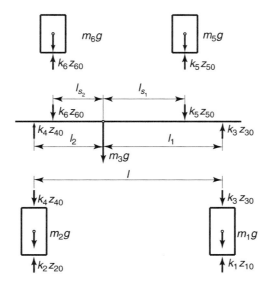

Figure 4.9   Equations of equilibrium.

from which it follows that

$$z_{10} = \frac{g}{k_1 l}[m_4 l_2 + m_1 l + m_5(l_1 + l_{s1}) + m_6(l_2 - l_{s2})],$$

$$z_{20} = \frac{g}{k_2 l}[m_3 l_1 + m_2 l + m_5(l_1 - l_{s1}) + m_6(l_2 + l_{s2})],$$

$$z_{30} = \frac{g}{k_3 l}[(m_3 + m_5 + m_6)l_2 + m_5 l_{s1} - m_6 l_{s2}],$$

$$z_{40} = \frac{g}{k_4 l}[(m_3 + m_5 + m_6)l_1 - m_5 l_{s1} + m_6 l_{s2}],$$

$$z_{50} = \frac{m_5 g}{k_5}, \quad z_{60} = \frac{m_6 g}{k_6}. \tag{4.1018}$$

For an arbitrary position, denoting the displacements with respect to the position of equilibrium by z_1, z_2, z_5, z_6 for the masses m_1, m_2, m_5, m_6, the displacement of the point C by z_3 and the angle of rotation of the suspended mass by ϕ, we obtain the forces represented in Figure 4.10. The theorem of momentum, written for the bodies of masses m_1, m_2, m_3, m_5, m_6, leads to the equations

$$m_1 \ddot{z}_1 = -k_1(z_1 - z_{10}) + k_3(z_3 + l_1\phi - z_1 - z_{30}) - m_1 g,$$

$$m_2 \ddot{z}_2 = -k_2(z_2 - z_{20}) + k_4(z_3 - l_2\phi - z_2 - z_{40}) - m_2 g,$$

$$m_3 \ddot{z}_3 = -k_3(z_3 + l_1\phi - z_1 - z_{30}) - k_4(z_3 - l_2\phi - z_2 - z_{40})$$
$$\qquad + k_5(z_5 - z_3 - l_{s1}\phi - z_{50}) + k_6(z_6 - z_3 + l_{s2}\phi - z_{60}) - m_3 g,$$

$$m_5 \ddot{z}_5 = -k_5(z_5 - z_3 - l_{s1}\phi - z_{50}) - m_5 g,$$

$$m_6 \ddot{z}_6 = -k_6(z_6 - z_3 + l_{s2}\phi - z_{60}) - m_6 g, \tag{4.1019}$$

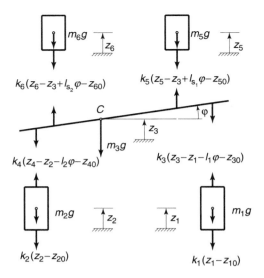

Figure 4.10   Equations of motion.

while the theorem of moment of momentum with respect to the center of gravity of the body of mass m_3 leads to the equation

$$J\ddot{\phi} = k_4 l_2 (z_3 - l_2\phi - z_2 - z_{40}) + k_5 l_{s1}(z_5 - z_3 - l_{s1}\phi - z_{50})$$
$$- k_3 l_1 (z_3 + l_1\phi - z_1 - z_{30}) - k_6 l_{s2}(z_6 - z_3 + l_{s2}\phi - z_{60}). \tag{4.1020}$$

Using the matrix notations,

$$\{\mathbf{z}\} = \begin{bmatrix} z_1 & z_2 & z_3 & \phi & z_5 & z_6 \end{bmatrix}^{\mathrm{T}}, \tag{4.1021}$$

$$[\mathbf{M}] = \begin{bmatrix} m_1 & 0 & 0 & 0 & 0 & 0 \\ 0 & m_2 & 0 & 0 & 0 & 0 \\ 0 & 0 & m_3 & 0 & 0 & 0 \\ 0 & 0 & 0 & J & 0 & 0 \\ 0 & 0 & 0 & 0 & m_5 & 0 \\ 0 & 0 & 0 & 0 & 0 & m_6 \end{bmatrix}, \tag{4.1022}$$

$$[\mathbf{K}] = \begin{bmatrix} k_1 + k_3 & 0 & -k_3 & k_3 l_1 & 0 & 0 \\ 0 & k_2 + k_4 & -k_4 & k_4 l_2 & 0 & 0 \\ -k_3 & -k_4 & k_2 + k_4 + k_5 + k_6 & k_3 l_1 + k_4 l_2 + k_5 l_{s1} - k_6 l_{s2} & -k_5 & -k_6 \\ -k_3 l_1 & k_4 l_2 & k_5 l_1 - k_4 l_2 + k_5 l_{s1} - k_6 l_{s2} & k_3 l_1^2 + k_4 l_2^2 + k_3 l_{s1}^2 + k_6 l_{s2}^2 & -k_5 l_{s1} & k_6 l_{s2} \\ 0 & 0 & -k_5 & -k_5 l_{s1} & k_5 & 0 \\ 0 & 0 & -k_6 & k_6 l_{s2} & 0 & k_6 \end{bmatrix}$$
$$\tag{4.1023}$$

and taking into account equation (4.1017), equation (4.1019), and equation (4.1020), we obtain the matrix differential equation

$$[\mathbf{M}]\{\ddot{\mathbf{z}}\} + [\mathbf{K}]\{\mathbf{z}\} = \{\mathbf{0}\}. \tag{4.1024}$$

The solution of this equation is of the form

$$\{\mathbf{z}\} = \{\mathbf{a}\} \cos(pt - \phi) \tag{4.1025}$$

and leads to the matrix equation

$$[-p^2[\mathbf{M}] + [\mathbf{K}]]\{\mathbf{a}\} = p^2\{\mathbf{a}\}, \tag{4.1026}$$

equivalent to the equation

$$[\mathbf{M}]^{-1}[\mathbf{K}]\{\mathbf{a}\} = p^2\{\mathbf{a}\}, \tag{4.1027}$$

which is a problem of eigenvalues and eigenvectors.

Solving the equation

$$\det[[\mathbf{K}] - p^2[\mathbf{M}]] = 0, \tag{4.1028}$$

we obtain the eigenvalues p_1^2, p_2^2, ..., p_6^2 and the eigenpulsations p_1, p_2, ..., p_6.

Corresponding to each eigenvalue, we obtain the eigenvectors $\{\mathbf{a}^{(i)}\}$, $i = \overline{1, 6}$, which define the modal matrix

$$[\mathbf{A}] = \left[\{\mathbf{a}^{(1)}\} \quad \{\mathbf{a}^{(2)}\} \quad \cdots \quad \{\mathbf{a}^{(6)}\}\right]. \tag{4.1029}$$

2. Numerical calculation
We obtain successively

$$[\mathbf{M}] = \begin{bmatrix} 30 & 0 & 0 & 0 & 0 & 0 \\ 0 & 30 & 0 & 0 & 0 & 0 \\ 0 & 0 & 450 & 0 & 0 & 0 \\ 0 & 0 & 0 & 300 & 0 & 0 \\ 0 & 0 & 0 & 0 & 60 & 0 \\ 0 & 0 & 0 & 0 & 0 & 60 \end{bmatrix}, \tag{4.1030}$$

$$[\mathbf{M}]^{-1} = \begin{bmatrix} 0.03333 & 0 & 0 & 0 & 0 & 0 \\ 0 & 0.03333 & 0 & 0 & 0 & 0 \\ 0 & 0 & 0.002222 & 0 & 0 & 0 \\ 0 & 0 & 0 & 0.003333 & 0 & 0 \\ 0 & 0 & 0 & 0 & 0.066667 & 0 \\ 0 & 0 & 0 & 0 & 0 & 0.066667 \end{bmatrix}, \tag{4.1031}$$

$$[\mathbf{K}] = \begin{bmatrix} 152000 & 0 & -12000 & 15000 & 0 & 0 \\ 0 & 154000 & -14000 & 17500 & 0 & 0 \\ -12000 & -14000 & 158000 & -2500 & -2000 & -2000 \\ 15000 & 17500 & -2500 & 42065 & -1200 & 1200 \\ 0 & 0 & -2000 & -1200 & 2000 & 0 \\ 0 & 0 & -2000 & 1200 & 0 & 2000 \end{bmatrix}, \tag{4.1032}$$

$$[\mathbf{M}]^{-1}[\mathbf{K}] = \begin{bmatrix} 5066.67 & 0 & -400 & 500 & 0 & 0 \\ 0 & 5133.33 & -466.67 & 583.33 & 0 & 0 \\ -26.67 & -31.11 & 351.11 & -5.56 & -4.44 & -4.44 \\ 50 & 58.33 & -8.33 & 140.22 & -4 & 4 \\ 0 & 0 & -33.33 & -20 & 33.33 & 0 \\ 0 & 0 & -33.33 & 20 & 0 & 33.33 \end{bmatrix}, \tag{4.1033}$$

$$p_1 = 6.22 \text{ s}^{-1}, \quad p_2 = 8.04 \text{ s}^{-1}, \quad p_3 = 13.13 \text{ s}^{-1},$$
$$p_4 = 14.26 \text{ s}^{-1}, \quad p_5 = 71.19 \text{ s}^{-1}, \quad p_6 = 41.69 \text{ s}^{-1}, \tag{4.1034}$$

$$[\mathbf{A}] = \begin{bmatrix} 0 & 0 & 0 & 0 & 1.0 & 0 \\ 0 & 0 & 0 & 0 & 0 & 1.0 \\ 0.5 & 0 & 0 & 0.2 & 0 & 0 \\ 0 & -0.6 & -0.2 & 0 & 0 & 0 \\ 0.7 & -0.5 & 0.7 & -0.7 & 0 & 0 \\ 0.6 & 0.7 & -0.7 & -0.7 & 0 & 0 \end{bmatrix}. \tag{4.1035}$$

The first mode of vibration defined by the eigenvector for the eigenpulsation p_1 corresponds to raising the vibrations of the suspended mass together with the displacement in phase of the chairs. The second and the third modes of vibration correspond to a motion of pitching, together with the motion in opposition to the phase of the chairs. The fourth mode of vibrations corresponds to a vibration of raise, together with the motion in opposition of the phase of the chairs. The last two modes of vibration correspond exclusively to the vibrations of the wheels.

Problem 4.10

We consider the rectangular plate in Figure 4.11, of dimensions $2l_1$, $2l_2$, of mass m and of moments of inertia $J_X = ml_2^2/3$, $J_Y = ml_1^2/3$, $J_Z = m(l_1^2 + l_2^2)/3$, suspended by the springs $A_i B_i$ of stiffness k_i, $i = \overline{1, 4}$.

As shown in Figure 4.11, the plate is in equilibrium under the action of the weight mg and of the deformed springs of deflections s_i, $i = \overline{1, 4}$.

Considering that the deflections s_i are relatively great with respect to the displacements of the plate when it is vibrating, knowing the lengths $L_i = A_{i0}B_i$ and the angles α_i, $i = \overline{1, 4}$, determine the following:

- the matrix differential equation of the linear vibrations;
- the eigenpulsations;
- the modal matrix.

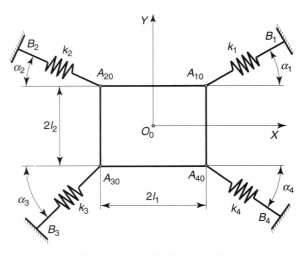

Figure 4.11   Problem 4.10.

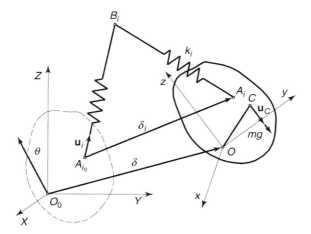

Figure 4.12 Small displacements of the rigid body.

Solution:

1. Theory

We consider a rigid solid the position of which is specified with respect to the fixed reference system O_0XYZ and to a system of reference $Oxyz$ rigidly linked to it (Fig. 4.12), so that at the position of equilibrium the mobile system coincides with the fixed one.

A small displacement of an arbitrary position of the rigid solid is defined by the linear displacement δ of the point O and by the rotation angle θ.

The rigid solid is acted upon by its own weight mg and is suspended by the springs A_iB_i, $i = \overline{1, n}$.

To construct the mathematical model of the linear solutions of the rigid solid, we introduce the following notations:

- $(\theta_X, \theta_Y, \theta_Z)$, $(\delta_X, \delta_Y, \delta_Z)$—projections of the vectors θ and δ on the axes of the system O_0XYZ;
- $\{\theta\}, \{\delta\}, \{\Delta\}$—column matrices

$$\{\theta\} = \begin{bmatrix} \theta_X & \theta_Y & \theta_Z \end{bmatrix}^T, \quad \{\delta\} = \begin{bmatrix} \delta_X & \delta_Y & \delta_Z \end{bmatrix}^T, \quad \{\Delta\} = \begin{bmatrix} \delta_X & \delta_Y & \delta_Z & \theta_X & \theta_Y & \theta_Z \end{bmatrix}^T; \tag{4.1036}$$

- δ_i—displacement $\mathbf{A}_{i0}\mathbf{A}_i$ of the end of the spring A_iB_i;
- $\mathbf{u}_i$—unit vector in the direction $\mathbf{A}_{i0}\mathbf{A}_i$ of the spring A_iB_i in the position of equilibrium of the solid;
- $\mathbf{r}_i$—position vector of the point A_{i0};
- x_i, y_i, z_i—coordinates of the point A_{i0} in the system O_0XYZ, respectively, the coordinates of the point A_i in the system $Oxyz$;
- $[\mathbf{r}_i]$—the matrix defined by

$$[\mathbf{r}_i] = \begin{bmatrix} 0 & -z_i & y_i \\ z_i & 0 & -x_i \\ -y_i & x_i & 0 \end{bmatrix}; \tag{4.1037}$$

- a_i, b_i, c_i—projections of the vector $\mathbf{u}_i$ in the system O_0XYZ;

- $\mathbf{m}_i^*$—the vector defined by the relation

$$\mathbf{m}_i^* = \mathbf{r}_i \cdot \mathbf{u}_i; \qquad (4.1038)$$

- d_i, e_i, f_i—the projections of the vector $\mathbf{m}_i^*$ on the axes of the trihedron O_0XYZ, that is, the quantities

$$d_i = y_i c_i - z_i b_i, \quad e_i = z_i a_i - x_i c_i, \quad f_i = x_i b_i - y_i a_i; \qquad (4.1039)$$

- $\{\mathbf{u}_i\}$, $\{\mathbf{m}_i^*\}$, $\{\mathbf{U}_i\}$—the column matrices given by the relations

$$\{\mathbf{u}_i\} = \begin{bmatrix} a_i & b_i & c_i \end{bmatrix}^\mathrm{T}, \quad \{\mathbf{m}_i^*\} = \begin{bmatrix} d_i & e_i & f_i \end{bmatrix}^\mathrm{T}, \quad \{\mathbf{U}_i\} = \begin{bmatrix} a_i & b_i & c_i & d_i & e_i & f_i \end{bmatrix}^\mathrm{T}; \qquad (4.1040)$$

- C—the center of gravity of the rigid solid;
- $\mathbf{u}_C$—the unit vector in the direction toward to the surface of the Earth;
- x_C, y_C, z_C—the coordinates of the center C in the system $Oxyz$, respectively, the coordinates of the point C_0 in the system O_0XYZ;
- $\mathbf{r}_C$—the position vector $\mathbf{O}_0\mathbf{C}_0$ of the point C_0;
- a_C, b_C, c_C—the projections of the vector $\mathbf{u}_C$ in the system O_0XYZ;
- d_C, e_C, f_C—parameters defined by the relations

$$d_C = y_C c_C - z_C b_C, \quad e_C = z_C a_C - x_C c_C, \quad f_C = x_C b_C - y_C a_C; \qquad (4.1041)$$

- $\{\mathbf{U}_C\}$—the column matrix

$$\{\mathbf{U}_C\} = \begin{bmatrix} a_C & b_C & c_C & d_C & e_C & f_C \end{bmatrix}^\mathrm{T}; \qquad (4.1042)$$

- δ_C—displacement of the point C;
- l_{i0}—the undeformed length of the spring $A_i B_i$;
- $[\mathbf{S}]$—the matrix defined by

$$[\mathbf{S}] = \begin{bmatrix} 0 & -mz_C & my_C \\ mz_C & 0 & -mx_C \\ -my_C & mx_C & 0 \end{bmatrix}; \qquad (4.1043)$$

- $[\mathbf{m}]$—the matrix

$$[\mathbf{m}] = \begin{bmatrix} m & 0 & 0 \\ 0 & m & 0 \\ 0 & 0 & m \end{bmatrix}; \qquad (4.1044)$$

- $[\mathbf{J}]$—the matrix of the moments of inertia

$$[\mathbf{J}] = \begin{bmatrix} J_{xx} & -J_{xy} & -J_{xz} \\ -J_{xy} & J_{yy} & -J_{yz} \\ -J_{xz} & -J_{yz} & J_{zz} \end{bmatrix}; \qquad (4.1045)$$

- $[\mathbf{M}]$—the matrix of inertia of the rigid solid

$$[\mathbf{M}] = \begin{bmatrix} [\mathbf{m}] & [\mathbf{S}]^\mathrm{T} \\ [\mathbf{S}] & [\mathbf{J}] \end{bmatrix}; \qquad (4.1046)$$

- T, V —the kinetic energy and the potential energy, respectively;
- V_a, V_C —the potential energy of the springs and the potential energy of the weight mg, respectively;
- $\{\partial T/\partial \dot{\boldsymbol{\Delta}}\}$. $\{\partial T/\partial \boldsymbol{\Delta}\}$, $\{\partial V/\partial \boldsymbol{\Delta}\}$ —the column matrices of the partial derivatives

$$\left\{\frac{\partial T}{\partial \dot{\boldsymbol{\Delta}}}\right\} = \left[\frac{\partial T}{\partial \dot{\delta}_X} \quad \frac{\partial T}{\partial \dot{\delta}_Y} \quad \frac{\partial T}{\partial \dot{\delta}_Z} \quad \frac{\partial T}{\partial \dot{\theta}_X} \quad \frac{\partial T}{\partial \dot{\theta}_Y} \quad \frac{\partial T}{\partial \dot{\theta}_Z}\right]^{\mathrm{T}},$$

$$\left\{\frac{\partial T}{\partial \boldsymbol{\Delta}}\right\} = \left[\frac{\partial T}{\partial \delta_X} \quad \frac{\partial T}{\partial \delta_Y} \quad \frac{\partial T}{\partial \delta_Z} \quad \frac{\partial T}{\partial \theta_X} \quad \frac{\partial T}{\partial \theta_Y} \quad \frac{\partial T}{\partial \theta_Z}\right]^{\mathrm{T}}, \qquad (4.1047)$$

$$\left\{\frac{\partial V}{\partial \boldsymbol{\Delta}}\right\} = \left[\frac{\partial V}{\partial \delta_X} \quad \frac{\partial V}{\partial \delta_Y} \quad \frac{\partial V}{\partial \delta_Z} \quad \frac{\partial V}{\partial \theta_X} \quad \frac{\partial V}{\partial \theta_Y} \quad \frac{\partial V}{\partial \theta_Z}\right]^{\mathrm{T}}.$$

By these notations, we may write

$$T = \frac{1}{2}\{\dot{\boldsymbol{\Delta}}\}[\mathbf{M}]\{\dot{\boldsymbol{\Delta}}\}, \quad V_a = \frac{1}{2}\sum_{i=1}^{n} k_i (A_i B_i - l_{i0})^2, \quad V_C = mg\,\boldsymbol{\delta}_C \mathbf{u}_C, \qquad (4.1048)$$

$$V = V_a + V_C. \qquad (4.1049)$$

Lagrange's equations have the matrix form

$$\frac{\mathrm{d}}{\mathrm{d}t}\left\{\frac{\partial T}{\partial \dot{\boldsymbol{\Delta}}}\right\} - \left\{\frac{\partial T}{\partial \boldsymbol{\Delta}}\right\} + \left\{\frac{\partial V}{\partial \boldsymbol{\Delta}}\right\} = \{\mathbf{0}\}; \qquad (4.1050)$$

taking into account the relation

$$\frac{\mathrm{d}}{\mathrm{d}t}\left\{\frac{\partial T}{\partial \dot{\boldsymbol{\Delta}}}\right\} = [\mathbf{M}]\{\ddot{\boldsymbol{\Delta}}\} \qquad (4.1051)$$

and the fact that $\{\partial T/\partial \boldsymbol{\Delta}\} = \{\mathbf{0}\}$, because it is a function of second degree in the components of the matrix $\{\dot{\boldsymbol{\Delta}}\}$, equation (4.1050) reads

$$[\mathbf{M}]\{\ddot{\boldsymbol{\Delta}}\} + \left\{\frac{\partial V_C}{\partial \boldsymbol{\Delta}}\right\} + \left\{\frac{\partial V_a}{\partial \boldsymbol{\Delta}}\right\} = \{\mathbf{0}\}. \qquad (4.1052)$$

The displacements $\boldsymbol{\delta}_C$, $\boldsymbol{\delta}_i$, $i = \overline{1, n}$, being small, can be expressed by the relations

$$\boldsymbol{\delta}_C = \boldsymbol{\delta} + \boldsymbol{\theta} \cdot \mathbf{r}_C, \quad \boldsymbol{\delta}_i = \boldsymbol{\delta} + \boldsymbol{\theta} \cdot \mathbf{r}_i, \quad i = \overline{1, n}, \qquad (4.1053)$$

so that

$$V_C = mg\{\mathbf{U}_C\}^{\mathrm{T}}\{\boldsymbol{\Delta}\}, \qquad (4.1054)$$

$$\left\{\frac{\partial V_C}{\partial \boldsymbol{\Delta}}\right\} = mg\{\mathbf{U}_C\}. \qquad (4.1055)$$

To calculate the column matrix $\{\partial V_a/\partial \boldsymbol{\Delta}\}$ we express first the length $A_i B_i$, taking into account the second relation (4.1053),

$$A_i B_i = \sqrt{(\mathbf{A}_i \mathbf{B}_i)^2} = \sqrt{(L_i \mathbf{u}_i - \boldsymbol{\delta}_i)^2}, \qquad (4.1056)$$

$$A_i B_i = \sqrt{(L_i \mathbf{u}_i - \boldsymbol{\delta} - \boldsymbol{\theta} \cdot \mathbf{r}_i)^2} \qquad (4.1057)$$

or

$$A_i B_i = [(L_i a_i - \delta_X - \theta_Y z_i + \theta_Z y_i)^2 + (L_i b_i - \delta_Y - \theta_Z x_i + \theta_X z_i)^2$$
$$+ (L_i c_i - \delta_Z - \theta_X y_i + \theta_Y x_i)^2]; \tag{4.1058}$$

by computing, it follows that

$$\left\{ \frac{\partial A_i B_i}{\partial \mathbf{\Delta}} \right\} = \frac{1}{A_i B_i} \left[-L_i \{\mathbf{U}_i\} + \begin{bmatrix} [\mathbf{I}] & -[\mathbf{r}_i] \\ [\mathbf{r}_i] & -[\mathbf{r}_i]^2 \end{bmatrix} \right] \{\mathbf{\Delta}\}, \tag{4.1059}$$

where $[\mathbf{I}]$ is the unit matrix of third order.

From relation (4.1057), expanding the binomial into series and neglecting the nonlinear terms, we obtain

$$A_i B_i = L_i \left[1 - 2\frac{\mathbf{u}_i}{L_i} (\delta - \theta \cdot \mathbf{r}_i) \right]^{\frac{1}{2}} = L_i - \{\mathbf{U}_i\}^{\mathrm{T}} \{\mathbf{\Delta}\}; \tag{4.1060}$$

taking into account the relation

$$s_i = L_i - l_{i0} \tag{4.1061}$$

and neglecting the nonlinear terms, it follows that

$$\frac{A_i B_i - l_{i0}}{A_i B_i} = \frac{s_i - \{\mathbf{U}_i\}^{\mathrm{T}} \{\mathbf{\Delta}\}}{L_i - \{\mathbf{U}_i\}^{\mathrm{T}} \{\mathbf{\Delta}\}} = \left[\frac{s_i}{L_i} - \frac{1}{L_i} \{\mathbf{U}_i\}^{\mathrm{T}} \{\mathbf{\Delta}\} \right] \left[1 + \frac{1}{L_i} \{\mathbf{U}_i\}^{\mathrm{T}} \{\mathbf{\Delta}\} \right] \tag{4.1062}$$

or

$$\frac{A_i B_i - l_{i0}}{A_i B_i} = \frac{s_i}{L_i} - \left(1 - \frac{s_i}{L_i} \right) \{\mathbf{U}_i\}^{\mathrm{T}} \{\mathbf{\Delta}\}. \tag{4.1063}$$

Finally, denoting by $[\mathbf{K}]$ the rigidity matrix

$$[\mathbf{K}] = \sum_{i=1}^{n} \frac{k_i s_i}{L_i} \begin{bmatrix} [\mathbf{I}] & [\mathbf{r}_i]^{\mathrm{T}} \\ [\mathbf{r}_i] & -[\mathbf{r}_i]^2 \end{bmatrix} + \sum_{i=1}^{n} \left(1 - \frac{s_i}{L_i} \right) \{\mathbf{U}_i\} \{\mathbf{U}_i\}^{\mathrm{T}} \tag{4.1064}$$

and taking into account the equilibrium equation

$$mg\{\mathbf{U}_C\} - \sum_{i=1}^{n} k_i s_i \{\mathbf{U}_i\} = \{\mathbf{0}\}, \tag{4.1065}$$

we get, from equation (4.1062), the matrix differential equation of the linear vibrations

$$[\mathbf{M}]\{\ddot{\mathbf{\Delta}}\} + [\mathbf{K}]\{\mathbf{\Delta}\} = \{\mathbf{0}\}. \tag{4.1066}$$

2. Numerical calculation
We obtain successively

$$J_X = 5 \text{ kg m}^2, \quad J_Y = 3.2 \text{ kg m}^2, \quad J_Z = 8.2 \text{ kg m}^2, \tag{4.1067}$$

$$x_C = 0, \quad y_C = 0, \quad z_C = 0, \quad [\mathbf{S}] = \begin{bmatrix} 0 & 0 & 0 \\ 0 & 0 & 0 \\ 0 & 0 & 0 \end{bmatrix}, \tag{4.1068}$$

$$[\mathbf{M}] = \begin{bmatrix} 60 & 0 & 0 & 0 & 0 & 0 \\ 0 & 60 & 0 & 0 & 0 & 0 \\ 0 & 0 & 60 & 0 & 0 & 0 \\ 0 & 0 & 0 & 5 & 0 & 0 \\ 0 & 0 & 0 & 0 & 3.2 & 0 \\ 0 & 0 & 0 & 0 & 0 & 8.2 \end{bmatrix}, \tag{4.1069}$$

$$x_1 = 0.3, \quad y_1 = 0.5, \quad z_1 = 0, \quad x_2 = -0.3, \quad y_2 = 0.5, \quad z_2 = 0,$$
$$x_3 = -0.3, \quad y_3 = -0.5, \quad z_3 = 0, \quad x_4 = 0, \quad y_4 = -0.5, \quad z_4 = 0, \tag{4.1070}$$

$$[\mathbf{r}_1] = \begin{bmatrix} 0 & 0 & 0.5 \\ 0 & 0 & -0.3 \\ -0.5 & 0.3 & 0 \end{bmatrix}, \quad [\mathbf{r}_2] = \begin{bmatrix} 0 & 0 & 0.5 \\ 0 & 0 & 0.3 \\ -0.5 & -0.3 & 0 \end{bmatrix},$$

$$[\mathbf{r}_3] = \begin{bmatrix} 0 & 0 & -0.5 \\ 0 & 0 & -0.3 \\ 0.5 & 0.3 & 0 \end{bmatrix}, \quad [\mathbf{r}_4] = \begin{bmatrix} 0 & 0 & -0.5 \\ 0 & 0 & -0.3 \\ 0.5 & 0.3 & 0 \end{bmatrix}, \tag{4.1071}$$

$$a_1 = \frac{\sqrt{3}}{2}, \quad b_1 = \frac{1}{2}, \quad c_1 = 0, \quad d_1 = 0, \quad e_1 = 0, \quad f_1 = -0.28301,$$

$$a_2 = -\frac{\sqrt{3}}{2}, \quad b_2 = \frac{1}{2}, \quad c_2 = 0, \quad d_2 = 0, \quad e_2 = 0, \quad f_2 = 0.28301,$$

$$a_3 = -\frac{\sqrt{3}}{2}, \quad b_3 = -\frac{1}{2}, \quad c_3 = 0, \quad d_3 = 0, \quad e_3 = 0, \quad f_3 = -0.28301, \tag{4.1072}$$

$$a_4 = \frac{\sqrt{3}}{2}, \quad b_4 = -\frac{1}{2}, \quad c_4 = 0, \quad d_4 = 0, \quad e_4 = 0, \quad f_4 = 0.28301,$$

$$[\mathbf{r}_1]^2 = \begin{bmatrix} -0.25 & 0.15 & 0 \\ 0.15 & -0.09 & 0 \\ 0 & 0 & -0.34 \end{bmatrix}, \quad [\mathbf{r}_2]^2 = \begin{bmatrix} -0.25 & 0.15 & 0 \\ 0.15 & -0.09 & 0 \\ 0 & 0 & -0.34 \end{bmatrix},$$

$$[\mathbf{r}_3]^2 = \begin{bmatrix} -0.25 & 0.15 & 0 \\ 0.15 & -0.09 & 0 \\ 0 & 0 & -0.34 \end{bmatrix}, \quad [\mathbf{r}_4]^2 = \begin{bmatrix} -0.25 & -0.15 & 0 \\ -0.15 & -0.09 & 0 \\ 0 & 0 & -0.34 \end{bmatrix}, \tag{4.1073}$$

$$\{\mathbf{U}_1\} = \begin{bmatrix} 0.86603 & 0.5 & 0 & 0 & 0 & -0.28301 \end{bmatrix}^{\mathrm{T}},$$
$$\{\mathbf{U}_2\} = \begin{bmatrix} -0.86603 & 0.5 & 0 & 0 & 0 & 0.28301 \end{bmatrix}^{\mathrm{T}},$$
$$\{\mathbf{U}_3\} = \begin{bmatrix} -0.86603 & -0.5 & 0 & 0 & 0 & -0.28301 \end{bmatrix}^{\mathrm{T}}, \tag{4.1074}$$
$$\{\mathbf{U}_4\} = \begin{bmatrix} 0.86603 & -0.5 & 0 & 0 & 0 & 0.28301 \end{bmatrix}^{\mathrm{T}},$$

$$\{\mathbf{U}_1\}\{\mathbf{U}_1\}^{\mathrm{T}} = \begin{bmatrix} 0.75 & 0.43301 & 0 & 0 & 0 & -0.24510 \\ 0.43301 & 0.25 & 0 & 0 & 0 & -0.14151 \\ 0 & 0 & 0 & 0 & 0 & 0 \\ 0 & 0 & 0 & 0 & 0 & 0 \\ 0 & 0 & 0 & 0 & 0 & 0 \\ -0.24510 & -0.14151 & 0 & 0 & 0 & 008010 \end{bmatrix},$$

$$\{\mathbf{U}_2\}\{\mathbf{U}_2\}^{\mathrm{T}} = \begin{bmatrix} 0.75 & -0.43301 & 0 & 0 & 0 & -0.24510 \\ -0.43301 & 0.25 & 0 & 0 & 0 & 0.14151 \\ 0 & 0 & 0 & 0 & 0 & 0 \\ 0 & 0 & 0 & 0 & 0 & 0 \\ 0 & 0 & 0 & 0 & 0 & 0 \\ -0.24510 & 0.14151 & 0 & 0 & 0 & 0.08010 \end{bmatrix},$$

$$\{U_3\}\{U_3\}^T = \begin{bmatrix} 0.75 & 0.43301 & 0 & 0 & 0 & 0.24510 \\ 0.43301 & 0.25 & 0 & 0 & 0 & 0.14151 \\ 0 & 0 & 0 & 0 & 0 & 0 \\ 0 & 0 & 0 & 0 & 0 & 0 \\ 0 & 0 & 0 & 0 & 0 & 0 \\ 0.24510 & 0.14151 & 0 & 0 & 0 & 0.08010 \end{bmatrix},$$

$$\{U_4\}\{U_4\}^T = \begin{bmatrix} 0.75 & -0.43301 & 0 & 0 & 0 & 0.24510 \\ -0.43301 & 0.25 & 0 & 0 & 0 & -0.14151 \\ 0 & 0 & 0 & 0 & 0 & 0 \\ 0 & 0 & 0 & 0 & 0 & 0 \\ 0 & 0 & 0 & 0 & 0 & 0 \\ 0.24510 & -0.14151 & 0 & 0 & 0 & 0.08010 \end{bmatrix}, \quad (4.1075)$$

$$\frac{k_1 s_1}{L_1}\begin{bmatrix} [\mathbf{I}] & [\mathbf{r}_1]^T \\ [\mathbf{r}_1] & -[\mathbf{r}_1]^2 \end{bmatrix} + k_1\left(1 - \frac{s_1}{L_1}\right)\{U_1\}\{U_1\}^T$$

$$= \begin{bmatrix} 6206.67 & 2829 & 0 & 0 & 0 & -2254.65 \\ 2829 & 2940 & 0 & 0 & 0 & -532.53 \\ 0 & 0 & 1306.67 & 653.33 & -392 & 0 \\ 0 & 0 & 653.33 & 326.67 & -196 & 0 \\ 0 & 0 & -392 & -196 & 117.6 & 0 \\ -2254.65 & -532.53 & 0 & 0 & 0 & 967.59 \end{bmatrix}, \quad (4.1076)$$

$$\frac{k_2 s_2}{L_2}\begin{bmatrix} [\mathbf{I}] & [\mathbf{r}_2]^T \\ [\mathbf{r}_2] & -[\mathbf{r}_2]^2 \end{bmatrix} + k_2\left(1 - \frac{s_2}{L_2}\right)\{U_2\}\{U_2\}^T$$

$$= \begin{bmatrix} 3266.67 & -1131.6 & 0 & 0 & 0 & -1293.86 \\ -1131.6 & 1960 & 0 & 0 & 0 & -22.19 \\ 0 & 0 & 1306.67 & 653.33 & 392 & 0 \\ 0 & 0 & 653.33 & 326.67 & -196 & 0 \\ 0 & 0 & 392 & -196 & 117.6 & 0 \\ -1293.86 & -22.19 & 0 & 0 & 0 & 653.39 \end{bmatrix}, \quad (4.1077)$$

$$\frac{k_3 s_3}{L_3}\begin{bmatrix} [\mathbf{I}] & [\mathbf{r}_3]^T \\ [\mathbf{r}_3] & -[\mathbf{r}_3]^2 \end{bmatrix} + k_3\left(1 - \frac{s_3}{L_3}\right)\{U_3\}\{U_3\}^T$$

$$= \begin{bmatrix} 1568 & 678.96 & 0 & 0 & 0 & 580.32 \\ 678.96 & 784 & 0 & 0 & 0 & 104.29 \\ 0 & 0 & 392 & -196 & 117.6 & 0 \\ 0 & 0 & -196 & 98 & -58.8 & 0 \\ 0 & 0 & 117.6 & -58.8 & 35.28 & 0 \\ 580.32 & 104.29 & 0 & 0 & 0 & 258.88 \end{bmatrix}, \quad (4.1078)$$

$$\frac{k_4 s_4}{L_4}\begin{bmatrix} [\mathbf{I}] & [\mathbf{r}_4]^T \\ [\mathbf{r}_4] & -[\mathbf{r}_4]^2 \end{bmatrix} + k_4\left(1 - \frac{s_4}{L_4}\right)\{U_4\}\{U_4\}^T$$

$$= \begin{bmatrix} 1148 & -436.47 & 0 & 0 & 0 & 443.06 \\ -436.47 & 644 & 0 & 0 & 0 & -25.04 \\ 0 & 0 & 392 & -196 & -117.6 & 0 \\ 0 & 0 & -196 & 98 & 58.8 & 0 \\ 0 & 0 & -117.6 & 58.8 & 35.28 & 0 \\ 443.06 & -25.04 & 0 & 0 & 0 & 214.02 \end{bmatrix}, \quad (4.1079)$$

$$[\mathbf{K}] = \sum_{i=1}^{4} \frac{k_i s_i}{L_i} \begin{bmatrix} [\mathbf{I}] & [\mathbf{r}_i]^{\mathrm{T}} \\ [\mathbf{r}_i] & -[\mathbf{r}_i]^2 \end{bmatrix} + \sum_{i=1}^{4} k_i \left(1 - \frac{s_i}{L_i}\right) \{\mathbf{U}_i\}\{\mathbf{U}_i\}^{\mathrm{T}}$$

$$= \begin{bmatrix} 12189.34 & 1939.89 & 0 & 0 & 0 & -2525.13 \\ 1939.89 & 6328 & 0 & 0 & 0 & -475.47 \\ 0 & 0 & 3397.34 & 914.66 & 0 & 0 \\ 0 & 0 & 914.66 & 849.34 & -392 & 0 \\ 0 & 0 & 0 & -392 & 305.76 & 0 \\ -2525.13 & -475.47 & 0 & 0 & 0 & 2094.08 \end{bmatrix}. \quad (4.1080)$$

The eigenpulsations are obtained from the equation

$$\begin{vmatrix} 12189.34 \\ -60p^2 & 1939.89 & 0 & 0 & 0 & -2525.13 \\ 1939.89 & \begin{matrix} 6328 \\ -60p^2 \end{matrix} & 0 & 0 & 0 & -475.47 \\ 0 & 0 & \begin{matrix} 3397.34 \\ -60p^2 \end{matrix} & 914.66 & 0 & 0 \\ 0 & 0 & 914.66 & \begin{matrix} 849.34 \\ -5p^2 \end{matrix} & -392 & 0 \\ 0 & 0 & 0 & -392 & \begin{matrix} 305.76 \\ -3.2p^2 \end{matrix} & 0 \\ -2525.13 & -475.47 & 0 & 0 & 0 & \begin{matrix} 2094.08 \\ -8.2p^2 \end{matrix} \end{vmatrix} = 0, \quad (4.1081)$$

from which

$$\begin{vmatrix} 12189.34 - 60p^2 & 1939.89 & -2525.13 \\ 1939.89 & 6328 - 60p^2 & -475.47 \\ -2525.13 & -475.47 & 2094.08 - 8.2p^2 \end{vmatrix}$$

$$\times \begin{vmatrix} 3397.34 - 60p^2 & 914.66 & 0 \\ 914.66 & 849.34 - 5p^2 & -392 \\ 0 & -392 & 305.76 - 3.2p^2 \end{vmatrix} = 0, \quad (4.1082)$$

that is,

$$-29520p^6 + 16649219.28p^4 - 2532108243.09p^2 + 115198062272.87 = 0 \quad (4.1083)$$

or

$$-960p^6 + 309158.72p^4 - 18112125.58p^2 + 104420926.76 = 0. \quad (4.1084)$$

It follows that

$$\begin{matrix} p_1 = 18.751, & p_2 = 10.934, & p_3 = 9.635, \\ p_4 = 567.485, & p_5 = 0.763, & p_6 = 0.761. \end{matrix} \quad (4.1085)$$

For the first three eigenpulsations, we use the system

$$\begin{matrix} (12189.34 - 60p^2)a_1 + 1939.89a_2 = 2525.13, \\ 1939.89a_1 + (6328 - 60p^2)a_2 = 475.47, \end{matrix} \quad (4.1086)$$

while for the last three eigenpulsations, we use the system

$$(3397.34 - 60p^2)b_1 + 914.66b_2 = 0,$$
$$914.66b_1 + (849.34 - 5p^2)b_2 = 392. \tag{4.1087}$$

The modal matrix reads

$$[\mathbf{A}] = \begin{bmatrix} -0.495 & 0.382 & 0.791 & 0 & 0 & 0 \\ -0.973 & 0.314 & -1.396 & 0 & 0 & 0 \\ 0 & 0 & 0 & 10^{-8} & -0.17843 & -0.17841 \\ 0 & 0 & 0 & 0.00024 & 0.65594 & 0.65591 \\ 0 & 0 & 0 & 1 & 1 & 1 \\ 1 & 1 & 1 & 0 & 0 & 0 \end{bmatrix}. \tag{4.1088}$$

Problem 4.11

Determine the efforts in the homogeneous, articulated, straight bars, of constant cross section from which a rigid solution is suspended.

Solution:

1. Theory

1.1. Generalities. Notations

Consider a rigid solid, as illustrated in Figure 4.13, suspended by the elastic straight bars $A_{0i}A_i$, $i = \overline{1, n}$, of constant cross section and spherical articulated (with spherical hinges) and the notations:

- O_0XYZ — the dextrorsum three-axes orthogonal fixed reference system;
- $Oxyz$ — the dextrorsum three-axes orthogonal reference system, rigidly linked to the solid;
- X_O, Y_O, Z_O — the coordinates of the point O in the system O_0XYZ;
- $\mathbf{F}, \mathbf{M}_O$ — the resultant and the resultant moment, respectively, of the external forces that act upon the body;

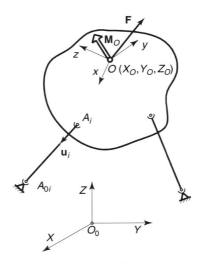

Figure 4.13   Problem 4.11.

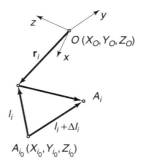

Figure 4.14 Small displacements.

- (F_x, F_y, F_z), (M_x, M_y, M_z)—projection of the vectors $\mathbf{F}$, $\mathbf{M}_O$ on the axes of the $Oxyz$-trihedron;
- l_i—length of the bar $A_{0i}A_i$;
- A_i—area of the cross section of the bar $A_{0i}A_i$;
- E_i—the longitudinal elasticity modulus of the bar $A_{0i}A_i$;
- k_i—the stiffness of the bar $A_{0i}A_i$

$$k_i = \frac{E_i A_i}{l_i};$$ (4.1089)

- $\boldsymbol{\delta}$—the displacement (small) of the point O (Fig. 4.14);
- $\boldsymbol{\theta}$—the rotation angle (small) of the rigid solid;
- $(\delta_x, \delta_y, \delta_z)$, $(\theta_x, \theta_y, \theta_z)$—the projections of the vectors $\boldsymbol{\delta}$ and $\boldsymbol{\theta}$ on the axes of the $Oxyz$-trihedron;
- $\boldsymbol{\delta}_i$—the displacement (small) of the point A_i;
- $\mathbf{u}_i$—the unit vector of the direction $\mathbf{A}_i\mathbf{A}_{0i}$;
- $\mathbf{r}_i$—the position vector of the point A_i;
- x_i, y_i, z_i—the coordinates of the point A_i in the $Oxyz$-system;
- a_i, b_i, c_i—projections of the unit vector $\mathbf{u}_i$ on the axes of the $Oxyz$-trihedron;
- d_i, e_i, f_i—projections of the vector $\mathbf{r}_i \cdot \mathbf{u}_i$ on the axes of the $Oxyz$-trihedron, that is,

$$d_i = y_i c_i - z_i b_i, \quad e_i = z_i a_i - x_i c_i, \quad f_i = x_i b_i - y_i a_i;$$ (4.1090)

- N_i—intensity of the effort $\mathbf{N}_i$ in the bar $A_{0i}A_i$;
- Δl_i—deformation of the bar $A_{0i}A_i$;
- $\{\mathbf{F}\}$, $\{\boldsymbol{\Delta}\}$, $\{\mathbf{U}_i\}$—column matrices defined by

$$\{\mathbf{F}\} = \begin{bmatrix} F_x & F_y & F_z & M_x & M_y & M_z \end{bmatrix}^{\mathrm{T}},$$
$$\{\boldsymbol{\Delta}\} = \begin{bmatrix} \delta_x & \delta_y & \delta_z & \theta_x & \theta_y & \theta_z \end{bmatrix}^{\mathrm{T}},$$ (4.1091)
$$\{\mathbf{U}_i\} = \begin{bmatrix} a_i & b_i & c_i & d_i & e_i & f_i \end{bmatrix}^{\mathrm{T}}.$$

1.2. Case in which none of the bars is deformed by the application of the external load $\mathbf{F}$, $\mathbf{M}_O$ With the above notations, we write the obvious relation

$$(l_i + \Delta l_i)^2 = (-l_i \mathbf{u}_i + \boldsymbol{\delta}_i)^2,$$ (4.1092)

from which, neglecting the nonlinear terms $(\Delta l_i)^2$, we obtain the relation

$$\Delta l_i = -\mathbf{u}_i \cdot \boldsymbol{\delta}_i. \tag{4.1093}$$

The displacement of the point A_i of the solid is small, so that it can be expressed by

$$\boldsymbol{\delta}_i = \boldsymbol{\delta} + \boldsymbol{\theta} \cdot \mathbf{r}_i; \tag{4.1094}$$

hence, using the mentioned notations, relation (4.1093) becomes

$$\Delta l_i = -\{\mathbf{U}_i\}^{\mathrm{T}}\{\boldsymbol{\Delta}\}. \tag{4.1095}$$

Under these conditions, the intensities of the efforts in the bars are

$$N_i = k_i \Delta l_i = -k_i \{\mathbf{U}_i\}^{\mathrm{T}}\{\boldsymbol{\Delta}\}, \quad i = \overline{1, n}; \tag{4.1096}$$

if $N_i > 0$ the bars are subjected to traction and if $N_i < 0$ they are subjected to compression.

The effort vector reads

$$\mathbf{N}_i = -k_i \{\mathbf{U}_i\}^{\mathrm{T}}\{\boldsymbol{\Delta}\}\mathbf{u}_i. \tag{4.1097}$$

Taking into account the previous notations and the equations of equilibrium

$$\sum_{i=1}^{n} \mathbf{N}_i + \mathbf{F} = \mathbf{0}, \quad \sum_{i=1}^{n} \mathbf{r}_i \cdot \mathbf{N}_i + \mathbf{M}_O = \mathbf{0}, \tag{4.1098}$$

we obtain the matrix equation

$$[\mathbf{K}]\{\boldsymbol{\Delta}\} = \{\mathbf{F}\}, \tag{4.1099}$$

where $[\mathbf{K}]$ is the stiffness matrix given by

$$[\mathbf{K}] = \sum_{i=1}^{n} k_i \{\mathbf{U}_i\}\{\mathbf{U}_i\}^{\mathrm{T}} = \sum_{i=1}^{n} k_i \begin{bmatrix} a_i^2 & a_i b_i & a_i c_i & a_i d_i & a_i e_i & a_i f_i \\ b_i a_i & b_i^2 & b_i c_i & b_i d_i & b_i e_i & b_i f_i \\ c_i a_i & c_i b_i & c_i^2 & c_i d_i & c_i e_i & c_i f_i \\ d_i a_i & d_i b_i & d_i c_i & d_i^2 & d_i e_i & d_i f_i \\ e_i a_i & e_i b_i & e_i c_i & e_i d_i & e_i^2 & e_i f_i \\ f_i a_i & f_i b_i & f_i c_i & f_i d_i & f_i e_i & f_i^2 \end{bmatrix}. \tag{4.1100}$$

Thus, equation (4.1099) gives the displacement $\{\boldsymbol{\Delta}\}$, and then the efforts in the bars are given by equation (4.1096)

Particular cases:

(a) The bars are parallel

We suppose in this case, that the bars are parallel to the Oz-axis and we get, successively

$$a_i = b_i = 0, \quad c_i = 1, \quad d_i = y_i, \quad e_i = -x_i, \quad f_i = 0, \tag{4.1101}$$

$$\{\mathbf{U}_i\} = \begin{bmatrix} c_i & d_i & e_i \end{bmatrix}^{\mathrm{T}}, \quad \{\boldsymbol{\Delta}\} = \begin{bmatrix} \delta_z & \theta_x & \theta_y \end{bmatrix}^{\mathrm{T}}, \quad \{\mathbf{F}\} = \begin{bmatrix} F_z & M_x & M_y \end{bmatrix}^{\mathrm{T}}, \tag{4.1102}$$

$$[\mathbf{K}] = \sum_{i=1}^{n} k_i \{\mathbf{U}_i\}\{\mathbf{U}_i\}^{\mathrm{T}} = \sum_{i=1}^{n} k_i \begin{bmatrix} c_i^2 & c_i d_i & c_i e_i \\ d_i c_i & d_i^2 & d_i e_i \\ e_i c_i & e_i d_i & e_i^2 \end{bmatrix}. \tag{4.1103}$$

(b) The bars are coplanar

We assume that the bars are situated in the Oxy-plane, so that

$$c_i = 0, \quad d_i = e_i = 0, \quad f_i = x_i b_i - y_i a_i, \tag{4.1104}$$

$$\{U_i\} = \begin{bmatrix} a_i & b_i & f_i \end{bmatrix}^T, \quad \{\Delta\} = \begin{bmatrix} \delta_x & \delta_y & \theta_z \end{bmatrix}^T, \quad \{F\} = \begin{bmatrix} F_x & F_y & M_z \end{bmatrix}^T, \tag{4.1105}$$

$$[K] = \sum_{i=1}^{n} k_i \{U_i\}\{U_i\}^T = \sum_{i=1}^{n} k_i \begin{bmatrix} a_i^2 & a_i b_i & a_i f_i \\ b_i a_i & b_i^2 & b_i f_i \\ f_i a_i & f_i b_i & f_i^2 \end{bmatrix}. \tag{4.1106}$$

(c) The bars are parallel and coplanar

In this case, we assume that the bars are situated in the Oz-plane and are parallel to the Oz-axis; it follows that

$$a_i = b_i = 0, \quad c_i = 1, \quad d_i = f_i = 0, \quad e_i = -x_i, \tag{4.1107}$$

$$\{U_i\} = \begin{bmatrix} c_i & e_i \end{bmatrix}^T, \quad \{\Delta\} = \begin{bmatrix} \delta_z & \theta_y \end{bmatrix}^T, \quad \{F\} = \begin{bmatrix} F_z & M_y \end{bmatrix}^T, \tag{4.1108}$$

$$[K] = \sum_{i=1}^{n} k_i \{U_i\}\{U_i\}^T = \sum_{i=1}^{n} k_i \begin{bmatrix} c_i^2 & c_i e_i \\ e_i c_i & e_i^2 \end{bmatrix}. \tag{4.1109}$$

(d) The bars are concurrent

In this case, the solid is reduced to the concurrence point, so that

$$\theta_x = \theta_y = \theta_z, \quad d_{i=0} = e_i = f_i, \tag{4.1110}$$

$$\{U_i\} = \begin{bmatrix} a_i & b_i & c_i \end{bmatrix}^T, \quad \{\Delta\} = \begin{bmatrix} \delta_x & \delta_y & \delta_z \end{bmatrix}^T, \tag{4.1111}$$

$$[K] = \sum_{i=1}^{n} k_i \{U_i\}\{U_i\}^T = \sum_{i=1}^{n} k_i \begin{bmatrix} a_i^2 & a_i b_i & a_i c_i \\ b_i a_i & b_i^2 & b_i c_i \\ c_i a_i & c_i b_i & c_i^2 \end{bmatrix}. \tag{4.1112}$$

(e) The bars are concurrent and coplanar

If the bars are situated in the Oxy-plane, we have

$$c_i = 0, \tag{4.1113}$$

$$\{U_i\} = \begin{bmatrix} a_i & b_i \end{bmatrix}^T, \quad \{\Delta\} = \begin{bmatrix} \delta_x & \delta_y \end{bmatrix}^T, \tag{4.1114}$$

$$[K] = \sum_{i=1}^{n} k_i \{U_i\}\{U_i\}^T = \sum_{i=1}^{n} k_i \begin{bmatrix} a_i^2 & a_i b_i \\ b_i a_i & b_i^2 \end{bmatrix}. \tag{4.1115}$$

1.3. Case in which the bars have errors of fabrication equal to $\Delta \tilde{l}_i$

In this case, relations (4.1096) and (4.1097) become

$$N_i = -k_i [\Delta \tilde{l}_i + \{U_i\}^T \{\Delta\}], \tag{4.1116}$$

$$\mathbf{N}_i = -k_i \mathbf{u}_i [\Delta \tilde{l}_i + \{U_i\}^T \{\Delta\}]. \tag{4.1117}$$

Using the notation

$$\{\tilde{F}\} = -k_i \Delta \tilde{l}_i \{U_i\}, \tag{4.1118}$$

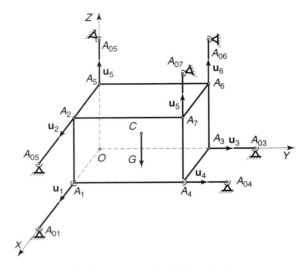

Figure 4.15   Application 2.1.

for where $\Delta \widetilde{l}_i$ corresponds to bars that are longer, the equation of equilibrium (4.1098) leads to the equation

$$[\mathbf{K}]\{\mathbf{\Delta}\} = \{\mathbf{F}\} + \{\widetilde{\mathbf{F}}\}. \tag{4.1119}$$

The rigidity matrix is also given by relation (4.1100).
In the case of temperature variations, the deviations that appear are given by

$$\Delta \overleftrightarrow{l}_i = l_i \alpha_i \Delta T, \tag{4.1120}$$

where α_i is the coefficient of linear dilatation, while ΔT is the temperature variation in Kelvin.

2. Numerical applications

Application 2.1. We consider the rigid solid in the form of a homogeneous parallelepiped (Fig. 4.15) of weight G and dimensions $2a$, $2b$, $2c$, suspended by seven homogeneous articulated straight bars, of the same length l and of the same stiffness k, the bars $A_1 A_{01}$, $A_2 A_{02}$ being parallel to the OX-axis, the bars $A_3 A_{03}$, $A_4 A_{04}$ being parallel to the OY-axis, while the bars $A_5 A_{05}$, $A_6 A_{06}$ and $A_7 A_{07}$ are parallel to the vertical OZ-axis. Assuming that the rigid solid is acted upon only by its own weight G, let us determine the efforts in the seven bars in the following cases:

(a) The bars have no fabrication errors.

(b) The bars $A_1 A_{01}$, $A_6 A_{06}$ have the fabrication errors $\Delta \widetilde{l}_1$, $\Delta \widetilde{l}_6$.

(c) The bar $A_4 A_{04}$ is heated by ΔT^0.

Solution of Application 2.1:

(a) It follows, successively, that

$$\{\mathbf{U}_1\} = \begin{bmatrix} 1 & 0 & 0 & 0 & 0 & 0 \end{bmatrix}^{\mathrm{T}}, \quad \{\mathbf{U}_2\} = \begin{bmatrix} 1 & 0 & 0 & 0 & 0.5 & 0 \end{bmatrix}^{\mathrm{T}},$$

$$\{\mathbf{U}_3\} = \begin{bmatrix} 0 & 1 & 0 & 0 & 0 & 0 \end{bmatrix}^{\mathrm{T}}, \quad \{\mathbf{U}_4\} = \begin{bmatrix} 0 & 1 & 0 & 0 & 0 & 1 \end{bmatrix}^{\mathrm{T}},$$

$$\{\mathbf{U}_5\} = \begin{bmatrix} 0 & 0 & 1 & 0 & 0 & 0 \end{bmatrix}^{\mathrm{T}}, \quad \{\mathbf{U}_6\} = \begin{bmatrix} 0 & 0 & 1 & 1 & 0 & 0 \end{bmatrix}^{\mathrm{T}},$$

$$\{\mathbf{U}_7\} = \begin{bmatrix} 0 & 0 & 1 & 1 & -1 & 0 \end{bmatrix}^{\mathrm{T}}, \tag{4.1121}$$

$$\{\mathbf{U}_1\}\{\mathbf{U}_1\}^{\mathrm{T}} = \begin{bmatrix} 1 & 0 & 0 & 0 & 0 & 0 \\ 0 & 0 & 0 & 0 & 0 & 0 \\ 0 & 0 & 0 & 0 & 0 & 0 \\ 0 & 0 & 0 & 0 & 0 & 0 \\ 0 & 0 & 0 & 0 & 0 & 0 \\ 0 & 0 & 0 & 0 & 0 & 0 \end{bmatrix}, \quad \{\mathbf{U}_2\}\{\mathbf{U}_2\}^{\mathrm{T}} = \begin{bmatrix} 1 & 0 & 0 & 0 & 0.5 & 0 \\ 0 & 0 & 0 & 0 & 0 & 0 \\ 0 & 0 & 0 & 0 & 0 & 0 \\ 0 & 0 & 0 & 0 & 0 & 0 \\ 0.5 & 0 & 0 & 0 & 0.25 & 0 \\ 0 & 0 & 0 & 0 & 0 & 0 \end{bmatrix},$$

$$\{\mathbf{U}_3\}\{\mathbf{U}_3\}^{\mathrm{T}} = \begin{bmatrix} 0 & 0 & 0 & 0 & 0 & 0 \\ 0 & 1 & 0 & 0 & 0 & 0 \\ 0 & 0 & 0 & 0 & 0 & 0 \\ 0 & 0 & 0 & 0 & 0 & 0 \\ 0 & 0 & 0 & 0 & 0 & 0 \\ 0 & 0 & 0 & 0 & 0 & 0 \end{bmatrix}, \quad \{\mathbf{U}_4\}\{\mathbf{U}_4\}^{\mathrm{T}} = \begin{bmatrix} 0 & 0 & 0 & 0 & 0 & 0 \\ 0 & 1 & 0 & 0 & 0 & 1 \\ 0 & 0 & 0 & 0 & 0 & 0 \\ 0 & 0 & 0 & 0 & 0 & 0 \\ 0 & 0 & 0 & 0 & 0 & 0 \\ 0 & 1 & 0 & 0 & 0 & 1 \end{bmatrix},$$

$$\{\mathbf{U}_5\}\{\mathbf{U}_5\}^{\mathrm{T}} = \begin{bmatrix} 0 & 0 & 0 & 0 & 0 & 0 \\ 0 & 0 & 0 & 0 & 0 & 0 \\ 0 & 0 & 1 & 0 & 0 & 0 \\ 0 & 0 & 0 & 0 & 0 & 0 \\ 0 & 0 & 0 & 0 & 0 & 0 \\ 0 & 0 & 0 & 0 & 0 & 0 \end{bmatrix}, \quad \{\mathbf{U}_6\}\{\mathbf{U}_6\}^{\mathrm{T}} = \begin{bmatrix} 0 & 0 & 0 & 0 & 0 & 0 \\ 0 & 0 & 0 & 0 & 0 & 0 \\ 0 & 0 & 1 & 1 & 0 & 0 \\ 0 & 0 & 1 & 1 & 0 & 0 \\ 0 & 0 & 0 & 0 & 0 & 0 \\ 0 & 0 & 0 & 0 & 0 & 0 \end{bmatrix},$$

$$\{\mathbf{U}_7\}\{\mathbf{U}_7\}^{\mathrm{T}} = \begin{bmatrix} 0 & 0 & 0 & 0 & 0 & 0 \\ 0 & 0 & 0 & 0 & 0 & 0 \\ 0 & 0 & 1 & 1 & -1 & 0 \\ 0 & 0 & 1 & 1 & -1 & 0 \\ 0 & 0 & -1 & -1 & 1 & 0 \\ 0 & 0 & 0 & 0 & 0 & 0 \end{bmatrix}, \tag{4.1122}$$

$$[\mathbf{K}] = k\sum_{i=1}^{7}\{\mathbf{U}_i\}\{\mathbf{U}_i\}^{\mathrm{T}} = 10^7 \begin{bmatrix} 2 & 0 & 0 & 0 & 0.5 & 0 \\ 0 & 2 & 0 & 0 & 0 & 1 \\ 0 & 0 & 3 & 2 & -1 & 0 \\ 0 & 0 & 2 & 2 & -1 & 0 \\ 0.5 & 0 & -1 & -1 & 1.25 & 0 \\ 0 & 1 & 0 & 0 & 0 & 1 \end{bmatrix}, \tag{4.1123}$$

$$\{\mathbf{F}\} = 200000\begin{bmatrix} 0 & 0 & -1 & -1 & 1 & 0 \end{bmatrix}^{\mathrm{T}}, \tag{4.1124}$$

$$[\mathbf{K}]^{-1} = 10^{-7} \begin{bmatrix} 0.6 & 0 & 0 & -0.2 & -0.4 & 0 \\ 0 & 1 & 0 & 0 & 0 & -1 \\ 0 & 0 & 1 & -1 & 0 & 0 \\ -0.2 & 0 & -1 & 1.9 & 0.8 & 0 \\ -0.4 & 0 & 0 & 0.8 & 1.6 & 0 \\ 0 & -1 & 0 & 0 & 0 & 2 \end{bmatrix}. \tag{4.1125}$$

$$\{\boldsymbol{\Delta}\} = [\mathbf{K}]^{-1}\{\mathbf{F}\} = \begin{bmatrix} 0.004 & 0 & 0 & -0.002 & 0.016 & 0 \end{bmatrix}^{\mathrm{T}}. \tag{4.1126}$$

$$N_1 = -k_1\{\mathbf{U}_1\}^{\mathrm{T}}\{\Delta\} = -40,000\ \mathrm{N}, \quad N_2 = -k_2\{\mathbf{U}_2\}^{\mathrm{T}}\{\Delta\} = -12,0000\ \mathrm{N},$$

$$N_3 = -k_3\{\mathbf{U}_3\}^{\mathrm{T}}\{\Delta\} = 0\ \mathrm{N}, \quad N_4 = -k_4\{\mathbf{U}_4\}^{\mathrm{T}}\{\Delta\} = 0\ \mathrm{N},$$

$$N_5 = -k_5\{\mathbf{U}_5\}^{\mathrm{T}}\{\Delta\} = 0\ \mathrm{N}, \quad N_6 = -k_6\{\mathbf{U}_6\}^{\mathrm{T}}\{\Delta\} = 20,000\ \mathrm{N},$$

$$N_7 = -k_7\{\mathbf{U}_7\}^{\mathrm{T}}\{\Delta\} = 180,000\ \mathrm{N}. \tag{4.1127}$$

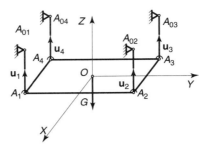

Figure 4.16   Application 2.2.

(b) We have, in this case,

$$\{\widetilde{\mathbf{F}}\} = -k_1\Delta\widetilde{l}_1\{\mathbf{U}_1\} - k_6\Delta\widetilde{l}_6\{\mathbf{U}_6\} = 200000\begin{bmatrix}-1 & 0 & -1 & -1 & 0 & 0\end{bmatrix}^{\mathrm{T}}, \quad (4.1128)$$

$$\{\mathbf{F}\} + \{\overleftrightarrow{\mathbf{F}}\} = 200000\begin{bmatrix}-1 & 0 & -2 & -2 & 1 & 0\end{bmatrix}^{\mathrm{T}}, \quad (4.1129)$$

$$\{\mathbf{\Delta}\} = [\mathbf{K}]^{-1}\{\{\mathbf{F}\} + \{\widetilde{\mathbf{F}}\}\} = \begin{bmatrix}-0.012 & 0 & 0 & -0.016 & 0.008 & 0\end{bmatrix}^{\mathrm{T}}, \quad (4.1130)$$

$$N_1 = -k_1[\Delta\widetilde{l}_1 + \{\mathbf{U}_1\}^{\mathrm{T}}\{\mathbf{\Delta}\}] = -80,000 \text{ N}, \quad N_2 = -k_2\{\mathbf{U}_2\}^{\mathrm{T}}\{\mathbf{\Delta}\} = 80,000 \text{ N},$$

$$N_3 = -k_3\{\mathbf{U}_3\}^{\mathrm{T}}\{\mathbf{\Delta}\} = 0 \text{ N}, \quad N_4 = -k_4\{\mathbf{U}_4\}^{\mathrm{T}}\{\mathbf{\Delta}\} = 0 \text{ N},$$

$$N_5 = -k_5\{\mathbf{U}_5\}^{\mathrm{T}}\{\mathbf{\Delta}\} = 160,000 \text{ N}, \quad N_6 = -k_6[\Delta\widetilde{l}_6 + \{\mathbf{U}_6\}^{\mathrm{T}}\{\mathbf{\Delta}\}] = -40,000 \text{ N},$$

$$N_7 = -k_7\{\mathbf{U}_7\}^{\mathrm{T}}\{\mathbf{\Delta}\} = 240,000 \text{ N}. \quad (4.1131)$$

(c) We obtain

$$\Delta\widetilde{l}_4 = l\alpha_4\Delta T = 0.012 \text{ m}, \quad (4.1132)$$

$$\{\widetilde{\mathbf{F}}\} = -k_4\Delta\widetilde{l}_4\{\mathbf{U}_4\} = 120,000\begin{bmatrix}0 & -1 & 0 & 0 & 0 & -1\end{bmatrix}^{\mathrm{T}}, \quad (4.1133)$$

$$\{\mathbf{F}\} + \{\widetilde{\mathbf{F}}\} = 40,000\begin{bmatrix}0 & -3 & -5 & -5 & 5 & -3\end{bmatrix}^{\mathrm{T}}, \quad (4.1134)$$

$$\{\mathbf{\Delta}\} = [\mathbf{K}]^{-1}\{\{\mathbf{F}\} + \{\widetilde{\mathbf{F}}\}\} = \begin{bmatrix}-0.004 & 0 & 0 & -0.002 & 0.016 & -0.012\end{bmatrix}^{\mathrm{T}}, \quad (4.1135)$$

$$N_1 = -k_1\{\mathbf{U}_1\}^{\mathrm{T}}\{\mathbf{\Delta}\} = 40,000 \text{ N}, \quad N_2 = -k_2\{\mathbf{U}_2\}^{\mathrm{T}}\{\mathbf{\Delta}\} = -40,000 \text{ N},$$

$$N_3 = -k_3\{\mathbf{U}_3\}^{\mathrm{T}}\{\mathbf{\Delta}\} = 0 \text{ N}, \quad N_4 = -k_4[\Delta\widetilde{l}_4 + \{\mathbf{U}_4\}^{\mathrm{T}}\{\mathbf{\Delta}\}] = 0 \text{ N},$$

$$N_5 = -k_5\{\mathbf{U}_5\}^{\mathrm{T}}\{\mathbf{\Delta}\} = 20,000 \text{ N}, \quad N_6 = -k_6\{\mathbf{U}_6\}\{\mathbf{\Delta}\} = -140,000 \text{ N},$$

$$N_7 = -k_7\{\mathbf{U}_7\}\{\mathbf{\Delta}\} = 180,000 \text{ N}. \quad (4.1136)$$

Application 2.2. A square horizontal plate of side $2l$ and weight G is suspended by four vertical bars of elastic stiffness k_1, k_2, k_3, k_4 (Fig. 4.16).
Determine the efforts in the bars in the following cases:
(a) The bars have no fabrication errors.
(b) The bar A_1A_{01} has a fabrication error given by $\Delta\widetilde{l}_1$. Numerical data: $l = 1$ m, $G = 200000$ N, $k_1 = 8 \times 10^6$ Nm^{-1}, $k_2 = 2 \times 10^6$ Nm^{-1}, $k_3 = 5 \times 10^6$ Nm^{-1}, $k_4 = 6 \times 10^6$ Nm^{-1}, $\Delta\widetilde{l}_1 = 0.02$ m.
Solution of Application 2.2: (a) It follows that

$$\{\mathbf{U}_1\} = \begin{bmatrix}1 & -l & -l\end{bmatrix}^{\mathrm{T}} = \begin{bmatrix}1 & -1 & -1\end{bmatrix}^{\mathrm{T}}, \quad \{\mathbf{U}_2\} = \begin{bmatrix}1 & l & -l\end{bmatrix}^{\mathrm{T}} = \begin{bmatrix}1 & 1 & -1\end{bmatrix}^{\mathrm{T}},$$

$$\{\mathbf{U}_3\} = \begin{bmatrix}1 & l & l\end{bmatrix}^{\mathrm{T}} = \begin{bmatrix}1 & 1 & 1\end{bmatrix}^{\mathrm{T}}, \quad \{\mathbf{U}_4\} = \begin{bmatrix}1 & -l & l\end{bmatrix}^{\mathrm{T}} = \begin{bmatrix}1 & -1 & 1\end{bmatrix}^{\mathrm{T}}, \quad (4.1137)$$

$$\{\mathbf{U}_1\}\{\mathbf{U}_1\}^{\mathrm{T}} = \begin{bmatrix} 1 & -1 & -1 \\ -1 & 1 & 1 \\ -1 & 1 & 1 \end{bmatrix}, \quad \{\mathbf{U}_2\}\{\mathbf{U}_2\}^{\mathrm{T}} = \begin{bmatrix} 1 & 1 & -1 \\ 1 & 1 & -1 \\ -1 & -1 & 1 \end{bmatrix},$$

$$\{\mathbf{U}_3\}\{\mathbf{U}_3\}^{\mathrm{T}} = \begin{bmatrix} 1 & 1 & 1 \\ 1 & 1 & 1 \\ 1 & 1 & 1 \end{bmatrix}, \quad \{\mathbf{U}_4\}\{\mathbf{U}_4\}^{\mathrm{T}} = \begin{bmatrix} 1 & -1 & 1 \\ -1 & 1 & -1 \\ 1 & -1 & 1 \end{bmatrix}, \tag{4.1138}$$

$$[\mathbf{K}] = \sum_{i=1}^{4} k_i \{\mathbf{U}_i\}\{\mathbf{U}_i\}^{\mathrm{T}} = 10^6 \begin{bmatrix} 21 & -7 & 1 \\ -7 & 21 & 5 \\ 1 & 5 & 21 \end{bmatrix}, \tag{4.1139}$$

$$\{\mathbf{F}\} = 200{,}000 \begin{bmatrix} -1 & 0 & 0 \end{bmatrix}^{\mathrm{T}}, \tag{4.1140}$$

$$[\mathbf{K}]^{-1} = 10^{-6} \begin{bmatrix} 0.054622 & 0.019958 & -0.007353 \\ 0.019958 & 0.057773 & -0.014706 \\ -0.007353 & -0.014706 & 0.051471 \end{bmatrix}, \tag{4.1141}$$

$$\{\mathbf{\Delta}\} = [\mathbf{K}]^{-1}\{\mathbf{F}\} = \begin{bmatrix} 0.010924 & 0.003992 & -0.001471 \end{bmatrix}^{\mathrm{T}}, \tag{4.1142}$$

$$N_1 = -k_1\{\mathbf{U}_1\}^{\mathrm{T}}\{\mathbf{\Delta}\} = -67{,}224 \text{ N}, \quad N_2 = -k_2\{\mathbf{U}_2\}^{\mathrm{T}}\{\mathbf{\Delta}\} = -32{,}774 \text{ N},$$

$$N_3 = -k_3\{\mathbf{U}_3\}^{\mathrm{T}}\{\mathbf{\Delta}\} = -67{,}225 \text{ N}, \quad N_4 = -k_4\{\mathbf{U}_4\}^{\mathrm{T}}\{\mathbf{\Delta}\} = -32{,}766 \text{ N}. \tag{4.1143}$$

(b) The rigidity matrix $[\mathbf{K}]$ and the matrix $\{\mathbf{F}\}$ remain the same. We calculate, successively,

$$\{\widetilde{\mathbf{F}}\} = -k_1\Delta\widetilde{l}_1\{\mathbf{U}_1\} = 160{,}000\begin{bmatrix} -1 & 1 & 1 \end{bmatrix}^{\mathrm{T}}, \tag{4.1144}$$

$$\{\mathbf{F}\} + \{\widetilde{\mathbf{F}}\} = 40{,}000\begin{bmatrix} -9 & 4 & 4 \end{bmatrix}^{\mathrm{T}}, \tag{4.1145}$$

$$\{\mathbf{\Delta}\} = [\mathbf{K}]^{-1}\{\{\mathbf{F}\} + \{\widetilde{\mathbf{F}}\}\} = \begin{bmatrix} -0.017647 & -0.000294 & 0.008529 \end{bmatrix}^{\mathrm{T}}, \tag{4.1146}$$

$$N_1 = -k_1[\Delta\widetilde{l}_1 + \{\mathbf{U}_1\}^{\mathrm{T}}\{\mathbf{\Delta}\}] = 47{,}056 \text{ N}, \quad N_2 = -k_2\{\mathbf{U}_2\}^{\mathrm{T}}\{\mathbf{\Delta}\} = 52{,}040 \text{ N},$$

$$N_3 = -k_3\{\mathbf{U}_3\}^{\mathrm{T}}\{\mathbf{\Delta}\} = 47{,}060 \text{ N}, \quad N_4 = -k_4\{\mathbf{U}_4\}^{\mathrm{T}}\{\mathbf{\Delta}\} = 52{,}944 \text{ N}. \tag{4.1147}$$

Application 2.3. Let us consider the rectangular plate in Figure 4.17 of dimensions $2a$, $2b$, suspended by the hinged bars $A_1 A_{01}$, $A_3 A_{03}$ parallel to the Ox-axis and by the bars $A_2 A_{02}$, $A_4 A_{04}$ parallel to the Oy-axis.

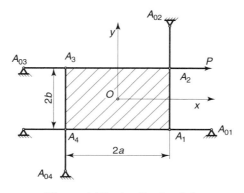

Figure 4.17   Application 2.3.

Knowing that the plate is acted upon at the point A_2 by the force P parallel to the Ox-axis and knowing the rigidities $k_1 = k$, $k_2 = k_3 = 2k$, $k_4 = 3k$, determine the efforts in the bars in the following cases:

(a) The bars have not fabrication errors.

(b) The bar $A_1 A_{01}$ has a fabrication error equal to $\Delta \tilde{l}_1$.

(c) The bar $A_1 A_{01}$ of length l_1 is heated by ΔT^0. Numerical data: $a = 0.5$ m, $b = 0.4$ m, $P = 10000$ N, $k = 10^6$ N m^{-1}, $\Delta \tilde{l}_1 = 0.01$ m, $\Delta T = 100$ K, $\alpha_1 = 12 \times 10^6$ deg^{-1}, $l_1 = 1$ m.

Solution of Application 2.3: (a) We have

$$\{U_1\} = \begin{bmatrix} 1 & 0 & b \end{bmatrix}^T = \begin{bmatrix} 1 & 0 & 0.4 \end{bmatrix}^T, \quad \{U_2\} = \begin{bmatrix} 0 & 1 & a \end{bmatrix}^T = \begin{bmatrix} 0 & 1 & 0.5 \end{bmatrix}^T,$$

$$\{U_3\} = \begin{bmatrix} -1 & 0 & b \end{bmatrix}^T = \begin{bmatrix} -1 & 0 & 0.4 \end{bmatrix}^T, \quad \{U_4\} = \begin{bmatrix} 0 & 1 & -a \end{bmatrix}^T = \begin{bmatrix} 0 & 1 & -0.5 \end{bmatrix}^T,$$

$$(4.1148)$$

$$\{U_1\}\{U_1\}^T = \begin{bmatrix} 1 & 0 & 0.4 \\ 0 & 0 & 0 \\ 0.4 & 0 & 0.16 \end{bmatrix}, \quad \{U_2\}\{U_2\}^T = \begin{bmatrix} 0 & 0 & 0 \\ 0 & 1 & 0.5 \\ 0 & 0.5 & 0.25 \end{bmatrix},$$

$$\{U_3\}\{U_3\}^T = \begin{bmatrix} 1 & 0 & -0.4 \\ 0 & 0 & 0 \\ -0.4 & 0 & 0.16 \end{bmatrix}, \quad \{U_4\}\{U_4\}^T = \begin{bmatrix} 0 & 0 & 0 \\ 0 & 1 & -0.5 \\ 0 & -0.5 & 0.25 \end{bmatrix}, \quad (4.1149)$$

$$[K] = \sum_{i=1}^{4} k_i \{U_i\}\{U_i\}^T = 10^6 \begin{bmatrix} 3 & 0 & -0.4 \\ 0 & 5 & -0.5 \\ -0.4 & -0.5 & 1.73 \end{bmatrix}, \quad (4.1150)$$

$$[K]^{-1} = 10^{-6} \begin{bmatrix} 0.344262 & 0.008197 & 0.081967 \\ 0.008197 & 0.206148 & 0.061475 \\ 0.081967 & 0.061475 & 0.614754 \end{bmatrix}, \quad (4.1151)$$

$$\{F\} = P \begin{bmatrix} 1 & 0 & -b \end{bmatrix}^T = 10{,}000 \begin{bmatrix} 1 & 0 & -0.4 \end{bmatrix}^T, \quad (4.1152)$$

$$\{\Delta\} = \begin{bmatrix} \delta_x & \delta_y & \theta_z \end{bmatrix}^T = [K]^{-1}\{F\} = \begin{bmatrix} 0.003115 & 0.000164 & -0.001639 \end{bmatrix}^T, \quad (4.1153)$$

$$N_1 = -k_1 \{U_1\}^T \{\Delta\} = -24{,}594 \text{ N}, \quad N_2 = -k_2 \{U_2\}^T \{\Delta\} = 1311 \text{ N},$$

$$N_3 = -k_3 \{U_3\}^T \{\Delta\} = 75{,}412 \text{ N}, \quad N_4 = -k_4 \{U_4\}^T \{\Delta\} = -24{,}505 \text{ N}. \quad (4.1154)$$

(b) We obtain

$$\{\tilde{F}\} = -k_1 \Delta \tilde{l}_1 \{U_1\} = 2000 \begin{bmatrix} -5 & 0 & -2 \end{bmatrix}^T, \quad (4.1155)$$

$$\{F\} + \{\tilde{F}\} = 8000 \begin{bmatrix} 0 & 0 & -1 \end{bmatrix}^T, \quad (4.1156)$$

$$\{\Delta\} = [K]^{-1}\{\{F\} + \{\tilde{F}\}\} = \begin{bmatrix} -0.000656 & -0.000492 & -0.004918 \end{bmatrix}^T, \quad (4.1157)$$

$$N_1 = -k_1 [\Delta \tilde{l}_1 + \{U_1\}^T \{\Delta\}] = -73{,}768 \text{ N}, \quad N_2 = -k_2 \{U_2\}^T \{\Delta\} = 5902 \text{ N},$$

$$N_3 = -k_3 \{U_3\}^T \{\Delta\} = 2622.4 \text{ N}, \quad N_4 = -k_4 \{U_4\}^T \{\Delta\} = 5901 \text{ N}. \quad (4.1158)$$

(c) It follows successively that

$$\Delta \tilde{l}_1 = l_1 \alpha_1 \Delta T = 0.0012 \text{ m}, \quad (4.1159)$$

$$\{\tilde{F}\} = -k_1 \Delta \tilde{l}_1 \{U_1\} = \begin{bmatrix} -12000 & 0 & -4800 \end{bmatrix}^T, \quad (4.1160)$$

$$\{F\} + \{\tilde{F}\} = \begin{bmatrix} -2000 & 0 & -8800 \end{bmatrix}^T, \quad (4.1161)$$

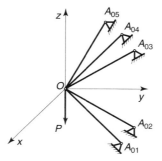

Figure 4.18 Application 2.4.

$$\{\mathbf{\Delta}\} = [\mathbf{K}]^{-1}\{\{\mathbf{F}\} + \{\widetilde{\mathbf{F}}\}\} = \begin{bmatrix} -0.001410 & -0.000557 & -0.005574 \end{bmatrix}^{\mathrm{T}}, \tag{4.1162}$$

$$N_1 = -k_1[\widetilde{\Delta l_1} + \{\mathbf{U}_1\}^{\mathrm{T}}\{\mathbf{\Delta}\}] = 24{,}396 \text{ N}, \quad N_2 = -k_2\{\mathbf{U}_2\}^{\mathrm{T}}\{\mathbf{\Delta}\} = 6688 \text{ N},$$

$$N_3 = -k_3\{\mathbf{U}_3\}^{\mathrm{T}}\{\mathbf{\Delta}\} = 1639.2 \text{ N}, \quad N_4 = -k_4\{\mathbf{U}_4\}^{\mathrm{T}}\{\mathbf{\Delta}\} = -6690 \text{ N}. \tag{4.1163}$$

Application 2.4. We consider the spatial system of articulated bars in Figure 4.18, concurrent at the articulation O, where the vertical force P situated on the Oz-axis is acting.

Knowing the rigidities of the bars $A_{0i}O$, $i = \overline{1,5}$, $k_1 = 2k$, $k_2 = 1.5k$, $k_3 = 2k$, $k_4 = 3k$, $k_5 = 2.5k$ and the direction cosines of their directions (a_i, b_i, c_i), $i = \overline{1,5}$, determine the efforts in the bars in the following cases:

(a) The bars have no fabrication errors.

(b) The bar $A_{01}O$ has a fabrication error equal to $\Delta \widetilde{l_1}$.

(c) The bar $A_{01}O$ of length l_1 is heated by ΔT^0. Numerical data: $P = 20000 \text{ N}$, $k = 10^6 \text{N m}^{-1}$, $\Delta \widetilde{l_1} = 0.02 \text{ m}$, $l_1 = 1 \text{ m}$, $\alpha_1 = 12 \times 10^{-6} \text{ deg}^{-1}$, $(a_1, b_1, c_1) = (3/5, 4/5, 0)$, $(a_2, b_2, c_2) = (2/3, 2/3, 1/3)$, $(a_3, b_3, c_3) = (0, 3/5, 4/5)$, $(a_4, b_4, c_4) = (-2/3, 2/3, 1/3)$, $(a_5, b_5, c_5) = (-3/5, 4/5, 0)$.

Solution of Application 2.4: (a) We have, successively,

$$\{\mathbf{U}_i\} = \begin{bmatrix} a_i & b_i & c_i \end{bmatrix}^{\mathrm{T}}, \quad i = \overline{1,5}, \tag{4.1164}$$

$$\{\mathbf{U}_1\}\{\mathbf{U}_1\}^{\mathrm{T}} = \begin{bmatrix} \dfrac{9}{25} & \dfrac{12}{25} & 0 \\[2mm] \dfrac{12}{25} & \dfrac{16}{25} & 0 \\[2mm] 0 & 0 & 0 \end{bmatrix}, \quad \{\mathbf{U}_2\}\{\mathbf{U}_2\}^{\mathrm{T}} = \begin{bmatrix} \dfrac{4}{9} & \dfrac{4}{9} & \dfrac{2}{9} \\[2mm] \dfrac{4}{9} & \dfrac{4}{9} & \dfrac{2}{9} \\[2mm] \dfrac{2}{9} & \dfrac{2}{9} & \dfrac{1}{9} \end{bmatrix},$$

$$\{\mathbf{U}_3\}\{\mathbf{U}_3\}^{\mathrm{T}} = \begin{bmatrix} 0 & 0 & 0 \\[2mm] 0 & \dfrac{9}{25} & \dfrac{12}{25} \\[2mm] 0 & \dfrac{12}{25} & \dfrac{16}{25} \end{bmatrix}, \quad \{\mathbf{U}_4\}\{\mathbf{U}_4\}^{\mathrm{T}} = \begin{bmatrix} \dfrac{4}{9} & -\dfrac{4}{9} & -\dfrac{2}{9} \\[2mm] -\dfrac{4}{9} & \dfrac{4}{9} & \dfrac{2}{9} \\[2mm] -\dfrac{2}{9} & \dfrac{2}{9} & \dfrac{1}{9} \end{bmatrix},$$

$$\{\mathbf{U}_5\}\{\mathbf{U}_5\}^{\mathrm{T}} = \begin{bmatrix} \dfrac{9}{25} & -\dfrac{12}{25} & 0 \\[2mm] -\dfrac{12}{25} & \dfrac{16}{25} & 0 \\[2mm] 0 & 0 & 0 \end{bmatrix}, \tag{4.1165}$$

$$[\mathbf{K}] = \sum_{i=1}^{5} k_i \{\mathbf{U}_i\}\{\mathbf{U}_i\}^{\mathrm{T}} = 10^6 \begin{bmatrix} 3.62 & -0.906667 & -0.333333 \\ -0.906667 & 5.6 & 1.96 \\ -0.333333 & 1.96 & 1.78 \end{bmatrix}, \tag{4.1166}$$

$$[\mathbf{K}]^{-1} = 10^{-6} \begin{bmatrix} 0.324021 & 0.119911 & -0.192715 \\ 0.119911 & 0.334921 & -0.391245 \\ -0.192715 & -0.391245 & 1.028696 \end{bmatrix}, \tag{4.1167}$$

$$\{\mathbf{F}\} = 20{,}000 \begin{bmatrix} 0 & 0 & -1 \end{bmatrix}^{\mathrm{T}}, \tag{4.1168}$$

$$\{\mathbf{\Delta}\} = \begin{bmatrix} \delta_x & \delta_y & \delta_z \end{bmatrix}^{\mathrm{T}} = [\mathbf{K}]^{-1}\{\mathbf{F}\} = \begin{bmatrix} 0.003854 & 0.007825 & -0.020574 \end{bmatrix}^{\mathrm{T}}, \tag{4.1169}$$

$$N_1 = -k_1\{\mathbf{U}_1\}^{\mathrm{T}}\{\mathbf{\Delta}\} = -17{,}144.8 \text{ N}, \quad N_2 = -k_2\{\mathbf{U}_2\}^{\mathrm{T}}\{\mathbf{\Delta}\} = -1392 \text{ N},$$

$$N_3 = -k_3\{\mathbf{U}_3\}^{\mathrm{T}}\{\mathbf{\Delta}\} = 23{,}528.4 \text{ N}, \quad N_4 = -k_4\{\mathbf{U}_4\}^{\mathrm{T}}\{\mathbf{\Delta}\} = 12{,}632 \text{ N},$$

$$N_5 = -k_5\{\mathbf{U}_5\}^{\mathrm{T}}\{\mathbf{\Delta}\} = -9869 \text{ N}. \tag{4.1170}$$

(b) It follows that

$$\{\widetilde{\mathbf{F}}\} = -k_1\Delta\widetilde{l}_1\{\mathbf{U}_1\} = 8000 \begin{bmatrix} -3 & -4 & 0 \end{bmatrix}^{\mathrm{T}}, \tag{4.1171}$$

$$\{\mathbf{F}\} + \{\widetilde{\mathbf{F}}\} = 4000 \begin{bmatrix} -6 & -8 & -5 \end{bmatrix}^{\mathrm{T}}, \tag{4.1172}$$

$$\{\mathbf{\Delta}\} = [\mathbf{K}]^{-1}\{\{\mathbf{F}\} + \{\widetilde{\mathbf{F}}\}\} = \begin{bmatrix} -0.007759 & -0.005770 & -0.003429 \end{bmatrix}^{\mathrm{T}}, \tag{4.1173}$$

$$N_1 = -k_1[\Delta\widetilde{l}_1 + \{\mathbf{U}_1\}^{\mathrm{T}}\{\mathbf{\Delta}\}] = -21{,}457.2 \text{ N}, \quad N_2 = -k_2\{\mathbf{U}_2\}^{\mathrm{T}}\{\mathbf{\Delta}\} = 15{,}243.5 \text{ N},$$

$$N_3 = -k_3\{\mathbf{U}_3\}^{\mathrm{T}}\{\mathbf{\Delta}\} = 12{,}410.4 \text{ N}, \quad N_4 = -k_4\{\mathbf{U}_4\}^{\mathrm{T}}\{\mathbf{\Delta}\} = 6309 \text{ N},$$

$$N_5 = -k_5\{\mathbf{U}_5\}^{\mathrm{T}}\{\mathbf{\Delta}\} = -98.5 \text{ N}. \tag{4.1174}$$

(c) We obtain the values

$$\Delta\widetilde{l}_1 = l_1\alpha_1\Delta T = 12 \times 10^{-4} \text{ m}, \tag{4.1175}$$

$$\{\widetilde{\mathbf{F}}\} = -k_1\Delta\widetilde{l}_1\{\mathbf{U}_1\} = \begin{bmatrix} -1440 & -1920 & 0 \end{bmatrix}^{\mathrm{T}}, \tag{4.1176}$$

$$\{\mathbf{F}\} + \{\widetilde{\mathbf{F}}\} = \begin{bmatrix} -1440 & -1920 & -20000 \end{bmatrix}^{\mathrm{T}}, \tag{4.1177}$$

$$\{\mathbf{\Delta}\} = [\mathbf{K}]^{-1}\{\{\mathbf{F}\} + \{\widetilde{\mathbf{F}}\}\} = \begin{bmatrix} 0.003157 & -0.008641 & -0.021048 \end{bmatrix}^{\mathrm{T}}, \tag{4.1178}$$

$$N_1 = -k_1[\Delta\widetilde{l}_1 + \{\mathbf{U}_1\}^{\mathrm{T}}\{\mathbf{\Delta}\}] = 7637.2 \text{ N}, \quad N_2 = -k_2\{\mathbf{U}_2\}^{\mathrm{T}}\{\mathbf{\Delta}\} = 16{,}008 \text{ N},$$

$$N_3 = -k_3\{\mathbf{U}_3\}^{\mathrm{T}}\{\mathbf{\Delta}\} = 44{,}046 \text{ N}, \quad N_4 = -k_4\{\mathbf{U}_4\}^{\mathrm{T}}\{\mathbf{\Delta}\} = 44{,}644 \text{ N},$$

$$N_5 = -k_5\{\mathbf{U}_5\}^{\mathrm{T}}\{\mathbf{\Delta}\} = 22{,}017.5 \text{ N}. \tag{4.1179}$$

Problem 4.12

Let us consider the continuous beam in Figure 4.19, where the sections have lengths l_k and rigidities EI_k, $k = \overline{1, n-1}$.

The beam is acted upon by given distributed loads and by given concentrated forces and moments. It is required to determine the reactions V_k, $k = \overline{1, n}$, in the supports.

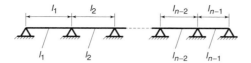

Figure 4.19 Problem 4.12.

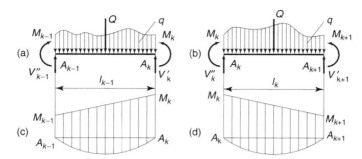

Figure 4.20 Isolation of the sections $A_{k-1}A_k$ and A_kA_{k+1}.

Solution:

1. Theory

By isolating the sections $A_{k-1}A_k$, A_kA_{k+1}, we obtain the representations in Figure 4.20a and b, where we have the notations:

- q, Q—given external loads;
- M_{k-1}, M_k, M_{k+1}—bending moments;
- V'_k, V'_{k+1}—reactions at the right of each section;
- V''_{k-1}, V''_k—reactions at the left of each section.

Figure 4.20c and d represents the loadings (bending moments) of the conjugate beams, while the bending moments given by the external loads q, Q are represented under the reference lines $A_{k-1}A_k$, A_kA_{k+1}. Denoting by $\widetilde{M}^r_{k-1}$, $\widetilde{M}^l_{k+1}$ the resultant moments of the external loading q with respect to the points A_{k-1} and A_{k+1}, respectively, it follows that the reactions V'_k, V''_k are given by

$$V'_k = \frac{1}{l_{k-1}}(M_{k-1} + \widetilde{M}^r_{k-1} - M_k), \quad V''_k = \frac{1}{l_k}(M_{k*1} + \widetilde{M}^l_{k*1} - M_k), \tag{4.1180}$$

so that the reaction at the support A_k

$$V_k = V'_k + V''_k \tag{4.1181}$$

reads

$$V_k = \frac{M_{k-1}}{l_{k-1}} - M_k\left(\frac{1}{l_{k-1}} + \frac{1}{l_k}\right) + \frac{M_{k+1}}{l_k} + \frac{\widetilde{M}^r_{k-1}}{l_{k-1}} + \frac{\widetilde{M}^l_{k+1}}{l_k}. \tag{4.1182}$$

Because the rotations ϕ'_k, ϕ''_k at the fixed support A_k for the two sections, respectively, are equal to the shearing forces divided by the rigidities EI_{k-1}, EI_k of the conjugate beams, it follows that

$$\phi'_k = \frac{1}{EI_{k-1}}\left(\frac{M_k l_{k-1}}{2}\frac{2l_{k-1}}{3} + \frac{M_{k-1}l_{k-1}}{2}\frac{l_{k-1}}{3} + S^r_{k-1}\right), \tag{4.1183}$$

$$\phi''_k = \frac{1}{EI_k}\left(\frac{M_k l_k}{2}\frac{2l_k}{3} + \frac{M_{k+1}l_{k+1}}{2}\frac{l_k}{3} + S^l_{k+1}\right), \tag{4.1184}$$

where by S_{k-1}^r, S_{k+1}^l we have denoted the static moments of the bending moments of the areas corresponding to the external loads q, Q.

The indices r, l specify the loadings to the right and at the left of the supports A_{k-1}, A_{k+1}, respectively.

Taking into account the relation

$$\phi_k' + \phi_k'' = 0, \tag{4.1185}$$

we obtain, from equation (4.1183) and equation (4.1184), the Clapeyron relation

$$\frac{M_{k-1}l_{k-1}}{I_{k-1}} + 2M_k\left(\frac{l_{k-1}}{I_{k-1}} + \frac{l_k}{I_k}\right) + \frac{M_{k+1}}{I_k} + 6\left(\frac{S_{k-1}^r}{l_{k-1}I_{k-1}} + \frac{S_{k+1}^l}{l_k I_k}\right) = 0. \tag{4.1186}$$

If we take into account that the moments at the supports A_1, A_n vanish ($M_1 = M_n = 0$) and if we use the notations

$$[\mathbf{A}] = \begin{bmatrix} 2\left(\frac{l_1}{I_1} + \frac{l_2}{I_2}\right) & \frac{l_2}{I_2} & 0 & 0 & \cdots & 0 & 0 & 0 \\ \frac{l_2}{I_2} & 2\left(\frac{l_2}{I_2} + \frac{l_3}{I_3}\right) & \frac{l_3}{I_3} & 0 & \cdots & 0 & 0 & 0 \\ 0 & \frac{l_3}{I_3} & 2\left(\frac{l_3}{I_3} + \frac{l_4}{I_4}\right) & 0 & \cdots & 0 & 0 & 0 \\ \cdots & \cdots & \cdots & \cdots & \cdots & & \cdots & \cdots \\ 0 & 0 & 0 & 0 & \cdots & \frac{l_{n-3}}{I_{n-3}} & 2\left(\frac{l_{n-3}}{I_{n-3}} + \frac{l_{n-2}}{I_{n-2}}\right) & \frac{l_{n-2}}{I_{n-2}} \\ 0 & 0 & 0 & 0 & \cdots & 0 & \frac{l_{n-2}}{I_{n-2}} & 2\left(\frac{l_{n-2}}{I_{n-2}} + \frac{l_{n-1}}{I_{n-1}}\right) \end{bmatrix}, \tag{4.1187}$$

$$\{\mathbf{B}\} = -6\begin{bmatrix} \dfrac{S_1^r}{l_1 I_1} + \dfrac{S_2^l}{l_2 I_2} \\[2mm] \dfrac{S_2^r}{l_2 I_2} + \dfrac{S_3^l}{l_3 I_3} \\[2mm] \dfrac{S_3^r}{l_3 I_3} + \dfrac{S_3^l}{l_3 I_3} \\[2mm] \vdots \\[2mm] \dfrac{S_{n-2}^r}{l_{n-2} I_{n-2}} + \dfrac{S_{n-1}^l}{l_{n-1} I_{n-1}} \end{bmatrix}, \tag{4.1188}$$

$$\{\mathbf{M}\} = \begin{bmatrix} M_2 & M_3 & \cdots & M_{n-1} \end{bmatrix}^T, \tag{4.1189}$$

$$\{\mathbf{V}\} = \begin{bmatrix} V_1 & V_2 & \cdots & V_n \end{bmatrix}^T, \tag{4.1190}$$

$$[\mathbf{C}] = \begin{bmatrix} \frac{1}{l_1} & 0 & 0 & 0 & \cdots & & & \\ -\left(\frac{1}{l_1} + \frac{1}{l_2}\right) & \frac{1}{l_2} & 0 & 0 & \cdots & & & \\ \frac{1}{l_2} & -\left(\frac{1}{l_2} + \frac{1}{l_3}\right) & \frac{1}{l_3} & 0 & \cdots & & & \\ \cdots & \cdots & \cdots & \cdots & \cdots & & \cdots & \cdots \\ 0 & 0 & 0 & 0 & \cdots & \frac{1}{l_{n-3}} & -\left(\frac{1}{l_{n-3}} + \frac{1}{l_{n-2}}\right) & \frac{1}{l_{n-2}} \\ 0 & 0 & 0 & 0 & \cdots & 0 & \frac{1}{l_{n-2}} & -\left(\frac{1}{l_{n-2}} + \frac{1}{l_{n-1}}\right) \\ 0 & 0 & 0 & 0 & \cdots & 0 & 0 & \frac{1}{l_{n-1}} \end{bmatrix}, \tag{4.1191}$$

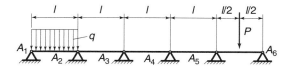

Figure 4.21   Numerical application.

$$\{D\} = \begin{bmatrix} \dfrac{\widetilde{M}_1^l}{l_1} \\[2ex] \dfrac{\widetilde{M}_1^r}{l_1} + \dfrac{\widetilde{M}_2^l}{l_2} \\[2ex] \dfrac{\widetilde{M}_2^r}{l_2} + \dfrac{\widetilde{M}_3^l}{l_3} \\[2ex] \vdots \\[2ex] \dfrac{\widetilde{M}_{n-2}^r}{l_{n-2}} + \dfrac{\widetilde{M}_{n-1}^l}{l_{n-1}} \\[2ex] \dfrac{\widetilde{M}_{n-1}^r}{l_{n-1}} \end{bmatrix}, \tag{4.1192}$$

then equation (4.1186) and equation (4.1182), for $k = \overline{1, n}$, may be written in the matrix form as

$$[A]\{M\} = \{B\}, \tag{4.1193}$$

$$\{V\} = [C]\{M\} + \{D\}, \tag{4.1194}$$

from which we obtain the solution

$$\{V\} = [C][A]^{-1}\{B\} + \{D\}. \tag{4.1195}$$

2. Numerical application

Figure 4.21 gives $n = 6$, $I_k = I = 256 \times 10^{-6}$ m^2, $k = \overline{1, 6}$, $l_k = l = 1$ m, $k = \overline{1, 6}$, $P = 20{,}000$ N, $q = 40{,}000$ N m^{-1}. The reactions V_k, $k = \overline{1,6}$, are required.
Solution of the numerical application: The matrices $[A]$ and $[C]$ are obtained, directly, from relations (4.1187) and (4.1191)

$$[A] = 3906.25 \begin{bmatrix} 4 & 1 & 0 & 0 \\ 1 & 4 & 1 & 0 \\ 0 & 1 & 4 & 1 \\ 0 & 0 & 1 & 4 \end{bmatrix}, \quad [C] = \begin{bmatrix} 1 & 0 & 0 & 0 \\ -2 & 1 & 0 & 0 \\ 1 & -2 & 1 & 0 \\ 0 & 1 & -2 & 1 \\ 0 & 0 & 1 & -2 \\ 0 & 0 & 0 & 1 \end{bmatrix}. \tag{4.1196}$$

The matrix $\{B\}$ is written first in the form

$$\{B\} = -\frac{6}{EI}\begin{bmatrix} S_1^r & 0 & 0 & S_6^l \end{bmatrix}^{\mathrm{T}}, \tag{4.1197}$$

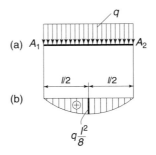

Figure 4.22   Section $A_1 A_2$.

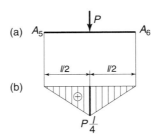

Figure 4.23   Section $A_5 A_6$.

and from Figure 4.22b and Figure 4.23b it follows that

$$S_1^r = \frac{ql^4}{24}, \tag{4.1198}$$

$$S_6^l = \frac{Pl^3}{16}, \tag{4.1199}$$

$$\{\mathbf{B}\} = \begin{bmatrix} -39062500 & 0 & 0 & -29296875 \end{bmatrix}^{\mathrm{T}}. \tag{4.1200}$$

Analogically, the matrix $\{\mathbf{D}\}$ is written first in the form

$$\{\mathbf{D}\} = \begin{bmatrix} \dfrac{\widetilde{M}_2^l}{l_1} & \dfrac{\widetilde{M}_1^r}{l_1} & 0 & 0 & \dfrac{\widetilde{M}_6^l}{l_5} & \dfrac{\widetilde{M}_5^r}{l_1} \end{bmatrix}^{\mathrm{T}}, \tag{4.1201}$$

and, because from Figure 4.22a and Figure 4.23a we have

$$\widetilde{M}_1^r = \widetilde{M}_2^l = \frac{ql^2}{2}, \tag{4.1202}$$

$$\widetilde{M}_5^r = \widetilde{M}_6^l = \frac{Pl}{2}, \tag{4.1203}$$

we obtain

$$\{\mathbf{D}\} = 10000 \begin{bmatrix} 2 & 2 & 0 & 0 & 1 & 1 \end{bmatrix}^{\mathrm{T}}. \tag{4.1204}$$

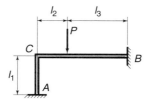

Figure 4.24   Problem 4.13.

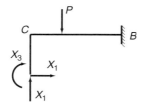

Figure 4.25   Basic system.

In the numerical case, from relation (4.1195) it follows that

$$\{\mathbf{V}\} = \begin{bmatrix} V_1 & V_2 & V_3 & V_4 & V_5 & V_6 \end{bmatrix}^{\mathrm{T}}$$
$$= \begin{bmatrix} -2000 & 9000 & -27500 & -25000 & 62500 & -20000 \end{bmatrix}^{\mathrm{T}}. \qquad (4.1205)$$

Problem 4.13

Let us determine, by the method of efforts, the reactions in the built-in sections A, B in Figure 4.24, assuming that the bars AC, CB have the same rigidity EI.

Numerical application: $EI = 2 \times 10^8$ N m^2, $l_1 = 0.5$ m, $l_2 = 0.4$ m, $l_3 = 0.6$ m, $P = 12{,}000$ N.

Solution:

1. Theory

Introducing at the built-in section A, the reactions forces X_1 and X_2 and the reaction moment X_3 (Fig. 4.25), we obtain the basic system, which is the bent beam ACB, built in at B and acted upon by the force P and by the unknown reactions X_1, X_2, X_3.

The external load P, the unit forces along the forces X_1 and X_2 and the unit moment in the direction of the moment X_3 produce on the basic system the diagrams of bending moments M_0, m_1, m_2 m_3, represented in Figure 4.26.

By means of these diagrams we calculate the coefficients of influence

$$\delta_{i0} = \sum \int \frac{m_i M_0}{EI} \mathrm{d}x, \qquad (4.1206)$$

$$\delta_{ij} = \sum \int \frac{m_i m_j}{EI} \mathrm{d}x. \qquad (4.1207)$$

Being given that the variations of the moments m_i are linear, we can also calculate them by Vereshchyagin's rule:

$$\delta_{i0} = \sum \frac{\Omega m_{iC}}{EI}, \qquad (4.1208)$$

$$\delta_{ij} = \sum \frac{\Omega_i m_{jC}}{EI}, \qquad (4.1209)$$

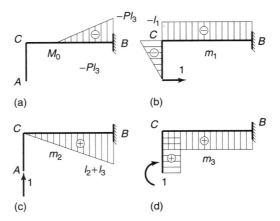

Figure 4.26   Diagrams of bending moments.

where Ω is the area of the moment surface of the diagram M_0, while m_{iC} is the moment of the diagram corresponding to the center of gravity of the surface Ω and m_i is the area of the surface of moments of the diagram m_i, while m_{jC} is the moment of the diagram m_j corresponding to the center of gravity of the surface of moments m_i, respectively.

2. Numerical application
It follows successively that

$$\delta_{10} = \frac{Pl_1 l_3^2}{2EI}, \quad \delta_{20} = -\frac{Pl_3^2(3l_2 + 2l_3)}{6EI}, \quad \delta_{30} = -\frac{Pl_3^2}{2EI}, \tag{4.1210}$$

$$\delta_{11} = \frac{l_1^2(l_1 + 3l_2 + 3l_3)}{3EI}, \quad \delta_{12} = \delta_{21} = -\frac{l_1(l_2 + l_3)^2}{2EI}, \quad \delta_{13} = \delta_{31} = -\frac{l_1(l_1 + 2l_2 + 2l_3)}{2EI},$$

$$\delta_{22} = \frac{(l_2 + l_3)^3}{3EI}, \quad \delta_{23} = \delta_{32} = \frac{(l_2 + l_3)^2}{2EI}, \quad \delta_{33} = \frac{l_1 + l_2 + l_3}{EI}. \tag{4.1211}$$

$$\delta_{10} = 3.24 \times 10^{-6} \text{ m}^2, \quad \delta_{20} = -8.64 \times 10^{-6} \text{ m}^2, \quad \delta_{30} = -6.48 \times 10^{-6}, \tag{4.1212}$$

$$\delta_{11} = 1.45833 \times 10^{-9} \text{ m N}^{-1}, \quad \delta_{12} = \delta_{21} = -1.25 \times 10^{-9} \text{ m N}^{-1},$$

$$\delta_{13} = \delta_{31} = -3.125 \times 10^{-9} \text{ N}^{-1}, \quad \delta_{22} = 1.66667 \times 10^{-9} \text{ m N}^{-1},$$

$$\delta_{23} = \delta_{32} = 2.5 \times 10^{9} \text{ N}^{-1}, \quad \delta_{33} = 7.5 \times 10^{-9} \text{N}^{-1} \text{ m}^{-1}. \tag{4.1213}$$

Using the notations

$$[\boldsymbol{\delta}] = \begin{bmatrix} \delta_{11} & \delta_{12} & \delta_{13} \\ \delta_{21} & \delta_{22} & \delta_{23} \\ \delta_{31} & \delta_{32} & \delta_{33} \end{bmatrix} = 10^{-9} \begin{bmatrix} 1.45833 & -1.25 & -3.125 \\ -1.25 & 1.66667 & 2.5 \\ -3.125 & 2.5 & 7.5 \end{bmatrix},$$

$$\{\boldsymbol{\delta}_0\} = \begin{bmatrix} \delta_{10} & \delta_{20} & \delta_{30} \end{bmatrix}^{\text{T}} = 10^{-6} \begin{bmatrix} 3.24 & -8.64 & -6.48 \end{bmatrix}^{\text{T}}, \quad \{\mathbf{X}\} = \begin{bmatrix} X_1 & X_2 & X_3 \end{bmatrix}^{\text{T}}, \tag{4.1214}$$

we obtain the matrix equation of condition

$$[\boldsymbol{\delta}]\{\mathbf{X}\} = -\{\boldsymbol{\delta}_0\}, \tag{4.1215}$$

from which we obtain

$$\{\mathbf{X}\} = -[\boldsymbol{\delta}]^{-1}\{\boldsymbol{\delta}_0\}. \tag{4.1216}$$

In our case,

$$[\delta]^{-1} = 1.53604 \times 10^9 \begin{bmatrix} 6.25003 & 1.5625 & 2.08334 \\ 1.5625 & 1.17185 & 0.26043 \\ 2.08334 & 0.26043 & 0.86805 \end{bmatrix}, \quad \{X\} = \begin{bmatrix} 10368.187 \\ 10368.071 \\ 1728.133 \end{bmatrix}. \quad (4.1217)$$

The reactions at B are

$$H_B = X_1 = 10{,}368.187 \text{ N}, \quad V_B = P - X_2 = 1631.929 \text{ N},$$
$$M_B = Pl_3 + X_1 l_1 - X_2(l_2 + l_3) - X_3 = 287.89 \text{ N m}. \quad (4.1218)$$

Observation 4.43 If $l_1 = l_2 = l_3 = l$, then we obtain the values

$$\delta_{10} = \frac{Pl^4}{2EI}, \quad \delta_{20} = -\frac{5Pl^4}{6EI}, \quad \delta_{30} = -\frac{Pl^2}{2EI}, \quad (4.1219)$$

$$\delta_{11} = \frac{7l^3}{3EI}, \quad \delta_{12} = \delta_{21} = -\frac{2l^3}{EI}, \quad \delta_{13} = \delta_{31} = -\frac{5l^2}{2EI},$$

$$\delta_{22} = \frac{8l^3}{3EI}, \quad \delta_{23} = \delta_{32} = \frac{2l^2}{EI}, \quad \delta_{33} = \frac{3l}{EI}. \quad (4.1220)$$

The condition for this is given by

$$\frac{l}{EI} \begin{bmatrix} \dfrac{7l^2}{3} & -2l^2 & -\dfrac{5l}{2} \\ -2l^2 & \dfrac{8l^2}{3} & 2l \\ -\dfrac{5l}{2} & 2l & 3 \end{bmatrix} \begin{bmatrix} X_1 \\ X_2 \\ X_3 \end{bmatrix} = -\frac{Pl^2}{EI} \begin{bmatrix} \dfrac{l^2}{2} \\ -\dfrac{5l^2}{6} \\ -\dfrac{l^2}{2} \end{bmatrix} \quad (4.1221)$$

or, equivalently, by

$$\begin{bmatrix} \dfrac{7l^2}{3} & -2l^2 & -\dfrac{5l}{2} \\ -2l^2 & \dfrac{8l^2}{3} & 2l \\ -\dfrac{5l}{2} & 2l & 3 \end{bmatrix} \begin{bmatrix} X_1 \\ X_2 \\ X_3 \end{bmatrix} = Pl \begin{bmatrix} -\dfrac{l^2}{2} \\ \dfrac{5l^2}{6} \\ \dfrac{l^2}{2} \end{bmatrix}, \quad (4.1222)$$

with the solution

$$\begin{bmatrix} X_1 & X_2 & X_3 \end{bmatrix}^T = \begin{bmatrix} \frac{P}{4} & \frac{7P}{16} & \frac{Pl}{12} \end{bmatrix}^T. \quad (4.1223)$$

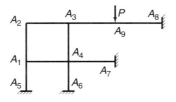

Figure 4.27 Problem 4.14.

Problem 4.14

Let us show that the plane frame in Figure 4.27 is with fixed knots and determine the reactions at the points A_5, A_6, A_7, A_8 by the method of displacements, knowing that the bars have the same rigidity EI and the same length, while $A_3 A_9 = A_9 A_8 = l$.
Numerical application for $l = 1$ m, $EI = 6 \times 10^8$ N m^2, $P = 12,000$ N.

Solution:

1. Theory
If we replace the elastic knots A_1, A_2, A_3, A_4 and the built-in ones A_5, A_6, A_7, A_8 by articulations, we obtain the structure in Figure 4.28, which has $b = 8$ bars and $n = 8$ articulations.
The structure in Figure 4.27 has $r = 12$ external constraints (three in each built-in section A_5, A_6, A_7, A_8). It follows thus that the expression $2n - (b + r) = -4$ is negative, so that the structure is with fixed knots.
Isolating an arbitrary bar $A_h A_j$ (Fig. 4.29), denoting by ϕ_h, ϕ_j, M_h, M_j the rotation angles and the moments at the ends of the bar, respectively, and using the method of the conjugate bar, we obtain the relations

$$M_{hj} = \frac{2EI}{l}(2\phi_h + \phi_j) + \frac{2(S_h - 2S_j)}{l^2}, \quad M_{jh} = \frac{2EI}{l}(2\phi_j + \phi_h) + \frac{2(S_j - 2S_h)}{l^2}, \quad (4.1224)$$

where by S_h, S_j we have denoted the static moments of the areas of the bending moments given by the external loads Q, q (Fig. 4.29).
In the case of Figure 4.27, these static moments vanish for all the bars, excepting the bar $A_3 A_8$ (Fig. 4.30), for which

$$S_3 = S_8 = \frac{Pl^3}{2}. \quad (4.1225)$$

To determine the unknown rotations ϕ_1, ϕ_2, ϕ_3, ϕ_4 at the knots A_1, A_2, A_3, A_4, we write the equilibrium equations that are obtained by isolating the knots, that is,

$$M_{12} + M_{14} + M_{15} = 0, \quad M_{21} + M_{23} = 0,$$
$$M_{32} + M_{34} + M_{38} = 0, \quad M_{41} + M_{43} + M_{46} + M_{47} = 0. \quad (4.1226)$$

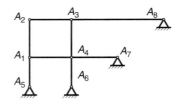

Figure 4.28 Resulting structure.

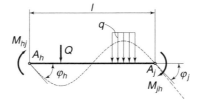

Figure 4.29 Isolation of the bar $A_h A_j$.

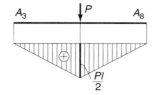

Figure 4.30 Diagram of bending moments for the bar A_3A_8.

Figure 4.31 Bar without external loads.

2. Computation relations

With the view to obtain the system of four equations with four unknowns from system (4.1226), we take into account that $\phi_5 = \phi_6 = \phi_7 = \phi_8 = 0$, obtaining thus the equalities

$$M_{12} = \frac{2EI(2\phi_1 + \phi_2)}{l}, \quad M_{14} = \frac{2EI(2\phi_1 + \phi_4)}{l}, \quad M_{15} = \frac{EI\phi_1}{l},$$

$$M_{21} = \frac{2EI(2\phi_2 + \phi_1)}{l}, \quad M_{23} = \frac{2EI(2\phi_2 + \phi_3)}{l}, \quad M_{31} = \frac{2EI(2\phi_1 + \phi_3)}{l}, \tag{4.1227}$$

$$M_{34} = \frac{2EI(2\phi_3 + \phi_4)}{l}, \quad M_{32} = \frac{2EI(2\phi_3 + \phi_2)}{l}, \quad M_{38} = \frac{2EI\phi_3}{l} - \frac{Pl}{4},$$

$$M_{41} = \frac{2EI(2\phi_4 + \phi_1)}{l}, \quad M_{43} = \frac{2EI(2\phi_4 + \phi_3)}{l}, \quad M_{46} = \frac{4EI\phi_4}{l}, \quad M_{47} = \frac{4EI\phi_4}{l},$$

so that system (4.1226), with the notation

$$[\mathbf{A}] = \begin{bmatrix} 6 & 1 & 0 & 1 \\ 1 & 4 & 1 & 0 \\ 0 & 1 & 5 & 1 \\ 1 & 0 & 1 & 8 \end{bmatrix}, \quad \{\boldsymbol{\phi}\} = \begin{bmatrix} \phi_1 & \phi_2 & \phi_3 & \phi_4 \end{bmatrix}^{\mathrm{T}}, \quad \{\mathbf{B}\} = \begin{bmatrix} 0 & 0 & \frac{Pl^2}{8} & 0 \end{bmatrix}^{\mathrm{T}}, \tag{4.1228}$$

becomes

$$[\mathbf{A}]\{\boldsymbol{\phi}\} = \{\mathbf{B}\} \tag{4.1229}$$

and has the solution

$$\{\boldsymbol{\phi}\} = [\mathbf{A}]^{-1}\{\mathbf{B}\}. \tag{4.1230}$$

The rotations ϕ_1, ϕ_2, ϕ_3, ϕ_4 being known now, from relations (4.1227), we determine the indicated moments and, moreover, the moments M_{51}, M_{64}, M_{74}, M_{83} by the formulae

$$M_{51} = \frac{2EI\phi_1}{l}, \quad M_{64} = M_{74} = \frac{2EI\phi_4}{l}, \quad M_{83} = \frac{Pl}{8} + \frac{EI\phi_1}{l}. \tag{4.1231}$$

For bars unloaded with external loads (Fig. 4.31), we obtain the reactions

$$V_h = V_j = \frac{M_{hj} + M_{jh}}{l}, \qquad (4.1232)$$

while for the bar $A_3 A_8$ (Fig. 4.32) we obtain the reactions

$$V_3' = \frac{M_{38} + M_{83} - Pl}{2l}, \qquad V_8 = \frac{M_{38} + M_{83} + Pl}{2l}. \qquad (4.1233)$$

On the basis of relation (4.1232), we may determine (Fig. 4.33) the reactions H_5, H_6, V_7, that is,

$$H_5 = \frac{M_{51} + M_{15}}{l}, \qquad H_6 = \frac{M_{64} + M_{46}}{l}, \qquad V_7 = \frac{M_{47} + M_{74}}{l}. \qquad (4.1234)$$

To determine the reactions V_5 and V_6, we isolate the parts in Figure 4.34; there result the successive relations

$$V_2 = \frac{M_{23} + M_{32}}{l}, \qquad V_1 = \frac{M_{14} + M_{41}}{l}, \qquad V_5 = -(V_1 + V_7),$$

$$V_3' = \frac{M_{38} + M_{83} - Pl}{2l}, \qquad V_4' = \frac{M_{47} + M_{74}}{l}, \qquad (4.1235)$$

$$V_6 = V_1 + V_2 - V_3' - V_4', \qquad (4.1236)$$

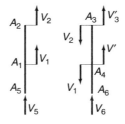

Figure 4.32   The bar $A_3 A_8$.

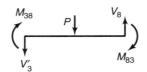

Figure 4.33   Calculation of the reactions H_5, H_6, and V_7.

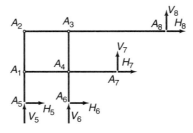

Figure 4.34   Determination of the reactions V_5 and V_6.

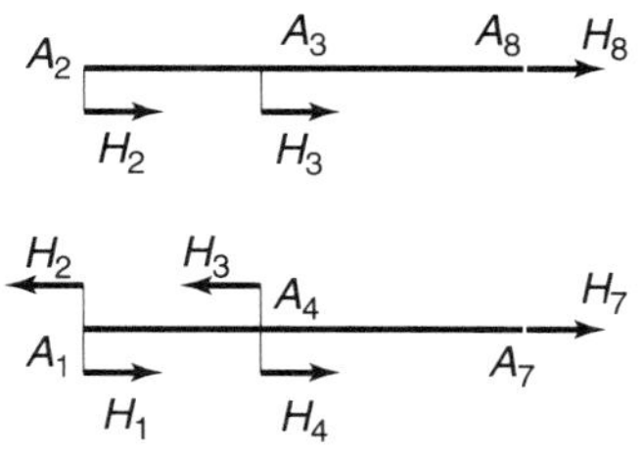

Figure 4.35 Determination of the reactions H_7 and H_8.

while, for the determination of the reactions H_7 and H_8, we isolate the parts in Figure 4.35 and there result the successive relations

$$H_2 = \frac{M_{12} + M_{21}}{l}, \quad H_3 = \frac{M_{34} + M_{43}}{l}, \quad H_8 = -(H_2 + H_3), \tag{4.1237}$$

$$H_1 = \frac{M_{15} + M_{51}}{l}, \quad H_4 = \frac{M_{46} + M_{64}}{l}, \quad H_7 = H_2 + H_3 - H_1 - H_4. \tag{4.1238}$$

In conclusion, we obtain the reactions:
- at the point A_5 — H_5, V_5, M_{51};
- at the point A_6 — H_6, V_6, M_{64};
- at the point A_7 — H_7, V_7, M_{74};
- at the point A_8 — H_8, V_8, M_{83}.

3. Numeric computation
We calculate successively

$$\{\mathbf{B}\} = \begin{bmatrix} 0 & 0 & 0.25 \times 10^{-6} & 0 \end{bmatrix}^{\mathrm{T}}, \tag{4.1239}$$

$$[\mathbf{A}]^{-1} = \begin{bmatrix} 0.178744 & -0.048309 & 0.014493 & -0.024155 \\ -0.048309 & 0.276570 & -0.057971 & 0.013285 \\ 0.014493 & -0.057971 & 0.217391 & -0.028986 \\ -0.024155 & 0.013285 & -0.028986 & 0.131643 \end{bmatrix}, \tag{4.1240}$$

$$\{\boldsymbol{\phi}\} = \begin{bmatrix} \phi_1 & \phi_2 & \phi_3 & \phi_4 \end{bmatrix}^{\mathrm{T}} = 10^{-9} \begin{bmatrix} 3.62325 & -14.49275 & 54.34775 & -7.2465 \end{bmatrix}^{\mathrm{T}}, \tag{4.1241}$$

$$M_{51} = 4.3479 \text{ N m}, \quad M_{64} = M_{74} = -8.6958 \text{ N m},$$

$$M_{83} = 152.17395 \text{ N m}, \quad M_{12} = -8.6955 \text{ N m}, \quad M_{15} = 2.17395 \text{ N m},$$

$$M_{14} = 0 \text{ N m}, \quad M_{21} = -30.4347 \text{ N m}, \quad M_{23} = 30.4347 \text{ N m},$$

$$M_{31} = 73.9131 \text{ N m}, \quad M_{34} = 121.7388 \text{ N m}, \quad M_{38} = -234.7827 \text{ N m},$$

$$M_{41} = 13.0437 \text{ N m}, \quad M_{43} = 47.8257 \text{ N m}, \quad M_{46} = -17.3916 \text{ N m},$$

$$M_{47} = 47.8257 \text{ N m}, \quad M_{32} = 113.0433 \text{ N m}, \tag{4.1242}$$

$$V_3' = -641.3 \text{ N}, \quad V_8 = 558.7 \text{ N}, \quad H_5 = 6.49 \text{ N}, \quad H_6 = -26.09 \text{ N},$$

$$V_7 = 39.13 \text{ N}, \quad V_2 = 143.5 \text{ N}, \quad V_1 = -13.04 \text{ N}, \quad V_5 = -26.09 \text{ N},$$

$$V_4' = 39.13 \text{ N}, \quad V_6 = 758.7 \text{ N}, \quad H_2 = -39.13 \text{ N}, \quad H_3 = 169.6 \text{ N},$$

$$H_8 = -130.5 \text{ N}, \quad H_1 = 6.52 \text{ N}, \quad H_4 = -26.09 \text{ N}, \quad H_7 = 150 \text{ N}. \tag{4.1243}$$

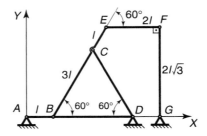

Figure 4.36   Problem 4.15.

Problem 4.15

Let us consider the plane articulated mechanism in Figure 4.36, where the crank AB is rotating with the constant angular velocity ω_1. For the position in Figure 4.36, determine the angular velocities ω_2, ω_3, ω_4, ω_5 and the angular accelerations ε_2, ε_3, ε_4, ε_5 of the bars BC, CD, EF, FG.

Numerical application for $\omega_1 = 100 \text{ s}^{-1}$, $l = 0.2 \text{ m}$.

Solution:

1. Theory

In an arbitrary position and in a more general case, the mechanism is represented in Figure 4.37. Denoting by l_1, l_2, l_2^*, l_3, l_4, l_5 the lengths of the bars AB, BC, BE, CD, EF, FG, from the vector equations

$$\mathbf{AB} + \mathbf{BC} + \mathbf{CD} = \mathbf{OD} - \mathbf{OA}, \quad \mathbf{AB} + \mathbf{BE} + \mathbf{EF} + \mathbf{FG} = \mathbf{OG} - \mathbf{OA}, \tag{4.1244}$$

projected on the axes OX and OY, we obtain the scalar equations

$$\begin{aligned}
l_1 \cos \phi_1 + l_2 \cos \phi_2 + l_3 \cos \phi_3 &= X_D - X_A, \\
l_1 \sin \phi_1 + l_2 \sin \phi_2 + l_3 \sin \phi_3 &= Y_D - Y_A, \\
l_1 \cos \phi_1 + l_2^* \cos \phi_2 + l_4 \cos \phi_4 + l_5 \cos \phi_5 &= X_G - X_A, \\
l_1 \sin \phi_1 + l_2^* \sin \phi_2 + l_4 \sin \phi_4 + l_5 \sin \phi_5 &= Y_G - Y_A.
\end{aligned} \tag{4.1245}$$

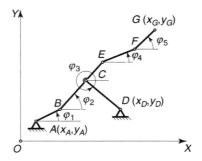

Figure 4.37   The general case.

Differentiating successively with respect to time relations (4.1225) and denoting by ω_i, ε_i the angular velocities and accelerations, respectively,

$$\omega_i = \dot{\phi}_i, \quad \varepsilon_i = \dot{\omega}_i, \quad i = \overline{1,5}, \tag{4.1246}$$

and knowing that $\dot{\omega}_1 = 0$, we obtain the systems of equations

$$-l_2\omega_2 \sin\phi_2 - l_3\omega_3 \sin\phi_3 = l_1\omega_1 \sin\phi_1,$$
$$l_2\omega_2 \cos\phi_2 + l_3\omega_3 \cos\phi_3 = -l_1\omega_1 \cos\phi_1,$$
$$-l_2^*\omega_2 \sin\phi_2 - l_4\omega_4 \sin\phi_4 - l_5\omega_5 \sin\phi_5 = l_1\omega_1 \sin\phi_1, \tag{4.1247}$$
$$l_2^*\omega_2 \cos\phi_2 + l_4\omega_4 \cos\phi_4 + l_5\omega_5 \cos\phi_5 = -l_1\omega_1 \cos\phi_1,$$

$$-l_2\varepsilon_2 \sin\phi_2 - l_3\varepsilon_3 \sin\phi_3 - l_2\omega_2^2 \cos\phi_2 - l_3\omega_3^2 \cos\phi_3 = l_1\omega_1^2 \cos\phi_1,$$
$$l_2\varepsilon_2 \cos\phi_2 + l_3\varepsilon_3 \cos\phi_3 - l_2\omega_2^2 \sin\phi_2 - l_3\omega_3^2 \sin\phi_3 = l_1\omega_1^2 \sin\phi_1,$$
$$-l_2^*\varepsilon_2 \sin\phi_2 - l_4\varepsilon_4 \sin\phi_4 - l_5\varepsilon_5 \sin\phi_5 - l_2^*\omega_2^2 \cos\phi_2 \tag{4.1248}$$
$$-l_4\omega_4^2 \cos\phi_4 - l_5\omega_5^2 \cos\phi_5 = l_1\omega_1^2 \cos\phi_1,$$
$$l_2^*\varepsilon_2 \cos\phi_2 + l_4\varepsilon_4 \cos\phi_4 + l_5\varepsilon_5 \cos\phi_5 - l_2^*\omega_2^2 \sin\phi_2$$
$$-l_4\omega_4^2 \sin\phi_4 - l_5\omega_5^2 \sin\phi_5 = l_1\omega_1^2 \sin\phi_1.$$

By using the notations

$$[\mathbf{A}] = \begin{bmatrix} -l_2 \sin\phi_2 & -l_3 \sin\phi_3 & 0 & 0 \\ l_2 \cos\phi_2 & l_3 \cos\phi_3 & 0 & 0 \\ -l_2^* \sin\phi_2 & 0 & -l_4 \sin\phi_4 & -l_5 \sin\phi_5 \\ l_2^* \cos\phi_2 & 0 & l_4 \cos\phi_4 & l_5 \cos\phi_5 \end{bmatrix}, \tag{4.1249}$$

$$\{\mathbf{B}\} = \begin{bmatrix} \sin\phi_1 & -\cos\phi_1 & \sin\phi_1 & -\cos\phi_1 \end{bmatrix}^T, \quad \{\boldsymbol{\omega}\} = \begin{bmatrix} \omega_2 & \omega_3 & \omega_4 & \omega_5 \end{bmatrix}^T, \tag{4.1250}$$

$$[\mathbf{A}_p] = \begin{bmatrix} -l_2 \cos\phi_2 & -l_3 \cos\phi_3 & 0 & 0 \\ -l_2 \sin\phi_2 & -l_3 \sin\phi_3 & 0 & 0 \\ -l_2^* \cos\phi_2 & 0 & -l_4 \cos\phi_4 & -l_5 \cos\phi_5 \\ -l_2^* \sin\phi_2 & 0 & -l_4 \sin\phi_4 & -l_5 \sin\phi_5 \end{bmatrix}, \tag{4.1251}$$

$$\{\mathbf{B}_p\} = \begin{bmatrix} \cos\phi_1 & \sin\phi_1 & \cos\phi_1 & \sin\phi_1 \end{bmatrix}^T,$$
$$\{\boldsymbol{\omega}^2\} = \begin{bmatrix} \omega_1^2 & \omega_2^2 & \omega_3^2 & \omega_4^2 \end{bmatrix}^T,$$
$$\{\boldsymbol{\varepsilon}\} = \begin{bmatrix} \varepsilon_1 & \varepsilon_2 & \varepsilon_3 & \varepsilon_4 \end{bmatrix}^T, \tag{4.1252}$$

the systems of equation (4.1247) and equation (4.1248) are written in the matrix form

$$[\mathbf{A}]\{\boldsymbol{\omega}\} = l_1\omega_1\{\mathbf{B}\}, \tag{4.1253}$$
$$[\mathbf{A}]\{\boldsymbol{\varepsilon}\} = l_1\omega_1^2\{\mathbf{B}_p\} - [\mathbf{A}_p]\{\boldsymbol{\omega}^2\}, \tag{4.1254}$$

obtaining thus the solutions

$$\{\boldsymbol{\omega}\} = l_1\omega_1[\mathbf{A}]^{-1}\{\mathbf{B}\}, \tag{4.1255}$$
$$\{\boldsymbol{\varepsilon}\} = l_1\omega_1^2[\mathbf{A}]^{-1}\{\mathbf{B}_p\} - [\mathbf{A}]^{-1}[\mathbf{A}_p]\{\boldsymbol{\omega}^2\}. \tag{4.1256}$$

2. Numerical calculation
The following values result:

$$l_1 = l, \quad l_2 = 3l, \quad l_2^* = 4l, \quad l_3 = 3l, \quad l_4 = 2l, \quad l_5 = 2\sqrt{3}l,$$

$$X_A = 0, \quad Y_A = 0, \quad X_G = 5l, \quad Y_G = 0, \quad X_D = 4l, \quad Y_D = 0,$$

$$\phi_1 = 0°, \quad \phi_2 = 60°, \quad \phi_3 = 300°, \quad \phi_4 = 0°, \quad \phi_5 = 270°, \tag{4.1257}$$

$$[\mathbf{A}] = \begin{bmatrix} -0.51962 & 0.51962 & 0 & 0 \\ 0.3 & 0.3 & 0 & 0 \\ -0.69282 & 0 & 0 & 0.69282 \\ 0.4 & 0 & 0.4 & 0 \end{bmatrix}, \tag{4.1258}$$

$$\{\mathbf{B}\} = \begin{bmatrix} 0.86603 & -0.5 & 0.86603 & -0.5 \end{bmatrix}^{\mathrm{T}}, \tag{4.1259}$$

$$[\mathbf{A}_p] = \begin{bmatrix} -0.3 & -0.3 & 0 & 0 \\ -0.51962 & 0.51962 & 0 & 0 \\ -0.4 & 0 & -0.4 & 0 \\ -0.69282 & 0 & 0 & 0.69282 \end{bmatrix}, \tag{4.1260}$$

$$\{\mathbf{B}_p\} = \begin{bmatrix} 0.5 & 0.86603 & 0.5 & 0.86603 \end{bmatrix}^{\mathrm{T}}, \tag{4.1261}$$

$$[\mathbf{A}]^{-1} = \begin{bmatrix} -0.962242 & 1.666667 & 0 & 0 \\ 0.962242 & 1.666667 & 0 & 0 \\ 0.962242 & -1.666667 & 0 & 2.5 \\ -0.962242 & 1.666667 & 1.44376 & 0 \end{bmatrix}, \tag{4.1262}$$

$$\{\boldsymbol{\omega}\} = \begin{bmatrix} -33.333 & 0 & 8.333 & -33.333 \end{bmatrix}^{\mathrm{T}}, \tag{4.1263}$$

$$\{\boldsymbol{\omega}^2\} = \begin{bmatrix} 1111.089 & 0 & 69.439 & 1111.089 \end{bmatrix}^{\mathrm{T}}, \tag{4.1264}$$

$$\{\boldsymbol{\varepsilon}\} = \begin{bmatrix} 2566.03 & 5131.99 & -280.61 & 4690.98 \end{bmatrix}^{\mathrm{T}}. \tag{4.1265}$$

Problem 4.16

We consider a mechanical system, the motion of which is defined by the matrix differential equation with constant coefficients

$$\{\dot{\mathbf{x}}\} = [\mathbf{A}]\{\mathbf{x}\} + [\mathbf{B}]\{\mathbf{u}\}, \tag{4.1266}$$

where

- $\{\mathbf{x}\} = \begin{bmatrix} x_1 & x_2 & \cdots & x_n \end{bmatrix}^{\mathrm{T}}$ is the state vector;
- $\{\mathbf{u}\} = \begin{bmatrix} u_1 & u_2 & \cdots & u_m \end{bmatrix}^{\mathrm{T}}$ is the command vector;
- $[\mathbf{A}] = [a_{ij}]_{1 \leq i, j \leq n}$ is the matrix of coefficients;
- $[\mathbf{B}] = [b_{ij}]_{\substack{1 \leq i \leq n \\ 1 \leq j \leq m}}$ is the command matrix.

Knowing that the matrix $[\mathbf{A}]$ has either positive solutions or complex ones with a positive real part, determine a command vector to make stable the motion with the aid of a reaction matrix.
Numerical application for

$$[\mathbf{A}] = \begin{bmatrix} 1 & 1 & 0 \\ 1 & 1 & 1 \\ 0 & 1 & 1 \end{bmatrix}, \quad [\mathbf{B}] = \begin{bmatrix} 0 \\ 0 \\ 1 \end{bmatrix}. \tag{4.1267}$$

Solution:

1. Theory

If the matrix $[\mathbf{A}]$ has all its eigenvalues either strictly negative or complex with a negative real part, then even the null command vector $\{\mathbf{u}\} = \{\mathbf{0}\}$ satisfies the condition that the motion be stable. If this condition is not fulfilled, then we may determine a command vector of the form

$$\{\mathbf{u}\} = [\mathbf{K}]\{\mathbf{x}\}, \tag{4.1268}$$

$[\mathbf{K}]$ being the reaction matrix, so that the motion is stable. To do this, the eigenvalues of the matrix $[\mathbf{A}] + [\mathbf{B}][\mathbf{K}]$ must be either negative or complex with the real part negative. To determine the matrix $[\mathbf{K}]$ that must fulfill these conditions, we may use the method of allocation of poles, by choosing convenient eigenvalues $\lambda_1, \lambda_2, \ldots, \lambda_n$ and obtaining the elements of the matrix $[\mathbf{K}]$ by means of the equations

$$\det[[\mathbf{A}] + [\mathbf{B}][\mathbf{K}] - \lambda[\mathbf{I}]] = 0, \quad \lambda = \lambda_1, \lambda_2, \ldots, \lambda_n. \tag{4.1269}$$

2. Numerical calculation

In the numerical case considered, the eigenvalues of the matrix $[\mathbf{A}]$ are given by the equation

$$\begin{vmatrix} 1 - \lambda & 1 & 0 \\ 1 & 1 - \lambda & 1 \\ 0 & 1 & 1 - \lambda \end{vmatrix} = 0, \tag{4.1270}$$

That is,

$$\lambda_1 = 1, \quad \lambda_{2,3} = 1 \pm \sqrt{2}; \tag{4.1271}$$

thus, in the absence of the command, the motion is unstable.

In the numerical case considered, the reaction matrix $[\mathbf{K}]$ is of the form

$$[\mathbf{K}] = \begin{bmatrix} \alpha_1 & \alpha_2 & \alpha_3 \end{bmatrix}, \tag{4.1272}$$

hence equation (4.1269) reads

$$\begin{vmatrix} 1 - \lambda & 1 & 0 \\ 1 & 1 - \lambda & 1 \\ \alpha_1 & 1 + \alpha_2 & 1 + \alpha_3 - \lambda \end{vmatrix} = 0 \tag{4.1273}$$

or

$$\lambda^3 - \lambda^2(3 + \alpha_3) + \lambda(-\alpha_2 + 2\alpha_3 + 1) + 1 - \alpha_1 + \alpha_2 = 0. \tag{4.1274}$$

If we allocate the poles

$$\lambda_1 = -1, \quad \lambda_2 = -2 + i, \quad \lambda_3 = -2 - i, \tag{4.1275}$$

then

$$\lambda_1 + \lambda_2 + \lambda_3 = -5, \quad \lambda_1\lambda_2 + \lambda_1\lambda_3 + \lambda_2\lambda_3 = 9, \quad \lambda_1\lambda_2\lambda_3 = -5 \tag{4.1276}$$

and we obtain the system

$$-5 = 3 + \alpha_3, \quad 9 = -\alpha_2 + 2\alpha_3 + 1, \quad -5 = \alpha_1 - \alpha_2 - 1, \tag{4.1277}$$

from which it follows that

$$\alpha_1 = -28, \quad \alpha_2 = -24, \quad \alpha_3 = -8; \tag{4.1278}$$

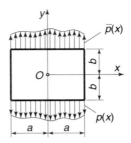

Figure 4.38   Problem 4.17.

as a conclusion, the reaction matrix is

$$[\mathbf{K}] = \begin{bmatrix} -28 & -24 & -8 \end{bmatrix}, \tag{4.1279}$$

so that the command becomes

$$u = -28x_1 - 24x_2 - 8x_3. \tag{4.1280}$$

Problem 4.17

Let a rectangular plate of dimensions $2a$ and $2b$ ($\lambda = a/b$, $\lambda' = 1/\lambda = b/a$) be subjected in the middle plane by the distributed loads

$$\bar{p}(x) = p(x) = b_0 + \sum_n b_n \cos \gamma_n x, \quad \gamma_n = \frac{n\pi}{a}, \quad n \in \mathbb{N}, \tag{4.1281}$$

distributed on $y = \pm b$, respectively, symmetrical with respect to both axes of coordinates (Fig. 4.38). The state of stress (σ_x and σ_y, normal stresses; τ_{xy}, tangential stress) may be expressed in the form

$$\sigma_x = \sum_n (-1)^n A_n \Phi_1(\gamma_n y) \cos \gamma_n x + \sum_m (-1)^m B_m \Phi_2'(\delta_m x) \cos \delta_m y,$$

$$\sigma_y = b_0 + \sum_n (-1)^n A_n \Phi_2(\gamma_n y) \cos \gamma_n x + \sum_m (-1)^m B_m \Phi_1'(\delta_m x) \cos \delta_m y, \tag{4.1282}$$

$$\tau_{xy} = \sum_n (-1)^n A_n \Phi_3(\gamma_n y) \sin \gamma_n x + \sum_m (-1)^m B_m \Phi_3'(\delta_m x) \sin \delta_m y,$$

where it has been denoted ($i = 1, 2, 3$)

$$\Phi_i(\gamma_n y) = \Theta_i(\nu\pi\zeta) \quad \text{for} \quad \nu = n\lambda', \quad n \in \mathbb{N}, \quad \zeta = \eta,$$

$$\Phi_i'(\delta_m x) = \Theta_i(\nu\pi\zeta) \quad \text{for} \quad \nu = m\lambda, \quad m \in \mathbb{N}, \quad \zeta = \xi, \tag{4.1283}$$

with

$$\xi = \frac{x}{a}, \quad \eta = \frac{y}{b}, \quad \delta_m = \frac{m\pi}{b}, \quad m \in \mathbb{N}. \tag{4.1284}$$

The functions $\Theta_i(\nu\pi\zeta)$ are defined by the relations

$$\Theta_1(\nu\pi\zeta) = \frac{\nu\pi}{\sinh \nu\pi}[(1 - \nu\pi \coth \nu\pi) \cosh \nu\pi\zeta + \nu\pi\zeta \sinh \nu\pi\zeta],$$

$$\Theta_2(\nu\pi\zeta) = \frac{\nu\pi}{\sinh \nu\pi}[(1 + \nu\pi \coth \nu\pi) \cosh \nu\pi\zeta - \nu\pi\zeta \sinh \nu\pi\zeta],$$

$$\Theta_3(\nu\pi\zeta) = -\frac{\nu\pi}{\sinh \nu\pi}(\nu\pi \coth \nu\pi \sinh \nu\pi\zeta - \nu\pi\zeta \cosh \nu\pi\zeta). \tag{4.1285}$$

The sequences of coefficients A_n and B_n are given by the system of equations with a double infinity of unknowns

$$\sum_i \mu_{mi}^2 A_i + \kappa(m\lambda) B_m = 0, \quad m, i \in \mathbb{N},$$

$$\sum_l \mu_{\ln}^2 B_l + \kappa'(n\lambda') A_n = (-1)^n b_n, \quad n, l \in \mathbb{N}, \tag{4.1286}$$

where we have introduced the rational function

$$\mu_{mn} = \frac{2\gamma_m \delta_m}{\gamma_n^2 + \delta_m^2}, \quad n, m \in \mathbb{N} \tag{4.1287}$$

and the hyperbolic functions

$$\kappa(m\lambda) = \Phi_1'(\delta_m a) = \left(\coth \delta_m a + \frac{\delta_m a}{\sinh^2 \delta_m a}\right) \delta_m a, \quad m \in \mathbb{N},$$

$$\kappa'(n\lambda') = \Phi_1(\gamma_n b) = \left(\coth \gamma_n b + \frac{\gamma_n b}{\sinh^2 \gamma_n b}\right) \gamma_n b, \quad n \in \mathbb{N}. \tag{4.1288}$$

To solve the system of infinite linear algebraic equations (4.1286) by approximate methods, we must prove the existence and the uniqueness of the solution, as well as its boundedness; thus we search whether the system is regular or not.

The system is completely regular if the conditions

$$\sum_i \mu_{mi}^2 < \kappa(m\lambda), \quad \sum_l \mu_{\ln}^2 < \kappa'(m\lambda') \tag{4.1289}$$

are fulfilled.

Solution: Let the expansions into Fourier series be given by

$$\Phi_3(\gamma_n y) = \sum_m (-1)^m \mu_{mn}^2 \cos \delta_m y, \quad \Phi_3'(\delta_m x) = \sum_n (-1)^n \mu_{mn}^2 \cos \gamma_n x. \tag{4.1290}$$

In particular, we get

$$\kappa(m\lambda) = \Phi_3'(\delta_m a) = \left(\coth \delta_m a - \frac{\delta_m a}{\sinh^2 \delta_m a}\right) \delta_m a, \quad m \in \mathbb{N},$$

$$\kappa'(n\lambda') = \Phi_3(\gamma_n b) = \left(\coth \gamma_n b - \frac{\gamma_n b}{\sinh^2 \gamma_n b}\right) \gamma_n b, \quad n \in \mathbb{N} \tag{4.1291}$$

Relations (4.1289) and (4.1290) lead to

$$\sum_i \mu_{mi}^2 = \kappa(m\lambda) - 2\left(\frac{\delta_m a}{\sinh \delta_m a}\right)^2, \quad \sum_l \mu_{\ln}^2 = \kappa'(n\lambda') - 2\left(\frac{\gamma_n b}{\sinh \gamma_n b}\right)^2. \tag{4.1292}$$

Thus, conditions (4.1288) become

$$2\left(\frac{\delta_m a}{\sinh \delta_m a}\right)^2 > 0, \quad 2\left(\frac{\gamma_n b}{\sinh \gamma_n b}\right)^2 > 0. \tag{4.1293}$$

We notice that these magnitudes tend to zero for $m \to \infty$ or $n \to \infty$. Hence, the system of equations (4.1286) is regular, but not completely regular.

We have

$$\rho_m = 1 - \frac{\sum\limits_i \mu_{mi}^2}{\kappa(m\lambda)} = \frac{2\left(\frac{\delta_m a}{\sinh \delta_m a}\right)^2}{\kappa(m\lambda)} = \frac{4\delta_m a}{\sinh 2\delta_m a + 2\delta_m a},$$

$$\rho_n' = \frac{4\gamma_n b}{\sinh 2\gamma_n b + 2\gamma_n b}. \tag{4.1294}$$

Asking that the solution of the infinite system of equations, the existence of which is assured for a regular system, be bounded and obtained by successive approximations, the free terms, that is, the Fourier coefficients b_n must satisfy the condition

$$\overline{b}_n = \frac{b_n}{\kappa_2'(n\lambda')} \le K\rho_n', \tag{4.1295}$$

where K is a positive constant, hence $\overline{b}_n$ must be of the same order of magnitude as ρ_n'. As a result, the type of external loads that may be taken into consideration is very restricted.

The solution of a regular system, however, is not necessarily unique. To study this problem, we make the change of variable

$$\overline{A}_n = \gamma_n^2 A_n, \quad \overline{B}_m = \delta_m^2 B_m, \quad m, n \in \mathbb{N}. \tag{4.1296}$$

Thus, system (4.1286) becomes

$$\sum_i \omega^2 \mu_{mi}^2 \overline{A}_i + \kappa(m\lambda)\overline{B}_m = 0, \quad \kappa'(m\lambda')\overline{A}_n + \sum_l \omega'^2 \mu_{ln}^2 \overline{B}_l = (-1)^n b_n, \tag{4.1297}$$

where we have denoted

$$\omega = \frac{m}{n}\lambda, \quad \omega' = \frac{1}{\omega} = \frac{n}{m}\lambda', \tag{4.1298}$$

eventually taking $n = i$ or $m = l$.

Let the expansions into Fourier series be given by

$$\Phi_1(\gamma_n y) = 2 + \sum_m (-1)^m \omega'^2 \mu_{mn}^2 \cos \delta_m y, \quad \Phi_1'(\delta_m x) = 2 + \sum_n (-1)^n \omega^2 \mu_{mn}^2 \cos \gamma_n x. \tag{4.1299}$$

Relations (4.1287) and (4.1298) allow us now to write

$$\sum_i \omega^2 \mu_{mi}^2 = \chi(m\lambda) - 2, \quad \sum_l \omega'^2 \mu_{ln}^2 = \chi'(n\lambda') - 2. \tag{4.1300}$$

Thus, we get

$$\rho_m = 1 - \frac{\sum\limits_i \omega^2 \mu_{mi}^2}{\kappa_2(m\lambda)} = \frac{2}{\kappa_2(m\lambda)} = \frac{2}{\delta_m a\left(\coth \delta_m a + \frac{\delta_m a}{\sinh^2 \delta_m a}\right)},$$

$$\rho_n' = \frac{2}{\kappa'(n\lambda')} = \frac{2}{\gamma_n b\left(\coth \gamma_n b + \frac{\gamma_n b}{\sinh^2 \gamma_n b}\right)}. \tag{4.1301}$$

Hence, the system of equations (4.1296) is regular too (not completely regular). Thus, the Fourier coefficients b_n must be of order of magnitude $1/n^2$ (ρ_m and ρ'_n tend to zero for $m \to \infty$ and for $n \to \infty$).

As, by a change of variable of form (4.1295), where $\gamma_n \to \infty$ and $\delta_m \to \infty$, together with $n \to \infty$ and $m \to \infty$, we have obtained also a regular system with bounded free terms, on the basis of a theorem of P. S. Bondarenko, we can affirm that the solution of both systems is unique.

It is also sufficient for system (4.1286) to have Fourier coefficients of order of magnitude $1/n^2$. Hence, we can consider any case of loading with a distributed load (we cannot make a calculation for a concentrated load; in this case, this force must be replaced by an equivalent distributed load on a certain interval).

To diminish the restriction imposed on the external loads, we will try a new change of variable, namely,

$$\overline{A}'_n = \gamma_n \overline{A}_n, \quad \overline{B}'_m = \delta_m \overline{B}_m, \quad m, n \in \mathbb{N}. \tag{4.1302}$$

System (4.1286) reads

$$\sum_i \omega \mu_{mi}^2 \overline{A}'_i + \kappa(m\lambda)\overline{B}'_m = 0, \quad \kappa'(n\lambda')\overline{A}'_n + \sum_l \omega' \mu_{\ln}^2 \overline{B}'_l = (-1)^n \gamma_n b_n, \tag{4.1303}$$

in this case. Taking into account

$$\sum_i \omega \mu_{mi}^2 = \sum_i \mu_{mi}(\omega \mu_{mi}) \le \sqrt{\sum_i \mu_{mi}^2 \sum_i \omega^2 \mu_{mi}^2}$$

$$= \sqrt{\kappa(m\lambda)[\kappa(m\lambda) - 2]} < \kappa(m\lambda) \tag{4.1304}$$

and

$$\sum_l \omega' \mu_{\ln}^2 \le \sqrt{\kappa'(n\lambda')[\kappa'(n\lambda') - 2]} < \kappa'(n\lambda'), \tag{4.1305}$$

we may affirm that system (4.1302) is regular too, obtaining the same conclusions as above. But the evaluations thus made are not strict; we try now to bring some improvements.

We notice that we may write

$$\sum_i \omega \mu_{mi}^2 = 4(m\lambda)^2 \sum_i \frac{i}{[i^2 + (m\lambda)^2]^2}. \tag{4.1306}$$

On the basis of some evaluations made by P. S. Bondarenko, who considers that the series above approximates a certain definite integral, we can write

$$\sum_i \frac{i}{[i^2 + (m\lambda)^2]^2} \le \begin{cases} f_1(m\lambda), & m\lambda \le 3, \\ f_2(m\lambda), & 3 < m\lambda \le 4, \\ f_3(m\lambda), & m\lambda > 4, \end{cases} \tag{4.1307}$$

where we denoted

$$f_1(m\lambda) = \frac{1}{[1 + (m\lambda)^2]^2} + \frac{1}{[4 + (m\lambda)^2]^2} + \frac{21 + (m\lambda)^2}{4[9 + (m\lambda)^2]^2} + \frac{32 + (m\lambda)^2}{4[16 + (m\lambda)^2]},$$

$$f_2(m\lambda) = \frac{1}{8(m\lambda)^2} + \frac{3 + (m\lambda)^2}{4[1 + (m\lambda)^2]^2} + \frac{2}{[4 + (m\lambda)^2]^2} + \frac{32 + (m\lambda)^2}{4[16 + (m\lambda)^2]}, \tag{4.1308}$$

$$f_3(m\lambda) = \frac{1}{4(m\lambda)^2} + \frac{3 + (m\lambda)^2}{4[1 + (m\lambda)^2]^2} + \frac{8 + (m\lambda)^2}{4[4 + (m\lambda)^2]}.$$

It follows that

$$\rho_m = 1 - \frac{\sum_i \omega \mu_{mi}^2}{\chi(m\lambda)} \geq 1 - \frac{4(m\lambda)^2 f_k(m\lambda)}{\chi(m\lambda)} = 1 - \frac{1}{\pi} \frac{(m\lambda)^2 f_k(m\lambda)}{\coth m\lambda + \frac{\pi m\lambda}{\sinh^2 \pi m\lambda}}, \qquad (4.1309)$$

for $k = 1, 2, 3$. The denominator of the last fraction is superunitary, being equal to the unity only for $m \to \infty$. Hence, we may write

$$\rho_m \geq 1 - \frac{4}{\pi}(m\lambda)^2 f_k(m\lambda). \qquad (4.1310)$$

The maximum of the function $(m\lambda)^2 f_k(m\lambda)$ is smaller or at most equal to the sum of the maximum values of each component fraction, for every variation interval of the argument $m\lambda$. We may thus write

$$\max[(m\lambda)^2 f_1(m\lambda)] \leq \frac{1}{4} + \frac{1}{9} + \frac{5}{24} + \frac{369}{2500}$$
$$< 0.250 + 0.112 + 0.210 + 0.148 = 0.720,$$
$$\max[(m\lambda)^2 f_2(m\lambda)] \leq \frac{1}{24} + \frac{27}{100} + \frac{18}{169} + \frac{1}{4}$$
$$< 0.042 + 0.270 + 0.108 + 0.250 = 0.670,$$
$$\max[(m\lambda)^2 f_3(m\lambda)] \leq \frac{1}{16} + \frac{76}{289} + \frac{1}{4}$$
$$< 0.065 + 0.265 + 0.250 = 0.580. \qquad (4.1311)$$

Thus,

$$\rho_m > 1 - \frac{4}{\pi}0.720 > 1 - 0.920 = 0.080 > 0, \qquad (4.1312)$$

for any m (for $m \to \infty$ too).

Analogically, we may show that

$$\rho_n' = 1 - \frac{\sum_l \omega' \mu_{\ln}^2}{\kappa'(n\lambda')} \geq 1 - \frac{4(n\lambda')^2 f_k(n\lambda')}{\kappa'(n\lambda')} > 0.080 > 0, \qquad (4.1313)$$

for any n (for $n \to \infty$ too).

Hence, the infinite system (4.1302) is completely regular. Its free terms, that is, the Fourier coefficients b_n must be all bounded; but we cannot consider loadings with concentrated moments (in this case, the Fourier coefficients b_n must be of the order of magnitude of n, so that they cannot all be bounded).

The linear system of algebraic equations may now be solved on sections (the first n equations with the first n unknowns), obtaining a result as accurate as we choose.

Let us now show that, from the infinite system of linear algebraic equations, we may obtain

$$A_n = \frac{1}{\kappa'(n\lambda')}\left[(-1)^n b_n - \sum_l \mu_{\ln}^2 B_l\right], \quad B_m = -\frac{1}{\kappa(m\lambda)}\sum_l \mu_{mi}^2 A_i. \qquad (4.1314)$$

Introducing A_n in the first group of equations (4.1286), we obtain the system

$$\sum_l a_{ml} B_l = c_m, \tag{4.1315}$$

with

$$a_{ml} = -\sum_i \frac{\mu_{mi}^2 \mu_{li}^2}{\kappa'(i\lambda')}, \quad a_{ml} = a_{lm}, \quad m \neq l,$$

$$a_{mm} = \kappa(m\lambda) - \sum_i \frac{\mu_{mi}^4}{\kappa'(i\lambda')}, \quad c_m = -\sum_k (-1)^k b_k \frac{\mu_{mk}^2}{\kappa'(k\lambda')}, \tag{4.1316}$$

while, introducing B_m in the second group of equations (4.1286), we obtain the system

$$\sum_i b_{ni} B_i = d_n, \tag{4.1317}$$

with

$$b_{ni} = -\sum_l \frac{\mu_{ln}^2 \mu_{li}^2}{\kappa(l\lambda)}, \quad b_{ni} = b_{in}, \quad n \neq i,$$

$$b_{nn} = \kappa'(n\lambda') - \sum_l \frac{\mu_{ln}^4}{\kappa(l\lambda)}, \quad d_n = (-1)^n b_n. \tag{4.1318}$$

We obtain that both systems are symmetric with respect to the principal diagonal. We obtain thus a system of equations for each sequence of unknown coefficients. These systems have, obviously, the same properties as system (4.1286) and may be similarly studied.

FURTHER READING

Acton FS (1990). Numerical Methods that Work. 4th ed. Washington: Mathematical Association of America.

Ackleh AS, Allen EJ, Hearfott RB, Seshaiyer P (2009). Classical and Modern Numerical Analysis: Theory, Methods and Practice. Boca Raton: CRC Press.

Atkinson KE (1989). An Introduction to Numerical Analysis. 2nd ed. New York: John Wiley & Sons, Inc.

Atkinson KE (1993). Elementary Numerical Analysis. 2nd ed. New York: John Wiley & Sons, Inc.

Atkinson K, Han W (2010). Theoretical Numerical Analysis: A Functional Analysis Framework. 3rd ed. New York: Springer-Verlag.

Bakhvalov N (1976). Méthodes Numérique. Moscou: Editions Mir (in French).

Berbente C, Mitran S, Zancu S (1997). Metode Numerice. Bucureşti: Editura Tehnică (in Romanian).

Bhatia R (1996). Matrix Analysis. New York: Springer-Verlag.

Burden RL, Faires L (2009). Numerical Analysis. 9th ed. Boston: Brooks/Cole.

Butt R (2009). Introduction to Numerical Analysis Using MATLAB. Boston: Jones and Bartlett Publishers.

Chapra SC (1996). Applied Numerical Methods with MATLAB for Engineers and Scientists. Boston: McGraw-Hill.

Cheney EW, Kincaid DR (1997). Numerical Mathematics and Computing. 6th ed. Belmont: Thomson.

Dahlquist G, Björck Å (1974). Numerical Methods. Englewood Cliffs: Prentice Hall.

Den Hartog JP (1961). Strength of Materials. New York: Dover Books on Engineering.

Démidovitch B, Maron I (1973). Éléments de Calcul Numérique. Moscou: Editions Mir (in French).

DiBenedetto E (2010). Classical Mechanics: Theory and Mathematical Modeling. New York: Springer-Verlag.

Epperson JF (2007). An Introduction to Numerical Methods and Analysis. Hoboken: John Wiley & Sons, Inc.

Fung YC, Tong P (2011). Classical and Computational Solid Mechanics. Singapore: World Scientific Publishing.

Golub GH, van Loan CF (1996). Matrix Computations. 3rd ed. Baltimore: John Hopkins University Press.

Greenbaum A, Chartier TP (2012). Numerical Methods: Design, Analysis, and Computer Implementation of Algorithms. Princeton: Princeton University Press.

Hamming RW (1987). Numerical Methods for Scientists and Engineers. 2nd ed. New York: Dover Publications.

Hamming RW (2012). Introduction to Applied Numerical Analysis. New York: Dover Publications.

Heinbockel JH (2006). Numerical Methods for Scientific Computing. Victoria: Trafford Publishing.

Hibbeler RC (2010). Mechanics of Materials. 8th ed. Englewood Cliffs: Prentice Hall.

Higham NJ (2002). Accuracy and Stability of Numerical Algorithms. 2nd ed. Philadelphia: SIAM.

Hildebrand FB (1987). Introduction to Numerical Analysis. 2nd ed. New York: Dover Publications.

Hoffman JD (1992). Numerical Methods for Engineers and Scientists. New York: McGraw-Hill.

Ionescu GM (2005). Algebră Liniară. Bucureşti: Editura Garamond (in Romanian).

Jazar RN (2008). Vehicle Dynamics: Theory and Applications. New York: Springer-Verlag.

Kharab A, Guenther RB (2011). An Introduction to Numerical Methods: A MATLAB Approach. 3rd ed. Boca Raton: CRC Press.

Kelley CT (1987). Iterative Methods for Linear and Nonlinear Equations. Philadelphia: SIAM.

Kleppner D, Kolenkow RJ (2010). An Introduction to Mechanics. Cambridge: Cambridge University Press.

Kress R (1996). Numerical Analysis. New York: Springer-Verlag.

Krîlov AN (1957). Lecţii de Calcule prin Aproximaţii. Bucureşti: Editura Tehnică (in Romanian).

Kunz KS (1957). Numerical Analysis. New York: McGraw-Hill.

Lange K (2010). Numerical Analysis for Statisticians. 2nd ed. New York: Springer-Verlag.

Lurie AI (2002). Analytical Mechanics. New York: Springer-Verlag.

Lurie AI (2005). Theory of Elasticity. New York: Springer-Verlag.

Mabie HH, Reinholtz CF (1987). Mechanisms and Dynamics of Machinery. 4th ed. New York: John Wiley & Sons, Inc.

Marinescu G (1974). Analiza Numerică. Bucureşti: Editura Academiei Române (in Romanian).

Meriam JL, Kraige LG (2012). Engineering Mechanics: Dynamics. Hoboken: John Wiley & Sons, Inc.

Otto SR, Denier JP (2005). An Introduction to Programming and Numerical Methods in MATLAB. London: Springer-Verlag.

Palm WJ III (2007). Mechanical Vibrations. Hoboken: John Wiley & Sons, Inc.

Pandrea N (2000). Elemente de Mecanica Solidului în Coordonate Plückeriene. Bucureşti: Editura Academiei Române (in Romanian).

Pandrea N, Pârlac S, Popa D (2001). Modele pentru Studiul Vibraţiilor Automobilelor. Piteşti: Tiparg (in Romanian).

Pandrea N, Popa D (2000). Mecanisme Teorie şi Aplicaţii CAD. Bucureşti: Editura Tehnică (in Romanian).

Pandrea N, Stănescu ND (2002). Mecanică. Bucureşti: Editura Didactică şi Pedagogică (in Romanian).

Postolache M (2006). Modelare Numerică. Teorie şi Aplicaţii. Bucureşti: Editura Fair Partners (in Romanian).

Press WH, Teukolski SA, Vetterling WT, Flannery BP (2007). Numerical Recipes: The Art of Scientific Computing. 3rd ed. Cambridge: Cambridge University Press.

Quarteroni A, Sacco R, Saleri F (2010). Numerical Mathematics. 2nd ed. Berlin: Springer-Verlag.

Ralston A, Rabinowitz P (2001). A First Course in Numerical Analysis. 2nd ed. New York: Dover Publications.

Reza F (1973). Spaţii Liniare. Bucureşti: Editura Didactică şi Pedagogică (in Romanian).

Ridgway Scott L (2011). Numerical Analysis. Princeton: Princeton University Press.

Salvadori MG, Baron ML (1962). Numerical Methods in Engineering. Englewood Cliffs: Prentice Hall.

Sauer T (2011). Numerical Analysis. 2nd ed. London: Pearson.

Simionescu I, Dranga M, Moise V (1995). Metode Numerice în Tehnică. Aplicaţii în FORTRAN. Bucureşti: Editura Tehnică (in Romanian).

Sinha AK (2010). Vibration of Mechanical Systems. Cambridge: Cambridge University Press.

Stănescu ND (2007). Metode Numerice. Bucureşti: Editura Didactică şi Pedagogică (in Romanian).

Stoer J, Bulirsh R (2010). Introduction to Numerical Analysis. 3rd ed. New York: Springer-Verlag.

Süli E, Mayers D (2003). An Introduction to Numerical Analysis. Cambridge: Cambridge University Press.

Trefethen LN, Bau D III (1997). Numerical Linear Algebra. Philadelphia: SIAM.

Udrişte C, Iftode V, Postolache M (1996). Metode Numerice de Calcul. Algoritmi şi Programe Turbo Pascal. Bucureşti: Editura Tehnică (in Romanian).

Voiévodine V (1980). Principes Numériques d'Algébre Linéare. Moscou: Editions Mir (in French).

Wilkinson JH (1988). The Algebraic Eigenvalue Problem. Oxford: Oxford University Press.

5

SOLUTION OF SYSTEMS OF NONLINEAR EQUATIONS

5.1 THE ITERATION METHOD (JACOBI)

Let us consider the equation[1]

$$\mathbf{F}(\mathbf{x}) = \mathbf{0},\tag{5.1}$$

where $\mathbf{F} : \mathcal{D} \subset \mathbb{R}^n \to \mathbb{R}^n$, $\mathbf{x} \in \mathbb{R}^n$.

In components, we have

$$f_1(x_1, x_2, \ldots, x_n) = 0, \quad f_2(x_1, x_2, \ldots, x_n) = 0, \ldots, f_n(x_1, x_2, \ldots, x_n).\tag{5.2}$$

Let us now write equation (5.1) in the form

$$\mathbf{x} = \mathbf{G}(\mathbf{x}),\tag{5.3}$$

where $\mathbf{G} : \mathcal{D} \subset \mathbb{R}^n \to \mathbb{R}^n$ or, in components,

$$x_1 = g_1(x_1, \ldots, x_n), \quad x_2 = g_2(x_1, \ldots, x_n), \ldots, x_n = g_n(x_1, \ldots, x_n).\tag{5.4}$$

We observe that, if $\mathbf{G}$ is a contraction, then the sequence of successive iterations

$$\mathbf{x}^{(0)} \in \mathcal{D} \quad \text{arbitrary}, \quad \mathbf{x}^{(1)} = \mathbf{G}(\mathbf{x}^{(0)}), \quad \mathbf{x}^{(2)} = \mathbf{G}(\mathbf{x}^{(1)}), \ldots, \mathbf{x}^{(n+1)} = \mathbf{G}(\mathbf{x}^{(n)}), \ldots, \quad n \in \mathbb{N}^* \tag{5.5}$$

where we assume that $\mathbf{x}^{(i)} \in \mathcal{D}$ for any $i \in \mathbb{N}^*$ is convergent, as proved by Banach's fixed-point theorem, because $\mathbb{R}^n$ is a Banach space with the usual Euclidean norm. The limit of this sequence is

$$\lim_{n \to \infty} \mathbf{x}^{(n)} = \overline{\mathbf{x}}\tag{5.6}$$

---

[1]The method is a generalization in the case of nonlinear systems for the Jacobi method in the case of linear systems of equations.

Numerical Analysis with Applications in Mechanics and Engineering, First Edition.
Petre Teodorescu, Nicolae-Doru Stănescu, and Nicolae Pandrea.
© 2013 The Institute of Electrical and Electronics Engineers, Inc. Published 2013 by John Wiley & Sons, Inc.

and satisfies the relation

$$\bar{\mathbf{x}} = \mathbf{G}(\bar{\mathbf{x}}). \tag{5.7}$$

Observation 5.1   If **G** is a contraction, then all the functions $g_i(\mathbf{x})$, $i = \overline{1, n}$, are contractions. Indeed, if **G** is a contraction, then there exists $q \in \mathbb{R}$, $0 < q < 1$, so that

$$\|\mathbf{G}(\mathbf{x}) - \mathbf{G}(\mathbf{y})\|_k \leq q\|\mathbf{x} - \mathbf{y}\|_k, \tag{5.8}$$

for any **x** and **y** of $\mathcal{D}$, $\|\ \|_k$ being the Euclidean norm on $\mathbb{R}^n$. Relation (5.8) may also be written in the form

$$\sqrt{\sum_{i=1}^{n} (g_i(\mathbf{x}) - g_i(\mathbf{y}))^2} \leq q \sqrt{\sum_{i=1}^{n} (x_i - y_i)^2}. \tag{5.9}$$

On the other hand,

$$\sum_{i=1}^{n} (g_i(\mathbf{x}) - g_i(\mathbf{y}))^2 \geq (g_j(\mathbf{x}) - g_j(\mathbf{y}))^2 \tag{5.10}$$

for any $j = \overline{1, n}$ and relation (5.9) leads to

$$|g_j(\mathbf{x}) - g_j(\mathbf{y})| \leq q \|\mathbf{x} - \mathbf{y}\|, \tag{5.11}$$

that is, $g_j : \mathcal{D} \subset \mathbb{R}^n \to \mathbb{R}$ is a contraction.

Observation 5.2   Let us suppose that $g_i : \mathcal{D} \subset \mathbb{R}^n \to \mathbb{R}$ is a contraction for any $i = \overline{1, n}$; it does not mean that $\mathbf{G} : \mathcal{D} \subset \mathbb{R}^n \to \mathbb{R}^n$ is also a contraction. Indeed, let us suppose that $n = 2$, so that

$$g_i(\mathbf{x}) = g_i(x_1, x_2) = \lambda x_i, \quad i = \overline{1, 2}, \quad 0 < \lambda < 1. \tag{5.12}$$

We have

$$|g_i(\mathbf{x}) - g_i(\mathbf{y})| = \lambda|x_1 - y_1| = \lambda\sqrt{(x_1 - y_1)^2}$$
$$\leq \lambda\sqrt{(x_1 - y_1)^2 + (x_2 - y_2)^2} = \lambda \|\mathbf{x} - \mathbf{y}\|, \tag{5.13}$$

so that g_i, $i = \overline{1, 2}$, are contractions.

On the other hand,

$$\|\mathbf{G}(\mathbf{x}) - \mathbf{G}(\mathbf{y})\| = \sqrt{(g_1(\mathbf{x}) - g_1(\mathbf{y}))^2 + (g_2(\mathbf{x}) - g_2(\mathbf{y}))^2}$$
$$= \sqrt{\lambda^2(x_1 - y_1)^2 + \lambda^2(x_1 - y_1)^2} = \lambda\sqrt{2}|x_1 - y_1|. \tag{5.14}$$

Let us now choose $\lambda > 1/\sqrt{2}$ and **x** and **y** so that

$$\mathbf{x} = \begin{bmatrix} x_1 & a \end{bmatrix}^\mathrm{T}, \quad \mathbf{y} = \begin{bmatrix} y_1 & a \end{bmatrix}^\mathrm{T}. \tag{5.15}$$

It follows that

$$\|\mathbf{x} - \mathbf{y}\| = \sqrt{(x_1 - y_1)^2} = |x_1 - y_1|, \tag{5.16}$$

hence the condition $\|\mathbf{G}(\mathbf{x}) - \mathbf{G}(\mathbf{y})\| \le q\,\|\mathbf{x} - \mathbf{y}\|$, $0 < q < 1$, leads to

$$q|x_1 - y_1| \ge \lambda\sqrt{2}|x_1 - y_1| > |x_1 - y_1|, \tag{5.17}$$

which is absurd.

Observation 5.3 Let us consider the Jacobian of $\mathbf{G}$,

$$\mathbf{J} = \begin{bmatrix} \dfrac{\partial g_1}{\partial x_1} & \dfrac{\partial g_1}{\partial x_2} & \cdots & \dfrac{\partial g_1}{\partial x_n} \\[2mm] \dfrac{\partial g_2}{\partial x_1} & \dfrac{\partial g_2}{\partial x_2} & \cdots & \dfrac{\partial g_2}{\partial x_n} \\[1mm] \cdots & \cdots & \cdots & \cdots \\[1mm] \dfrac{\partial g_n}{\partial x_1} & \dfrac{\partial g_n}{\partial x_2} & \cdots & \dfrac{\partial g_n}{\partial x_n} \end{bmatrix}, \tag{5.18}$$

and one of the norms $\|\,\|_\infty$ or $\|\,\|_1$. Proceeding as in the one-dimensional case, it follows that if

$$\|\mathbf{J}\|_\infty = \max_{i=\overline{1,n}} \sum_{j=1}^{n} \left|\frac{\partial g_i}{\partial x_j}\right| < 1 \text{ on } \mathcal{D} \tag{5.19}$$

or if

$$\|\mathbf{J}\|_1 = \max_{j=\overline{1,n}} \sum_{i=1}^{n} \left|\frac{\partial g_j}{\partial x_i}\right| < 1 \text{ on } \mathcal{D}, \tag{5.20}$$

respectively, then the function $\mathbf{G}$ is a contraction and the sequence of successive iterations is convergent.

5.2 NEWTON'S METHOD

Let the equation[2] be

$$\mathbf{f}(\mathbf{x}) = \mathbf{0}, \tag{5.21}$$

where $\mathbf{f} : \mathcal{D} \subset \mathbb{R}^n \to \mathbb{R}^n$, and let us denote by $\overline{\mathbf{x}}$ its solution.

We suppose that

$$\mathbf{f} = \begin{bmatrix} f_1 & f_2 & \cdots & f_n \end{bmatrix}^{\mathrm{T}}, \tag{5.22}$$

the functions f_i, $i = \overline{1,n}$, being of class C^1 on $\mathcal{D}$. We also suppose that the determinant of Jacobi's matrix does not vanish at $\overline{\mathbf{x}}$,

$$\det \mathbf{J} = \begin{vmatrix} \dfrac{\partial f_1}{\partial x_1} & \dfrac{\partial f_1}{\partial x_2} & \cdots & \dfrac{\partial f_1}{\partial x_n} \\[2mm] \dfrac{\partial f_2}{\partial x_1} & \dfrac{\partial f_2}{\partial x_2} & \cdots & \dfrac{\partial f_2}{\partial x_n} \\[1mm] \cdots & \cdots & \cdots & \cdots \\[1mm] \dfrac{\partial f_n}{\partial x_1} & \dfrac{\partial f_n}{\partial x_2} & \cdots & \dfrac{\partial f_n}{\partial x_n} \end{vmatrix}_{\mathbf{x}=\overline{\mathbf{x}}} \ne 0. \tag{5.23}$$

[2]This method is the generalization of the Newton method presented in Chapter 2.

It follows that there exists a neighborhood $\mathcal{V}$ of $\bar{\mathbf{x}}$ so that $\det \mathbf{J} \neq 0$ on $\mathcal{V}$.

Let us consider an arbitrary point $\mathbf{x} \in \mathcal{V}$. There exists $\mathbf{J}^{-1}(\mathbf{x})$ under these conditions, and we may define a recursive sequence, so that

$$\mathbf{x}^{(0)} \in \mathcal{V} \text{ arbitrary}, \quad \mathbf{x}^{(k)} = \mathbf{x}^{(k-1)} - \mathbf{J}^{-1}(\mathbf{x}^{(k-1)})\mathbf{f}(\mathbf{x}), \quad k \in \mathbb{N}^*, \tag{5.24}$$

with the condition $\mathbf{x}^{(i)} \in \mathcal{V}, i \in \mathbb{N}$.

Theorem 5.1   Let $\mathbf{f} : \mathcal{D} \subset \mathbb{R}^n \to \mathbb{R}^n$ and equation (5.21) with the solution $\bar{\mathbf{x}}$. Let us suppose that $\det \mathbf{J}(\bar{\mathbf{x}}) \neq 0$ too. If there exists the real constants α, β, and γ so that

$$\left\| \mathbf{J}^{-1}\left(\mathbf{x}^{(0)}\right) \right\| \leq \alpha, \tag{5.25}$$

$$\left\| \mathbf{x}^{(1)} - \mathbf{x}^{(0)} \right\| \leq \gamma, \tag{5.26}$$

$$\sum_{i=1}^{n} \sum_{j=1}^{n} \left\| \frac{\partial^2 f_i}{\partial x_i \partial y_j} \right\| < \beta; \quad i = \overline{1, n}; \quad j = \overline{1, n}, \tag{5.27}$$

$$2n\alpha\beta\gamma < 1, \tag{5.28}$$

then the recurrent sequence defined by relation (5.24) is convergent to the solution $\bar{\mathbf{x}}$ of equation (5.21).

Demonstration. It is analogous to that of the Theorem 2.5.

As stopping conditions for the iterative process we use

$$\left\| \mathbf{x}^{(k)} - \mathbf{x}^{(k-1)} \right\| < \varepsilon, \tag{5.29}$$

$$\left\| \mathbf{f}\left(\mathbf{x}^{(k)}\right) \right\| < \varepsilon, \tag{5.30}$$

where $\|\ \|$ is one of the canonical norms of the matrix. Sometimes, we use both conditions (5.29) and (5.30) together. A variant of condition (5.29) is given by

$$\left\| \mathbf{x}^{(k)} - \mathbf{x}^{(k-1)} \right\| < \varepsilon, \quad \text{if } \left\| \mathbf{x}^{(k)} \right\| \leq 1, \tag{5.31}$$

$$\frac{\left\| \mathbf{x}^{(k)} - \mathbf{x}^{(k-1)} \right\|}{\left\| \mathbf{x}^{(k)} \right\|} < \varepsilon, \quad \text{if } \left\| \mathbf{x}^{(k)} \right\| > 1. \tag{5.32}$$

5.3   THE MODIFIED NEWTON METHOD

If the matrix $\mathbf{J}^{-1}$ is continuous on a neighborhood of the solution $\bar{\mathbf{x}}$ and if the start vector $\mathbf{x}^{(0)}$ is sufficiently close to $\bar{\mathbf{x}}$, that is, it fulfills the conditions of Theorem 5.1, then we may replace the sequence of iterations

$$\mathbf{x}^{(k+1)} = \mathbf{x}^{(k)} - \mathbf{J}^{-1}(\mathbf{x}^{(k)})\mathbf{f}(\mathbf{x}^{(k)}) \tag{5.33}$$

by the sequence

$$\mathbf{x}^{(k+1)} = \mathbf{x}^{(k)} - \mathbf{J}^{-1}(\mathbf{x}^{(0)})\mathbf{f}(\mathbf{x}^{(k)}), \tag{5.34}$$

obtaining thus a variant of Newton's method[3]; this variant has the advantage in that the calculation of the inverse $\mathbf{J}^{-1}$ at each iteration step is no more necessary.

---

[3]It is the generalization of the modified Newton method discussed in Chapter 2.

5.4   THE NEWTON–RAPHSON METHOD

Let us consider the system of nonlinear equations[4]

$$\mathbf{f}(\mathbf{x}) = \mathbf{0} \tag{5.35}$$

for which an approximation $\mathbf{x}^{(0)}$ of the solution $\bar{\mathbf{x}}$ is known.

Let us now determine the variation

$$\boldsymbol{\delta}^{(0)} = \begin{bmatrix} \delta_1 & \delta_2 & \cdots & \delta_n \end{bmatrix}^{\mathrm{T}}, \tag{5.36}$$

so that $\mathbf{x}^{(0)} + \boldsymbol{\delta}^{(0)}$ be a solution of equation (5.35). Expanding the components f_i, $i = \overline{1, n}$, of the vector function $\mathbf{f}$ into a Taylor series around $\mathbf{x}^{(0)}$, we have

$$f_i(\mathbf{x}^0) + \delta_1^{(0)} \left.\frac{\partial f_i}{\partial x_1}\right|_{\mathbf{x}=\mathbf{x}^{(0)}} + \delta_2^{(0)} \left.\frac{\partial f_i}{\partial x_2}\right|_{\mathbf{x}=\mathbf{x}^{(0)}} + \cdots + \delta_n^{(0)} \left.\frac{\partial f_i}{\partial x_n}\right|_{\mathbf{x}=\mathbf{x}^{(0)}} + \cdots + = 0, \quad i = \overline{1, n}. \tag{5.37}$$

We neglect the terms of higher order in relation (5.37), obtaining thus a linear system of n equations with n unknowns

$$\delta_1^{(0)} \left.\frac{\partial f_1}{\partial x_1}\right|_{\mathbf{x}=\mathbf{x}^{(0)}} + \delta_2^{(0)} \left.\frac{\partial f_1}{\partial x_2}\right|_{\mathbf{x}=\mathbf{x}^{(0)}} + \cdots + \delta_n^{(0)} \left.\frac{\partial f_1}{\partial x_n}\right|_{\mathbf{x}=\mathbf{x}^{(0)}} = -f_1(\mathbf{x}^0), \ldots,$$

$$\delta_1^{(0)} \left.\frac{\partial f_n}{\partial x_1}\right|_{\mathbf{x}=\mathbf{x}^{(0)}} + \delta_2^{(0)} \left.\frac{\partial f_n}{\partial x_2}\right|_{\mathbf{x}=\mathbf{x}^{(0)}} + \cdots + \delta_n^{(0)} \left.\frac{\partial f_n}{\partial x_n}\right|_{\mathbf{x}=\mathbf{x}^{(0)}} = -f_n(\mathbf{x}^0). \tag{5.38}$$

By solving this system, we obtain the values $\delta_i^{(0)}$, $i = \overline{1, n}$. The new approximation of the solution is

$$\mathbf{x}^{(1)} = \mathbf{x}^{(0)} + \boldsymbol{\delta}^{(0)} \tag{5.39}$$

and the procedure continues, obtaining successively $\boldsymbol{\delta}^{(1)}$, $\mathbf{x}^{(2)}$, $\boldsymbol{\delta}^{(2)}$, $\mathbf{x}^{(3)}$, and so on.

5.5   THE GRADIENT METHOD

Let the equation be

$$\mathbf{f}(\mathbf{x}) = \mathbf{0}, \tag{5.40}$$

where $\mathbf{f} : \mathbb{R}^n \to \mathbb{R}^n$ is at least of class C^1 on a domain $\mathcal{D} \subset \mathbb{R}^n$, while $\mathbf{x} = \begin{bmatrix} x_1 & x_2 & \cdots & x_n \end{bmatrix}^{\mathrm{T}}$. Equation (5.40) may also be written in the form of a system with n unknowns

$$f_1(x_1, \ldots, x_n) = 0, \quad f_2(x_1, \ldots, x_n) = 0, \ldots, \quad f_n(x_1, \ldots, x_n) = 0. \tag{5.41}$$

Let us consider the function

$$U(\mathbf{x}) = \sum_{i=1}^{n} f_i^2(x_1, x_2, \ldots, x_n). \tag{5.42}$$

---

[4]It is easy to prove that the Newton method is equivalent to the Newton–Raphson method; moreover, they lead to the same results.

We observe that the solution $\bar{\mathbf{x}}$ of equation (5.40) is solution of the equation

$$U(\mathbf{x}) = 0 \tag{5.43}$$

too and reciprocally. We thus reduce the problem of solving equation (5.40) to an equivalent problem of determination of the absolute minimum of the function $U(\mathbf{x})$.

Let us denote by $\mathbf{x}^{(0)}$ the first approximation of the solution of equation (5.40), or the first approximation of the absolute minimum of function (5.42). We will draw through $\mathbf{x}^{(0)}$ the level hypersurface of the function $U(\mathbf{x}) = U(\mathbf{x}^{(0)})$ (Fig. 5.1). We will go along the normal to this hypersurface at the point P_0 until it pierces another hypersurface $U(\mathbf{x}) = U(\mathbf{x}^{(1)})$ where it meets the point P_1 of coordinate $\mathbf{x}^{(1)}$ with $U(\mathbf{x}^{(1)}) < U(\mathbf{x}^{(0)})$. Starting now from the point P_1 along the normal to the hypersurface $U(\mathbf{x}) = U(\mathbf{x}^{(1)})$, we obtain the point P_2 corresponding to the intersection of the normal with the hypersphere $U(\mathbf{x}) = U(\mathbf{x}^{(2)})$, where $U(\mathbf{x}^{(2)}) < U(\mathbf{x}^{(1)})$. Let this point of coordinate be $\mathbf{x}^{(2)}$. The procedure continues, obtaining thus the sequence of points $P_1, P_2, P_3, \ldots, P_n$ for which we have the sequence of relations

$$U(\mathbf{x}^{(1)}) > U(\mathbf{x}^{(2)}) > U(\mathbf{x}^{(3)}) > \cdots > U(\mathbf{x}^{(n)}) > \cdots \tag{5.44}$$

it follows that the sequence of points $P_1, P_2, \ldots, P_n, \ldots$ approaches the point P, which realizes the minimum value of the function $U(\mathbf{x})$.

The triangle OP_0P_1 leads to

$$\mathbf{x}^{(1)} = \mathbf{x}^{(0)} - \lambda_0 \nabla U(\mathbf{x}^{(0)}), \tag{5.45}$$

where ∇U means the gradient of the function U

$$\nabla U(\mathbf{x}) = \left[\frac{\partial U}{\partial x_1} \quad \frac{\partial U}{\partial x_2} \quad \cdots \quad \frac{\partial U}{\partial x_n} \right]^{\mathrm{T}}. \tag{5.46}$$

Let the function now be

$$\phi(\lambda_0) = U(\mathbf{x}^{(0)} - \lambda_0 \nabla U(\mathbf{x}^{(0)})). \tag{5.47}$$

We must search that value of the parameter λ_0 for which the function $\phi(\lambda_0)$ will be minimum, from which it follows that

$$\frac{\partial \phi}{\partial \lambda_0} = 0 \tag{5.48}$$

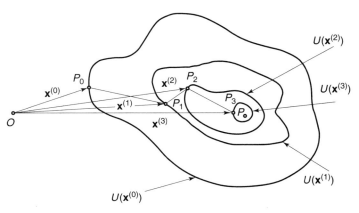

Figure 5.1   The gradient method.

or

$$\frac{\partial}{\partial \lambda_0} U(\mathbf{x}^{(0)} - \lambda_0 \nabla U(\mathbf{x}^{(0)})) = 0, \qquad (5.49)$$

λ_0 being the smallest positive solution of equation (5.49).

On the other hand, we have

$$\phi(\lambda_0) = \sum_{i=1}^{n} f_i^2(\mathbf{x}^{(0)} - \lambda_0 \nabla U(\mathbf{x}^{(0)})) = 0. \qquad (5.50)$$

Expanding the functions f_i into a Taylor series, supposing that $\lambda_0 \ll 1$ and neglecting the nonlinear terms in λ_0, we obtain the relation

$$\phi(\lambda_0) = \sum_{i=1}^{n} f_i^2 \left[\mathbf{x}^{(0)} - \lambda_0 \sum_{j=1}^{n} \left(\frac{\partial f_i(\mathbf{x}^{(0)})}{\partial x_j} \frac{\partial U(\mathbf{x}^{(0)})}{\partial x_j} \right) \right]. \qquad (5.51)$$

Condition (5.48) of minimum may be now written in the form

$$2 \sum_{i=1}^{n} \left\{ \left[f_i(\mathbf{x}^{(0)}) - \lambda_0 \sum_{j=1}^{n} \left(\frac{\partial f_i(\mathbf{x}^{(0)})}{\partial x_j} \frac{\partial U(\mathbf{x}^{(0)})}{\partial \mathbf{x}_j} \right) \right] \sum_{j=1}^{n} \left(\frac{\partial f_i(\mathbf{x}^{(0)})}{\partial x_j} \frac{\partial U(\mathbf{x}^{(0)})}{\partial x_j} \right) \right\} = 0, \qquad (5.52)$$

from which it follows that

$$\lambda_0 = \frac{\sum_{i=1}^{n} \left[f_i(\mathbf{x}^{(0)}) \sum_{j=1}^{n} \left(\frac{\partial f_i(\mathbf{x}^{(0)})}{\partial x_j} \frac{\partial f_i(\mathbf{x}^{(0)})}{\partial x_j} \right) \right]}{\sum_{i=1}^{n} \left[\sum_{j=1}^{n} \left(\frac{\partial f_i(\mathbf{x}^{(0)})}{\partial x_j} \frac{\partial f_i(\mathbf{x}^{(0)})}{\partial x_j} \right) \right]^2}. \qquad (5.53)$$

From the definition of the function $U(\mathbf{x})$ we have

$$\frac{\partial U}{\partial x_j} = \frac{\partial}{\partial x_j} \sum_{i=1}^{n} f_i^2(\mathbf{x}) = 2 \sum_{i=1}^{n} \left(f_i(\mathbf{x}) \frac{\partial f_i(\mathbf{x})}{\partial x_j} \right), \qquad (5.54)$$

$$\nabla U(\mathbf{x}) = 2 \left[\sum_{i=1}^{n} f_i(\mathbf{x}) \frac{\partial f_i(\mathbf{x})}{\partial x_1} \cdots \sum_{i=1}^{n} f_i(\mathbf{x}) \frac{\partial f_i(\mathbf{x})}{\partial x_n} \right]^{\mathrm{T}} = 2 \mathbf{J}(\mathbf{x}) \mathbf{f}(\mathbf{x}), \qquad (5.55)$$

where we have denoted the Jacobian of the vector function $\mathbf{f}$ by $\mathbf{J}(\mathbf{x})$,

$$\mathbf{J}(\mathbf{x}) = \begin{bmatrix} \dfrac{\partial f_1}{\partial x_1} & \dfrac{\partial f_1}{\partial x_2} & \cdots & \dfrac{\partial f_1}{\partial x_n} \\ \cdots & \cdots & \cdots & \cdots \\ \dfrac{\partial f_n}{\partial x_1} & \dfrac{\partial f_n}{\partial x_2} & \cdots & \dfrac{\partial f_n}{\partial x_n} \end{bmatrix}. \qquad (5.56)$$

We denote the scalar product by $\langle \cdot, \cdot \rangle$

$$\langle \mathbf{x}, \mathbf{y} \rangle = \mathbf{x}^{\mathrm{T}} \mathbf{y}, \qquad (5.57)$$

where

$$\mathbf{x} = \begin{bmatrix} x_1 & \cdots & x_n \end{bmatrix}^{\mathrm{T}}, \quad \mathbf{y} = \begin{bmatrix} y_1 & \cdots & y_n \end{bmatrix}^{\mathrm{T}}, \tag{5.58}$$

so that relation (5.53) may be written in a more compact form

$$2\lambda_0 = \frac{\langle \mathbf{f}(\mathbf{x}^{(0)}), \mathbf{J}(\mathbf{x}^{(0)})\mathbf{J}^{\mathrm{T}}(\mathbf{x}^{(0)})\mathbf{f}(\mathbf{x}^{(0)}) \rangle}{\langle \mathbf{J}(\mathbf{x}^{(0)})\mathbf{J}^{\mathrm{T}}(\mathbf{x}^{(0)})\mathbf{f}(\mathbf{x}^{(0)}), \mathbf{J}(\mathbf{x}^{(0)})\mathbf{J}^{\mathrm{T}}(\mathbf{x}^{(0)})\mathbf{f}(\mathbf{x}^{(0)}) \rangle}. \tag{5.59}$$

Relation (5.45) now becomes

$$\mathbf{x}^{(1)} = \mathbf{x}^{(0)} - 2\lambda_0 \mathbf{J}^{\mathrm{T}}(\mathbf{x}^{(0)})\mathbf{f}(\mathbf{x}^{(0)}). \tag{5.60}$$

Using the recurrence relation

$$\mathbf{x}^{(k+1)} = \mathbf{x}^{(k)} - 2\lambda_k \mathbf{J}^{\mathrm{T}}(\mathbf{x}^{(k)})\mathbf{f}(\mathbf{x}^{(k)}), \tag{5.61}$$

we thus obtain the sequence of vectors $\mathbf{x}^{(1)}, \ldots, \mathbf{x}^{(k)}, \ldots$, where

$$2\lambda_k = \frac{\langle \mathbf{f}(\mathbf{x}^{(k)}), \mathbf{J}(\mathbf{x}^{(k)})\mathbf{J}^{\mathrm{T}}(\mathbf{x}^{(k)})\mathbf{f}(\mathbf{x}^{(k)}) \rangle}{\langle \mathbf{J}(\mathbf{x}^{(k)})\mathbf{J}^{\mathrm{T}}(\mathbf{x}^{(k)})\mathbf{f}(\mathbf{x}^{(k)}), \mathbf{J}(\mathbf{x}^{(k)})\mathbf{J}^{\mathrm{T}}(\mathbf{x}^{(k)})\mathbf{f}(\mathbf{x}^{(k)}) \rangle}. \tag{5.62}$$

5.6   THE METHOD OF ENTIRE SERIES

Instead of solving the system of equations

$$f_k(x_1, x_2, \ldots, x_n) = 0, \quad k = \overline{1, n}, \tag{5.63}$$

we will solve the system formed by the equations

$$F_k(x_1, x_2, \ldots, x_n, \lambda) = 0, \quad k = \overline{1, n}, \tag{5.64}$$

where F_k, $k = \overline{1, n}$, are analytic on a neighborhood of the solution $\overline{\mathbf{x}}$, while λ is a real parameter.

The functions $F_k(\mathbf{x}, \lambda)$ fulfill the condition that the solution of system (5.64) is known for $\lambda = 0$, while for $\lambda = 1$ we have $F_k(\mathbf{x}, 1) = f_k(\mathbf{x})$, $k = \overline{1, n}$. Moreover, F_k, $k = \overline{1, n}$, are analytic in λ.

Moreover, we also suppose that for $0 \leq \lambda \leq 1$ system (5.64) admits an analytic solution $\mathbf{x}(\lambda)$, while $\overline{\mathbf{x}} = \mathbf{x}(0)$ is an isolated solution of system (5.63).

Expanding into a Taylor series the solution $x_j(\lambda)$ around 0, we have

$$x_j(\lambda) = x_j(0) + \lambda x_j'(0) + \frac{\lambda^2}{2!} x_j''(0) + \cdots, \quad j = \overline{1, n}. \tag{5.65}$$

Differentiating relation (5.64) with respect to λ, we obtain

$$\sum_{j=1}^{n} \frac{\partial F_k}{\partial x_j} x_j'(\lambda) + \frac{\partial F_k}{\partial \lambda} = 0, \quad k = \overline{1, n}. \tag{5.66}$$

If we denote by $\overline{\mathbf{x}}^{(0)} = \overline{\mathbf{x}}(0)$ the solution for $\lambda = 0$, then relation (5.66) leads to

$$\sum_{j=1}^{n} \frac{\partial F_k(\overline{\mathbf{x}}^{(0)}, 0)}{\partial x_j} x_j'(0) + \frac{\partial F_k(\overline{\mathbf{x}}^{(0)}, 0)}{\partial \lambda} = 0, \quad k = \overline{1, n}, \tag{5.67}$$

and if

$$\det \left[\frac{\partial F_k\left(\overline{\mathbf{x}}^{(0)}, 0\right)}{\partial x_j} \right] \neq 0, \tag{5.68}$$

then from equation (5.67) we obtain the values $x_j'(0)$, $j = \overline{1, n}$.

Differentiating once more expression (5.66) with respect to λ, we get

$$\sum_{j=1}^{n} \frac{\partial F_k}{\partial x_j} x_j''(\lambda) + \sum_{j=1}^{n} \sum_{l=1}^{n} \frac{\partial^2 F_k}{\partial x_j \partial x_l} x_j'(\lambda) x_l'(\lambda)$$

$$+ 2 \sum_{j=1}^{n} \frac{\partial^2 F_k}{\partial x_j \partial \lambda} x_j'(\lambda) + \frac{\partial^2 F_k}{\partial \lambda^2} = 0, \quad k = \overline{1, n}. \tag{5.69}$$

Making now $\lambda = 0$, expression (5.69) becomes

$$\sum_{j=1}^{n} \frac{\partial F_k(\overline{\mathbf{x}}^{(0)}, 0)}{\partial x_j} x_j''(0) + \sum_{j=1}^{n} \sum_{l=1}^{n} \frac{\partial^2 F_k(\overline{\mathbf{x}}^{(0)}, 0)}{\partial x_j \partial x_l} x_j'(0) x_l'(0)$$

$$+ 2 \sum_{j=1}^{n} \frac{\partial^2 F_k(\overline{\mathbf{x}}^{(0)}, 0)}{\partial x_j \partial \lambda} x_j'(0) + \frac{\partial^2 F_k(\overline{\mathbf{x}}^{(0)}, 0)}{\partial \lambda^2} = 0, \quad k = \overline{1, n}; \tag{5.70}$$

because the values $x_j'(0)$, $j = \overline{1, n}$, are known, it follows that $x_j''(0)$ are determined from equation (5.70).

Obviously, the procedure of differentiation may continue now with relation (5.69), solving $x_j'''(0)$, and so on.

The solution of system (5.63) is thus given by expression (5.65).

5.7   NUMERICAL EXAMPLE

Example 5.1   Let us consider the nonlinear system

$$50x_1 + x_1^2 + x_2^2 + x_2^3 = 52, \quad 50x_2 + x_1^3 + x_2^4 = 52, \tag{5.71}$$

which has the obvious solution $x_1 = 1$ and $x_2 = 1$.

To determine the solution by Jacobi's method, we write this system in the form

$$x_1 = 1.04 - 0.02x_1^2 - 0.02x_2^3 = g_1(x_1, x_2), \quad x_2 = 1.04 - 0.02x_1^3 - 0.02x_2^4 = g_2(x_1, x_2). \tag{5.72}$$

The Jacobi matrix is given by

$$\mathbf{J} = \begin{bmatrix} \dfrac{\partial g_1}{\partial x_1} & \dfrac{\partial g_1}{\partial x_2} \\[2mm] \dfrac{\partial g_2}{\partial x_1} & \dfrac{\partial g_2}{\partial x_2} \end{bmatrix} = \begin{bmatrix} -0.04x_1 & -0.06x_2^2 \\[2mm] -0.06x_1^2 & -0.08x_2^3 \end{bmatrix} \tag{5.73}$$

and we observe that $\|J\| < 1$ for a neighborhood of the solution $\begin{bmatrix} 1 & 1 \end{bmatrix}^{\mathrm{T}}$.

Let use choose as vector of start

$$\mathbf{x}^{(0)} = \begin{bmatrix} 1.05 & 0.92 \end{bmatrix}^{\mathrm{T}}. \tag{5.74}$$

The relation of recurrence reads

$$\begin{bmatrix} x_1^{(n+1)} \\ x_2^{(n+1)} \end{bmatrix} = \begin{bmatrix} 1.04 - 0.02\left(x_1^{(n)}\right)^2 - 0.02(x_2^{(n)})^3 \\ 1.04 - 0.02(x_1^{(n)})^3 - 0.02(x_2^{(n)})^4 \end{bmatrix}, \tag{5.75}$$

the calculations being given in Table 5.1.

To apply Newton's method, we write

$$\mathbf{F}(\mathbf{x}) = \begin{bmatrix} f_1\left(x_1, x_2\right) \\ f_2(x_1, x_2) \end{bmatrix} = \begin{bmatrix} 50x_1 + x_1^2 + x_2^3 - 52 \\ 50x_2 + x_1^3 + x_2^3 - 52 \end{bmatrix}, \tag{5.76}$$

so that the Jacobian is

$$\mathbf{J}(\mathbf{x}) = \begin{bmatrix} 50 + 2x_1 & 3x_2^2 \\ 3x_1^2 & 50 + 4x_2^3 \end{bmatrix}, \tag{5.77}$$

from which

$$\mathbf{J}^{-1}(\mathbf{x}) = \frac{1}{(50 + 2x_1)(50 + 4x_2^3) - 9x_1^2 x_2^2} \begin{bmatrix} 50 + 4x_2^3 & -3x_2^2 \\ -3x_1^2 & 50 + 2x_1 \end{bmatrix}. \tag{5.78}$$

The recurrence formula reads

$$\mathbf{x}^{(n+1)} = \mathbf{x}^{(n)} - \mathbf{J}^{-1}(\mathbf{x}^{(n)})\mathbf{F}(\mathbf{x}^{(n)}), \tag{5.79}$$

the calculation being systematized in Table 5.2.

In the case of the modified Newton method, the recurrence relation reads

$$\mathbf{x}^{(n+1)} = \mathbf{x}^{(n)} - \mathbf{J}^{-1}(\mathbf{x}^{(0)})\mathbf{F}(\mathbf{x}^{(n)}), \tag{5.80}$$

where

$$\mathbf{J}^{-1}(\mathbf{x}^{(0)}) = \begin{bmatrix} 0.019252 & -0.000920 \\ -0.001199 & 0.018884 \end{bmatrix}, \tag{5.81}$$

The calculations are given in Table 5.3.

TABLE 5.1   Solution of Equation (5.71) by Jacobi's Method

Step	$x_1^{(n)}$	$x_2^{(n)}$
0	1.05	0.92
1	1.002376	1.002520
2	0.999753	0.999655
3	1.000031	1.000042
4	0.999996	0.999995
5	1.000000	1.000001

TABLE 5.2   Solution of Equation (5.71) by Newton's Method

Step	$x_1^{(n)}$	$x_2^{(n)}$	$\mathbf{J}^{-1}(x^n)$		$\mathbf{F}(x^{(n)})$
0	1.05	0.92	$\begin{bmatrix} 0.019252 & -0.000920 \\ -0.001199 & 0.018884 \end{bmatrix}$		$\begin{bmatrix} 2.381188 \\ -4.125982 \end{bmatrix}$
1	1.000361	1.000770	$\begin{bmatrix} 0.019252 & -0.001075 \\ -0.001072 & 0.018575 \end{bmatrix}$		$\begin{bmatrix} 0.021084 \\ 0.042667 \end{bmatrix}$
2	1.000001	1.000000			

TABLE 5.3   Solution of Equation (5.71) by Newton's Modified Method

Step	$x_1^{(n)}$	$x_2^{(n)}$	$\mathbf{F}(x^{(n)})$
0	1.05	0.92	$\begin{bmatrix} 2.381188 \\ -4.125982 \end{bmatrix}$
1	1.000361	1.000770	$\begin{bmatrix} 0.021084 \\ 0.042667 \end{bmatrix}$
2	0.999994	0.999990	$\begin{bmatrix} -0.000342 \\ -0.000558 \end{bmatrix}$
3	1.000000	1.000000	

The problem is put to see if Newton's method has been correctly applied, that is, if the conditions of Theorem 5.1 are fulfilled. We thus calculate successively

$$\left\| \mathbf{J}^{-1}(\mathbf{x}_0) \right\|_\infty = \left\| \begin{bmatrix} 0.019252 & -0.000920 \\ -0.001199 & 0.018884 \end{bmatrix} \right\|_\infty = 0.020172 = \alpha, \tag{5.82}$$

$$\left\| \mathbf{x}^{(1)} - \mathbf{x}^{(0)} \right\|_\infty = \left\| \begin{bmatrix} 1.000361 & -1.05 \\ 1.000770 & -0.92 \end{bmatrix} \right\|_\infty = 0.08077 = \beta, \tag{5.83}$$

$$\sum_{i=1}^{2} \sum_{j=1}^{2} \left\| \left[\frac{\partial^2 f_i}{\partial x_i \partial x_j} \right] \right\|_\infty = \left\| \begin{bmatrix} 2 & 0 \\ 0 & 6x_2 \end{bmatrix} \right\|_\infty + \left\| \begin{bmatrix} 6x_1 & 0 \\ 0 & 12x_2^2 \end{bmatrix} \right\|_\infty. \tag{5.84}$$

Choosing now a neighborhood of the point $(1, 1)$, given by

$$\left\| \mathbf{x} - \begin{bmatrix} 1 \\ 1 \end{bmatrix} \right\|_\infty < 0.1, \tag{5.85}$$

we deduce

$$\sum_{i=1}^{2} \sum_{j=1}^{2} \left\| \left[\frac{\partial^2 f_i}{\partial x_i \partial x_j} \right] \right\|_\infty = |6x_2| + |12x_2^2| < 6 \times 1.1 + 12 \times 1.1^2 = 21.12 = \gamma. \tag{5.86}$$

It follows that the relation

$$2n\alpha\beta\gamma = 2 \times 2 \times 0.020172 \times 0.08077 \times 21.12 = 0.1376 < 1; \tag{5.87}$$

hence, Newton's method has been correctly applied.

Let us now pass to the solving of system (5.71) by means of the Newton–Raphson method. To do this, we successively calculate

$$\frac{\partial f_1}{\partial x_1} = 50 + 2x_1, \quad \frac{\partial f_1}{\partial x_2} = 3x_2^2, \quad \frac{\partial f_2}{\partial x_1} = 3x_1^2, \quad \frac{\partial f_2}{\partial x_2} = 50 + 4x_2^3, \tag{5.88}$$

$$\frac{\partial f_1}{\partial x_1}\bigg|_{\mathbf{x}=\mathbf{x}^{(0)}} = 52.1, \quad \frac{\partial f_1}{\partial x_2}\bigg|_{\mathbf{x}=\mathbf{x}^{(0)}} = 2.5392, \quad \frac{\partial f_2}{\partial x_1}\bigg|_{\mathbf{x}=\mathbf{x}^{(0)}} = 3.3075,$$

$$\frac{\partial f_2}{\partial x_2}\bigg|_{\mathbf{x}=\mathbf{x}^{(0)}} = 53.114752, \quad f_1(\mathbf{x}^{(0)}) = 2.381188, \quad f_2(\mathbf{x}^{(0)}) = -4.125982 \tag{5.89}$$

and obtain the system

$$52.1\delta_1^{(0)} + 2.5392\delta_2^{(0)} = -2.381188, \quad 3.3075\delta_1^{(0)} + 53.114752\delta_2^{(0)} = 4.125982, \tag{5.90}$$

with the solution

$$\delta_1^{(0)} = -0.049641, \quad \delta_2^{(0)} = 0.080772, \tag{5.91}$$

so that

$$\mathbf{x}^{(1)} = \mathbf{x}^{(0)} + \begin{bmatrix} \delta_1^{(0)} \\ \delta_2^{(0)} \end{bmatrix} = \begin{bmatrix} 1.000359 \\ 1.000772 \end{bmatrix}. \tag{5.92}$$

In the following step, we have

$$\frac{\partial f_1}{\partial x_1}\bigg|_{\mathbf{x}=\mathbf{x}^{(0)}} = 52.000718, \quad \frac{\partial f_1}{\partial x_2}\bigg|_{\mathbf{x}=\mathbf{x}^{(0)}} = 3.004634, \quad \frac{\partial f_2}{\partial x_1}\bigg|_{\mathbf{x}=\mathbf{x}^{(0)}} = 3.002154,$$

$$\frac{\partial f_2}{\partial x_2}\bigg|_{\mathbf{x}=\mathbf{x}^{(0)}} = 54.009271, \quad f_1(\mathbf{x}^{(0)}) = 0.020986, \quad f_2(\mathbf{x}^{(0)}) = 0.042769, \tag{5.93}$$

the system

$$52.000718\delta_1^{(1)} + 3.004634\delta_2^{(1)} = -0.020986, \quad 3.002154\delta_1^{(1)} + 54.009271\delta_2^{(1)} = -0.042769, \tag{5.94}$$

and the solution

$$\delta_1^{(1)} = -0.000359, \quad \delta_2^{(1)} = -0.000772. \tag{5.95}$$

It follows that

$$\mathbf{x}^{(2)} = \mathbf{x}^{(1)} + \begin{bmatrix} \delta_1^{(1)} \\ \delta_2^{(1)} \end{bmatrix} = \begin{bmatrix} 1.000000 \\ 1.000000 \end{bmatrix}. \tag{5.96}$$

We observe that the Newton and Newton–Raphson methods lead to the same solution (in the limits of the calculation approximates). As a matter of fact, the two methods are equivalent.

Let us now pass to the solution of system (5.71) by means of the gradient method.

We calculate successively

$$\mathbf{J}(\mathbf{x}) = \begin{bmatrix} 50 + 2x_1 & 3x_2^2 \\ 3x_1^2 & 50 + 4x_2^3 \end{bmatrix}, \tag{5.97}$$

$$\mathbf{J}^T(\mathbf{x}) = \begin{bmatrix} 50 + 2x_1 & 3x_1^2 \\ 3x_2^2 & 50 + 4x_2^3 \end{bmatrix}, \tag{5.98}$$

$$\mathbf{F}(\mathbf{x}) = \begin{bmatrix} 50x_1 + x_1^2 + x_2^3 - 52 \\ 50x_2 + x_1^3 + x_2^4 - 52 \end{bmatrix}, \tag{5.99}$$

$$\mathbf{J}^T(\mathbf{x})\mathbf{F}(\mathbf{x}) = \begin{bmatrix} (50 + 2x_1)(50x_1 + x_1^2 + x_2^3 - 52) + 3x_1^2(50x_2 + x_1^3 + x_2^4 - 52) \\ 3x_2^2(50x_1 + x_1^2 + x_2^3 - 52) + (50 + 4x_2^3)(50x_2 + x_1^3 + x_2^4 - 52) \end{bmatrix}, \tag{5.100}$$

$$\mathbf{J}(\mathbf{x})\mathbf{J}^T(\mathbf{x}) = \begin{bmatrix} (50 + 2x_1)^2 + 9x_2^4 & 3x_1^2(50 + 2x_1) \\ 3x_1^2(50 + 2x_1) + 3x_2^2(50 + 4x_2)^3 & 9x_4^4 + (50 + 4x_2^3)^2 \end{bmatrix}, \tag{5.101}$$

The calculations are contained in Table 5.4.
Let us consider the system

$$\mathbf{F}(\mathbf{x}, \lambda) = \begin{bmatrix} 50x_1 + \lambda(x_1^2 + x_2^3) - 52 \\ 50x_2 + \lambda(x_1^3 + x_2^4) - 52 \end{bmatrix} = \begin{bmatrix} 0 \\ 0 \end{bmatrix}, \tag{5.102}$$

where λ is a real parameter. For $\lambda = 1$ we obtain system (5.71), while for $\lambda = 0$, the solution of system (5.102) becomes obvious

$$\mathbf{x}(0) = \begin{bmatrix} 1.04 \\ 1.04 \end{bmatrix}. \tag{5.103}$$

We observe that the conditions asked by the method of entire series are fulfilled.

TABLE 5.4   The Solution of Equation (5.71) by the Gradient Method

Step	$\mathbf{x}^{(n)}$	$2\lambda_n$
0	$\begin{bmatrix} 1.05 \\ 0.92 \end{bmatrix}$	0.0003957
1	$\begin{bmatrix} 1.0076065 \\ 1.0043272 \end{bmatrix}$	0.0003189
2	$\begin{bmatrix} 1.0004987 \\ 0.9995063 \end{bmatrix}$	0.0004063
3	$\begin{bmatrix} 1.0000230 \\ 1.0000285 \end{bmatrix}$	0.0003117
4	$\begin{bmatrix} 1.0000002 \\ 1.0000002 \end{bmatrix}$	0.0003126

We have

$$\frac{\partial F_1}{\partial x_1} = 50 + 2\lambda x_1, \quad \frac{\partial F_1}{\partial x_2} = 3\lambda x_2^2, \quad \frac{\partial F_2}{\partial x_1} = 3\lambda x_1^2, \quad \frac{\partial F_2}{\partial x_2} = 50 + 4\lambda x_2^3, \quad (5.104)$$

$$\frac{\partial F_1(\mathbf{x}^{(0)}, 0)}{\partial x_1} = 50, \quad \frac{\partial F_1(\mathbf{x}^{(0)}, 0)}{\partial x_2} = 0, \quad \frac{\partial F_2(\mathbf{x}^{(0)}, 0)}{\partial x_1} = 0, \quad \frac{\partial F_2(\mathbf{x}^{(0)}, 0)}{\partial x_2} = 50, \quad (5.105)$$

$$\frac{\partial F_1}{\partial \lambda} = x_1^2 + x_2^3, \quad \frac{\partial F_2}{\partial \lambda} = x_1^3 + x_2^4, \quad (5.106)$$

$$\frac{\partial F_1(\mathbf{x}^{(0)}, 0)}{\partial \lambda} = 1.04^2 + 1.04^3 = 2.206464, \quad \frac{\partial F_2(\mathbf{x}^{(0)}, 0)}{\partial \lambda} = 1.04^3 + 1.04^4 = 2.29472256,$$

$$(5.107)$$

where

$$\mathbf{x}^{(0)} = \mathbf{x}(0) = \begin{bmatrix} 1.04 \\ 1.04 \end{bmatrix}. \quad (5.108)$$

It follows that the system

$$50x_1'(0) + 2.206464 = 0, \quad 50x_2'(0) + 2.29472256 = 0, \quad (5.109)$$

with the solution

$$x_1'(0) = -0.04412928, \quad x_2'(0) = -0.045894451. \quad (5.110)$$

On the other hand,

$$\frac{\partial^2 F_1}{\partial x_1^2} = 2\lambda, \quad \frac{\partial^2 F_1}{\partial x_1 \partial x_2} = 0, \quad \frac{\partial^2 F_2}{\partial x_1 \partial x_2} = 0, \quad \frac{\partial^2 F_2}{\partial x_2^2} = 12\lambda x_2^2, \quad (5.111)$$

$$\frac{\partial^2 F_1}{\partial x_1 \partial \lambda} = 2x_1, \quad \frac{\partial^2 F_1}{\partial x_2 \partial \lambda} = 3x_2^2, \quad \frac{\partial^2 F_2}{\partial x_1 \partial \lambda} = 3x_1^2, \quad \frac{\partial^2 F_2}{\partial x_2 \partial \lambda} = 4x_2^3, \quad (5.112)$$

$$\frac{\partial^2 F_1}{\partial \lambda^2} = 0, \quad \frac{\partial^2 F_2}{\partial \lambda^2} = 0, \quad (5.113)$$

$$\frac{\partial^2 F_1(\mathbf{x}^{(0)}, 0)}{\partial x_1^2} = 0, \quad \frac{\partial^2 F_2(\mathbf{x}^{(0)}, 0)}{\partial x_2^2} = 0, \quad (5.114)$$

$$\frac{\partial^2 F_1(\mathbf{x}^{(0)}, 0)}{\partial x_1 \partial \lambda} = 2.08, \quad \frac{\partial^2 F_1(\mathbf{x}^{(0)}, 0)}{\partial x_2 \partial \lambda} = 3.2448,$$

$$(5.115)$$

$$\frac{\partial^2 F_2(\mathbf{x}^{(0)}, 0)}{\partial x_1 \partial \lambda} = 3.2448, \quad \frac{\partial^2 F_2(\mathbf{x}^{(0)}, 0)}{\partial x_2 \partial \lambda} = 4.499456.$$

There follows the system

$$50x_1''(0) - 0.481414433 = 0, \quad 50x_2''(0) - 0.699381501 = 0, \quad (5.116)$$

with the solution

$$x_1''(0) = 0.009628288, \quad x_2''(0) = 0.01398763. \quad (5.117)$$

We obtain the values

$$x_1 \approx x_1(0) + x_1'(0) + \frac{1}{2}x_1''(0) = 1.000684864,$$

$$(5.118)$$

$$x_2 \approx x_2(0) + x_2'(0) + \frac{1}{2}x_2''(0) = 1.001099364.$$

5.8 APPLICATIONS

Problem 5.1

Let us consider the plane articulated mechanism in Figure 5.2, where the dimensions $OA = l_1$, $AB = l_2$, $BC = l_3$, $AD = l_2^*$, $DE = l_4$, $EF = l_5$, the angle α, the coordinates X_C, Y_C, X_F, Y_F and the initial position $\phi_i = \phi_i^\circ$, $i = \overline{1,5}$, are known.
  Determine and represent graphically the functions $\phi_i(\phi_1)$, $i = \overline{2,5}$.
  Numerical application: $l = 0.2$ m, $l_1 = l$, $l_2 = 3l$, $l_3 = 3l$, $l_2^* = 4l$, $l_4 = 2l$, $l_5 = 2l\sqrt{3}$, $\alpha = 0°$, $X_C = 4l$, $Y_C = 0$, $X_F = 5l$, $Y_F = 0$, $\phi_1^\circ = 0°$, $\phi_2^\circ = 60°$, $\phi_3^\circ = 60°$, $\phi_4^\circ = 0°$, $\phi_5^\circ = -90°$, $\omega = 100$ s^{-1}, the imposed precision being $\varepsilon = 0.0001$, while the variation of the angle ϕ_1 is $\Delta\phi_1 = 1°$.

Solution:

  1. Theory
The vector equations

$$\mathbf{OA} + \mathbf{AB} + \mathbf{BC} = \mathbf{OC}, \quad \mathbf{OA} + \mathbf{AD} + \mathbf{DE} + \mathbf{EF} = \mathbf{OF}, \quad (5.119)$$

projected on the axes OX, OY, the notations

$$\begin{aligned}
f_1 &= l_1 \cos\phi_1 + l_2 \cos\phi_2 + l_3 \cos\phi_3 - X_C, \\
f_2 &= l_1 \sin\phi_1 + l_2 \sin\phi_2 + l_3 \sin\phi_3 - Y_C, \\
f_3 &= l_1 \cos\phi_1 + l_2^* \cos(\phi_2 + \alpha) + l_4 \cos\phi_4 + l_5 \cos\phi_5 - X_F, \\
f_4 &= l_1 \sin\phi_1 + l_2^* \sin(\phi_2 + \alpha) + l_4 \sin\phi_4 + l_5 \sin\phi_5 - Y_F,
\end{aligned} \quad (5.120)$$

being used, lead to the system of nonlinear equations

$$f_i(\phi_2, \phi_3, \phi_4, \phi_5) = 0, \quad i = \overline{2,5}; \quad (5.121)$$

we must determine the unknowns ϕ_2, ϕ_3, ϕ_4, ϕ_5 in function of the angle ϕ_1.

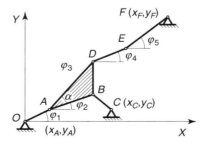

Figure 5.2 Problem 5.1.

Denoting by [**J**] the Jacobian

$$[\mathbf{J}] = \begin{bmatrix} -l_2 \sin \phi_2 & -l_3 \sin \phi_3 & 0 & 0 \\ l_2 \cos \phi_2 & l_3 \cos \phi_3 & 0 & 0 \\ -l_2^* \sin(\phi_2 + \alpha) & 0 & -l_4 \sin \phi_4 & -l_5 \sin \phi_5 \\ l_2^* \cos(\phi_2 + \alpha) & 0 & l_4 \cos \phi_4 & l_5 \cos \phi_5 \end{bmatrix} \qquad (5.122)$$

and by $\{\phi\}$, $\{\mathbf{f}\}$, $\{\Delta\phi\}$ the column matrices

$$\{\phi\} = \begin{bmatrix} \phi_2 & \phi_3 & \phi_4 & \phi_5 \end{bmatrix}^T, \ \{\mathbf{f}\} = \begin{bmatrix} f_2 & f_3 & f_4 & f_5 \end{bmatrix}^T, \ \{\Delta\phi\} = \begin{bmatrix} \Delta\phi_2 & \Delta\phi_3 & \Delta\phi_4 & \Delta\phi_5 \end{bmatrix}^T,$$
$$(5.123)$$

we obtain the equation
$$[\mathbf{J}]\{\Delta\phi\} = -\{\mathbf{f}\}, \qquad (5.124)$$

from which, by means of the known initial values ϕ_i°, $i = \overline{1,5}$, we determine $\{\Delta\phi\}$; then $\{\phi\} \mapsto \{\phi^\circ\} + \{\Delta\phi\}$, and the iteration process is continued until $|\Delta\phi_i| < \varepsilon$, $i = \overline{2,5}$, ε becomes the imposed precision.

After determination of the angles ϕ_i, $i = \overline{2,5}$, an increment $\Delta\phi_1 = 1°$ of the angle ϕ_1 is given; the values known from the previous step are considered to be approximate values for ϕ_i, $i = \overline{2,5}$, and the iteration process is taken again.

2. Numerical calculation

The results of the simulation are presented in Table 5.5 and graphically are plotted in the diagrams of Figure 5.3, Figure 5.4, Figure 5.5, and Figure 5.6.

Problem 5.2

We consider the rigid solid in Figure 5.7 suspended by six bars $A_{0i}A_i$, $i = \overline{1,6}$, spherical articulated and having lengths variable in time

$$l_i(t) = l_{0i} + s_i(t), \quad s_i(0) = 0, \quad i = \overline{1,6}. \qquad (5.125)$$

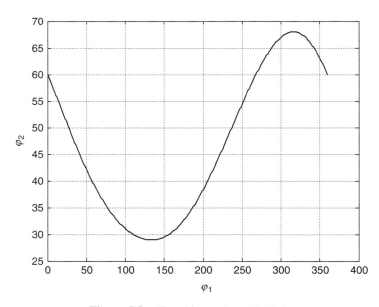

Figure 5.3   Time history $\phi_2 = \phi_2(\phi_1)$.

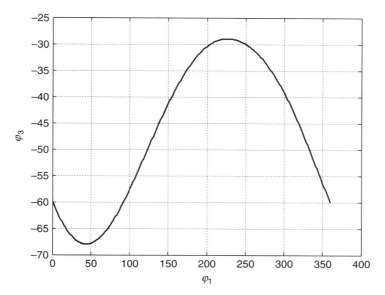

Figure 5.4   Time history $\phi_3 = \phi_3(\phi_1)$.

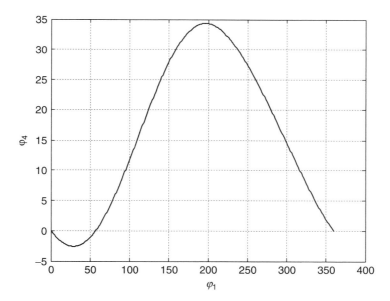

Figure 5.5   Time history $\phi_4 = \phi_4(\phi_1)$.

In particular, this may be the mechanical model of a Stewart platform.

The position of the rigid solid with respect to a fixed frame of reference O_0XYZ is defined by the position of the frame of reference rigidly linked to the body $Oxyz$, by the coordinates X_O, Y_O, Z_O of the point O and by the Bryan angles ψ, θ, ϕ, respectively.

Knowing the coordinates x_i, y_i, z_i of the points A_i, $i = \overline{1,6}$, in the system $Oxyz$, the coordinates X_{0i}, Y_{0i}, Z_{0i} of the points A_{0i}, $i = \overline{1,6}$, in the system O_0XYZ, the functions $s_i(t)$, $i = \overline{1,6}$, the initial position X_O°, Y_O°, Z_O°, ψ°, θ°, ϕ°, the error ε and the step Δt, determine the functions $X_O(t)$, $Y_O(t)$, $Z_O(t)$, $\psi(t)$, $\theta(t)$, $\phi(t)$ and represent them graphically.

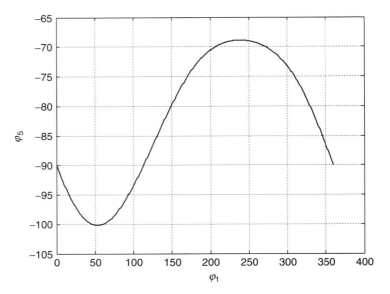

Figure 5.6   Time history $\phi_5 = \phi_5(\phi_1)$.

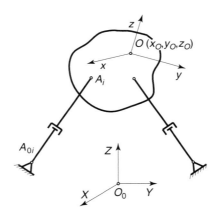

Figure 5.7   Problem 5.2.

Numerical application (Fig. 5.8): $l = 1$ m; $l_{0i} = l$, $i = \overline{1,6}$; $s_1(t) = (1/100) \sin \pi t$; $s_i(t) = 0$, $i = \overline{2,6}$; the coordinates of the points A_{0i}, A_i are given in Table 5.6.

We know $X_O^\circ = Y_O^\circ = Z_O^\circ = 0$ m, $\psi^\circ = \theta^\circ = \phi^\circ = 0$ rad, $\varepsilon = 10^{-6}$, $\Delta t = 0.05$ s too.

Solution:

1. Theory

   1.1. Notations

      We denote

      - X_i, Y_i, Z_i—the coordinates of the points A_i, $i = \overline{1,6}$ in the system $O_0 XYZ$;
      - $\{\mathbf{R}_i\}$, $\{\mathbf{R}_O\}$, $\{\mathbf{r}_i\}$, $i = \overline{1,6}$—column matrices defined by the relations

$$\{\mathbf{R}_i\} = \begin{bmatrix} X_i & Y_i & Z_i \end{bmatrix}^{\mathrm{T}}, \quad \{\mathbf{R}_O\} = \begin{bmatrix} X_O & Y_O & Z_O \end{bmatrix}^{\mathrm{T}}, \quad \{\mathbf{r}_i\} = \begin{bmatrix} x_i & y_i & z_i \end{bmatrix}^{\mathrm{T}};$$
$$(5.126)$$

TABLE 5.5   Results of the Simulation

$\phi_1[°]$	$\phi_2[°]$	$\phi_3[°]$	$\phi_4[°]$	$\phi_5[°]$
0.000000	60.000000	−60.000000	0.000000	−90.000000
10.000000	56.481055	−63.073225	−1.425165	−93.194507
20.000000	52.744084	−65.497920	−2.303616	−95.958155
30.000000	49.001803	−67.131160	−2.561647	−98.101199
40.000000	45.423080	−67.906509	−2.163048	−99.505742
50.000000	42.122571	−67.829804	−1.112080	−100.129729
60.000000	39.165924	−66.961696	0.551096	−99.994181
70.000000	36.582735	−65.396930	2.758832	−99.163908
80.000000	34.380507	−63.247016	5.424664	−97.729573
90.000000	32.556126	−60.628613	8.450173	−95.794641
100.000000	31.103960	−57.657128	11.729479	−93.467451
110.000000	30.020982	−54.444041	15.151752	−90.857173
120.000000	29.309571	−51.096361	18.602544	−88.072056
130.000000	28.978502	−47.716900	21.964860	−85.218490
140.000000	29.042278	−44.404335	25.120966	−82.399651
150.000000	29.518760	−41.252238	27.955835	−79.712771
160.000000	30.425042	−38.346622	30.362862	−77.244546
170.000000	31.771829	−35.762068	32.251753	−75.065015
180.000000	33.557310	−33.557310	33.557310	−73.221345
190.000000	35.762068	−31.771829	34.246675	−71.733836
200.000000	38.346622	−30.425042	34.322340	−70.596343
210.000000	41.252238	−29.518760	33.819449	−69.781847
220.000000	44.404335	−29.042278	32.798103	−69.251836
230.000000	47.716900	−28.978502	31.333094	−68.966865
240.000000	51.096361	−29.309571	29.503898	−68.895743
250.000000	54.444041	−30.020982	27.386860	−69.021894
260.000000	57.657128	−31.103960	25.050335	−69.346594
270.000000	60.628613	−32.556126	22.552622	−69.889466
280.000000	63.247016	−34.380507	19.942121	−70.686657
290.000000	65.396930	−36.582735	17.259152	−71.786823
300.000000	66.961696	−39.165924	14.539060	−73.244478
310.000000	67.829804	−42.122571	11.816457	−75.109848
320.000000	67.906509	−45.423080	9.130485	−77.414403
330.000000	67.131160	−49.001803	6.530785	−80.152359
340.000000	65.497920	−52.744084	4.083089	−83.261374
350.000000	63.073225	−56.481055	1.872281	−86.609758
360.000000	60.000000	−60.000000	0.000000	−90.000000

- $[\psi]$, $[\theta]$, $[\phi]$—rotation matrices

$$[\psi] = \begin{bmatrix} 1 & 0 & 0 \\ 0 & \cos\psi & -\sin\psi \\ 0 & \sin\psi & \cos\psi \end{bmatrix}, \quad [\theta] = \begin{bmatrix} \cos\theta & 0 & \sin\theta \\ 0 & 1 & 0 \\ -\sin\theta & 0 & \cos\theta \end{bmatrix},$$

$$[\phi] = \begin{bmatrix} \cos\phi & -\sin\phi & 0 \\ \sin\phi & \cos\phi & 0 \\ 0 & 0 & 1 \end{bmatrix}; \tag{5.127}$$

- $[\mathbf{U}_\psi]$, $[\mathbf{U}_\theta]$, $[\mathbf{U}_\phi]$—matrices given by the relations

$$[\mathbf{U}_\psi] = \begin{bmatrix} 0 & 0 & 0 \\ 0 & 0 & -1 \\ 0 & 1 & 0 \end{bmatrix}, \quad [\mathbf{U}_\theta] = \begin{bmatrix} 0 & 0 & 1 \\ 0 & 0 & 0 \\ -1 & 0 & 0 \end{bmatrix}, \quad [\mathbf{U}_\phi] = \begin{bmatrix} 0 & -1 & 0 \\ 1 & 0 & 0 \\ 0 & 0 & 0 \end{bmatrix};$$

(5.128)

- $[\mathbf{A}]$—rotation matrix

$$[\mathbf{A}] = [\mathbf{\psi}][\mathbf{\theta}][\mathbf{\phi}];$$

(5.129)

- $[\mathbf{A}_\psi]$, $[\mathbf{A}_\theta]$, $[\mathbf{A}_\phi]$—partial derivatives of the rotation matrix, which are written in the form

$$[\mathbf{A}_\psi] = [\mathbf{U}_\psi][\mathbf{A}], \quad [\mathbf{A}_\theta] = [\mathbf{A}][\mathbf{\phi}]^{\mathrm{T}}[\mathbf{U}_\theta][\mathbf{\phi}], \quad [\mathbf{A}_\phi] = [\mathbf{A}][\mathbf{U}_\phi];$$

(5.130)

- f_i, $i = \overline{1,6}$—functions of variables X_O, Y_O, Z_O, ψ, θ, ϕ, defined by the relations

$$\{f_i\} = [\{\mathbf{R}_i\}^{\mathrm{T}} - \{\mathbf{R}_{0i}\}^{\mathrm{T}}]\{\{\mathbf{R}_i\} - \{\mathbf{R}_{0i}\}\} - (l_{0i} + s_i)^2, \quad i = \overline{1,6};$$

(5.131)

- $\{\mathbf{f}\}$—the column matrix

$$\{\mathbf{f}\} = \begin{bmatrix} f_1 & f_2 & f_3 & f_4 & f_5 & f_6 \end{bmatrix}^{\mathrm{T}};$$

(5.132)

- $\{\mathbf{q}\}$, $\{\Delta\mathbf{q}\}$—the column matrices

$$\{\mathbf{q}\} = \begin{bmatrix} X_O & Y_O & Z_O & \psi & \theta & \phi \end{bmatrix}^{\mathrm{T}},$$

$$\{\Delta\mathbf{q}\} = \begin{bmatrix} \Delta X_O & \Delta Y_O & \Delta Z_O & \Delta\psi & \Delta\theta & \Delta\phi \end{bmatrix}^{\mathrm{T}};$$

(5.133)

- $[\mathbf{B}_i]$—matrix given by the relation

$$[\mathbf{B}_i] = \begin{bmatrix} [\mathbf{A}_\psi]\{\mathbf{r}_i\} & [\mathbf{A}_\theta]\{\mathbf{r}_i\} & [\mathbf{A}_\phi]\{\mathbf{r}_i\} \end{bmatrix}, \quad i = \overline{1,6}.$$

(5.134)

1.2. Computation relations

The column matrices $\{\mathbf{R}_i\}$, $\{\mathbf{R}_O\}$, $\{\mathbf{r}_i\}$ are dependent on the relation

$$\{\mathbf{R}_i\} = \{\mathbf{R}_O\} + [\mathbf{A}]\{\mathbf{r}_i\}, \quad i = \overline{1,6}.$$

(5.135)

The conditions

$$(\mathbf{A}_{0i}\mathbf{A}_i)^2 = (l_{01} + s_i)^2, \quad i = \overline{1,6}$$

(5.136)

are transcribed in the system of nonlinear equations

$$f_i = 0, \quad i = \overline{1,6},$$

(5.137)

the solution of which leads to the equation

$$[\mathbf{J}]\{\Delta\mathbf{q}\} = -\{\mathbf{f}\},$$

(5.138)

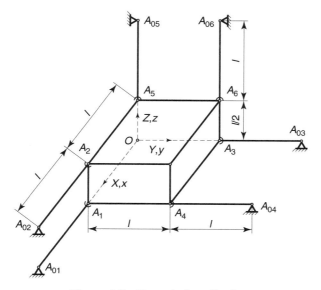

Figure 5.8   Numerical application.

TABLE 5.6   Coordinates of the Points A_{0i}, A_i, $i = \overline{1, 6}$.

i	X_{0i}	Y_{0i}	Z_{0i}	x_i	y_i	z_i
1	$2l$	0	0	l	0	0
2	$2l$	0	$l/2$	l	0	$l/2$
3	0	$2l$	0	0	l	0
4	l	$2l$	0	l	l	0
5	0	0	$3l/2$	0	0	$l/2$
6	0	l	$3l/2$	0	l	$l/2$

[**J**] being the Jacobian of the system, which, with the given notations, reads

$$[\mathbf{J}] = 2 \begin{bmatrix} \left[\{\mathbf{R}_1\}^T - \{\mathbf{R}_{01}\}^T \right] \left[[\mathbf{I}] \quad [\mathbf{B}_1] \right] \\ \left[\{\mathbf{R}_2\}^T - \{\mathbf{R}_{02}\}^T \right] \left[[\mathbf{I}] \quad [\mathbf{B}_2] \right] \\ \cdots\cdots \\ \left[\{\mathbf{R}_6\}^T - \{\mathbf{R}_{06}\}^T \right] \left[[\mathbf{I}] \quad [\mathbf{B}_6] \right] \end{bmatrix}. \tag{5.139}$$

We calculate successively
- the values of the functions s_i;
- the matrices $[\boldsymbol{\psi}]$, $[\boldsymbol{\theta}]$, $[\boldsymbol{\phi}]$, $[\mathbf{A}]$, $[\mathbf{A}_\psi]$, $[\mathbf{A}_\theta]$, $[\mathbf{A}_\phi]$;
- the matrices $\{\mathbf{R}_i\}$;
- the values of the functions f_i, $i = \overline{1, 6}$, and the column matrix $\{\mathbf{f}\}$;
- the matrices $[\mathbf{B}_i]$, $i = \overline{1, 6}$;
- the Jacobian $[\mathbf{J}]$;
- the column matrix $\{\Delta\mathbf{q}\}$;
- the column matrix $\{\mathbf{q}\}$ that becomes $\{\mathbf{q}\} + \{\Delta\mathbf{q}\}$;

- in a cyclic manner, until $|\Delta q_i| < \varepsilon$, $i = \overline{1, 6}$;
- the parameter t becomes $t + \Delta t$, and the calculation is taken again, the approximate values of the matrix $\{\mathbf{q}\}$ being those given at the previous step.

2. Numerical calculation

The motion is periodic with the period $T = 2\pi/\pi = 2$ s, while the results are transcribed in Figure. 5.9, Figure 5.10, Figure 5.11, Figure 5.12, Figure 5.13, and Figure 5.14.

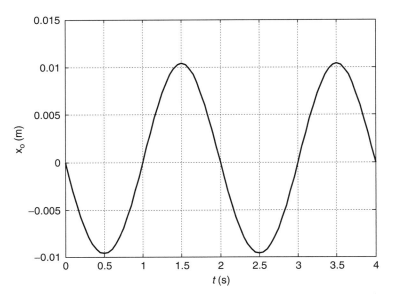

Figure 5.9   Time history $X_O(t)$.

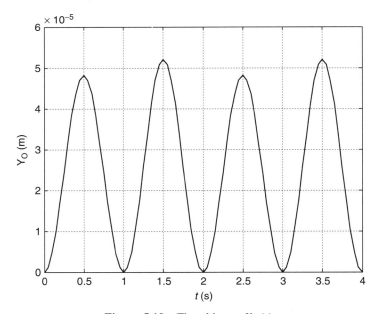

Figure 5.10   Time history $Y_O(t)$.

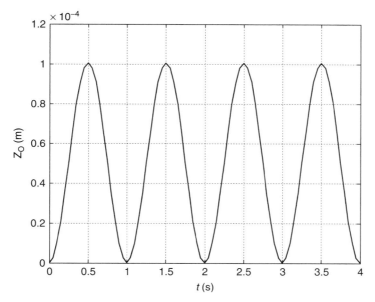

Figure 5.11   Time history $Z_O(t)$.

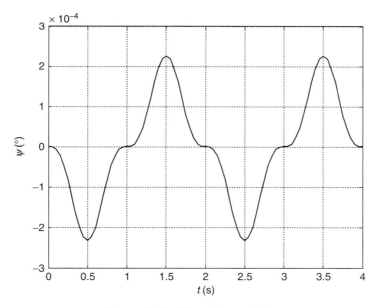

Figure 5.12   Time history $\psi(t)$.

Problem 5.3

Let us consider the planetary gear in Figure 5.15, with an angular axial tripod coupling to the gear box, and with an angular coupling to the wheel in the ball joint C.

The motion is transmitted from the tulip axle (body 1) by contacts between the ramps of the tulip $B_i A_i$, $i = \overline{1, 3}$, symmetrical parallel to the rotation axis and to the arms of the tripod $O_2 A_i$, $i = \overline{1, 3}$, axisymmetric and normal to the axle $O_2 C$ disposed.

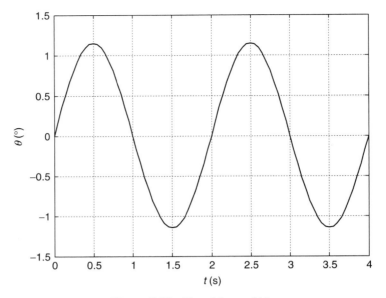

Figure 5.13   Time history $\theta(t)$.

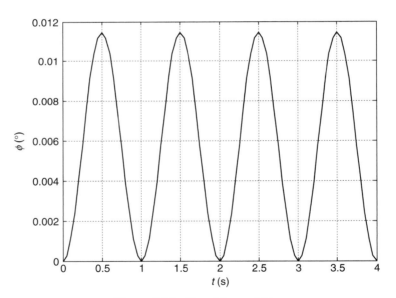

Figure 5.14   Time history $\phi(t)$.

On the rotation axis of the tulip, we consider the point O_0, so chosen as to have $O_2C = O_0C = l$. The fixed reference system $O_0x_0y_0z_0$ is so chosen that the O_0z_0-axis coincides with the rotation axis; as well, we choose the mobile reference system rigidly linked to the tulip $O_0x_1y_1z_1$, so that the O_0z_1-axis coincides with the O_0z_0-axis, while the O_0x_1-axis be parallel with O^*C_1 and intersects the ramp B_1A_1.

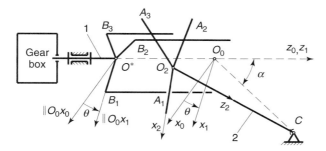

Figure 5.15 Problem 5.3.

We denote by θ the rotation angle of the tulip (the angle between the axes O_0x_0 and O_0x_1); knowing the distances $O^*B_1 = O^*B_2 = O^*B_3 = r$, the angle α (the angle between the O_0z_0-axis and the O_2C-line), the length l and the coordinates X_C, Y_C of the point C in the system $O_0x_0y_0z_0$, determine

- the variation of the angle γ (the angle between O_2C and the O_0z_0-axis), as a function of the angle θ;
- the variation of the coordinates ξ, η, ζ of the point O_2 in the reference system $O_0x_1y_1z_1$;
- the variation of the coordinates ξ_0, η_0, ζ_0 of the point O_2 in the reference system $O_0x_0y_0z_0$ as a function of the angle θ;
- the projections of the trajectory of the point O_2 on each of the planes $O_0x_1y_1$ and $O_0x_0y_0$.

Numerical application: $r = 0.04$ m, $l = 0.2$ m, $\alpha = 30°$, $X_C = 0$ m, $Y_C = -0.1$ m.

Solution:

1. Theory

We choose the system of reference $O_2x_2y_2z_2$, so that the O_2x_2-axis coincides with the straight line O_2A_1, while the O_2z-axis coincides with the straight line O_2C, and denoting by x_{1i}, y_{1i}, z_{1i}, x_{2i}, y_{2i}, z_{2i} the coordinates of the points A_i, $i = \overline{1,3}$, in each of the systems $O_0x_1y_1z_1$, $O_2x_2y_2z_2$, we write the relations

$$\begin{bmatrix} x_{1i} \\ y_{1i} \\ z_{1i} \end{bmatrix} = \begin{bmatrix} \xi \\ \eta \\ \zeta \end{bmatrix} + [\mathbf{A}_{21}] \begin{bmatrix} x_{2i} \\ y_{2i} \\ z_{2i} \end{bmatrix}, \quad i = \overline{1,3}, \tag{5.140}$$

where $[\mathbf{A}_{21}]$ is the rotation matrix of the system $O_2x_2y_2z_2$, with respect to the system $O_0x_1y_1z_1$

$$[\mathbf{A}_{21}] = \begin{bmatrix} \alpha_1 & \alpha_2 & \alpha_3 \\ \beta_1 & \beta_2 & \beta_3 \\ \gamma_1 & \gamma_2 & \gamma_3 \end{bmatrix}. \tag{5.141}$$

Taking into account the relations

$$\begin{bmatrix} x_{1i} \\ y_{1i} \\ z_{1i} \end{bmatrix} = \begin{bmatrix} r\cos\delta_i \\ r\sin\delta_i \\ z_{1i} \end{bmatrix}, \quad \begin{bmatrix} x_{2i} \\ y_{2i} \\ z_{2i} \end{bmatrix} = \begin{bmatrix} \mu_i\cos\delta_i \\ \mu_i\sin\delta_i \\ 0 \end{bmatrix}, \tag{5.142}$$

where

$$\delta_i = \frac{2}{3}(i-1)\pi, \quad \mu_i = O_2 A_i, \quad i = \overline{1,3}, \tag{5.143}$$

from equation (5.140) we obtain the relations

$$r \cos \delta_i = \xi + \mu_i (\alpha_1 \cos \delta_i + \alpha_2 \sin \delta_i), \tag{5.144}$$

$$r \sin \delta_i = \eta + \mu_i (\beta_1 \cos \delta_i + \beta_2 \sin \delta_i), \tag{5.145}$$

$$z_{1i} = \zeta + \mu_i (\gamma_1 \cos \delta_i + \gamma_2 \sin \delta_i). \tag{5.146}$$

By eliminating the parameter μ_i of equation (5.144) and equation (5.145), we obtain

$$\begin{aligned}
\xi(\beta_1 \cos \delta_i + \beta_2 \sin \delta_i) &- \eta(\alpha_1 \cos \delta_i + \alpha_2 \sin \delta_i) \\
&= \frac{r}{2}[(\beta_1 - \alpha_2) + (\beta_1 + \alpha_2) \cos \delta_i + (\beta_2 - \alpha_1) \sin \delta_i], \quad i = \overline{1,3}
\end{aligned} \tag{5.147}$$

and taking into account the equalities

$$\sum_{i=1}^{3} \sin \delta_i = \sum_{i=1}^{3} \cos \delta_i = \sum_{i=1}^{3} \sin 2\delta_i = \sum_{i=1}^{3} \cos 2\delta_i = 0, \tag{5.148}$$

by summation of relation (5.147), we obtain the condition

$$\alpha_2 = \beta_1; \tag{5.149}$$

by adding and subtracting relation (5.147) for $i = 2, 3$, we obtain the system

$$\xi \beta_1 - \eta \alpha_1 = r \beta_1, \quad \xi \beta_2 - \eta \alpha_2 = \frac{r}{2}(\alpha_1 - \beta_2), \tag{5.150}$$

from which we obtain the unknowns

$$\xi = \frac{r}{2\gamma_3}[-2\beta_1 \alpha_1 + \alpha_1(\alpha_1 - \beta_2)], \quad \eta = \frac{r\beta_1}{2\gamma_3}(\alpha_1 - 3\beta_2). \tag{5.151}$$

By means of Euler's angles ψ, γ, ϕ condition (5.149) becomes $\psi = -\phi$, and the rotation matrix takes the form

$$[\mathbf{A}_{21}] = \begin{bmatrix} \cos^2 \phi + \sin^2 \cos \gamma & -\sin \phi \cos \phi (1 - \cos \gamma) & -\sin \phi \sin \gamma \\ -\sin \phi \cos \phi(1 - \cos \gamma) & \sin^2 \phi + \cos^2 \phi \cos \gamma & -\cos \phi \sin \gamma \\ \sin \phi \sin \gamma & \cos \phi \sin \gamma & \cos \gamma \end{bmatrix}, \tag{5.152}$$

while the coordinates ξ, η are given by

$$\xi = \frac{r(1 - \cos \gamma)}{2 \cos \gamma}(\cos 3\phi \cos \phi + \cos \gamma \sin 3\phi \sin \phi), \tag{5.153}$$

$$\eta = \frac{r(1 - \cos \gamma)}{2 \cos \gamma}(-\cos 3\phi \sin \phi + \cos \gamma \sin 3\phi \cos \phi). \tag{5.154}$$

Starting from the vector relation

$$\mathbf{O_0O_2} + \mathbf{O_2C} = \mathbf{O_0C},\tag{5.155}$$

denoting by $[\boldsymbol{\theta}]$ the rotation matrix from the system $O_0x_0y_0z_0$ to the system $O_0x_1y_1z_1$

$$[\boldsymbol{\theta}] = \begin{bmatrix} \cos\theta & -\sin\theta & 0 \\ \sin\theta & \cos\theta & 0 \\ 0 & 0 & 1 \end{bmatrix},\tag{5.156}$$

and denoting by β the angle defined by the relations

$$\cos\beta = \frac{X_C}{\sqrt{X_C^2 + Y_C^2}}, \quad \sin\beta = \frac{Y_C}{\sqrt{X_C^2 + Y_C^2}},\tag{5.157}$$

we obtain the matrix equation

$$\begin{bmatrix} \xi \\ \eta \\ \zeta \end{bmatrix} + [\mathbf{A}_{21}]\begin{bmatrix} 0 \\ 0 \\ l \end{bmatrix} = [\boldsymbol{\theta}]^T \begin{bmatrix} l\sin\alpha\cos\beta \\ l\sin\alpha\sin\beta \\ l\cos\alpha \end{bmatrix},\tag{5.158}$$

from which the scalar relations

$$\frac{r(1-\cos\gamma)}{2\cos\gamma}(\cos 3\phi\cos\phi + \cos\gamma\sin 3\phi\sin\phi) - l\sin\gamma\sin\phi = l\sin\alpha\cos(\theta - \beta),\tag{5.159}$$

$$\frac{r(1-\cos\gamma)}{2\cos\gamma}(-\cos 3\phi\sin\phi + \cos\gamma\sin 3\phi\cos\phi) - 1\sin\gamma\cos\phi = l\sin\alpha\sin(\theta - \beta),\tag{5.160}$$

$$\zeta + l\cos\gamma = l\cos\alpha\tag{5.161}$$

are obtained.

Summing relations (5.159) and (5.160), multiplied by $\sin\phi$, $\cos\phi$, $\cos\phi$, $-\sin\phi$, and using the notation

$$\lambda = \frac{r}{2l},\tag{5.162}$$

we obtain the equations

$$f_1(\phi,\gamma) = \lambda(1 - \cos\gamma)\sin 3\phi - \sin\gamma - \sin\alpha\sin(\phi - \theta + \beta) = 0,\tag{5.163}$$

$$f_2(\phi,\gamma) = \lambda(1 - \cos\gamma)\cos 3\phi - \sin\alpha\cos\gamma\cos(\phi - \theta + \beta) = 0,\tag{5.164}$$

the solving of which leads to $\phi(\theta)$, $\gamma(\theta)$.

2. Numerical calculation

For $\theta = 0$ we obtain the approximate values $\gamma = \alpha$, $\phi = 0$ and because $\beta = 3\pi/2$, from equation (5.163) and equation (5.164) we obtain by the Newton–Raphson method, the results plotted into the diagrams in Figure 5.16 and Figure 5.17; then, from relations (5.153), (5.154), and (5.161), we obtain the results plotted in Figure 5.18, Figure 5.19, Figure 5.20, and Figure 5.21.

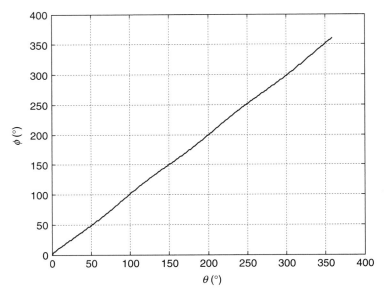

Figure 5.16   Time history $\phi = \phi(\theta)$.

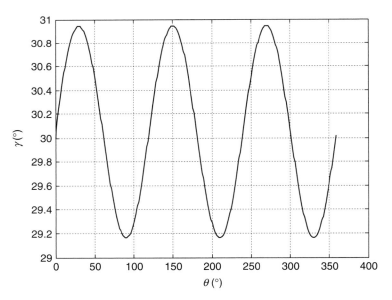

Figure 5.17   Time history $\gamma = \gamma(\theta)$.

To calculate ϕ and γ, we have taken into account that

$$\begin{bmatrix} \Delta\phi \\ \Delta\gamma \end{bmatrix} = - \begin{bmatrix} A_{11} & A_{12} \\ A_{21} & A_{22} \end{bmatrix}^{-1} \begin{Bmatrix} f_1 \\ f_2 \end{Bmatrix}, \tag{5.165}$$

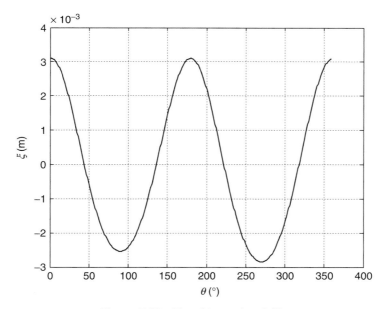

Figure 5.18   Time history $\xi = \xi(\theta)$.

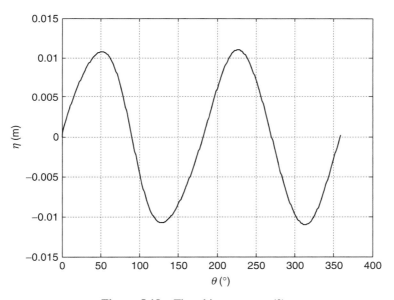

Figure 5.19   Time history $\eta = \eta(\theta)$.

where

$$
\begin{aligned}
A_{11} &= 3\lambda(1 - \cos\gamma)\cos 3\phi - \sin\alpha\cos(\phi - \theta + \beta), \\
A_{12} &= \lambda\sin\gamma\sin 3\phi - \cos\gamma, \\
A_{21} &= -3\lambda(1 - \cos\gamma)\sin 3\phi + \sin\alpha\cos\gamma\sin(\phi - \theta + \beta), \\
A_{22} &= \lambda\sin\gamma\cos 3\phi + \sin\alpha\sin\gamma\cos(\phi - \theta + \beta).
\end{aligned}
\tag{5.166}
$$

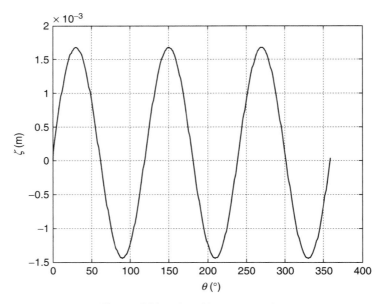

Figure 5.20 Time history $\zeta = \zeta(\theta)$.

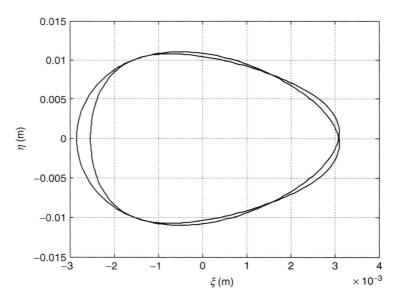

Figure 5.21 Variation $\eta = \eta(\xi)$.

For the diagrams $\xi_0(\theta)$, $\eta_0(\theta)$, $\zeta_0(\eta)$ we take into account the relations

$$\xi_0 = \xi \cos \theta - \eta \sin \theta, \quad \eta_0 = \xi \sin \theta + \eta \cos \theta, \quad \zeta_0 = l(\cos \alpha - \cos \gamma); \qquad (5.167)$$

and the diagrams in Figure 5.22, Figure 5.23, Figure 5.24, Figure 5.25 are obtained.

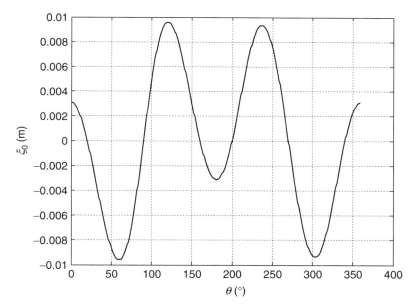

Figure 5.22   Time history $\xi_0 = \xi_0(\theta)$.

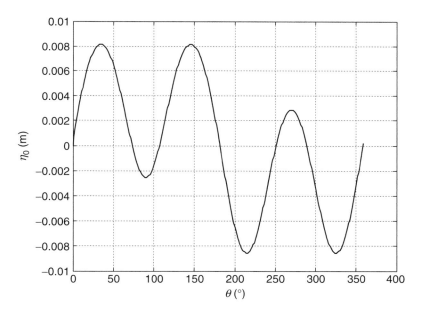

Figure 5.23   Time history $\eta_0 = \eta_0(\theta)$.

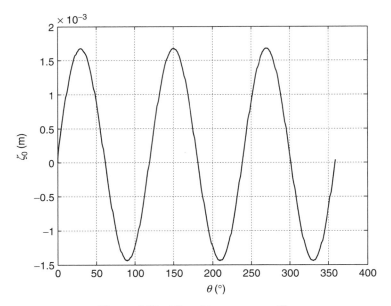

Figure 5.24   Time history $\zeta_0 = \zeta_0(\theta)$.

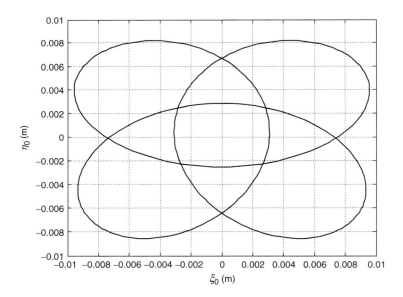

Figure 5.25   Variation $\eta_0 = \eta_0(\xi_0)$.

FURTHER READING

Acton FS (1990). Numerical Methods that Work. 4th ed. Washington: Mathematical Association of America.

Ackleh AS, Allen EJ, Hearfott RB, Seshaiyer P (2009). Classical and Modern Numerical Analysis: Theory, Methods and Practice. Boca Raton: CRC Press.

Atkinson KE (1989). An Introduction to Numerical Analysis. 2nd ed. New York: John Wiley & Sons, Inc.

Atkinson K, Han W (2010). Theoretical Numerical Analysis: A Functional Analysis Framework. 3rd ed. New York: Springer-Verlag.

Bakhvalov N (1976). Méthodes Numérique. Moscou: Editions Mir (in French).

Berbente C, Mitran S, Zancu S (1997). Metode Numerice. Bucureşti: Editura Tehnică (in Romanian).

Burden RL, Faires L (2009). Numerical Analysis. 9th ed. Boston: Brooks/Cole.

Butt R (2009). Introduction to Numerical Analysis Using MATLAB. Boston: Jones and Bartlett Publishers.

Chapra SC (1996). Applied Numerical Methods with MATLAB for Engineers and Scientists. Boston: McGraw-Hill.

Cheney EW, Kincaid DR (1997). Numerical Mathematics and Computing. 6th ed. Belmont: Thomson.

Cira O, Măruşter Ş (2008). Metode Numerice pentru Ecuaţii Neliniare. Bucureşti: Editura Matrix Rom (in Romanian).

Dahlquist G, Björck Å (1974). Numerical Methods. Englewood Hills: Prentice Hall.

Démidovitch B, Maron I (1973). Éléments de Calcul Numérique. Moscou: Editions Mir (in French).

Dennis JE Jr, Schnabel RB (1987). Numerical Methods for Unconstrained Optimization and Nonlinear Equations. Philadelphia: SIAM.

DiBenedetto E (2010). Classical Mechanics: Theory and Mathematical Modeling. New York: Springer-Verlag.

Fung YC, Tong P (2011). Classical and Computational Solid Mechanics. Singapore: World Scientific Publishing.

Gautschi W (1997). Numerical Analysis: An Introduction. Boston: Birkhäuser.

Greenbaum A, Chartier TP (2012). Numerical Methods: Design, Analysis, and Computer Implementation of Algorithms. Princeton: Princeton University Press.

Hamming RW (1987). Numerical Methods for Scientists and Engineers. 2nd ed. New York: Dover Publications.

Heinbockel JH (2006). Numerical Methods for Scientific Computing. Victoria: Trafford Publishing.

Hildebrand FB (1987). Introduction to Numerical Analysis. 2nd ed. New York: Dover Publications.

Hoffman JD (1992). Numerical Methods for Engineers and Scientists. New York: McGraw-Hill.

Kharab A, Guenther RB (2011). An Introduction to Numerical Methods: A MATLAB Approach. 3rd ed. Boca Raton: CRC Press.

Kleppner D, Kolenkow RJ (2010). An Introduction to Mechanics. Cambridge: Cambridge University Press.

Kress R (1996). Numerical Analysis. New York: Springer-Verlag.

Krîlov AN (1957). Lecţii de Calcule prin Aproximaţii. Bucureşti: Editura Tehnică (in Romanian).

Kunz KS (1957). Numerical Analysis. New York: McGraw-Hill.

Lurie AI (2002). Analytical Mechanics. New York: Springer-Verlag.

Mabie HH, Reinholtz CF (1987). Mechanisms and Dynamics of Machinery. 4th ed. New York: John Wiley & Sons, Inc.

Meriam JL, Kraige LG (2012). Engineering Mechanics: Dynamics. Hoboken: John Wiley & Sons, Inc.

Pandrea N (2000). Elemente de Mecanica Solidului în Coordonate Plückeriene. Bucureşti: Editura Academiei Române (in Romanian).

Pandrea N, Pârlac S, Popa D (2001). Modele pentru Studiul Vibraţiilor Automobilelor. Piteşti: Tiparg (in Romanian).

Pandrea N, Popa D (2000). Mecanisme. Teorie şi Aplicaţii CAD. Bucureşti: Editura Tehnică (in Romanian).

Pandrea N, Stănescu ND (2002). Mecanică. Bucureşti: Editura Didactică şi Pedagogică (in Romanian).

Popovici P, Cira O (1992). Rezolvarea Numerică a Ecuaţiilor Neliniare. Timişoara: Editura Signata (in Romanian).

Postolache M (2006). Modelare Numerică. Teorie şi Aplicaţii. Bucureşti: Editura Fair Partners (in Romanian).

Press WH, Teukolski SA, Vetterling WT, Flannery BP (2007). Numerical Recipes: The Art of Scientific Computing. 3rd ed. Cambridge: Cambridge University Press.

Quarteroni A, Sacco R, Saleri F (2010). Numerical Mathematics. 2nd ed. Berlin: Springer-Verlag.

Ralston A, Rabinowitz P (2001). A First Course in Numerical Analysis. 2nd ed. New York: Dover Publications.

Ridgway Scott L (2011). Numerical Analysis. Princeton: Princeton University Press.

Salvadori MG, Baron ML (1962). Numerical Methods in Engineering. Englewood Cliffs: Prentice-Hall Inc.

Sauer T (2011). Numerical Analysis. 2nd ed. London: Pearson.

Simionescu I, Dranga M, Moise V (1995). Metode Numerice în Tehnică. Aplicaţii în FORTRAN. Bucureşti: Editura Tehnică (in Romanian).

Stănescu ND (2007). Metode Numerice. Bucureşti: Editura Didactică şi Pedagogică (in Romanian).

Süli E, Mayers D (2003). An Introduction to Numerical Analysis. Cambridge: Cambridge University Press.

Udrişte C, Iftode V, Postolache M (1996). Metode Numerice de Calcul. Algoritmi şi Programe Turbo Pascal. Bucureşti: Editura Tehnică (in Romanian).

6

INTERPOLATION AND APPROXIMATION OF FUNCTIONS

6.1 LAGRANGE'S INTERPOLATION POLYNOMIAL

Definition 6.1 Let $[a, b]$, $-\infty < a < b < \infty$, be an interval of the real axis and $x_0, x_1, \ldots, x_n$, $n + 1$ interior points of the segment $[a, b]$, with

$$a \leq x_0 < x_1 < x_2 < \cdots < x_{n-1} < x_n = b. \tag{6.1}$$

The points x_i, $i = \overline{0, n}$, are called *interpolation knots*.

Let us consider a function $f : [a, b] \to \mathbb{R}$ for which we know the values

$$y_i = f(x_i), \quad i = \overline{0, n}. \tag{6.2}$$

We wish to construct a polynomial[1] function $L(x)$, for which the values at the interpolation knots x_i, $i = \overline{0, n}$, coincide with the values of the function f at the very same points, that is,

$$y_i = L(x_i), \quad i = \overline{0, n}. \tag{6.3}$$

Theorem 6.1 Let $f : [a, b] \to \mathbb{R}$, the interpolation knots x_i, $i = \overline{0, n}$, and the values of the function f at the points x_i, that is, $y_i = f(x_i)$, $i = \overline{0, n}$. Under these conditions, there exists a polynomial $L_n(x)$ of degree n at the most which is unique and the values of which coincide with the values of the function f at the interpolation knots.

---

[1]The polynomial was discovered by Edward Waring (circa 1736–1798) in 1779, then by Leonhard Euler (1707–1783) in 1783, and published by Joseph Louis Lagrange (1736–1813) in 1795.

Numerical Analysis with Applications in Mechanics and Engineering, First Edition.
Petre Teodorescu, Nicolae-Doru Stănescu, and Nicolae Pandrea.
© 2013 The Institute of Electrical and Electronics Engineers, Inc. Published 2013 by John Wiley & Sons, Inc.

Demonstration. Let us consider a polynomial $\psi_i(x)$ with the property

$$\psi_i(x_j) = \delta_{ij}, \tag{6.4}$$

where δ_{ij} is Kronecker's symbol

$$\delta_{ij} = \begin{cases} 1 \text{ for } i = j \\ 0 \text{ for } i \neq j. \end{cases} \tag{6.5}$$

It follows that the polynomial $\psi_i(x)$ may be written in the form

$$\psi_i(x) = C_i(x - x_0)(x - x_1) \cdots (x - x_{i-1})(x - x_{i+1}) \cdots (x - x_n), \tag{6.6}$$

where C_i is given by the condition

$$\psi_i(x_i) = C_i(x_i - x_0) \cdots (x_i - x_{i-1})(x_i - x_{i+1}) \cdots (x_i - x_n) = 1. \tag{6.7}$$

We obtain

$$C_i = \frac{1}{(x_i - x_0) \cdots (x_i - x_{i-1})(x_i - x_{i+1}) \cdots (x_i - x_n)}, \tag{6.8}$$

hence

$$\psi_i(x) = \frac{(x - x_0) \cdots (x - x_{i-1})(x - x_{i+1}) \cdots (x - x_n)}{(x_i - x_0) \cdots (x_i - x_{i-1})(x_i - x_{i+1}) \cdots (x_i - x_n)}. \tag{6.9}$$

Let us construct the polynomial $L_n(x)$ in the form

$$L_n(x) = \sum_{i=0}^{n} \psi_i(x) y_i. \tag{6.10}$$

We have

$$L_n(x_j) = \sum_{i=0}^{n} \psi_i(x_j) y_i = \psi_j(x_j) y_j = y_j. \tag{6.11}$$

Because $\psi_i(x)$, $i = \overline{0, n}$, are polynomials of nth degree, it follows that $L_n(x)$ has a degree n at the most. Formula (6.10) may also be written in the form

$$L_n(x) = \sum_{i=0}^{n} \frac{(x - x_0) \cdots (x - x_{i-1})(x - x_{i+1}) \cdots (x - x_n)}{(x_i - x_0) \cdots (x_i - x_{i-1})(x_i - x_{i+1}) \cdots (x_i - x_n)} y_i. \tag{6.12}$$

We will show that $L_n(x)$ is unique. Let us suppose that there exists another polynomial $\Lambda_n(x)$ such that $\Lambda_n(x_i) = y_i$, the degree of $\Lambda_n(x)$ being n at the most. Let us consider the polynomial

$$D_n(x) = L_n(x) - \Lambda_n(x), \tag{6.13}$$

which is of degree n at the most (as a difference of two polynomials of degrees equal to n at the most), and let us assume that

$$D_n(x_i) = 0, \quad i = \overline{0, n}. \tag{6.14}$$

It follows that the polynomial $D_n(x)$ of degree n at the most has at least $n + 1$ real roots, $x_0, x_1, \ldots,$ x_n. It follows that the polynomial $D_n(x)$ vanishes identically, hence

$$L_n(x) = \Lambda_n(x),\tag{6.15}$$

where $L_n(x)$ is unique.

Definition 6.2   The polynomial $L_n(x)$ given by formula (6.12) is called *Lagrange's interpolation polynomial*.

Observation 6.1   Let us denote by $P_{n+1}(x)$ the polynomial

$$P_{n+1}(x) = \prod_{i=0}^{n}(x - x_i).\tag{6.16}$$

Under these conditions, we have

$$L_n(x) = P_{n+1}(x)\sum_{i=0}^{n}\frac{y_i}{(x - x_i)P'_{n+1}(x_i)}.\tag{6.17}$$

Demonstration. We may successively write

$$L_n(x) = \sum_{i=0}^{n}\frac{(x - x_0)\cdots(x - x_{i-1})(x - x_{i+1})\cdots(x - x_n)}{(x_i - x_0)\cdots(x_i - x_{i-1})(x_i - x_{i+1})\cdots(x_i - x_n)}\frac{x - x_i}{x - x_i}y_i$$

$$= P_{n+1}(x)\sum_{i=0}^{n}\frac{y_i}{(x - x_i)}\frac{1}{(x_i - x_0)\cdots(x_i - x_{i-1})(x_i - x_{i+1})\cdots(x_i - x_n)}.\tag{6.18}$$

On the other hand,

$$P'_{n+1}(x) = \sum_{i=0}^{n}(x - x_0)\cdots(x - x_{i-1})(x - x_{i+1})\cdots(x - x_n)\tag{6.19}$$

and it follows that

$$P'_{n+1}(x_i) = (x_i - x_0)\cdots(x_i - x_{i-1})(x_i - x_{i+1})\cdots(x_i - x_n).\tag{6.20}$$

Formula (6.18), in which we replace relation (6.20), leads to relation (6.17), which had to be proved.

Observation 6.2   The polynomial $L_n(x)$ may also be written in the form

$$L_n(x) = a_n x^n + a_{n-1}x^{n-1} + \cdots + a_1 x + a_0\tag{6.21}$$

and condition (6.3) implies a system of $n + 1$ linear equations with $n + 1$ unknowns $a_0, a_1, \ldots, a_n$:

$$\begin{cases} a_n x_0^n + a_{n-1}x_0^{n-1} + \cdots + a_1 x_0 + a_0 = y_0, \\ \vdots \\ a_n x_n^n + a_{n-1}x_n^{n-1} + \cdots + a_1 x_n + a_0 = y_n. \end{cases}\tag{6.22}$$

The determinant of the system matrix

$$\Delta = \begin{vmatrix} x_0^n & x_0^{n-1} & \cdots & x_0 & 1 \\ x_1^n & x_1^{n-1} & \cdots & x_1 & 1 \\ \cdots & \cdots & \cdots & \cdots & \cdots \\ x_n^n & x_n^{n-1} & \cdots & x_n & 1 \end{vmatrix}, \tag{6.23}$$

is of the Vandermonde type, the value of which,

$$\Delta = (x_1 - x_2) \cdots (x_1 - x_n)(x_2 - x_3) \cdots (x_2 - x_n) \cdots (x_{n-1} - x_n) = \prod_{i<j}(x_i - x_j), \tag{6.24}$$

does not vanish because $x_i \neq x_j$ for $i \neq j$. Hence, it follows that system (6.22) has a unique solution so that Lagrange's polynomial does exist and is unique.

Theorem 6.2 (Evaluation of the Error for Lagrange's Polynomial). Let $f : [a, b] \to \mathbb{R}$ of class C^{n+1} on $[a, b]$ and let us denote by M the value

$$M = \sup_{x \in [a,b]} |f^{(n+1)}(x)|. \tag{6.25}$$

Let $x_0, x_1, \ldots, x_n$ be the $n + 1$ interpolation knots on $[a, b]$ and let $y_i = f(x_i)$, $i = \overline{0, n}$. $L_n(x)$, Lagrange's polynomial, satisfy $L_n(x_i) = y_i$, $i = \overline{0, n}$. Under these conditions, we have

$$|f(x) - L_n(x)| \leq \frac{M}{(n+1)!}|P_{n+1}(x)|. \tag{6.26}$$

Demonstration. Let us denote by $\theta : [a, b] \to \mathbb{R}$ an auxiliary function

$$\theta(x) = f(x) - L_n(x) - \lambda P_{n+1}(x), \quad \lambda \in \mathbb{R}. \tag{6.27}$$

We observe that

$$\theta(x_i) = f(x_i) - L_n(x_i) - \lambda P_{n+1}(x_i) = 0, \quad i = \overline{0, n}; \tag{6.28}$$

hence, $\theta(x)$ has at least $n + 1$ roots in the interval $[a, b]$. Let us choose $\lambda \in \mathbb{R}$ so that $\theta(x)$ admits a $(n + 2)$th root also on $[a, b]$, and let us denote this root by $\overline{x}$. In this case,

$$\theta(\overline{x}) = f(\overline{x}) - L_n(\overline{x}) - \lambda P_{n+1}(\overline{x}) = 0; \tag{6.29}$$

hence

$$\lambda = \frac{f(\overline{x}) - L_n(\overline{x})}{P_{n+1}(\overline{x})}. \tag{6.30}$$

Let us arrange the $n + 2$ roots of θ in increasing order. The intervals $[x_0, x_1]$, $[x_1, x_2]$, $\ldots$, $[x_j, \overline{x}]$, $[\overline{x}, x_{j+1}]$, $\ldots$, $[x_{n-1}, x_n]$ are thus obtained. The function $\theta(x)$ vanishes at the ends of each of these intervals for the value λ given by relation (6.30). Applying Rolle's theorem for each of these intervals, it follows that the function $\theta'(x)$ has at least $n + 1$ distinct roots. Analogically, it follows that $\theta''(x)$ has at least n distinct roots, $\ldots$, and the function $\theta^{(n+1)}(x)$ has at least one root ζ; hence,

$$\theta^{(n+1)}(\zeta) = 0. \tag{6.31}$$

Differentiating $n + 1$ times the function θ in relation (6.27) and taking into account that

$$L_n^{(n+1)}(x) = 0, \quad P_{n+1}^{(n+1)} = (n + 1)!, \tag{6.32}$$

because $L_n(x)$ is a polynomial of degree n at the most while $P_{n+1}(x)$ is a polynomial of $(n + 1)$th degree, we get

$$\theta^{(n+1)}(x) = f^{(n+1)}(x) - \lambda(n + 1)!, \tag{6.33}$$

from which

$$f^{(n+1)}(\zeta) - \lambda(n + 1)! = 0; \tag{6.34}$$

hence

$$\lambda = \frac{f^{(n+1)}(\zeta)}{(n + 1)!}. \tag{6.35}$$

Equating relations (6.30) and (6.35), we get

$$f(\overline{x}) - L_n(\overline{x}) = \frac{f^{(n+1)}(\zeta)}{(n + 1)!} P_{n+1}(\overline{x}) \tag{6.36}$$

and because $\overline{x}$ is arbitrary, it follows that

$$|f(x) - L_n(x)| = \frac{1}{(n + 1)!} |f^{(n+1)}(\zeta)| |P_{n+1}(x)|. \tag{6.37}$$

Passing on to the supremum after ζ on $[a, b]$, we obtain

$$|f(x) - L_n(x)| \leq \frac{1}{(n + 1)!} \sup_{\zeta \in [a,b]} |f^{(n+1)}(\zeta)| |P_{n+1}(x)| = \frac{M}{(n + 1)!} |P_{n+1}(x)|, \tag{6.38}$$

and the theorem is proved.

6.2   TAYLOR POLYNOMIALS

We remember a well-known theorem of analysis.

Theorem 6.3 (Taylor[2]). Let us consider $f : I \rightarrow \mathbb{R}$, where I is an interval of the real axis, and x and $\overline{x}$ are two elements of I. If f is of class C^{n+1} on I, then the relation

$$f(\overline{x}) = f(x) + \frac{(\overline{x} - x)^1}{1!} f'(x) + \cdots + \frac{(\overline{x} - x)^n}{n!} f^{(n)}(x) + \frac{(\overline{x} - x)^{n+1}}{(n + 1)!} f^{(n+1)}(\zeta) \tag{6.39}$$

exists, where ζ is a point between x and $\overline{x}$.

Observation 6.3   Relation (6.39) leads to an approximate formula for the calculation of $f(\overline{x})$, that is,

$$f(\overline{x}) \approx f(x) + \frac{(\overline{x} - x)^1}{1!} f'(x) + \frac{(\overline{x} - x)^2}{2!} f''(x) + \cdots$$

$$+ \frac{(\overline{x} - x)^n}{n!} f^{(n)}(x) = \sum_{k=0}^{n} \frac{(\overline{x} - x)^k}{k!} f^{(k)}(x). \tag{6.40}$$

[2]Brook Taylor (1685–1731) stated this theorem in 1712.

6.3   FINITE DIFFERENCES: GENERALIZED POWER

Let there be a function $f : \mathbb{R} \to \mathbb{R}$.

Definition 6.3   We call step a fixed value $h = \Delta x$ of the increment of the argument of the function f.

Definition 6.4   The expression

$$\Delta y = \Delta f(x) = f(x + \Delta x) - f(x) \tag{6.41}$$

is called *first difference of the function f*. In general, the difference of order n of the function f is defined by

$$\Delta^n y = \Delta(\Delta^{n-1} y), \tag{6.42}$$

where $n \geq 2$.

Proposition 6.1   Let

$$P_n(x) = a_0 x^n + a_1 x^{n-1} + \cdots + a_n \tag{6.43}$$

be a polynomial of nth degree, where $a_i \in \mathbb{R}$, $i = \overline{0, n}$, and h is the step. Under these conditions,

(i) $\Delta^k P_n(x)$ is a polynomial of degree $n - k$, $1 \leq k \leq n$, the dominant coefficient of which is given by

$$a_0^{(k)} = a_0 n(n - 1) \cdots (n - k + 1) h^k; \tag{6.44}$$

(ii) for $k = n$, we have

$$a_0^{(n)} = a_0 n! h^n; \tag{6.45}$$

(iii) if $k > n$, then

$$\Delta^k P_n(x) = 0. \tag{6.46}$$

Demonstration

(i) Successively, we may write

$$\begin{aligned}
\Delta P_n(x) &= P_n(x + h) - P_n(x) \\
&= a_0(x + h)^n + a_1(x + h)^{n-1} + \cdots + a_n - a_0 x^n - a_1 x^{n-1} - \cdots - a_n \\
&= a_0 x^n + C_n^1 a_0 x^{n-1} h + \cdots + a_1 x^{n-1} + \cdots + a_n - a_0 x^n - a_1 x^{n-1} - \cdots - a_n \\
&= C_n^1 a_0 x^{n-1} h + \cdots;
\end{aligned} \tag{6.47}$$

hence, $\Delta P_n(x)$ is a polynomial of degree $n - 1$, the dominant coefficient of which is

$$a_0^{(1)} = C_n^1 a_0 h = n a_0 h. \tag{6.48}$$

Then

$$\begin{aligned}
\Delta^2 P_n(x) &= \Delta(\Delta P_n(x)) = n a_0 h(x + h)^{n-1} + \cdots - n a_0 h x^{n-1} - \cdots \\
&= n a_0 h C_{n-1}^1 x^{n-2} h + \cdots = n(n - 1) a_0 h^2 x^{n-2} + \cdots,
\end{aligned} \tag{6.49}$$

and hence $\Delta^2 P_n(x)$ is a polynomial of degree $n - 2$, the dominant coefficient of which is given by

$$a_0^{(2)} = n(n - 1)a_0 h^2. \tag{6.50}$$

We can thus show that $\Delta^k P_n(x)$ is a polynomial of degree $n - k$, $1 \leq k \leq n$, the dominant coefficient of which is given by (6.44).

(ii) It is a particular case of (i) for $k = n$. It follows that $\Delta^n P_n(x)$ is a polynomial of degree 0 (hence a constant), its value being given by

$$\Delta^n P_n(x) = a_0 n! h^n. \tag{6.51}$$

(iii) Let $k = n + 1$. We have

$$\Delta^k P_n(x) = \Delta(\Delta^n P_n(x)) = \Delta(a_0 n! h^n) = 0 \tag{6.52}$$

and, in general, the finite difference of a constant is zero and the proposition is proved.

Proposition 6.2 Finite differences have the following properties:

(i) If f and g are two functions and a and b two real constants, then

$$\Delta(af + bg) = a\,\Delta f + b\,\Delta g. \tag{6.53}$$

(ii) The relation

$$\Delta^m(\Delta^n y) = \Delta^{m+n} y \tag{6.54}$$

exists for any $m, n \in \mathbb{N}^*$ ($\mathbb{N}^* = \mathbb{N} - \{0\} = 1, 2, 3, \ldots$).

(iii) If we write

$$f(x + \Delta x) = f(x) + \Delta f(x) = (1 + \Delta)f(x), \tag{6.55}$$

then the relation

$$f(x + n\Delta x) = (1 + \Delta)^n f(x) = \sum_{k=0}^{n} C_n^k \Delta^k f(x) \tag{6.56}$$

holds for any $n \in \mathbb{N}^*$.

Demonstration

(i) We have

$$\begin{aligned}
\Delta(af + bg) &= af(x + \Delta x) + bg(x + \Delta x) - af(x) - bg(x) \\
&= a[f(x + \Delta x) - f(x)] + b[g(x + \Delta x) - g(x)] \\
&= a\,\Delta f + b\,\Delta g.
\end{aligned} \tag{6.57}$$

(ii) Let $n \in \mathbb{N}^*$ arbitrary be fixed. If $m = 1$, then we have

$$\Delta^m(\Delta^n y) = \Delta(\Delta^n y) = \Delta^{1+n} y = \Delta^{m+n} y \tag{6.58}$$

corresponding to the definition of the finite difference. Let us suppose that relation (6.54) is valid for $n \in \mathbb{N}^*$ arbitrary and $m \in \mathbb{N}^*$ and let us write it for $m + 1$. We have

$$\Delta^{m+1}(\Delta^n y) = \Delta[\Delta^m(\Delta^n y)] = \Delta(\Delta^{m+n} y) = \Delta^{m+1+n} y \qquad (6.59)$$

and, conforming to the principle of mathematical induction, it follows that the property (ii) holds for any $m, n \in \mathbb{N}^*$.

(iii) For $n = 1$ we have

$$f(x + \Delta x) = f(x) + \Delta f(x) = (1 + \Delta) f(x), \qquad (6.60)$$

while for $n = 2$ we may write

$$f(x + 2\Delta x) = (1 + \Delta) f(x + \Delta x) = (1 + \Delta)^2 f(x). \qquad (6.61)$$

Let us suppose that relation (6.56) holds for n and let us show that it holds for $n + 1$ too. We have

$$f[x + (n+1)\Delta x] = (1 + \Delta) f(x + n\Delta x) = (1 + \Delta)(1 + \Delta)^n f(x) = (1 + \Delta)^{n+1} f(x) \qquad (6.62)$$

and, conforming to the principle of mathematical induction, the property is valid for any $n \in \mathbb{N}^*$.

Corollary 6.1 We may write

$$\Delta^n f(x) = f(x + n\Delta x) - C_n^1 f[x + (n-1)\Delta x] + C_n^2 f[x + (n-2)\Delta x] + \cdots + (-1)^n f(x) \qquad (6.63)$$

for any $n \in \mathbb{N}^*$.

Demonstration. Indeed,

$$\begin{aligned}
\Delta^n f(x) &= [(1 + \Delta) - 1]^n f(x) = \sum_{k=0}^{n} C_n^k (-1)^k (1 + \Delta)^{n-k} f(x) \\
&= \sum_{k=0}^{n} (-1)^k f[x + (n-k)\Delta x] = f(x + n\Delta x) - C_n^1 f[x + (n-1)\Delta x] \\
&\quad + C_n^2 f[x + (n-2)\Delta x] + \cdots + (-1)^n f(x).
\end{aligned} \qquad (6.64)$$

Proposition 6.3 Let I be an open interval of the real axis and $f : I \to \mathbb{R}$ of class C^∞ on I. Let us denote the step by $h = \Delta x$. Under these conditions,

$$\Delta^n f(x) = (\Delta x)^n f^{(n)}(x + n\xi\Delta x), \qquad (6.65)$$

where $0 < \xi < 1$.

Demonstration. We proceed by induction after n. For $n = 1$ we get

$$\Delta f(x) = \Delta x f'(x + \xi\Delta x), \qquad (6.66)$$

which is just Lagrange's theorem of finite increments. Let us suppose that the statement holds for n and let us show that it is valid for $n + 1$ too. We have

$$\begin{aligned}
\Delta^{n+1} f(x) &= \Delta(\Delta^n f(x)) = \Delta^n f(x + \Delta x) - \Delta^n f(x) \\
&= (\Delta x)^n [f^{(n)}(x + \Delta x + n\xi_1\Delta x) - f^{(n)}(x + n\xi_1\Delta x)] \\
&= (\Delta x)^n (\Delta x) f^{(n+1)}(x + n\xi_1\Delta x + \lambda\Delta x),
\end{aligned} \qquad (6.67)$$

the last relation being the result of the application of Lagrange's theorem, while $\lambda \in (0, 1)$. Let us denote

$$\xi = \frac{n\xi_1 + \lambda}{n + 1} \in (0, 1); \tag{6.68}$$

hence

$$\Delta^{n+1} f(x) = (\Delta x)^{n+1} f^{(n+1)}[x + (n + 1)\xi \Delta x]. \tag{6.69}$$

Corresponding to the principle of mathematical induction, the property is valid for any $n \in \mathbb{N}^*$.

Corollary 6.2   In the above conditions, there exists the relation

$$f^{(n)}(x) = \lim_{\Delta x \to 0} \frac{\Delta^n f(x)}{(\Delta x)^n}. \tag{6.70}$$

Demonstration. We pass to the limit for $\Delta x \to 0$ in the relation

$$f^{(n)}(x + n\xi \Delta x) = \frac{\Delta^n f(x)}{(\Delta x)^n}, \tag{6.71}$$

with $0 < \xi < 1$, and obtain just the requested relation.

Observation 6.4

(i) Let there be a system of equidistant points x_i, $i = \overline{0, n}$, for which

$$\Delta x_i = x_{i+1} - x_i = h = ct, \quad i = \overline{0, n - 1}, \tag{6.72}$$

and let us denote by y_i, $i = \overline{0, n}$ the values of the function at the points x_i. We may write the relations

$$\Delta y_i = y_{i+1} - y_i, \quad i = \overline{0, n - 1}, \tag{6.73}$$

$$\Delta^2 y_i = \Delta y_{i+1} - \Delta y_i = y_{i+1} - 2y_{i+1} + y_i, \quad i = \overline{0, n - 2}, \tag{6.74}$$

and, in general,

$$\Delta^k y_i = \Delta^{k-1} y_{i+1} - \Delta^{k-1} y_i, \quad i = \overline{0, n - k}. \tag{6.75}$$

On the other hand,

$$y_{i+1} = y_i + \Delta y_i = (1 + \Delta) y_i, \quad i = \overline{0, n - 1}, \tag{6.76}$$

$$y_{i+2} = y_{i+1} + \Delta y_{i+1} = (1 + \Delta) y_{i+1} = (1 + \Delta)^2 y_i, \quad i = \overline{0, n - 2}, \tag{6.77}$$

and, in general,

$$y_{i+k} = (1 + \Delta)^k y_i, \quad i = \overline{0, n - k}. \tag{6.78}$$

Hence, it follows that

$$y_{i+k} = \sum_{j=0}^{k} C_k^j \Delta^j y_i = y_i + C_k^1 \Delta y_i + \cdots + \Delta^k y_i. \tag{6.79}$$

(ii) We can calculate

$$\Delta^k y_i = [(1 + \Delta) - 1]^k y_i = \sum_{j=0}^{k} C_k^j (-1)^j (1 + \Delta)^{k-j} y_i$$

$$= (1 + \Delta)^k y_i - C_k^1 (1 + \Delta)^{k-1} y_i + C_n^2 (1 + \Delta)^{k-2} y_i + \cdots + (-1)^k C_k^k y_i$$

(6.80)

and, taking into account relation (6.78), we obtain

$$\Delta^k y_i = y_{i+k} - C_k^1 y_{i+k-1} + C_k^2 y_{i+k-2} + \cdots + (-1)^k y_i.$$

(6.81)

Usually, we put the finite differences as, for example, in Table 6.1.

Definition 6.5   We denote by generalized power of order n the product

$$x^{(n)} = x(x - h)(x - 2h) \cdots [x - (n - 1)h].$$

(6.82)

Proposition 6.4   The relation

$$\Delta^k x^{(n)} = n(n - 1) \cdots [n - (k - 1)h]h^k x^{(n-k)}$$

(6.83)

holds for $k \in \mathbb{N}^*$.

Demonstration. Let us consider firstly that $k = 1$. We have

$$\Delta x^{(n)} = (x + h)^{(n)} - x^{(n)} = (x + h)x(x - h) \cdots [x - (n - 2)h]$$
$$- x(x - h) \cdots [x - (n - 2)h][x - (n - 1)h]$$
$$= x(x - h) \cdots [x - (n - 2)h]nh = nhx^{(n-1)}.$$

(6.84)

It follows that

$$\Delta^2 x^{(n)} = nh\Delta x^{(n-1)} = nh[(x + h)^{(n-1)} - x^{(n-1)}]$$
$$= nh\{(x + h)x \cdots [x - (n - 3)h] - x(x - h) \cdots [x - (n - 2)h]\}$$
$$= nhx(x - h) \cdots [x - (n - 3)h]h(n - 1) = n(n - 1)h^2 x^{(n-2)},$$

(6.85)

for $k = 2$. Let us suppose that the relation holds for k and let us show that it remains valid for $k + 1$. We have

$$\Delta^k x^{(n)} = n(n - 1) \cdots [n - (k - 1)]h^k x^{(n-k)}$$

(6.86)

TABLE 6.1   Table of the Finite Differences

x	y	Δy	$\Delta^2 y$	$\ldots$	$\Delta^{n-3} y$	$\Delta^{n-2} y$	$\Delta^{n-1} y$	$\Delta^n y$
x_0	y_0	Δy_0	$\Delta^2 y_0$	$\ldots$	$\Delta^{n-3} y_0$	$\Delta^{n-2} y_0$	$\Delta^{n-1} y_0$	$\Delta^n y_0$
x_1	y_1	Δy_1	$\Delta^2 y_1$	$\ldots$	$\Delta^{n-3} y_1$	$\Delta^{n-2} y_1$	$\Delta^{n-1} y_1$	
x_2	y_2	Δy_2	$\Delta^2 y_2$	$\ldots$	$\Delta^{n-3} y_2$	$\Delta^{n-2} y_2$		
x_3	y_3	Δy_3	$\Delta^2 y_3$	$\ldots$	$\Delta^{n-3} y_3$			
$\ldots$	$\ldots$	$\ldots$	$\ldots$	$\ldots$				
x_{n-2}	y_{n-2}	Δy_{n-2}	$\Delta^2 y_{n-2}$					
x_{n-1}	y_{n-1}	Δy_{n-1}						
x_n	y_n							

$$
\begin{aligned}
\Delta^{k+1} x^{(n)} &= n(n-1) \cdots [n - (k-1)] h^k [(x+h)^{(n-k)} - x^{(n-k)}] \\
&= n(n-1) \cdots [n - (k-1)] h^k \{(x+h)x \cdots [x - (n-k-2)] \\
&\quad - x(x-h) \cdots [x - (n-k-1)h]\} \\
&= n(n-1) \cdots [n - (k-1)] h^k x(x-h) \cdots [x - (n-k-2)h](n-k)h \\
&= n(n-1) \cdots (n-k) h^{k+1} x^{(n-k-1)}
\end{aligned}
\tag{6.87}
$$

and, conforming to the principle of mathematical induction, property (6.83) is valid for any $k \in \mathbb{N}^*$.

Observation 6.5 If $h = 0$, then the generalized power coincides with the normal power.

6.4 NEWTON'S INTERPOLATION POLYNOMIALS

Proposition 6.5 Let us consider the function $f : [a, b] \to \mathbb{R}$ and an equidistant system of knots[3]

$$
x_i = x_0 + ih, \quad i = \overline{0, n},
\tag{6.88}
$$

where h is the constant interpolation step. If $y_i = f(x_i)$, $i = \overline{0, n}$, then there exists a polynomial $P_n(x)$ of degree n at the most so that $P_n(x_i) = y_i$ and

$$
P_n = y_0 + \frac{q}{1!} \Delta y_0 + \frac{q(q-1)}{2!} \Delta^2 y_0 + \cdots + \frac{q(q-1) \ldots [q - (n-1)]}{n!} \Delta^n y_0,
\tag{6.89}
$$

where

$$
q = \frac{x - x_0}{h}.
\tag{6.90}
$$

Demonstration. Let us search the polynomial P_n in the form

$$
P_n = a_0 + a_1(x - x_0) + a_2(x - x_0)(x - x_1) + \cdots + a_n(x - x_0) \cdots (x - x_{n-1})
\tag{6.91}
$$

or, equivalently,

$$
P_n = a_0 + a_1(x - x_0)^{(1)} + a_2(x - x_0)^{(2)} + \cdots + a_n(x - x_0)^{(n)}.
\tag{6.92}
$$

The condition $P_n(x_i) = y_i$ is equivalent to the condition

$$
\Delta^k P_n(x_0) = \Delta^k y_0, \quad k \geq 0.
\tag{6.93}
$$

For $k = 0$, we obtain

$$
P_n(x_0) = y_0,
\tag{6.94}
$$

from which

$$
a_0 = y_0.
\tag{6.95}
$$

For $k = 1$ we have

$$
\Delta P_n(x) = 1! a_1 h + 2 a_2 h(x - x_0)^{(1)} + \cdots + n a_n h(x - x_0)^{(n-1)},
\tag{6.96}
$$

[3]Newton's interpolation polynomials were described by Isaac Newton in a letter to Smith in 1675; a letter to Oldenburg in 1676; in *Methodus Differentialis* in 1711; in *Regula Differentiarum* written in 1676 and discovered in the twentieth century; and in *Philosophiae Naturalis Principia Mathematica*, published in 1687.

obtaining

$$\Delta P_n(x_0) = 1!a_1 h, \tag{6.97}$$

hence

$$a_1 = \frac{\Delta y_0}{1!h}. \tag{6.98}$$

For $k = 2$ we have

$$\Delta^2 P_n(x) = 1 \times 2 \times a_2 h^2 + 2 \times 3 \times a_3 h^2 (x - x_0)^{(1)} + \cdots + n(n-1)a_n h^2 (x - x_0)^{(n-2)} \tag{6.99}$$

and we get

$$\Delta^2 P_n(x_0) = 2!a_2 h^2, \tag{6.100}$$

from which

$$a_2 = \frac{\Delta^2 y_0}{2!h^2}. \tag{6.101}$$

Step by step, we obtain

$$a_k = \frac{\Delta^k y_0}{k!h^k}, \quad k = \overline{0, n}, \tag{6.102}$$

and the polynomial $P_n(x)$ may now be written as

$$P_n(x) = y_0 + \frac{\Delta y_0}{1!h}(x - x_0)^{(1)} + \frac{\Delta^2 y_0}{2!h^2}(x - x_0)^{(2)} + \cdots + \frac{\Delta^n y_0}{n!h^n}(x - x_0)^{(n)}. \tag{6.103}$$

We now verify that $P_n(x)$ is an interpolation polynomial, that is,

$$P_n(x_k) = y_k, \quad k = \overline{0, n}. \tag{6.104}$$

Observing that

$$(x_k - x_0)^{(k+p)} = 0, \tag{6.105}$$

for any $p \in \mathbb{N}^*$, it follows that $P_n(x_k)$ may be written in the form

$$P_n(x_k) = y_0 + \frac{\Delta y_0}{1!h}(x_k - x_0)^{(1)} + \frac{\Delta^2 y_0}{2!h^2}(x_k - x_0)^{(2)} + \cdots + \frac{\Delta^k y_0}{k!h^k}(x_k - x_0)^{(k)}. \tag{6.106}$$

Then

$$x_k - x_0 = kh, \quad x_k - x_1 = (k-1)h, \quad x_k - x_2 = (k-2)h, \quad \ldots, \quad x_k - x_{k-1} = h \tag{6.107}$$

and formula (6.106) is now written as

$$P_n(x_k) = y_0 + \frac{\Delta y_0}{1!h}kh + \frac{\Delta^2 y_0}{2!h^2}k(k-1)h^2 + \cdots + \frac{\Delta^k y_0}{k!h^k}h^k k(k-1) \cdots 1. \tag{6.108}$$

Because

$$\frac{k(k-1)\cdots[k-(p-1)]}{p!} = C_k^p, \tag{6.109}$$

relation (6.108) becomes

$$P_n(x_k) = y_0 + C_k^1 \Delta y_0 + C_k^2 \Delta^2 y_0 + \cdots + C_k^k \Delta^k y_0. \tag{6.110}$$

But we know that

$$y_k = (1 + \Delta)^k y_0 \tag{6.111}$$

and it follows that

$$P_n(x_k) = (1 + \Delta)^k y_0 = y_k. \tag{6.112}$$

We calculate

$$\frac{(x - x_0)^k}{h^k} = \frac{(x - x_0)(x - x_1) \cdots (x - x_{k-1})}{h^k} = \frac{x - x_0}{h} \frac{x - x_1}{h} \cdots \frac{x - x_{k-1}}{h}. \tag{6.113}$$

But

$$\frac{x - x_0}{h} = q, \quad \frac{x - x_1}{h} = \frac{x - x_0 - h}{h} = q - 1, \quad \ldots, \quad \frac{x - x_{k-1}}{h} = \frac{x - x_0 - (k-1)h}{h} = q - (k-1) \tag{6.114}$$

and, taking into account the relation (6.103), we obtain the relation (6.89); hence the proposition is proved.

Definition 6.6   The polynomial $P_n(x)$ is called *Newton's polynomial* or *Newton's forward polynomial*.

Observation 6.6   Newton's formula (6.89) is inconvenient for x contiguous to the value x_n (x situated in the inferior part of the finite difference table); therefore, another Newton's polynomial beginning with x_n is necessary.

Observation 6.7   Because

$$f_k^{(k)} = \lim_{\Delta x \to 0} \frac{\Delta^k f(x)}{(\Delta x)^k}, \tag{6.115}$$

corresponding to the demonstrations in Section 6.3 and considering that

$$\lim_{h \to 0} \frac{\Delta^k y_0}{h^k} = y^{(k)}(x_0), \tag{6.116}$$

it follows that

$$f^{(k)} = y^{(k)}(x_0), \tag{6.117}$$

so that Newton's polynomial is transformed into the formula of expansion into a Taylor series.

Proposition 6.6   Let $f : [a, b] \to \mathbb{R}$ and the equidistant interpolation knots $x_i = x_0 + ih$, $i = \overline{0, n}$. Let us denote by y_i the values of the function f at the points x_i, $y_i = f(x_i)$, $i = \overline{0, n}$. Under these conditions, the polynomial of degree n at the most, given by

$$P_n(x) = y_n + \frac{q}{1!} \Delta y_{n-1} + \frac{q(q+1)}{2!} \Delta^2 y_{n-2} + \cdots + \frac{q(q+1) \cdots (q+n-1)}{n!} \Delta^n y_0, \tag{6.118}$$

is an interpolation polynomial with

$$q = \frac{x - x_n}{h}. \tag{6.119}$$

Demonstration.   We seek the polynomial $P_n(x)$ in the form

$$P_n(x) = a_0 + a_1(x - x_n) + a_2(x - x_n)(x - x_{n-1}) + \cdots + a_n(x - x_n)(x - x_{n-1}) \cdots (x - x_1). \tag{6.120}$$

The condition $P_n(x_i) = y_i$ is equivalent to the condition

$$\Delta^i P_n(x_{n-i}) = \Delta^i y_{n-i}. \tag{6.121}$$

Relation (6.120) may also be written in the form

$$P_n(x) = a_0 + a_1(x - x_n)^{(1)} + a_2(x - x_{n-1})^{(2)} + \cdots + a_n(x - x_1)^{(n)}. \tag{6.122}$$

We obtain

$$P_n(x_n) = a_0, \tag{6.123}$$

for $i = 0$ in relation (6.121), from which

$$a_0 = y_n. \tag{6.124}$$

If we make $i = 1$ in the same relation, then it follows that

$$\Delta P_n(x_{n-1}) = \Delta y_{n-1}, \tag{6.125}$$

where

$$\Delta P_n(x_{n-1}) = 1 \times a_1 \times h; \tag{6.126}$$

hence,

$$a_1 = \frac{\Delta y_{n-1}}{1!h}. \tag{6.127}$$

On the other hand,

$$\Delta^2 P_n(x) = 1 \times 2 \times a_2 h^2 + 2 \times 3a_3 h^2(x - x_{n-2})^{(1)} + \cdots + n(n-1)(x - x_1)^{(n-2)}; \tag{6.128}$$

making $x = x_{n-2}$, we obtain

$$\Delta^2 P_n(x_{n-2}) = 2!a_2 h^2. \tag{6.129}$$

But

$$\Delta^2 P_n(x_{n-2}) = \Delta^2 y_{n-2}, \tag{6.130}$$

corresponding to relation (6.121) for $i = 2$ so that it follows that

$$a_2 = \frac{\Delta^2 y_{n-2}}{2!h^2}. \tag{6.131}$$

Step by step, we obtain

$$a_i = \frac{\Delta^i y_{n-i}}{i!h^i}, \quad i = \overline{0, n}. \tag{6.132}$$

Newton's polynomial becomes

$$P_n(x) = y_n + \frac{\Delta y_{n-1}}{1!h}(x - x_n)^{(1)} + \frac{\Delta^2 y_{n-2}}{2!h^2}(x - x_{n-1})^{(2)} + \cdots + \frac{\Delta^n y_0}{n!h^n}(x - x_1)^{(n)}. \tag{6.133}$$

$P_n(x)$ is an interpolation polynomial, that is,

$$P_n(x_i) = y_i, \quad i = \overline{0, n}. \tag{6.134}$$

Firstly, let us observe that

$$(x - x_{n-k})^{(k+p)} = 0,$$ (6.135)

for any $p \in \mathbb{N}^*$; hence,

$$P_n(x_i) = y_n + \frac{\Delta y_{n-1}}{1!h}(x_i - x_n)^{(1)} + \frac{\Delta^2 y_{n-2}}{2!h}(x_i - x_{n-1})^{(2)} + \cdots + \frac{\Delta^{n-i} y_i}{(n-i)!h^{n-i}}(x_i - x_{i+1})^{(n-i)}.$$ (6.136)

Then

$$x_i - x_n = (i - n)h, \quad x_i - x_{n-1} = (i - n + 1)h, \quad \ldots, \quad x_i - x_{i+1} = -h$$ (6.137)

and relation (6.136) reads

$$P_n(x_i) = y_n + \frac{(i-n)h}{1!h}\Delta y_{n-1} + \frac{(i-n)(i-n+1)h^2}{2!h^2}\Delta^2 y_{n-2} + \cdots$$
$$+ \frac{(i-n)(i-n+1)\cdots(-1)h^{n-i}}{(n-i)!h^{n-i}}\Delta^{n-i} y_i.$$ (6.138)

On the other hand,

$$\frac{i-n}{1!} = -\frac{n-i}{1!} = -C_{n-i}^1, \quad \frac{(i-n)(i-n+1)\cdots(-1)}{2!}$$
$$= \frac{(n-i)(n-i-1)}{2!} = C_{n-i}^2, \quad \ldots,$$ (6.139)
$$\frac{(i-n)(i-n+1)\cdots(-1)}{(n-i)!} = (-1)^{n-i}\frac{(n-i)!}{(n-i)!} = (-1)^{n-i}C_{n-i}^{n-i}$$

and relation (6.138) leads to

$$P_n(x_i) = y_n - C_{n-i}^1\Delta y_{n-1} + C_{n-i}^2\Delta^2 y_{n-2} + \cdots + (-1)^{n-i}C_{n-i}^{n-i}\Delta^{n-i}y_i = y_i,$$ (6.140)

corresponding to Section 6.3.

We have

$$\frac{x - x_n}{h} = q, \quad \frac{x - x_{n-1}}{h} = \frac{x - x_n + h}{h} = q + 1, \quad \frac{x - x_{n-2}}{h} = \frac{x - x_n + 2h}{h} = q + 2, \quad \ldots,$$
$$\frac{x - x_1}{h} = \frac{x - x_n + (n-1)h}{h} = q + (n-1)$$ (6.141)

and relation (6.133) leads to relation (6.118), which had to be proved.

Definition 6.7   The polynomial $P_n(x)$ is called *Newton's polynomial* or *Newton's backward polynomial*.

Observation 6.8   Newton's formula (6.118) is used for values contiguous to x_n (situated in the inferior part of the finite differences table).

Observation 6.9

(i) We know that the Lagrange interpolation polynomial is unique; hence, Newton's polynomials are in fact Lagrange polynomials written differently.

(ii) The error in case of the Lagrange polynomial is given by

$$|f(x) - L_n(x)| = \frac{|f^{(n+1)}(\zeta)|}{(n+1)!}|P_{n+1}(x)|, \tag{6.142}$$

where ζ is a point situated in the interval $[a, b]$, while

$$P_{n+1}(x) = (x - x_0)(x - x_1) \cdots (x - x_n). \tag{6.143}$$

Considering that

$$P_{n+1}(x) = qh(q-1)h \cdots (q-n)h = q(q-1)\cdots(q-n)h^{n+1}, \tag{6.144}$$

where we used Newton's forward polynomial and the relation

$$f^{(n+1)}(\zeta) = \lim_{h \to 0} \frac{\Delta^{n+1} f(\zeta)}{h^{n+1}}, \tag{6.145}$$

relation (6.144) becomes

$$|f(x) - P_n(x)| \approx \frac{\Delta^{n+1} f(\zeta)}{(n+1)! h^{n+1}} q^{[n+1]} h^{n+1} \approx \frac{\Delta^{n+1} y_0 q^{[n+1]}}{(n+1)!}. \tag{6.146}$$

Analogically, for Newton's backward polynomial we have

$$P_{n+1} = qh(q+1)h \cdots (q+n)h = q(q+1)\cdots(q+n)h^{n+1} \tag{6.147}$$

and it follows that

$$|f(x) - P_n(x)| \approx \frac{\Delta^{n+1} f(\zeta)}{(n+1)! h^{n+1}}(q+n)^{(n+1)} h^{n+1} \approx \frac{\Delta^{n+1} y_0 (q+n)^{(n+1)}}{(n+1)!}. \tag{6.148}$$

6.5 CENTRAL DIFFERENCES: GAUSS'S FORMULAE, STIRLING'S FORMULA, BESSEL'S FORMULA, EVERETT'S FORMULAE

Let us consider the function $f : [a, b] \to \mathbb{R}$ and $2n + 1$ equidistant points in the interval $[a, b]$. We denote these points by $x_{-n}, x_{-n+1}, \ldots, x_{-1}, x_0, x_1, \ldots, x_{n-1}, x_n$ and denote by h the step

$$h = x_{i+1} - x_i = \text{const}, \quad i = \overline{-n, n-1}. \tag{6.149}$$

Theorem 6.4 (Gauss's first formula[4]). Under the above conditions and denoting

$$q = \frac{x - x_0}{h} \tag{6.150}$$

and $y_i = f(x_i)$, $i = \overline{-n, n}$, there exists a unique interpolation polynomial of degree $2n$ at the most, the expression of which is

---

[4]Carl Friedrich Gauss (1777–1855) gave these formulae in 1812, in a lecture on interpolation.

$$P(x) = y_0 + q\Delta y_0 + \frac{q(q-1)}{2!}\Delta^2 y_{-1} + \frac{(q+1)q(q-1)}{3!}\Delta^3 y_{-1}$$

$$+ \frac{(q+1)q(q-1)(q-2)}{4!}\Delta^4 y_{-2} + \frac{(q+2)(q+1)q(q-1)(q-2)}{5!}\Delta^5 y_{-2} \quad (6.151)$$

$$+ \cdots + \frac{(q+n-1)\cdots(q+1)q(q-1)\cdots(q-n)}{(2n)!}\Delta^{2n} y_{-n}.$$

Demonstration. In the case of Gauss's polynomial, the conditions are

$$\Delta^k P(x_i) = \Delta^k y_i, \quad i = \overline{-n, n}, \quad k = \overline{0, 2n}. \quad (6.152)$$

We require the polynomial in the form

$$P(x) = a_0 + a_1(x - x_{-1})^{(-1)} + a_2(x - x_{-1})^{(2)} + a_3(x - x_{-2})^{(3)}$$

$$+ a_4(x - x_{-2})^{(4)} + \cdots + a_{2n-1}(x - x_{-n})^{(2n-1)} + a_{2n}(x - x_{-n})^{(2n)}. \quad (6.153)$$

Proceeding as with Newton's polynomials, conditions (6.152) lead to

$$a_0 = y_0, \quad a_1 = \frac{\Delta y_0}{1!h}, \quad a_2 = \frac{\Delta^2 y_{-1}}{2!h^2}, \quad a_3 = \frac{\Delta^3 y_{-1}}{3!h^3}, \quad a_4 = \frac{\Delta^4 y_{-2}}{4!h^4}, \quad \ldots, \quad a_{2n} = \frac{\Delta^{2n} y_{-n}}{(2n)!h^{2n}}.$$
$$(6.154)$$

Taking into account equation (6.150) and equation (6.154) and replacing in relation (6.153), we get formula (6.151), which had to be proved. As for Newton's polynomials, we may show that $P(x)$ is an interpolation polynomial.

Observation 6.10 The first Gauss formula may also be written in the form

$$P(x) = y_0 + q^{(1)}\Delta y_0 + \frac{q^{(2)}}{2!}\Delta^2 y_{-1} + \frac{(q+1)^{(3)}}{3!}\Delta^3 y_{-1}$$

$$+ \frac{(q+1)^{(4)}}{4!}\Delta^4 y_{-2} + \cdots + \frac{(q+n-1)^{(2n)}}{(2n)!}\Delta^{2n} y_{-n}. \quad (6.155)$$

Definition 6.8 The finite differences Δy_{-1}, Δy_0, and $\Delta^2 y_{-1}$ are called *central differences*. For an arbitrary i between $-n+1$ and 0, we call central differences the finite differences Δy_{i-1}, Δy_i, and $\Delta^2 y_{i-1}$.

Theorem 6.5 (Gauss's Second Formula). Under the conditions of Theorem 6.4, the interpolation polynomial may be written in the form

$$P(x) = y_0 + q^{(1)}\Delta y_{-1} + \frac{(q+1)^{(2)}}{2!}\Delta^2 y_{-1} + \frac{(q+1)^{(3)}}{3!}\Delta^3 y_{-2}$$

$$+ \frac{(q+2)^{(4)}}{4!}\Delta^4 y_{-2} + \cdots + \frac{(q+n)^{(2n)}}{(2n)!}\Delta^{2n} y_{-n}. \quad (6.156)$$

Demonstration. It is analogous to the demonstrations of the first Gauss formula and the Newton polynomials.

Corollary 6.3 (The Stirling Formula[5]). Under the conditions of Theorem 6.4, the interpolation polynomial reads

$$
P(x) = y_0 + q\frac{\Delta y_{-1} + \Delta y_0}{2} + \frac{q^2}{2}\Delta^2 y_{-1} + \frac{q(q^2 - 1)}{3!}\frac{\Delta^3 y_{-2} + \Delta^3 y_{-1}}{2}
$$

$$
+ \frac{q^2(q^2 - 1)}{4!}\Delta^4 y_{-2} + \frac{q(q^2 - 1^2)(q^2 - 2^2)}{5!}\frac{\Delta^5 y_{-3} + \Delta^5 y_{-2}}{2} \tag{6.157}
$$

$$
+ \cdots + \frac{q^2(q^2 - 1^2)\cdots[q^2 - (n - 1)^2]}{(2n)!}\Delta^{2n} y_{-n}.
$$

Demonstration. Formula (6.157) is the arithmetic mean of relations (6.151) and (6.156).

For Bessel's formulae[6] we start from Gauss second formula, in which we take as initial values x_1 and, correspondingly, $y_1 = f(x_1)$. We have

$$
\frac{x - x_1}{h} = q - 1 \tag{6.158}
$$

and, replacing q by $q - 1$, we obtain

$$
P(x) = y_1 + (q - 1)\Delta y_0 + \frac{q(q - 1)}{2!}\Delta^2 y_0 + \frac{q(q - 1)(q - 2)}{3!}\Delta^3 y_{-1}
$$

$$
+ \frac{(q + 1)q(q - 1)(q - 2)}{4!}\Delta^4 y_{-1} + \frac{(q + 1)q(q - 1)(q - 2)(q - 3)}{5!}\Delta^5 y_{-2}
$$

$$
+ \cdots + \frac{(q + n - 2)(q + n - 3)\cdots(q - n)}{(2n - 1)!}\Delta^{2n-1} y_{-(n-1)} \tag{6.159}
$$

$$
+ \frac{(q + n - 1)(q + n - 2)\cdots(q - n)}{(2n)!}\Delta^{2n} y_{-(n-1)}.
$$

To obtain the first interpolation formula of Bessel, we take the arithmetic mean between relation (6.159) and the first interpolation formula of Gauss, resulting in

$$
P(x) = \frac{y_0 + y_1}{2} + \left(q - \frac{1}{2}\right)\Delta y_0 + \frac{q(q - 1)}{2!}\frac{\Delta^2 y_{-1} + \Delta^2 y_0}{2} + \frac{\left(q - \frac{1}{2}\right)q(q - 1)}{3!}\Delta^3 y_{-1}
$$

$$
+ \frac{q(q - 1)(q + 1)(q - 2)}{4!}\frac{\Delta^4 y_{-2} + \Delta^4 y_{-1}}{2} + \frac{\left(q - \frac{1}{2}\right)q(q - 1)(q + 1)(q - 2)}{5!}\Delta^5 y_{-2}
$$

$$
+ \frac{q(q - 1)(q + 1)(q - 2)(q + 2)(q - 3)}{6!}\frac{\Delta^6 y_{-3} + \Delta^6 y_{-2}}{2} + \cdots
$$

$$
+ \frac{q(q - 1)(q + 1)(q - 2)(q + 2)\cdots(q - n)(q + n - 1)}{(2n)!}\frac{\Delta^{2n} y_{-n} + \Delta^{2n} y_{-n+1}}{2}
$$

$$
+ \frac{\left(q - \frac{1}{2}\right)q(q - 1)(q + 1)(q - 2)(q + 2)\cdots(q - n)(q + n - 1)}{(2n + 1)!}\Delta^{2n+1} y_{-n}, \tag{6.160}
$$

---

[5]In 1719, James Stirling (1692–1770) discussed some Newton's interpolation formulae in *Methodus Differentialis*. In 1730, Stirling published a more elaborate booklet on the topic.
[6]Friedrich Wilhelm Bessel (1784–1846) published these formulae in 1824.

where

$$q = \frac{x - x_0}{h}. \tag{6.161}$$

The polynomial $P(x)$ in formula (6.160) coincides with $f(x)$ at the points $x_{-n}, x_{-n+1}, \ldots, x_n, x_{n+1}$, that is, at $2n + 2$ points.

If we consider the particular case $n = 1$, then we obtain the quadratic interpolation formula of Bessel

$$P(x) = y_0 + q \Delta y_0 + \frac{q(q-1)}{4} (\Delta y_1 - \Delta y_{-1}). \tag{6.162}$$

Let us observe that in Bessel's formula (6.160) all the terms that contain differences of odd order have the factor $(q - 1/2)$. If we choose $q = 1/2$, then we obtain Bessel's dichotomy formula

$$P\left(\frac{x_0 + x_1}{2}\right) = \frac{y_0 + y_1}{2} - \frac{1}{8} \frac{\Delta^2 y_{-1} + \Delta^2 y_0}{2} + \frac{3}{128} \frac{\Delta^4 y_{-2} + \Delta^4 y_{-1}}{2}$$

$$- \frac{5}{1024} \frac{\Delta^4 y_{-3} + \Delta^4 y_{-2}}{2} + \cdots \tag{6.163}$$

$$+ (-1)^n \frac{[1 \times 3 \times 5 \times \cdots \times (2n-1)]^2}{2^{2n}(2n)!} \frac{\Delta^{2n} y_{-n} + \Delta^{2n} y_{-n+1}}{2}.$$

If we denote

$$q_1 = q - \frac{1}{2}, \tag{6.164}$$

then Bessel's formula reads

$$P(x) = \frac{y_0 + y_1}{2} + q_1 \Delta y_0 + \frac{q_1^2 - \frac{1}{4}}{2!} \frac{\Delta^2 y_{-1} + \Delta^2 y_0}{2} + \frac{q_1 \left(q_1^2 - \frac{1}{4}\right)}{3!} \Delta^3 y_{-1}$$

$$+ \frac{\left(q_1^2 - \frac{1}{4}\right)\left(q_1^2 - \frac{9}{4}\right)}{4!} \frac{\Delta^4 y_{-2} + \Delta^4 y_{-1}}{2} + \frac{q \left(q_1^2 - \frac{1}{4}\right)\left(q_1^2 - \frac{9}{4}\right)}{5!} \Delta^5 y_{-2}$$

$$+ \frac{\left(q_1^2 - \frac{1}{4}\right)\left(q_1^2 - \frac{9}{4}\right)\left(q_1^2 - \frac{25}{4}\right)}{6!} \frac{\Delta^6 y_{-3} + \Delta^6 y_{-2}}{2} + \cdots$$

$$+ \frac{\left(q_1^2 - \frac{1}{4}\right)\left(q_1^2 - \frac{9}{4}\right) \cdots \left[q_1^2 - \frac{(2n-1)^2}{4}\right]}{(2n)!} \frac{\Delta^{2n} y_{-n} + \Delta^{2n} y_{-n+1}}{2}$$

$$+ \frac{q_1 \left(q_1^2 - \frac{1}{4}\right)\left(q_1^2 - \frac{9}{4}\right) \cdots \left[q_1^2 - \frac{(2n-1)^2}{4}\right]}{(2n+)!} \Delta^{2n+} y_{-n+1}, \tag{6.165}$$

where

$$q_1 = \frac{x - \dfrac{x_0 + x_1}{2}}{h}. \tag{6.166}$$

Definition 6.9 We define the operator δ by the relations

$$\delta f(x) = f\left(x + \frac{h}{2}\right) - f\left(x - \frac{h}{2}\right), \quad \delta^{k+1} f(x) = \delta^k f\left(x + \frac{h}{2}\right) - \delta^k f\left(x - \frac{h}{2}\right), \tag{6.167}$$

where $k \geq 1$, $k \in \mathbb{N}$.

Observation 6.11

(i) Calculating $\delta^2 f(x)$, we obtain

$$\delta^2 f(x) = \delta f\left(x + \frac{h}{2}\right) - \delta f\left(x - \frac{h}{2}\right) = f(x+h) - 2f(x) + f(x-h). \qquad (6.168)$$

(ii) Proceeding by induction, it follows immediately that if k is an even number, then in the calculation of $\delta^k y_p$ supplementary intermediate points do not appear. Indeed, if $k = 2$, we have seen above that the affirmation is true. Let us suppose that the affirmation is true for $k = 2l$ and let us show that it remains true for $k = 2l + 2$, $l \in \mathbb{N}$, $l \geq 1$. We have

$$\delta^{2l+2} y_p = \delta^{2l-2} y_{p+1} - 2\delta^{2l-2} y_p + \delta^{2l-2} y_{p-1} \qquad (6.169)$$

and, because all the terms on the right side do not introduce new supplementary points besides the given ones $x_{-n}, x_{-n+1}, \ldots, x_n$, the affirmation is proved.

Starting from the first formula of Gauss and writing all the finite differences as a function of $\delta^k y_0$ and $\delta^k y_1$, we obtain the first Everett formula[7]

$$P(x) = (1-q)y_0 - \frac{q(q-1)(q-2)}{3!}\delta^2 y_0 - \frac{(q+1)q(q-1)(q-2)(q-3)}{5!}\delta^4 y_0 - \cdots$$

$$- \frac{(q+n-1)(q+n-2)\cdots(q-n-1)}{(2n+1)!}\delta^{2n} y_0 + q y_1 + \frac{(q+1)q(q-1)}{3!}\delta^2 y_1$$

$$+ \frac{(q+2)(q+1)q(q-1)(q-2)}{5!}\delta^4 y_1 + \cdots + \frac{(q+n)(q+n-1)\cdots(q-n)}{(2n+1)!}\delta^{2n} y_1. \qquad (6.170)$$

Observation 6.12

(i) The expression $\delta y_{p+1/2}$ reads

$$\delta y_{p+\frac{1}{2}} = f(x_p + h) - f(x_p) = y_{p+1} - y_p. \qquad (6.171)$$

(ii) Proceeding as with Observation 6.11, we deduce that $\delta^k y_{p+1/2}$ does not introduce supplementary points if k is a natural odd number.

The first Gauss formula may also be written in the form

$$P(x) = y_0 + \frac{q+1}{2!}\delta y_{\frac{1}{2}} + \frac{(q+2)(q+1)q(q-1)}{4!}\delta^3 y_{\frac{1}{2}} + \cdots$$

$$+ \frac{(q+n+1)(q+n)\cdots(q-n)}{(2n+2)!}\delta^{2n+1} y_{\frac{1}{2}} - \frac{q(q-1)}{2!}\delta y_{-\frac{1}{2}}$$

$$- \frac{(q+1)q(q-1)(q-2)}{4!}\delta^3 y_{-\frac{1}{2}} - \cdots$$

$$- \frac{(q+n)(q+n-1)\cdots(q-n-1)}{(2n+2)!}\delta^{2n+1} y_{-\frac{1}{2}}, \qquad (6.172)$$

called the *second interpolation formula of Everett* or the *interpolation formula of Steffensen*.[8]

[7]Joseph Davis Everett (1831–1904) published his formulae in 1900.
[8]The formula is called after Johan Frederik Steffensen (1873–1961) who presented it in 1950.

6.6   DIVIDED DIFFERENCES

Definition 6.10   Let there be $f : I \subset \mathbb{R} \to \mathbb{R}$, I interval of the real axis, and the division points $x_1, x_2, \ldots, x_n$. The values of the function at these points are $y_i = f(x_i)$, $i = \overline{1, n}$. We define the divided differences by the relations

$$[x_i, x_j] = f(x_i; x_j) = \frac{f(x_j) - f(x_i)}{x_j - x_i}, \tag{6.173}$$

$$[x_i, x_j, x_k] = f(x_i; x_j; x_k) = \frac{f(x_j; x_k) - f(x_i; x_j)}{x_k - x_i}, \tag{6.174}$$

and, in general, by

$$[x_{i_1}, x_{i_2}, \ldots, x_{i_{k+1}}] = f(x_{i_1}; x_{i_2}; \ldots; x_{i_{k+1}}) = \frac{f(x_{i_2}; \ldots; x_{i_{k+1}}) - f(x_{i_1}; \ldots; x_{i_k})}{x_{i_{k+1}} - x_{i_1}}, \tag{6.175}$$

where $i_l \in \{1, 2, \ldots, n\}$, $l = \overline{1, k + 1}$.

Theorem 6.6   There exists the relation

$$f(x_1; \ldots; x_k) = \sum_{\substack{j=1 \\ j \neq i}}^{k} \frac{f(x_j)}{\prod(x_j - x_i)}. \tag{6.176}$$

Demonstration. We proceed by induction. For $k = 1$, we have

$$f(x_1) = f(x_1) \tag{6.177}$$

which is true.

For $k = 2$, we obtain

$$f(x_1; x_2) = \frac{f(x_2)}{x_2 - x_1} + \frac{f(x_1)}{x_1 - x_2} = \frac{f(x_2) - f(x_1)}{x_2 - x_1}, \tag{6.178}$$

which is the definition of divided differences.

Let us suppose now that the affirmation is valid for any $i \leq k$ and let us show that it exists for $k + 1$. We have

$$f(x_1; \ldots; x_{k+1}) = \frac{f(x_2; \ldots; x_{k+1}) - f(x_1; \ldots; x_k)}{x_{k+1} - x_1}$$

$$= \frac{1}{x_{k+1} - x_1} \left[\sum_{j=2}^{k+1} \frac{f(x_j)}{\prod_{\substack{2 \leq i \leq k+1 \\ i \neq j}} (x_j - x_i)} - \sum_{j=1}^{k} \frac{f(x_j)}{\prod_{\substack{1 \leq i \leq k \\ i \neq j}} (x_j - x_i)} \right], \tag{6.179}$$

corresponding to the induction hypothesis.

We calculate the coefficient of $f(x_j)$, that is,

$$c_j = \frac{1}{x_{k+1} - x_1} \left[\frac{1}{\displaystyle\prod_{\substack{2 \le i \le k+1 \\ i \ne j}} (x_j - x_i)} - \frac{1}{\displaystyle\prod_{\substack{1 \le i \le k \\ i \ne j}} (x_j - x_i)} \right] \tag{6.180}$$

$$= \frac{(x_j - x_1) - (x_j - x_{k+1})}{(x_{k+1} - x_1) \displaystyle\prod_{\substack{1 \le i \le k+1 \\ i \ne j}} (x_j - x_i)} = \frac{1}{\displaystyle\prod_{\substack{1 \le i \le k+1 \\ i \ne j}} (x_j - x_i)}$$

and the theorem is proved.

Observation 6.13

(i) The divided differences are linear operators, that is,

$$\left(\sum_{i=1}^{l} \alpha_i f_i \right) (x_1; \ldots ; x_k) = \sum_{i=1}^{l} \alpha_i f_i (x_1; \ldots ; x_k). \tag{6.181}$$

(ii) A divided difference is an even function with respect to its arguments.

We may construct Table 6.2 of divided differences in the following form.

Observation 6.14

(i) If $x_2 = x_1 + \varepsilon$, then

$$f(x_1; x_2) = \frac{f(x_1 + \varepsilon) - f(x_1)}{\varepsilon} \tag{6.182}$$

and it follows that

$$f(x; x) = \lim_{\varepsilon \to 0} \frac{f(x + \varepsilon) - f(x)}{\varepsilon} = f'(x). \tag{6.183}$$

(ii) In general,

$$f(x; x; \ldots ; x) = \frac{1}{k!} f^{(k)}(x), \tag{6.184}$$

where x appears k times in the left part of formula (6.184).

TABLE 6.2 Table of Divided Differences

x_1	$f(x_1)$				
		$f(x_1; x_2)$			
x_2	$f(x_2)$		$f(x_1; x_2; x_3)$		
		$f(x_2; x_3)$		$f(x_1; x_2; x_3; x_4)$	
x_3	$f(x_3)$		$f(x_2; x_3; x_4)$		$f(x_1; x_2; x_3; x_4; x_5)$	$\ldots$
		$f(x_3; x_4)$		$f(x_2; x_3; x_4; x_5)$	
x_4	$f(x_4)$		$f(x_3; x_4; x_5)$		
$\ldots$	$\ldots$	$\ldots$	$\ldots$	$\ldots$	$\ldots$	$\ldots$
x_n	$f(x_n)$				

The demonstration is made by induction. For $k = 1$, the affirmation has been given at point (i). Let us suppose that the affirmation holds for k and that it remains valid for $k + 1$. We may write

$$f(x; \ldots ; x; x)_{k+1 \text{ times}} = \lim_{\varepsilon \to 0} f(x; x + \varepsilon; \ldots ; x + (k+1)\varepsilon)$$

$$= \lim_{\varepsilon \to 0} \frac{f(x + \varepsilon; \ldots ; x + (k+1)\varepsilon) - f(x; \ldots ; x + k\varepsilon)}{x + (k+1)\varepsilon - x} \tag{6.185}$$

$$= \frac{1}{k+1} \frac{f^{(k+1)}(x)}{k!} = \frac{f^{(k+1)}(x)}{(k+1)!},$$

the affirmation thus being proved.

(iii) There exists the relation

$$\frac{\mathrm{d}}{\mathrm{d}x} f(x_1; \ldots ; x_n; x) = f(x_1; \ldots ; x_n; x; x). \tag{6.186}$$

(iv) If $u_1, \ldots, u_p$ are differentiable functions of x, then

$$\frac{\mathrm{d}}{\mathrm{d}x} f(x_1; \ldots ; x_n; u_1; \ldots ; u_p) = \sum_{i=1}^{p} f(x_1; \ldots ; x_n; u_1; \ldots ; u_p; u_i) \frac{\mathrm{d}u_i}{\mathrm{d}x}. \tag{6.187}$$

(v) We may write

$$\frac{\mathrm{d}^r}{\mathrm{d}x^r} f(x_1; \ldots ; x_n; x) = \frac{1}{r!} f(x_1; \ldots ; x_n; x; \ldots ; x), \tag{6.188}$$

where x appears r times on the right side.

Theorem 6.7   Let $x_0, x_1, \ldots, x_n$ be distinct internal points of a connected domain $\mathcal{D}$ included in the complex plane and $f : \mathcal{D} \to \mathbb{C}$ holomorphic. Under these conditions,

$$[x_0; x_1; \ldots ; x_n] = \frac{1}{2\pi \mathrm{i}} \oint_C \frac{f(z)\mathrm{d}z}{(z - x_0) \cdots (z - x_n)}, \tag{6.189}$$

where C is a rectifiable contour in the complex plane, contained in $\mathcal{D}$, which contains in its interior the points $x_0, x_1, \ldots, x_n$.

Demonstration.   Let

$$I = \frac{1}{2\pi \mathrm{i}} \oint_C \frac{f(z)\mathrm{d}z}{(z - x_0) \cdots (z - x_n)}, \tag{6.190}$$

where C is passed through in the positive sense. We apply the residue theorem, knowing that the function under the integral admits the poles of the first order $x_0, x_1, \ldots, x_n$; it follows that

$$I = \sum_{k=0}^{n} \frac{f(x_k)}{\prod_{\substack{i=0 \\ i \neq k}}^{n} (x_k - x_i)}, \tag{6.191}$$

the last expression being $[x_0; x_1; \ldots ; x_n]$, in conformity with Theorem 6.6.

Observation 6.15

(i) It follows that Theorem 6.7 is true in the domain of holomorphy of the function $f(z)$ too; hence, the representation remains valid, immaterial of the choice of the points x_i in the domain bounded by the curve C, in particular, if these points coincide.

(ii) If we denote by L the length of the curve C, then we have

$$|[x_0; x_1; \ldots; x_n]| \leq \frac{L}{2\pi} \frac{\max\limits_{z \in C}|f(z)|}{\min\limits_{z \in C}|(z - x_0) \cdots (z - x_n)|}. \tag{6.192}$$

Theorem 6.8 (Hermite). Let $f : \mathcal{D} \to \mathbb{C}$ analytic, $\mathcal{D}$ connected, with z_k, $k = \overline{1, \nu}$, interpolation knots of multiplicity orders p_k, $\sum_{k=0}^{\nu} p_k = n + 1$. Under these conditions, we have

$$f(x) = \sum_{k=1}^{\nu} \left[\sum_{k=0}^{p_k-1} \left[\sum_{s=0}^{m} \frac{f^{(m)}(z_k)}{(p_k - m - 1)!(m - s)!} \frac{d^{m-s}}{dz^{m-s}} \left[\frac{(z - z_k)^{p_k}}{Q(z)} \right] \Big|_{z=z_k} \frac{Q(x)}{(x - z_k)^{s+1}} \right] \right] \tag{6.193}$$

$$+ Q(x)[x_0; x_1; \ldots x_n],$$

where x_0, x_1, $\ldots$, x_n are the interpolation knots z_1, $\ldots$, z_ν too, but counted as many times as indicated by the multiplicity order, $x = x_0$, while Q will be specified later.

Demonstration. From Theorem 6.7, we have

$$[x_0; x_1; \ldots; x_n] = \frac{1}{2\pi i} \oint_C \frac{f(z)dz}{(z - z_0)^{p_0} \cdots (z - z_\nu)^{p_\nu}}. \tag{6.194}$$

Let us choose the curves C_k in the form of circles of radii r_k, sufficiently small, centered at z_k, and interior to the domain bounded by the curve C. It follows that formula (6.194) may be written in the form

$$[x_0; x_1; \ldots; x_n] = \frac{1}{2\pi i} \oint_{C_k} \frac{f(z)dz}{(z - z_0)^{p_0} \cdots (z - z_\nu)^{p_\nu}}. \tag{6.195}$$

We denote

$$q(z) = \prod_{k=0}^{\nu} (z - z_k)^{p_k}, \tag{6.196}$$

$$I_k = \frac{1}{2\pi i} \oint_{C_k} \left[\frac{(z - z_k)^{p_k}}{q(z)} f(z) \right] \frac{1}{(z - z_k)^{p_k}} dz. \tag{6.197}$$

The function $(z - z_k)^{p_k} f(z)/q(z)$ is holomorphic in the circle bounded by C_k.
From Cauchy's theorem, we have

$$I_k = \frac{1}{(p_k - 1)!} \frac{d^{p_k-1}}{dz^{p_k-1}} \left[\frac{(z - z_k)^{p_k}}{q(z)} f(z) \right] \Big|_{z=z_k}. \tag{6.198}$$

Applying now Leibniz's formula of differentiation of a product of functions, follows that

$$I = \sum_{k=0}^{\nu} \left\{ \sum_{m=0}^{p_k-1} \left[\frac{f^{(m)}(z_k)}{(p_k - m - 1)!} \frac{d^m}{dz^m} \left[\frac{(z - z_k)^{p_k}}{q(z)} \right] \Big|_{z=z_k} \right] \right\}. \tag{6.199}$$

We denote

$$Q(z) = \frac{q(z)}{z - x} \prod_{k=1}^{\nu} (z - z_k)^{p_k} \tag{6.200}$$

and have

$$I = \sum_{k=0}^{\nu} \left\{ \sum_{m=0}^{p_k - 1} \left[\frac{f^{(m)}(z_k)}{(p_k - m - 1)!} \frac{\mathrm{d}^m}{\mathrm{d}z^m} \left[\frac{(z - z_k)^{p_k}}{Q(z)} \frac{1}{z - x} \right] \Bigg|_{z = z_k} \right] \right\}. \tag{6.201}$$

We make $k = 0$ and apply once more Leibniz's formula to relation (6.201), obtaining

$$I = \frac{f(x)}{Q(x)} - \sum_{k=1}^{\nu} \left\{ \sum_{m=0}^{p_k - 1} \left[\frac{f^{(m)}(z_k)}{(p_k - m - 1)!} \sum_{s=0}^{m} \frac{1}{(m - s)!} \frac{\mathrm{d}^m}{\mathrm{d}z^m} \left[\frac{(z - z_k)^{p_k}}{Q(z)} \frac{1}{z - x} \right] \Bigg|_{z = z_k} \right] \right\} \tag{6.202}$$
$$= [x_0; x_1; \ldots ; x_n],$$

that is, Hermite's formula, the theorem thus being proved.

6.7 NEWTON-TYPE FORMULA WITH DIVIDED DIFFERENCES

Lemma 6.1 If $P(x)$ is a polynomial of nth degree, then its divided difference of $(n + 1)$th order satisfies the relation

$$P(x; x_0; x_1; \ldots ; x_n) = 0, \tag{6.203}$$

where the knots x_i, $i = \overline{0, n}$, are distinct.

Demonstration. From the definition, we have

$$P(x; x_0) = \frac{P(x) - P(x_0)}{x - x_0}, \tag{6.204}$$

which is a polynomial of $(n - 1)$th degree.

Further,

$$P(x; x_0; x_1) = \frac{P(x; x_0) - P(x_0; x_1)}{x - x_1} \tag{6.205}$$

is a polynomial of $(n - 2)$th order. Moreover, it follows that $x - x_1$ divides $P(x; x_0) - P(x_0; x_1)$.

Proceeding step by step, we obtain $P(x; x_0; \ldots ; x_{n-1})$, which is a polynomial of zeroth degree, that is, a constant, which will be denoted by C. Finally,

$$P(x; x_0; x_1; \ldots ; x_n) = \frac{C - C}{x - x_n} = 0, \tag{6.206}$$

hence the lemma is proved.

A consequence for the Lagrange interpolation polynomial is immediately obtained. Indeed, if $P(x)$ is a Lagrange interpolation polynomial for which $P(x_i) = y_i$, $i = \overline{0, n}$, then

$$P(x; x_0; x_1; \ldots ; x_n) = 0. \tag{6.207}$$

On the other hand,

$$P(x) = P(x_0) + (x - x_0) \frac{P(x) - P(x_0)}{x - x_0} = P(x_0) + P(x; x_0)(x - x_0). \tag{6.208}$$

Proceeding step by step, it follows that

$$
\begin{aligned}
P(x) &= P(x_0) + P(x; x_0)(x - x_0) \\
&= P(x_0) + P(x_0; x_1)(x - x_0) + P(x; x_0; x_1)(x - x_0)(x - x_1) \\
&= P(x_0) + P(x_0; x_1)(x - x_0) + P(x; x_0; x_1)(x - x_0)(x - x_1) \\
&\quad + P(x; x_0; x_1; x_2)(x - x_0)(x - x_1)(x - x_2) \\
&= \cdots = P(x_0) + P(x_0; x_1)(x - x_0) + P(x; x_0; x_1)(x - x_0)(x - x_1) + \cdots \\
&\quad + P(x_0; x_1; \ldots; x_n)(x - x_0) \ldots (x - x_{n-1}) \\
&\quad + P(x; x_0; x_1; \ldots; x_n)(x - x_0) \ldots (x - x_{n-1})(x - x_n),
\end{aligned}
\tag{6.209}
$$

where we have marked the last term too, even if this one is equal to zero.

Definition 6.11   The expression

$$
\begin{aligned}
P(x) &= y_0 + [x_0, x_1](x - x_0) + [x_0, x_1, x_2](x - x_0)(x - x_1) + \cdots \\
&\quad + [x_0, x_1, \ldots, x_n](x - x_0) \cdots (x - x_{n-1})
\end{aligned}
\tag{6.210}
$$

is called *Newton-type formula* with divided differences.

6.8 INVERSE INTERPOLATION

The determination of the value x for which the function takes a certain value y is considered in the frame of the inverse interpolation.

Two cases may occur:

- the division points are equidistant;
- the division points are arbitrary.

Let us begin with the first case. Newton's forward interpolation polynomial leads to

$$
y = y_0 + \frac{q}{1!} \Delta y_0 + \frac{q(q-1)}{2!} \Delta^2 y_0 + \cdots + \frac{q(q-1) \cdots (q-n+1)}{n!} \Delta^n y_0;
\tag{6.211}
$$

that is,

$$
y = y(q).
\tag{6.212}
$$

The problem consists in solving equation (6.211), because if we know q and the relation

$$
q = \frac{x - x_0}{h},
\tag{6.213}
$$

h being the interpolation step, then it results automatically in the required value of x.

We start with an initial approximation of the solution and customarily we take

$$
q_0 = \frac{y - y_0}{\Delta y_0},
\tag{6.214}
$$

the solution obtained from equation (6.211) by neglecting the nonlinear terms.

If f is of class $C^{n+1}([a, b])$, $[a, b]$ being the interval that contains the points of division, while f is the function that connects the values x_i and $y_i = f(x_i)$, $i = \overline{0, n}$, then the iterative sequence given by the relation

$$
q_{p+1} = \frac{y - y_0}{\Delta y_0} - \frac{q_p(q_p - 1)}{2! \Delta y_0} - \cdots - \frac{q_p(q_p - 1) \cdots (q_p - n + 1)}{n!} \Delta^n y_0, \quad p \in \mathbb{N},
\tag{6.215}
$$

where q_0 is definite by equation (6.214), is convergent to $\bar{q}$, the solution of equation (6.211), the problem thus being solved.

If the knots are arbitrary, then instead of constructing the Lagrange polynomial that gives y as a function of x, we construct the Lagrange polynomial that gives x as a function of y, that is,

$$x = \sum_{i=0}^{n} \frac{(y - y_0) \cdots (y - y_{i-1})(y - y_{i+1}) \cdots (y - y_n)}{(y_i - y_0) \cdots (y_i - y_{i-1})(y_i - y_{i+1}) \cdots (y_i - y_n)} y_i \tag{6.216}$$

or

$$x = x_0 + [y_0, y_1](y - y_0) + [y_0, y_1, y_2](y - y_0)(y - y_1) + \cdots \\ + [y_0, y_1, \ldots, y_n](y - y_0)(y - y_1) \cdots (y - y_{n-1}), \tag{6.217}$$

the problem being solved by a simple numerical replacement.

Obviously, this method may be applied in the case of equidistant knots also.

6.9 DETERMINATION OF THE ROOTS OF AN EQUATION BY INVERSE INTERPOLATION

The method of determination of the roots of an equation by inverse interpolation is an application of the preceding paragraph.

The idea consists in construction of a table of values with knots that are equidistant or not and in finding the value $\bar{x}$ for which $f(\bar{x}) = 0$ at a certain interval.

An application consists in the determination of the eigenvalues of a matrix.

Let us consider the characteristic equation written in the form

$$D(\lambda) = \begin{vmatrix} a_{11} - \lambda & a_{12} & \cdots & a_{1n} \\ a_{21} & a_{22} - \lambda & \cdots & a_{2n} \\ \cdots & \cdots & \cdots & \cdots \\ a_{n1} & a_{n2} & \cdots & a_{nn} - \lambda \end{vmatrix} = 0, \tag{6.218}$$

and let us give to λ the values $0, 1, 2, \ldots, n$, resulting in $D(0), D(1), \ldots, D(n)$.

By using Newton's forward formula, we obtain

$$D(\lambda) = D(0) + \lambda \Delta D(0) + \frac{\lambda(\lambda - 1)}{2!} \Delta^2 D(0) + \cdots + \frac{\lambda(\lambda - 1) \cdots (\lambda - n + 1)}{n!} \Delta^n D(0). \tag{6.219}$$

On the other hand,

$$\frac{\lambda(\lambda - 1) \cdots (\lambda - r + 1)}{n!} = \sum_{p=1}^{r} c_{pr} \lambda^p, \quad r = \overline{1, n}, \tag{6.220}$$

so that expression (6.219) reads

$$D(\lambda) = D(0) + \sum_{p=1}^{n} \left(\lambda^p \sum_{i=p}^{n} c_{pi} \Delta^i D(0) \right), \tag{6.221}$$

thus obtaining Markoff's formula.

If, instead of the values $0, 1, \ldots, n$, we choose the values $a, a + h, \ldots, a + nh$, then Markoff's formula takes the form

$$D(\lambda) = D(a) + \sum_{p=1}^{n} \left[(\lambda - a)^p \sum_{i=p}^{n} c_{pi} h^i \Delta^i D(a) \right]. \tag{6.222}$$

Let us consider, for example, that the matrix $\mathbf{A}$ is given by

$$\mathbf{A} = \begin{bmatrix} 1 & 0 & 3 \\ 1 & 2 & -1 \\ 0 & 3 & 1 \end{bmatrix}; \tag{6.223}$$

then

$$D(0) = \begin{vmatrix} 1 & 0 & 3 \\ 1 & 2 & -1 \\ 0 & 3 & 1 \end{vmatrix} = 14, \quad D(1) = \begin{vmatrix} 0 & 0 & 3 \\ 1 & 1 & -1 \\ 0 & 3 & 0 \end{vmatrix} = 9,$$

$$\tag{6.224}$$

$$D(2) = \begin{vmatrix} -1 & 0 & 3 \\ 1 & 0 & -1 \\ 0 & 3 & -1 \end{vmatrix} = 6, \quad D(3) = \begin{vmatrix} -2 & 0 & 3 \\ 1 & -1 & -1 \\ 0 & 3 & -2 \end{vmatrix} = -1,$$

$$\frac{\lambda}{1!} = \lambda, \quad \frac{\lambda(\lambda - 1)}{2!} = \frac{\lambda^2}{2} - \frac{\lambda}{2}, \quad \frac{\lambda(\lambda - 1)(\lambda - 2)}{3!} = \frac{\lambda^3}{6} - \frac{\lambda^2}{2} + \frac{\lambda}{3}, \tag{6.225}$$

$$c_{11} = 1, \quad c_{12} = -\frac{1}{2}, \quad c_{22} = \frac{1}{2}, \quad c_{13} = \frac{1}{3}, \quad c_{23} = -\frac{1}{2}, \quad c_{33} = \frac{1}{6}. \tag{6.226}$$

We thus construct Table 6.3, the table of finite differences.
We obtain

$$\begin{aligned} D(\lambda) &= D(0) + \lambda(c_{11}\Delta D(0) + c_{12}\Delta^2 D(0) + c_{13}\Delta^3 D(0)) \\ &\quad + \lambda^2(c_{22}\Delta^2 D(0) + c_{23}\Delta^3 D(0)) + \lambda^3 c_{33}\Delta^3 D(0) \\ &= 14 - 8\lambda + 4\lambda^2 - \lambda^3. \end{aligned} \tag{6.227}$$

Let the function $f : \mathbb{R} \to \mathbb{R}$, $f(\lambda) = -\lambda^3 + 4\lambda^2 - 8\lambda + 14$, the derivative of which is $f'(\lambda) = -3\lambda^2 + 8\lambda - 8$. The equation $f'(\lambda) = 0$ has no real roots, and hence the function $f(\lambda)$ is strictly decreasing on $\mathbb{R}$. It follows that the equation $f(\lambda) = 0$ has a single real root; because $D(2) > 0$, $D(3) < 0$, we may state that this root is between 2 and 3.

Refining this interval a little, we find that the root is between 2.7 and 3, a situation for which Table 6.4 of finite differences has been created.

TABLE 6.3   The Table of Finite Differences

λ	D	ΔD	$\Delta^2 D$	$\Delta^3 D$
0	14	−5	2	−6
1	9	−3	−4	
2	6	−7		
3	−1			

TABLE 6.4   Table of Finite Differences

λ	$f(\lambda)$	Δf	$\Delta^2 f$	$\Delta^3 f$
2.7	1.877	−0.869	−0.088	−0.006
2.8	1.008	−0.957	−0.094	
2.9	0.051	−1.051		
3.0	−1			

We choose $\lambda_0 = 2.9$, which corresponds to $q_0 = 2$. We have

$$q_1 = \frac{0 - 1.877}{-0.869} - \frac{2 \times 1}{2! \times (-0.869)} \times (-0.088) - \frac{2 \times 1 \times 0}{3! \times (-0.869)} \times (-0.006) = 2.05869,$$

$$q_2 = 2.04945, \quad q_3 = 2.05093, \quad q_4 = 2.05069, \quad q_5 = 2.05073,$$ (6.228)

from which we obtain the root of the equation $f(\lambda) = 0$, that is,

$$\overline{\lambda} \approx 2.7 + 0.1 q_5 = 2.905,$$ (6.229)

for which

$$f(\overline{\lambda}) = 0.00073.$$ (6.230)

6.10   INTERPOLATION BY SPLINE FUNCTIONS

Let us consider a function $f : [a, b] \to \mathbb{R}$ and an approximation of the same by an interpolation polynomial P such that $P(x_i) = f(x_i) = y_i$, $i = \overline{0, n}$, x_i being the interpolation knots. For higher values of n, there is a better chance for the degree of the interpolation polynomial to increase (obviously, remaining n at the most). But, a polynomial of a higher degree has a deep oscillatory character as can be seen in Figure 6.1. Because of this oscillation property, interpolation polynomials of high degree are avoided.

An alternative used to obtain interpolation functions is to divide the interval $[a, b]$ in a finite set of subintervals, using for each subinterval another interpolation polynomial. We thus obtain a piecewise interpolation. Let us observe that such a method does not guarantee the differentiability of the approximation function at the ends of the subintervals. Usually, it is required that the approximation function be of the same class of differentiability as the original function. Practically, if the approximation function is of class C^2 on $[a, b]$, then it is sufficient for most situations. Usually, we use on each subinterval polynomial functions of third degree; hence, we realize a cubical spline interpolation.

Definition 6.12   Let $f : [a, b] \to \mathbb{R}$ and the interpolation knots be

$$a = x_0 < x_1 < \cdots < x = b.$$ (6.231)

A cubical spline for the function f is a function S that satisfies the following conditions:

(a) $S_j = S|_{[x_j, x_{j+1}]}$ is a polynomial of degree at the most 3 for each $j = \overline{0, n - 1}$;
(b) $S(x_j) = f(x_j)$ for any $j = \overline{0, n}$;
(c) $S_{j+1}(x_{j+1}) = S_j(x_{j+1})$ for any $j = \overline{0, n - 2}$;
(d) $S'(x_{j+1}) = S'_j(x_{j+1})$ for $j = \overline{0, n - 2}$;

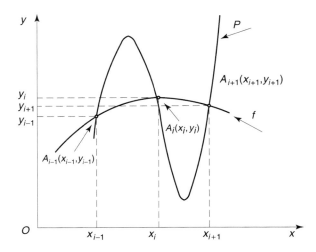

Figure 6.1   The oscillatory character of polynomials of high degree.

(e) $S''_{j+1}(x_{j+1}) = S''_j(x_{j+1})$ for $j = \overline{0, n-2}$;

(f) the following boundary conditions are satisfied:

- or $S''(x_0) = S''(x_n) = 0$ (the so-called condition of free boundary),
- or $S'(x_0) = f'(x_0)$ and $S'(x_n) = f'(x_n)$ (the so-called condition of imposed boundary).

Observation 6.16   We have to determine n polynomials of third degree S_j, $j = \overline{0, n-1}$. As any polynomial of third degree has four coefficients, it follows that the interpolation by spline functions is equivalent to the determination of $4n$ coefficients. Condition (b) of Definition 6.12 leads to $n+1$ equations, the condition (c) leads to $n-1$ equations, condition (d) implies $n-1$ equations, while the condition (e) leads to $n-1$ equations. We thus have $4n-2$ equations to which are added the two equations of point (f) for free or imposed frontier. A system of $4n$ equations with $4n$ unknowns are thus obtained.

Observation 6.17   Let us choose the polynomials S_j, $j = \overline{0, n-1}$, in the form

$$S_j(x) = a_j + b_j(x - x_j) + c_j(x - x_j)^2 + d_j(x - x_j)^3. \tag{6.232}$$

Immediately, we notice that

$$S_j(x_j) = S(x_j) = f(x_j) = a_j, \quad j = \overline{0, n-1}. \tag{6.233}$$

On the other hand,

$$a_{j+1} = S_{j+1}(x_{j+1}) = S_j(x_{j+1}), \tag{6.234}$$

hence

$$a_{j+1} = a_j + b_j(x_{j+1} - x_j) + c_j(x_{j+1} - x_j)^2 + d_j(x_{j+1} - x_j)^3, \quad j = \overline{0, n-1}, \tag{6.235}$$

where we have assumed that

$$a_n = f(x_n). \tag{6.236}$$

Defining

$$b_n = S'(x_n) \tag{6.237}$$

and observing that

$$S'_j(x) = b_j + 2c_j(x - x_j) + 3d_j(x - x_j), \tag{6.238}$$

from which

$$S'(x_j) = b_j, \quad j = \overline{0, n - 1}, \tag{6.239}$$

we obtain

$$b_{j+1} = b_j + 2c_j(x_{j+1} - x_j) + 3d_j(x_{j+1} - x_j)^2, \quad j = \overline{0, n - 1}, \tag{6.240}$$

from condition (d).
   Finally, defining

$$c_n = \frac{S''(x_n)}{2} \tag{6.241}$$

and applying the condition (e), we obtain the relation

$$c_{j+1} = c_j + 3d_j(x_{j+1} - x_j). \tag{6.242}$$

Relation (6.242) leads to

$$d_j = \frac{c_{j+1} - c_j}{3(x_{j+1} - x_j)}; \tag{6.243}$$

replacing in relations (6.235) and (6.240), we obtain

$$a_{j+1} = a_j + b_j(x_{j+1} - x_j) + \frac{(x_{j+1} - x_j)^2}{3}(2c_j + c_{j+1}), \tag{6.244}$$

$$b_{j+1} = b_j + (x_{j+1} - x)(c_j + c_{j+1}), \tag{6.245}$$

for $j = \overline{0, n - 1}$. Eliminating b_j between the last two relations, it follows that the system

$$
\begin{aligned}
(x_j - x_{j-1})c_{j-1} &+ 2(x_{j+1} - x_{j-1})c_j + (x_{j+1} - x_j)c_{j+1} \\
&= \frac{3}{(x_{j+1} - x_j)}(a_{j+1} - a_j) - \frac{3}{x_j - x_{j-1}}(a_j - a_{j-1}), \quad j = \overline{1, n - 1}
\end{aligned}
\tag{6.246}
$$

the unknowns being c_j, $j = \overline{0, n}$; this system is a linear one.

Theorem 6.9   If $f : [a, b] \rightarrow \mathbb{R}$, then f has a unique natural interpolation spline, which is a unique interpolation spline that satisfies the free boundary conditions $S''(a) = S''(b) = 0$.

Demonstration.   The free boundary conditions imply

$$c_n = \frac{S''(x_n)}{2} = 0, \tag{6.247}$$

$$0 = S''(x_0) = 2c_0 + 6d_0(x_0 - x_0), \quad c_0 = 0. \tag{6.248}$$

System (6.246) determines the matrix

$$
\begin{bmatrix}
1 & 0 & 0 & \cdots & 0 & 0 \\
x_1 - x_0 & 2\left(x_2 - x_0\right) & x_1 - x_0 & \cdots & 0 & 0 \\
0 & x_2 - x_1 & 2(x_3 - x_1) & \cdots & 0 & 0 \\
\cdots & \cdots & \cdots & \cdots & \cdots & \cdots \\
0 & 0 & 0 & \cdots & 2(x_n - x_{n-2}) & x_n - x_{n-1} \\
0 & 0 & 0 & \cdots & 0 & 1
\end{bmatrix},
\tag{6.249}
$$

the determinant of which is nonzero.

Observation 6.18   We can describe an algorithm for the determination of a natural spline interpolation function as follows:

- for $i = \overline{1, n-1}$, calculate $\alpha_i = 3[f(x_{i+1})(x_i - x_{i-1}) - f(x_i)(x_{i+1} - x_{i-1}) + f(x_{i-1})$
  $(x_{i+1} - x_i)]/[(x_{i+1} - x_i)(x_i - x_{i-1})]$;
- set $\beta_0 = 1, \quad \gamma_0 = 0, \quad \delta_0 = 0$;
- for $i = \overline{1, n-1}$, calculate $\beta_i = 2(x_{i+1} - x_{i-1}) - (x_i - x_{i-1})\gamma_{i-1}, \quad \gamma_i = (1/\beta_i)(x_{i+1} - x_i)$,
  $\delta_i = (1/\beta_i)[\alpha_i - (x_i - x_{i-1})\delta_{i-1}]$;
- set $\beta_n = 1, \delta_n = 0, c_n = \delta_n$;
- for $j = \overline{n-1, 0}$, calculate $c_j = \delta_j - \gamma_j c_{j+1}, \quad b_j = [f(x_{j+1}) - f(x_j)]/(x_{j+1} - x_j)$
  $-[(x_{j+1} - x_j)(c_{j+1} + 2c_j)]/3, \quad d_j = (c_{j+1} - c_j)/3(x_{j+1} - x_j)$;
- the natural spline interpolation function reads
  $S_j(x) = f(x_j) + b_j(x - x_j) + c_j(x - x_j)^2 + d_j(x - x)^3, \quad j = \overline{0, n-1}$.

Theorem 6.10   If $f : [a, b] \to \mathbb{R}$, then f admits a unique spline interpolation function that satisfies the imposed boundary conditions $S'(a) = f'(a)$ and $S'(b) = f'(b)$.

Demonstration. Because

$$
S'(a) = S'(x_0) = b_0,
\tag{6.250}
$$

equation (6.244), written for $j = 0$, implies

$$
f'(a) = \frac{a_1 - a_0}{x_1 - x_0} - \frac{x_1 - x_0}{3}(2c_0 + c_1),
\tag{6.251}
$$

from which

$$
2(x_1 - x_0)c_0 + (x_1 - x_0)c_1 = \frac{3}{x_1 - x_0}(a_1 - a_0) - 3f'(a).
\tag{6.252}
$$

Analogically,

$$
f'(b) = b_n = b_{n-1} + (x_n - x_{n-1})(c_{n-1} + c_n)
\tag{6.253}
$$

and equation (6.244), written for $j = n - 1$, leads to

$$
\begin{aligned}
f'(b) &= \frac{a_n - a_{n-1}}{x_n - x_{n-1}} - \frac{x_n - x_{n-1}}{3}(2c_{n-1} + c_n) + (x_n - x_{n-1})(c_{n-1} + c_n) \\
&= \frac{a_n - a_{n-1}}{x_n - x_{n-1}} + \frac{x_n - x_{n-1}}{3}(c_{n-1} + 2c_n),
\end{aligned}
\tag{6.254}
$$

from which

$$
(x_n - x_{n-1})c_{n-1} + 2(x_n - x_{n-1})c_n = 3f'(b) - \frac{3}{x_n - x_{n-1}}(a_n - a_{n-1}).
\tag{6.255}
$$

The system formed by equation (6.246), equation (6.252), and equation (6.255) is a linear system, the matrix of which is

$$
\begin{bmatrix}
2(x_1 - x_0) & x_1 - x_0 & 0 & \cdots & 0 & 0 \\
0 & 2(x_2 - x_0) & x_1 - x_0 & \cdots & 0 & 0 \\
0 & x_2 - x_1 & 2(x_3 - x_1) & \cdots & \cdots & \cdots \\
\cdots & \cdots & \cdots & \cdots & \cdots & \cdots \\
0 & 0 & 0 & \cdots & 2(x_n - x_{n-2}) & x_n - x_{n-1} \\
0 & 0 & 0 & \cdots & x_{n-1} - x_{n-2} & 2(x_n - x_{n-1})
\end{bmatrix}. \qquad (6.256)
$$

The determinant of this matrix does not vanish, hence its solution is unique.

Observation 6.19 In this case too, we may give an algorithm to determine the cubical spline interpolation function with the imposed boundary conditions as follows:

– set $\alpha_0 = [3(f(x_1) - f(x_0))]/x_1 - x_0 - 3f'(x_0)$,
  $\alpha_n = 3f'(x_n) - [3(f(x_n) - f(x_{n-1}))]/x_n - x_{n-1}$;
– for $i = \overline{1, n-1}$, calculate $\alpha_i = 3[f(x_{i+1})(x_i - x_{i-1}) - f(x_i)(x_{i+1} - x_{i-1}) + f(x_{i-1})(x_{i+1} - x_i)]/[(x_{i+1} - x_i)(x_i - x_{i-1})]$;
– set $\beta_0 = 2(x_1 - x_0)$, $\gamma_0 = 1/2$, $\delta_0 = \alpha_0/2(x_1 - x_0)$, $b_0 = f'(x_0)$;
– for $i = \overline{1, n-1}$, calculate $\beta_i = 2(x_{i+1} - x_{i-1}) - (x_i - x_{i-1})\gamma_{i-1}$, $\gamma_i = (1/\beta_i)(x_{i+1} - x_i)$, $\delta_i = (1/\beta_i)[\alpha_i - (x_i - x_{i-1})\delta_{i-1}]$;
– set $\beta_n = (x_n - x_{n-1})(2 - \gamma_{n-1})$, $\delta_n = (1/\beta_n)[\alpha_n - (x_n - x_{n-1})\delta_{n-1}]$, $c_n = \delta_n$;
– for $j = \overline{n-1, 0}$, calculate $c_j = \delta_j - \gamma_j c_{j+1}$, $b_j = \{[f(x_{j+1}) - f(x_j)]/x_{j+1} - x_j\} - \{[(x_{j+1} - x_j)(c_{j+1} + 2c_j)]/3\}$, $d_j = (c_{j+1} - c_j)/3(x_{j+1} - x_j)$;
– the cubical spline interpolation function is given by
  $S_j(x) = f(x_j) + b_j(x - x_j) + c_j(x - x_j)^2 + d_j(x - x_j)^3$, $j = \overline{0, n-1}$.

6.11   HERMITE'S INTERPOLATION

Definition 6.13 Let $[a, b]$ be an interval of the real axis, with $n + 1$ distinct points in this interval $x_0, x_1, \ldots, x_n$ and m_i, $i = \overline{0, n}$, $n + 1$ integers associated to the points x_i. We denote by m the value

$$
m = \max_{0 \le i \le n} m_i. \qquad (6.257)
$$

Let a function $f : [a, b] \to \mathbb{R}$, f at least of class C^m on the interval $[a, b]$. The polynomial P of minimum degree, which satisfies

$$
\frac{d^k P(x_i)}{dx^k} = \frac{d^k f(x_i)}{dx^k} \qquad (6.258)
$$

for any $i = \overline{0, n}$ and $k = \overline{0, m_i}$ is called *approximation osculating polynomial of the function f* on the interval $[a, b]$.

Observation 6.20 The degree of the approximation osculating polynomial P will be at the most

$$
M = \sum_{i=0}^{n} m_i + n, \qquad (6.259)
$$

because the number of conditions that must be satisfied is $\sum_{i=0}^{n} m_i + n + 1$ and a polynomial of degree M has $M + 1$ coefficients that are deduced from these conditions.

Observation 6.21

(i) If $n = 0$, then the approximation osculating polynomial P becomes just the Taylor polynomial of degree m_0 for f at x_0.

(ii) If $m_i = 0$ for $i = \overline{0, n}$, then the approximation osculating polynomial P coincides with Lagrange's interpolation polynomial at the interpolation knots $x_0, x_1, \ldots, x_n$.

Theorem 6.11 If $f \in C^1([a, b])$, $f : [a, b] \to \mathbb{R}$ and $x_0, x_1, \ldots, x_n$ are $n + 1$ distinct points in $[a, b]$, then the unique polynomial[9] of minimum degree, which coincides with f at the knots x_i, $i = \overline{0, n}$, and the derivative of which coincides with f' at the very same points x_i is given by

$$H_{2n+1}(x) = \sum_{j=0}^{n} f(x_j) H_{n,j}(x) + \sum_{j=0}^{n} f'(x_j) \widehat{H}_{n,j}(x), \tag{6.260}$$

where

$$H_{n,j}(x) = [1 - 2(x - x_j) L'_{n,j}(x_j)] L^2_{n,j}(x) \tag{6.261}$$

and

$$\widehat{H}_{n,j}(x) = (x - x_j) L^2_{n,j}(x), \tag{6.262}$$

while $L_{n,j}$ represents the polynomial coefficient of degree n and order j, that is,

$$L_{n,j} = \frac{(x - x_0) \cdots (x - x_{j-1})(x - x_{j+1}) \cdots (x - x_n)}{(x_j - x_0) \cdots (x_j - x_{j-1})(x_j - x_{j+1}) \cdots (x_j - x_n)}. \tag{6.263}$$

If $f \in C^{2n+2}([a, b])$, then the following expression of the approximation osculating polynomial error

$$f(x) - H_{2n+1}(x) = \frac{(x - x_0)^2 \cdots (x - x_n)^2}{(2n + 2)!} f^{(2n+2)}(\xi), \tag{6.264}$$

where ξ is a point situated between a and b, exists.

Demonstration. It is similar to the proof of the existence and uniqueness of the Lagrange polynomial, formula (6.264) being obtained in an analogous way as the formula of the error in case of the Lagrange polynomial.

6.12 CHEBYSHEV'S POLYNOMIALS

Definition 6.14 Let $f : [a, b] \to \mathbb{R}$ be a real function of real variable. We call deviation from zero of the function $f(x)$ on the segment $[a, b]$ the greatest value of the modulus of the function f on the very same interval.

Lemma 6.2 Let $x \in [-1, 1]$ and

$$T_n(x) = \cos(n \arccos x). \tag{6.265}$$

Under these conditions,

---

[9]The name of the polynomial is given in honor of Charles Hermite (1822–1901).

(i) $T_n(x)$ represents a polynomial[10] of degree n in x, the dominant coefficient of which is equal to 2^{n-1};

(ii) all the roots of the equation $T_n(x) = 0$ are distinct and in the interval $[-1, 1]$;

(iii) the maximal value of the polynomial $T_n(x)$ on the interval $[-1, 1]$ is equal to 1 and exists for

$$x_k = \cos \frac{2k\pi}{n}, \quad k = 0, 1, \ldots, \left(\frac{n}{2}\right) + 1; \tag{6.266}$$

(iv) the minimal value of the polynomial $T_n(x)$ on the interval $[-1, 1]$ is equal to -1 and exists for

$$x_l = \cos \frac{(2l+1)\pi}{n}, \quad l = 0, 1, \ldots, \left(\frac{n-1}{2}\right) + 1. \tag{6.267}$$

Demonstration. From Moivre's formula

$$(\cos \alpha + i \sin \alpha)^n = \cos n\alpha + i \sin n\alpha, \quad n \in \mathbb{N}^*; \tag{6.268}$$

considering

$$(\cos \alpha + i \sin \alpha)^n = \cos^n \alpha + i C_n^1 \cos^{n-1} \alpha \sin \alpha - C_n^2 \cos^{n-2} \alpha \sin^2 \alpha + \cdots + i^n \sin^n \alpha, \tag{6.269}$$

we obtain

$$\cos n\alpha = \cos^n \alpha - C_n^2 \cos^{n-2} \alpha \sin^2 \alpha + C_n^4 \cos^{n-4} \alpha \sin^4 \alpha - \cdots \tag{6.270}$$

Choosing now

$$\alpha = \arccos x, \tag{6.271}$$

hence

$$\cos \alpha = x, \quad \sin \alpha = \sqrt{1 - x^2}, \tag{6.272}$$

formula (6.270) leads to

$$T_n(x) = \cos(n \arccos x) = x^n - C_n^2 x^{n-2}(1 - x^2) + C_n^4 x^{n-4}(1 - x^2)^2 - \cdots \tag{6.273}$$

It follows that T_n is a polynomial of degree n at the most.

(i) On the other hand, the coefficient of x^n is given by

$$1 + C_n^2 + C_n^4 + \cdots = 2^{n-1}, \tag{6.274}$$

so that the point (i) of the lemma is proved.

(ii) The following equation

$$\cos \phi = 0 \tag{6.275}$$

leads to the solutions

$$\phi = \frac{2k - 1}{2}\pi, \quad k \in \mathbb{Z}. \tag{6.276}$$

It follows that

$$T_n(x) = \cos(n \arccos x) = 0 \tag{6.277}$$

[10]The polynomials are named after Pafnuty Lvovich Chebysev (1821–1894) who introduced them in 1854.

if and only if

$$n \arccos x = \frac{2k-1}{2}\pi, \quad x = \cos\left(\frac{2k-1}{2n}\pi\right), \quad k \in \mathbb{Z}. \tag{6.278}$$

Giving the values 1, 2, 3, $\ldots$, n to k, we get n distinct roots of the equation $T_n(x) = 0$, that is,

$$x_1 = \cos\left(\frac{\pi}{2n}\right), \quad x_2 = \cos\left(\frac{3\pi}{2n}\right), \quad x_3 = \cos\left(\frac{5\pi}{2n}\right), \quad \ldots, \quad x_n = \cos\left(\frac{2n-1}{2n}\pi\right). \tag{6.279}$$

(iii) From (6.265) it follows that

$$-1 \leq T_n(x) \leq 1. \tag{6.280}$$

The condition $T_n(x) = 1$ leads to

$$n \arccos x = 2k\pi, \quad k \in \mathbb{Z}, \tag{6.281}$$

obtaining immediately relation (6.266).

(iv) It is analogous to point (iii), the condition $T_n(x) = -1$ leading to

$$n \arccos x = (2k+1)\pi, \quad k \in \mathbb{Z}. \tag{6.282}$$

Definition 6.15   The polynomials $K_n(x) = 2^{1-n}T_n(x)$, $x \in [-1, 1]$, are called *Chebyshev's polynomials*.

Theorem 6.12   (Chebyshev)

(i) The deviation from zero of the polynomial

$$Q(x) = x^n + a_1 x^{n-1} + a_2 x^{n-2} + \cdots + a_{n-1}x + a_n \tag{6.283}$$

cannot be less then 2^{1-n} on the interval $[-1, 1]$ and it is equal to 2^{1-n} only for Chebyshev's polynomial $K_n(x)$.

(ii) There exists a unique polynomial of degree n with the dominant coefficient equal to 1, the deviation of which on the segment $[-1, 1]$ is equal to 2^{1-n}, this polynomial being, obviously, $K_n(x)$.

Demonstration

(i) Let us suppose, per absurdum, that there would exist a polynomial $Q(x)$ of the form (6.283) for which the deviation from zero would be less than 2^{1-n}. This means that for any $x \in [-1, 1]$, we have

$$-\frac{1}{2^{n+1}} < Q(x) < \frac{1}{2^{n+1}} \tag{6.284}$$

or, equivalently,

$$Q(x) - \frac{1}{2^{n+1}} < 0, \quad Q(x) + \frac{1}{2^{n+1}} > 0. \tag{6.285}$$

Let us consider the polynomial

$$P(x) = Q(x) - K_n(x). \qquad (6.286)$$

Because the coefficients of the terms of maximal degree are equal to 1 both for $Q(x)$ and for $K_n(x)$, it follows that $P(x)$ is a polynomial of degree $n-1$ at the most. On the other hand, from formulae (6.266) and (6.267) it follows that

$$P(1) = Q(1) - K_n(1) < 0,$$

$$P\left[\cos\left(\frac{\pi}{n}\right)\right] = Q\left[\cos\left(\frac{\pi}{n}\right)\right] - K_n\left[\cos\left(\frac{\pi}{n}\right)\right] > 0,$$

$$P\left[\cos\left(\frac{2\pi}{n}\right)\right] = Q\left[\cos\left(\frac{2\pi}{n}\right)\right] - K_n\left[\cos\left(\frac{2\pi}{n}\right)\right] < 0, \qquad (6.287)$$

$$P\left[\cos\left(\frac{3\pi}{n}\right)\right] = Q\left[\cos\left(\frac{3\pi}{n}\right)\right] - K_n\left[\cos\left(\frac{3\pi}{n}\right)\right] > 0, \ldots$$

This means that for $x = 1$, $x = \cos(2\pi/n)$, $x = \cos(4\pi/n)$, ..., the polynomial $P(x)$ is negative, while for $x = \cos(\pi/n)$, $x = \cos(3\pi/n)$, ..., the polynomial $P(x)$ is positive. It follows that the polynomial $P(x)$ has at least one root between 1 and $\cos(\pi/n)$, at least one root between $x = \cos(\pi/n)$ and $x = \cos(2\pi/n)$, ..., at least one root between $x = \cos[(n-1)\pi/n]$ and $x = \cos\pi = 1$. Hence, the polynomial $P(x)$ has at least n roots. But $P(x)$ is of degree $n-1$ at the most. That means that $P(x) = 0$, hence $Q(x) = K_n(x)$.

(ii) Let us assume now, per absurdum too, that there exists a polynomial $Q(x)$ of degree n at the most, the dominant coefficient of which is equal to 1 and for which the deviation from zero on the segment $[-1, 1]$ is equal to 2^{1-n}. Let

$$P(x) = Q(x) - K_n(x), \qquad (6.288)$$

which obviously is a polynomial of degree $n-1$ at the most. For the polynomial $P(x)$ we may state that it has nonpositive values at the points $x = 1$, $x = \cos(2\pi/n)$, $x = \cos(4\pi/n)$, ..., while at the points $x = \cos(\pi/n)$, $x = \cos(3\pi/n)$, ... it has nonnegative ones. It follows that on each interval $[-1, \cos((n-1)\pi/n)]$, $[\cos((n-1)\pi/n), \cos((n-2)\pi/n)]$, ..., $[\cos(3\pi/n), \cos(2\pi/n)]$, $[\cos(2\pi/n), \cos(\pi/n)]$, $[\cos(\pi/n), 1]$ the equation $P(x) = 0$ has at least one root. But, although we have n intervals, the number of roots of the equation $P(x) = 0$ may be less than n because a root may be the common extremity of two neighboring intervals. Let us now consider such a case, for example, the case in which the root is $\bar{x} = \cos(\pi/n)$. This means that in the interval $[\cos(2\pi/n), 1]$ the equation $P(x) = 0$ has a single root, that is, $\bar{x}$. Because of this, it follows that the curve $y = P(x)$ is tangential to the Ox-axis at the point $\bar{x} = \cos(\pi/n)$. If not, then the curve $y = P(x)$ pierces the Ox-axis at the point $\bar{x}$ and $P(x)$ becomes positive either on the interval $(\cos(2\pi/n), \cos(\pi/n))$ or on the interval $(\cos(\pi/n), 1)$. But $P(x)$ is a continuous function and $P(\cos(2\pi/n)) < 0$, $P(1) < 0$, and hence the equation $P(x) = 0$ has the second root on the interval $[\cos(2\pi/n), 1]$, which is a contradiction, from which the curve $y = P(x)$ is tangential to the Ox-axis at the point $\bar{x}$. This means that $\bar{x}$ is a double root of the equation $P(x) = 0$. Let us suppose now that $\bar{x}$ is not a double root of the equation $P(x) = 0$. Hence, the equation may be written in the form

$$\left[x - \cos\left(\frac{\pi}{n}\right)\right] P_1(x) = 0, \qquad (6.289)$$

where the polynomial $P_1(x)$ is of degree $n-2$ at the most and $P_1(\bar{x}) \neq 0$. But $P_1(x)$ is a continuous function so that it has a constant sign in a neighborhood V of $\bar{x}$. But the polynomial

$$P(x) = \left[x - \cos\left(\frac{\pi}{n}\right)\right] P_1(x) \qquad (6.290)$$

changes the sign on V, together with the factor $x - \cos(\pi/n)$; it means that the curve $y = P(x)$ pierces the axis Ox at the point $\overline{x}$, which is not possible. Hence, if $\overline{x} = \cos(\pi/n)$ is a root of the equation $P(x) = 0$, then it is at least a double one. It follows that on each interval of the form $[\cos(k\pi/n), \cos((k-1)\pi/n)]$, $k = \overline{1, n-1}$, we have at least one root of the equation $P(x) = 0$ (if it is in the interior of the interval, then it is at least a single one; if it is at one of the frontiers (excepting the ends -1 and 1 where one has no roots) it is at least a double one). The equation $P(x) = 0$ will thus have at least n roots (distinct or not), $P(x)$ being a polynomial of degree $n - 1$ at the most. It follows that $P(x)$ is an identical zero polynomial and the point (ii) of the theorem is proved.

6.13 MINI–MAX APPROXIMATION OF FUNCTIONS

Let the function $f : [a, b] \to \mathbb{R}$ and its approximate $g : [a, b] \to \mathbb{R}$. We suppose that both f and g are at least of class C^0 on the interval $[a, b]$. The mini–max principle requires that the approximation function g satisfies the condition

$$\max_{x \in [a,b]} |f(x) - g(x)| = \text{minimum}. \tag{6.291}$$

Observation 6.22 Condition (6.291) is incomplete at least for one reason: the kind of function we require for the approximate g is not specified. Usually, g is required in the set of polynomial functions.

Let us consider on the interval $[a, b]$ a division formed by the points $x_0, x_1, \ldots, x_n$ so that $x_i < x_{i+1}$, $i = \overline{0, n-1}$, and let $g : [a, b] \to \mathbb{R}$ the approximate of the function f, which we require in the form of a polynomial $P_n(x)$ of degree n at the most. The mini–max principle given by relation (6.291) is thus written in the form

$$\max_{x \in [a,b]} |f(x) - P_n(x)| = \text{minimum}. \tag{6.292}$$

In this case, the required polynomial $P_n(x)$ will have the smallest deviation from the function f on the interval $[a, b]$. We also require that the polynomial $P_n(x)$ pass through the interpolation knots x_i, that is,

$$P_n(x_i) = y_i, \quad y_i = f(x_i), \quad i = \overline{0, n}. \tag{6.293}$$

In contrast to the interpolations considered until now, the interpolation knots are not known. We minimize error (6.292) by an adequate choice of knots. Lagrange's interpolation leads to

$$|f(x) - P_n(x)| = \frac{|f^{(n+1)}(\xi)|}{(n+1)!} |(x - x_0)(x - x_1) \cdots (x - x_n)|, \tag{6.294}$$

where ξ is a point situated between a and b, while f is at least of class C^{n+1} on $[a, b]$. Let us consider the product

$$R_{n+1}(x) = (x - x_0)(x - x_1) \cdots (x - x_n) \tag{6.295}$$

and let us make the change of variable

$$x = \frac{b - a}{2} u + \frac{b + a}{2}, \tag{6.296}$$

so that the interval $[a, b]$ is transformed into the interval $[-1, 1]$. It follows that

$$R_{n+1}(u) = \left(\frac{b - a}{2}\right)^{n+1} (u - u_0)(u - u_1) \cdots (u - u_n). \tag{6.297}$$

As we know from Chebyshev's polynomials, the minimum of the product $R_{n+1}(u)$, which is a polynomial of $(n+1)$th degree in u, is realized if u_i, $i = \overline{0, n}$, are just the zeros of Chebyshev's polynomial $K_{n+1}(u)$. We may write

$$R_{n+1}(u) \geq \left(\frac{b-a}{2}\right)^{n+1} \frac{1}{2^n},$$

(6.298)

and formula (6.294) leads to

$$|f(x) - P_n(x)| \geq \frac{|f^{(n+1)}(\xi)|}{(n+1)!} \left(\frac{b-a}{2}\right)^{n+1} \frac{1}{2^n}.$$

(6.299)

On the other hand, the roots of Chebyshev's polynomial $K_{n+1}(u)$ are

$$u_0 = \cos\left[\frac{2(n+1)-1}{2(n+1)}\pi\right], \quad u_1 = \cos\left[\frac{2n-1}{2(n+1)}\pi\right], \quad \ldots, \quad u_n = \cos\left[\frac{\pi}{2(n+1)}\right], \quad (6.300)$$

so that the interpolation knots will be

$$x_i = \frac{b-a}{2}u_i + \frac{b+a}{2}.$$

(6.301)

Hence, it follows that among all the polynomials of degree n at the most, the one that minimizes error (6.292) is the one constructed with the abscissas of the knots given by the roots of Chebyshev's polynomial $K_{n+1}(x)$, of degree $n+1$.

6.14   ALMOST MINI–MAX APPROXIMATION OF FUNCTIONS

Let us give a somewhat new formulation to the mini–max optimization criterion. Instead of

$$\max_{x \in [a,b]} |f(x) - P_n(x)| = \text{minimum},$$

(6.302)

where f is a real function defined on $[a, b]$, at least of class C^0 on $[a, b]$, while $P_n(x)$ is a polynomial of degree n at the most, we will require

$$\max_{x \in [a,b]} |f(x) - P_n(x)| \leq \varepsilon,$$

(6.303)

where ε is a positive error a priori imposed. We reduce the problem to the interval $[-1, 1]$, with its generality not being changed. We also suppose that f is analytic on $[-1, 1]$, that is, f may be expanded into a convergent power series

$$f(x) = \sum_{k=0}^{\infty} b_k x^k.$$

(6.304)

Lemma 6.3   The Chebyshev polynomials constitute the basis for the vector space of real polynomials.

Demonstration.   The idea consists in showing that every polynomial $P(x)$ may be written as a linear combination of the polynomials $K_n(x)$, $n \in \mathbb{N}$. The demonstration is made by induction after n. The affirmation is true for $n = 0$, because 1 is Chebyshev's polynomial $K_0(x)$. Let us suppose that the affirmation holds for any polynomial x^k, $k \le n$, and let us state it for x^{n+1}. The polynomial $x^{n+1} - K_{n+1}(x)$ is of degree n at the most for which we can write

$$x^{n+1} - K_{n+1}(x) = \alpha_0 K_0(x) + \alpha_1 K_1(x) + \cdots + \alpha_n K_n(x), \tag{6.305}$$

with $\alpha_i \in \mathbb{R}$, $i = \overline{0, n}$. It follows that x^{n+1} can also be written as a combination of Chebyshev polynomials and, by mathematical induction, the lemma is proved.

Taking into account Lemma 6.3, it follows that relation (6.304) may be written by means of the Chebyshev polynomials as follows:

$$f(x) = \sum_{k=0}^{\infty} a_k K_k(x). \tag{6.306}$$

Truncating series (6.306) at $k = n$, we get

$$P_n(x) = \sum_{k=0}^{n} a_k K_k(x) \tag{6.307}$$

and criterion (6.303) leads to

$$|f(x) - P_n(x)| = \left| \sum_{k=n+1}^{\infty} a_k K_k(x) \right| < \sum_{k=n+1}^{\infty} |a_k||K_k(x)| \le \sum_{k=n+1}^{\infty} |a_k| \frac{1}{2^{k-1}} < \sum_{k=n+1}^{\infty} |a_k| < \varepsilon. \tag{6.308}$$

Instead of the infinite sum $\sum_{k=n+1}^{\infty} |a_k|$ we usually consider the approximation $\sum_{k=n+1}^{N} |a_k|$ so that condition (6.303) now reads

$$\sum_{k=n+1}^{N} |a_k| < \varepsilon. \tag{6.309}$$

Definition 6.16   The polynomial $P_n(x)$ thus obtained is called an *almost mini−max polynomial for the function f*.

Observation 6.23

   (i) The almost mini−max polynomial $P_n(x)$ of the function f may be different from the mini−max polynomial constructed in Section 6.13.

  (ii) We know that the mini−max polynomial minimizes the error, but this minimal error is not known. Using the almost mini−max polynomial, the error is less than $\varepsilon > 0$ imposed a priori.

6.15   APPROXIMATION OF FUNCTIONS BY TRIGONOMETRIC FUNCTIONS (FOURIER)

Definition 6.17

   (i) Let $\mathcal{H}$ be a fixed Hilbert space. We call basis in $\mathcal{H}$ a system $\mathcal{B} = \{e_i\}_{i \in I}$ linearly independent of elements in $\mathcal{H}$ for which the Hilbert subspace generated by it is dense in $\mathcal{H}$.

  (ii) We call orthonormal basis in $\mathcal{H}$ (total or complete orthonormal system) any basis $\mathcal{B}$ of $\mathcal{H}$ for which we have for any two elements e_i and e_j of $\mathcal{B}$,

$$\langle e_i, e_j \rangle = \delta_{ij}, \tag{6.310}$$

where $\langle \cdot, \cdot \rangle$ is the scalar product on $\mathcal{H}$, while δ_{ij} is Kronecker's symbol

$$\delta_{ij} = \begin{cases} 1 \text{ for } i = j, \\ 0 \text{ otherwise.} \end{cases} \tag{6.311}$$

(iii) Let $\mathcal{H}$ be a Hilbert space with an orthonormal basis $\mathcal{B} = \{e_n\}_{n \geq 1}$. For any arbitrary $u \in \mathcal{H}$, we call generalized Fourier coefficients of u relative to $\mathcal{B}$ the numbers

$$c_n = \langle u, e_n \rangle, \quad n \geq 1, \tag{6.312}$$

while the series $\sum_{n > 1} c_n e_n$ is called *generalized Fourier series*[11] of u relative to $\mathcal{B}$.

Theorem 6.13 (Generalization of Dirichlet's Theorem). Let $\mathcal{H}$ be a Hilbert space with an orthonormal basis $\mathcal{B} = \{e\}_{n \geq 1}$. For any $u \in \mathcal{H}$, its generalized Fourier series relative to $\mathcal{B}$ is convergent in $\mathcal{H}$, its sum being equal to u. The numerical series $\sum_{u \geq 1} |c_n|^2$ is convergent, its sum being equal to $\|u\|^2$.

Demonstration. We must show that

$$\lim_{n \to \infty} \left\| u - \sum_{i=1}^{n} c_i e_i \right\| = 0, \tag{6.313}$$

$$\lim_{n \to \infty} \left(\|u\|^2 - \sum_{i=1}^{n} |c_i|^2 \right) = 0, \tag{6.314}$$

respectively. Let

$$u_n = \sum_{i=1}^{n} c_i e_i, \quad n \geq 1, \tag{6.315}$$

where c_i given by equation (6.312) are the Fourier coefficients of u relative to the basis $\mathcal{B}$. Let $k \in \mathbb{N}$, $1 \leq k \leq n$, arbitrary. We may write

$$\langle u_n, e_k \rangle = \sum_{i=1}^{n} c_i \langle e_i, e_k \rangle = \sum_{i=1}^{n} c_i \delta_{ij} = c_k = \langle u, e_k \rangle, \tag{6.316}$$

that is,

$$\langle u_n - u, e_k \rangle = 0. \tag{6.317}$$

Let $n \geq 1$, arbitrary but fixed, and let us denote by $\mathcal{H}_n$ the vector subspace of $\mathcal{H}$, generated by the elements $e_1, e_2, \ldots, e_n$. It follows that $u_n - u \in \mathcal{H}_n^{\perp}$ for any $n \geq 1$. But $\mathcal{H}_n$ is a subspace of finite dimension (dim $\mathcal{H}_n = n$), hence a closed set in $\mathcal{H}$. Moreover, u_n is the projection of u on $\mathcal{H}_n$. Because

$$\|u - u_n\|^2 + \|u_n - v\|^2 = \|u - v\|^2, \tag{6.318}$$

---

[11] The series is called after Jean Baptiste Joseph Fourier (1768–1830) who published his results in *Mémoire sur la propagation de la chaleur dans les corps solides* in 1807 and then in *Théorie analytique de la chaleur* in 1822. The first steps in this field were made by Leonhard Euler (1707–1783), Jean-Baptiste le Rond d'Alembert (1717–1783), and Daniel Bernoulli (1700–1782).

corresponding to Pythagoras's theorem, it follows that

$$\|u - u_n\| \le \|u - v\|. \tag{6.319}$$

Let $\varepsilon > 0$ be fixed. Because the subspace generated by $\mathcal{B}$ in $\mathcal{H}$ is dense, it follows that there exists $v \in \mathcal{H}$, a finite linear combination of elements of $\mathcal{B}$ such that

$$\|u - v\| < \varepsilon. \tag{6.320}$$

It follows that there exists a natural number $N(\varepsilon)$ such that $v \in \mathcal{H}_n$ for any $n \ge N(\varepsilon)$, and from (6.319) and (6.320) we obtain

$$\|u - u_n\| < \varepsilon \tag{6.321}$$

too for any $n \ge N(\varepsilon)$. We have shown that $u_n \to u$ in $\mathcal{H}$, that is,

$$\sum_{i=1}^{\infty} c_i e_i = u. \tag{6.322}$$

On the other hand,

$$\|u\|^2 = \langle u_n, u_n \rangle = \left\langle \sum_{i=1}^{n} c_i e_i, \sum_{j=1}^{n} c_j e_j \right\rangle = \sum_{i=1}^{n} \sum_{j=1}^{n} c_i \bar{c}_j \delta_{ij} = \sum_{i=1}^{n} |c_i|^2, \tag{6.323}$$

a relation valid for any $n \ge 1$. Making $n \to \infty$ and considering that $\|u_n\| \to \|u\|$, it follows that

$$\sum_{i=1}^{\infty} |c_i|^2 = \|u\|^2. \tag{6.324}$$

Definition 6.18   Relation (6.324) is called *the relation or the equality of Parseval.*

Corollary 6.4

(i) If the basis $\mathcal{B}$ is fixed and $u \in \mathcal{H}$, then the Fourier expansion of u is unique.

(ii) For any $n \ge 1$ we have Bessel's inequality

$$\sum_{i=1}^{n} |c_i|^2 \le \|u\|^2 \tag{6.325}$$

and

$$\lim_{n \to \infty} c_n = 0. \tag{6.326}$$

(iii) Let $\mathcal{H} = L^2_{[-\pi, \pi]}$, that is, the space of real square integrable functions, on which the scalar product

$$\langle f, g \rangle = \int_{-\pi}^{\pi} f(x)g(x)\mathrm{d}x \tag{6.327}$$

has been defined, and let us consider as orthonormal basis in $\mathcal{H}$ the sequence

$$e_1 = \frac{1}{\sqrt{2\pi}}, \quad e_2 = \frac{1}{\sqrt{\pi}}\cos x, \quad e_3 = \frac{1}{\sqrt{\pi}}\sin x, \quad e_4 = \frac{1}{\sqrt{\pi}}\cos 2x, \quad e_5 = \frac{1}{\sqrt{\pi}}\sin 2x, \ \ldots \tag{6.328}$$

Under these conditions, for $u : [-\pi, \pi] \to \mathbb{R}$, $u \in \mathcal{H}$, the generalized Fourier coefficients of u relative to the orthonormal basis $\mathcal{B} = \{e\}_{n \geq 1}$ are

$$c_1 = \sqrt{\frac{\pi}{2}} a_0, \quad c_2 = a_1\sqrt{\pi}, \quad c_3 = b_1\sqrt{\pi}, \quad c_4 = a_2\sqrt{\pi}, \quad c_5 = b_2\sqrt{\pi}, \quad \ldots, \tag{6.329}$$

where

$$a_n = \frac{1}{\pi} \int_{-\pi}^{\pi} u(x) \cos(nx)\,\mathrm{d}x, \quad b_n = \frac{1}{\pi} \int_{-\pi}^{\pi} u(x) \sin(nx)\,\mathrm{d}x, \quad n \geq 0. \tag{6.330}$$

Parseval's equality now reads

$$\frac{a_0^2}{2} + \sum_{i=1}^{\infty} (a_i^2 + b_i^2) = \frac{1}{\pi} \int_{\pi}^{\pi} u^2(x)\,\mathrm{d}x. \tag{6.331}$$

(iv) (Dirichlet's theorem) If the periodic function $f(x)$ of period 2π satisfies Dirichlet's conditions in the interval $(-\pi, \pi)$, that is,

(a) f is uniformly bounded on $(-\pi, \pi)$, that is, there exists $M > 0$ and finite such that $|f(x)| \leq M$ for any $x \in (-\pi, \pi)$, and

(b) f has a finite number of strict extremes, then, at each point of continuity $x \in (-\pi, \pi)$, the function $f(x)$ may be expanded into a trigonometric Fourier series

$$f(x) = \frac{a_0}{2} + \sum_{i=1}^{\infty} [a_i \cos(ix) + b_i \sin(ix)], \tag{6.332}$$

where the Fourier coefficients a_i and b_i are given by

$$a_i = \frac{1}{\pi} \int_{-\pi}^{\pi} f(x) \cos(ix)\,\mathrm{d}x, \quad i = 0, 1, \ 2, \ \ldots, \tag{6.333}$$

$$b_i = \frac{1}{\pi} \int_{-\pi}^{\pi} f(x) \sin(ix)\,\mathrm{d}x, \quad i = 1, \ 2, \ \ldots, \tag{6.334}$$

respectively. If $x \in (-\pi, \pi)$ is a point of discontinuity for the function $f(x)$, then the sum $S(x)$ of the Fourier series (6.332) attached to f reads

$$S(x) = \frac{f(x - 0) + f(x + 0)}{2}. \tag{6.335}$$

At the ends, we have

$$S(-\pi) = S(\pi) = \frac{f(-\pi + 0) + f(\pi + 0)}{2}. \tag{6.336}$$

Demonstration

(i) Let us suppose, per absurdum, that the expansion is not unique, that is,

$$u = \sum_{i=1}^{\infty} c_i e_i \text{ and } u = \sum_{i=1}^{\infty} d_i e_i, \tag{6.337}$$

where there exists at least $i \in \mathbb{N}^*$ such that $c_i \neq d_i$. Let $v_n = \sum_{i=1}^{n} d_i e_i$. It follows that $\langle v_n, e_i \rangle = d_i$ for any $i \leq n$, making $n \to \infty$; because $v_n \to u$ it also follows that $\langle u, e_i \rangle = d_i$, that is, $d_i = c_i$ for any $i \geq 1$.

(ii) The relations are obvious, taking into account Parseval's equality.

(iii) We successively have

$$c_1 = \langle u, e_1 \rangle = \int_{-\pi}^{\pi} u(x) \frac{1}{\sqrt{2\pi}} dx = \sqrt{\frac{\pi}{2}} a_0, \tag{6.338}$$

$$c_2 = \langle u, e_2 \rangle = \int_{-\pi}^{\pi} u(x) \frac{1}{\sqrt{\pi}} \cos x dx = \sqrt{\pi} a_1, \tag{6.339}$$

$$c_3 = \langle u, e_3 \rangle = \int_{-\pi}^{\pi} u(x) \frac{1}{\sqrt{\pi}} \sin x dx = \sqrt{\pi} b_1 \tag{6.340}$$

and, in general, all the requested relations are satisfied. Parseval's equality becomes

$$\int_{-\pi}^{\pi} u^2(x) dx = \sum_{i=1}^{n} |c_i|^2 = \frac{\pi}{2} a_0^2 + \pi \sum_{i=1}^{\infty} (a_i^2 + b_i^2) = \pi \left[\frac{a_0^2}{2} + \sum_{i=1}^{\infty} (a_i^2 + b_i^2) \right], \tag{6.341}$$

that is, relation (6.331).

(iv) Obviously, a function f that satisfies Dirichlet's conditions is a function of $L_{[-\pi,\pi]}^2$ and the theorem is proved. At the points of discontinuity, the Fourier series is replaced by relations (6.335) and (6.336), respectively, which may or not satisfy equality (6.332).

Observation 6.24

(i) If the function $f(x)$ is even, $f(x) = f(-x)$, then $b_i = 0$, for any $i \in \mathbb{N}^*$ and the Fourier series becomes

$$f(x) = \frac{a_0}{2} + \sum_{i=1}^{\infty} a_i \cos(ix), \quad a_i = \frac{2}{\pi} \int_0^{\pi} f(x) \cos(ix) dx, \quad i \in \mathbb{N}. \tag{6.342}$$

(ii) If the function $f(x)$ is odd $f(-x) = -f(x)$, then $a_i = 0$, $i \in \mathbb{N}$, and the Fourier series reads

$$f(x) = \sum_{i=1}^{\infty} b_i \sin(ix), \quad b_i = \frac{2}{\pi} \int_0^{\pi} f(x) \sin(ix) dx, \quad i \in \mathbb{N}. \tag{6.343}$$

(iii) If the function $f(x)$ satisfies Dirichlet's conditions on the interval $(-l, l)$, then we have the expansion

$$f(x) = \frac{a_0}{2} + \sum_{i=1}^{\infty} \left[a_i \cos\left(\frac{\pi i}{l} x\right) + b_i \sin\left(\frac{\pi i}{l} x\right) \right], \tag{6.344}$$

where

$$a_i = \frac{1}{l} \int_{-l}^{l} f(x) \cos\left(\frac{\pi i}{l} x\right) dx, \quad i = 0, 1, 2, \dots, \tag{6.345}$$

$$b_i = \frac{1}{l} \int_{-l}^{l} f(x) \sin\left(\frac{\pi i}{l} x\right) dx, \quad i = 1, 2, 3, \dots \tag{6.346}$$

(iv) If the function $f(x)$ satisfies Dirichlet's conditions on a finite interval (a, b), then we make the change of variable

$$x = \alpha z + \beta, \tag{6.347}$$

so that

$$a = -\alpha \pi + \beta, \quad b = \alpha \pi + \beta, \tag{6.348}$$

from which

$$\beta = \frac{a+b}{2}, \quad \alpha = \frac{b-a}{2\pi}. \tag{6.349}$$

Transformation (6.347) may be written as

$$x = \frac{b-a}{2\pi} z + \frac{b+a}{2}. \tag{6.350}$$

Let us consider now the case in which the function f is given numerically, that is, we know the values

$$y_i = f(x_i), \tag{6.351}$$

with x_i, $i = \overline{0, n}$, division knots, $x_i \in [-\pi, \pi]$. We denote by $S(x)$ the series

$$S(x) = \frac{a_0}{2} + \sum_{k=1}^{m} a_k \cos(kx) + \sum_{k=1}^{m} b_k \sin(kx). \tag{6.352}$$

The coefficients a_i, $i = \overline{0, n}$, and b_i, $i = \overline{1, n}$, are determined by the condition of minimal error

$$\varepsilon_f = \sum_{i=0}^{n} [y_i - S(x_i)]^2 = \text{minimum}. \tag{6.353}$$

There result the conditions

$$\frac{\partial \varepsilon_f}{\partial a_j} = 0, \quad j = \overline{0, m}; \quad \frac{\partial \varepsilon_f}{\partial b_j} = 0, \quad j = \overline{1, m}. \tag{6.354}$$

Taking into account that

$$\frac{\partial S(x_i)}{\partial a_0} = \frac{1}{2}, \quad \frac{\partial S(x_i)}{\partial a_j} = \cos(jx_i), \quad \frac{\partial S(x_i)}{\partial b_j} = \sin(jx_i), \quad j = \overline{1, \ m}, \tag{6.355}$$

Equation (6.353) and equation (6.354) lead to the system

$$\sum_{i=0}^{n} y_i = \sum_{i=0}^{n} S(x_i), \quad \sum_{i=0}^{n} y_i \cos(jx_i) = \sum_{i=0}^{n} S(x_i)\cos(jx_i), \quad \sum_{i=0}^{n} y_i \sin(jx_i) = \sum_{i=0}^{n} S(x_i)\sin(jx_i),$$

$$j = \overline{1, \ m}. \tag{6.356}$$

The system is compatible if

$$n + 1 \geq 2m + 1. \tag{6.357}$$

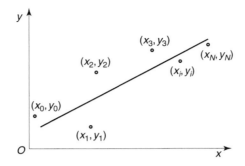

Figure 6.2 Discrete approximation by the least squares.

6.16 APPROXIMATION OF FUNCTIONS BY THE LEAST SQUARES

An idea to consider the approximation function $g(x)$ for a given function $f(x)$ is that of writing the approximate in the form of a finite linear combination of certain functions[12] $\Phi = \{\phi_i\}_{i=\overline{1,n}}$ that satisfy certain properties. Under these conditions, the approximate $g(x)$ will be of the form

$$g(x) = \sum_{i=1}^{n} c_i \phi_i(x), \tag{6.358}$$

where c_i, $i = \overline{1, n}$ are real constants. Thus, once the set Φ is chosen, the problem is reduced to the determination of the constants c_i, $i = \overline{1, n}$. These constants result from the condition that the graph of the approximate $g(x)$ be sufficiently near the set $M = \{(x_i, y_i), i = \overline{1, N}\}$. The nearness of the approximate $g(x)$ to the set M is calculated by means of a norm, which usually is

$$\|f\|_2 = \sqrt{\int_a^b f^2(x)\mathrm{d}x} \tag{6.359}$$

for $f \in C^0([a, b])$ and

$$\|f\|_2 = \sqrt{\sum_{i=0}^{n} |f(x_i)|^2} \tag{6.360}$$

for the discrete case, respectively.

The problem of approximation of a given function f by a linear combination of the functions of the set Φ may be seen as a problem of determination of the constants c_i, $i = \overline{1, n}$, which minimize the expression

$$\left\| f - \sum_{i=1}^{n} c_i \phi_i \right\| = \text{minimum.} \tag{6.361}$$

Definition 6.19 If the norm in relation (6.361) is one of norms (6.359) or (6.360), then the approximation of the function $f(x)$ by

$$g(x) = \sum_{i=1}^{n} c_i \phi_i(x) \tag{6.362}$$

is called *approximation by the least square*.

---

[12]The first description of the least squares method was given by Carl Friedrich Gauss (1777–1855) in *Theoria motus corporum coelestium in sectionibus conicis Solem ambientum* in 1809.

Let us suppose, at the beginning, that we have a sequence of values (x_i, y_i), $i = \overline{0, N}$, as a result of the application of an unknown function $f(x)$ on the distinct values x_i, $i = \overline{0, N}$ (Fig. 6.2). We require a straight line that realizes the best approximation. The problem is thus reduced to the minimization of the function

$$E(a, b) = \sum_{i=0}^{N} [y_i - (ax_i + b)]^2, \tag{6.363}$$

where a and b are the parameters of the straight line

$$(d) : y = ax + b. \tag{6.364}$$

For minimizing expression (6.363), it is necessary that

$$\frac{\partial E(a, b)}{\partial a} = 0, \quad \frac{\partial E(a, b)}{\partial b} = 0 \tag{6.365}$$

or, otherwise,

$$\frac{\partial}{\partial a} \sum_{i=0}^{N} [y_i - (ax_i + b)]^2 = 0, \quad \frac{\partial}{\partial b} \sum_{i=0}^{N} [y_i - (ax_i + b)]^2 = 0. \tag{6.366}$$

System (6.366) is equivalent with

$$a \sum_{i=0}^{N} x_i^2 + b \sum_{i=0}^{N} x_i = \sum_{i=0}^{N} x_i y_i, \quad a \sum_{i=0}^{N} x_i + b(N + 1) = \sum_{i=0}^{N} y_i \tag{6.367}$$

and has the solution

$$a = \frac{(N + 1) \left(\sum_{i=0}^{N} x_i y_i \right) - \left(\sum_{i=0}^{N} x_i \right) \left(\sum_{i=0}^{N} y_i \right)}{(N + 1) \left(\sum_{i=0}^{N} x_i^2 \right) - \left(\sum_{i=0}^{N} x_i \right)^2}, \quad b = \frac{\left(\sum_{i=0}^{N} x_i^2 \right) \left(\sum_{i=0}^{N} y_i \right) - \left(\sum_{i=0}^{N} x_i y_i \right) \left(\sum_{i=0}^{N} x_i \right)}{(N + 1) \left(\sum_{i=0}^{N} x_i^2 \right) - \left(\sum_{i=0}^{N} x_i \right)^2}. \tag{6.368}$$

Considering that $d^2 E(a, b)$ is everywhere positive definite, it follows that the function $E(a, b)$ is convex; hence, the previous critical point given by relation (6.368) is a point of global minimum.

Let us pass now to the general case in which the approximate g is a polynomial of nth degree

$$g(x) = a_0 + a_1 x + a_2 x^2 + \cdots + a_n x^n, \tag{6.369}$$

with $n < N$. The problem is obviously reduced to the determination of the coefficients $a_0, a_1, \ldots, a_n$, which minimize the expression

$$E(a_l) = \sum_{i=0}^{N} [y_i - g(x_i)]^2 = \sum_{i=0}^{N} y_i^2 - 2 \sum_{i=0}^{N} \left(\sum_{j=0}^{n} a_j x_i^j \right) y_i + \sum_{i=0}^{N} \left(\sum_{j=0}^{n} a_j x_i^j \right)^2 \tag{6.370}$$

$$= \sum_{i=0}^{N} y_i^2 - 2 \sum_{j=0}^{n} a_j \left(\sum_{i=0}^{N} y_i x_i^j \right) + \sum_{j=0}^{n} \sum_{k=0}^{n} a_j a_k \left(\sum_{i=0}^{N} x_i^{j+k} \right).$$

To minimize $E(a_l)$ it is necessary that

$$\frac{\partial E}{\partial a_l} = 0, \quad \text{for } l = \overline{0, n}. \tag{6.371}$$

There result the equations

$$-2 \sum_{i=0}^{N} y_i x_i^j + 2 \sum_{k=0}^{n} a_k \sum_{i=0}^{N} x_i^{j+k} = \frac{\partial E}{\partial a_j} = 0, \quad j = \overline{0, n}. \tag{6.372}$$

We obtain the determined compatible system

$$a_0 \sum_{i=0}^{N} x_i^0 + a_1 \sum_{i=0}^{N} x_i^1 + a_2 \sum_{i=0}^{N} x_i^2 + \cdots + a_n \sum_{i=0}^{N} x_i^n = \sum_{i=0}^{N} y_i x_i^0,$$

$$a_0 \sum_{i=0}^{N} x_i^1 + a_1 \sum_{i=0}^{N} x_i^2 + a_2 \sum_{i=0}^{N} x_i^3 + \cdots + a_n \sum_{i=0}^{N} x_i^{n+1} = \sum_{i=0}^{N} y_i x_i^1, \quad \ldots, \tag{6.373}$$

$$a_0 \sum_{i=0}^{N} x_i^n + a_1 \sum_{i=0}^{N} x_i^{n+1} + a_2 \sum_{i=0}^{N} x_i^{n+2} + \cdots + a_n \sum_{i=0}^{N} x_i^{2n} = \sum_{i=0}^{N} y_i x_i^n.$$

Because the error is a convex function, it follows that the solution of system (6.373) is a point of global minimum.

6.17   OTHER METHODS OF INTERPOLATION

6.17.1   Interpolation with Rational Functions

The interpolation with polynomials has at least one disadvantage, that is, for $x \to \pm\infty$ the values of the polynomials become infinite too.

Many times, we know, practically, some information about the real function, concerning its behavior at $\pm\infty$, as, for instance, it has a certain oblique asymptote, it is bounded, and so on.

For this reason, we may choose as approximate function a rational one

$$R(x) = \frac{P(x)}{Q(x)}, \tag{6.374}$$

where P and Q are polynomials of mth and nth degree, respectively.

We may write

$$R(x) = \frac{a_0 x^m + a_1 x^{m-1} + \cdots + a_m}{b_0 x^n + b_1 x^{n-1} + \cdots + b_n}. \tag{6.375}$$

Because b_0 may be a common factor, we may choose $b_0 = 1$ such that expression (6.375) takes the form

$$R(x) = \frac{a_0 x^m + a_1 x^{m-1} + \cdots + a_m}{x^n + b_1 x^{n-1} + \cdots + b_n}. \tag{6.376}$$

We have $m + n + 1$ unknown coefficients $(a_0, \ldots, a_m, b_1, \ldots, b_n)$ to determine in relation (6.376) so that $m + n + 1$ division points are necessary.

If, for instance, we know that the function has an oblique asymptote of the form $y = cx + d$, then we obtain the values $m = n + 1$, $a_0 = c$, $a_1 - b_1 c = d$, the number of division points necessary to determine the coefficients thus being reduced.

6.17.2   The Method of Least Squares with Rational Functions

We may also give in this case a criterion of optimization, that is,

$$\sum_{i=1}^{N}\left[y_i - \frac{P\left(x_i\right)}{Q(x_i)}\right]^2 = \text{minimum.} \tag{6.377}$$

Proceeding as with the method of least squares, it follows that the coefficients of the polynomials $P(x)$ and $Q(x)$ will be determined by equations of the form

$$\sum_{i=1}^{N}\left\{\left[y_i - \frac{P\left(x_i\right)}{Q(x_i)}\right]\frac{\frac{\partial P(x_i)}{\partial a_j}}{Q(x_i)}\right\} = 0, \quad \sum_{i=1}^{N}\left\{\left[y_i - \frac{P\left(x_i\right)}{Q(x_i)}\right]\frac{P(x_i)}{Q^2(x_i)}\frac{\partial Q(x_i)}{\partial b_k}\right\} = 0, \tag{6.378}$$

where $j = \overline{0, m}$, $k = \overline{1, n}$, while N is the number of the division points at which we know the values of the function.

Unfortunately, system (6.378) is a nonlinear one so that the calculation of the coefficients of the polynomials $P(x)$ and $Q(x)$ become difficult.

6.17.3   Interpolation with Exponentials

We may require an approximate of the function $f(x)$ in the form

$$g(x) = C_1 e^{\alpha_1 x} + C_2 e^{\alpha_2 x} + \cdots + C_p e^{\alpha_p x}, \tag{6.379}$$

thus introducing $2p$ unknowns C_i, α_i, $i = \overline{1, p}$.

These unknowns are deduced by the conditions

$$f(x_i) = y_i = g(x_i), \quad i = \overline{0, 2p - 1}. \tag{6.380}$$

Two cases may occur:

(i) The exponents are known, that is, we know the values α_i, $i = \overline{1, p}$. In this case, because the exponentials are linearly independent, we obtain a linear system of p equations with p unknowns C_i, $i = \overline{1, p}$, compatible determined, of the form

$$\begin{aligned}
C_1 e^{\alpha_1 x_1} + C_2 e^{\alpha_2 x_1} + \cdots + C_p e^{\alpha_p x_1} &= y_1, \\
C_1 e^{\alpha_1 x_2} + C_2 e^{\alpha_2 x_2} + \cdots + C_p e^{\alpha_p x_2} &= y_2, \ldots, \\
C_1 e^{\alpha_1 x_p} + C_2 e^{\alpha_2 x_p} + \cdots + C_p e^{\alpha_p x_p} &= y_p.
\end{aligned} \tag{6.381}$$

(ii) The exponents are unknown. If the division points are equidistant, then we apply Prony's method.[13] To do this, we observe that the exponential

$$e^{\alpha_i j} = (e^{\alpha_i})^j = \rho_i^j \tag{6.382}$$

satisfies, for any $i = \overline{0, k - 1}$, a relation of the form

$$y(j + k) + C_{k-1} y(j + k - 1) + C_{k-2} y(j + k - 2) + \cdots + C_0 y(j) = 0, \tag{6.383}$$

[13] The method was introduced by Gaspard Clair François Marie Riche de Prony (1755–1839) in 1795.

where we have supposed that the division points are $x_j = j - 1$; this may be always made, eventually, in a scalar way on the Ox-axis. In relation (6.383), the coefficients C_i, $i = \overline{0, k-1}$, are constant real numbers. The characteristic equation is of the form

$$\rho^k + C_{k-1}\rho^{k-1} + C_{k-2}\rho^{k-2} + \cdots + C_0 = 0. \tag{6.384}$$

We remark that the original function $f(x)$ satisfies equation (6.383), that is,

$$f(j + k) + C_{k-1}f(j + k - 1) + C_{k-2}f(j + k - 2) + \cdots + C_0 f(j) = 0, \quad j = \overline{1, n - k}. \tag{6.385}$$

From the last relation, there result the values of the constants C_0, ..., C_{k-1}, while from relation (6.384) we obtain the roots ρ_0, ..., ρ_{k-1}, the interpolation exponentials being of the form

$$g(x) = C_0 e^{\rho_0 x} + C_1 e^{\rho_1 x} + \cdots + C_{k-1} e^{\rho_{k-1} x}. \tag{6.386}$$

If certain parameters are imposed, for example, we know α_0, then the number of unknowns diminishes so that equation (6.384) now has an imposed root $\rho_0 = \alpha_0$.

6.18 NUMERICAL EXAMPLES

Example 6.1 Let us consider the following table of data.

x_i	$y_i = f(x_i)$
0	-2
1	-3
2	-16
3	-35
4	-30

We solve the problem to determine the Lagrange interpolation polynomial.
From the relation

$$L_4(x) = \sum_{i=0}^{4} \left(\prod_{\substack{j=0 \\ j \neq i}}^{4} \frac{x - x_j}{x_i - x_j} \right) y_i, \tag{6.387}$$

we deduce

$$L_4(x) = \frac{(x - 1)(x - 2)(x - 3)(x - 4)}{(0 - 1)(0 - 2)(0 - 3)(0 - 4)}(-2) + \frac{x(x - 2)(x - 3)(x - 4)}{(1 - 0)(1 - 2)(1 - 3)(1 - 4)}(-3)$$

$$+ \frac{x(x - 1)(x - 3)(x - 4)}{(2 - 0)(2 - 1)(2 - 3)(2 - 4)}(-16) + \frac{x(x - 1)(x - 2)(x - 4)}{(3 - 0)(3 - 1)(3 - 2)(3 - 4)}(-35)$$

$$+ \frac{x(x - 1)(x - 2)(x - 3)}{(4 - 0)(4 - 1)(4 - 2)(4 - 3)}(-30) \tag{6.388}$$

$$= x^4 - 5x^3 + 2x^2 + x - 2.$$

Example 6.2 Let the function $f : [-1, \infty) \to [0, \infty)$,

$$f(x) = \sqrt{x + 1}. \tag{6.389}$$

We wish to determine approximations of $\sqrt{1.1}$ and $\sqrt{0.89}$, by means of the expansions into a Taylor series of the function f.

Because

$$f'(x) = \frac{(x+1)^{-\frac{1}{2}}}{2}, \quad f''(x) = -\frac{(x+1)^{-\frac{3}{2}}}{2^2}, \quad f'''(x) = \frac{1 \times 3}{2^3}(x+1)^{-\frac{5}{2}}, \quad \ldots,$$

$$f^{(n)}(x) = \frac{(-1)^{n+1}(2n-3)!!}{2^n}(x+1)^{\frac{1-2n}{2}}, \quad n \geq 2,$$

(6.390)

we deduce

$$f'(0) = \frac{1}{2}, \quad f''(0) = -\frac{1}{2^2}, \quad f'''(0) = \frac{1 \times 3}{2^3}, \quad \ldots,$$

$$f^{(n)}(0) = \frac{(-1)^{n+1}(2n-3)!!}{2^n}, \quad n \geq 2,$$

(6.391)

obtaining the expansion into a Taylor series around the origin

$$f(x) = f(0) + \frac{1}{2}\frac{x}{1!} + \sum_{k=2}^{n} \frac{x^k}{k!}\frac{(-1)^{k+1}(2k-3)!!}{2^k}$$

$$+ \frac{x^{n+1}}{(n+1)!}\frac{(-1)^{n+2}(2n-1)!!}{2^{n+1}}(1+\xi)^{-\frac{1+2n}{2}},$$

(6.392)

where ξ is a point situated between 0 and x.

For an approximate calculation of $\sqrt{1.1}$ we have $x = 0.1$ and it follows that

$$f(0.1) \approx f(0) = 1,$$

(6.393)

$$f(0.1) \approx f(0) + \frac{0.1}{2 \times 1!} = 1.05,$$

(6.394)

$$f(0.1) \approx f(0) + \frac{0.1}{2 \times 1!} - \frac{0.1^2}{2^2 \times 2!} = 1.04875,$$

(6.395)

$$f(0.1) \approx f(0) + \frac{0.1}{2 \times 1!} - \frac{0.1^2}{2^2 \times 2!} + \frac{0.1^3 \times 3}{2^3 \times 3!} = 1.0488125,$$

(6.396)

$$f(0.1) \approx f(0) + \frac{0.1}{2 \times 1!} - \frac{0.1^2}{2^2 \times 2!} + \frac{0.1^3 \times 3}{2^3 \times 3!} - \frac{0.1^4 \times 3 \times 5}{2^4 \times 4!} = 1.048808594.$$

(6.397)

The exact value is

$$\sqrt{1.1} = 1.048808848,$$

(6.398)

so that approximation (6.397) gives six exact decimal digits.

For $\sqrt{0.89}$ we must take $x = -0.11$, and we obtain

$$f(-0.11) \approx f(0) = 1,$$

(6.399)

$$f(-0.11) \approx f(0) - \frac{0.11}{2 \times 1!} = 0.945, \tag{6.400}$$

$$f(-0.11) \approx f(0) - \frac{0.11}{2 \times 1!} - \frac{0.11^2}{2^2 \times 2!} = 0.9434875, \tag{6.401}$$

$$f(-0.11) \approx f(0) - \frac{0.11}{2 \times 1!} - \frac{0.11^2}{2^2 \times 2!} - \frac{0.11^3 \times 3}{2^3 \times 3!} = 0.943404312, \tag{6.402}$$

$$f(-0.11) \approx f(0) - \frac{0.11}{2 \times 1!} - \frac{0.11^2}{2^2 \times 2!} - \frac{0.11^3 \times 3}{2^3 \times 3!} - \frac{0.11^4 \times 3 \times 5}{2^4 \times 4!} = 0.943398593. \tag{6.403}$$

On the other hand,
$$\sqrt{0.89} = 0.943398113, \tag{6.404}$$

and hence approximation (6.403) that uses the first four derivatives of the function f leads to six exact decimal digits.

Example 6.3   For the function $f : [-1, 3] \to \mathbb{R}$ we know the following values.

x_i	$y_i = f(x_i)$
-1	6
0	3
1	-2
2	9
3	78

We wish to determine approximate values for $f(-0.9)$ and $f(2.8)$ using forward and backward Newton's interpolation polynomials, respectively.

To do this, we construct Table 6.5 of finite differences.

In the case of forward Newton's polynomial, the value of q is given by

$$q = \frac{x - x_0}{h} = \frac{-0.9 + 1}{1} = 0.1 \tag{6.405}$$

and we have

$$\begin{aligned} P(q) = {} & y_0 + \frac{q}{1!} \Delta y_0 + \frac{q(q-1)}{2!} \Delta^2 y_0 \\ & + \frac{q(q-1)(q-2)}{3!} \Delta^3 y_0 + \frac{q(q-1)(q-2)(q-3)}{4!} \Delta^4 y_0, \end{aligned} \tag{6.406}$$

TABLE 6.5   Table of Finite Differences

x_i	y_i	Δy_i	$\Delta^2 y_i$	$\Delta^3 y_i$	$\Delta^4 y_i$
-1	6	-3	-2	18	24
0	3	-5	16	42	
1	-2	11	58		
2	9	69			
3	78				

from which

$$f(-0.9) \approx P(0.1) = 5.8071. \tag{6.407}$$

For the backward Newton's polynomial we may write

$$q = \frac{x - x_n}{h} = \frac{2.8 - 3}{1} = -0.2, \tag{6.408}$$

$$
\begin{aligned}
P(q) = y_4 &+ \frac{q}{1!} \Delta y_3 + \frac{q(q+1)}{2!} \Delta^2 y_2 \\
&+ \frac{q(q+1)(q+2)}{3!} \Delta^3 y_1 + \frac{q(q+1)(q+2)(q+3)}{4!} \Delta^4 y_0,
\end{aligned} \tag{6.409}
$$

hence

$$f(2.8) \approx P(-0.2) = 56.7376. \tag{6.410}$$

Example 6.4   Let the function $f : [-3, 3] \to \mathbb{R}$ be given by the following table of values.

x_i	$y_i = f(x_i)$
-3	68
-2	42
-1	18
0	2
1	0
2	18
3	62

We wish to have an approximate value for $f(0.5)$.
We construct Table 6.6 of finite differences.
We have

$$x_0 = 0, \quad x_{-1} = -1, \quad x_{-2} = -2, \quad x_{-3} = -3, \quad x_1 = 1, \quad x_2 = 2, \quad x_3 = 3, \tag{6.411}$$

$$h = 1, \quad q = \frac{x - x_0}{h} = 0.5. \tag{6.412}$$

TABLE 6.6   Table of Finite Differences

x_i	$y_i = f(x_i)$	Δy_i	$\Delta^2 y_i$	$\Delta^3 y_i$	$\Delta^4 y_i$	$\Delta^5 y_i$	$\Delta^6 y_i$
-3	68	-26	2	6	0	0	0
-2	42	-24	8	6	0	0	
-1	18	-16	14	6	0		
0	2	-2	20	6			
1	0	18	26				
2	18	44					
3	62						

If we apply Gauss's first formula, then we obtain

$$
\begin{aligned}
f(0.5) \approx y_0 + \frac{q}{1!}\Delta y_0 + \frac{q(q-1)}{2!}\Delta^2 y_{-1} + \frac{(q+1)q(q-1)}{3!}\Delta^3 y_{-1} \\
+ \frac{(q+1)q(q-1)(q-2)}{4!}\Delta^4 y_{-2} + \frac{(q+2)(q+1)q(q-1)(q-2)}{5!}\Delta^5 y_{-2} \\
+ \frac{(q+2)(q+1)q(q-1)(q-2)(q-3)}{6!}\Delta^6 y_{-3}
\end{aligned}
\tag{6.413}
$$

$$= -1.125.$$

The use of the second Gauss's formula leads to the relation

$$
\begin{aligned}
f(0.5) \approx y_0 + \frac{q^{(1)}}{1!}\Delta y_{-1} + \frac{(q+1)^{(2)}}{2!}\Delta^2 y_{-1} + \frac{(q+1)^{(3)}}{3!}\Delta^3 y_{-2} \\
+ \frac{(q+2)^{(4)}}{4!}\Delta^4 y_{-2} + \frac{(q+2)^{(5)}}{5!}\Delta^5 y_{-3} + \frac{(q+3)^{(6)}}{6!}\Delta^6 y_{-3}
\end{aligned}
\tag{6.414}
$$

$$= -1.125.$$

Analogically, we may use the formulae of Stirling, Bessel, or Everrett.

Example 6.5 Let us consider the function $f : [0, 1] \rightarrow \mathbb{R}$,

$$f(x) = e^x, \tag{6.415}$$

as well as the intermediary points

$$x_0 = 0, \quad x_1 = 0.5, \quad x_2 = 1. \tag{6.416}$$

The values of the function f at these points are

$$f(0) = 1, \quad f(0.5) = 1.64872, \quad f(1) = 2.71828. \tag{6.417}$$

If we wish to determine the natural cubic spline interpolation polynomial, then we shall calculate successively

$$\alpha_1 = \frac{3[f(x_2)(x_1 - x_0) - f(x_1)(x_2 - x_0) + f(x_0)(x_2 - x_1)]}{(x_2 - x_1)(x_1 - x_0)} = 2.52504, \tag{6.418}$$

$$\beta_0 = 1, \quad \gamma_0 = 0, \quad \delta_0 = 0, \tag{6.419}$$

$$\beta_1 = 2(x_2 - x_0) - (x_1 - x_2)\gamma_0 = 2, \tag{6.420}$$

$$\gamma_1 = \frac{1}{\beta_1}(x_2 - x_1) = 0.25, \tag{6.421}$$

$$\delta_1 = \frac{1}{\beta_1}[\alpha_1 - (x_1 - x_0)\delta_0] = 1.26252, \tag{6.422}$$

$$\beta_2 = 1, \quad \delta_2 = 0, \quad c_2 = 0, \tag{6.423}$$

$$c_1 = \delta_1 - \gamma_1 c_2 = 0, \tag{6.424}$$

$$b_1 = \frac{f(x_2) - f(x_1)}{x_2 - x_1} - \frac{(x_2 - x_1)(c_2 + 2c_1)}{3} = 1.71828, \tag{6.425}$$

$$d_1 = \frac{c_2 - c_1}{3(x_2 - x_1)} = -0.84168, \tag{6.426}$$

$$b_0 = \frac{f(x_1) - f(x_0)}{x_1 - x_0} - \frac{(x_1 - x_0)(c_1 + 2c_0)}{3} = 1.08702, \tag{6.427}$$

$$d_0 = \frac{c_1 - c_0}{3(x_1 - x_0)} = 0.84168. \tag{6.428}$$

We obtain the natural cubic spline interpolation polynomial in the form

$$S(x) = \begin{cases} 1 + 1.08702x + 0.84168x^3, & \text{for } x \in [0, 0.5] \\ 1.64872 + 1.71828(x - 0.5) + 1.26252(x - 0.5)^2 \\ \quad -0.84168(x - 0.5)^3, & \text{for } x \in [0.5, 1] \end{cases} \tag{6.429}$$

If we wish to determine the cubic spline interpolation polynomial with an imposed frontier, then we must take into account that

$$f'(0) = 1, \quad f'(0.5) = 1.64872, \quad f'(1) = 2.71828, \tag{6.430}$$

obtaining the answer

$$S(x) = \begin{cases} 1 + x + 0.48895x^2 \text{ for } x \in [0, 0.5] \\ 1.64872 + 1.64785(x - 0.5) + 0.80677(x - 0.5)^2 \\ \quad +0.35155(x - 0.5)^3 \text{ for } x \in [0.5, 1] \end{cases} \tag{6.431}$$

Example 6.6   Let us consider the function $f : [0, 4] \to \mathbb{R}$,

$$f(x) = \frac{\sin x}{3 + x + \sin x} \tag{6.432}$$

and the interpolation knots

$$x_0 = 0, \quad x_1 = 1, \quad x_2 = 2, \quad x_3 = 3, \quad x_4 = 4. \tag{6.433}$$

If we realize the interpolation of this function by interpolation polynomials, then the limit to infinite of any such polynomial will be $\pm\infty$, in contradiction to

$$\lim_{x \to \pm\infty} f(x) = 0. \tag{6.434}$$

We realize the interpolation by rational functions and let

$$R(x) = \frac{P(x)}{Q(x)} \tag{6.435}$$

be such a function.
From relation (6.434), we deduce

$$\deg P < \deg Q \tag{6.436}$$

and, because we have five interpolation points, we may take

$$P(x) = a_1 x + a_0, \quad Q(x) = b_2 x^2 + b_1 x + b_0, \tag{6.437}$$

with $b_2 \neq 0$, $a_i \in \mathbb{R}$, $i = 0, 1$, $b_i \in \mathbb{R}$, $i = \overline{0, 2}$.

It follows that the linear system

$$\frac{a_0}{b_0} = f(0) = 0, \quad \frac{a_1 + a_0}{b_2 + b_1 + b_0} = f(1) = 0.17380, \quad \frac{2a_1 + a_0}{4b_2 + 2b_1 + b_0} = f(2) = 0.15388,$$

$$\frac{3a_1 + a_0}{9b_2 + 3b_1 + b_0} = f(3) = 0.02298, \quad \frac{4a_1 + a_0}{16b_2 + 4b_1 + b_0} = f(4) = -0.12122 \tag{6.438}$$

which is equivalent to,

$$\begin{aligned} &a_0 = 0, \quad a_1 - 0.17380b_0 - 0.17380b_1 - 0.17380b_2 = 0, \\ &2a_1 - 0.15388b_0 - 0.30776b_1 - 0.61552b_2 = 0, \\ &3a_1 - 0.02298b_0 - 0.06894b_1 - 0.20682b_2 = 0, \\ &4a_1 + 0.12122b_0 + 0.48488b_1 + 1.93952b_2 = 0. \end{aligned} \tag{6.439}$$

System (6.439) is compatible indeterminate. We shall determine its general solution. To do this, we consider that $a_1 = \lambda$, where λ is a real parameter. It follows that the system

$$0.15388b_0 + 0.30776b_1 + 0.61552b_2 = 2\lambda, \quad 0.02298b_0 + 0.06894b_1 + 0.20682b_2 = 3\lambda,$$

$$0.12122b_0 + 0.48488b_1 + 1.93952b_2 = -4\lambda, \tag{6.440}$$

with the solution

$$b_0 = -1065.4\lambda, \quad b_1 = 820.29\lambda, \quad b_2 = -140.55\lambda. \tag{6.441}$$

We deduce

$$R(x) = \frac{\lambda x}{-140.55\lambda x^2 + 820.29\lambda x - 1065\lambda} = \frac{x}{-140.55x^2 + 820.29x - 1065}, \quad \lambda \neq 0. \tag{6.442}$$

Example 6.7   Let us consider the function $f : [-1, 1] \to \mathbf{R}$,

$$f(x) = \frac{1}{1 + x^2}, \tag{6.443}$$

called the *Runge function*, for which let us choose two systems of knots of interpolation. The first system will contain four equidistant interpolation knots, that is,

$$x_0 = -1, \quad x_1 = -\frac{1}{3}, \quad x_2 = \frac{1}{3}, \quad x_3 = 1, \tag{6.444}$$

while the second system will have as interpolation knots the roots of the Chebyshev polynomial $K_4(x)$, that is,

$$\bar{x}_0 = -\sqrt{\frac{2 + \sqrt{2}}{4}}, \quad \bar{x}_1 = -\sqrt{\frac{2 - \sqrt{2}}{4}}, \quad \bar{x}_2 = \sqrt{\frac{2 - \sqrt{2}}{4}}, \quad \bar{x}_3 = \sqrt{\frac{2 + \sqrt{2}}{4}}. \tag{6.445}$$

---

[14]The function was presented by Carl David Tolmé Runge (1856–1927) in 1901.

TABLE 6.7   The Values of the Interpolation Knots and of Function (6.443) at These Knots

x	$f(x)$	x	$f(x)$
$x_0 = -1$	0.5	$\bar{x}_0 = -0.9238795$	0.5395043
$x_1 = -0.3333333$	0.9	$\bar{x}_1 = -0.3826834$	0.8722604
$x_2 = 0.3333333$	0.9	$\bar{x}_2 = 0.3826834$	0.8722604
$x_3 = 1$	0.5	$\bar{x}_3 = 0.9238795$	0.5395043

We shall construct interpolation polynomials corresponding to each system of knots and shall verify that the deviation is minimum in the case of the second system of interpolation knots for various numbers of interpolation knots.

The Lagrange polynomial that passes through the interpolation knots z_i, $i = \overline{0, 3}$, reads

$$
\begin{aligned}
L_3(x) = & \frac{(x - z_1)(x - z_2)(x - z_3)}{(z_0 - z_1)(z_0 - z_2)(z_0 - z_3)} y_0 \\
& + \frac{(x - z_0)(x - z_2)(x - z_3)}{(z_1 - z_0)(z_1 - z_2)(z_1 - z_3)} y_1 \\
& + \frac{(x - z_0)(x - z_1)(x - z_3)}{(z_2 - z_0)(z_2 - z_1)(z_2 - z_3)} y_2 + \frac{(x - z_0)(x - z_1)(x - z_2)}{(z_3 - z_0)(z_3 - z_1)(z_3 - z_2)} y_3,
\end{aligned}
\tag{6.446}
$$

where $y_i = f(z_i)$, $i = \overline{0, 3}$.

We construct Table 6.7 with the values of the interpolation knots and of function (6.443) at these knots.

The Lagrange polynomial for the first system of interpolation knots reads

$$
L_3^{(1)}(x) = -0.45x^2 + 0.95.
\tag{6.447}
$$

The Lagrange polynomial for the second set of interpolation knots is

$$
L_3^{(2)}(x) = -0.4705883x^2 + 0.9411765.
\tag{6.448}
$$

In general, calculating the values of the function f and of the polynomials $L_n^{(1)}(x)$ and $L_n^{(2)}(x)$ on the interval $[-1, 1]$ with the step $\Delta x = 0.001$, we have determined the values in Table 6.8.

We have denoted by ε_{eq} the maximum deviation for equidistant points, by P_{eq} the points at which this deviation takes place, by ε_{Ch} the maximum deviation with Chebyshev knots, and by P_{Ch} the points at which the maximum deviation with Chebyshev knots takes place.

We observe that for the interpolation knots given by the roots of the Chebyshev polynomial the error is stable at values of order 10^{-15}; for equidistant interpolation knots, the error is unbounded; thus, the oscillatory character of the polynomials of higher degree is established.

6.19   APPLICATIONS

Problem 6.1

Let us consider the planar linkage in Figure 6.3, where $OA = d$, $OC = c$, $AB = a$, $BC = b$, and $CM = \lambda BC$; the polynomials of first, second, and third degree, that approximate, in the sense of the least squares, the trajectory of the point M if the positions of the points M_i, specified by the angles

$$
\phi_i = -\frac{3\pi}{4} + (i - 1)\frac{\pi}{4}, \quad i = \overline{1, 7},
\tag{6.449}
$$

are known, have to be determined.

TABLE 6.8   Deviation

n	ε_{eq}	P_{eq}	ε_{Ch}	P_{Ch}
4	0.058359	±0.701	0.058824	0
5	0.022282	±0.827	0.012195	±1
6	0.014091	±0.851	0.10101	0
7	0.006873	±0.894	0.002092	±1
8	0.004273	±0.905	0.001733	0
9	0.002258	±0.925	0.000359	±1
10	0.001425	±0.931	0.000297	0
11	0.000791	±0.943	0.00062	±1
12	0.000501	±0.947	0.00051	0
13	0.00029	±0.954	0.00001	±1
14	0.0001815	±0.957	88×10^{-7}	0
15	0.0001061	±0.962	18×10^{-7}	±1
16	6.73×10^{-5}	±0.964	1.5×10^{-6}	0
17	3.99×10^{-5}	±0.968	3.11×10^{-7}	±1
18	2.54×10^{-5}	±0.969	2.58×10^{-7}	0
19	1.52×10^{-5}	±0.972	5.34×10^{-8}	±1
20	9.67×10^{-6}	±0.973	4.42×10^{-8}	0
25	8.84×10^{-7}	±0.980	2.70×10^{-10}	±1
30	8.79×10^{-8}	±0.984	6.57×10^{-12}	0
35	1.92×10^{-8}	±0.979	4.02×10^{-14}	±0.964
40	4.13×10^{-7}	±0.989	1.78×10^{-15}	±0.082
45	9.37×10^{-6}	±0.991	1.22×10^{-15}	±0.052
50	0.0003145	±0.988	1.22×10^{-15}	±0.319
60	0.365949	±0.994	1.67×10^{-15}	±0.163
70	218.546	±0.990	1.67×10^{-15}	±0.035
80	171416	±0.995	1.67×10^{-15}	±0.056
90	2.03×10^8	±0.996	1.55×10^{-15}	±0.753
100	1.47×10^{11}	±0.998	2×10^{-15}	±0.054
200	1.42×10^{41}	±0.998	2.78×10^{-15}	±0.544
300	3.95×10^{70}	±0.999	2.66×10^{-15}	±0.043
400	4.67×10^{100}	±0.999	3.33×10^{-15}	±0.320
500	4.23×10^{130}	±0.999	3.66×10^{-15}	±0.445

Solution:

1. Theory
Denoting by X_C, Y_C the coordinates of the point C, as well as $OC^2 = c^2$, $CB^2 = b^2$, we obtain the equations

$$X_C^2 + Y_C^2 = c^2, \tag{6.450}$$

$$[X_C - (d + a \cos \phi)]^2 + (Y_C - a \sin \phi)^2 = b^2, \tag{6.451}$$

from which, by subtracting and using the notation

$$f = \frac{c^2 + a^2 + d^2 + 2ad \cos \phi - b^2}{2}, \tag{6.452}$$

we get the equation of first degree

$$X_C(d + a \cos \phi) + Y_C a \sin \phi = f. \tag{6.453}$$

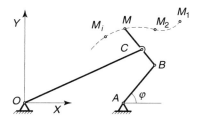

Figure 6.3   Problem 6.1.

Further, using the notations

$$h = \frac{fa \sin \phi}{a^2 + d^2 + 2ad \cos \phi}, \quad k = \frac{c^2(d + a \cos \phi)^2 - f^2}{a^2 + d^2 + 2ad \cos \phi}, \tag{6.454}$$

equation (6.450) and equation (6.453) lead to the equation

$$Y_C^2 - 2hY_C - k = 0, \tag{6.455}$$

the solution of which is

$$Y_C = h + \sqrt{h^2 + k}; \tag{6.456}$$

also, from equation (6.453) we obtain

$$X_C = \frac{f - Y_C a \sin \phi}{d + a \cos \phi}. \tag{6.457}$$

Denoting then by X, Y the coordinates of the point M, there result

$$X = (1 - \lambda)X_C + \lambda(d + a \cos \phi), \tag{6.458}$$

$$Y = (1 - \lambda)Y_C + \lambda a \sin \phi. \tag{6.459}$$

Numerical application for $a = l$, $b = c = 3l$, $d = 2l$, $l = 1$, $\lambda = 1/3$ (with a positive value for λ, it follows, on the basis of a known relation in the affine geometry, that the point M is between C and B).

2. Numerical calculation

Relations (6.449), (6.452), (6.454), (6.456), (6.457), (6.458), and (6.459) lead to the values in Table 6.9.

Successively, the polynomials

$$Y = 2.405819 - 0.496319X, \tag{6.460}$$

$$Y = 2.220796 + 0.377282X - 0.390308X^2, \tag{6.461}$$

$$Y = 2.209666 + 0.773455X - 0.888467X^2 + 0.147989X^3 \tag{6.462}$$

are obtained (Fig. 6.4).

Problem 6.2

Let there be a mechanism with the plane follower of translation as shown in Figure 6.5; the mechanism is used for admission and evacuation of gas at heat engines.

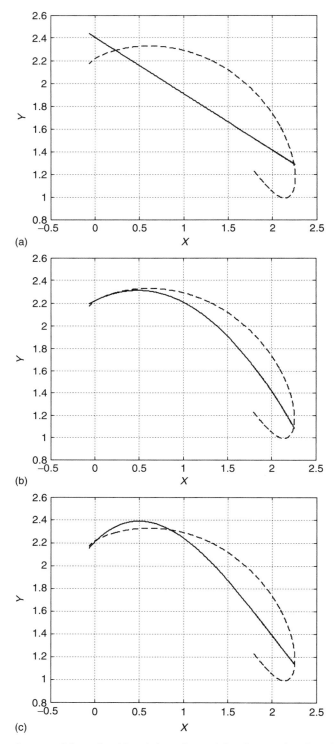

(a)

(b)

(c)

Figure 6.4   The trajectory of the point M and the polynomials of approximations by the least square method: (a) of first degree, (b) of second degree, (c) of third degree (the dashed line represents the original function).

TABLE 6.9   Numerical Results

i	ϕ_i	X_{Ci}	Y_{Ci}	X_i	Y_i
1	-2.356194	2.041879	2.197892	1.792217	1.229559
2	-1.570796	2.244990	1.989980	2.163327	0.993320
3	-0.785398	2.024246	2.214143	2.251866	1.240393
4	0.000000	1.500000	2.598076	2.000000	1.732051
5	0.785398	0.682861	2.921250	1.357610	2.183202
6	1.570796	-0.244990	2.989980	0.503340	2.326653
7	2.356194	-0.748985	2.904999	-0.068359	2.172368

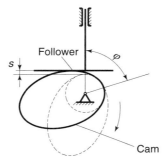

Figure 6.5   Problem 6.2.

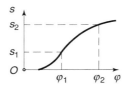

Figure 6.6   The displacement of the follower versus the rotation angle of the cam.

If the motion law $s = s(\phi)$ of the follower, where s is the displacement and ϕ is the rotation angle of the cam, is piecewise polynomial, then the cam is called *polydine* (Fig. 6.6).

Let us determine, on the interval $[\phi_1, \phi_2]$, the Hermitic polynomial of minimal degree, which verifies the conditions

$$s_i(\phi_i) = s(\phi_i), \quad \widetilde{v}_i = \frac{ds}{d\phi}\Big|_{\phi=\phi_i}, \quad \widetilde{a}_i = \frac{d^2 s}{d\phi^2}\Big|_{\phi=\phi_i}, \quad i = 1, \ 2. \tag{6.463}$$

Solution:

1. Theory

Because there are six conditions, it means that the polynomial is of fifth degree and may be written in the form

$$s = b_0 + b_1 \Phi + b_2 \Phi^2 + b_3 \Phi^3 + b_4 \Phi^4 + b_5 \Phi^5, \tag{6.464}$$

where

$$\Phi = \frac{\phi - \phi_1}{\phi - \phi_0}, \quad \Phi \in [0, 1]. \tag{6.465}$$

Moreover, taking into account conditions (6.463), polynomial (6.464) reads

$$s = s_1 P_1(\Phi) + s_2 P_2(\Phi) + (\phi_2 - \phi_1)[\tilde{v}_1 P_3(\Phi) + \tilde{v}_2 P_4(\Phi)](\phi_2 - \phi_1)^2[\tilde{a}_1 P_5(\Phi) + \tilde{a}_2 P_6(\Phi)], \tag{6.466}$$

where $P_i(\Phi)$, $i = \overline{1,6}$, are polynomials of fifth degree in Φ, which satisfy the conditions

$$\begin{aligned}
&P_1(0) = 1, \ P_1(1) = 1, \ P_1'(0) = P_1'(1) = 0, \ P_1''(0) = P_1''(1) = 0, \ P_2(0) = 0, \ P_2(1) = 1, \\
&P_2'(0) = P_2'(1) = 0, \ P_2''(0) = P_2''(1) = 0, \ P_3(0) = P_3(1) = 0, \ P_3'(0) = 1, \ P_3'(1) = 1, \\
&P_3''(0) = P_3''(1) = 0, \ P_4(0) = P_4(1) = 0, \ P_4'(0) = 0, \ P_4'(1) = 1, \ P_4''(0) = P_4''(1) = 0, \\
&P_5(0) = P_5(1) = 0, \ P_5'(0) = P_5'(1) = 0, \ P_5''(0) = 1, \ P_5''(1) = 0, \ P_6(0) = P_6(1) = 0, \\
&P_6'(0) = P_6'(1) = 0, \ P_6''(0) = 0, \ P_6''(1) = 1. \tag{6.467}
\end{aligned}$$

If we express the polynomial $P_i(\Phi)$ and its derivatives in the form

$$\begin{aligned}
P_i(\Phi) &= c_{0i} + c_{1i}\Phi + c_{2i}\Phi^2 + \cdots + c_{5i}\Phi^5, \\
P_i'(\Phi) &= c_{1i} + 2c_{2i}\Phi + 3c_{3i}\Phi^2 + 4c_{4i}\Phi^3 + 5c_{5i}\Phi^4, \\
P_i''(\Phi) &= 2c_{2i} + 6c_{3i}\Phi + 12c_{4i}\Phi^2 + 20c_{5i}\Phi^3, \ i = \overline{1,6}, \tag{6.468}
\end{aligned}$$

then conditions (6.467) lead to the system

$$c_{3i} + c_{4i} + c_{5i} = \alpha_i, \ 3c_{3i} + 4c_{4i} + 5c_{5i} = \beta_i, \ 6c_{3i} + 12c_{4i} + 20c_{5i} = \gamma_i, \ i = \overline{1,\ 6}, \tag{6.469}$$

where the constants α_i, β_i, γ_i and c_{0i}, c_{1i}, c_{2i}, determined for each case, are given in Table 6.10. The solution

$$c_{3i} = \frac{20\alpha_i - 8\beta_i + \gamma_i}{2}, \quad c_{4i} = -15\alpha_i + 7\beta_i - \gamma_i, \quad c_{5i} = \frac{12\alpha_i - 6\beta_i + \gamma_i}{2} \tag{6.470}$$

is obtained from system (6.469), using the data of Table 6.10; numerical results are given in Table 6.11.

Thus, the six polynomials read

$$\begin{aligned}
&P_1(\Phi) = 1 - 10\Phi^3 + 15\Phi^4 - 6\Phi^5, \quad P_2(\Phi) = 10\Phi^3 - 15\Phi^4 + 6\Phi^5, \\
&P_3(\Phi) = \Phi - 6\Phi^3 + 8\Phi^4 - 3\Phi^5, \quad P_4(\Phi) = -4\Phi^3 + 7\Phi^4 - 3\Phi^5, \\
&P_5(\Phi) = \frac{1}{2}\Phi^2 - \frac{3}{2}\Phi^3 + \frac{3}{2}\Phi^4 - \frac{1}{2}\Phi^5, \quad P_6(\Phi) = \frac{1}{2}\Phi^3 - \Phi^4 + \frac{1}{2}\Phi^5. \tag{6.471}
\end{aligned}$$

Particular case: $\phi_1 = 0$ rad, $s_1 = 0$ mm, $\phi_2 = 1$ rad, $s_2 = h = 7$ mm, $\tilde{v}_1 = \tilde{v}_2 = 0$, $\tilde{a}_1 = \tilde{a}_2 = 0$.
2. Particular case
The answer

$$s = h P_2(\Phi) = h\left(10\frac{\phi^3}{\phi_2^3} - 15\frac{\phi^4}{\phi_2^4} + 6\frac{\phi^5}{\phi_2^5}\right) = 7(10\phi^3 - 15\phi^4 + 6\phi^5) \tag{6.472}$$

is obtained and the diagram is shown in Figure 6.7.

Problem 6.3

Let us consider the quadrangular mechanism in Figure 6.8, where $AB = a$, $OA = b$, $BC = CM = OC = c$.

It is required to determine the distance Y_0 so that the straight line $Y - Y_0 = 0$ approximates the trajectory of the point M on the interval $\phi \in [-\pi/2, \pi/2]$ in the sense of the mini−max method.

TABLE 6.10   The Values c_{0i}, c_{1i}, c_{2i}, α_i, β_i, and γ_i

i	c_{0i}	c_{1i}	c_{2i}	α_i	β_i	γ_i
1	1	0	0	-1	-1	0
2	0	1	0	1	1	0
3	0	0	0	-1	-1	0
4	0	0	0	0	0	1
5	0	0	1/2	$-1/2$	$-1/2$	-1
6	0	0	0	0	0	1

TABLE 6.11   The Values c_{3i}, c_{4i}, and c_{5i}

i	c_{3i}	c_{4i}	c_{5i}
1	-10	15	-6
2	10	-15	6
3	-6	8	-3
4	-4	7	-3
5	$-3/2$	3/2	$-1/2$
6	1/2	-1	1/2

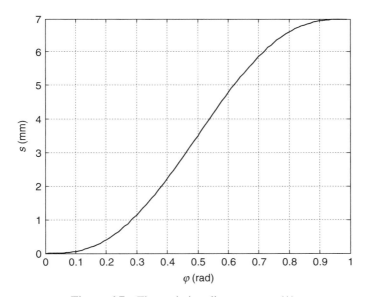

Figure 6.7   The variation diagram $s = s(\phi)$.

Solution:

1. Theoretical aspects

Let us consider the function $y = y(x)$, the graphic of which is symmetric on the interval $[-a, a]$ (Fig. 6.9). We wish to determine the straight line $y - y_0 = 0$, which approximates this curve in the sense of the mini−max method.

Let us choose, for example,

$$y_{0i} = y(0) + \Delta y_i; \tag{6.473}$$

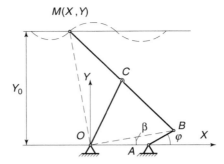

Figure 6.8   Problem 6.3.

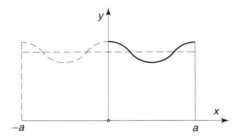

Figure 6.9   Theoretical aspects.

we then calculate

$$\max|y(x_i) - y_{0i}| = y^i_{\max}. \tag{6.474}$$

We construct a table such as the following for each Δy_i.

x	$y^i_{\max}$
0	0.2
0.01	0.3
0.02	0.5
$\vdots$	$\vdots$
a	0.01

The above table has been created for $\Delta y = 0.2$.
We thus obtain a sequence of data of the following form.

Δy_i	$y^i_{\max}$
0	0.5
0.01	0.8
$\vdots$	$\vdots$
0.5	0.125
$\vdots$	$\vdots$

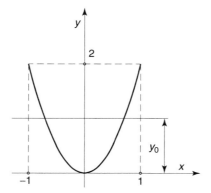

Figure 6.10   Function (6.477).

The minimum in this table is obtained (in the case given by us) for $\Delta y_i = 0.5$ and has the value

$$y^i_{max} = 0.125 = \text{minimum}. \tag{6.475}$$

We deduce the required straight line of the equation

$$y_0 - y(0) = 0.125. \tag{6.476}$$

Sometimes, the problem may be solved analytically also.
Let there be a function (Fig. 6.10) with

$$y = 2x^2, \quad x \in [-1, 1], \tag{6.477}$$

for which we consider

$$y_0 < f(1) = 2. \tag{6.478}$$

It follows immediately that

$$g(x) = |y_0 - 2x^2| = \begin{cases} y_0 - 2x^2 \text{ for } |x| \le \dfrac{y_0}{\sqrt{2}}, \\ 2x^2 - y_0 \text{ for } |x| > \dfrac{y_0}{\sqrt{2}}. \end{cases} \tag{6.479}$$

In the first case of formula (6.479), we deduce $g_{max} = y_0$, while in the second case we have $g_{max} = 2 - y_0$.
It follows that the required straight line is given by

$$y_0 = 1, \quad y - 1 = 0. \tag{6.480}$$

Let us return to the problem in Figure 6.8. The triangle OBM is rectangular at O so that there result the relations

$$OM = \sqrt{BM^2 - OB^2} = \sqrt{4c^2 - (a^2 + c^2 + 2ac \cos \phi)}. \tag{6.481}$$

Thus, also result

$$\cos \beta = \frac{b + a \cos \phi}{\sqrt{a^2 + b^2 + 2ab \cos \phi}}, \quad \sin \beta = \frac{a \sin \phi}{\sqrt{a^2 + b^2 + 2ab \cos \phi}}; \tag{6.482}$$

hence

$$X_M = OM \cos \left(\frac{\pi}{2} + \beta \right) = -\frac{a \sin \phi \sqrt{4c^2 - (a^2 + b^2 + 2ab \cos \phi)}}{\sqrt{a^2 + b^2 + 2ab \cos \phi}}, \tag{6.483}$$

$$Y_M = OM \sin \left(\frac{\pi}{2} + \beta \right) = \frac{(b + a \cos \phi) \sqrt{4c^2 - (a^2 + b^2 + 2ab \cos \phi)}}{\sqrt{a^2 + b^2 + 2ab \cos \phi}}. \tag{6.484}$$

Because $X_M(-\phi) = -X_M(\phi)$, $Y_M(-\phi) = Y_M(\phi)$, it follows that the trajectory of the point M is symmetric with respect to the OY-axis.

Numerical application for $a = 0.1$ m, $b = 0.2$ m, $c = 0.25$ m.

2. Numerical calculation

Expressions (6.483) and (6.484) become

$$X_M = -\frac{0.1 \sin \phi \sqrt{0.2 - 0.04 \cos \phi}}{\sqrt{0.05 + 0.04 \cos \phi}}, \tag{6.485}$$

$$Y_M = \frac{(0.2 + 0.1 \cos \phi) \sqrt{0.2 - 0.04 \cos \phi}}{\sqrt{0.05 + 0.04 \cos \phi}}. \tag{6.486}$$

Denoting now

$$\phi = \frac{\pi}{2} \phi^*, \quad \phi^* \in [-1, 1], \tag{6.487}$$

we obtain the following table of values.

ϕ^*	X_M	Y_M
-1	0.200000	0.400000
-0.9	0.183292	0.400183
-0.8	0.164973	0.400529
-0.7	0.145533	0.400825
-0.6	0.125354	0.400968
-0.5	0.104726	0.400934
-0.4	0.083858	0.400758
-0.3	0.062893	0.400505
-0.2	0.041912	0.400251
-0.1	0.020947	0.400067
0	0.000000	0.400000
0.1	-0.020947	0.400067
0.2	-0.041912	0.400251
0.3	-0.062893	0.400505
0.4	-0.083858	0.400758
0.5	-0.104726	0.400934
0.6	-0.125354	0.400968
0.7	-0.145533	0.400825
0.8	-0.164973	0.400529
0.9	-0.183292	0.400183
1	-0.200000	0.400000

We consider now the step

$$\Delta Y = 10^{-6} \text{ m} \tag{6.488}$$

and the interval $0.4 \text{ m} \leq Y \leq 0.401 \text{ m}$.

For each Y we have constructed a table of the following form (in this case the table has been created for $Y = 0.4 \text{ m}$)

X_M^i	Y_M^i	$|Y_M^i - Y|$
0.200000	0.400000	0.000000
0.183292	0.400183	0.000183
0.164973	0.400529	0.000529
0.145533	0.400825	0.000825
0.125354	0.400968	0.000968
0.104726	0.400934	0.000934
0.083858	0.400758	0.000758
0.062893	0.400505	0.000505
0.041912	0.400251	0.000251
0.020947	0.400067	0.000067
0.000000	0.400000	0.000000
−0.020947	0.400067	0.000067
−0.041912	0.400251	0.000251
−0.062893	0.400505	0.000505
−0.083858	0.400758	0.000758
−0.104726	0.400934	0.000934
−0.125354	0.400968	0.000968
−0.145533	0.400825	0.000825
−0.164973	0.400529	0.000529
−0.183292	0.400183	0.000183
−0.200000	0.400000	0.000000

From the above table, it follows

$$\max |Y_M^i - Y| = 0.000968. \tag{6.489}$$

Analyzing each table, we deduce the value

$$\min \max |Y_M^i - Y| = 0.000484 \tag{6.490}$$

obtained for

$$Y_0 = 0.400484 \text{ m}; \tag{6.491}$$

hence, the equation of the required straight line is

$$Y - 0.400484 = 0. \tag{6.492}$$

In Figure 6.11 the trajectory of the point M has been drawn (with a continuous line), as also the straight line (6.492) (with a broken line).

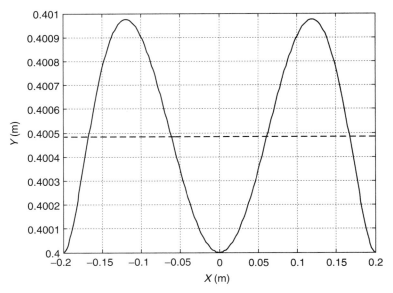

Figure 6.11   Trajectory of the point M (continuous line) and its approximation by the straight line (6.492) (broken line).

FURTHER READING

Acton FS (1990). Numerical Methods that Work. 4th ed. Washington: Mathematical Association of America.

Ackleh AS, Allen EJ, Hearfott RB, Seshaiyer P (2009). Classical and Modern Numerical Analysis: Theory, Methods and Practice. Boca Raton: CRC Press.

Atkinson KE (1989). An Introduction to Numerical Analysis. 2nd ed. New York: John Wiley & Sons, Inc.

Atkinson KE (1993). Elementary Numerical Analysis. 2nd ed. New York: John Wiley & Sons, Inc.

Atkinson K, Han W (2010). Theoretical Numerical Analysis: A Functional Analysis Framework. 3rd ed. New York: Springer-Verlag.

Bakhvalov N (1976). Méthodes Numérique. Moscou: Editions Mir (in French).

Berbente C, Mitran S, Zancu S (1997). Metode Numerice. Bucureşti: Editura Tehnică (in Romanian).

Bloch S (1951). Angenäherte Synthese von Mechanismen. Berlin: Verlag Technik (in German).

Burden RL, Faires L (2009). Numerical Analysis. 9th ed. Boston: Brooks/Cole.

Butt R (2009). Introduction to Numerical Analysis Using MATLAB. Boston: Jones and Bartlett Publishers.

Chapra SC (1996). Applied Numerical Methods with MATLAB for Engineers and Scientists. Boston: McGraw-Hill.

Cheney EW, Kincaid DR (1997). Numerical Mathematics and Computing. 6th ed. Belmont: Thomson.

Dahlquist G, Björck Å (1974). Numerical Methods. Englewood Cliffs: Prentice Hall.

Démidovitch B, Maron I (1973). Éléments de Calcul Numérique. Moscou: Editions Mir (in French).

DiBenedetto E (2010). Classical Mechanics: Theory and Mathematical Modeling. New York: Springer-Verlag.

Epperson JF (2007). An Introduction to Numerical Methods and Analysis. Hoboken: John Wiley & Sons, Inc.

Fung YC, Tong P (2011). Classical and Computational Solid Mechanics. Singapore: World Scientific Publishing.

Golub GH, van Loan CF (1996). Matrix Computations. 3rd ed. Baltimore: John Hopkins University Press.

Greenbaum A, Chartier TP (2012). Numerical Methods: Design, Analysis, and Computer Implementation of Algorithms. Princeton: Princeton University Press.

Hamming RW (1987). Numerical Methods for Scientists and Engineers. 2nd ed. New York: Dover Publications.

Hamming RW (2012). Introduction to Applied Numerical Analysis. New York: Dover Publications.

Heinbockel JH (2006). Numerical Methods for Scientific Computing. Victoria: Trafford Publishing.

Hildebrand FB (1987). Introduction to Numerical Analysis. 2nd ed. New York: Dover Publications.

Hoffman JD (1992). Numeical Methods for Engineers and Scientists. New York: McGraw-Hill.

Kharab A, Guenther RB (2011). An Introduction to Numerical Methods: A MATLAB Approach. 3rd ed. Boca Raton: CRC Press.

Kleppner D, Kolenkow RJ (2010). An Introduction to Mechanics. Cambridge: Cambridge University Press.

Kress R (1996). Numerical Analysis. New York: Springer-Verlag.

Krîlov AN (1957). Lecţii de Calcule prin Aproximaţii. Bucureşti: Editura Tehnică (in Romanian).

Kunz KS (1957). Numerical Analysis. New York: McGraw-Hill.

Lange K (2010). Numerical Analysis for Statisticians. 2nd ed. New York: Springer-Verlag.

Lurie AI (2002). Analytical Mechanics. New York: Springer-Verlag.

Mabie HH, Reinholtz CF (1987). Mechanisms and Dynamics of Machinery. 4th ed. New York: John Wiley & Sons, Inc.

Marciuk GI (1983). Metode de Analiză Numerică. Bucureşti: Editura Academiei Române (in Romanian).

Marciuk GI, Şaidurov VV (1981). Creşterea Preciziei Soluţiilor în Scheme cu Diferenţe. Bucureşti: Editura Academiei Române (in Romanian).

Meriam JL, Kraige LG (2012). Engineering Mechanics: Dynamics. Hoboken: John Wiley & Sons, Inc.

Otto SR, Denier JP (2005). An Introduction to Programming and Numerical Methods in MATLAB. London: Springer-Verlag.

Pandrea N (2000). Elemente de Mecanica Solidului în Coordonate Plückeriene. Bucureşti: Editura Academiei Române (in Romanian).

Pandrea N, Pârlac S, Popa D (2001). Modele pentru Studiul Vibraţiilor Automobilelor. Piteşti: Tiparg (in Romanian).

Pandrea N, Popa D (2000). Mecanisme. Teorie şi Aplicaţii CAD. Bucureşti: Editura Tehnică (in Romanian).

Pandrea N, Stănescu ND (2002). Mecanică. Bucureşti: Editura Didactică şi Pedagogică (in Romanian).

Postolache M (2006). Modelare Numerică. Teorie şi Aplicaţii. Bucureşti: Editura Fair Partners (in Romanian).

Press WH, Teukolski SA, Vetterling WT, Flannery BP (2007). Numerical Recipes: The Art of Scientific Computing. 3rd ed. Cambridge: Cambridge University Press.

Quarteroni A, Sacco R, Saleri F (2010). Numerica Mathematics. 2nd ed. Berlin: Springer-Verlag.

Ralston A, Rabinowitz P (2001). A First Course in Numerical Analysis. 2nd ed. New York: Dover Publications.

Reza F (1973). Spaţii Liniare. Bucureşti: Editura Didactică şi Pedagogică p. 4 (in Romanian).

Ridgway Scott L (2011). Numerical Analysis. Princeton: Princeton University Press. pp. 1–8, 10.

Rivière B (2008). Discontinuous Galerkin Methods for Solving Elliptic and Parabolic Equations: Theory and Implementation. Philadelphia: SIAM. 9.

Salvadori MG, Baron ML (1962). Numerical Methods in Engineering. Englewood Cliffs: Prentice Hall.

Sauer T (2011). Numerical Analysis. 2nd ed. London: Pearson.

Simionescu I, Dranga M, Moise V (1995). Metode Numerice în Tehnică. Aplicaţii în FORTRAN. Bucureşti: Editura Tehnică (in Romanian).

Stănescu ND (2007). Metode Numerice. Bucureşti: Editura Didactică şi Pedagogică (in Romanian).

Stoer J, Bulirsh R (2010). Introduction to Numerical Analysis. 3rd ed. New York: Springer-Verlag.

Süli E, Mayers D (2003). An Introduction to Numerical Analysis. Cambridge: Cambridge University Press.

Udrişte C, Iftode V, Postolache M (1996). Metode Numerice de Calcul. Algoritmi şi Programe Turbo Pascal. Bucureşti: Editura Tehnică (in Romanian).

7

NUMERICAL DIFFERENTIATION AND INTEGRATION

7.1 INTRODUCTION

The numerical differentiation is used if the function to differentiate is defined in a numerical form by its values y_i at the knots x_i,

$$y_i = f(x_i), \ i = \overline{0, n}, \tag{7.1}$$

with $f : \mathcal{D} \subset \mathbb{R} \to \mathbb{R}$, or if the expression of the function is very complicated and difficult to use, or if the function is the solution of an equation or of a system of equations.

The operation of differentiation is, in general, avoided, because it increases the small errors. Such an example is given in Figure 7.1, where the function f has been drawn by an unbroken line, while its approximate $\overline{f}$ has been drawn by a broken one. The function and its approximate pass through the points $A_{i-1}(x_{i-1}, y_{i-1})$, $A_i(x_i, y_i)$, $A_{i+1}(x_{i+1}, y_{i+1})$. The straight line (τ) is tangent to the graph of the function f at the point $A_{i-1}(x_{i-1}, y_{i-1})$, while the straight line (τ_1) marks the tangent to the graph of the approximate $\overline{f}$ at the very same point $A_{i-1}(x_{i-1}, y_{i-1})$. Thus we obtain the relation

$$\tan \alpha = f'(x_{i-1}), \ \tan \alpha_1 = \overline{f}'(x_{i-1}) \tag{7.2}$$

and in the figure, we observe that the error is $|\tan \alpha - \tan \alpha_1|$.

7.2 NUMERICAL DIFFERENTIATION BY MEANS OF AN EXPANSION INTO A TAYLOR SERIES

Let $f : [a, b] \to \mathbb{R}$ be of class $C^3([a, b])$ and let

$$a = x_0 < x_1 < x_2 < \cdots < x_n = b \tag{7.3}$$

Numerical Analysis with Applications in Mechanics and Engineering, First Edition.
Petre Teodorescu, Nicolae-Doru Stănescu, and Nicolae Pandrea.
© 2013 The Institute of Electrical and Electronics Engineers, Inc. Published 2013 by John Wiley & Sons, Inc.

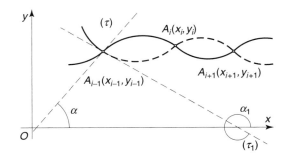

Figure 7.1   Numerical differentiation.

be a division of the interval $[a, b]$. Let us denote by h the magnitude

$$h = x_i - x_{i-1} \tag{7.4}$$

and by h_1 the magnitude

$$h_1 = x_{i+1} - x_i. \tag{7.5}$$

In the general case, $h \neq h_1$ and we may write

$$h_1 = h\alpha, \tag{7.6}$$

where $\alpha \in \mathbb{R}_+^*$.

Let us consider now the expansion into a Taylor series of the function f around the point x_i

$$f(x) = f(x_i) + \frac{x - x_i}{1!} f'(x_i) + \frac{(x - x_i)^2}{2!} f''(x_i) + \frac{(x - x_i)^3}{3!} f'''(\xi), \tag{7.7}$$

where ξ is a point situated between x and x_i. We may also write

$$\xi = x_i + \theta(x - x_i), \tag{7.8}$$

where $\theta \in (0, 1)$. It follows that

$$f(x) = f(x_i) + \frac{x - x_i}{1!} f'(x_i) + \frac{(x - x_i)^2}{2!} f''(x_i) + \frac{(x - x_i)^3}{3!} f'''[x_i + \theta(x - x_i)]. \tag{7.9}$$

Let us now consider the values $x = x_{i-1}$ and $x = x_{i+1}$, $i = \overline{1, n-1}$. We thus obtain

$$f(x_{i+1}) = f(x_i) + \frac{\alpha h}{1!} f'(x_i) + \frac{(\alpha h)^2}{2!} f''(x_i) + \frac{(\alpha h)^3}{3!} f'''(\xi_i), \tag{7.10}$$

with ξ_i situated between x_i and x_{i+1}, and

$$f(x_{i-1}) = f(x_i) - \frac{h}{1!} f'(x_i) + \frac{h^2}{2!} f''(x_i) - \frac{h^3}{3!} f'''(\zeta_i), \tag{7.11}$$

where ζ_i is situated between x_{i-1} and x_i, respectively.

We will now subtract the last two relations one from another, obtaining

$$f(x_{i+1}) - f(x_{i-1}) = \frac{(\alpha + 1)h}{1!} f'(x_i) + \frac{h^2(\alpha^2 - 1)}{2!} f''(x_i)$$

$$+ \frac{(\alpha h)^3}{3!} f'''(\xi_i) + \frac{h^3}{3!} f'''(\zeta_i), \qquad (7.12)$$

from which

$$f'(x_i) = \frac{1}{(\alpha + 1)h} (f(x_{i+1}) - f(x_{i-1})) + \frac{(1 - \alpha)h}{2!} f''(x_i)$$

$$- \frac{h^2}{3!(\alpha + 1)} (\alpha^3 f'''(\xi_i) + f'''(\zeta_i)). \qquad (7.13)$$

Observation 7.1   If $f : [a, b] \to \mathbb{R}$ is at least of class $C^3([a, b])$, then we may consider

$$f'(x_i) \approx \frac{1}{(\alpha + 1)h} (f(x_{i+1}) - f(x_{i-1})). \qquad (7.14)$$

We add now relation (7.10) to relation (7.11) multiplied by α. It follows that

$$f(x_{i+1}) + \alpha f(x_{i-1}) = (1 + \alpha) f(x_i) + \frac{\alpha h^2}{2!} f''(x_i)(1 + \alpha)$$

$$+ \frac{(\alpha h)^3}{3!} f'''(\xi_i) - \frac{\alpha h^3}{3!} f'''(\zeta_i), \qquad (7.15)$$

from which

$$f''(x_i) = \frac{2}{\alpha(\alpha + 1)h^2} \left[f(x_{i+1}) + \alpha f(x_{i-1}) - (1 + \alpha) f(x_i) \right.$$

$$\left. - \frac{(\alpha h)^3}{3!} f'''(\xi_i) - \frac{\alpha h^3}{3!} f'''(\zeta_i) \right]. \qquad (7.16)$$

Observation 7.2   In the same conditions as at the Observation 7.1, we can use the approximate formula

$$f''(x_i) \approx \frac{2}{\alpha(\alpha + 1)h^2} [\alpha f(x_{i-1}) - (1 + \alpha) f(x_i) + f(x_{i+1})]. \qquad (7.17)$$

Proposition 7.1   Let $f : [a, b] \to \mathbb{R}$ be at least of class $C^3([a, b])$. Under these conditions:

(i) the approximation error of $f'(x_i)$ obtained by using formula (7.14) is

$$\varepsilon_{f'} = \frac{(1 - \alpha)h}{2!} f''(x_i) - \frac{h^2}{3!(1 + \alpha)} (\alpha^3 f'''(\xi_i) + f'''(\zeta_i)); \qquad (7.18)$$

(ii) the approximation error of $f''(x_i)$ obtained by using formula (7.17) is

$$\varepsilon_{f''} = \frac{h}{3(\alpha + 1)} (\alpha^2 f'''(\xi_i) - f'''(\zeta_i)). \qquad (7.19)$$

Demonstration. It is immediate, using formulae (7.13) and (7.16), respectively.

Corollary 7.1 If the knots are equidistant ($\alpha = 1$), then

(i) formula (7.14) of approximation of the derivative of first order $f'(x_i)$ takes the form

$$f'(x_i) \approx \frac{f(x_{i+1}) - f(x_{i-1})}{2h}, \tag{7.20}$$

the error being

$$\varepsilon_{f'} = -\frac{h^2}{12}(f'''(\xi_i) + f'''(\zeta_i)); \tag{7.21}$$

(ii) formula (7.17) of approximation of the derivative of second order $f''(x_i)$ reads

$$f''(x_i) \approx \frac{f(x_{i-1}) - 2f(x_i) + f(x_{i+1})}{h^2}, \tag{7.22}$$

the error being

$$\varepsilon_{f''} = \frac{h}{6}(f'''(\xi_i) - f'''(\zeta_i)). \tag{7.23}$$

Corollary 7.2 If $f : [a, b] \to \mathbb{R}$, $f \in C^3([a, b])$ and the interpolation knots are equidistant, then we denote

$$M = \sup_{x \in [a,b]} f'''(x), \quad m = \inf_{x \in [a,b]} f'''(x). \tag{7.24}$$

In this case,

$$|\varepsilon_{f'}| \leq \frac{h^2}{6} \max\{|M|, |m|\}, \tag{7.25}$$

$$|\varepsilon_{f''}| \leq \frac{h}{6}|M - m|. \tag{7.26}$$

Observation 7.3 We use the approximate formulae

$$f'(x_0) \approx \frac{-3f(x_0) + 4f(x_1) - f(x_2)}{x_2 - x_0}, \tag{7.27}$$

$$f'(x_n) \approx \frac{3f(x_n) - 4f(x_{n-1}) + f(x_{n-2})}{x_n - x_{n-2}}. \tag{7.28}$$

for the points x_0 and x_n.

7.3 NUMERICAL DIFFERENTIATION BY MEANS OF INTERPOLATION POLYNOMIALS

Let the function be $f : [a, b] \to \mathbb{R}$ and the equidistant interpolation knots x_i, $i = \overline{0, n}$, so that

$$x_{i+1} - x_i = h = \text{const}, \ i = \overline{0, n-1}. \tag{7.29}$$

We also denote by $P(q)$ Newton's interpolation polynomial, where $q = (x - x_0)/h$ for x in the superior part of the finite differences table and where $q = (x - x_n)/h$ for x in the inferior part of the finite differences table. We approximate the derivative $f'(x) = df/dx$ by the derivative of Newton's polynomial at the very same point

$$f'(x) \approx \frac{dP}{dx}. \tag{7.30}$$

We mention that we may write

$$
\begin{aligned}
\frac{dP}{dx} &= \frac{dP}{dq}\frac{dq}{dx} = \frac{1}{h}\frac{dP}{dq}, \\
\frac{d^2 P}{dx^2} &= \frac{d}{dx}\left(\frac{dP}{dx}\right) = \frac{1}{h}\frac{d}{dx}\left(\frac{dP}{dq}\right) = \frac{1}{h^2}\frac{d^2 P}{dq^2}, \cdots, \\
\frac{d^k P}{dx^k} &= \frac{1}{h^k}\frac{d^k P}{dq^k}, \cdots
\end{aligned} \tag{7.31}
$$

Lemma 7.1 Let $x^{(n)}$ be the generalized power of nth order. Under these conditions

$$\frac{d^k}{dx^k}x^{(n)} = n(n-1)\cdots(n-k+1)x^{(n-k)}. \tag{7.32}$$

Demonstration. We have

$$\Delta x^{(n)} = nhx^{(n-1)} \tag{7.33}$$

and

$$\frac{d}{dx}x^{(n)} = \lim_{h\to 0}\frac{\Delta x^{(n)}}{h} = nx^{(n-1)}. \tag{7.34}$$

Step by step, we obtain formula (7.32).

Let $P(q)$ be Newton's forward polynomial

$$P(q) = y_0 + \frac{q^{(1)}}{1!}\Delta y_0 + \frac{q^{(2)}}{2!}\Delta^2 y_0 + \cdots + \frac{q^{(n)}}{n!}\Delta^n y_0. \tag{7.35}$$

Under these conditions, assuming that $q = (x - x_0)/h$, Lemma 7.1 leads to

$$
\begin{aligned}
\frac{dP}{dx} &= \frac{1}{h}\left[\Delta y_0 + \frac{2q^{(1)}}{2!}\Delta^2 y_0 + \frac{3q^{(2)}}{3!}\Delta^3 y_0 + \cdots + \frac{nq^{(n-1)}}{n!}\Delta^n y_0\right] \\
&= \frac{1}{h}\left[\Delta y_0 + \frac{q^{(1)}}{1!}\Delta^2 y_0 + \frac{q^{(2)}}{2!}\Delta^3 y_0 + \cdots + \frac{q^{(n-1)}}{(n-1)!}\Delta^n y_0\right],
\end{aligned} \tag{7.36}
$$

$$
\begin{aligned}
\frac{d^2 P}{dx^2} &= \frac{1}{h^2}\left[\Delta^2 y_0 + \frac{2q^{(1)}}{2!}\Delta^3 y_0 + \frac{3q^{(2)}}{3!}\Delta^4 y_0 + \cdots + \frac{(n-1)q^{(n-2)}}{(n-1)!}\Delta^n y_0\right] \\
&= \frac{1}{h^2}\left[\Delta^2 y_0 + \frac{q^{(1)}}{1!}\Delta^3 y_0 + \frac{q^{(2)}}{2!}\Delta^4 y_0 + \cdots + \frac{q^{(n-2)}}{(n-2)!}\Delta^n y_0\right].
\end{aligned} \tag{7.37}
$$

In general, we may write

$$\frac{d^k P}{dx^k} = \frac{1}{h^k}\left[\Delta^k y_0 + \frac{q^{(1)}}{2!}\Delta^{k+1} y_0 + \frac{q^{(2)}}{2!}\Delta^{k+2} y_0 + \cdots + \frac{q^{(n-k)}}{(n-k)!}\Delta^n y_0\right]. \tag{7.38}$$

Let us consider now Newton's backward polynomial

$$P(q) = y_n + \frac{q^{(1)}}{1!}\Delta y_{n-1} + \frac{(q+1)^{(2)}}{2!}\Delta^2 y_{n-2} + \cdots + \frac{(q+n-1)^{(n)}}{n!}\Delta^n y_0. \qquad (7.39)$$

Applying again Lemma 7.1 with $q = (x - x_n)/h$, we have

$$\frac{dP}{dx} = \frac{1}{h}\left[\Delta y_{n-1} + \frac{2(q+1)^{(1)}}{2!}\Delta^2 y_{n-2} + \cdots + \frac{n(q+n-1)^{(n-1)}}{n!}\Delta^n y_0\right]$$

$$= \frac{1}{h}\left[\Delta y_{n-1} + \frac{(q+1)^{(1)}}{1!}\Delta^2 y_{n-2} + \cdots + \frac{(q+n-1)^{(n-1)}}{(n-1)!}\Delta^n y_0\right], \qquad (7.40)$$

$$\frac{d^2P}{dx^2} = \frac{1}{h^2}\left[\Delta^2 y_{n-2} + \frac{2(q+2)^{(1)}}{2!}\Delta^3 y_{n-3} + \cdots + \frac{(n-1)(q+n-1)^{(n-2)}}{(n-1)!}\Delta^n y_0\right]$$

$$= \frac{1}{h^2}\left[\Delta^2 y_{n-2} + \frac{(q+2)^{(1)}}{1!}\Delta^3 y_{n-3} + \cdots + \frac{(q+n-1)^{(n-2)}}{(n-2)!}\Delta^n y_0\right] \qquad (7.41)$$

and, in general,

$$\frac{d^kP}{dx^k} = \frac{1}{h^k}\left[\Delta^k y_{n-k} + \frac{(q+k)^{(1)}}{2!}\Delta^{k+1} y_{n-k-1} + \cdots + \frac{(q+n-1)^{(n-k)}}{(n-k)!}\Delta^n y_0\right]. \qquad (7.42)$$

7.4 INTRODUCTION TO NUMERICAL INTEGRATION

We want to calculate the integrals

$$I = \int_a^b f(x)dx, \qquad (7.43)$$

where $-\infty \le a < b \le \infty$, f being integrable on $[a, b]$.
  In general, two situations exist

The first case is that of a proper integral (7.43), which will be considered at this place.

The second case assumes that the integral (7.43) is an improper one. Several techniques exist to transform an improper integral into a proper one, or to approximate with an imposed precision the value of the improper integral.

If the interval $[a, b]$ is an infinite one, that is, if the integral (7.43) has one of the forms

$$I = \int_{-\infty}^b f(x)dx, \ I = \int_a^\infty f(x)dx, \ I = \int_{-\infty}^\infty f(x)dx, \qquad (7.44)$$

then we may use the following techniques to calculate the improper integrals:

• the change of variable which may lead to the transformation of the infinite interval $(-\infty, b]$, $[a, \infty)$ or $(-\infty, \infty)$ into an interval of finite length;

- the separation of the integral in two integrals of the form

$$\int_{-\infty}^{b} f(x)dx = \int_{-\infty}^{b_1} f(x)dx + \int_{b_1}^{b} f(x)dx,$$

$$\int_{a}^{\infty} f(x)dx = \int_{a}^{a_1} f(x)dx + \int_{\infty}^{a_1} f(x)dx, \qquad (7.45)$$

$$\int_{-\infty}^{\infty} f(x)dx = \int_{-\infty}^{a_2} f(x)dx + \int_{a_2}^{b_2} f(x)dx + \int_{\infty}^{b_2} f(x)dx.$$

The idea is that if $|a_i|$, $|b_i|$, $i = \overline{1,2}$ are sufficient great, then the improper integrals $\int_{-\infty}^{b_1} f(x)dx$, $\int_{a_1}^{\infty} f(x)dx$, $\int_{-\infty}^{a_2} f(x)dx$ and $\int_{b_2}^{\infty} f(x)dx$ may be neglected, the values of the integrals in formula (7.45) being given by

$$\int_{-\infty}^{b} f(x)dx \approx \int_{b_1}^{b} f(x)dx, \quad \int_{a}^{\infty} f(x)dx \approx \int_{a}^{a_1} f(x)dx, \quad \int_{-\infty}^{\infty} f(x)dx \approx \int_{a_2}^{b_2} f(x)dx.$$
$$(7.46)$$

A question rises: what can we understand by $|a_i|$, $|b_i|$, $i = \overline{1,2}$, sufficient great? In general, the answer to this question is based on the following considerations: we may analytically show that the improper integrals neglected $\int_{-\infty}^{b_1} f(x)dx$, $\int_{a_1}^{\infty} f(x)dx$, $\int_{-\infty}^{a_2} f(x)dx$ and $\int_{b_2}^{\infty} f(x)dx$ may be less than an ε a priori given for $|a_i|$, $|b_i|$, $i = \overline{1,2}$, sufficient great in modulus, or we calculate the integrals

$$\int_{b_1}^{b} f(x)dx, \quad \int_{d_1}^{b_1} f(x)dx, \quad d_1 \ll b_1, \qquad (7.47)$$

$$\int_{a}^{a_1} f(x)dx, \quad \int_{a_1}^{c_1} f(x)dx, \quad c_1 \gg a_1, \qquad (7.48)$$

$$\int_{a_2}^{b_2} f(x)dx, \quad \int_{c_2}^{a_2} f(x)dx, \quad \int_{b_2}^{d_2} f(x)dx, \quad c_2 \ll a_2, d_2 \gg b_2, \qquad (7.49)$$

and we show that

$$\left| \frac{\int_{a_1}^{b_1} f(x)\,dx}{\int_{b_1}^{b} f(x)dx} \right| \ll 1, \quad \left| \frac{\int_{a_1}^{c_1} f(x)\,dx}{\int_{a}^{a_1} f(x)dx} \right| \ll< 1, \quad \frac{\left| \int_{c_2}^{a_2} f(x)\,dx \right| + \left| \int_{b_2}^{d_2} f(x)\,dx \right|}{\left| \int_{a_2}^{b_2} f(x)\,dx \right|} \ll 1; \quad (7.50)$$

- if the asymptotic behavior of $f(x)$ that is, we know that the functions $g_1(x)$ and $g_2(x)$ so that

$$\lim_{x \to \infty} \frac{f(x)}{g_1(x)} = \mu_1, \quad \lim_{x \to -\infty} \frac{f(x)}{g_2(x)} = \mu_2, \qquad (7.51)$$

where μ_1 and μ_2 are two finite real values, then we may write the approximate relations

$$\int_{-\infty}^{a} f(x)dx \approx \mu_2 \int_{-\infty}^{a_1} g_2(x)dx + \int_{a_1}^{a} f(x)dx,$$

$$\int_{b}^{\infty} f(x)dx \approx \mu_2 \int_{b}^{b_1} f(x)dx + \int_{b_1}^{\infty} g_1(x)dx,$$

$$\int_{-\infty}^{\infty} f(x)dx = \mu_2 \int_{-\infty}^{a_2} g_2(x)dx + \int_{a_2}^{b_2} f(x)dx + \mu_1 \int_{b_2}^{\infty} g_1(x)dx; \qquad (7.52)$$

- a last method to solve the problem of the improper integral on an infinite interval is that by a change of variable, which transforms the infinite limit into a finite one. But, in many cases, this technique introduces a singularity.

The last situation that may appear for the integral (7.43) is that in which the interval $[a, b]$ is bounded, but

$$\lim_{x \to a} f(x)\mathrm{d}x = \pm\infty \quad \text{or} \quad \lim_{x \to b} f(x)\mathrm{d}x = \pm\infty. \tag{7.53}$$

There are several methods to avoid the singularities, that is:

- their elimination, by using the integration by parts, the change of variable etc.;
- the use of certain Gauss type quadrature formulae, which eliminate some types of singularities, using other polynomials as Legendre ones;
- the use of Gauss type quadrature formulae with Legendre polynomials, because the calculation of the values of the function f at the points a and b is not necessary;
- the division of the integral in several integrals of the form

$$\int_a^b f(x)\mathrm{d}x = \int_a^{a+\varepsilon_1} f(x)\mathrm{d}x + \int_{a+\varepsilon_1}^{b-\varepsilon_2} f(x)\mathrm{d}x + \int_{b-\varepsilon_2}^b f(x)\mathrm{d}x, \tag{7.54}$$

  using a very small integration step for the first and the last integral in the right member, which leads to a very great time of calculation;
- the transformation of the finite interval in an infinite one by a certain change of variable, the new integral thus obtained being easier to calculate.

7.5   THE NEWTON–CÔTES QUADRATURE FORMULAE

We begin with a definition.

Definition 7.1   A quadrature formula is a numerical procedure by which the value of a definite integral is approximated by using information about the integrand only at certain points in which this one is definite.

Let N be a nonzero natural number and the integral

$$I = \int_0^N f(x)\mathrm{d}x. \tag{7.55}$$

Observation 7.4   Any integral of the form

$$I = \int_a^b g(u)\mathrm{d}u, \tag{7.56}$$

with $-\infty < a < b < \infty$, may be brought to form (7.55) by using the change of variable

$$u = a + \frac{b-a}{N}x, \; \mathrm{d}u = \frac{b-a}{N}\mathrm{d}x. \tag{7.57}$$

Indeed,

$$I = \int_a^b g(u)\mathrm{d}u = \int_0^N g\left(a + \frac{b-a}{N}x\right)\frac{b-a}{N}\mathrm{d}x, \tag{7.58}$$

where

$$f(x) = g\left(a + \frac{b-a}{N}x\right)\frac{b-a}{N}.$$

(7.59)

Let us further denote by

$$y_i = f(i), \ i = \overline{0, N},$$

(7.60)

the values of the function f of equation (7.55) at the points i and by $L_N(x)$ the Lagrange polynomial corresponding to the function f on the interval $[0, N]$ and to the division points $x_i = i, \ i = \overline{0, N}$. We replace the integral (7.55) by the approximate value

$$I \approx \int_0^N L_N(x)\mathrm{d}x.$$

(7.61)

On the other hand, we have

$$L_N(x) = \sum_{i=0}^N \frac{(x-0)(x-1)\cdots(x-i+1)(x-i-1)\cdots(x-N)}{(i-0)(i-1)\cdots(i-i+1)(i-i-1)\cdots(i-N)}y_i$$

(7.62)

or, equivalently,

$$L_N(x) = \sum_{i=0}^N \phi_i(x_i)y_i,$$

(7.63)

where the notations are obvious. Replacing relation (7.63) in the formula (7.61), we get

$$I \approx \int_0^N \sum_{i=0}^N \phi_i(x)y_i\mathrm{d}x = \sum_{i=0}^N y_i \int_0^N \phi_i(x)\mathrm{d}x = \sum_{i=0}^N c_i^{(N)}y_i,$$

(7.64)

where

$$c_i^{(N)} = \int_0^N \phi_i(x)\mathrm{d}x.$$

(7.65)

Definition 7.2 The formula

$$I \approx \sum_{i=0}^N c_i^{(N)}y_i$$

(7.66)

is called the *Newton–Côtes quadrature formula*.[1]

Proposition 7.2 (Error in the Newton–Côtes Quadrature Formula). If the function f is of class C^{N+1} and if we denote

$$M = \sup_{x\in[0,N]} |f^{(N+1)}(x)|,$$

(7.67)

then the formula

$$\left|I - \sum_{i=0}^N c_i^{(N)}y_i\right| \leq \frac{M}{(N+1)!}\int_0^N |x(x-1)\cdots(x-N)|\mathrm{d}x$$

(7.68)

takes place.

[1]The formula is named after Sir Isaac Newton (1642–1727) and Roger Côtes (1682–1716).

Demonstration. If from the error formula of Lagrange's polynomial

$$|f(x) - L_N(x)| \leq \frac{M}{(N+1)!} |x(x-1) \cdots (x-N)|, \tag{7.69}$$

we pass to integration, then

$$\left| I - \sum_{i=0}^{N} c_i^{(N)} y_i \right| = \left| \int_0^N f(x)\, dx - \int_0^N L_N(x) dx \right|$$

$$= \left| \int_0^N \left[f(x) - L_N(x) \right] dx \right| \leq \int_0^N |f(x) - L_N(x)| dx$$

$$\leq \int_0^N \left| \frac{M}{(N+1)!} x(x-1) \cdots (x-N) \right| dx$$

$$\leq \frac{M}{(N+1)!} \int_0^N |x(x-1) \cdots (x-N)| dx \tag{7.70}$$

and the proposition is stated.

Observation 7.5   We can write the exact formula

$$I - \sum_{i=0}^{N} c_i^{(N)} y_i = \frac{f^{(N+1)}(\xi)}{(N+1)!} \int_0^N x(x-1) \cdots (x-N) dx \tag{7.71}$$

too, obtained analogically as equation (7.68), taking into account the expression of the rest in Lagrange's polynomial, ξ being a point between 0 and N.

7.6   THE TRAPEZOID FORMULA

This formula is a particular case of the Newton–Côtes quadrature formula for $N = 1$.
    Let the integral be

$$I_i = \int_{x_i}^{x_{i+1}} f(x) dx, \tag{7.72}$$

where $f : [x_i, x_{i+1}] \to \mathbb{R}$, $x_i \neq x_{i+1}$, f at least of class C^0 on $[x_i, x_{i+1}]$. We make the change of variable

$$x = x_i + (x_{i+1} - x_i)u, \; dx = (x_{i+1} - x_i)du \tag{7.73}$$

and the integral (7.72) now reads

$$I_i = \int_0^1 F(u) du, \tag{7.74}$$

with

$$F(u) = f[x_i + (x_{i+1} - x_i)u](x_{i+1} - x_i). \tag{7.75}$$

Taking into account the discussion in Section 7.5, we have

$$I_i \approx c_0^{(1)} y_0 + c_1^{(1)} y_1, \tag{7.76}$$

where

$$y_0 = F(0) = f(x_i)(x_{i+1} - x_i), \quad y_1 = F(1) = f(x_{i+1})(x_{i+1} - x_i), \tag{7.77}$$

$$c_0^{(1)} = \int_0^1 \frac{x-1}{0-1} dx = \int_0^1 (1-x) dx = x - \frac{x^2}{2} \Big|_0^1 = \frac{1}{2},$$

$$c_1^{(1)} = \int_0^1 \frac{x-0}{1-0} dx = \int_0^1 x dx = \frac{x^2}{2} \Big|_0^1 = \frac{1}{2}. \tag{7.78}$$

It follows that

$$I_i \approx \frac{x_{i+1} - x_i}{2} (f(x_i) + f(x_{i+1})). \tag{7.79}$$

Definition 7.3 Relation (7.79) is called the trapezoid formula.

Observation 7.6 Relation (7.79) means that the area under the curve $y = f(x)$, equal to the integral I_i, is approximated by the area of the trapezium hatched in Figure 7.2.

Let $f : [a, b] \to \mathbb{R}$ be of class C^2 on $[a, b]$. Let us assume that the interval $[a, b]$ is divided into n equal parts so that

$$a = x_0 < x_1 < x_2 \cdots < x_n = b, \; x_{j+1} - x_j = h = \frac{b-a}{n}, \; j = \overline{0, n-1}. \tag{7.80}$$

Applying the trapezoid formula on each interval $[x_j, x_{j+1}]$ and summing, we obtain

$$I = \int_a^b f(x) dx = \sum_{j=0}^{n-1} \int_{x_j}^{x_{j+1}} f(x) dx \approx \sum_{j=0}^n \frac{x_{j+1} - x_j}{2} (f(x_{j+1}) + f(x_j))$$

$$= \frac{h}{2} [(f(a) + f(x_1)) + (f(x_1) + f(x_2)) + \cdots + (f(x_{n-1}) + f(b))], \tag{7.81}$$

that is,

$$I \approx \frac{h}{2} \left(f(a) + f(b) + 2 \sum_{j=1}^{n-1} f(x_j) \right). \tag{7.82}$$

Definition 7.4 Formula (7.82) is called the generalized trapezoid formula.

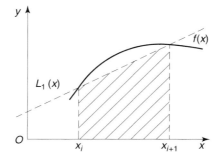

Figure 7.2 The trapezoid formula.

Proposition 7.3 (The Error in the Generalized Trapezoid Formula). If $f : [a, b] \to \mathbb{R}$, is of class C^2 on $[a, b]$, then the relation

$$\int_a^b f(x)dx - \frac{h}{2}\left(f(a) + f(b) + 2\sum_{j=1}^{n} f(x_j) \right) = -\frac{(b-a)^2}{12u^2}f''(\xi) \tag{7.83}$$

holds, where ξ is a point situated between a and b, while x_j, $j = \overline{0, n}$, is an equidistant division of the interval $[a, b]$, with $x_0 = a$, $x_n = b$ and $x_{j+1} - x_j = h = (b-a)/n$.

Demonstration. Let us calculate the error on each interval of the form $[x_j, x_{j+1}]$, $j = \overline{0, n-1}$. Taking into account Observation 7.4, we have

$$\varepsilon_j(f(x)) = \varepsilon_j(F(u)) = \frac{F''(\zeta)}{2!}\int_0^1 x(x-1)dx, \tag{7.84}$$

where $\zeta \in [0, 1]$, while

$$\int_0^1 x(x-1)dx = \frac{x^3}{3} - \frac{x^2}{2}\Big|_0^1 = -\frac{1}{6}. \tag{7.85}$$

Relation (7.84) now becomes

$$\varepsilon_j(f(x)) = -\frac{F''(\zeta)}{12}. \tag{7.86}$$

Formula (7.75) leads to

$$F''(u) = (x_{j+1} - x_j)^3 f''[x_j + (x_{j+1} - x_j)u] \tag{7.87}$$

and taking into account that $x_{j+1} - x_j = h$, relation (7.86) reads

$$\varepsilon_j(f(x)) = -\frac{h^3}{12}f''(\xi_j), \tag{7.88}$$

where ξ_j is a point in the interval $[x_j, x_{j+1}]$. We have

$$\varepsilon_{[a,b]}(f(x)) = \sum_{j=0}^{n-1} \varepsilon_j(f(x)) = -\frac{h^3}{12}\sum_{j=0}^{n-1} f''(\xi_j) \tag{7.89}$$

on the entire interval $[a, b]$. Because $f \in C^2([a, b])$, there exists $\xi \in [a, b]$ so that

$$f''(\xi) = \frac{1}{n}\sum_{j=0}^{n-1} f''(\xi_j) \tag{7.90}$$

and relation (7.89) becomes

$$\varepsilon_{[a,b]}(f(x)) = -\frac{(b-a)^3}{12n^2}f''(\xi_j), \tag{7.91}$$

the relation (7.83), which had to be demonstrated.

Corollary 7.3   In the conditions of Proposition 7.3, denoting

$$M = \sup_{x \in [a,b]} |f''(x)|, \tag{7.92}$$

there exists the inequality

$$|\varepsilon_{[a,b]}(f(x))| \le \frac{M}{12u^2}(b-a)^3. \tag{7.93}$$

Demonstration.   From relation (7.91) we obtain immediately

$$|\varepsilon_{[a,b]}(f(x))| = \frac{(b-a)^3}{12u^2}|f''(\xi)| \le \frac{(b-a)^3}{12n^2} \sup_{\xi \in [a,b]} |f''(\xi)| = \frac{M}{12u^2}(b-a)^3. \tag{7.94}$$

Observation 7.7   We observe that, by increasing the number of division points (increasing n) the error $\varepsilon_{[a,b]}(f(x))$ diminishes in direct proportion to n^2. This method of increasing the precision may not always be used, because the growth of n leads to the increasing of the calculation time.

7.7   SIMPSON'S FORMULA

This formula is a particular case of the Newton–Côtes formula[2] for $N = 2$.
Let $f : [a, b] \to \mathbb{R}$, be of class C^0 on $[a, b]$, and let a division of the interval be $[a, b]$ so that

$$a = x_0 < x_1 < \cdots < x_{2n} = b, \, x_{i+1} - x_i = h = \frac{b-a}{2n}, \, i = \overline{0, 2n-1}. \tag{7.95}$$

Let us consider the integral

$$I_{2i} = \int_{x_{2i}}^{x_{2i+2}} f(x)\mathrm{d}x \tag{7.96}$$

and let us make the change of variable

$$x = x_{2i} + \frac{x_{2i+2} - x_{2i}}{2}u, \, \mathrm{d}x = \frac{x_{2i+2} - x_{2i}}{2}\mathrm{d}u. \tag{7.97}$$

The integral (7.96) now reads

$$I_{2i} = \int_0^2 F(u)\mathrm{d}u, \tag{7.98}$$

where

$$F(u) = f\left(x_{2i} + \frac{x_{2i+2} - x_{2i}}{2}u\right)\frac{x_{2i+2} - x_{2i}}{2}. \tag{7.99}$$

Corresponding to the Section 7.5, we have

$$I_{2i} \approx c_0^{(2)}y_0 + c_1^{(2)}y_1 + c_2^{(2)}y_2, \tag{7.100}$$

---

[2]The method was introduced by Thomas Simpson (1710–1761) in 1750. The method was also known by Bonaventura Francesco Cavalieri (1598–1647) since 1639, Johannes Kepler (1571–1630) since 1609, and James Gregory (1638–1675) since 1668 in the book *The Universal Part of Geometry*.

where

$$y_0 = F(0) = hf(x_{2i}), \ y_1 = F(1) = hf(x_{2i+1}), \ y_2 = F(2) = hf(x_{2i+2}), \qquad (7.101)$$

$$c_0^{(2)} = \int_0^2 \frac{(x-1)(x-2)}{(0-1)(0-2)} dx = \int_0^2 \frac{x^2 - 3x + 2}{2} dx = \left. \frac{x^3}{6} - \frac{3x^2}{4} + x \right|_0^2 = \frac{1}{3},$$

$$c_1^{(2)} = \int_0^2 \frac{x(x-2)}{(1-0)(1-2)} dx = \int_0^2 \frac{2x - x^2}{1} dx = \left. x^2 - \frac{x^3}{3} \right|_0^2 = \frac{4}{3}, \qquad (7.102)$$

$$c_2^{(2)} = \int_0^2 \frac{x(x-1)}{(2-0)(2-1)} dx = \int_0^2 \frac{x^2 - x}{2} dx = \left. \frac{x^3}{6} - \frac{x^2}{4} + x \right|_0^2 = \frac{1}{3}.$$

We thus obtain

$$I_{2i} \approx \frac{h}{3}(f(x_{2i}) + 4f(x_{2i+1}) + f(x_{2i+2})). \qquad (7.103)$$

Definition 7.5   Formula (7.103) is called *Simpson's formula*.

Observation 7.8   Geometrically, relation (7.103) shows that the integral I, equal to the area under the curve $f(x)$, is approximated by the area hatched in Figure 7.3 and which is under the $L_2(x)$.

Applying Simpson's formula on each interval $[x_{2j}, x_{2j+2}]$, with $j = \overline{0, n-1}$ and summing, we obtain

$$I = \int_a^b f(x)dx \approx \sum_{j=0}^{n-1} I_{2j} = \frac{h}{3}\sum_{j=0}^{n-1}(y_{2j} + 4y_{2j+1} + y_{2j+2})$$

$$= \frac{h}{3}[y_0 + y_{2n} + 4(y_1 + y_3 + \cdots + y_{2n-1}) + 2(y_2 + y_4 + \cdots + y_{2n-2})]. \qquad (7.104)$$

Definition 7.6   Formula (7.104) is called the *generalized Simpson formula*.

Proposition 7.4 (The Error in the Generalized Simpson Formula). If $f : [a, b] \to \mathbb{R}$, f of class C^4 on $[a, b]$, while x_j, $j = \overline{0, 2n}$, is an equidistant division of the interval $[a, b]$, with $x_0 = a$, $x_{2n} = b$ and $x_{j+1} - x_j = h = (b-a)/(2n)$, then takes place the relation

$$\int_a^b f(x)dx - \frac{h}{3}[y_0 + y_{2n} + 4(y_1 + \cdots + y_{2n-1}) + 2(y_2 + \cdots + y_{2n-2})] = -\frac{(b-a)^5}{2880n^4} y^{(4)}(\xi),$$

$$\qquad (7.105)$$

where $\xi \in [a, b]$.

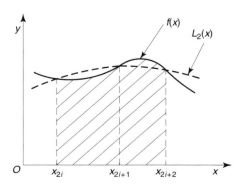

Figure 7.3   The Simpson formula.

Demonstration. Let us consider the interval $[x_{2j}, x_{2j+2}]$ for which the error is

$$\varepsilon_{2j}(f(x)) = \int_{x_{2j}}^{x_{2j+1}+h} f(x)dx - \frac{h}{3}(y_{2j} + 4y_{2j+1} + y_{2j+2}) \tag{7.106}$$

or, equivalently,

$$\varepsilon_{2j}(f(x)) = \int_{x_{2j}-h}^{x_{2j+1}+h} f(x)dx - \frac{h}{3}[y(x_{2j} - h) + 4y(x_{2j+1}) + y(x_{2j+2} + h)], \tag{7.107}$$

ε_{2j} being a function of h. We have

$$\frac{d\varepsilon_{2j}}{dh} = y(x_{2j+1} + h) + y(x_{2j+1} - h) - \frac{1}{3}[y(x_{2j+1} - h) + 4y(x_{2j+1}) + y(x_{2j+1} + h)]$$
$$- \frac{h}{3}\left[-\frac{dy\,(x_{2j+1} - h)}{dh} + \frac{dy(x_{2j+1} + h)}{dh}\right] \tag{7.108}$$

and it follows that

$$\frac{d\varepsilon_{2j}}{dh} = \frac{2}{3}[y(x_{2j+1} + h) + y(x_{2j+1} - h)] - \frac{4}{3}y(x_{2j+1})$$
$$- \frac{h}{3}\left[-\frac{dy\,(x_{2j+1} - h)}{dh} + \frac{dy(x_{2j+1} + h)}{dh}\right]. \tag{7.109}$$

Further,

$$\frac{d^2\varepsilon_{2j}}{dh^2} = \frac{2}{3}\left[\frac{dy\,(x_{2j+1} + h)}{dh} - \frac{dy(x_{2j+1} - h)}{dh}\right] - \frac{1}{3}\left[-\frac{dy\,(x_{2j+1} - h)}{dh} + \frac{dy(x_{2j+1} + h)}{dh}\right]$$
$$- \frac{h}{3}\left[\frac{d^2y\,(x_{2j+1} - h)}{dh^2} + \frac{d^2y(x_{2j+1} + h)}{dh^2}\right], \tag{7.110}$$

that is,

$$\frac{d^2\varepsilon_{2j}}{dh^2} = -\frac{1}{3}\left[-\frac{dy\,(x_{2j+1} - h)}{dh} - \frac{dy(x_{2j+1} + h)}{dh}\right] - \frac{h}{3}\left[\frac{d^2y\,(x_{2j+1} - h)}{dh^2} + \frac{d^2y(x_{2j+1} + h)}{dh^2}\right]. \tag{7.111}$$

Analogically,

$$\frac{d^2\varepsilon_{2j}}{dh^2} = \frac{1}{3}\left[\frac{d^2y\,(x_{2j+1} - h)}{dh^2} + \frac{d^2y(x_{2j+1} + h)}{dh^2}\right] - \frac{1}{3}\left[\frac{d^2y\,(x_{2j+1} - h)}{dh^2} + \frac{d^2y(x_{2j+1} + h)}{dh^2}\right]$$
$$- \frac{h}{3}\left[-\frac{d^3y\,(x_{2j+1} - h)}{dh^3} + \frac{d^3y(x_{2j+1} + h)}{dh^3}\right]$$
$$= -\frac{h}{3}\left[\frac{d^3y\,(x_{2j+1} + h)}{dh^3} - \frac{d^3y(x_{2j+1} - h)}{dh^3}\right]. \tag{7.112}$$

Applying Lagrange's finite increments formula to the function $d^3 y / dh^3$ on the interval $[y(x_{2j+1} - h), y(x_{2j+1} + h)]$, it follows that the existence of an intermediate point $\xi_{2j} \in (x_{2j+1} - h, x_{2j+1} + h)$ so that

$$\frac{d^3 y(x_{2j+1} + h)}{dh^3} - \frac{d^3 y(x_{2j+1} - h)}{dh^3} = 2h \frac{d^4 y(\xi_{2j})}{dh^4}, \tag{7.113}$$

hence

$$\frac{d^3 \varepsilon_{2j}}{dh^3} = -\frac{2h^2}{3} \frac{d^4 y(\xi_{2j})}{dh^4}. \tag{7.114}$$

On the other hand, we have

$$\varepsilon_{2j}(0) = 0, \quad \frac{d\varepsilon_{2j}(0)}{dh} = 0, \quad \frac{d^2 \varepsilon_{2j}(0)}{dh^2} = 0 \tag{7.115}$$

and, by successive integration of formula (7.114) between 0 and h, we obtain

$$\frac{d^2 \varepsilon_{2j}(h)}{dh^2} = \frac{d^2 \varepsilon_{2j}(0)}{dh^2} + \int_0^h \frac{d^3 \varepsilon_{2j}(\tau)}{d\tau^3} d\tau = -2 \frac{d^4 y(\xi_{2j})}{dh^4} \int_0^h \tau^2 d\tau = -\frac{2}{9} h^3 \frac{d^4 y(\xi_{2j})}{dh^4}, \tag{7.116}$$

$$\frac{d\varepsilon_{2j}(h)}{dh} = \frac{d\varepsilon_{2j}(0)}{dh} + \int_0^h \frac{d^2 \varepsilon_{2j}(\tau)}{d\tau^2} d\tau = -\frac{2}{9} \frac{d^4 y(\xi_{2j})}{dh^4} \int_0^h \tau^3 d\tau = -\frac{1}{18} h^4 \frac{d^4 y(\xi_{2j})}{dh^4}, \tag{7.117}$$

$$\varepsilon_{2j}(h) = \varepsilon_{2j}(0) + \int_0^h \frac{d\varepsilon_{2j}(\tau)}{d\tau} d\tau = -\frac{1}{18} \frac{d^4 y(\xi_{2j})}{dh^4} \int_0^h \tau^4 d\tau = -\frac{1}{90} h^5 \frac{d^4 y(\xi_{2j})}{dh^4}. \tag{7.118}$$

It follows that

$$\varepsilon_{2j}(h) = -\frac{h^5}{90} y^{(4)}(\xi_{2j}), \tag{7.119}$$

where $\xi_{2j} \in (x_{2j}, x_{2j+2})$.

Summing on the entire interval $[a, b]$, we obtain the error

$$\varepsilon_{[a,b]}(f(x)) = -\frac{h^5}{90} \sum_{j=0}^{n-1} y^{(4)}(\xi_{2j}). \tag{7.120}$$

Because f is of class C^4 on $[a, b]$, there exists $\xi \in [a, b]$ so that

$$\frac{1}{n} \sum_{j=0}^{n-1} y^{(4)}(\xi_{2j}) = y^{(4)}(\xi) \tag{7.121}$$

and expression (7.120) of the error reads

$$\varepsilon_{[a,b]}(f(x)) = -\frac{nh^5}{90} y^{(4)}(\xi). \tag{7.122}$$

Taking into account that $h = (b - a)/(2n)$, the last formula leads to

$$\varepsilon_{[a,b]}(f(x)) = -\frac{n}{90} \frac{(b-a)^5}{32n^5} y^{(4)}(\xi) = -\frac{(b-a)^5}{2880n^4} y^{(4)}(\xi), \tag{7.123}$$

that is, relation (7.105) which had to be stated.

Corollary 7.4   In the conditions of Proposition 7.4, denoting

$$M = \sup_{x \in [a,b]} |f^{(4)}(x)|, \tag{7.124}$$

the relation

$$|\varepsilon_{[a,b]}(f(x))| \le \frac{M}{2880 n^4}(b-a)^5 \tag{7.125}$$

is valid

Demonstration. From equation (7.123) it follows that

$$|\varepsilon_{[a,b]} f(x)| = \frac{(b-a)^5}{2880 n^4}|y^{(4)}(\xi)| \le \frac{(b-a)^5}{2880 n^4} \sup_{\xi \in [a,b]} |f^{(4)}(\xi)| = \frac{M(b-a)^5}{2880 n^4}. \tag{7.126}$$

Observation 7.9   If the number n of the division points increases, then the error decreases in direct proportion to n^4. But the growth of n cannot be as great as we wish, because the calculation time may increase too much.

7.8   EULER'S AND GREGORY'S FORMULAE

Definition 7.7   We define the operators ∇, E, D, J called operator of backward differentiation, operator of shifting, operator of differentiation, and operator of integration, respectively, by the formulae

$$\nabla f(x) = f(x) - f(x-h), \tag{7.127}$$

$$\mathrm{E}f(x) = f(x+h), \tag{7.128}$$

$$\mathrm{D}f(x) = f'(x), \tag{7.129}$$

$$\mathrm{J}f(x) = \int_x^{x+h} f(t)\mathrm{d}t, \tag{7.130}$$

where h is the division step.

Observation 7.10

(i) There exist the immediate relations

$$\mathrm{E}^P f(x) = f(x+ph),\ p \in \mathbb{N}, \tag{7.131}$$

$$\mathrm{DJ}f(x) = \mathrm{JDf}(x), \tag{7.132}$$

$$\mathrm{DJ} = \mathrm{JD} = \Delta, \tag{7.133}$$

$$\mathrm{D}^{-1}f(x) = F(x) + C, \tag{7.134}$$

where $F(x)$ is a primitive of $f(x)$, while C is a constant,

$$\Delta \mathrm{D}^{-1}f(x) = \mathrm{Jf}(x), \tag{7.135}$$

$$\Delta = \mathrm{E} - 1,\ \nabla = 1 - \mathrm{E}^{-1}, \tag{7.136}$$

where 1 is the identity operator, $1f(x) = f(x)$,

$$DJ = JD = E - 1,$$ (7.137)

$$\Delta^p = E^p \nabla^p = (E - 1)^p = E^p - C_p^1 E^{p-1} + C_p^2 E^{p-2} - \cdots + (-1)^{p-1} C_p^{p-1} E + (-1)^p,$$ (7.138)

$$\nabla^p y_k = y_k - C_k^1 y_{k-1} + C_p^2 y_{k-2} - \cdots + (-1)^{p-1} y_{k-p+1} + (-1)^p y_{k-p},$$ (7.139)

$$(1 - \nabla)(1 + \nabla + \nabla^2 + \cdots + \nabla^p) = 1 - \nabla^{p+1},$$ (7.140)

$$(1 - \nabla)^{-1} = 1 + \nabla + \nabla^2 + \cdots + \nabla^p + \cdots = \sum_{i=0}^{\infty} \nabla^i.$$ (7.141)

(ii) If the function f is a polynomial of nth degree, then

$$(1 - \nabla)^{-1} = 1 + \nabla + \nabla^2 + \cdots + \nabla^n.$$ (7.142)

Let us consider the sum

$$\sum_{l=m}^{k-1} f(x_0 + lh) = f(x_m) + f(x_{m+1}) + \cdots + f(x_{k-1}) = y_m + y_{m+1} + \cdots y_{k-1},$$ (7.143)

where $y_i = f(x_i)$, $i \in \mathbb{N}$.

The problem is connected to finding a function $F(x)$ with the property $\Delta F(x) = f(x)$. Indeed, if we find such a function $F(x)$, then

$$\sum_{l=m}^{k-1} f(x_0 + lh) = F(x_{m+1}) - F(x_m) + F(x_{m+2}) - F(x_{m+1}) + \cdots$$
$$+ F(x_k) - F(x_{k-1}) = F(x_k) - F(x_m).$$ (7.144)

Writing $F(x) = \Delta^{-1} f(x)$, we have

$$\Delta^{-1} f(x_k) = C + \sum_{l=m}^{k-1} f(x_l),$$ (7.145)

$$\sum_{l=l_0}^{k-1} f(x_l) = \Delta^{-1} f(x_k) - \Delta^{-1} f(x_{l_0}),$$ (7.146)

where C is a constant, while l_0 is an integer for which $m \leq l_0 \leq k$.

If f is a polynomial, then

$$\sum_{l=0}^{p-1} f(x_l) = (1 + E + E^2 + \cdots + E^{p-1}) f(x_0) = \frac{E^p - 1}{E - 1} f(x_0)$$
$$= \left[\frac{(1 + \Delta)^p - 1}{\Delta} \right] f(x_0) = \left[p + \frac{p(p-1)}{2!} \Delta + \frac{p(p-1)(p-2)}{3!} \Delta^2 \right.$$
$$\left. + \cdots + \frac{p(p-1)\cdots(p-n+1)}{n!} \Delta^n \right] f(x_0),$$ (7.147)

where n is its degree.

Let us remark that the formula is useful for n small in comparison with p.

Taking into account the identity

$$DJ\Delta^{-1} = 1, \tag{7.148}$$

obtained from equation (7.133), it follows that

$$hf(x) = \left(\frac{hD}{e^{hD} - 1}\right) Jf(x). \tag{7.149}$$

Definition 7.8   The coefficients B_i of the expansion

$$\frac{t}{e^t - 1} = \sum_{i=0}^{\infty} \frac{B_i}{i!} t^i \tag{7.150}$$

are called *Bernoulli's numbers*.[3]

Bernoulli's numbers verify the property

$$B_1 = -\frac{1}{2}, \ B_{2p+1} = 0, \ p \in \mathbb{N}, \ P \neq 0. \tag{7.151}$$

Hence it follows that expression (7.149) now becomes

$$hf(x) = \sum_{i=0}^{\infty} \frac{B_i}{i!} h^i D^i Jf(x) \tag{7.152}$$

or

$$hf(x) = \int_x^{x+h} f(t)dt + \sum_{i=1}^{\infty} \frac{B_i}{i!} h^i D^i Jf(x). \tag{7.153}$$

If we take into account that

$$D^i Jf(x) = D^{i-1}(f(x+h) - f(x)), \tag{7.154}$$

then relation (7.153) becomes

$$f(x) = \frac{1}{h} \int_x^{x+h} f(t)dt + \sum_{i=1}^{\infty} \frac{B_i}{i!} h^{i-1}(f^{(i-1)}(x+h) + f^{(i-1)}(x)) \tag{7.155}$$

or, equivalently,

$$\sum_{l=0}^{p-1} f(x_l) = \frac{1}{h} \int_{x_0}^{x_p} f(t)dt + \sum_{i=1}^{\infty} \frac{B_i}{i!} h^{i-1}(f^{(i-1)}(x_p) + f^{(i-1)}(x_0)), \tag{7.156}$$

called the *first Euler formula* or the *first Euler–Maclaurin formula*.[4]

---

[3]The numbers are called after Jacob Bernoulli (1654–1705) who used them in the book *Ars Conjectandi* published in 1713. The numbers are also known by Seki Takakazu (Seki Kōwa) (1642–1708).

[4]The formulae were called after Leonhard Euler (1707–1783) and Colin Maclaurin (1698–1746) who discovered them in 1735.

If we take into account equation (7.151), then relation (7.156) reads

$$\sum_{l=0}^{p-1} f(x_l) = \frac{1}{h} \int_{x_0}^{x_p} f(t)dt + \frac{1}{2}(f(x_0) + f(x_p))$$

$$+ \sum_{i=1}^{\infty} \frac{B_{2i}}{(2i)!} h^{2i-1}(f^{(2i-1)}(x_p) + f^{(2i-1)}(x_0)). \tag{7.157}$$

Obviously, if f is a polynomial, then the infinite sum on the right side becomes a finite one.

Analogically, we obtain also the second Euler formula or the second Euler–Maclaurin formula, in the form

$$\sum_{l=0}^{p-1} f\left(x_l + \frac{h}{2}\right) = \frac{1}{h} \int_{x_0}^{x_p} f(t)dt - \sum_{i=1}^{\infty} \frac{(1-2^{1-2i})B_{2i}}{(2i)!} h^{2i-1}(f^{(2i-1)}(x_p) + f^{(2i-1)}(x_0)). \tag{7.158}$$

In the first Euler formula we express the derivatives at the point x_0 by forward differences, while the derivatives at the point x_p by the backward differences in the form

$$hf'(x_0) = y_0 - \frac{1}{2}\Delta^2 y_0 + \frac{1}{3}\Delta^3 y_0 - \frac{1}{4}\Delta^4 y_0 + \frac{1}{5}\Delta^5 y_0 - \cdots,$$

$$hf'(x_p) = \nabla y_p + \frac{1}{2}\nabla^2 y_p + \frac{1}{3}\nabla^3 y_p + \frac{1}{4}\nabla^4 y_p + \frac{1}{5}\nabla^5 y_p + \cdots,$$

$$h^3 f'''(x_0) = \Delta^3 y_0 - \frac{3}{2}\Delta^4 y_0 + \frac{7}{4}\Delta^5 y_0 - \cdots,$$

$$h^3 f'''(x_p) = \nabla^3 y_p + \frac{3}{2}\nabla^4 y_p + \frac{7}{4}\nabla^5 y_p \cdots, \tag{7.159}$$

then we obtain Gregory's formula[5]

$$\int_{x_0}^{x_p} f(t)dt = h\left(\frac{1}{2}y_0 + y_1 + y_2 + \cdots + y_{p-1} + \frac{1}{2}y_p\right)$$

$$- \frac{h}{12}(\nabla y_p - \Delta y_0) - \frac{h}{24}(\nabla^2 y_p + \Delta^2 y_0) - \frac{19h}{720}(\nabla^3 y_p - \Delta^3 y_0)$$

$$+ \frac{3h}{180}(\nabla^4 y_p + \Delta^4 y_0) - \frac{863h}{60480}(\nabla^5 y_p - \Delta^5 y_0) - \cdots \tag{7.160}$$

7.9 ROMBERG'S FORMULA

Let us suppose that the error in the calculation of the integral

$$I = \int_a^b f(x)dx \tag{7.161}$$

---

[5]The formula was discovered by James Gregory (1638–1675) in 1670.

may be written in the form

$$E = Ch^p f^{(p)}(\xi), \tag{7.162}$$

where integration step is h, C is a positive constant that does not depend on h, p is a natural nonzero number, while $\xi \in (a, b)$.

If we calculate the integral (7.161) with the integration steps h_1 and h_2, then the errors are

$$E_1 = I - I_1 = Ch_1^p f^{(p)}(\xi_1), \tag{7.163}$$

$$E_2 = I - I_2 = Ch_2^p f^{(p)}(\xi_2). \tag{7.164}$$

Let us remark that, in general, $\xi_1 \neq \xi_2$.

Let us suppose that $f^{(p)}(\xi_1) \approx f^{(p)}(\xi_2)$. Under these conditions, the integral I may be approximated by Richardson's formula of extrapolation[6]

$$I = \frac{h_1^p I_2 - h_2^p I_1}{h_1^p - h_2^p} = I_2 + \frac{I_2 - I_1}{\left(\frac{h_1}{h_2}\right)^p - 1}. \tag{7.165}$$

If, for example, $h_2 = \lambda h_1$, then

$$I = \frac{I_2 - \lambda^p I_1}{1 - \lambda^p} = I_2 + \frac{I_2 - I_1}{\left(\frac{1}{\lambda}\right)^p - 1}. \tag{7.166}$$

Usually, we consider $h_2 = h_1/2$ and it follows that

$$I = \frac{2^p I_2 - I_1}{2^p - 1} = I_2 + \frac{I_2 - I_1}{2^p - 1}. \tag{7.167}$$

On the other hand, the error in the trapezium formula may be put in the form

$$E = C_1 h^2 + C_2 h^4 + \cdots + C_p h^{2p} + (b - a)h^{2p+2} + \frac{B_{2p+2}}{(2p+2)!} f^{(2p+2)}(\xi), \tag{7.168}$$

where B_{2k} are Bernoulli's numbers.

Suppose now that the integration step is chosen of the form

$$h_n = \frac{b - a}{2^n}, \tag{7.169}$$

and let us denote by $I_n^{(0)}$ the value of the integral, calculated with the step h_n. We apply Richardson's extrapolation formula, in which $I_{n+1}^{(0)}$ is the value of the same integral with a halved step. We obtain the approximation

$$I_n^{(1)} = \frac{2^n I_{n+1}^{(0)} - I_n^{(0)}}{2^n - 1}. \tag{7.170}$$

The procedure may continue and we obtain the general recurrence formulae

$$I_n^{(p)} = \frac{4^p I_{n+1}^{(p-1)} - I_n^{(p-1)}}{4^p - 1}, \tag{7.171}$$

$$I_0^{(p)} = \frac{4^p I_1^{(p-1)} - I_0^{(p-1)}}{4^p - 1}. \tag{7.172}$$

[6]The formula was published by Lewis Fry Richardson (1881–1953) in 1910.

TABLE 7.1   Table of the Romberg Procedure

$I_0^{(0)}$				
$I_1^{(0)}$	$I_0^{(1)}$			
$I_2^{(0)}$	$I_1^{(1)}$	$I_0^{(2)}$		
$I_3^{(0)}$	$I_2^{(1)}$	$I_1^{(2)}$	$I_0^{(3)}$	
$\vdots$	$\vdots$	$\vdots$	$\vdots$	$\vdots$

Using these formulae, the approximation $I_1^{(p)}$ has an error of the order h^{2p+2}, so that, for example, in expression (7.168) of the error for $I_1^{(1)}$, the term $C_1 h^2$ does not appear any longer.

This procedure is called the *Romberg procedure*. [7]

Usually, we work in a table form, where the integrals are put as shown in Table 7.1.

7.10   CHEBYSHEV'S QUADRATURE FORMULAE

In the Newton–Côtes formulae the division knots have been arbitrarily chosen, the only condition imposed being that of their equidistance. If this condition is not put and we choose certain points as division knots, then we obtain Chebyshev's quadrature formulae.[8]

Let us consider the integral

$$I = \int_{-1}^{1} f(x)\,dx \tag{7.173}$$

and let us write the relation

$$I \approx \sum_{i=1}^{n} A_i f(x_i), \tag{7.174}$$

where A_i are certain constants, and x_i are the division knots. Obviously, the relation (7.174) is an equality only in certain cases.

In the case of Chebyshev's quadrature formulae, the following conditions are put:

(a) the constants A_i, $i = \overline{1, n}$, are equal, that is

$$A_1 = A_2 = \cdots = A_n = A; \tag{7.175}$$

(b) the quadrature formula (7.174) is exact for any polynomial till the degree n inclusive.

Observation 7.11

(i) Let us write the quadrature formula (7.174) for the polynomial $f(x) = 1$. We obtain

$$I = \int_{-1}^{1} dx = 2; \tag{7.176}$$

taking into account the condition a in Section 7.10, it follows that

$$I = A_1 + A_2 + \cdots + A_n = nA, \tag{7.177}$$

---

[7]Werner Romberg (1909–2003) published the procedure in 1955. In fact, the procedure is an application of the Richardson extrapolation on the trapezoid formula.
[8]The formula was called in honor of Pafnuty Lvovich Chebyshev (1821–1894).

from which

$$A_1 = A_2 = \cdots = A_n = A = \frac{2}{n}. \tag{7.178}$$

(ii) Because the polynomials $1, x, x^2, \ldots, x^n$ form a basis for the vector space of polynomials of degree at most n, it follows that we must verify the condition b in Section 7.10 for these polynomials only. But

$$\int_{-1}^{1} x^k dx = \frac{x^{k+1}}{k+1} \bigg|_{-1}^{1} = \frac{1 - (-1)^{k+1}}{k+1} \tag{7.179}$$

and we obtain the system

$$x_1 + x_2 + \cdots + x_n = 0, \; x_1^1 + x_2^2 + \cdots + x_n^2 = \frac{2}{3} \times \frac{n}{2}, \quad x_1^3 + x_2^3 + \cdots + x_n^3 = 0, \ldots,$$

$$x_1^k + x_2^k + \cdots + x_n^k = \frac{1 - (-1)^{k+1}}{k+1} \times \frac{n}{2}, \ldots, x_1^n + x_2^n + \cdots + x_n^n = \frac{1 - (-1)^{n+1}}{n+1} \times \frac{n}{2}. \tag{7.180}$$

The solving of system (7.180) in the unknowns $x_1, x_2, \ldots, x_n$ is equivalent to the solving of an algebraic equation of degree n. A question arises: are the solutions of system (7.180) real and contained in the interval $[-1, 1]$? The answer to this question is positive only for $n \leq 7$ and $n = 9$.[9] It has been shown that for $n = 8$ and $n \geq 10$ system (7.180) has not only real roots, hence Chebyshev's method cannot be applied.

Observation 7.12 Let the integral be

$$J = \int_{a}^{b} F(u) du \tag{7.181}$$

for which we make the change of variable

$$u = \frac{b+a}{2} + \frac{b-a}{2}x, \quad du = \frac{b-a}{2} dx. \tag{7.182}$$

It follows that

$$J = \int_{a}^{b} F(u) du = \int_{-1}^{1} F\left(\frac{b+a}{2} + \frac{b-a}{2}x\right) \frac{b-a}{2} dx; \tag{7.183}$$

denoting

$$f(x) = F\left(\frac{b+a}{2} + \frac{b-a}{2}x\right) \frac{b-a}{2}, \tag{7.184}$$

we obtain form (7.173). The quadrature formula now reads

$$\int_{a}^{b} F(u) du \approx \frac{2}{n} \frac{b-a}{2} \sum_{i=1}^{n} F(u_i) = \frac{b-a}{n} \sum_{i=1}^{n} F(u_i), \tag{7.185}$$

---

[9]This result belongs to Francis Begnaud Hildebrand (1915–2002) who published it in *Introduction to Numerical Analysis* in 1956.

where

$$u_i = \frac{b+a}{2} + \frac{b-a}{2} x_i. \tag{7.186}$$

7.11 LEGENDRE'S POLYNOMIALS

Let us consider an interval $[a, b] \subset \mathbb{R}$ and let f and g be two functions of class at least C^n on $[a, b]$. The obvious relation

$$\int_a^b f(x)g^{(n)}(x)\mathrm{d}x = f(x)g^{(n-1)}(x)\mathrm{d}x|_a^b - f'(x)g^{(n-2)}(x)|_a^b + f''(x)g^{(n-3)}(x)|_a^b$$

$$- \cdots + (-1)^{n-1} f^{(n-1)}(x)g(x)|_a^b + (-1)^n \int_a^b f^{(n)}(x)g(x)\mathrm{d}x \tag{7.187}$$

takes place in these conditions. We will particularize relation (7.187) taking for $f(x)$ any polynomial $Q(x)$ of degree at most $n-1$ and for $g(x)$ the polynomial $A_n(x-a)^n(x-b)^n$, $A_n \in \mathbb{R}$. Because the degree of $Q(x)$ is at most $n-1$, we get

$$Q^{(n)}(x) = 0, \quad \int_a^b Q^{(n)}(x)g(x)\mathrm{d}x = 0. \tag{7.188}$$

From

$$g(x) = A_n(x-a)^n(x-b)^n \tag{7.189}$$

we obtain

$$\begin{aligned} g(a) = g'(a) = g''(a) = \cdots = g^{n-1}(a) = 0, \\ g(b) = g'(b) = g''(b) = \cdots = g^{n-1}(b) = 0 \end{aligned} \tag{7.190}$$

and relation (7.187) is reduced now to

$$A_n \int_a^b Q(x)\frac{\mathrm{d}^n}{\mathrm{d}x^n}[(x-a)^n(x-b)^n]\mathrm{d}x = 0. \tag{7.191}$$

Let us now denote P_n the polynomial of degree n by P_n, given by

$$P_n(x) = A_n \frac{\mathrm{d}^n}{\mathrm{d}x^n}[(x-a)^n(x-b)^n]. \tag{7.192}$$

On the other hand, $Q(x)$ is an arbitrary polynomial of degree at most $n-1$, so that for $Q(x)$ we may take the polynomials of a basis of the vector space of the polynomials of degree at most $n-1$, that is the polynomials $1, x, x^2, \ldots, x^{n-1}$. We may write

$$\int_a^b P_n(x) = 0, \quad \int_a^b x P_n(x) = 0, \ldots, \quad \int_a^b x^{n-1} P_n(x) = 0. \tag{7.193}$$

We observe that we may also write the relation

$$\int_a^b P_m(x)P_n(x)\mathrm{d}x = 0, \quad m \neq n. \tag{7.194}$$

Indeed, let us suppose that $m < n$; we may consider that $P_m(x)$ is one of the polynomials $Q(x)$ of degree at most $n - 1$.

Observation 7.13 Relation (7.194) means that the sequence $\{P_n(x)\}_{x \in \mathbb{N}}$ is a sequence of orthogonal polynomials on $[a, b]$.

Observation 7.14 The polynomials P_n are unique, with the exception of a multiplicative constant. Indeed, let us suppose that there exists a sequence $\left\{ \prod_n (x) \right\}_{n \in \mathbb{N}}$ of orthogonal polynomials too. We may write the relations

$$\int_a^b Q(x) \prod_n (x) \mathrm{d}x = 0, \quad \int_a^b Q(x) P_n(x) \mathrm{d}x = 0, \quad \int_a^b Q(x) C_n P_n(x) \mathrm{d}x = 0, \tag{7.195}$$

where C_n is an arbitrary constant, while $Q(x)$ is an arbitrary polynomial of degree at most equal to $n - 1$. From the first and the third relation (7.195) we obtain

$$\int_a^b \left(C_n P_n (x) - \prod_n (x) \right) Q(x) \mathrm{d}x = 0. \tag{7.196}$$

We choose the constant C_n so that the polynomial $C_n P_n(x) - \prod_n(x)$ does have a degree at most $n - 1$ and we take

$$Q(x) = C_n P_n(x) - \prod_n(x). \tag{7.197}$$

We obtain the expression

$$\int_a^b \left(C_n P_n (x) - \prod_n (x) \right)^2 \mathrm{d}x = 0, \tag{7.198}$$

hence,

$$C_n P_n(x) - \prod_n(x) = 0, \tag{7.199}$$

that is, $\{P_n(x)\}_{n \in \mathbb{N}}$ are uniquely determined excepting a multiplicative constant.

Definition 7.9 The sequence of polynomials[10]

$$P_n(x) = \frac{1}{2^n n!} \frac{\mathrm{d}^n}{\mathrm{d}x^n} [(x^2 - 1)^n] \tag{7.200}$$

is called the *sequence of Legendre polynomials*.

Theorem 7.1 Let $\{P_n(x)\}_{n \in \mathbb{N}}$ be the sequence of Legendre polynomials and let $R_n(x)$ be the polynomials

$$R_n(x) = 2^n n! P_n(x). \tag{7.201}$$

---

[10]These polynomials were introduced by Adrien–Marie Legendre (1752–1833) in *Recherches sur la figure des planètes* published in 1784.

Under these conditions, the following affirmations hold:

(i) for any $n \in \mathbb{N}$

$$P_n(1) = 1; \tag{7.202}$$

(ii) for any $n \in \mathbb{N}$

$$P_n(-1) = (-1)^n; \tag{7.203}$$

(iii) all the real roots of Legendre's polynomials $P_n(x)$ are in the interval $(-1, 1)$ for any $n \in \mathbb{N}$;

(iv) for any $n \in \mathbb{N}$ we have

$$(x^2 - 1)R_n'(x) = nx R_n(x) - 2n^2 R_{n-1}(x); \tag{7.204}$$

(v) for any $n \in \mathbb{N}$ we have

$$R_{n+1}(x) = 2(2n + 1)x R_n(x) - 4n^2 R_{n-1}(x); \tag{7.205}$$

(vi) the sequence of the polynomials $R_n(x)$ forms a Sturm sequence.

Demonstration.

(i) We rewrite the Legendre polynomial (7.200) by means of the Leibniz formula

$$\frac{d^n}{dx^n}(uv) = \frac{d^n u}{dx^n}v + C_n^1 \frac{d^{n-1}u}{dx^{n-1}}\frac{dv}{dx} + C_n^2 \frac{d^{n-2}u}{dx^{n-2}}\frac{d^2 v}{d^2 x} + \cdots + u\frac{d^n v}{dx^n}, \tag{7.206}$$

assuming

$$u = (x - 1)^n, \quad v = (x + 1)^n. \tag{7.207}$$

It follows that

$$P_n(x) = \frac{1}{2^n n!}\{[(x - 1)^n]^{(n)}(x + 1)^n + C_n^1[(x - 1)^n]^{(n-1)}[(x + 1)^n]'$$
$$+ C_n^2[(x - 1)^n]^{(n-2)}[(x + 1)^n]'' + \cdots + (x - 1)^n[(x + 1)^n]^{(n)}\}. \tag{7.208}$$

But

$$[(x - 1)^n]^{(k)}|_{x=1} = 0, \quad k = \overline{1, n - 1}, \quad [(x - 1)^n]^{(n)} = n! \tag{7.209}$$

and

$$[(x + 1)^n]^{(k)}|_{x=-1} = 0, \quad k = \overline{1, n - 1}, \quad [(x + 1)^n]^{(n)} = n!. \tag{7.210}$$

Relation (7.208) leads to

$$P_n(1) = \frac{1}{2^n n!}n!(1 + 1)^n = 1. \tag{7.211}$$

(ii) From equation (7.208) we get

$$P_n(-1) = \frac{1}{2^n n!}n!(-1 - 1)^n = (-1)^n. \tag{7.212}$$

(iii) Let us observe that the polynomial $(x^2 - 1)^n$ and its $n - 1$ successive derivatives vanish at the points $x = -1$ and $x = 1$. Taking into account Rolle's theorem, under these conditions, the first derivative will have a real root in the interval $(-1, 1)$. The first derivative vanishes at three points $x = -1$, $x = 1$ and at a point between -1 and 1 and it follows that the second derivative will have two distinct roots in the interval $(-1, 1)$. Applying Rolle's theorem, step by step, it follows that the $(n - 1)$th derivative has $n - 1$ distinct roots in the interval $(-1, 1)$, hence $P_n(x)$ has n distinct roots in the interval $(-1, 1)$.

(iv) Let us write

$$R_n(x) = [(x^2 - 1)^{n-1}(x^2 - 1)]^{(n)}, \tag{7.213}$$

a relation to which we apply Leibniz's formula (7.206) with

$$u = (x^2 - 1)^{n-1}, \quad v = x^2 - 1. \tag{7.214}$$

It follows that

$$R_n(x) = [(x^2 - 1)^{n-1}]^{(n)}(x^2 - 1) + 2nx[(x^2 - 1)^{n-1}]^{(n-1)} + n(n-1)[(x^2 - 1)^{n-1}]^{(n-2)}. \tag{7.215}$$

Now, we write

$$R_n(x) = [(x^2 - 1)^n]^{(n)} = 2n[(x^2 - 1)^{n-1}x]^{(n-1)} \tag{7.216}$$

and apply again Leibniz's formula (7.206) with

$$u = (x^2 - 1)^{n-1}, \quad v = x, \tag{7.217}$$

obtaining

$$R_n(x) = 2nx[(x^2 - 1)^{n-1}]^{(n-1)} + 2n(n-1)[(x^2 - 1)^{n-1}]^{(n-2)}. \tag{7.218}$$

Multiplying relation (7.215) by 2 and subtracting relation (7.218), we get

$$R_n(x) = 2(x^2 - 1)R'_{n-1}(x) + 2nx R_{n-1}(x). \tag{7.219}$$

On the other hand,

$$R'_n(x) = [(x^2 - 1)^n]^{(n-1)} = 2n[(x^2 - 1)^{n-1}x]^{(n)}, \tag{7.220}$$

and we may again apply Leibniz's formula (7.206) with

$$u = (x^2 - 1)^{n-1}, \quad v = x, \tag{7.221}$$

Resulting in

$$R'_n(x) = 2nx R'_{n-1}(x) + 2n^2 R_{n-1}(x). \tag{7.222}$$

Multiplying relation (7.219) by nx and relation (7.222) by $x^2 - 1$ and subtracting the results thus obtained one of the other, we obtain

$$(x^2 - 1)R'_n(x) = nx R_n(x) - 2n^2 R_{n-1}(x), \tag{7.223}$$

that is, relation (7.204) which had to be stated.

(v) We make $n \mapsto n + 1$ in relation (7.219) it follows that

$$R_{n+1}(x) = 2(x^2 - 1)R_n'(x) + 2(n + 1)xR_n(x) \tag{7.224}$$

or, equivalently,

$$2(x^2 - 1)R_n'(x) = R_{n+1}(x) - 2(n + 1)xR_n(x). \tag{7.225}$$

We multiply relation (7.223) by 2 and subtract expression (7.225) from the result thus obtained, that is,

$$0 = 2nxR_n(x) + 2(n + 1)xR_n(x) - R_{n+1}(x) - 4n^2R_{n-1}(x) \tag{7.226}$$

or

$$R_{n+1}(x) = 2(2n + 1)xR_n(x) - 4n^2R_{n-1}(x), \tag{7.227}$$

that is, relation (7.205) which had to be stated.

(vi) The last polynomial $R_n(x)$ preserves a constant sign (i.e., $R_0(x)$), because it is a constant. Two neighboring polynomials $R_k(x)$ and $R_{k+1}(x)$ cannot simultaneously vanish, because taking into account equation (7.227), $R_{k-1}(x)$ would vanish too, and step by step $R_0(x)$ would also vanish, which is absurd. If $R_n(x) = 0$, then from equation (7.227) we obtain

$$R_{n+1}(x_0) = -4n^2R_{n-1}(x_0), \tag{7.228}$$

hence

$$R_{n+1}(x_0)R_{n-1}(x_0) < 0. \tag{7.229}$$

Let x_0 be a root of $R_n(x)$. From equation (7.223) we obtain

$$(x_0^2 - 1)R_n'(x_0) = nx_0R_n(x_0) - 2n^2R_{n-1}(x_0) \tag{7.230}$$

and because $R_n(x_0) = 0$, it follows that

$$(1 - x_0^2)R_n'(x_0) = 2n^2R_{n-1}(x_0). \tag{7.231}$$

But $x_0 \in (-1, 1)$, because the roots of Legendre's polynomial

$$P_n(x) = \frac{1}{2^n n!}R_n(x) \tag{7.232}$$

are in the interval $(-1, 1)$, hence

$$1 - x_0^2 > 0. \tag{7.233}$$

From equation (7.231) and equation (7.233) it follows that $R_n'(x_0)$ and $R_{n-1}(x_0)$ have the same sign. It follows that $R_n(x)$ forms a Sturm sequence.

7.12   GAUSS'S QUADRATURE FORMULAE

Let $f : [-1, 1] \to \mathbb{R}$ and the quadrature formula[11] be

$$I = \int_{-1}^{1} f(x)\mathrm{d}x \approx \sum_{i=1}^{n} A_i f(x_i). \tag{7.234}$$

We wish that formula (7.234) be exact for polynomials of a maximum possible degree N. Because we have $2n$ unknowns, that is, the constants $A_1, A_2, \ldots, A_n$ and the knots $x_1, x_2, \ldots, x_n$ of the division, it follows that

$$N = 2n - 1, \tag{7.235}$$

because a polynomial of degree $2n - 1$ has $2n$ coefficients. Proceeding as at Chebyshev's quadrature formulae, it follows that it is sufficient to satisfy relation (7.234) only for the polynomials 1, x, x^2, x^3, $\ldots$, x^{2n-1}, because they form a basis in the vector space of the polynomials of degree at most $2n - 1$.

On the other hand,

$$\int_{-1}^{1} x^k \mathrm{d}x = \frac{1 - (-1)^{k+1}}{k + 1} \tag{7.236}$$

and it follows that the system

$$
\begin{aligned}
A_1 + A_2 + \cdots + A_n &= \int_{-1}^{1} \mathrm{d}x = 2, \\
A_1 x_1 + A_2 x_2 + \cdots + A_n x_n &= \int_{-1}^{1} x\,\mathrm{d}x = 0, \\
A_1 x_1^2 + A_2 x_2^2 + \cdots + A_n x_n^2 &= \int_{-1}^{1} x^2\,\mathrm{d}x = \frac{2}{3}, \ldots, \\
A_1 x_1^k + A_2 x_2^k + \cdots + A_n x_n^k &= \int_{-1}^{1} x^k\,\mathrm{d}x = \frac{1 - (-1)^{k+1}}{k + 1}, \ldots, \\
A_1 x_1^{2n-1} + A_2 x_2^{2n-1} + \cdots + A_n x_n^{2n-1} &= \int_{-1}^{1} x^{2n-1}\,\mathrm{d}x = 0.
\end{aligned} \tag{7.237}
$$

Let us consider that

$$f(x) = x^k P_n(x), \quad k = \overline{0, n - 1}, \tag{7.238}$$

where $P_n(x)$ is Legendre's polynomial of degree n. Taking into account the properties of the Legendre polynomial, we have

$$\int_{-1}^{1} x^k P_n(x)\mathrm{d}x = 0, \quad k = \overline{0, n - 1}, \tag{7.239}$$

and from formula (7.234) we get

$$\int_{-1}^{1} x^k P_n(x)\mathrm{d}x = \sum_{i=1}^{n} A_i x_i^k P_n(x_i), \quad k = \overline{0, n - 1}. \tag{7.240}$$

Equating the last two relations, it follows that x_i are the roots of Legendre's polynomial of nth degree, all these roots being real, distinct, and situated in the interval $(-1, 1)$.

[11]The method was developed by Carl Friedrich Gauss (1777–1855) in *Methodus nova integralium valores per approximationem inveniendi* in 1815. The method is also known as Gauss–Legendre quadrature.

We select now the first n equations from system (7.237), which form a linear system of n equations with n unknowns, that is, the coefficients A_1, A_2, ..., A_n. The determinant of this system is a Vandermonde one,

$$\Delta = \prod_{\substack{i,j=1 \\ i<j}}^{n} (x_i - x_j) \neq 0, \tag{7.241}$$

because the roots x_i of Legendre's polynomial $P_n(x)$ are distinct. It thus follows that the system has a unique solution.

Observation 7.15   If we have to calculate

$$J = \int_a^b F(u)\mathrm{d}u, \tag{7.242}$$

then, by a change of variable

$$u = \frac{b+a}{2} + \frac{b-a}{2}x, \quad \mathrm{d}u = \frac{b-a}{2}\mathrm{d}x, \tag{7.243}$$

we obtain

$$J = \int_{-1}^{1} F\left(\frac{b+a}{2} + \frac{b-a}{2}x\right)\frac{b-a}{2}\mathrm{d}x; \tag{7.244}$$

denoting

$$f(x) = F\left(\frac{b+a}{2} + \frac{b-a}{2}x\right)\frac{b-a}{2}, \tag{7.245}$$

we obtain form (7.234) of the integral,

$$\int_a^b F(u)\mathrm{d}u = \frac{b-a}{2}\sum_{i=1}^{n} A_i F\left(\frac{b+a}{2} + \frac{b-a}{2}x_i\right), \tag{7.246}$$

where x_i are the roots of the Legendre polynomial.

7.13   ORTHOGONAL POLYNOMIALS

Let us denote by $\mathbb{R}[X]$ the set of the polynomials with real coefficients in the indeterminate X.
We define the scalar product on $\mathbb{R}[X]$ by

$$\langle P(x), Q(x) \rangle = \int_a^b P(x)Q(x)\rho(x)\mathrm{d}x, \tag{7.247}$$

where $\rho(x)$ is a weight function.

Definition 7.10   We say that the polynomials P and Q are orthogonal if and only if $\langle P, Q \rangle = 0$, where the scalar product $\langle, \rangle$ has been defined by relation (7.247).

Observation 7.16   Starting from the sequence of polynomials $1, x, x^2, \ldots$, we construct a sequence of orthogonal polynomials $P_0, P_1, \ldots, P_n$, with the help of the Gramm–Schmidt procedure. Thus, we have

$$P_0 = 1, \quad P_1 = x - \frac{\langle x, P_0 \rangle}{\|P_0\|^2}P_0, \ldots, \quad P_n = x^n - \sum_{i=1}^{n-1} \frac{\langle x^n, P_i \rangle}{\|P_i\|^2}P_i, \ldots, \tag{7.248}$$

where $\| \; \|$ marks the norm defined by

$$\|P\| = \sqrt{\langle P, P \rangle}. \tag{7.249}$$

We may thus construct various sequences of orthogonal polynomials.

7.13.1 Legendre Polynomials

In the case of Legendre's polynomials, we choose $a = -1$, $b = 1$, $\rho(x) = 1$; It follows that

$$P_0 = 1, \tag{7.250}$$

$$P_1 = x - \frac{\langle x, 1 \rangle}{\|P_0\|^2} \times 1 = x, \tag{7.251}$$

$$P_2 = x^2 - \frac{\langle x^2, 1 \rangle}{\|P_0\|^2} \times 1 - \frac{\langle x^2, x \rangle}{\|P_1\|} \times x = x^2 - \frac{1}{3}, \tag{7.252}$$

$$P_3 = x^3 - \frac{\langle x^3, 1 \rangle}{\|P_0\|^2} \times 1 - \frac{\langle x^3, x \rangle}{\|P_1\|^2} \times x - \frac{\langle x^3, x^2 - \frac{1}{3} \rangle}{\|P_2\|^2} \times \left(x^2 - \frac{1}{3} \right) = x^3 - \frac{3}{5}x, \; \ldots \tag{7.253}$$

7.13.2 Chebyshev Polynomials

We define the Chebyshev polynomials by $a = -1$, $b = 1$, $\rho(x) = 1/\sqrt{1 - x^2}$.
Because

$$I_k = \int_{-1}^{1} \frac{x^k}{\sqrt{1 - x^2}} dx = (-x^{k-1}\sqrt{1 - x^2})|_{-1}^{1} + \int_{-1}^{1} (k - 1)x^{k-2}\sqrt{1 - x^2} dx$$

$$= (k - 1)\int_{-1}^{1} \frac{x^{k-2} dx}{\sqrt{1 - x^2}} - (k - 1)\int_{-1}^{1} \frac{x^k dx}{\sqrt{1 - x^2}} = (k - 1)I_{k-2} - (k - 1)I_k, \tag{7.254}$$

we obtain

$$kI_k = (k - 1)I_{k-2}, \tag{7.255}$$

that is,

$$I_k = \frac{k - 1}{k} I_{k-2}. \tag{7.256}$$

On the other hand,

$$I_0 = \int_{-1}^{1} \frac{dx}{\sqrt{1 - x^2}} = \pi, \tag{7.257}$$

$$I_1 = \int_{-1}^{1} \frac{x \, dx}{\sqrt{1 - x^2}} = 0, \tag{7.258}$$

hence

$$I_{2p+1} = 0, \quad p \in \mathbb{N}, \tag{7.259}$$

$$I_2 = \frac{1}{2}I_0 = \frac{\pi}{2}, \quad I_4 = \frac{3}{4}I_2 = \frac{3\pi}{8}, \; \ldots \;,$$

$$I_{2p} = \frac{2p - 1}{2p} I_{2p-2} = \frac{(2p - 1)!!}{(2p)!!} \pi. \tag{7.260}$$

We obtain the Chebyshev polynomials in the form

$$P_0 = 1, \tag{7.261}$$

$$P_1 = x - \frac{\langle x, 1 \rangle}{\|P_0\|^2} \times 1 = x, \tag{7.262}$$

$$P_2 = x^2 - \frac{\langle x^2, 1 \rangle}{\|P_0\|^2} \times 1 - \frac{\langle x^2, x \rangle}{\|P_1\|^2} \times x = x^2 - \frac{1}{2}, \tag{7.263}$$

$$P_3 = x^3 - \frac{\langle x^3, 1 \rangle}{\|P_0\|^2} \times 1 - \frac{\langle x^3, x \rangle}{\|P_1\|^2} \times x - \frac{\langle x^3, x^2 - \frac{1}{2} \rangle}{\|P_2\|^2} \times \left(x^2 - \frac{1}{2} \right) = x^3 - \frac{3}{4}x, \; \ldots \tag{7.264}$$

7.13.3 Jacobi Polynomials

In case of the Jacobi polynomials,[12] $a = -1$, $b = 1$, $\rho(x) = (1 - x)^\alpha (1 + x)^\beta$, $\alpha > -1$, $\beta > -1$, α, β integers.

We observe that we obtain various sequences of orthogonal polynomials, depending on the choice of the parameters α and β. If $\alpha = \beta = 0$, then we get Legendre's polynomials.

Let us take $\alpha = \beta = 1$. We have

$$P_0 = 1, \tag{7.265}$$

$$P_1 = x - \frac{\langle x, 1 \rangle}{\|P_0\|^2} \times 1 = x, \tag{7.266}$$

$$P_2 = x^2 - \frac{\langle x^2, 1 \rangle}{\|P_0\|^2} \times 1 - \frac{\langle x^2, x \rangle}{\|P_1\|^2} x = x^2 - \frac{1}{5}, \tag{7.267}$$

$$P_3 = x^3 - \frac{\langle x^3, 1 \rangle}{\|P_0\|^2} \times 1 - \frac{\langle x^3, x \rangle}{\|P_1\|^2} \times x - \frac{\langle x^3, x^2 - \frac{1}{5} \rangle}{\|P_2\|^2} \times \left(x^2 - \frac{1}{5} \right) = x^3 - \frac{3}{7}x, \; \ldots \tag{7.268}$$

7.13.4 Hermite Polynomials

In the case of the Hermite polynomials[13] we have $a = -\infty$, $b = \infty$, $\rho(x) = \exp(-x^2)$.
We may write

$$I_k = \int_{-\infty}^{\infty} x^k e^{-x^2} dx = \left(-\frac{x^{k-1}}{2} e^{-x^2} \right) \Big|_{-\infty}^{\infty} + (k - 1) \int_{-\infty}^{\infty} \frac{x^{k-2}}{2} e^{-x^3} dx = \frac{k - 1}{2} I_{k-2}. \tag{7.269}$$

On the other hand,

$$I_0 = \int_{-\infty}^{\infty} e^{-x^2} dx = \sqrt{\pi}, \tag{7.270}$$

$$I_1 = \int_{-\infty}^{\infty} x e^{-x^2} dx = 0; \tag{7.271}$$

---

[12]These polynomials were introduced by Carl Gustav Jacob Jacobi (1804–1851).
[13]These polynomials were named in honor of Charles Hermite (1822–1901) who studied them in *Sur un nouveau développement en série de fonctions* in 1864. They were also studied by Pierre–Simon Laplace (1749–1827) in a memoir since 1810 and Chebyshev in *Sur le développement des fonctions à une seulle variable* in 1859.

hence, it follows that

$$I_{2p+1} = 0, \quad p \in \mathbb{N}, \tag{7.272}$$

$$I_0 = \sqrt{\pi}, \quad I_2 = \frac{1}{2}I_0 = \frac{\sqrt{\pi}}{2}, \quad I_4 = \frac{3}{4}\sqrt{\pi}, \ldots,$$

$$I_{2p} = \frac{2p-1}{2}I_{2p-2} = \frac{(2p-1)!!}{2^p}\sqrt{\pi}, \ldots \tag{7.273}$$

We obtain the Hermite polynomials

$$P_0 = 1, \tag{7.274}$$

$$P_1 = x - \frac{\langle x, 1 \rangle}{\|P_0\|^2} \times 1 = x, \tag{7.275}$$

$$P_2 = x^2 - \frac{\langle x^2, 1 \rangle}{\|P_0\|^2} \times 1 - \frac{\langle x^2, x \rangle}{\|P_1\|^2} \times x = x^2 - \frac{1}{2}, \tag{7.276}$$

$$P_3 = x^3 - \frac{\langle x^3, 1 \rangle}{\|P_0\|^2} \times 1 - \frac{\langle x^3, x \rangle}{\|P_1\|^2} \times x - \frac{\langle x^3, x^2 - \frac{1}{2} \rangle}{\|P_2\|^2} \times \left(x^2 - \frac{1}{2} \right) = x^3 - \frac{3}{2}x, \ldots \tag{7.277}$$

7.13.5   Laguerre Polynomials

The Laguerre polynomials[14] are defined by $a = 0$, $b = \infty$, $\rho(x) = e^{-x}x^\alpha$, α integer.

Obviously, we obtain various sequences of Laguerre polynomials as function of the exponent α. We may consider the case $\alpha = 1$.

Taking into account that

$$I_k = \int_0^\infty x^k x e^{-x} dx = (-x^{k+1}e^{-x})|_0^\infty + (k+1)\int_0^\infty x^{k-1}xe^{-x}dx = (k+1)I_{k-1}, \tag{7.278}$$

$$I_0 = \int_0^\infty xe^{-x}dx = (-xe^{-x})|_0^\infty + \int_0^\infty e^{-x}dx = 1, \tag{7.279}$$

we get

$$I_1 = 2I_0 = 2, \quad I_2 = 3I_1 = 6, \ldots, \quad I_k = (k+1)I_k = (k+1)!. \tag{7.280}$$

We obtain thus Laguerre's polynomials

$$P_0 = 1, \tag{7.281}$$

$$P_1 = x - \frac{\langle x, 1 \rangle}{\|P_0\|^2} \times 1 = x - 2, \tag{7.282}$$

$$P_2 = x^2 - \frac{\langle x^2, 1 \rangle}{\|P_0\|^2} \times 1 - \frac{\langle x^2, x - 2 \rangle}{\|P_1\|^2} \times (x - 2) = x^2 - 6x + 6, \tag{7.283}$$

$$P_3 = x^3 - \frac{\langle x^3, 1 \rangle}{\|P_0\|^2} \times 1 - \frac{\langle x^3, x - 2 \rangle}{\|P_1\|^2} \times (x - 2) - \frac{\langle x^3, x^2 - 6x + 6 \rangle}{\|P_2\|^2} \times (x^2 - 6x + 6) \cdots$$

$$= x^3 - 12x^2 + 36x - 24, \tag{7.284}$$

[14]They are called after Edmond Nicolas Laguerre (1834–1886) who studied them in 1879.

7.13.6   General Properties of the Orthogonal Polynomials

Let us begin with a remark.

Observation 7.17

(i) The complex roots λ_1, λ_2, ..., λ_n of the polynomials P_j, $j = \overline{1, m}$, given by formulae (7.248), satisfy the relation

$$\lambda_k = \frac{\langle x Q_i, Q_i \rangle}{\| Q_i \|^2}, \quad k = \overline{1, \ n},$$ (7.285)

in which

$$Q_i(x) = \prod_{\substack{l=1 \\ l \neq i}}^{n} (x - \lambda_l), \quad i = \overline{1, \ n}.$$ (7.286)

Indeed, if λ_k is a root of $P_n(x)$, then

$$P_n(x) = (x - \lambda_k) Q_k(x);$$ (7.287)

from the orthogonality condition

$$\langle Q_k, P_n \rangle = 0$$ (7.288)

we get

$$0 = \langle Q_k, P_n \rangle = \langle Q_k, x Q_k \rangle - \langle Q_k, \lambda_k Q_k \rangle,$$ (7.289)

that is, a relation equivalent to equation (7.285).

(ii) The scalar product defined by relation (7.247) has the property of symmetry, that is, we have the relation

$$\langle xP, Q \rangle = \langle P, xQ \rangle.$$ (7.290)

Proposition 7.5   If the scalar product considered in relation (7.248) satisfies the condition (7.285), then the polynomials P_0, P_1, ..., P_m verify the relations

$$P_0(x) = 1, \quad P_1(x) = x - \alpha_0, \ \ldots,$$
$$P_{i+1}(x) = (x - \alpha_i) P_i(x) - \beta_i P_{i-1}(x), \quad i = \overline{1, \ m-1},$$ (7.291)

where

$$\alpha_i = \frac{\langle x P_i, P_i \rangle}{\| P_i \|^2}, \quad i = \overline{1, \ m-1},$$ (7.292)

$$\beta_i = \frac{\| P_i \|^2}{\| P_{i-1} \|^2}, \quad i = \overline{1, \ m-1}.$$ (7.293)

Demonstration.   The first relations (7.291) result directly from formulae (7.248).
Let it now be $m \geq 2$, and for any $i = \overline{1, m-1}$, let us consider

$$Q_{i+1}(x) = (x - \alpha_i) P_i(x) - \beta_1 P_{i-1}(x),$$ (7.294)

with P_{i-1} and P_i given by relation (7.248).

Because P_{i-1} and P_i are orthogonal, we get

$$\langle Q_{i+1}, P_i \rangle = \langle x P_i, P_i \rangle - \alpha_i \| P_i \|^2. \tag{7.295}$$

Moreover,

$$\langle Q_{i+1}, P_{i+1} \rangle = \langle P_i, x P_i \rangle - \beta_i \| P_{i-1} \|^2 = \langle P_i, x P_{i-1} - P_i \rangle = 0, \tag{7.296}$$

because x^i does not appear in the difference $x P_{i-1} - P_i x^i$, while P_i is orthogonal to the polynomials $1, x, x^2, \ldots, x^{i-1}$.

On the other hand, for any $k = \overline{0, i-2}$, the polynomial P_i is orthogonal to the polynomials P_k and $x P_k$; hence

$$\langle Q_{i+1}, P_k \rangle = \langle P_i, x P_k \rangle - \alpha_i \langle P_i, P_k \rangle - \beta_i \langle P_{i-1}, P_k \rangle = 0. \tag{7.297}$$

We thus deduce that the polynomial Q_{i+1} is orthogonal to all the polynomials of degree strictly less than i and is of the form

$$Q_{i+1}(x) = x^{i+1} + R(x), \tag{7.298}$$

where the degree of R is at most equal to i.

On the other hand, the polynomials $P_0, P_1, \ldots, P_i$ form an orthogonal basis for the space of polynomials of degree at most equal to i, so that $R(x)$ will be written in the form

$$R(x) = \sum_{k=0}^{i} \frac{\langle R, P_k \rangle}{\| P_k \|^2} P_k. \tag{7.299}$$

From the relation

$$\langle x^{i+1}, P_k \rangle + \langle R, P_k \rangle = \langle Q_{i+1}, P_k \rangle = 0, \quad k = \overline{0, \ i}, \tag{7.300}$$

we deduce

$$\langle R, P_k \rangle = -\langle x^{i+1}, P_k \rangle, \tag{7.301}$$

hence, $Q_{i+1} = P_{i+1}$, the proposition being stated.

Theorem 7.2 If the scalar product (7.247) satisfies the conditions of symmetry (7.290), then the roots of the polynomial P_n constructed with relation (7.247) and denoted by $\lambda_1, \lambda_2, \ldots, \lambda_n$ are real, distinct, and verify the relations

$$\lambda_i = \frac{\langle x L_i, L_i \rangle}{\| L_i \|^2}, \quad i = \overline{1, \ n}, \tag{7.302}$$

in which

$$L_i(x) = \prod_{\substack{k=1 \\ k \neq i}}^{n} \frac{x - \lambda_k}{\lambda_i - \lambda_k}. \tag{7.303}$$

Demonstration. Because

$$\langle x Q_j, Q_j \rangle = \langle Q_j, x Q_j \rangle = \overline{\langle x Q_j, Q_j \rangle}, \tag{7.304}$$

where the upper bar marks the complex conjugate, taking into account Proposition 7.5 we deduce that the roots are real and distinct.

If the coefficients of the polynomials P_n are real numbers, then the complex roots of these polynomials are conjugate two by two, which means that the polynomial P_n is written in the form

$$P_n(x) = [(x-a)^2 + b^2]R(x), \tag{7.305}$$

where a and b are real numbers, while R is a polynomial with real coefficients of degree $n-2$.

We may write successively

$$0 = \langle P_n, R \rangle = \langle [(x-a)^2 + b^2]R, R \rangle = \langle (x-a)^2 R, R \rangle + b^2 \langle R, R \rangle$$

$$= \|(x-a)R\|^2 + b^2 \|R\|^2 > 0, \tag{7.306}$$

which is absurd.

If the polynomial P would have a multiple real root a, then

$$P_n(x) = (x-a)^2 R(x), \tag{7.307}$$

where R is a polynomial of degree $n-2$, which may have a as root.

We have

$$0 = \langle P_n, R \rangle = \langle (x-a)^2 R, R \rangle = \|(x-a)R\|^2 > 0 \tag{7.308}$$

obtaining again a contradiction.

Formula (7.302) is a consequence of Proposition 7.5.

7.14   QUADRATURE FORMULAE OF GAUSS TYPE OBTAINED BY ORTHOGONAL POLYNOMIALS

We have calculated in the previous paragraph various orthogonal polynomials till the third degree. Let P be such a polynomial of degree 3, and denote by x_1, x_2 and x_3 its real and distinct roots.

We search a quadrature formula of the form

$$\int_a^b f(x)\mathrm{d}x \approx A_1 f(x_1) + A_2 f(x_2) + A_3 f(x_3), \tag{7.309}$$

where A_1, A_2 and A_3 are constants; the formula is exact for polynomials of maximum possible degree.

We have

$$\int_a^b \mathrm{d}x = b - a, \quad \int_a^b x\,\mathrm{d}x = \frac{b^2 - a^2}{2}, \quad \int_a^b x^2\,\mathrm{d}x = \frac{b^3 - a^3}{3}, \tag{7.310}$$

obtaining thus a linear system of three equations with three unknowns

$$A_1 + A_2 + A_3 = b - a,$$

$$A_1 x_1 + A_2 x_2 + A_3 x_3 = \frac{b^2 - a^2}{2}, \tag{7.311}$$

$$A_1 x_1^2 + A_2 x_2^2 + A_3 x_3^2 = \frac{b^3 - a^3}{3}.$$

We deduce the values A_1, A_2, and A_3 from system (7.311).

Obviously, if we wish to have a quadrature formula at n points, then we consider the polynomial P_n with the roots $x_1, x_2, \ldots, x_n$; it follows that the system

$$A_1 + A_2 + \cdots + A_n = b - a, \quad A_1x_1 + A_2x_2 + \cdots + A_nx_n = \frac{b^2 - a^2}{2}, \ldots,$$

$$A_1x_1^{n-1} + A_2x_2^{n-1} + \cdots + A_nx_n^{n-1} = \frac{b^n - a^n}{n}. \tag{7.312}$$

7.14.1 Gauss–Jacobi Quadrature Formulae

The Jacobi polynomial of second degree is given (the case $\alpha = \beta = 1$) by

$$P_2(x) = x^2 - \frac{1}{5}; \tag{7.313}$$

it has the roots

$$x_1 = -\sqrt{\frac{1}{5}}, \quad x_2 = \sqrt{\frac{1}{5}} \tag{7.314}$$

and it follows that the system

$$A_1 + A_2 = 2, \quad -A_1\sqrt{\frac{1}{5}} + A_2\sqrt{\frac{1}{5}} = 0, \tag{7.315}$$

with the solution $A_1 = A_2 = 1$. We obtain the Gauss–Jacobi quadrature formula

$$\int_{-1}^{1} f(x)dx \approx f\left(-\sqrt{\frac{1}{5}}\right) + f\left(\sqrt{\frac{1}{5}}\right). \tag{7.316}$$

Considering now the Jacobi polynomial of third degree (the case $\alpha = \beta = 1$)

$$P_3(x) = x^3 - \frac{3}{7}x, \tag{7.317}$$

we obtain the roots

$$x_1 = -\sqrt{\frac{3}{7}}, \quad x_2 = 0, \quad x_3 = \sqrt{\frac{3}{7}} \tag{7.318}$$

and the system

$$A_1 + A_2 + A_3 = 2, \quad -A_1\sqrt{\frac{3}{7}} + A_3\sqrt{\frac{3}{7}} = 0, \quad \frac{3}{7}A_1 + \frac{3}{7}A_3 = \frac{2}{3}, \tag{7.319}$$

with the solution

$$A_1 = \frac{7}{9}, \quad A_2 = \frac{4}{9}, \quad A_3 = \frac{7}{9}. \tag{7.320}$$

It follows that the Gauss–Jacobi quadrature formula

$$\int_{-1}^{1} f(x)dx \approx \frac{7}{9}f\left(-\sqrt{\frac{3}{7}}\right) + \frac{4}{9}f(0) + \frac{7}{9}f\left(\sqrt{\frac{3}{7}}\right). \tag{7.321}$$

7.14.2 Gauss–Hermite Quadrature Formulae

A formula of the form

$$\int_{-\infty}^{\infty} e^{-x^2} f(x) dx \approx \sum_{i=1}^{n} A_i f(x_i) \tag{7.322}$$

is searched; this one is exact for f polynomial of the maximum possible degree.

The Hermite polynomials $P_1(x) = x$ has the root $x_1 = 0$, so that formula (7.322) becomes

$$\int_{-\infty}^{\infty} e^{-x^2} f(x) dx \approx A_1 f(0). \tag{7.323}$$

Choosing $f(x) = 1$, we obtain

$$\int_{-\infty}^{\infty} e^{-x^2} dx = \sqrt{\pi} = A_1 \tag{7.324}$$

and the first Gauss–Hermite quadrature formula reads

$$\int_{-\infty}^{\infty} e^{-x^2} dx = \sqrt{\pi} f(0). \tag{7.325}$$

Let us consider now the Hermite polynomial $P_2(x) = x^2 - 1/2$, with the roots

$$x_1 = -\sqrt{\frac{1}{2}}, \quad x_2 = \sqrt{\frac{1}{2}}; \tag{7.326}$$

the quadrature formula is now of the form

$$\int_{-\infty}^{\infty} e^{-x^2} f(x) dx \approx A_1 f\left(-\sqrt{\frac{1}{2}}\right) + A_2 f\left(\sqrt{\frac{1}{2}}\right). \tag{7.327}$$

Taking $f(x) = 1$ and $f(x) = x$, we obtain the linear algebraic system

$$\int_{-\infty}^{\infty} e^{-x^2} dx = \sqrt{\pi} = A_1 + A_2, \quad \int_{-\infty}^{\infty} x e^{-x^2} dx = 0 = -A_1\sqrt{\frac{1}{2}} + A_2\sqrt{\frac{1}{2}}, \tag{7.328}$$

with the solution

$$A_1 = A_2 = \frac{\sqrt{\pi}}{2}; \tag{7.329}$$

it follows that the second Gauss–Hermite quadrature formula

$$\int_{-\infty}^{\infty} e^{-x^2} f(x) dx \approx \frac{\sqrt{\pi}}{2} f\left(-\sqrt{\frac{1}{2}}\right) + \frac{\sqrt{\pi}}{2} f\left(\sqrt{\frac{1}{2}}\right). \tag{7.330}$$

For a Gauss–Hermite quadrature formula in three points, one starts from the Hermite polynomial $P_3(x) = x^3 - 3x/2$, the roots of which are

$$x_1 = -\sqrt{\frac{3}{2}}, \quad x_2 = 0, \quad x_3 = \sqrt{\frac{3}{2}}. \tag{7.331}$$

From

$$\int_{-\infty}^{\infty} e^{-x^2} f(x) dx \approx A_1 f(x_1) + A_2 f(x_2) + A_3 f(x_3), \tag{7.332}$$

choosing $f(x) = 1$, $f(x) = x$, and $f(x) = x^2$, we obtain the linear algebraic system

$$\int_{-\infty}^{\infty} e^{-x^2} dx = \sqrt{\pi} = A_1 + A_2 + A_3,$$

$$\int_{-\infty}^{\infty} x e^{-x^2} dx = 0 = -A_1\sqrt{\frac{3}{2}} + A_3\sqrt{\frac{3}{2}}, \qquad (7.333)$$

$$\int_{-\infty}^{\infty} x^2 e^{-x^2} dx = \frac{\sqrt{\pi}}{2} = \frac{3}{2}A_1 + \frac{3}{2}A_3,$$

with the solution

$$A_1 = \frac{\sqrt{\pi}}{6}, \quad A_2 = \frac{2\sqrt{\pi}}{3}, \quad A_3 = \frac{\sqrt{\pi}}{6}; \qquad (7.334)$$

it thus results the Gauss–Hermite quadrature formula

$$\int_{-\infty}^{\infty} e^{-x^2} f(x) dx \approx \frac{\sqrt{\pi}}{6} f\left(-\sqrt{\frac{3}{2}}\right) + \frac{2\sqrt{\pi}}{3} f(0) + \frac{\sqrt{\pi}}{6} f\left(\sqrt{\frac{3}{2}}\right). \qquad (7.335)$$

7.14.3 Gauss–Laguerre Quadrature Formulae

We take the quadrature formulae of the form (for $\alpha = 1$)

$$\int_0^{\infty} x e^{-x} f(x) dx \approx \sum_{i=1}^{n} A_i f(x_i). \qquad (7.336)$$

For the Laguerre polynomial $P_1(x) = x - 2$ we find the root $x_1 = 2$ and formula (7.336) becomes

$$\int_0^{\infty} x e^{-x} f(x) dx \approx A_1 f(2). \qquad (7.337)$$

Choosing $f(x) = 1$, it follows that the equation

$$\int_0^{\infty} x e^{-x} dx = 1 = A_1; \qquad (7.338)$$

thus we obtain the Gauss–Laguerre quadrature formula

$$\int_0^{\infty} x e^{-x} f(x) dx \approx f(2). \qquad (7.339)$$

In the case of the Laguerre polynomial $P_2(x) = x^2 - 6x + 6$, the roots being

$$x_1 = 3 - \sqrt{3}, \quad x_2 = 3 + \sqrt{3}, \qquad (7.340)$$

we obtain the relation

$$\int_0^{\infty} x e^{-x} f(x) dx \approx A_1 f(3 - \sqrt{3}) + A_2 f(3 + \sqrt{3}). \qquad (7.341)$$

Taking now $f(x) = 1$ and $f(x) = x$, it follows that the linear algebraic system

$$\int_0^\infty x e^{-x} dx = 1 = A_1 + A_2,$$

$$\int_0^\infty x^2 e^{-x} dx = 2 = A_1(3 - \sqrt{3}) + A_2(3 + \sqrt{3}),$$

(7.342)

with the solution

$$A_1 = \frac{1 + \sqrt{3}}{2\sqrt{3}}, \quad A_2 = \frac{\sqrt{3} - 1}{2\sqrt{3}}.$$

(7.343)

We obtain the Gauss–Laguerre quadrature formula

$$\int_0^\infty x e^{-x} f(x) dx \approx \frac{1 + \sqrt{3}}{2\sqrt{3}} f(3 - \sqrt{3}) + \frac{\sqrt{3} - 1}{2\sqrt{3}} f(3 + \sqrt{3}).$$

(7.344)

Let the Laguerre polynomial now be $P_3(x) = x^3 - 12x^2 + 36x - 24$, the roots of which are

$$x_1 \approx 0.9358, \quad x_2 \approx 3.3050, \quad x_3 \approx 7.7598.$$

(7.345)

The quadrature formula reads

$$\int_0^\infty x e^{-x} f(x) dx \approx A_1 f(x_1) + A_2 f(x_2) + A_3 f(x_3).$$

(7.346)

Choosing $f(x) = 1$, $f(x) = x$, and $f(x) = x^2$, it follows that the linear algebraic system

$$\int_0^\infty x e^{-x} dx = 1 = A_1 + A_2 + A_3,$$

$$\int_0^\infty x^2 e^{-x} dx = 2 = A_1 x_1 + A_2 x_2 + A_3 x_3,$$

$$\int_0^\infty x^3 e^{-x} dx = 6 = A_1 x_1^2 + A_2 x_2^2 + A_3 x_3^2,$$

(7.347)

from which we obtain the values

$$A_1 = 0.589, \quad A_2 = 0.391, \quad A_3 = 0.020.$$

(7.348)

The Gauss–Laguerre quadrature formula reads

$$\int_0^\infty x e^{-x} f(x) dx = 0.589 f(0.9358) + 0.391 f(3.3050) + 0.020 f(7.7598).$$

(7.349)

7.15   OTHER QUADRATURE FORMULAE

7.15.1   Gauss Formulae with Imposed Points

We present now the theory in the case in which a point of division is imposed, so that

$$\int_{-1}^{1} f(x)\mathrm{d}x = C_0 f(x_0) + \sum_{i=1}^{n} C_i f(x_i), \tag{7.350}$$

where the division point x_0 is the imposed point.

Let us remark that $2n + 1$ parameters remain to be determined, that is, the points x_i, $i = \overline{1, n}$, and the coefficients $C_0, C_1, \ldots, C_n$.

Proceeding as in the Gauss method, we have

$$\int_{-1}^{1} \mathrm{d}x = 2 = C_0 + \sum_{i=1}^{n} C_i, \qquad \int_{-1}^{1} x\,\mathrm{d}x = 0 = C_0 x_0 + \sum_{i=1}^{n} C_i x_i,$$

$$\int_{-1}^{1} x^2 \mathrm{d}x = \frac{2}{3} = C_0 x_0^2 + \sum_{i=1}^{n} C_i x_i^2, \ldots,$$

$$\int_{-1}^{1} x^{2n-1} \mathrm{d}x = 0 = C_0 x_0^{2n-1} + \sum_{i=1}^{n} C_i x_i^{2n-1}, \tag{7.351}$$

$$\int_{-1}^{1} x^{2n} \mathrm{d}x = \frac{2}{2n+1} = C_0 x_0^{2n} + \sum_{i=1}^{n} C_i x_i^{2n}.$$

Multiplying by x_0 each such relation (unless the last one) and subtracting from the following one, we obtain

$$-2 = \sum_{i=1}^{n} C_i (x_i - x_0) = \sum_{i=1}^{n} C_i x_i - x_0 \sum_{i=1}^{n} C_i,$$

$$\frac{2}{3} = \sum_{i=1}^{n} C_i x_i (x_i - x_0) = \sum_{i=1}^{n} C_i x_i^2 - x_0 \sum_{i=1}^{n} C_i x_i,$$

$$-\frac{2}{3} = \sum_{i=1}^{n} C_i x_i^2 (x_i - x_0) = \sum_{i=1}^{n} C_i x_i^3 - x_0 \sum_{i=1}^{n} C_i x_i^2, \ldots, \tag{7.352}$$

$$\frac{2}{2n+1} = \sum_{i=1}^{n} C_i x_i^{2n-1}(x_i - x_0) = \sum_{i=1}^{n} C_i x_i^{2n} - x_0 \sum_{i=1}^{n} C_i x_i^{2n-1}.$$

From the first relation (7.352), we find

$$\sum_{i=1}^{n} C_i x_i = -2 + x_0 \sum_{i=1}^{n} C_i, \tag{7.353}$$

which replaced in the second relation (7.352), leads to

$$\sum_{i=1}^{n} C_i x_i^2 = \frac{2}{3} - 2x_0 + x_0^2 \sum_{i=1}^{n} C_i. \tag{7.354}$$

Step by step, we deduce

$$\sum_{i=1}^{n} C_i x_i^k = P_k(x_0) + x_0^k \sum_{i=1}^{n} C_i, \tag{7.355}$$

where P_k is a polynomial of $(k-1)$th degree.

On the other hand, from the first relation (7.351), we obtain

$$\sum_{i=1}^{n} C_i = 2 - C_0, \tag{7.356}$$

so that expression (7.355) becomes

$$\sum_{i=1}^{n} C_i x_i^k = P_k(x_0) + (2 - C_0) x_0^k. \tag{7.357}$$

The problem has been reduced to Gauss quadrature in which the terms that define the sums $\sum_{i=1}^{n} C_i x_i^k$ are no more equal to $\int_{-1}^{1} x^k dx$, but to the expressions at the right of relation (7.357). We find the same interpolation knots, but the constants $C_0, C_1, \ldots, C_n$ are other ones now.

Similarly, we discuss the case in which more points are imposed.

7.15.2   Gauss Formulae in which the Derivatives of the Function Also Appear

A formula in which the derivatives of the function also appear is of the form

$$\int_{-1}^{1} f(x) dx = C_1 f(x_1) + \cdots + C_p f(x_p) + D_1 f'(x_1') + \cdots \\ + D_r f'(x_r') + E_1 f''(x_1'') + \cdots + E_s f''(x_s'') + \cdots \tag{7.358}$$

Such a relation may or may not have certain imposed points, but we must be careful because the system which is obtained may be without solutions.

As a first example, let us consider a Gauss formula of the form

$$\int_{-1}^{1} f(x) dx = Cf(y) + Df'(y), \tag{7.359}$$

where the unknowns are C, D, and y. We have

$$\int_{-1}^{1} dx = 2 = C, \quad \int_{-1}^{1} x \, dx = 0 = Cy + D, \quad \int_{-1}^{1} x^2 dx = \frac{2}{3} = Cy^2 + 2Dy. \tag{7.360}$$

From the first relation (7.360) it follows that $C = 2$, and from the second one we get $D = -Cy = -2y$, which replaced in the last expression (7.360), leads to

$$\frac{2}{3} = 2y^2 - 2y^2 = 0, \tag{7.361}$$

which is absurd; hence, we cannot have such a Gauss formula.

Let us now search a Gauss formula of the form

$$\int_{-1}^{1} f(x) dx = Cf(-1) + Df(1) + Ef'(y), \tag{7.362}$$

in which the unknowns are C, D, E, and y. We have

$$\int_{-1}^{1} dx = 2 = C + D, \quad \int_{-1}^{1} x\,dx = 0 = -C + D + E,$$
$$\int_{-1}^{1} x^2\,dx = \frac{2}{3} = C + D + 2Ey, \quad \int_{-1}^{1} x^3\,dx = 0 = -C + D + 3Ey^2. \tag{7.363}$$

It follows that successively

$$C = 2 - D, \quad E = C - D = 2 - 2D, \tag{7.364}$$

$$\frac{2}{3} = 2 + 2(2 - 2D)y, \quad 2D - 2 + 3(2 - 2D)y^2 = 0, \tag{7.365}$$

from which

$$y = \frac{1}{3(D-1)}, \quad y^2 = \frac{1}{9(D-1)^2}, \tag{7.366}$$

$$y^2 = \frac{2 - 2D}{3(2 - 2D)} = \frac{1}{3}. \tag{7.367}$$

For $y = 1/\sqrt{3}$, we obtain the values

$$(D-1)^2 = \frac{1}{3}, \quad D = 1 + \frac{1}{\sqrt{3}}, \quad \text{or} \quad D = 1 - \frac{1}{\sqrt{3}}, \tag{7.368}$$

$$E = -\frac{2}{\sqrt{3}} \quad \text{or} \quad E = \frac{2}{\sqrt{3}}, \tag{7.369}$$

$$C = 1 - \frac{1}{\sqrt{3}} \quad \text{or} \quad C = 1 + \frac{1}{\sqrt{3}} \tag{7.370}$$

as well as the quadrature formulae

$$\int_{-1}^{1} f(x)dx = \left(1 - \frac{1}{\sqrt{3}}\right) f(-1) + \left(1 + \frac{1}{\sqrt{3}}\right) f(1) - \frac{2}{\sqrt{3}} f'\left(\frac{1}{\sqrt{3}}\right), \tag{7.371}$$

$$\int_{-1}^{1} f(x)dx = \left(1 + \frac{1}{\sqrt{3}}\right) f(-1) + \left(1 - \frac{1}{\sqrt{3}}\right) f(1) + \frac{2}{\sqrt{3}} f'\left(\frac{1}{\sqrt{3}}\right). \tag{7.372}$$

For $y = -1/\sqrt{3}$, the formulae read

$$\int_{-1}^{1} f(x)dx = \left(1 - \frac{1}{\sqrt{3}}\right) f(-1) + \left(1 + \frac{1}{\sqrt{3}}\right) f(1) - \frac{2}{\sqrt{3}} f'\left(-\frac{1}{\sqrt{3}}\right), \tag{7.373}$$

$$\int_{-1}^{1} f(x)dx = \left(1 + \frac{1}{\sqrt{3}}\right) f(-1) + \left(1 - \frac{1}{\sqrt{3}}\right) f(1) + \frac{2}{\sqrt{3}} f'\left(-\frac{1}{\sqrt{3}}\right). \tag{7.374}$$

7.16 CALCULATION OF IMPROPER INTEGRALS

We will exemplify, in this paragraph, the methods described in Section 7.4 for the calculation of the improper integrals.

We consider the integral

$$I = \int_0^\infty \frac{dx}{(x+2)\sqrt{x+1}}. \tag{7.375}$$

The integral may be written in the form

$$I = \int_0^\infty xe^{-x} \frac{dx}{xe^{-x}(x+2)\sqrt{x+1}}; \tag{7.376}$$

we may apply the Gauss–Laguerre quadrature formula

$$I \approx 0.589 f(0.9358) + 0.391 f(3.3050) + 0.020 f(7.7598), \tag{7.377}$$

where

$$f(x) = \frac{e^x}{x(x+2)\sqrt{x+1}}. \tag{7.378}$$

It follows that

$$f(0.9358) \approx 0.667, \quad f(3.3050) \approx 0.749, \quad f(7.7598) \approx 10.459, \tag{7.379}$$

$$I \approx 0.895. \tag{7.380}$$

By the change of variable

$$x = u - 2, \quad dx = du, \tag{7.381}$$

it follows that

$$I = \int_2^\infty \frac{du}{u\sqrt{u-1}}. \tag{7.382}$$

By a new change of variable

$$u = \frac{1}{v}, \quad du = -\frac{1}{v^2}dv, \tag{7.383}$$

the integral takes the form

$$I = \int_{\frac{1}{2}}^0 \frac{-\frac{1}{v^2}dv}{\frac{1}{v}\sqrt{\frac{1}{v}-1}} = \int_0^{\frac{1}{2}} \frac{dv}{\sqrt{v(v-1)}}. \tag{7.384}$$

By a new change of variable

$$v = \frac{w+1}{4}, \quad dv = \frac{1}{4}dw, \tag{7.385}$$

it follows that

$$I = \int_{-1}^1 \frac{dw}{\sqrt{w+1}\sqrt{3-w}}. \tag{7.386}$$

We may apply the Gauss quadrature formula in three points, obtaining

$$I \approx \frac{5}{9} f\left(-\sqrt{\frac{3}{5}}\right) + \frac{8}{9} f(0) + \frac{5}{9} f\left(\sqrt{\frac{3}{5}}\right), \tag{7.387}$$

where

$$f(w) = \frac{1}{\sqrt{w+1}\sqrt{3-w}}, \tag{7.388}$$

$$f\left(-\sqrt{\frac{3}{5}}\right) \approx 0.9734, \quad f(0) \approx 0.5774, \quad f\left(\sqrt{\frac{3}{5}}\right) \approx 0.5032, \tag{7.389}$$

$$I \approx 1.3336. \tag{7.390}$$

If we wish to apply the Gauss–Jacobi quadrature formula in three points, we calculate successively

$$f\left(-\sqrt{\frac{3}{7}}\right) \approx 1.5147, \quad f(0) \approx 0.5774, \quad f\left(\sqrt{\frac{3}{7}}\right) \approx 0.3946, \tag{7.391}$$

$$I \approx \frac{7}{9} f\left(-\sqrt{\frac{3}{7}}\right) + \frac{4}{9} f(0) + \frac{7}{9} f\left(\sqrt{\frac{3}{7}}\right) \approx 1.7416. \tag{7.392}$$

Returning to relation (7.382) of the integral, we observe that the asymptotic behavior of the function

$$f(u) = \frac{1}{u\sqrt{u-1}} \tag{7.393}$$

is given by the function

$$g(u) = \frac{1}{u\sqrt{u}} = u^{-\frac{3}{2}}. \tag{7.394}$$

Calculating $(a > 0)$

$$\int_a^\infty g(u)du = \left(-2u^{-\frac{1}{2}}\right)\Big|_a^\infty = \frac{2}{\sqrt{a}}, \tag{7.395}$$

we observe that the integral (7.395) may be made as small as we wish by conveniently choosing a. For example, let, $a = 100$. We may write

$$\int_2^\infty \frac{du}{u\sqrt{u-1}} = \int_2^{100} \frac{du}{u\sqrt{u-1}} + \int_{100}^\infty \frac{du}{u\sqrt{u-1}} \approx \int_2^{100} \frac{du}{u\sqrt{u-1}} + \int_{100}^\infty \frac{du}{u^{\frac{3}{2}}}$$

$$= 0.2 + \int_2^{100} \frac{du}{u\sqrt{u-1}}. \tag{7.396}$$

By the change of variable

$$u = 49v + 51, \quad du = 49dv, \tag{7.397}$$

the last integral (7.396) becomes

$$\int_2^{100} \frac{du}{u\sqrt{u-1}} = \int_{-1}^1 \frac{49dv}{(49v+51)\sqrt{49v+50}}. \tag{7.398}$$

Applying the Gauss quadrature formula in three points to the last integral

$$f(v) = \frac{49}{(49v + 51)\sqrt{49v + 50}}, \tag{7.399}$$

$$f\left(-\sqrt{\frac{3}{5}}\right) \approx 1.0823, \quad f(0) \approx 0.1359, \quad f\left(\sqrt{\frac{3}{5}}\right) \approx 0.0587, \tag{7.400}$$

we get

$$\int_{-1}^{1} \frac{49\,dv}{(49v + 51)\sqrt{49v + 50}} \approx 0.7455, \tag{7.401}$$

$$I \approx 0.9455. \tag{7.402}$$

In form (7.384), this integral may be easily calculated; it has the value

$$I = (\arcsin(2v))|_0^{\frac{1}{2}} = \frac{\pi}{2} \approx 1.5708. \tag{7.403}$$

We remark that the values thus obtained are sensibly different from the exact value (7.403). The precision may be improved by using Gauss quadrature formulae in several points; but we are thus led to an increased calculation time.

7.17 KANTOROVICH'S METHOD

The idea of this method[15] consists in writing

$$I = \int_a^b f(x)dx \tag{7.404}$$

in the form

$$I = \int_a^b g(x)dx + \int_a^b (f(x) - g(x))dx, \tag{7.405}$$

where the first integral is directly calculated, while the second one is calculated by numerical formulae.

Let us return, by exemplifying, to the example of the preceding paragraph written in the form

$$I = \int_0^{\frac{1}{2}} \frac{dx}{\sqrt{x}\sqrt{1 - x}}. \tag{7.406}$$

The function

$$f(x) = \frac{1}{\sqrt{x}\sqrt{1 - x}} \tag{7.407}$$

is not defined for $x = 0$.

We expand into series the function

$$\phi(x) = \frac{1}{\sqrt{1 - x}} \tag{7.408}$$

---

[15]The method was described by Leonid Vitaliyevich Kantorovich (1912–1986).

around $x = 0$; it follows that

$$\phi(x) = 1 + \frac{1}{2}x + \frac{3}{4}x^2 + \frac{5}{16}x^3 + \frac{35}{128}x^4 + \cdots \qquad (7.409)$$

We get

$$I = \int_0^{\frac{1}{2}} x^{-\frac{1}{2}}\,dx + \frac{1}{2}\int_0^{\frac{1}{2}} x^{\frac{1}{2}}\,dx + \frac{3}{8}\int_0^{\frac{1}{2}} x^{\frac{3}{2}}\,dx + \frac{5}{16}\int_0^{\frac{1}{2}} x^{\frac{5}{2}}\,dx + \frac{35}{128}\int_0^{\frac{1}{2}} x^{\frac{7}{2}}\,dx + J$$

$$= 1.5691585 + J, \qquad (7.410)$$

where J is the integral

$$J = \int_0^{\frac{1}{2}} \left[\frac{1}{\sqrt{1-x}} - \left(1 + \frac{1}{2}x + \frac{3}{8}x^2 + \frac{5}{16}x^3 + \frac{35}{128}x^4 + \cdots \right) \right] dx. \qquad (7.411)$$

This last integral is no more an improper one and may be calculated as usual, for example, by the trapezoid formula with the step $h = 0.1$.

Denoting

$$\psi(x) = \frac{1}{\sqrt{1-x}} - \left(1 + \frac{1}{2}x + \frac{3}{8}x^2 + \frac{5}{16}x^3 + \frac{35}{128}x^4 \right), \qquad (7.412)$$

we have

$$\psi(0) = 0, \quad \psi(0.1) = 2.7 \times 10^{-6}, \quad \psi(0.2) = 9.65 \times 10^{-5}, \qquad (7.413)$$

$$\psi(0.3) = 8.263 \times 10^{-4}, \quad \psi(0.4) = 0.0039944, \quad \psi(0.5) = 0.0143112,$$

$$J \approx \frac{0.1}{2}[\psi(0) + 2(\psi(0.1) + \psi(0.2) + \psi(0.3) + \psi(0.4)) + \psi(0.5)] = 0.001208. \qquad (7.414)$$

It follows that

$$I \approx 1.50916 + 0.00121 = 1.57037, \qquad (7.415)$$

which is a value very close to the exact one $I = \pi/2$.

7.18   THE MONTE CARLO METHOD FOR CALCULATION OF DEFINITE INTEGRALS

Hereafter, we consider firstly the one-dimensional case, generalizing then for the multidimensional case.

7.18.1   The One-Dimensional Case

Let us suppose that we must calculate the integral

$$I = \int_a^b f(x)\,dx, \qquad (7.416)$$

where a and b are two finite real numbers, $a < b$, while f is continuous and positive on $[a, b]$.

With the change of variable

$$x = a + (b-a)t, \quad dx = (b-a)dt, \qquad (7.417)$$

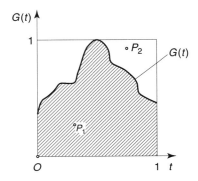

Figure 7.4   The Monte Carlo method in the one-dimensional case.

the integral I reads

$$I = \int_0^1 F(t)\mathrm{d}t, \tag{7.418}$$

where

$$F(t) = (b-a)f(a+(b-a)t), \tag{7.419}$$

Let

$$M = \max_{t\in[0,1]} F(t), \tag{7.420}$$

so that the integral I may be put in the form

$$I = M\int_0^1 \frac{F(t)}{M}\mathrm{d}t = M\int_0^1 G(t)\mathrm{d}t. \tag{7.421}$$

The function G is definite on the interval $[0, 1]$ and takes values in the same interval. Graphically, this is shown in Figure 7.4.

Denoted by A the hatched area in Figure 7.4, it follows that the integral I has the form

$$I = MA. \tag{7.422}$$

Obviously, if the value M given by relation (7.420) is difficult to determine, then, we may take a covering value for M.

Hence, it follows that the determination of the value of the integral has been reduced to the determination of the area A. To do this, we generate pairs (x, y) of aleatory numbers, uniformly distributed in the interval $[0, 1]$, resulting in the points $P_1(x_1, y_1)$, $P_2(x_2, y_2)$, ..., $P_n(x_n, y_n)$. We index the entire variable s by 0. If the point $P_i(x_i, y_i)$ is in the interior of the hatched area (the case of the point P_1 in Fig. 7.4), then the variable s is incremented by a unit; in the opposite case (the case of the point P_2 in Fig. 7.4), the variable s remains unchanged. Finally, the area A is approximated by the formula

$$A \approx \frac{s}{n}, \tag{7.423}$$

where n is the number of generatings. Obviously,

$$A = \lim_{n\to\infty} \frac{s}{n}. \tag{7.424}$$

Observation 7.18

(i) If the function f changes of sign in the interval $[a, b]$, then we divide the interval $[a, b]$ in subintervals on which the function f keeps a constant sign; thus we apply the described method on each such interval.

(ii) If $F(t)$ is negative on the interval $[0, 1]$, then we choose

$$M = \min_{t \in [0,1]} F(t) \tag{7.425}$$

and it follows that $G : [0, 1] \to [0, 1]$; the procedure may be applied.

7.18.2   The Multidimensional Case

Let the function be

$$y = f(x_1, x_2, \ldots, x_n), \tag{7.426}$$

continuous on the closed domain $\mathcal{D}$ of $\mathbb{R}^n$ and the integral

$$I = \iint_{\mathcal{D}} \cdots \int f(x_1, x_2, \ldots, x_n) dx_1\, dx_2 \cdots dx_n. \tag{7.427}$$

The domain $\mathcal{D}$ may be included in the n-dimensional hyperparallelepiped

$$[a_1, b_1] \times [a_2, b_2] \times \cdots \times [a_n, b_n] \supseteq \mathcal{D} \tag{7.428}$$

We make the change of variable

$$x_i = a_i + (b_i - a_i)\xi_i, \quad i = \overline{1, n}, \tag{7.429}$$

from which

$$\frac{D(x_1, x_2, \ldots, x_n)}{D(\xi_1, \xi_2, \ldots, \xi_n)} = \begin{vmatrix} b_1 - a_1 & 0 & \cdots & 0 \\ 0 & b_2 - a_2 & \cdots & 0 \\ \cdots & \cdots & \cdots & \cdots \\ 0 & 0 & \cdots & b_n - a_n \end{vmatrix} = \prod_{i=1}^{n}(b_i - a_i); \tag{7.430}$$

the integral I becomes

$$I = \iint_{\mathcal{E}} \cdots \int F(\xi_1, \xi_2, \ldots, \xi_n) d\xi_1\, d\xi_2 \cdots d\xi_n, \tag{7.431}$$

where $\mathcal{E}$ marks the n-dimensional hypercube

$$\mathcal{E} = [0, 1] \times [0, 1] \times \cdots \times [0, 1], \tag{7.432}$$

while

$$F(\xi_1, \xi_2, \ldots, \xi_n) = \prod_{i=1}^{n}(b_i - a_i) f(a_1 + (b_1 - a_1)\xi_1, \ldots, a_n + (b_n - a_n)\xi_n). \tag{7.433}$$

We generate groups of n aleatory numbers uniformly distributed in the interval $[0, 1]$. Let $g = (g_1, g_2, \ldots, g_n)$ be such a group. The point $P(g_1, g_2, \ldots, g_n)$ may be found in the interior of the transform of the domain $\mathcal{D}$ by the changes of variables (7.429), case in which it must be taken in consideration with the value $F(g_1, g_2, \ldots, g_n)$. Let us denote by S the set of all the points of this kind obtained by N generations of groups of aleatory uniformly distributed numbers. We define the value

$$y_{\text{med}} = \frac{1}{|S|} \sum_{g \in S} F(g), \tag{7.434}$$

where $|S|$ is the cardinal number of S, $F(g) = F(g_1, g_2, \ldots, g_n)$, while $g = (g_1, g_2, \ldots, g_n)$ is the group of n uniformly distributed aleatory numbers. For the integral I follows that the approximate value

$$I \approx \frac{1}{N} \sum_{g \in S} F(g). \tag{7.435}$$

If the function $F(\xi_1, \xi_2, \ldots, \xi_n)$ is positive, then we may consider the integral (7.433) as defining the volume of the body in a $(n + 1)$-dimensional space given by

$$0 \le \xi_i \le 1, \quad i = \overline{1, \, n}, \quad 0 \le y \le F(\xi). \tag{7.436}$$

We may find a real positive number B for which $0 \le F(\xi) \le B$. We introduce variable

$$\eta = \frac{1}{B} y, \tag{7.437}$$

so that the integral I now becomes

$$I = \iint_{\mathcal{E} \times [0,1]} \cdots \int d\xi_1 \, d\xi_2 \cdots d\xi_n d\eta \tag{7.438}$$

and is equal to the volume of a hypercylinder interior to the $(n + 1)$-dimensional hypercube given by $\mathcal{E} \times [0, 1]$.

Now, we also generate groups of uniformly distributed aleatory numbers in the interval $[0, 1]$; but, in this case, a group will contain $n + 1$ uniformly distributed aleatory numbers. If we denote by S the set of groups which define points in the interior of the hypercylinder, then

$$I \approx B \frac{|S|}{N}, \tag{7.439}$$

where N is the number of generations of such groups.

Observation 7.19

(i) If as a consequence of the generation of a group of aleatory numbers it follows that a point is raised on the frontier of the domain, then this may be considered as a valid point, which is definite by a group of, or on the contrary, it is possible to not take it into consideration. Obviously, immaterial of how we consider such a point, passing to the limit for the number of generations $N \to \infty$, we obtain the searched value of the integral.

(ii) The method supposes that we may determine if a group g is a part or not a part of the set S. If the frontier of the domain $\mathcal{D}$ is described by complicated expressions, then the validation of a group g may take sufficient time, so that the method is quite slow.

7.19 NUMERICAL EXAMPLES

Example 7.1 Let us consider the function $f : [0, 3] \to \mathbb{R}$,

$$f(x) = e^x(\sin x + \cos^2 x), \tag{7.440}$$

for which the values in the following table are known.

x_i	$y_i = f(x_i)$
0	1
0.5	2.060204
1.2	3.530421
1.8	6.203722
2.3	11.865576
3.0	22.520007

We wish to determine approximations for the values of the derivatives $f'(x)$ and $f''(x)$ in the interior division knots and to compare these values with the real values.

The derivative of the function f is given by

$$f'(x) = e^x(\sin x + \cos x + x\cos^2 x - \sin 2x), \tag{7.441}$$

$$f''(x) = e^x(2\cos x + \cos^2 x - 2\sin 2x - 2\cos 2x). \tag{7.442}$$

For the knot $x_1 = 0.5$ we have

$$h = x_1 - x_0 = 0.5, \quad h_1 = x_2 - x_1 = 0.7 = 1.4h \tag{7.443}$$

and it follows that

$$f'(x) \approx \frac{1}{(\alpha + 1)h}(f(x_2) - f(x_0)) = \frac{1}{(1.4 + 1)0.5}(3.530421 - 1) = 2.10868 \tag{7.444}$$

$$f''(x) \approx \frac{1}{\alpha(\alpha + 1)h}(f(x_2) - f(x_0) - (1 + \alpha)f(x_1))$$

$$= \frac{2}{1.4 \times 2.4 \times 0.5}(3.530421 + 1.4 \times 1 - 2.4 \times 2.060204) = -0.01675. \tag{7.445}$$

The exact values are

$$f'(x) = 2.11974, \quad f''(x_1) = -0.39278. \tag{7.446}$$

The calculations are given in the following table.

x_i	y_i	approx $f'(x_i)$	exact $f'(x_i)$	approx $f''(x_i)$	exact $f''(x_i)$
0	1		2		1
0.5	2.060204	2.10868	2.11974	−0.01675	−0.39278
1.2	3.530411	3.18732	2.49087	2.53636	3.25332
1.8	6.203722	9.09290	7.50632	7.49259	13.76763
2.3	11.865576	13.59690	15.13127	3.24742	13.19643
3.0	22.520007		8.24769		47.43018

Example 7.2   Let $f : [0, 4] \to \mathbb{R}$,

$$f(x) = \frac{\sin x}{1 + \cos^2 x} \tag{7.447}$$

and the equidistant division knots $x_0 = 0$, $x_1 = 1$, $x_2 = 2$, $x_3 = 3$, $x_4 = 4$.

Approximate values of the derivatives $f'(x_i)$, $f''(x_i)$, $i = \overline{1, 3}$, as well as of the derivatives $f'(0.5)$, $f''(0.4)$, $f'(3.7)$, $f''(3.73)$ are asked.

We construct the table of finite differences.

x_i	$y_i = f(x_i)$	Δy_i	$\Delta^2 y_i$	$\Delta^3 y_i$	$\Delta^4 y_i$
0	0	0.651330	−0.527588	−0.299956	1.229384
1	0.651330	0.123742	−0.827544	0.929824	
2	0.775072	−0.703802	0.102280		
3	0.071270	−0.601522			
4	−0.530252				

If we use an expansion into a Taylor series, then we obtain the following results:

$$f'(1) \approx \frac{f(2) - f(0)}{2} = 0.387536,$$

$$f'(2) \approx \frac{f(3) - f(1)}{2} = -0.290030, \tag{7.448}$$

$$f'(3) \approx \frac{f(4) - f(2)}{2} = -0.652662,$$

$$f''(1) \approx \frac{f(0) + f(2) - 2f(1)}{1^2} = -0.527588,$$

$$f''(2) \approx \frac{f(1) + f(3) - 2f(2)}{1^2} = -0.827544, \tag{7.449}$$

$$f''(3) \approx \frac{f(2) + f(4) - 2f(3)}{1^2} = 0.102280.$$

The Newton forward and backward interpolation polynomials read

$$P_1(q_1) = y_0 + \frac{q_1^{(1)}}{1!} \Delta y_0 + \frac{q_1^{(2)}}{2!} \Delta^2 y_0 + \frac{q_1^{(3)}}{3!} \Delta^3 y_0 + \frac{q_1^{(4)}}{4!} \Delta^4 y_0, \tag{7.450}$$

$$P_2(q_2) = y_4 + \frac{q_2^{(1)}}{1!} \Delta y_3 + \frac{(q_2 + 1)^{(2)}}{2!} \Delta^2 y_2 + \frac{(q_2 + 2)^{(3)}}{3!} \Delta^3 y_1 + \frac{(q_2 + 3)^{(4)}}{4!} \Delta^4 y_2, \tag{7.451}$$

respectively, where

$$q_1 = \frac{x - x_0}{h}, \quad q_2 = \frac{x - x_n}{h}. \tag{7.452}$$

We deduce the following values:

- for $x = 0.5$:

$$q_1 = \frac{0.5 - 0}{1} = 0.5, \tag{7.453}$$

$$f'(0.5) \approx \frac{1}{1} \left[\Delta y_0 + \frac{q_1^{(1)}}{1!} \Delta^2 y_0 + \frac{q_1^{(2)}}{2!} \Delta^3 y_0 + \frac{q_1^{(3)}}{3!} \Delta^4 y_0 \right] = 0.501867; \tag{7.454}$$

- for $x = 0.4$:

$$q = \frac{0.4 - 0}{1} = 0.4, \tag{7.455}$$

$$f''(0.4) \approx \frac{1}{1^2} \left[\Delta^2 y_0 + \frac{q_1^{(1)}}{1!} \Delta^3 y_0 + \frac{q_1^{(2)}}{2!} \Delta^4 y_0 \right] = -0.801243; \tag{7.456}$$

- for $x = 3.7$:

$$q_2 = \frac{3.7 - 0}{1} = -0.3, \tag{7.457}$$

$$f'(3.7) \approx \frac{1}{1} \left[\Delta y_3 + \frac{(q_2 + 1)^{(1)}}{1!} \Delta^2 y_2 + \frac{(q_2 + 2)^{(2)}}{2!} \Delta^3 y_1 + \frac{(q_2 + 3)^{(3)}}{3!} \Delta^4 y_0 \right] = 0.681654, \tag{7.458}$$

- for $x = 3.73$:

$$q_2 = \frac{3.73 - 4}{1} = -0.27, \tag{7.459}$$

$$f'(3.73) \approx \frac{1}{1^2} \left[\Delta^2 y_2 + \frac{(q_2 + 2)^{(1)}}{1!} \Delta^3 y_1 + \frac{(q_2 + 3)^{(2)}}{2!} \Delta^4 y_0 \right] = 4.614004. \tag{7.460}$$

On the other hand,

$$f'(x) = \frac{\cos x (2 + \sin^2 x)}{(1 + \cos^2 x)^2}, \tag{7.461}$$

$$f''(x) = \frac{\sin x (1 + 7\cos^2 x - 4\sin^2 x)}{(1 + \cos^2 x)^3} \tag{7.462}$$

and the exact values of the function and of its first two derivative are given in the following table.

x	$f(x)$	$f'(x)$	$f''(x)$
0	0	0.5	0
0.4	0.2102684	0.876641	0.422211
0.5	0.270839	0.624515	0.534146
1	0.651330	0.876641	0.405069
2	0.775072	−0.854707	−0.294121
3	0.071270	−0.510032	0.142858
3.7	−0.308174	−0.654380	−0.596319
3.73	−0.328049	−0.670677	−0.633525
4	−0.530252	−0.8255541	−0.697247

These two examples show:

- (i) the method that uses the expansion into a Taylor series is more precise than the one which uses interpolation polynomials;
- (ii) the derivative of first order is more precisely calculated as that of second order;
- (iii) the numerical derivative does not offer a good precision.

Example 7.3   Let

$$I = \int_1^2 x \sin dx. \tag{7.463}$$

We shall give approximations of the integral I using various numerical methods. The integral I may be directly calculated, obtaining the value

$$I = (-x \cos x + \sin x)|_1^2 = 1.4404224. \tag{7.464}$$

To apply the trapezium method, we take the division step $h = 0.1$, obtaining the following data.

x_i	$y_i = f(x_i)$
1	0.8414710
1.1	0.9803281
1.2	1.1184469
1.3	1.2526256
1.4	1.3796296
1.5	1.4962425
1.6	1.5993178
1.7	1.6858302
1.8	1.7529257
1.9	1.7979702
2.0	1.8185949

It follows that

$$I \approx \frac{0.1}{2}(f(1) + 2(f(1,1) + f(1,2) + \cdots + f(1,9)) + f(2)) = 1.4393350. \tag{7.465}$$

The same problem may be solved by using Simpson's formula obtaining

$$I \approx \frac{0.1}{3}(f(1) + 2(f(1.2) + f(1.4) + f(1.6) + f(1.8)) \\ + 4(f(1.1) + f(1.3) + f(1.5) + f(1.7) + f(1.9)) + f(2)) = 1.4404233. \tag{7.466}$$

Let us consider the transformation

$$x = \frac{1}{2}y + \frac{3}{2}, \quad dx = \frac{1}{2}dy. \tag{7.467}$$

Now, the integral I reads

$$I = \int_{-1}^{1} \frac{y+3}{2} \sin\left(\frac{y+3}{2}\right) \frac{dy}{2}. \tag{7.468}$$

We shall determine the Chebyshev quadrature formulae for the cases $n = 2$, $n = 3$, and $n = 4$, applying them to the integral (7.468).

In the case $n = 2$ we obtain

$$A_1 = A_2 = 1 \tag{7.469}$$

and the system

$$x_1 + x_2 = 0, \quad x_1^2 + x_2^2 = \frac{2}{3}, \tag{7.470}$$

which it results in Chebyshev's formula

$$I = \int_{-1}^{1} f(x)dx \approx f\left(-\frac{1}{\sqrt{3}}\right) + f\left(\sqrt{\frac{1}{3}}\right) \tag{7.471}$$

and, numerically,

$$I \approx 1.440144. \tag{7.472}$$

If $n = 3$, then we deduce the values

$$A_1 = A_2 = A_3 = \frac{2}{3} \tag{7.473}$$

and the system

$$x_1 + x_2 + x_3 = 0, \quad x_1^2 + x_2^2 + x_3^2 = 1, \quad x_1^3 + x_2^3 + x_3^3 = 0, \tag{7.474}$$

with the solution

$$x_1 = -\sqrt{\frac{1}{2}}, \quad x_2 = 0, \quad x_3 = \sqrt{\frac{1}{2}}. \tag{7.475}$$

Chebyshev's formula reads

$$I = \int_{-1}^{1} f(x)dx \approx \frac{2}{3}\left[f\left(-\sqrt{\frac{1}{2}}\right) + f(0) + f\left(\sqrt{\frac{1}{2}}\right)\right], \tag{7.476}$$

leading to the value

$$I \approx 1.440318. \tag{7.477}$$

Finally, in the case $n = 4$ we obtain the values

$$A_1 = A_2 = A_3 = A_4 = \frac{1}{2} \tag{7.478}$$

and the system

$$\begin{aligned} x_1 + x_2 + x_3 + x_4 = 0, \quad & x_1^2 + x_2^2 + x_3^2 + x_4^2 = \frac{4}{3}, \\ x_1^3 + x_2^3 + x_3^3 + x_4^3 = 0, \quad & x_1^4 + x_2^4 + x_3^4 + x_4^4 = \frac{4}{5}, \end{aligned} \tag{7.479}$$

with the solution

$$x_1 = -0.79466, \quad x_2 = -0.18759, \quad x_3 = 0.18759, \quad x_4 = 0.79466. \tag{7.480}$$

The integral I will have the value

$$I = \int_{-1}^{1} f(x)dx \approx 0.5(f(-0.79466) + f(-0.18759) + f(0.18759) + f(0.79466)), \tag{7.481}$$

hence

$$I \approx 1.440422. \tag{7.482}$$

The same integral I at equation (7.468) may be calculated by quadrature formulae of Gauss type. To do this, we determine firstly the Legendre polynomials:

$$P_0(x) = 1, \tag{7.483}$$

$$P_1(x) = \frac{1}{2 \times 1!} \frac{d^2(x^2 - 1)}{dx} = x, \tag{7.484}$$

$$P_2(x) = \frac{1}{2^2 \times 2!} \frac{d^2[(x^2 - 1)^2]}{dx^2} = \frac{1}{2}(3x^2 - 1), \tag{7.485}$$

$$P_3(x) = \frac{1}{2^3 \times 3!} \frac{d^3[(x^2 - 1)^3]}{dx^3} = \frac{1}{2}(5x^3 - 3x), \tag{7.486}$$

$$P_4(x) = \frac{1}{2^4 \times 4!} \frac{d^4[(x^2 - 1)^4]}{dx^4} = \frac{1}{8}(35x^4 - 30x^2 + 3), \ldots \tag{7.487}$$

The roots of these polynomials are

- for $P_1(x)$:

$$x_1 = 0; \tag{7.488}$$

- for $P_2(x)$:

$$x_1 = -\sqrt{\frac{1}{3}}, \quad x_2 = \sqrt{\frac{1}{3}}; \tag{7.489}$$

- for $P_3(x)$:

$$x_1 = -\sqrt{\frac{3}{5}}, \quad x_2 = 0, \quad x_3 = \sqrt{\frac{3}{5}}; \tag{7.490}$$

- for $P_4(x)$:

$$x_1 = -\sqrt{\frac{30 + \sqrt{480}}{70}}, \quad x_2 = -\sqrt{\frac{30 - \sqrt{480}}{70}}, \quad x_3 = -\sqrt{\frac{30 - \sqrt{480}}{70}}, \quad x_4 = \sqrt{\frac{30 + \sqrt{480}}{70}}. \tag{7.491}$$

In the case $n = 2$ we obtain the system

$$A_1 + A_2 = 2, \quad -A_1\sqrt{\frac{1}{3}} + A_2\sqrt{\frac{1}{3}} = 0, \tag{7.492}$$

with the solution

$$A_1 = 1, \quad A_2 = 1; \tag{7.493}$$

it results in the quadrature formula

$$I = \int_{-1}^{1} f(x)dx \approx f\left(-\sqrt{\frac{1}{3}}\right) + f\left(\sqrt{\frac{1}{3}}\right), \tag{7.494}$$

which is Chebyshev's quadrature formula (7.471), leading to the same value (7.472) for I.

In the case $n = 3$ we obtain the system

$$A_1 + A_2 + A_3 = 2, \quad -\sqrt{\frac{3}{5}}A_1 + \sqrt{\frac{3}{5}}A_3 = 0, \quad \frac{3}{5}A_1 + \frac{2}{5}A_3 = \frac{2}{3}, \tag{7.495}$$

with the solution

$$A_1 = \frac{5}{9}, \quad A_2 = \frac{8}{9}, \quad A_3 = \frac{5}{9} \tag{7.496}$$

and the formula

$$I = \int_{-1}^{1} f(x)dx \approx \frac{5}{9}f\left(-\sqrt{\frac{3}{5}}\right) + \frac{8}{9}f(0) + \frac{5}{9}f\left(\sqrt{\frac{3}{5}}\right), \tag{7.497}$$

from which

$$I \approx 1.440423. \tag{7.498}$$

For $n = 4$ we obtain the system

$$A_1 + A_2 + A_3 + A_4 = 2, \quad A_1 x_1 + A_2 x_2 + A_3 x_3 + A_4 x_4 = 0,$$
$$A_1 x_1^2 + A_2 x_2^2 + A_3 x_3^2 + A_4 x_4^2 = \frac{2}{3}, \quad A_1 x_1^3 + A_2 x_2^3 + A_3 x_3^3 + A_4 x_4^3 = 0, \tag{7.499}$$

with x_1, x_2, x_3, and x_4 given by equation (7.491). The solution of this system is

$$A_1 = A_4 = \frac{x_3^2 - \frac{1}{3}}{x_3^2 - x_4^2} = 0.3478548, \quad A_2 = A_3 = \frac{x_4^2 - \frac{1}{3}}{x_4^2 - x_3^2} = 0.6521452, \tag{7.500}$$

leading to the quadrature formula

$$I = \int_{-1}^{1} f(x)dx \approx 0.3478548 f(x_1) + 0.6521452 f(x_2)$$
$$+ 0.6521452 f(x_3) + 0.3478548 f(x_4) \tag{7.501}$$
$$= 0.3478548[f(-0.8611363) + f(0.8611363)]$$
$$+ 0.6521452[f(-0.3399810) + f(0.3399810)],$$

from which

$$I \approx 1.440422. \tag{7.502}$$

Another possibility of determination of the integral (7.463) is by the use of the Monte Carlo method. To do this, we denote by $f(x)$ the function $f : [1, 2] \to \mathbb{R}$,

$$f(x) = x \sin x, \tag{7.503}$$

the derivative of which is

$$f'(x) = \sin x - x \cos x. \tag{7.504}$$

The equation $f'(x) = 0$ leads to

$$x = \tan x, \tag{7.505}$$

without solution in the interval $[1, 2]$.

Moreover, $f'(x) > 0$ for any $x \in [1, 2]$. We deduce that the maximum value of the function f takes place at the point 2, while the minimum value of the same function takes place at the point 1; we may write

$$\max f = f(2) = 1.818595, \quad \min f = f(1) = 0.841471. \tag{7.506}$$

We shall generate pairs of aleatory numbers (a, b), where a is an aleatory number uniformly distributed in the interval $[1, 2]$, while b is an aleatory number uniformly distributed in the interval $[0, 2]$. The value b is then compared with $f(a)$. If $b < f(a)$, then the pair (a, b) is taken into consideration; otherwise it is eliminated.

We have made 1000 generations of the following form.

Step	a	b	$f(a)$	Counter
1	1.644	1.958	1.639597	0
2	1.064	1.622	0.930259	0
3	1.622	1.414	1.619874	1
4	1.521	0.606	1.519115	2
5	1.212	0.600	1.134820	3
6	1.303	1.086	1.256556	3
7	1.856	0.872	1.781026	4
8	1.648	1.648	1.643091	4
9	1.713	0.702	1.695709	5
10	1.000	1.288	0.841471	5

We obtained the result

$$I \approx 1.456. \tag{7.507}$$

To apply Euler's or Gregory's formulae, we may calculate first Bernoulli's numbers. Writing

$$e^t - 1 = t + \frac{t^2}{2!} + \frac{t^3}{3!} + \frac{t^4}{4!} + \frac{t^5}{5!} + \cdots \tag{7.508}$$

and

$$\frac{t}{e^t - 1} = B_0 + B_1 t + \frac{B_2}{2!} t^2 + \frac{B_3}{3!} t^3 + \frac{B_4}{4!} t^4 + \frac{B_5}{5!} t^5 + \cdots, \tag{7.509}$$

it follows that

$$t = \left(B_0 + B_1 t + \frac{B_2}{2} t^2 + \frac{B_3}{6} t^3 + \frac{B_4}{24} t^4 + \frac{B_5}{120} t^5 + \cdots \right)$$
$$\times \left(t + \frac{t^2}{2} + \frac{t^3}{6} + \frac{t^4}{24} + \frac{t^5}{120} + \cdots \right), \tag{7.510}$$

hence

$$B_0 = 1, \quad \frac{B_0}{2} + B_1 = 0, \quad \frac{B_0}{6} + \frac{B_1}{2} + \frac{B_2}{2} = 0,$$
$$\frac{B_0}{24} + \frac{B_1}{6} + \frac{B_2}{4} + \frac{B_3}{6} = 0, \quad \frac{B_0}{120} + \frac{B_1}{24} + \frac{B_2}{12} + \frac{B_3}{12} + \frac{B_4}{24} = 0, \ldots, \tag{7.511}$$

from which

$$B_0 = 1, \quad B_1 = -\frac{1}{2}, \quad B_2 = \frac{1}{6}, \quad B_3 = 0, \quad B_4 = -\frac{1}{30}, \ldots \tag{7.512}$$

On the other hand,

$$f'(x) = x \cos x + \sin x, \tag{7.513}$$

$$f''(x) = -x \sin x + 2 \cos x, \tag{7.514}$$

$$f'''(x) = -x \cos x - 3 \sin x. \tag{7.515}$$

The first formula of Euler leads to

$$\int_1^2 f(x)\mathrm{d}x \approx h \sum_{i=0}^9 f(x_i) - h \sum_{i=1}^4 \frac{B_i}{i!} h^{i-1} [f^{(i-1)}(2) + f^{(i-1)}(1)], \tag{7.516}$$

where

$$f(2) = 1.8185949, \quad f(1) = 0.8414710, \tag{7.517}$$

$$f'(2) = 0.077004, \quad f'(1) = 1.381773, \tag{7.518}$$

$$f''(2) = -2.650889, \quad f''(1) = 0.239134, \tag{7.519}$$

$$f'''(2) = -1.895599, \quad f'''(1) = -3.064715. \tag{7.520}$$

It follows that

$$I \approx 1.38428. \tag{7.521}$$

Analogically, we may use the second formula of Euler or Gregory's formula too.
We have seen that the value of the considered integral, calculated by the trapezium method is

$$I_2 \approx 1.4393350. \tag{7.522}$$

If we would use only the points 1.0, 1.2, 1.4, 1.6, 1.8, and 2.0, then the value of the integral, calculated by the trapezium method too, would be

$$I_1 \approx \frac{0.2}{2}(f(1) + 2(f(1.2) + f(1.4) + f(1.6) + f(1.8)) + f(2)) = 1.4360706. \tag{7.523}$$

The Richardson extrapolation formula leads to the value

$$I = I_2 + \frac{I_2 - I_1}{2^2 - 1} = 1.440423. \tag{7.524}$$

7.20 APPLICATIONS

Problem 7.1

Let us consider the forward eccentric with pusher rod (Fig. 7.5) of a heat engine; the motion law of the valve is given by $\bar{s} = \bar{s}(\phi)$, where ϕ is the rotation angle of the cam.
Let us determine

- the law of motion of the follower;
- the parametric equations of the cam;
- the variation of the curvature radius of the cam, in numerical values.

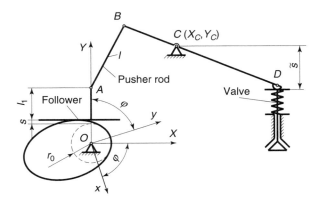

Figure 7.5   Distribution mechanism.

We know

$$
\widetilde{s} =
\begin{cases}
0 \text{ for } \phi \in \left[0, \dfrac{\pi}{2}\right) \\[2mm]
h(1 + \cos 2\phi) \text{ for } \phi \in \left[\dfrac{\pi}{2}, \dfrac{3\pi}{2}\right], \\[2mm]
0 \text{ for } \phi \in \left(\dfrac{3\pi}{2}, 2\pi\right]
\end{cases}
\tag{7.525}
$$

$h = 4$ mm, $CD = a = 3$ mm, $CB = b = 20$ mm, $AB = l = 70$ mm, $l_1 = 30.72$ mm, $r_0 = 10$ mm, $X_C = 30$ mm, $Y_C = 110$ mm.

Solution:

1. Theory
Denoting by θ the rotation angle of the rocker BD, we obtain the relation

$$
\theta = \arcsin \frac{\widetilde{s}}{a}.
\tag{7.526}
$$

The coordinates of the points A, B in the OXY-system (Fig. 7.5) read

$$
\begin{aligned}
X_A &= 0, \quad Y_A = r_0 + l_1 + s, \\
X_B &= X_C - b \cos \theta, \quad Y_B = Y_C + b \sin \theta;
\end{aligned}
\tag{7.527}
$$

under these conditions, taking into account the relations

$$
(X_C - b)^2 + (Y_C - r_0 - l_1)^2 - l^2 = 0
\tag{7.528}
$$

and using the notations

$$
\alpha = b \sin \theta + Y_C - r_0 - l_1,
\tag{7.529}
$$

$$
\beta = 2b[(Y_C - r_0 - l_1) \sin \theta + X_C(1 - \cos \theta)],
\tag{7.530}
$$

the relation

$$
(X_B - X_A)^2 + (Y_B - Y_A)^2 - l^2 = 0
\tag{7.531}
$$

leads to the equation

$$
s^2 - 2\alpha s + \beta = 0,
\tag{7.532}
$$

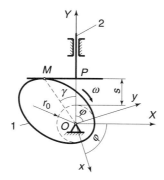

Figure 7.6   Parametric equations of the cam.

the solution of which

$$s = \alpha - \sqrt{\alpha^2 - \beta}$$

(7.533)

represents the law of motion of the follower.

The numerical solution is obtained by giving to the angle ϕ values from degree to degree and by calculating the values of the parameters θ_i, α_i, β_i, s_i, $i = \overline{0, 360}$, by means of relations (7.526), (7.529), (7.530), and (7.533).

To establish the parametric equations of the cam in the proper system of axes (Fig. 7.6), the relation between the absolute velocity $\mathbf{v}_{M_2}$, the transportation velocity $\mathbf{v}_{M_1}$, and the relative velocity $\mathbf{v}_{M_2 M_1}$ of the point M_2 is written in the form

$$\mathbf{v}_{M_2} = \mathbf{v}_{M_1} + \mathbf{v}_{M_2 M_1};$$

(7.534)

projecting on the Oy-axis, we obtain

$$\omega \frac{\mathrm{d}s}{\mathrm{d}\phi} = \omega OM \sin \gamma$$

(7.535)

or

$$MP = \frac{\mathrm{d}s}{\mathrm{d}\phi},$$

(7.536)

where ω is the angular velocity of the cam. Under these conditions, the coordinates x, y of the point M are

$$x = -(r_0 + s) \sin \phi - \frac{\mathrm{d}s}{\mathrm{d}\phi} \cos \phi,$$

(7.537)

$$y = (r_0 + s) \cos \phi - \frac{\mathrm{d}s}{\mathrm{d}\phi} \sin \phi,$$

(7.538)

while the curvature radius

$$R = \frac{\left[\left(\frac{\mathrm{d}x}{\mathrm{d}\phi} \right)^2 + \left(\frac{\mathrm{d}y}{\mathrm{d}\phi} \right)^2 \right]^{\frac{3}{2}}}{\frac{\mathrm{d}^2 x}{\mathrm{d}\phi^2} \frac{\mathrm{d}y}{\mathrm{d}\phi} - \frac{\mathrm{d}^2 y}{\mathrm{d}\phi^2} \frac{\mathrm{d}x}{\mathrm{d}\phi}}$$

(7.539)

becomes

$$R = r + s + \frac{\mathrm{d}^2 s}{\mathrm{d}\phi^2}.$$

(7.540)

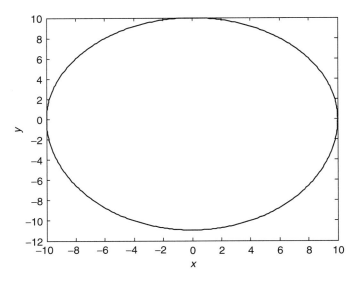

Figure 7.7   Representation of the cam.

2. Numerical calculation

For a numerical calculation, we give to the angle ϕ_i, $i = \overline{0, 360}$, values from degree in degree; thus we calculate successively the parameters $\widetilde{s}_i$, θ_i, α_i, β_i, s_i, x_i, y_i, R_i by means of relations (7.525), (7.526), (7.529), (7.530), (7.533), (7.537), (7.538), and (7.540), where for the derivatives $ds/d\phi$, $d^2s/d\phi^2$ we use finite differences

$$\frac{ds}{d\phi}\Big|_{\phi=\phi_i} = \frac{s_{i+1} - s_{i-1}}{2}\frac{180}{\pi}, \tag{7.541}$$

$$\frac{d^2s}{d\phi^2}\Big|_{\phi=\phi_i} = (s_{i+1} - 2s_i + s_{i-1})\left(\frac{180}{\pi}\right)^2. \tag{7.542}$$

The results obtained for $\phi = 0°$, $\phi = 10°$, ..., $\phi = 360°$ are given in Table 7.2.

The representation of the cam is given in Figure 7.7.

If the radius r_0 of the basis circle is small, then it is possible that the curvature radius becomes negative; the cam is no more useful from a technical point of view in this case. To avoid this situation, we increase the radius r_0 of the basis circle.

Problem 7.2

Let the equation of nondamped free nonlinear vibrations be

$$\ddot{x} + f(x) = 0, \tag{7.543}$$

where $f(x)$ is an odd function

$$f(x) = \begin{cases} \dfrac{p^2 x^n}{l^{n+1}} & \text{if } x \geq 0 \\ \dfrac{p^2}{l^{n+1}}(-1)^{n-1}x^n & \text{if } x < 0 \end{cases}. \tag{7.544}$$

It is asked to show that the period of vibrations is given by

$$T_n = \frac{4}{p}\sqrt{\frac{(n+1)l^{n-1}}{2A^{n-1}}}I_n, \tag{7.545}$$

TABLE 7.2   Numerical Results

ϕ_i	$\widetilde{s}_i$	θ_i	α_i	β_i	s_i	$\dfrac{ds}{d\phi}$	$\dfrac{d^2s}{d\phi^2}$	x_i	y_i	R_i
0	0.000	0.000	69.280	0.000	0.000	0.000	0.000	0.000	10.000	10.000
10	0.000	0.000	69.280	0.000	0.000	0.000	0.000	−1.736	9.848	10.000
20	0.000	0.000	69.280	0.000	0.000	0.000	0.000	−3.420	9.397	10.000
30	0.000	0.000	69.280	0.000	0.000	0.000	0.000	−5.000	8.660	10.000
40	0.000	0.000	69.280	0.000	0.000	0.000	0.000	−6.428	7.660	10.000
50	0.000	0.000	69.280	0.000	0.000	0.000	0.000	−7.660	6.428	10.000
60	0.000	0.000	69.280	0.000	0.000	0.000	0.000	−8.660	5.000	10.000
70	0.000	0.000	69.280	0.000	0.000	0.000	0.000	−9.397	3.420	10.000
80	0.000	0.000	69.280	0.000	0.000	0.000	0.000	−9.848	1.736	10.000
90	0.000	0.000	69.280	0.000	0.000	0.008	0.931	−10.000	−0.008	10.931
100	0.241	0.080	69.308	3.890	0.028	0.318	1.750	−9.820	−2.055	11.778
110	0.936	0.312	69.389	15.105	0.109	0.599	1.430	−9.295	−4.020	11.539
120	2.000	0.667	69.513	32.326	0.233	0.807	0.937	−8.458	−5.816	11.170
130	3.305	1.102	69.665	53.512	0.385	0.919	0.330	−7.365	−7.379	10.715
140	4.695	1.565	69.826	76.135	0.547	0.920	−0.318	−6.075	−8.671	10.229
150	6.000	2.000	69.978	97.464	0.700	0.810	−0.931	−4.648	−9.671	9.769
160	7.064	2.355	70.102	114.904	0.824	0.602	−1.432	−3.137	−10.377	9.393
170	7.759	2.587	70.183	126.311	0.906	0.320	−1.760	−1.578	−10.796	9.146
180	8.000	2.668	70.211	130.278	0.934	0.000	−1.874	0.000	−10.934	9.060
190	7.759	2.587	70.183	126.311	0.906	−0.320	−1.760	1.578	−10.796	9.146
200	7.064	2.355	70.102	114.904	0.824	−0.602	−1.432	3.137	−10.377	9.393
210	6.000	2.000	69.978	97.464	0.700	−0.810	−0.931	4.648	−9.671	9.769
220	4.695	1.565	69.826	76.135	0.547	−0.920	−0.318	6.075	−8.671	10.229
230	3.305	1.102	69.665	53.512	0.385	−0.919	0.330	7.365	−7.379	10.715
240	2.000	0.667	69.513	32.326	0.233	−0.807	0.937	8.458	−5.816	11.170
250	0.936	0.312	69.389	15.105	0.109	−0.599	1.430	9.295	−4.020	11.539
260	0.241	0.080	69.308	3.890	0.028	−0.318	1.750	9.820	−2.055	11.778
270	0.000	0.000	69.280	0.000	0.000	−0.008	0.931	10.000	−0.008	10.931
280	0.000	0.000	69.280	0.000	0.000	0.000	0.000	9.848	1.736	10.000
290	0.000	0.000	69.280	0.000	0.000	0.000	0.000	9.397	3.420	10.000
300	0.000	0.000	69.280	0.000	0.000	0.000	0.000	8.660	5.000	10.000
310	0.000	0.000	69.280	0.000	0.000	0.000	0.000	7.660	6.428	10.000
320	0.000	0.000	69.280	0.000	0.000	0.000	0.000	6.428	7.660	10.000
330	0.000	0.000	69.280	0.000	0.000	0.000	0.000	5.000	8.660	10.000
340	0.000	0.000	69.280	0.000	0.000	0.000	0.000	3.420	9.397	10.000
350	0.000	0.000	69.280	0.000	0.000	0.000	0.000	1.736	9.848	10.000
360	0.000	0.000	69.280	0.000	0.000	0.000	0.000	0.000	10.000	10.000

where

$$I_n = \int_0^1 \frac{d\beta}{\sqrt{1 - \beta^{n+1}}}, \tag{7.546}$$

for the initial conditions are

$$t = 0, \quad x = A, \quad \dot{x} = 0. \tag{7.547}$$

Determine numerically the periods T_1, T_2, T_3, T_4, T_5 for $A = l/\lambda$, λ positive.

Solution:

1. Theory
The differential equation (7.543), written in the form

$$\dot{x}\,d(\dot{x}) + f(x)dx = 0, \tag{7.548}$$

is integrated in the form

$$\frac{\dot{x}^2}{2} + \int_0^x f(\xi)d\xi = C_1, \tag{7.549}$$

the integration constant C_1 being specified by the initial conditions in the form

$$C_1 = \int_0^A f(\xi)d\xi, \tag{7.550}$$

from which relation (7.549) becomes

$$\dot{x}^2 = 2\int_x^A f(\xi)d\xi. \tag{7.551}$$

From the very beginning, the velocity $\dot{x}$ is negative, hence

$$\dot{x} = -\sqrt{2\int_x^A f(\xi)d\xi}, \tag{7.552}$$

so that

$$dt = -\frac{dx}{\sqrt{2\int_x^A f(\xi)d\xi}}, \tag{7.553}$$

hence

$$t = -\int_0^x \frac{d\eta}{\sqrt{2\int_\eta^A f(\xi)d\xi}} + C_2. \tag{7.554}$$

Taking into account the initial given conditions, it follows that

$$C_2 = \int_0^A \frac{d\eta}{\sqrt{2\int_\eta^A f(\xi)d\xi}}, \tag{7.555}$$

from which the relation becomes

$$t = \int_x^A \frac{d\eta}{\sqrt{2\int_\eta^A f(\xi)d\xi}}. \tag{7.556}$$

For $x = 0$ in equation (7.556), we obtain the time $T/4$ (a quarter of the period), therefore

$$T = 4 \int_0^A \frac{d\eta}{\sqrt{2 \int_\eta^A f(\xi)d\xi}};$$ (7.557)

replacing $f(\xi)$ by $(p^2/l^{n+1})\xi^n$, we obtain

$$T = \frac{4}{p} \sqrt{\frac{(n+1)l^{n+1}}{2}} \int_0^A \frac{d\eta}{\sqrt{A^{n+1} - \eta^{n+1}}},$$ (7.558)

so that the substitution $\eta = A\beta$ leads to

$$T = \frac{4}{p} \sqrt{\frac{(n+1)l^{n+1}}{2A^{n+1}}} I_n,$$ (7.559)

where I_n is the integral (7.546).

2. Numerical results

Numerically, we obtain the values:
- with Gauss formula in two points

$$I_1 = 1.328412, \quad T_1 = 5.3137 \frac{\lambda}{p}, \quad I_2 = 1.202903,$$

$$T_2 = 5.8930 \frac{\lambda^{\frac{3}{2}}}{p}, \quad I_3 = 1.139060, \quad T_3 = 6.3977 \frac{\lambda^2}{p},$$ (7.560)

$$I_4 = 1.099923, \quad T_4 = 6.9565 \frac{\lambda^{\frac{5}{2}}}{p}, \quad I_5 = 1.073808, \quad T_5 = 7.4603 \frac{\lambda^3}{p};$$

- with Gauss formula in three points

$$I_1 = 1.395058, \quad T_1 = 5.5802 \frac{\lambda}{p}, \quad I_2 = 1.259053,$$

$$T_2 = 6.1681 \frac{\lambda^{\frac{3}{2}}}{p}, \quad I_3 = 1.187340, \quad T_3 = 6.7166 \frac{\lambda^2}{p},$$ (7.561)

$$I_4 = 1.143415, \quad T_4 = 7.2316 \frac{\lambda^{\frac{5}{2}}}{p}, \quad I_5 = 1.113941, \quad T_5 = 7.7176 \frac{\lambda^3}{p};$$

- with Gauss formula in four points

$$I_1 = 1.434062, \quad T_1 = 5.7362 \frac{\lambda}{p}, \quad I_2 = 1.290703,$$

$$T_2 = 6.3231 \frac{\lambda^{\frac{3}{2}}}{p}, \quad I_3 = 1.214628, \quad T_3 = 6.8710 \frac{\lambda^2}{p},$$ (7.562)

$$I_4 = 1.167633, \quad T_4 = 7.3848 \frac{\lambda^{\frac{5}{2}}}{p}, \quad I_5 = 1.135837, \quad T_5 = 7.8693 \frac{\lambda^3}{p}.$$

Problem 7.3

We consider the equation of nondamped free vibrations

$$\ddot{x} + f(x) = 0, \tag{7.563}$$

where

$$f(x) = \begin{cases} f_1(x), & \text{if } x \leq 0, \\ f_2(x), & \text{if } x > 0, \end{cases} \tag{7.564}$$

and

$$f_1(0) = f_2(0) = 0, \quad f_1(x) \leq 0. \tag{7.565}$$

Show that the period is given by

$$T = 2 \int_{A_1}^{0} \frac{d\eta}{\sqrt{2 \int_{\eta}^{A_1} f_1(\xi) d\xi}} + 2 \int_{0}^{A_2} \frac{d\eta}{\sqrt{2 \int_{\eta}^{A_2} f_2(\xi) d\xi}}, \tag{7.566}$$

where the distance A_1 is specified by the equation

$$\int_{-A_1}^{0} f(x) dx + \int_{0}^{A_2} f(x) dx = 0, \tag{7.567}$$

for the initial conditions

$$t = 0, \quad x = A_2, \quad \dot{x} = 0, \quad A_2 > 0. \tag{7.568}$$

Numerical application for $A_2 = 0.25$ and

$$f(x) = \begin{cases} -6x^2 & \text{if } x \leq 0, \\ 6x + 64x^3 & \text{if } x > 0. \end{cases} \tag{7.569}$$

Solution:

1. Theory
Applying the theorem of kinetic energy and work on the interval BC (Fig. 7.8) and observing that the kinetic energy at the points B and C vanishes, we obtain relation (7.567).

Starting from the point B (Fig. 7.8), the particle travels through the direction BO in the time interval t_2 given by the relation (7.556) of Problem 7.2, where x is replaced by 0, $f(x)$ by $f_2(x)$ and A by A_2, so that

$$t_2 = \int_{0}^{A_2} \frac{d\eta}{\sqrt{2 \int_{\eta}^{A_2} f_2(\xi) d\xi}}. \tag{7.570}$$

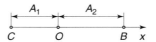

Figure 7.8   Problem 7.3.

In the study of the motion from the point C toward the point O, we obtain

$$\frac{\dot{x}^2}{2} + \int_0^x f_1(\xi)d\xi = C_1, \tag{7.571}$$

the initial conditions $t = 0$, $x = -A_1$, $\dot{x} = 0$ leading to

$$C_1 = \int_0^{A_1} f_1(\xi)d\xi, \tag{7.572}$$

so that

$$\dot{x}^2 = 2\int_x^{-A_1} f_1(\xi)d\xi; \tag{7.573}$$

because the velocity is $\dot{x} > 0$, it follows that

$$\dot{x} = \sqrt{2\int_x^{-A_1} f_1(\xi)d\xi}, \tag{7.574}$$

from which

$$t = \int_0^x \frac{d\eta}{\sqrt{2\int_\eta^{-A_1} f_1(\xi)d\xi}} + C_2. \tag{7.575}$$

The initial conditions lead, successively, to

$$C_2 = -\int_0^{-A_1} \frac{d\eta}{\sqrt{2\int_\eta^{-A_1} f_1(\xi)d\xi}}, \tag{7.576}$$

$$t = \int_{-A_1}^x \frac{d\eta}{\sqrt{2\int_\eta^{-A_1} f_1(\xi)d\xi}}, \tag{7.577}$$

obtaining the time of traveling through the distance CO (equal to the time corresponding to the distance OC)

$$t_1 = \int_{-A_1}^0 \frac{d\eta}{\sqrt{2\int_\eta^{-A_1} f_1(\xi)d\xi}}. \tag{7.578}$$

Summing the times t_1 and t_2 given by relations (7.578) and (7.570), we obtain half of the period $(T/2)$, hence the relation (7.566).

2. Numerical calculation

Relations (7.567) and (7.569) lead to

$$\int_{-A_1}^0 (-6x^2)dx + \int_0^{A_2} (6x + 64x^3)dx = 0, \tag{7.579}$$

$$-2A_1^3 + 3A_2^2 + 16A_2^4 = 0; \tag{7.580}$$

because $A_2 = 0.25$, it follows that $A_1 = 0.5$, so that we obtain successively

$$\int_\eta^{-A_1} f_1(\xi)d\xi = 2(\eta^3 + 0.125), \tag{7.581}$$

$$\int_\eta^{A_2} f_2(\xi)d\xi = 0.25 - 3\eta^2 - 16\eta^4, \tag{7.582}$$

$$T = 2\int_{-0.5}^0 \frac{d\eta}{\sqrt{4(\eta^3 + 0.125)}} + 2\int_0^{0.25} \frac{d\eta}{\sqrt{2(0.25 - 3\eta^2 - 16\eta^4)}}, \tag{7.583}$$

so that

$$T = 2.668799 \text{ s}, \tag{7.584}$$

where, for the calculation of the integrals we use Gauss formula in four points.

Problem 7.4

Let us consider the crankshaft mechanism in Figure 7.9, where:

- the crank OA has the length r, while the moment of inertia with respect to the point O is equal to J_1;
- the shaft AB is a homogeneous bar of length l, of constant cross section, of mass m_2 and moment of inertia with respect to the center of gravity $J_2 = m_2 l^2/12$;
- the rocker in B has the mass m_3.

The crank OA is acted by a moment M

$$M = \begin{cases} M_0 & \text{if } 0 \le \phi \le \pi, \\ -M_0 & \text{if } \pi < \phi \le 2\pi, \end{cases} \tag{7.585}$$

and the motion of the mechanism is in a phased regimen, the mean angular velocity of the crank being ω_m.

We ask to determine

- the variation of the angular velocity ω of the crank OA as function of the angle ϕ;
- the irregularity degree δ_0 of the motion;
- the moment of inertia J_v of a fly wheel rigidly linked to the crank OA, so that the irregularity degree δ be equal to $\delta_0/4$.

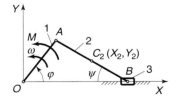

Figure 7.9   Problem 7.4.

Numerical application: $\omega_m = 100$ rad s^{-1}, $r = 0.04$ m, $l = 0.2$ m, $J_1 = 0.00016$ kg m^2, $m_2 = 1.2$ kg, $J_2 = 0.004$ kg m^2, $m_3 = 0.8$ kg, $M_0 = 4$ N m.

Solution:

1. Theory

Denoting by X_2, Y_2 the coordinates of the point C_2 and by X_3 the distance OB, the kinetic energy of the mechanism is

$$T = \frac{1}{2}J_1\omega^2 + \frac{1}{2}J_2\left(\frac{d\psi}{d\phi}\right)^2\omega^2 + \frac{1}{2}m_2\left[\left(\frac{dX_2}{d\phi}\right)^2 + \left(\frac{dY_2}{d\phi}\right)^2\right]\omega^2 + \frac{1}{2}m_3\left(\frac{dX_3}{d\phi}\right)^2\omega^2 \qquad (7.586)$$

or with the notation

$$J_{red}(\phi) = J_1 + J_2\left(\frac{d\psi}{d\phi}\right)^2 + m_2\left[\left(\frac{dX_2}{d\phi}\right)^2 + \left(\frac{dY_2}{d\phi}\right)^2\right] + m_3\left(\frac{dX_3}{d\phi}\right)^2, \qquad (7.587)$$

$$T = \frac{1}{2}J_{red}(\phi)\omega^2. \qquad (7.588)$$

The numerical computation of the moment of inertia $J_{red}(\phi)$ is made by the successive relations

$$\psi = \arcsin\left(\frac{r\sin\phi}{l}\right), \qquad (7.589)$$

$$\frac{d\psi}{d\phi} = \frac{r\cos\phi}{l\cos\psi}, \qquad (7.590)$$

$$\frac{dX_2}{d\phi} = -r\sin\phi - \frac{l}{2}\frac{d\psi}{d\phi}\sin\psi, \qquad (7.591)$$

$$\frac{dY_2}{d\phi} = \frac{l}{2}\frac{d\psi}{d\phi}\cos\psi, \qquad (7.592)$$

$$\frac{dX_3}{d\phi} = -r\sin\phi - l\frac{d\psi}{d\phi}\sin\psi. \qquad (7.593)$$

Applying the theorem of the kinetic energy between the position in which $\phi = 0$, $J_{red}(0) = J_1 + m_2 r^2/3$, $\omega(0) = \omega_0$ and an arbitrary position, we obtain the equality

$$J_{red}(\phi)\omega^2 - J_0\omega_0^2 = 2L(\phi), \qquad (7.594)$$

where

$$L(\phi) = \int_0^\phi M\,d\phi = \begin{cases} M_0\phi & \text{if } 0 \le \phi \le \pi, \\ M_0(2\pi - \phi) & \text{if } \pi < \phi \le 2\pi. \end{cases} \qquad (7.595)$$

The motion is periodic, because $L(2\pi) = 0$, $L(2\pi) = L(0)$, the period being $\phi_d = 2\pi$. From equation (7.594), we deduce

$$\omega(\phi) = \sqrt{\frac{2L(\phi) + J_0\omega_0^2}{J_{red}(\phi)}}, \qquad (7.596)$$

while the mean angular velocity is given by

$$\omega_m = \frac{1}{2\pi}\int_0^{2\pi}\sqrt{\frac{2L(\phi) + J_0\omega_0^2}{J_{red}(\phi)}}\,d\phi. \qquad (7.597)$$

From equation (7.597), we obtain the unknown ω_0.

We take as approximate value of start $\omega = \omega_m$, and with the notation

$$F(\omega_0) = \frac{1}{2\pi} \int_0^{2\pi} \sqrt{\frac{2L(\phi) + J_0\omega_0^2}{J_{red}(\phi)}} \, d\phi - \omega_m, \tag{7.598}$$

applying Newton's method, it follows that

$$\Delta\omega_0 = -\frac{\displaystyle\int_0^{2\pi} \sqrt{\frac{2L(\phi) + J_0\omega_0^2}{J_{red}(\phi)}} \, d\phi - 2\pi\omega_m}{\displaystyle\int_0^{2\pi} \sqrt{\frac{J_{red}(\phi)}{2L(\phi) + J_0\omega_0^2}} \frac{J_0\omega_0}{J_{red}(\phi)} \, d\phi} \tag{7.599}$$

and the iterative process continues till $|\Delta\omega_0| < 0.01$.

From the graphic representation of the function $\omega(\phi)$, we obtain the values ω_{min}, ω_{max} and it follows that

$$\delta = \frac{\omega_{max} - \omega_{min}}{\omega_m}. \tag{7.600}$$

Adding the fly wheel of moment of inertia J_v, relation (7.598) becomes

$$F(\omega_0) = \frac{1}{2\pi} \int_0^{2\pi} \sqrt{\frac{2L(\phi) + (J_0 + J_v)\omega_0^2}{J_{red}(\phi) + J_v}} \, d\phi - \omega_m. \tag{7.601}$$

We consider $\Delta J_v = J_0/10$ and we calculate ω_0, ω_{min}, ω_{max}, δ for the set of values ΔJ_v, $2\Delta J_v$, $\dots$, comparing δ with $\delta_0/4$. The function $\delta(J_v)$ is decreasing.

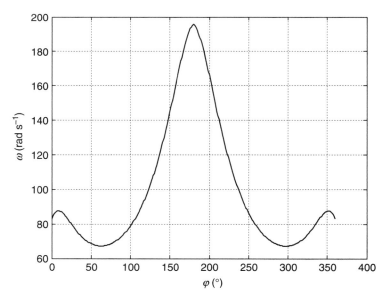

Figure 7.10 Diagram $\omega = \omega(\phi)$.

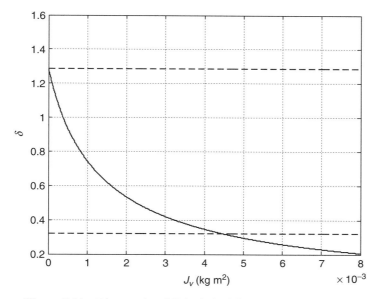

Figure 7.11   Diagram $\delta = \delta(J_v)$; dashed lines mark δ_0 and $\delta_0/4$.

2. Numerical calculation

We obtain the results plotted in the diagrams in Figure 7.10 and Figure 7.11.

It follows that

$$\omega_{min} = 67.2455 \text{ rad s}^{-1}, \quad \omega_{max} = 195.8535 \text{ rad s}^{-1}, \quad \delta_0 = 1.2861, \quad J_v \approx 4.5 \text{ kg m}^2. \quad (7.602)$$

FURTHER READING

Acton FS (1990). Numerical Methods that Work. 4th ed. Washington: Mathematical Association of America.

Ackleh AS, Allen EJ, Hearfott RB, Seshaiyer P (2009). Classical and Modern Numerical Analysis: Theory, Methods and Practice. Boca Raton: CRC Press.

Atkinson KE (1989). An Introduction to Numerical Analysis. 2nd ed. New York: John Wiley & Sons, Inc.

Atkinson KE (2003). Elementary Numerical Analysis. 2nd ed. New York: John Wiley & Sons, Inc.

Bakhvalov N (1976). Méthodes Numérique. Moscou: Editions Mir (in French).

Berbente C, Mitran S, Zancu S (1997). Metode Numerice. Bucureşti: Editura Tehnică (in Romanian).

Burden RL, Faires L (2009). Numerical Analysis. 9th ed. Boston: Brooks/Cole.

Butt R (2009). Introduction to Numerical Analysis Using MATLAB. Boston: Jones and Bartlett Publishers.

Chapra SC (1996). Applied Numerical Methods with MATLAB for Engineers and Scientists. Boston: McGraw-Hill.

Cheney EW, Kincaid DR (1997). Numerical Mathematics and Computing. 6th ed. Belmont: Thomson.

Dahlquist G, Björck Å (1974). Numerical Methods. Englewood Cliffs: Prentice Hall.

Davis JD, Rabinowitz P (2007). Methods of Numerical Integration. 2nd ed. New York: Dover Publications.

Démidovitch B, Maron I (1973). Éléments de Calcul Numérique. Moscou: Editions Mir (in French).

DiBenedetto E (2010). Classical Mechanics: Theory and Mathematical Modeling. New York: Springer-Verlag.

Epperson JF (2007). An Introduction to Numerical Methods and Analysis. Hoboken: John Wiley & Sons, Inc.

Fung YC, Tong P (2011). Classical and Computational Solid Mechanics. Singapore: World Scientific Publishing.

Gautschi W (1997). Numerical Analysis: An Introduction. Boston: Birkhäuser.

Greenbaum A, Chartier TP (2012). Numerical Methods: Design, Analysis, and Computer Implementation of Algorithms. Princeton: Princeton University Press.

Hamming RW (1987). Numerical Methods for Scientists and Engineers. 2nd ed. New York: Dover Publications.

Hamming RW (2012). Introduction to Applied Numerical Analysis. New York: Dover Publications.

Heinbockel JH (2006). Numerical Methods for Scientific Computing. Victoria: Trafford Publishing.

Hildebrand FB (1987). Introduction to Numerical Analysis. 2nd ed. New York: Dover Publications.

Hoffman JD (1992). Numerical Methods for Engineers and Scientists. New York: McGraw-Hill.

Kharab A, Guenther RB (2011). An Introduction to Numerical Methods: A MATLAB Approach. 3rd ed. Boca Raton: CRC Press.

Kleppner D, Kolenkow RJ (2010). An Introduction to Mechanics. Cambridge: Cambridge University Press.

Kress R (1996). Numerical Analysis. New York: Springer-Verlag.

Krîlov AN (1957). Lecţii de Calcule prin Aproximaţii. Bucureşti: Editura Tehnică (in Romanian).

Kunz KS (1957). Numerical Analysis. New York: McGraw-Hill.

Lange K (2010). Numerical Analysis for Statisticians. 2nd ed. New York: Springer-Verlag.

Lurie AI (2002). Analytical Mechanics. New York: Springer-Verlag.

Mabie HH, Reinholtz CF (1987). Mechanisms and Dynamics of Machinery. 4th ed. New York: John Wiley & Sons, Inc.

Marciuk GI (1983). Metode de Analiză Numerică. Bucureşti: Editura Academiei Române (in Romanian).

Meriam JL, Kraige LG (2012). Engineering Mechanics: Dynamics. Hoboken: John Wiley & Sons, Inc.

Otto SR, Denier JP (2005). An Introduction to Programming and Numerical Methods in MATLAB. London: Springer-Verlag.

Palm WJ III (2007). Mechanical Vibrations. Hoboken: John Wiley & Sons, Inc.

Pandrea N, Popa D (2000). Mecanisme. Teorie şi Aplicaţii CAD. Bucureşti: Editura Tehnică (in Romanian).

Pandrea N (2000). Elemente de Mecanica Solidului în Coordonate Plückeriene. Bucureşti: Editura Academiei Române (in Romanian).

Pandrea N, Stănescu ND (2002). Mecanică. Bucureşti: Editura Didactică şi Pedagogică (in Romanian).

Postolache M (2006). Modelare Numerică. Teorie şi Aplicaţii. Bucureşti: Editura Fair Partners (in Romanian).

Press WH, Teukolski SA, Vetterling WT, Flannery BP (2007). Numerical Recipes: The Art of Scientific Computing. 3rd ed. Cambridge: Cambridge University Press.

Quarteroni A, Sacco R, Saleri F (2010). Numerical Mathematics. 2nd ed. Berlin: Springer-Verlag.

Ralston A, Rabinowitz P (2001). A First Course in Numerical Analysis. 2nd ed. New York: Dover Publications.

Ridgway Scott L (2011). Numerical Analysis. Princeton: Princeton University Press.

Salvadori MG, Baron ML (1962). Numerical Methods in Engineering. Englewood Cliffs: Prentice Hall.

Sauer T (2011). Numerical Analysis. 2nd ed. London: Pearson.

Simionescu I, Dranga M, Moise V (1995). Metode Numerice în Tehnică. Aplicaţii în FORTRAN. Bucureşti: Editura Tehnică (in Romanian).

Sinha AK (2010). Vibration of Mechanical Systems. Cambridge: Cambridge University Press.

Stănescu ND (2007). Metode Numerice. Bucureşti: Editura Didactică şi Pedagogică (in Romanian).

Stoer J, Bulirsh R (2010). Introduction to Numerical Analysis. 3rd ed. New York: Springer-Verlag.

Süli E, Mayers D (2003). An Introduction to Numerical Analysis. Cambridge: Cambridge University Press.

Udrişte C, Iftode V, Postolache M (1996). Metode Numerice de Calcul. Algoritmi şi Programe Turbo Pascal. Bucureşti: Editura Tehnică (in Romanian).

8

INTEGRATION OF ORDINARY DIFFERENTIAL EQUATIONS AND OF SYSTEMS OF ORDINARY DIFFERENTIAL EQUATIONS

This chapter presents the numerical methods for the integration of ordinary differential equations and of systems of differential equations. We thus present Euler's method, Taylor's method, the Runge–Kutta methods, the multistep methods, and the predictor–corrector methods. Finally, we close the chapter with some applications.

8.1 STATE OF THE PROBLEM

Let us consider the ordinary differential equation

$$\frac{\mathrm{d}\mathbf{x}}{\mathrm{d}t} = \mathbf{f}(t, \mathbf{x}), \tag{8.1}$$

where $\mathbf{x} \in \mathbb{R}^n$, $\mathbf{f} : \mathbb{R}^{n+1} \to \mathbb{R}$, and $t \in I$, with I interval on the real axis. We shall attach to equation (8.1) the initial condition

$$\mathbf{x}(t_0) = \mathbf{x}^0. \tag{8.2}$$

Relations (8.1) and (8.2) form the so-called Cauchy problem or the problem with initial values, which can be written in detail as

$$\frac{\mathrm{d}x_1}{\mathrm{d}t} = f_1(t, x_1, x_2, \ldots, x_n), \quad \frac{\mathrm{d}x_2}{\mathrm{d}t} = f_2(t, x_1, x_2, \ldots, x_n), \ldots, \quad \frac{\mathrm{d}x_n}{\mathrm{d}t} = f_n(t, x_1, x_2, \ldots, x_n), \tag{8.3}$$

to which we add

$$x_1(t_0) = x_1^0, \quad x_2(t_0) = x_2^0, \ldots, \quad x_n(t_0) = x_n^0. \tag{8.4}$$

Equation (8.1), to which we added the initial condition (8.2), is equivalent to the differential equation system (8.3), to which we add the initial conditions (8.4). It follows that we can thus treat the most general case of Cauchy problems (8.1) and (8.2).

Numerical Analysis with Applications in Mechanics and Engineering, First Edition.
Petre Teodorescu, Nicolae-Doru Stănescu, and Nicolae Pandrea.
© 2013 The Institute of Electrical and Electronics Engineers, Inc. Published 2013 by John Wiley & Sons, Inc.

The first question is to find the conditions under which Cauchy problems (8.1) and (8.2) have solutions, and especially solutions that are unique.

Theorem 8.1 (Of Existence and Uniqueness; Cauchy–Lipschitz[1]). Let $\mathbf{f} : I \times G \subset \mathbb{R} \times \mathbb{R}^n$ be continuous and Lipschitzian. Under these conditions, for any $t_0 \in I$ and $\mathbf{x}^0 \in G$, fixed, there exists a neighborhood $I_0 \times J_0 \times G_0 \in V_{\mathbb{R}^{n+2}}(t_0, t_0, \mathbf{x}_0)$ (i.e., a neighborhood in $\mathbb{R}^{n+2}$ for $(t_0, t_0, \mathbf{x}_0)$) with the propriety that $I_0 \times J_0 \times G_0 \subset I \times I \times G$ and that there exists a unique a function $\boldsymbol{\alpha} \in C^0 \left(I_0 \times J_0 \times G_0 \right)$ with the properties

$$\frac{d\boldsymbol{\alpha}(t \tau \boldsymbol{\xi}^0)}{dt} = \mathbf{f}(t, \boldsymbol{\alpha}(t \tau \boldsymbol{\xi}^0)), \tag{8.5}$$

for any $t \in I_0$, and

$$\boldsymbol{\alpha}(\tau, \tau, \boldsymbol{\xi}^0) = \boldsymbol{\xi}^0, \tag{8.6}$$

for any $(\tau, \boldsymbol{\xi}^0) \in (J_0 \times G_0)$.

Definition 8.1 We say that Cauchy problems (8.1) and (8.2) are correctly stated if

   (i) there exists a unique solution $\mathbf{x} = \mathbf{x}(t)$ of problems (8.1) and (8.2);

   (ii) there exists $\varepsilon > 0$ with the property that the problem

$$\frac{d\mathbf{z}}{dt} = \mathbf{f}(t, \mathbf{z}) + \boldsymbol{\delta}(t), \quad \mathbf{z}(0) = \mathbf{z}^0 = \mathbf{x}^0 + \boldsymbol{\varepsilon}^0 \tag{8.7}$$

admits a unique solution $\mathbf{z} = \mathbf{z}(t)$ for any $\boldsymbol{\varepsilon}^0$ with $\|\boldsymbol{\varepsilon}^0\| < \varepsilon$ and $\|\boldsymbol{\delta}(t)\| < \varepsilon$;

   (iii) there exists a constant $K > 0$ such that

$$\|\mathbf{z}(t) - \mathbf{x}(t)\| < K\varepsilon \tag{8.8}$$

for any $t \in I$.

Definition 8.2 Cauchy problem (8.7) is named the perturbed problem associated to Cauchy problems (8.1) and (8.2).

Corollary 8.1 Cauchy problems (8.1) and (8.2) are correctly stated problems under the conditions of the Cauchy–Lipschitz theorem.

Demonstration. The corollary is obvious considering ε, $\boldsymbol{\varepsilon}^0$ such that we do not leave the domain $I \times G$.

If we abandon the Lipschitz condition in the Cauchy–Lipschitz theorem, then we can prove only the existence of the solution of the Cauchy problem.

Theorem 8.2 (Of Existence; Peano[2]). Let $\mathbf{f} : I \times G \subset \mathbb{R} \times \mathbb{R}^n \to \mathbb{R}$ be continuous in $I \times G$. Under these conditions, for any $(t_0, \mathbf{x}^0) \in I \times G$ there exists a solution of Cauchy problems (8.1) and (8.2).

---

[1]The theorem is also known as Picard–Lindelöf theorem. It was called after Charles Émile Picard (1856–1941), Ernst Leonard Lindelöf (1870–1946), Rudolf Otto Sigismund Lipschitz (1832–1903), and Augustin–Louis Cauchy (1789–1857).
[2]Giuseppe Peano (1858–1932) proved this theorem in 1886.

Observation 8.1

(i) The Cauchy–Lipschitz and Peano theorems assure the existence and uniqueness or only the existence of the solution of the Cauchy problem, respectively, in a neighborhood of the initial conditions. In general, the solution can be extended without problems to intervals long enough, but there is no rule in this sense.

(ii) If we consider the ordinary differential equation

$$\frac{d^n y}{dt^n} = f\left(t, y, \frac{dy}{dt}, \frac{d^2 y}{dt^2}, \ldots, \frac{d^{n-1} y}{dt^{n-1}}\right),$$
(8.9)

with the conditions

$$y(0) = y_0, \quad \frac{dy}{dt}(0) = y_0', \quad \ldots, \quad \frac{d^{n-1} y}{dt^{n-1}}(0) = y_0^{(n-1)},$$
(8.10)

then, using the notations

$$x_1 = y, \quad x_2 = \frac{dy}{dt}, \quad \ldots, \quad x_n = \frac{d^{n-1} y}{dt^{n-1}},$$
(8.11)

we obtain the system

$$\frac{dx_2}{dt} = x_1, \quad \frac{dx_3}{dt} = x_2, \quad \ldots, \quad \frac{dx_{n-1}}{dt} = x_{n-2}, \quad \frac{dx_n}{dt} = f(t, x_1, x_2, \ldots, x_n),$$
(8.12)

for which the initial conditions are

$$x_1(0) = x_1^0 = y_0, \quad x_2(0) = x_2^0 = y_0', \quad \ldots, \quad x_n(0) = x_n^0 = y_0^{(n-1)}.$$
(8.13)

It thus follows that equation (8.9) is not a special case and that it can be considered in the frame of the general Cauchy problems (8.1) and (8.2).

(iii) The Cauchy–Lipschitz and Peano theorems give us sufficient conditions for the existence and uniqueness or only for the existence of the solution of Cauchy problems (8.1) and (8.2), respectively. Therefore, it does not mean that, if the hypotheses of these theorems are not satisfied, then the Cauchy problem has no solution or that the solution is not unique.

Let us consider, for instance, the problem of a ball that falls on the surface of the Earth, the restitution coefficient being k. The mechanical problem is simple, and if we denote by h_0 the initial height of the ball, then it will collide with the Earth, at a speed $v_0 = \sqrt{2gh_0}$; after the collision, it will have the speed $v' = v_1 = kv_0$ (Fig. 8.1). The new height reached by the ball is $h_1 = v_1^2/2g = kh_0$ and the process can continue, the ball jumping lesser and lesser. During the time when the ball is in the air the mathematical problem is simple, the equation of motion being

$$\ddot{x} = -g.$$
(8.14)

The inconveniences appear at the collision between the ball and the Earth, when the velocity vector presents discontinuities in both modulus and sense. Obviously, none of the previous theorems can be applied, although the problem has a unique solution.

(iv) As we observed, the Cauchy–Lipschitz or Peano theorems can be applied on some subintervals (the time in which the ball is in the air), the solution being obtained piecewise.

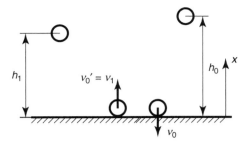

Figure 8.1   The collision between a ball and the surface of the Earth.

8.2 EULER'S METHOD

The goal of the method[3] is to obtain an approximation of the solution of the Cauchy problem

$$\frac{\mathrm{d}x}{\mathrm{d}t} = f(t, x), \quad t \in [t_0, t_f], \quad x(t_0) = x^0, \tag{8.15}$$

considered as a correct stated problem.

Let the interval $[t_0, t_f]$ be divided by $N + 1$ equidistant points (including the limit ones),

$$t_i = t_0 + ih, \quad h = \frac{t_f - t_0}{N}, \quad i = 0, 1, \dots, N. \tag{8.16}$$

We shall assume that the unique solution $x = x(t)$ is at least of class C^2 in the interval $[t_0, t_f]$ and we shall use the Taylor theorem

$$x(t_{i+1}) = x(t_i + h) = x(t_i) + h\frac{\mathrm{d}x(t_i)}{\mathrm{d}t} + \frac{h^2}{2}\frac{\mathrm{d}^2x(\xi_i)}{\mathrm{d}t^2}, \tag{8.17}$$

where $\xi_i \in (t_i, t_{i+1})$. Relation (8.17) holds for all $i = 0, 1, \dots, N - 1$. Writing relation (8.15) for $t = t_i$,

$$\frac{\mathrm{d}x(t_i)}{\mathrm{d}t} = f(t_i, x(t_i)) \tag{8.18}$$

and replacing expression (8.18) in equation (8.17), we obtain

$$x(t_{i+1}) = x(t_i + h) = x(t_i) + hf(t_i, x(t_i)) + \frac{h^2}{2}\frac{\mathrm{d}^2x(\xi_i)}{\mathrm{d}t^2}. \tag{8.19}$$

There results the equation

$$\frac{x(t_{i+1}) - x(t_i)}{h} = f(t_i, x(t_i)) + \frac{h}{2}\frac{\mathrm{d}^2x(\xi_i)}{\mathrm{d}t^2}. \tag{8.20}$$

Because x is of class C^2 in the interval $[t_0, t_f]$, we deduce that, for a small h, the expression $(h/2)\mathrm{d}^2x(\xi_i)/\mathrm{d}t^2$ is small enough to be neglected in relation (8.20); hence, we obtain

$$\frac{x(t_{i+1}) - x(t_i)}{h} \approx f(t_i, x(t_i)). \tag{8.21}$$

[3]Leonhard Euler (1707–1783) published this method in *Institutionum calculi integralis* in 1768–1770.

Denoting

$$w_0 = x(t_0), \quad w_{i+1} = w_i + hf(t_i, w_i), \tag{8.22}$$

we get

$$w_i \approx x(t_i) \tag{8.23}$$

for all $i = 0, 1, \ldots, N$.

Definition 8.3 Expression (8.22) is named the equation with finite differences associated to Euler's method.

Observation 8.2 Euler's method can be easily generalized to the n-dimensional case, resulting in the following algorithm:

- inputs N, t_0, t_f, $\mathbf{x}(t_0) = \mathbf{x}^{(0)}$, $\mathbf{w}^{(0)} = \mathbf{x}^{(0)}$;
- calculate $h = \dfrac{t_f - t_0}{N}$;
- for i from 1 to N
  - calculate $t_i = t_0 + ih$;
  - calculate $\mathbf{w}^{(i)} = \mathbf{w}^{(i-1)} + h\mathbf{f}(t_{i-1}, \mathbf{w}^{(i-1)})$.

Lemma 8.1 Let $x \in \mathbb{R}$, $x \geq -1$, and $m \in \mathbb{N}^*$ arbitrary. Under these conditions exists the inequality

$$0 \leq (1+x)^m \leq e^{mx}. \tag{8.24}$$

Demonstration. The first relation (8.24) is evident. For the second one, we shall proceed by induction. For $m = 1$, the relation becomes (the case $m = 0$ is evident)

$$1 + x \leq e^x. \tag{8.25}$$

Let us consider the function

$$g : [-1, \infty) \to \mathbb{R}, \quad g(x) = e^x - x - 1, \tag{8.26}$$

for which

$$g'(x) = e^x - 1, \quad g''(x) = e^x > 0. \tag{8.27}$$

The equation $g'(x) = 0$ has the unique solution $x = 0$, which is a point of minimum and $g(0) = 0$, such that the relation (8.25) is true for any $x \in [-1, \infty)$. Let us assume that expression (8.24) is true for $m \in \mathbb{N}$ and let us prove it for $m + 1$. We have

$$(1+x)^{m+1} = (1+x)(1+x)^m \leq (1+x)e^{mx} \leq e^x e^{mx} = e^{(m+1)x}. \tag{8.28}$$

Taking into account the principle of mathematical induction, it follows that equation (8.24) is true for any $m \in \mathbb{N}$.

Lemma 8.2 If m and n are two real positive numbers and $\{a_i\}_{i=\overline{0,k}}$ is a finite set of real numbers with $a_0 \geq 0$, which satisfies the relation

$$a_{i+1} \leq (1+m)a_i + n, \quad i = \overline{0, k-1}, \tag{8.29}$$

then

$$a_{i+1} \le e^{(i+1)m} \left(\frac{n}{m} + a_0 \right) - \frac{n}{m}, \quad i = \overline{0, k-1}. \tag{8.30}$$

Demonstration. We shall use the induction after i. For $i = 0$, we have

$$a_1 \le (1+m)a_0 + n; \tag{8.31}$$

applying Lemma 8.1, we obtain

$$a_1 \le e^m a_0 + n. \tag{8.32}$$

We shall prove that

$$e^m a_0 + n \le e^m \left(\frac{n}{m} + a_0 \right) - \frac{n}{m}. \tag{8.33}$$

The last relation reads equivalently in the form

$$n \le e^m \frac{n}{m} - \frac{n}{m}, \quad 1 + m \le e^m, \tag{8.34}$$

obviously true from Lemma 8.1. Let us suppose that the affirmation is true for i and let us prove it for $i+1$. We can write

$$a_{i+1} \le (1+m)a_i + n \le (1+m)e^{im} \left(\frac{n}{m} + a_0 \right) - \frac{n}{m}. \tag{8.35}$$

We shall prove that

$$(1+m)e^{im} \left(\frac{n}{m} + a_0 \right) - \frac{n}{m} \le e^{(i+1)m} \left(\frac{n}{m} + a_0 \right) - \frac{n}{m}, \tag{8.36}$$

meaning that $1 + m \le e^m$ is obviously true. The lemma is completely proved.

Theorem 8.3 (Determination of the Error in Euler's Method). Let $x(t)$ be the unique solution of Cauchy problem (8.15) and w_i, $i = \overline{0, N}$, the approximations of the values of the solution obtained using Euler's method for a certain $N > 0$, $N \in \mathbb{N}$. If x is defined in a convex set $\mathcal{D}$, if it is Lipschitzian in $\mathcal{D}$, of constant L, and if there is $M \in \mathbf{R}$, $M > 0$, such that

$$\left| \frac{d^2 x}{dt^2} \right| \le M; \quad (\forall) t \in [t_0, t_f], \tag{8.37}$$

then

$$|x(t_i) - w_i| \le \frac{hM}{2L} [e^{L(t_i - t_0)} - 1] \tag{8.38}$$

for $i = \overline{0, N}$.

Demonstration. For $i = 0$ we obtain

$$0 = |x(t_0) - w_0| \le \frac{hM}{2L} (e^{L \cdot 0} - 1) = 0 \tag{8.39}$$

and the theorem is true.

On the other hand,

$$x(t_{i+1}) = x(t_i) + hf(t_i, x(t_i)) + \frac{h^2}{2} \frac{d^2 x(t_i + \theta_i h)}{dt^2}, \tag{8.40}$$

where $\theta_i \in (0, 1)$, $i = \overline{0, N-1}$ and

$$w_{i+1} = w_i + hf(t_i, w_i), \quad i = \overline{0, N-1}. \tag{8.41}$$

It successively results in

$$|x(t_{i+1}) - w_{i+1}| = \left| x(t_i) - w_i + hf(t_i, x(t_i)) - hf(t_i, w_i) + \frac{h^2}{2} \frac{d^2 x(t_i + \theta_i h)}{dt^2} \right|$$

$$\leq |x(t_i) - w_i| + h|f(t_i, x(t_i)) - f(t_i, w_i)| + \frac{h^2}{2} \left| \frac{d^2 x(t_i + \theta_i h)}{dt^2} \right| \tag{8.42}$$

$$\leq |x(t_i) - w_i|(1 + hL) + \frac{h^2 M}{2}.$$

Now applying Lemma 8.2 with $a_j = |x(t_j) - w_j|$, $j = \overline{0, N}$, $m = hL$, $n = h^2 M/2$, expression (8.42) leads to

$$|x(t_{i+1}) - w_{i+1}| \leq e^{(i+1)hL} \left[|x(t_0) - w_0| + \frac{hM}{2L} \right] - \frac{hM}{2L}. \tag{8.43}$$

Taking into account that $x(t_0) = w_0 = x_0$ and $(i + 1)h = t_{i+1} - t_0$, relation (8.43) leads us to expression (8.38) that we had to prove.

Observation 8.3   Relation (8.38) shows that the bound of the error depends linearly on the size of the division step h. In conclusion, a better approximation of the solution is obtained by decreasing the division step.

8.3   TAYLOR METHOD

We shall consider the Cauchy problem

$$\frac{dx}{dt} = f(t, x(t)), \quad t \in [t_0, t_f], \quad x(t_0) = x_0, \tag{8.44}$$

considered as a correct stated one, and we shall assume that the function $x = x(t)$, the solution of the problem, is at least of class C^{n+1} in the interval $[t_0, t_f]$.

Using the expansion of the function $x = x(t)$ into a Taylor series, we can write the relation

$$x(t_{i+1}) = x(t_i) + h \frac{dx(t_i)}{dt} + \frac{h^2}{2} \frac{d^2 x(t_i)}{dt^2} + \cdots + \frac{h^n}{n!} \frac{d^n x(t_i)}{dt^n} + \frac{h^{n+1}}{(n+1)!} \frac{d^{n+1} x(\xi_i)}{dt^n}, \tag{8.45}$$

in which ξ_i is an intermediary point between t_i and t_{i+1}, $\xi_i \in (t_i, t_{i+1})$, t_i are the nodes of an equidistant division of the interval $[t_0, t_f]$, h is the step of the division, $h = (t_f - t_0)/N$, $t_i = t_0 + ih$, $i = \overline{1, N}$, and N is the number of points of the division.

On the other hand, we have

$$\frac{dx}{dt} = f(t, x(t)), \tag{8.46}$$

$$\frac{d^2x}{dt^2} = \frac{\partial f(t, x(t))}{\partial t} + \frac{\partial f(t, x(t))}{\partial x} \frac{dx}{dt}$$

$$= \frac{\partial f(t, x(t))}{\partial t} + \frac{\partial f(t, x(t))}{\partial x} f(t, x(t)) = \frac{df(t, x(t))}{dt} = f'(t, x(t)), \tag{8.47}$$

$$\frac{d^3x}{dt^3} = \frac{d}{dt}\left(\frac{df(t, x(t))}{dt}\right) = \frac{\partial f'(t, x(t))}{\partial t} + \frac{\partial f'(t, x(t))}{\partial x} \frac{dx(t)}{dt}$$

$$= \frac{\partial f'(t, x(t))}{\partial t} + \frac{\partial f'(t, x(t))}{\partial x} f(t, x(t)) \tag{8.48}$$

$$= \frac{d^2 f(t, x(t))}{dt^2} = f''(t, x(t)).$$

and, in general,

$$\frac{d^k x(t)}{dt^k} = \frac{dx^{(k-1)}(t)}{dt} = \frac{df^{(k-2)}(t, x(t))}{dt} = f^{(k-1)}(t, x(t)). \tag{8.49}$$

Replacing these derivatives in equation (8.45), it follows that

$$x(t_{i+1}) = x(t_i) + hf(t_i, x(t_i)) + \frac{h^2}{2} f'(t_i, x(t_i)) + \cdots$$

$$+ \frac{h^n}{n!} f^{(n-1)}(t_i, x(t_i)) + \frac{h^{n+1}}{(n+1)!} f^{(n)}(\xi_i, x(\xi_i)). \tag{8.50}$$

Renouncing to the remainder, we obtain the equation with finite differences

$$w_0 = x(t_0) = x_0, \quad w_{i+1} = w_i + hT^{(n)}(t_i, w_i), \quad i = \overline{0, N-1}, \tag{8.51}$$

where

$$T^{(n)}(t_i, w_i) = f(t_i, w_i) + \frac{h}{2} f'(t_i, w_i) + \cdots + \frac{h^{n-1}}{n!} f^{(n-1)}(t_i, w_i). \tag{8.52}$$

Definition 8.4 Relation (8.51) is called the *equation with differences* associated to the nth-order Taylor's method.

Observation 8.4 Euler's method is in fact the first-order Taylor's method.

8.4 THE RUNGE–KUTTA METHODS

The Runge–Kutta method[4] implies the obtaining of the values c_1, α_1, and β_1, such that $c_1 f(t + \alpha_1, x + \beta_1)$ approximates $T^{(2)}(t, x) = f(t, x) + (h/2)f'(t, x)$ with an error at most equal to $\mathcal{O}(h^2)$, which is the truncation error for the second-order Taylor's method.

On the other hand,

$$f'(t, x(t)) = \frac{df}{dt}(t, x(t)) = \frac{\partial f}{\partial t}(t, x(t)) + \frac{\partial f}{\partial x}(t, x(t))x'(t), \tag{8.53}$$

where

$$x'(t) = f(t, x(t)), \tag{8.54}$$

---

[4]The methods were developed by Carl David Tolmé Runge (1856–1927) and Martin Wilhelm Kutta (1867–1944) in 1901.

hence

$$T^{(2)}(t, x(t)) = f(t, x(t)) + \frac{h}{2} \frac{\partial t}{\partial x}(t, x(t)) + \frac{h}{2} \frac{\partial t}{\partial x}(t, x(t)) f(t, x(t)). \tag{8.55}$$

Expanding into a Taylor series $c_1 f(t + \alpha_1, x + \beta_1)$ around (t, x), we obtain

$$c_1 f(t + \alpha_1, x + \beta_1) = c_1 f(t, x) + c_1 \alpha_1 \frac{\partial f}{\partial t}(t, x) + c_1 \beta_1 \frac{\partial f}{\partial t}(t, x) + c_1 R_2(t + \alpha_1, x + \beta_1), \tag{8.56}$$

where the rest $R_2(t + \alpha_1, x + \beta_1)$ reads

$$R_2(t + \alpha_1, x + \beta_1) = \frac{\alpha_1^2}{2} \frac{\partial^2 f}{\partial t^2}(\tau, \xi) + \alpha_1 \beta_1(\tau, \xi) + \frac{\beta_1^2}{2} \frac{\partial^2 f}{\partial x^2}(\tau, \xi). \tag{8.57}$$

Identifying the coefficients of f and of its derivatives in formulae (8.55) and (8.56), we find the system

$$c_1 = 1, \quad c_1 \alpha_1 = \frac{h}{2}, \quad c_1 \beta_1 = \frac{h}{2} f(t, x), \tag{8.58}$$

the solution of which is

$$c_1 = 1, \quad \alpha_1 = \frac{h}{2}, \quad \beta_1 = \frac{h}{2} f(t, x). \tag{8.59}$$

Therefore, it follows that

$$T^{(2)}(t, x) = f\left(t + \frac{h}{2}, x + \frac{h}{2} f(t, x)\right) - R_2\left(t + \frac{h}{2}, x + \frac{h}{2} f(t, x)\right), \tag{8.60}$$

where

$$R_2\left(t + \frac{h}{2}, x + \frac{h}{2} f(t, x)\right) = \frac{h^2}{8} \frac{\partial^2 f}{\partial t^2}(\tau, \xi) + \frac{h^2}{4} f(t, x) \frac{\partial^2 f}{\partial t \partial x}(\tau, \xi)$$
$$+ \frac{h^2}{8} [f(t, x)]^2 \frac{\partial^2 f}{\partial x^2}(\tau, \xi). \tag{8.61}$$

Observation 8.5 If all second-order partial derivatives of f are bounded, then $R_2[t + (h/2), x + (h/2) f(t, x)]$ will be of order $\mathcal{O}(h^2)$.

Definition 8.5 The method with differences obtained from Taylor's method by replacing $T^2(t, x)$ is called the *Runge–Kutta method* of the mean point.

The mean point method is given by the relations

$$\mathbf{w}_0 = \mathbf{x}(t_0) = \mathbf{x}_0, \quad \mathbf{w}_{i+1} = \mathbf{w}_i + h\mathbf{f}\left(t_i + \frac{h}{2}, \mathbf{w}_i + \frac{h}{2}\mathbf{f}(t_i, \mathbf{w}_i)\right), \quad i = \overline{0, N-1}. \tag{8.62}$$

Definition 8.6

(i) If we approximate

$$T^{(2)}(t, x(t)) = f(t, x(t)) + \frac{h}{2} \frac{\partial f}{\partial x}(t, x(t)) + \frac{h^2}{6} \frac{\partial^2 f}{\partial x^2}(t, x(t)) \tag{8.63}$$

by an expression of the form

$$T^{(2)}(t, x(t)) \approx c_1 f(t, x(t)) + c_2 f(t + \alpha_2, x + \delta_2 f(t, x(t))) \tag{8.64}$$

so that the error is of order $\mathcal{O}(h^2)$, and if we choose the parameters

$$c_1 = c_2 = \frac{1}{2}, \quad \alpha_2 = \delta_2 = h, \tag{8.65}$$

then we obtain the modified Euler method for which the equation with differences reads

$$\mathbf{w}_0 = \mathbf{x}(t_0) = \mathbf{x}_0, \quad \mathbf{w}_{i+1} = \mathbf{w}_i + \frac{h}{2}[\mathbf{f}(t_i, \mathbf{w}_i) + \mathbf{f}(t_{i+1}, \mathbf{w}_i + h\mathbf{f}(t_i, \mathbf{w}_i))], \quad i = \overline{0, N-1}. \tag{8.66}$$

(ii) Under the same conditions, choosing

$$c_1 = \frac{1}{4}, \quad c_2 = \frac{3}{4}, \quad \alpha_2 = \delta_2 = \frac{2}{3}h, \tag{8.67}$$

we obtain Heun's method,[5] for which the equation with differences is of the form

$$\mathbf{w}_0 = \mathbf{x}(t_0) = \mathbf{x}_0,$$
$$\mathbf{w}_{i+1} = \mathbf{w}_i + \frac{h}{4}\left[\mathbf{f}\left(t_i, \mathbf{w}_i\right) + 3\mathbf{f}\left(t_i + \frac{2}{3}h, \mathbf{w}_i + \frac{2}{3}h\mathbf{f}\left(t_i, \mathbf{w}_i\right)\right)\right], \quad i = \overline{0, N-1}. \tag{8.68}$$

Analogically, the higher order Runge–Kutta formulae are established:
– the third-order Runge–Kutta method for which the equation with differences is

$$\mathbf{w}_0 = \mathbf{x}(t_0) = \mathbf{x}_0, \quad \mathbf{K}_1 = h\mathbf{f}(t_i, \mathbf{w}_i), \quad \mathbf{K}_2 = h\mathbf{f}\left(t_i + \frac{h}{2}, \mathbf{w}_i + \frac{\mathbf{K}_1}{2}\right),$$
$$\mathbf{K}_3 = h\mathbf{f}(t_i + h, \mathbf{w}_i + 2\mathbf{K}_2 + \mathbf{K}_1), \quad \mathbf{w}_{i+1} = \mathbf{w}_i + \frac{1}{6}(\mathbf{K}_1 + 4\mathbf{K}_2 + \mathbf{K}_3); \tag{8.69}$$

– the fourth-order Runge–Kutta method for which the equation with differences reads

$$\mathbf{w}_0 = \mathbf{x}(t_0) = \mathbf{x}_0, \quad \mathbf{K}_1 = h\mathbf{f}(t_i, \mathbf{w}_i), \quad \mathbf{K}_2 = h\mathbf{f}\left(t_i + \frac{h}{2}, \mathbf{w}_i + \frac{\mathbf{K}_1}{2}\right),$$
$$\mathbf{K}_3 = h\mathbf{f}\left(t_i + h, \mathbf{w}_i + \frac{\mathbf{K}_2}{2}\right), \quad \mathbf{K}_4 = h\mathbf{f}(t_i + h, \mathbf{w}_i + \mathbf{K}_3),$$
$$\mathbf{w}_{i+1} = \mathbf{w}_i + \frac{1}{6}(\mathbf{K}_1 + 2\mathbf{K}_2 + 2\mathbf{K}_3 + \mathbf{K}_4); \tag{8.70}$$

– the sixth-order Runge–Kutta method for which the equation with differences has the form

$$\mathbf{w}_0 = \mathbf{x}(t_0) = \mathbf{x}_0, \quad \mathbf{K}_1 = h\mathbf{f}(t_i, \mathbf{w}_i), \quad \mathbf{K}_2 = h\mathbf{f}\left(t_i + \frac{h}{2}, \mathbf{w}_i + \frac{\mathbf{K}_1}{3}\right),$$
$$\mathbf{K}_3 = h\mathbf{f}\left(t_i + \frac{2h}{5}, \mathbf{w}_i + \frac{1}{25}\left(6\mathbf{K}_2 + 4\mathbf{K}_1\right)\right),$$
$$\mathbf{K}_4 = h\mathbf{f}\left(t_i + h, \mathbf{w}_i + \frac{1}{4}\left(15\mathbf{K}_3 - 12\mathbf{K}_2 + \mathbf{K}_1\right)\right),$$
$$\mathbf{K}_5 = h\mathbf{f}\left(t_i + \frac{2h}{3}, \mathbf{w}_i + \frac{2}{81}\left(4\mathbf{K}_4 - 25\mathbf{K}_3 + 45\mathbf{K}_2 + 3\mathbf{K}_1\right)\right),$$
$$\mathbf{K}_6 = h\mathbf{f}\left(t_i + \frac{4h}{5}, \mathbf{w}_i + \frac{1}{75}\left(8\mathbf{K}_4 + 10\mathbf{K}_3 + 36\mathbf{K}_2 + 6\mathbf{K}_1\right)\right),$$
$$\mathbf{w}_{i+1} = \mathbf{w}_i + \frac{1}{192}(23\mathbf{K}_1 + 125\mathbf{K}_3 - 81\mathbf{K}_5 + 125\mathbf{K}_6). \tag{8.71}$$

[5] After Karl L. W. M. Heun (1859–1929) who published it in 1900.

Definition 8.7   The local error is the absolute value of the difference between the approximation at a division point and the exact solution at the same point of the Cauchy problem that has as initial value the approximation at the previous division point.

Observation 8.6   If $y(t)$ is the solution of the Cauchy problem

$$\dot{y}(t) = f(t, y), \quad t_0 \leq t \leq t_f, \quad y(t_0) = w_i, \tag{8.72}$$

where w_i is the approximate value obtained using the method with differences, then the local error at the point t_{i+1} has the expression

$$\varepsilon_{i+1}(h) = |y(t_{i+1}) - w_{i+1}|. \tag{8.73}$$

In various problems, we can apply methods that exert some control on the error too. One of these methods is the Runge–Kutta–Fehlberg method[6] for which the algorithm is the following:

- inputs $\varepsilon > 0$, t_0, $\mathbf{w}_0 = \mathbf{x}(t_0) = \mathbf{x}_0$, $h = \varepsilon^{1/4}$, t_f;
- $i = 0$;
- while $t_i + h \leq t_f$
- calculate

$$\mathbf{w}_0 = \mathbf{x}(t_0) = \mathbf{x}_0, \quad \mathbf{K}_1 = h\mathbf{f}(t_i, \mathbf{w}_i), \quad \mathbf{K}_2 = h\mathbf{f}\left(t_i + \frac{h}{2}, \mathbf{w}_i + \frac{1}{3}\mathbf{K}_1\right), \quad \mathbf{K}_1 = h\mathbf{f}(t_i, \mathbf{w}_i),$$

$$\mathbf{K}_2 = h\mathbf{f}\left(t_i + \frac{h}{4}, \mathbf{w}_i + \frac{1}{4}\mathbf{K}_1\right), \quad \mathbf{K}_3 = h\mathbf{f}\left(t_i + \frac{3h}{8}, \mathbf{w}_i + \frac{3}{32}\mathbf{K}_1 + \frac{9}{32}\mathbf{K}_2\right),$$

$$\mathbf{K}_4 = h\mathbf{f}\left(t_i + \frac{12}{13}h, \mathbf{w}_i + \frac{1932}{2197}\mathbf{K}_1 - \frac{7200}{2197}\mathbf{K}_2 + \frac{7296}{2197}\mathbf{K}_3\right),$$

$$\mathbf{K}_5 = h\mathbf{f}\left(t_i + h, \mathbf{w}_i + \frac{439}{216}\mathbf{K}_1 - 8\mathbf{K}_2 + \frac{3680}{513}\mathbf{K}_3 - \frac{845}{4104}\mathbf{K}_4\right),$$

$$\mathbf{K}_6 = h\mathbf{f}\left(t_i + \frac{h}{2}, \mathbf{w}_i - \frac{8}{27}\mathbf{K}_1 + 2\mathbf{K}_2 - \frac{3544}{2565}\mathbf{K}_3 + \frac{1859}{4104}\mathbf{K}_4 - \frac{11}{40}\mathbf{K}_5\right);$$

- calculate

$$\mathbf{w}_{i+1} = \mathbf{w}_i + \frac{25}{216}\mathbf{K}_1 + \frac{1408}{2565}\mathbf{K}_3 + \frac{2197}{4104}\mathbf{K}_4 - \frac{1}{5}\mathbf{K}_5,$$

$$\overline{\mathbf{w}}_{i+1} = \mathbf{w}_i + \frac{16}{135}\mathbf{K}_1 + \frac{6656}{12825}\mathbf{K}_3 + \frac{28561}{56430}\mathbf{K}_4 - \frac{9}{50}\mathbf{K}_5 + \frac{2}{55}\mathbf{K}_6;$$

- calculate

$$\mathbf{r}_{i+1} = \frac{1}{h}(\overline{\mathbf{w}}_{i+1} - \mathbf{w}_i), \quad \delta = 0,84\left(\frac{\varepsilon}{\|\mathbf{r}_{i+1}\|}\right)^{\frac{1}{4}};$$

- if $\delta \leq 0.1$, then $h := 0.1h$;
- if $\delta \geq 4$, then $h := 4h$;
- if $0.1 < \delta < 4$, then $h := \delta h$;
- if $\|\mathbf{r}_{i+1}\| \leq \varepsilon$, then $i := i + 1$.

In this case, $\mathbf{w}_i$ approximates $\mathbf{x}_i(t)$ with a local error at most ε.

---

[6]The algorithm was presented by Erwin Fehlberg (1891–1979) in *Classical fifth-, sixth-, seventh-, and eighth-order Runge–Kutta formulae with stepsize control* in 1968.

8.5 MULTISTEP METHODS

The methods presented before required only the knowledge of the value x_i at the point t_i to determine numerically the value x_{i+1} at the point t_{i+1}. Therefore, it was necessary to return only one step to determine the new value; it means that we discussed one-step methods. The following methods use approximations of the solutions in more previous points to determine the approximate solution at the present division point.

Definition 8.8   It is called the *multistep method* for the determination of the approximate $\mathbf{w}_i$ of the solution of the Cauchy problem

$$\dot{\mathbf{x}}(t) = \mathbf{f}(t, \mathbf{x}), \quad t_0 \le t \le t_f, \quad \mathbf{x}(t_0) = \mathbf{x}_0, \tag{8.74}$$

at the division point t_{i+1}, by using the equations with finite differences, which can be represented in the form

$$\begin{aligned}
\mathbf{w}_{i+1} &= a_{m-1}\mathbf{w}_i + a_{m-2}\mathbf{w}_{i-1} + \cdots + a_0\mathbf{w}_{i+1-m} \\
&\quad + h[b_m\mathbf{f}(t_{i+1}, \mathbf{w}_{i+1}) + b_{m-1}(t_{i+1}, \mathbf{w}_{i+1}) + \cdots + b_0\mathbf{f}(t_{i+1-m}, \mathbf{w}_{i+1-m})], \\
&\quad i = m - 1, \ldots, N - 1,
\end{aligned} \tag{8.75}$$

where N is the number of the division steps of the interval $[t_0, t_f]$, h is the division step of the same interval, $h = (t_f - t_0)/N$, $m > 1$, and in addition

$$\mathbf{w}_0 = \mathbf{x}(t_0) = \mathbf{x}_0, \quad \mathbf{w}_1 = \mathbf{x}(t_1) = \mathbf{x}_1, \ldots, \quad \mathbf{w}_{m-1} = \mathbf{x}(t_{m-1}) = \mathbf{x}_{m-1}. \tag{8.76}$$

Definition 8.9

  (i) If $b_m = 0$, then the method is called *explicit* or *open* because relation (8.75) is an explicit equation to determine $\mathbf{w}_{i+1}$.
  (ii) If $b_m \ne 0$, then the method is called *implicit* or *closed* because $\mathbf{w}_{i+1}$ appears in both members of expression (8.75).

Observation 8.7   The start values $\mathbf{w}_0$, $\mathbf{w}_1$, ..., $\mathbf{w}_{m-1}$ must be specified according to formula (8.76); that is, they must be the exact values of the function $\mathbf{x} = \mathbf{x}(t)$ at the points t_0, $t_1 = t_0 + h$, ..., $t_{m-1} = t_0 + (m-1)h$, or they can be determined using a one-step method starting from the value $\mathbf{w}_0 = \mathbf{x}(t_0) = \mathbf{x}_0$.
The most used technique to obtain multistep methods starts from the evident equality

$$\mathbf{x}(t_{i+1}) = \mathbf{x}(t_i) + \int_{t_i}^{t_{i+1}} \mathbf{f}(t, \mathbf{x}(t))dt. \tag{8.77}$$

Owing to the fact that the integral at the right hand part of relation (8.77) cannot be calculated because the solution $\mathbf{x}(t)$ is not known, we replace $\mathbf{f}(t, \mathbf{x}(t))$ by an interpolation polynomial $\mathbf{P}(t)$ that is determined as a function of the known values $(t_0, \mathbf{w}_0)$, $(t_1, \mathbf{w}_1)$, ..., $(t_i, \mathbf{w}_i)$, where $\mathbf{w}_j = \mathbf{x}(t_j)$, $j = \overline{0, i}$. Relation (8.77) now becomes

$$\mathbf{x}(t_{i+1}) \approx \mathbf{x}(t_i) + \int_{t_i}^{t_{i+1}} \mathbf{P}(t)dt. \tag{8.78}$$

8.6 ADAMS'S METHOD

In the equation[7]

$$\frac{dx}{dt} = f(t, x), \tag{8.79}$$

we replace the function $f(t, x)$ by the first five terms of Newton's polynomial

$$N_5(q) = x_0 + \frac{q}{1!}\Delta x_0 + \frac{q(q-1)}{2!}\Delta^2 x_0 + \frac{q(q-1)(q-2)}{3!}\Delta^3 x_0$$
$$+ \frac{q(q-1)(q-2)(q-3)}{4!}\Delta^4 x_0, \tag{8.80}$$

in which $q = (t - t_0)/h$, $h = (t_f - t_0)/N$, N being the number of the division points in the interval $\lfloor t_0, t_f \rfloor$, $t = t_0 + qh$, $dt = hdq$. Integrating, it follows that

$$x_1 - x_0 = \int_{x_0}^{x_0+h} f(t, x)dt = h\int_0^1 f(t, x)dq$$
$$= h\left(x_0 + \frac{1}{2}\Delta x_0 - \frac{1}{12}\Delta^2 x_0 - \frac{1}{24}\Delta^3 x_0 - \frac{19}{720}\Delta^4 x_0\right), \tag{8.81}$$

$$x_2 - x_0 = \int_{x_0}^{x_0+2h} f(t, x)dt = h\int_0^2 f(t, x)dq$$
$$= h\left(2x_0 + 2\Delta x_0 + \frac{1}{3}\Delta^2 x_0 - \frac{1}{90}\Delta^4 x_0\right), \tag{8.82}$$

$$x_3 - x_0 = \int_{x_0}^{x_0+3h} f(t, x)dt = h\int_0^3 f(t, x)dq$$
$$= h\left(3x_0 + \frac{9}{2}\Delta x_0 + \frac{9}{4}\Delta^2 x_0 + \frac{3}{8}\Delta^3 x_0 - \frac{3}{80}\Delta^4 x_0\right), \tag{8.83}$$

$$x_4 - x_0 = \int_{x_0}^{x_0+4h} f(t, x)dt = h\int_0^4 f(t, x)dq$$
$$= h\left(4x_0 + 8\Delta x_0 + \frac{20}{3}\Delta^2 x_0 + \frac{8}{3}\Delta^3 x_0 + \frac{14}{45}\Delta^4 x_0\right). \tag{8.84}$$

The calculation involves successive approximations:

– approximation 1:

$$x_1^{(1)} = x_0 + f(t_0, \ x_0), \ \ \Delta f(t_0, x_0) = f(t_1, x_1^{(1)}) - f(t_0, x_0); \tag{8.85}$$

[7]The method was presented by John Couch Adams (1819–1892). It appears for the first time in a letter written by F. Bashforth in 1855.

– approximation 2:

$$x_1^{(2)} = x_0 + hf(t_0, x_0) + \frac{1}{2}h\Delta f(t_0, x_0),$$

$$x_2^{(1)} = x_0 + 2hf(t_0, x_0) + 2h\Delta f(t_0, \; x_0), \qquad (8.86)$$

$$\Delta f(t_0, x_0) = f(t_1, x_1^{(2)}) - f(t_0, \; x_0),$$

$$\Delta^2 f(t_0, x_0) = f(t_2, x_2^{(1)}) - 2f(t_1, x_1^{(2)}) + f(t_0, \; x_0);$$

– approximation 3:

$$x_1^{(3)} = x_0 + hf(t_0, x_0) + \frac{1}{2}h\Delta f(t_0, x_0) - \frac{1}{12}h\Delta^2 f(t_0, x_0),$$

$$x_2^{(2)} = x_0 + 2hf(t_0, x_0) + 2h\Delta f(t_0, x_0) + \frac{1}{3}h\Delta^2 f(t_0, x_0),$$

$$x_3^{(1)} = x_0 + 3hf(t_0, x_0) + \frac{9}{2}h\Delta f(t_0, \; x_0) + \frac{9}{4}h\Delta^2 f(t_0, x_0), \qquad (8.87)$$

$$\Delta f(t_0, x_0) = f(t_1, x_1^{(3)}) - f(t_0, \; x_0),$$

$$\Delta^2 f(t_0, x_0) = f(t_2, x_2^{(2)}) - 2f(t_1, x_1^{(3)}) + 3f(t_0, \; x_0),$$

$$\Delta^3 f(t_0, x_0) = f(t_3, x_3^{(1)}) - 3f(t_2, x_2^{(2)}) + 3f(t_1, x_1^{(3)}) - f(t_0, \; x_0);$$

– approximation 4:

$$x_1^{(4)} = x_0 + hf(t_0, x_0) + \frac{1}{2}h\Delta f(t_0, x_0) - \frac{1}{12}h\Delta^2 f(t_0, x_0) + \frac{1}{24}h\Delta^3 f(t_0, \; x_0),$$

$$x_2^{(3)} = x_0 + 2hf(t_0, x_0) + 2h\Delta f(t_0, x_0) + \frac{1}{2}h\Delta^2 f(t_0, \; x_0),$$

$$x_3^{(2)} = x_0 + 3hf(t_0, x_0) + \frac{9}{2}h\Delta f(t_0, x_0) + \frac{9}{4}h\Delta^2 f(t_0, x_0) + \frac{1}{8}h\Delta^3 f(t_0, \; x_0),$$

$$x_4^{(1)} = x_0 + 4hf(t_0, x_0) + 8h\Delta f(t_0, x_0) + \frac{20}{3}h\Delta^2 f(t_0, x_0) + \frac{8}{3}h\Delta^3 f(t_0, \; x_0),$$

$$\Delta f(t_0, x_0) = f(t_1, \; x_1^{(4)}) - f(t_0, \; x_0), \quad \Delta^2 f(t_0, x_0) = f(t_2, x_2^{(3)}) - 2f(t_1, x_1^{(4)}) + f(t_0, x_0),$$

$$\Delta^3 f(t_0, x_0) = f(t_3, x_3^{(2)}) - 3f(t_2, x_2^{(3)}) + 3f(t_1, x_1^{(4)}) - f(t_0, \; x_0),$$

$$\Delta^4 f(t_0, x_0) = f(t_4, x_4^{(1)}) - 4f(t_3, x_3^{(2)}) + 6f(t_2, x_2^{(3)}) - 4f(t_1, x_1^{(4)}) + f(t_0, \; x_0);$$

$$(8.88)$$

– approximation 5:

$$x_1^{(5)} = x_0 + hf(t_0, x_0) + \frac{1}{2}h\Delta f(t_0, x_0) - \frac{1}{12}h\Delta^2 f(t_0, x_0)$$

$$+ \frac{1}{24}h\Delta^3 f(t_0, x_0) - \frac{19}{720}h\Delta^4 f(t_0, x_0),$$

$$x_2^{(4)} = x_0 + 2hf(t_0, x_0) + 2h\Delta f(t_0, x_0) + \frac{1}{3}h\Delta^2 f(t_0, x_0) - \frac{1}{90}h\Delta^4 f(t_0, x_0)$$

$$x_3^{(3)} = x_0 + 3hf(t_0, x_0) + \frac{9}{2}h\Delta f(t_0, x_0) + \frac{9}{4}h\Delta^2 f(t_0, x_0)$$

$$+ \frac{3}{8}h\Delta^3 f(t_0, x_0) - \frac{3}{80}h\Delta^4 f(t_0, x_0),$$

$$x_4^{(2)} = x_0 + 4hf(t_0, x_0) + 8h\Delta f(t_0, x_0) + \frac{20}{3}h\Delta^2 f(t_0, x_0)$$

$$+ \frac{8}{3}h\Delta^3 f(t_0, x_0) + \frac{14}{45}h\Delta^4 f(t_0, x_0),$$

$$\Delta f(t_0, x_0) = f(t_1, x_1^{(5)}) - f(t_0, x_0),$$

$$\Delta^2 f(t_0, x_0) = f(t_2, x_2^{(4)}) - 2f(t_1, x_1^{(5)}) + f(t_0, x_0),$$

$$\Delta^3 f(t_0, x_0) = f(t_3, x_3^{(3)}) - 3f(t_2, x_2^{(4)}) + 3f(t_1, x_1^{(5)}) - f(t_0, x_0),$$

$$\Delta^4 f(t_0, x_0) = f(t_4, x_4^{(2)}) - 4f(t_3, x_3^{(3)}) + 6f(t_2, x_2^{(4)}) - 4(t_1, x_1^{(5)}) + f(t_0, x_0). \tag{8.89}$$

The values x_1, x_2, x_3, x_4 are calculated repeatedly according to formula (8.86), formula (8.87), formula (8.88), and formula (8.89) until the difference between two successive iterations decreases under an imposed value.

We now replace the function $f(t, x)$ by Newton's polynomial

$$N_5^*(q) = f(t_i, x_i) + \frac{q}{1!}\Delta f(t_{i-1}, x_{i-1}) + \frac{q(q+1)}{2!}\Delta^2 f(t_{i-2}, x_{i-2})$$

$$+ \frac{q(q+1)(q-2)}{3!}\Delta^3 f(t_{i-3}, x_{i-3}) + \frac{q(q+1)(q-2)(q-3)}{4!}\Delta^4 f(t_{i-4}, x_{i-4}), \tag{8.90}$$

where $q = (t - t_i)/h$. Thus, it follows that

$$\int_{t_i}^{t_{i+1}} f(t, x)\mathrm{d}t = h\int_0^1 f(t, x)\mathrm{d}q. \tag{8.91}$$

Integrating, we deduce Adams's formula

$$x_{i+1} = x_i + hf(t_i, x_i) + \frac{1}{2}h\Delta f(t_{i-1}, x_{i-1}) + \frac{5}{12}h\Delta^2 f(t_{i-2}, x_{i-2})$$

$$+ \frac{3}{8}h\Delta^3 f(t_{i-3}, x_{i-3}) + \frac{251}{720}h\Delta^4 f(t_{i-4}, x_{i-4}), \quad i = 4, 5, \ldots \tag{8.92}$$

8.7   THE ADAMS–BASHFORTH METHODS

To deduce the recurrent formula of the Adams–Bashforth method,[8] we shall start from the relation

$$f(t_i + qh) = f(t_i) + \frac{q}{1!}\Delta f(t_{i-1}) + \frac{q(q+1)}{2!}\Delta^2 f(t_{i-2}) + \frac{q(q-1)(q-2)}{3!}\Delta^3 f(t_{i-3}) + \cdots \tag{8.93}$$

[8]The methods were published by John Couch Adams (1819–1892) and Francis Bashforth (1819–1912) in *An Attempt to Test the Theories of Capillary Action by Comparing the Theoretical and Measured Forms of Drops of Fluid, with an Explanation of the Method of Integration Employed in Constructing the Tables which Give the Theoretical Forms of Such Drops* in 1882.

It follows that

$$\int_{t_i}^{t_{i+1}} P(t)dt = h \int_0^1 f(t_i + qh)dq; \tag{8.94}$$

using expression (8.93), we obtain

$$\int_{t_i}^{t_{i+1}} P(t)dt = h \int_0^1 f(t_i)dq + \frac{h}{1}\Delta f(t_{i-1}) \int_0^1 q\,dq + \frac{h}{2!}\Delta^2 f(t_{i-2}) \int_0^1 q(q+1)dq + \cdots$$

$$+ \frac{h}{r!}\Delta^r f(t_{i-r}) \int_0^1 q(q+1)\cdots(q+r-1)dq + \cdots \tag{8.95}$$

Calculating the integrals and limiting ourselves to the terms up to $\Delta^r f(t_{i-r})$, we deduce the expression

$$\int_{t_i}^{t_{i+1}} P(t)dt = hf(t_i) + \frac{h}{2}\Delta f(t_{i-1}) + \frac{5h}{12}\Delta^2 f(t_{i-2}) + \frac{3h}{8}\Delta^3 f(t_{i-3}) + \frac{251h}{720}\Delta^4 f(t_{i-4}) + \cdots \tag{8.96}$$

Thus, it results in the recurrent relation for the Adams–Bashforth method

$$x_{i+1} = x_i + hf(t_i) + \frac{h}{2}\Delta f(t_{i-1}) + \frac{5h}{12}\Delta^2 f(t_{i-2}) + \frac{3h}{8}\Delta^3 f(t_{i-3}) + \frac{251h}{720}\Delta^4 f(t_{i-4}) + \cdots \tag{8.97}$$

Depending on the degree r of the interpolation polynomial, we deduce different Adams–Bashforth formulae:

– for $r = 1$:

$$x_{i+1} = x_i + \frac{h}{2}[3f(t_i, x_i) - f(t_{i-1}, x_{i-1})]; \tag{8.98}$$

– for $r = 2$:

$$x_{i+1} = x_i + \frac{h}{12}[23f(t_i, x_i) - 16f(t_{i-1}, x_{i-1}) + 5f(t_{i-2}, x_{i-2})]; \tag{8.99}$$

– for $r = 3$:

$$x_{i+1} = x_i + \frac{h}{24}[55f(t_i, x_i) - 59f(t_{i-1}, x_{i-1}) + 37f(t_{i-2}, x_{i-2}) - 9f(t_{i-3}, x_{i-3})]; \tag{8.100}$$

– for $r = 4$:

$$x_{i+1} = x_i + \frac{h}{720}[1901f(t_i, x_i) - 2774f(t_{i-1}, x_{i-1})$$
$$+ 2616f(t_{i-2}, x_{i-2}) - 1274f(t_{i-3}, x_{i-3}) + 251f(t_{i-4}, x_{i-4})]. \tag{8.101}$$

The most used methods are those of the third, fourth, and fifth order, for which the recurrent relations read as follows:

– the third-order Adams–Bashforth method:

$$\mathbf{w}_0 = \mathbf{x}(t_0) = \mathbf{x}_0, \quad \mathbf{w}_1 = \mathbf{x}(t_1) = \mathbf{x}_1, \quad \mathbf{w}_2 = \mathbf{x}(t_2) = \mathbf{x}_2,$$
$$\mathbf{w}_{i+1} = \mathbf{w}_i + \frac{h}{12}[23\mathbf{f}(t_i, \mathbf{w}_i) - 16\mathbf{f}(t_{i-1}, \mathbf{w}_{i-1}) + 5\mathbf{f}(t_{i-2}, \mathbf{w}_{i-2})]; \tag{8.102}$$

– the fourth-order Adams–Bashforth method:

$$\mathbf{w}_0 = \mathbf{x}(t_0) = \mathbf{x}_0, \quad \mathbf{w}_1 = \mathbf{x}(t_1) = \mathbf{x}_1, \quad \mathbf{w}_2 = \mathbf{x}(t_2) = \mathbf{x}_2, \quad \mathbf{w}_3 = \mathbf{x}(t_3) = \mathbf{x}_3,$$
$$\mathbf{w}_{i+1} = \mathbf{w}_i + \frac{h}{24}[55f(t_i, \mathbf{w}_i) - 59f(t_{i-1}, \mathbf{w}_{i-1}) + 37f(t_{i-2}, \mathbf{w}_{i-2}) - 9f(t_{i-3}, \mathbf{w}_{i-3})]; \tag{8.103}$$

– the fifth-order Adams–Bashforth method:

$$\mathbf{w}_0 = \mathbf{x}(t_0) = \mathbf{x}_0, \quad \mathbf{w}_1 = \mathbf{x}(t_1) = \mathbf{x}_1, \quad \mathbf{w}_2 = \mathbf{x}(t_2) = \mathbf{x}_2, \quad \mathbf{w}_3 = \mathbf{x}(t_3) = \mathbf{x}_3,$$
$$\mathbf{w}_4 = \mathbf{x}(t_4) = \mathbf{x}_4, \quad \mathbf{w}_{i+1} = \mathbf{w}_i + \frac{h}{720}[1901f(t_i, \mathbf{w}_i) - 2774f(t_{i-1}, \mathbf{w}_{i-1}) \tag{8.104}$$
$$+ 2616f(t_{i-2}, \mathbf{w}_{i-2}) - 1274f(t_{i-3}, \mathbf{w}_{i-3}) + 251f(t_{i-4}, \mathbf{w}_{i-4})].$$

Observation 8.8   The start values $\mathbf{w}_0, \mathbf{w}_1, \ldots$ are obtained using a one-step method.

8.8   THE ADAMS–MOULTON METHODS

Writing the interpolation polynomial $P(t)$ in the form

$$P(t) = f(t_{i+1}) + \frac{q-1}{1!}\Delta f(t_i) + \frac{(q-1)q}{2!}\Delta^2 f(t_{i-1})$$
$$+ \frac{(q-1)q(q+1)}{3!}\Delta^3 f(t_{i-2}) + \frac{(q-1)q(q+1)(q+2)}{4!}\Delta^4 f(t_{i-3}) \tag{8.105}$$
$$+ \cdots + \frac{(q-1)q(q+1)\ldots(q+r-2)}{r!}\Delta^r f(t_{i-r+1}),$$

it results, by integration, in

$$\int_{t_i}^{t_{i+1}} P(t)dt = hf(t_{i+1}) - \frac{h}{2}\Delta f(t_i) - \frac{h}{12}\Delta^2 f(t_{i-1}) - \frac{h}{24}\Delta^3 f(t_{i-2}) + \frac{19h}{720}\Delta^4 f(t_{i-3}) - \cdots \tag{8.106}$$

Limiting the number of terms in the right-hand side of formula (8.106), we obtain the following particular expressions:

– for $r = 1$:
$$\mathbf{x}_{i+1} = \mathbf{x}_i + 0.5h[\mathbf{f}(t_{i+1}, \mathbf{x}_{i+1}) + \mathbf{f}(t_i, \mathbf{x}_i)]; \tag{8.107}$$

– for $r = 2$:
$$\mathbf{x}_{i+1} = \mathbf{x}_i + \frac{h}{12}[5\mathbf{f}(t_{i+1}, \mathbf{x}_{i+1}) + 8\mathbf{f}(t_i, \mathbf{x}_i) - \mathbf{f}(t_{i-1}, \mathbf{x}_{i-1})]; \tag{8.108}$$

– for $r = 3$:
$$\mathbf{x}_{i+1} = \mathbf{x}_i + \frac{h}{24}[9\mathbf{f}(t_{i+1}, \mathbf{x}_{i+1}) + 19\mathbf{f}(t_i, \mathbf{x}_i) - 5\mathbf{f}(t_{i-1}, \mathbf{x}_{i-1}) + \mathbf{f}(t_{i-2}, \mathbf{x}_{i-2})]; \tag{8.109}$$

– for $r = 4$:

$$\mathbf{x}_{i+1} = \mathbf{x}_i + \frac{h}{720}[251\mathbf{f}(t_{i+1}, \mathbf{x}_{i+1}) + 646\mathbf{f}(t_i, \mathbf{x}_i) \tag{8.110}$$
$$- 246\mathbf{f}(t_{i-1}, \mathbf{x}_{i-1}) + 106\mathbf{f}(t_{i-2}, \mathbf{x}_{i-2}) - 19\mathbf{f}(t_{i-3}, \mathbf{x}_{i-3})].$$

The most used Adams–Moulton methods[9] are those of the third, fourth, and fifth order for which the equations with differences read as follows:

– the third-order Adams–Moulton method:

$$\mathbf{w}_0 = \mathbf{x}_0(t_0) = \mathbf{x}_0, \quad \mathbf{w}_1 = \mathbf{x}(t_1) = \mathbf{x}_1,$$
$$\mathbf{w}_{i+1} = \mathbf{w}_i + \frac{h}{12}[5\mathbf{f}(t_{i+1}, \mathbf{w}_{i+1}) + 8\mathbf{f}(t_i, \mathbf{w}_i) - \mathbf{f}(t_{i-1}, \mathbf{w}_{i-1})]; \tag{8.111}$$

– the fourth-order Adams–Moulton method:

$$\mathbf{w}_0 = \mathbf{x}_0(t_0) = \mathbf{x}_0, \quad \mathbf{w}_1 = \mathbf{x}(t_1) = \mathbf{x}_1, \quad \mathbf{w}_2 = \mathbf{x}(t_2) = \mathbf{x}_2,$$
$$\mathbf{w}_{i+1} = \mathbf{w}_i + \frac{h}{24}[9\mathbf{f}(t_{i+1}, \mathbf{w}_{i+1}) + 19\mathbf{f}(t_i, \mathbf{w}_i) - 5\mathbf{f}(t_{i-1}, \mathbf{w}_{i-1}) + \mathbf{f}(t_{i-2}, \mathbf{w}_{i-2})]; \tag{8.112}$$

– the fifth-order Adams–Moulton method:

$$\mathbf{w}_0 = \mathbf{x}_0(t_0) = \mathbf{x}_0, \quad \mathbf{w}_1 = \mathbf{x}(t_1) = \mathbf{x}_1, \quad \mathbf{w}_2 = \mathbf{x}(t_2) = \mathbf{x}_2, \quad \mathbf{w}_3 = \mathbf{x}(t_3) = \mathbf{x}_3,$$
$$\mathbf{w}_{i+1} = \mathbf{w}_i + \frac{h}{720}[251\mathbf{f}(t_{i+1}, \mathbf{w}_{i+1}) + 646\mathbf{f}(t_i, \mathbf{w}_i) \tag{8.113}$$
$$- 264\mathbf{f}(t_{i-1}, \mathbf{w}_{i-1}) + 106\mathbf{f}(t_{i-2}, \mathbf{w}_{i-2}) - 19\mathbf{f}(t_{i-3}, \mathbf{w}_{i-3})].$$

Observation 8.9

(i) Unlike the Adams–Bashforth methods in which the required value $\mathbf{w}_{i+1}$ appears only on the left side of the equality, in the Adams–Moulton formulae this appears both on the left and right sides of the equal sign. It follows that, at each step, it is necessary to solve an equation of the form

$$\mathbf{w}_{i+1} = \mathbf{w}_i + h[c_0\mathbf{f}(t_{i+1}, \mathbf{w}_{i+1}) + c_1\mathbf{f}(t_i, \mathbf{w}_i) + \cdots], \tag{8.114}$$

where $c_0, c_1, \ldots$ are the coefficients that appear in the respective Adams–Moulton formula.

(ii) Equation (8.114) is solved by successive approximations using the recurrent formula

$$\mathbf{w}_{i+1}^{(k)} = \mathbf{w}_i + h[c_0\mathbf{f}(t_{i+1}, \mathbf{w}_{i+1}^{(k-1)}) + c_1\mathbf{f}(t_i, \mathbf{w}_i) + \cdots], \tag{8.115}$$

an expression that can also be written in the form

$$\mathbf{w}_{i+1}^{(k)} = \mathbf{w}_{i+1} + hc_0\mathbf{f}(t_{i+1}, \mathbf{w}_{i+1}^{(k-1)}) - hc_0\mathbf{f}(t_i, \mathbf{w}_i), \tag{8.116}$$

obtained by subtraction of equation (8.114) from equation (8.115).

---

[9]Forest Ray Moulton (1872–1952) published these methods in New Methods in *Exterior Ballistics* in 1926.

(iii) If the function $\mathbf{f}$ is Lipschitzian in the second variable and if there exists $L > 0$ so as to have for any $\mathbf{y}$ and $\mathbf{z}$

$$\|\mathbf{f}(t, \mathbf{y})\| - \|\mathbf{f}(t, \mathbf{z})\| \le L\|\mathbf{y} - \mathbf{z}\|, \tag{8.117}$$

then expression (8.116) can be written as

$$\|\mathbf{w}_{i+1}^{(k)} - \mathbf{w}_{i+1}\| \le hc_0 L\|\mathbf{w}_{i+1}^{(k-1)} - \mathbf{w}_{i+1}\|. \tag{8.118}$$

The last formula offers us the sufficient condition for the convergence of the iterative procedure

$$hc_0 L < 1 \quad \text{or} \quad h < \frac{1}{c_0 L}. \tag{8.119}$$

8.9 PREDICTOR–CORRECTOR METHODS

Definition 8.10 A predictor–corrector method is a linear combination between an explicit multi-step method and an implicit multistep one, the first realizing a predetermination of the value $\mathbf{x}_{i+1}$ function of the previous values $\mathbf{x}_i, \mathbf{x}_{i-1}, \ldots$, and the second realizing a more correct evaluation of the value $\mathbf{x}_{i+1}$.

Observation 8.10 The corrector formula can be applied more times until the difference between two successive iterations $\mathbf{x}_{i+1}^{(k)}$ and $\mathbf{x}_{i+1}^{(k+1)}$ becomes less than an imposed value ε, that is,

$$\|\mathbf{x}_{i+1}^{(k+1)} - \mathbf{x}_i^{(k)}\| < \varepsilon. \tag{8.120}$$

We shall now present a few most used predictor–corrector methods.

8.9.1 Euler's Predictor–Corrector Method

In this case, the formula with differences reads

$$\mathbf{w}_0 = \mathbf{x}(t_0) = \mathbf{x}_0, \mathbf{w}_{i+1}^{\text{pred}} = \mathbf{w}_i + h\mathbf{f}(t_i, \mathbf{w}_i),$$
$$\mathbf{w}_{i+1}^{\text{cor}} = \mathbf{w}_i + 0.5h[\mathbf{f}(t_i, \mathbf{w}_i) + \mathbf{f}(t_{i+1}, \mathbf{w}_{i+1}^{\text{pred}}). \tag{8.121}$$

8.9.2 Adams's Predictor–Corrector Methods

These methods consist of an Adams–Bashforth method with the role of predictor for $\mathbf{w}_{i+1}$ and of an Adams–Moulton method with the role of corrector, both methods having the same order.

We obtain

– the third-order predictor–corrector Adams's algorithm for which the equations with differences read

$$\mathbf{w}_0 = \mathbf{x}(t_0) = \mathbf{x}_0, \quad \mathbf{w}_1 = \mathbf{x}(t_1) = \mathbf{x}_1, \quad \mathbf{w}_2 = \mathbf{x}(t_2) = \mathbf{x}_2,$$

$$\mathbf{w}_{i+1}^{\text{pred}} = \mathbf{w}_i + \frac{h}{12}[23\mathbf{f}(t_i, \mathbf{w}_i) - 16\mathbf{f}(t_{i-1}, \mathbf{w}_{i-1}) + 5\mathbf{f}(t_{i-2}, \mathbf{w}_{i-2})], \tag{8.122}$$

$$\mathbf{w}_i^{\text{cor}} = \mathbf{w}_i + \frac{h}{12}[5\mathbf{f}(t_{i+1}, \mathbf{w}_{i+1}^{\text{pred}}) + 8\mathbf{f}(t_i, \mathbf{w}_i^{\text{pred}}) - \mathbf{f}(t_{i-1}, \mathbf{w}_{i-1}^{\text{pred}});$$

– the fourth-order predictor–corrector Adams's algorithm for which the equations with differences are

$$\mathbf{w}_0 = \mathbf{x}(t_0) = \mathbf{x}_0, \quad \mathbf{w}_1 = \mathbf{x}(t_1) = \mathbf{x}_1, \quad \mathbf{w}_2 = \mathbf{x}(t_2) = \mathbf{x}_2, \quad \mathbf{w}_3 = \mathbf{x}(t_3) = \mathbf{x}_3,$$

$$\mathbf{w}_{i+1}^{\text{pred}} = \mathbf{w}_i + \frac{h}{24}[55\mathbf{f}(t_i, \mathbf{w}_i) - 59\mathbf{f}(t_{i-1}, \mathbf{w}_{i-1}) + 37\mathbf{f}(t_{i-2}, \mathbf{w}_{i-2}) - 9\mathbf{f}(t_{i-3}, \mathbf{w}_{i-3})], \quad (8.123)$$

$$\mathbf{w}_{i+1}^{\text{cor}} = \mathbf{w}_i + \frac{h}{24}[9\mathbf{f}(t_{i+1}, \mathbf{w}_{i+1}^{\text{pred}}) + 19\mathbf{f}(t_i, \mathbf{w}_i^{\text{pred}}) - 5\mathbf{f}(t_{i-1}, \mathbf{w}_{i-1}^{\text{pred}}) + \mathbf{f}(t_{i-2}, \mathbf{w}_{i-2}^{\text{pred}})];$$

– the fifth-order predictor–corrector Adams's algorithm for which the equations with differences have the expressions

$$\mathbf{w}_0 = \mathbf{x}(t_0) = \mathbf{x}_0, \quad \mathbf{w}_1 = \mathbf{x}(t_1) = \mathbf{x}_1, \quad \mathbf{w}_2 = \mathbf{x}(t_2) = \mathbf{x}_2, \quad \mathbf{w}_3 = \mathbf{x}(t_3) = \mathbf{x}_3,$$

$$\mathbf{w}_4 = \mathbf{x}(t_4) = \mathbf{x}_4, \quad \mathbf{w}_{i+1}^{\text{pred}} = \mathbf{w}_i + \frac{h}{720}[1901\mathbf{f}(t_i, \mathbf{w}_i) - 2774\mathbf{f}(t_{i-1}, \mathbf{w}_{i-1}) + 2616\mathbf{f}(t_{i-2}, \mathbf{w}_{i-2})$$

$$- 1274\mathbf{f}(t_{i-3}, \mathbf{w}_{i-3}) + 646\mathbf{f}(t_{i-4}, \mathbf{w}_{i-4})],$$

$$- 264\mathbf{f}(t_{i-1}, \mathbf{w}_{i-1}^{\text{pred}}) + 106\mathbf{f}(t_{i-2}, \mathbf{w}_{i-2}^{\text{pred}}) - 19\mathbf{f}(t_{i-3}, \mathbf{w}_{i-3}^{\text{pred}})].$$

$$(8.124)$$

The most used is the fourth-order predictor–corrector algorithm.

8.9.3 Milne's Fourth-Order Predictor–Corrector Method

For this method,[10] the equations with differences read

$$\mathbf{w}_0 = \mathbf{x}(t_0) = \mathbf{x}_0, \quad \mathbf{w}_1 = \mathbf{x}(t_1) = \mathbf{x}_1, \quad \mathbf{w}_2 = \mathbf{x}(t_2) = \mathbf{x}_2, \quad \mathbf{w}_3 = \mathbf{x}(t_3) = \mathbf{x}_3,$$

$$\mathbf{w}_{i+1}^{\text{pred}} = \mathbf{w}_{i-3} + \frac{4}{3}h[2\mathbf{f}(t_i, \mathbf{w}_i) + 2\mathbf{f}(t_{i-2}, \mathbf{w}_{i-2}) - \mathbf{f}(t_{i-1}, \mathbf{w}_{i-1})], \quad (8.125)$$

$$\mathbf{w}_{i+1}^{\text{cor}} = \mathbf{w}_{i-1} + \frac{h}{3}[\mathbf{f}(t_{i+1}, \mathbf{w}_{i+1}) + 4\mathbf{f}(t_i, \mathbf{w}_i) + \mathbf{f}(t_{i-1}, \mathbf{w}_{i-1})].$$

8.9.4 Hamming's Predictor–Corrector Method

The equations with differences are, in this case,[11]

$$\mathbf{w}_0 = \mathbf{x}(t_0) = \mathbf{x}_0, \quad \mathbf{w}_1 = \mathbf{x}(t_1) = \mathbf{x}_1, \quad \mathbf{w}_2 = \mathbf{x}(t_2) = \mathbf{x}_2, \quad \mathbf{w}_3 = \mathbf{x}(t_3) = \mathbf{x}_3,$$

$$\mathbf{w}_{i+1}^{\text{pred}} = \mathbf{w}_{i-3} + \frac{4}{3}h[2\mathbf{f}(t_i, \mathbf{w}_i) + 2\mathbf{f}(t_{i-2}, \mathbf{w}_{i-2}) - \mathbf{f}(t_{i-1}, \mathbf{w}_{i-1})], \quad (8.126)$$

$$\mathbf{w}_{i+1}^{\text{cor}} = \frac{9}{8}\mathbf{w}_i - \frac{1}{8}\mathbf{w}_{i-2} + \frac{3h}{8}[\mathbf{f}(t_{i+1}, \mathbf{w}_{i+1}^{\text{pred}}) + 2\mathbf{f}(t_i, \mathbf{w}_i) - \mathbf{f}(t_{i-1}, \mathbf{w}_{i-1})].$$

[10]The method was presented by William Edmund Milne (1890–1971) in *Numerical Calculus* in 1949.
[11]The method was described by Richard Wesley Hamming (1915–1998) in *Numerical Methods for Scientists and Engineers* in 1962.

8.10   THE LINEAR EQUIVALENCE METHOD (LEM)

The linear equivalence method (LEM) was introduced by Ileana Toma to study the nonlinear ordinary differential systems depending on the parameters in a classical linear frame.

The method is presented only for homogeneous nonlinear differential operators with constant coefficients, although it can be—and was—applied in more general cases.

Consider, therefore, the system

$$\mathcal{F}(\mathbf{y}) = \dot{\mathbf{y}} - \mathbf{f}(\mathbf{y}) = \mathbf{0}, \quad \mathbf{f}(\mathbf{y}) = [f_j(\mathbf{y})]_{j=\overline{1,n}}, \quad f_j(\mathbf{y}) = \sum_{|\mu|=1}^{\infty} f_{j\mu} \mathbf{y}^{\mu}, \quad f_{j\mu} \in \mathbb{R}, \tag{8.127}$$

to which are associated the arbitrary Cauchy conditions

$$\mathbf{y}(t_0) = \mathbf{y}_0, \quad t_0 \in \mathbb{R}. \tag{8.128}$$

The main idea of LEM consists of an exponential mapping depending on n parameters— $\xi = (\xi_1, \xi_2, \dots, \xi_n) \in \mathbb{R}^n$—namely,

$$v(x, \xi) \equiv e^{\langle \xi, y \rangle}. \tag{8.129}$$

Multiplying equation (8.127) by v, and then differentiating it with respect to t and replacing the derivatives $\dot{y}_j$ from the nonlinear system gives

(a) the first LEM equivalent:

$$\mathcal{L}v(x, \xi) \equiv \frac{\partial v}{\partial t} - \langle \xi, \mathbf{f}(D) \rangle v = 0, \tag{8.130}$$

a linear partial differential equation, always of first order with respect to x, accompanied by the obvious condition

$$v(t_0, \xi) = e^{\langle \xi, y_0 \rangle}, \quad \xi \in \mathbb{R}^n. \tag{8.131}$$

The usual notation $f_j(D_\xi)$ stands for the formal operator

$$f_j(D_\xi) = \sum_{|\mu|=1}^{\infty} f_\mu \frac{\partial^{|\mu|}}{\partial \xi^{\mu}}. \tag{8.132}$$

The formal scalar product in (8.130) is expressed as

$$\sum_{j=1}^{n} \xi_j f_j(D_\xi) \equiv \langle \xi, \mathbf{f}(D) \rangle. \tag{8.133}$$

Searching now for the unknown function v in the class of analytic with respect to ξ functions,

$$v(t, \xi) = 1 + \sum_{|\gamma|=1}^{\infty} v_\gamma(t) \frac{\xi^{\gamma}}{\gamma!} \tag{8.134}$$

is obtained.

(b) the second LEM equivalent:

$$\delta \mathbf{V} \equiv \frac{d\mathbf{V}}{dt} - \mathbf{A}\mathbf{V} = 0, \quad \mathbf{V} = (\mathbf{V}_j)_{j\in\mathbb{N}}, \quad \mathbf{V}_j = (v_{\boldsymbol{\gamma}})_{|\boldsymbol{\gamma}|=j}, \tag{8.135}$$

which must be solved under the Cauchy conditions

$$\mathbf{V}(t_0) = (\mathbf{y}_0^{\boldsymbol{\gamma}})_{|\boldsymbol{\gamma}|\in\mathbb{N}}. \tag{8.136}$$

The LEM matrix $\mathbf{A}$ is always column-finite; in the case of a polynomial operator, $\mathbf{A}$ is also row-finite. The cells $\mathbf{A}_{ss}$ on the main diagonal are square, of $s+1$ rows and columns, and are generated by those $f_{j\boldsymbol{\mu}}$, for which $|\boldsymbol{\mu}| = 1$. The other cells $\mathbf{A}_{k,k+s}$ contain only those $f_{j\boldsymbol{\mu}}$ with $|\boldsymbol{\mu}| = s+1$. More precisely, the diagonal cells contain the coefficients of the linear part; on the next upper diagonal we find cells containing the coefficients of the second degree in $\mathbf{y}$, and so on. In the case of polynomial operators of degree m, the associated LEM matrix is band-diagonal, the band being made up of m lines.

We can express the LEM matrix as

$$\mathbf{A}(t) = \begin{bmatrix} \mathbf{A}_{11} & \mathbf{A}_{12} & \mathbf{A}_{13} & \cdots & \mathbf{A}_{1m} & \mathbf{A}_{1,m+1} & \cdots \\ \mathbf{0} & \mathbf{A}_{22} & \mathbf{A}_{23} & \cdots & \mathbf{A}_{2m} & \mathbf{A}_{2,m+1} & \cdots \\ \mathbf{0} & \mathbf{0} & \mathbf{A}_{33} & \cdots & \mathbf{A}_{3m} & \mathbf{A}_{3,m+1} & \cdots \\ \cdots & \cdots & \cdots & \cdots & \cdots & \cdots & \cdots \end{bmatrix}. \tag{8.137}$$

It should be mentioned that this particular form of the LEM matrix is also conserved if the method is applied to nonhomogeneous ordinary differential systems with variable coefficients. This form permits the calculus by block partitioning, which represents a considerable simplification.

It was proved that any analytic with respect to $\boldsymbol{\xi}$ solution of linear problems (8.130) and (8.131) is of the exponential form (8.129), with $\mathbf{y}$ solution of the nonlinear initial problems (8.127) and (8.128).

Starting from this essential fact, we can establish various representations of the solution of nonlinear ordinary differential systems.

Theorem 8.4   The solution of the nonlinear initial problem

(i) coincides with the first n components of the infinite vector

$$\mathbf{V}(t) = e^{\mathbf{A}(t-t_0)}\mathbf{V}_0, \tag{8.138}$$

where the exponential matrix

$$e^{\mathbf{A}(t-t_0)} = \mathbf{I} + \frac{(t-t_0)}{1!}\mathbf{A} + \frac{(t-t_0)^2}{2!}\mathbf{A}^2 + \cdots + \frac{(t-t_0)^n}{n!}\mathbf{A}^n + \cdots \tag{8.139}$$

can be computed by block partitioning, each step involving finite sums;

(ii) coincides with the series

$$y_j(t) = y_{j0} + \sum_{l=1}^{\infty} \sum_{|\boldsymbol{\gamma}|=l} u_{j\boldsymbol{\gamma}}(t) y_0^{\boldsymbol{\gamma}}, \quad j = \overline{1, n}, \tag{8.140}$$

where $u_{j\boldsymbol{\gamma}}(t)$ are solutions of the finite linear ordinary differential systems

$$\frac{d\mathbf{U}_k}{dt} = \mathbf{A}_{1k}^{\mathrm{T}}\mathbf{U}_1 + \mathbf{A}_{2k}^{\mathrm{T}}\mathbf{U}_2 + \cdots + \mathbf{A}_{kk}^{\mathrm{T}}\mathbf{U}_k, \quad k = \overline{1, l}, \quad \mathbf{U}_s(t) = [u_{\boldsymbol{\gamma}}(t)]_{|\boldsymbol{\gamma}|=s}. \tag{8.141}$$

which satisfy the Cauchy conditions

$$\mathbf{U}_1(t_0) = \mathbf{e}_j, \quad \mathbf{U}_s(t_0) = \mathbf{0}, \quad s = \overline{2, l}. \tag{8.142}$$

T standing for transposed.

The above theorem generalizes a similar one, stated for polynomial ordinary differential systems. The corresponding result is very much alike a solution of a linear ordinary differential system with constant coefficients. There is more: the computation is even easier because of the fact that the eigen values of the diagonal cells are always known. The generalized representation (8.140) is the normal LEM representation and it was used in many applications requiring the qualitative behavior of the solution.

8.11 CONSIDERATIONS ABOUT THE ERRORS

The integration error is obviously of the order $\mathcal{O}(h)$ for Euler's method.

Taylor's method has the advantage that the order of the error is $\mathcal{O}(h^n)$, but it has the disadvantage that it needs the calculus of the derivatives of the function $\mathbf{f}(t, \mathbf{x}(t))$.

In the case of the Runge–Kutta type methods the error is of the order $\mathcal{O}(h^{p+1})$, where p is the order of the method.

Butcher stated that between the number of evaluations of the function $\mathbf{f}$ at each step and the truncation error's order, there is a link of the following form:

- for two evaluations of the function $\mathbf{f}$, the truncation error is of the order $\mathcal{O}(h^2)$;
- for three evaluations, the truncation error is of the order $\mathcal{O}(h^3)$;
- for four or five evaluations, the truncation error is of the order $\mathcal{O}(h^4)$;
- for six evaluations, the truncation error is of the order $\mathcal{O}(h^5)$;
- for seven evaluations, the truncation error is of the order $\mathcal{O}(h^6)$;
- for eight or more evaluations of the function $\mathbf{f}$, the truncation error is of the order $\mathcal{O}(h^{n-2})$, where n is the number of evaluations.

Proceeding as with the evaluation of the error in the case of Lagrange's interpolation polynomials, we obtain the following estimations of the errors in the case of multistep methods:

- for the second-order Adams–Bashforth method,

$$\varepsilon_x = \frac{5h^3}{12}M_2, \quad M_2 = \sup_{\xi \in [t_0, t_f]} |f''(\xi, x(\xi))|; \tag{8.143}$$

- for the third-order Adams–Bashforth method,

$$\varepsilon_x = \frac{3h^4}{8}M_3, \quad M_3 = \sup_{\xi \in [t_0, t_f]} |f^{(3)}(\xi, x(\xi))|; \tag{8.144}$$

- for the fourth-order Adams–Bashforth method,

$$\varepsilon_x = \frac{251h^5}{720}M_4, \quad M_4 = \sup_{\xi \in [t_0, t_f]} |f^{(4)}(\xi, x(\xi))|; \tag{8.145}$$

– for the fifth-order Adams–Bashforth method,

$$\varepsilon_x = \frac{85h^6}{288} M_5, \quad M_5 = \sup_{\xi \in [t_0, t_f]} |f^{(5)}(\xi, x(\xi))|; \tag{8.146}$$

– for the second-order Adams–Moulton method,

$$\varepsilon_x = \frac{h^3}{12} M_2, \quad M_2 = \sup_{\xi \in [t_0, t_f]} |f''(\xi, x(\xi))|; \tag{8.147}$$

– for the third-order Adams–Moulton method,

$$\varepsilon_x = \frac{h^4}{24} M_3, \quad M_3 = \sup_{\xi \in [t_0, t_f]} |f^{(3)}(\xi, x(\xi))|; \tag{8.148}$$

– for the fourth-order Adams–Moulton method,

$$\varepsilon_x = \frac{19h^5}{720} M_4, \quad M_4 = \sup_{\xi \in [t_0, t_f]} |f^{(4)}(\xi, x(\xi))|; \tag{8.149}$$

– for the fifth-order Adams–Moulton method,

$$\varepsilon_x = \frac{3h^6}{16} M_5, \quad M_5 = \sup_{\xi \in [t_0, t_f]} |f^{(5)}(\xi, x(\xi))|. \tag{8.150}$$

We can easily observe that the Adams–Moulton methods are more precise than the same-order Adams–Bashforth methods.

8.12 NUMERICAL EXAMPLE

Example Let us consider the Cauchy problem

$$\dot{x} = \frac{dx}{dt} = x + e^t (2\cos 2t - \sin t), \quad t \in [0, 2], \quad x(0) = 1, \tag{8.151}$$

the solution of which, obviously, is

$$x(t) = e^t (\sin 2t + \cos t). \tag{8.152}$$

We shall determine the numerical solution of this Cauchy problem by various methods, with the step $h = 0.1$.

In the case of Euler's method, the calculation relation is

$$w^{(i)} = w^{(i-1)} + hf(t_{i-1}, w^{(i-1)}), \quad i = \overline{1, 20}, \tag{8.153}$$

where

$$f(t, w) = w + e^t (2\cos 2t - \sin t). \tag{8.154}$$

It results in Table 8.1.

TABLE 8.1   Solution of Problem (8.151) with Euler's Method

Step	t_i	$x_i = x(t_i)$	$f(t_{i-1}, w_{i-1})$	w_i
0	0.0	1.000000	–	1.000000
1	0.1	1.319213	3.000000	1.300000
2	0.2	1.672693	3.355949	1.635595
3	0.3	2.051757	3.642913	1.999886
4	0.4	2.444231	3.829149	2.382801
5	0.5	2.834240	3.880586	2.770860
6	0.6	3.202145	3.762036	3.147063
7	0.7	3.524655	3.438735	3.490937
8	0.8	3.775141	2.878185	3.778755
9	0.9	3.924192	2.052280	3.983983
10	1.0	3.940421	0.939656	4.077949
11	1.1	3.791535	−0.471815	4.030767
12	1.2	3.445687	−2.182478	3.812520
13	1.3	2.873060	−4.178426	3.394677
14	1.4	2.047695	−6.429262	2.751751
15	1.5	0.949478	−8.886245	1.863126
16	1.6	−0.433755	−11.481013	0.715025
17	1.7	−2.104107	−14.125068	−0.697482
18	1.8	−4.051585	−16.710208	−2.368502
19	1.9	−6.252297	−19.110082	−4.279511
20	2.0	−8.666988	−21.183026	−6.397813

Another possibility to solve problem (8.151) is the use of Taylor's method. We shall use Taylor's method of second order, for which we have

$$T^{(2)}(t_i, w_i) = f(t_i, w) + \frac{h}{2} f'(t_i, w_i), i = \overline{0, 19}, \tag{8.155}$$

$$f'(t, x) = \frac{df(t, x)}{dt} = x + e^t(4\cos 2t - 4\sin 2t - 2\sin t - \cos t), \tag{8.156}$$

$$w_{i+1} = w_i + hT^{(2)}(t_i, w_i), \quad i = \overline{0, 19}. \tag{8.157}$$

The numerical results are given in Table 8.2.
If we solve the same Cauchy problem by Euler's modified method, then we have the relation

$$w_{i+1} = w_i + \frac{h}{2}[f(t_i, w_i) + f(t_{i+1}, w_i + hf(t_i, w_i))], \quad i = \overline{0, 19}, \tag{8.158}$$

resulting in Table 8.3.
The solution of Cauchy problems (8.151) and (8.152) by Heun's method leads to the relation

$$w_i = w_i + \frac{h}{4}\left[f(t_i, w_i) + 3f\left(t_i + \frac{2}{3}h, w_i + \frac{2}{3}hf(t_i, w_i)\right)\right] \tag{8.159}$$

and to the data in Table 8.4. Another way to treat Cauchy problems (8.151) and (8.152) is that of the Runge–Kutta method.

TABLE 8.2 Solution of Problem (8.151) with Taylor's Second-Order Method

Step	t_i	$f(t_i, w_i)$	$f'(t_i, w_i)$	$T^{(2)}(t_i, w_i)$	w_i
0	0.0	3.000000	4.000000	3.200000	1.000000
1	0.1	3.375949	3.453994	3.548649	1.320000
2	0.2	3.682182	2.589898	3.811677	1.674865
3	0.3	3.885295	1.376238	3.954107	2.056033
4	0.4	3.949228	−0.207727	3.938842	2.451443
5	0.5	3.836504	−2.168613	3.728074	2.845327
6	0.6	3.509807	−4.495524	3.285031	3.218135
7	0.7	2.933886	−7.156876	2.576043	3.546638
8	0.8	2.077767	−10.097625	1.572886	3.804242
9	0.9	0.917204	−13.237152	0.255346	3.961531
10	1.0	−0.562699	−16.468063	−1.386102	3.987065
11	1.1	−2.364790	−19.656143	−3.347597	3.848455
12	1.2	−4.477250	−22.641732	−5.609337	3.513696
13	1.3	−6.871177	−25.242758	−8.133315	2.952762
14	1.4	−9.498565	−27.259588	−10.861545	2.139430
15	1.5	−12.290864	−28.481849	−13.714956	1.053276
16	1.6	−15.158313	−28.697264	−16.593176	−0.318220
17	1.7	−17.990263	−27.702427	−19.375385	−1.977537
18	1.8	−20.656655	−25.315371	−21.922424	−3.915076
19	1.9	−23.010834	−21.389601	−24.080314	−6.107318
20	2.0	−24.893818	−15.829130	−25.685275	−8.515350

TABLE 8.3 Solution of Problem (8.151) with the Modified Euler Method

Step	t_i	$f(t_i, w_i) + f(t_{i+1}, w_i + hf(t_i, w_i))$	w_i
0	0.0	6.355949	1.000000
1	0.1	6.355949	1.317797
2	0.2	7.036236	1.669609
3	0.3	7.543491	2.046784
4	0.4	7.808220	2.437195
5	0.5	7.756849	2.825037
6	0.6	7.314545	3.190765
7	0.7	6.408693	3.511199
8	0.8	4.973017	3.759850
9	0.9	2.952235	3.907462
10	1.0	0.307146	3.922819
11	1.1	−2.980065	3.773816
12	1.2	−6.900502	3.428791
13	1.3	−11.413518	2.858115
14	1.4	−16.442287	2.036000
15	1.5	−21.870334	0.942484
16	1.6	−27.539431	−0.434488
17	1.7	−33.249253	−2.096950
18	1.8	−38.759174	−4.034909
19	1.9	−43.792562	−6.224537
20	2.0	−48.043864	−8.626730

TABLE 8.4   Solution of Equation (8.151) by Heun's Method

Step	t_i	x_i	w_i
0	0.0	1.000000	1.000000
1	0.1	1.3192132	1.3185770
2	0.2	1.6726927	1.6714575
3	0.3	2.0517570	2.0500182
4	0.4	2.4442311	2.4421527
5	0.5	2.8342401	2.8320649
6	0.6	3.2021455	3.2002036
7	0.7	3.5246551	3.5233706
8	0.8	3.7751413	3.7750360
9	0.9	3.9241925	3.9258857
10	1.0	3.9404206	3.9446252
11	1.1	3.7915355	3.7990486
12	1.2	3.4456868	3.4573757
13	1.3	2.8730600	2.8898418
14	1.4	2.0476947	2.0705108
15	1.5	0.9494781	0.9792638
16	1.6	−0.4337552	−0.3961070
17	1.7	−2.1041065	−2.0577838
18	1.8	−4.0515853	−3.9958985
19	1.9	−6.2522972	−6.1867206
20	2.0	−8.6669884	−8.5911995

Thus, for the Runge–Kutta method of third order we apply the relations

$$K_1 = hf(t_i, w_i), \quad K_2 = hf\left(t_i + \frac{h}{2}, w_i + \frac{K_1}{2}\right), \quad K_3 = hf(t_i + h, w_i + 2K_2 + K_1), \quad (8.160)$$

$$w_{i+1} = w_i + \frac{1}{6}(K_1 + 4K_2 + K_3), \tag{8.161}$$

the results being given in Table 8.5. Analogically, for the Runge–Kutta method of fourth order we have the relations

$$K_1 = hf(t_i, w_i), \quad K_2 = hf\left(t_i + \frac{h}{2}, w_i + \frac{K_1}{2}\right), \quad K_3 = hf\left(t_i + \frac{h}{2}, w_i + \frac{K_2}{2}\right),$$
$$K_4 = hf(t_i + h, w_i + K_3), \tag{8.162}$$

$$w_{i+1} = w_i + \frac{1}{6}(K_1 + 2K_2 + 2K_3 + K_4), \tag{8.163}$$

while for the Runge–Kutta method of sixth order we may write

$$K_1 = hf(t_i, w_i), \quad K_2 = hf\left(t_i + \frac{h}{2}, w_i + \frac{K_1}{3}\right),$$

$$K_3 = hf\left(t_i + \frac{2h}{5}, w_i + \frac{1}{25}\left(6K_2 + 4K_3\right)\right),$$

$$K_4 = hf\left(t_i + h, w_i + \frac{1}{4}\left(15K_3 - 12K_2 + K_1\right)\right),$$

TABLE 8.5 Solution of Equation (8.151) by the Runge–Kutta Method of Third Order

Step	x_i	w_i
0	1.0000000	1.0000000
1	1.3192132	1.3291972
2	1.6726927	1.6949971
3	2.0517570	2.0887387
4	2.4442311	2.4981579
5	2.8342401	2.9071609
6	3.2021455	3.2957409
7	3.5246551	3.6400730
8	3.7751413	3.9128210
9	3.9241925	4.0836843
10	3.9404206	4.1202083
11	3.7915355	3.9888704
12	3.4456868	3.6564447
13	2.8730600	3.0916307
14	2.0476947	2.2669173
15	0.9494781	1.1606331
16	−0.4337552	−0.2408872
17	−2.1041065	−1.9411070
18	−4.0515853	−3.9311771
19	−6.2522972	−6.1880339
20	−8.6669884	−8.6728551

$$K_5 = hf\left(t_i + \frac{2}{3}h, w_i + \frac{2}{81}\left(4K_4 - 25K_3 + 45K_2 + 3K_1\right)\right),$$

$$K_6 = hf\left(t_i + \frac{4}{5}h, w_i + \frac{1}{75}\left(8K_4 + 10K_3 + 36K_2 + 6K_1\right)\right), \tag{8.164}$$

$$w_{i+1} = w_i + \frac{1}{192}(23K_1 + 125K_3 - 8K_5 + 12K_6). \tag{8.165}$$

The results are given in Table 8.6 and Table 8.7.

The solution of Cauchy problems (8.151) and (8.152) by the Runge–Kutta–Fehlberg method leads to the data in Table 8.8.

We may study the problem by using the multistep methods too.

Thus, Adams method leads to the results in Table 8.9. For Adams–Bashforth methods of the third, fourth, and fifth order we obtain the data in Table 8.10, Table 8.11, and Table 8.12, respectively.

The use of the Adams–Moulton methods of third, fourth, and fifth order leads to the results in Table 8.13, Table 8.14, and Table 8.15, respectively.

If we use the predictor–corrector methods, then it results

- for Euler's predictor–corrector method the data in Table 8.16;
- for Adams's predictor–corrector method the data in Table 8.17, Table 8.18, and Table 8.19;
- for Milne's predictor–corrector method of fourth order the data in Table 8.20;
- for Hamming's predictor–corrector method the data in Table 8.21.

TABLE 8.6   Solution of Equation (8.151) by the Runge–Kutta Method of Fourth Order

Step	x_i	w_i
0	1.0000000	1.0000000
1	1.3192132	1.3192130
2	1.6726927	1.6726923
3	2.0517570	2.0517565
4	2.4442311	2.4442305
5	2.8342401	2.8342396
6	3.2021455	3.2021451
7	3.5246551	3.5246551
8	3.7751413	3.7751417
9	3.9241925	3.9241937
10	3.9404206	3.9404228
11	3.7915355	3.7915390
12	3.4456868	3.4456919
13	2.8730600	2.8730670
14	2.0476947	2.0477038
15	0.9494781	0.9494898
16	−0.4337552	−0.4337406
17	−2.1041065	−2.1040888
18	−4.0515853	−4.0515641
19	−6.2522972	−6.2522725
20	−8.6669884	−8.6669599

TABLE 8.7   Solution of Equation (8.151) by the Runge–Kutta Method of Sixth Order

Step	x_i	w_i
0	1.0000000	1.0000000
1	1.3192132	1.3192132
2	1.6726927	1.6726927
3	2.0517570	2.0517570
4	2.4442311	2.4442311
5	2.8342401	2.8342402
6	3.2021455	3.2021455
7	3.5246551	3.5246551
8	3.7751413	3.7751413
9	3.9241925	3.9241926
10	3.9404206	3.9404208
11	3.7915355	3.7915357
12	3.4456868	3.4456871
13	2.8730600	2.8730603
14	2.0476947	2.0476951
15	0.9494781	0.9494786
16	−0.4337552	−0.4337547
17	−2.1041065	−2.1041059
18	−4.0515853	−4.0515846
19	−6.2522972	−6.2522964
20	−8.6669884	−8.6669876

TABLE 8.8   Solution of Equation (8.151) by the Runge–Kutta–Fehlberg Method

t	w	x
0.0000000	1.0000000	1.0000000
0.0316228	1.0968461	1.0968461
0.1469862	1.4814837	1.4814836
0.2666438	1.9231489	1.9231488
0.4162211	2.5081341	2.5081341
0.5210182	2.9141284	2.9141283
0.6250856	3.2883041	3.2883041
0.7170764	3.5733095	3.5733096
0.8010931	3.7773744	3.7773745
0.8799701	3.9039488	3.9039489
0.9551846	3.9516312	3.9516314
1.0276254	3.9171714	3.9171716
1.0979024	3.7965716	3.7965719
1.1664726	3.5854933	3.5854937
1.2337016	3.2794283	3.2794287
1.2998982	2.8737670	2.8737676
1.3653372	2.3638101	2.3638107
1.4302756	1.7447325	1.7447331
1.4949669	1.0114991	1.0114998
1.5596750	0.1587110	0.1587118
1.6246911	−0.8196561	−0.8196552
1.6903571	−1.9307042	−1.9307032
1.7571028	−3.1834262	−3.1834251
1.8255128	−4.5902733	−4.5902721
1.8964618	−6.1705045	−6.1705032
1.9714434	−7.9585369	−7.9585354

8.13   APPLICATIONS

Problem 8.1

Study the motion of a rigid solid with a point constrained to move without friction on a given curve (Fig. 8.2). As numerical application, let us consider a body formed (Fig. 8.3) from a homogeneous cube $ABDE\,A'B'D'E'$ of mass m and edge l and a bar OG of length l and negligible mass, G being the center of the square $ABDE$. The point O moves without friction on the cylindrical curve Γ of equations

$$X_0 = l\cos\xi_1, \quad Y_0 = l\sin\xi_1, \quad Z_0 = kl\xi_1. \tag{8.166}$$

Knowing that the mass m, the length l, and the parameter k have the values

$$m = 12\ \text{kg}, \quad l = 0.1\ \text{m}, \quad k = 0.1, \tag{8.167}$$

and that the initial conditions of the attached Cauchy problem are (for $t = 0$)

$$\xi_1 = 0\ \text{m}, \quad \xi_5 = 0\ \text{m s}^{-1}, \quad \psi = 0\ \text{rad}, \quad \theta = 0.001\ \text{rad}, \quad \phi = 0\ \text{rad}, \quad \omega_x = 0\ \text{rad s}^{-1},$$
$$\omega_y = 0\ \text{rad s}^{-1}, \quad \omega_z = 0\ \text{rad s}^{-1},$$

$$\tag{8.168}$$

draw the variables $\xi_i(t)$, $i = \overline{1,8}$.

TABLE 8.9 Solution of Equation (8.151) by the Adams Method

Step	t	x	$f(t_i, w_i)$	Δf	$\Delta^2 f$	$\Delta^3 f$	$\Delta^4 f$	w
0	0.0	1.00000	3.00000	0.37516	−0.07031	−0.03352	−0.00265	1.00000
1	0.1	1.31921	3.37516	0.30485	−0.10384	−0.03617	−0.00145	1.31921
2	0.2	1.67269	3.68001	0.20101	−0.14001	−0.03762	0.00024	1.67269
3	0.3	2.05176	3.88102	0.06100	−0.17764	−0.03739	0.00208	2.05176
4	0.4	2.44423	3.94202	−0.11664	−0.21502	−0.03530	0.00429	2.44423
5	0.5	2.83424	3.82538	−0.33166	−0.25033	−0.03102	0.00678	2.83420
6	0.6	3.20215	3.49371	−0.58199	−0.28134	−0.02424	0.00940	3.20204
7	0.7	3.52466	2.91173	−0.86333	−0.30558	−0.01484	0.01209	3.52448
8	0.8	3.77514	2.04839	−1.16892	−0.32042	−0.00275	0.01473	3.77487
9	0.9	3.92419	0.87948	−1.48934	−0.32317	0.01198	0.01714	3.92381
10	1.0	3.94042	−0.60986	−1.81251	−0.31120	0.02912	0.01916	3.93990
11	1.1	3.79154	−2.42238	−2.12371	−0.28208	0.04827	0.02060	3.79087
12	1.2	3.44569	−4.54609	−2.40579	−0.23381	0.06887	0.02125	3.44486
13	1.3	2.87306	−6.95188	−2.63960	−0.16494	0.09012	0.02092	2.87206
14	1.4	2.04769	−9.59148	−2.80454	−0.07482	0.11104	0.01942	2.04652
15	1.5	0.94948	−12.39601	−2.87935	0.03622	0.13046	0.01658	0.94813
16	1.6	−0.43376	−15.27536	−2.84313	0.16668	0.14704	0.01229	−0.43527
17	1.7	−2.10411	−18.11850	−2.67646	0.31372	0.15933		
18	1.8	−4.05159	−20.79496	−2.36274	0.47305			
19	1.9	−6.25230	−23.15770	−1.88970				
20	2.0	−8.66699	−25.04739					

TABLE 8.10   Solution of Equation (8.151) by the Adams–Bashforth Method of Third Order

Step	x_i	w_i
0	1.00000	1.00000
1	1.31921	1.31921
2	1.67269	1.67269
3	2.05176	2.05301
4	2.44423	2.44707
5	2.83424	2.83887
6	3.20215	3.20874
7	3.52466	3.53335
8	3.77514	3.78599
9	3.92419	3.93717
10	3.94042	3.95539
11	3.79154	3.80823
12	3.44569	3.46373
13	2.87306	2.89191
14	2.04769	2.06669
15	0.94948	0.96783
16	−0.43376	−0.41696
17	−2.10411	−2.08986
18	−4.05159	−4.04092
19	−6.25230	−6.24627
20	−8.66699	−8.66659

**TABLE 8.11 Solution of Equation (8.151) by the
Adams–Bashforth Method of Fourth Order**

Step	x_i	w_i
0	1.00000	1.00000
1	1.31921	1.31921
2	1.67269	1.67269
3	2.05176	2.05176
4	2.44423	2.44433
5	2.83424	2.83441
6	3.20215	3.20233
7	3.52466	3.52478
8	3.77514	3.77513
9	3.92419	3.92394
10	3.94042	3.93980
11	3.79154	3.79041
12	3.44569	3.44391
13	2.87306	2.87047
14	2.04769	2.04414
15	0.94948	0.94479
16	−0.43376	−0.43971
17	−2.10411	−2.11146
18	−4.05159	−4.06043
19	−6.25230	−6.26269
20	−8.66699	−8.67894

**TABLE 8.12 Solution of Equation (8.151) by the
Adams–Bashforth Method of Fifth Order**

Step	x_i	w_i
0	1.00000	1.00000
1	1.31921	1.31921
2	1.67269	1.67269
3	2.05176	2.05176
4	2.44423	2.44423
5	2.83424	2.83420
6	3.20215	3.20204
7	3.52466	3.52448
8	3.77514	3.77487
9	3.92419	3.92381
10	3.94042	3.93990
11	3.79154	3.79087
12	3.44569	3.44486
13	2.87306	2.87206
14	2.04769	2.04652
15	0.94948	0.94813
16	−0.43376	−0.43527
17	−2.10411	−2.10577
18	−4.05159	−4.05338
19	−6.25230	−6.25418
20	−8.66699	−8.66892

TABLE 8.13   Solution of Equation (8.151) by the Adams–Moulton Method of Third Order

Step	x_i	w_i
0	1.00000	1.00000
1	1.31921	1.31921
2	1.67269	1.67255
3	2.05176	2.05145
4	2.44423	2.44372
5	2.83424	2.83351
6	3.20215	3.20118
7	3.52466	3.52345
8	3.77514	3.77369
9	3.92419	3.92250
10	3.94042	3.93852
11	3.79154	3.78946
12	3.44569	3.44349
13	2.87306	2.87081
14	2.04769	2.04548
15	0.94948	0.94739
16	−0.43376	−0.43561
17	−2.10411	−2.10562
18	−4.05159	−4.05264
19	−6.25230	−6.25278
20	−8.66699	−8.66680

TABLE 8.14   Solution of Equation (8.151) by the Adams–Moulton Method of Fourth Order

Step	x_i	w_i
0	1.00000	1.00000
1	1.31921	1.31921
2	1.67269	1.67269
3	2.05176	2.05175
4	2.44423	2.44422
5	2.83424	2.83422
6	3.20215	3.20213
7	3.52466	3.52465
8	3.77514	3.77515
9	3.92419	3.92423
10	3.94042	3.94049
11	3.79154	3.79165
12	3.44569	3.44586
13	2.87306	2.87330
14	2.04769	2.04802
15	0.94948	0.94990
16	−0.43376	−0.43323
17	−2.10411	−2.10347
18	−4.05159	−4.05084
19	−6.25230	−6.25143
20	−8.66699	−8.66601

TABLE 8.15   Solution of Equation (8.151) by the Adams–Moulton Method of Fifth Order

Step	x_i	w_i
0	1.00000	1.00000
1	1.31921	1.31921
2	1.67269	1.67269
3	2.05176	2.05176
4	2.44423	2.44423
5	2.83424	2.83425
6	3.20215	3.20216
7	3.52466	3.52467
8	3.77514	3.77516
9	3.92419	3.92422
10	3.94042	3.94046
11	3.79154	3.79158
12	3.44569	3.44574
13	2.87306	2.87313
14	2.04769	2.04777
15	0.94948	0.94956
16	−0.43376	−0.43366
17	−2.10411	−2.10400
18	−4.05159	−4.05148
19	−6.25230	−6.25219
20	−8.66699	−8.66688

TABLE 8.16   Solution of Equation (8.151) by Euler's Predictor–Corrector Method

Step	x_i	w_i^{pred}	w_i^{corr}
0	1.000000000	1.000000000	1.000000000
1	1.319213234	1.300000000	1.317797459
2	1.672692659	1.655172121	1.669609276
3	2.051756990	2.037301965	2.046783846
4	2.444231072	2.434388485	2.437194823
5	2.834240148	2.830692770	2.825037271
6	3.202145482	3.206658671	3.190764509
7	3.524655087	3.539008168	3.511199171
8	3.775141261	3.801043935	3.759850010
9	3.924192475	3.963187530	3.907461783
10	3.940420612	3.993775235	3.922819068
11	3.791535483	3.860124570	3.773815798
12	3.445686849	3.529872878	3.428790709
13	2.873060026	2.972575236	2.858114788
14	2.047694688	2.161532373	2.036000413
15	0.949478141	1.075800882	0.942483717
16	−0.433755206	−0.297681859	−0.434487826
17	−2.104106532	−1.961945934	−2.096950472
18	−4.051585254	−3.907918108	−4.034909166
19	−6.252297191	−6.112558023	−6.224537284
20	−8.666988414	−8.537342587	−8.626730488

TABLE 8.17   Solution of Equation (8.151) by Adams's Predictor–Corrector Method of Third Order

Step	x_i	w_i^{pred}	w_i^{corr}
0	1.000000000	1.000000000	1.000000000
1	1.319213234	1.319213234	1.319213234
2	1.672692659	1.672692659	1.672692659
3	2.051756990	2.053006306	2.051661525
4	2.444231072	2.445469036	2.444025281
5	2.834240148	2.835416070	2.833912943
6	3.202145482	3.203185641	3.201689577
7	3.524655087	3.525480687	3.524068322
8	3.775141261	3.775667889	3.774427807
9	3.924192475	3.924333295	3.923363951
10	3.940420612	3.940090450	3.939497056
11	3.791535483	3.790655697	3.790546062
12	3.445686849	3.444190896	3.444670252
13	2.873060026	2.870899572	2.872064424
14	2.047694688	2.044846047	2.046777180
15	0.949478141	0.945948761	0.948703618
16	−0.433755206	−0.437920555	−0.434315861
17	−2.104106532	−2.108820265	−2.104378926
18	−4.051585254	−4.056712629	−4.051494673
19	−6.252297191	−6.257653609	−6.251772462
20	−8.666988414	−8.672338860	−8.665966364

TABLE 8.18   Solution of Equation (8.151) by Adams's Predictor–Corrector Method of Fourth Order

Step	x_i	w_i^{pred}	w_i^{corr}
0	1.000000000	1.000000000	1.000000000
1	1.319213234	1.319213234	1.319213234
2	1.672692659	1.672692659	1.672692659
3	2.051756990	2.051756990	2.051756990
4	2.444231072	2.444325646	2.444229802
5	2.834240148	2.834290471	2.834239769
6	3.202145482	3.202142622	3.202148906
7	3.524655087	3.524590325	3.524665906
8	3.775141261	3.775008126	3.775163759
9	3.924192475	3.923986977	3.924231579
10	3.940420612	3.940142130	3.940481805
11	3.791535483	3.791187569	3.791624671
12	3.445686849	3.445277980	3.445810180
13	2.873060026	2.872604252	2.873223668
14	2.047694688	2.047212125	2.047904558
15	0.949478141	0.948995244	0.949739603
16	−0.433755206	−0.434205656	−0.433437678
17	−2.104106532	−2.104485777	−2.103729696
18	−4.051585254	−4.051849311	−4.051147446
19	−6.252297191	−6.252398041	−6.251798643
20	−8.666988414	−8.666875667	−8.666431527

TABLE 8.19   Solution of Equation (8.151) by Adams's Predictor–Corrector Method of Fifth Order

Step	x_i	w_i^{pred}	w_i^{corr}
0	1.000000000	1.000000000	1.000000000
1	1.319213234	1.319213234	1.319213234
2	1.672692659	1.672692659	1.672692659
3	2.051756990	2.051756990	2.051756990
4	2.444231072	2.444231072	2.444231072
5	2.834240148	2.834199636	2.834241554
6	3.202145482	3.202095487	3.202148720
7	3.524655087	3.524595924	3.524660533
8	3.775141261	3.775074728	3.775149304
9	3.924192475	3.924120543	3.924203459
10	3.940420612	3.940346215	3.940434826
11	3.791535483	3.791462325	3.791553128
12	3.445686849	3.445619382	3.445708016
13	2.873060026	2.873003382	2.873084668
14	2.047694688	2.047654547	2.047722600
15	0.949478141	0.949460545	0.949508941
16	−0.433755206	−0.433744107	−0.433722093
17	−2.104106532	−2.104060787	−2.104071874
18	−4.051585254	−4.051499477	−4.051550007
19	−6.252297191	−6.252166980	−6.252262480
20	−8.666988414	−8.666810798	−8.666955499

TABLE 8.20   Solution of Equation (8.151) by Milne's Predictor–Corrector Method of Fourth Order

Step	x_i	w_i^{pred}	w_i^{corr}
0	1.000000000	1.000000000	1.000000000
1	1.319213234	1.319213234	1.319213234
2	1.672692659	1.672692659	1.672692659
3	2.051756990	2.051756990	2.051756990
4	2.444231072	2.444313815	2.444232221
5	2.834240148	2.834284533	2.834241933
6	3.202145482	3.202140594	3.202149027
7	3.524655087	3.524591299	3.524660029
8	3.775141261	3.775009983	3.775148704
9	3.924192475	3.923986136	3.924202128
10	3.940420612	3.940134740	3.940433506
11	3.791535483	3.791168274	3.791551327
12	3.445686849	3.445241097	3.445706520
13	2.873060026	2.872542757	2.873083141
14	2.047694688	2.047118841	2.047721888
15	0.949478141	0.948862029	0.949508855
16	−0.433755206	−0.434386680	−0.433720655
17	−2.104106532	−2.104722840	−2.104068978
18	−4.051585254	−4.052149724	−4.051544739
19	−6.252297191	−6.252768644	−6.252254840
20	−8.666988414	−8.667321559	−8.666944624

TABLE 8.21   Solution of Equation (8.151) by Hamming's Predictor–Corrector Method of Fourth Order

Step	x_i	w_i^{pred}	w_i^{corr}
0	1.000000000	1.000000000	1.000000000
1	1.319213234	1.319213234	1.319213234
2	1.672692659	1.672692659	1.672692659
3	2.051756990	2.051756990	2.051756990
4	2.444231072	2.444313815	2.444229732
5	2.834240148	2.834283869	2.834239485
6	3.202145482	3.202140273	3.202148436
7	3.524655087	3.524590804	3.524665679
8	3.775141261	3.775008426	3.775164256
9	3.924192475	3.923986924	3.924233399
10	3.940420612	3.940141921	3.940485639
11	3.791535483	3.791187804	3.791631306
12	3.445686849	3.445279364	3.445820481
13	2.873060026	2.872607655	2.873238554
14	2.047694688	2.047218551	2.047924973
15	0.949478141	0.949005833	0.949766481
16	−0.433755206	−0.434189654	−0.433403459
17	−2.104106532	−2.104463036	
18	−4.051585254	−4.051818467	−4.051096382
19	−6.252297191	−6.252357753	−6.251738441
20	−8.666988414	−8.666824674	−8.666362041

Solution:

1. Theory

Let us consider the rigid solid in Figure 8.2, in which its point O moves on the curve Γ, and let $O_0 X_0 Y_0 Z_0$ be a fixed reference system, $Oxyz$ the movable system of the principal axes of inertia, and C the weight center of the rigid solid.

Further on, we use the notations:

- X_O, Y_O, Z_O, the co-ordinates of the point O in the fixed reference system;
- $\mathbf{r}_C$, the vector **OC**;
- x_C, y_C, z_C, the co-ordinates of the point C in the system $Oxyz$;
- m, the mass of the rigid solid;
- J_x, J_y, J_z, the principal moments of inertia;
- the parametric equations of the curve Γ, given by

$$X_O = f_1(\lambda), \quad Y_O = f_2(\lambda), \quad Z_O = f_3(\lambda), \quad \text{where } \lambda \in \mathbb{R}; \qquad (8.169)$$

- $Ox_0'y_0'z_0'$, a reference system with the origin at O and with the axes parallel to those of the system $O_0 X_0 Y_0 Z_0$, respectively;
- ψ, θ, ϕ, the Euler angles, which define the position of the system $Oxyz$ relative to the system $Ox_0'y_0'z_0'$;
- $\mathbf{F}$, the resultant of the forces that act upon the rigid solid;
- $\mathbf{M}_O$, the resultant moment of the given forces at O.

Considering that the parameters ψ, θ, ϕ, λ and their derivatives $\dot{\psi}$, $\dot{\theta}$, $\dot{\phi}$, $\dot{\lambda}$, the inertial parameters m, J_x, J_y, J_z, x_C, y_C, z_C, and also the torsor of the forces $\{\mathbf{F}, \mathbf{M}_O\}$ at the moment $t = 0$ are known,

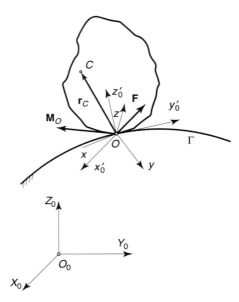

Figure 8.2   The rigid solid, a point of which is constrained to move without friction on a given curve.

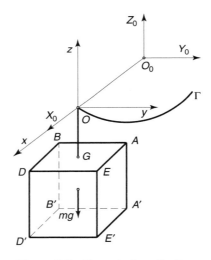

Figure 8.3   Numerical application.

determine the motion, respectively, the functions of time $\psi = \psi(t)$, $\theta = \theta(t)$, $\phi = \phi(t)$, $\lambda = \lambda(t)$, $X_O(t)$, $Y_O(t)$, $Z_O(t)$.

The theorem of momentum can be written in the vector form

$$m[\mathbf{a}_O + \boldsymbol{\varepsilon} \times \mathbf{r}_C + \boldsymbol{\omega} \times (\boldsymbol{\omega} \times \mathbf{r}_C)] = \mathbf{F} + N_1\boldsymbol{v} + N_2\boldsymbol{\beta}, \tag{8.170}$$

where

- $\mathbf{a}_O$ is the acceleration of the point O;
- $\boldsymbol{\varepsilon}$ is the angular acceleration of the rigid solid;
- $\boldsymbol{\omega}$ is the angular velocity of the rigid solid;

- $\mathbf{v}$, $\boldsymbol{\beta}$ are the unit vectors of the principal normal and of the binormal, respectively, to the curve Γ;
- N_1, N_2 are the reactions in the direction of the principal normal and in the direction of the binormal, respectively, to the curve Γ.

The theorem of moment of momentum relative to the point O, in the vector form, reads

$$\mathbf{r}_C \times m\mathbf{a}_O + [J_x \varepsilon_x - (J_y - J_z)\omega_y \omega_z]\mathbf{i}$$
$$+ [J_y \varepsilon_y - (J_z - J_x)\omega_z \omega_x]\mathbf{j} + [J_z \varepsilon_z - (J_x - J_y)\omega_x \omega_y]\mathbf{k} = \mathbf{M}_O, \tag{8.171}$$

where

- ω_x, ω_y, ω_z are the projections of the vector $\boldsymbol{\omega}$ onto the axes of the system $Oxyz$;
- ε_x, ε_y, ε_z are the projections of the vector $\boldsymbol{\varepsilon}$ onto the axes of the system $Oxyz$.

If $\mathbf{T}_1$ is a tangent vector at the point O to the curve Γ, then from relation (8.170), by a dot product of both members by $\mathbf{T}_1$, we can eliminate the reactions N_1 and N_2, obtaining

$$m\{\mathbf{T}_1 \cdot \mathbf{a}_O + \mathbf{T}_1 \cdot (\boldsymbol{\varepsilon} \times \mathbf{r}_C) + \mathbf{T}_1 \cdot [\boldsymbol{\omega} \times (\boldsymbol{\omega} \times \mathbf{r}_C)]\} = \mathbf{T}_1 \cdot \mathbf{F}. \tag{8.172}$$

As we shall see soon, the system consisting of equations (8.171) and (8.172) can be transformed in a system of eight first-order differential equations, from which the parameters ψ, θ, ϕ, λ are finally deduced.

To pass from the system $O_0 X_0 Y_0 Z_0$ to the system $Oxyz$, the rotation matrix $[\mathbf{R}]$ is written in the form

$$[\mathbf{R}] = [\boldsymbol{\phi}][\boldsymbol{\theta}][\boldsymbol{\psi}], \tag{8.173}$$

where

$$[\boldsymbol{\phi}] = \begin{bmatrix} \cos\phi & \sin\phi & 0 \\ -\sin\phi & \cos\phi & 0 \\ 0 & 0 & 1 \end{bmatrix}, \quad [\boldsymbol{\theta}] = \begin{bmatrix} 1 & 0 & 0 \\ 0 & \cos\theta & \sin\theta \\ 0 & -\sin\theta & \cos\theta \end{bmatrix}, \quad [\boldsymbol{\psi}] = \begin{bmatrix} \cos\psi & \sin\psi & 0 \\ -\sin\psi & \cos\psi & 0 \\ 0 & 0 & 1 \end{bmatrix}. \tag{8.174}$$

The vector $\mathbf{T}_1$, tangent to the curve, and the acceleration $\mathbf{a}_O$ have the matrix expressions

$$\{\mathbf{T}_1\} = \begin{bmatrix} T_{1x} \\ T_{1y} \\ T_{1z} \end{bmatrix} = \begin{bmatrix} f_1'(\lambda) \\ f_2'(\lambda) \\ f_3'(\lambda) \end{bmatrix}, \tag{8.175}$$

$$\{\mathbf{a}_O\} = \begin{bmatrix} a_{Ox} \\ a_{Oy} \\ a_{Oz} \end{bmatrix} = \ddot{\lambda}\{\mathbf{T}_1\} + \dot{\lambda}^2\{\mathbf{T}_2\}, \tag{8.176}$$

where

$$\{\mathbf{T}_2\} = \begin{bmatrix} T_{2x} \\ T_{2y} \\ T_{2z} \end{bmatrix} = \begin{bmatrix} f_1''(\lambda) \\ f_2''(\lambda) \\ f_3''(\lambda) \end{bmatrix}, \tag{8.177}$$

in the system $O_0 X_0 Y_0 Z_0$. On the basis of these notations, we calculate the dot product $m\mathbf{T}_1 \cdot \mathbf{a}_O$ and we obtain

$$m\mathbf{T}_1 \cdot \mathbf{a}_O = \ddot{\lambda} A_{14} + \dot{\lambda}^2 A_{15}, \tag{8.178}$$

where

$$A_{14} = m(T_{1x}^2 + T_{1y}^2 + T_{1z}^2), \quad A_{15} = m(T_{1x}T_{2x} + T_{1y}T_{2y} + T_{1z}T_{2z}). \tag{8.179}$$

Further on, the calculation is made in the system $Oxyz$ because the vectors $\boldsymbol{\varepsilon}$, $\boldsymbol{\omega}$, $\mathbf{r}_C$, $\mathbf{F}$, $\mathbf{M}_O$ are represented in this system. Hence, we calculate successively

$$\{\mathbf{T}_1^*\} = [\mathbf{R}]\{\mathbf{T}_1\}, \quad \{\mathbf{T}_2^*\} = [\mathbf{R}]\{\mathbf{T}_2\}, \tag{8.180}$$

$$\{\mathbf{a}_O^*\} = \ddot{\lambda}\{\mathbf{T}_1^*\} + \dot{\lambda}^2\{\mathbf{T}_2^*\}. \tag{8.181}$$

The components ω_x, ω_y, ω_z of the angular velocity are given by the relations

$$\omega_x = \dot{\psi}\sin\theta\sin\phi + \dot{\theta}\cos\phi, \quad \omega_y = \dot{\psi}\sin\theta\cos\phi - \dot{\theta}\sin\phi, \quad \omega_z = \dot{\psi}\cos\theta + \dot{\phi}, \tag{8.182}$$

from which it follows that

$$\dot{\psi} = \frac{1}{\sin\theta}(\omega_x\sin\phi + \omega_y\cos\phi), \quad \dot{\theta} = \omega_x\cos\phi - \omega_y\sin\phi, \quad \dot{\phi} = \omega_z - \frac{\cos\theta}{\sin\theta}(\omega_x\sin\phi + \omega_y\cos\phi). \tag{8.183}$$

Further on, using the matrix notations

$$\{\mathbf{r}_C\} = \begin{bmatrix} x_C \\ y_C \\ z_C \end{bmatrix}, \tag{8.184}$$

$$[\boldsymbol{\omega}] = \begin{bmatrix} 0 & -\omega_z & \omega_y \\ \omega_z & 0 & -\omega_x \\ -\omega_y & \omega_x & 0 \end{bmatrix}, \tag{8.185}$$

$$\{\mathbf{F}\} = \begin{bmatrix} F_x \\ F_y \\ F_z \end{bmatrix}, \quad \{\mathbf{M}_O\} = \begin{bmatrix} M_{Ox} \\ M_{Oy} \\ M_{Oz} \end{bmatrix}, \tag{8.186}$$

and the scalar notations

$$A_{11} = m(y_C T_{1z}^* - z_C T_{1y}^*), \quad A_{12} = m(z_C T_{1x}^* - x_C T_{1z}^*), \quad A_{13} = m(x_C T_{1y}^* - y_C T_{1x}^*), \tag{8.187}$$

$$B_1 = -A_{15}\dot{\lambda}^2 - m\{\mathbf{T}_1^*\}^T[\boldsymbol{\omega}]^2\{\mathbf{r}_C\} + \{\mathbf{T}_1^*\}^T\{\mathbf{F}\}, \tag{8.188}$$

too, we obtain the relation

$$A_{11}\varepsilon_x + A_{12}\varepsilon_y + A_{13}\varepsilon_z + A_{14}\ddot{\lambda} = B_1, \tag{8.189}$$

from equation (8.182). Taking into account relations (8.180) and (8.181), we get for equation (8.171), the matrix formulation

$$\begin{bmatrix} m\ddot{\lambda}\left(y_C T_{1z}^* - z_C T_{1y}^*\right) + m\dot{\lambda}^2(y_C T_{2z}^* - z_C T_{2y}^*) + J_x\varepsilon_x - (J_y - J_z)\omega_y\omega_z \\ m\ddot{\lambda}(z_C T_{1x}^* - x_C T_{1z}^*) + m\dot{\lambda}^2(z_C T_{2x}^* - x_C T_{2z}^*) + J_y\varepsilon_y - (J_z - J_x)\omega_z\omega_x \\ m\ddot{\lambda}(x_C T_{1y}^* - y_C T_{1x}^*) + m\dot{\lambda}^2(x_C T_{2y}^* - y_C T_{2x}^*) + J_z\varepsilon_z - (J_x - J_y)\omega_x\omega_y \end{bmatrix} = \begin{bmatrix} M_{Ox} \\ M_{Oy} \\ M_{Oz} \end{bmatrix}; \tag{8.190}$$

using the scalar notations

$$\begin{aligned} B_2 &= M_{Ox} - m\dot{\lambda}^2(y_C T_{2z}^* - z_C T_{2y}^*) + (J_y - J_z)\omega_y\omega_z, \\ B_3 &= M_{Oy} - m\dot{\lambda}^2(z_C T_{2x}^* - x_C T_{2z}^*) + (J_z - J_x)\omega_z\omega_x, \\ B_4 &= M_{Oz} - m\dot{\lambda}^2(x_C T_{2y}^* - y_C T_{2x}^*) + (J_x - J_y)\omega_x\omega_y, \end{aligned} \tag{8.191}$$

we get the system

$$A_{11}\ddot{\lambda} + J_x\varepsilon_x = B_2, \quad A_{12}\ddot{\lambda} + J_y\varepsilon_y = B_3, \quad A_{13}\ddot{\lambda} + J_z\varepsilon_z = B_4. \tag{8.192}$$

Equations (8.189) and (8.192) form a linear system of four equations with four unknowns $\ddot{\lambda}$, ε_x, ε_y, ε_z. Finally, if we denote

$$C = \frac{B_1 - \dfrac{A_{11}B_2}{J_x} - \dfrac{A_{12}B_3}{J_y} - \dfrac{A_{13}B_4}{J_z}}{A_{14} - \dfrac{A_{11}^2}{J_x} - \dfrac{A_{12}^2}{J_y} - \dfrac{A_{13}^2}{J_z}}, \tag{8.193}$$

then we obtain, from equations (8.189) and (8.192), the system of four differential equations

$$\ddot{\lambda} = C, \quad \varepsilon_x = \frac{1}{J_x}(B_2 - A_{11}C), \quad \varepsilon_y = \frac{1}{J_y}(B_2 - A_{12}C), \quad \varepsilon_z = \frac{1}{J_z}(B_4 - A_{13}C). \tag{8.194}$$

To determine the parameters that are involved in the problem, we have to couple the equations of the kinematic system (8.183) with the equations of system (8.194). Thus, it results in a system of seven differential equations of first and second order. To apply the fourth-order Runge–Kutta method, the system must contain only first-order differential equations. With the notations

$$\lambda = \xi_1, \quad \psi = \xi_2, \quad \theta = \xi_3, \quad \phi = \xi_4, \quad \dot{\lambda} = \xi_5, \quad \omega_x = \xi_6, \quad \omega_y = \xi_7, \quad \omega_z = \xi_8, \tag{8.195}$$

we obtain, from relations (8.183) and (8.194), the following system of eight first-order differential equations

$$\dot{\xi}_1 = \xi_5, \quad \dot{\xi}_2 = \frac{1}{\sin\xi_3}(\xi_6\sin\xi_4 + \xi_7\cos\xi_4), \quad \dot{\xi}_3 = \xi_6\cos\xi_4 - \xi_7\sin\xi_4,$$
$$\dot{\xi}_4 = \xi_8 - \frac{\cos\xi_3}{\sin\xi_3}(\xi_6\sin\xi_4 + \xi_7\cos\xi_4),$$
$$\dot{\xi}_5 = C, \quad \dot{\xi}_6 = \frac{1}{J_x}(B_2 - A_{11}C), \tag{8.196}$$
$$\dot{\xi}_7 = \frac{1}{J_y}(B_2 - A_{12}C), \quad \dot{\xi}_8 = \frac{1}{J_z}(B_4 - A_{13}C).$$

Taking into account that the initial conditions are known (or can be deduced), we choose the integration step Δt and apply the fourth-order Runge–Kutta method to determine the numerical results. At each step of the method, we proceed with the calculations in the following manner:

- the matrices $\{\mathbf{T}_1\}$ and $\{\mathbf{T}_2\}$ with relations (8.175) and (8.177);
- the parameters A_{14} and A_{15} with relations (8.179);
- the rotation matrix with relations (8.173) and (8.174);
- the matrices $\{\mathbf{T}_1^*\}$ and $\{\mathbf{T}_2^*\}$ with relations (8.180);
- the matrix $[\boldsymbol{\omega}]$ with relation (8.185);
- the expression B_1 with relation (8.188);
- the parameters B_2, B_3, B_4 with relations (8.191);
- the parameter C with relation (8.193).

2. Numerical calculation

The principal axes of inertia determine the system $Oxyz$, where $Ox \| BD$, $Oy \| AB$, $Oz \| AA'$. In this reference frame, the co-ordinates of the gravity center C are

$$x_C = 0, \quad y_C = 0, \quad z_C = -\frac{3}{2}l. \tag{8.197}$$

The principal moments of inertia read

$$J_x = mz_C^2 + \frac{ml^2}{6} = \frac{29}{12}ml^2, \quad J_y = mz_C^2 + \frac{ml^2}{6} = \frac{29}{12}ml^2, \quad J_z = \frac{ml^2}{6}. \tag{8.198}$$

The force $\mathbf{F}$ is given by the weight $\mathbf{G}$, which, in the system $O_0X_0Y_0Z_0$, has the expression

$$\{\mathbf{F}_0\} = mg \begin{bmatrix} 0 \\ 0 \\ -1 \end{bmatrix}. \tag{8.199}$$

The rotation matrix reads

$$[\mathbf{R}] = \begin{bmatrix} c\xi_2 c\xi_4 - s\xi_2 c\xi_3 s\xi_4 & s\xi_2 c\xi_4 + c\xi_2 c\xi_3 s\xi_4 & s\xi_3 s\xi_4 \\ -c\xi_2 s\xi_4 - s\xi_2 c\xi_3 c\xi_4 & -s\xi_2 s\xi_4 + c\xi_2 c\xi_3 c\xi_4 & s\xi_3 c\xi_4 \\ s\xi_2 s\xi_3 & -c\xi_2 s\xi_3 & c\xi_3 \end{bmatrix}, \tag{8.200}$$

from which, if we take into account the relation

$$\{\mathbf{F}\} = [\mathbf{R}]\{\mathbf{F}_0\}, \tag{8.201}$$

we obtain the expression

$$\{\mathbf{F}\} = -mg \begin{bmatrix} \sin \xi_3 \sin \xi_4 \\ \sin \xi_3 \cos \xi_4 \\ \cos \xi_3 \end{bmatrix}. \tag{8.202}$$

For the moment $\mathbf{M}_O = \mathbf{OC} \times \mathbf{F}$, we obtain the matrix representation

$$\{\mathbf{M}_O\} = \frac{3}{2}mgl \sin \xi_3 \begin{bmatrix} -\cos \xi_4 \\ \sin \xi_4 \\ 0 \end{bmatrix}. \tag{8.203}$$

The graphic results obtained after the simulation are captured in Figure 8.4.

This problem may be solved by a method of multibody type, as will be seen in Problem 8.4; but it is necessary to solve an algebraic-differential system of equations, having the advantage of obtaining the reactions at the same time.

Problem 8.2

Study the motion of a rigid solid having a point constrained to move without friction on a given surface (Fig. 8.5). As numerical application, let us consider the body formed (Fig. 8.6) by a homogeneous cube $ABDE\,A'B'D'E'$ of mass m and edge l and a bar OG of length l and neglected mass, G being the center of the square $ABDE$. The point O moves without friction on the plane of equations

$$X_0 = \xi_1, \quad Y_0 = \xi_2, \quad Z_0 = l - \xi_1 - \xi_2. \tag{8.204}$$

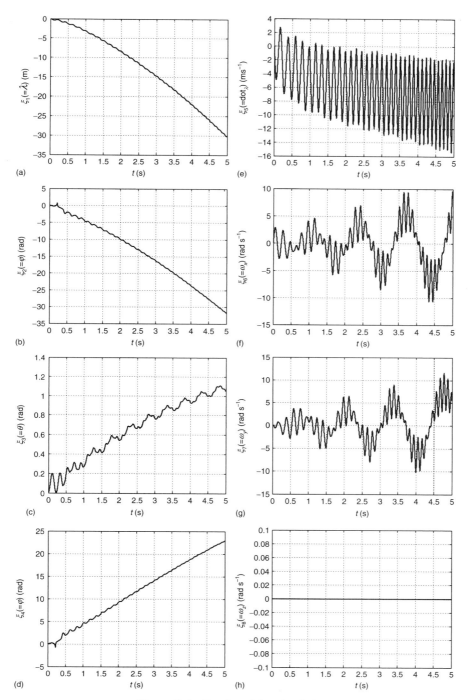

Figure 8.4   Results of the simulation.

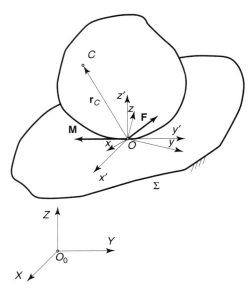

Figure 8.5   The rigid solid with a point constrained to move without friction on a given surface.

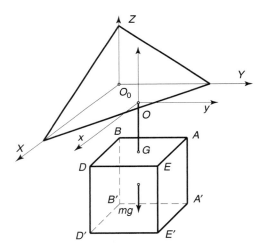

Figure 8.6   Numerical application.

Knowing that

$$m = 12 \text{ kg}, \quad l = 0.1 \text{ m}, \tag{8.205}$$

and that the initial conditions are given by (for $t = 0$)

$$\xi_1 = 0 \text{ m}, \quad \xi_2 = 0 \text{ m}, \quad \dot{\xi}_1 = 0 \text{ m s}^{-1}, \quad \dot{\xi}_2 = 0 \text{ m s}^{-1}, \quad \psi = 0 \text{ rad},$$
$$\theta = 0.001 \text{ rad}, \quad \phi = 0 \text{ rad}, \tag{8.206}$$
$$\omega_x = 0 \text{ rad/s}, \quad \omega_y = 0 \text{ rad s}^{-1}, \quad \omega_z = 0 \text{ rad s}^{-1},$$

we search the graphical representation of the variations of the variables $\xi_i(t)$, $i = \overline{1, 10}$.

Solution:

1. Theory

Let us consider a rigid solid (Fig. 8.5), the point O of which is constrained to move on the surface Σ. We shall consider

- the three-orthogonal system O_0XYZ;
- the three-orthogonal system $Oxyz$ of the principal axes of inertia, relative to the point O of the rigid solid;
- the three-orthogonal system $Ox'y'z'$ having the axes parallel to those of the three-orthogonal system O_0XYZ.

The following are known:

- the equations of the surface Σ

$$X = X(\xi_1, \xi_2), \quad Y = Y(\xi_1, \xi_2), \quad Z = Z(\xi_1, \xi_2), \tag{8.207}$$

where ξ_1 and ξ_2, respectively, are two real parameters;
- the mass and the principal moments of inertia of the rigid solid: m and J_x, J_y, and J_z, respectively;
- the resultant of the given forces $\mathbf{F}(F_x, F_y, F_z)$ and the resultant moment $\mathbf{M}(M_x, M_y, M_z)$ of the given forces;
- the position vector of the gravity center $\mathbf{r}_C(x_C, y_C, z_C)$.

In addition, we shall define the Euler angles:

$$\psi = \xi_3, \quad \theta = \xi_4, \quad \phi = \xi_5. \tag{8.208}$$

We wish to determine

- the motion and the functions of time $\xi_i = \xi_i(t)$, $i = 1, 2, \ldots, 5$;
- the normal reaction $\mathbf{N} = \mathbf{N}(t)$.

Applying the theorem of momentum in the form of the theorem of gravity center's motion, we obtain the vector relation

$$m[\mathbf{a}_O + \boldsymbol{\varepsilon} \times \mathbf{r}_C + \boldsymbol{\omega} \times (\boldsymbol{\omega} \times \mathbf{r}_C)] = \mathbf{F} + \mathbf{N}. \tag{8.209}$$

The theorem of the moment of momentum leads to

$$m\mathbf{r}_C \times \mathbf{a}_O + \mathbf{J}\boldsymbol{\varepsilon} + \boldsymbol{\omega} \times \mathbf{J}\boldsymbol{\omega} = \mathbf{M}. \tag{8.210}$$

The passing from the fixed system O_0XYZ to the movable system $Oxyz$, rigidly linked to the rigid solid, is made by the matrix

$$[\mathbf{P}] = [\boldsymbol{\phi}][\boldsymbol{\theta}][\boldsymbol{\psi}] = [\boldsymbol{\xi}_5][\boldsymbol{\xi}_4][\boldsymbol{\xi}_3], \tag{8.211}$$

where

$$[\boldsymbol{\phi}] = \begin{bmatrix} \cos\phi & \sin\phi & 0 \\ -\sin\phi & \cos\phi & 0 \\ 0 & 0 & 1 \end{bmatrix}, \quad [\boldsymbol{\theta}] = \begin{bmatrix} 1 & 0 & 0 \\ 0 & \cos\theta & \sin\theta \\ 0 & -\sin\theta & \cos\theta \end{bmatrix}, \quad [\boldsymbol{\psi}] = \begin{bmatrix} \cos\psi & \sin\psi & 0 \\ -\sin\psi & \cos\psi & 0 \\ 0 & 0 & 1 \end{bmatrix}.$$

$$\tag{8.212}$$

Making the calculation, we find

$$[\mathbf{P}] = \begin{bmatrix} c\xi_3 c\xi_5 - s\xi_3 c\xi_4 s\xi_5 & s\xi_3 c\xi_5 + c\xi_3 c\xi_4 s\xi_5 & s\xi_4 s\xi_5 \\ -c\xi_3 s\xi_5 - s\xi_3 c\xi_4 c\xi_5 & -s\xi_3 s\xi_5 + c\xi_3 c\xi_4 c\xi_5 & s\xi_4 c\xi_5 \\ s\xi_3 s\xi_4 & -c\xi_3 s\xi_4 & c\xi_4 \end{bmatrix}, \tag{8.213}$$

where the functions cosine and sine are marked by c and s, respectively.

We make the following notations:

$$\dot{\xi}_1 = \xi_6, \quad \dot{\xi}_2 = \xi_7, \quad \omega_x = \xi_8, \quad \omega_y = \xi_9, \quad \omega_z = \xi_{10}, \tag{8.214}$$

$$\{\mathbf{r}\} = \begin{bmatrix} X \\ Y \\ Z \end{bmatrix}, \quad \{\mathbf{r}_1\} = \begin{bmatrix} \dfrac{\partial X}{\partial \xi_1} \\ \dfrac{\partial Y}{\partial \xi_1} \\ \dfrac{\partial Z}{\partial \xi_1} \end{bmatrix}, \quad \{\mathbf{r}_2\} = \begin{bmatrix} \dfrac{\partial X}{\partial \xi_2} \\ \dfrac{\partial Y}{\partial \xi_2} \\ \dfrac{\partial Z}{\partial \xi_2} \end{bmatrix}, \tag{8.215}$$

$$\{\mathbf{r}_{11}\} = \begin{bmatrix} \dfrac{\partial^2 X}{\partial \xi_1^2} \\ \dfrac{\partial^2 Y}{\partial \xi_1^2} \\ \dfrac{\partial^2 Z}{\partial \xi_1^2} \end{bmatrix}, \quad \{\mathbf{r}_{12}\} = \begin{bmatrix} \dfrac{\partial^2 X}{\partial \xi_1 \partial \xi_2} \\ \dfrac{\partial^2 Y}{\partial \xi_1 \partial \xi_2} \\ \dfrac{\partial^2 Z}{\partial \xi_1 \partial \xi_2} \end{bmatrix}, \quad \{\mathbf{r}_{22}\} = \begin{bmatrix} \dfrac{\partial^2 X}{\partial \xi_2^2} \\ \dfrac{\partial^2 Y}{\partial \xi_2^2} \\ \dfrac{\partial^2 Z}{\partial \xi_2^2} \end{bmatrix}, \tag{8.216}$$

$$\{\mathbf{R}_1\} = [\mathbf{P}]\{\mathbf{r}_1\}, \quad \{\mathbf{R}_2\} = [\mathbf{P}]\{\mathbf{r}_2\}, \quad \{\mathbf{R}_{11}\} = [\mathbf{P}]\{\mathbf{r}_{11}\}, \quad \{\mathbf{R}_{12}\} = [\mathbf{P}]\{\mathbf{r}_{12}\}, \quad \{\mathbf{R}_{22}\} = [\mathbf{P}]\{\mathbf{r}_{22}\}, \tag{8.217}$$

$$\{\mathbf{r}_C\} = \begin{bmatrix} x_C \\ y_C \\ z_C \end{bmatrix}, \quad \{\boldsymbol{\omega}\} = \begin{bmatrix} \xi_8 \\ \xi_9 \\ \xi_{10} \end{bmatrix}, \quad \{\boldsymbol{\varepsilon}\} = \begin{bmatrix} \dot{\xi}_8 \\ \dot{\xi}_9 \\ \dot{\xi}_{10} \end{bmatrix}, \tag{8.218}$$

$$[\mathbf{r}_C] = \begin{bmatrix} 0 & -z_C & y_C \\ z_C & 0 & -x_C \\ -y_C & x_C & 0 \end{bmatrix}, \quad [\boldsymbol{\omega}] = \begin{bmatrix} 0 & -\xi_{10} & \xi_9 \\ \xi_{10} & 0 & -\xi_8 \\ -\xi_9 & \xi_8 & 0 \end{bmatrix}, \quad [\mathbf{J}] = \begin{bmatrix} J_x & 0 & 0 \\ 0 & J_y & 0 \\ 0 & 0 & J_z \end{bmatrix}, \tag{8.219}$$

$$\{\mathbf{a}_O\} = \begin{bmatrix} a_{Ox} & a_{Oy} & a_{Oz} \end{bmatrix}^{\mathrm{T}}, \quad \{\mathbf{A}_O\} = [\mathbf{P}]\{\mathbf{a}_O\}. \tag{8.220}$$

Considering that $\mathbf{r}_1 \perp \mathbf{N}$, $\mathbf{r}_2 \perp \mathbf{N}$, $\mathbf{a}_O$ are expressed in the system $O_0 XYZ$ and $\boldsymbol{\varepsilon}$, $\mathbf{r}_C$, $\boldsymbol{\omega}$, $\mathbf{F}$ in the system $Oxyz$, from equation (8.209) there result the matrix relations

$$\begin{aligned} m\{\mathbf{r}_1\}^{\mathrm{T}}\{\mathbf{a}_O\} + m\{\boldsymbol{\varepsilon}\}^{\mathrm{T}}[\mathbf{r}_C]\{\mathbf{R}_1\} &= \{\mathbf{R}_1\}^{\mathrm{T}}\{\mathbf{F}\} - m\{\mathbf{R}_1\}^{\mathrm{T}}[\boldsymbol{\omega}]^2\{\mathbf{r}_C\}, \\ m\{\mathbf{r}_2\}^{\mathrm{T}}\{\mathbf{a}_O\} + m\{\boldsymbol{\varepsilon}\}^{\mathrm{T}}[\mathbf{r}_C]\{\mathbf{R}_2\} &= \{\mathbf{R}_2\}^{\mathrm{T}}\{\mathbf{F}\} - m\{\mathbf{R}_2\}^{\mathrm{T}}[\boldsymbol{\omega}]^2\{\mathbf{r}_C\}, \end{aligned} \tag{8.221}$$

where

$$\{\mathbf{a}_O\} = \{\mathbf{r}_1\}\ddot{\xi}_1 + \{\mathbf{r}_2\}\ddot{\xi}_2 + \{\mathbf{r}_{11}\}\dot{\xi}_1^2 + \{\mathbf{r}_{22}\}\dot{\xi}_2^2 + 2\{\mathbf{r}_{12}\}\dot{\xi}_1\dot{\xi}_2 \tag{8.222}$$

or

$$\{\mathbf{a}_O\} = \{\mathbf{r}_1\}\dot{\xi}_6 + \{\mathbf{r}_2\}\dot{\xi}_7 + \{\mathbf{r}_{11}\}\xi_6^2 + \{\mathbf{r}_{22}\}\xi_7^2 + 2\{\mathbf{r}_{12}\}\xi_6\xi_7. \tag{8.223}$$

It follows that

$$\{\mathbf{A}_O\} = \{\mathbf{R}_1\}\dot{\xi}_6 + \{\mathbf{R}_2\}\dot{\xi}_7 + \{\mathbf{R}_{11}\}\xi_6^2 + \{\mathbf{R}_{22}\}\xi_7^2 + 2\{\mathbf{R}_{12}\}\xi_6\xi_7 \tag{8.224}$$

too.

We denote

$$A_{11} = m\{\mathbf{r}_1\}^T\{\mathbf{r}_1\}, \quad A_{12} = m\{\mathbf{r}_1\}^T\{\mathbf{r}_2\}, \quad A_{13} = m(y_C R_{1z} - z_C R_{1y}), \quad A_{14} = m(z_C R_{1x} - x_C R_{1z}),$$
$$A_{15} = m(x_C R_{1y} - y_C R_{1x}), \quad A_{21} = m\{\mathbf{r}_2\}^T\{\mathbf{r}_1\}, \quad A_{22} = m\{\mathbf{r}_2\}^T\{\mathbf{r}_2\}, \quad A_{23} = m(y_C R_{2z} - z_C R_{2y}),$$
$$A_{24} = m(z_C R_{2x} - x_C R_{2z}), \quad A_{25} = m(x_C R_{2y} - y_C R_{2x}),$$

$$(8.225)$$

$$B_1 = \{\mathbf{R}_1\}^T\{\mathbf{F}\} - m\{\mathbf{R}_1\}^T[\boldsymbol{\omega}]^2\{\mathbf{r}_C\} - m\{\mathbf{r}_1\}^T\{\mathbf{r}_{11}\}\xi_6^2 - m\{\mathbf{r}_1\}^T\{\mathbf{r}_{22}\}\xi_7^2 - 2m\{\mathbf{r}_1\}^T\{\mathbf{r}_{12}\}\xi_6\xi_7,$$
$$B_2 = \{\mathbf{R}_2\}^T\{\mathbf{F}\} - m\{\mathbf{R}_2\}^T[\boldsymbol{\omega}]^2\{\mathbf{r}_C\} - m\{\mathbf{r}_2\}^T\{\mathbf{r}_{11}\}\xi_6^2 - m\{\mathbf{r}_2\}^T\{\mathbf{r}_{11}\}\xi_7^2 - 2m\{\mathbf{r}_2\}^T\{\mathbf{r}_{12}\}\xi_6\xi_7.$$

$$(8.226)$$

From equation (8.209) we obtain the equations

$$A_{11}\dot\xi_6 + A_{12}\dot\xi_7 + A_{13}\dot\xi_8 + A_{14}\dot\xi_9 + A_{15}\dot\xi_{10} = B_1,$$
$$A_{21}\dot\xi_6 + A_{22}\dot\xi_7 + A_{23}\dot\xi_8 + A_{24}\dot\xi_9 + A_{25}\dot\xi_{10} = B_2.$$

$$(8.227)$$

In the matrix form, relation (8.210) reads

$$m[\mathbf{r}_C]\{\mathbf{A}_O\} + [\mathbf{J}]\{\boldsymbol{\varepsilon}\} + [\boldsymbol{\omega}][\mathbf{J}]\{\boldsymbol{\omega}\} = \{\mathbf{M}\} \tag{8.228}$$

or

$$m[\mathbf{r}_C]\{\mathbf{R}_1\}\dot\xi_6 + m[\mathbf{r}_C]\{\mathbf{R}_2\}\dot\xi_7 + [\mathbf{J}]\{\boldsymbol{\varepsilon}\} = \{\mathbf{M}\} - [\boldsymbol{\omega}][\mathbf{J}]\{\boldsymbol{\omega}\} - m[\mathbf{r}_C]\{\mathbf{R}_{11}\}\xi_6^2$$
$$- m[\mathbf{r}_C]\{\mathbf{R}_{22}\}\xi_7^2 - 2m[\mathbf{r}_C]\{\mathbf{R}_{12}\}\xi_6\xi_7. \tag{8.229}$$

If we denote

$$B_3 = M_x + (J_y - J_z)\xi_9\xi_{10} - m(y_C R_{11z} - z_C R_{11y})\xi_6^2$$
$$- m(y_C R_{22z} - z_C R_{22y})\xi_7^2 - 2m(y_C R_{12z} - z_C R_{12y})\xi_6\xi_7,$$
$$B_4 = M_y + (J_z - J_x)\xi_{10}\xi_8 - m(z_C R_{11x} - x_C R_{11z})\xi_6^2$$
$$- m(z_C R_{22x} - x_C R_{22z})\xi_7^2 - 2m(z_C R_{12x} - x_C R_{12z})\xi_6\xi_7,$$
$$B_5 = M_z + (J_x - J_y)\xi_8\xi_9 - m(x_C R_{11y} - y_C R_{11x})\xi_6^2$$
$$- m(x_C R_{22y} - y_C R_{22x})\xi_7^2 - 2m(x_C R_{12y} - y_C R_{12x})\xi_6\xi_7,$$

$$(8.230)$$

then we obtain the system

$$A_{13}\dot\xi_6 + A_{23}\dot\xi_7 + J_x\dot\xi_8 = B_3, \quad A_{14}\dot\xi_6 + A_{24}\dot\xi_7 + J_y\dot\xi_9 = B_4,$$
$$A_{15}\dot\xi_6 + A_{25}\dot\xi_7 + J_z\dot\xi_{10} = B_5.$$

$$(8.231)$$

Solving the linear system formed by equations (8.227) and (8.231), it follows that

$$\dot\xi_i = D_i, \quad i = 6, 7, \ldots, 10. \tag{8.232}$$

From the known relations

$$\omega_x = \dot\psi \sin\theta \sin\phi + \dot\theta \cos\phi, \quad \omega_y = \dot\psi \sin\theta \cos\phi - \dot\theta \sin\phi, \quad \omega_z = \dot\psi \cos\theta + \dot\phi, \tag{8.233}$$

which form a system of three equations with the unknowns $\dot\psi$, $\dot\theta$, and $\dot\phi$, it follows that

$$\dot\psi = \frac{1}{\sin\theta}(\omega_x \sin\phi + \omega_y \cos\phi), \quad \dot\theta = \omega_x \cos\phi - \omega_y \sin\phi,$$
$$\dot\phi = \omega_z - \frac{\cos\theta}{\sin\theta}(\omega_x \sin\phi + \omega_y \cos\phi). \tag{8.234}$$

With the notations

$$D_1 = \xi_6, \quad D_2 = \xi_7, \quad D_3 = \frac{1}{\sin\xi_4}(\xi_8\sin\xi_5 + \xi_9\cos\xi_5), \quad D_4 = \xi_8\cos\xi_5 - \xi_9\sin\xi_5,$$

$$D_5 = \xi_{10} - \frac{\cos\xi_4}{\sin\xi_4}(\xi_8\sin\xi_5 + \xi_9\cos\xi_5),$$

(8.235)

it results in the system of first-order differential equations

$$\dot{\xi}_i = D_i, \quad i = 1, 2, \ldots, 10.$$

(8.236)

To apply the fourth-order Runge–Kutta method, it is necessary that at each step we execute the following calculations:

- the rotation matrix with relation (8.213);
- $\{\mathbf{r}_1\}$, $\{\mathbf{r}_2\}$, $\{\mathbf{r}_{11}\}$, $\{\mathbf{r}_{12}\}$, $\{\mathbf{r}_{22}\}$, with relations (8.215) and (8.216);
- $\{\mathbf{R}_1\}$, $\{\mathbf{R}_2\}$, $\{\mathbf{R}_{11}\}$, $\{\mathbf{R}_{12}\}$, $\{\mathbf{R}_{22}\}$, with relations (8.217);
- $\{\mathbf{r}_C\}$, $\{\boldsymbol{\omega}\}$, $[\mathbf{r}_C]$, $[\boldsymbol{\omega}]$, with relations (8.218) and (8.219);
- A_{11}, A_{12}, A_{13}, A_{14}, A_{15}, A_{21}, A_{22}, A_{23}, A_{24}, A_{25}, B_1, B_2, with relations (8.225) and (8.226);
- B_3, B_4, B_5, with relations (8.230);
- the linear system formed by equations (8.227) and (8.231), obtaining the parameters D_i, $i = 6, 7, \ldots, 10$;
- D_i, $i = 1, 2, \ldots, 5$, with relations (8.235).

2. Numerical calculation

Proceeding as in the previous application, we get

- the co-ordinates of the gravity center C of the body

$$x_C = 0, \quad y_C = 0, \quad z_C = -\frac{3}{2}l;$$

(8.237)

- the principal moments of inertia

$$J_x = mz_C^2 + \frac{ml^2}{6} = \frac{29}{12}ml^2, \quad J_y = mz_C^2 + \frac{ml^2}{6} = \frac{29}{12}ml^2, \quad J_z = \frac{ml^2}{6};$$

(8.238)

- the rotation matrix

$$\mathbf{P} = \begin{bmatrix} c\xi_3 c\xi_5 - s\xi_3 c\xi_4 s\xi_5 & s\xi_3 c\xi_5 + c\xi_3 c\xi_4 s\xi_5 & s\xi_4 s\xi_5 \\ -c\xi_3 s\xi_5 - s\xi_3 c\xi_4 c\xi_5 & -s\xi_3 s\xi_5 + c\xi_3 c\xi_4 c\xi_5 & s\xi_4 c\xi_5 \\ s\xi_3 s\xi_4 & -c\xi_3 s\xi_4 & c\xi_4 \end{bmatrix};$$

(8.239)

- the matrix expression of the force $\mathbf{F}$, in the system $Oxyz$,

$$\{\mathbf{F}\} = -mg \begin{bmatrix} \sin\xi_4\sin\xi_5 \\ \sin\xi_4\cos\xi_5 \\ \cos\xi_4 \end{bmatrix};$$

(8.240)

- the matrix expression of the moment $\mathbf{M}_O = \mathbf{OC} \times \mathbf{F}$,

$$\{\mathbf{M}_O\} = \frac{3}{2}mgl\sin\xi_4 \begin{bmatrix} -\cos\xi_5 \\ \sin\xi_5 \\ 0 \end{bmatrix}.$$

(8.241)

Integrating the obtained system of differential equations by the fourth-order Runge–Kutta method, we get the numerical results plotted into diagrams (Fig. 8.7).

This problem may be solved by a multibody-type method too, as seen in Problem 8.3; also, in this case we have to solve an algebraic-differential system of equations, with the advantage of obtaining, at the same time, the reactions.

Problem 8.3

We consider the parallelepiped $ABCD\,A'B'C'D'$ (Fig. 8.8) of dimensions $AD = 2a$, $AB = 2b$, $BB' = 2c$ and of mass m, with the vertex A situated without friction on the cylindrical surface

$$Z = 1 - x^2. \tag{8.242}$$

Knowing that the parallelepiped is acted on only by its own weight mg, while the O_0Z-axis is vertical, with the initial conditions $t = 0$, $X_O = X_O^0$, $Y_O = Y_O^0$, $Z_O = Z_O^0$, $\psi = \psi^0$, $\theta = \theta^0$, $\phi = \phi^0$, O being the gravity center, and ψ, θ, ϕ being Bryan's angles, let us determine

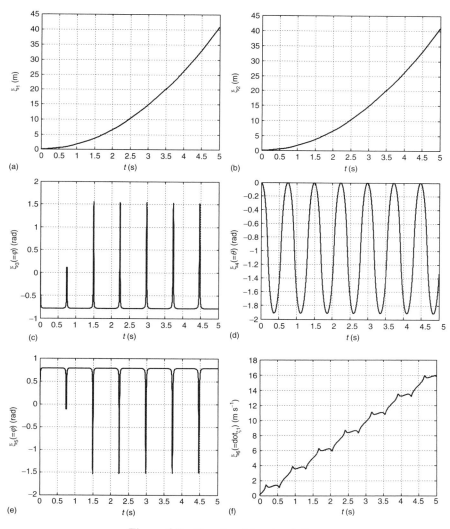

Figure 8.7   Results of the simulation.

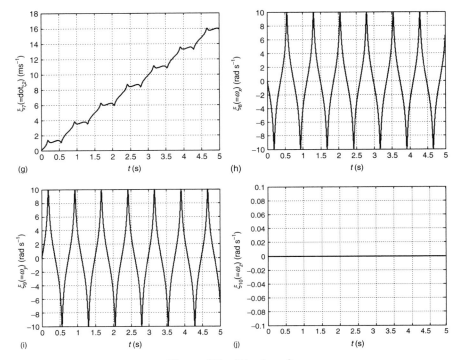

Figure 8.7   (*Continued*)

- the trajectory of the point A;
- the trajectory of the point O;
- the reaction at A.

Numerical application for $a = 0.3$ m, $b = 0.2$ m, $c = 0.1$ m, $X_O^0 = 0.1$ m, $Y_O^0 = 0.2$ m, $Z_O^0 = 0.74$ m, $m = 100$ kg, $\psi^0 = 0$ rad, $\theta^0 = 0$ rad, $\phi^0 = 0$ rad, $\dot{\psi}^0 = 0$ rad s^{-1}, $\dot{\theta}^0 = 0$ rad s^{-1}, $\dot{\phi}^0 = 0$ rad s^{-1}.

Solution:

1. Theory

   1.1. Kinematic relations

   We consider the frame of reference $Oxyz$ rigidly linked to the parallelepiped, the axes Ox, Oy, Oz being parallel to AD, AB, BB', respectively, and the frame of reference $Ox'y'z'$ with the axes Ox', Oy', Oz', parallel to the axes O_0X, O_0Y, O_0Z.

   If, from the position $Ox'y'z'$ we attain the position $Oxyz$, by successive rotations of angles ψ, θ, ϕ, specified in the schema

$$Ox'y'z' \xrightarrow[\text{angle } \psi]{\text{axis } Ox'} Ox'y''z'' \xrightarrow[\text{angle } \theta]{\text{axis } Oy''} Ox'''y''z \xrightarrow[\text{angle } \phi]{\text{axis } Oz} Oxyz,$$

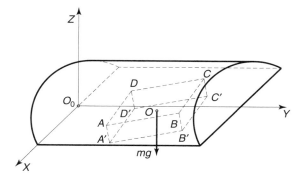

Figure 8.8   Problem 8.3.

where ψ, θ, ϕ are Bryan's angles, then the partial rotation matrices are

$$[\mathbf{\psi}] = \begin{bmatrix} 1 & 0 & 0 \\ 0 & \cos\psi & -\sin\psi \\ 0 & \sin\psi & \cos\psi \end{bmatrix}, \quad [\mathbf{\theta}] = \begin{bmatrix} \cos\theta & 0 & \sin\theta \\ 0 & 1 & 0 \\ -\sin\theta & 0 & \cos\theta \end{bmatrix},$$

$$[\mathbf{\phi}] = \begin{bmatrix} \cos\phi & -\sin\phi & 0 \\ \sin\phi & \cos\phi & 0 \\ 0 & 0 & 1 \end{bmatrix}, \tag{8.243}$$

while the matrix of the system $Oxyz$ with respect to the system O_0XYZ is

$$[\mathbf{A}] = [\mathbf{\psi}][\mathbf{\theta}][\mathbf{\phi}]. \tag{8.244}$$

Associating to the matrices $[\mathbf{\psi}]$, $[\mathbf{\theta}]$, $[\mathbf{\phi}]$ the antisymmetric matrices

$$[\mathbf{U}_\psi] = \begin{bmatrix} 0 & 0 & 0 \\ 0 & 0 & -1 \\ 0 & 1 & 0 \end{bmatrix}, \quad [\mathbf{U}_\theta] = \begin{bmatrix} 0 & 0 & 1 \\ 0 & 0 & 0 \\ -1 & 0 & 0 \end{bmatrix}, \quad [\mathbf{U}_\phi] = \begin{bmatrix} 0 & -1 & 0 \\ 1 & 0 & 0 \\ 0 & 0 & 0 \end{bmatrix}, \tag{8.245}$$

we obtain the derivatives $[\mathbf{\psi}_p]$, $[\mathbf{\theta}_p]$, $[\mathbf{\phi}_p]$ from the relations

$$[\mathbf{\psi}_p] = [\mathbf{U}_\psi][\mathbf{\psi}] = [\mathbf{\psi}][\mathbf{U}_\psi], \quad [\mathbf{\theta}_p] = [\mathbf{U}_\theta][\mathbf{\theta}] = [\mathbf{\theta}][\mathbf{U}_\theta], \quad [\mathbf{\phi}_p] = [\mathbf{U}_\phi][\mathbf{\phi}] = [\mathbf{\phi}][\mathbf{U}_\phi]; \tag{8.246}$$

thus, the partial derivatives $[\mathbf{A}_\psi]$, $[\mathbf{A}_\theta]$, $[\mathbf{A}_\phi]$ of the matrix $[\mathbf{A}]$ are

$$[\mathbf{A}_\psi] = [\mathbf{U}_\psi][\mathbf{A}], \quad [\mathbf{A}_\theta] = [\mathbf{A}][\mathbf{\phi}]^{\mathrm{T}}[\mathbf{U}_\theta][\mathbf{\phi}], \quad [\mathbf{A}_\phi] = [\mathbf{A}][\mathbf{U}_\phi], \tag{8.247}$$

while the derivative with respect to time of the matrix $[\mathbf{A}]$ is

$$[\dot{\mathbf{A}}] = \dot{\psi}[\mathbf{A}_\psi] + \dot{\theta}[\mathbf{A}_\theta] + \dot{\phi}[\mathbf{A}_\phi]. \tag{8.248}$$

The square matrix $[\omega]$ of the angular velocity with respect to the frame $Oxyz$ is antisymmetric and we deduce the relation

$$[\omega] = [A]^T[\dot{A}] = \begin{bmatrix} 0 & -\omega_z & \omega_y \\ \omega_z & 0 & -\omega_x \\ -\omega_y & \omega_x & 0 \end{bmatrix}, \tag{8.249}$$

from which it follows that

$$\{\omega\} = [Q]\{\dot{\beta}\}, \tag{8.250}$$

where

$$\{\omega\} = \begin{bmatrix} \omega_x & \omega_y & \omega_z \end{bmatrix}^T, \quad \{\beta\} = \begin{bmatrix} \dot{\psi} & \dot{\theta} & \dot{\phi} \end{bmatrix}^T, \tag{8.251}$$

$$[Q] = \begin{bmatrix} \cos\theta\cos\phi & \sin\phi & 0 \\ -\cos\theta\sin\phi & \cos\phi & 0 \\ \sin\theta & 0 & 1 \end{bmatrix}. \tag{8.252}$$

Moreover, we obtain

$$[Q_\theta] = \begin{bmatrix} -\sin\theta\cos\phi & 0 & 0 \\ \sin\theta\sin\phi & 0 & 0 \\ \cos\theta & 0 & 0 \end{bmatrix}, \quad [Q_\phi] = \begin{bmatrix} -\cos\theta\sin\phi & \cos\phi & 0 \\ -\cos\theta\cos\phi & -\sin\phi & 0 \\ 0 & 0 & 0 \end{bmatrix}, \tag{8.253}$$

$$[\dot{Q}] = \dot{\theta}[Q_\theta] + \dot{\phi}[Q_\phi]. \tag{8.254}$$

1.2. The constraints matrix

In the frame of reference $Oxyz$, the point A has the co-ordinates a, $-b$, c; denoting by X_A, Y_A, Z_A the co-ordinates of the same point in the frame O_0XYZ, we obtain the matrix equation

$$\begin{bmatrix} X_A \\ Y_A \\ Z_A \end{bmatrix} = \begin{bmatrix} X_O \\ Y_O \\ Z_O \end{bmatrix} + [A] \begin{bmatrix} a \\ -b \\ c \end{bmatrix}, \tag{8.255}$$

or

$$\{R_A\} = \{R_O\} + [A]\{r_A\}, \tag{8.256}$$

where

$$\{R_A\} = \begin{bmatrix} X_A & Y_A & Z_A \end{bmatrix}^T, \quad \{R_O\} = \begin{bmatrix} X_O & Y_O & Z_O \end{bmatrix}^T, \quad \{r_A\} = \begin{bmatrix} a & -b & c \end{bmatrix}^T. \tag{8.257}$$

Writing equation (8.242) in the general form

$$f(X, Y, Z) = 0, \tag{8.258}$$

we must verify the relation

$$f(X_A, Y_A, Z_A) = 0. \tag{8.259}$$

Differentiating with respect to time equation (8.259), it follows that

$$\{f_p\}^T \begin{bmatrix} \dot{X}_A \\ \dot{Y}_A \\ \dot{Z}_A \end{bmatrix} = 0, \tag{8.260}$$

where

$$\{\mathbf{f}_p\} = \begin{bmatrix} \dfrac{\partial f}{\partial X} & \dfrac{\partial f}{\partial Y} & \dfrac{\partial f}{\partial Z} \end{bmatrix}^{\mathrm{T}}. \tag{8.261}$$

Differentiating with respect to time relation (8.256) and taking into account the successive relations

$$[\dot{\mathbf{A}}]\{\mathbf{r}_A\} = [\mathbf{A}][\boldsymbol{\omega}]\{\mathbf{r}_A\} = [\mathbf{A}][\mathbf{r}_A]^{\mathrm{T}}\{\boldsymbol{\omega}\}, \tag{8.262}$$

where

$$[\mathbf{r}_A] = \begin{bmatrix} 0 & -c & -b \\ c & 0 & -a \\ b & a & 0 \end{bmatrix}, \tag{8.263}$$

we obtain

$$\{\dot{\mathbf{R}}_A\} = \{\dot{\mathbf{R}}_O\} + [\mathbf{A}][\mathbf{r}_A]^{\mathrm{T}}[\mathbf{Q}]\{\dot{\boldsymbol{\beta}}\}; \tag{8.264}$$

equation (8.260), with the notations

$$[\mathbf{B}] = \{\mathbf{f}_p\}^{\mathrm{T}} \begin{bmatrix} [\mathbf{I}] & [\mathbf{A}][\mathbf{r}_A]^{\mathrm{T}}[\mathbf{Q}] \end{bmatrix}, \tag{8.265}$$

$$\{\mathbf{q}\} = \begin{bmatrix} X_O & Y_O & Z_O & \psi & \theta & \phi \end{bmatrix}^{\mathrm{T}}, \tag{8.266}$$

becomes

$$[\mathbf{B}]\{\dot{\mathbf{q}}\} = 0, \tag{8.267}$$

where $[\mathbf{B}]$ is the constraints matrix.

1.3. The matrix differential equation of the motion

The kinetic energy T of the rigid solid reads

$$T = \frac{1}{2}m\{\dot{\mathbf{R}}_O\}^{\mathrm{T}}\{\dot{\mathbf{R}}_O\} + \frac{1}{2}\{\boldsymbol{\omega}\}^{\mathrm{T}}[\mathbf{J}]\{\boldsymbol{\omega}\}, \tag{8.268}$$

where $[\mathbf{J}]$ is the matrix of the moments of inertia with respect to the axes Ox, Oy, Oz

$$[\mathbf{J}] = \begin{bmatrix} J_{xx} & -J_{xy} & -J_{xz} \\ -J_{yx} & J_{yy} & -J_{yz} \\ -J_{zx} & -J_{zy} & J_{zz} \end{bmatrix}. \tag{8.269}$$

In the considered case $J_{xy} = J_{xz} = J_{yz} = 0$ and

$$J_{xx} = \frac{m}{3}(b^2 + c^2), \quad J_{yy} = \frac{m}{3}(a^2 + c^2), \quad J_{zz} = \frac{m}{3}(a^2 + b^2). \tag{8.270}$$

Applying Lagrange's equations and using the notations

$$[\mathbf{m}] = \begin{bmatrix} m & 0 & 0 \\ 0 & m & 0 \\ 0 & 0 & m \end{bmatrix}, \quad [\mathbf{M}] = \begin{bmatrix} [\mathbf{m}] & [\mathbf{0}] \\ [\mathbf{0}] & [\mathbf{Q}]^{\mathrm{T}}[\mathbf{J}][\mathbf{Q}] \end{bmatrix},$$

$$\{\mathbf{F}\} = \begin{bmatrix} 0 & 0 & -mg & 0 & 0 & 0 \end{bmatrix}^{\mathrm{T}},$$

$$[\boldsymbol{\Delta}] = \begin{bmatrix} \{\dot{\boldsymbol{\beta}}\}^{\mathrm{T}}[\mathbf{Q}_\psi]^{\mathrm{T}}[\mathbf{J}][\mathbf{Q}] \\ \{\dot{\boldsymbol{\beta}}\}^{\mathrm{T}}[\mathbf{Q}_\theta]^{\mathrm{T}}[\mathbf{J}][\mathbf{Q}] \\ \{\dot{\boldsymbol{\beta}}\}^{\mathrm{T}}[\mathbf{Q}_\phi]^{\mathrm{T}}[\mathbf{J}][\mathbf{Q}] \end{bmatrix}, \quad \{\widetilde{\mathbf{F}}_{\boldsymbol{\beta}}\} = [[\dot{\mathbf{Q}}]^{\mathrm{T}}[\mathbf{J}][\mathbf{Q}] + [\mathbf{Q}]^{\mathrm{T}}[\mathbf{J}][\dot{\mathbf{Q}}] + [\boldsymbol{\Delta}]]\{\dot{\boldsymbol{\beta}}\},$$

$$\{\widetilde{\mathbf{F}}\} = \begin{bmatrix} 0 & 0 & 0 & \{\widetilde{\mathbf{F}}_{\boldsymbol{\beta}}\}^{\mathrm{T}} \end{bmatrix}^{\mathrm{T}}, \tag{8.271}$$

we obtain the matrix differential equation

$$[\mathbf{M}]\{\ddot{\mathbf{q}}\} = \{\mathbf{F}\} + \{\widetilde{\mathbf{F}}\} + \lambda[\mathbf{B}]^{\mathrm{T}}. \tag{8.272}$$

Equation (8.272) together with Equation (8.267), differentiated with respect to time, form the equation

$$\begin{bmatrix} [\mathbf{M}] & -[\mathbf{B}]^{\mathrm{T}} \\ [\mathbf{B}] & 0 \end{bmatrix} \begin{bmatrix} \{\ddot{\mathbf{q}}\} \\ \lambda \end{bmatrix} = \begin{bmatrix} \{\mathbf{F}\} + \{\widetilde{\mathbf{F}}\} \\ -[\dot{\mathbf{B}}]\{\dot{\mathbf{q}}\} \end{bmatrix}, \tag{8.273}$$

from which we obtain $\{\ddot{\mathbf{q}}\}$, λ; then, by the Runge–Kutta method, we get the new values for $\{\mathbf{q}\}$ and $\{\dot{\mathbf{q}}\}$.

2. Numerical calculation

With the initial values we calculate, successively, $[\boldsymbol{\psi}]$, $[\boldsymbol{\theta}]$, $[\boldsymbol{\phi}]$, $[\mathbf{A}_\psi]$, $[\mathbf{A}_\theta]$, $[\mathbf{A}_\phi]$, $[\dot{\mathbf{A}}]$, $[\mathbf{Q}]$, $[\mathbf{Q}_\psi]$, $[\mathbf{Q}_\theta]$, $[\mathbf{Q}_\phi]$, $[\dot{\mathbf{Q}}]$ by relations (8.243) and (8.244) and then the co-ordinates X_A, Y_A, Z_A by relation (8.225) and

$$\{\mathbf{f}_p\} = \begin{bmatrix} 2X_A & 0 & 1 \end{bmatrix}^{\mathrm{T}}, \tag{8.274}$$

as well as the matrix $[\mathbf{B}]$ by relation (8.265).

Hereafter, from equation (8.264) we obtain $\dot{X}_A$, $\dot{Y}_A$, $\dot{Z}_A$; we may thus calculate

$$\{\dot{\mathbf{f}}_p\} = \begin{bmatrix} 2\dot{X}_A & 0 & 0 \end{bmatrix}^{\mathrm{T}}, \tag{8.275}$$

and

$$[\dot{\mathbf{B}}] = \{\dot{\mathbf{f}}_p\}^{\mathrm{T}} \big[[\mathbf{I}] \quad [\mathbf{A}][\mathbf{r}_A]^{\mathrm{T}}[\mathbf{Q}]\big] + \{\mathbf{f}_p\}^{\mathrm{T}} \big[[\mathbf{0}] \quad [\dot{\mathbf{A}}][\mathbf{r}_A]^{\mathrm{T}}[\mathbf{Q}] + [\mathbf{A}][\mathbf{r}_A]^{\mathrm{T}}[\dot{\mathbf{Q}}]\big], \tag{8.276}$$

and then the matrices $[\boldsymbol{\Delta}]$, $\{\widetilde{\mathbf{F}}_\beta\}$, $\{\mathbf{F}\}$, by relation (8.271), where $[\mathbf{Q}_\psi] = [\mathbf{0}]$.

Finally, from equation (8.273) we calculate $\{\ddot{\mathbf{q}}\}$, λ; then, by the Runge–Kutta method we determine the new values $\{\mathbf{q}\}$, $\{\dot{\mathbf{q}}\}$, the iteration process being then taken again.

We obtain the diagrams in Figure 8.9.

For the reaction, it follows that

$$\{\mathbf{N}_A\} = \lambda\{\mathbf{f}_p\} = \lambda\begin{bmatrix} 2X_A & 0 & 1 \end{bmatrix}^{\mathrm{T}}, \tag{8.277}$$

hence

$$N_A = \lambda\sqrt{4X_A^2 + 1}. \tag{8.278}$$

The graphic is drawn in Figure 8.10.

Problem 8.4

Let $ABCD\,A'B'C'D'$ in Figure 8.8 be the parallelepiped discussed in Problem 8.3, where the point A is situated without friction on the curve of equations

$$X^2 + Z - 1 = 0, \quad X^2 + (Y-1)^2 - 1 = 0. \tag{8.279}$$

Assuming the same data as in Problem 8.3 and the initial conditions $X_O^0 = -0.3$ m, $Y_O^0 = 2.2$ m, $Z_O^0 = 0.9$ m, $\psi^0 = 0$ rad, $\theta^0 = 0$ rad, $\phi^0 = 0$ rad, $\dot{\psi}^0 = 0$ rad s^{-1}, $\dot{\theta}^0 = 0$ rad s^{-1}, $\dot{\phi}^0 = 0$ rad s^{-1}, let us determine

- the trajectory of the point O;
- the reaction at A.

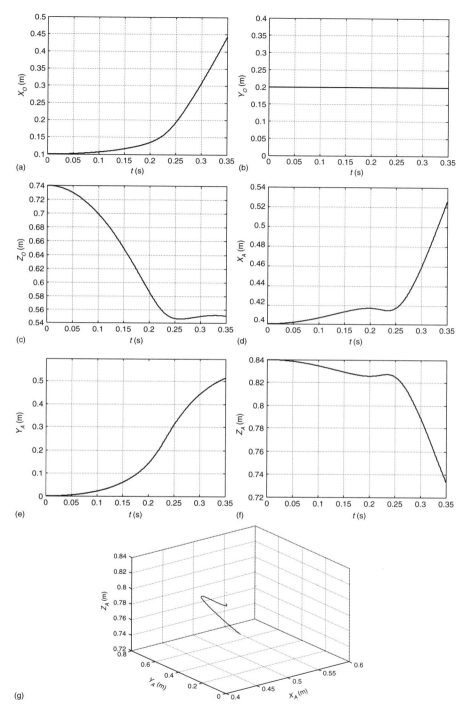

Figure 8.9   Variation diagrams.

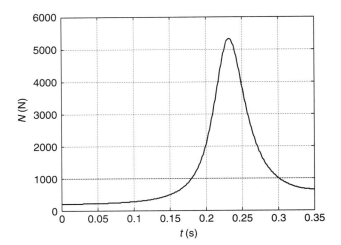

Figure 8.10   The diagram $N_A = N_A(t)$.

Solution:

1. Theory

In this case, the calculation algorithm remains, in principle, the same as that in the previous problem; the constraints matrix becomes

$$[\mathbf{B}] = \begin{bmatrix} \{\mathbf{f}_{1_p}\}^{\mathrm{T}} \begin{bmatrix} [\mathbf{I}] & [\mathbf{A}][\mathbf{r}_A]^{\mathrm{T}}[\mathbf{Q}] \end{bmatrix} \\ \{\mathbf{f}_{2_p}\}^{\mathrm{T}} \begin{bmatrix} [\mathbf{I}] & [\mathbf{A}][\mathbf{r}_A]^{\mathrm{T}}[\mathbf{Q}] \end{bmatrix} \end{bmatrix}, \tag{8.280}$$

where

$$\{\mathbf{f}_{1_p}\} = \begin{bmatrix} 2X_A & 0 & 1 \end{bmatrix}^{\mathrm{T}}, \quad \{\mathbf{f}_{2_p}\} = \begin{bmatrix} 2X_A & 2Y_A - 2 & 0 \end{bmatrix}^{\mathrm{T}}, \tag{8.281}$$

$$\{\dot{\mathbf{f}}_{1_p}\} = \begin{bmatrix} 2\dot{X}_A & 0 & 0 \end{bmatrix}^{\mathrm{T}}, \quad \{\dot{\mathbf{f}}_{2_p}\} = \begin{bmatrix} 2\dot{X}_A & 2\dot{Y}_A & 0 \end{bmatrix}^{\mathrm{T}}. \tag{8.282}$$

It follows the calculation algorithm, so that
  – we determine the matrices $[\boldsymbol{\psi}]$, $[\boldsymbol{\theta}]$, $[\boldsymbol{\phi}]$, $[\mathbf{A}]$, $[\mathbf{A}_\psi]$, $[\mathbf{A}_\theta]$, $[\mathbf{A}_\phi]$, $[\dot{\mathbf{A}}]$, $[\mathbf{Q}]$, $[\mathbf{Q}_\psi]$, $[\mathbf{Q}_\theta]$, $[\mathbf{Q}_\phi]$;
  – we determine the matrices $\{\mathbf{R}_A\}$, $\{\dot{\mathbf{R}}_A\}$

$$\{\mathbf{R}_A\} = \{\mathbf{R}_O\} + [\mathbf{A}]\{\mathbf{r}_A\}, \quad \{\dot{\mathbf{R}}_A\} = \{\dot{\mathbf{R}}_O\} + [\mathbf{A}][\mathbf{r}_A]^{\mathrm{T}}[\mathbf{Q}]\{\dot{\boldsymbol{\beta}}\}; \tag{8.283}$$

  – we determine the constraints matrix by relation (8.280) and its derivative by the relation

$$[\dot{\mathbf{B}}] = \begin{bmatrix} \{\dot{\mathbf{f}}_{1_p}\}^{\mathrm{T}} \begin{bmatrix} [\mathbf{I}] & [\mathbf{A}][\mathbf{r}_A]^{\mathrm{T}}[\mathbf{Q}] \end{bmatrix} + \{\mathbf{f}_{1_p}\}^{\mathrm{T}} \begin{bmatrix} [\mathbf{0}] & [\dot{\mathbf{A}}][\mathbf{r}_A]^{\mathrm{T}}[\dot{\mathbf{Q}}] + [\mathbf{A}][\mathbf{r}_A]^{\mathrm{T}}[\dot{\mathbf{Q}}] \end{bmatrix} \\ \{\dot{\mathbf{f}}_{2_p}\}^{\mathrm{T}} \begin{bmatrix} [\mathbf{I}] & [\mathbf{A}][\mathbf{r}_A]^{\mathrm{T}}[\mathbf{Q}] \end{bmatrix} + \{\mathbf{f}_{2_p}\}^{\mathrm{T}} \begin{bmatrix} [\mathbf{0}] & [\dot{\mathbf{A}}][\mathbf{r}_A]^{\mathrm{T}}[\dot{\mathbf{Q}}] + [\mathbf{A}][\mathbf{r}_A]^{\mathrm{T}}[\dot{\mathbf{Q}}] \end{bmatrix} \end{bmatrix}; \tag{8.284}$$

  – we calculate the matrices $[\mathbf{M}]$, $\{\widetilde{\mathbf{F}}\}$ by the relations

$$[\mathbf{m}] = \begin{bmatrix} m & 0 & 0 \\ 0 & m & 0 \\ 0 & 0 & m \end{bmatrix}, \quad [\mathbf{M}] = \begin{bmatrix} [\mathbf{m}] & [\mathbf{0}] \\ [\mathbf{0}] & [\mathbf{Q}]^{T}[\mathbf{J}][\mathbf{Q}] \end{bmatrix}, \quad [\boldsymbol{\Delta}] = \begin{bmatrix} \{\dot{\boldsymbol{\beta}}\}^{\mathrm{T}}[\mathbf{Q}_\psi]^{\mathrm{T}}[\mathbf{J}][\mathbf{Q}] \\ \{\dot{\boldsymbol{\beta}}\}^{\mathrm{T}}[\mathbf{Q}_\theta]^{\mathrm{T}}[\mathbf{J}][\mathbf{Q}] \\ \{\dot{\boldsymbol{\beta}}\}^{\mathrm{T}}[\mathbf{Q}_\phi]^{\mathrm{T}}[\mathbf{J}][\mathbf{Q}] \end{bmatrix},$$

$$\{\mathbf{F}_\beta\}^{\mathrm{T}} = [[\dot{\mathbf{Q}}]^{\mathrm{T}}[\mathbf{J}][\mathbf{Q}] + [\mathbf{Q}]^{\mathrm{T}}[\mathbf{J}][\dot{\mathbf{Q}}] + [\boldsymbol{\Delta}]]\{\dot{\boldsymbol{\beta}}\}, \quad \{\widetilde{\mathbf{F}}\} = \begin{bmatrix} 0 & 0 & 0 & \{\widetilde{\mathbf{F}}_\beta\}^{\mathrm{T}} \end{bmatrix}^{\mathrm{T}}; \tag{8.285}$$

– we calculate $\{\ddot{\mathbf{q}}\}$, λ_1, λ_2 from the equation

$$\begin{bmatrix} [\mathbf{M}] & -[\mathbf{B}]^{\mathrm{T}} \\ [\mathbf{B}] & [\mathbf{0}] \end{bmatrix} \begin{bmatrix} \{\ddot{\mathbf{q}}\} \\ \lambda_1 \\ \lambda_2 \end{bmatrix} = \begin{bmatrix} \{\mathbf{F}\} + \{\tilde{\mathbf{F}}\} \\ -[\dot{\mathbf{B}}]\{\dot{\mathbf{q}}\} \end{bmatrix}, \tag{8.286}$$

and then the new values of the matrices $\{\mathbf{q}\}$, $\{\dot{\mathbf{q}}\}$ by means of the Runge–Kutta method. The reaction N_A reads

$$\{N_A\} = \lambda_1\{\mathbf{f}_{1p}\} + \lambda_2\{\mathbf{f}_{2p}\}, \tag{8.287}$$

$$N_A = \sqrt{\lambda_1^2\{\mathbf{f}_{1p}\}^{\mathrm{T}}\{\mathbf{f}_{1p}\} + \lambda_2^2\{\mathbf{f}_{2p}\}^{\mathrm{T}}\{\mathbf{f}_{2p}\} + 2\lambda_1\lambda_2\{\mathbf{f}_{1p}\}^{\mathrm{T}}\{\mathbf{f}_{2p}\}}. \tag{8.288}$$

2. Numerical calculation
We obtain the numerical results plotted in the diagrams in Figure 8.11 and Figure 8.12.

Problem 8.5

Let us consider the system formed by n bodies, hung in a vertical plane and linked to one another in series (Fig. 8.13). Study the motion of this system. As numerical application, consider the system formed by four bodies (Fig. 8.14) for which

$n = 4$, $m_1 = 10$ kg, $m_2 = 8$ kg, $m_3 = 50$ kg, $m_4 = 16$ kg, $l_1 = 4$ m, $l_2 = 0.5$ m,
$l_3 = 0.5$ m, $l_4 = 0.7$ m, $r_1 = 2$ m, $r_2 = 0.25$ m, $r_3 = 0.25$ m, $r_4 = 0.35$ m,
$J_1 = 13.3333$ kg m^2, $J_2 = 0.1666$ kg m^2, $J_3 = 1.0416$ kg m^2, $J_4 = 0.6533$ kg m^2.
$$\tag{8.289}$$

The initial conditions are (for $t = 0$)

$\theta_1^0 = 0$ rad, $\theta_2^0 = 1$ rad, $\theta_3^0 = 3.12414$ rad, $\theta_4^0 = 3.12414$ rad, $\dot{\theta}_1^0 = 0$ rad s^{-1},
$\dot{\theta}_2^0 = 0.25$ rad s^{-1}, $\dot{\theta}_3^0 = 0$ rad s^{-1}, $\dot{\theta}_4^0 = 0$ rad s^{-1}.
$$\tag{8.290}$$

Solution:

1. Theory
The following are known:
- the masses of the n bodies m_i, $i = 1, \ldots, n$;
- the moments of inertia relative to the gravity centers C_i of the bodies, calculated with respect to an axis perpendicular to the plane of the motion and denoted by J_i, $i = 1, \ldots, n$;
- the lengths of the bodies calculated from the link point to the previous body to the link point to the next body, denoted by l_i, $i = 1, \ldots, n$;
- the distances from the link point to the previous body to the gravity center, denoted by r_i, $i = 1, \ldots, n$.

We are required to
- establish the equations of motion of the bodies;
- the numerical integration of these equations.

To establish the equations of motion, we shall use the second-order Lagrange equations, which, in the general case of the holonomic constraints and assuming that the forces derive from a function of force, read

$$\frac{\mathrm{d}}{\mathrm{d}t}\left(\frac{\partial T}{\partial \dot{q}_i}\right) - \frac{\partial T}{\partial q_i} + \frac{\partial V}{\partial q_i} = 0, \tag{8.291}$$

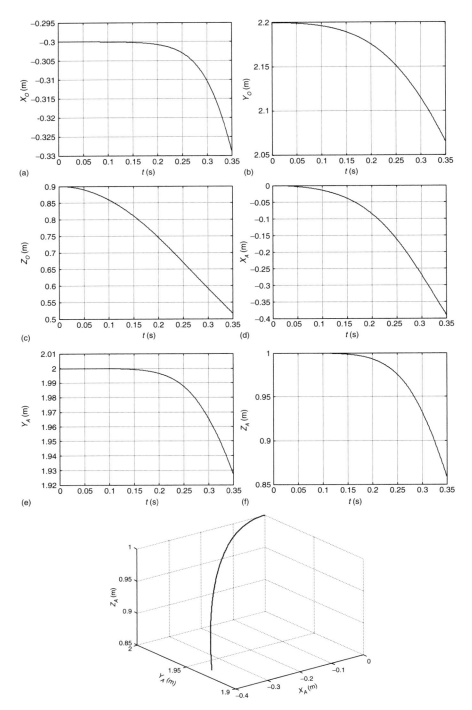

Figure 8.11   Variation diagrams.

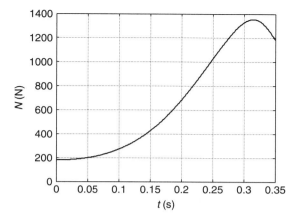

Figure 8.12 The diagram $N_A = N_A(t)$.

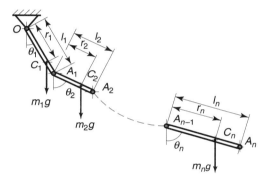

Figure 8.13 Problem 8.5.

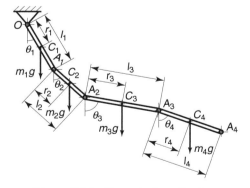

Figure 8.14 Numerical application.

where T denotes the kinetic energy of the system, V represents the potential energy, and q_i, $i = \overline{1, n}$, is a generalized co-ordinate of the system.

In this case, the kinetic energy is given by the relation

$$T = \sum_{i=1}^{n} T_i, \tag{8.292}$$

where T_i, $i = 1, 2, \ldots, n$, are the kinetic energies of the component bodies of the system. These read

$$T_i = \frac{1}{2} m_i v_{C_i}^2 + \frac{1}{2} J_i \dot{\theta}_i^2, \tag{8.293}$$

where v_{C_i} is the velocity of the gravity center of the body i, given by the relation

$$v_{C_i}^2 = \dot{x}_{C_i}^2 + \dot{y}_{C_i}^2. \tag{8.294}$$

We obtain

$$T = \frac{1}{2} \sum_{i=1}^{n} \left\{ m_i \left[\sum_{j=1}^{i-1} l_j^2 \dot{\theta}_j^2 + r_i^2 \dot{\theta}_i^2 + 2 \sum_{j=1}^{i-2} \sum_{k=j+1}^{i-1} l_j l_k \dot{\theta}_j \dot{\theta}_k \cos\left(\theta_k - \theta_j\right) \right. \right.$$
$$\left. \left. + 2 \sum_{j=1}^{i-1} l_j r_i \dot{\theta}_j \dot{\theta}_k \cos\left(\theta_i - \theta_j\right) \right] + J_i \dot{\theta}_i^2 \right\}. \tag{8.295}$$

Taking into account that the only forces that act are the weights of the bodies, the potential energy of the system takes the form

$$\begin{aligned} V = &-m_1 g r_1 \cos\theta_1 - m_2 g(l_1 \cos\theta_1 + r_2 \cos\theta_2) \\ &- m_3 g(l_1 \cos\theta_1 + l_2 \cos\theta_2 + r_3 \cos\theta_3) - \cdots \\ &- m_n g(l_1 \cos\theta_1 + l_2 \cos\theta_2 + l_3 \cos\theta_3 + \cdots + l_{n-1} \cos\theta_{n-1} + r_n \cos\theta_n). \end{aligned} \tag{8.296}$$

With the notations

$$J_{ii} = J_i + m_i r_i^2 + \left(\sum_{j=i+1}^{n} m_j \right) l_i^2, \tag{8.297}$$

$$a_i = m_i r_i + \left(\sum_{j=i+1}^{n} m_j \right) l_i, \tag{8.298}$$

$$[\mathbf{J}] = \begin{bmatrix} J_{11} & a_2 l_1 \cos\left(\theta_1 - \theta_2\right) & \cdots & a_n l_1 \cos(\theta_1 - \theta_n) \\ a_2 l_1 \cos(\theta_1 - \theta_2) & J_{22} & \cdots & a_n l_2 \cos(\theta_2 - \theta_n) \\ \cdots & \cdots & \cdots & \cdots \\ a_n l_1 \cos(\theta_1 - \theta_n) & a_n l_2 \cos(\theta_2 - \theta_n) & \cdots & J_{nn} \end{bmatrix}, \tag{8.299}$$

$$[\mathbf{A}] = \begin{bmatrix} 0 & a_2 l_1 \sin\left(\theta_1 - \theta_2\right) & \cdots & a_n l_1 \sin(\theta_1 - \theta_n) \\ -a_2 l_1 \sin(\theta_1 - \theta_2) & 0 & \cdots & a_n l_2 \sin(\theta_2 - \theta_n) \\ \cdots & \cdots & \cdots & \cdots \\ -a_n l_1 \sin(\theta_1 - \theta_n) & -a_n l_2 \sin(\theta_2 - \theta_n) & \cdots & 0 \end{bmatrix}, \tag{8.300}$$

$$[\mathbf{K}] = \begin{bmatrix} g a_1 & 0 & \cdots & 0 \\ 0 & g a_2 & \cdots & 0 \\ \cdots & \cdots & \cdots & \cdots \\ 0 & 0 & \cdots & g a_n \end{bmatrix}, \tag{8.301}$$

$$\{\boldsymbol{\theta}\} = \begin{bmatrix} \theta_1 & \theta_2 & \cdots & \theta_n \end{bmatrix}^{\mathrm{T}}, \quad \{\ddot{\boldsymbol{\theta}}\} = \begin{bmatrix} \ddot{\theta}_1 & \ddot{\theta}_2 & \cdots & \ddot{\theta}_n \end{bmatrix}^{\mathrm{T}}, \quad \{\dot{\boldsymbol{\theta}}^2\} = \begin{bmatrix} \dot{\theta}_1^2 & \dot{\theta}_2^2 & \cdots & \dot{\theta}_n^2 \end{bmatrix}^{\mathrm{T}},$$
$$\{\sin\boldsymbol{\theta}\} = \begin{bmatrix} \sin\theta_1 & \sin\theta_2 & \cdots & \sin\theta_n \end{bmatrix}^{\mathrm{T}},$$

$$\tag{8.302}$$

where the elements of the matrices $[\mathbf{J}]$, $[\mathbf{A}]$, and $[\mathbf{K}]$ are given by the formulae

$$J_{pq} = \begin{cases} J_{pp} & \text{for } p = q, \\ a_q l_p \cos(\theta_p - \theta_q) & \text{for } p < q, \\ J_{qp} & \text{for } p > q, \end{cases} \qquad (8.303)$$

$$A_{pq} = \begin{cases} 0 & \text{for } p = q, \\ a_q l_p \sin(\theta_p - \theta_q) & \text{for } p < q, \\ -A_{pq} & \text{for } p > q, \end{cases} \qquad (8.304)$$

and

$$K_{pq} = \begin{cases} g a_p & \text{for } p = q, \\ 0 & \text{for } p \neq q, \end{cases} \qquad (8.305)$$

respectively, and the system of equations of motion reads

$$[\mathbf{J}]\{\ddot{\boldsymbol{\theta}}\} + [\mathbf{A}]\{\dot{\boldsymbol{\theta}}^2\} + [\mathbf{K}]\{\sin\boldsymbol{\theta}\} = \{\mathbf{0}\}. \qquad (8.306)$$

Relation (8.306) can be written in the form

$$\{\ddot{\boldsymbol{\theta}}\} = -[\mathbf{J}]^{-1}[\mathbf{A}]\{\dot{\boldsymbol{\theta}}\}^2 - [\mathbf{J}]^{-1}[\mathbf{K}]\{\sin\boldsymbol{\theta}\}. \qquad (8.307)$$

With the notations

$$\theta_1 = \xi_1, \quad \theta_2 = \xi_2, \ldots, \quad \theta_n = \xi_n, \quad \dot\theta_1 = \xi_{n+1}, \quad \dot\theta_2 = \xi_{n+2}, \ldots, \quad \dot\theta_n = \xi_{2n}, \qquad (8.308)$$

$$[\mathbf{B}] = [\mathbf{J}]^{-1}[\mathbf{A}], \qquad (8.309)$$

$$[\mathbf{L}] = [\mathbf{J}]^{-1}[\mathbf{K}], \qquad (8.310)$$

we obtain the system

$$\frac{d\xi_i}{dt} = \begin{cases} \xi_{n+i} & \text{for } i \leq n, \\ -\displaystyle\sum_{j=1}^{n} B_{i-n,j}\xi_{n+j}^2 - \sum_{j=1}^{n} L_{i-n,j}\sin\xi_j & \text{for } i > n. \end{cases} \qquad (8.311)$$

2. Numerical calculation

In the case of the numerical application, we obtain, with the aid of the fourth-order Runge–Kutta method, the numerical results plotted in the diagrams in Figure 8.15.

Problem 8.6

Let the kinematic schema in Figure 8.16 be of a torque converter of G. Constantinescu.[12]

It is composed of the principal axle 1, the floating lever 2, the connection bars 3, $\tilde{3}$, and the bars 4, $\tilde{4}$. The principal axle is articulated to the floting lever at the point A, the last one acting the connection bars by the multiple articulation B. The connection bars are acting the bars 4, $\tilde{4}$ by the articulations D, $\tilde{D}$. The bars 4, $\tilde{4}$ are hinged at the fixed point E. Thus, the motion of rotation of the principal axle 1 is transformed into the oscillatory plane-parallel motion of the lever 2, and this is transformed, by means of a coupling system, into a motion of rotation in the same sense of the secondary axle 5. In Figure 8.16, the simplest system of coupling, formed by the ratchet wheel 5 and the ratchets 6, $\tilde{6}$, has been chosen.

---

[12]After George "Gogu" Constantinescu (1881–1965) who created the theory of sonics in *A Treatise of Transmission of Power by Vibrations* in 1918. This torque converter is an invention of G. Constantinescu.

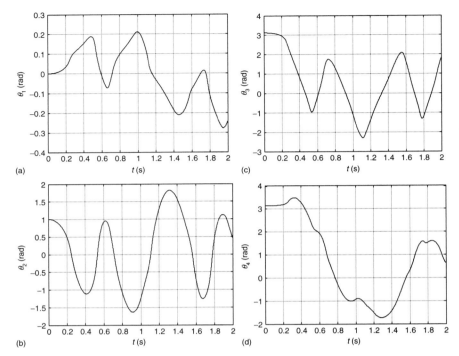

Figure 8.15 Results of the simulation.

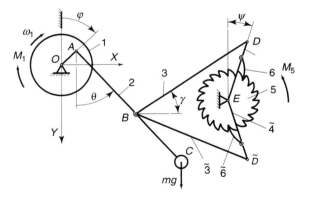

Figure 8.16 Torque converter of G. Constantinescu.

The following are known:

– the distances $OA = a$, $AB = b$, $AC = l$, $BD = B\widetilde{D} = c$, $ED = E\widetilde{D} = d$, x_E, y_E;
– the moment of inertia J_1 and the mass m;
– the motor torque

$$M_1 = M_0 - k\omega^2;$$ (8.312)

– the resistant torque

$$M_5 = \begin{cases} \widetilde{M}_5 & \text{if } \dot{\psi} \geq 0, \\ -\widetilde{M}_5 & \text{if } \dot{\psi} < 0; \end{cases}$$ (8.313)

– the initial conditions (which have to be consistent with position and velocity constraint equations, see below) $t = 0$, $\phi = \phi_0$, $\theta = \theta_0$, $\gamma = \gamma_0$, $\psi = \psi_0$, $\dot{\phi} = \dot{\theta} = \dot{\gamma} = \dot{\psi} = 0$.

It is required to determine and represent graphically

- $\omega_1(t)$, $\omega_5(t) = |\dot{\psi}|$;
- the trajectory of the point B.

Numerical application: $l = 0.3$ m, $a = 0.015$ m, $b = 0.15$ m, $c = 0.25$ m, $d = \sqrt{b^2 - a^2}$, $x_E = \sqrt{c^2 - d^2}$, $y_E = d$, $m = 3$ kg, $J_1 = 0.1$ kg m^3, $M_0 = 3.2$ Nm, $k = 2 \times 10^{-5}$ Nms^2, $M_5 = 20$ Nm, $\phi_0 = -\pi/2$, $\theta_0 = \arg\tan(a/d)$, $\gamma_0 = \arg\tan(d/\sqrt{c^2 - d^2})$, $\psi_0 = 0$ rad, $\dot{\phi} = \dot{\theta} = \dot{\gamma} = \dot{\psi} = 0$ rad s^{-1}.

Solution:

1. Theory

The chosen mechanical model is that in which the bodies 3, $\tilde{3}$, 4, $\tilde{4}$ have no mass, while the one-directional system formed by these bars leads (approximately) to a symmetry of the motion of the bars 4, $\tilde{4}$.

Under these conditions, we study the motion of the mechanism with two degrees of freedom, formed by the elements 1, 2, 3, 4, 5, the bar 4 being acted on by the torque M_5, given by relation (8.313).

We obtain the equations of constraints

$$a \sin\phi + b \sin\theta + c \cos\gamma - d \sin\psi = X_E, \quad -a \cos\phi + b \cos\theta - c \sin\gamma + d \cos\psi = Y_E; \tag{8.314}$$

by differentiation with respect to time, denoting by $[\mathbf{B}]$ the matrix of constraints

$$[\mathbf{B}] = \begin{bmatrix} a \cos\phi & b \cos\theta & -c \sin\gamma & -d \cos\psi \\ a \sin\phi & -b \sin\theta & -c \cos\gamma & -d \sin\psi \end{bmatrix} \tag{8.315}$$

and by $\{\mathbf{q}\}$ the column matrix of the generalized co-ordinates

$$\{\mathbf{q}\} = \begin{bmatrix} \phi & \theta & \gamma & \psi \end{bmatrix}^{\mathrm{T}}, \tag{8.316}$$

we obtain the equation of constraints

$$[\mathbf{B}]\{\dot{\mathbf{q}}\} = \{\mathbf{0}\}. \tag{8.317}$$

The kinetic energy T of the system reads

$$T = \frac{1}{2}[J_1 \dot{\phi}^2 + m(\dot{X}_C^2 + \dot{Y}_C^2)] \tag{8.318}$$

or

$$T = \frac{1}{2}[(J_1 + ma^2)\dot{\phi}^2 + ml^2\dot{\theta}^2 + 2mal\,\dot{\phi}\dot{\theta}\cos(\phi + \theta)]. \tag{8.319}$$

Using Lagrange's equations, we write successively the relations

$$\frac{\mathrm{d}}{\mathrm{d}t}\left(\frac{\partial T}{\partial \dot{\phi}}\right) = (J_1 + ma^2)\ddot{\phi} + mal\,\ddot{\theta}\cos(\phi + \theta) - mal(\dot{\phi} + \dot{\theta})\sin(\phi + \theta), \tag{8.320}$$

$$\frac{\partial T}{\partial \phi} = -mal\,\dot{\phi}\dot{\theta}\sin(\phi + \theta), \tag{8.321}$$

$$\frac{d}{dt}\left(\frac{\partial T}{\partial \dot{\theta}}\right) = ml^2\ddot{\theta} + mal\,\ddot{\phi}\cos(\phi + \theta) - mal\,\dot{\phi}(\dot{\phi} + \dot{\theta})\sin(\phi + \theta), \tag{8.322}$$

$$\frac{\partial T}{\partial \theta} = -mal\,\dot{\phi}\dot{\theta}\sin(\phi + \theta), \tag{8.323}$$

$$\frac{d}{dt}\left(\frac{\partial T}{\partial \dot{\gamma}}\right) = \frac{d}{dt}\left(\frac{\partial T}{\partial \dot{\psi}}\right) = 0, \quad \frac{\partial T}{\partial \gamma} = \frac{\partial T}{\partial \psi} = 0; \tag{8.324}$$

because the generalized forces are

$$Q_\phi = M_1 + mg\sin\phi, \quad Q_\theta = -mgl\sin\theta, \quad Q_\psi = -M_5, \tag{8.325}$$

Lagrange's equations, which are of the form

$$\frac{d}{dt}\left(\frac{\partial T}{\partial \dot{q}_k}\right) - \frac{\partial T}{\partial \dot{q}_k} = Q_k + B_{1k}\lambda_1 + B_{2k}\lambda_2, \tag{8.326}$$

B_{1k}, B_{2k} being the elements of the matrix $[\mathbf{B}]$, while λ_1, λ_2 are Lagrange's multipliers, are written in the matrix form

$$[\mathbf{M}]\{\ddot{\mathbf{q}}\} = \{\mathbf{F}\} + \{\widetilde{\mathbf{F}}\} + [\mathbf{B}]^T\{\boldsymbol{\lambda}\}, \tag{8.327}$$

where

$$[\mathbf{M}] = \begin{bmatrix} J_1 + ma^2 & mal\cos(\phi + \theta) & 0 & 0 \\ mal\cos(\phi + \theta) & ml^2 & 0 & 0 \\ 0 & 0 & 0 & 0 \\ 0 & 0 & 0 & 0 \end{bmatrix}, \tag{8.328}$$

$$\{\mathbf{F}\} = \begin{bmatrix} Q_\phi & Q_\theta & 0 & Q_\psi \end{bmatrix}^T, \tag{8.329}$$

$$\{\widetilde{\mathbf{F}}\} = mal\begin{bmatrix} \dot{\theta}^2 & \dot{\phi}^2 & 0 & 0 \end{bmatrix}^T \sin(\phi + \theta), \tag{8.330}$$

$$\{\boldsymbol{\lambda}\} = \begin{bmatrix} \lambda_1 & \lambda_2 \end{bmatrix}^T. \tag{8.331}$$

If to the differential equation (8.327) we add equation (8.317), differentiated with respect to time, we obtain the matrix differential equation

$$\begin{bmatrix} [\mathbf{M}] & -[\mathbf{B}]^T \\ [\mathbf{B}] & [\mathbf{0}] \end{bmatrix}\begin{bmatrix} \{\ddot{\mathbf{q}}\} \\ \{\boldsymbol{\lambda}\} \end{bmatrix} = \begin{bmatrix} \{\mathbf{F}\} + \{\widetilde{\mathbf{F}}\} \\ -[\dot{\mathbf{B}}]\{\dot{\mathbf{q}}\} \end{bmatrix}, \tag{8.332}$$

where

$$[\dot{\mathbf{B}}] = \begin{bmatrix} -a\dot{\phi}\sin\phi & -b\dot{\theta}\sin\theta & -c\dot{\gamma}\cos\gamma & d\dot{\psi}\sin\psi \\ a\dot{\phi}\cos\phi & -b\dot{\theta}\cos\theta & c\dot{\gamma}\sin\gamma & -d\dot{\psi}\cos\psi \end{bmatrix}. \tag{8.333}$$

For the given initial conditions, from equation (8.332) we determine the matrices $\{\mathbf{q}\}$, $\{\boldsymbol{\lambda}\}$; then, by the Runge–Kutta numerical method, we determine the new values of the matrices $\{\mathbf{q}\}$, $\{\dot{\mathbf{q}}\}$, which become the initial conditions for the following integration step.

This problem is a particular one in the class of drift and constraint stabilization.

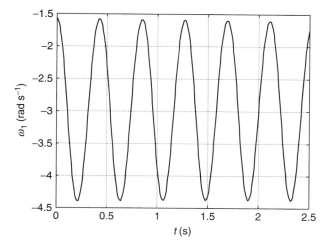

Figure 8.17   Variation of $\omega_1 = \omega_1(t)$.

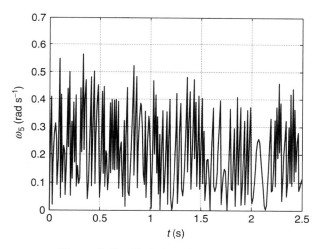

Figure 8.18   Variation of $\omega_5 = \omega_5(t)$.

2. Numerical calculation

On the basis of the calculation algorithm constructed by means of relations (8.312), (8.313), (8.315), (8.316), (8.323), (8.329), (8.330), (8.331), (8.333), and (8.332) as well as of the relations

$$X_B = a \sin \phi + b \sin \theta, \quad Y_B = -a \cos \phi + b \cos \theta, \tag{8.334}$$

the results plotted in the diagrams in Figure 8.17, Figure 8.18, and Figure 8.19 have been obtained.

Problem 8.7

We consider the toroidal wheel of radius r_0 and balloon radius r, which, under the influence of the weight mg, is rolling without sliding on a horizontal plane.

Knowing that, at the initial moment, the wheel axis is inclined by the angle θ_0 with respect to the vertical and that the angular velocity is parallel to the rotation axis of the wheel and has the value ω_0, let us determine

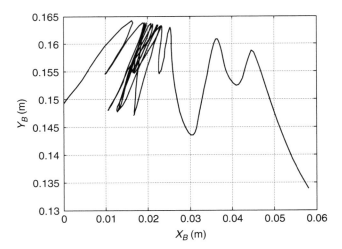

Figure 8.19   Variation of $Y_B = Y_B(X_B)$.

- the variation in time of the inclination angle of the wheel axis with respect to the vertical;
- the trajectory of the point of contact wheel-plane;
- the variation in time of the contact forces wheel-plane.

Numerical   application: $r_0 = 0.3$ m, $r = 0.05$ m, $m = 20$ kg, $J_x = J_y = 0.9$ kg m^2, $J_z = 1.8$ kg m^2, $\theta_0 = 5\pi/12$ rad.

Solution:

1. Theory

   1.1. Equations of the torus

   We consider the circle of radius r situated in the plane $Oy'z$ (Fig. 8.20), the center C of it being chosen so as to have $y'_C = -r_0$.

   The $Oy'z$-plane is obtained by rotation with the angle η of the Oyz-plane around the Oz-axis.

   By the notations in Figure 8.20, the co-ordinates of a point of the circle in the system $Ox'y'z$ are

   $$x' = 0, \quad y' = -(r_0 + r\cos\xi), \quad z' = r\sin\xi. \tag{8.335}$$

   By rotating the circle, we obtain the torus, the parametric equations of which are obtained, in the $Oxyz$-frame, from the relation

   $$\begin{bmatrix} x \\ y \\ z \end{bmatrix} = \begin{bmatrix} \cos\eta & -\sin\eta & 0 \\ \sin\eta & \cos\eta & 0 \\ 0 & 0 & 1 \end{bmatrix} \begin{bmatrix} 0 \\ -(r_0 + r\cos\xi) \\ r\sin\xi \end{bmatrix}; \tag{8.336}$$

   it follows that

   $$x = (r_0 + r\cos\xi)\sin\eta, \quad y = -(r_0 + r\cos\xi)\cos\eta, \quad z = r\sin\xi. \tag{8.337}$$

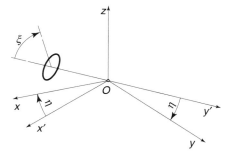

Figure 8.20   Equations of the torus.

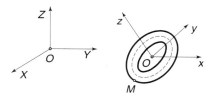

Figure 8.21   Conditions of tangency of the torus with the plane.

1.2. Conditions of tangency of the torus with the plane

We take as rolling plane the horizontal O_0XY-plane (Fig. 8.21) and we choose as rotation angles Euler's angles ψ, θ, ϕ, to which correspond the partial rotation matrices

$$[\psi] = \begin{bmatrix} \cos\psi & -\sin\psi & 0 \\ \sin\psi & \cos\psi & 0 \\ 0 & 0 & 1 \end{bmatrix}, \quad [\theta] = \begin{bmatrix} 1 & 0 & 0 \\ 0 & \cos\theta & -\sin\theta \\ 0 & \sin\theta & \cos\theta \end{bmatrix},$$

$$[\phi] = \begin{bmatrix} \cos\phi & -\sin\phi & 0 \\ \sin\phi & \cos\phi & 0 \\ 0 & 0 & 1 \end{bmatrix}, \tag{8.338}$$

and the rotation matrix $[\mathbf{A}]$ of the frame $Oxyz$ with respect to the frame O_0XYZ

$$[\mathbf{A}] = [\psi][\theta][\phi]. \tag{8.339}$$

Denoting by $\{\mathbf{r}\}$, $\{\mathbf{r}_\xi\}$, $\{\mathbf{r}_\eta\}$ the matrices

$$\{\mathbf{r}\} = \begin{bmatrix} (r_0 + r\cos\xi)\sin\eta \\ -(r_0 + r\cos\xi)\cos\eta \\ r\sin\xi \end{bmatrix}, \quad \{\mathbf{r}_\xi\} = \begin{bmatrix} -r\sin\xi\sin\eta \\ r\sin\xi\cos\eta \\ r\cos\xi \end{bmatrix},$$

$$\{\mathbf{r}_\eta\} = \begin{bmatrix} (r_0 + r\cos\xi)\cos\eta \\ (r_0 + r\cos\xi)\sin\eta \\ 0 \end{bmatrix}, \tag{8.340}$$

the tangency conditions at the point M are written in the form

$$\begin{bmatrix} 0 & 0 & 1 \end{bmatrix}[\mathbf{A}]\{\mathbf{r}_\xi\} = 0, \quad \begin{bmatrix} 0 & 0 & 1 \end{bmatrix}[\mathbf{A}]\{\mathbf{r}_\eta\} = 0; \tag{8.341}$$

hence, we obtain the equations

$$\sin\theta\sin(\phi+\eta)=0, \quad \sin\theta\sin\xi\cos(\phi+\eta)+\cos\theta\cos\xi=0, \tag{8.342}$$

from which it follows that

$$\eta=-\phi, \quad \xi=\theta-\frac{\pi}{2}. \tag{8.343}$$

1.3. Initial conditions

If we choose the frame of reference O_0XYZ, so that the contact point at the initial moment is O_0, the Ox-axis is parallel to the O_0Y-axis, while the Oz-axis is normal to the O_0Y-axis, then, at the initial moment, the conditions

$$\psi=\frac{\pi}{2}, \quad \theta=\theta_0, \quad \phi=0, \quad [\mathbf{A}]=\begin{bmatrix} 0 & -1 & 0 \\ 1 & 0 & 0 \\ 0 & 0 & 1 \end{bmatrix}\begin{bmatrix} 1 & 0 & 0 \\ 0 & \cos\theta_0 & -\sin\theta_0 \\ 0 & \sin\theta_0 & \cos\theta_0 \end{bmatrix},$$

$$\{\mathbf{r}\}=\begin{bmatrix} 0 \\ -(r_0+r\sin\theta_0) \\ -r\cos\theta_0 \end{bmatrix}, \tag{8.344}$$

are fulfilled; also, from the contact equation at O_0

$$\begin{bmatrix} 0 \\ 0 \\ 0 \end{bmatrix}=\begin{bmatrix} X_O \\ Y_O \\ Z_O \end{bmatrix}+[\mathbf{A}]\{\mathbf{r}\}, \tag{8.345}$$

we obtain the initial conditions

$$X_O=-r_0\cos\theta_0, \quad Y_O=0, \quad Z_O=r_0\sin\theta_0+r. \tag{8.346}$$

From the conditions specified in the enunciation, it also follows that at the initial moment

$$\dot\psi=\dot\theta=0, \quad \dot\phi=\omega_0, \tag{8.347}$$

while, from the condition of rolling without sliding, we get

$$\begin{bmatrix} \dot X_O \\ \dot Y_O \\ \dot Z_O \end{bmatrix}+[\mathbf{A}][\mathbf{r}]^{\mathrm{T}}[\mathbf{Q}]\begin{bmatrix} \dot\psi \\ \dot\theta \\ \dot\phi \end{bmatrix}=\{\mathbf{0}\}; \tag{8.348}$$

knowing that

$$[\mathbf{r}]=\begin{bmatrix} 0 & r\cos\theta_0 & -(r_0+r\sin\theta_0) \\ -r\cos\theta_0 & 0 & 0 \\ r_0+r\sin\theta_0 & 0 & 0 \end{bmatrix},$$

$$[\mathbf{Q}]=\begin{bmatrix} \sin\phi\sin\theta & \cos\phi & 0 \\ \cos\phi\sin\theta & -\sin\phi & 0 \\ \cos\theta & 0 & 1 \end{bmatrix}=\begin{bmatrix} 0 & 1 & 0 \\ \sin\theta_0 & 0 & 0 \\ \cos\theta & 0 & 1 \end{bmatrix}, \tag{8.349}$$

we obtain the initial conditions

$$\dot X_O=\dot Y_O=0, \quad \dot Z_O=-(r_0+r\sin\theta_0)\omega_0. \tag{8.350}$$

1.4. The constraints matrix

Taking into account relation (8.343), from the last relation (8.340) we get

$$\{r\} = \begin{bmatrix} -(r_0 + r\sin\theta)\sin\phi \\ -(r_0 + r\sin\theta)\cos\phi \\ -r\cos\theta \end{bmatrix};$$

(8.351)

with the notations

$$[r] = \begin{bmatrix} 0 & r\cos\theta & -(r_0 + r\sin\theta)\cos\phi \\ -r\cos\theta & 0 & (r_0 + r\sin\theta)\sin\phi \\ (r_0 + r\sin\theta)\cos\phi & -(r_0 + r\sin\theta)\sin\phi & 0 \end{bmatrix}, \quad (8.352)$$

from equation (8.348) we obtain the constraints matrix

$$[\mathbf{B}] = \begin{bmatrix} [\mathbf{I}] & [\mathbf{A}][r]^T[\mathbf{Q}] \end{bmatrix}.$$

(8.353)

The derivative with respect to time of the constraints matrix is

$$[\dot{\mathbf{B}}] = \begin{bmatrix} [\mathbf{0}] & [\dot{\mathbf{A}}][r]^T[\mathbf{Q}] + [\mathbf{A}][\dot{r}]^T[\mathbf{Q}] + [\mathbf{A}][r]^T[\dot{\mathbf{Q}}] \end{bmatrix}, \quad (8.354)$$

where

$$[\dot{r}] = \begin{bmatrix} 0 & -\dot{z} & \dot{y} \\ \dot{z} & 0 & -\dot{x} \\ -\dot{y} & \dot{x} & 0 \end{bmatrix}, \quad (8.355)$$

$$\dot{x} = -r\dot{\theta}\cos\theta\sin\phi - \dot{\phi}(r_0 + r\sin\theta)\cos\phi, \quad \dot{y} = -r\dot{\theta}\cos\theta\sin\phi + \dot{\phi}(r_0 + r\sin\theta)\sin\phi,$$
$$\dot{z} = -r\dot{\theta}\sin\theta.$$

(8.356)

2. Numerical calculation

As has been shown in Problem 8.6, the matrix differential equation of the motion is

$$\begin{bmatrix} [\mathbf{M}] & -[\mathbf{B}]^T \\ [\mathbf{B}] & [\mathbf{0}] \end{bmatrix} \begin{bmatrix} \{\ddot{q}\} \\ \{\lambda\} \end{bmatrix} = \begin{bmatrix} \{\mathbf{F}\} + \{\widetilde{\mathbf{F}}\} \\ -[\dot{\mathbf{B}}]\{\dot{q}\} \end{bmatrix}, \quad (8.357)$$

where

$$[\mathbf{m}] = \begin{bmatrix} m & 0 & 0 \\ 0 & m & 0 \\ 0 & 0 & m \end{bmatrix}, \quad [\mathbf{J}] = \begin{bmatrix} J_x & 0 & 0 \\ 0 & J_y & 0 \\ 0 & 0 & J_z \end{bmatrix}, \quad (8.358)$$

$$[\mathbf{Q}] = \begin{bmatrix} \sin\phi\sin\theta & \cos\phi & 0 \\ \cos\phi & -\sin\phi & 0 \\ \cos\theta & 0 & 1 \end{bmatrix}, \quad (8.359)$$

$$[\mathbf{M}] = \begin{bmatrix} [\mathbf{m}] & [\mathbf{0}] \\ [\mathbf{0}] & [\mathbf{Q}]^T[\mathbf{J}][\mathbf{Q}] \end{bmatrix}, \quad (8.360)$$

$$\{q\} = \begin{bmatrix} X_O & Y_O & Z_O & \psi & \theta & \phi \end{bmatrix}^T, \quad \{\lambda\} = \begin{bmatrix} \lambda_1 & \lambda_2 & \lambda_3 \end{bmatrix}^T, \quad (8.361)$$

$$\{\mathbf{F}\} = \begin{bmatrix} 0 & 0 & -mg & 0 & 0 & 0 \end{bmatrix}^T, \quad (8.362)$$

$$\{\boldsymbol{\beta}\} = \begin{bmatrix} \psi & \theta & \phi \end{bmatrix}^T, \quad (8.363)$$

$$[\mathbf{U}_\psi] = [\mathbf{U}_\phi] = \begin{bmatrix} 0 & -1 & 0 \\ 1 & 0 & 0 \\ 0 & 0 & 0 \end{bmatrix}, \quad [\mathbf{U}_\theta] = \begin{bmatrix} 0 & 0 & 0 \\ 0 & 0 & -1 \\ 0 & 1 & 0 \end{bmatrix}, \tag{8.364}$$

$$[\mathbf{Q}_\psi] = [\mathbf{0}], \quad [\mathbf{Q}_\theta] = \begin{bmatrix} \sin\phi\cos\theta & 0 & 0 \\ \cos\phi\cos\theta & 0 & 0 \\ -\sin\theta & 0 & 0 \end{bmatrix}, \quad [\mathbf{Q}_\phi] = \begin{bmatrix} \cos\phi\sin\theta & -\sin\phi & 0 \\ -\sin\phi\sin\theta & -\cos\phi & 0 \\ 0 & 0 & 0 \end{bmatrix}, \tag{8.365}$$

$$[\mathbf{\Delta}] = \begin{bmatrix} \{\dot{\boldsymbol{\beta}}\}^T [\mathbf{Q}_\psi]^T [\mathbf{J}][\mathbf{Q}] \\ \{\dot{\boldsymbol{\beta}}\}^T [\mathbf{Q}_\theta]^T [\mathbf{J}][\mathbf{Q}] \\ \{\dot{\boldsymbol{\beta}}\}^T [\mathbf{Q}_\phi]^T [\mathbf{J}][\mathbf{Q}] \end{bmatrix}, \tag{8.366}$$

$$[\dot{\mathbf{Q}}] = \dot\theta[\mathbf{Q}_\psi] + \dot\phi[\mathbf{Q}_\phi], \quad [\mathbf{A}_\psi] = [\mathbf{U}_\psi][\mathbf{A}], \quad [\mathbf{A}_\theta] = [\mathbf{A}][\phi]^T[\mathbf{U}_\theta][\phi], \quad [\mathbf{A}_\phi] = [\mathbf{A}][\mathbf{U}_\phi], \tag{8.367}$$

$$\{\widetilde{\mathbf{F}}_\beta\} = [[\dot{\mathbf{Q}}]^T[\mathbf{J}][\mathbf{Q}] + [\mathbf{Q}]^T[\mathbf{J}][\dot{\mathbf{Q}}] + [\mathbf{\Delta}]]\{\dot{\boldsymbol{\beta}}\}, \quad \{\widetilde{\mathbf{F}}\} = \begin{bmatrix} 0 & 0 & 0 & \{\widetilde{\mathbf{F}}_\beta\}^T \end{bmatrix}^T. \tag{8.368}$$

By solving equation (8.357), we determine the functions $X_O(t)$, $Y_O(t)$, $Z_O(t)$, $\psi(t)$, $\theta(t)$, $\phi(t)$. The variation of the inclination angle θ is given in Figure 8.22.

The trajectory of the contact point is obtained by means of the co-ordinates X, Y, $Z = 0$, which are obtained from the relation

$$\begin{bmatrix} X \\ Y \\ Z \end{bmatrix} = \begin{bmatrix} X_O \\ Y_O \\ Z_O \end{bmatrix} + [\mathbf{A}]\{\mathbf{r}\}; \tag{8.369}$$

it results in the trajectory in Figure 8.23.

The reaction of contact has the components along the axes $O_0 X$, $O_0 Y$, $O_0 Z$

$$R_X = \lambda_1, \quad R_Y = \lambda_2, \quad R_Z = \lambda_3; \tag{8.370}$$

thus, the force tangent to the wheel is

$$F_t = \frac{\dot{X}\lambda_1 + \dot{Y}\lambda_2}{\sqrt{\dot{X}^2 + \dot{Y}^2}}, \tag{8.371}$$

while the force in the plane of contact, normal to the tangent at the wheel, is

$$F_n = \frac{\dot{Y}\lambda_1 - \dot{X}\lambda_2}{\sqrt{\dot{X}^2 + \dot{Y}^2}}. \tag{8.372}$$

The variation in time of the forces R_Z, F_t, F_n is given in Figure 8.24, Figure 8.25, and Figure 8.26.

Problem 8.8

(Postcritical behavior of the cantilever beam). Let us consider a cantilever beam of length l, acted upon by the constant axial force P (Fig. 8.27). The mathematical model of the problem may be expressed in the nonlinear general form

$$\frac{dy}{ds} = \sin\theta, \quad \frac{d\theta}{ds} = \alpha^2(f - y), \quad \alpha^2 = \frac{P}{EI}, \tag{8.373}$$

where $ds = \sqrt{(dx)^2 + (dy)^2}$, Ox is the direction along the bar axis, O corresponds to the bar left end, Oy is the transverse axis, θ is the rotation of the bar cross section, and EI is the constant

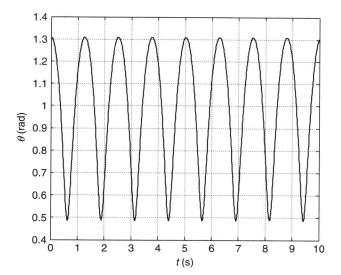

Figure 8.22   The variation $\theta = \theta(t)$.

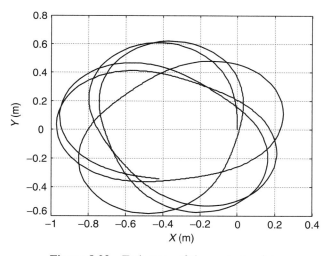

Figure 8.23   Trajectory of the contact point.

bending rigidity of the bar (E is the modulus of longitudinal elasticity, I is the moment of inertia of the cross section with respect to the neutral axis). The solution must be found under null Cauchy conditions

$$y(0) = 0, \quad \theta(0) = 0. \tag{8.374}$$

We firstly perform the change of function

$$\widetilde{y}(x) = y(x) - f, \tag{8.375}$$

and then apply the LEM mapping, which in this case will depend on two parameters

$$v(x, \sigma, \xi) = \mathrm{e}^{\sigma \widetilde{y}(s) + \xi \theta(s)}; \tag{8.376}$$

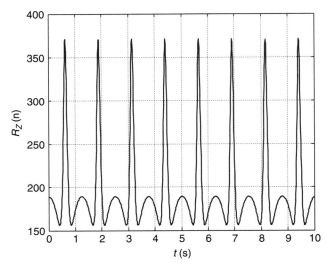

Figure 8.24   The variation $R_Z = R_Z(t)$.

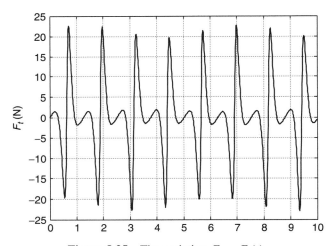

Figure 8.25   The variation $F_t = F_t(t)$.

this leads to the first linear partial differential equation, equivalent to equation (8.373), the first LEM equivalent

$$\frac{\partial v}{\partial x} = \sigma \sin D_\xi v - \alpha^2 \xi \frac{\partial v}{\partial \sigma}. \tag{8.377}$$

By $\sin D_\xi$, we mean the operator obtained by formally replacing the powers of θ with derivatives with respect to ξ of the same order in the expansion of $\sin \theta$.

Considering for v a series expansion in σ and ξ, we get the second LEM equivalent

$$\frac{dv_{ij}}{ds} = i \sum_{k=1}^{\infty} \frac{(-1)^{k+1}}{(2k-1)!} v_{i-1,j+2k-1} - j\alpha^2 v_{i+1,j-1}. \tag{8.378}$$

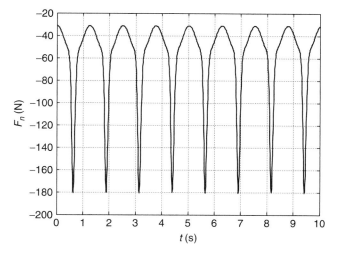

Figure 8.26   The variation $F_n = F_n(t)$.

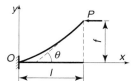

Figure 8.27   Problem 8.8.

Applying Theorem 8.4, we get the following normal LEM representation

$$y(x) \equiv -f(\cos \alpha x - 1) - f^2 \alpha^2 \Phi(\alpha x) - f^4 \alpha^4 \Psi(\alpha x), \tag{8.379}$$

where $\Psi(\alpha x)$ is analytic in αx and $\Phi(\alpha x)$ is given by

$$\Phi(\alpha x) = \frac{1}{16} \left[\frac{1}{4} (\cos 3\alpha x - \cos \alpha x) + \alpha x \sin \alpha x \right]. \tag{8.380}$$

To equation (8.379) we apply the condition $y(l) = f$, meaning that the bar length remains still l if the shortening is neglected in postcritical behavior. This gives

$$\cos \alpha l + (\alpha f)^2 \Phi(\alpha l) \equiv 0, \tag{8.381}$$

in fact, an approximate relationship depending on the parameters f and α.

From equation (8.381), by elementary computation we obtain

$$\frac{f}{l} \cong \frac{4}{\alpha l} \sqrt{\frac{2 \cot \alpha l}{\sin 2\alpha l - 2\alpha l}}, \quad \frac{\pi}{2} < \alpha l < \pi, \tag{8.382}$$

which is, in fact, a direct LEM representation of the postcritical values of f/l as a function of the supraunitary ratio P/P_{cr} ($P_{cr} = \pi^2 EI/(4l^2)$ is the critical force). It will be marked by LEM.

Considering for α the following expansion

$$\alpha = \alpha_0 + \alpha_1 f + \alpha_2 \frac{f^2}{2!} + \cdots \equiv \sum_{j=0}^{\infty} \alpha_j \frac{f^j}{j!}, \tag{8.383}$$

and, introducing it in equation (8.381), a power series in f appears that must vanish identically. Determining the coefficients α_j up to $j = 2$, we obtain

$$\frac{\alpha}{\alpha_0} \cong 1 + 16\alpha_0^2 f^2, \tag{8.384}$$

from which another approximate LEM formula for the postcritical values of f/l, marked by LEM$_1$ is finally deduced:

$$\frac{f}{l} \cong \frac{8}{\pi} \sqrt{\sqrt{\frac{P}{P_{\mathrm{cr}}}} - 1}. \tag{8.385}$$

We can also relate the dimensionless quantities αl and αf by taking

$$(\alpha f)^2 = \sum_{j=0}^{\infty} p_j \frac{(\alpha - \alpha_0)^j l^j}{j!}; \tag{8.386}$$

introducing this in formula (8.381) again leads to a series in αl, whose coefficients must vanish. Going as far as $j = 1$, we obtain the following approximating value for αf

$$(\alpha f)^2 \cong 16(\alpha - \alpha_0)l, \tag{8.387}$$

and from equation (8.381) we get a third formula for the postcritical cantilever bar, marked by LEM$_2$,

$$\frac{f}{l} \cong \frac{8}{\pi} \sqrt{\frac{P_{\mathrm{cr}}}{P}} \sqrt{\sqrt{\frac{P}{P_{\mathrm{cr}}}} - 1}, \tag{8.388}$$

which coincides with Schneider's formula.

The form of these formulae suggests a comparison with Grashof's formula (marked by G)

$$\frac{f}{l} \cong \frac{8}{\pi} \sqrt{\frac{P}{P_{\mathrm{cr}}}} \sqrt{\sqrt{\frac{P}{P_{\mathrm{cr}}}} - 1}, \tag{8.389}$$

established from the well-known form of the solution of the cantilever problem by using elliptic integrals.

The LEM representation for y was also used to get good postcritical formulae for other quantities of interest, such as δ/l, where $\delta = l - x(l)$, the displacement of the bar along its straight axis, and $\theta(l)$.

In Table 8.22 the values of the ratio f/l, expressed by elliptic integrals (exact solution), are compared

$$\frac{f}{l} = \frac{2k}{K(k)}, \quad k = \frac{\sin \theta l}{2}, \quad K(k) = \frac{\pi}{2} \sqrt{\frac{P}{P_{\mathrm{cr}}}}, \tag{8.390}$$

with LEM, LEM$_1$, LEM$_2$, and G.

TABLE 8.22   The Values of the Ratio f/l Computed Comparatively by Using Three LEM Variants, Grashof's Formula, and Elliptic Integrals

P/P_{cr}	1.004	1.015	1.035	1.063	1.102	1.152	1.215	1.293
Exact solution	0.110	0.220	0.324	0.422	0.514	0.594	0.662	0.720
LEM	0.110	0.220	0.324	0.422	0.516	0.601	0.676	0.741
LEM_1	0.116	0.220	0.329	0.435	0.541	0.642	0.738	0.829
LEM_2 (Schneider)	0.114	0.220	0.335	0.448	0.563	0.689	0.814	0.942
G	0.114	0.221	0.341	0.462	0.596	0.740	0.898	1.072

This comparison is emphasized for $1 < P/P_{cr} < 1.3$, the formulae approximating the postcritical behavior of the cantilever bar being ordered with respect to their "goodness."

The mean square errors with respect to the exact solution are 0.24% for LEM, 1.36% for LEM_1, 2.67% for LEM_2 (Schneider), and 4.22% for G. These results point out that LEM leads to quite simple formulae, which give very good approximations for the ratio f/l, and that it is, in any case, much better than Grashof's formula. Similar conclusions can be drawn for the ratio δ/l and for $\theta(l)$.

We can conclude that the method presented here provides direct approximate formulae for f/l, δ/l, and $\theta(l)$ in the case of the cantilever bar, as well as critical values for the loads, considering various hypotheses.

It must also be mentioned that this method, based on LEM, does not depend on some particular mechanical interpretation. Using the same pattern, we can obtain similar results for various cases of loading and support.

FURTHER READING

Acton FS (1990). Numerical Methods that Work. 4th ed. Washington: Mathematical Association of America.

Ackleh AS, Allen EJ, Hearfott RB, Seshaiyer P (2009). Classical and Modern Numerical Analysis: Theory, Methods and Practice. Boca Raton: CRC Press.

Atkinson KE (1989). An Introduction to Numerical Analysis. 2nd ed. New York: John Wiley & Sons, Inc.

Atkinson KE (2003). Elementary Numerical Analysis. 2nd ed. Hoboken: John Wiley & Sons, Inc.

Babuška I, Práger M, Vitásek E (1966). Numerical Processes in Differential Equations. Prague: SNTI.

Bakhvalov N (1976). Méthodes Numérique. Moscou: Editions Mir (in French).

Boyce WE, DiPrima RC (2008). Elementary Differential Equations and Boundary Value Problems. 9th ed. Hoboken: John Wiley & Sons, Inc.

Burden RL, Faires L (2009). Numerical Analysis. 9th ed. Boston: Brooks/Cole.

Chapra SC (1996). Applied Numerical Methods with MATLAB for Engineers and Scientists. Boston: McGraw-Hill.

Cheney EW, Kincaid DR (1997). Numerical Mathematics and Computing. 6th ed. Belmont: Thomson.

Constantinescu G (1985). Teoria sonicității. București: Editura Academiei (in Romanian).

Dahlquist G, Björck Å (1974). Numerical Methods. Englewood Cliffs: Prentice Hall.

Démidovitch B, Maron I (1973). Éléments de Calcul Numérique. Moscou: Editions Mir (in French).

Den Hartog JP (1961). Strength of Materials. New York: Dover Books on Engineering.

DiBenedetto E (2010). Classical Mechanics: Theory and Mathematical Modeling. New York: Springer-Verlag.

Epperson JF (2007). An Introduction to Numerical Methods and Analysis. Hoboken: John Wiley & Sons, Inc.

Fung YC, Tong P (2011). Classical and Computational Solid Mechanics. Singapore: World Scientific Publishing.

Gautschi W (1997). Numerical Analysis: An Introduction. Boston: Birkhäuser.

Godunov SK, Reabenki VS (1977). Scheme de Calcul cu Diferenţe Finite. Bucureşti: Editura Tehnică (in Romanian).

Greenbaum A, Chartier TP (2012). Numerical Methods: Design, Analysis, and Computer Implementation of Algorithms. Princeton: Princeton University Press.

Hamming RW (1987). Numerical Methods for Scientists and Engineers. 2nd ed. New York: Dover Publications.

Hamming RW (2012). Introduction to Applied Numerical Analysis. New York: Dover Publications.

Heinbockel JH (2006). Numerical Methods for Scientific Computing. Victoria: Trafford Publishing.

Hibbeler RC (2010). Mechanics of Materials. 8th ed. Englewood Cliffs: Prentice Hall.

Hildebrand FB (1987). Introduction to Numerical Analysis. 2nd ed. New York: Dover Publications.

Hoffman JD (1992). Numerical Methods for Engineers and Scientists. New York: McGraw-Hill.

Iserles A (2008). A first Course in the Numerical Analysis of Differential Equations. 2nd ed. Cambridge: Cambridge University Press.

Ixaru LG (1979). Metode Numerice pentru Ecuaţii Diferenţiale cu Aplicaţii. Bucureşti: Editura Academiei Române (in Romanian).

Jazar RN (2008). Vehicle Dynamics: Theory and Applications. New York: Springer-Verlag.

Kharab A, Guenther RB (2011). An Introduction to Numerical Methods: A MATLAB Approach. 3rd ed. Boca Raton: CRC Press.

Kleppner D, Kolenkow RJ (2010). An Introduction to Mechanics. Cambridge: Cambridge University Press.

Kress R (1996). Numerical Analysis. New York: Springer-Verlag.

Kunz KS (1957). Numerical Analysis. New York: McGraw-Hill.

Levine L (1964). Methods for Solving Engineering Problems Using Analog Computers. New York: McGraw-Hill.

Lurie AI (2002). Analytical Mechanics. New York: Springer-Verlag.

Mabie HH, Reinholtz CF (1987). Mechanisms and Dynamics of Machinery. 4th ed. New York: John Wiley & Sons, Inc.

Lurie AI (2005). Theory of Elasticity. New York: Springer-Verlag.

Marciuk GI (1983). Metode de Analiză Numerică. Bucureşti: Editura Academiei Române (in Romanian).

Marciuk GI, Şaidurov VV (1981). Creşterea Preciziei Soluţiilor în Scheme cu Diferenţe. Bucureşti: Editura Academiei Române (in Romanian).

Marinescu G (1974). Analiza Numerică. Bucureşti: Editura Academiei Române (in Romanian).

Meriam JL, Kraige LG (2012). Engineering Mechanics: Dynamics. Hoboken: John Wiley & Sons, Inc.

Otto SR, Denier JP (2005). An Introduction to Programming and Numerical Methods in MATLAB. London: Springer-Verlag.

Palm WJ III (2007). Mechanical Vibrations. Hoboken: John Wiley & Sons, Inc.

Pandrea N (2000). Elemente de Mecanica Solidului în Coordonate Plückeriene. Bucureşti: Editura Academiei Române (in Romanian).

Pandrea N, Pârlac S, Popa D (2001). Modele pentru Studiul Vibraţiilor Automobilelor. Piteşti: Tiparg (in Romanian).

Pandrea N, Popa D (2000). Mecanisme. Teorie şi Aplicaţii CAD. Bucureşti: Editura Tehnică (in Romanian).

Pandrea N, Stănescu ND (2002). Mecanică. Bucureşti: Editura Didactică şi Pedagogică (in Romanian).

Press WH, Teukolski SA, Vetterling WT, Flannery BP (2007). Numerical Recipes: The Art of Scientific Computing. 3rd ed. Cambridge: Cambridge University Press.

Quarteroni A, Sacco R, Saleri F (2010). Numerical Mathematics. 2nd ed. Berlin: Springer-Verlag.

Ralston A, Rabinowitz P (2001). A First Course in Numerical Analysis. 2nd ed. New York: Dover Publications.

Ridgway Scott L (2011). Numerical Analysis. Princeton: Princeton University Press.

Salvadori MG, Baron ML (1962). Numerical Methods in Engineering. Englewood Cliffs: Prentice Hall.

Sauer T (2011). Numerical Analysis. 2nd ed. London: Pearson.

Simionescu I, Dranga M, Moise V (1995). Metode Numerice în Tehnică. Aplicaţii în FORTRAN. Bucureşti: Editura Tehnică (in Romanian).

Sinha AK (2010). Vibration of Mechanical Systems. Cambridge: Cambridge University Press.

Soare M, Teodorescu PP, Toma I (2010). Ordinary Differential Equations with Applications to Mechanics. Dordrecht: Springer-Verlag.

Stănescu ND (2007). Metode Numerice. Bucureşti: Editura Didactică şi Pedagogică (in Romanian).

Stănescu ND, Munteanu L, Chiroiu V, Pandrea N (2007). Sisteme Dinamice: Teorie şi Aplicaţii. Volume 1. Bucureşti: Editura Academiei Române (in Romanian).

Stănescu ND, Munteanu L, Chiroiu V, Pandrea N (2011). Sisteme Dinamice. Teorie şi Applicaţii. Volume 2. Bucureşti: Editura Academiei Române (in Romanian).

Stoer J, Bulirsh R (2010). Introduction to Numerical Analysis. 3rd ed. New York: Springer-Verlag.

Stuart AM, Humphries AR (1998). Dynamical Systems and Numerical Analysis. Cambridge: Cambridge University Press.

Süli E, Mayers D (2003). An Introduction to Numerical Analysis. Cambridge: Cambridge University Press.

Teodorescu PP (2008). Mechanical Systems: Classical Models. Volume 2: Mechanics of Discrete and Continuous Systems. Dordrecht: Springer-Verlag.

Teodorescu PP (2009). Mechanical Systems: Classical Models. Volume 3: Analytical Mechanics. Dordrecht: Springer-Verlag.

Toma I (2008). Metoda Echivalenţei Lineare şi Aplicaţiile Ei în Mecanică. Bucureşti: Editura Tehnică (in Romanian).

Udrişte C, Iftode V, Postolache M (1996). Metode Numerice de Calcul. Algoritmi şi Programe Turbo Pascal. Bucureşti: Editura Tehnică (in Romanian).

9

INTEGRATION OF PARTIAL DIFFERENTIAL EQUATIONS AND OF SYSTEMS OF PARTIAL DIFFERENTIAL EQUATIONS

9.1 INTRODUCTION

Many problems of science and technique lead to partial differential equations. The mathematical theories of such equations, especially of the nonlinear ones, are very intricate, such that their numerical study becomes inevitable.

To classify the partial differential equations, we may use various criteria, that is,

- considering the order of the derivatives, we have equations of first order, second order, or nth order;
- considering the linearity character, we have linear, quasilinear, or nonlinear equations;
- considering the influence of the integration domain at a point, we have equations of elliptic, parabolic, or hyperbolic type;
- considering the types of limit conditions, we get Dirichlet, Neumann, or mixed problems.

The partial differential equations which will be dealt with further are mostly the usual equations, the existence and the uniqueness of the solution being assured.

9.2 PARTIAL DIFFERENTIAL EQUATIONS OF FIRST ORDER

The partial differential equations of first order have the general form

$$\sum_{i=1}^{n} a_i(x_1, x_2, \ldots, x_n, u) \frac{\partial u}{\partial x_i} = b(x_1, x_2, \ldots, x_n, u), \tag{9.1}$$

where u is the unknown function, x_i, $i = \overline{1, n}$, are the independent variables, while a_i, $i = \overline{1, n}$, and b are functions that do not depend on the partial derivatives $\partial u/\partial x_i$, $i = \overline{1, n}$.

Numerical Analysis with Applications in Mechanics and Engineering, First Edition.
Petre Teodorescu, Nicolae-Doru Stănescu, and Nicolae Pandrea.
© 2013 The Institute of Electrical and Electronics Engineers, Inc. Published 2013 by John Wiley & Sons, Inc.

Definition 9.1

(i) If the functions a_i, $i = \overline{1, n}$, and b do not depend on the unknown function u, then the equation is linear.

(ii) If the function b is identically zero, $b \equiv 0$, then the equation is called *homogeneous*.

The solution of equation (9.1) is reduced to the solving of a system of n ordinary differential equations

$$\frac{dx_1}{a_1(x_1, \ldots, x_n, u)} = \frac{dx_2}{a_2(x_1, \ldots, x_n, u)} = \cdots = \frac{dx_n}{a_n(x_1, \ldots, x_n, u)} = \frac{du}{b(x_1, \ldots, x_n, u)}. \quad (9.2)$$

Definition 9.2   System (9.2) is called a *characteristic system*.

In general, the solution of equation (9.1) is an n-dimensional hypersurface in a domain $\mathcal{D}_{n+1} \subset \mathbb{R}^{n+1}$, the solution being of the form $F(x_1, \ldots, x_n, u) = 0$, or of the form $u = f(x_1, \ldots, x_n)$.

In the case of the Cauchy problem, the n-dimensional integral hypersurface pierces an $(n-1)$-dimensional hypersurface Γ, contained in the $(n+1)$-dimensional definition domain, the hypersurface Γ being the intersection of two n-dimensional hypersurfaces,

$$F_1(x_1, \ldots, x_n, u) = 0; \quad F_2 = (x_1, \ldots, x_n, u) = 0. \quad (9.3)$$

The solution of system (9.2) depends on n arbitrary constants C_i, $i = \overline{1, n}$, and is of the form

$$\phi_i(x_1, \ldots x_n, u) = C_i, \quad i = \overline{1, n}. \quad (9.4)$$

Definition 9.3   The hypersurfaces $\phi_i(x_1, \ldots x_n, u) = C_i, i = \overline{1, n}$, are called *characteristic hypersurfaces* and depend on one parameter.

Relations (9.3) and (9.4) form a system of $n + 2$ equations from which $n + 1$ variables x_1, x_2, $\ldots$, x_n, u are expressed as functions of C_i, $i = \overline{1, n}$; introducing in the last equation, we obtain

$$\Phi(C_i, \ldots, C_n) = 0. \quad (9.5)$$

From equations (9.4) and (9.5) we get the solution

$$\Phi(C_1, \ldots, C_n) = \Phi(\phi_1, \ldots, \phi_n) \equiv F(x_1, \ldots, x_n, u) = 0 \quad (9.6)$$

To solve the problem numerically, we proceed as follows. We seek the solution in the domain $\mathcal{D}_{n+1} \subset \mathbb{R}^{n+1}$, which contains the hypersurface Γ of equation (9.3). We divide conveniently the hypersurface Γ, observing that the values at the knots represent initial conditions for the system of differential equation (9.2).

If $b \equiv 0$, then the system (9.2) is simpler and reads

$$\frac{dx_1}{a_1(x_1, \ldots, x_n, u_0)} = \cdots = \frac{dx_n}{a_n(x_1, \ldots, x_n, u_0)}, \quad (9.7)$$

where $u = u_0 = $ const is a first integral of the system.

There are two possibilities to tackle a numerical solution. The first implies the use of explicit schemata, while the second implies the use of implicit schemata.

9.2.1 Numerical Integration by Means of Explicit Schemata

The first step, in this case, consists of discretization of the partial differential equation, that is, dividing the domain by means of a calculation net and by replacing the partial differential equation by a new and simpler equation. The simplest method is based on finite differences.

Let us deal with this method for a simple problem, that is, the partial differential equation of first order with two independent variables

$$a_1(x_1, x_2, u)\frac{\partial u}{\partial x_1} + a_2(x_1, x_2, u)\frac{\partial u}{\partial x_2} = b(x_1, x_2, u); \quad x_1 \in [0, l_1]; \quad x_2 \in [0, l_2]. \tag{9.8}$$

To solve equation (9.8), there are necessary initial conditions of the form

$$u(x_1, 0) = f(x_1). \tag{9.9}$$

Sometimes, limit conditions of the form

$$u(0, x_2) = g_0(x_2), \quad u(l_1, x_2) = g_1(x_2) \tag{9.10}$$

are put, where the functions f, g_0, and g_1 are known.

The numerical solution of equation (9.8) implies the division of the rectangular domain $[0, l_1] \times [0, l_2]$ by means of a net with equal steps on each axis, denoted by h and k for the variables x_1 and x_2, respectively (Fig. 9.1).

Using the expansion of the function $u(x_1, x_2)$ into a Taylor series around the point $A(x_1^i, x_2^j)$, we get

$$u(x_1^{i-1}, x_2^j) = u(x_1^i, x_2^j) - h\frac{\partial(x_1^i, x_2^j)}{\partial x_1} + \mathcal{O}(h^2), \tag{9.11}$$

$$u(x_1^i, x_2^{j+1}) = u(x_1^i, x_2^j) + k\frac{\partial(x_1^i, x_2^j)}{\partial x_2} + \mathcal{O}(k^2), \tag{9.12}$$

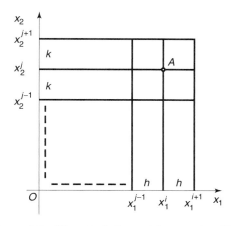

Figure 9.1   The calculation net for equation (9.8).

where $x_1^i = ih$, $i = \overline{0, I}$, $x_2^j = jk$, $j = \overline{0, J}$, $h = l_1/I$, $k = l_2/J$. It follows that

$$\frac{\partial u(x_1^i, x_2^j)}{\partial x_1} = \frac{u(x_1^i, x_2^j) - u(x_1^{i-1}, x_2^j)}{h} + \mathcal{O}(h), \tag{9.13}$$

$$\frac{\partial u(x_1^i, x_2^j)}{\partial x_2} = \frac{u(x_1^i, x_2^{j+1}) - u(x_1^i, x_2^j)}{k} + \mathcal{O}(k). \tag{9.14}$$

Neglecting $\mathcal{O}(h)$ and $\mathcal{O}(k)$, in equations (9.13) and (9.14), we obtain the equation with finite differences

$$a_1(x_1^i, x_2^j, u(x_1^i, x_2^j)) \frac{u(x_1^i, x_2^j) - u(x_1^{i-1}, x_2^j)}{h}$$
$$+ a_2(x_1^i, x_2^j, u(x_1^i, x_2^j)) \frac{u(x_1^i, x_2^{j+1}) - u(x_1^i, x_2^j)}{k} = b(x_1^i, x_2^j, u(x_1^i, x_2^j)). \tag{9.15}$$

Let us now consider the waves propagation equation

$$\frac{\partial u}{\partial t} + a\frac{\partial u}{\partial x} = 0, \quad x \in [0, 1], \quad t \in [0, T], \tag{9.16}$$

where a is a positive constant.

Applying the previous theory, we obtain the equation in finite differences

$$V(x^i, t^{j+1}) = V(x^i, t^j) + c[V(x^{i-1}, t^j) - V(x^i, t^j)], \quad i = \overline{1, I}, \quad j = \overline{1, J}, \tag{9.17}$$

where $V(x^i, t^j)$ means the approximate value of the function $u(x^i, t^j)$, $x^i = ih$, $t^j = jk$, $h = 1/I$, $k = T/J$.

Definition 9.4   The number c of relation (9.17), the expression of which is

$$c = \frac{ak}{h} \tag{9.18}$$

bears the name of Courant.[1]

Equation (9.16) is equivalent to the system

$$\frac{dt}{1} = \frac{dx}{a}, \tag{9.19}$$

which leads to the first integral

$$x - at = C_1, \tag{9.20}$$

where C_1 is a constant; hence, the exact solution of the problem is

$$u = \phi(x - at), \tag{9.21}$$

where ϕ is an arbitrary function.

---

[1]The number appears in Courant–Friedrichs–Lewy condition of convergence, called after Richard Courant (1888–1972), Kurt O Friedrichs (1901–1982) and Hans Lewy (1904–1988) who published it in 1928.

If $c = 1$, then the schema is

$$V(x^i, t^{j+1}) = V(x^{i-1}, t^j). \tag{9.22}$$

Definition 9.5 We say that a method with finite differences is convergent if the solution obtained by means of the equation with differences converges to the exact solution, when the norm of the net tends to zero.

Observation 9.1

(i) No schema is unconditionally stable or unstable.

(ii) The schema given in the previous example is stable for $0 < c \leq 1$.

(iii) A better approximation of the derivative $\partial u(x^i, t^j)/\partial x$ by using central differences

$$\frac{\partial u(x^i, t^j)}{\partial x} = \frac{u(x^{i+1}, t^j) - u(x^{i-1}, t^j)}{2h} + \mathcal{O}(h^2) \tag{9.23}$$

leads to an unstable schema for any Courant number c.

An often used explicit schema is the Lax–Wendroff[2] schema for which, in the case of the previous example, the equation with differences reads

$$V(x^i, t^{j+1}) = (1 - c^2)V(x^i, t^j) - \frac{c}{2}(1 - c)V(x^{i+1}, t^j) + \frac{c}{2}(1 + c)V(x^{i-1}, t^j), \tag{9.24}$$

its order of accuracy being $\mathcal{O}(h^2)$. Let us note that for $c = 1$ the Lax–Wendroff schema leads to the exact solution $V(x^i, t^{j+1}) = V(x^{i-1}, t^j)$.

9.2.2 Numerical Integration by Means of Implicit Schemata

The implicit schemata avoid the disadvantage of the conditional convergence that appears in case of the explicit schemata.

In case of implicit schemata, the space derivative is approximated by using the approximate values $V(x^i, t^{j+1})$ and not the $V(x^i, t^j)$ ones. Thus, we may write

$$\frac{\partial u(x^i, t^{j+1})}{\partial x} = \frac{u(x^{i+1}, t^{j+1}) - u(x^i, t^{j+1})}{h} + \mathcal{O}(h). \tag{9.25}$$

In our example, the equation with finite differences takes the form

$$V(x^i, t^{j+1}) = \frac{cV(x^{i+1}, t^{j+1}) + V(x^i, t^j)}{1 + c}, \quad i = 1, 2, \ldots, \tag{9.26}$$

which is unconditionally convergent.

Another schema often used in the case of the considered example is that of Wendroff, for which the equation with differences reads

$$V(x^i, t^{j+1}) = V(x^{i-1}, t^j) + \frac{1 - c}{1 + c}[V(x^i, t^j) - V(x^{i-1}, t^j)]. \tag{9.27}$$

[2]After Peter David Lax (1926–) and Burton Wendroff (1930–) who presented the method in 1960.

9.3   PARTIAL DIFFERENTIAL EQUATIONS OF SECOND ORDER

Let us consider the quasi-linear partial differential equation of second order

$$\sum_{i=1}^{n} a_i(x_1, \ldots, x_n, u) \frac{\partial^2 u}{\partial x_i^2} + \sum_{i=1}^{n} b_i(x_1, \ldots, x_n, u) \frac{\partial u}{\partial x_i} + c(x_1, \ldots, x_n, u) = 0, \tag{9.28}$$

written in a canonical form (it does not contain mixed partial derivatives).

Equation (9.28) is

- of elliptic type if all the coefficients $a_i(x_1, \ldots, x_n, u)$, $i = \overline{1, n}$, have the same sign;
- of parabolic type if there exists an index j, $1 \leq j \leq n$, so that $a_j(x_1, \ldots, x_n, u) = 0$, $a_i(x_1, \ldots, x_n, u) \neq 0$ for $i \neq j$, $1 \leq i \leq n$, and $b_j(x_1, \ldots, x_n, u) \neq 0$;
- of hyperbolic type if all the coefficients $a_i(x_1, \ldots, x_n, u)$ have the same sign, excepting one, which is of opposite sign.

Observation 9.2

(i) In case of an equation of elliptic type, an arbitrary point of the domain is influenced by all the points of any of its neighborhood. For the reason of reciprocal influence, a problem of elliptic type is numerically solved simultaneously for all the points of the domain. Moreover, the limit conditions are conditions of closed frontiers.

(ii) If the equation is of parabolic type, then we can numerically go on in the direction x_j for which $a_j(x_1, \ldots, x_n, u) = 0$. Equation (9.28) is now written in the form

$$b_j(x_1, \ldots, x_n, u) \frac{\partial u}{\partial x_j} = F\left(x_1, \ldots, x_n, u, \frac{\partial u}{\partial x_i}, \frac{\partial^2 u}{\partial x_i^2}\right), \quad i = \overline{1, n}, \quad i \neq j. \tag{9.29}$$

The problem is now solved only for the points situated on the hypersurfaces $x_j = $ const and not for all the points of the domain.

(iii) In the case of hyperbolic equations, there exist points, which do not influence each other. The numerical solution must take this fact into account. Moreover, there exist several distinct characteristic directions along which we may go on starting from a certain initial state. In the case of these equations, we may have not only initial conditions but boundary conditions too.

9.4   PARTIAL DIFFERENTIAL EQUATIONS OF SECOND ORDER OF ELLIPTIC TYPE

We consider Poisson's equation[3]

$$\nabla^2 u(x, y) = \frac{\partial^2 u}{\partial x^2}(x, y) + \frac{\partial^2 u}{\partial y^2}(x, y) = f(x, y), \tag{9.30}$$

where $(x, y) \in \mathcal{D}$, $\mathcal{D}$ rectangular domain,

$$\mathcal{D} = \{(x, y) | \quad a < x < b, \quad c < y < d\}, \tag{9.31}$$

[3]The equation was studied by Siméon Denis Poisson (1781–1840) in 1818.

with the boundary condition

$$u(x, y) = g(x, y), \quad (x, y) \in \partial D. \tag{9.32}$$

Observation 9.3 If $f(x, y)$ and $g(x, y)$ are continuous, then problem (9.30) with the boundary conditions (9.32) has a unique solution.

We divide the interval $[a, b]$ in n equal subintervals of length h and the interval $[c, d]$ in m equal subintervals of length k, so that

$$h = \frac{b - a}{n}, \quad k = \frac{d - c}{m}. \tag{9.33}$$

Thus, the rectangle D will be covered by a net grid with vertical and horizontal lines which pass through the points x_i, $i = \overline{0, n}$, and y_j, $j = \overline{0, m}$, where

$$x_i = a + ih, \quad i = \overline{0, n}, \tag{9.34}$$

$$y_i = c + jk, \quad j = \overline{0, m}. \tag{9.35}$$

Let a knot be $A_{ij}(x_i, y_j)$, $i = \overline{1, n - 1}$, $j = \overline{1, m - 1}$, from the inside of the net. We may expand the function $u(x, y)$ into a Taylor series in the x-variable, around x_i, obtaining

$$\frac{\partial^2 u}{\partial x^2}(x_i, y_j) = \frac{u(x_{i+1}, y_j) - 2u(x_i, y_j) + u(x_{i-1}, y_j)}{h^2} - \frac{h^2}{12}\frac{\partial^4 u}{\partial x^4}(\xi_i, y_j), \tag{9.36}$$

where ξ_i is an intermediary value between x_{i-1} and x_{i+1}. Analogically, expanding the function $u(x, y)$ into a Taylor series in the y-variable, around y_j, it follows that

$$\frac{\partial^2 u}{\partial y^2}(x_i, y_j) = \frac{u(x_i, y_{j+1}) - 2u(x_i, y_j) + u(x_i, y_{j-1})}{h^2} - \frac{k^2}{12}\frac{\partial^4 u}{\partial y^4}(x_i, \eta_j), \tag{9.37}$$

with η_j, in this case being an intermediary point between y_{j-1} and y_j.

By means of formulae (9.36) and (9.37), problems (9.30) and (9.32) become

$$\frac{u(x_{i+1}, y_j) - 2u(x_i, y_j) + u(x_{i-1}, y_j)}{h^2} + \frac{u(x_i, y_{j+1}) - 2u(x_i, y_j) + u(x_i, y_{j-1})}{k^2}$$

$$= f(x_i, y_j) + \frac{h^4}{12}\frac{\partial^4 u}{\partial x^4}(x_i, y_j) + \frac{k^4}{12}\frac{\partial^4 u}{\partial y^4}(x_i, y_j), \quad i = \overline{1, n - 1}, \quad j = \overline{1, m - 1}, \tag{9.38}$$

$$u(x_0, y_j) = g(x_0, y_j), \quad j = \overline{0, m}, \tag{9.39}$$

$$u(x_n, y_j) = g(x_n, y_j), \quad j = \overline{0, m}, \tag{9.40}$$

$$u(x_i, y_0) = g(x_i, y_0), \quad i = \overline{1, n - 1}, \tag{9.41}$$

$$u(x_i, y_m) = g(x_i, y_m), \quad i = \overline{1, n - 1}. \tag{9.42}$$

Observation 9.4 The local truncation error is of order $\mathcal{O}(h^2 + k^2)$.

We use the notation

$$w_{ij} = u(x_i, y_j), \quad i = \overline{0, n}, \quad j = \overline{0, m}; \tag{9.43}$$

and take into account that h and k are sufficiently small to rewrite formulae (9.38)–(9.42) in the form

$$2\left[\left(\frac{h}{k}\right)^2 + 1\right]w_{ij} - (w_{i+1,j} + w_{i-1,j}) - \left(\frac{h}{k}\right)^2(w_{i,j+1} + w_{i,j-1}) = -h^2 f(x_i, y_j), \qquad (9.44)$$

$$w_{0,j} = g(x_0, y_j), \quad j = \overline{0, m}, \qquad (9.45)$$

$$w_{n,j} = g(x_n, y_j), \quad j = \overline{0, m}, \qquad (9.46)$$

$$w_{i,0} = g(x_i, y_0), \quad i = \overline{1, n-1}, \qquad (9.47)$$

$$w_{i,m} = g(x_i, y_m), \quad i = \overline{1, n-1}. \qquad (9.48)$$

Equation (9.44), equation (9.45), equation (9.46), equation (9.47)and equation (9.48) lead to a system of $(n-1)(m-1)$ linear equations with $(n-1)(m-1)$ unknowns, that is, $w_{i,j} = u(x_i, y_j)$, $i = \overline{1, n-1}$, $j = \overline{1, m-1}$.

Numbering the knots of the net again, so that

$$A_{i,j} = A_l, \qquad (9.49)$$

where

$$l = i + (m-1-j)(n-1), \quad i = \overline{1, n-1}, \quad j = \overline{1, m-1} \qquad (9.50)$$

and noting

$$w_{i,j} = w_l, \qquad (9.51)$$

we may write the system of $(n-1)(m-1)$ equations with $(n-1)(m-1)$ unknowns in a matrix form.

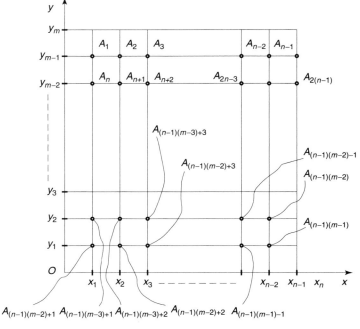

Figure 9.2 The numbering of the internal knots of the net.

Observation 9.5 The renumbering creates a succession of the internal knots of the net, starting from left up to right lateral as shown in Figure 9.2.

The algorithm of the finite differences for problems (9.30) and (9.32) reads

- given m, n, a, b, c, d, ε, $g(x, y)$, $f(x, y)$;
- calculate $h = (b - a)/n$, $k = (d - c)/m$;
- for i from 0 to n calculate $x_i = a + ih$;
- for j from 0 to m calculate $y_j = c + jk$;
- for i from 1 to $n - 1$ do
    - for j from 1 to $m - 1$ do
        - calculate $w_{i,j}^{(0)} = 0$;
- calculate $\lambda = (h^2/k^2)$;
- set $l = 1$;
- repeat
    - calculate
    $$w_{1,m-1}^{(l)} = [1/2(\lambda + 1)]\left[-h^2 f\left(x_1, y_{m-1}\right) + g(x_0, y_{m-1}) + \lambda g(x_1, y_m)\right.$$
    $$\left. + \lambda w_{1,m-2}^{(l-1)} + w_{2,m-1}^{(l-1)}\right];$$
    - for i from 2 to $n - 2$ calculate
    $$w_{i,m-1}^{(l)} = [1/2(\lambda + 1)]\left[-h^2 f\left(x_i, y_{m-1}\right) + \lambda g(x_i, y_m) + w_{i-1,m-1}^{(l)}\right.$$
    $$\left. + w_{i+1,m-1}^{(l-1)} + \lambda w_{i,m-2}^{(l-1)}\right];$$
    - calculate
    $$w_{n-1,m-1}^{(l)} = [1/2(\lambda + 1)]\left[-h^2 f\left(x_{n-1}, y_{m-1}\right) + g(x_n, y_{m-1}) + \lambda g(x_{n-1}, y_m)\right.$$
    $$\left. + w_{n-2,m-1}^{(l)} + \lambda w_{n-1,m-2}^{(l-1)}\right];$$
    - for j from $m - 2$ to 2 do
        - calculate
        $$w_{1,j}^{(l)} = [1/2(\lambda + 1)]\left[-h^2 f\left(x_1, y_j\right) + g(x_0, y_j) + \lambda w_{1,j+1}^{(l)} + \lambda w_{1,j-1}^{(l-1)} + w_{2,j}^{(l-1)}\right];$$
    - for i from 2 to $n - 2$ do
        - calculate
        $$w_{i,j}^{(l)} = [1/2(\lambda + 1)]\left[-h^2 f\left(x_i, y_j\right) + w_{i-1,j}^{(l)} + \lambda w_{i,j+1}^{(l)} + w_{i+1,j}^{(l-1)} + \lambda w_{i,j-1}^{(l-1)}\right];$$
    - calculate
    $$w_{n-1,j}^{(l)} = [1/2(\lambda + 1)]\left[-h^2 f\left(x_{n-1}, y_j\right) + g(x_n, y_j) + w_{n-2,j}^{(l)} + \lambda w_{n-1,j}^{(l)} + \lambda w_{n-1,j-1}^{(l-1)}\right];$$
    - calculate
    $$w_{1,1}^{(l)} = [1/2(\lambda + 1)]\left[-h^2 f\left(x_1, y_1\right) + g(x_0, y_1) + \lambda g(x_1, y_0) + \lambda w_{1,2}^{(l)} + w_{2,1}^{(l-1)}\right];$$
    - for i from 2 to $n - 2$ do
        - calculate
        $$w_{i,1}^{(l)} = [1/2(\lambda + 1)]\left[-h^2 f\left(x_1, y_1\right) + g(x_i, y_0) + w_{i-1,1}^{(l)} + \lambda w_{i,2}^{(l)} + w_{i+1,1}^{(l-1)}\right];$$
    - calculate
    $$w_{n-1,1}^{(l)} = [1/2(\lambda + 1)][-h^2 f(x_{n-1}, y_1) + g(x_n, y_1) + \lambda g(x_{n-1}, y_0)$$
    $$+ w_{n-2,1}^{(l)} + \lambda w_{n-1,2}^{(l)}]$$
    - set $b = $ true;
    - for i from 1 to $n - 1$ do
        - for j from 1 to $m - 1$ do
            - if $|w_{i,j}^{(l)} - w_{i,j}^{(l-1)}| \geq \varepsilon$
                then $b = $ false;
    - if $b = $ false

then $l = l + 1$;
  – until $b =$ true.

At the end, $w_{i,j}$ approximates $u(x_i, y_j)$ for $i = \overline{1, n-1}$, $j = \overline{1, m-1}$.

Observation 9.6 The solving of the linear system has been previously made by the Gauss–Seidel method.

9.5 PARTIAL DIFFERENTIAL EQUATIONS OF SECOND ORDER OF PARABOLIC TYPE

We consider the partial differential equation of second order of parabolic type of the form

$$\frac{\partial u}{\partial t}(x, t) - \alpha^2 \frac{\partial^2 u}{\partial x^2}(x, t) = 0, \quad 0 \le x \le l, \quad t > 0, \tag{9.52}$$

with the initial and on the frontier conditions

$$u(x, 0) = f(x), \quad 0 \le x \le l, \tag{9.53}$$

$$u(0, t) = u(l, t) = 0, \quad t > 0. \tag{9.54}$$

We begin by choosing two net constants h and k, where

$$h = \frac{l}{m}, \quad m \in \mathbb{N}. \tag{9.55}$$

Thus, the knots of the net are (x_i, t_j), where

$$x_i = ih, \quad i = \overline{0, m}, \tag{9.56}$$

$$t_j = jk, \quad j = 0, 1, \dots \tag{9.57}$$

Expanding into a Taylor series, we obtain the formulae with differences

$$\frac{\partial u}{\partial t}(x_i, t_j) = \frac{u(x_i, t_j + k) - u(x_i, t_j)}{k} - \frac{k}{2} \frac{\partial^2 u}{\partial x^2}(x_i, \tau_j), \tag{9.58}$$

where $\tau_j \in (t_j, t_{j+1})$ and

$$\frac{\partial^2 u}{\partial x^2}(x_i, t_j) = \frac{u(x_i + h, t_j) - 2u(x_i, t_j) + u(x_i - h, t_j)}{h^2} - \frac{h^2}{2} \frac{\partial^4 u}{\partial x^4}(\xi_i, t_j), \tag{9.59}$$

where ξ_i is a point between x_{i-1} and x_{i+1}. Replacing expressions (9.58) and (9.59) in equation (9.52), we obtain the linear system

$$\frac{w_{i,j+1} - w_{i,j}}{k} - \alpha^2 \frac{w_{i+1,j} - 2w_{i,j} + w_{i-1,j}}{h^2} = 0, \quad i = \overline{1, m-1}, \quad j = 1, 2, \dots, \tag{9.60}$$

where w_{ij} is the approximate of $u(x_i, t_j)$.

Observation 9.7 The truncation error is of the order $\mathcal{O}(h + k^2)$.

From equation (9.60) we get

$$w_{i,j+1} = \left(1 - \frac{2\alpha^2 k}{h^2}\right) w_{i,j} + \alpha^2 \frac{k}{h^2}(w_{i+1,j} + w_{i-1,j}), \quad i = \overline{1, m-1}, \quad j = 1, 2, \ldots \quad (9.61)$$

Condition (9.53) leads to

$$w_{i,0} = f(x_i), \quad i = \overline{0, m}. \tag{9.62}$$

With these values, we can determine $w_{i,1}$, $i = \overline{1, m-1}$. From the frontier condition (9.54) we obtain

$$w_{0,1} = w_{m,1} = 0. \tag{9.63}$$

Applying now the above described procedure with the known values $w_{i,1}$, it follows that we can determine the other values $w_{i,2}$, $w_{i,3}$, $\ldots$, $w_{i,m-1}$. We obtain a tridiagonal quadratic matrix of order $m - 1$ associated to the linear system, the form of which is

$$\mathbf{A} = \begin{bmatrix} 1 - 2\lambda & \lambda & 0 & 0 & \cdots & 0 & 0 & 0 \\ \lambda & 1 - 2\lambda & \lambda & 0 & \cdots & 0 & 0 & 0 \\ 0 & \lambda & 1 - 2\lambda & \lambda & \cdots & 0 & 0 & 0 \\ \cdots & \cdots & \cdots & \cdots & \cdots & \cdots & & \cdots \\ 0 & 0 & 0 & 0 & \cdots & 0 & 1 - 2\lambda & \lambda \\ 0 & 0 & 0 & 0 & \cdots & 0 & \lambda & 1 - 2\lambda \end{bmatrix}, \tag{9.64}$$

where

$$\lambda = \alpha^2 \frac{k}{h^2}. \tag{9.65}$$

If we now denote

$$\mathbf{w}^{(j)} = \begin{bmatrix} w_{1,j} \\ w_{2,j} \\ \vdots \\ w_{m-1,j} \end{bmatrix}, \quad j = 1, 2, \ldots, \tag{9.66}$$

$$\mathbf{w}^{(0)} = \begin{bmatrix} f(x_1) \\ f(x_2) \\ \vdots \\ f(x_{m-1}) \end{bmatrix}, \tag{9.67}$$

then the approximate solution of problems (9.52)–(9.54) is given by the matrix equation

$$\mathbf{w}^{(0)} = \mathbf{A}\mathbf{w}^{(j-1)}, \quad j = 1, 2, \ldots \tag{9.68}$$

Definition 9.6 The technique that has been presented is called *the method with differences forward*.

If we denote the error in the representation of the initial data $\mathbf{w}^{(0)}$ by $\boldsymbol{\varepsilon}^{(0)}$, then $\mathbf{w}^{(1)}$ reads

$$\mathbf{w}^{(1)} = \mathbf{A}(\mathbf{w}^{(0)} + \boldsymbol{\varepsilon}^{(0)}) = \mathbf{A}\mathbf{w}^{(0)} + \mathbf{A}\boldsymbol{\varepsilon}^{(0)}, \tag{9.69}$$

so that the representation error of $\mathbf{w}^{(1)}$ is given by $\mathbf{A}\boldsymbol{\varepsilon}^{(0)}$. Step by step we obtain the representation error $\mathbf{A}^n\boldsymbol{\varepsilon}^{(0)}$ of $\mathbf{w}^{(n)}$. Hence, the method is stable if and only if

$$\|\mathbf{A}^n\boldsymbol{\varepsilon}^{(0)}\| \leq \|\boldsymbol{\varepsilon}^{(0)}\|, \quad n = 1, 2, \ldots \tag{9.70}$$

This implies $\|\mathbf{A}^n\| \leq 1$, where $\|\|$ denotes any of the canonical norms; it follows that the spectral radius of the matrix $\mathbf{A}^n$ must be at most equal to unity

$$\rho(\mathbf{A}^n) = [\rho(\mathbf{A})]^n \leq 1. \tag{9.71}$$

This happens if all the eigenvalues of the matrix $\mathbf{A}$ are at most equal to unity.

On the other hand, the eigenvalues of the matrix $\mathbf{A}$ are given by

$$\mu_i = 1 - 4\lambda\sin^2\left(\frac{\pi i}{2m}\right), \quad i = \overline{1, m-1}, \tag{9.72}$$

while the stability condition

$$\left|1 - 4\lambda\sin^2\left(\frac{\pi i}{2m}\right)\right| \leq 1, \quad i = \overline{1, m-1}, \tag{9.73}$$

leads to

$$0 \leq 1 - 4\lambda\sin^2\left(\frac{\pi i}{2m}\right) \leq \frac{1}{2}, \quad i = \overline{1, m-1}. \tag{9.74}$$

Making now $m \to \infty$ (or its equivalent, $h \to 0$), we get

$$\lim_{m \to \infty} \sin^2\left[\frac{(m-1)\pi}{2m}\right] = 1, \tag{9.75}$$

hence the searched condition is

$$0 \leq \lambda = \alpha^2 \frac{k}{h^2} \leq \frac{1}{2}. \tag{9.76}$$

The previous presented schema is thus conditioned stable.

A nonconditioned stable schema starts from the relation

$$\frac{\partial u}{\partial t}(x_i, t_j) = \frac{u(x_i, t_j) - u(x_i, t_{j-1})}{k} + \frac{k}{2}\frac{\partial^2 u}{\partial t^2}(x_i, \tau_j), \tag{9.77}$$

where τ_j is a point between t_{j-1} and t_j, as well as from formula (9.59). We obtain

$$\frac{w_{i,j} - w_{i,j-1}}{k} - \alpha^2 \frac{w_{i+1,j} - 2w_{i,j} + w_{i-1,j}}{h^2} = 0, \quad w_{ij} \approx u(x_i, t_j). \tag{9.78}$$

Definition 9.7   The above presented method is called *the method with differences backward.*

Equation (9.78) is written in the form

$$(1 + 2\lambda)w_{i,j} - \lambda w_{i+1,j} - \lambda w_{i-1,j} = w_{i,j-1}, \quad i = \overline{1, m-1}, \quad j = 1, 2, \ldots \tag{9.79}$$

Because $w_{i,0} = f(x_i)$, $i = \overline{1, m-1}$, and $w_{m,0} = w_{0,j} = 0$, $j = 1, 2, \ldots$, the linear system takes the matrix form

$$\mathbf{A}\mathbf{w}^{(j)} = \mathbf{w}^{(j-1)}, \tag{9.80}$$

where the matrix $\mathbf{A}$ is

$$
\mathbf{A} = \begin{bmatrix}
1+2\lambda & -\lambda & 0 & 0 & \cdots & 0 & 0 & 0 \\
-\lambda & 1+2\lambda & -\lambda & 0 & \cdots & 0 & 0 & 0 \\
0 & -\lambda & 1+2\lambda & -\lambda & \cdots & 0 & 0 & 0 \\
\cdots & \cdots & \cdots & \cdots & \cdots & \cdots & \cdots & \cdots \\
0 & 0 & 0 & 0 & \cdots & 0 & 1+2\lambda & -\lambda \\
0 & 0 & 0 & 0 & \cdots & 0 & -\lambda & 1+2\lambda
\end{bmatrix}. \tag{9.81}
$$

The solving algorithm of problems (9.52)–(9.54) is as follows:

- given $m > 0$, k, $N > 0$, $T = kN$, l;
- calculate $h = (l/m)$;
- for i from 0 to m do
    - calculate $x_i = ih$;
- calculate $\lambda = \alpha^2(k/h^2)$;
- for i from 1 to $m-1$ do
    - calculate $w_{i,0} = f(x_i)$;
- for j from 1 to N do
    - calculate $w_{0,j} = w_{m,j} = 0$;
- calculate $l_1 = 1 + 2\lambda$, $u_1 = -(\lambda/l_1)$;
- for n from 2 to $m-2$ do
    - calculate $l_n = 1 + 2\lambda + \lambda u_{n-1}$, $u_n = -(\lambda/l_n)$;
- calculate $l_{m-1} = 1 + 2\lambda + \lambda u_{n-2}$;
- for j from 0 to N do
    - calculate $z_1 = w_{1,j}/l_1$;
- for n from 2 to $m-1$ do
    - calculate $z_n = [(w_{n,j} + \lambda z_{n-1})/l_n]$;
- calculate $w_{m-1,j+1} = z_{m-1}$;
- for n from $m-2$ to 1 do
    - calculate $w_{n,j+1} = z_n w_{n+1,j+1}$.

The values $w_{i,j}$ approximate $u(x_i, t_j)$, $i = \overline{0, m}$, $j = \overline{0, N}$.

In the case of the above described algorithm, the matrix $\mathbf{A}$ has the eigenvalues

$$
\mu_i = 1 + 4\lambda \sin^2\left(\frac{i\pi}{2m}\right), \quad i = \overline{1, m-1}, \tag{9.82}
$$

all of them being positive and superunitary. Thus, it follows that the eigenvalues of the matrix $\mathbf{A}^{-1}$ are positive and subunitary, and hence the method with differences backward is unconditioned stable.

Using for $\partial u(x_i, t_j)/\partial t$, the formula with central differences

$$
\frac{\partial u}{\partial t}(x_i, t_j) = \frac{u(x_i, t_{j+1}) - u(x_i, t_{j-1})}{2k} - \frac{k^2}{6}\frac{\partial^3 u}{\partial t^3}(x_i, \tau_j), \tag{9.83}
$$

where τ_j is between t_{j-1} and t_{j+1}, and for $\partial^2 u(x_i, t_j)/\partial x^2$, formula (9.59), we obtain the approximating system

$$
\frac{w_{i,j+1} - w_{i,j-1}}{2k} - \alpha^2 \frac{w_{i+1,j} - 2w_{i,j} + w_{i-1,j}}{h^2} = 0, \quad w_{ij} \approx u(x_i, t_j). \tag{9.84}
$$

Definition 9.8   The method put in evidence by relation (9.84) bears the name of Richardson.[4]

Observation 9.8
    (i) The error of Richardson's method is of order $\mathcal{O}(h^2 + k^2)$.
    (ii) The Richardson method is conditioned stable.

An unconditioned stable method leads to the equation with finite differences

$$\frac{w_{i,j+1} - w_{i,j}}{k} - \frac{\alpha^2}{2}\left[\frac{w_{i+1,j} - 2w_{i,j} + w_{i-1,j}}{h^2} + \frac{w_{i+1,j+1} - 2w_{i,j+1} + w_{i-1,j+1}}{h^2}\right] = 0. \quad (9.85)$$

Definition 9.9   The method given by formula (9.85) is called *the Crank–Nicolson method*.

Observation 9.9   The truncation error in the Crank–Nicolson method is of order $\mathcal{O}(h^2 + k^2)$.
The Crank–Nicolson system may be written in a matrix form

$$\mathbf{A}\mathbf{w}^{(j+1)} = \mathbf{B}\mathbf{w}^{(j)}, \quad j = 0, 1, 2, \ldots, \quad (9.86)$$

the matrices **A** and **B** being given by

$$\mathbf{A} = \begin{bmatrix} 1+\lambda & -\frac{\lambda}{2} & 0 & 0 & \cdots & 0 & 0 & 0 \\ -\frac{\lambda}{2} & 1+\lambda & -\frac{\lambda}{2} & 0 & \cdots & 0 & 0 & 0 \\ 0 & -\frac{\lambda}{2} & 1+\lambda & -\frac{\lambda}{2} & \cdots & 0 & 0 & 0 \\ \cdots & \cdots & \cdots & \cdots & \cdots & \cdots & & \cdots \\ 0 & 0 & 0 & 0 & \cdots & 0 & 1+\lambda & -\frac{\lambda}{2} \\ 0 & 0 & 0 & 0 & \cdots & 0 & -\frac{\lambda}{2} & 1+\lambda \end{bmatrix}, \quad (9.87)$$

$$\mathbf{B} = \begin{bmatrix} 1-\lambda & \frac{\lambda}{2} & 0 & 0 & \cdots & 0 & 0 & 0 \\ \frac{\lambda}{2} & 1-\lambda & \frac{\lambda}{2} & 0 & \cdots & 0 & 0 & 0 \\ 0 & \frac{\lambda}{2} & 1-\lambda & \frac{\lambda}{2} & \cdots & 0 & 0 & 0 \\ \cdots & \cdots & \cdots & \cdots & \cdots & \cdots & & \cdots \\ 0 & 0 & 0 & 0 & \cdots & 0 & 1-\lambda & \frac{\lambda}{2} \\ 0 & 0 & 0 & 0 & \cdots & 0 & \frac{\lambda}{2} & 1-\lambda \end{bmatrix}. \quad (9.88)$$

The solving Crank–Nicolson algorithm[5] of solving problems (9.52)–(9.54) is as follows:

  – given: $m > 0$, $k > 0$, $N > 0$, $T = kN$, l;
  – calculate $h = (l/m)$;
  – for i from 0 to m do
      – calculate $x_i = ih$;
  – for j from 0 to N do
      – calculate $t_j = jk$;

---

[4]After Lewis Fry Richardson (1881–1953) who presented it in 1922.
[5]John Crank (1916–2006) and Phyllis Nicolson (1917–1968) published this algorithm in *A Practical Method for Numerical Evaluation of Solutions of Partial Differential Equations of the Heat Conduction Type* in 1947.

- calculate $\lambda = \alpha^2(k/h^2)$;
- for i from 1 to $m - 1$ do
  - calculate $w_{i,0} = f(x_i)$;
- for j from 1 to N do
  $$w_{0,j} = w_{m,j} = 0;$$
  - calculate $l_1 = 1 + \lambda$, $u_1 = -(\lambda/2l_1)$;
- for n from 2 to $m - 2$ do
  - calculate $l_n = 1 + \lambda + \lambda(u_n - 1/2)$, $u_n = -(\lambda/2l_n)$;
- calculate $l_{m-1} = 1 + \lambda + \lambda(u_{m-2}/2)$;
- for j from 0 to $N - 1$ do
  - calculate $z_1 = [(1 - \lambda)w_{1,j} + (\lambda/2)w_{2,j}]/l_1$;
- for n from 2 to $m - 1$ do
  - calculate $z_n = [(1 - \lambda)w_{n,j} + (\lambda/2)w_{n+1,j} + (\lambda/2)w_{n-1,j} + (\lambda/2)z_{n-1}]/l_n$;
- calculate $w_{m-1,j+1} = z_{m-1}$;
- for n from $m - 2$ to 1 do
  - calculate $w_{n,j+1} = z_n - u_n w_{n+1,j+1}$.

Finally, $w_{i,j}$ approximate $u(x_i, t_j)$, $i = \overline{0, m}$, $j = \overline{0, N}$.

9.6 PARTIAL DIFFERENTIAL EQUATIONS OF SECOND ORDER OF HYPERBOLIC TYPE

We start from the equation

$$\frac{\partial^2 u}{\partial t^2}(x, t) - \alpha^2 \frac{\partial^2 u}{\partial x^2}(x, t) = 0, \quad 0 < x < l, \quad t > 0, \tag{9.89}$$

to which the conditions

$$u(0, t) = u(l, t) = 0, \quad t > 0, \tag{9.90}$$

$$u(x, 0) = f(x), \quad 0 \le x \le l, \tag{9.91}$$

$$\frac{\partial u}{\partial t}(x, 0) = g(x), \quad 0 \le x \le l. \tag{9.92}$$

are added; α is a real constant in equation (9.89).

Let us choose a nonzero natural number m and a time step $k > 0$ and denote

$$h = \frac{l}{m}. \tag{9.93}$$

Thus, the knots (x_i, t_j) of the net are given by

$$x_i = ih, \quad i = \overline{0, m}, \tag{9.94}$$

$$t_j = jk, \quad j = 0, 1, \quad \ldots \tag{9.95}$$

Let $A_{i,j}(x_i, t_j)$ be an interior point of the net. We can write the relation

$$\frac{\partial^2 u}{\partial t^2}(x_i, t_j) - \alpha^2 \frac{\partial^2 u}{\partial x^2}(x_i, t_j) = 0 \tag{9.96}$$

at this point. Using the central differences of second order, we can write

$$\frac{\partial^2 u}{\partial t^2}(x_i, t_j) = \frac{u(x_i, t_{j+1}) - 2u(x_i, t_j) + u(x_i, t_{j-1})}{k^2} - \frac{k^2}{12} \frac{\partial^4 u}{\partial t^4}(x_i, \tau_j), \tag{9.97}$$

where τ_j is an intermediary value between t_{j-1} and t_{j+1}, and

$$\frac{\partial^2 u}{\partial t^2}(x_i, t_j) = \frac{u(x_{i+1}, t_j) - 2u(x_i, t_j) + u(x_{i-1}, t_j)}{k^2} - \frac{h^2}{12}\frac{\partial^4 u}{\partial x^4}(\xi_i, t_j), \tag{9.98}$$

where $\xi_i \in (x_{i-1}, x_{i+1})$. It follows that

$$\frac{u(x_i, t_{j+1}) - 2u(x_i, t_j) + u(x_i, t_{j-1})}{k^2} - \alpha^2 \frac{u(x_{i+1}, t_j) - 2u(x_i, t_j) + u(x_{i-1}, t_j)}{k^2}$$

$$= \frac{1}{12}\left[k^2 \frac{\partial^4 u}{\partial t^4}(x_i, \tau_j) - \alpha^2 h^2 \frac{\partial^4 u}{\partial x^4}(\xi_i, t_j) \right], \tag{9.99}$$

which will be approximated by

$$\frac{w_{i,j+1} - 2w_{i,j} + w_{i,j-1}}{k^2} - \alpha^2 \frac{w_{i+1,j} - 2w_{i,j} + w_{i-1,j}}{h^2} = 0. \tag{9.100}$$

Denoting

$$\lambda = \frac{\alpha k}{h}, \tag{9.101}$$

we obtain

$$w_{i,j+1} - 2w_{i,j} + w_{i,j-1} - \lambda^2 w_{i+1,j} + 2\lambda^2 w_{i,j} - \lambda^2 w_{i-1,j} = 0 \tag{9.102}$$

from equation (9.100), or equivalently,

$$w_{i,j+1} = 2(1 - \lambda^2)w_{i,j} + \lambda^2(w_{i+1,j} + w_{i-1,j}) - w_{i,j-1} = 0, \quad i = \overline{1, m-1}, \quad j = 1, 2, \dots \tag{9.103}$$

The frontier conditions (9.90) are

$$w_{0,j} = w_{m,j} = 0, \quad j = 1, 2, \dots, \tag{9.104}$$

while the initial conditions (9.91) lead to

$$w_{i,0} = f(x_i), \quad i = \overline{1, m-1}. \tag{9.105}$$

We obtain the matrix equation

$$\mathbf{w}^{(j+1)} = \mathbf{A}\mathbf{w}^{(j)} - \mathbf{w}^{(j-1)}, \tag{9.106}$$

where

$$\mathbf{w}^{(k)} = \begin{bmatrix} w_{1,k} \\ w_{2,k} \\ \vdots \\ w_{m-1,k} \end{bmatrix}, \tag{9.107}$$

$$\mathbf{A} = \begin{bmatrix} 2\left(1 - \lambda^2\right) & \lambda^2 & 0 & 0 & \cdots & 0 & 0 & 0 \\ \lambda^2 & 2(1 - \lambda^2) & \lambda^2 & 0 & \cdots & 0 & 0 & 0 \\ 0 & \lambda^2 & 2(1 - \lambda^2) & \lambda^2 & \cdots & 0 & 0 & 0 \\ \cdots & \cdots & \cdots & \cdots & \cdots & \cdots & \cdots & \cdots \\ 0 & 0 & 0 & 0 & \cdots & 0 & 2(1 - \lambda^2) & \lambda^2 \\ 0 & 0 & 0 & 0 & \cdots & 0 & \lambda^2 & 2(1 - \lambda^2) \end{bmatrix}. \tag{9.108}$$

Observation 9.10 We notice that to determine $\mathbf{w}^{(j+1)}$, the values $\mathbf{w}^{(j)}$ and $\mathbf{w}^{(j-1)}$ that create difficulties for $j = 0$ are necessary, because the values $w_{1,j}$, $j = 1, 2, \ldots$, must be determined by condition (9.92).

Usually, $\partial u / \partial t$ is replaced by the expression with differences backward

$$\frac{\partial u}{\partial t}(x_i, 0) = \frac{u(x_i, t_1) - u(x_i, t_0)}{k} - k^2 \frac{\partial^2 u}{\partial t^2}(x_i, \tau_i), \tag{9.109}$$

where $\tau_i \in (0, k)$. Thus, it follows that

$$w_{i,1} = w_{i,0} + kg(x_i), \quad i = \overline{1, m}, \tag{9.110}$$

which leads to the error $\mathcal{O}(k)$ in the initial data.

On the other hand, the local truncation error for equation (9.103) is of order $\mathcal{O}(h^2 + k^2)$; we wish to have an error of order $\mathcal{O}(k^2)$ for the initial data. We have

$$\frac{u(x_i, t_1) - u(x_i, t_0)}{k} = \frac{\partial u}{\partial t}(x_i, 0) + \frac{k}{2} \frac{\partial^2 u}{\partial t^2}(x_i, 0) + \frac{k^2}{6} \frac{\partial^3 u}{\partial t^3}(x_i, \tau_i), \tag{9.111}$$

where $\tau_i \in (0, k)$.

Supposing that equation (9.89) takes place on the initial interval too, that is, we may write

$$\frac{\partial^2 u}{\partial t^2}(x_i, 0) - \alpha^2 \frac{\partial^2 u}{\partial x^2}(x_i, 0) = 0, \quad i = \overline{0, m}, \tag{9.112}$$

and if there also exists $f''(x)$, then we may write

$$\frac{\partial^2 u}{\partial t^2}(x_i, 0) = \alpha^2 \frac{\partial^2 u}{\partial x^2}(x_i, 0) = \alpha^2 \frac{d^2 f(x_i)}{dx^2} = \alpha^2 f''(x_i). \tag{9.113}$$

But

$$f''(x_i) = \frac{f(x_{i+1}) - 2f(x_i) + f(x_{i-1})}{h^2} - \frac{h^2}{12} f^{(4)}(\xi_i), \tag{9.114}$$

where ξ_i is between x_{i-1} and x_{i+1}, while $f \in C^4$ ([0, l]), and we obtain

$$\frac{u(x_i, t_1) - u(x_i, 0)}{k} = g(x_i) + \frac{k\alpha^2}{2h^2}[f(x_{i+1}) - 2f(x_i) + f(x_{i-1})] + \mathcal{O}(h^2 + k^2). \tag{9.115}$$

We get successively

$$u(x_i, t_1) = u(x_i, 0) + kg(x_i) + \frac{\lambda^2}{2}[f(x_{i+1}) - 2f(x_i) + f(x_{i-1})] + O(k^3 + h^2 k^2)$$

$$= (1 - \lambda^2)f(x_i) + \frac{\lambda^2}{2} f(x_{i+1}) + \frac{\lambda^2}{2} f(x_{i-1}) + kg(x_i) + \mathcal{O}(k^3 + h^2 k^2). \tag{9.116}$$

It follows that the determination of the values $w_{i,1}$, $i = \overline{1, m-1}$, can be made by means of the relation

$$w_{i,1} = (1 - \lambda^2)f(x_i) + \frac{\lambda^2}{2} f(x_{i+1}) + \frac{\lambda^2}{2} f(x_{i-1}) + kg(x_i). \tag{9.117}$$

Thus, the algorithm with finite differences used to solve problems (9.89)–(9.92) is

- given: m, $N > 0$, $k > 0$, l, α, $f(x)$, $g(x)$;
- calculate $h = (l/m)$, $T = kN$, $\lambda = (\alpha k/h)$;
- for i from 0 to m do
  - calculate $x_i = ih$;
- for j from 0 to N do
  - calculate $t_j = j \times k$;
- for j from 1 to N do
  - calculate $w_{0,j} = w_{m,j} = 0$;
- for i from 0 to m do
  - calculate $w_{i,0} = f(x_i)$;
- for i from 1 to $m - 1$ do
  - calculate $w_{i,1} = (1 - \lambda^2)f(x_i) + (\lambda^2/2)(f(x_{i+1}) + f(x_{i-1})) + kg(x_i)$;
- for j from 1 to $N - 1$ do
  - for i from 1 to $m - 1$ do
    - calculate $w_{i,j-1} = 2(1 - \lambda^2)w_{i,j} - \lambda^2(w_{i+1,j} + w_{i-1,j}) - w_{i,j-1}$.

Thus, $w_{i,j}$ approximate $u(x_i, t_j)$, $i = \overline{0, m}$, $j = \overline{0, N}$.

9.7 POINT MATCHING METHOD

This method[6] has been developed at the middle of the twentieth century. We will present it in the two-dimensional case for partial differential equations of elliptic type, particularly for biharmonic equations (we may use it on the same way for polyharmonic equations too). The method fits well with the plane problem of the theory of elasticity, formulated for a plane domain D.

Some methods of calculation (e.g., the variational methods) allow to obtain, with an approximation as good as we wish, the searched function (solution of the partial differential equation) and its derivatives at any point of the domain D. Other methods (finite differences method, nets method, relaxation method, etc.) allow to obtain an appropriate value of the searched function at a finite number of points in the interior of the domain, satisfying the boundary conditions also at a finite number of points.

We can imagine a method of calculation that uses ideas from both types of methods. The method consists in searching an analytic function of a form as simple as possible, which does verify the partial differential equation at any point of D, excepting the boundary, where this does occur at a finite number of points.

We will thus search a biharmonic function

$$F(x, y) = \sum_{i=2}^{n} P_i(x, y), \tag{9.118}$$

where $P_i(x, y)$ are biharmonic polynomials ($\Delta\Delta P_i = 0$) of ith degree, $i = 2, 3, \ldots$ We notice that such a polynomial implies four arbitrary constants, except $P_2(x, y)$, which contain only three such constants. Thus, $F(x, y)$ contains $4n - 5$ arbitrary constants.

At a point of the boundary, we may put two conditions, that is, for the function F (or for its tangential derivative $\partial F/\partial s$) and for the normal derivative $\partial F/\partial n$. Hence, for a point of the contour we get two conditions for the constants to determine. If we put boundary conditions at $2n - 3$ points of the contour, we find a system of $4n - 6$ equations, with $4n - 5$ unknowns, which will determine the coefficients of the biharmonic polynomial. One of these constants must be taken arbitrary.

---

[6]Also known as collocation method. It was introduced by Leonid Vitaliyevich Kantorovich (1912–1986) in 1934.

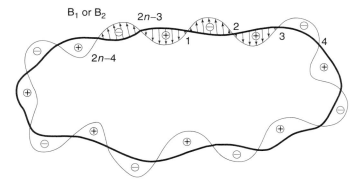

Figure 9.3   Point matching method.

Let $\mathcal{B}'_1$ and $\mathcal{B}'_2$ be the distribution of the real boundary conditions and $\mathcal{B}''_1$ and $\mathcal{B}''_2$ the boundary conditions obtained after calculation (Fig. 9.3). The differences $\mathcal{B}_1 = \mathcal{B}'_1 - \mathcal{B}''_1$, $\mathcal{B}_2 = \mathcal{B}'_2 - \mathcal{B}''_2$ must be as small as possible, so that the error in the determination of the biharmonic function will also be as small as possible. The calculation of the error may be made from case to case from the physical point of view.

As an advantage, we mention that contour can be a complicated one and that one gets an analytical expansion for the solution.

Besides elementary representations (biharmonic polynomials), we may also use other functions, adequate for some particular problems.

We have to solve a system of linear algebraic equations, so that various methods of calculation can be used.

In fact, the method considered above is a collocation method.

9.8   VARIATIONAL METHODS

Let us consider the functional

$$I(y) = \int\limits_{x_0}^{x_1} f(x, y, y')\mathrm{d}x,$$ (9.119)

where f is a function continuous, together with its derivatives till the second order inclusive, in a domain of $\mathbb{R}^3$, $y = y(x)$ is continuous with continuous derivative $y' = \mathrm{d}y/\mathrm{d}x$ and $y(x_0) = y_0$, $y(x_1) = y_1$. It follows that the function f verifies Euler's equation

$$\frac{\partial f}{\partial y} - \frac{\mathrm{d}}{\mathrm{d}x}\frac{\partial f}{\partial y'} = 0.$$ (9.120)

If the functional is of the form

$$I(y) = \int \cdots \int f\left(x_1, x_2, \ldots, x_n, y, \frac{\partial f}{\partial x_1}, \frac{\partial f}{\partial x_2}, \ldots, \frac{\partial f}{\partial x_n}\right) \mathrm{d}x_1\mathrm{d}x_2 \cdots \mathrm{d}x_n,$$ (9.121)

then Euler's equation reads

$$\frac{\partial f}{\partial y} - \frac{\mathrm{d}}{\mathrm{d}x_1}\frac{\partial f}{\partial \dfrac{\partial y}{\partial x_1}} - \frac{\mathrm{d}}{\mathrm{d}x_2}\frac{\partial f}{\partial \dfrac{\partial y}{\partial x_2}} - \cdots - \frac{\mathrm{d}}{\mathrm{d}x_n}\frac{\partial f}{\partial \dfrac{\partial y}{\partial x_n}} = 0.$$ (9.122)

In the general case, we consider the equation

$$Lu = f, \tag{9.123}$$

where L is an autoadjoint positive linear operator, with the domain of definition $\mathcal{D}$ in the Hilbert space $\mathcal{H}$, the dot product $\langle , \rangle$ which has values (the operator) in $\mathcal{H}$, $u \in \mathcal{D}$, while $f \in \mathcal{H}$.

Proposition 9.1 If the solution of problem (9.123) exists, then this one assures the minimum of the functional

$$I(u) = \langle Lu, u \rangle - 2\langle u, f \rangle. \tag{9.124}$$

Demonstration. Let $\bar{u}$ be the solution of problem (9.123) and $v \in \mathcal{D}$ arbitrary and nonzero. If c is a real nonzero number, then we consider

$$v_c = \bar{u} + cv \tag{9.125}$$

and we may write

$$I(v_c) = \langle L(\bar{u} + cv), \bar{u} + cv \rangle - 2\langle \bar{u} + cv, f \rangle. \tag{9.126}$$

Because L is autoadjoint, we have

$$I(v_c) = I(\bar{u}) + 2c\langle L\bar{u} - f, v \rangle + c^2 \langle Lv, v \rangle, \tag{9.127}$$

obtaining thus

$$I(v_c) = I(\bar{u}) + c^2 \langle Lv, v \rangle; \tag{9.128}$$

because L is positive, it follows that

$$I(v_c) > I(\bar{u}) \tag{9.129}$$

for any $c \neq 0$. Hence $\bar{u}$ minimizes the functional $I(u)$.

Proposition 9.2 If $\bar{u} \in \mathcal{H}$ minimizes the functional $I(u)$ and $\bar{u} \in \mathcal{D}$, then $L\bar{u} = f$.

Demonstration. Let $v \in \mathcal{D}$ be arbitrary. Because $w = \alpha u + \beta v \in \mathcal{D}$, with α and β constant, taking into account that the functional $I(u)$ attains its minimum at $\bar{u}$, we get

$$I(\bar{u} + cv) \geq I(\bar{u}). \tag{9.130}$$

If L is symmetric, then from equation (9.130) we obtain

$$2c\langle L\bar{u} - f, v \rangle + c^2 \langle Lv, v \rangle \geq 0; \tag{9.131}$$

with necessity, and it follows that

$$\langle L\bar{u} - f, v \rangle = 0, \tag{9.132}$$

that is, $L\bar{u} - f$ is orthogonal on any element of $\mathcal{D}$, hence

$$L\bar{u} - f = 0. \tag{9.133}$$

9.8.1 Ritz's Method

In the frame of this method,[7] we consider the problem

$$Lu = f, \tag{9.134}$$

in Hilbert's space $\mathcal{H}$, with the scalar product$\langle , \rangle$; $\mathcal{D}$ is the domain of definition of L, considered dense in $\mathcal{H}$, while L is a positive definite autoadjoint operator.

The problem is equivalent to the finding of the element $\bar{u} \in \mathcal{D}$, which minimizes the functional

$$I(u) = \langle Lu, u \rangle - 2\langle f, u \rangle. \tag{9.135}$$

To ensure the existence of the solution, we consider a new scalar product in $\mathcal{H}$, defined by

$$\langle u, v \rangle_L = \langle Lu, v \rangle, \quad u, v \in \mathcal{D}, \tag{9.136}$$

the norm being given by

$$\|u\|_L = \sqrt{\langle u, u \rangle_L}. \tag{9.137}$$

Definition 9.10 We call energetic space defined by the operator L, the space obtained by the completing of $\mathcal{D}$ by the norm $\| \|_L$. We denote this space by $\mathcal{H}_L$.

We may write

$$I(u) = \langle u, u \rangle_L - 2\langle f, u \rangle, \quad u \in \mathcal{D}. \tag{9.138}$$

Because L is positive definite, that is,

$$\langle Lu, u \rangle = \langle u, u \rangle_L \geq c^2 \|u\|^2, \quad u \in \mathcal{D}, \tag{9.139}$$

with c constant, $c > 0$, the by completing $\mathcal{D}$ to $\mathcal{H}_L$, it follows that $\langle u, u \rangle_L \geq c^2 \|u\|$, for any $u \in \mathcal{H}_L$.

On the other hand,

$$|\langle u, f \rangle| \leq \|u\| \|f\| \leq \frac{1}{c} \|u\|_L \|f\| = B\|u\|_L, \tag{9.140}$$

so that $\langle u, f \rangle$ is bounded, and we may apply Ritz's theorem. It follows that there exists $u_0 \in \mathcal{H}_L$, so that for any $u \in \mathcal{H}_L$ we have

$$\langle u, f \rangle = \langle u, u_0 \rangle_L. \tag{9.141}$$

Thus, the functional reads

$$I(u) = \langle u, u \rangle_L - 2\langle f, u \rangle = \langle u, u \rangle_L - 2\langle u, u_0 \rangle_L = \|u - u_0\|_L^2 - \|u_0\|_L^2, \tag{9.142}$$

with $u \in \mathcal{H}_L$; hence it attains its minimum for $u = u_0$.

Definition 9.11 The element $u_0 \in \mathcal{H}_L$ bears the name of generalized solution of the equation $Lu = f$.

Observation 9.11 If $u_0 \in \mathcal{D}$, then u_0 is the classical solution of problem (9.134).

[7]After Walther Ritz (1878–1909) who published this method in 1909.

We will consider a sequence of finite dimensional subspaces $\mathcal{H}_k \subseteq \mathcal{H}_L$ given by the parameters $k_1, k_2, \ldots$, so that $k_i \to 0$, for $i \to \infty$.

Definition 9.12   We say that the sequence $\{\mathcal{H}_k\}$ is complete in $\mathcal{H}_L$ if for any $u \in \mathcal{H}_L$ and $\varepsilon > 0$ there exists $\overline{k} = \overline{k}(u, \varepsilon) > 0$, so that

$$\inf_{v \in \mathcal{H}_k} \|u - v\|_L < \varepsilon, \tag{9.143}$$

for any $k < \overline{k}$.

From the previous definition we deduce that if $\{\mathcal{H}_k\}$ is complete, then any element $u \in \mathcal{H}_L$ may be approximated with any precision that we may wish with elements of $\mathcal{H}_k$.

We will ask to determine the element $u^k \in \mathcal{H}_k$, which minimizes the functional $I(u)$ in $\mathcal{H}_k$.

Proposition 9.3   In the above conditions, the sequence $\{u^k\}$ of Ritz's approximations for the solution of the equation $Lu = f$ converges to the generalized solution of this problem.

Demonstration. For $v \in \mathcal{H}_k$ we have

$$\|u_0 - u^k\|_L^2 = I(u^k) - I(u_0) \le I(v) - I(u_0) = \|u_0 - v\|_L^2. \tag{9.144}$$

Because v is arbitrary, we may write

$$\|u_0 - u^k\|_L^2 \le \inf_{v \in \mathcal{H}_k} \|u_0 - v\|_L^2 \xrightarrow[k \to 0]{} 0. \tag{9.145}$$

If a basis of the space $\mathcal{H}_k$ formed by the functions $\phi_1^k, \phi_2^k, \ldots, \phi_{n_k}^k$ (n_k being the dimension of the space $\mathcal{H}_k$) is known, then the problem of the determination of $u^k \in \mathcal{H}_k$ is equivalent to the determination of the coefficients $c_1, c_2, \ldots, c_{n_k}$ in the expansion

$$u^k = c_1 \phi_1^k + c_2 \phi_2^k + \cdots + c_{n_k} \phi_{n_k}^k. \tag{9.146}$$

We obtain the system

$$\mathbf{A}\mathbf{c} = \mathbf{g}, \tag{9.147}$$

where

$$\mathbf{c} = \begin{bmatrix} c_1 & \cdots & c_{n_k} \end{bmatrix}^T, \tag{9.148}$$

$$\mathbf{g} = \begin{bmatrix} g_1 & \cdots & g_{n_k} \end{bmatrix}^T, \quad g_i = \langle f, \phi_i^k \rangle, \quad i = \overline{1, n_k}, \tag{9.149}$$

$$\mathbf{A} = [a_{ij}]_{i,j = \overline{1, n_k}}, \quad a_{ij} = \langle \phi_i^k, \phi_j^k \rangle, \quad i, j = \overline{1, n_k}. \tag{9.150}$$

If $\phi_i^k \in \mathcal{D}$, $i = \overline{1, n_k}$, then we may also write

$$a_{ij} = \langle L\phi_i^k, \phi_j^k \rangle, \quad i, j = \overline{1, n_k}. \tag{9.151}$$

Let us remark that the matrix $\mathbf{A}$ is symmetric and positive definite, because

$$\langle \mathbf{A}v, v \rangle = \sum_{i=1}^{n_k} \sum_{j=1}^{n_k} a_{ij} v_i v_j = \left\langle \sum_{i=1}^{n_k} v_i \phi_i^k, \sum_{j=1}^{n_k} v_j \phi_j^k \right\rangle_L \ge c^2 \left\| \sum_{i=1}^{n_k} v_i \phi_i^k \right\|^2 \ge 0. \tag{9.152}$$

Observation 9.12 It is possible that the functions ϕ_1^k, ϕ_2^k, ..., $\phi_{n_k}^k$ do not verify the limit conditions imposed to problem (9.134). This is due to the completion of the space to $\mathcal{H}_L$.

Definition 9.13

    (i) The limit conditions which are obligatory satisfied by the functions of the domain $\mathcal{D}$, and are not obligatory satisfied by the functions of the energetic space $\mathcal{H}_L$ are called *natural conditions for the operator* L.

    (ii) The limit conditions which are obligatory satisfied by the functions of the energetic space $\mathcal{H}_L$ are called *essential conditions*.

Observation 9.13 In the frame of Ritz's method we choose bases in the energetic space; it follows that the functions ϕ_i^k, $i = \overline{1, n_k}$, are not subjected to the natural conditions.

9.8.2 Galerkin's Method

In the frame of Ritz's method it has been asked that the operator L be autoadjoint and positive definite, which represents a limitation of this method.

In the case of Galerkin's method[8] we solve the operational equation

$$Lu = f \tag{9.153}$$

in a Hilbert space $\mathcal{H}$, $f \in \mathcal{H}$, while the domain $\mathcal{D}$ of definition of L is dense in $\mathcal{H}$.

We write L in the form

$$L = L_0 + K, \tag{9.154}$$

where L_0 is a positive definite symmetric operator with L_0^{-1} total continuous in $\mathcal{H}$, while the domain $\mathcal{D}_K$ of definition of K satisfies the relation $\mathcal{D}_F \supseteq \mathcal{D}_{L_0}$, where $\mathcal{D}_{L_0}$ is the domain of definition of L_0.

We also introduce now the energetic space $\mathcal{H}_{L_0}$ of the operator L_0, with the scalar product $\langle u, v \rangle_{L_0}$ and the norm $\|u\|_{L_0}^2 = \langle u, u \rangle_{L_0}$.

Let us perform a scalar product of relation (9.135) and an arbitrary function $v \in \mathcal{D}_{L_0}$. We obtain

$$\langle L_0 u, v \rangle + \langle K u, v \rangle = \langle f, v \rangle \tag{9.155}$$

or

$$\langle u, v \rangle_{L_0} + \langle K u, v \rangle = \langle f, v \rangle. \tag{9.156}$$

Definition 9.14 We call the generalized solution of equation (9.135) a function $u_0 \in \mathcal{H}_{L_0}$, which satisfies relation (9.156) for any $v \in \mathcal{H}_{L_0}$.

Observation 9.14 If $u_0 \in \mathcal{D}_{L_0}$, then, because

$$\langle u, v \rangle_{L_0} = \langle L_0 u, v \rangle, \tag{9.157}$$

it follows that

$$\langle L_0 u_0 + K u_0 - f, v \rangle = 0 \tag{9.158}$$

and because $\mathcal{D}_{L_0}$ is dense in $\mathcal{H}$, we deduce that u_0 satisfies equation (9.153).

---

[8]Boris Grigoryevich Galerkin (1871–1945) described the method in 1915.

Also, we now construct the spaces $\mathcal{H}_k \subseteq \mathcal{H}_{L_0}$ and the bases ϕ_1^k, ϕ_2^k, $\ldots$, $\phi_{n_k}^k$, the approximation of the solution being

$$u^k = \sum_{i=1}^{n_k} c_i \phi_i^k, \tag{9.159}$$

where the coefficients c_i, $i = \overline{1, n_k}$, are chosen so that u^k do verify relation (9.156) for any $v \in \mathcal{H}_k$. On the other hand, because $v \in \mathcal{H}_k$, we deduce that v is written in the form

$$v = \sum_{i=1}^{n_k} b_i \phi_i^k; \tag{9.160}$$

hence, u^k is determined by the system of equations

$$\langle u^k, \phi_i^k \rangle_{L_0} + \langle K u^k, \phi_i^k \rangle = \langle f, \phi_i^k \rangle, \quad i = \overline{1, n_k}. \tag{9.161}$$

The last system may be put in the form

$$\mathbf{Ac} = \mathbf{g}, \tag{9.162}$$

where

$$\mathbf{A} = [a_{ij}]_{i, j = \overline{1, n_k}}, \quad a_{ij} = \langle \phi_i^k, \phi_j^k \rangle_{L_0} + \langle K \phi_i^k, \phi_j^k \rangle, \quad i, j = \overline{1, n_k}, \tag{9.163}$$

$$\mathbf{g} = \begin{bmatrix} g_1 & \cdots & g_{n_k} \end{bmatrix}^T, \quad g_i = \langle f, \phi_i^k \rangle, \quad i = \overline{1, n_k}, \tag{9.164}$$

$$\mathbf{c} = \begin{bmatrix} c_1 & \cdots & c_{n_k} \end{bmatrix}^T. \tag{9.165}$$

Observation 9.15 If $K = 0$, then Galerkin's method becomes Ritz's method.

Observation 9.16 We consider that there exists the operator L_0^{-1}, bounded and defined on the whole space $\mathcal{H}$. Equation (9.153) is now equivalent to

$$u + L_0^{-1} K u = L_0^{-1} f. \tag{9.166}$$

We denote by $\mathcal{H}_1$ the Hilbert space with the scalar product

$$\langle u, v \rangle_1 = \langle L u_0, L_0 v \rangle \tag{9.167}$$

and the norm

$$\|u\|_1 = \|L_0 u\|. \tag{9.168}$$

We also now construct the subspaces $\mathcal{H}_k$, finite dimensional but included in $\mathcal{H}_1$ and of bases ψ_i^k, $i = \overline{1, n_k}$, and search the approximate solution in the form

$$u^k = \sum_{i=1}^{n_k} c_i \psi_i^k, \tag{9.169}$$

where c_i, $i = \overline{1, n_k}$, are obtained from the system

$$\langle u^k, \psi_i^k \rangle_1 + \langle L_0^{-1} K u^k, \psi_i^k \rangle_1 = \langle L_0^{-1} f, \psi_i^k \rangle_1, \quad i = \overline{1, n_k}. \tag{9.170}$$

9.8.3 Method of the Least Squares

Let the operational equation be

$$Lu = f, \tag{9.171}$$

in the Hilbert space $\mathcal{H}$ and let $\mathcal{H}_k$ be dimensional finite subspaces of $\mathcal{H}$ with the bases $\phi_i^k, i = \overline{1, n_k}$, and with $\mathcal{H}_k \subseteq \mathcal{D}$.

Starting from the relations

$$\frac{\partial}{\partial c_i} \|Lu - f\| = 0, \quad i = \overline{1, n_k}, \tag{9.172}$$

we obtain system (9.147) in which

$$\mathbf{A} = [a_{ij}]_{i, j = \overline{1, n_k}}, \quad a_{ij} = \langle L\phi_i^k, L\phi_j^k \rangle, \quad i, j = \overline{1, n_k}, \tag{9.173}$$

$$\mathbf{g} = \begin{bmatrix} g_1 & \cdots & g_{n_k} \end{bmatrix}^T, \quad g_i = \langle f, L\phi_i^k \rangle, \quad i = \overline{1, n_k}, \tag{9.174}$$

$$\mathbf{c} = \begin{bmatrix} c_1 & \cdots & c_{n_k} \end{bmatrix}^T, \tag{9.175}$$

the approximate solution being

$$u^k = \sum_{i=1}^{n_k} c_i \phi_i^k. \tag{9.176}$$

The approximate solution u^k converges to the exact solution of equation (9.171), if that equation has a unique solution, the sequence of subspaces $L\mathcal{H}_k$ is complete in $\mathcal{D}$, while the operator L^{-1} does exist and is bounded.

Observation 9.17 The problem is put that the limit solution verifies the limit conditions of problem (9.171). There are two possibilities of tackling this problem:
  (i) we impose the functions of the space $\mathcal{H}_k$ to verify the limit conditions; but the method is difficult to apply;
  (ii) if $Lu = f$ in $\mathcal{D}$ and $L_i u = f_i$ on $\partial \mathcal{D}_i, i = \overline{1, p}$, are the problems and the limit conditions, then we consider the functional

$$I_k(u) = \|Lu - f\|^2 + \sum_{i=1}^{n_k} c_i(k) \|L_i u - f_i\|^2, \tag{9.177}$$

where $c_i(k), i = \overline{1, n_k}$, are positive functions of parameter k. If the solution is smooth, then

$$c_i(k) = k^{-2\left(2m - m_i - \frac{1}{2}\right)}, \quad i = \overline{1, n_k}, \tag{9.178}$$

where $2m$ is the order of the partial differential equation $Lu = f$, while m_i is the order of the highest order derivative in the operator $L_i, i = \overline{1, p}$.

We now search the approximations u^k as solutions of the variational problem

$$\inf_{v \in \mathcal{H}_k} I_k(v) = I_k(u^k). \tag{9.179}$$

9.9 NUMERICAL EXAMPLES

Example 9.1 Let us consider the equation of wave propagation

$$\frac{\partial u}{\partial t} + a\frac{\partial u}{\partial x} = 0, \quad x \in [0, 1], \quad t \in [0, T], \tag{9.180}$$

where a is a positive constant.

Applying the theory of numerical integration of partial differential equations of first order using explicit schemata, we obtain the equations with finite differences

$$V(x^i, t^{j+1}) = V(x^i, t^j) + c[V(x^{i-1}, t^j) - V(x^i, t^j)], \quad i = \overline{1, I}, \quad j = \overline{1, J}, \tag{9.181}$$

where by $V(x^i, t^j)$ has been denoted by the approximate value of the function $u(x^i, t^j)$, $x^i = ih$, $t^j = jk$, $h = 1/I$, $k = I/J$.

Equation (9.180) is equivalent to the system

$$\frac{dt}{1} = \frac{dx}{a} \tag{9.182}$$

which leads to the first integral

$$x - at = C_1, \tag{9.183}$$

where C_1 is a constant; hence the exact solution of the problem is

$$u = \phi(x - at), \tag{9.184}$$

where ϕ is an arbitrary function.

If $C = 1$, then it follows that the schema

$$V(x^i, t^{j+1}) = V(x^{i-1}, t^j). \tag{9.185}$$

Example 9.2 Let the partial differential equation be

$$\frac{\partial u}{\partial t} + \frac{\partial u}{\partial x} = 0 \tag{9.186}$$

for which the initial and boundary conditions are

$$u(x, 0) = 0, \quad 0 < x \le 1, \quad u(0, t) = 1, \quad t \ge 0. \tag{9.187}$$

At the initial moment $t = 0$ the function u is identically null for all the values x in the domain, excepting $x = 0$ for which $u = 1$.

We wish to obtain the equation with differences for problem (9.186), $t \le 1$, with the steps $h = 0.1$, $k = 0.1$.

We shall apply relation (9.185) from Example 9.1.

It follows that

$$V(x^i, t^0) = 0, \quad i > j, \tag{9.188}$$

$$V(x^0, t^j) = 1, \quad j \ge 0, \tag{9.189}$$

$$V(x^i, t^{j+1}) = V(x^{i-1}, t^j), \quad i \ge 1, \quad j \ge 0, \quad i \le 10, \quad j \le 9 \tag{9.190}$$

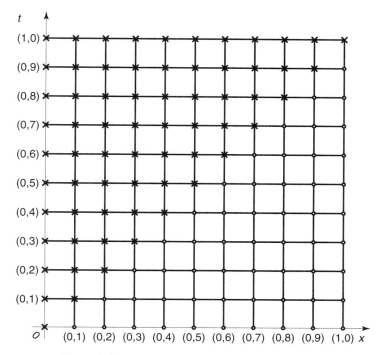

Figure 9.4   Numerical solution of problem (9.186).

and the solution

$$V(x^i, t^j) = \begin{cases} 1 \text{ for } i \le j \\ 0 \text{ otherwise} \end{cases}. \tag{9.191}$$

Graphically, the situation is given in Figure 9.4, wherein the points where $V(x^i, t^j) = 1$ have been marked by a star, while the points where $V(x^i, t^j) = 0$ have been marked by a circle.

Let us observe that for $c = 1$ the Lax–Wendroff schema leads to the exact solution $V(x^i, t^{j+1}) = V(x^{i-1}, t^j)$, as in this example.

Example 9.3   The equation with finite differences for Example 9.1 are now of the form (using implicit schemata)

$$V(x^i, t^{j+1}) = \frac{cV(x^{i+1}, t^{j+1}) + V(x^i, t^j)}{1 + c}, \quad i = 1, 2, \ldots \tag{9.192}$$

which is unconditioned convergent.

Another schema often used in case of Example 9.1 is the Wendroff schema for which the equation with differences reads

$$V(x^i, t^{j+1}) = V(x^{i-1}, t^j) + \frac{1 - c}{1 + c}[V(x^i, t^j) - V(x^{i-1}, t^j)]. \tag{9.193}$$

Example 9.4   Returning to Example 9.2 and using the implicit schemata (9.186) and (9.187) from Example 9.3 for $c = 1$, we obtain the same results as in Figure 9.4.

Example 9.5   Let the problem of elliptic type be

$$\frac{\partial^2 u}{\partial x^2} + \frac{\partial^2 u}{\partial y^2} = 0, \quad 0 < x < 1, \quad 0 < y < 1 \tag{9.194}$$

with the boundary conditions

$$u(x, 0) = 0, \quad u(x, 1) = x, \quad 0 \le x \le 1, \tag{9.195}$$

$$u(0, y) = 0, \quad u(1, y) = y, \quad 0 \le y \le 1, \tag{9.196}$$

the exact solution of which is

$$u(x, y) = xy. \tag{9.197}$$

Using a system with $n = 5$, $m = 5$, we will determine the numerical solution of the problem. In the case of our problem

$$h = \frac{1-0}{5} = 0.2, \quad k = \frac{1-0}{5} = 0.2, \quad \frac{h}{k} = 1, \tag{9.198}$$

and the linear approximating system

$$4w_{i,j} - w_{i+1,j} - w_{i-1,j} - w_{i,j+1} - w_{i,j-1} = 0, \quad i = \overline{1,4}, \quad j = \overline{1,4}, \tag{9.199}$$

$$w_{0,j} = 0, \quad j = \overline{0,5}, \tag{9.200}$$

$$w_{5,j} = 0.2j, \quad j = \overline{0,5}, \tag{9.201}$$

$$w_{i,0} = 0, \quad i = \overline{1,4}, \tag{9.202}$$

$$w_{i,m} = 0.2i, \quad i = \overline{1,4}. \tag{9.203}$$

Renumbering the knots as in Figure 9.5, it follows that the linear system

$$4w_{13} - w_{14} - w_9 = w_{0,1} + w_{1,0} = 0, \quad 4w_9 - w_{10} - w_5 - w_{13} = w_{0,2} = 0,$$

$$4w_5 - w_6 - w_1 - w_9 = w_{0,3} = 0, \quad 4w_1 - w_2 - w_5 = w_{0,4} + w_{1,5} = 0 + 0.2 = 0.2,$$

$$4w_{14} - w_{15} - w_{13} - w_{10} = w_{2,0} = 0, \quad 4w_{10} - w_{11} - w_9 - w_6 - w_{14} = 0,$$

$$4w_6 - w_7 - w_5 - w_2 - w_{10} = 0, \quad 4w_2 - w_3 - w_1 - w_{10} = w_{2,5} = 0.4,$$

$$4w_{15} - w_{16} - w_{14} - w_{11} = w_{3,0} = 0, \quad 4w_{11} - w_{12} - w_{10} - w_7 - w_{15} = 0,$$

$$4w_7 - w_8 - w_6 - w_3 - w_{11} = 0, \quad 4w_3 - w_4 - w_2 - w_7 = w_{3,5} = 0.6,$$

$$4w_{16} - w_{15} - w_{12} = w_{5,1} + w_{4,0} = 0.2 + 0 = 0.2,$$

$$4w_{12} - w_{11} - w_8 - w_{16} = w_{5,2} = 0.4,$$

$$4w_8 - w_7 - w_4 - w_{12} = w_{5,3} = 0.6,$$

$$4w_4 - w_3 - w_8 = w_{5,4} + w_{4,5} = 0.8 + 0.8 = 1.6. \tag{9.204}$$

The solution of this system is

$$w_1 = 0.16, \quad w_2 = 0.32, \quad w_3 = 0.48, \quad w_4 = 0.64, \quad w_5 = 0.12, \quad w_6 = 0.24,$$

$$w_7 = 0.36, \quad w_8 = 0.48, \quad w_9 = 0.08, \quad w_{10} = 0.16, \quad w_{11} = 0.24, \tag{9.205}$$

$$w_{12} = 0.32, \quad w_{13} = 0.04, \quad w_{14} = 0.08, \quad w_{15} = 0.12, \quad w_{16} = 0.16.$$

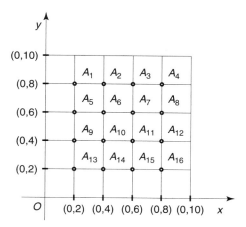

Figure 9.5   Numbering of the knots for problem (9.196).

We observe that the numerical solution coincides with the exact solution and this is because

$$\frac{\partial^4 u}{\partial x^4} = 0, \quad \frac{\partial^4 u}{\partial y^4} = 0; \tag{9.206}$$

hence the truncation error vanishes at each step.

Example 9.6   Let the problem of elliptic type be

$$\frac{\partial^2 u}{\partial x^2} + \frac{\partial^2 u}{\partial y^2} = 0, \quad 0 < x < 1, \quad 0 < y < 1 \tag{9.207}$$

with the boundary conditions

$$
\begin{aligned}
u(x, 0) &= 0, & u(x, 1) &= \sin(\pi x)\sinh 1, & 0 &\le x \le 1, \\
u(0, y) &= 0, & u(x, 0) &= 0, & 0 &\le y \le 1
\end{aligned}
\tag{9.208}
$$

the solution of which is

$$u(x, y) = \sin(\pi x)\sinh(\pi y). \tag{9.209}$$

Using the algorithm presented for the differential equations of elliptic type with $n = 6, m = 6$, and the stopping condition given by $\varepsilon = 10^{-10}$, we will determine the approximate numerical solution of the problem, as well as the error with respect to the exact solution $|u(x_i, y_j) - w_{i,j}^{(l)}|$, $i = \overline{1, n}$, $j = \overline{1, m}$, while l is given by the algorithm.
We have

$$f(x, y) = 0 \text{ for } (x, y) \in [0, 1] \times [0, 1], \tag{9.210}$$

$$g(x, y) = \begin{cases} 0 \text{ for } y = 0, & x = 0 \text{ or } x = 1 \\ \sin(\pi x)\sinh(\pi) \text{ for } j = m \end{cases} \tag{9.211}$$

or written in the form

$$g(x_i, y_j) = \begin{cases} 0 \text{ for } j = 0, & i = 0 \text{ or } i = n \\ \sin(\pi x)\sinh(1) \text{ for } j = m \end{cases}. \tag{9.212}$$

The results of the program are given in Table 9.1 in which $l = 80$.

TABLE 9.1   Numerical Solution of Problems (9.207) and (9.208)

i	j	x_i	y_j	$w_{i,j}^{(80)}$	$u(x_i, y_j)$	$\|u(x_i, y_j) - w_{i,j}^{(80)}\|$
1	1	0.1667	0.1667	0.28665	0.27393	0.01272
1	2	0.1667	0.3333	0.65011	0.62468	0.02542
1	3	0.1667	0.5000	1.18776	1.15065	0.03711
1	4	0.1667	0.6667	2.04367	1.99935	0.04433
1	5	0.1667	0.8333	3.44719	3.40881	0.03837
2	1	0.3333	0.1667	0.49649	0.47446	0.02204
2	2	0.3333	0.3333	1.12602	1.08198	0.04404
2	3	0.3333	0.5000	2.05726	1.99298	0.06428
2	4	0.3333	0.6667	3.53975	3.46297	0.07678
2	5	0.3333	0.8333	5.97070	5.90423	0.06647
3	1	0.5000	0.1667	0.57330	0.54785	0.02545
3	2	0.5000	0.3333	1.30021	1.24937	0.05085
3	3	0.5000	0.5000	2.37552	2.30130	0.07422
3	4	0.5000	0.6667	4.08735	3.99869	0.08865
3	5	0.5000	0.8333	6.89437	6.81762	0.07675
4	1	0.6667	0.1667	0.49649	0.47446	0.02204
4	2	0.6667	0.3333	1.12602	1.08198	0.04404
4	3	0.6667	0.5000	2.05726	1.99298	0.06428
4	4	0.6667	0.6667	3.53975	3.46297	0.07678
4	5	0.6667	0.8333	5.97070	5.90423	0.06647
5	1	0.8333	0.1667	0.28665	0.27393	0.01272
5	2	0.8333	0.3333	0.65011	0.62468	0.03711
5	3	0.8333	0.5000	1.18776	1.15065	0.03711
5	4	0.8333	0.6667	2.04367	1.99935	0.04433
5	5	0.8333	0.8333	3.44719	3.40881	0.03837

Example 9.7   Let the problem of parabolic type be

$$\frac{\partial u}{\partial t} - \frac{\partial^2 u}{\partial x^2} = 0, \quad 0 < x < \pi, \quad t > 0 \tag{9.213}$$

with the initial and boundary conditions

$$u(x, 0) = \sin x, \tag{9.214}$$

$$u(0, t) = u(\pi, t) = 0 \tag{9.215}$$

the exact solution of which is

$$u(x, t) = e^{-t} \sin x. \tag{9.216}$$

Considering $m = 20$, from which $h = \pi/20$ and $k = 0.01$, we search the approximate of the problem for $t = 0.5$, which will be compared with the exact solution.

We shall solve the same problem for $h = \pi/20$ and $k = 0.1$.

The results are given in Table 9.2.

The numerical and the exact solutions in the second case are given in Table 9.3.

We observe that the method presented is not stable in the second case studied above.

TABLE 9.2   Solution of Equation (9.213) in the First Case

i	x_i	$u(x_i, 0.5)$	$w_{i,50}$	$\lvert u(x_i, 0.5)\rvert - w_{i,50}$
0	0	0	0	0
1	0.157079633	0.094882299	0.094742054	0.000140245
2	0.314159265	0.187428281	0.187151245	0.000277037
3	0.471238898	0.275359157	0.274952150	0.000407007
4	0.628318531	0.356509777	0.355982821	0.000526955
5	0.7853981463	0.428881942	0.428248014	0.000633928
6	0.942477796	0.490693611	0.489968319	0.000725292
7	1.099557429	0.540422775	0.539623979	0.000798796
8	1.256637061	0576844936	0.575992305	0.000852632
9	1.413716694	0.599063261	0.598177788	0.000885473
10	1.570796327	0.606530660	0.605634150	0.000896510
11	1.727875959	0.599063261	0.598177788	0.000885473
12	1.884955592	0.576844936	0.575992305	0.000852632
13	2.042035225	0.540422775	0.539623979	0.000798796
14	2.199114858	0.490693611	0.489968319	0.0007252925
15	2.356194490	0.428881942	0.428248014	0.000633928
16	2.513274123	0.356509777	0.355982821	0.000526955
17	2.670353756	0.275359157	0.274952150	0.000407007
18	2.827433388	0.187428281	0.187151245	0.000277037
19	2.984513021	0.094882299	0.094742054	0.000140245
20	3.141592654	0	0	0

TABLE 9.3   Solution of Equation (9.213) in the Second Case

i	x_i	$u(x_i, 0.5)$	$w_{i,5}$	$\lvert u(x_i, 0.5)\rvert - w_{i,5}$
0	0	0	0	0
1	0.157079633	0.094882299	0.092478468	0.002403832
2	0.314159265	0.187428281	0.182679809	0.004748473
3	0.471238898	0.275359157	0.268382966	0.006976191
4	0.628318531	0.356509777	0.347477645	0.009032132
5	0.7853981463	0.428881942	0.418016274	0.010865672
6	0.942477796	0.490693611	0.478261948	0.012431663
7	1.099557429	0.540422775	0.526731229	0.013691545
8	1.256637061	0576844936	0.562230640	0.014614296
9	1.413716694	0.599063261	0.582886066	0.015177195
10	1.570796327	0.606530660	0.591164279	0.015366381
11	1.727875959	0.599063261	0.582886066	0.015177195
12	1.884955592	0.576844936	0.562230640	0.014614296
13	2.042035225	0.540422775	0.526731229	0.013691545
14	2.199114858	0.490693611	0.478261948	0.012431663
15	2.356194490	0.428881942	0.418016270	0.010865672
16	2.513274123	0.356509777	0.347477645	0.009032132
17	2.670353756	0.275359157	0.268382966	0.006976191
18	2.827433388	0.187428281	0.182679809	0.004748473
19	2.984513021	0.094882299	0.092478468	0.002403832
20	3.141592654	0	0	0

Example 9.8   Let the problem of parabolic type be

$$\frac{\partial u}{\partial t} - \frac{\partial^2 u}{\partial t^2} = 0, \quad 0 < x < \pi, \quad t > 0 \tag{9.217}$$

with the initial and boundary conditions

$$u(x, 0) = \sin x, \tag{9.218}$$

$$u(0, t) = u(\pi, t) = 0 \tag{9.219}$$

the exact solution of which is

$$u(x, t) = e^{-t} \sin x. \tag{9.220}$$

Considering $m = 20$, from which $h = \pi/20$ and $k = 0.1$ we will determine the approximate solution of the problem for $t = 0.5$, which will be compared with the exact solution using the method with backward differences.

By means of the presented algorithm, the results are given in Table 9.4.

Example 9.9   Let the problem of parabolic type be

$$\frac{\partial u}{\partial t} - \frac{\partial^2 u}{\partial t^2} = 0, \quad 0 < x < \pi, \quad t > 0 \tag{9.221}$$

with the initial and boundary conditions

$$u(x, 0) = \sin x, \tag{9.222}$$

$$u(0, t) = u(\pi, t) = 0 \tag{9.223}$$

TABLE 9.4   Solution of Problem (9.217)

i	x_i	$u(x_i, 0.5)$	$w_{i,5}$	$|u(x_i, 0.5)| - w_{i,5}$
0	0	0	0	0
1	0.157079633	0.094882299	0.097224254	0.002341955
2	0.314159265	0.187428281	0.192054525	0.004626243
3	0.471238898	0.275359157	0.282155775	0.006796618
4	0.628318531	0.356509777	0.365309415	0.008799638
5	0.7853981463	0.428881942	0.439467923	0.010585981
6	0.942477796	0.490693611	0.502805274	0.012111662
7	1.099557429	0.540422775	0.553761889	0.013339114
8	1.256637061	0576844936	0.591083049	0.014238113
9	1.413716694	0.599063261	0.613849783	0.014786522
10	1.570796327	0.606530660	0.621501498	0.014970838
11	1.727875959	0.599063261	0.613849783	0.014786522
12	1.884955592	0.576844936	0.591083049	0.014238113
13	2.042035225	0.540422775	0.553761889	0.013339114
14	2.199114858	0.490693611	0.502805274	0.012111662
15	2.356194490	0.428881942	0.439467923	0.010585981
16	2.513274123	0.356509777	0.365309415	0.008799638
17	2.670353756	0.275359157	0.282155775	0.006796618
18	2.827433388	0.187428281	0.192054525	0.004626243
19	2.984513021	0.094882299	0.097224254	0.002341955
20	3.141592654	0	0	0

the exact solution of which is

$$u(x, t) = e^{-t} \sin x. \tag{9.224}$$

Considering $m = 20$, where $h = \pi/20$ and $k = 0.1$, we will determine the approximate solution of the problem for $t = 0.5$, which will be compared with the exact solution by using the Crank–Nicolson method.

The results are given in Table 9.5.

Example 9.10 Let the problem of hyperbolic type be

$$\frac{\partial^2 u}{\partial t^2} - \frac{\partial^2 u}{\partial x^2} = 0, \quad 0 < x < 1, \quad t > 0 \tag{9.225}$$

with the conditions

$$u(0, t) = u(1, t) = 0, \quad t > 0, \tag{9.226}$$

$$u(x, 0) = \sin(\pi x), \quad 0 \le x \le 1, \tag{9.227}$$

$$\frac{\partial u}{\partial t}(x, 0) = 0, \quad 0 \le x \le 1; \tag{9.228}$$

the exact solution is

$$u(x, t) = \sin(\pi x) \cos(\pi t). \tag{9.229}$$

TABLE 9.5   Solution of Problem (9.221)

i	x_i	$u(x_i, 0.5)$	$w_{i,5}$	$|u(x_i, 0.5)| - w_{i,5}$
0	0	0	0	0
1	0.157079633	0.094882299	0.094940434	0.000058135
2	0.314159265	0.187428281	0.187543119	0.00114838
3	0.471238898	0.275359157	0.275527871	0.00168713
4	0.628318531	0.356509777	0.356728211	0.000218434
5	0.7853981463	0.428881942	0.429144720	0.000262777
6	0.942477796	0.490693611	0.490994261	0.000300649
7	1.099557429	0.540422775	0.540753893	0.000331118
8	1.256637061	0576844936	0.577198371	0.000353434
9	1.413716694	0.599063261	0.599430308	0.000367048
10	1.570796327	0.606530660	0.606902283	0.000371623
11	1.727875959	0.599063261	0.599430308	0.000367048
12	1.884955592	0.576844936	0.577198371	0.000353434
13	2.042035225	0.540422775	0.540753893	0.000331118
14	2.199114858	0.490693611	0.490994261	0.000300649
15	2.356194490	0.428881942	0.429144720	0.000262777
16	2.513274123	0.356509777	0.356728211	0.000218434
17	2.670353756	0.275359157	0.275527871	0.000168713
18	2.827433388	0.187428281	0.187543119	0.000114838
19	2.984513021	0.094882299	0.094940434	0.000058135
20	3.141592654	0	0	0

TABLE 9.6   Solution of Equation (9.225)

i	x_i	$u(x_i, 0.5)$	$w_{i,60}$	$\|u(x_i, 0.5)\| - w_{i,60}$
0	0	0	0	0
1	0.05	−0.048340908	−0.051663969	0.003323061
2	0.10	−0.095491503	−0.102101248	0.006609746
3	0.15	−0.140290780	−0.150138925	0.009848145
4	0.20	−0.181635632	−0.193803147	0.012167515
5	0.25	−0.218508012	−0.234218363	0.015710350
6	0.30	−0.250000000	−0.266551849	0.16551849
7	0.35	−0.275336158	−0.292401548	0.017065390
8	0.40	−0.293892626	−0.311103275	0.017210649
9	0.45	−0.305212482	−0.313895800	0.008683318
10	0.50	−0.309016994	−0.299780167	0.009236827
11	0.55	−0.305212482	−0.278282952	0.026929531
12	0.60	−0.293892626	−0.259112488	0.034780138
13	0.65	−0.275336158	−0.241810622	0.033525536
14	0.70	−0.250000000	−0.218502651	0.031497349
15	0.75	−0.218508012	−0.189734816	0.028773196
16	0.80	−0.181635632	−0.158609575	0.023026057
17	0.85	−0.140290780	−0.122055771	0.018235009
18	0.90	−0.095491503	−0.083173084	0.012318419
19	0.95	−0.048340908	−0.042127931	0.006212977
20	1.00	0	0	0

Using the algorithm of finite differences for $h = 0.05$, $k = 0.01$, $T = 0.5$, we will determine the approximate solution, which will be compared with the exact solution.

The results are given in Table 9.6.

9.10   APPLICATIONS

Problem 9.1

Let be a square deep beam of side, acted upon on the upper side by a uniform distributed normal load and by the reactions which act as tangential loadings parabolically distributed (Fig. 9.6a). One asks to calculate the corresponding state of stress.

Solution:
We decompose the loading in two cases, using the properties of symmetry with respect to the Ox-axis. We have thus to solve the problem in Figure 9.6b, with properties of skew symmetry with respect to Ox; the case in Figure 9.6c is symmetric with respect to Ox and represents a simple compression, for which the state of stress is given by (σ_x, σ_y – normal stresses, τ_{xy} – tangential stress)

$$\sigma_x = 0, \quad \sigma_y = -\frac{p}{2}, \quad \tau_{xy} = 0. \tag{9.230}$$

For the first case, we use the Airy biharmonic function $F(x, y)$, the second derivatives of which give the state of stress in the form

$$\sigma_x = \frac{\partial^2 F}{\partial y^2}, \quad \sigma_y = \frac{\partial^2 F}{\partial x^2}, \quad \tau_{xy} = -\frac{\partial^2 F}{\partial x \partial y}; \tag{9.231}$$

we notice that $F(x, y)$ must be even with respect to x and odd with respect to y, so that we take the function of the form (the polynomials are obtained from the general form, putting the condition of biharmonicity)

$$
\begin{aligned}
F(x, y) &= P_3(x, y) + P_5(x, y) + P_7(x, y) + P_9(x, y) + P_{11}(x, y) \\
&= \gamma_3 x^2 y + \delta_3 y^3 + \gamma_5(x^4 y - x^2 y^3) + \delta_5(y^5 - 5x^2 y^3) \\
&\quad + \gamma_7 \left(x^6 y - \frac{10}{3} x^4 y^3 + x^2 y^5 \right) + \delta_7 \left(y^7 - 14x^2 y^5 + \frac{35}{3} x^4 y^3 \right) \\
&\quad + \gamma_9(x^8 y - 7x^6 y^3 + 7x^4 y^5 - x^2 y^7) + \delta_9(y^9 - 27x^2 y^7 + 63x^4 y^5 \\
&\quad - 21x^6 y^3) + \gamma_{11} \left(x^{10} y - 12x^8 y^3 + \frac{126}{5} x^6 y^5 - 12x^4 y^7 + x^2 y^9 \right);
\end{aligned} \tag{9.232}
$$

hence the state of stress is given by

$$
\begin{aligned}
\sigma_x &= 6\delta_3 y - 6\gamma_5 x^2 y + \delta_5(20y^3 - 30x^2 y) + \gamma_7(-20x^4 y + 20x^2 y^3) \\
&\quad + \delta_7(42y^5 - 280x^2 y^3 + 70x^4 y) + \gamma_9(-42x^6 y + 140x^4 y^3 - 42x^2 y^5) \\
&\quad + \delta_9(72y^7 - 1134x^2 y^5 + 1260x^4 y^3 - 126x^6 y) \\
&\quad + \gamma_{11}(-72x^8 y + 504x^6 y^3 - 504x^4 y^5 + 72x^2 y^7), \\
\sigma_y &= 2\gamma_3 y + \gamma_5(12x^2 y - 2y^3) - 10\delta_5 y^3 + \gamma_7(30x^4 y - 40x^2 y^3 + 2y^5) \\
&\quad + \delta_7(-28y^5 + 140x^2 y^3) + \gamma_9(56x^6 y - 210x^4 y^3 + 84x^2 y^5 - 2y^7) \\
&\quad + \delta_9(-54y^7 + 756x^2 y^5 - 630x^4 y^3) \\
&\quad + \gamma_{11}(90x^8 y - 672x^6 y^3 + 756x^4 y^5 - 144x^2 y^7 + 2y^9), \\
\tau_{xy} &= -2\gamma_3 x + \gamma_5(-4x^3 + 6xy^2) + 30\delta_5 xy^2 + \gamma_7(-6x^5 + 40x^3 y^2 - 10xy^4) \\
&\quad + \delta_7(140xy^4 - 140x^3 y^2) + \gamma_9(-8x^7 + 126x^5 y^2 - 140x^3 y^4 + 14xy^6) \\
&\quad + \delta_9(378xy^6 - 1260x^3 y^4 + 378x^5 y^2) \\
&\quad + \gamma_{11}(-10x^9 + 288x^7 y^2 - 756x^5 y^4 + 336x^3 y^6 - 18xy^8). \tag{9.233}
\end{aligned}
$$

We put conditions at 16 points of the contour. Because of the symmetry, there remain five distinct points (Fig. 9.6b). The conditions

$$
\sigma_x(a, 0) = 0, \quad \tau_{xy}(0, a) = 0 \tag{9.234}
$$

are identically satisfied. We then have ($\tau_{yx} = \tau_{xy}$)

$$
\sigma_y(0, a) = \sigma_y \left(\frac{a}{2}, a \right) = \sigma_y(a, a) = -0.5p, \quad \tau_{yx} \left(\frac{a}{2}, a \right) = \tau_{yx}(a, a) = 0,
$$
$$
\sigma_x \left(a, \frac{a}{2} \right) = \sigma_x(a, a) = 0, \quad \tau_{xy}(a, 0) = 0.75p, \quad \tau_{xy} \left(a, \frac{a}{2} \right) = 0.5625p; \tag{9.235}
$$

we notice that at the point (a, a), three conditions must be satisfied, because of the symmetry of the stress tensor, hence of the tangential stresses.

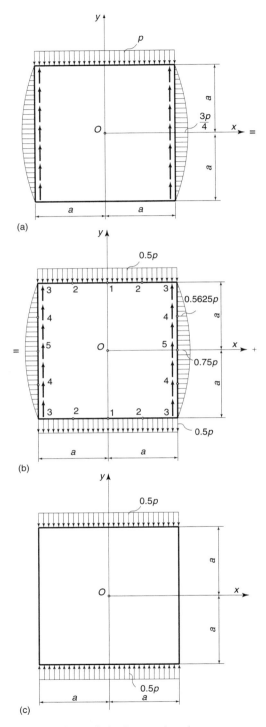

Figure 9.6   Square deep beam.

We find thus following system of nine linear equations for the nine arbitrary parameters ($\alpha_1 = \gamma_3 a$, $\alpha_2 = \delta_3 a$, $\alpha_3 = \gamma_5 a^3$, $\alpha_4 = \delta_5 a^3$, $\alpha_5 = \gamma_7 a^5$, $\alpha_6 = \delta_7 a^5$, $\alpha_7 = \gamma_9 a^7$, $\alpha_8 = \delta_9 a^7$, $\alpha_9 = \gamma_{11} a^9$),

$$\alpha_1 - \alpha_3 - 5\alpha_4 + \alpha_5 - 14\alpha_6 - \alpha_7 - 27\alpha_8 + \alpha_9 = -0.25p,$$

$$2\alpha_1 + \alpha_3 - 10\alpha_4 - 6.125\alpha_5 + 7\alpha_6 + 6.75\alpha_7 + 95.625\alpha_8 + 3.1016\alpha_9 = -0.5p,$$

$$\alpha_1 + 5\alpha_3 - 5\alpha_4 - 4\alpha_5 + 56\alpha_6 - 36\alpha_7 + 36\alpha_8 + 16\alpha_9 = -0.25p,$$

$$\alpha_1 - 2.5\alpha_3 - 15\alpha_4 + 0.1875\alpha_5 - 52.5\alpha_6 + 6.625\alpha_7 - 13.3125\alpha_8 - 11.6055\alpha_9 = 0,$$

$$\alpha_1 - \alpha_3 - 15\alpha_4 - 12\alpha_5 + 4\alpha_7 + 252\alpha_8 + 80\alpha_9 = 0,$$

$$3\alpha_2 - 3\alpha_3 - 12.5\alpha_4 - 7.5a_5 + 1.3125\alpha_6 - 4.8125\alpha_7 + 59.625\alpha_8 + 11.8125\alpha_9 = 0,$$

$$3\alpha_2 - 3\alpha_3 - 5\alpha_4 - 84\alpha_6 + 28\alpha_7 + 36\alpha_8 = 0,$$

$$\alpha_1 + 2\alpha_3 + 3\alpha_5 + 4\alpha_7 + 5\alpha_9 = -0.375p,$$

$$2\alpha_1 + 2.5\alpha_3 - 7.5\alpha_4 - 3.375\alpha_5 + 26.25\alpha_6 - 14.9688\alpha_7 - 21.6563\alpha_8 - 19.9297\alpha_9 = -0.5625p. \tag{9.236}$$

By solving the system (we use one of the methods that have been presented in Section 4.5), we get

$$\gamma_3 = -0.347100\frac{p}{a}, \quad \delta_3 = -0.083952\frac{p}{a}, \quad \gamma_5 = 0.009407\frac{p}{a^3},$$

$$\delta_5 = -0.014571\frac{p}{a^3}, \quad \gamma_7 = -0.009264\frac{p}{a^5}, \quad \delta_7 = -0.003585\frac{p}{a^5}, \tag{9.237}$$

$$\gamma_9 = -0.003837\frac{p}{a^7}, \quad \delta_9 = 0.000376\frac{p}{a^7}, \quad \gamma_{11} = -0.000654\frac{p}{a^9},$$

the function $F(x, y)$ being thus completely determined.

Taking into account the state of stress (9.230) and formulae (9.233), we get finally ($\xi = x/a$, $\eta = y/a$)

$$\sigma_x = [(-0.504 + 0.380\xi^2 - 0.064\xi^4 + 0.113\xi^6 + 0.047\xi^8)\eta$$
$$+ (-0.291 + 0.819\xi^2 - 0.064\xi^4 - 0.329\xi^6)\eta^3$$
$$+ (-0.151 - 0.265\xi^2 + 0.329\xi^4)\eta^5 + (0.027 - 0.047\xi^3)\eta^7]p,$$

$$\sigma_y = [-0.500 + (-0.695 + 0.113\xi^2 - 0.278\xi^4 - 0.215\xi^6 - 0.059\xi^8)\eta$$
$$+ (0.127 - 0.132\xi^2 + 0.570\xi^4 + 0.439\xi^6)\eta^3 + (0.082 - 0.038\xi^2 - 0.494\xi^4)\eta^5 \tag{9.238}$$
$$+ (-0.013 + 0.094\xi^2)\eta^7 - 0.001\eta^9]p,$$

$$\tau_{xy} = [0.695\xi - 0.638\xi^3 + 0.056\xi^5 + 0.031\xi^7 + 0.006\xi^9$$
$$+ (-0.381\xi + 0.131\xi^3 - 0.338\xi^5 - 0.189\xi^7)\eta^2$$
$$+ (-0.409\xi + 0.063\xi^3 + 0.494\xi^5)\eta^4 + (0.088\xi - 0.221\xi^3)\eta^6 + 0.012\xi\eta^8]p.$$

We obtain thus on the contour a distribution of stresses from which we subtract the distribution of the external loading; it follows that

• on the sides $\xi = \pm 1$:

$$\sigma_x(\pm 1, \eta) = (-0.028\eta + 0.135\eta^3 - 0.087\eta^5 - 0.020\eta^7)p$$

$$= -0.02\eta(1 - \eta^2)(0.25 - \eta^2)(5.6 + \eta^2)p,$$

$$\tau_{xy}(\pm 1, \eta) = \mp(0.027\eta^2 - 0.148\eta^4 + 0.133\eta^6 - 0.012\eta^8)p$$

$$\cong \mp 0.012\eta^2(1 - \eta^2)(0.25 - \eta^2)(9.7 - \eta^2)p;$$

(9.239)

• on the sides $\eta = \pm 1$:

$$\sigma_y(\xi, \pm 1) = \pm(0.037\xi^2 - 0.202\xi^4 + 0.224\xi^6 - 0.059\xi^8)p$$

$$\cong \pm 0.05\xi^2(1 - \xi^2)(0.25 - \xi^2)(2.55 - \xi^2)p,$$

$$\tau_{yx}(\xi, \pm 1) = (0.005\xi - 0.065\xi^3 + 0.212\xi^5 - 0.158\xi^7 + 0.006\xi^9)p$$

$$\cong 0.006\xi(1 - \xi^2)(0.25 - \xi^2)(0.15 - \xi^2)(25 - \xi^2)p.$$

(9.240)

We represent these parasite stresses in Figure 9.7. Although Saint–Venant's principle cannot be applied, because the deep beam has equal dimensions, a negligible state of stress takes place in the interior (the stresses are very small with respect to the loading). We can make an elementary verification, approximating the loading by parabolically distributed loads and using methods

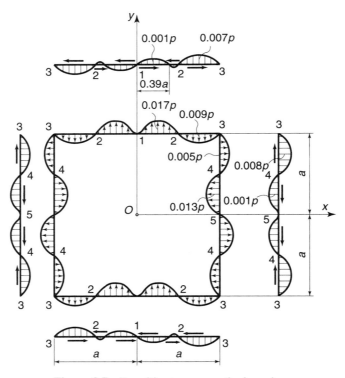

Figure 9.7 Parasitic stresses on the boundary.

of strength of materials. The bending moments at the vertical cross sections 2–2 and 1–1 are (covering)

$$M_{2-2} = -2\frac{2}{3}0.01p\frac{a}{2}\frac{a}{4} = -\frac{1}{6}0.01pa^2,$$

$$M_{1-1} = -2\frac{2}{3}0.01p\frac{a}{2}\frac{3a}{4} + 2\frac{2}{3}0.02p\frac{a}{2}\frac{a}{4} = -\frac{1}{6}0.01pa^2;$$

(9.241)

hence, we get (the strength modulus is $W = (1/6)(2a)^2 = 2a^2/3$)

$$\sigma_{\max} = \mp0.0025p.$$

(9.242)

We can thus see that the error is not greater then 1.7% of the maximum external load, which takes place at four points of the contour.

We may consider that the relations (9.238) give the searched state of stress, which we represent in Figure 9.8a and Figure 9.8b. The broken line in Figure 9.8a corresponds to the linear distribution obtained in strength of materials (Navier's formula).

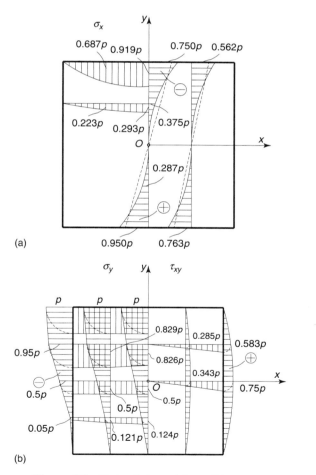

Figure 9.8 State of stress (a) σ_x; (b) σ_y, τ_{xy}.

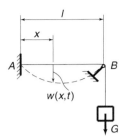

Figure 9.9   Problem 9.2.

Problem 9.2

We consider a thread of length l and density ρ, the cross section of which is constant of area equal to A. The spring is fixed at A (Fig. 9.9) and passes over a small pulley at B, at the other end of the thread holding a weight G.

The partial differential equation of the free transverse vibrations of the thread is

$$\frac{\partial^2 w}{\partial x^2} - \frac{1}{c^2}\frac{\partial^2 w}{\partial t^2} = 0, \qquad (9.243)$$

where $w(x, t)$ is the deflection, while c is a constant

$$c = \sqrt{\frac{G}{\rho A}}; \qquad (9.244)$$

knowing the initial conditions

$$t = 0, \quad w(x, 0) = 4h_0\left(\frac{x}{l} - \frac{x^2}{l^2}\right), \quad \frac{\partial w(x, 0)}{\partial t} = 0, \qquad (9.245)$$

determine
- the exact solution, integrating the equation by Fourier's method;
- a numerical solution, integrating with finite differences and compare the results.

Numerical application: $A = 10^{-6}$ m², $\rho = 10^4$ kg m⁻³, $l = 2$ m, $h_0 = 2 \times 10^{-2}$ m, $G = 10^{-2}$ N.

Solution:
1. Solution by the Fourier method
We consider a solution of the form

$$w(x, t) = Y(x)\cos(pt - \phi) \qquad (9.246)$$

and expression (9.243) leads to the differential equation

$$Y'' + \frac{p^2}{c^2}Y = 0, \qquad (9.247)$$

from which we obtain

$$Y(x) = B\cos\left(\frac{p}{c}x\right) + D\sin\left(\frac{p}{c}x\right); \qquad (9.248)$$

taking into account the boundary conditions

$$w(0, t) = w(l, t) = 0, \qquad (9.249)$$

we obtain

$$\sin\left(\frac{p}{c}l\right) = 0, \tag{9.250}$$

which leads to the eigenvalues

$$p_k = k\pi\frac{c}{l}, \quad k = 1, 2, \ldots \tag{9.251}$$

Under these conditions, the general solution takes the form

$$w(x, t) = \sum_{k=1}^{\infty} D_k \sin\left(\frac{k\pi x}{l}\right)\cos(p_k t - \phi_k), \tag{9.252}$$

the constants D_k, ϕ_k being given by

$$D_k \cos\phi_k = \frac{2}{l}\int_0^l w(x, 0)\sin\left(\frac{k\pi x}{l}\right)dx, \quad D_k \sin\phi_k = \frac{2}{l}\int_0^l \frac{\partial w(x, 0)}{\partial t}\sin\left(\frac{k\pi x}{l}\right)dx. \tag{9.253}$$

We obtain the results

$$\phi_k = 0, \quad D_k = \frac{16h_0}{k^3\pi^3}(1 - \cos k\pi), \tag{9.254}$$

from which the solution

$$w(x, t) = \frac{32h_0}{\pi^3}\sum_{i=1}^{\infty}\frac{\sin\left((2i-1)\frac{\pi x}{l}\right)\cos p_{2i-1}t}{(2i-1)^3}. \tag{9.255}$$

2. Numerical calculation

We apply the theory presented for the partial differential equations of second order of hyperbolic type for

$$\alpha = c, \quad f(x) = 4h_0\left(\frac{x}{l} - \frac{x^2}{l^2}\right), \quad g(x) = 0. \tag{9.256}$$

The results for $x = l/2$ are plotted in Figure 9.10

Problem 9.3

Let us consider the bar BC of length l (Fig. 9.11), of density ρ, of modulus of longitudinal elasticity E, having a constant area A of the cross section; the bar is built-in at B, the end C being free.

The partial differential equation of the free transverse vibrations of the bar reads

$$\frac{\partial^4 w}{\partial x^4} + \frac{A\rho}{EI}\frac{\partial^2 w}{\partial t^2} = 0, \tag{9.257}$$

where $w(x, t)$ is the deflection (Fig. 9.11), and I is the principal moment of inertia of the cross section of the bar with respect to the neutral axis (normal to Bx and Bw). Being given the initial conditions

$$t = 0, \quad w(x, 0) = h_0\frac{f_1(\beta_1)f_4\left(\beta_1\frac{x}{l}\right) - f_2(\beta_1)f_3\left(\beta_1\frac{x}{l}\right)}{|f_1(\beta_1)f_4(\beta_1) - f_2(\beta_1)f_3(\beta_1)|}, \quad \frac{\partial w(x, 0)}{\partial t} = 0, \tag{9.258}$$

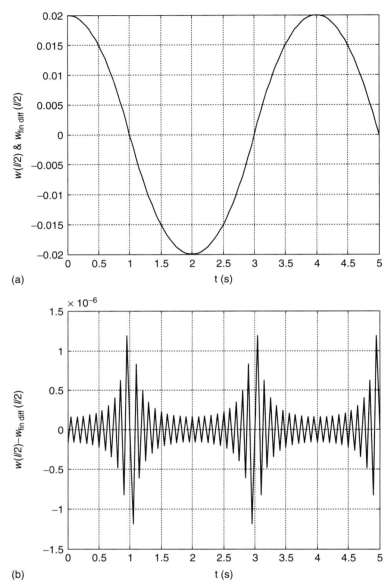

(a)

(b)

Figure 9.10 (a) The analytic $w(l/2)$ calculated with 20 terms and the numerical $w(l/2)$ versus time; (b) the error.

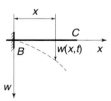

Figure 9.11 Problem 9.3.

where f_1, f_2, f_3, f_4 are Krylov's functions

$$f_1(z) = \frac{\cosh z + \cos z}{2}, \quad f_2(z) = \frac{\sinh z + \sin z}{2},$$

$$f_3 = \frac{\cosh z - \cos z}{2}, \quad f_4 = \frac{\sinh z - \sin z}{2}, \qquad (9.259)$$

while β_1 is the smallest positive solution of the equation

$$\cosh \beta \cos \beta + 1 = 0, \qquad (9.260)$$

determine:

- the exact solution, integrating the equation by Fourier's method;
- a numerical solution, integrating by means of finite differences and compare the results for $x = l/2$.

Numerical application: $\rho = 7800 \text{ kg m}^{-3}$, $l = 1 \text{ m}$, $A = 6 \times 10^{-4} \text{ m}^2$, $I = 5 \times 10^{-9} \text{ m}^4$, $E = 2 \times 10^{11} \text{ N m}^{-2}$, $h_0 = 0.02 \text{ m}$.

Solution:

1. Solution by Fourier's method

Let us consider a solution of the form

$$w(x, t) = Y(x) \cos(pt - \phi); \qquad (9.261)$$

from equation (9.257) we obtain the differential equation

$$Y^{(iv)} - \alpha^4 Y = 0, \qquad (9.262)$$

where

$$\alpha^4 = p^2 \frac{\rho A}{EI}. \qquad (9.263)$$

The solution of equation (9.262) and its derivatives Y', Y'', Y''' satisfy the matrix equation

$$\begin{bmatrix} Y(x) \\ \dfrac{Y'(x)}{\alpha} \\ \dfrac{Y''(x)}{\alpha^2} \\ \dfrac{Y'''(x)}{\alpha^3} \end{bmatrix} = \begin{bmatrix} f_1(\alpha x) & f_2(\alpha x) & f_3(\alpha x) & f_4(\alpha x) \\ f_4(\alpha x) & f_1(\alpha x) & f_2(\alpha x) & f_3(\alpha x) \\ f_3(\alpha x) & f_4(\alpha x) & f_1(\alpha x) & f_2(\alpha x) \\ f_2(\alpha x) & f_3(\alpha x) & f_4(\alpha x) & f_1(\alpha x) \end{bmatrix} \begin{bmatrix} Y(0) \\ \dfrac{Y'(0)}{\alpha} \\ \dfrac{Y''(0)}{\alpha^2} \\ \dfrac{Y'''(0)}{\alpha^3} \end{bmatrix}. \qquad (9.264)$$

Observing from Figure 9.11 that the conditions that take place for the bar at the ends are

$$Y(0) = Y'(0) = 0, \quad Y''(l) = Y'''(l) = 0, \qquad (9.265)$$

we obtain from the expression (9.264) the homogenous equations in $Y''(0)$, $Y'''(0)$

$$\alpha f_1(\alpha l) Y''(0) + f_2(\alpha l) Y'''(0) = 0, \quad \alpha f_4(\alpha l) Y''(0) + f_1(\alpha l) Y'''(0) = 0. \qquad (9.266)$$

The system (9.266) admits a nontrivial solution if

$$f_1^2(\beta) - f_2(\beta) f_4(\beta) = 0, \qquad (9.267)$$

where

$$\beta = \alpha l. \tag{9.268}$$

Taking into account equation (9.259), equation (9.267) becomes

$$\cosh \beta \cos \beta + 1 = 0, \tag{9.269}$$

with the solutions β_1, β_2, ..., β_n, ..., so that, from equation (9.263) and equation (9.268) we deduce the eigenpulsations

$$p_n = \frac{\beta_n^2}{l^2} \sqrt{\frac{EI}{\rho A}}. \tag{9.270}$$

Taking into account relations (9.264), (9.266), and (9.270), the functions $Y_n(x)$ read

$$Y_n(x) = D_n \Phi_n(x), \tag{9.271}$$

where D_n are constants, while $\Phi_n(x)$ are the eigenfunctions

$$\Phi_n(x) = f_1(\beta_n) f_4 \left(\beta_n \frac{x}{l} \right) - f_2(\beta_n) f_3 \left(\beta_n \frac{x}{l} \right), \tag{9.272}$$

with the property of orthogonality

$$\int_0^l \Phi_n(x) \Phi_m(x) \mathrm{d}x = 0, \quad \text{if } m \neq n. \tag{9.273}$$

Under these conditions, the general solution is

$$w(x, t) = \sum_{n=1}^{\infty} D_n \Phi_n(x) \cos(p_n t - \phi_n), \tag{9.274}$$

where D_n and ϕ_n are given by

$$D_n \cos \phi_n = \frac{\int_0^l w(x, t) \Phi_n(x) \mathrm{d}x}{\int_0^l \Phi_n^2(x) \mathrm{d}x}, \quad D_n \sin \phi_n = \frac{\int_0^l \frac{\partial w(x,0)}{\partial t} \Phi_n(x) \mathrm{d}x}{p_n^2 \int_0^l \Phi_n^2(x) \mathrm{d}x}. \tag{9.275}$$

In the considered case, with the conditions (9.258), it follows that

$$\phi_n = 0, \quad n \geq 0, \quad D_n = 0, \quad n \geq 1, \tag{9.276}$$

$$D_1 = \frac{h_0}{|f_1(\beta_1) f_4(\beta_1) - f_2(\beta_1) f_3(\beta_1)|}, \tag{9.277}$$

where $\beta_1 \approx 1.875$, $p_1 = \beta_1^2 \sqrt{EI/(\rho A)}/l^2$, hence

$$w(x, t) = h_0 \frac{f_1(\beta_1) f_4 \left(\beta_1 \frac{x}{l} \right) - f_2(\beta_1) f_3 \left(\beta_1 \frac{x}{l} \right)}{|f_1(\beta_1) f_4(\beta_1) - f_2(\beta_1) f_3(\beta_1)|} \cos p_1 t. \tag{9.278}$$

2. Numerical calculation
We consider the domain

$$[0, l] \times [0, T] \subset \mathbb{R}^2, \tag{9.279}$$

the number of division points being m and n, respectively.
We may write

$$h = \frac{l}{m}, \quad k = \frac{T}{n}. \tag{9.280}$$

From the relation

$$w(x, k) = w(x, 0) + k \frac{\partial w(x, 0)}{\partial t} + \mathcal{O}(k^2) \tag{9.281}$$

we obtain

$$w_{i,1} \approx w_{i,0} + k \frac{\partial w(x_i, 0)}{\partial t} + w_{i,0}, \quad i = \overline{0, m}. \tag{9.282}$$

On the other hand, the conditions

$$Y''(l) = Y'''(l) = 0, \tag{9.283}$$

are put; we take into account that

$$\begin{aligned}
Y(l - h) &= Y(l) - hY'(l) + \mathcal{O}(h^4), \\
Y(l - 2h) &= Y(l) - 2hY'(l) + \mathcal{O}(h^4), \\
Y(l - 2h) &= Y(l - h) - hY'(l - h) + \mathcal{O}(h^4),
\end{aligned} \tag{9.284}$$

from which

$$Y'(l) = Y'(l - h) = Y'(l - 2h), \tag{9.285}$$

and that

$$Y'(l) \approx \frac{w_{m-1,j} - w_{m,j}}{h}, \tag{9.286}$$

$$Y'(l - h) \approx \frac{w_{m-2,j} - w_{m-1,j}}{h}, \tag{9.287}$$

$$Y'(l - 2h) \approx \frac{w_{m-3,j} - w_{m-2,j}}{h}, \tag{9.288}$$

we are led to

$$w_{m-1,j} = 2w_{m-2,j} - w_{m-3,j}, \quad w_{m,j} = 2w_{m-1,j} - w_{m-2,j}. \tag{9.289}$$

On the other hand,

$$\frac{\partial^4 w}{\partial x^4} \approx \frac{w_{i+2,j} - 4w_{i+1,j} + 6w_{i,j} - 4w_{i-1,j} + w_{i-2,j}}{h^4}, \tag{9.290}$$

$$\frac{\partial^2 w}{\partial t^2} \approx \frac{w_{i,j+1} - 2w_{i,j} + w_{i,j-1}}{k^2}, \tag{9.291}$$

so that equation (9.257) takes the form

$$w_{i,j+1} = 2w_{i,j} - w_{i,j-1} - \lambda^2(w_{i+2,j} - 4w_{i+1,j} + 6w_{i,j} - 4w_{i-1,j} + w_{i-2,j}), \tag{9.292}$$

in finite differences, where

$$\lambda^2 = \frac{A\rho}{EI}\frac{k^2}{h^4}. \tag{9.293}$$

By formula (9.292), we may calculate the values w at the points A, B, and C, marked in Figure 9.12.

The values w for the points of type D or E cannot be calculated by this formula. We apply the formula (9.289) for these points and we obtain:

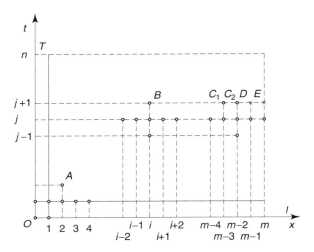

Figure 9.12   Working schema.

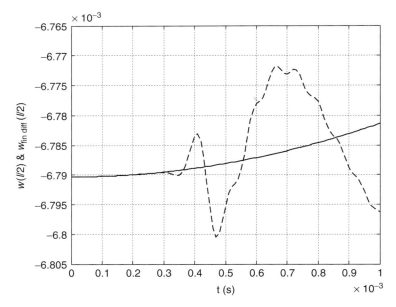

Figure 9.13   The analytic $w(l/2)$ (continuous line) and numerical $w(l/2)$ (dashed line) versus time.

- for the point D

$$w_{m-1,j+1} = 2w_{m-2,j+1} - w_{m-3,j+1} \qquad (9.294)$$

or

$$w_D = 2w_{C_1} - w_{C_2}; \qquad (9.295)$$

- for the point E

$$w_{m,j+1} = 2w_{m-1,j+1} - w_{m-2,j+1} \qquad (9.296)$$

or

$$w_E = 2w_D - w_{C_1}. \qquad (9.297)$$

The results obtained for $x = l/2$ are plotted in Figure 9.13.

FURTHER READING

Acton FS (1990). Numerical Methods that Work. 4th ed. Washington: Mathematical Association of America.

Atkinson K, Han W (2010). Theoretical Numerical Analysis: A Functional Analysis Framework. 3rd ed. New York: Springer-Verlag.

Babuška I, Práger M, Vitásek E (1966). Numerical Processes in Differential Equations. Prague: SNTI.

Bakhvalov N (1976). Méthodes Numérique. Moscou: Editions Mir (in French).

Boyce WE, DiPrima RC (2008). Elementary Differential Equations and Boundary Value Problems. 9th ed. Hoboken: John Wiley & Sons, Inc.

Burden RL, Faires L (2009). Numerical Analysis. 9th ed. Boston: Brooks/Cole.

Cheney EW, Kincaid DR (1997). Numerical Mathematics and Computing. 6th ed. Belmont: Thomson.

Dahlquist G, Björck Å (1974). Numerical Methods. Englewood Cliffs: Prentice Hall.

Den Hartog JP (1961). Strength of Materials. New York: Dover Books on Engineering.

Epperson JF (2007). An Introduction to Numerical Methods and Analysis. Hoboken: John Wiley & Sons, Inc.

Farlow SJ (1982). Partial Differential Equations for Scientists and Engineers. New York: John Wiley & Sons, Inc.

Gockenbach MS (2010). Partial Differential Equations: Analytical and Numerical Methods. 2nd ed. Philadelphia: SIAM.

Godunov SK, Reabenki VS (1977). Scheme de Calcul cu Diferenţe Finite. Bucureşti: Editura Tehnică (in Romanian).

Golub GH, van Loan CF (1996). Matrix Computations. 3rd ed. Baltimore: John Hopkins University Press.

Greenbaum A, Chartier TP (2012). Numerical Methods: Design, Analysis, and Computer Implementation of Algorithms. Princeton: Princeton University Press.

Grossmann C, Roos HG, Stynes M (2007). Numerical Treatment of Partial Differential Equations. Berlin: Springer-Verlag.

Heinbockel JH (2006). Numerical Methods for Scientific Computing. Victoria: Trafford Publishing.

Hibbeler RC (2010). Mechanics of Materials. 8th ed. Englewood Cliffs: Prentice Hall.

Hoffman JD (1992). Numerical Methods for Engineers and Scientists. New York: McGraw-Hill.

Iserles A (2008). A First Course in the Numerical Analysis of Differential Equations. 2nd ed. Cambridge: Cambridge University Press.

Ixaru LG (1979). Metode Numerice pentru Ecuaţii Diferenţiale cu Aplicaţii. Bucureşti: Editura Academiei Române (in Romanian).

Kharab A, Guenther RB (2011). An Introduction to Numerical Methods: A MATLAB Approach. 3rd ed. Boca Raton: CRC Press.

Kunz KS (1957). Numerical Analysis. New York: McGraw-Hill.

Lurie AI (2005). Theory of Elasticity. New York: Springer-Verlag.

Marciuk GI (1983). Metode de Analiză Numerică. Bucureşti: Editura Academiei Române (in Romanian).

Marciuk GI, Şaidurov VV (1981). Creşterea Preciziei Soluţiilor în Scheme cu Diferenţe. Bucureşti: Editura Academiei Române (in Romanian).

Marinescu G (1974). Analiza Numerică. Bucureşti: Editura Academiei Române (in Romanian).

Palm WJ III (2007). Mechanical Vibrations. Hoboken: John Wiley & Sons, Inc.

Pandrea N, Pârlac S (2000). Vibraţii Mecanice: Teorie şi Aplicaţii din Domeniile Autovehiculelor Rutiere şi din Domeniul Prelucrărilor Mecanice. Piteşti: Editura Universităţii din Piteşti (in Romanian)

Press WH, Teukolski SA, Vetterling WT, Flannery BP (2007). Numerical Recipes: The Art of Scientific Computing. 3rd ed. Cambridge: Cambridge University Press.

Quarteroni A, Sacco R, Saleri F (2010). Numerical Mathematics. 2nd ed. Berlin: Springer-Verlag.

Rivière B (2008). Discontinuous Galerkin Methods for Solving Elliptic and Parabolic Equations: Theory and Implementation. Philadelphia: SIAM.

Salvadori MG, Baron ML (1962). Numerical Methods in Engineering. Englewood Cliffs: Prentice Hall.

Samarski A, Andréev V (1978). Méthodes aux Différences pour Équations Elliptiques. Moscou: Editions Mir (in French).

Sauer T (2011). Numerical Analysis. 2nd ed. London: Pearson.

Shabana AA (2011). Computational Continuum Mechanics. 2nd ed. Cambridge: Cambridge University Press.

Simionescu I, Dranga M, Moise V (1995). Metode Numerice în Tehnică. Aplicaţii în FORTRAN. Bucureşti: Editura Tehnică (in Romanian).

Sinha AK (2010). Vibration of Mechanical Systems. Cambridge: Cambridge University Press.

Smith GD (1986). Numerical Solution of Partial Differential Equations: Finite Difference Methods. 3rd ed. Oxford: Oxford University Press.

Stănescu ND (2007). Metode Numerice. Bucureşti: Editura Didactică şi Pedagogică (in Romanian).

Stănescu ND, Munteanu L, Chiroiu V, Pandrea N (2007). Sisteme Dinamice: Teorie şi Aplicaţii. Volume 1. Bucureşti: Editura Academiei Române (in Romanian).

Stănescu ND, Munteanu L, Chiroiu V, Pandrea N (2011). Sisteme Dinamice. Teorie şi Applicaţii. Volume 2. Bucureşti: Editura Academiei Române (in Romanian).

Teodorescu PP, Nicorovici NAP (2010). Applications of the Theory of Groups in Mechanics and Physics. Dordrecht: Kluwer Academic Publishers.

Teodorescu PP (2008). Mechanical Systems: Classical Models. Volume 2: Mechanics of Discrete and Continuous Systems. Dordrecht: Springer-Verlag.

Teodorescu PP (2009). Mechanical Systems: Classical Models. Volume 3: Analytical Mechanics. Dordrecht: Springer-Verlag.

Udrişte C, Iftode V, Postolache M (1996). Metode Numerice de Calcul. Algoritmi şi Programe Turbo Pascal. Bucureşti: Editura Tehnică (in Romanian).

10

OPTIMIZATIONS

10.1 INTRODUCTION

Definition 10.1 A method of optimization solves the problem of determination of the minimum (maximum) of an objective (purpose) function U, where $U : \mathcal{D} \subset \mathbb{R}^n \to \mathbb{R}$.

Observation 10.1 Because the determination of the maximum of the objective function U is equivalent to the determination of the minimum of the function $-U$, it follows that we may limit ourselves to the determination of the minimum of the objective function.

In general, in case of optimization problems, the global minimum is of interest. Such a point of global minimum will be found between the points of local minimum; it can be unique or multiple (i.e., there exists only one point at which the function U takes its least value in $\mathcal{D}$, or there are several such points, possibly even an infinity).

For a local minimum $\bar{\mathbf{x}}$ of the function U we can write

$$\nabla U(\bar{\mathbf{x}}) = 0, \quad \nabla^2 U(\bar{\mathbf{x}}) > 0, \tag{10.1}$$

where ∇U is the gradient of U, that is,

$$\nabla U(\bar{\mathbf{x}}) = \left.\frac{\partial U}{\partial x_1}\right|_{\mathbf{x}=\bar{\mathbf{x}}} \mathbf{i}_1 + \cdots + \left.\frac{\partial U}{\partial x_n}\right|_{\mathbf{x}=\bar{\mathbf{x}}} \mathbf{i}_n, \tag{10.2}$$

and where $\mathbf{x} = (x_1, \ldots, x_n)^{\mathrm{T}}$ is a point of $\mathcal{D} \subset \mathbb{R}^n$, $\mathbf{i}_1, \ldots, \mathbf{i}_n$ are the unit vectors of the coordinate axes in $\mathbb{R}^n$, while $\nabla^2 U$ is the Hessian matrix

$$\nabla^2 U(\bar{\mathbf{x}}) = \begin{bmatrix} \dfrac{\partial^2 U}{\partial x_1^2} & \dfrac{\partial^2 U}{\partial x_1 \partial x_2} & \cdots & \dfrac{\partial^2 U}{\partial x_1 \partial x_n} \\ \cdots & \cdots & \cdots & \cdots \\ \dfrac{\partial^2 U}{\partial x_n \partial x_1} & \dfrac{\partial^2 U}{\partial x_n \partial x_2} & \cdots & \dfrac{\partial^2 U}{\partial x_n^2} \end{bmatrix}_{\mathbf{x}=\bar{\mathbf{x}}}. \tag{10.3}$$

Numerical Analysis with Applications in Mechanics and Engineering, First Edition.
Petre Teodorescu, Nicolae-Doru Stănescu, and Nicolae Pandrea.
© 2013 The Institute of Electrical and Electronics Engineers, Inc. Published 2013 by John Wiley & Sons, Inc.

Definition 10.2   Conditions (10.1) are called *optimality conditions*.

Observation 10.2

(i) The optimality conditions are sufficient for $\bar{\mathbf{x}}$ to be a global minimum for the function U, but they are not necessary.

(ii) The condition $\nabla^2 U(\bar{\mathbf{x}}) > 0$ requires that the Hessian matrix be positive definite at the point $\bar{\mathbf{x}}$.

To determine the global minimum of the function U, we can proceed intuitively in two modes:

- we start with different points $\mathbf{x}^{(0)}$, determining in each case the minimum of the function U; the point $\bar{\mathbf{x}}$ is that which leads to the least value between the minima previously obtained;
- we determine a local minimum; if, by a perturbation, the algorithm returns us to the same point, then it may be a serious candidate for the global minimum.

The classification of the optimization methods can be made after several criteria as

- from the point of view of the restrictions imposed to the variables we have optimization problems with or without restrictions;
- from the point of view of the objective function we may have linear optimization problems for which both the objective function and the restrictions are linear and nonlinear optimization problems in the opposite case;
- from the point of view of the calculation of the derivatives we encounter (i) optimization methods of Newton type, where the Hessian matrix $\nabla^2 U(\bar{\mathbf{x}})$ and the gradient vector ∇U are calculated, (ii) optimization methods of quasi-Newton type and optimization methods with conjugate gradients, where only the partial derivatives of first order are calculated, and (iii) optimization methods where no partial derivatives are calculated.

The optimization methods are iterative ones. They determine the value $\bar{\mathbf{x}}$ as a limit of a sequence $\mathbf{x}^{(0)}, \mathbf{x}^{(1)}, \ldots, \mathbf{x}^{(k)}, \ldots$ defined iteratively by the relation

$$\mathbf{x}^{(k+1)} = \mathbf{x}^{(k)} + \alpha_k \mathbf{p}^{(k)}, \quad k = 0, \ 1, \ \ldots, \tag{10.4}$$

where $\mathbf{p}^{(k)}$ is a direction of decreasing of the objective function U by the step k, while α_k is a positive real number such that

$$U(\mathbf{x}^{(k+1)}) < U(\mathbf{x}^{(k)}), \quad k = 0, \ 1, \ \ldots \tag{10.5}$$

The point $\mathbf{x}^{(0)} \in \mathcal{D}$ is necessary to start the algorithm.

10.2   MINIMIZATION ALONG A DIRECTION

Let us consider the function $f : \mathbb{R} \rightarrow \mathbb{R}$, the minimum of which we wish to determine.
  There can appear two situations:

- the derivative f' may be analytically determined. In this case, we have to solve the equation $f'(x) = 0$ and to verify which of its solutions are local minima. The global minimum will, obviously, be the smallest value of these local minima and will correspond to one or several points at which $f'(x) = 0$;
- the derivative f' cannot be analytically determined. In this case, we have to go through two steps:

(a) localization of the minimum, that is, the determination of an interval (a, b) of the real axis that contains the point of minimum;

(b) reduction of the length of the interval (a, b) until it has a length strictly smaller than an imposed value ε

$$|b - a| < \varepsilon. \tag{10.6}$$

Observation 10.3   Let us denote the representation error of the numbers in the computer by ε_m, that is, the minimal distance between two numbers, which can be represented in the computer, for which the two representations differ. Under these conditions, ε must fulfill the relation

$$\varepsilon \geq \sqrt{\varepsilon_m}. \tag{10.7}$$

Indeed, let a be a point sufficiently near to the point of minimum, so that

$$f'(a) \approx 0. \tag{10.8}$$

Taylor's relation around the point a leads to

$$f(b) \approx f(a) + \frac{(b - a)^2}{2!} f''(a). \tag{10.9}$$

The values a and b must satisfy the relation

$$|f(b) - f(a)| > \varepsilon_m |f(a)|, \tag{10.10}$$

so that the representations of $f(a)$ and $f(b)$ be different. We thus deduce

$$|b - a| \approx \sqrt{2\varepsilon_m \frac{|f(a)|}{|f''(a)|}} = |a| \sqrt{\varepsilon_m} \sqrt{2 \frac{|f(a)|}{a^2 |f''(a)|}}. \tag{10.11}$$

Moreover, if $\sqrt{2|f(a)|/(a^2 f''(a))}$ is of order $\mathcal{O}(1)$, then $|b - a|$ is of order $\mathcal{O}(|a|\sqrt{\varepsilon_m})$ and the condition

$$|b - a| < \varepsilon |a| \tag{10.12}$$

leads to equation (10.7).

10.2.1   Localization of the Minimum

To localize the minimum of a function $f : \mathbb{R} \to \mathbb{R}$, at least three points are necessary.

Considering three points a, b and c, so that $a < b < c$, the minimum x_m is situated in the interval (a, c) if $f(a) > f(b)$ and $f(b) < f(c)$.

If we have two values a and b, with $a < b$ and $f(a) > f(b)$, we use the following algorithm for the localization of the minimum:

– given: a, b, $a < b$, $f(a) > f(b)$;
– calculate $f_a = f(a)$, $f_b = f(b)$;
– repeat
  – calculate $c = b + k(b - a)$, $f_c = f(c)$;
  – if $f_c > f_b$
      then $x_m \in (a, c)$; stop;
      else
          – calculate $a = b$, $b = c$, $f_a = f_b$, $f_b = f_c$;
      until false.

Observation 10.4

(i) Usually, the searching step is not taken constant ($k = 1$), but it increases from one step to another, so that the localization of the minimum does take place as fast as possible

$$h_{j+1} = kh_j, \quad k > 1.$$
(10.13)

(ii) The algorithm may be improved by using a parabolic interpolation. Thus, a parabola passes through the points $A(a, f(a))$, $B(b, f(b))$ and $C(c, f(c))$, whose equation is

$$g(x) = \frac{(x - b)(x - c)}{(a - b)(a - c)} f(a) + \frac{(x - a)(x - c)}{(b - a)(b - c)} f(b) + \frac{(x - a)(x - b)}{(c - a)(c - b)} f(c)$$

$$= d_2 x^2 + d_1 x + d_0.$$
(10.14)

Let us denote the point of minimum of this parabola by

$$x^* = -\frac{d_1}{2d_2}.$$
(10.15)

The following situations may occur:

- $x^* > c$. In this case it requires that x^* not be very far from the point c, so that $|x^* - c| < \lambda |c - b|$, where we may take, for example, $\lambda = 50$;
- $x^* < a$. The situation is similar to the previous one, replacing the point c by the point a;
- $x^* \in (b, c)$, $f(b) > f(x^*)$, $f(x^*) < c$. It follows that the minimum of the function is between the points b and c;
- $x^* \in (a, b)$, $f(a) > f(x^*)$, $f(x^*) < f(b)$. The case is analogous to the preceding one, the minimum of the function f now taking place between a and b;
- $x^* \in (b, c)$, $f(a) \leq f(x^*)$ or $f(x^*) \geq f(c)$. The algorithm fails;
- $x^* \in (a, b)$, $f(a) \leq f(x^*)$, $f(x^*) \geq f(b)$. The algorithm fails.

10.2.2 Determination of the Minimum

There are two ways to solve the problem.

The first method supposes the reduction of the interval in which the minimum has been localized by successive steps, until the point of minimum is obtained with the desired accuracy. The method has the advantage of reliability (the point of minimum has been correctly determined), but also the disadvantage of a slow convergence.

A second method to determine a point of minimum consists in replacing the function $f(x)$ by another function $g(x)$, which does pass through certain points, common with $f(x)$, and hence to be $g(x_i) = f(x_i)$ for certain x_i of the interval in which the minimum takes place; it requires now the minimum of the function $g(x)$. The method has the advantage of a faster convergence as in case of the previous one, but also the disadvantage of eventually leading to great errors if the point of minimum of the function $g(x)$ is not in the considered interval. Usually, we take a parabola for $g(x)$, because only three points are necessary to determine it.

In connection with the first method, let us present the golden section algorithm[1] in the following:

- given: $a < b < c$, $f(a) > f(b)$, $f(b) < f(c)$, $\varepsilon > \sqrt{\varepsilon_m}$, $w = 0.38197$;

---

[1]The algorithm was presented by Jack Carl Kiefer (1924–1981) in 1953.

- calculate $w_1 = 1 - w$, $x_0 = a$, $x_3 = c$, $f_0 = f(a)$, $f_3 = f(c)$;
- if $|c - a| > |b - a|$
    then $x_1 = b$, $x_2 = b + w|c - b|$;
    else $x_2 = b$, $x_1 = b - w|b - a|$;
- calculate $f_1 = f(x_1)$, $f_2 = f(x_2)$;
- while $|x_3 - x_0| > \varepsilon|x_1 + x_2|$ do
    - if $f_2 < f_1$
        then $x_0 = x_1$, $x_1 = x_2$, $x_2 = w_1 x_1 + w x_3$, $f_0 = f_1$, $f_1 = f_2$, $f_2 = f(x_2)$;
        else $x_3 = x_2$, $x_2 = x_1$, $x_1 = w_1 x_2 + w x_0$, $f_3 = f_2$, $f_2 = f_1$, $f_1 = f(x_1)$;
    - if $f_1 < f_2$
        then $x_{\min} = x_1$, $f_{\min} = f_1$;
        else $x_{\min} = x_2$, $f_{\min} = f_2$.

The idea of the golden section algorithm is based on considerations which we further show. Let us consider three points a, b and c with

$$a < b < c, \quad f_a = f(a) > f(b) = f_b, \quad f_b < f_c = f(c). \tag{10.16}$$

Let

$$w = \frac{b - a}{c - a}, \quad 1 - w = \frac{c - b}{c - a}. \tag{10.17}$$

We shall try to find a point $x \in (a, c)$ so as to diminish the interval in which the minimum will be determined. We suppose also that (b, c) is an interval of length greater than (a, c) and that x is in (b, c). Let us denote

$$z = \frac{x - b}{c - a}. \tag{10.18}$$

The point of minimum will be either in the interval (a, x) or in the interval (b, c). We may write

$$\frac{x - a}{c - a} = w + z, \quad \frac{c - b}{c - a} = 1 - w. \tag{10.19}$$

Imposing the condition of equality of the two ratios of (10.19) (the most unfavorable case), it follows that the relation

$$z = 1 - 2w. \tag{10.20}$$

But the same method has been used also for the determination of the point b at the previous step

$$\frac{x - b}{c - b} = \frac{b - a}{c - a} = w, \tag{10.21}$$

from which we may successively deduce

$$x - b = w(c - b) = z(c - a), \quad 1 - w = \frac{c - b}{c - a} = \frac{z}{w}. \tag{10.22}$$

We thus obtained the equation

$$w^2 - 3w + 1 = 0, \tag{10.23}$$

which has the solution (w must be in the interval $(0, 1)$)

$$w = \frac{3 - \sqrt{5}}{2} \approx 0.38197; \tag{10.24}$$

hence, it follows that the position of the point x

$$x = b + w(c - b) = c - (1 - w)(c - b).$$ (10.25)

We will present Brent's algorithm[2] of the second method:

> - given: a, c, $f(a)$, $f(c)$, n_{max}, $w = 0.381966$, ε;
> - calculate $b = c$, $f_b = f_c$, $u = b$, $f_u = f_b$;
> - if $f_b < f_a$
>   then $t = b$, $f_t = f_b$, $v = a$, $f_v = f_a$;
>   else $t = a$, $f_t = f_a$, $v = b$, $f_v = f_b$;
> - set $i = 1$, $\delta u = 0$, $\delta x = b - a$;
> - calculate $x = 0.5(b + a)$, $f_x = f(x)$;
> - while $(b - a) > \varepsilon(2|x| + 1)$ and $i \leq n_{max}$ do
>   - calculate $x_m = 0.5(b + a)$;
>   - if $|\delta x| > 0, 5\delta u$ or $u - a < \varepsilon(2|x| + 1)$ or $b - u < \varepsilon(2|x| + 1)$
>   then
>   - if $x > x_m$
>   then $\delta_x = w(a - x)$;
>   else $\delta_x = w(b - x)$, $\delta_u = \max(|b - x|, |a - x|)$;
>   else $r = (x - t)(f_x - f_v)$, $q = (x - v)(f_x - f_t)$, $p = (x - v)q - (x - t)r$,
> $\delta_x = -0.5\frac{p}{q-r}$, $\delta_u = |\delta_x|$;
>   - calculate $f_u = f(u)$, $u = x + \delta_x$;
>   - if $f_u \leq f_x$
>   then
>   - if $u \geq x$
>   then $a = x$;
>   else $b = x$;
>   - calculate $v = t$, $t = x$, $x = u$, $f_v = f_t$, $f_t = f_x$, $f_x = f_u$;
>   else
>   - if $u < x$
>   then $a = u$;
>   else $b = u$;
>   - if $f_u \leq f_t$ or $t = x$
>   then $v = t$, $t = u$, $f_v = f_t$, $f_t = f_u$;
>   else
>   - if $f_u \leq f_v$ or $v = x$ or $x = t$
>   then $v = u$, $f_v = f_u$;
>   - set $i = i + 1$.

Brent's algorithm uses six points a, b, u, v, t, x, not necessarily distinct, which have the following meanings: a and b are the points of the limits of the interval which contains the minimum; x is the point at which the function f takes the smallest value until a given moment; t is the value previous to x; v is the value previous to t, while u is the point at which the function f has been calculated last time. The parabolic interpolation is made through the points $(x, f(x))$, $(t, f(t))$ and $(v, f(v))$.

Brent's algorithm combines the assurance of the first method with the speed of the parabolic interpolation. To do this, we must take certain precautions so that the parabolic interpolation can be accepted, that is:

- the calculated minimum be in the interval (a, b);

---

[2]Richard Pierce Brent (1946–) published this algorithm (also known as *Brent's method*) in 1973.

- the displacement with respect to the last value which approximates the minimum of f be at most equal to half of the previous displacement, to be sure that we have a convergent process;
- the calculated point of minimum u is not be very near to another value previously calculated, that is, $|u - p| > \varepsilon_p$.

10.3   CONJUGATE DIRECTIONS

A method to determine the minimum of a function $U : \mathbb{R}^n \to \mathbb{R}^n$ may be conceived as a repetition of the method of one-dimensional search along the directions $\mathbf{i}_1, \mathbf{i}_2, \ldots, \mathbf{i}_n$, not necessarily in this order. We thus determine a partial minimum of the function U, realizing the minimization of this function along the direction $\mathbf{i}_{j_1}$; let U_1 be this minimum. We minimize then along the direction $\mathbf{i}_{j_2}$, resulting in the minimum U_2 and so on until $\mathbf{i}_{j_n}$, obtaining the minimum U_n. In the above procedure, we have $j_k \in \{1, 2, \ldots, n\}$ and $\mathbf{i}_{j_k} \neq \mathbf{i}_{j_l}$ for $j_k \neq j_l$, $k = \overline{1, n}$, $l = \overline{1, n}$. Moreover, there exists the sequence of inequalities

$$U_1 \geq U_2 \geq \cdots \geq U_n. \tag{10.26}$$

The algorithm is as follows:

– given: $\mathbf{x}^{(0)}$, $U(\mathbf{x})$;
– for j from 1 to n do $\mathbf{x}^{(j)} = \min_{\alpha \in \mathbf{R}}[U(\mathbf{x}^{(j-1)} + \alpha \mathbf{i}_j)]$.

Definition 10.3   The method considered above is called *the method of one-dimensional search*.

Observation 10.5   The method is very simple, but has the disadvantage that either the minimum is not found or the time of work of the algorithm is sufficiently great to be inefficient.

The problem is put to determine other more efficient displacement directions.

Definition 10.4   The decreasing directions for which the method of one-dimensional search converges are called *conjugate directions*.

Let us suppose that $U(\mathbf{x})$ is twice differentiable with continuous derivatives. We may define the quadratic form

$$\phi(\mathbf{x}) = U(\mathbf{x}^{(k)}) + \begin{bmatrix} x_1 - x_1^{(k)} & \cdots & x_n - x_n^{(k)} \end{bmatrix} \begin{bmatrix} \dfrac{\partial U}{\partial x_1} \\ \vdots \\ \dfrac{\partial U}{\partial x_n} \end{bmatrix}_{\mathbf{x}=\mathbf{x}^{(k)}}$$

$$+ \frac{1}{2}\begin{bmatrix} x_1 - x_1^{(k)} & \cdots & x_n - x_n^{(k)} \end{bmatrix} \begin{bmatrix} \dfrac{\partial^2 U}{\partial x_1^2} & \cdots & \dfrac{\partial^2 U}{\partial x_1 \partial x_n} \\ \cdots & \cdots & \cdots \\ \dfrac{\partial^2 U}{\partial x_n \partial x_1} & \cdots & \dfrac{\partial^2 U}{\partial x_n^2} \end{bmatrix}_{\mathbf{x}=\mathbf{x}_k^{(k)}} \begin{bmatrix} x_1 - x_1^{(k)} \\ \vdots \\ x_n - x_n^{(k)} \end{bmatrix}. \tag{10.27}$$

We observe that the quadratic form ϕ coincides with the three terms of the expansion into a Taylor series of the function $U(\mathbf{x})$ about $\mathbf{x}^{(k)}$. The previous expression may be written in the form

$$\phi(\mathbf{x}) = U(\mathbf{x}^{(k)}) + (\mathbf{x} - \mathbf{x}^{(k)})\nabla U(\mathbf{x})|_{\mathbf{x}=\mathbf{x}^{(k)}} + \frac{1}{2}(\mathbf{x} - \mathbf{x}^{(k)})\nabla^2 U(\mathbf{x})|_{\mathbf{x}=\mathbf{x}^{(k)}} \tag{10.28}$$

too. Moreover

$$\nabla\phi(\mathbf{x}) = \nabla U(\mathbf{x})|_{\mathbf{x}=\mathbf{x}^{(k)}} + \nabla^2 U(\mathbf{x})|_{\mathbf{x}=\mathbf{x}^{(k)}}(\mathbf{x} - \mathbf{x}^{(k)}). \tag{10.29}$$

Let us denote by $\mathbf{p}^{(k)}$ the conjugate directions. The point $\mathbf{x}^{(k)}$ is the point which minimizes the function $\phi(\mathbf{x}^{(k-1)} + \alpha\mathbf{p}^{(k-1)})$, hence $\nabla U(\mathbf{x})|_{\mathbf{x}=\mathbf{x}^{(k)}}$ must be normal to the direction $\mathbf{p}^{(k-1)}$, which is written in the form

$$[\mathbf{p}^{(k-1)}]^T \nabla U(\mathbf{x})|_{\mathbf{x}=\mathbf{x}^{(k)}} = 0. \tag{10.30}$$

Moreover, the gradient of the function $U(\mathbf{x})$, calculated at $\mathbf{x} = \mathbf{x}^{(k+1)}$, must be normal to the direction $\mathbf{p}^{(k-1)}$, otherwise $\mathbf{p}^{(k-1)}$ would not be a conjugate direction of minimization. Hence,

$$[\mathbf{p}^{(k-1)}]^T \nabla U(\mathbf{x})|_{\mathbf{x}=\mathbf{x}^{(k+1)}} = 0 \tag{10.31}$$

and equation (10.29) leads to

$$\nabla\Phi(\mathbf{x}) = \nabla U(\mathbf{x})|_{\mathbf{x}=\mathbf{x}^{(k+1)}} + \nabla^2 U(\mathbf{x})|_{\mathbf{x}=\mathbf{x}^{(k+1)}}(\mathbf{x} - \mathbf{x}^{(k+1)}). \tag{10.32}$$

Subtracting relations (10.32) and (10.29) one from the other, we get

$$\nabla U(\mathbf{x})|_{\mathbf{x}=\mathbf{x}^{(k+1)}} - \nabla U(\mathbf{x})|_{\mathbf{x}=\mathbf{x}^{(k)}} + [\nabla^2 U(\mathbf{x})|_{\mathbf{x}=\mathbf{x}^{(k+1)}} - \nabla^2 U(\mathbf{x})|_{\mathbf{x}=\mathbf{x}^{(k)}}](\mathbf{x} - \mathbf{x}^{(k+1)})$$
$$+ \nabla^2 U(\mathbf{x})|_{\mathbf{x}=\mathbf{x}^{(k)}}(\mathbf{x}^{(k)} - \mathbf{x}^{(k+1)}) = \mathbf{0}. \tag{10.33}$$

Taking now into account that $\mathbf{x}^{(k+1)}$ has been determined by the displacement along the conjugate direction $\mathbf{p}^{(k)}$, it follows that

$$\nabla U(\mathbf{x})|_{\mathbf{x}=\mathbf{x}^{(k+1)}} = \nabla U(\mathbf{x})|_{\mathbf{x}=\mathbf{x}^{(k)}} + \nabla^2 U(\mathbf{x})|_{\mathbf{x}=\mathbf{x}^{(k)}}(\mathbf{x}^{(k+1)} - \mathbf{x}^{(k)})$$
$$= \nabla U(\mathbf{x})|_{\mathbf{x}=\mathbf{x}^{(k)}} + \alpha_k \nabla^2 U(\mathbf{x})|_{\mathbf{x}=\mathbf{x}^{(k)}} \mathbf{p}^{(k)}, \tag{10.34}$$

with $\alpha_k \in \mathbb{R}$. Taking into account formulae (10.29) and (10.30), the product of the last relation and $[\mathbf{p}^{(k-1)}]^T$ leads to

$$[\mathbf{p}^{(k-1)}]^T \nabla^2 U(\mathbf{x})|_{\mathbf{x}=\mathbf{x}^{(k)}}[\mathbf{p}^{(k)}] = 0. \tag{10.35}$$

Definition 10.5   Two directions which satisfy condition (10.35) are called G -*conjugate directions*.

Observation 10.6

(i) If ϕ is a quadratic form, then its minimum is obtained after n displacements along n conjugate directions defined by relation (10.35). Therefore, it is requested that at each minimization stage of ϕ along the direction $\mathbf{p}^{(k)}$, the minimum must be determined so that

$$[\mathbf{p}^{(k)}]^T \nabla U(\mathbf{x})|_{\mathbf{x}=\mathbf{x}^{(k)}} = 0. \tag{10.36}$$

(ii) If the function U is not a quadratic form, then its minimum is not obtained after n displacements, but we arrive sufficiently near to it.

10.4 POWELL'S ALGORITHM

The Powell algorithm[3] gives a procedure to determine n conjugate directions without using the matrix $\nabla^2 U(\mathbf{x})$ and is as follows:

- given: $\mathbf{x}^{(0)}$, $U(\mathbf{x})$, ε, n, $iter$;
- for l from 1 to $iter$ do
  - for j from 1 to n do
    - set $\mathbf{p}^{(j)} = \mathbf{i}_j$;
  - for k from 1 to $n-1$ do
    - for i from 1 to n do
      - determine $\mathbf{x}^{(i)}$ so that $\min_{\alpha \in \mathbf{R}}[U(\mathbf{x}^{(i-1)} + \alpha \mathbf{p}^{(i)})]$;
    - for i from 1 to $n-1$ do $\mathbf{p}^{(i)} = \mathbf{p}^{(i+1)}$;
    - set $\mathbf{p}^{(n)} = \mathbf{p}^{(n)} - \mathbf{x}^{(0)}$;
    - determine $\mathbf{x}^{(0)}$ so that $\min_{\alpha \in \mathbf{R}}[U(\mathbf{x}^n) + \alpha \mathbf{p}^{(n)}]$;
  - if $|U - U_0| < \varepsilon(1 - |U|)$
        then stop (the minimum has been determined).

Powell showed that, for a quadratic form ϕ, k iterations lead to a set of directions $\mathbf{p}^{(i)}$, of which the latter k iterations are G-conjugate if the minimizations along the directions $\mathbf{p}^{(i)}$ have been exactly made.

In the frame of the algorithm, an iteration means $n+1$ minimizations made along the directions $\mathbf{p}^{(1)}$, $\mathbf{p}^{(2)}$, ..., $\mathbf{p}^{(n)}$ and $\mathbf{p}^{(n)} - \mathbf{x}^{(0)}$.

Powell's algorithm has the tendency to lead to linearly dependent directions. To avoid this phenomenon, we have two possibilities, that is:

- either we use new initial positions for the directions $\mathbf{p}^{(j)} = \mathbf{i}_j$ after $n+1$ iterations;
- or we renounce to the direction $\mathbf{p}^{(j)}$ which has produced the greatest decrease of the function $U(\mathbf{x})$.

10.5 METHODS OF GRADIENT TYPE

The methods of gradient type are characterized by the use of the gradient of the function to be optimized, $\nabla U(\mathbf{x})$.

10.5.1 The Gradient Method

This method rises from the observation that the given $n-1$-dimensional hypersurfaces of equations

$$U(\mathbf{x}) = C_i = \text{const}, \quad i = 1, \ 2, \ \ldots, \tag{10.37}$$

are disposed so that the constants C_i take more and more greater values when we go along the positive direction of the gradient.

Definition 10.6 The hypersurfaces defined by relation (10.37) bear the name of level surfaces of the function U.

[3]Michael James David Powell (1936–) purposed this method in 1964.

The gradient method supposes the construction of the sequence of iterations

$$\mathbf{x}^{(0)} \text{ arbitrary}, \quad \mathbf{x}^{(k+1)} = \mathbf{x}^{(k)} + \alpha_k \nabla U(\mathbf{x}^{(k)}), \tag{10.38}$$

where

$$U(\mathbf{x}^{(k)}) > U(\mathbf{x}^{(k+1)}). \tag{10.39}$$

Let us notice that the direction $\mathbf{p}^{(k)} = -\nabla U(\mathbf{x}^{(k)})$ is a direction of decreasing of the value of the function $U(\mathbf{x})$ at the point $\mathbf{x}^{(k)}$ (as a matter of fact, it is the direction of maximum decreasing for the function $U(\mathbf{x})$ at the point $\mathbf{x}^{(k)}$).

The real value α_k is determined by using one of the methods previously emphasized. Moreover, if the value α_k is exactly determined, then between the gradients of the points $\mathbf{x}^{(k)}$ and $\mathbf{x}^{(k+1)}$ there exist the relations

$$\nabla U(\mathbf{x}^{(k)}) \perp \nabla U(\mathbf{x}^{(k+1)}) \Rightarrow [\nabla U(\mathbf{x}^{(k)})]^{\mathrm{T}} \nabla U(\mathbf{x}^{(k+1)}) = 0. \tag{10.40}$$

Definition 10.7 If the value of the scalar α_k is exactly determined at each step k, then we say that the gradient method uses an optimal step or a Cauchy step.

Any algorithm which uses the gradient of the objective function $U(\mathbf{x})$ has the following structure:

– given: $\mathbf{x}^{(0)}$, $U(\mathbf{x})$, $\nabla U(\mathbf{x})$, ε, iter;
– set
$\mathbf{x} = \mathbf{x}^{(0)}$, $U_k = U(\mathbf{x}^{(0)})$, $\nabla U(\mathbf{x}^{(k)}) = \nabla U(\mathbf{x}^{(0)})$, $\mathbf{p} = \nabla U(\mathbf{x}^{(k)})$;
– for i from 1 to iter do
  – determine $\mathbf{x}$ so that $\min_{\alpha \in \mathbf{R}}[\mathbf{x}^{(k)} + \alpha \mathbf{p}]$;
  – set
$U_{k+1} = U(\mathbf{x})$, $\nabla U(\mathbf{x}^{(k+1)}) = \nabla U(\mathbf{x})$;
  – if $U_{k+1} \geq U_k$
    then the algorithm failed; stop;
    else perform test of convergence; actualize decreasing direction $\mathbf{p}$;
  – set $U_k = U_{k+1}$.

Observation 10.7

(i) A one-dimensional minimization method may be chosen, for example, Brent's method.

(ii) The gradient method does not require an exact calculus for the one-dimensional minimization. Therefore, we must specify a certain sufficiency criterion to determine the one-dimensional minimum. An idea is that of using the directional derivative in the form

$$|[\mathbf{p}^{(k)}]^{\mathrm{T}} \nabla U[\mathbf{x}^{(k)} + \alpha_k \mathbf{p}^{(k)}]| \leq \eta |[\mathbf{p}^{(k)}]^{\mathrm{T}} \nabla U(\mathbf{x}^{(k)})|, \quad 0 \leq \eta \leq 1. \tag{10.41}$$

Thus, for $\eta = 0$ it follows that $[\mathbf{p}^{(k)}]^{\mathrm{T}} \nabla U(\mathbf{x}^{(k+1)}) = 0$, hence the unidirectional minimization has been exactly made.

We may impose also a condition of sufficient decreasing in the form

$$\nabla U(\mathbf{x}^{(k+1)}) - \nabla U(\mathbf{x}^{(k)}) \leq -\mu \alpha_k [\nabla U(\mathbf{x}^{(k)})]^{\mathrm{T}} \mathbf{p}^{(k)}. \tag{10.42}$$

In general, we take

$$10^{-5} \leq \mu \leq 10^{-1}, \quad \mu < \eta < 1. \tag{10.43}$$

(iii) Concerning the convergence test, we may use many criteria. One of the criteria is defined by the relation

$$\|\mathbf{x}^{(k+1)} - \mathbf{x}^{(k)}\| \le \varepsilon(1 + \|\mathbf{x}^{(k+1)}\|). \tag{10.44}$$

A second criterion reads

$$\|U(\mathbf{x}^{(k+1)}) - U(\mathbf{x}^{(k)})\| \le \varepsilon(1 + \|U(\mathbf{x}^{(k+1)})\|). \tag{10.45}$$

Sometimes one uses a criterion of the form

$$\|\nabla U(\mathbf{x}^{(k+1)})\| \le \varepsilon, \tag{10.46}$$

but its fulfillment does not necessarily mean that U has a minimum at that point (it can be a point of maximum or a mini−max one).

10.5.2   The Conjugate Gradient Method

Let us consider the quadratic form

$$\phi(\mathbf{x}) = \nabla U(\mathbf{x}^{(k)}) + [\mathbf{x} - \mathbf{x}^{(k)}]^T \nabla U(\mathbf{x}^{(k)}) + \frac{1}{2}[\mathbf{x} - \mathbf{x}^{(k)}]^T \nabla^2 U(\mathbf{x}^{(k)})[\mathbf{x} - \mathbf{x}^{(k)}] \tag{10.47}$$

and a point $\mathbf{x}^{(k+1)}$ for which we can write

$$\begin{aligned} \nabla\phi(\mathbf{x}^{(k+1)}) &= \nabla U(\mathbf{x}^{(k)}) + \nabla^2 U(\mathbf{x}^{(k)})[\mathbf{x}^{(k+1)} - \mathbf{x}^{(k)}] \\ &= \nabla U(\mathbf{x}^{(k)}) + \alpha_k \nabla^2 U(\mathbf{x}^{(k)})\mathbf{p}^{(k)}, \end{aligned} \tag{10.48}$$

where

$$\mathbf{x}^{(k+1)} = \mathbf{x}^{(k)} + \alpha_k \mathbf{p}^{(k)}, \tag{10.49}$$

while the decreasing directions are given by

$$\mathbf{p}^{(k+1)} = -\nabla U(\mathbf{x}^{(k+1)}) + \beta_k \mathbf{p}^{(k)}. \tag{10.50}$$

Imposing the condition that the directions $\mathbf{p}^{(k)}$ and $\mathbf{p}^{(k+1)}$ be G -conjugate

$$[\mathbf{p}^{(k+1)}]^T \nabla^2 U(\mathbf{x}^{(k)})\mathbf{p}^{(k)} = 0, \tag{10.51}$$

transposing relation (10.50)

$$[\mathbf{p}^{(k+1)}]^T = -[\nabla U(\mathbf{x}^{(k+1)})]^T + \beta_k[\mathbf{p}^{(k)}]^T \tag{10.52}$$

and multiplying it at the right by $\nabla^2 U(\mathbf{x}^{(k)})\mathbf{p}^{(k)}$, we get

$$\beta_k = \frac{[\nabla U(\mathbf{x}^{(k+1)})]^T \nabla^2 U(\mathbf{x}^{(k)})\mathbf{p}^{(k)}}{[\mathbf{p}^{(k)}]^T \nabla^2 U(\mathbf{x}^{(k)})\mathbf{p}^{(k)}}. \tag{10.53}$$

Multiplying relation (10.52) by $\nabla^2 U(\mathbf{x}^{(k)})\mathbf{p}^{(k+1)}$, it now follows that

$$[\mathbf{p}^{(k+1)}]^T \nabla^2 U(\mathbf{x}^{(k)})\mathbf{p}^{(k+1)} = -[\nabla U(\mathbf{x}^{(k+1)})]^T \nabla^2 U(\mathbf{x}^{(k)})\mathbf{p}^{(k+1)}, \tag{10.54}$$

where we take into account relation (10.51).

On the other hand, formula (10.48) leads to

$$\nabla^2 U(\mathbf{x}^{(k)})\mathbf{p}^{(k)} = \frac{\nabla U(\mathbf{x}^{(k+1)}) - \nabla U(\mathbf{x}^{(k)})}{\alpha_k}, \tag{10.55}$$

relation which holds if $\nabla U(\mathbf{x}^{(k+1)})$ and $\nabla U(\mathbf{x}^{(k)})$ are normal to each other, hence

$$[\nabla U(\mathbf{x}^{(k+1)})]^T \nabla U(\mathbf{x}^{(k)}) = 0. \tag{10.56}$$

Relation (10.53) leads now to

$$\beta_k = -\frac{[\nabla U(\mathbf{x}^{(k+1)})]^T \nabla^2 U(\mathbf{x}^{(k)})\mathbf{p}^{(k)}}{[\nabla U(\mathbf{x}^{(k)})]^T \nabla^2 U(\mathbf{x}^{(k)})\mathbf{p}^{(k)}} = \frac{[\nabla U(\mathbf{x}^{(k+1)})]^T \nabla U(\mathbf{x}^{(k+1)})}{[\nabla U(\mathbf{x}^{(k)})]^T \nabla U(\mathbf{x}^{(k)})}. \tag{10.57}$$

Multiplying relation (10.48) by $[\nabla U(\mathbf{x}^{(k+1)})]^T$ and by $[\nabla U(\mathbf{x}^{(k)})]^T$ and imposing condition (10.56) of perpendicularity of the vectors $\nabla U(\mathbf{x}^{(k)})$ and $\nabla U(\mathbf{x}^{(k+1)})$, we obtain

$$\alpha_k = -\frac{[\nabla U(\mathbf{x}^{(k)})]^T \nabla U(\mathbf{x}^{(k)})\mathbf{p}^{(k)}}{[\nabla U(\mathbf{x}^{(k)})]^T \nabla^2 U(\mathbf{x}^{(k)})\mathbf{p}^{(k)}} = \frac{[\nabla U(\mathbf{x}^{(k+1)})]^T \nabla U(\mathbf{x}^{(k+1)})}{[\nabla U(\mathbf{x}^{(k+1)})]^T \nabla^2 U(\mathbf{x}^{(k)})\mathbf{p}^{(k)}}. \tag{10.58}$$

On the other hand, the value α_k of equation (10.48) is the value obtained from the approximation $\min U_{\alpha \in \mathbf{R}}[\mathbf{x}^{(k)} + \alpha \mathbf{p}^{(k)}]$. Indeed, it is sufficient to show that the vectors $\mathbf{p}^{(k)}$ and $\nabla U(\mathbf{x}^{(k+1)})$ are normal to each other

$$[\mathbf{p}^{(k)}]^T \nabla U(\mathbf{x}^{(k+1)}) = 0. \tag{10.59}$$

But, from equation (10.48), equation (10.50), and equation (10.54) it follows that

$$[\mathbf{p}^{(k)}]^T \nabla U(\mathbf{x}^{(k+1)}) = \beta_{k-1} [\mathbf{p}^{(k-1)}]^T \nabla U(\mathbf{x}^{(k)}). \tag{10.60}$$

We thus deduce that if at the previous step the one-dimensional search has been exactly made, that is, α_{k-1} has been determined so that $\mathbf{p}^{(k+1)}$ and $\nabla U(\mathbf{x}^{(k)})$ be normal to each other, then we have relation (10.59) too.

Observation 10.8   We have thus obtained the G-conjugate directions $\mathbf{p}^{(k)}$ for which it has not been necessary to know the Hessian matrix, but for which it is necessary that the weights α_k be exactly calculated.

We use several variants to determine β_k, that is:

- the Fletcher–Reeves method[4] for which

$$\beta_k = \frac{[\nabla U(\mathbf{x}^{(k+1)})]^T \nabla U(\mathbf{x}^{(k+1)})}{[\nabla U(\mathbf{x}^{(k)})]^T \nabla U(\mathbf{x}^{(k)})}; \tag{10.61}$$

- the Polak–Ribière method[5] given by

$$\beta_k = \frac{[\nabla U(\mathbf{x}^{(k+1)})]^T \mathbf{y}^{(k)}}{[\nabla U(\mathbf{x}^{(k)})]^T \nabla U(\mathbf{x}^{(k)})}, \quad \mathbf{y}^{(k)} = \nabla U(\mathbf{x}^{(k+1)}) - \nabla U(\mathbf{x}^{(k)}); \tag{10.62}$$

[4]Roger Fletcher and C. M. Reeves published it in 1964.
[5]The method was presented by E. Polak and G. Ribière in 1969.

- the Hestenes–Stiefel method[6] characterized by

$$\beta_k = \frac{[\nabla U(\mathbf{x}^{(k+1)})]^T \mathbf{y}^{(k)}}{[\nabla U(\mathbf{x}^{(k)})]^T \mathbf{p}^{(k)}}, \quad \mathbf{y}^{(k)} = \nabla U(\mathbf{x}^{(k+1)}) - \nabla U(\mathbf{x}^{(k)}). \tag{10.63}$$

The most robust of these three methods is the Polak–Ribière method.

10.5.3 Solution of Systems of Linear Equations by Means of Methods of Gradient Type

Let the linear system be

$$\mathbf{Ax} = \mathbf{b}, \tag{10.64}$$

where $\mathbf{A}$ is a positive definite symmetric matrix

$$\mathbf{A}^T = \mathbf{A}, \quad \mathbf{x}^T \mathbf{Ax} > 0, \quad (\forall) \ \mathbf{x} \neq \mathbf{0}. \tag{10.65}$$

The solution of system (10.64) is equivalent to the minimization of the quadratic form

$$U(\mathbf{x}) = \langle \mathbf{x}, \mathbf{Ax} \rangle - 2 \langle \mathbf{x}, \mathbf{b} \rangle, \tag{10.66}$$

whereby $\langle \cdot, \cdot \rangle$ we denoted the dot product given by

$$\langle \mathbf{y}, \mathbf{z} \rangle = \mathbf{y}^T \mathbf{z}. \tag{10.67}$$

The gradient of $U(\mathbf{x})$ is expressed by

$$\nabla U(\mathbf{x}) = -2(\mathbf{b} - \mathbf{Ax}), \tag{10.68}$$

for the symmetric matrix $\mathbf{A}$, while the Hessian reads

$$\nabla^2 U(\mathbf{x}) = 2\mathbf{A}. \tag{10.69}$$

If we denote by $\bar{\mathbf{x}}$ the solution of system (10.64), then

$$\nabla U(\bar{\mathbf{x}}) = 0, \quad \nabla^2 U(\mathbf{x}) = 2\mathbf{A}, \tag{10.70}$$

hence the function U has a minimum at $\bar{\mathbf{x}}$. Moreover, if $\mathbf{p}$ is a decreasing direction, then we also have

$$\begin{aligned} U(\mathbf{x} + \alpha \mathbf{p}) &= \langle \mathbf{x} + \alpha \mathbf{p}, \mathbf{A}(\mathbf{x} + \alpha \mathbf{p}) \rangle - 2 \langle \mathbf{x} + \alpha \mathbf{p}, \mathbf{b} \rangle \\ &= U(\mathbf{x}) + 2\alpha \langle \mathbf{p}, \mathbf{Ax} - b \rangle + \alpha^2 \langle \mathbf{p}, \mathbf{Ap} \rangle. \end{aligned} \tag{10.71}$$

On the other hand,

$$\langle \mathbf{p}, \mathbf{Ap} \rangle > 0, \tag{10.72}$$

because $\mathbf{A}$ is a positive definite matrix; hence, $U(\mathbf{x} + \alpha \mathbf{p})$ has a minimum for $\alpha = \bar{\alpha}$, obtained from

$$\frac{dU(\mathbf{x} + \alpha \mathbf{p})}{d\alpha} = 0, \tag{10.73}$$

[6]Magnus Rudolph Hestenes (1906–1991) and Eduard L. Stiefel (1909–1978) published the method in 1952.

that is,

$$2\langle \mathbf{p}, \mathbf{Ax} - \mathbf{b} \rangle + 2\alpha \langle \mathbf{p}, \mathbf{Ap} \rangle = 0, \tag{10.74}$$

from which

$$\overline{\alpha} = \frac{\langle \mathbf{p}, \mathbf{b} - \mathbf{Ax} \rangle}{\langle \mathbf{p}, \mathbf{b} - \mathbf{Ap} \rangle}. \tag{10.75}$$

For $\alpha = \overline{\alpha}$ it follows that the minimum of the function $U(\mathbf{x} + \overline{\alpha}\mathbf{p})$ along the direction $\mathbf{p}$

$$U(\mathbf{x} + \overline{\alpha}\mathbf{p}) = U(\mathbf{x}) + \overline{\alpha}[2\langle \mathbf{p}, \mathbf{Ax} - \mathbf{b} \rangle + \overline{\alpha}\langle \mathbf{p}, \mathbf{Ap} \rangle] = U(\mathbf{x}) - \frac{\langle \mathbf{p}, \mathbf{b} - \mathbf{Ax} \rangle^2}{\langle \mathbf{p}, \mathbf{Ap} \rangle}. \tag{10.76}$$

Observation 10.9

(i) Using the method of the gradient for which the decreasing direction is

$$\mathbf{p} = -\nabla U(\mathbf{x}), \tag{10.77}$$

we then obtain the following algorithm:

– given: $\mathbf{x}^{(0)}$, $\mathbf{A}$, $\mathbf{b}$, iter, ε;
– set $i = 1$; norm $= 1$; $\mathbf{x} = \mathbf{x}^{(0)}$;
– while norm $> \varepsilon$ and $i \leq iter$ do
  – calculate $\mathbf{p} = \mathbf{b} - \mathbf{Ax}$, norm $= \sqrt{\langle \mathbf{p}, \mathbf{p} \rangle}$; $\alpha = \text{norm}^2 / \langle \mathbf{p}, \mathbf{Ap} \rangle$, $\mathbf{x} = \mathbf{x} + \alpha\mathbf{p}$, $i = i + 1$.

(ii) If we apply the Fletcher–Reeves method, then we obtain the algorithm:

– given: $\mathbf{x}^{(0)}$, $\mathbf{A}$, $\mathbf{b}$, iter, ε, δ;
– set $\mathbf{r}^{(0)} = \mathbf{b} - \mathbf{Ax}^{(0)}$, $\mathbf{p}^{(0)} = \mathbf{r}^{(0)}$;
– for k from 0 to iter $- 1$ do
  – if $\sqrt{\langle \mathbf{p}^{(k)}, \mathbf{p}^{(k)} \rangle} < \delta$
    then stop;
  – calculate $\alpha_k = \frac{\langle \mathbf{r}^{(k)}, \mathbf{r}^{(k)} \rangle}{\langle \mathbf{p}^{(k)}, \mathbf{Ap}^{(k)} \rangle}$, $\mathbf{x}^{(k+1)} = \mathbf{x}^{(k)} + \alpha_k \mathbf{p}^{(k)}$, $\mathbf{r}^{(k+1)} = \mathbf{r}^{(k)} - \alpha_k \mathbf{Ap}^{(k)}$;
  – if $\langle \mathbf{r}^{(k+1)}, \mathbf{r}^{(k+1)} \rangle < \varepsilon$
    then stop;
  – calculate $\beta_k = \frac{\langle \mathbf{r}^{(k+1)}, \mathbf{r}^{(k+1)} \rangle}{\langle \mathbf{r}^{(k)}, \mathbf{Ar}^{(k)} \rangle}$, $\mathbf{p}^{(k+1)} = \mathbf{r}^{(k+1)} + \beta_k \mathbf{p}^{(k)}$.

10.6   METHODS OF NEWTON TYPE

The methods of Newton type use the Hessian matrix $\nabla^2 U(\mathbf{x})$.

10.6.1   Newton's Method

The Newton method approximates the objective function $U(\mathbf{x})$, at an arbitrary iteration k, by a quadratic form

$$\phi_k(\mathbf{x}) = U(\mathbf{x}^{(k)}) + [\mathbf{x} - \mathbf{x}^{(k)}]^T \nabla U(\mathbf{x}^{(k)}) + \frac{1}{2}[\mathbf{x} - \mathbf{x}^{(k)}]^T \nabla^2 U(\mathbf{x}^{(k)})[\mathbf{x} - \mathbf{x}^{(k)}]. \tag{10.78}$$

If the Hessian matrix $\nabla^2 U(\mathbf{x}^{(k)})$ is positive definite, then the quadratic form $\phi_k(\mathbf{x})$ has a minimum $\mathbf{x} = \bar{\mathbf{x}}$, hence

$$\phi_k(\mathbf{x}) - \phi_k(\bar{\mathbf{x}}) > 0 \qquad (10.79)$$

in a neighborhood of $\bar{\mathbf{x}}$. Moreover, the point of minimum $\bar{\mathbf{x}}$ is a stationary point, hence the gradient of $\phi_k(\mathbf{x})$ vanishes at this point

$$\nabla \phi_k(\bar{\mathbf{x}}) = 0. \qquad (10.80)$$

We may write the approximate relation

$$\phi_k(\mathbf{x}) - \phi_k(\bar{\mathbf{x}}) \approx \frac{1}{2}[\mathbf{x} - \bar{\mathbf{x}}]^T \nabla^2 U(\mathbf{x}^{(k)})[\mathbf{x} - \bar{\mathbf{x}}]. \qquad (10.81)$$

Equation (10.80) may be solved using Newton's method, which leads to the definition of the iterative sequence

$$\mathbf{x}^{(0)} \text{ arbitrary}, \quad \mathbf{x}^{(k+1)} = \mathbf{x}^{(k)} - [\nabla^2 U(\mathbf{x}^{(k)})]^{-1} \nabla U(\mathbf{x}^{(k)}). \qquad (10.82)$$

Definition 10.8   The decreasing direction $\mathbf{p}^{(k)}$, defined by

$$\mathbf{p}^{(k)} = -[\nabla^2 U(\mathbf{x}^{(k)})]^{-1} \nabla U(\mathbf{x}^{(k)}), \quad [\nabla U(\mathbf{x}^{(k)})]^T \mathbf{p}^{(k)} < 0, \qquad (10.83)$$

bears the name of Newton direction.

Observation 10.10

(i) The affirmation $\mathbf{x}^{(0)}$ arbitrary in relation (10.82) must be understood as $\mathbf{x}^{(0)}$ being an arbitrary point in a sufficiently small neighborhood of the exact solution, which is valid in any Newton method.

(ii) If the Hessian matrix $\nabla^2 U(\mathbf{x}^{(k)})$ is not positive definite, then it may happen that $\nabla U(\mathbf{x}^{(k+1)})$ be greater in value as $\nabla U(\mathbf{x}^{(k)})$, that is, the direction $\mathbf{p}^{(k)}$ is no more a decreasing direction.

(iii) If $U(\mathbf{x})$ has flat zones, in other words if it can be approximated by a hyperplane, then in these zones the Hessian matrix $\nabla^2 U(\mathbf{x})$ vanishes and the method cannot be applied. For these zones it would be necessary to determine, instead of the Hessian $\nabla^2 U(\mathbf{x})$, another positive definite matrix to may continue the procedure.

Various algorithms have been conceived to eliminate such inconveniences; one such algorithmis the algorithm of the trust region, which is presented as follows:

- given: $\mathbf{x}^{(0)}$, $U(\mathbf{x})$, $\nabla U(\mathbf{x})$, $\nabla^2 U(\mathbf{x})$, μ, η, γ_1, γ_2, δ_0, λ_0, ε, ε_p, iter, n_p;
- set $\mathbf{x} = \mathbf{x}^{(0)}$, $\delta = \delta_0$, $\lambda = \lambda_0$, $U_k = U(\mathbf{x}^{(0)})$, $\nabla U(\mathbf{x}) = \nabla \check{U}(\mathbf{x}^{(0)})$, $\nabla^2 U(\mathbf{x}^{(k)}) = \nabla^2 U(\mathbf{x}^{(0)})$, $\phi_k(\mathbf{x}) = U_k$;
- for k from 1 to iter do
  - set $d = 1$, $i_p = 1$;
  - while $|d| > \varepsilon_p |\lambda| + 10^{-5}$ and $i_p < n_p$ do
    - calculate the Cholesky factorization of $\nabla U(\mathbf{x}^{(k)}) + \lambda \mathbf{I} = \mathbf{R}^T \mathbf{R}$;
    - solve the system $\mathbf{R}^T \mathbf{R} \mathbf{p}^{(k)} = -\nabla U(\mathbf{x}^{(k)})$;
    - solve the system $\mathbf{R}^T \mathbf{q} = -\mathbf{p}^{(k)}$;
    - calculate $d = (\|p^{(k)}\|/\|q\|)^2 ((\|\mathbf{p}^{(k)}\|/\delta) - 1)$, $\lambda = \lambda + d$, $i_p = i_p + 1$;
    - calculate $\mathbf{x}^{(k+1)} = \mathbf{x}^{(k)} + \mathbf{p}^{(k)}$, $U_{k+1} = U(\mathbf{x}^{(k+1)})$, $\phi_{k+1} = U_k + [\mathbf{p}^{(k)}]^T \nabla U(\mathbf{x}^{(k+1)}) + 1/2[\mathbf{p}^{(k)}]^T \nabla^2 U(\mathbf{x}^{(k+1)}) \mathbf{p}^{(k)}$, $d = U_{k+1} - U_k$;

- if $|d| < \varepsilon |U_{k+1}|$
    then stop (the minimum has been found);
- calculate $r_k = d/\phi(\mathbf{x}^{(k+1)}) - \phi(\mathbf{x}^{(k)})$;
- if $r_k > \mu$
    then $\mathbf{x}^{(k+1)} = \mathbf{x}^{(k)}$;
- if $r_k \leq \mu$
    then $\delta = \gamma_1 \delta$;
    else
- if $r_k > \eta$
    then $\delta = \gamma_2 \delta$.

Observation 10.11

(i) The usual values for each of the parameters μ, η, γ_1, and γ_2 are as follows

$$\mu = 0.25, \quad \eta = 0.75, \quad \gamma_1 = 0.5, \quad \gamma_2 = 2. \tag{10.84}$$

(ii) The algorithm establishes a trust region in the model, that is, a region in which $U(\mathbf{x})$ may be good approximated by a quadratic form $\phi_k(\mathbf{x})$. This zone is a hypersphere of center $\mathbf{x}^{(k)}$ and radius δ_k; we try the point of minimum for $\phi_k(\mathbf{x})$ in this hypersphere. This minimum is not taken into consideration if it does not belong to the interior of the hypersphere.

(iii) The length of the hypersphere radius which defines the trust zone at the step $k+1$ is calculated as a function of the previous value and of the ratio r_k between the effective reduction of the hypersphere radius and the planed one

$$r_k = \frac{U(\mathbf{x}^{(k+1)}) - U(\mathbf{x}^{(k)})}{\phi(\mathbf{x}^{(k+1)}) - \phi(\mathbf{x}^{(k)})}. \tag{10.85}$$

If r_k is small, then $\delta_{k+1} < \delta_k$, otherwise we consider $\delta_{k+1} > \delta_k$.

(iv) The searching Newton direction $\mathbf{p}^{(k)}$ is determined by the relation

$$[\nabla^2 U(\mathbf{x}^{(k)}) + \lambda \mathbf{I}] \, \mathbf{p}^{(k)} = -\nabla U(\mathbf{x}^{(k)}), \tag{10.86}$$

where λ is a parameter which assures that the matrix $\nabla^2 U(\mathbf{x}^{(k)}) + \lambda \mathbf{I}$ be positive definite so as to avoid the cases in Observation 10.10.

(v) The Cholesky decomposition is not imperatively necessary, but increases the calculation velocity to solve system (10.86) in case of the positive definite matrix $\nabla^2 U(\mathbf{x}^{(k)}) + \lambda \mathbf{I}$.

10.6.2 Quasi-Newton Method

The quasi-Newton method approximates the Hessian matrix $\nabla^2 U(\mathbf{x})$ by a positive definite symmetric matrix $\mathbf{B}$.

The equation which determinates the decreasing direction $\mathbf{p}^{(k)}$ is now written in the form

$$\mathbf{B}_k \mathbf{p}^{(k)} = -\nabla U(\mathbf{x}), \tag{10.87}$$

while $\mathbf{x}^{(k+1)}$ is determined by the relation

$$\mathbf{x}^{(k+1)} = \mathbf{x}^{(k)} + \alpha_k \mathbf{p}^{(k)}, \tag{10.88}$$

where α_k results from the condition of minimum of the function of one variable $U[\mathbf{x}^{(k)} + \alpha_k \mathbf{p}^{(k)}]$.

It remains to solve the problem of bringing up-to-date the matrix $\mathbf{B}_k$ in the matrix $\mathbf{B}_{k+1}$. There exist several methods, the most known being:

- the Davidon–Fletcher–Powell[7] method for which

$$\mathbf{B}_{k+1} = \mathbf{B}_k + \frac{\mathbf{z}^{(k)}[\mathbf{y}^{(k)}]^T + \mathbf{y}^{(k)}[\mathbf{z}^{(k)}]^T}{[\mathbf{y}^{(k)}]^T[\mathbf{x}^{(k+1)} - \mathbf{x}^{(k)}]} - \frac{[\mathbf{z}^{(k)}]^T[\mathbf{x}^{(k+1)} - \mathbf{x}^{(k)}]}{\{[\mathbf{y}^{(k)}]^T[\mathbf{x}^{(k+1)} - \mathbf{x}^{(k)}]\}^2} \mathbf{y}^{(k)}[\mathbf{y}^{(k)}]^T,$$

$$\mathbf{z}^{(k)} = \mathbf{y}^{(k)} + \alpha_k \nabla U(\mathbf{x}^{(k)}), \quad \mathbf{y}^{(k)} = \nabla U(\mathbf{x}^{(k+1)}) - \nabla U(\mathbf{x}^{(k)}); \tag{10.89}$$

- the Broyden–Fletcher–Goldfarb–Shanno method in which

$$\mathbf{B}_{k+1} = \mathbf{B}_k + \frac{\mathbf{y}^{(k)}[\mathbf{y}^{(k)}]^T}{[\mathbf{y}^{(k)}]^T[\mathbf{x}^{(k+1)} - \mathbf{x}^{(k)}]} - \frac{\mathbf{B}_k[\mathbf{x}^{(k+1)} - \mathbf{x}^{(k)}][\mathbf{x}^{(k+1)} - \mathbf{x}^{(k)}]^T\mathbf{B}_k}{[\mathbf{x}^{(k+1)} - \mathbf{x}^{(k)}]^T\mathbf{B}_k[\mathbf{x}^{(k+1)} - \mathbf{x}^{(k)}]},$$

$$\mathbf{y}^{(k)} = \nabla U(\mathbf{x}^{(k+1)}) - \nabla U(\mathbf{x}^{(k)}). \tag{10.90}$$

We may write

$$\mathbf{x}^{(k+1)} = \mathbf{x}^{(k)} - \alpha_k \mathbf{B}_k^{-1} \nabla U(\mathbf{x}^{(k)}) \tag{10.91}$$

too, while formulae (10.89) and (10.90) also give the inverse $\mathbf{B}_{k+1}^{-1}$ as a function of $\mathbf{B}_k^{-1}$. Thus:
- the Davidon–Fletcher–Powell method gives

$$\mathbf{B}_{k+1}^{-1} = \mathbf{B}_k^{-1} + \frac{[\mathbf{x}^{(k+1)} - \mathbf{x}^{(k)}][\mathbf{x}^{(k+1)} - \mathbf{x}^{(k)}]^T}{[\mathbf{y}^{(k)}]^T[\mathbf{x}^{(k+1)} - \mathbf{x}^{(k)}]} - \frac{\mathbf{B}_k^{-1}\mathbf{y}^{(k)}[\mathbf{y}^{(k)}]^T\mathbf{B}_k^{-1}}{[\mathbf{y}^{(k)}]^T\mathbf{B}_k^{-1}\mathbf{y}^{(k)}}; \tag{10.92}$$

- the Broyden–Fletcher–Goldfarb–Shanno[8] method leads to

$$\mathbf{B}_{k+1}^{-1} = \frac{\mathbf{B}_k^{-1} - \mathbf{B}_k^{-1}\mathbf{y}^{(k)}[\mathbf{x}^{(k+1)} - \mathbf{x}^{(k)}]^T + [\mathbf{x}^{(k+1)} - \mathbf{x}^{(k)}][\mathbf{y}^{(k)}]^T\mathbf{B}_k^{-1}}{[\mathbf{y}^{(k)}]^T[\mathbf{x}^{(k+1)} - \mathbf{x}^{(k)}]}$$

$$+ \frac{[\mathbf{x}^{(k+1)} - \mathbf{x}^{(k)}][\mathbf{y}^{(k)}]^T\mathbf{B}_k^{-1}\mathbf{y}^{(k)}[\mathbf{x}^{(k+1)} - \mathbf{x}^{(k)}]^T}{\{[\mathbf{y}^{(k)}]^T[\mathbf{x}^{(k+1)} - \mathbf{x}^{(k)}]\}^2} + \frac{[\mathbf{x}^{(k+1)} - \mathbf{x}^{(k)}][\mathbf{x}^{(k+1)} - \mathbf{x}^{(k)}]^T}{[\mathbf{y}^{(k)}]^T[\mathbf{x}^{(k+1)} - \mathbf{x}^{(k)}]}. \tag{10.93}$$

10.7 LINEAR PROGRAMMING: THE SIMPLEX ALGORITHM

10.7.1 Introduction

Let a linear system of m equations with n unknowns be

$$\mathbf{Ax} = b. \tag{10.94}$$

Definition 10.9 Two linear systems are called *equivalent* if any solution of the first system is a solution of the second system too and reciprocal.

Definition 10.10 We call elementary transformation applied on a linear system as any one of the following:

- the multiplication of an equation by a nonzero number;
- the change of the order of two equations;

[7]William C. Davidon, Roger Fletcher and Michael James David Powell published the method in 1958 and 1964.
[8]Charles George Broyden (1933–2011), Roger Fletcher, Donald Goldfarb and David Shanno published the method in 1970.

- the multiplication of an equation by a nonzero number, the addition of the result to another equation, and the replacing of the latter equation by the equation thus obtained.

Observation 10.12

(i) Each of the above operation determines an operation on the enlarged matrix of the system. These transformations are equivalent to the multiplication of the extended matrix at the left by certain matrices.

Thus, considering the matrix

$$
\mathbf{M}_1 = \begin{bmatrix} 1 & \cdots & 0 & \cdots & 0 \\ \cdots & \cdots & \cdots & \cdots & \cdots \\ 0 & \cdots & \alpha & \cdots & 0 \\ \cdots & \cdots & \cdots & \cdots & \cdots \\ 0 & \cdots & 0 & \cdots & 1 \end{bmatrix}, \quad \mathbf{M}_1 \in M_m(\mathbb{R}), \tag{10.95}
$$

which differs from the unit matrix only by the element α situated at the position (i, i), $\alpha \neq 0$, the multiplication at the left of the extended matrix by $\mathbf{M}_1$ has as effect, the multiplication of the row i of the extended matrix by α.

If we multiply the extended matrix at left by the matrix $\mathbf{M}_2$ given by

$$
\mathbf{M}_2 = \begin{bmatrix} 1 & \cdots & 0 & \cdots & 0 & \cdots & 0 \\ \cdots & \cdots & \cdots & \cdots & \cdots & \cdots & \cdots \\ 0 & \cdots & 0 & \cdots & 1 & \cdots & 0 \\ \cdots & \cdots & \cdots & \cdots & \cdots & \cdots & \cdots \\ 0 & \cdots & 1 & \cdots & 0 & \cdots & 0 \\ \cdots & \cdots & \cdots & \cdots & \cdots & \cdots & \cdots \\ 0 & \cdots & 0 & \cdots & 0 & \cdots & 1 \end{bmatrix}, \quad \mathbf{M}_2 \in M_m(\mathbb{R}), \tag{10.96}
$$

which differs from the unit matrix of order m by the elements at the positions (i, i) and (i, j) replaced by 0 and by the elements at the positions (i, j) and (j, i) replaced by 1, then the product $\mathbf{M}_2\overline{\mathbf{A}}$, where $\overline{\mathbf{A}}$ is the extended matrix has as effect, the interchange of the rows i and j of the extended matrix $\overline{\mathbf{A}}$.

Let us now consider the matrix

$$
\mathbf{M}_3 = \begin{bmatrix} 1 & \cdots & 0 & \cdots & 0 & \cdots & 0 \\ \cdots & \cdots & \cdots & \cdots & \cdots & \cdots & \cdots \\ 0 & \cdots & 1 & \cdots & \alpha & \cdots & 0 \\ \cdots & \cdots & \cdots & \cdots & \cdots & \cdots & \cdots \\ 0 & \cdots & 0 & \cdots & 1 & \cdots & 0 \\ \cdots & \cdots & \cdots & \cdots & \cdots & \cdots & \cdots \\ 0 & \cdots & 0 & \cdots & 0 & \cdots & 0 \end{bmatrix}, \quad \mathbf{M}_3 \in M_m(\mathbb{R}), \tag{10.97}
$$

which differs from the unit matrix by the element at the position (i, j), which has the value $\alpha \neq 0$; then the product $\mathbf{M}_3\overline{\mathbf{A}}$ has as effect, the multiplication of the row j by α and the addition of it to the row i.

(ii) The elementary operations lead, obviously, to equivalent systems.

Definition 10.11 A system is called *explicit* if the matrix of the system contains all the columns of the unit matrix of order m (the number of the equations of the system).

Observation 10.13

(i) The columns of the unit matrix may be found at any position in the matrix **A** of the system.

(ii) A developed linear system has the number of unknowns at least equal to the number of equations, that is, $m \leq n$.

Definition 10.12   The variables, the coefficients of which form the columns of the unit matrix are called *principal or basic variables*. The other variables of the system are called *secondary or nonbasic variables*.

Observation 10.14   A compatible system may be developed so as to have exactly m columns of the unit matrix. To do this, it is sufficient to effect the elementary transformations presented in a certain order.

Definition 10.13

(i) A solution of system (10.94) in which the $n - m$ secondary variables vanish is called *basic solution*.

(ii) A basic solution is called *nondegenerate* if it has exactly m nonzero components (the principal variables have nonzero values) and degenerate in the opposite case.

10.7.2   Formulation of the Problem of Linear Programming

Definition 10.14

(i) A problem of linear programming is a problem which requires the minimization (maximization) of the function

$$f(x_1, \ x_2, \ \ldots, \ x_n) = \text{minimum (maximum)} \tag{10.98}$$

if

$$f_i(x_1, x_2, \ldots, x_n) \leq b_i, \quad i = \overline{1, p},$$
$$f_j(x_1, x_2, \ldots, x_n) \geq b_j, \quad j = \overline{p + 1, q},$$
$$f_k(x_1, x_2, \ldots, x_n) = b_k, \quad k = \overline{q + 1, r} \tag{10.99}$$

and

$$x_l \geq 0, \quad l = \overline{1, \ m_1},$$
$$x_h \leq 0, \quad h = \overline{m_1 + 1, \ m_2},$$
$$x_t \ \text{arbitrary}, \quad t = \overline{m_2 + 1, \ m}, \tag{10.100}$$

the functions f, f_i, f_j, and f_k being linear.

(ii) Conditions (10.99) are called *the restrictions of the problem*, while the vector $\mathbf{x} = [x_1 \ \ldots \ x_n]^T$, which verifies the system of restrictions, is called *possible solution of the linear programming problem*.

(iii) The possible solution $\bar{\mathbf{x}}$ which verifies conditions (10.100) too is called *admissible solution of the linear programming problem*.

(iv) The admissible solution which realizes the extremum of function (10.98) is called *optimal solution or optimal program*.

The linear programming may be written in a matrix form

$$\mathbf{A}x S \mathbf{b}, \quad \mathbf{x} > \mathbf{0}, \quad f = \mathbf{C}^T\mathbf{x} = \text{minimum (maximum)}, \tag{10.101}$$

in which

$$\mathbf{A} = [a_{ij}]_{\substack{i=\overline{1,m}, \\ j=\overline{1,n}}}, \quad \mathbf{b} = \begin{bmatrix} b_1 & \cdots & b_n \end{bmatrix}^{\mathrm{T}}, \quad \mathbf{C} = \begin{bmatrix} c_1 & \cdots & c_n \end{bmatrix}^{\mathrm{T}}, \tag{10.102}$$

and where S takes the place of one of the signs $\leq$, $=$, or $\geq$.

Let us observe that the second relation (10.101) puts the condition that all variables be non-negative. This can be always obtained, as will be seen later.

Definition 10.15

(i) A problem of linear programming is of standard form if all the restrictions are equations and if we impose conditions of non-negativeness to all variables.

(ii) A problem of linear programming is of canonical form if all the restrictions are inequalities of the same sense and if conditions of non-negativeness are imposed to all variables.

Observation 10.15

(i) A program of standard form reads

$$\mathbf{A}\mathbf{x} = \mathbf{b}, \quad \mathbf{x} \geq \mathbf{0}, \quad f = \mathbf{C}^{\mathrm{T}}\mathbf{x}. \tag{10.103}$$

(ii) A program of canonical form is written

$$\mathbf{A}\mathbf{x} \geq \mathbf{b}, \quad \mathbf{x} \geq \mathbf{0}, \quad \mathbf{C}^{\mathrm{T}}\mathbf{x} = \text{minimum} \tag{10.104}$$

or

$$\mathbf{A}\mathbf{x} \leq \mathbf{b}, \quad \mathbf{x} \geq \mathbf{0}, \quad \mathbf{C}^{\mathrm{T}}\mathbf{x} = \text{maximum}. \tag{10.105}$$

(iii) A program may be brought to a standard or to a canonical form by using the following elementary transformations:

- an inequality of a certain sense may be transformed into an opposite sense by multiplication with -1;
- a negative variable may be transformed in a positive one by its multiplication with -1;
- a variable, let us say x_k, $x_k \in \mathbb{R}$, is written in the form

$$x_k = x_k^{(1)} - x_k^{(2)}, \tag{10.106}$$

  where $x_k^{(1)} \geq 0$, $x_k^{(2)} \geq 0$;
- an equality is expressed by means of two inequalities; so

$$a_{i1}x_1 + a_{i2}x_2 + \cdots + a_{in}x_n = b_i \tag{10.107}$$

  is written in the form

$$a_{i1}x_1 + a_{i2}x_2 + \cdots + a_{in}x_n \leq b_i, \quad a_{i1}x_1 + a_{i2}x_2 + \cdots + a_{in}x_n \geq b_i; \tag{10.108}$$

- the inequalities are transformed in equalities by means of the compensation variables; thus

$$a_{i1}x_1 + a_{i2}x_2 + \cdots + a_{in}x_n \leq b_i \tag{10.109}$$

becomes

$$a_{i1}x_1 + a_{i2}x_2 + \cdots + a_{in}x_n + y = b_i, \quad y \geq 0, \tag{10.110}$$

while

$$a_{i1}x_1 + a_{i2}x_2 + \cdots + a_{in}x_n \geq b_i \tag{10.111}$$

is transformed in

$$a_{i1}x_1 + a_{i2}x_2 + \cdots + a_{in}x_n - y = b_i, \quad y \geq 0. \tag{10.112}$$

10.7.3   Geometrical Interpretation

In the space $\mathbb{R}^n$, an equality of the restrictions system defines a hyperplane, while an inequality defines a half-space. We thus define a convex polyhedron in the space $\mathbb{R}^n$, and if the optimum is unique, then it will be situated at one of the vertices of this polyhedron.

The objective function, written in the form

$$f(\mathbf{x}) = c_1 x_1 + c_2 x_2 + \cdots + c_n x_n = \lambda, \quad \lambda \in \mathbb{R}, \tag{10.113}$$

defines a pencil of hyperplanes, while for $\lambda = 0$ we obtain a hyperplane which passes through the origin.

Definition 10.16

(i) The hyperplanes of the pencil (10.113) are called *level hyperplanes*.
(ii) The hyperplanes become straight lines in $\mathbb{R}^2$ and are called *level straight lines*.

Observation 10.16   The objective function has the same value at points situated on the same level hyperplane.

10.7.4   The Primal Simplex Algorithm

Definition 10.17   A linear program is said to be in primal admissible form if it is given by the relations

$$\text{maximum (minimum)}\mathbf{f}(\mathbf{x}) = f_0 + \sum_{k \in K} a_{0k} x_k, \tag{10.114}$$

$$x_i + \sum_{k \in K} a_{ik} x_k = b_i, \quad i \in I, \tag{10.115}$$

$$x_k \geq 0, \quad x_i \geq 0, \quad k \in K, \quad i \in I, \tag{10.116}$$

where K is the set of indices of secondary variables, while I marks the set of indices of principal variables.

Observation 10.17 Obviously, any linear program may be brought to the primal admissible form by means of the elementary transformations presented above.

Let a program be in the primal admissible form and an admissible basic solution corresponding to this form. The Simplex algorithm[9] realizes a partial examination of the list of the basic solutions of the system of restrictions, having scope to find an optimal basic solution or to demonstrate the inexistence of such a solution.

Let us assume that after r steps the program takes its primal admissible form

$$f = f_0^{(r)} + \sum_{k \in K^{(r)}} a_{0k} x_k, \tag{10.117}$$

$$x_i = \sum_{k \in K^{(r)}} a_{ik} x_k = b_i, \quad i \in I^{(r)}, \tag{10.118}$$

$$x_k \geq 0, \quad x_i \geq 0, \quad k \in K^{(r)}, \quad i \in I^{(r)}, \tag{10.119}$$

where the upper index r marks the iteration step.

There are four operations to perform:

- application of the optimality criterion. If $a_{0k} \geq 0$ for all $k \in K^{(r)}$, then the linear program has the basic solution obtained at the step r and the algorithm stops; in the opposite case, we pass to the following stage;

- application of the entrance criterion. At this stage, we determine the secondary unknown x_h, which becomes a principal variable and is given by

$$a_{0h} = \min_{k \in K^{(r)}} a_{0k} < 0. \tag{10.120}$$

If all $a_{ih} \leq 0$, $i \in I^{(r)}$, then the program does not have an optimal solution and the algorithm stops; in the opposite case, we pass to the following stage;

- application of the exit criterion. We determine the principal variable x_j, which becomes secondary by the relations

$$\frac{x_j}{a_{jh}} = \min_{\substack{i \in I^{(r)} \\ a_{ih} > 0}} \frac{b_i}{a_{ih}}; \tag{10.121}$$

- we make a pivoting with the pivot a_{jh} to obtain the column of the unit matrix on the column h.

Usually, we use tables.

	x_1	$\cdots$	x_i	$\cdots$	x_m	x_{m+1}	$\cdots$	x_k	$\cdots$	x_n	
	0	$\cdots$	0	$\cdots$	0	a_{01}	$\cdots$	a_{0k}	$\cdots$	a_{0n}	$-f_0$
x_1	1	$\cdots$	0	$\cdots$	0	$a_{1,m+1}$	$\cdots$	a_{1k}	$\cdots$	a_{1n}	b_1
$\cdots$	$\cdots$	$\cdots$	$\cdots$	$\cdots$	$\cdots$	$\cdots$	$\cdots$	$\cdots$	$\cdots$	$\cdots$	$\cdots$
x_i	0	$\cdots$	1	$\cdots$	0	$a_{i,m+1}$	$\cdots$	$a_{i,k}$	$\cdots$	$a_{i,n}$	b_i
$\cdots$	$\cdots$	$\cdots$	$\cdots$	$\cdots$	$\cdots$	$\cdots$	$\cdots$	$\cdots$	$\cdots$	$\cdots$	$\cdots$
x_m	0	$\cdots$	0	$\cdots$	1	$a_{m,m+1}$		$a_{m,k}$		$a_{m,n}$	b_m

[9]The algorithm was purposed by George Bernard Dantzig (1914–2005) in 1947.

10.7.5   The Dual Simplex Algorithm

Definition 10.18   Let the problem of linear programming in canonical form be

$$a_{11}x_1 + a_{12}x_2 + \cdots + a_{1n}x_n \geq b_1, \quad a_{21}x_1 + a_{22}x_2 + \cdots + a_{2n}x_n \geq b_2, \quad \ldots ,$$

$$a_{m1}x_1 + a_{m2}x_2 + \cdots + a_{mn}x_n \geq b_m, \tag{10.122}$$

$$x_1 \geq 0, \quad x_2 \geq 0, \quad \ldots , \quad x_n \geq 0, \tag{10.123}$$

$$\text{minimum} f = c_1 x_1 + c_2 x_2 + \cdots + c_n x_n. \tag{10.124}$$

By definition, the dual of this problem is

$$a_{11}y_1 + a_{21}y_2 + \cdots + a_{m1}y_m \leq c_1, \quad a_{12}y_1 + a_{22}y_2 + \cdots + a_{2n}y_m \leq c_2, \quad \ldots ,$$

$$a_{1n}y_1 + a_{2n}y_2 + \cdots + a_{mn}y_m \leq c_n, \tag{10.125}$$

$$y_1 \geq 0, \quad y_2 \geq 0, \quad \ldots , \quad y_m \geq 0, \tag{10.126}$$

$$\max g = b_1 y_1 + \cdots + b_m y_m. \tag{10.127}$$

Observation 10.18   The dual problem is obtained from the primal problem as follows:

- to each restriction of the system of restrictions (10.122) we associate a dual variable y_i;
- the variable y_i does not have a sign restriction if the corresponding restriction of (10.122) is an equality and has a restriction in case of inequality; thus, for $\geq$ corresponds $y_i \geq 0$, for $\leq$ corresponds $y_i \leq 0$ and for $=$ corresponds y_i arbitrary;
- to each variable x_i we associate a restriction in which the coefficients of the variables $y_1, \ldots ,$ y_m are the coefficients of the variable x_i of system (10.122), while the free terms are c_i;
- the dual restriction associated to x_i is $\leq$ if $x_i \geq 0$, is $\geq$ if $x_i \leq 0$ and is $=$ for any x_i;
- the minimum of the objective function of the primal problem is transformed in the maximum of the objective function of the dual problem;
- the objective function of the dual problem is obtained by means of the free terms of the initial restrictions (10.122).

Definition 10.19   A linear program is in an explicit dual admissible form if

$$x_i + \sum_{k \in K} a_{ik} x_k = b_i, \quad i \in I, \tag{10.128}$$

$$x_i \geq 0, \quad x_k \geq 0, \quad i \in I, \quad k \in K, \tag{10.129}$$

$$f_0 + \sum_{k \in K} a_{0k} x_k = \text{minimum.} \tag{10.130}$$

Let us suppose that at the step r, the linear program is expressed by the relations

$$x_i + \sum_{k \in K} a_{ik} x_k = b_i, \quad i \in I^{(r)}, \tag{10.131}$$

$$x_i \geq 0, \quad x_k \geq 0, \quad i \in I^{(r)}, \quad k \in K^{(r)}, \tag{10.132}$$

$$f_0 + \sum_{k \in K^{(r)}} a_{0k} x_k = \text{minimum.} \tag{10.133}$$

For the step $r + 1$, we have to pass through the stages:

- application of the optimality criterion. At this stage we establish if $b_i \geq 0$ for all $i \in I^{(r)}$. If the answer is yes, then the solution is optimal; in the opposite case, we pass to the following stage;
- application of the exit criterion. We determine the unknown x_j, which becomes secondary by the condition

$$b_j = \min_{i \in I^{(r)}} b_i, \tag{10.134}$$

and we verify if all the elements $a_{jk} \geq 0$, with $k \in K^{(r)}$. If yes, then the problem does not have an admissible solution; in the opposite case, we pass to the following step;
- application of the entrance criterion. We determine the unknown x_h, which becomes a principal variable. This results from the condition

$$\frac{a_{0h}}{a_{jh}} = \min_{\substack{k \in K^{(r)} \\ a_{jk} < 0}} \left| \frac{a_{0k}}{a_{jk}} \right|; \tag{10.135}$$

that effects the pivoting with the element a_{jh}.

10.8 CONVEX PROGRAMMING

Definition 10.20 Let X be a convex set and f a function $f : X \to \mathbb{R}$. We say that the function f is convex (or convex in Jensen's sense) if for any $\alpha \in (0, 1)$ and any x_1, x_2 of X we have

$$f(\alpha x_1 + (1 - \alpha)x_2) \leq f(x_1) + (1 - \alpha) f(x_2). \tag{10.136}$$

Observation 10.19

(i) If f is differentiable, then, instead relation (10.136), we may consider the inequality

$$f(x) \geq f(x^*) + \langle f(x^*), x - x^* \rangle, \tag{10.137}$$

where $\langle \cdot, \cdot \rangle$ marks the scalar product.

(ii) If $f : I \subset \mathbb{R} \to \mathbb{R}$, I being an interval, let us consider the expansion into a Taylor series

$$f(x) = f(x^*) + f'(x^*)(x - x^*) + \frac{1}{2} f''(\xi)(x - x^*)^2, \tag{10.138}$$

where ξ is a point between x and x^*. The convexity condition of f leads to the inequality $f''(x) \geq 0$, for any $x \in I$.

(iii) In the case $f : \mathcal{D} \subset \mathbb{R}^n \to \mathbb{R}$, it requires that the matrix of the derivatives of second order be semi-positive definite, that is,

$$\begin{bmatrix} x_1 & x_2 & \cdots & x_n \end{bmatrix} \begin{bmatrix} \dfrac{\partial^2 f}{\partial x_1^2} & \dfrac{\partial^2 f}{\partial x_1 \partial x_2} & \cdots & \dfrac{\partial^2 f}{\partial x_1 \partial x_n} \\[2mm] \dfrac{\partial^2 f}{\partial x_2 \partial x_1} & \dfrac{\partial^2 f}{\partial x_2^2} & \cdots & \dfrac{\partial^2 f}{\partial x_2 \partial x_n} \\[2mm] \cdots & \cdots & \cdots & \cdots \\[2mm] \dfrac{\partial^2 f}{\partial x_n \partial x_1} & \dfrac{\partial^2 f}{\partial x_n \partial x_2} & \cdots & \dfrac{\partial^2 f}{\partial x_n^2} \end{bmatrix} \begin{bmatrix} x_1 \\ x_2 \\ \vdots \\ x_n \end{bmatrix} \geq 0, \qquad (10.139)$$

for any $\mathbf{x} \in \mathcal{D}$.

The problem of convex programming requires determining the minimum of $f(\mathbf{x})$, $f : \mathcal{D} \subset \mathbb{R}^n \to \mathbb{R}$ in the condition of a restriction of the form $g_i(\mathbf{x}) \leq 0$, $i = \overline{1, m}$.

If we denote by $\mathcal{E}$ the admissible set

$$\mathcal{E} = \{\mathbf{x} \in \mathcal{D} | g_i(\mathbf{x}) \leq 0, i = \overline{1, m}\}, \qquad (10.140)$$

then the problem of convex programming requires the determination of the value $\inf_{\mathbf{x} \in \mathcal{E}} f(\mathbf{x})$.

We define Lagrange's function by

$$\mathcal{L}(\mathbf{x}, \boldsymbol{\lambda}) = f(\mathbf{x}) + \sum_{i=1}^{m} \lambda_i g_i(\mathbf{x}), \qquad (10.141)$$

where

$$\boldsymbol{\lambda} = \begin{bmatrix} \lambda_1 & \lambda_2 & \cdots & \lambda_m \end{bmatrix}^{\mathrm{T}} \qquad (10.142)$$

is a vector of non-negative components $\lambda_i > 0$, $i = \overline{1, m}$.

We suppose that the condition of regularity is fulfilled too, in the sense that there exists at least a point $\boldsymbol{\xi} \in \mathcal{E}$ at which the inequalities $g_i(\mathbf{x}) \leq 0$ become strict, that is,

$$g_i(\boldsymbol{\xi}) < 0, \quad i = \overline{1, m}. \qquad (10.143)$$

The Kuhn–Tucker theorem states that to ensure the minimum of the function f by $\mathbf{x}^*$ it is sufficient (and necessary if the condition of regularity is fulfilled) that the vector $\boldsymbol{\lambda} = [\lambda_1 \, \lambda_2 \, \cdots \, \lambda_m]^{\mathrm{T}}$ does exist so as to have

$$\mathcal{L}(\mathbf{x}^*, \boldsymbol{\lambda}) \leq \mathcal{L}(\mathbf{x}^*, \boldsymbol{\lambda}^*) \leq \mathcal{L}(\mathbf{x}, \boldsymbol{\lambda}^*) \qquad (10.144)$$

for all $\mathbf{x} \in \mathcal{D}$ and $\boldsymbol{\lambda} > \mathbf{0}$ ($\lambda_1 > 0$, $\lambda_2 > 0$, ..., $\lambda_m > 0$).

The point $(\mathbf{x}^*, \boldsymbol{\lambda}^*) \in \mathcal{D} \times \mathbb{R}_+^m$ is called *saddle point for Lagrange's function* and fulfills the condition

$$\lambda_i^* g_i(\mathbf{x}^*) = 0, \quad i = \overline{1, m}. \qquad (10.145)$$

Moreover,

$$\mathcal{L}(\mathbf{x}^*, \boldsymbol{\lambda}^*) = f(\mathbf{x}^*). \qquad (10.146)$$

Let us suppose that Lagrange's function has the saddle point $(\mathbf{x}^*, \boldsymbol{\lambda}^*)$ and let us consider the function

$$\phi(\boldsymbol{\lambda}) = \inf_{\mathbf{x} \in \mathcal{D}} \mathcal{L}(\mathbf{x}, \boldsymbol{\lambda}), \quad \boldsymbol{\lambda} \geq \mathbf{0} \qquad (10.147)$$

for which $\phi(\boldsymbol{\lambda}^*) = f(\mathbf{x}^*)$. Now, let the function be $\overline{f} : \mathbb{R}^n \to \mathbb{R}$, given by

$$\overline{f}(\mathbf{x}) = \begin{cases} \infty & \text{if } \mathbf{x} \notin \mathcal{E}, \\ f(\mathbf{x}) & \text{if } \mathbf{x} \in \mathcal{E}. \end{cases} \tag{10.148}$$

Definition 10.21   Let us define the dual problem of the convex programming

$$\inf_{\mathbf{x} \in \mathcal{E}} f(\mathbf{x}), \tag{10.149}$$

that is the problem

$$\inf_{\mathbf{x} \in \mathcal{D}} \overline{f}(\mathbf{x}). \tag{10.150}$$

We have

$$f(\mathbf{x}^*) = \min_{\mathbf{x} \in \mathcal{D}} \overline{f}(\mathbf{x}) = \max_{\boldsymbol{\lambda} > 0} \phi(\boldsymbol{\lambda}), \tag{10.151}$$

hence, instead of searching $f(\mathbf{x}^*) = \min_{\mathbf{x} \in \mathcal{D}} \overline{f}(\mathbf{x})$, we may determine $\max_{\boldsymbol{\lambda} > 0} \phi(\boldsymbol{\lambda})$.

10.9   NUMERICAL METHODS FOR PROBLEMS OF CONVEX PROGRAMMING

We present hereafter some methods of convex programming.

10.9.1   Method of Conditional Gradient

For the point $\overline{\mathbf{x}}$ of the admissible set $\mathcal{E}$, we consider the problem

$$\min_{\mathbf{x} \in \mathcal{E}} [f(\overline{\mathbf{x}}) + \langle f(\overline{\mathbf{x}}), \mathbf{x} - \overline{\mathbf{x}} \rangle]. \tag{10.152}$$

If $\mathbf{x}^0$ is the solution of this problem, then, on the segment of a line which joints the points $\overline{\mathbf{x}}$ and $\mathbf{x}^0$, that is, for the points

$$\mathbf{x} = (1 - \alpha)\overline{\mathbf{x}} + \alpha\mathbf{x}^0, \tag{10.153}$$

we search the point of minimum of f, that is, we solve the problem

$$\min_{\alpha \in [0, 1]} [f(\overline{\mathbf{x}} + \alpha(\mathbf{x}^0 - \overline{\mathbf{x}}))]; \tag{10.154}$$

let us suppose that this minimum is attained for $\alpha = \overline{\alpha}$. Under these conditions, we continue the procedure with the point

$$\mathbf{x}^1 = \overline{\mathbf{x}} + \overline{\alpha}(\mathbf{x}^0 - \overline{\mathbf{x}}). \tag{10.155}$$

10.9.2   Method of Gradient's Projection

The idea of the method of gradient's projection consists in the displacement along the antigradient's direction $-\nabla f(\overline{\mathbf{x}})$ by a step so as to not go out of the domain of admissible solutions. If h is the length of the step (which depends on any iteration step), then we calculate

$$\mathbf{x}^0 = \overline{\mathbf{x}} - \nabla f(\overline{\mathbf{x}}); \tag{10.156}$$

we solve the problem

$$\min_{\mathbf{x} \in \mathcal{E}} \left[\frac{1}{2} \langle \mathbf{x} - \mathbf{x}^0, \mathbf{x} - \mathbf{x}^0 \rangle \right], \tag{10.157}$$

continuing the procedure with the point of minimum thus obtained.

10.9.3 Method of Possible Directions

Let $\mathbf{x}$ be an admissible point and let us define the set of active restrictions at the point $\mathbf{x}$, denoted by $S(\mathbf{x})$ as being the set of all indices i for which $g_i(\mathbf{x}) = 0$.

At the point $\overline{\mathbf{x}}$, we will search a direction $\mathbf{x}$, which make an obtuse angle with ∇f as well as with the external normals to the active restrictions $\nabla g_i(\overline{\mathbf{x}})$, $i \in S(\overline{\mathbf{x}})$. This choice leads to the diminishing of the function to be minimized and ensures to remain in the interior of $\mathcal{E}$, if we impose the conditions

$$\langle \nabla f(\overline{\mathbf{x}}), \mathbf{x} \rangle + \beta \| \nabla f(\overline{\mathbf{x}}) \| \leq 0, \tag{10.158}$$

$$\langle \nabla g_i(\overline{\mathbf{x}}), \mathbf{x} \rangle + \beta \| \nabla g_i(\overline{\mathbf{x}}) \| \leq 0, \quad i \in S(\overline{\mathbf{x}}), \tag{10.159}$$

where the factor β has to be minimized. Usually, we introduce also a normalization condition of the form

$$\langle \mathbf{x}, \mathbf{x} \rangle \leq 1 \tag{10.160}$$

or

$$-1 \leq x_j \leq 1, \quad j = \overline{1, \ n}. \tag{10.161}$$

Once the direction $\mathbf{x}$ is determined, we pass to the solving of the problem of one-directional minimization

$$\min_{\beta}[f(\overline{\mathbf{x}} + \beta \mathbf{x})], \quad \text{with } g_i(\overline{\mathbf{x}} + \beta \mathbf{x}) \leq 0, \quad i \in S(\overline{\mathbf{x}}). \tag{10.162}$$

10.9.4 Method of Penalizing Functions

In the frame of penalizing functions method, we introduce a term in the function to be minimized, which penalizes the non compliance of a restriction. Let us consider

$$\Phi(\mathbf{x}) = \sum_{i=1}^{m} [\max\{g_i(\mathbf{x}), 0\}]^2 \tag{10.163}$$

and let us search the minimum of the function $f(\mathbf{x}) + r\Phi(\mathbf{x})$, where r is a sufficiently great positive number.

10.10   QUADRATIC PROGRAMMING

Let us consider the programming problem

$$\min f(\mathbf{x}) = \min \left[\frac{1}{2} \sum_{j=1}^{n} \sum_{k=1}^{n} c_{jk} x_j x_k + \sum_{j=1}^{n} d_j x_j \right], \tag{10.164}$$

$$\sum_{j=1}^{n} a_{ij} x_j \geq b_i, \quad i = \overline{1, m}, \tag{10.165}$$

or in a matrix form,

$$\min f(x) = \min \left[\frac{1}{2} \langle \mathbf{x}, \mathbf{Cx} \rangle + \langle \mathbf{D}, \mathbf{x} \rangle \right], \tag{10.166}$$

$$\mathbf{Ax} \geq \mathbf{b}, \tag{10.167}$$

where $\mathbf{C} \in \mathcal{M}_n(\mathbb{R})$ is symmetric and positive definite, $\mathbf{A} \in \mathcal{M}_{m,n}(\mathbb{R})$, $\mathbf{D} \in \mathcal{M}_{n,1}(\mathbb{R})$, $\mathbf{b} \in \mathcal{M}_{m,1}(\mathbb{R})$.
  Lagrange's function is of the form

$$\mathcal{L} = \frac{1}{2} \langle \mathbf{x}, \mathbf{Cx} \rangle + \langle \mathbf{D}, \mathbf{x} \rangle + \langle \boldsymbol{\lambda}, \mathbf{b} - \mathbf{Ax} \rangle, \tag{10.168}$$

the saddle point being searched for $\boldsymbol{\lambda} \geq \mathbf{0}$.
  The optimality criterion

$$\mathcal{L}(\mathbf{x}^*, \boldsymbol{\lambda}^*) \leq \mathcal{L}(\mathbf{x}, \boldsymbol{\lambda}^*) \tag{10.169}$$

leads to

$$\frac{\partial \mathcal{L}(\mathbf{x}, \boldsymbol{\lambda}^*)}{\partial \mathbf{x}}\Big|_{\mathbf{x}=\mathbf{x}^*} = \mathbf{0} \tag{10.170}$$

or

$$\mathbf{Cx}^* + \mathbf{D} - \mathbf{A}^\mathsf{T} \boldsymbol{\lambda}^* = \mathbf{0}. \tag{10.171}$$

The inequality

$$\mathcal{L}(\mathbf{x}^*, \boldsymbol{\lambda}) \leq \mathcal{L}(\mathbf{x}^*, \boldsymbol{\lambda}^*) \tag{10.172}$$

leads to

$$\mathbf{Ax}^* \geq \mathbf{b}, \tag{10.173}$$

$$\lambda_i^*(b_i - (\mathbf{Ax})_i) = 0, \quad i = \overline{1, m}. \tag{10.174}$$

Moreover,

$$\lambda_i^* \geq 0, \quad i = \overline{1, m}. \tag{10.175}$$

It follows that if the pair $(\mathbf{x}^*, \boldsymbol{\lambda}^*)$ satisfies conditions (10.171), (10.173), (10.174), and (10.175), then $\mathbf{x}^*$ is the solution for problems (10.166), (10.167), while $\boldsymbol{\lambda}^*$ is the solution for the dual problem.
  We suppose that the rows of the matrix $\mathbf{A}$ are linearly independent (it means that the restrictions (10.165) are independent). In relation (10.174), we have denoted by $(\mathbf{Ax})_i$ the element on the row i and column 1 in the product $\mathbf{Ax}$.
  The system of restrictions (10.167) defines a polyhedrical set with faces of various dimensions. Each face contains only admissible points, which satisfy a system of equations

$$\mathbf{A}_I \mathbf{x} = \mathbf{b}_I \tag{10.176}$$

where $\mathbf{A}_I$ is the matrix obtained from the matrix $\mathbf{A}$ by retaining only the rows of the set I, that is, the matrix of rows $(\mathbf{A})_i$, $i \in I$, $I = \{i_1, i_2, \ldots, i_l\}$; analogically for the matrix $\mathbf{b}_I$.
  On the other hand, the minimum $\mathbf{x}^*$ is found on a face of the polyhedron, in particular on an edge or at its vertex.
  Let us suppose that there exists the admissible point $\bar{\mathbf{x}}$ for which we have the set $I = \{i_1, i_2, \ldots, i_l\}$, the rows of the matrix $\mathbf{A}_I$ are independent, while $\bar{\mathbf{x}}$ satisfies relation (10.176). There may occur two situations.

    (i) The point $\bar{\mathbf{x}}$ gives the minimum of the function f with the restrictions (10.176). It follows that there exist the factors $\bar{\lambda}_i$, $i \in I$, for which

$$\frac{\partial}{\partial \mathbf{x}}[f(\mathbf{x}) + \bar{\boldsymbol{\lambda}}_I(\mathbf{b}_I - \mathbf{A}_I \mathbf{x})]_{\mathbf{x}=\bar{\mathbf{x}}} = \mathbf{0}, \tag{10.177}$$

    that is,

$$\mathbf{C}\bar{\mathbf{x}} + \mathbf{D} - \mathbf{A}_I^\mathsf{T} \bar{\boldsymbol{\lambda}}_I = \mathbf{0}. \tag{10.178}$$

From relation (10.178), we determine the vector $\overline{\boldsymbol{\lambda}}_I$; if all its components $\overline{\lambda}_I$, $i \in I$ are non-negative, then the algorithm stops, because the searched solution $\mathbf{x}^* = \overline{\mathbf{x}}$ has been found. But, if there exists an index $i_k \in I$ for which $\overline{\lambda}_{i_k} < 0$, then i_k is eliminated from the set I, resulting in

$$I = \{i_1, \ldots, i_{k-1}, i_k, \ldots, i_l\}, \tag{10.179}$$

that is, we pass to a new face of the polyhedral set.

(ii) The function f attains its minimum in the set of solutions (10.176), at a point $\mathbf{x}_0 \neq \overline{\mathbf{x}}$. In this case, we write

$$\mathbf{z} = \mathbf{x}_0 - \overline{\mathbf{x}}, \tag{10.180}$$

$$g_i = -(\mathbf{Ax})_i = -\sum_{j=1}^{n} a_{ij} z_j, \quad i \notin I, \tag{10.181}$$

$$\Delta_i = (\mathbf{Ax})_i - b_i = \sum_{j=1}^{n} a_{ij} \overline{x}_j - b_i, \quad i \notin I \tag{10.182}$$

and determine

$$\varepsilon_0 = \min_{g_i > 0} \frac{\Delta_i}{g_i}. \tag{10.183}$$

We choose

$$\overline{\varepsilon} = \min\{\varepsilon_0, 1\}. \tag{10.184}$$

If $\overline{\varepsilon} = 1$, then the displacement has been made at the point $\mathbf{x}_0$, the set I being preserved. If $\overline{\varepsilon} < 1$, then this minimum has been attained for an index i' which did not belong to the set and the set I must be brought up-to-date by adding this index also

$$I = \{i_1, i_2, \ldots, I_l, i'\}; \tag{10.185}$$

we replace thus the point $\overline{\mathbf{x}}$ by the point $\overline{\mathbf{x}} + \overline{\varepsilon}\mathbf{x}_0$.

Let us notice that for the determination of $\mathbf{x}^{(0)}$, that is, of the start point, we must solve the linear system

$$\mathbf{Cx} + \mathbf{D} - \mathbf{A}_I^T\boldsymbol{\lambda}_I = \mathbf{0}, \quad \mathbf{A}_I\mathbf{x} = \mathbf{b}_I. \tag{10.186}$$

10.11 DYNAMIC PROGRAMMING

Let us consider the optimal control problem for the system[10]

$$\frac{d\varphi}{dt} = \mathbf{f}(\varphi, \mathbf{u}), \quad 0 \leq t \leq T, \quad \varphi(0) = \varphi_0, \tag{10.187}$$

where

$$\varphi = \begin{bmatrix} \phi_1 & \phi_2 & \cdots & \phi_n \end{bmatrix}^T, \quad \mathbf{f} = \begin{bmatrix} f_1 & f_2 & \cdots & f_n \end{bmatrix}^T,$$

$$\mathbf{u} = \begin{bmatrix} u_1 & u_2 & \cdots & u_m \end{bmatrix}^T, \quad n \in \mathbb{N}, \quad m \in \mathbb{N}, \quad n \geq 1, \quad m \geq 1, \tag{10.188}$$

[10]The concept of dynamic programming was introduced by Richard E. Bellman (1920–1984) in 1953.

The admissible commands are given by $\mathbf{u} = \mathbf{u}(t)$ and are piecewise continuous, $\mathbf{u}(t) \in \mathcal{U}$, where $\mathcal{U}$ is a closed set.

In the class of the admissible commands we must find a command $\mathbf{u}(t)$ to which corresponds the solution $\varphi(t)$ of problem (10.187) for which the functional

$$F(\mathbf{u}) = \int_0^T f_0(\varphi, \mathbf{u})dt \qquad (10.189)$$

be minimum.

To do this, we apply Bellman's principle[11] which states that the optimal command, at any moment, does not depend on the previous history of the system, but is determined only by the goal of the command and by the state of the system at that moment.

Denoting

$$Q(\varphi, t) = \min_{\mathbf{u} \in \mathcal{U}} \int_t^T f_0(\varphi(\tau), \mathbf{u}(\tau))d\tau, \qquad (10.190)$$

Bellman's optimality principle leads to the notation

$$Q(\varphi(t), t) = \min_{\mathbf{u}} \left\{ \int_t^{t+\Delta t} f_0(\varphi(\tau), \mathbf{u}(\tau)) d\tau + \min_{\mathbf{u}} \int_{t+\Delta t}^T f_0(\varphi(\tau), \mathbf{u}(\tau))d\tau \right\}. \qquad (10.191)$$

But

$$\int_{t+\Delta t}^T f_0(\varphi(\tau), \mathbf{u}(\tau))d\tau = Q(\boldsymbol{\xi} + \Delta\boldsymbol{\xi}, t + \Delta t), \qquad (10.192)$$

where

$$\Delta\boldsymbol{\xi} = \int_t^{t+\Delta t} \mathbf{f}(\varphi, \mathbf{u})d\tau. \qquad (10.193)$$

Let us suppose that both terms between brackets in relation (10.191) may be expanded into a Taylor series and let us make $\Delta t \to 0$. It follows that Bellman's equation

$$-\frac{\partial Q}{\partial t} = \min \left[f_0(\varphi, \mathbf{u}) + \left\langle \mathbf{f}(\varphi, \mathbf{u}), \frac{\partial Q}{\partial \varphi} \right\rangle \right], \qquad (10.194)$$

$$Q(\varphi, T) = 0. \qquad (10.195)$$

If the minimum in the right side of relation (10.194) is attained at only one point $\mathbf{u}^*$, then $\mathbf{u}^*$ is function of φ and $\partial Q / \partial \varphi$, that is,

$$\mathbf{u}^* = \mathbf{u}^* \left(\varphi, \frac{\partial Q}{\partial \varphi} \right). \qquad (10.196)$$

Introducing this result in relation (10.194), it follows that a nonlinear system of the form

$$-\frac{\partial Q}{\partial t} = f_0 \left(\varphi, \mathbf{u}^* \left(\varphi, \frac{\partial Q}{\partial \varphi} \right) \right) + \left\langle \mathbf{f} \left(\varphi, \mathbf{u}^* \left(\varphi, \frac{\partial Q}{\partial \varphi} \right) \right), \frac{\partial Q}{\partial \varphi} \right\rangle. \qquad (10.197)$$

[11]Richard E. Bellman (1920–1984) stated this principle in 1952.

If $\mathbf{u}^*$ is a function of φ and t, then system (10.197) is a hyperbolic one, with the characteristics oriented from $t = 0$ to $t = T$.

Let us consider a process described by a system of difference equations

$$\varphi_{i+1} = \mathbf{g}(\varphi_i, \mathbf{u}_i), \quad i = \overline{0, N-1}. \tag{10.198}$$

We must minimize the functional

$$F(\mathbf{u}) = \sum_{i=0}^{N-1} f_0(\varphi_i, \mathbf{u}_i), \tag{10.199}$$

the solution of which depends on the initial state φ_0 and on the number of steps N. If we denote the searched optimal value by $Q_N(\varphi_0)$, then the problem of minimum leads to the relation

$$Q_N(\varphi_0) = \min_{\mathbf{u}_0} \min_{[\mathbf{u}_1, \mathbf{u}_2, \dots, \mathbf{u}_{N-1}]} \left[f_0(\varphi_0, \mathbf{u}_0) + \sum_{i=1}^{N-1} f_0(\varphi_i, \mathbf{u}_i) \right]. \tag{10.200}$$

But

$$\sum_{i=1}^{N-1} f_0(\varphi_i, \mathbf{u}_i) = Q_{N-1}(\varphi_1), \tag{10.201}$$

obtaining thus

$$Q_N(\varphi_0) = \min_{\mathbf{u}_0} [f_0(\varphi_0, \mathbf{u}_0) + Q_N(\varphi_1)]. \tag{10.202}$$

Step by step, we get the recurrence relations

$$Q_{N-j}(\varphi_j) = \min_{\mathbf{u}_j \in \mathcal{U}} [f_0(\varphi_j, \mathbf{u}_j) + Q_{N-j-1}(\varphi_{j+1})], \quad j = \overline{0, N-2}, \quad \varphi_{j+1} = \mathbf{g}(\varphi_j, \mathbf{u}_j),$$

$$Q_{N-1}(\varphi_j) = \min_{\mathbf{u}_{N-1} \in \mathcal{U}} f_0(\varphi_{N-1}, \mathbf{u}_{N-1}), \quad \varphi_{N-11} = \mathbf{g}(\varphi_{N-2}, \mathbf{u}_{N-2}). \tag{10.203}$$

If φ_{N-1} is known, then from (10.180) we get $\mathbf{u}_{N-2}, \dots, \mathbf{u}_0$ and $Q_N(\varphi_0)$.

10.12   PONTRYAGIN'S PRINCIPLE OF MAXIMUM

Let us consider the system of ordinary differential equations

$$\frac{d\varphi}{dt} = \mathbf{f}(\varphi, \mathbf{u}), \quad 0 \leq t \leq T, \tag{10.204}$$

where

$$\varphi = \begin{bmatrix} \phi_1 & \phi_2 & \cdots & \phi_n \end{bmatrix}^T, \quad \mathbf{f} = \begin{bmatrix} f_1 & f_2 & \cdots & f_n \end{bmatrix}^T, \quad \mathbf{u} = \begin{bmatrix} u_1 & u_2 & \cdots & u_n \end{bmatrix}^T, \tag{10.205}$$

and to which we add the limit conditions

$$\varphi(0) \in S_0, \quad \varphi(T) \in S_1, \tag{10.206}$$

where S_0 and S_1 are given manifolds in the Euclidian space $\mathcal{E}_n$.

The problem requires that, being given a closed set $\mathcal{U} \subset \mathcal{E}_n$, do determine a moment T and a command $\mathbf{u} = \mathbf{u}(t) \in \mathcal{U}$ piecewise continuous, for which the trajectory $\varphi = \varphi(t, \mathbf{u})$ do satisfy the conditions (10.204) and (10.206), as well as

$$F(\mathbf{u}) = \int_0^T f_0(\varphi, \mathbf{u}) dt = \text{minimum}. \tag{10.207}$$

We will suppose that:

- the functions $\mathbf{f}(\varphi, \mathbf{u})$ are definite and continuous in the doublet $(\varphi, \mathbf{u})$, together with the partial derivatives $\partial f_i / \partial \phi_j$, $i, j = \overline{1, n}$;
- the manifolds S_0 and S_1 are given by the relations

$$S_0 = \{\varphi | \phi_i(0) = \phi_i^0; i = \overline{1, n}\}, \tag{10.208}$$

$$S_1 = \{\varphi | h_k(\varphi(t)) = 0; k = \overline{1, l}, l \leq n\}, \tag{10.209}$$

where $h_k(\mathbf{x})$ are functions with continuous partial derivatives; supplementary, $\nabla h_k(\mathbf{x})$, $k = \overline{1, l}$, contains linearly independent components for any $\mathbf{x} \in S_1$.

Let us remark that if $l = n$, then we get the optimal control problem (10.204), (10.206), (10.207) with fixed right end. Condition (10.208) mean fixation of the left end. If $S_1 = \mathcal{E}_n$, then we have an optimal control problem with a mobile right end, while if $0 < l < n$, then we have a problem with a mobile right end. Immaterial of whether the right end is fixed, free or mobile, the dimension of the manifold S_1 is equal to $n - 1$.

Theorem 10.1 (Pontryagin[12]). Let the system be of ordinary differential equations

$$\frac{d\varphi}{dt} = \mathbf{f}(\varphi, \mathbf{u}), \quad \mathbf{u} \in \mathcal{U}, \quad S_0 = \{\varphi(0) = \varphi^0\}, \quad S_1 = \{h_k(\varphi(T)) = 0, \quad k = \overline{1, l}\} \tag{10.210}$$

for which the above conditions are fulfilled. Let $\{\varphi(t), \mathbf{u}(t)\}$, $0 \leq t \leq T$ be the optimal process that leads the system from the state φ^0 in the state $\varphi^1 \in S_1$, and let us introduce Hamilton's function

$$H(\varphi, \boldsymbol{\psi}, \mathbf{u}) = \sum_{i=0}^n \psi_i f_i(\varphi, \mathbf{u}). \tag{10.211}$$

Under these conditions, there exists the nontrivial vector function

$$\boldsymbol{\psi}(t) = \begin{bmatrix} \psi_1(t) & \psi_2(t) & \cdots & \psi_n(t) \end{bmatrix}^T, \quad \psi_0 = \text{const} \leq 0, \tag{10.212}$$

which satisfies the system of equations

$$\frac{\partial \psi_i}{\partial t} = -\frac{\partial H(\varphi(t), \boldsymbol{\psi}, \mathbf{u}(t))}{\partial \phi_i}, \quad i = \overline{1, n}, \tag{10.213}$$

with the limit conditions

$$\psi_i(T) = \sum_{k=1}^l \gamma_k \frac{\partial h_k(\varphi(T))}{\partial \phi_i}, \quad i = \overline{1, n}, \tag{10.214}$$

[12]Lev Semenovich Pontryagin (1908–1988) formulated this principle in 1956.

where $\gamma_1, \ldots, \gamma_l$ are numbers such that, at any moment $0 \le t \le T$ verifies the condition of maximum

$$H(\varphi(t), \boldsymbol{\psi}(t), \mathbf{u}(t)) = \max_{\mathbf{u} \in \mathcal{U}} H(\varphi(t), \boldsymbol{\psi}(t), \mathbf{u}). \tag{10.215}$$

If the moment T is not fixed, then the following relation takes place

$$H_T = H(\varphi(T), \boldsymbol{\psi}(T), \mathbf{u}(T)) = 0. \tag{10.216}$$

The classical problem of the variational calculus consists in the minimization of the functional

$$F = \int_0^T f_0 \left(\phi, \frac{d\phi}{dt}, t \right) dt \tag{10.217}$$

in the class of the functions sectionally smooth, which satisfy the limit conditions $\phi(0) \in S_0$, $\phi(T) \in S_1$, is a particular case of problems (10.204), (10.206), (10.207), that is, to find the minimum of the functional

$$F = \int_{t_0}^T f_0(\phi, u, t) dt, \tag{10.218}$$

with the condition

$$\frac{d\phi}{dt} = u. \tag{10.219}$$

10.13   PROBLEMS OF EXTREMUM

Hereby, we will denote a Hilbert space over the field of real numbers by $\mathcal{H}$, and the scalar product and the norm in $\mathcal{H}$ by $\langle \cdot, \cdot \rangle_{\mathcal{H}}$ and $\| \| _{\mathcal{H}}$, respectively. Let $\pi(u, v)$ be a symmetric and continuous bilinear form and $L(u)$ a linear form continuous in $\mathcal{H}$. We also denote by $\mathcal{D} \subset \mathcal{H}$ a convex and closed set.

We define the quadratic functional

$$F(v) = \pi(v, v) + 2L(v), \tag{10.220}$$

where $\pi(v, v)$ is positive definite on $\mathcal{H}$, that is, there exists $c > 0$ with the property

$$\pi(v, v) \ge c \|v\|_{\mathcal{H}}^2, \tag{10.221}$$

for any $v \in \mathcal{H}$.

Under these conditions there exists an uniquely determined element $u \in \mathcal{D}$, which is the solution of the problem

$$F(u) = \inf_{u \in \mathcal{D}} F(v). \tag{10.222}$$

Theorem 10.2   If the above conditions are fulfilled, then $u \in \mathcal{D}$ is a solution of problem (10.222) if and only if for any $v \in \mathcal{D}$ we have

$$\pi(u, v - u) \ge L(v - u). \tag{10.223}$$

Demonstration. The necessity results from the following considerations. If u is a solution of problem (10.222), then for any $v \in \mathcal{D}$ and $\theta \in (0, 1)$ we have

$$F(u) \leq F((1 - \theta)u + \theta v), \tag{10.224}$$

where we take into account that $\mathcal{D}$ is convex.

From equation (10.224), we obtain

$$\frac{F(u + \theta(v - u)) + F(u)}{\theta} \geq 0 \tag{10.225}$$

and passing to the limit for $\theta \to 0$, it follows that

$$\lim_{\theta \to 0} \frac{F(u + \theta(v - u)) + F(u)}{\theta} = \lim_{\theta \to 0} 2[\pi(u, v - u) - L(v - u)]$$

$$+ \lim_{\theta \to 0} \theta \pi(v - u, v - u) = 2[\pi(u, v - u) - L(v - u)] \geq 0 \tag{10.226}$$

for any $v \in \mathcal{D}$.

Let us now show the sufficiency. Because $F(u)$ is convex, then for any $v \in \mathcal{D}$ and any $\theta \in (0, 1)$ subsists the inequality

$$F((1 - \theta)u + \theta v) \leq (1 - \theta)F(u) + \theta F(v), \tag{10.227}$$

from which it follows that

$$F(v) - F(u) \geq \frac{F((1 - \theta)u + \theta v) - F(u)}{\theta}. \tag{10.228}$$

We pass to the limit for $\theta \to 0$ and it follows that

$$F(u) \leq F(v) \tag{10.229}$$

for any $v \in \mathcal{D}$, hence the theorem is proved.

Observation 10.20   If we write $v = u \pm \phi$ with $\phi \in \mathcal{D}$ arbitrary, then

$$\pi(u, \phi) \geq L(\phi), \quad -\pi(u, \phi) \geq -L(\phi), \tag{10.230}$$

hence u is a solution of problem (10.222) if and only if, for any $\phi \in \mathcal{D}$, we have

$$\pi(u, \phi) = L(\phi), \tag{10.231}$$

that is, Euler's equation for the variational problem

$$F(u) = \inf_{v \in \mathcal{D}} F(v). \tag{10.232}$$

10.14 NUMERICAL EXAMPLES

Example 10.1   Let the function be $f : [0, 2] \to \mathbb{R}$,

$$f(x) = \frac{x^5}{5} - x. \tag{10.233}$$

We wish to localize the minimum of this function knowing $a = 0$, $b = 0.8$, $c = 2$. First of all we use the linear algorithm of localization of the minimum and have

$$a = 0 < 0.8 = b, \tag{10.234}$$

$$f(a) = 0, \quad f(b) = \frac{0.8^5}{5} - 0.8 = -0.734464, \quad f(a) > f(b). \tag{10.235}$$

Let

$$k = 1.1 \tag{10.236}$$

and calculate

$$c_1 = b + k(b - a) = 1.68, \tag{10.237}$$

$$f(c_1) = \frac{1.68^5}{5} - 1.68 = 0.99656 > 0, \quad f(c_1) > f(b). \tag{10.238}$$

It follows that the point of minimum is in the interval $[0, 1.68]$.

On the other hand, the parabola which passes through the points $A(0, 0)$, $B(0.8, -0.734464)$, $C(2, 4.4)$ is of equation

$$L_2(x) = 2.5984x^2 - 2.9968x \tag{10.239}$$

and attains its minimum at the point

$$x^* = \frac{2.9968}{2 \times 2.5984} = 0.576663. \tag{10.240}$$

Moreover,

$$f(x^*) = -0.563909 < f(2) = 4.4, \tag{10.241}$$

$$f(x^*) = -0.563909 > f(0.8) = -0.734464; \tag{10.242}$$

hence, the point of minimum of the function f is in the interval $[0.8, 2]$.

To determine the minimum, we may use the algorithm of the golden section, the results being specified in the Table 10.1.

We may also use the Brent algorithm, the calculation being given in Table 10.2.

In both cases the precision is

$$\varepsilon = 10^{-3}. \tag{10.243}$$

Example 10.2   Let us consider the function $U : D \subset \mathbb{R}^3 \to \mathbb{R}$,

$$U(x) = U(x, y, z) = 2x^2 + 5y^2 + 5z^2 + 2xy - 4xz - 4yz, \tag{10.244}$$

where

$$D = \{(x, y, z) \in \mathbb{R}^3 | x^2 + 2y^2 + z^2 \le 2\}. \tag{10.245}$$

Let $\mathbf{p}^{(1)}$ be the direction given by

$$\mathbf{p}^{(1)} = \begin{bmatrix} 1 & 2 & 3 \end{bmatrix}^{\mathsf{T}}. \tag{10.246}$$

TABLE 10.1 Determination of the Minimum of Function (10.233) by Means of the Algorithm of the Golden Section

Step	x_0	x_1	x_2	x_3	$f(x_0)$	$f(x_1)$	$f(x_2)$	$f(x_3)$
0	0.000	0.800	1.258	2.000	0.000	−0.735	−0.627	4.400
1	0.000	0.494	0.800	1.258	0.000	−0.489	−0.734	−0.627
2	0.494	0.800	0.975	1.258	−0.489	−0.734	−0.799	−0.627
3	0.800	0.975	1.083	1.258	−0.734	−0.799	−0.785	−0.627
4	0.800	0.908	0.975	1.083	−0.734	−0.785	−0.799	−0.785
5	0.908	0.975	1.016	1.083	−0.785	−0.799	−0.799	−0.785
6	0.975	1.016	1.042	1.083	−0.799	−0.799	−0.796	−0.785
7	0.975	1.001	1.016	1.042	−0.799	−0.800	−0.799	−0.796
8	0.975	0.991	1.001	1.016	−0.799	−0.800	−0.800	−0.799
10	0.991	1.001	1.007	1.016	−0.800	−0.800	−0.800	−0.799
11	0.991	0.997	1.001	1.007	−0.800	−0.800	−0.800	−0.800

TABLE 10.2 Determination of the Minimum of Function (10.233) by Brent's Algorithm

Step	a	b	u	v	t	x	f_a	f_b	f_u	f_v	f_t	f_x
0	0.000	2.000	2.000	2.000	0.000	1.000	0.000	4.400	4.400	4.400	0.000	−0.800
1	0.000	1.382	1.382	1.382	0.000	1.000	0.000	4.400	4.400	4.400	0.000	−0.800
2	0.618	1.382	0.618	0.000	0.618	1.000	0.000	4.400	−0.374	0.000	−0.374	−0.800
3	0.618	1.146	1.146	0.618	1.146	1.000	0.000	4.400	−0.600	−0.374	−0.600	−0.800
4	0.854	1.146	0.854	1.146	0.854	1.000	0.000	4.400	−0.751	−0.600	−0.751	−0.800
5	0.854	1.056	1.056	0.854	1.056	1.000	0.000	4.400	−0.763	−0.751	−0.763	−0.800
6	0.944	1.056	0.944	1.056	0.944	1.000	0.000	4.400	−0.793	−0.763	−0.793	−0.800
7	0.944	1.021	1.021	0.944	1.021	1.000	0.000	4.400	−0.794	−0.793	−0.794	−0.800
8	0.979	1.021	0.979	1.021	0.979	1.000	0.000	4.400	−0.799	−0.794	−0.799	−0.800
9	0.979	1.008	1.008	0.979	1.008	1.000	0.000	4.400	−0.799	−0.799	−0.799	−0.800

We wish to determine the other G-conjugate directions too, as well as the minimum of the function U.

To do this, we calculate the Hessian matrix

$$\nabla^2 U(\mathbf{x}) = \begin{bmatrix} \dfrac{\partial^2 U}{\partial x^2} & \dfrac{\partial^2 U}{\partial x \partial y} & \dfrac{\partial^2 U}{\partial x \partial z} \\[2mm] \dfrac{\partial^2 U}{\partial x \partial y} & \dfrac{\partial^2 U}{\partial y^2} & \dfrac{\partial^2 U}{\partial y \partial z} \\[2mm] \dfrac{\partial^2 U}{\partial x \partial z} & \dfrac{\partial^2 U}{\partial y \partial z} & \dfrac{\partial^2 U}{\partial z^2} \end{bmatrix} = \begin{bmatrix} 4 & 2 & -4 \\ 2 & 10 & -4 \\ -4 & -4 & 10 \end{bmatrix}. \tag{10.247}$$

The second G-conjugate direction is determined by the relation

$$\begin{bmatrix} 1 & 2 & 3 \end{bmatrix} \begin{bmatrix} 4 & 2 & -4 \\ 2 & 10 & -4 \\ -4 & -4 & 10 \end{bmatrix} \begin{bmatrix} p_{12} \\ p_{22} \\ p_{23} \end{bmatrix} = 0, \tag{10.248}$$

which leads to the equation

$$-4p_{21} + 10p_{22} + 18p_{23} = 0; \tag{10.249}$$

we choose

$$p_{21} = 2, \quad p_{22} = -1, \quad p_{23} = 1. \tag{10.250}$$

We have obtained

$$\mathbf{p}^{(2)} = \begin{bmatrix} 2 & -1 \end{bmatrix}^{\mathrm{T}}. \tag{10.251}$$

The last G -conjugate direction is given by the relation

$$\begin{bmatrix} 2 & -1 & 1 \end{bmatrix} \begin{bmatrix} 4 & 2 & -4 \\ 2 & 10 & -4 \\ -4 & -4 & 10 \end{bmatrix} \begin{bmatrix} p_{31} \\ p_{32} \\ p_{33} \end{bmatrix} = 0, \tag{10.252}$$

from which

$$2p_{31} - 10p_{32} + 6p_{33} = 0. \tag{10.253}$$

We choose

$$p_{31} = 2, \quad p_{32} = 1, \quad p_{33} = 1, \tag{10.254}$$

hence

$$\mathbf{p}^{(3)} = \begin{bmatrix} 2 & 1 & 1 \end{bmatrix}^{\mathrm{T}}. \tag{10.255}$$

We take as start point the value

$$\mathbf{x}^{(0)} = \begin{bmatrix} 1 & 0 & 1 \end{bmatrix}^{\mathrm{T}}. \tag{10.256}$$

The expression

$$U(\mathbf{x}^{(0)} + \alpha \mathbf{p}^{(1)}) = U\left(\begin{bmatrix} 1 + \alpha \\ 2\alpha \\ 1 + 3\alpha \end{bmatrix}\right) = 35\alpha^2 + 14\alpha + 3 \tag{10.257}$$

becomes minimum for

$$\alpha = -\frac{1}{5} \tag{10.258}$$

and it follows that

$$\mathbf{x}^{(1)} = \mathbf{x}^{(0)} + \alpha \mathbf{p}^{(1)} = \begin{bmatrix} \frac{4}{5} & -\frac{2}{5} & \frac{2}{5} \end{bmatrix}^{\mathrm{T}}. \tag{10.259}$$

We calculate

$$U(\mathbf{x}^{(1)} + \alpha \mathbf{p}^{(2)}) = U\left(\begin{bmatrix} \frac{4}{5} + 2\alpha \\ -\frac{2}{5} - \alpha \\ \frac{2}{5} + \alpha \end{bmatrix}\right) = 26\alpha^2 + \frac{104}{5}\alpha + \frac{104}{25}. \tag{10.260}$$

The minimum of this expression is attained for

$$\alpha = -\frac{2}{5}, \tag{10.261}$$

from which

$$\mathbf{x}^{(2)} = \mathbf{x}^{(1)} + \alpha \mathbf{p}^{(2)} = \begin{bmatrix} 0 & 0 & 0 \end{bmatrix}^{\mathrm{T}} \tag{10.262}$$

Finally, the expression

$$U(\mathbf{x}^{(2)} + \alpha \mathbf{p}^{(3)}) = U\left(\begin{bmatrix} 2\alpha \\ \alpha \\ \alpha \end{bmatrix}\right) = 10\alpha^2 \tag{10.263}$$

attains its minimum for

$$\alpha = 0 \tag{10.264}$$

and it follows that

$$\mathbf{x}^{(3)} = \mathbf{x}^{(2)} + \alpha \mathbf{p}^{(3)} = \begin{bmatrix} 0 & 0 & 0 \end{bmatrix}^T = \mathbf{x}^{(2)}. \tag{10.265}$$

The point of minimum of the function U is given by $\mathbf{x}^{(3)}$, while the minimum value of U is

$$U_{\min} = U(\mathbf{x}^{(3)}) = 0. \tag{10.266}$$

Example 10.3   Let us consider the function $U : \mathbb{R}^3 \rightarrow \mathbb{R}$,

$$U(\mathbf{x}) = U(x, y, z) = e^{x^2}(y^2 + z^2), \tag{10.267}$$

for which we wish to calculate the minimum by Powell's algorithm. We know

$$\varepsilon = 10^{-2}, \quad \text{iter} = 3, \tag{10.268}$$

$$\mathbf{x}^{(0)} = \begin{bmatrix} 2 & 1 & -3 \end{bmatrix}^T. \tag{10.269}$$

We have

$$U(\mathbf{x}^{(k-1)} + \alpha \mathbf{p}^{(k)}) = U\left(\begin{bmatrix} x^{(k-1)} + \alpha p_1^{(k)} \\ y^{(k-1)} + \alpha p_2^{(k)} \\ z^{(k-1)} + \alpha p_3^{(k)} \end{bmatrix}\right)$$

$$= e^{(x^{(k-1)} + \alpha p_1^{(k)})^2}[(y^{(k-1)} + \alpha p_2^{(k)})^2 + (z^{(k-1)} + \alpha p_3^{(k)})^2] \tag{10.270}$$

$$\frac{dU(\mathbf{x}^{(k-1)} + \alpha \mathbf{p}^{(k)})}{d\alpha}$$

$$= e^{(x^{(k-1)} + \alpha p_1^{(k)})^2} \begin{bmatrix} 2\left(x^{(k-1)} + \alpha p_1^{(k)}\right) p_1^{(k)} + (y^{(k-1)} + \alpha p_2^{(k)})^2 + (z^{(k-1)} + \alpha p_3^{(k)})^2 \\ +2p_2^{(k)}(y^{(k-1)} + \alpha p_2^{(k)}) + 2p_3^{(k)}(z^{(k-1)} + \alpha p_3^{(k)}) \end{bmatrix}$$

$$= e^{(x^{(k-1)} + \alpha p_1^{(k)})^2} F(\alpha). \tag{10.271}$$

The value $\alpha_{\min}$ which minimizes the expression (10.271) is obtained by solving the equation of second degree

$$F(\alpha) = 0. \tag{10.272}$$

The directions $\mathbf{p}^{(1)}$, $\mathbf{p}^{(2)}$ and $\mathbf{p}^{(3)}$ are

$$\mathbf{p}^{(1)} = \begin{bmatrix} 1 & 0 & 0 \end{bmatrix}^T, \quad \mathbf{p}^{(2)} = \begin{bmatrix} 0 & 1 & 0 \end{bmatrix}^T, \quad \mathbf{p}^{(3)} = \begin{bmatrix} 0 & 0 & 1 \end{bmatrix}^T. \tag{10.273}$$

We have

$$U(\mathbf{x}^{(0)} + \alpha \mathbf{p}^{(1)}) = U\left(\begin{bmatrix} 2+\alpha \\ 1 \\ -3 \end{bmatrix}\right) = 10e^{(2+\alpha)^2}, \tag{10.274}$$

$$\frac{dU(\mathbf{x}^{(0)} + \alpha \mathbf{p}^{(1)})}{d\alpha} = 20e^{(2+\alpha)^2(2+\alpha)}, \tag{10.275}$$

from which

$$\alpha_{min} = -2, \tag{10.276}$$

$$\mathbf{x}^{(1)} = \mathbf{x}^{(0)} - 2\mathbf{p}^{(1)} = \begin{bmatrix} 0 & 1 & -3 \end{bmatrix}^{\mathsf{T}}. \tag{10.277}$$

We calculate now

$$U(\mathbf{x}^{(1)} + \alpha \mathbf{p}^{(2)}) = U\left(\begin{bmatrix} 0 \\ 1+\alpha \\ -3 \end{bmatrix}\right) = 10 + 2\alpha + \alpha^2, \tag{10.278}$$

$$\frac{dU(\mathbf{x}^{(1)} + \alpha \mathbf{p}^{(2)})}{d\alpha} = 2\alpha + 2, \tag{10.279}$$

such that

$$\alpha_{min} = -1, \tag{10.280}$$

$$\mathbf{x}^{(2)} = \mathbf{x}^{(1)} - \mathbf{p}^{(2)} = \begin{bmatrix} 0 & 0 & -3 \end{bmatrix}^{\mathsf{T}}. \tag{10.281}$$

Finally, we also find

$$U(\mathbf{x}^{(2)} + \alpha \mathbf{p}^{(3)}) = U\left(\begin{bmatrix} 0 \\ 0 \\ -3 \end{bmatrix} + \alpha\right) = 9 - 6\alpha + \alpha^2 \tag{10.282}$$

so that

$$\alpha_{min} = 3, \tag{10.283}$$

$$\mathbf{x}^{(3)} = \mathbf{x}^{(2)} + 3\mathbf{p}^{(3)} = \begin{bmatrix} 0 & 0 & 0 \end{bmatrix}^{\mathsf{T}}. \tag{10.284}$$

On the other hand, the new value $\mathbf{p}^{(3)}$ is given by

$$\mathbf{p}^{(3)} = \mathbf{x}^{(3)} - \mathbf{x}^{(2)} = \begin{bmatrix} 0 & 0 & 3 \end{bmatrix}^{\mathsf{T}}; \tag{10.285}$$

we have

$$U(\mathbf{x}^{(3)} + \alpha \mathbf{o}^{(3)}) = U\left(\begin{bmatrix} 0 \\ 0 \\ 3\alpha \end{bmatrix}\right) = 9\alpha^2, \tag{10.286}$$

from which

$$\alpha_{min} = 0, \tag{10.287}$$

$$\mathbf{x}^{(4)} = \mathbf{x}^{(3)} = \begin{bmatrix} 0 & 0 & 0 \end{bmatrix}^{\mathsf{T}}. \tag{10.288}$$

But

$$\|\mathbf{x}^{(4)} - \mathbf{x}^{(3)}\| = 0 < \varepsilon, \tag{10.289}$$

such that the point of minimum is determined by

$$\mathbf{x}_{\min} = \begin{bmatrix} 0 & 0 & 0 \end{bmatrix}^T, \tag{10.290}$$

the minimum value of the function U being

$$U_{\min} = U(\mathbf{x}_{\min}) = 0. \tag{10.291}$$

Example 10.4 Let us consider again the function U of Example 10.3, for which we will calculate the minimum using gradient type methods.

We begin by the gradient method. Therefore, we calculate

$$\nabla U(\mathbf{x}) = \begin{bmatrix} 2xe^{x^2}\left(y^2 + z^2\right) \\ 2ye^{x^2} \\ 2ze^{x^2} \end{bmatrix} \tag{10.292}$$

and it follows that

$$\nabla U(\mathbf{x}^{(0)}) = \begin{bmatrix} 40e^4 \\ 2e^4 \\ -6e^4 \end{bmatrix}, \tag{10.293}$$

this being the first direction $\mathbf{p}^{(1)}$.

The scalar α_0 minimizes the expression

$$U(\mathbf{x}^{(0)} + \alpha_0 \mathbf{p}^{(1)}) = U\left(\begin{bmatrix} 2 + 40\alpha_0 e^4 \\ 1 + 2\alpha_0 e^4 \\ -3 - 6\alpha_0 e^4 \end{bmatrix}\right) = e^{(2+40\alpha_0 e^4)^2}(10 + 40\alpha_0^2 e^8 + 40\alpha_0 e^4). \tag{10.294}$$

But

$$U'(\alpha_0) = e^{(2+40\alpha_0 e^4)^2}(3200e^{12}\alpha_0^2 + 3280\alpha_0 e^8 + 840e^4) \tag{10.295}$$

and the equation $U'(\alpha_0) = 0$ leads to

$$\alpha_{01} = -\frac{21}{40e^4} \quad \text{or} \quad \alpha_{02} = -\frac{1}{2e^4}. \tag{10.296}$$

Then

$$U(\alpha_{01}) = \frac{e^{361}}{40}, \quad U(\alpha_{02}) = 0, \tag{10.297}$$

so that we choose $\alpha_0 = \alpha_{02}$.

It follows that

$$\mathbf{x}^{(1)} = \mathbf{x}^{(0)} - \frac{1}{2e^4}\mathbf{p}^{(1)} = \begin{bmatrix} 2 \\ 1 \\ -3 \end{bmatrix} - \begin{bmatrix} 20 \\ 1 \\ -3 \end{bmatrix} = \begin{bmatrix} -18 \\ 0 \\ 0 \end{bmatrix}. \tag{10.298}$$

We calculate

$$\nabla U(\mathbf{x}^{(1)}) = \begin{bmatrix} 0 \\ 0 \\ 0 \end{bmatrix}; \tag{10.299}$$

hence, the sequence $\mathbf{x}^{(k)}$ becomes constant $\mathbf{x}^{(k)} = \mathbf{x}^{(1)}$, $k \geq 2$.

If we wish to solve the problem by methods of conjugate gradient, then we calculate:

- for the Fletcher–Reeves method:

$$\beta_1 = \frac{[\nabla U(\mathbf{x}^{(1)})]^T[\nabla U(\mathbf{x}^{(1)})]}{[\nabla U(\mathbf{x}^{(0)})]^T[\nabla U(\mathbf{x}^{(0)})]} = 0; \tag{10.300}$$

- for the Polak–Ribière method:

$$\mathbf{y}^{(0)} = \nabla U(\mathbf{x}^{(1)}) - \nabla U(\mathbf{x}^{(0)}) = \begin{bmatrix} -40e^4 \\ -2e^4 \\ 6e^4 \end{bmatrix}, \tag{10.301}$$

$$\beta_0 = \frac{[\nabla U(\mathbf{x}^{(1)})]^T\mathbf{y}^{(0)}}{[\nabla U(\mathbf{x}^{(0)})]^T[\nabla U(\mathbf{x}^{(0)})]} = 0; \tag{10.302}$$

- for the Hestenes–Stiefel method:

$$\beta_0 = \frac{[\nabla U(\mathbf{x}^{(1)})]^T\mathbf{y}^{(0)}}{[(\mathbf{y}^{(0)})]^T\mathbf{p}^{(0)}} = 0, \tag{10.303}$$

$$\mathbf{p}^{(1)} = -\nabla U(\mathbf{x}^{(1)}) - \beta_0\mathbf{p}^{(0)} = \begin{bmatrix} 0 \\ 0 \\ 0 \end{bmatrix}. \tag{10.304}$$

We observe that in all cases, we obtain the same constant sequence $\mathbf{x}^{(k)} = \mathbf{x}^{(1)}$, $k \geq 2$, hence $U_{min} = 0$.

Comparing the Example 10.3 and Example 10.4, we see that we do not obtain the same points of minimum. This may be explained by the fact that the function U has an infinity of points of minimum characterized by $x \in \mathbb{R}$ arbitrary, $y = 0$, $z = 0$.

Example 10.5   We wish to solve the linear system

$$5x_1 + 2x_2 + 2x_3 = 11, \quad 2x_1 + 5x_2 + 2x_3 = 14, \quad 2x_1 + 2x_2 + 5x_3 = 11, \tag{10.305}$$

using methods of gradient type and starting with

$$\mathbf{x}^{(0)} = \begin{bmatrix} -1 & 1 & 0 \end{bmatrix}^T. \tag{10.306}$$

We know the values

$$\varepsilon = 10^{-3}, \quad \delta = 10^{-1}, \quad \text{iter} = 10. \tag{10.307}$$

We have

$$\mathbf{A} = \begin{bmatrix} 5 & 2 & 2 \\ 2 & 5 & 2 \\ 2 & 2 & 5 \end{bmatrix}, \quad \mathbf{b} = \begin{bmatrix} 11 \\ 14 \\ 11 \end{bmatrix}. \tag{10.308}$$

The matrix $\mathbf{A}$ is positive definite because

$$\begin{bmatrix} x_1 & x_2 & x_3 \end{bmatrix}^T[\mathbf{A}]\begin{bmatrix} x_1 \\ x_2 \\ x_3 \end{bmatrix} = (x_1 + 2x_2)^2 + (x_2 + 2x_3)^2 + (x_3 + 2x_1)^2. \tag{10.309}$$

The data are given in Table 10.3.

TABLE 10.3   Solution of System (10.305) by the Gradient Method

Step	x	p	$\langle \mathbf{p}, \mathbf{p} \rangle$	$(\mathbf{p}, \mathbf{Ap})$	α
0	$\begin{bmatrix} -1 \\ 0 \\ 1 \end{bmatrix}$	$\begin{bmatrix} 14.00000 \\ 14.00000 \\ 8.00000 \end{bmatrix}$	456.00000	3960.00000	0.11515
1	$\begin{bmatrix} 0.61212 \\ 1.61212 \\ 1.92121 \end{bmatrix}$	$\begin{bmatrix} 0.87273 \\ 0.87273 \\ -3.05455 \end{bmatrix}$	10.85355	35.98810	0.30159
2	$\begin{bmatrix} 0.87532 \\ 1.87532 \\ 1.00000 \end{bmatrix}$	$\begin{bmatrix} 0.87273 \\ 0.87273 \\ 0.49870 \end{bmatrix}$	1.77201	15.38850	0.11515
3	$\begin{bmatrix} 0.97582 \\ 1.97582 \\ 1.05743 \end{bmatrix}$	$\begin{bmatrix} 0.05440 \\ 0.05440 \\ -0.19041 \end{bmatrix}$	0.04218	0.13985	0.30159
4	$\begin{bmatrix} 0.99223 \\ 1.99223 \\ 1.00000 \end{bmatrix}$	$\begin{bmatrix} 0.05440 \\ 0.05440 \\ 0.03109 \end{bmatrix}$	0.00689	0.05980	0.11515
5	$\begin{bmatrix} 0.99849 \\ 1.99849 \\ 1.00358 \end{bmatrix}$	$\begin{bmatrix} 0.00339 \\ 0.00339 \\ -0.01187 \end{bmatrix}$	0.00016	0.00054	0.30159
6	$\begin{bmatrix} 0.99952 \\ 1.99952 \\ 1.00000 \end{bmatrix}$	$\begin{bmatrix} 0.00339 \\ 0.00339 \\ 0.00194 \end{bmatrix}$	0.00003	0.00023	0.11515
7	$\begin{bmatrix} 0.99991 \\ 1.99991 \\ 1.00000 \end{bmatrix}$	$\begin{bmatrix} 0.00021 \\ 0.00021 \\ -0.00074 \end{bmatrix}$	0.00000	0.00000	0.30159
8	$\begin{bmatrix} 0.99997 \\ 1.99997 \\ 1.00000 \end{bmatrix}$	–	–	–	–

If we apply the Fletcher–Reeves method, then we obtain the data given in Table 10.4.

Example 10.6   Let the function be $U : \mathbb{R}^3 \to \mathbb{R}$,

$$U(\mathbf{x}) = U(x, y, z) = 5x^2 + 5y^2 + 5z^2 + 4xy + 4yz + 4xz, \tag{10.310}$$

for which we wish to determine the minimum, using Newton type methods.
    We know

$$\varepsilon = 10^{-2}, \tag{10.311}$$

$$\mathbf{B}_0 = \begin{bmatrix} 1 & 0 & 0 \\ 0 & 1 & 0 \\ 0 & 0 & 1 \end{bmatrix} = \mathbf{I}_3, \tag{10.312}$$

while the start vector is

$$\mathbf{x}^{(0)} = \begin{bmatrix} 1 & -1 & 1 \end{bmatrix}^{\mathrm{T}}. \tag{10.313}$$

TABLE 10.4   Solution of System (10.305) by the Fletcher–Reeves Method

Step	x	p	r	$\langle \mathbf{p}, \mathbf{p} \rangle$	α	β
0	$\begin{bmatrix} -1.00000 \\ 0.00000 \\ 1.00000 \end{bmatrix}$	$\begin{bmatrix} 14.00000 \\ 14.00000 \\ 8.00000 \end{bmatrix}$	$\begin{bmatrix} 14.00000 \\ 14.00000 \\ 8.00000 \end{bmatrix}$	456.00000	0.11515	0.00274
1	$\begin{bmatrix} 0.61212 \\ 1.61212 \\ 1.92121 \end{bmatrix}$	$\begin{bmatrix} 0.91110 \\ 0.91110 \\ -3.03262 \end{bmatrix}$	$\begin{bmatrix} 0.87273 \\ 0.87273 \\ -3.05455 \end{bmatrix}$	10.85698	0.30572	0.03963
2	$\begin{bmatrix} 0.89067 \\ 1.89067 \\ 0.99407 \end{bmatrix}$	$\begin{bmatrix} 0.81331 \\ 0.81331 \\ 0.34682 \end{bmatrix}$	$\begin{bmatrix} 0.77720 \\ 0.77720 \\ 0.46700 \end{bmatrix}$	1.44323	0.11769	0.00126
3	$\begin{bmatrix} 0.98638 \\ 1.98638 \\ 1.03488 \end{bmatrix}$	$\begin{bmatrix} 0.02660 \\ 0.02660 \\ -0.11950 \end{bmatrix}$	$\begin{bmatrix} 0.02557 \\ 0.02557 \\ -0.11994 \end{bmatrix}$	0.01570	0.28084	0.06347

We calculate

$$\nabla U(\mathbf{x}) = \begin{bmatrix} 10x + 4y + 4z \\ 10y + 4x + 4z \\ 10z + 4x + 4y \end{bmatrix}, \tag{10.314}$$

$$\nabla U^2(\mathbf{x}) = \begin{bmatrix} 10 & 4 & 4 \\ 4 & 10 & 4 \\ 4 & 4 & 10 \end{bmatrix}. \tag{10.315}$$

The matrix $\nabla U^2(\mathbf{x})$ is positive definite because

$$\begin{bmatrix} x_1 & x_2 & x_3 \end{bmatrix} \begin{bmatrix} 10 & 4 & 4 \\ 4 & 10 & 4 \\ 4 & 4 & 10 \end{bmatrix} \begin{bmatrix} x_1 \\ x_2 \\ x_3 \end{bmatrix} = 2[(x + 2y)^2 + (y + 2z)^2 + (x + 2x)^2]. \tag{10.316}$$

Moreover,

$$[\nabla^2 U(\mathbf{x})]^{-1} = \frac{1}{648} \begin{bmatrix} 84 & -24 & -24 \\ -24 & 84 & -24 \\ -24 & -24 & 84 \end{bmatrix}. \tag{10.317}$$

In the case of Newton's method we obtain the sequence of iterations

$$\mathbf{x}^{(k+1)} = \mathbf{x}^{(k)} - [\nabla^2 U(\mathbf{x})]^{-1} \nabla U(\mathbf{x}^{(k)}) = \begin{bmatrix} -\dfrac{8}{27}x_1^{(k)} + \dfrac{4}{27}x_2^{(k)} + \dfrac{4}{27}x_3^{(k)} \\ \dfrac{4}{27}x_1^{(k)} - \dfrac{8}{27}x_2^{(k)} + \dfrac{4}{27}x_3^{(k)} \\ \dfrac{4}{27}x_1^{(k)} + \dfrac{4}{27}x_2^{(k)} - \dfrac{8}{27}x_3^{(k)} \end{bmatrix}. \tag{10.318}$$

The calculations are given in Table 10.5.

TABLE 10.5   Determination of the Minimum of the Function U by Newton's Method

Step	x_1	x_2	x_3
0	1.000000	−1.000000	1.000000
1	−0.296296	0.592593	−0.296296
2	0.131687	−0.263374	0.131687
3	−0.058528	0.117055	−0.058528
4	0.026012	−0.052025	0.026012
5	−0.011561	0.023122	−0.011561
6	0.005138	−0.010276	0.005138
7	−0.002284	0.004567	−0.002284
8	0.001015	−0.002030	0.001015
9	−0.000451	0.000902	−0.000451
10	0.000200	−0.000401	0.000200
11	−0.000089	0.000178	−0.000089
12	0.000040	−0.000079	0.000040
13	−0.000018	0.000035	−0.000018
14	0.000008	−0.000016	0.000008
15	−0.000003	0.000007	−0.000003
16	0.000002	−0.000003	0.000002
17	0.000001	0.000001	−0.000001
18	0.000000	−0.000001	0.000000
19	−0.000000	0.000000	−0.000000
20	0.000000	−0.000000	0.000000

In the case of Davidon–Fletcher–Powell method we have successively

$$\mathbf{B}_0 \mathbf{p}^{(0)} = -\nabla U(\mathbf{x}^{(0)}), \qquad \begin{bmatrix} 1 & 0 & 0 \\ 0 & 1 & 0 \\ 0 & 0 & 1 \end{bmatrix} \begin{bmatrix} p_1^{(0)} \\ p_2^{(0)} \\ p_3^{(0)} \end{bmatrix} = - \begin{bmatrix} 10 \\ -2 \\ 10 \end{bmatrix}, \qquad (10.319)$$

$$\mathbf{p}_0 = \begin{bmatrix} -10 & 2 & -10 \end{bmatrix}^{\mathrm{T}}, \qquad (10.320)$$

$$U(\mathbf{x}^{(0)} + \alpha \mathbf{p}^{(0)}) = U\left(\begin{bmatrix} 1 - 10\alpha \\ -1 + 2\alpha \\ 1 - 10\alpha \end{bmatrix} \right) = 1260\alpha^2 - 204\alpha + 11. \qquad (10.321)$$

This expression is minimized for

$$\alpha_0 = \frac{17}{210} \qquad (10.322)$$

and it follows that

$$\mathbf{x}^{(1)} = \mathbf{x}^{(0)} + \alpha_0 \mathbf{p}^{(0)} = \begin{bmatrix} \dfrac{4}{21} & -\dfrac{88}{105} & \dfrac{4}{21} \end{bmatrix}, \qquad (10.323)$$

$$\mathbf{y}^{(0)} = \nabla U(\mathbf{x}^{(1)}) - \nabla U(\mathbf{x}^{(0)}) = \begin{bmatrix} -\dfrac{374}{35} \\ -\dfrac{34}{7} \\ -\dfrac{374}{35} \end{bmatrix}, \qquad (10.324)$$

$$\mathbf{z}^{(0)} = \mathbf{y}^{(0)} + \alpha_0 \nabla U(\mathbf{x}^{(0)}) = \begin{bmatrix} -\dfrac{374}{35} \\ -\dfrac{34}{7} \\ -\dfrac{374}{35} \end{bmatrix} + \dfrac{17}{10} \begin{bmatrix} 10 \\ -2 \\ 10 \end{bmatrix} = \begin{bmatrix} \dfrac{221}{35} \\ -\dfrac{289}{35} \\ \dfrac{221}{35} \end{bmatrix}, \tag{10.325}$$

$$\mathbf{B}_1 = \mathbf{B}_0 + \dfrac{\mathbf{z}^{(0)}[\mathbf{y}^{(0)}]^T + \mathbf{y}^{(0)}[\mathbf{z}^{(0)}]^T}{[\mathbf{y}^{(0)}]^T[\mathbf{x}^{(1)} - \mathbf{x}^{(0)}]} - \dfrac{[\mathbf{z}^{(0)}]^T[\mathbf{x}^{(1)} - \mathbf{x}^{(0)}]}{\{[\mathbf{y}^{(0)}]^T[\mathbf{x}^{(1)} - \mathbf{x}^{(0)}]\}^2} \mathbf{y}^{(0)}[\mathbf{y}^{(0)}]^T$$

$$= \begin{bmatrix} -7.171836 & 4.971392 & -8.171836 \\ 4.971392 & 1.971425 & 4.971392 \\ 8.171021 & 0.114249 & 9.171021 \end{bmatrix}. \tag{10.326}$$

Obviously, the procedure may continue.

The application of the Broyden–Fletcher–Goldfarb–Shanno method is completely similar. The minimum of the function $U(\mathbf{x})$ is obtained for

$$\mathbf{x}_{\min} = 0, \quad U(\mathbf{x}_{\min}) = 0. \tag{10.327}$$

Example 10.7 Let the problem of linear programming be

$$\operatorname{maxim}(2x_1 - x_2) = ?, \tag{10.328}$$

with the restrictions

$$x_1 + x_2 \le 5, \quad x_2 - x_1 \le 4, \quad x_2 - x_1 \ge -3, \quad x_2 + \dfrac{4}{3}x_1 \ge 4. \tag{10.329}$$

Having only two variables x_1 and x_2, we can associate the straight lines

$$d_1 : x_1 + x_2 + 5 = 0, \quad d_2 : x_2 - x_1 - 4 = 0, \quad d_3 : x_2 - x_1 + 3 = 0, \quad d_4 : x_2 + \dfrac{4}{3}x_1 - 4 = 0, \tag{10.330}$$

represented in Figure 10.1.

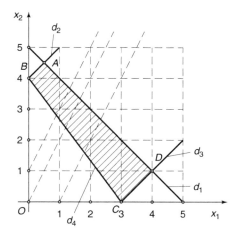

Figure 10.1 Geometric solution of the problem of linear programming (10.328) and (10.329).

These lines define the quadrilateral $ABCD$, its vertices having the coordinates

$$A(0.5, 4.5), \quad B(0, 4), \quad C(3, 0), \quad D(4, 1). \tag{10.331}$$

The function $f : \mathbb{R}^2 \to \mathbb{R}$,

$$f(x_1, x_2) = 2x_1 - x_2 \tag{10.332}$$

has in these points, the values

$$f(A) = -3.5, \quad f(B) = -8, \quad f(C) = 6, \quad f(D) = 7, \tag{10.333}$$

the maximum value taking place at the point D.

It follows that the solution of problem (10.328) and (10.329) is

$$\text{maxim}(2x_1 - x_2) = 7. \tag{10.334}$$

The same problem (10.328) and (10.329) to which we add the conditions $x_i \geq 0$, $i = 1, 2$, may be solved by the primal Simplex algorithm.

Thus, the system of restriction (10.329) will be replaced by the system

$$x_1 + x_2 + x_3 = 5, \quad x_2 - x_1 + x_4 = 4, \quad x_1 - x_2 + x_5 = 3,$$

$$\frac{4}{3}x_1 + x_2 - x_6 + x_7 = 4, \quad x_i \geq 0, \quad i = \overline{1, \ 7}, \tag{10.335}$$

while problem (10.328) will be replaced by

$$\text{minim } f(\mathbf{x}) = \text{minim } (x_2 - 2x_1) = ?. \tag{10.336}$$

We construct the Simplex table.

	x_1	x_2	x_3	x_4	x_5	x_6	x_7	
	-2	1	0	0	0	0	0	0
x_3	1	1	1	0	0	0	0	5
x_4	-1	1	0	1	0	0	0	4
x_5	1	-1	0	0	1	0	0	3
x_7	$\dfrac{4}{3}$	1	0	0	0	-1	1	4

A basic solution is

$$x_1 = 0, \quad x_2 = 0, \quad x_3 = 5, \quad x_4 = 4, \quad x_5 = 3, \quad x_6 = 0, \quad x_7 = 4. \tag{10.337}$$

At the first iteration, x_1 enters in the basis and x_5 exits from the basis (it is possible for the exit of x_7 too, because $3/1 = 4/(4/3)!$).

It follows that the new table

	x_1	x_2	x_3	x_4	x_5	x_6	x_7	
	0	-1	0	0	2	0	0	6
x_3	0	2	1	0	-1	0	0	2
x_4	0	0	0	1	1	0	0	7
x_1	1	-1	0	0	1	0	0	3
x_7	0	$\dfrac{7}{3}$	0	0	$-\dfrac{4}{3}$	-1	1	0

The new basic solution reads

$$x_1 = 3, \quad x_2 = 0, \quad x_3 = 2, \quad x_4 = 7, \quad x_5 = 0, \quad x_6 = 0, \quad x_7 = 0. \tag{10.338}$$

In the next step, x_2 enters in the basis instead x_3 and we obtain the new Simplex table.

	x_1	x_2	x_3	x_4	x_5	x_6	x_7	
	0	0	$\dfrac{1}{2}$	0	$\dfrac{3}{2}$	0	0	7
x_2	0	2	1	0	-1	0	0	2
x_4	0	0	0	1	1	0	0	7
x_1	1	0	$\dfrac{1}{2}$	0	$\dfrac{1}{2}$	0	0	4
x_7	0	0	$-\dfrac{7}{6}$	0	$-\dfrac{1}{6}$	-1	1	$-\dfrac{7}{3}$

It follows that the solution

$$x_1 = 4, \quad x_2 = 1, \quad x_3 = 0, \quad x_4 = 7, \quad x_5 = 0, \quad x_6 = \frac{7}{3}, \quad x_7 = 0. \tag{10.339}$$

We observe that the anomaly which appears in the last line of the Simplex table, that is, the solution $x_6 = 0$, $x_7 = -7/3$ is due to the modality of transformation of the last relation (10.329) in the last equality (10.335). Indeed, we would obtain

$$\frac{4}{3}x_1 + x_2 \geq 4, \quad \frac{4}{3}x_1 + x_2 - x_6 = 4, \tag{10.340}$$

but not the unit column corresponding to x_6. In this situation, we have written $x_6 \mapsto x_6 - x_7$ to obtain the unit column for the variable x_7. In fact, this has been only a trick to start the Simplex algorithm.

Analogically, we can use the dual Simplex algorithm, obviously after the transformation of problem (10.335) and (10.336) in the dual problem.

10.15   APPLICATIONS

Problem 10.1

Let us consider the model of half of an automotive in Figure 10.2, formed of the bar AB of length $l_1 + l_2$ and of the nonlinear springs 1 and 2. The forces in the two springs are given by $f_1(z)$ and $f_2(z)$, respectively, where z is the elongation, while the functions f_1 and f_2 are odd in the variable z. The weight of the bar is G, its center of gravity C being at the distance l_1 with respect to A, while its moment of inertia with respect to this center is J. We suppose that the rotation θ of the bar AB is small and that the springs have the same length in the nondeformed state.

Determine the positions of equilibrium of the bar.

Numerical application for $G = 5000\,\text{N}$, $f_1(z) = f_2(z) = f(z)$, $f(z) = kz^p$, $p = 1$ or $p = 3$, $k = 25000\,\text{N/m}^p$, $l_1 = 1.5\,\text{m}$, $l_2 = 2.5\,\text{m}$.

Solution:

1. Theoretical aspects
   The system has two degrees of freedom: the displacement x of the center of gravity C and the rotation θ of the bar. We have denoted the position of the bar in the absence of any deformation by $A_0 B_0$.

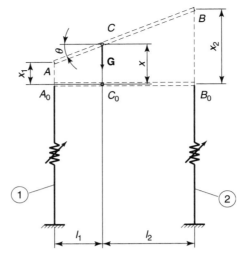

Figure 10.2 Theoretical model.

There result the displacements x_1 and x_2 of the ends A and B, respectively, in the form

$$x_1 = x - l_1\theta, \quad x_2 = x + l_2\theta. \tag{10.341}$$

The theorem of momentum leads to the equation

$$G + f_1(x - l_1\theta) + f_2(x + l_2\theta) = 0, \tag{10.342}$$

while the theorem of moment of momentum, with respect to the center of gravity C allows to write

$$f_1(x - l_1\theta)l_1 - f_2(x + l_2\theta)l_2 = 0. \tag{10.343}$$

The two equations (10.342) and (10.343) may be put together in the equation

$$U(\mathbf{x}) = U(x, \theta) = 0, \tag{10.344}$$

where

$$U(x, \theta) = [G + f_1(x - l_1\theta) + f_2(x + l_2\theta)]^2 + [l_1 f_1(x - l_1\theta) + l_2 f_2(x + l_2\theta)]^2. \tag{10.345}$$

If the system formed by equation (10.342) and equation (10.343) has a solution, then equation (10.344) has a solution too and reciprocally. The determination of the solution of equation (10.344) is equivalent, in this case, to the determination of the minimum of the function U, given by expression (10.345).

2. Numerical case

For $p = 1$, we have successively

$$f_1(x - l_1\theta) = 25000(x - 1.5\theta), \tag{10.346}$$

$$f_2(x + l_2\theta) = 25000(x + 2.5\theta), \tag{10.347}$$

the function U being of the form

$$U(x, \theta) = [5000 + 2500(x - 1.5\theta) + 25000(x + 2.5\theta)]^2$$
$$+ \{1.5[25000(x - 1.5\theta)] - 2.5[25000(x + 2.5\theta)]\}^2 \qquad (10.348)$$

or equivalent,

$$U(x, \theta) = (5000 + 50000x + 25000\theta)^2 + (-25000x - 212500\theta)^2. \qquad (10.349)$$

It follows that

$$U(x, \theta) = 3.125 \times 10^9 x^2 + 4.578125 \times 10^{10}\theta^2 + 1.3125 \times 10^{10}x\theta$$
$$+ 5 \times 10^8 x + 2.5 \times 10^8\theta + 2.5 \times 10^7, \qquad (10.350)$$

with the solution

$$\theta = -0.011 \text{ rad}, \quad x = -0.094 \text{ m}. \qquad (10.351)$$

For $p = 3$, we obtain

$$U(x, \theta) = [5000 + 2500(x - 1.5\theta)^3 + 25000(x + 2.5\theta)^3]^2$$
$$+ \{1.5[25000(x - 1.5\theta)^3] - 2.5[25000(x + 2.5\theta)^3]\}^2, \qquad (10.352)$$

with the solution

$$\theta = 0.0196 \text{ rad}, \quad x = -0.47064 \text{ m}. \qquad (10.353)$$

Problem 10.2

Let us consider the linear program

$$\min \mathbf{c}^T \mathbf{x} \qquad (10.354)$$

with the restrictions

$$\mathbf{Bx} = \mathbf{b}, \quad \mathbf{x} \geq \mathbf{0}, \qquad (10.355)$$

where $\mathbf{x} \in \mathcal{M}_{n,1}(\mathbb{R})$, $\mathbf{b} \in \mathcal{M}_{m,1}(\mathbb{R})$, $\mathbf{c} \in \mathcal{M}_{n,1}(\mathbb{R})$, $\mathbf{B} \in \mathcal{M}_{mn}(\mathbb{R})$.
Let us solve this program in the case $m = n - 1$, while $\mathbf{B}$ is a full rank matrix.

Solution: Because $\mathbf{B}$ is a full rank matrix, it follows that the components of the vector $\mathbf{x}$ may be written as a function of only one component, assumed as x_1, that is,

$$x_2 = \alpha_2 x_1 + \beta_2, \quad \ldots, \quad x_n = \alpha_n x_1 + \beta_n. \qquad (10.356)$$

The function

$$f(\mathbf{x}) = \mathbf{c}^T \mathbf{x} \qquad (10.357)$$

now takes the form

$$f(\mathbf{x}) = c_1 x_1 + \cdots + c_n x_n = ax_1 + b, \qquad (10.358)$$

that is, it becomes a linear function in a single unknown x_1.
If $a \geq 0$, then obviously,

$$\min f = f(0) = b. \qquad (10.359)$$

If $a < 0$, then one considers relation (10.356). If the coefficients α_i, $i = \overline{2, n}$ are positive, then expression (10.356) does not introduce any restriction on the variable x_1 and the program does not have an optimal solution. If there exist negative coefficients α_j, then from

$$x_j = \alpha_j x_1 + \beta_j, \quad x_j \geq 0, \tag{10.360}$$

we deduce

$$\alpha_j x_1 + \beta_j \geq 0, \tag{10.361}$$

hence

$$x_1 \leq -\frac{\beta_j}{\alpha_j}. \tag{10.362}$$

If there exists at least a strictly negative β_j, then there results x_1 strictly negative and the linear program does not have an optimal solution.

It follows that in the case $a < 0$, the necessary and sufficient condition to have an optimal solution for the program consists in the existence of at least expression (10.356) with $\alpha_j < 0$ and in the condition that the expressions of this form have strictly positive coefficients β_j.

Let us remark that if relation (10.359) takes place, then the linear program has an optimal solution if and only if all the values $\beta_i \geq 0$, $i = \overline{2, n}$.

FURTHER READING

Ackleh AS, Allen EJ, Hearfott RB, Seshaiyer P (2009). Classical and Modern Numerical Analysis: Theory, Methods and Practice. Boca Raton: CRC Press.

Atkinson K, Han W (2010). Theoretical Numerical Analysis: A Functional Analysis Framework. 3rd ed. New York: Springer-Verlag.

Baldick R (2009). Applied Optimization: Formulation and Algorithms for Engineering Systems. Cambridge. Cambridge University Press.

Berbente C, Mitran S, Zancu S (1997). Metode Numerice. Bucureşti: Editura Tehnică (in Romanian).

Boyd S, Vandenberghe L (2004). Convex Optimization. Cambridge: Cambridge University Press.

Cheney EW, Kincaid DR (1997). Numerical Mathematics and Computing. 6th ed. Belmont: Thomson.

Chong EKP, Żak SH (2008). An Introduction to Optimization. 3rd ed. Hoboken: John Wiley & Sons, Inc.

Dahlquist G, Björck Å (1974). Numerical Methods. Englewood Cliffs: Prentice Hall.

Dennis JE Jr, Schnabel RB (1987). Numerical Methods for Unconstrained Optimization and Nonlinear Equations. Philadelphia: SIAM.

Diwekar U (2010). Introduction to Applied Optimization. 2nd ed. New York: Springer-Verlag.

Fletcher R (2000). Practical Methods of Optimizations. 2nd ed. New York: John Wiley & Sons, Inc.

Golub GH, van Loan CF (1996). Matrix Computations. 3rd ed. Baltimore: John Hopkins University Press.

Griva I, Nash SG, Sofer A (2008). Linear and Nonlinear Optimization. 2nd ed. Philadelphia: SIAM.

Hamming RW (2012). Introduction to Applied Numerical Analysis. New York: Dover Publications.

Hoffman JD (1992). Numerical Methods for Engineers and Scientists. New York: McGraw-Hill.

Jazar RN (2008). Vehicle Dynamics: Theory and Applications: New York: Springer-Verlag.

Kharab A, Guenther RB (2011). An Introduction to Numerical Methods: A MATLAB Approach. 3rd ed. Boca Raton: CRC Press.

Kleppner D, Kolenkow RJ (2010). An Introduction to Mechanics. Cambridge: Cambridge University Press.

Lange K (2010a). Numerical Analysis for Statisticians. 2nd ed. New York: Springer-Verlag.

Lanczos C (1949). The Variational Principles of Mechanics. Toronto: University of Toronto Press.

Lange K (2010b). Optimization. New York: Springer-Verlag.

Lawden DF (2006). Analytical Methods of Optimization. 2nd ed. New York: Dover Publications.

Luenberger DG (1997). Optimization by Vector Space Methods. New York: John Wiley & Sons, Inc.

Lurie AI (2002). Analytical Mechanics. New York: Springer-Verlag.

Marciuk GI (1983). Metode de Analiză Numerică. Bucureşti: Editura Academiei Române (in Romanian).

Meriam JL, Kraige LG (2012). Engineering Mechanics: Dynamics. Hoboken: John Wiley & Sons, Inc.

Nocedal J, Wright SJ (2006). Numerical Optimization. 2nd ed. New York: Springer-Verlag.

Pandrea N, Pârlac S, Popa D (2001). Modele pentru Studiul Vibraţiilor Automobilelor. Piteşti: Tiparg (in Romanian).

Rao SS (2009). Engineering Optimization: Theory and Practice. 3rd ed. Hoboken: John Wiley & Sons, Inc.

Ridgway Scott L (2011). Numerical Analysis. Princeton: Princeton University Press.

Ruszczyński A (2006). Nonlinear Optimization. Princeton: Princeton University Press.

Sauer T (2011). Numerical Analysis. 2nd ed. London: Pearson.

Stănescu ND (2007). Metode Numerice. Bucureşti: Editura Didactică şi Pedagogică (in Romanian).

Süli E, Mayers D (2003). An Introduction to Numerical Analysis. Cambridge: Cambridge University Press.

Venkataraman P (2009). Applied Optimization with MATLAB Programming. 2nd ed. Hoboken: John Wiley & Sons, Inc.

INDEX

Numerical Analysis with Applications in Mechanics and Engineering, First Edition.
Petre Teodorescu, Nicolae-Doru Stănescu, and Nicolae Pandrea.
© 2013 The Institute of Electrical and Electronics Engineers, Inc. Published 2013 by John Wiley & Sons, Inc.